INCOME STATEMENT, STATEMENT OF OWNER'S EQUITY, BALANCE SHEET, and STATEMENT OF CASH FLOWS

Income Statement, Statement of Owner's Equity, Balance Sheet, and Statement of Cash Flows for Roland Consultancy

Roland Consultancy
Statement of Cash Flows
For the Month Ended December 31, 2014

Cash flows from operating activities:		
Net income		$ 8,400
Adjustments to reconcile net income to net cash flows from operating activities:		
(Increase) in accounts receivable	$ (4,000)	
(Increase) in supplies	(2,000)	
Increase in accounts payable	2,400	(3,600)
Net cash flows from operating activities		$ 4,800
Cash flows from investing activities:		
Purchase of land	$ (40,000)	
Purchase of building	(100,000)	
Net cash flows used by investing activities		(140,000)
Cash flows from financing activities:		
Investments by owner	$ 200,000	
Withdrawals	(2,400)	
Net cash flows from financing activities		197,600
Net increase (decrease) in cash		$ 62,400
Cash at beginning of month		0
Cash at end of month		$ 62,400

Roland Consultancy
Income Statement
For the Month Ended December 31, 2014

Revenues:		
Consulting fees		$14,000
Expenses:		
Equipment rental expense	$2,800	
Wages expense	1,600	
Utilities expense	1,200	
Total expenses		5,600
Net income		$ 8,400

Roland Consultancy
Statement of Owner's Equity
For the Month Ended December 31, 2014

T. Roland, capital, December 1, 2014	$ 0
Investment by T. Roland	200,000
Net income for the month	8,400
Subtotal	$208,400
Less withdrawals	2,400
T. Roland, capital, December 31, 2014	$206,000

Roland Consultancy
Balance Sheet
December 31, 2014

Assets		Liabilities	
Cash	$ 62,400	Accounts payable	$ 2,400
Accounts receivable	4,000	Total liabilities	$ 2,400
Supplies	2,000		
Land	40,000	**Owner's Equity**	
Buildings	100,000	T. Roland, capital	206,000
		Total liabilities and	
Total assets	$208,400	owner's equity	$208,400

STUDY NOTE: *Notice the sequence in which these statements are prepared: income statement, statement of owner's equity, balance sheet, and finally, the statement of cash flows.*

LIQUIDITY RATIOS

Current ratio	$$\dfrac{\text{Current Assets}}{\text{Current Liabilities}}$$	Measures short-term debt-paying ability	**Chapter 5, LO3**
Quick ratio	$$\dfrac{\text{Cash + Marketable Securities + Receivables}}{\text{Current Liabilities}}$$	Measures short-term debt-paying ability	**Chapter 16, LO3**
Receivables turnover	$$\dfrac{\text{Net Sales}}{\text{Average Accounts Receivable}}$$	Average number of times receivables are turned into cash during an accounting period	**Chapter 9, LO4**
Days' sales uncollected	$$\dfrac{\text{365 Days}}{\text{Receivables Turnover}}$$	Average number of days a company must wait to receive payment for credit sales or to collect accounts receivable	**Chapter 9, LO4**
Inventory turnover	$$\dfrac{\text{Costs of Goods Sold}}{\text{Average Inventory}}$$	Number of times a company's average inventory is sold during an accounting period	**Chapter 16, LO3**
Days' inventory on hand	$$\dfrac{\text{Days in Accounting Period}}{\text{Inventory Turnover}}$$	Average number of days taken to sell inventory on hand	**Chapter 16, LO3**
Payables turnover	$$\dfrac{\text{Costs of Goods Sold} \pm \text{Change in Merchandise Inventory}}{\text{Average Accounts Payable}}$$	Average number of times a company pays its accounts payable in an accounting period	**Chapter 11, LO6**
Days' payable	$$\dfrac{\text{365 Days}}{\text{Payables Turnover}}$$	Average number of days a company takes to pay its accounts payable	**Chapter 11, LO6**

PROFITABILITY RATIOS

Profit margin	$$\dfrac{\text{Net Income}}{\text{Revenues}}$$	Percentage of each sales dollar that contributes to net income	**Chapter 5, LO3**
Asset turnover	$$\dfrac{\text{Revenues}}{\text{Average Total Assets}}$$	How efficiently assets are used to produce sales	**Chapter 5, LO3**
Return on assets	$$\dfrac{\text{Net Income}}{\text{Average Total Assets}}$$	How efficiently a company uses its assets to produce income, or the amount earned on each dollar of assets invested	**Chapter 5, LO3**
Return on equity	$$\dfrac{\text{Net Income}}{\text{Average Owner's Equity}}$$	Relates the amount earned by a business to the owner's investment in the business	**Chapter 5, LO3**

LONG-TERM SOLVENCY RATIOS

Debt to equity ratio	$$\dfrac{\text{Total Liabilities}}{\text{Total Equity}}$$	Proportion of a company's assets financed by creditors and the proportion financed by the owner	**Chapter 5, LO3**
Interest coverage ratio	$$\dfrac{\text{Income Before Income Taxes + Interest Expense}}{\text{Interest Expense}}$$	Degree of protection a company has from default on interest payments	**Chapter 14, LO9**

CASH FLOW ADEQUACY RATIOS

Cash flow yield	$$\dfrac{\text{Net Cash Flows from Operating Activities}}{\text{Net Income}}$$	Measures a company's ability to generate operating cash flows in relation to net income	**Chapter 15, LO5**
Cash flows to sales	$$\dfrac{\text{Net Cash Flows from Operating Activities}}{\text{Sales}}$$	Ratio of net cash flows from operating activities to sales	**Chapter 15, LO5**
Cash flows to assets	$$\dfrac{\text{Net Cash Flows from Operating Activities}}{\text{Average Total Assets}}$$	Measures the ability of assets to generate operating cash flows	**Chapter 15, LO5**
Free cash flow	Net Cash Flows from Operating Activities – Dividends – Net Capital Expenditures	Measures the amount of cash that remains after deducting the funds a company must commit to continue operating at its planned level	**Chapter 15, LO5**

MARKET STRENGTH RATIOS

Price/ earnings ratio	$$\dfrac{\text{Market Price per Share}}{\text{Earnings per Share}}$$	Measures investors' confidence in a company's future; a means of comparing stock values	**Chapter 13, LO8**
Dividend yield	$$\dfrac{\text{Dividends per Share}}{\text{Market Price per Share}}$$	Measures a stock's current return to an investor or stockholder	**Chapter 13, LO8**

Principles of Financial Accounting

TWELFTH EDITION

Principles of Financial Accounting

TWELFTH EDITION

Belverd E. Needles, Jr., Ph.D., C.P.A., C.M.A.
DePaul University

Marian Powers, Ph.D.
Northwestern University

SOUTH-WESTERN
CENGAGE Learning

Australia • Brazil • Japan • Korea • Mexico • Singapore • Spain • United Kingdom • United States

SOUTH-WESTERN
CENGAGE Learning·

Principles of Financial Accounting, 12e

Belverd Needles and Marian Powers

Senior Vice President, LRS/Acquisitions & Solutions Planning: Jack W. Calhoun

Editorial Director, Business & Economics: Erin Joyner

Editor-in-Chief: Rob Dewey

Executive Editor: Sharon Oblinger

Development Editor: Krista Kellman

Editorial Assistant: A.J. Smiley

Sr. Brand Manager: Kristen Hurd

Sr. Market Development Manager: Natalie Livingston

Sr. Marketing Communications Manager: Sarah Greber

Marketing Coordinator: Eileen Corcoran

Sr. Content Project Manager: Tim Bailey

Media Editor: Lysa Kosins

Manufacturing Planner: Doug Wilke

Production Service: Cenveo Publisher Services

Sr. Art Director: Stacy Jenkins Shirley

Internal and Cover Designer: Craig Ramsdell

Cover Image: © Martin Marraud/Getty Images

Rights Acquisition Director: Audrey Pettengill

For product information and technology assistance, contact us at **Cengage Learning Customer & Sales Support, 1-800-354-9706**

For permission to use material from this text or product, submit all requests online at **www.cengage.com/permissions**

Further permissions questions can be emailed to **permissionrequest@cengage.com**

ExamView® is a registered trademark of eInstruction Corp.

The financial statements are included for illustrative and education purposes only. Nothing herein should be construed as financial advice.

Except where otherwise noted, all content in this title is © Cengage Learning.

Library of Congress Control Number: 2012950475

ISBN-13: 978-1-133-93928-3
ISBN-10: 1-133-93928-7

South-Western
5191 Natorp Boulevard
Mason, OH 45040
USA

Cengage Learning is a leading provider of customized learning solutions with office locations around the globe, including Singapore, the United Kingdom, Australia, Mexico, Brazil, and Japan. Locate your local office at: **www.cengage.com/global**

Cengage Learning products are represented in Canada by Nelson Education, Ltd.

For your course and learning solutions, visit **www.cengage.com**
Purchase any of our products at your local college store or at our preferred online store **www.cengagebrain.com**

Printed in the United States of America
1 2 3 4 5 6 7 16 15 14 13 12

BRIEF CONTENTS

CONTENTS

CONTENTS

LATEST RESEARCH ON STUDENT LEARNING

We talked to over 150 instructors and discovered that current textbooks did not effectively:

- Help students logically process information
- Build on what students already know in a carefully guided sequence
- Reinforce core accounting concepts throughout the chapters
- Help students see how the pieces of accounting fit together

The Needles/Powers series addresses these challenges by creating a better solution for you. This includes new features and a brand new structure for enhanced learning.

We have worked hard to create a textbook that mirrors the way you learn!

A LOGICAL METHODOLOGY TO BUILDING KNOWLEDGE: THE THREE SECTION APPROACH

Needles/Powers' *Principles of Financial Accounting* continuously evolves to meet the needs of today's learner. As a result of our research, the chapters in Needles/Powers have been organized into a **Three Section Approach**, which helps students more easily digest the content.

ThreeSection APPROACH

1. The first section is **Concepts** and focuses on the overarching accounting concepts that require consistent reiteration throughout the course.

2. With a clear understanding of the concepts, you can proceed to the second section, **Accounting Applications**. Here, you can practice the application of accounting procedures with features like "Apply It!" and a new transaction analysis model, which breaks down the transaction in a simple, visual format.

3. Finally, move to section three, **Business Applications**. This section illustrates how the concepts and procedures are used to make business decisions. Real company examples are used throughout the chapter to show the relevance of accounting.

"I think this new chapter structure would be much easier for students to read and comprehend."

Shannon Ogden
Black River Technical College

TriLevel PROBLEM

TriLevel Problems within CengageNOW mirror the Three Section Approach and connect the sections—Concepts, Accounting Applications, and Business Applications. In this way, the problems teach you to think holistically about an accounting issue.

Breaking Down the Three Section Approach

SECTION 1: CONCEPTS

In Section 1, students experience the **Concepts** related to each chapter. In this case, *concepts* are the overarching accounting concepts that need to be reinforced throughout the accounting course, such as revenue recognition, the matching rule, valuation, classification, and disclosure.

Every chapter's Section 1 reinforces these key concepts so that once students understand the concepts, they can apply them to every aspect of the accounting system—from measuring to processing to communicating information about a business. This is a clear and logical way to present accounting.

SECTION 1 | CONCEPTS

CONCEPTS
- Accrual accounting (matching principle)
- Valuation
- Disclosure

RELEVANT LEARNING OBJECTIVE

LO 1 Define receivables, and explain the allowance method for valuation of receivables as an application of accrual accounting.

LO 1 Concepts Underlying Notes and Accounts Receivable

The most common receivables are *accounts receivable* and *notes receivable*. The *allowance method* is used to apply *accrual accounting* to the *valuation* of accounts receivable. Proper *disclosure* in the financial statements and the notes to them is important for users of the statements to interpret them.

Accounts Receivable

Accounts receivable are short-term financial assets that arise from sales on credit and are often called **trade credit**. Terms of trade credit usually range from 5 to 60 days, depending on industry practice, and may allow customers to pay in installments. Credit sales or loans not made in the ordinary course of business, such as those made to employees, officers, or owners, should appear separately under asset titles like Receivables from Employees. Exhibit 1 shows the level of accounts receivable in selected industries.

"It does a very good job in explaining each concept and reinforcing each one by giving specific examples."

Paul Jaijairam
Bronx Community College

In Section 2, students learn the accounting procedures and the technical **application** of concepts. Students can apply the fundamental concepts they have already learned in Section 1. Section 2 includes things like recording business transactions and creating financial statements.

SECTION 2

ACCOUNTING APPLICATIONS
- Estimate uncollectible accounts and uncollectible accounts expense using
  - Percentage of net sales method
  - Accounts receivable aging method
- Write off uncollectible accounts
- Make common calculations for notes receivable

RELEVANT LEARNING OBJECTIVES

LO 2 Apply the allowance method of accounting for uncollectible accounts.

LO 3 Make common calculations for Notes Receivable

ACCOUNTING APPLICATIONS

LO 2 Uncollectible Accounts

The allowance account is necessary because the specific uncollectible accounts will not be identified until later. It is not like another contra account, Accumulated Depreciation, whose purpose is to show how much of the plant and equipment cost has been allocated as an expense to previous periods.

If management takes an optimistic view and projects a small loss from uncollectible accounts, the resulting net accounts receivable will be larger than if management takes a pessimistic view. The net income will also be larger under the optimistic view because the estimated expense will be smaller. The company's accountant makes an estimate based on past experience and current economic conditions. For example, losses from uncollectible accounts are normally expected to be greater in a recession than during a period of economic growth. The final decision on the amount of the expense will depend on objective information, such as the accountant's analyses, and on certain qualitative factors, such as how investors, bankers, creditors, and others view the performance of the debtor company. Regardless of the qualitative considerations, the estimated losses from uncollectible accounts should be realistic.

Two common methods of estimating uncollectible accounts expense are the percentage of net sales method and the accounts receivable aging method.

Percentage of Net Sales Method

The basis for the **percentage of net sales method** is the amount of this year's *net sales* that will not be collected. The answer determines the amount of uncollectible accounts expense for the year.

Uncollectible Accounts: The Percentage of Net Sales Method

Transaction The following balances represent Varta Company's ending figures for 2014:

"Section 2 walks through the accounting procedures very well. I like the use of a visual plus the narrative to explain the procedures."

Gerald Childs
Waukesha County Technical College

With a solid foundation of the fundamental accounting concepts as well as how to apply these concepts when performing accounting procedures, students are now ready for Section 3: **Business Applications**. This section teaches students how accounting information is used to make business decisions. Included here are topics like using ratios to evaluate a company's performance.

SECTION 3

BUSINESS APPLICATIONS

BUSINESS APPLICATIONS
- Receivables turnover
- Days' sales uncollected
- Financing receivables
  - Factoring of accounts receivable
  - Securitization of accounts receivable
  - Discounting of accounts receivable
- Ethics

RELEVANT LEARNING OBJECTIVE

LO 4 Show how to evaluate the level of receivables, and identify alternative means of financing receivables.

BUSINESS APPLICATIONS

LO 4 Evaluating the Level of Accounts Receivable and Ethical Ramifications

Receivables are an important asset for any company that sells on credit. For them, it is critical to manage the level of receivables. Two common measures of the effect of a company's credit policies are *receivables turnover* and *days' sales uncollected*. Further, many companies manage their receivables by using various means to finance them. Finally, the judgments in estimating uncollectible accounts are a temptation for unethical behavior.

Receivables Turnover

The **receivables turnover** shows how many times, on average, a company turned its receivables into cash during a period. It reflects the relative size of a company's accounts receivable and the success of its credit and collection policies. It may also be affected by external factors, such as seasonal conditions and interest rates.

The receivables turnover is computed by dividing net sales by the average accounts receivable (net of allowances). Theoretically, the numerator should be net credit sales; but since the amount of net credit sales is rarely available in public reports, investors use total net sales. Using data from **Nike**'s annual report, we can compute the company's receivables turnover in 2011 as follows (dollar amounts are in millions).

RATIO

Receivables Turnover: How Many Times Did the Company Collect Its Accounts Receivable During an Accounting Period?

$$\text{Receivables Turnover} = \frac{\text{Net Sales}}{\text{Average Accounts Receivable}}$$

$$\frac{\$20{,}962}{(\$3{,}138 + \$2{,}650)/2} = \frac{\$20{,}962}{\$2{,}894} = 7.2 \text{ times*}$$

* Rounded

"This is a nice and useful touch to help students tie everything together. The theory can be dry at times, so this recap helps engage the students' attention again."

Dennis Mullen
City College of San Francisco

EXAMPLES, ACTIVITIES, AND PRACTICE

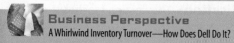

Business Perspective
A Whirlwind Inventory Turnover—How Does Dell Do It?

Dell Computer Corporation turns its inventory over every 10 days. How can it do this when other computer companies have inventory on hand for 60 days or even longer? Technology and good inventory management are a big part of the answer.

Dell's speed from order to delivery sets the standard for the computer industry. Consider that a computer ordered by 9 A.M. can be delivered the next day by 9 P.M. How can Dell do this when it does not start ordering components and assembling computers until a customer places an order? First, Dell's suppliers keep components warehoused just minutes from Dell's factories, making efficient, just-in-time operations possible. Dell also saves time by sending an e-mail message for some finished products to a shipper, such as **United Parcel Service**, and the shipper picks up the product from a supplier and schedules it to arrive with the PC. In addition to contributing to a high inventory turnover, this practice saves Dell in freight costs. Dell is showing the world how to run a business in the cyber age by selling more than $39 million worth of computers a day on its website.⁶

◀ **Business Perspective**
Throughout the chapter, **Business Perspective** features keep students engaged by providing real business context and examples from well-known companies including **Google, CVS, Boeing, Ford Motor Company, Microsoft, L.L. Bean,** and **The Walt Disney Company**.

BUSINESS INSIGHT
Sung's Grill

Sung's Grill is a popular neighborhood restaurant. Its business has increased substantially over the past year, and Emma Sung, the restaurant's owner, has had to hire more cashiers, waiters, and kitchen help. She has become concerned about possible theft of cash and food inventory, and she is looking for ways to prevent it. She is also concerned about whether the restaurant's sales and other transactions are being recorded properly. She is particularly concerned about the accuracy of the restaurant's financial statements, because she is considering applying for a bank loan so that she can open a second restaurant. To obtain a loan, she will have to present Sung's Grill's financial statements to the bank.

1. CONCEPT ▶ Why is each of the five components of internal control important to the faithful representation of a company's operations in its financial statements?

2. ACCOUNTING APPLICATION ▶ How can Sung's Grill maintain control over its cash?

3. BUSINESS APPLICATION ▶ How can Sung's Grill's bank and other users of its financial statements be confident that the restaurant has an adequate system of internal control?

TriLevel Problem

Sung's Grill

The beginning of this chapter focused on Emma Sung, the owner of Sung's Grill, who was looking for ways to ensure that the restaurant's assets were protected and that all its transactions were recorded properly. Complete the following requirements in order to answer the questions posed at the beginning of the chapter.

Section 1: Concepts
Why is each of the five components of internal control important to the faithful representation of a company's operations in its financial statements?

Section 2: Accounting Applications
How can Sung's Grill maintain control over its cash?

In order to have better control over cash, Emma Sung has established several rules for cashiers. Match each of the internal controls with the control activities that follow. (*Hint:* Some may have more than one answer.)

Business Insight and TriLevel Problem ▲
Each chapter opens with a **Business Insight** that shows how a small company would use accounting information to make decisions. The Business Insight poses three questions—each of which will be answered in one of the three sections of the chapter. At the end of each chapter, a NEW **TriLevel Problem** revisits the Business Insight company to tie the three sections together.

Apply It! and Try It! ▶
Apply It! activities throughout the chapter illustrate and solve a short exercise and then reference end-of-chapter assignments where students can go to **Try It!** This provides students with an example to reference as they are working to complete homework, making getting started less intimidating.

APPLY IT!

Assume that on December 1, 2014, a company receives a 90-day, 8 percent, $5,000 note and that the company prepares financial statements monthly.

1. What is the maturity date of the note?
2. How much interest will be earned on the note if it is paid when due?
3. What is the maturity value of the note?
4. If the company's fiscal year ends on December 31, describe the adjusting entry that would be made, including the amount.
5. How much interest will be earned on this note in 2015?

SOLUTION

1. Maturity date is March 1, 2015, determined as follows.

Days remaining in December (31 − 1)	30
Days in January	31
Days in February	28
Days in March	1
Total days	90

2. Interest: $5,000 × 8/100 × 90/365 = $98.63*
3. Maturity value: $5,000 + $98.63 = $5,098.63
4. An adjusting entry to accrue 30 days of interest income in the amount of $32.88* ($5,000 × 8/100 × 30/365) would be needed.
5. Interest earned in 2015: $65.75 ($98.63 − $32.88)
   * Rounded

TRY IT! SE6, SE7, SE8, E8A, E9A, E10A, E11A, E8B, E9B, E10B, E11B

Notes Receivable Calculations

SE8. On August 25, Intercontinental Company received a 90-day, 9 percent note in settlement of an account receivable in the amount of $20,000. Determine the maturity date, amount of interest on the note, and maturity value. (Round to the nearest cent.)

Business Transaction Model ▶

A new business transaction model for all financial accounting chapters involving transactions visually guides students step-by-step through accounting for business transactions as follows:

- Statement of the transaction
- Analysis of the effect on the accounts
- Application of double-entry accounting in T accounts
- Illustration of the journal entry (linked to the T account showing the relationships between the methods and featuring account ing equations)
- Comments that offer supporting explanations regarding the significance of the transaction (often looping back to the concepts covered in Section 1)

Purchase of an Asset on Credit

Transaction On July 5, Blue Design Studio receives the office supplies ordered on July 2 and an invoice for $5,200.

Analysis The journal entry to record the purchase of office supplies on credit
- ▲ *increases* the asset account *Office Supplies* with a debit
- ▲ *increases* the liability account *Accounts Payable* with a credit

Application of Double Entry

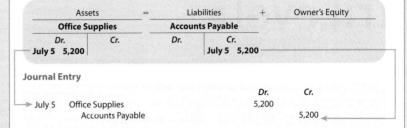

Assets	=	Liabilities	+	Owner's Equity

Office Supplies		Accounts Payable	
Dr.	Cr.	Dr.	Cr.
July 5 5,200			July 5 5,200

Journal Entry

		Dr.	Cr.
July 5	Office Supplies	5,200	
	Accounts Payable		5,200

Comment Office supplies in this transaction are *classified* as an asset (prepaid expense) because they will not be used up in the current month and thus will benefit future periods. The credit is *classified* as Accounts Payable because there is a delay between the time of the purchase and the time of payment.

RATIO

Profit Margin: How Much Income Does Each Dollar of Sales Generate?

Income Statement Numbers · **Statement of Cash Flows Number** · **Balance Sheet Numbers**

Revenues · Net Income · Cash Flows from Operating Activities · Total Assets · Total Liabilities · Total Equity

$$\text{Profit Margin} = \frac{\text{Net Income}}{\text{Revenues}}$$

$$= \frac{\$71,524}{\$1,248,624}$$

$$= 0.057, \text{ or } 5.7\%$$

Advertising Agencies	5.8
Scheduled Air Transportation	1.1
Clothing Stores	4.2
Grocery Stores	1.4
Industrial Machinery Manufacturing	6.0
Computer and Peripheral Equipment Manufacturing	7.4

0 1 2 3 4 5 6 7 8

■ Service Industries ■ Merchandising Industries ■ Manufacturing Industries

Based on Bizmin Industry Financial Report, December 2011.

◀ Ratio Analysis Model

A new framework for teaching how to analyze company information and make informed decisions simplifies ratio analysis as follows:

- Key question regarding company performance (which the ratio answers)
- Elements of the financial statements that are needed to compute the ratio (focusing on revenue and net income from the income statement, cash flows from operating activities from the statement of cash flows, and total assets, total liabilities, and total equity from the balance sheet)
- Formula for the ratio (which links to the related elements of the financial statements)
- Computation/example
- Graph of industry averages
- Comments that explain what the ratio means (whether it's good or bad)

NEW TriLevel Problems within CengageNOW follow the same Three Section Approach the book employs by including *Concepts, Accounting Applications,* and *Business Applications*. The problems reinforce and apply overarching concepts while also tying the three sections together to give students a complete understanding.

Transaction Analysis

The process of assigning business transactions to accounts is called [Select ▾].

One of the most important classification issues in accounting is the difference between an asset and a their cost is classified as an [Select ▾]. If the items will be used in the future, they are classified as

Travis Services is an office cleaning company. Consider Travis Services' transactions during its first mo

(a)	Received cash from Stanley Travis, in exchange for stock, $18,680.
(b)	Performed services for a client on account, $6,530.
(c)	Purchased equipment with cash, $12,920.
(d)	Performed services for a customer who paid cash, $7,150.
(e)	Purchased supplies with cash, $3,480.

Use the following T accounts to record these transactions. You will need to record the transactions in bottom) on the debit or credit side of the T account, whichever is appropriate.

Cash	Accounts Receivable	Supplies

Equipment	Fees Earned	Common Stock

As supplies are used, Travis Services debits Supplies Expense and credits Supplies.

Stanley Travis would like to charge Supplies Expense when the supplies are purchased. He wants to

a. "Great idea. By increasing expenses Travis Services income is lowered and that translates to lo
b. "Accounting rules dictate that purchases that are consumed in future periods be classified as a purposes."

© Cengage Learning 2014

"Any time the students are engaged in the learning process and have to actively participate, I think they enhance their retention of the material. The ability to relate this to an actual company (whether real or not) allows students to see this information in practice."

Chuck Smith
Iowa Western Community College

96% of instructors surveyed said that the TriLevel Problem adequately coached students through thinking about an issue.

"The [TriLevel Problem] links procedure to the creation and use of information, and closes that loop between what students are doing and why it is useful."

Andy Williams
Edmonds Community College

"It reviews everything students have learned in a format they will find useful, and it links the three areas together. I love this. Each one ending with a business application."

Joan Ryan
Clackamas Community College

NEW CENGAGENOW FEATURES
HELP STUDENTS MAKE CONNECTIONS

NEW Blueprint Problems ▶

In CengageNOW, these problems cover primary learning objectives and help students understand the fundamental accounting concepts and their associated building blocks—not just memorize the formulas or journal entries required for a single concept. *Blueprint Problems* include rich feedback and explanations, providing students with an excellent learning resource.

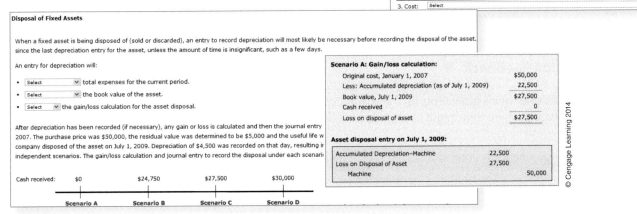

Blueprint Problem: Predetermined, overapplied, and underapplied overhead

The Nature of Overhead

Recall that unit costs include direct materials, direct labor, and overhead. The costs for direct materials and dire production or sales, and some overhead costs are unknown until the end of the period or early in the next per to determine unit costs, because overhead costs are not always directly related to units produced. Therefore, the beginning of the year, and applied to production throughout the year. This requires three steps:

1. Calculate the predetermined overhead rate.
2. Apply the overhead throughout the year.
3. Reconcile the applied and actual overhead at the end of the year.

Predetermined Overhead Rate

The overhead costs are allocated to jobs using a common measure related to each job. This measure is called should reflect the consumption or use of the overhead costs. There are basically three types of drivers (or acti

To calculate the predetermined overhead rate, you must first estimate the overhead costs for the year, as wel

Match the type of driver with its cause.

Driver	Cause
1. Volume:	Select
2. Time:	Select
3. Cost:	Select

Disposal of Fixed Assets

When a fixed asset is being disposed of (sold or discarded), an entry to record depreciation will most likely be necessary before recording the disposal of the asset. since the last depreciation entry for the asset, unless the amount of time is insignificant, such as a few days.

An entry for depreciation will:

- Select ⌄ total expenses for the current period.
- Select ⌄ the book value of the asset.
- Select ⌄ the gain/loss calculation for the asset disposal.

After depreciation has been recorded (if necessary), any gain or loss is calculated and then the journal entry 2007. The purchase price was $50,000, the residual value was determined to be $5,000 and the useful life w company disposed of the asset on July 1, 2009. Depreciation of $4,500 was recorded on that day, resulting ir independent scenarios. The gain/loss calculation and journal entry to record the disposal under each scenario

Cash received:	$0	$24,750	$27,500	$30,000
	Scenario A	Scenario B	Scenario C	Scenario D

Scenario A: Gain/loss calculation:

Original cost, January 1, 2007	$50,000
Less: Accumulated depreciation (as of July 1, 2009)	22,500
Book value, July 1, 2009	$27,500
Cash received	0
Loss on disposal of asset	$27,500

Asset disposal entry on July 1, 2009:

Accumulated Depreciation–Machine	22,500	
Loss on Disposal of Asset	27,500	
Machine		50,000

NEW Blueprint Connections ▲

Blueprint Connections in CengageNOW build upon concepts covered and introduced within the *Blueprint Problems*. These scenario-based exercises help reinforce students' knowledge of the concept.

NEW Animated Activities ▶

Animated Activities in CengageNOW are videos that guide students through selected core topics using a realistic company example to illustrate how the concepts relate to the everyday activities of a business.

Assets	February 26, 2016	February 27, 2015
Current assets:		
Cash and cash equivalents	$ 1,183,587	$ 1,096,100
Short-term investment securities	605,608	431,476
Merchandise inventories	1,968,907	1,759,703
Other current assets	315,736	276,066
Total current assets	4,073,838	3,563,345
Long-term investment securities	121,446	132,860
Property and equipment, net	1,116,297	1,119,292
Other assets	334,612	336,633
Total assets	$ 5,646,193	$ 5,152,130

NEW Check My Work Feedback ▼

Written feedback is now available when students click on "Check My Work" in CengageNOW to provide students with valuable guidance as they work through homework items.

Incorrect

▼ Additional Feedback

Rework the formula above to solve for Fixed Costs:

Fixed Costs = Sales - Variable Costs - Operating Income

Now consider what happens to this formula when Operating Income is equal to zero.

© Cengage Learning 2014

NEW Post-submission Feedback ▼

After students have submitted their assignments for a grade in CengageNOW, they can go back and see the correct answers to better understand where they might have gotten off track.

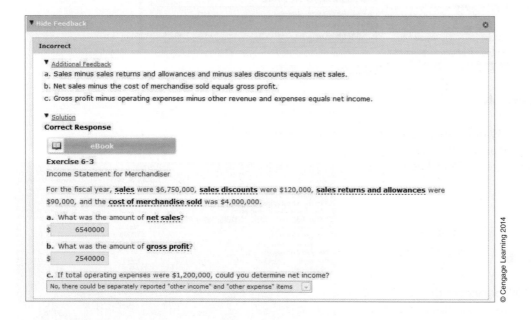

▼ Hide Feedback

Incorrect

▼ Additional Feedback
a. Sales minus sales returns and allowances and minus sales discounts equals net sales.
b. Net sales minus the cost of merchandise sold equals gross profit.
c. Gross profit minus operating expenses minus other revenue and expenses equals net income.

▼ Solution
Correct Response

📖   eBook

Exercise 6-3

Income Statement for Merchandiser

For the fiscal year, **sales** were $6,750,000, **sales discounts** were $120,000, **sales returns and allowances** were $90,000, and the **cost of merchandise sold** was $4,000,000.

a. What was the amount of **net sales**?
$ 6540000

b. What was the amount of **gross profit**?
$ 2540000

c. If total operating expenses were $1,200,000, could you determine net income?
No, there could be separately reported "other income" and "other expense" items

© Cengage Learning 2014

NEW Apply It Demos

These demonstration videos in CengageNOW will help students complete end-of-chapter questions from Section 2.

ACKNOWLEDGMENTS

In developing and refining the twelfth edition of *Principles of Financial Accounting*, we wanted to ensure that we were creating a textbook that truly reflected the way we teach accounting. To do so, we asked for feedback from over 150 professors, other professional colleagues, and students. We want to recognize those who made special contributions to our efforts in preparing this edition through their reviews, suggestions, and participation in surveys, interviews, and focus groups. We cannot begin to say how grateful we are for the feedback from the many instructors who have generously shared their responses and teaching experiences with us.

John G. Ahmad, *Northern Virginia Community College*

Robert Almon, *South Texas College*

Elizabeth Ammann, *Lindenwood University*

Paul Andrew, *SUNY, Morrisville*

Ryan Andrew, *Columbia College Chicago*

Sidney Askew, *Borough of Manhattan Community College*

Joe Atallah, *Irvine Valley College*

Shele Bannon, *Queensborough Community College*

Michael Barendse, *Grossmont College*

Beverly R. Beatty, *Anne Arundel Community College*

Robert Beebe, *Morrisville State College*

Teri Bernstein, *Santa Monica College*

Cynthia Bird, *Tidewater Community College*

David B. Bojarsky, *California State University*

Linda Bolduc, *Mount Wachusett Community College*

John Bongorno, *Cuyahoga Community College*

Anna Boulware, *St. Charles Community College*

Amy Bourne, *Oregon State University*

Thomas Branton, *Alvin Community College*

Billy Brewster, *University of Texas at Arlington*

Nina E. Brown, *Tarrant County College*

Tracy L. Bundy, *University of Louisiana at Lafayette*

Jacqueline Burke, *Hofstra University*

Marci L. Butterfield, *University of Utah*

Charles Caliendo, *University of Minnesota*

Gerald Childs, *Waukesha County Technical College*

James J. Chimenti, *Jamestown Community College*

Alice Chu, *Golden West College*

Sandra Cohen, *Columbia College*

Lisa Cole, *Johnson County Community College*

Debora Constable, *Georgia Perimeter College*

Barry Cooper, *Borough of Manhattan Community College*

Cheryl Copeland, *California State University, Fresno*

Susan Cordes, *Johnson County Community College*

Meg Costello, *Oakland Community College*

Richard Culp, *Ball State University*

Sue Cunningham, *Rowan Cabarrus Community College*

Robin D'Agati, *Palm Beach State College*

Emmanuel Danso, *Palm Beach State College*

Robert Derstine, *Kutztown University*

Michael Dole, *Marquette University*

Jap Efendi, *University of Texas at Arlington*

Dustin Emhart, *North Georgia Technical College*

Denise M. English, *Boise State University*

Michael Farina, *Cerritos College*

J. Thomas Franco, *Wayne County Community College*

Dean Gray, *Reedley College*

Timothy Green, *North Georgia Technical College*

Timothy Griffin, *Hillsborough Community College*

Teri Grimmer, *Portland Community College*

Michael J. Gurevitz, *Montgomery College*

Qian Hao, *Wilkes University*

Sara Harris, *Arapahoe Community College*

Syed Hasan, *George Mason University*

Wendy Heltzer, *DePaul University*

Merrily Hoffman, *San Jacinto College*

Shanelle Hopkins, *Carroll Community College*

David Hossain, *California State University, Los Angeles*

Phillip Imel, *NOVA Community College, Annadale*

ThankGod O. Imo, *Tompkins Cortland Community College*

Paul Jaijairam, *Bronx Community College*

Gene Johnson, *Clark College*

Howard A. Kanter, *DePaul University*

Irene Kim, *George Washington University*

Christopher Kinney, *Mount Wachusett Community College*

Gordon Klein, *University of California, Los Angeles*

Shirly A. Kleiner, *Johnson County Community College*

Leon Korte, *University of South Dakota*

Lynn Krausse, *Bakersfield College*

Les Kren, *University of Wisconsin, Milwaukee*

Donnie Kristof-Nelson, *Edmonds Community College*

Christopher Kwak, *De Anza College*

Richard Lau, *California State University, Los Angeles*

Suzanne R. Laudadio, *Durham Technical Community College*

George Leonard, *St. Petersburg College*

Lydia Leporte, *Tidewater Community College*

Hui Lin, *DePaul University*

Joseph Lipari, *Montclair State*

Xiang Liu, *California State University, San Bernardino*

Angelo Luciano, *Columbia College*

Susan Lueders, *DePaul University*

Cathy Lumbattis, *Southern Illinois University*

Sakthi Mahenthiran, *Butler University*

Eileen Marutzky, *DePaul University*

Robert Maxwell, *College of the Canyons*

Mark McCarthy, *DePaul University*

Clarice McCoy, *Brookhaven College*

Terra McGhee, *University of Texas at Arlington*

Florence McGovern, *Bergen Community College*

Cheryl McKay, *Monroe County Community College*

John McQuilkin, *Roger Williams University*

Jeanette Milius, *Iowa Western Community College*

Jeanne K. Miller, *Cypress College*

Rita Mintz, *Calhoun Community College*

Jill Mitchell, *Northern Virginia Community College, Annandale*

Odell Moon, *Victor Valley College*

Kathleen Moreno, *Abraham Baldwin Agricultural College*

Walter Moss, *Cuyahoga Community College*

Dennis Mullen, *City College of San Francisco*

Elizabeth A. Murphy, *DePaul University*

Penny Nunn, *Henderson Community College*

Christopher O'Byrne, *Cuyamaca College*

Shannon Ogden, *Black River Technical College*

Glenn Pate, *Palm Beach State College*

Sy Pearlman, *California State University, Long Beach*

Rama Ramamurthy, *College of William & Mary*

Lawrence A. Roman, *Cuyahoga Community College*

Gregg Romans, *Ivy Tech Community College*

Joan Ryan, *Clackamas Community College*

Donna B. Sanders, *Guilford Technical Community College*

Regina Schultz, *Mount Wachusett Community College*

Jay Semmel, *Broward College*

Andreas Simon, *California Polytechnic State University*

Jaye Simpson, *Tarrant County College*

Alice Sineath, *Forsyth Technical Community College*

Kimberly Sipes, *Kentucky State University*

Chuck Smith, *Iowa Western Community College*

Robert K. Smolin, *Citrus College*

Jennifer Sneed, *Arkansas State University, Newport*

Lyle Stelter, *Dakota County Technical College*

Rhonda Stone, *Black River Technical College*

Gracelyn Stuart-Tuggle, *Palm Beach State College – Boca Raton*

Linda Tarrago, *Hillsborough Community College*

Steve Teeter, *Utah Valley University*

Don Trippeer, *SUNY Oneonta*

Robert Urell, *Irvine Valley College*

La Vonda Ramey, *Schoolcraft College*

Patricia Walczak, *Lansing Community College*

Scott Wandler, *University of New Orleans*

Chris Widmer, *Tidewater Community College*

Andy Williams, *Edmonds Community College*

Wanda Wong, *Chabot College*

Ronald Zhao, *Monmouth University*

Teri Zuccaro, *Clarke University*

We also wish to express deep appreciation to colleagues at DePaul University, who have been extremely supportive and encouraging.

Finally, very important to the quality of this book are our Developmental Editor, Krista Kellman; Executive Editor, Sharon Oblinger; and Senior Market Development Manager, Natalie Livingston.

ABOUT THE AUTHORS

Belverd E. Needles, Jr., received B.B.A. and M.B.A. degrees from Texas Tech University and his Ph.D. degree from the University of Illinois at Urbana-Champaign. He teaches financial accounting, managerial accounting, and auditing at DePaul University, where he is an internationally recognized expert in international accounting and education. He has published in leading journals and is the author or editor of more than 20 books and monographs. His current research relates to international financial reporting, performance measurement, and corporate governance of high-performance companies in the United States, Europe, India, and Australia. His textbooks are used throughout the world and have received many awards, including (in 2008) the McGuffey Award from the Text and Academic Authors Association. Active in many academic and professional organizations, he is immediate past Vice-President-Education of the American Accounting Association. He has received the Distinguished Alumni Award from Texas Tech University, the Illinois CPA Society Outstanding Educator Award and its Life-Time Achievement Award, the Joseph A. Silvoso Faculty Award of Merit from the Federation of Schools of Accountancy, the Ledger & Quill Award of Merit, and the Ledger & Quill Teaching Excellence Award. He was named Educator of the Year by the American Institute of CPAs, Accountant of the Year for Education by the national honorary society Beta Alpha Psi, and Outstanding International Accounting Educator by the American Accounting Association. He has received the Excellence in Teaching Award from DePaul University.

Marian Powers received her B.S. degree from Chicago State University and her Ph.D. degree from University of Illinois at Urbana-Champaign. In addition to the Kellogg School of Management at Northwestern University, she has taught financial accounting at the University of Illinois, Chicago, and at the Lake Forest Graduate School of Management. Internationally recognized as a dynamic teacher in executive education, she specializes in teaching nonfinancial managers how to read and understand internal and external financial reports, including the impact of international financial reporting standards (IFRS). Her current research relates to international financial reporting, performance measurement, and corporate governance of high-performance companies in the United States, Europe, India, and Australia. Her research has been published in leading journals. Her textbooks, coauthored with Belverd E. Needles, Jr., are used throughout the world and have received many awards, including the Textbook Excellence Award and the McGuffey Award from the Text and Academic Authors Association. She has also coauthored three interactive multimedia software products. She currently serves on the Board of the CPA Endowment Fund of Illinois and is immediate past-chair of the Board of Governors of the Winnetka Community House. She is a member of International Association of Accounting Education and Research, and Illinois CPA Society. She has served on the Board of Directors of the Illinois CPA Society, the Educational Foundation of Women in Accounting, and both the national as well as Chicago chapters of ASWA.

Principles of Financial Accounting

TWELFTH EDITION

CHAPTER 1
Accounting Principles and the Financial Statements

BUSINESS INSIGHT
Keep-Fit Center

On January 1, 2014, Jenny Mullin, an experienced fitness coach, started a business called Keep-Fit Center, which offers classes and private instruction in aerobics, yoga, and Pilates. By December 31, 2014, the center had generated $375,500, and its clients were praising its excellent service. Jenny is now considering expanding the business. She would need a bank loan and, to qualify, both she and the bank would have to use various financial measures to determine the business's ability to repay the loan (i.e., its profitability and liquidity). Whether a business is small, like Keep-Fit Center, or large, like **CVS**, the same financial measures are used to evaluate it.

1. CONCEPT ▶ *What is* accounting, *and what are the concepts that underlie it?*

2. ACCOUNTING APPLICATION ▶ *What are three financial statements that Keep-Fit Center will need to present in a way that is useful to Jenny and to the bank?*

3. BUSINESS APPLICATION ▶ *How do these financial statements help Jenny Mullin, as owner of Keep-Fit Center, measure progress toward the company's two main financial goals of profitability and liquidity? What additional financial statement information would be useful?*

LEARNING OBJECTIVES

LO 1 Define *accounting*, and explain the concepts underlying accounting measurement.

LO 2 Define *financial position*, and state the accounting equation.

LO 3 Identify the four basic financial statements and their interrelationships.

LO 4 Explain how generally accepted accounting principles (GAAP) and international financial reporting standards (IFRS) relate to financial statements and the independent CPA's report, and identify the organizations that influence GAAP.

LO 5 Identify the users of accounting information, and identify business goals, activities, and performance measures.

LO 6 Explain the importance of ethics in financial reporting.

Andresr/Shutterstock.com

CONCEPTS

LO 1 Concepts Underlying Accounting Measurement

Accounting is an information system that measures, processes, and communicates financial information about a business.[1] Accountants focus on the needs for financial information, whether the decision makers are inside or outside a business or other economic entity. An **economic entity** is a unit that exists independently, such as a business, hospital, or a governmental body. Accountants supply the information decision makers need to make "reasoned choices among alternative uses of scarce resources in the conduct of business and economic activities."[2] As shown in Exhibit 1, accounting is a link between business activities and decision makers.

- Accounting measures business activities by recording data about them for future use.
- The data are stored until needed and then processed to become useful information.
- The information is communicated through reports to decision makers.
- Based on information from accounting, decision makers take actions that affect subsequent business activities.

In other words, data about business activities are the input to the accounting system, and useful information for decision makers is the output.

Exhibit 1
Accounting as an Information System

© Cengage Learning 2014

Financial and Managerial Accounting

Accounting's role of measuring, processing, and communicating financial information is usually divided into financial accounting and managerial accounting. Although the functions of financial accounting and managerial accounting overlap, they can be distinguished by the principal users of their information.

Financial Accounting *External* decision makers use **financial accounting** to evaluate how well the business has achieved its goals. These reports, called **financial statements**, are a central feature of accounting. **CVS**, whose stock is traded on the New York Stock Exchange, sends its financial statements to its owners (called *stockholders*), its banks and other creditors, and government regulators. Financial statements report on a business's financial performance and are used extensively both inside and outside a business to evaluate its financial success.

It is important to distinguish accounting from bookkeeping and management information systems.

- **Bookkeeping** is the process of recording financial transactions and keeping financial records. It is mechanical and repetitive, yet an important part of accounting that is usually handled by computers.
- **Management information systems (MIS)** consist of the interconnected subsystems, including accounting, that provide the information needed to run a business.

Managerial Accounting *Internal* decision makers use information provided by **managerial accounting** about operating, investing, and financing activities. Managers and employees need information about how they have done in the past and what they can expect in the future. For example, **Gap, Inc.**, a retail clothing business, needs an operating report that tells how much was sold at each store and what costs were incurred, and it needs a budget that projects each store's sales and costs for the next year.

Accounting Measurement

To make an *accounting measurement*, the accountant must answer four basic questions:

- What is measured?
- When should the measurement be made?
- What value should be placed on what is measured?
- How should what is measured be classified?

Accountants debate the answers to these questions constantly, and the answers change as new knowledge and practice require. But the basis of today's accounting practice rests on a number of widely accepted concepts and conventions. We begin by focusing on the first question: What is measured? We discuss the other three questions in the next chapter.

Business Transactions **Business transactions** are economic events that affect a business's financial position. Businesses can have hundreds or even thousands of transactions every day. These transactions are the raw material of accounting reports.

A transaction can be an exchange of value (a purchase, sale, payment, collection, or loan) between two or more parties. A transaction also can be an economic event that does not involve an exchange. Some examples of nonexchange transactions are losses from fire, flood, explosion, and theft; physical wear and tear on machinery and equipment; and the day-by-day accumulation of interest.

To be recorded, a transaction must relate directly to a business entity. Suppose a customer buys toothpaste from **CVS** but buys shampoo from a competing store because CVS is out of shampoo. The transaction in which the toothpaste was sold is entered in CVS's records. However, the purchase of the shampoo is not entered in CVS's records because, even though it indirectly affects CVS economically (by losing a sale), it does not involve a direct exchange of value between CVS and the customer.

Money Measure All business transactions are recorded in terms of money. This concept is called **money measure**. Of course, nonfinancial information may also be recorded, but a business's transactions and activities are measured through the recording of monetary amounts. Money is the only factor common to all business transactions, and thus it is the only unit of measure capable of producing financial data that can be compared. The monetary unit a business uses depends on the country in which the business resides. For example, in the United States, the basic unit of money is the dollar. In China, it is the yuan; in Japan, the yen; in the European Union (EU), the euro; and in the United Kingdom, the pound. In international transactions, exchange rates must be used to translate from one currency to another. An **exchange rate** is the value of one currency in terms of another. For example, a British person purchasing goods from a U.S. company like **CVS** and paying in U.S. dollars must exchange British pounds for U.S. dollars before making payment. In effect, currencies are goods that can be bought and sold.

Exhibit 2 illustrates the exchange rates for several currencies in dollars. It shows the exchange rate for British pounds as $1.59 per pound on a particular date. Like the prices of many goods, currency prices change daily according to supply and demand. For example, a year and a half earlier, the exchange rate for British pounds was $1.63.

Exhibit 2
Examples of Foreign Exchange Rates

Country	Price in $U.S.	Country	Price in $U.S.
Australia (dollar)	1.07	Hong Kong (dollar)	0.13
Brazil (real)	0.58	Japan (yen)	0.012
Britain (pound)	1.59	Mexico (peso)	0.08
Canada (dollar)	1.00	Russia (ruble)	0.03
European Union (euro)	1.32	Singapore (dollar)	0.79

Source: The Wall Street Journal, February 18, 2012.

STUDY NOTE: *For accounting purposes, a business is always separate and distinct from its owners, creditors, and customers.*

Separate Entity   For accounting purposes, a business organization is a **separate entity**, distinct not only from its creditors and customers but also from its owners. It should have its own set of financial records, and its records and reports should refer only to its own affairs.

For example, Just Because Flowers Company should have a bank account separate from the account of Molly Dar, the owner. Molly Dar may own a home, a car, and other property, and she may have personal debts; but these are not the resources or debts of Just Because Flowers. Molly Dar may own another business, say a stationery shop. If she does, she should have a completely separate set of records for each business.

Forms of Business Organization

The three basic forms of business organization recognized as separate entities are the sole proprietorship, the partnership, and the corporation.

Sole Proprietorship   A **sole proprietorship** is a business owned by one person.* The owner takes all the profits or losses of the business and is liable for all its obligations. As Exhibit 3 shows, sole proprietorships represent the largest number of businesses in the United States, but typically they are the smallest in size.

STUDY NOTE: *A key disadvantage of a partnership is the unlimited liability of its owners. Unlimited liability can be avoided by organizing the business as a corporation or, in some states, by forming what is known as a limited liability partnership (LLP).*

Partnership   A **partnership** is like a sole proprietorship in most ways, but it has two or more owners. The partners share the profits and losses of the business according to a prearranged formula. Generally, any partner can obligate the business to another party, and the personal resources of each partner can be called on to pay the obligations. A partnership must be dissolved if the ownership changes, as when a partner leaves or dies. If the business is to continue as a partnership after this occurs, a new partnership must be formed.

Corporation   Both the sole proprietorship and the partnership are convenient ways of separating the owners' commercial activities from their personal activities. Legally,

---

*Accounting for a sole proprietorship is simpler than accounting for a partnership or corporation. For that reason, we focus on the sole proprietorship in the early part of this book. At critical points, however, we call attention to the essential differences between accounting for a sole proprietorship and accounting for a partnership or corporation.

Oleg V. Ivanov/Shutterstock.com

Because this surf shop is a partnership, the owners share the profits and losses of the business, and their personal resources can be called on to pay the obligations of the business.

however, there is no economic separation between the owners and the businesses. A **corporation**, on the other hand, is a business unit chartered by the state and legally separate from its owners (the stockholders). The **stockholders**, whose ownership is represented by shares of stock, do not directly control the corporation's operations. Instead, they elect a board of directors to run the corporation for their benefit. In exchange for their limited involvement in the corporation's operations, stockholders enjoy **limited liability**; that is, their risk of loss is limited to the amount they paid for their shares. Thus, stockholders are often willing to invest in risky, but potentially profitable, activities. Also, because stockholders can sell their shares without dissolving the corporation, the life of a corporation is unlimited and not subject to the whims or health of a proprietor or a partner.

The characteristics of corporations make them very efficient in amassing capital, which enables them to grow extremely large. As Exhibit 3 shows, even though corporations are fewer in number than sole proprietorships and partnerships, they contribute much more to the U.S. economy in monetary terms. For example, in 2011, **ExxonMobil** generated more revenues than all but 28 of the world's countries.[3]

Exhibit 3
Number and Receipts (Revenues) of U.S. Proprietorships, Partnerships, and Corporations

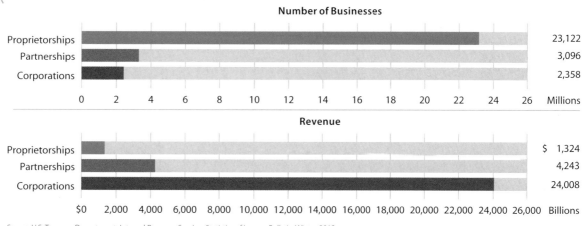

Number of Businesses

Proprietorships	23,122
Partnerships	3,096
Corporations	2,358

0 2 4 6 8 10 12 14 16 18 20 22 24 26 Millions

Revenue

Proprietorships	$ 1,324
Partnerships	4,243
Corporations	24,008

$0 2,000 4,000 6,000 8,000 10,000 12,000 14,000 16,000 18,000 20,000 22,000 24,000 26,000 Billions

Source: U.S. Treasury Department, Internal Revenue Service, *Statistics of Income Bulletin*, Winter 2012.

© Aija / iStockphoto.com

Business Perspective
Are Most Corporations Big or Small Businesses?

Most people think of corporations as large national or global companies whose shares of stock are held by thousands of people and institutions. Indeed, corporations can be huge and have many stockholders. However, of the approximately 4 million corporations in the United States, only about 15,000 have stock that is publicly bought and sold. The vast majority of corporations are small businesses privately held by a few stockholders. Illinois alone has more than 250,000 corporations. Thus, the study of corporations is just as relevant to small businesses as it is to large ones.

APPLY IT!

Match each description with the appropriate term. (*Hint*: Terms may be used more than once.)

1. Owners have limited liability
2. Requires an exchange of value between two or more parties
3. Owned by only one person
4. Multiple co-owners
5. An amount associated with a business transaction
6. Management appointed by board of directors
7. Distinct from customers, lenders, and owners
8. Biggest segment of the economy

a. Business transactions
b. Corporation(s)
c. Money measure
d. Partnership
e. Sole proprietorship
f. Separate entity

SOLUTION

1. b; 2. a; 3. e; 4. d; 5.c; 6. b; 7. f; 8. b

TRY IT! SE1, SE2, E1A, E2A, E3A, E12A, E1B, E2B, E3B, E12B

LO 2 Concepts Underlying Financial Position

Financial position refers to a company's economic resources, such as cash, inventory, and buildings, and the claims against those resources at a particular time. Another term for claims is *equities*.

Every company has two types of equities: creditors' equities, such as bank loans, and owner's equity. The sum of these equities equals a company's resources:

$$\text{Economic Resources} = \text{Creditors' Equities} + \text{Owner's Equity}$$

In accounting terminology, economic resources are called *assets* and creditors' equities are called *liabilities*. So the equation can be written like this:

$$\text{Assets} = \text{Liabilities} + \text{Owner's Equity}$$

This equation is known as the **accounting equation (A = L + OE)**. The two sides of the equation must always be equal, or "in balance," as shown in Exhibit 4. To evaluate the financial effects of business activities, it is important to understand their effects on this equation.

Exhibit 4
The Accounting Equation

A = L + OE

© Cengage Learning 2014

Assets

Assets are the economic resources that are expected to benefit the company's future operations. Certain kinds of assets—for example, cash and money that customers owe to the company (called *accounts receivable*)—are monetary items. Other assets—inventories (goods held for sale), land, buildings, and equipment—are nonmonetary, physical items. Still other assets—the rights granted by patents, trademarks, and copyrights—are nonphysical.

Liabilities

Liabilities are a business's present obligations to pay cash, transfer assets, or provide services to other entities in the future. Among these obligations are amounts owed to suppliers for goods or services bought on credit (called *accounts payable*), borrowed money (e.g., money owed on bank loans), salaries and wages owed to employees, taxes owed to the government, and services to be performed.

Liabilities are claims recognized by law. That is, the law gives creditors the right to force the sale of a company's assets if the company fails to pay its debts. Creditors have rights over owners and must be paid before the owners receive anything, even if the payment of debt uses up all the assets.

Owner's Equity

Owner's equity represents the claims by the owner of a business to the assets of the business. Theoretically, owner's equity is what would be left if all liabilities were paid, and it is sometimes said to equal **net assets**. By rearranging the accounting equation, we can define owner's equity this way:

$$\text{Owner's Equity} = \text{Assets} - \text{Liabilities}$$

Owner's equity is affected by the owner's investments in and withdrawals from the business and by the business's revenues and expenses.

- **Owner's investments** are assets that the owner puts into the business (e.g., by transferring cash from a personal bank account to the business's bank account). In this case, the assets (cash) of the business increase, and the owner's equity in those assets also increases.
- **Withdrawals** are assets that the owner takes out of the business (e.g., by transferring cash from the business's bank account to a personal bank account). In this case, the assets of the business decrease, as does the owner's equity in the business.

Simply stated, **revenues** and **expenses** are the increases and decreases in owner's equity that result from operating a business.

- ▲ For example, the amounts customers pay (or agree to pay in the future) to Keep-Fit Center for its exercise service are revenues for Keep-Fit. Keep-Fit's assets (cash or accounts receivable) increase, as does its owner's equity in those assets.
- ▼ On the other hand, the amount Keep-Fit must pay out (or agree to pay out) for rent and wages to instructors so that it can provide its service are expenses. In this case, the assets (cash) decrease or the liabilities (accounts payable) increase, and the owner's equity decreases.

Generally, a company is successful if its revenues exceed its expenses.

- ▲ When revenues exceed expenses, the difference is called **net income**.
- ▼ When expenses exceed revenues, the difference is called **net loss**.

In summary, owner's equity is the accumulated net income (revenues − expenses) minus withdrawals over the life of the business.

APPLY IT!

Stevenson Company had assets of $140,000 and liabilities of $60,000 at the beginning of the year, and assets of $200,000 and liabilities of $70,000 at the end of the year. During the year, $20,000 was invested in the business, and withdrawals of $24,000 were made. What amount of net income did the company earn during the year?

Beginning of the year

Assets	=	Liabilities	+	Owner's Equity
$140,000	=	$60,000	+	$ 80,000

During the year

		Investment	+	20,000
		Withdrawals	−	24,000
		Net income		?

End of year

$200,000	=	$70,000	+	$130,000

SOLUTION

Net income = $54,000

Start by finding the owner's equity at the beginning of the year: $140,000 − $60,000 = $80,000

Then find the owner's equity at the end of the year: $200,000 − $70,000 = $130,000

Then determine net income by calculating how the transactions during the year led to the owner's equity amount at the end of the year: $80,000 + $20,000 − $24,000 + net income = $130,000; net income = $54,000

TRY IT! SE3, SE4, SE5, SE6, E4A, E5A, E4B, E5B

SECTION 2

ACCOUNTING APPLICATIONS

RELEVANT LEARNING OBJECTIVES

LO 3 Identify the four basic financial statements and their interrelationships.

LO 4 Explain how generally accepted accounting principles (GAAP) and international financial reporting standards (IFRS) relate to financial statements and the independent CPA's report, and identify the organizations that influence GAAP.

LO 3 Financial Statements

Financial statements are the primary means of communicating accounting information about a business to those who have an interest in the business. These statements model the business enterprise in financial terms. As is true of all models, however, financial statements are not perfect pictures of the real thing. Four major financial statements are used to communicate accounting information: the income statement, the statement of owner's equity, the balance sheet, and the statement of cash flows. Exhibit 5 presents an overview of these four financial statements and their interrelationships. The following sections examine them in more detail.

Income Statement

The **income statement** summarizes the revenues earned and expenses incurred by a business over an accounting period. Many people consider it the most important financial report because it shows whether a business achieved its profitability goal—that is, whether it earned an acceptable income. Exhibit 6 shows that Roland Consultancy had revenues of $14,000. From this amount, total expenses of $5,600 were deducted to arrive at net income of $8,400. To show the period to which the statement applies, it is dated "For the Month Ended December 31, 2014."

Statement of Owner's Equity

The **statement of owner's equity** shows the changes in owner's equity over an accounting period. In Exhibit 7, beginning owner's equity is zero because Roland Consultancy began operations in this period. During the month, the owner, Tom Roland, invested $200,000 in the business, and the company earned an income (as shown on the income statement) of $8,400. Withdrawals of $2,400 by the owner are deducted from this amount, leaving an ending balance of $206,000.

Balance Sheet

The purpose of a **balance sheet** is to show the financial position of a business on a certain date, usually the end of the month or year. For this reason, it often is called the *statement of financial position*. It's important to note that the date on the balance sheet is a single date, whereas the dates on the other three statements cover a period of time, such as a month, quarter, or year. The balance sheet presents a view of the business as the holder of resources, or assets, that are equal to the claims against those assets. The claims consist of the company's liabilities and the owner's equity. Exhibit 8 shows that Roland Consultancy has several categories of assets, which total $208,400. These assets equal the total liabilities of $2,400 plus the owner's equity of $206,000. Notice that the amount of the owner's capital account on the balance sheet comes from the ending balance on the statement of owner's equity.

Exhibit 5
Financial Statement Relationships

Exhibit 6
Income Statement for Roland Consultancy

Roland Consultancy
Income Statement
For the Month Ended December 31, 2014

Revenues:		
Consulting fees earned		$14,000
Expenses:		
Equipment rental expense	$2,800	
Wages expense	1,600	
Utilities expense	1,200	
Total expenses		5,600
Net income		$ 8,400

Exhibit 7
Statement of Owner's Equity for Roland Consultancy

Roland Consultancy
Statement of Owner's Equity
For the Month Ended December 31, 2014

T. Roland, capital, December 1, 2014	$ 0
Investment by T. Roland	200,000
Net income for the month	8,400
Subtotal	$208,400
Less withdrawals	2,400
T. Roland, capital, December 31, 2014	$206,000

Exhibit 8
Balance Sheet for Roland Consultancy

Roland Consultancy
Balance Sheet
December 31, 2014

Assets		**Liabilities**	
Cash	$ 62,400	Accounts payable	$ 2,400
Accounts receivable	4,000	Total liabilities	$ 2,400
Supplies	2,000		
Land	40,000	**Owner's Equity**	
Buildings	100,000	T. Roland, capital	206,000
Total assets	$208,400	Total liabilities and owner's equity	$208,400

Statement of Cash Flows

Whereas the income statement focuses on a company's profitability, the **statement of cash flows** focuses on *liquidity*, that is, balancing the inflows and outflows of cash to enable it to operate and pay its bills when they are due. **Cash flows** are the inflows and outflows of cash into and out of a business. Net cash flows are the difference between the inflows and outflows.

As you can see in Exhibit 9, the statement of cash flows is organized according to three major business activities.

- **Cash flows from operating activities:** The first section of Exhibit 9 shows the cash produced by business operations. Roland's operating activities produced net cash flows of $4,800 (liquidity) compared to net income of $8,400 (profitability). The company used cash to increase accounts receivable and supplies. However, by borrowing funds, it increased accounts payable. This is not a good trend, which Roland should try to reverse in future months.
- **Cash flows from investing activities:** Roland used cash to expand by purchasing land and a building.
- **Cash flows from financing activities:** Roland obtained most of its cash from the owner, who then made a small cash withdrawal.

Overall, Roland had a net increase in cash of $62,400, due in large part to the investment by the owner. In future months, Roland must generate more cash through operations.

Exhibit 9
Statement of Cash Flows for Roland Consultancy

Roland Consultancy
Statement of Cash Flows
For the Month Ended December 31, 2014

Cash flows from operating activities:		
Net income		$ 8,400
Adjustments to reconcile net income to net cash flows from operating activities:		
(Increase) in accounts receivable	$ (4,000)	
(Increase) in supplies	(2,000)	
Increase in accounts payable	2,400	(3,600)
Net cash flows from operating activities		$ 4,800
Cash flows from investing activities:		
Purchase of land	$ (40,000)	
Purchase of building	(100,000)	
Net cash flows used by investing activities		(140,000)
Cash flows from financing activities:		
Investments by owner	$ 200,000	
Withdrawals	(2,400)	
Net cash flows from financing activities		197,600
Net increase (decrease) in cash		$ 62,400
Cash at beginning of month		0
Cash at end of month		$ 62,400

Note: Parentheses indicate a cash outflow.

The statement of cash flows is related directly to the other three financial statements. Notice that net income comes from the income statement and that withdrawals come from the statement of owner's equity. The other items in the statement represent changes in the balance sheet accounts: accounts receivable, supplies, accounts payable, land, and buildings.

Relationships Among the Financial Statements

STUDY NOTE: *Notice the sequence in which these statements are prepared: income statement, statement of owner's equity, balance sheet, and finally, the statement of cash flows.*

Exhibit 10 illustrates the relationships among the four financial statements for Roland Consultancy. Notice the similarity of the headings at the top of each statement. Each identifies the company and the kind of statement. The income statement, the statement of owner's equity, and the statement of cash flows indicate the period to which they apply; the balance sheet gives the specific date to which it applies.

Exhibit 10

Income Statement, Statement of Owner's Equity, Balance Sheet, and Statement of Cash Flows for Roland Consultancy

Roland Consultancy
Statement of Cash Flows
For the Month Ended December 31, 2014

Cash flows from operating activities:		
Net income	$ 8,400	
Adjustments to reconcile net income to net cash flows from operating activities:		
(Increase) in accounts receivable	$ (4,000)	
(Increase) in supplies	(2,000)	
Increase in accounts payable	2,400	(3,600)
Net cash flows from operating activities		$ 4,800
Cash flows from investing activities:		
Purchase of land	$ (40,000)	
Purchase of building	(100,000)	
Net cash flows used by investing activities		(140,000)
Cash flows from financing activities:		
Investments by owner	$ 200,000	
Withdrawals	(2,400)	
Net cash flows from financing activities		197,600
Net increase (decrease) in cash		$ 62,400
Cash at beginning of month		0
Cash at end of month		$ 62,400

Roland Consultancy
Income Statement
For the Month Ended December 31, 2014

Revenues:		
Consulting fees		$14,000
Expenses:		
Equipment rental expense	$2,800	
Wages expense	1,600	
Utilities expense	1,200	
Total expenses		5,600
Net income		$ 8,400

Roland Consultancy
Statement of Owner's Equity
For the Month Ended December 31, 2014

T. Roland, capital, December 1, 2014	$ 0
Investment by T. Roland	200,000
Net income for the month	8,400
Subtotal	$208,400
Less withdrawals	2,400
T. Roland, capital, December 31, 2014	$206,000

Roland Consultancy
Balance Sheet
December 31, 2014

Assets		Liabilities	
Cash	$ 62,400	Accounts payable	$ 2,400
Accounts receivable	4,000	Total liabilities	$ 2,400
Supplies	2,000		
Land	40,000	**Owner's Equity**	
Buildings	100,000	T. Roland, capital	206,000
		Total liabilities and	
Total assets	$208,400	owner's equity	$208,400

Complete the following financial statements by determining the amounts that correspond to the letters. (Assume no new investments by owners.)

Income Statement

Revenues	$2,775
Expenses	(a)
Net income	$ (b)

Statement of Owner's Equity

Beginning balance	$7,250
Net income	(c)
Less withdrawals	500
Ending balance	$7,500

Balance Sheet

Total assets	$ (d)
Total liabilities	$4,000
Owner's equity	(e)
Total liabilities and owner's equity	$ (f)

SOLUTION

Net income links the income statement and the statement of owner's equity. The ending balance of owner's equity links the statement of owner's equity and the balance sheet.

Thus, start with (c), which must equal $750 ($7,250 + $750 − $500 = $7,500). Then, (b) equals (c), or $750. Thus, (a) must equal $2,025 ($2,775 − $2,025 = $750). Because (e) equals $7,500 (ending balance from the statement of owner's equity), (f) must equal $11,500 ($4,000 + $7,500 = $11,500). Finally, (d) must equal (f), or $11,500.

TRY IT! SE7, SE8, E6A, E7A, E8A, E9A, E10A, E11A, E6B, E7B, E8B, E9B, E10B, E11B

LO 4 Generally Accepted Accounting Principles

To ensure that financial statements are understandable to their users, a set of **generally accepted accounting principles (GAAP)** has been developed to provide guidelines for financial accounting. "Generally accepted accounting principles encompass the conventions, rules, and procedures necessary to define accepted accounting practice at a particular time."[4] In other words, GAAP arises from wide agreement on the theory and practice of accounting at a particular time. These "principles" evolve to meet the needs of decision makers, and they change as circumstances change or as better methods are developed.

In this book, we present accounting practice, or GAAP, as it is today, and we try to explain the reasons or theory on which the practice is based. Accounting is a discipline that is always growing, changing, and improving. However, it may take years for new accounting discoveries to be implemented. As a result, you may encounter practices that seem contradictory. In some cases, we point out new directions in accounting.

GAAP and the Independent CPA's Report

Many companies of all sizes have their financial statements audited by an independent **certified public accountant (CPA)**. *Independent* means that the CPA is not an employee of the company being audited and has no financial or other compromising ties to it. CPAs are licensed by all states to protect the public by ensuring the quality of professional service. The firms listed in Exhibit 11 employ about 25 percent of all CPAs.

Exhibit 11
Large International Certified Public Accounting Firms

Firm	Home Office	Some Major Clients
Deloitte & Touche	New York	General Motors, Procter & Gamble
Ernst & Young	New York	Coca-Cola, McDonald's
KPMG	New York	General Electric, Xerox
PricewaterhouseCoopers	New York	ExxonMobil, IBM, Ford

An **audit** is an examination of a company's financial statements and the accounting systems, controls, and records that produced them. The purpose of the audit is to ascertain that the financial statements have been prepared in accordance with generally accepted accounting principles. If the independent CPA is satisfied that this standard has been met, his or her report contains the following language:

> *In our opinion, the financial statements . . . present fairly, in all material respects . . . in conformity with generally accepted accounting principles . . .*

This wording emphasizes that accounting and auditing are not exact sciences. The auditor can render only an opinion about whether the financial statements *present fairly* or conform *in all material respects* to GAAP. The auditor's report does not preclude minor or immaterial errors in the financial statements. However, a favorable report from the auditor does imply that, on the whole, investors and creditors can rely on the financial statements. In other words, the audit lends credibility to a set of financial statements. Auditors offer opinions, based on testing, about the fairness of the presentation of a company's financial information, but they cannot attest to the absolute accuracy of such information.

Historically, auditors have enjoyed a strong reputation for competence and independence. The independent audit has been an important factor in the worldwide growth of financial markets.

Organizations That Issue Accounting Standards

Two organizations issue accounting standards that are used in the United States: the FASB and the IASB.

- The **Financial Accounting Standards Board (FASB)** has been designated by the Securities and Exchange Commission (SEC) to issue *Statements of Financial Accounting Standards*. The FASB organizes these statements including any amendments, interpretations, or other references to them into a topical U.S. GAAP compendium called an American Standard Codification (ASC). This codification, which is available through the FASB website, makes it easy to find all references to a particular topic, such as revenues, in one place.

- The **International Accounting Standards Board (IASB)**, which issues **international financial reporting standards (IFRS)**, is becoming increasingly important because of the acceptance of its standards in many financial markets throughout the world. The SEC now allows foreign companies to use these standards in the United States rather than having to convert their statements to U.S. GAAP. The SEC is also presently considering allowing U.S. public companies to use IFRS.

Other Organizations That Influence GAAP

Many other organizations directly or indirectly influence GAAP:

- The **Public Company Accounting Oversight Board (PCAOB)**, a governmental body created by the Sarbanes-Oxley Act, has wide powers to determine the standards that auditors must follow. The PCAOB regulates audits of public companies registered with the SEC.
- The **American Institute of Certified Public Accountants (AICPA)**, a professional association, influences accounting practice through the activities of its senior technical committees. In addition to endorsing standards issued by the FASB, the AICPA has determined that standards issued by the IASB are also of high quality

International Perspective
IFRS The Arrival of International Financial Reporting Standards in the United States

Over the next few years, international financial reporting standards (IFRS) will become much more important in the United States and globally. The International Accounting Standards Board (IASB) has been working with the Financial Accounting Standards Board (FASB) and similar boards in other nations to achieve identical or nearly identical standards worldwide under what is called the convergence project. IFRS are now required in many parts of the world, including Europe, Canada, and parts of Asia. The Securities and Exchange Commission (SEC) allows foreign registrants in the United States to use IFRS. This is a major development because in the past, the SEC required foreign registrants to explain how the standards used in their statements differed from U.S. standards. This change affects approximately 10 percent of all public U.S. companies. In addition, the SEC may in the near future allow U.S. companies to use IFRS.[5]

and are thus acceptable for use in the United States.* The AICPA is the primary professional organization of certified public accountants.

- The **Securities and Exchange Commission (SEC)**, a governmental agency, has the legal power to set and enforce accounting practices for companies whose securities are offered for sale to the general public.
- The **Governmental Accounting Standards Board (GASB)**, a separate but related body to the FASB, issues accounting standards for state and local governments.
- The **Internal Revenue Service (IRS)** interprets and enforces the tax laws that specify the rules for determining taxable income. In some cases, the rules conflict with good accounting practice, but they are nonetheless important.

Professional Conduct

The code of professional ethics of the American Institute of Certified Public Accountants (and adopted, with variations, by each state) governs the conduct of CPAs. Fundamental to this code is the responsibility of CPAs to clients, creditors, investors, and anyone else who relies on their work. The code requires CPAs to act with:

- **Integrity**: Be honest and candid and subordinate personal gain to service and the public trust.
- **Objectivity**: Be impartial and intellectually honest.
- **Independence**: Avoid all relationships that impair or appear to impair objectivity.

Research shows that these are the attributes that business decision makers and the investing public most closely associate with CPAs.[6] The accountant must also exercise **due care** in all activities, carrying out professional responsibilities with competence and diligence. For example, an accountant must not accept a job for which he or she is not qualified, even at the risk of losing a client to another firm, and careless work is unacceptable. These broad principles are supported by more specific rules that public accountants must follow. For instance, with certain exceptions, client information must be kept strictly confidential. Accountants who violate the rules can be disciplined or even suspended from practice.

The **Institute of Management Accountants (IMA)**, the primary professional association of managerial accountants, also has a code of professional conduct. It emphasizes that managerial accountants have a responsibility:

- To be competent in their jobs
- To keep information confidential except when authorized or legally required to disclose it
- To maintain integrity and avoid conflicts of interest
- To communicate information objectively and without bias[7]

APPLY IT!

Match the common acronym with its description.

1. GAAP
2. IFRS
3. CPA
4. FASB
5. IASB
6. PCAOB
7. AICPA
8. SEC

a. Sets U.S. accounting standards
b. Audits financial statements
c. Established by the Sarbanes-Oxley Act
d. Sets international accounting standards
e. Established by the FASB
f. Established by the IASB
g. Influences accounting standards through member CPAs
h. Receives audited financial statements of public companies

SOLUTION

1. e; 2. f; 3. b; 4. a; 5. d; 6. c; 7. g; 8. h

TRY IT! E13A, E14A, E13B, E14B

---

*Established in January 2007, the Private Company Financial Reporting Committee of the AICPA is charged with amending FASB accounting standards so that they better suit the needs of private companies, especially as they relate to the cost or benefit of implementing certain standards. A Blue-Ribbon Committee established by the FASB, AICPA, and other organizations is currently studying this issue. Its recommendations could ultimately result in two sets of standards, one for private companies and one for public companies.

BUSINESS APPLICATIONS

LO 5 Decision Makers: The Users of Accounting Information

As shown in Exhibit 12, the people who use accounting information to make decisions fall into three categories: managers (internal users of accounting information), outsiders who have a direct financial interest in the business, and outsiders who have an indirect financial interest. These categories apply to governmental and not-for-profit organizations as well as to profit-oriented ventures.

Exhibit 12
The Users of Accounting Information

Management

Management is responsible for ensuring that a company meets its goals of profitability and liquidity. All companies pursue these goals by engaging in operating, investing, and financing activities. Making decisions about these activities is the basic function of managers; and to make good decisions, they must have timely and valid accounting information.

To make good decisions, Jenny Mullin at Keep-Fit Center and other owners and managers need answers to such questions as:

■ What were the company's earnings during the past quarter?
■ Is the rate of return to the owners adequate?
■ Does the company have enough cash?
■ Which products or services are most profitable?

Users with a Direct Financial Interest

Most companies periodically publish financial statements that report their success in meeting the goals of profitability and liquidity. These statements, discussed earlier, show what has happened in the past and are important indicators of what will happen in the future. Many people outside a company, particularly investors and creditors and potential investors and creditors, study these statements carefully.

Investors **Investors**, like Jenny Mullin, owner of the Keep-Fit Center, and the stockholders who have invested in **CVS**, have a direct financial interest in the success of their companies. They depend on financial statements to evaluate how their businesses have performed. A thorough study of a company's financial statements helps potential investors judge the prospects for a profitable investment.

Creditors **Creditors**, those who lend money or deliver goods and services before being paid, are interested mainly in whether a company will have the cash to pay interest charges and to repay the debt on time. They study a company's cash flow to determine its liquidity; they also look at its profitability. Banks, finance companies, mortgage companies, securities firms, insurance firms, suppliers, and other lenders must analyze a company's financial position before they make a loan.

Users with an Indirect Financial Interest

In recent years, governmental and public groups have become one of the largest and most important users of accounting information. These groups include tax authorities and regulatory agencies.

Tax Authorities Government at every level is financed through the collection of taxes. Companies and individuals pay many kinds of taxes, including federal, state, and city income taxes; Social Security and other payroll taxes; excise taxes; and sales taxes. Proper reporting is generally a matter of law and can be very complicated.

Regulatory Agencies Most companies must report periodically to one or more regulatory agencies at the federal, state, and local levels. For example, all publicly traded corporations must report periodically to the Securities and Exchange Commission (SEC). This body, set up by Congress to protect the public, regulates the issuing, buying, and selling of stocks in the United States.

Other Groups Other groups with an indirect financial interest in accounting information include the following:

- **Labor unions:** As they prepare for contract negotiations with a company, labor unions study the company's financial statements. A company's income and expenses often play an important role in these negotiations.
- **Advisors of investors and creditors:** Financial analysts, brokers, underwriters, lawyers, economists, and the financial press all have an indirect interest in the financial performance and prospects of a business.
- **Consumer groups, customers, and the general public:** The public has become more concerned about financing and earnings as well as about the effects that corporations have on inflation, the environment, social issues, and the quality of life.
- **Economic planners:** The President's Council of Economic Advisers and the Federal Reserve Board use aggregated accounting information to set and evaluate economic policies and programs.

Governmental and Not-for-Profit Organizations

More than 30 percent of the U.S. economy is generated by governmental and not-for-profit organizations (hospitals, universities, professional organizations, and charities). The managers of these diverse entities need accounting information and knowledge of how to use it. Their functions include raising funds from investors (including owners), creditors, taxpayers, and donors and deploying scarce resources. They must also plan how to pay for operations and to repay creditors on a timely basis. In addition, they have an obligation to report their financial performance to legislators, boards, and donors, as well as to deal with tax authorities, regulators, and labor unions. Although most of the examples in this text focus on business enterprises, the same basic principles apply to governmental and not-for-profit organizations.

Business Goals and Activities

A **business** is an economic unit that aims to sell goods and services at prices that will provide an adequate return to its owners. The list that follows contains the names of some well-known businesses and the principal goods or services that they sell. These businesses have similar goals and engage in similar activities, as shown in Exhibit 13.

Wal-Mart Corp.	Comprehensive discount goods
Reebok International Ltd.	Athletic footwear and clothing
Best Buy Co.	Consumer electronics, personal computers
Wendy's International Inc.	Food service
Starbucks Corp.	Coffee and related service
Southwest Airlines Co.	Passenger airline service

Exhibit 13
Business Goals and Activities

© Cengage Learning 2014

The two major goals of all businesses are profitability and liquidity.

- **Profitability** is the ability to earn enough income to attract and hold investment capital.
- **Liquidity** is the ability to have enough cash to pay debts when they are due.

To succeed and even survive, a company must meet both goals. For example, **Toyota** may sell many cars at a price that earns a profit, but if its customers do not pay quickly enough to enable Toyota to pay its suppliers and employees, the company may not meet the goal of liquidity, which could force it into bankruptcy.

All businesses, including Jenny Mullin's Keep-Fit Center, pursue their goals by engaging in operating, investing, and financing activities.

- **Operating activities** include buying, producing, and selling goods and services; hiring managers and other employees; and paying taxes.
- **Investing activities** involve spending a company's capital in ways that will help it achieve its goals. They include buying resources for operating the business, such as land, buildings, and equipment, and selling those resources when they are no longer needed.
- **Financing activities** involve obtaining adequate funds to begin operating the business and to continue operating it. They include obtaining capital from creditors, such as banks and suppliers, and from the company's owners. They also include repaying creditors and paying a return to the owners.

Business Perspective
What Does CVS Have to Say About Itself?

CVS, a major drug store chain, describes the company's progress in meeting its major business objectives as follows:

- **Liquidity:** "We generated $4.6 billion in free cash for the year, exceeding our goal, and returned more than $3.5 billion to our shareholders in the form of dividends and share repurchases."

- **Profitability:** "2011 was a year of great accomplishment for CVS Caremark. We executed successfully on a number of key initiatives across the Company and reported solid financial results, delivering on our promises. Our retail business continued to post strong top- and bottom-line results, and our PBM enjoyed strong revenue growth, another very successful selling season, and great progress on several important initiatives."[8]

CVS's main business activities are shown at the right.

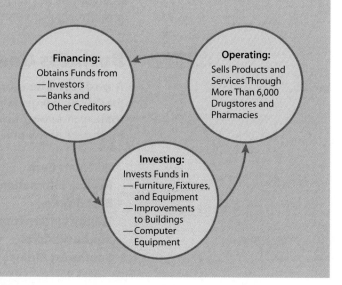

Financial Analysis

CASH FLOW

Financial analysis is the use of financial statements to determine that a business is well managed and is achieving its goals. The effectiveness of financial analysis depends on the use of relevant performance measures and financial ratios.

To be relevant, **performance measures** must be well aligned with the two major goals of business—profitability and liquidity. Profitability is commonly measured in net income, and cash flows are a common measure of liquidity. For example, in 2011, **CVS** had net income of $3,457 million and cash flows from operating activities of $5,856 million. These figures indicate that CVS was both profitable and liquid. In 2008, however, **General Motors** curtailed spending on new auto and truck models because its earnings were negative and, even worse, its cash flows were negative. Its cash flow problem led to its bankruptcy and a government bailout in 2009. Clearly, General Motors was not meeting either its profitability or liquidity goals.

Financial ratios show how the elements of financial statements relate to each other. They allow for comparisons from one period to another and from one company to another. For example, to assess Keep-Fit Center's profitability, it would be helpful to consider the ratio of its earnings to total assets, and for liquidity, the ratio of its cash flows to total assets.

APPLY IT!

Match the terms that follow with the definitions or the type of user of accounting information. (*Hint:* Some answers may be used more than once.)

1. Managerial accounting
2. Management
3. Financial accounting
4. Investing activities
5. Regulatory agencies
6. Financing activities
7. Profitability
8. Tax authorities
9. Investors
10. Liquidity
11. Creditors
12. Operating activities

a. A business goal
b. Engaged in by all businesses
c. Financial information developed for external users
d. Internal user
e. Direct external user
f. Indirect external user
g. Accounting information used by management

SOLUTION

1. g; 2. d; 3. c; 4. b; 5. f; 6. b; 7. a; 8. f; 9. e; 10. a; 11. e; 12. b

TRY IT! SE9, E12A, E13A, E12B, E13B

LO 6 Ethical Financial Reporting

Ethics is a code of conduct that applies to everyday life. It addresses the question of whether actions are right or wrong. Actions—whether ethical or unethical, right or wrong—are the product of individual decisions. Thus, when an organization uses false advertising, cheats customers, pollutes the environment, or treats employees unfairly, the management and other employees have made a conscious decision to act in this manner.

Ethics is especially important in preparing financial reports because users of these reports must depend on the good faith of the people involved in their preparation. Users have no other assurance that the reports are accurate and fully disclose all relevant facts.

The intentional preparation of misleading financial statements is called **fraudulent financial reporting**.[9] It can result from:

- Distortion of records (e.g., the manipulation of inventory records)
- Falsified transactions (e.g., fictitious sales)
- Misapplication of various accounting principles

There are a number of motives for fraudulent reporting—for instance, to cover up financial weakness to obtain a higher price when a company is sold; to meet the expectations of investors, owners, and financial analysts; or to obtain a loan. The incentive can also be personal gain, such as additional compensation, promotion, or avoidance of penalties for poor performance.

Whatever the motive for fraudulent financial reporting, it can have dire consequences, as the accounting scandals at **Enron Corporation** and **WorldCom** in 2001 and 2002, respectively, attest. Unethical financial reporting and accounting practices at those two major corporations caused thousands of people to lose their jobs, their investment incomes, and their pensions. They also resulted in prison sentences and fines for the corporate executives who were involved.

In response to these scandals, the **Sarbanes-Oxley Act** of 2002 regulates financial reporting of public companies and their auditors. This legislation requires chief executives and chief financial officers of all publicly traded U.S. companies to swear that, based on their knowledge, their quarterly statements and annual reports filed with the Securities and Exchange Commission (SEC) are accurate and complete. Violation can result in criminal penalties.

Management expresses its duty to ensure that financial reports are not false or misleading in the management report that appears in the company's annual report. For example, in its management report, **Target Corporation** makes the following statement:

> *Management is responsible for the consistency, integrity, and presentation of the information in the Annual Report.*[10]

However, it is accountants, not management, who physically prepare and audit financial reports. They must apply accounting concepts in such a way as to present a fair view of a company's operations and financial position and to avoid misleading the readers of their reports. Accountants have a responsibility—not only to the profession but also to employers, clients, and society as a whole—to ensure that their reports provide accurate, reliable information. The historically high regard for the accounting profession is evidence that most accountants have upheld the ethics of the profession.

APPLY IT!

Match each definition with the appropriate terms that follow.

1. The intentional preparation of misleading financial statements.
2. A code of conduct that applies to everyday life.
3. Regulates financial reporting of public companies and their auditors.
4. Has a duty to ensure that financial reports are not false or misleading.

a. Ethics
b. Fraudulent financial reporting
c. Management
d. Sarbanes-Oxley Act

SOLUTION

1. b; 2. a; 3. d; 4. c

TRY IT! SE10, E15A, E15B

TriLevel Problem

Keep-Fit Center

The beginning of this chapter focused on Keep-Fit Center. The owner, Jenny Mullin, was considering expanding the business. Complete the following requirements in order to answer the questions posed at the beginning of the chapter.

Section 1: Concepts
What is accounting *and what are the concepts that underlie it?*

Section 2: Accounting Applications
What are three financial statements that Keep-Fit Center will need to present in a way that is useful to Mullin and to the bank?

To answer this question, use the financial statement items and amounts listed below from the records of Keep-Fit Center for the year ended April 30, 2014, the company's first year of operations, and prepare the following:

- income statement
- statement of owner's equity
- balance sheet

For examples of the statements, refer to Exhibit 10.

Accounts payable	$ 19,000
Accounts receivable	104,000
Cash	111,000
Equipment	47,000
Fees revenue	375,000
Investment by J. Mullin	100,000
Marketing expense	18,000
Salaries expense	172,000
Salaries payable	78,000
Rent expense	91,000
Supplies	2,000
Supplies expense	6,000
Utilities expense	11,000
Withdrawals	10,000

Section 3: Business Applications
How do these financial statements help Jenny Mullin, as owner of Keep-Fit Center, measure progress toward the company's two main financial goals of profitability and liquidity? What additional financial statement information would be useful?

SOLUTION

Section 1: Concepts
Accounting is an information system that measures, processes, and communicates financial information about a business useful to internal and external decision makers. Accounting achieves its objectives by *measuring* the effects of *business transactions* on specific business *entities* in terms of *money*. It summarizes the results in financial statements based on the equation: *Assets = Liabilities + Owner's Equity* (A = L + OE).

Section 2: Accounting Applications

Jenny Mullin needs to provide the bank with an income statement, statement of owner's equity, and balance sheet for Keep-Fit Center.

	A	B	C	D	E
1			Keep-Fit Center		
2			Income Statement		
3			For the Year Ended April 30, 2014		
4	Revenues:				
5		Fees revenues			$375,000
6					
7	Expenses:				
8		Marketing expense		$ 18,000	
9		Rent expense		91,000	
10		Salaries expense		172,000	
11		Supplies expense		6,000	
12		Utilities expense		11,000	
13	Total expenses				298,000
14	Net income				$ 77,000
15					

	A	B	C	D	E
1			Keep-Fit Center		
2			Statement of Owner's Equity		
3			For the Year Ended April 30, 2014		
4		J. Mullin, capital, May 1, 2013			$ —
5		Investment by J. Mullin			100,000
6		Net income for the year			77,000
7		Subtotal			$177,000
8		Less withdrawals			10,000
9		J. Mullin, capital, April 30, 2014			$167,000
10					

	A	B	C	D	E
1			Keep-Fit Center		
2			Balance Sheet		
3			April 30, 2014		
4	Assets		Liabilities		
5	Cash	$111,000	Accounts payable	$19,000	
6	Accounts receivable	104,000	Salaries payable	78,000	
7	Supplies	2,000	Total liabilities		$ 97,000
8	Equipment	47,000			
9			Owner's Equity		
10		—	J. Mullin, capital		167,000
11	Total assets	$264,000	Total liabilities and owner's equity		$264,000
12					

Section 3: Business Applications

The income statement shows that Keep-Fit Center earned $77,000 after expenses were deducted from fees revenue. Further, it may be observed that this $77,000 of net income is very good when compared to total assets of $264,000 and owner's equity on the balance sheet. Thus, it can be concluded that Keep-Fit Center is profitable. It would be useful to see Keep-Fit Center's statement of cash flows to better evaluate its liquidity.

Chapter Review

Define *accounting*, and explain the concepts underlying accounting measurement. **LO 1**

Accounting is an information system that measures, processes, and communicates financial information about a business. It provides the information necessary to make choices among alternative uses of scarce resources in the conduct of business and economic activities.

Managerial accounting focuses on the preparation of information primarily for internal use by management. Financial accounting is concerned with the development and use of reports that are communicated to those outside the business as well as to management.

The accountant must determine what is measured, when the measurement should be made, what value should be placed on what is measured, and how to classify what is measured. The objects of accounting measurement are business transactions. Financial accounting uses a money measure to gauge the impact of these transactions on a business entity.

The three basic forms of business organization are the sole proprietorship, the partnership, and the corporation. A sole proprietorship is a business owned by one person. A partnership is like a sole proprietorship in most ways, but it has two or more owners. A corporation is a business unit chartered by the state and legally separate from its owners (the stockholders).

Define *financial position*, and state the accounting equation. **LO 2**

Financial position refers to a company's economic resources and the claims against those resources at a particular time. The accounting equation shows financial position as Assets = Liabilities + Owner's Equity. Business transactions affect financial position by decreasing or increasing assets, liabilities, and owner's equity in such a way that the accounting equation is always in balance.

Identify the four basic financial statements and their interrelationships. **LO 3**

The four basic financial statements are the income statement, the statement of owner's equity, the balance sheet, and the statement of cash flows. They are the primary means by which accountants communicate the financial condition and activities of a business to those who have an interest in the business.

Explain how generally accepted accounting principles (GAAP) and international financial reporting standards (IFRS) relate to financial statements and the independent CPA's report, and identify the organizations that influence GAAP. **LO 4**

Acceptable accounting practice consists of the conventions, rules, and procedures that make up generally accepted accounting principles. GAAP are essential to the preparation and interpretation of financial statements and the independent CPA's report. Foreign companies registered in the United States may use international financial reporting standards (IFRS).

Among the organizations that influence the formulation of GAAP are the Public Company Accounting Oversight Board, the Financial Accounting Standards Board, the American Institute of Certified Public Accountants, the Securities and Exchange Commission, and the Internal Revenue Service.

All accountants are required to follow a code of professional ethics. Accountants must act with integrity, objectivity, and independence, and exercise due care in all their activities.

The board of directors is responsible for the overall direction of the corporation for the benefit of the stockholders.

Identify the users of accounting information, and identify business goals, activities, and performance measures.

Accounting provides information to managers of all institutions and to individuals with a direct financial interest in those institutions, including present or potential investors and creditors. Accounting information is also important to those with an indirect financial interest in the business—tax authorities, regulatory agencies, and economic planners.

A business is an economic entity that engages in operating, investing, and financing activities to achieve goals of profitability and liquidity.

Explain the importance of ethics in financial reporting. **LO 6**

Ethical financial reporting is important to the well-being of a company. Fraudulent financial reports can have serious consequences for many people.

Key Terms

accounting 2 (LO1)
accounting equation
  (A = L + OE) 6 (LO2)
American Institute of Certified Public
  Accountants (AICPA) 13 (LO4)
assets 6 (LO2)
audit 12 (LO4)
balance sheet 8 (LO3)
bookkeeping 3 (LO1)
business 17 (LO5)
business transactions 3 (LO1)
cash flows 10 (LO3)
certified public accountant
  (CPA) 12 (LO4)
corporation 5 (LO1)
creditors 16 (LO5)
due care 14 (LO4)
economic entity 2 (LO1)
ethics 19 (LO6)
exchange rate 4 (LO1)
expenses 7 (LO2)
financial accounting 2 (LO1)
Financial Accounting Standards
  Board (FASB) 13 (LO4)
financial analysis 18 (LO5)
financial position 6 (LO2)
financial ratios 18 (LO5)

financial statements 2 (LO1)
financing activities 17 (LO5)
fraudulent financial
  reporting 19 (LO6)
generally accepted accounting
  principles (GAAP) 12 (LO4)
Governmental Accounting Standards
  Board (GASB) 14 (LO4)
income statement 8 (LO3)
independence 14 (LO4)
Institute of Management
  Accountants (IMA) 14 (LO4)
integrity 14 (LO4)
Internal Revenue Service
  (IRS) 14 (LO4)
International Accounting Standards
  Board (IASB) 13 (LO4)
international financial reporting
  standards (IFRS) 13 (LO4)
investing activities 17 (LO5)
investors 16 (LO5)
liabilities 6 (LO2)
limited liability 5 (LO1)
liquidity 17 (LO5)
management 15 (LO5)
management information
  systems (MIS) 3 (LO1)

managerial accounting 3 (LO1)
money measure 3 (LO1)
net assets 7 (LO2)
net income 7 (LO2)
net loss 7 (LO2)
objectivity 14 (LO4)
operating activities 17 (LO5)
owner's equity 7 (LO2)
owner's investments 7 (LO2)
partnership 4 (LO1)
performance measures 18 (LO5)
profitability 17 (LO5)
Public Company Accounting
  Oversight Board (PCAOB) 13 (LO4)
revenues 7 (LO2)
Sarbanes-Oxley Act 19 (LO6)
Securities and Exchange
  Commission (SEC) 14 (LO4)
separate entity 4 (LO1)
sole proprietorship 4 (LO1)
statement of cash flows 10 (LO3)
statement of owner's equity 8 (LO3)
stockholders 5 (LO1)
withdrawals 7 (LO2)

Chapter Assignments

DISCUSSION QUESTIONS

LO **1**   **DQ1.** What makes accounting a valuable discipline?

LO **1**   **DQ2. CONCEPT** ▶ Are all economic events business transactions?

LO **1**   **DQ3.** Sole proprietorships, partnerships, and corporations differ legally; how and why does accounting treat them alike?

LO **2**   **DQ4.** How are expenses and withdrawals similar, and how are they different?

LO **4**   **DQ5.** How do generally accepted accounting principles (GAAP) differ from the laws of mathematics?

LO **5**   **DQ6.** Why do managers in governmental and not-for-profit organizations need to understand financial information as much as managers in profit-seeking businesses?

LO **5**   **DQ7.** In what ways are **CVS** and **Southwest Airlines** comparable? Not comparable?

LO **6**   **DQ8. BUSINESS APPLICATION** ▶ What are some unethical ways in which a business may do its accounting or prepare its financial statements?

SHORT EXERCISES

LO **1**   **Accounting Concepts**

SE1. CONCEPT ▶ Indicate whether each of the following words or phrases relates most closely to (a) a business transaction, (b) a separate entity, or (c) a money measure:

1. Partnership
2. U.S. dollar
3. Payment of an expense
4. Sole proprietorship
5. Sale of an asset

LO **1**   **Forms of Business Organization**

SE2. Match the descriptions that follow with the appropriate forms of business organization.

1. Most numerous
2. Commands most revenues
3. Has two or more co-owners
4. Has stockholders
5. Is owned by only one person
6. Has a board of directors

a. Sole proprietorship
b. Partnership
c. Corporation

LO **2**   **The Accounting Equation**

SE3. Determine the amount missing from each accounting equation that follows.

	Assets	=	Liabilities	+	Owner's Equity
1.	?		$100,000		$140,000
2.	$312,000		$168,000		?
3.	$584,000		?		$384,000

LO **2**   **The Accounting Equation**

SE4. Use the accounting equation to answer each question that follows.

1. Ambria Company's assets are $240,000, and its liabilities are $90,000. What is the amount of its owner's equity?
2. Dao Company's liabilities equal one-fifth of the total assets. The owner's equity is $40,000. What is the amount of the liabilities?

LO **2**   **The Accounting Equation**

SE5. Use the accounting equation to answer each question that follows.

1. At the beginning of the year, Palette Company's assets were $90,000, and its owner's equity was $50,000. During the year, assets increased by $30,000 and liabilities increased by $5,000. What was the owner's equity at the end of the year?
2. At the beginning of the year, Carmines Company had liabilities of $100,000 and owner's equity of $96,000. If assets increased by $40,000 and liabilities decreased by $30,000, what was the owner's equity at the end of the year?

LO **2**   **The Accounting Equation and Net Income**

SE6. Vivaldi Company had assets of $280,000 and liabilities of $120,000 at the beginning of the year, and assets of $400,000 and liabilities of $140,000 at the end of the year. During the year, the owner invested an additional $40,000 in the business, and the company made withdrawals of $48,000. What amount of net income did the company earn during the year?

LO **3**   **Preparation and Completion of a Balance Sheet**

SE7. Use the following accounts and balances to prepare a balance sheet with the accounts in proper order for Manteno Company at June 30, 2014, using Exhibit 8 as a model:

Accounts Receivable	$ 3,200	Building	$44,000
Wages Payable	1,400	Cash	?
Owner's Capital	57,400		

LO **3**   **Preparation of Financial Statements**

SE8. Randall Company engaged in activities during the first year of its operations that resulted in the following: service revenue, $4,800; expenses, $2,450; and withdrawals, $410. In addition, the year-end balances of selected accounts were as follows: Cash, $1,890; Other Assets, $1,000; Accounts Payable, $450; and Owner's Capital, $2,440. Prepare Randall's income statement, statement of owner's equity, and balance sheet (assume the year ends on December 31, 2014). (*Hint:* You must solve for the beginning balance of Owner's Equity for 2014.)

LO **5**   **Accounting and Business Enterprises**

SE9. Match the terms that follow with the appropriate definitions.

1. Accounting
2. Profitability
3. Liquidity
4. Financing activities
5. Investing activities
6. Operating activities
7. Financial accounting
8. Managerial accounting
9. Ethics
10. Fraudulent financial reporting

a. The process of producing accounting information for the internal use of a company's management
b. Having enough cash available to pay debts when they are due
c. Activities of management engaged to obtain adequate funds for beginning and continuing to operate a business

d. The process of generating and communicating accounting information in the form of financial statements to decision makers outside the organization
e. Activities of management engaged to spend capital in ways that are productive and will help a business achieve its objectives
f. The ability to earn enough income to attract and hold investment capital
g. An information system that measures, processes, and communicates financial information about an identifiable economic entity
h. The intentional preparation of misleading financial statements
i. Activities of management engaged to operate the business
j. A code of conduct that addresses whether actions are right or wrong

LO 6   **Ethics and Accounting**

SE10. BUSINESS APPLICATION ▶ Match the descriptions that follow with the appropriate terms.

1. Preparation of financial statements that mislead the public.
2. An important underpinning of financial reporting.
3. A law that strengthened financial reporting of public companies and their auditors.
4. Have a duty to prepare financial reports that are not false or misleading.

a. Ethics
b. Fraudulent financial reporting
c. Accountants
d. Sarbanes-Oxley Act

EXERCISES: SET A

LO 1   **Business Transactions**

E1A. CONCEPT ▶ Austin owns and operates a minimart. Which of Austin's actions described below are business transactions? Explain why any other actions are not considered business transactions.

1. Austin reduces the price of a gallon of milk in order to match the price offered by a competitor.
2. Austin pays a high school student cash for cleaning up the driveway behind the market.
3. Austin fills his son's car with gasoline in payment for his son's restocking the vending machines and the snack food shelves.
4. Austin pays interest to himself on a loan he made to the business three years ago.

LO 1   **Accounting Concepts**

E2A. CONCEPT ▶ Financial accounting uses money measures to gauge the impact of business transactions on a separate business entity. Indicate whether each of the following words or phrases relates most closely to (a) a business transaction, (b) a separate entity, or (c) a money measure.

1. U.S. dollars
2. Indian rupees
3. Partnership
4. Receipt of cash
5. Sole proprietorship
6. Corporation
7. Sales of products
8. Owner's investments
9. Japanese yen
10. Purchase of supplies

LO 1   **Money Measure**

E3A. CONCEPT ▶ You have been asked to compare the sales and assets of four companies that make computer chips to determine which company is the largest in each category. You have gathered the following data, but they cannot be used for direct comparison because each company's sales and assets are in its own currency:

Company (Currency)	Sales	Assets
Abril Chip (U.S. dollar)	2,000,000	1,300,000
Dao (Hong Kong dollar)	5,000,000	2,400,000
Aiko (Japanese yen)	350,000,000	250,000,000
Orca (euro)	3,000,000	3,900,000

Assuming that the exchange rates in Exhibit 2 are current and appropriate, convert all the figures to U.S. dollars (multiply amount by exchange rate) and determine which company is the largest in sales and which is the largest in assets.

LO 2   **The Accounting Equation**

E4A. Use the accounting equation to answer each question that follows. Show any calculations you make.

1. Oshkosh Company's assets are $400,000, and its owner's equity is $155,000. What is the amount of its liabilities?
2. Salvatore Company's liabilities and owner's equity are $72,000 and $79,500, respectively. What is the amount of the assets?
3. Radisson Company's liabilities equal one-third of the total assets, and owner's equity is $160,000. What is the amount of its liabilities?
4. At the beginning of the year, Sun Company's assets were $275,000, and its owner's equity was $150,000. During the year, assets increased $75,000 and liabilities decreased $22,500. What is the owner's equity at the end of the year?

LO 2   **Owner's Equity and the Accounting Equation**

E5A. Daiichi Company's total assets and liabilities at the beginning and end of the year follow.

	Assets	Liabilities
Beginning of the year	$175,000	$ 68,750
End of the year	275,000	162,500

Determine Daiichi's net income or loss for the year under each of the following alternatives:

1. The owner made no investments in or withdrawals from the business during the year.
2. The owner made no investments in the business but withdrew $27,500 during the year.
3. The owner invested $16,250 in the business but made no withdrawals during the year.
4. The owner invested $12,500 in the business and withdrew $27,500 during the year.

LO 3   **Identification of Accounts**

E6A.

1. Indicate whether each of the following accounts is an asset (A), a liability (L), or a part of owner's equity (OE):
   a. Building   e. Cash
   b. Salaries Payable   f. Accounts Payable
   c. Accounts Receivable   g. Equipment
   d. Owner's Capital
2. Indicate whether each account that follows would be shown on the income statement (IS), the statement of owner's equity (OE), or the balance sheet (BS).
   a. Commissions Earned   e. Supplies Expense
   b. Automobile   f. Accounts Payable
   c. Utilities Expense   g. Withdrawals
   d. Land

LO 3   **Preparation of a Balance Sheet**

E7A. Listed in random order are some of Oxford Services Company's account balances as of December 31, 2014.

Accounts Payable	$ 50,000	Accounts Receivable	$62,500
Building	112,500	Cash	25,000
J. Oxford, Capital	212,500	Equipment	50,000
Supplies	12,500		

Place the balances in proper order and prepare a balance sheet similar to the one in Exhibit 8.

LO 3   **Preparation and Integration of Financial Statements**

E8A. Dukakis Company had the following accounts and balances during 2014: Service Revenue, $13,200; Rent Expense, $1,200; Wages Expense, $8,340; Advertising Expense, $1,350; Utilities Expense, $900; and Withdrawals, $700. In addition, the year-end balances of selected accounts were as follows: Cash, $1,550; Accounts Receivable, $750; Supplies, $100; Land, $1,000; Accounts Payable, $450; Investment by Owner, $1,240; and beginning capital balance of $1,000.

    Prepare Dukakis's income statement, statement of owner's equity, and balance sheet (assume the year ends on December 31, 2014). (*Hint:* You must first solve for the net income and ending balances of owner's equity for 2014.)

LO 3   **Statement of Cash Flows**

E9A. Arlington Service Company began the year 2014 with cash of $55,900. In addition to earning a net income of $32,500 and making cash withdrawals of $19,500, Arlington Service borrowed $78,000 from the bank and purchased equipment with $117,000 of cash. Also, Accounts Receivable increased by $7,800, and Accounts Payable increased by $11,700.

    Determine the amount of cash on hand at December 31, 2014, by preparing a statement of cash flows similar to the one in Exhibit 9.

LO 3   **Statement of Owner's Equity**

E10A. ACCOUNTING CONNECTION ▶ Information from Mrs. Shah's Cookies' statement of owner's equity for 2014 follows.

Withdrawals	$ 0
Net income	?
Owner's equity, January 31, 2014	159,490
Owner's equity, January 31, 2013	102,403

Prepare Mrs. Shah's Cookies' statement of owner's equity. You will need to solve for the amount of net income. What is owner's equity? Why might the owner decide not to make any withdrawals from the company?

LO 3   **Preparation and Integration of Financial Statements**

E11A. Complete the financial statements that follow by determining the amounts that correspond to the letters. (Assume no new investments by owners.)

Income Statement	
Revenues	$11,100
Expenses	(a)
Net income	$ (b)
Statement of Owner's Equity	
Beginning balance	$29,000
Net income	(c)
Less withdrawals	2,000
Ending balance	$30,000
Balance Sheet	
Total assets	$ (d)
Total liabilities	$16,000
Owner's equity (T. Proviso, capital)	(e)
Total liabilities and owner's equity	$ (f)

LO **1, 5**   **Users of Accounting Information and Forms of Business Organization**

E12A. Avalon Pharmacy has recently been formed to develop a new type of drug treatment for cancer. Previously a partnership, Avalon has now become a corporation. Describe the various groups that will have an interest in Avalon's financial statements. What is the difference between a partnership and a corporation? What advantages does the corporate form have over the partnership form of business organization?

LO **4, 5**   **The Nature of Accounting**

E13A. Match the terms that follow with the appropriate descriptions.

1. Communication
2. Business transactions
3. Investors
4. Financial Accounting Standards Board (FASB)
5. Creditors
6. Management
7. Bookkeeping
8. Securities and Exchange Commission (SEC)
9. Money measure
10. Sarbanes-Oxley Act
11. Financial statements
12. Management information system

a. The recording of all business transactions in terms of money
b. A process by which information is exchanged between individuals through a common system of symbols, signs, or behavior
c. The process of identifying and assigning values to business transactions

d. Legislation requiring CEOs and CFOs to swear that any reports they file with the SEC are accurate and complete
e. Show how well a company is meeting the goals of profitability and liquidity
f. Collectively, the people who have overall responsibility for operating a business and meeting its goals
g. People who commit money to earn a financial return
h. The interconnected subsystems that provide the information needed to run a business
i. The most important body for developing and issuing rules on accounting practice, called *Statements of Financial Accounting Standards*
j. An agency set up by Congress to protect the public by regulating the issuing, buying, and selling of stocks
k. Economic events that affect a business's financial position
l. People or businesses to whom money is due

LO **4**   **Accounting Abbreviations**

E14A. Identify the accounting meaning of each of the following abbreviations: CPA, IRS, PCAOB, GAAP, FASB, SEC, GASB, IASB, IMA, and AICPA.

LO **6**   **Ethics and Accounting**

E15A.   BUSINESS APPLICATION ▶ Match the descriptions that follow with the appropriate terms.

1. Responsible for the ethical preparation of financial statements
2. Preparation of financial statements that mislead the public
3. Underlies both management's and accountants' actions in preparing financial statements
4. A law related to regulation of financial reporting of public companies and their auditors following the Enron scandal
5. Has overall responsibility for ensuring that financial reports are not false or misleading

a. Accountants
b. Ethics
c. Fraudulent financial reporting
d. Management
e. Sarbanes-Oxley Act

EXERCISES: SET B

Visit the textbook companion web site at www.cengagebrain.com to access Exercise Set B for this chapter.

PROBLEMS

LO **3, 5**   **Preparation and Interpretation of Financial Statements**

P1. A list of financial statement items follows.

Utilities expense	Accounts payable
Building	Rent expense
Owner's capital	Withdrawals
Net income	Fees earned
Land	Cash
Equipment	Supplies
Revenues	Wages expense
Accounts receivable	

REQUIRED

1. Indicate whether each item is found on the income statement (IS), statement of owner's equity (OE), and/or balance sheet (BS).
2. **BUSINESS APPLICATION** ▶ Which statement is most closely associated with the goal of profitability?

LO **3**   **Integration of Financial Statements**

✔ 1f: Total liabilities and owner's equity: $4,600

P2. The following three independent sets of financial statements have several amounts missing:

Income Statement	Set A	Set B	Set C
Revenues	$1,100	$ (g)	$ 240
Expenses	(a)	5,200	(m)
Net income	$ (b)	$ (h)	$ 80
Statement of Owner's Equity			
Beginning balance	$2,900	$24,400	$ 340
Net income	(c)	1,600	(n)
Less withdrawals	200	(i)	(o)
Ending balance	$3,000	$ (j)	$ (p)
Balance Sheet			
Total assets	$ (d)	$31,000	$ (q)
Total liabilities	$1,600	$ 5,000	(r)
Owner's capital	(e)	(k)	380
Total liabilities and owner's equity	$ (f)	$ (l)	$ 380

REQUIRED

1. Complete each set of financial statements by determining the missing amounts that correspond to the letters.
2. **ACCOUNTING CONNECTION** ▶ Why is it necessary to prepare the income statement prior to the balance sheet?

LO **3, 5**

SPREADSHEET

✔ 1: Total net income: $79,200
✔ 1: Total assets: $136,800

Preparation and Interpretation of Financial Statements

P3. Fuel Designs' financial accounts follow. The company has just completed its tenth year of operations ended December 31, 2014.

Accounts Payable	$ 3,600
Accounts Receivable	4,500
Cash	71,700
Commission Sales Revenue	400,000
Commissions Expense	225,000
Commissions Payable	22,700
Equipment	59,900
Marketing Expense	20,100
Office Rent Expense	36,000
Owner's Capital, December 31, 2013	64,300
Supplies	700
Supplies Expense	2,600
Telephone and Computer Expenses	5,100
Wages Expense	32,000
Withdrawals	33,000

REQUIRED

1. Prepare Fuel Designs' income statement, statement of owner's equity, and balance sheet. There were no investments by the owner during the year.
2. **ACCOUNTING CONNECTION** ▶ The owner is considering expansion. What other financial statement would be useful to the owner in assessing whether the company's operations are generating sufficient funds to support the expenses? Why would it be useful?

LO **3, 5**

SPREADSHEET

✔ 1: Total net income: $1,600
✔ 1: Total assets: $27,300

Preparation and Interpretation of Financial Statements

P4. The accounts of Frequent Ad, an agency that develops marketing materials for print, radio, and television, follow. The agency's first year of operations just ended on January 31, 2014.

Accounts Payable	$ 19,400
Accounts Receivable	24,600
Advertising Service Revenue	159,200
A. Francis, Capital	5,000*
Cash	1,800
Equipment Rental Expense	37,200
Marketing Expense	4,500
Office Rent Expense	10,800
Salaries Expense	86,000
Salaries Payable	1,300
Supplies	900
Supplies Expense	19,100
Withdrawals	0

*Represents the initial investment by the owner.

REQUIRED

1. Prepare Frequent Ad's income statement, statement of owner's equity, and balance sheet.
2. **BUSINESS APPLICATION** ▶ Review the financial statements and comment on the financial challenges Frequent Ad faces.

LO **3, 4, 5**   **Use and Interpretation of Financial Statements**

P5. Athena Riding Club's financial statements follow.

Athena Riding Club
Income Statement
For the Month Ended November 30, 2014

Revenues:		
Riding lesson revenue	$4,650	
Locker rental revenue	1,450	
Total revenues		$6,100
Expenses:		
Salaries expense	$1,125	
Feed expense	750	
Utilities expense	450	
Total expenses		2,325
Net income		$3,775

Athena Riding Club
Statement of Owner's Equity
For the Month Ended November 30, 2014

Owner's capital, October 31, 2014	$35,475
Investment by owner	6,000
Net income for the month	3,775
Subtotal	$45,250
Less withdrawals	2,400
Owner's capital, November 30, 2014	$42,850

Athena Riding Club
Balance Sheet
November 30, 2014

Assets		**Liabilities**	
Cash	$ 6,700	Accounts payable	$11,250
Accounts receivable	900	**Owner's Equity**	
Supplies	750	Owner's capital	42,850
Land	15,750		
Building	22,500		
Horses	7,500		
Total assets	$54,100	Total liabilities and owner's equity	$54,100

Athena Riding Club
Statement of Cash Flows
For the Month Ended November 30, 2014

Cash flows from operating activities:		
Net income		$3,775
Adjustments to reconcile net income to net cash flows from operating activities:		
Increase in accounts receivable	$ (400)	
Increase in supplies	(550)	
Increase in accounts payable	400	(550)
Net cash flows from operating activities		$3,225
Cash flows from investing activities:		
Purchase of horses	$(2,000)	
Sale of horses	1,000	
Net cash flows from investing activities		(1,000)
Cash flows from financing activities:		
Investment by owner	$ 6,000	
Cash withdrawals	(2,400)	
Net cash flows from financing activities		3,600
Net increase in cash		$5,825
Cash at beginning of month		875
Cash at end of month		$6,700

REQUIRED

1. **ACCOUNTING CONNECTION** ▶ Explain how Athena Riding Club's four statements relate to each other.
2. **BUSINESS APPLICATION** ▶ Which statements are most closely associated with the goals of liquidity and profitability? Why?
3. **BUSINESS APPLICATION** ▶ If you were the owner of this business, how would you evaluate the company's performance? Give specific examples.
4. **ACCOUNTING CONNECTION** ▶ If you were a banker considering Athena Riding Club for a loan, why might you want the company to be audited by an independent CPA? What would the audit tell you?

ALTERNATE PROBLEMS

LO **3, 5**   **Preparation and Interpretation of Financial Statements**

P6. A list of financial statement items follows.

Wages expense
Equipment
Equipment rental expense
Net income
Land
Owner's capital
Revenues
Accounts receivable

Accounts payable
Rent expense
Withdrawals
Fees earned
Cash
Supplies
Utilities expense

REQUIRED

1. Indicate whether each item is found on the income statement (IS), statement of owner's equity (OE), and/or balance sheet (BS).
2. **BUSINESS APPLICATION** ▶ Which statement is most closely associated with the goal of profitability?

LO **3**

✔ 1f: Total liabilities and owner's equity: $9,380

Integration of Financial Statements

P7. Three independent sets of financial statements with several amounts missing follow.

Income Statement	Set A	Set B	Set C
Revenues	$2,400	$ (g)	$ 480
Expenses	(a)	10,000	(m)
Net income	$ (b)	$ (h)	$ 296
Statement of Owner's Equity			
Beginning balance	$5,800	$48,800	$ 480
Net income	(c)	3,200	(n)
Less withdrawals	400	(i)	(o)
Ending balance	$6,180	$ (j)	$ (p)
Balance Sheet			
Total assets	$ (d)	$60,000	$ (q)
Total liabilities	$3,200	$10,000	$ (r)
Owner's capital	(e)	(k)	560
Total liabilities and owner's equity	$ (f)	$ (l)	$1,160

REQUIRED

1. Complete each set of financial statements by determining the amounts that correspond to the letters.
2. **ACCOUNTING CONNECTION** ▶ In what order is it necessary to prepare the financial statements and why?

LO **3, 5**

SPREADSHEET

✔ 1: Total net income: $111,000
✔ 1: Total assets: $151,500

Preparation and Interpretation of Financial Statements

P8. Sears Labs' financial accounts follow. The company has just completed its third year of operations ended November 30, 2014.

Accounts Payable	$ 7,400
Accounts Receivable	9,100
Cash	141,600
Design Service Revenue	248,000
Marketing Expense	19,700
Office Rent Expense	18,200
Owner's Capital, November 30, 2013	70,400
Salaries Expense	96,000
Salaries Payable	2,700
Supplies	800
Supplies Expense	3,100
Withdrawals	40,000

REQUIRED

1. Prepare Sears Labs' income statement, statement of owner's equity, and balance sheet. There were no investments by the owner during the year.
2. **BUSINESS APPLICATION** ▶ Evaluate the company's ability to meet its bills when they come due.

LO **1, 3**

SPREADSHEET

✔ 1: Total net income: $20,600
✔ 1: Total assets: $45,000

Preparation and Interpretation of Financial Statements

P9. Bachino's Pizza's accounts follow. The company has just completed its first year of operations ended September 30, 2014.

Accounts Payable	$ 21,000
Accounts Receivable	26,400
Cash	5,200
Delivery Truck Rent Expense	14,400
Equipment	12,600
Equipment Rental Expense	5,800
Marketing Expense	3,000
Owner's Capital	4,000*
Pizza Revenue	164,000
Salaries Expense	112,000
Salaries Payable	1,400
Supplies	800
Supplies Expense	8,200
Withdrawals	2,000

*Represents the initial investment by the owner.

REQUIRED

1. Prepare Bachino's Pizza's income statement, statement of owner's equity, and balance sheet.
2. Why would Bachino's Pizza's owner set his business up as a sole proprietorship and not a partnership? Discuss how profits and obligations are shared in the two forms of business organizations.

LO **3, 4, 5**

Use and Interpretation of Financial Statements

P10. Aqua Swimming Club's financial statements follow.

Aqua Swimming Club
Income Statement
For the Month Ended November 30, 2014

Revenues:		
Swimming lesson revenue	$4,650	
Locker rental revenue	1,275	
Total revenues		$5,925
Expenses:		
Salaries expense	$1,125	
Supplies expense	750	
Utilities expense	450	
Total expenses		2,325
Net income		$3,600

Aqua Swimming Club
Statement of Owner's Equity
For the Month Ended November 30, 2014

Owner's capital, October 31, 2014	$34,975
Investment by owner	5,000
Net income for the month	3,600
Subtotal	$43,575
Less withdrawals	2,400
Owner's capital, November 30, 2014	$41,175

(*Continued*)

Aqua Swimming Club
Balance Sheet
November 30, 2014

Assets		Liabilities	
Cash	$ 7,125	Accounts payable	$13,350
Accounts receivable	900	**Owner's Equity**	
Supplies	750	Owner's capital	41,175
Land	15,750		
Building	22,500		
Equipment	7,500		
Total assets	$54,525	Total liabilities and owner's equity	$54,525

Aqua Swimming Club
Statement of Cash Flows
For the Month Ended November 30, 2014

Cash flows from operating activities:		
Net income		$3,600
Adjustments to reconcile net income to net cash flows from operating activities:		
Increase in accounts receivable	$ (400)	
Increase in supplies	(550)	
Increase in accounts payable	400	(550)
Net cash flows from operating activities		$3,050
Cash flows from investing activities:		
Sale of equipment	$ 2,000	
Purchase of equipment	(1,000)	
Net cash flows from investing activities		1,000
Cash flows from financing activities:		
Investment by owner	$ 5,000	
Cash withdrawals	(2,400)	
Net cash flows from financing activities		2,600
Net increase in cash		$6,650
Cash at beginning of month		475
Cash at end of month		$7,125

REQUIRED

1. **ACCOUNTING CONNECTION** ▶ Explain how Aqua Swimming Club's four statements relate to each other.
2. **BUSINESS APPLICATION** ▶ Which statements are most closely associated with the goals of liquidity and profitability? Why?
3. **BUSINESS APPLICATION** ▶ If you were the owner of this business, how would you evaluate the company's performance? Give specific examples.
4. **ACCOUNTING CONNECTION** ▶ If you were a banker considering Aqua Swimming Club for a loan, why might you want the company to be audited by an independent CPA? What would the audit tell you?

CASES

LO 5 **Conceptual Understanding: Business Activities and Management Functions**

C1. Costco Wholesale Corporation is America's largest membership retail company. According to its letter to stockholders:

> For the first time [in 2011], four of our locations had more than $300 million in annual sales, including one which had more than $400 million in sales. This rate of

top line revenue per building stands out in the retail industry and results from our ongoing focus on value—that winning combination of quality and price on every item we sell that, we believe, sets Costco apart from many of its competitors.[11]

To achieve its strategy, Costco must organize its management by functions that relate to the principal activities of a business. Discuss the three basic activities Costco will engage in to achieve its goals, and suggest some examples of each. What is the role of Costco's management? What functions must its management perform to carry out these activities?

LO 2   **Conceptual Understanding: Concept of an Asset**

C2. CONCEPT ▶ **Southwest Airlines Co.** is one of the most successful airlines in the United States. One of its annual reports contained this statement:

We are a company of People, not Planes. That is what distinguishes us from other airlines and other companies. At Southwest Airlines, People are our most important asset.[12]

Are employees considered assets in the financial statements? Why or why not? Discuss in what sense Southwest considers its employees to be assets.

LO 4   **Conceptual Understanding: Generally Accepted Accounting Principles**

C3. Fidelity Investments Company is a well-known mutual fund investment company. It makes investments worth billions of dollars in companies listed on the New York Stock Exchange and other stock markets. Generally accepted accounting principles (GAAP) are very important for Fidelity's investment analysts. What are generally accepted accounting principles? Why are financial statements that have been prepared in accordance with GAAP and audited by an independent CPA useful for Fidelity's investment analysts? What organizations influence GAAP? Explain how they do so.

LO 3   **Interpreting Financial Reports: Analysis of Four Basic Financial Statements**

C4. Refer to the **CVS** annual report in the Supplement to Chapter 16 to answer the questions below. Keep in mind that every company, while following basic principles, adapts financial statements and terminology to its own special needs. Therefore, the complexity of CVS's financial statements and the terminology in them will differ somewhat from the financial statements in the text.

1. What names does CVS give to its four basic financial statements? (Note that the word *consolidated* in the names of the financial statements means that these statements combine those of several companies owned by CVS.)
2. Prove that the accounting equation works for CVS on December 31, 2011 by finding the amounts for the following equation: Assets = Liabilities + Stockholders' Equity.
3. What were the total revenues of CVS for the year ended December 31, 2011?
4. Was CVS profitable in the year ended December 31, 2011? How much was net income (loss) in that year, and did it increase or decrease from the year ended December 31, 2010?
5. Did the company's cash and cash equivalents increase from December 31, 2010 to December 31, 2011? If so, by how much? In what two places in the statements can this number be found or computed?
6. Did cash flows from operating activities, cash flows from investing activities, and cash flows from financing activities increase or decrease from years 2010 to 2011?
7. Who is the auditor for the company? Why is the auditor's report that accompanies the financial statements important?

LO 5   **Comparison Analysis: Performance Measures and Financial Statements**

CASH FLOW

C5. BUSINESS APPLICATION ▶ Refer to the **CVS** annual report and the financial statements of **Southwest Airlines Co.** in the Supplement to Chapter 16 to answer the questions that follow.

(Continued)

1. Which company is larger in terms of assets and in terms of revenues? What do you think is the best way to measure the size of a company?
2. Which company is more profitable in terms of net income? What is the trend of profitability over the past three years for both companies?
3. Which company has more cash? Which increased its cash the most in the last year? Which has more liquidity as measured by cash flows from operating activities?

LO 6   **Ethical Dilemma: Professional Situations**

C6. BUSINESS APPLICATION ▶ Discuss the ethical choices in the situations below. In each instance, describe the ethical dilemma, determine the alternative courses of action, and tell what you would do.

1. You are the payroll accountant for a small business. A friend asks you how much another employee is paid per hour.
2. As an accountant for the branch office of a wholesale supplier, you discover that several of the receipts the branch manager has submitted for reimbursement as selling expenses actually stem from nights out with his spouse.
3. You are an accountant in the purchasing department of a construction company. When you arrive home from work on December 22, you find a large ham in a box marked "Happy Holidays—It's a pleasure to work with you." The gift is from a supplier who has bid on a contract your employer plans to award next week.
4. As an auditor with one year's experience at a local CPA firm, you are expected to complete a certain part of an audit in 20 hours. Because of your lack of experience, you know you cannot finish the job within that time. Rather than admit this, you are thinking about working late to finish the job and not telling anyone.
5. You are a tax accountant at a local CPA firm. You help your neighbor fill out her tax return, and she pays you $200 in cash. Because there is no record of this transaction, you are considering not reporting it on your tax return.
6. The accounting firm for which you work as a CPA has just won a new client, a firm in which you own 200 shares of stock that you received as an inheritance from your grandmother. Because it is only a small number of shares and you think the company will be very successful, you are considering not disclosing the investment.

Continuing Case: Annual Report Project

C7. Choose a company in which you are interested, and obtain its most recent annual report online at the company's website. Click on *Investor Relations*; then, select *Annual Report* or *SEC Form 10-K*. (*Hint:* When performing a search, use "*company name investor relations*" to avoid the customer-oriented home page.)

1. Identify the company by writing a summary that includes the following elements:
   - Name of the chief executive officer
   - Location of the home office
   - Ending date of latest fiscal year
   - Description of the company's principal products or services
   - Main geographic area of activity
   - Name of the company's independent accountants (auditors). In your own words, explain what the accountants said about the company's financial statements.

2. Identify the company's four financial statements. What differences, if any, do you see in the titles given to the statements as compared to those used in the chapter? Trace the interrelationships of the statements.
3. Show that the accounting equation (Assets = Liabilities + Stockholders' Equity) is in balance for the most recent year.

CHAPTER 2
Analyzing and Recording Business Transactions

BUSINESS INSIGHT
Paws and Hoofs Clinic

After graduating from veterinary school, Jim Wright started the Paws and Hoofs Clinic. On his second day of business, he received a standing order from Quarter Horse Stables to examine its horses on a monthly basis for one year. The fee for the service was to be $500 per visit, or $6,000 for the year. Confident that his agreement with Quarter Horse Stables will work out, Jim is thinking of including the $6,000 he expects to receive in his financial statements. He believes that doing so would be a good advertisement for his business, but he must answer the following questions to determine if this is acceptable practice.

***1.* CONCEPT** ▶ *How will the concepts of recognition, valuation, and classification help Wright record the transaction properly?*

***2.* ACCOUNTING APPLICATION** ▶ *How does one enter business transactions, which are economic events, in the accounting records?*

***3.* BUSINESS APPLICATION** ▶ *Can a business transaction benefit a business even though no cash is received when the transaction takes place?*

LEARNING OBJECTIVES

LO 1 Explain how the concepts of recognition, valuation, and classification apply to business transactions.

LO 2 Explain the double-entry system and the usefulness of T accounts in analyzing business transactions.

LO 3 Demonstrate how the double-entry system is applied to common business transactions.

LO 4 Prepare a trial balance, and describe its value and limitations.

LO 5 Record transactions in the general journal, and post transactions to the ledger.

LO 6 Explain why ethical financial reporting depends on proper recording of business transactions.

LO 7 Show how the timing of transactions affects cash flows and liquidity.

SECTION 1

CONCEPTS

CONCEPTS
- Recognition
- Valuation
- Classification

RELEVANT LEARNING OBJECTIVE

LO 1 Explain how the concepts of recognition, valuation, and classification apply to business transactions.

LO 1 Concepts Underlying Business Transactions

Business transactions are economic events that should be recorded in the accounting records. As illustrated in Exhibit 1, the concepts of *recognition*, *valuation*, and *classification* underlie all business transactions.

Exhibit 1
Concepts Underlying Business Transactions

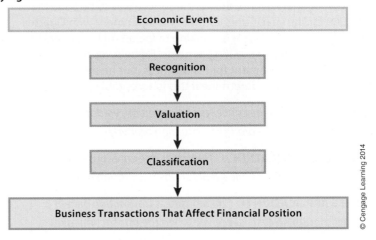

© Cengage Learning 2014

Recognition

Recognition refers to the decision as to *when* to record a business transaction. Usually, companies set specific recognition policies, such as recognizing revenue when title to goods passes or a service is provided. For example, for Paws and Hoofs Clinic that was introduced at the beginning of the chapter, Jim needs to know when to record the $6,000 fee in his financial statements. The resolution of this issue is important because the date on which a transaction is recorded affects amounts in the financial statements.

Valuation

Valuation is the process of assigning a monetary amount to business transactions and the resulting assets and liabilities. Generally accepted accounting principles state that all business transactions should be valued at *fair value* when they occur. **Fair value**

International Perspective
IFRS The Challenge of Fair Value Accounting

The measurement of fair value is a major success of the International Accounting Standards Board (IASB) and the Financial Accounting Standards Board (FASB) convergence project to merge U.S. GAAP with international financial reporting standards (IFRS).[1] After initially recording an asset at cost, fair value is the price at which an asset *could* be sold (or a liability settled) in a current transaction between independent parties. It is not the actual, or historical, price at which the asset was acquired or the liability assumed. Because it represents the price in a hypothetical transaction, fair value is often difficult to measure and subject to judgment. For example, when there is no ready market for an asset—as might be the case for used factory equipment—the potential selling price may not be easy to determine.

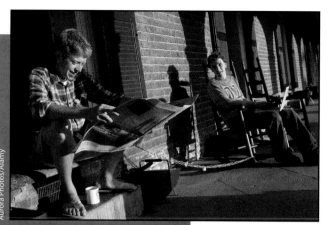

Aurora Photos/Alamy

Barter transactions, in which exchanges are made but no cash changes hands, can make valuation complicated. For example, if an office supply company provides a year's supply of computer paper to a local newspaper in exchange for an advertisement in the weekly paper, the value of the transaction equals the fair value of the items being traded.

is the *exchange price* of an actual or potential business transaction between market participants.[2] Recording transactions at the exchange price at the point of recognition is called the **cost principle**. The cost, or exchange price, is used because it is verifiable. For example, when Jim performs the service for Quarter Horse Stables, he and Quarter Horse Stables will record the transaction in their respective records at the agreed-upon price.

Normally, the value of an asset remains at its initial fair value or cost until the asset is sold, expires, or is consumed. However, if a change in the fair value of the asset (or liability) occurs, an adjustment may be required. Different fair-value rules apply to different classes of assets. For example, a building or equipment remains at cost unless convincing evidence exists that the fair value is less than cost. In this case, a loss is recorded to reduce the value from its cost to fair value. Investments, on the other hand, are often accounted for at fair value, regardless of whether fair value is greater or less than cost.

Classification

Classification is the process of assigning all the transactions in which a business engages to appropriate categories, or accounts. Classification of debts can affect a company's ability to borrow money, and classification of purchases can affect its income. One of the most important classification issues in accounting is the difference between an expense and an asset, both represented by debits in the accounts. For example, if Jim buys medicines that are used immediately at the Paws and Hoofs Clinic, their cost is classified as an expense. If the medicines will be used in the future, they are classified as assets. Similarly, if **CVS** buys paper towels to resell to customers, the cost would be recorded as an asset in the Inventory account. If the paper towels are used for cleaning in the store today, the cost is an expense.

As we explain later in the chapter, proper classification depends not only on correctly analyzing the effect of each transaction but also on maintaining a system of accounts that reflects that effect.

APPLY IT! ▶

Three major issues underlie every accounting transaction: recognition, valuation, and classification. Match each of these issues to the statements that are most closely associated with the issue. A company:

1. Records a piece of equipment at the price paid for it.

2. Records the purchase of the equipment on the day on which it takes ownership.

3. Records the equipment as an asset because it will benefit future periods.

SOLUTION

1. valuation
2. recognition
3. classification

TRY IT! SE1, SE2, SE3, E1A, E1B

ACCOUNTING APPLICATIONS

LO 2 Double-Entry System

Accounting is a very old discipline. Forms of it have been essential to commerce for more than 5,000 years. Accounting, in a version close to what we know today, gained widespread use in the 1400s, especially in Italy, where it was instrumental in the development of shipping, trade, construction, and other forms of commerce. This system of double-entry bookkeeping, i.e., *recording, valuing,* and *classifying* business transactions, was documented by the famous Italian mathematician, scholar, and philosopher Fra Luca Pacioli. In 1494, Pacioli published his most important work, *Summa de Arithmetica, Geometrica, Proportioni et Proportionalita,* which contained a detailed description of accounting as practiced in that age. This book became the most widely read book on mathematics in Italy and firmly established Pacioli as the "Father of Accounting." Goethe, the famous German poet and dramatist, referred to double-entry bookkeeping as "one of the finest discoveries of the human intellect."

What is the significance of the double-entry system? The system is based on the *principle of duality,* which means that every economic event has two aspects—such as effort and reward, sacrifice and benefit, source and use—that offset, or balance, each other. In the **double-entry system**, each transaction must be recorded with at least one debit and one credit, and the total amount of the debits must equal the total amount of the credits. All accounting systems, no matter how sophisticated, are based on the principle of duality.

Accounts

Accounts are the basic storage units for accounting data and are used to accumulate amounts from similar transactions. An accounting system has a separate account for each asset, each liability, and each component of owner's equity, including revenues and expenses. Managers must be able to refer to accounts so that they can study their company's financial history and plan for the future. A very small company may need only a few dozen accounts; a multinational corporation may need thousands.

An account title should describe what is recorded in the account. However, account titles can be rather confusing. For example, Wages Expense and Salaries Expense are both titles for labor expenses. Moreover, many account titles change over time as preferences and practices change.

Chart of Accounts

In a manual accounting system, each account is kept on a separate page or card. These pages or cards are placed together in a book or file called the **general ledger**. In computerized systems, accounts are maintained electronically. However, accountants still refer to the group of accounts as the *general ledger,* or simply the *ledger.*

To help identify accounts in the ledger and make them easy to find, the accountant often numbers them. A list of these numbers with the corresponding account titles is called a **chart of accounts**. A chart of accounts is a table of contents for the ledger. Typically, it lists accounts in the order in which they appear in the ledger, which is usually the order in which they appear in the financial statements. The numbering scheme allows for some flexibilitiy. A very simple chart of accounts appears in Exhibit 2. The first digit in the account number identifies the major financial statement *classification*—that is, an asset account begins with the digit 1, a liability account begins with a 2, and so forth. The second and third digits identify individual accounts. The gaps in the sequence of numbers allow the accountant to expand the number of accounts within the classification.

Exhibit 2
Chart of Accounts for a Small Business

Account Number	Account Name	Description
		Assets
111	Cash	Money and any medium of exchange (coins, currency, checks, money orders, and money on deposit in a bank)
112	Notes Receivable	Promissory notes (written promises to pay definite sums of money at fixed future dates) due from others
113	Accounts Receivable	Amounts due from others for revenues or sales on credit (sales on account)
116	Office Supplies	Prepaid expense; office supplies purchased and not used
117	Prepaid Rent	Prepaid expense; rent paid in advance and not used
118	Prepaid Insurance	Prepaid expense; insurance purchased and not expired
141	Land	Property owned for use in the business
142	Buildings	Structures owned for use in the business
143	Accumulated Depreciation—Buildings	Total of periodic allocation of the cost of buildings to expense; deducted from Buildings
146	Office Equipment	Office equipment owned for use in the business
147	Accumulated Depreciation—Office Equipment	Total of periodic allocation of the cost of office equipment to expense; deducted from Office Equipment
		Liabilities
211	Notes Payable	Promissory notes due to others
212	Accounts Payable	Amounts due to others for purchases on credit
213	Unearned Revenue	Unearned revenue; advance deposits for services to be provided in the future
214	Wages Payable	Amounts due to employees for wages earned and not paid
		Owner's Equity
311	Owner's Capital	Owner's investments in a company and claims against company assets derived from profitable operations
313	Withdrawals	Distributions of assets (usually cash) that reduce owner's capital
314	Income Summary	Temporary account used at the end of the accounting period to summarize the revenues and expenses for the period
		Revenues
411	Service Revenue	Amounts earned from services
		Expenses
511	Wages Expense	Amounts earned by employees
512	Utilities Expense	Amounts for utilities, such as water, electricity, and gas, used
513	Telephone Expense	Amounts of telephone services used
514	Rent Expense	Amounts of property and buildings rent used
515	Insurance Expense	Amounts for insurance expired
517	Office Supplies Expense	Amounts for office supplies used
518	Depreciation Expense—Buildings	Amount of buildings' cost allocated to expense
520	Depreciation Expense—Office Equipment	Amount of office equipment cost allocated to expense

The T Account

The T account is a good place to begin the study of the double-entry system. Such an account has the following three parts:

- a title, which identifies the asset, liability, or owner's equity account
- a left side, which is called the **debit** side
- a right side, which is called the **credit** side

The **T account**, so called because it resembles the letter *T*, is a tool used to analyze transactions and is not part of the accounting records. It looks like this:

Title of Account	
Debit	Credit
(left) side	(right) side

STUDY NOTE: *It is important to realize that debit simply means "left side" and credit simply means "right side." Do not let preconceived ideas about what debit and credit mean affect your understanding.*

Any entry made on the left side of the account is a debit, and any entry made on the right side is a credit. The terms *debit* (abbreviated Dr., from the Latin *debere*) and *credit* (abbreviated Cr., from the Latin *credere*) are simply the accountant's words for "left" and "right" (*not* for "increase" or "decrease"). We present a more formal version of the T account, the ledger account form, later in this chapter.

The T Account Illustrated Suppose a company had several transactions during the month that involved the receipt or payment of cash. These transactions can be summarized in the Cash account by recording receipts on the left (debit) side of a T account and payments on the right (credit) side.

Cash	
Dr.	*Cr.*
100,000	70,000
3,000	400
	1,200
103,000	71,600
Bal. **31,400**	

The cash receipts on the left total $103,000. (The total is written in smaller, blue figures so that it cannot be confused with an actual debit entry.) The cash payments on the right side total $71,600. These totals are simply working totals, or **footings**. Footings, which are calculated at the end of each month, are an easy way to determine cash on hand. The difference between the total debit footing and the total credit footing is called the **account balance** (or *balance*). If the balance is a debit, it is written on the left side. If it is a credit, it is written on the right side. Notice that the Cash account has a debit balance of $31,400 ($103,000 – $71,600). This is the amount of cash the business has on hand at the end of the month.

Rules of Double-Entry Accounting

The double-entry system follows two rules:

- Every transaction affects at least two accounts.
- Total debits must equal total credits.

In other words, for every transaction, one or more accounts must be debited, or entered on the left side of a T account, and one or more accounts must be credited, or entered on the right side of a T account, and the total dollar amount of the debits must equal the total dollar amount of the credits.

Look again at the accounting equation:

Assets = Liabilities + Owner's Equity

▲ If a debit *increases* assets, then a credit must be used to *increase* liabilities or owner's equity because they are on opposite sides of the equal sign.

▼ Likewise, if a credit *decreases* assets, then a debit must be used to *decrease* liabilities or owner's equity.

These rules can be shown as follows.

Assets		=	Liabilities		+	Owner's Equity	
Debit for increases (+)	Credit for decreases (−)		Debit for decreases (−)	Credit for increases (+)		Debit for decreases (−)	Credit for increases (+)

One of the more difficult points is the application of double-entry rules to the components of owner's equity. Remember that withdrawals and expenses are deductions from owner's equity. Thus, transactions that *increase* withdrawals or expenses *decrease* owner's equity. Consider this expanded version of the accounting equation:

						Owner's Equity					
Assets	=	Liabilities	+	Owner's Capital	−	Withdrawals	+	Revenues	−	Expenses

Assets		=	Liabilities		+	Owner's Capital		−	Withdrawals		+	Revenues		−	Expenses	
+ (Dr.)	− (Cr.)		− (Dr.)	+ (Cr.)		− (Dr.)	+ (Cr.)		+ (Dr.)	− (Cr.)		− (Dr.)	+ (Cr.)		+ (Dr.)	− (Cr.)

STUDY NOTE: *To remember the normal balances and the rules of debit and credit, use the acronym AWE: Assets, Withdrawals, and Expenses are always increased by debits. All other accounts are increased by credits.*

Normal Balance

The **normal balance** of an account is its usual balance and is the side (debit or credit) that increases the account. Exhibit 3 summarizes the normal account balances of the major account categories.

Exhibit 3
Normal Account Balances of Major Account Categories

Account Category	Increases Recorded by		Normal Balance	
	Debit	Credit	Debit	Credit
Assets	×		×	
Liabilities		×		×
Owner's Equity:				
Owner's Capital		×		×
Withdrawals	×		×	
Revenues		×		×
Expenses	×		×	

Owner's Equity Accounts

Exhibit 4 illustrates how owner's equity accounts relate to each other and to the financial statements. The distinctions among these accounts are important for both legal purposes and financial reporting. Owner's capital represents the original investments by the owner plus (or minus) income earned (or losses incurred) by the business minus withdrawals made by the owner.

Exhibit 4
Relationships of
Owner's Equity
Accounts

The Accounting Cycle

As Exhibit 5 shows, the **accounting cycle** is a series of steps that measure and communicate useful information to decision makers. These steps follow.

- **Step 1.** *Analyze* business transactions from source documents.
- **Step 2.** *Record* the transactions by entering them in the general journal.

Exhibit 5
Overview of the Accounting Cycle

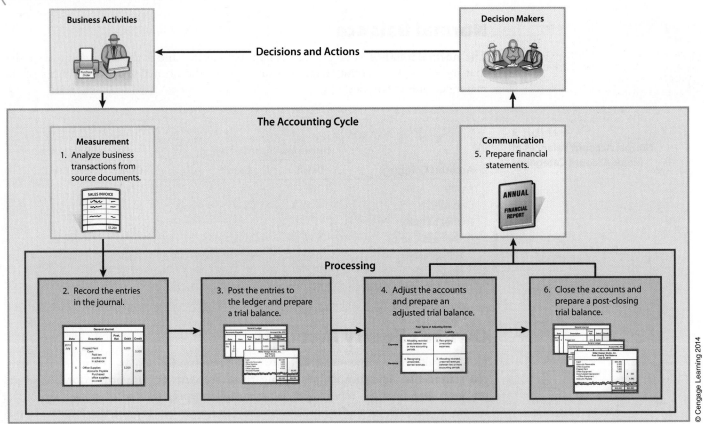

■ **Step 3.** *Post* the journal entries to the ledger, and prepare a trial balance.
■ **Step 4.** *Adjust* the accounts, and prepare an adjusted trial balance.
■ **Step 5.** *Prepare* financial statements.
■ **Step 6.** *Close* the accounts, and prepare a post-closing trial balance.

Note that Steps 3, 4, and 6 entail preparation of trial balances, which are explained later in this chapter. The remainder of this chapter examines Steps 1–3 in detail.

APPLY IT!

You are given the following list of accounts with dollar amounts:

D. Logan, Withdrawals	$ 75	Cash	$625
Accounts Payable	200	D. Logan, Capital	400
Wages Expense	150	Fees Revenue	250

Insert the account title at the top of the corresponding T account that follows and enter the dollar amount as a normal balance in the account. Then show that the accounting equation is in balance.

SOLUTION

Cash	Accounts Payable	D. Logan, Capital	D. Logan, Withdrawals	Fees Revenue	Wages Expense
625	200	400	75	250	150

Assets = Liabilities + Owner's Equity
$625 = $200 + ($400 − $75 + $250 − $150)
$625 = $200 + $425
$625 = $625

TRY IT! SE4, E2A, E3A, E2B, E3B

LO3 Business Transaction Analysis

In the next few pages, we illustrate the first three steps of the accounting cycle by showing how to apply the double-entry system to some common business transactions. **Source documents**—invoices, receipts, checks, or contracts—support the details of a transaction.

Here, we focus on the transactions of a small firm, Blue Design Studio. To walk through every step of recording business transactions, each transaction will be broken into the following parts:

■ **Transaction:** The date and a description of the transaction are provided.
■ **Analysis:** The transaction is analyzed to determine which accounts are affected.
■ **Application of Double-Entry:** T accounts show how the transaction affects the accounting equation. Note that this is *not* part of the accounting records but is undertaken before recording a transaction in order to understand the effects of the transaction.
■ **Journal Entry:** A **journal entry** is a notation that records a single transaction in the chronological accounting record known as a **journal** (sometimes called the *book of original entry* because it is where transactions first enter the accounting records).

STUDY NOTE: *T accounts are used to understand and visualize the double-entry effects of a transaction on the accounting equation. They help in recording the journal entry.*

Each entry must be in proper **journal form**, which, as illustrated below, is a way of recording a transaction with the date, debit account, and debit amount shown on one line, and the credit account (indented) and credit amount shown on the next line. The amounts are shown in their respective debit and credit columns.

		Dr.	Cr.
Date	Debit Account Name	Amount	
	Credit Account Name		Amount

■ **Comment:** Comments that offer supporting explanations will help you apply the rules of double-entry accounting.

Owner's Investment to Form the Business

Transaction On July 1, Joan Blue invests $40,000 in cash to form Blue Design Studio.

Analysis The journal entry to record an owner's investment in the business

▲ *increases* the asset account *Cash* with a debit

▲ *increases* the owner's equity account *J. Blue, Capital* with a credit

Application of Double Entry

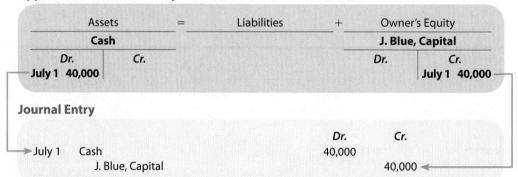

Comment If Joan Blue had invested assets other than cash in the business, the debit would be *classified* as the appropriate asset account (for example, Equipment).

Economic Event That Is Not a Business Transaction

Event On July 1, Joan orders $5,200 of office supplies for Blue Design Studio.

Comment When an economic event is not a business transaction, it is not *recognized* and no entry is made. In this case, there is no confirmation that the supplies have been shipped or that title has passed.

Prepayment of Expenses in Cash

Transaction On July 3, Joan rents an office for Blue Design Studio. She pays $3,200 for two months' rent in advance.

Analysis The journal entry to record the prepayment of office rent in cash

▲ *increases* the asset account *Prepaid Rent* with a debit

▼ *decreases* the asset account *Cash* with a credit

Application of Double Entry

Comment A prepaid expense is *classified* as an asset because the expenditure will benefit future operations. This transaction does not affect the totals of assets or liabilities and owner's equity because it simply trades one asset for another asset. If the company had paid only July's rent, the owner's equity account *Rent Expense* would be *recognized* and debited because the total benefit of the expenditure would be used up in the current month.

Purchase of an Asset on Credit

Transaction On July 5, Blue Design Studio receives the office supplies ordered on July 2 and an invoice for $5,200.

Analysis The journal entry to record the purchase of office supplies on credit

- ▲ *increases* the asset account *Office Supplies* with a debit
- ▲ *increases* the liability account *Accounts Payable* with a credit

Application of Double Entry

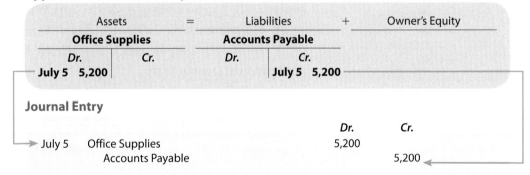

Comment Office supplies in this transaction are *classified* as an asset (prepaid expense) because they will not be used up in the current month and thus will benefit future periods. The credit is *classified* as Accounts Payable because there is a delay between the time of the purchase and the time of payment.

Purchase of an Asset Partly in Cash and Partly on Credit

Transaction On July 6, Joan purchases office equipment totaling $16,320 for Blue Design Studio. Joan pays $13,320 in cash and agrees to pay the rest next month.

Analysis The journal entry to record the purchase of office equipment in cash and on credit

▲ *increases* the asset account *Office Equipment* with a debit

▼ *decreases* the asset account *Cash* with a credit

▲ *increases* the liability account *Accounts Payable* with a credit

Application of Double Entry

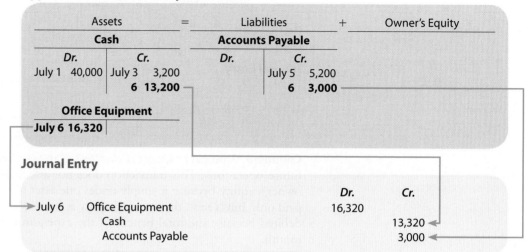

Comment As this transaction illustrates, assets may be paid for partly in cash and partly on credit. A journal entry in which more than two accounts are involved is called a **compound entry** because a portion of the entry is properly *classified* in two or more accounts.

Payment of a Liability

Transaction On July 9, Blue Design Studio makes a partial payment of $2,600 for the amount owed for the office supplies received on July 5.

Analysis The journal entry to record a payment of a liability

▼ *decreases* the liability account *Accounts Payable* with a debit

▼ *decreases* the asset account *Cash* with a credit

Application of Double Entry

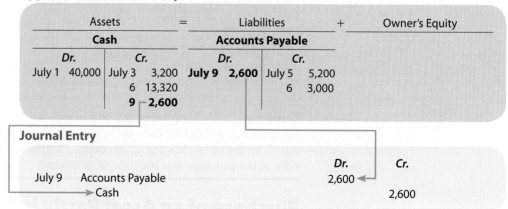

Comment Note that the office supplies, which were *recognized* and recorded when they were purchased on July 5, are not part of the July 9 transaction.

Revenue in Cash

Transaction On July 10, Blue Design Studio performs a service for an investment advisor by designing a series of brochures and collects a $2,800 fee in cash.

Analysis The journal entry to record revenue received in cash

- ▲ *increases* the asset account *Cash* with a debit
- ▲ *increases* the owner's equity account *Design Revenue* with a credit

Application of Double Entry

Comment For this transaction, revenue is *recognized* when the service is provided and the cash is received.

Revenue on Credit

Transaction On July 15, Blue Design Studio performs a service for a department store by designing a TV commercial. The company bills for the $9,600 fee now but will collect it later.

Analysis The journal entry to record revenue billed to a customer

- ▲ *increases* the asset account *Accounts Receivable* with a debit
- ▲ *increases* the owner's equity account *Design Revenue* with a credit

Accounts Receivable is used to indicate the customer's obligation until it is paid.

Application of Double Entry

Comment In this case, there is a delay between the time revenue is earned and the time the cash is received. Revenues are *recognized* and recorded at the time they are earned and billed regardless of when cash is received.

Revenue Collected in Advance

Transaction On July 19, Blue Design Studio accepts a $1,400 advance fee as a deposit on a series of brochures to be designed.

Analysis The journal entry to record revenue received in advance

▲ *increases* the asset account *Cash* with a debit

▲ *increases* the liability account *Unearned Design Revenue* with a credit

Application of Double Entry

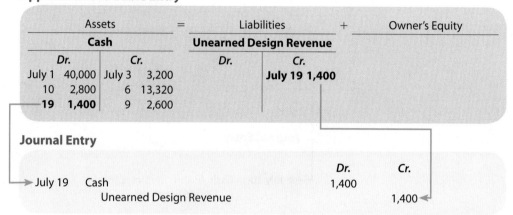

Comment In this case, cash is received before the fees are earned. Unearned Design Revenue is *recognized* and *classified* as a liability because the firm must either provide the service or return the deposit.

Collection on Account

Transaction On July 22, Blue Design Studio receives $5,000 cash from customer previously billed on July 15.

Analysis The journal entry to record the collection of an account receivable from a customer previously billed

▲ *increases* the asset account *Cash* with a debit

▼ *decreases* the asset account *Accounts Receivable* with a credit

Application of Double Entry

Comment Note that the revenue related to this transaction was *recognized* and recorded on July 15. Thus, no revenue is recognized at this time.

Business Perspective
No Dollar Amount: How Can That Be?

Determining the value of a sale or purchase transaction isn't difficult when the value equals the amount of cash that changes hands. However, barter transactions, in which exchanges are made but no cash changes hands, can make valuation more complicated. Barter transactions are quite common in business today. Here are some examples:

- A consulting company provides its services to an auto dealer in exchange for the loan of a car for a year.
- An office supply company provides a year's supply of computer paper to a local weekly newspaper in exchange for an advertisement in 52 issues of the newspaper.
- Two Internet companies each provide an advertisement and link to the other's website on their own websites.

Determining the value of these transactions is a matter of determining the fair value of the items being traded.

© Cengage Learning 2014

Expense Paid in Cash

Transaction On July 26, Blue Design Studio pays $4,800 for four weeks of employee wages.

Analysis The journal entry to record this cash expense

▲ *increases* the owner's equity account *Wages Expense* with a debit

▼ *decreases* the asset account *Cash* with a credit

Application of Double Entry

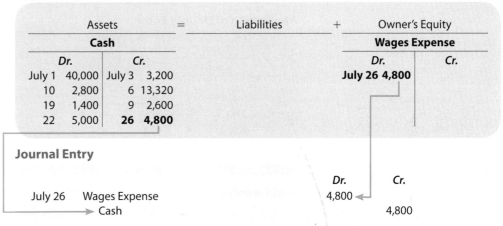

Assets		=	Liabilities	+	Owner's Equity	
Cash					**Wages Expense**	
Dr.	Cr.				Dr.	Cr.
July 1 40,000	July 3 3,200				**July 26 4,800**	
10 2,800	6 13,320					
19 1,400	9 2,600					
22 5,000	**26 4,800**					

Journal Entry

		Dr.	Cr.
July 26	Wages Expense	4,800	
	Cash		4,800

Comment Wages Expense will appear on the income statement as a deduction from revenues.

Expense to Be Paid Later

Transaction On July 30, Blue Design Studio receives but does not pay the utility bill that is due next month for $680.

Analysis The journal entry to record this cash expense

▲ *increases* the owner's equity account *Utilities Expense* with a debit

▲ *increases* the liability account *Accounts Payable* with a credit

Application of Double Entry

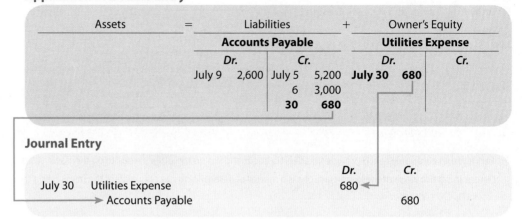

Journal Entry

		Dr.	Cr.
July 30	Utilities Expense	680	
	Accounts Payable		680

Comment The expense is *recognized* and recorded if the benefit has been received and the amount is owed, even if the cash is not to be paid until later.

Withdrawals

Transaction On July 31, Blue Design Studio withdraws $2,800 in cash.

Analysis The journal entry to record a cash withdrawal

▲ *increases* the owner's equity account *Withdrawals* with a debit

▼ *decreases* the asset account *Cash* with a credit

Application of Double Entry

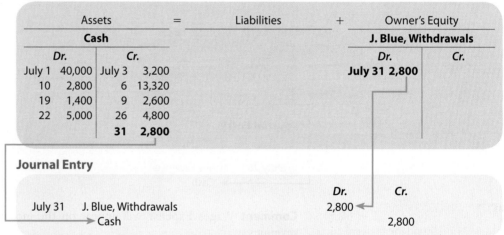

Journal Entry

		Dr.	Cr.
July 31	J. Blue, Withdrawals	2,800	
	Cash		2,800

Comment Cash payments to owners are not *classified* as expenses but as withdrawals.

Summary of Transactions

Exhibit 6 uses the accounting equation to summarize the transactions of Blue Design Studio. Note that the income statement accounts appear under owner's equity and that the transactions in the Cash account will be reflected on the statement of cash flows.

Exhibit 6
Summary of Transactions of Blue Design Studio

| | Assets | | | = | | Liabilities | | | + | | Owner's Equity | | |

Cash

	Dr.			Cr.
July 1	40,000	July 3	3,200
10	2,800	6	13,320
19	1,400	9	2,600
22	5,000	26	4,800
		31	2,800
	49,200		**26,720**
Bal.	**22,480**		

Accounts Payable

	Dr.			Cr.
July 9	2,600	July 5	5,200
		6	3,000
		30	680
	2,600		**8,880**
		Bal.	**6,280**

J. Blue, Capital

	Dr.		Cr.
		July 1	40,000

J. Blue, Withdrawals

	Dr.		Cr.
July 31	2,800	

> This account links to the statement of cash flows.

Accounts Receivable

	Dr.			Cr.
July 15	9,600	July 22	5,000
Bal.	**4,600**		

Unearned Design Revenue

	Dr.			Cr.
		July 19	1,400

Design Revenue

	Dr.		Cr.
		July 10	2,800
		15	9,600
		Bal.	**12,400**

Office Supplies

	Dr.		Cr.
July 5	5,200	

Wages Expense

	Dr.		Cr.
July 26	4,800	

Prepaid Rent

	Dr.		Cr.
July 3	3,200	

Utilities Expense

	Dr.		Cr.
July 30	680	

Office Equipment

	Dr.		Cr.
July 6	16,320	

> These accounts link to the income statement.

Assets	=	Liabilities	+	Owner's Equity
$51,800	=	$7,680	+	$44,120

APPLY IT!

The following accounts are applicable to Kathy's Nail Salon, a company that provides manicures and pedicures:

1. Cash
2. Accounts Receivable
3. Supplies
4. Equipment
5. Accounts Payable
6. Services Revenue
7. Wages Expense
8. Rent Expense

For Kathy's Nail Salon, enter the number corresponding to the proper account for each debit and credit for the following transactions:

		Debit	Credit
a.	Made a rent payment for the current month.	8	1
b.	Received cash from customers for current services.		
c.	Agreed to accept payment next month from a client for current services.		
d.	Purchased supplies on credit.		
e.	Purchased a new chair and table for cash.		
f.	Made a payment on accounts payable.		

SOLUTION

		Debit	Credit
a.	Made a rent payment for the current month.	8	1
b.	Received cash from customers for current services.	1	6
c.	Agreed to accept payment next month from a client for current services.	2	6
d.	Purchased supplies on credit.	3	5
e.	Purchased a new chair and table for cash.	4	1
f.	Made a payment on accounts payable.	5	1

TRY IT! SE2, SE5, SE6, E4A, E5A, E6A, E7A, E8A, E4B, E5B, E6B, E7B, E8B

LO 4 The Trial Balance

The **trial balance**, prepared periodically, is a device used to ensure that the total of debits and credits in the accounts are equal, meaning that the accounts balance. Exhibit 7 shows a trial balance for Blue Design Studio. It was prepared from the accounts in Exhibit 6.

Exhibit 7
Trial Balance

Blue Design Studio
Trial Balance
July 31, 2014

	Debit	Credit
Cash	22,480	
Accounts Receivable	4,600	
Office Supplies	5,200	
Prepaid Rent	3,200	
Office Equipment	16,320	
Accounts Payable		6,280
Unearned Design Revenue		1,400
J. Blue, Capital		40,000
J. Blue, Withdrawals	2,800	
Design Revenue		12,400
Wages Expense	4,800	
Utilities Expense	680	
	60,080	60,080

© Cengage Learning 2014

Preparation and Use of a Trial Balance

Although a trial balance may be prepared at any time, it is usually prepared on the last day of the accounting period. The steps involved in preparing a trial balance follow.

- **Step 1.** List each account that has a balance, with debit balances in the left column and credit balances in the right column. Accounts are listed in the following order: assets, liabilities, owner's capital, withdrawals, revenues, and expenses.
- **Step 2.** Add each column.
- **Step 3.** Compare the totals of the columns.

Once in a while, a transaction leaves an account with a balance that isn't "normal." For example, when a company overdraws its bank account, its Cash account (an asset) will show a credit balance instead of a debit balance. The "abnormal" balance should be copied into the trial balance columns as it stands, as a debit or a credit.

The trial balance proves whether the accounts are in balance. *In balance* means that the total of all debits recorded equals the total of all credits recorded. But the trial balance does not prove that the transactions were analyzed correctly or recorded in the proper accounts. For example, the trial balance does not show that a debit should have been made in Office Supplies rather than in Office Equipment. And the trial balance does not detect whether transactions have been omitted, because equal debits and credits will have been omitted. Also, if an error of the same amount is made in both a debit and a credit, it will not be evident in the trial balance. The trial balance proves only that the debits and credits in the accounts are in balance.

Finding Trial Balance Errors

If the debit and credit balances in a trial balance are not equal, look for one or more of the following errors:

- A debit was entered in an account as a credit, or vice versa.
- The balance of an account was computed incorrectly.
- An error was made in carrying the account balance to the trial balance.
- The trial balance was summed incorrectly.

Other than simply adding the columns incorrectly, the two most common mistakes in preparing a trial balance are:

- Recording an account as a credit when it usually carries a debit balance, or vice versa. This mistake causes the trial balance to be out of balance by an amount divisible by 2.
- Transposing two digits when transferring an amount to the trial balance (for example, entering $23,459 as $23,549). This error causes the trial balance to be out of balance by an amount divisible by 9.

So, if a trial balance is out of balance and the addition of the columns is correct, determine the amount by which the trial balance is out of balance and divide it first by 2 and then by 9. If the amount is divisible by 2, look in the trial balance for an amount that is equal to the quotient. If you find such an amount, chances are it's in the wrong column. If the amount is divisible by 9, trace each amount back to the T account balance, checking carefully for a transposition error. If neither of these techniques is successful in identifying the error, first recompute the balance of each T account. Then, if you still have not found the error, retrace each posting to the journal or the T account.

APPLY IT!

Prepare a trial balance for Dras Company from the following list of accounts (in alphabetical order) as of March 31, 2014. Compute the balance of cash.

Accounts Payable	$ 9
Accounts Receivable	5
Building	10
Cash	?
Dras, Capital	16
Equipment	2
Land	1
Inventory	3

SOLUTION

Dras Company
Trial Balance
March 31, 2014

Cash	$ 4	
Accounts Receivable	5	
Inventory	3	
Land	1	
Building	10	
Equipment	2	
Accounts Payable		$ 9
Dras, Capital		16
Totals	$25	$25

TRY IT! SE7, E9A, E10A, E11A, E12A, E9B, E10B, E11B, E12B

LO5 Recording and Posting Transactions

Earlier in the chapter, we described how transactions are analyzed according to the rules of double entry and how a trial balance is prepared. Recall in Exhibit 5, transaction analysis and preparation of a trial balance appear at several points in the process. Two intermediate steps are recording the entry in the general journal and posting the entry to the ledger. In this section, we demonstrate how these steps are accomplished in a manual accounting system.

General Journal

STUDY NOTE: *The journal is a chronological record of transactions.*

Although transactions can be entered directly into the ledger accounts, identifying individual transactions or finding errors is difficult because the debit is recorded in one account and the credit in another. The solution is to record all transactions chronologically in a journal, which, as we noted earlier, is where transactions first enter the accounting records. Later, the debit and credit portions of each transaction are transferred to the appropriate accounts in the ledger.

Most businesses have more than one kind of journal. The simplest and most flexible kind is the **general journal**. Businesses may also have several special-purpose journals, each for recording a common transaction, such as credit sales, credit purchases, cash receipts, and cash disbursements. At this point, we cover only the general journal. Exhibit 8, which displays two of the transactions of Blue Design Studio, shows the format for recording entries in a general journal.

Exhibit 8
The General Journal

A = L + SE
+ 3,200
− 3,200

A = L + SE
+ 5,200   + 5,200

	General Journal			Page 1	
Date	**Description**	**Post. Ref.**	**Debit**	**Credit**	
2014 July	3 Prepaid Rent		3,200		
	Cash			3,200	
	Paid two months' rent in advance				
	5 Office Supplies		5,200		
	Accounts Payable			5,200	
	Purchase of office supplies on credit				

As you can see in Exhibit 8, the entries in a general journal include the following information about each transaction:

- **Date:** The year appears on the first line of the first column, the month on the next line of the first column, and the day in the second column opposite the month. For subsequent entries on the same page for the same month and year, the month and year can be omitted.
- **Accounts:** The names of the accounts debited and credited appear in the Description column. The names of the accounts that are debited are placed next to the left margin opposite the dates; on the line below, the names of the accounts credited are indented.
- **Amounts:** The debit amounts appear in the Debit column opposite the accounts that are debited, and the credit amounts appear in the Credit column opposite the accounts credited.
- **Explanation:** An explanation of each transaction appears in the Description column below the account names. An explanation should be brief but sufficient to identify the transaction.
- **Account numbers:** The account numbers appear in the Post. Ref. (posting reference) column, if they apply.

At the time the transactions are recorded, nothing is placed in the Post. Ref. column. Later, if the company uses account numbers to identify accounts in the ledger, the account numbers are filled in. They provide a convenient cross-reference from the general journal to the ledger and indicate that the entry has been *posted* to the ledger. If the accounts are not numbered, the accountant uses a checkmark (✓) to signify that the entry has been posted.

General Ledger

STUDY NOTE: *A T account is a means of quickly analyzing a set of transactions. It is simply an abbreviated version of a ledger account. Ledger accounts, which provide more information, are used in the accounting records.*

The general journal is used to record the details of each transaction. The general ledger is used to update each account.

The Ledger Account Form The T account is a simple, direct means of recording transactions. In practice, a somewhat more complicated form of the account is needed to record more information. The **ledger account form** is a form of the account that contains four columns for dollar amounts, as is illustrated in Exhibit 9.

Exhibit 9
Accounts Payable in the General Ledger

General Ledger							
Accounts Payable						Account No. 212	
						Balance	
Date		Item	Post. Ref.	Debit	Credit	Debit	Credit
2014 July	5		J1		5,200		5,200
	6		J1		3,000		8,200
	9		J1	2,600			5,600
	30		J2		680		6,280

© Cengage Learning 2014

The account title and number appear at the top of the account form. As in the journal, the transaction date appears in the first two columns. The Item column is rarely used to identify transactions because explanations already appear in the journal. The Post. Ref. column is used to note the journal page on which the original entry for the transaction can be found. The dollar amount is entered in the appropriate Debit or Credit column, and a new account balance is computed in the last two columns opposite each entry. The advantage of this account form over the T account is that the current balance of the account is readily available.

Posting After transactions have been entered in the journal, they must be transferred to the ledger. This process is called **posting**. Posting is usually done after several entries have been made—for example, at the end of each day or less frequently, depending on the number of transactions. As Exhibit 10 shows, each amount in the Debit column of the journal is transferred to the Debit column of the appropriate account in the ledger, and each amount in the Credit column of the journal is transferred to the Credit column of the appropriate account in the ledger.

The steps in the posting process follow.

- **Step 1:** In the ledger, locate the debit account named in the journal entry.
- **Step 2:** Enter the date of the transaction in the ledger and, in the Post. Ref. column, the journal page number from which the entry comes.
- **Step 3:** In the Debit column of the ledger account, enter the amount of the debit as it appears in the journal.
- **Step 4:** Calculate the account balance and enter it in the appropriate Balance column.
- **Step 5:** Enter in the Post. Ref. column of the journal the account number to which the amount has been posted.

The same five steps are repeated in posting the credit side of the journal entry. As noted earlier, in addition to serving as an easy reference between the journal entry and the ledger account, the entry in the Post. Ref. column of the journal (Step 5) indicates that the entry has been posted to the ledger.

Exhibit 10
Posting from the General Journal to the Ledger

$$A = L + SE$$
$$+680 \quad -680$$

General Journal — Page 2

Date		Description	Post. Ref.	Debit	Credit
2014 July	30	Utilities Expense	512	680	
		Accounts Payable	212		680
		Received bill from utility company			

General Ledger

Accounts Payable — Account No. 212

Date		Item	Post. Ref.	Debit	Credit	Balance Debit	Balance Credit
2014 July	5		J1		5,200		5,200
	6		J1		3,000		8,200
	9		J1	2,600			5,600
	30		J2		680		6,280

General Ledger

Utilities Expense — Account No. 512

Date		Item	Post. Ref.	Debit	Credit	Balance Debit	Balance Credit
2014 July	30		J2	680		680	

© Cengage Learning 2014

Some Notes on Presentation

Exhibit 11 offers some guidance on how to format financial statements, trial balances, journals, and ledgers in accordance with common accounting conventions.

Exhibit 11
Formatting Guidelines

BLUE DESIGN STUDIO'S FINANCIAL HIGHLIGHTS

Cash	$22,480
Accounts receivable	4,600
Office supplies	5,200
Prepaid rent	3,200
Office equipment	16,320
Total assets	$51,800

❶ A ruled line appears in financial reports before each subtotal and total to indicate that the amounts above are added or subtracted. It is common practice to use a double line under a final total to show that it has been verified.

❷ Dollar signs ($) are required in all financial statements and other schedules. On these reports, a dollar sign should be placed before the first amount in each column and before the first amount in a column following a ruled line. Dollar signs in the same column are aligned. Dollar signs are not used in journals and ledgers.

❸ On normal unruled paper, commas and decimal points are used when recording dollar amounts. On the paper used in journals and ledgers, commas and decimal points are unnecessary because ruled columns are provided to properly align dollars and cents. Commas, dollar signs, and decimal points are also unnecessary in electronic spreadsheets. In this book, because most problems and illustrations are in whole dollar amounts, the cents column usually is omitted. When accountants deal with whole dollars, they often use a dash in the cents column to indicate whole dollars rather than taking the time to write zeros.

❹ Account names are capitalized when referenced in text or listed in work documents like the journal or ledger. In financial statements, however, only the first word of an account name is capitalized.

© Cengage Learning 2014

APPLY IT!

Prepare journal entries to record the following transactions. Use the following account numbers—Cash, 111; Supplies, 114; and Accounts Payable, 212—to show in the Post Ref. columns that the entries have been posted:

June 4 Purchased supplies for $40 on credit.
      8 Paid for the supplies purchased on June 4.

SOLUTION

Date		Description	Post. Ref.	Debit	Credit
June	4	Supplies	114	40	
		Accounts Payable	212		40
		Purchased supplies on credit			
	8	Accounts Payable	212	40	
		Cash	111		40
		Paid amount due for supplies			

TRY IT! SE8, SE9, SE10, E8A, E13A, E14A, E8B, E13B, E14B

Accounting uses a double-entry system to record business transactions based on source documents. Each transaction is recorded in a journal and then posted to the ledger. The final step of the transaction analysis is the preparation of the trial balance. As depicted in Exhibit 12, business transactions can affect all components of the accounting equation.

Exhibit 12
Transaction Effects on Accounting Equation

	Assets		=	Liabilities	+	Owner's Equity				
Transaction	Cash	+ Other Assets				Owner's Capital	− Withdrawals	+ Revenues	− Expenses
1. Owner's cash investment	+					+			
2. Prepayment of expenses in cash	−	+							
3. Purchase of an asset on credit		+		+					
4. Purchase of an asset partly on credit and partly in cash	−	+		+					
5. Payment of liability	−			−					
6. Revenue received in cash	+							+	
7. Revenue on credit		+						+	
8. Revenue collected in advance	+			+					
9. Collection on account	+	−							
10. Expense paid in cash	−								+
11. Expense to be paid later				+					+
12. Withdrawal by owner	−						+		

BUSINESS APPLICATIONS

LO 6 Ethical Financial Reporting and Business Transactions

Financial statements result from the recording of business transactions. Users of these financial statements have a right to expect that all business transactions have been recorded and reflected properly in the statements. Thus, *recognition*, *valuation*, and *classification* as specified under generally accepted accounting principles are important factors in ethical financial reporting. These guidelines help managers meet their obligation to their company's owners and to their creditors. Many of the most egregious financial reporting frauds result from violations of these guidelines, as the following examples show.

- **Computer Associates** violated the guidelines for recognition when it kept its books open a few days after the end of a reporting period so revenues could be counted a quarter earlier than they should have been. In all, the company prematurely reported $3.3 billion in revenues from 363 software contracts. When the SEC ordered the company to stop the practice, Computer Associates' stock price dropped by 43 percent in a single day.
- Among its many other transgressions, **Enron Corporation** violated the guidelines for valuation when it transferred, to related companies, assets at far more than their actual value.
- By a simple violation of the guidelines for classification, **WorldCom** (now **MCI**, a component of **Verizon**) perpetrated the largest financial fraud in history. Over a period of several years, the company recorded as assets its expenditures that should have been classified as expenses, understating expenses and overstating income by more than $10 billion.

Recognition

The *recognition* issue can be particularly difficult to resolve. To illustrate some of the factors involved, suppose a company wants to purchase an office desk. The following events take place:

- **Event 1:** An employee sends a purchase request for the desk to the purchasing department.
- **Event 2:** The purchasing department sends a purchase order to the supplier.
- **Event 3:** The supplier ships the desk.
- **Event 4:** The company receives the desk.
- **Event 5:** The company receives the bill from the supplier.
- **Event 6:** The company pays the bill.

A transaction should be recorded when title to merchandise passes from the supplier to the purchaser and creates an obligation to pay. A purchase should usually not be recognized (recorded) before the title is transferred because, until that point, the vendor has not fulfilled its contractual obligation and the buyer has no liability. Thus, depending on the details of the shipping agreement for the desk, the transaction should be recognized (recorded) at the time of either Event 3 or 4. We generally use this guideline in this book. However, many small businesses that have simple accounting systems do not record a transaction until they receive a bill (Event 5) or pay it (Event 6), because these are the implied points of title transfer. The predetermined time at which a transaction should be recorded is the **recognition point**.

Although purchase requests and purchase orders (Events 1 and 2) are economic events, they do not affect a company's financial position, and they are not recognized in the accounting records. Even the most important economic events may not be recognized in the accounting records.

Business Perspective
Accounting Policies: Where Do You Find Them?

The Boeing Company, one of the world's largest makers of airliners, takes orders for planes years in advance. Although it is an important economic event to both Boeing and the buyer, neither the buyer nor the seller would record the event as a transaction. So, how do you know when companies record sales or purchase transactions? The answer to this question and others about companies' accounting policies can be found in the Summary of Significant Accounting Policies in their annual reports. For example, in that section of its annual report, Boeing states: "We recognize sales for commercial airplane deliveries as each unit is completed and accepted by the customer."[3]

Here are some more examples of economic events that should and should not be recorded as business transactions:

Events That Are *Not* Recorded as Transactions	Events That *Are* Recorded as Transactions
• A customer inquires about the availability of a product	• A customer buys a product.
• A company hires a new employee.	• A company pays an employee for work performed.
• A company signs a contract to provide a service in the future.	• A company performs a service.

Consider an advertising agency that is planning a major advertising campaign for a client. Employees may work on the plan several hours a day for a number of weeks. They add value to the plan as they develop it. Should this added value be recognized as the plan is being developed or at the time it is completed? Usually, the increase in value is recorded at the time the plan is finished and the client is billed for it. However, the agency and the client may agree that the client will be billed at key points during its development. In that case, a transaction is recorded at each billing.

APPLY IT!

For each of the following ethical situations involving business transactions, indicate what accounting concept has been violated or whether there is no violation:

1. A sales transaction is recorded on the last day of the fiscal year because the customer indicates that she will be in next week to sign the agreement.
2. A purchase of an insurance policy is recorded as an asset (instead of as an expense) because it will be used in future periods.
3. A laser printer, in excellent condition, that is purchased at a garage sale for $50 is recorded at its estimated value of $150.

SOLUTION

1. Recognition concept: violated
2. Classification concept: no violation
3. Valuation concept: violated

TRY IT! SE1, SE2, SE11, E1A, E15A, E1B, E15B

LO7 Cash Flows and the Timing of Transactions

To avoid financial distress, a company must be able to pay its bills on time. Because the timing of cash flows is critical to maintaining adequate liquidity to pay bills, managers and other users of financial information must understand the difference between transactions that generate immediate cash and those that do not. Consider the transactions of Blue Design Studio shown in Exhibit 13. Most of them involve either an inflow or outflow of cash.

Blue's Cash account has more transactions than any of its other accounts. Look at the transactions of July 10, 15, and 22 in Exhibit 13:

- July 10: Blue received a design revenue payment in cash of $2,800.
- July 15: The firm billed a customer $9,600 for a service it had already performed.
- July 22: The firm received a partial payment of $5,000 from the customer, but it had not received the remaining $4,600 by the end of the month.

Because Blue incurred expenses in providing this service, it must pay careful attention to its cash flows and liquidity.

One way Blue can manage its expenditures is to rely on its creditors to give it time to pay. Compare the transactions of July 3, 5, and 9 in Exhibit 13.

- July 3: Blue prepaid rent of $3,200. That immediate cash outlay may have caused a strain on the business.
- July 5: The firm received an invoice for office supplies in the amount of $5,200. In this case, it took advantage of the opportunity to defer payment.
- July 9: The firm paid $2,600, but it deferred paying the remaining $2,600 until after the end of the month.

Of course, Blue expects to receive the rest of the cash from the customer that it billed on July 15, and it must eventually pay the rest of what it owes on the office supplies. In the meantime, the firm must perform a delicate balancing act with its cash flows to ensure that it achieves the goal of liquidity so that it can grow and be profitable.

Exhibit 13
Transactions of Blue Design Studio

© Cengage Learning 2014

Large companies face the same challenge but often on a much greater scale. For example, it can take **Boeing** a number of years to plan and make the aircraft that customers order. At the end of 2011, Boeing had net orders of $103 billion and a backlog of orders totaling $356 billion.[4] Think of the cash outlays Boeing must make before it delivers the planes and collects payment for them. To maintain liquidity, Boeing's management must carefully plan the company's needs for cash.

APPLY IT!

A company engaged in the following transactions:

Oct. 1   Performed services for cash, $1,050.
2   Paid expenses in cash, $550.
3   Incurred expenses on credit, $750.

Oct. 4   Performed services on credit, $900.
5   Paid on account, $350.
6   Collected on account, $600.

Record these transactions using the T accounts below (remember to add the correct titles to the T accounts). Determine the cash balance after these transactions, the amount still to be received, and the amount still to be paid.

SOLUTION

Cash balance after transactions: $1,050 + $600 − $550 − $350 = $750

Amount still to be received: $900 − $600 = $300

Amount still to be paid: $750 − $350 = $400

TRY IT! SE12, E16A, E16B

TriLevel Problem

Paws and Hoofs Clinic

The beginning of this chapter focused on Paws and Hoofs Clinic and the standing order for monthly service that Quarter Horse Stables placed with Paws and Hoofs. Jim Wright, the clinic's owner, was confident of receiving $6,000 in fees over the course of the year and was thinking of including the fees in his financial statements. Complete the following requirements in order to answer the questions posed at the beginning of the chapter.

Section 1: Concepts
How will the concepts of recognition, valuation, and classification help Wright to record the transaction properly?

Section 2: Accounting Applications
How does one enter business transactions, which are economic events, in the accounting records?

Jim Wright needs to record the clinic's business transactions in the accounting records. Paws and Hoofs Clinic engaged in the following economic events during May 2014:

May 1 Jim Wright invested $20,000 in cash to form Paws and Hoofs Clinic.
2 Made an agreement to provide $6,000 in services over the next year to Quarter Horse Stables.
3 Paid $600 in advance for two months' rent of an office.
9 Purchased medical supplies for $400 in cash.
12 Purchased $4,000 of equipment on credit; made a 25 percent down payment.
15 Delivered a calf for a fee of $350 on credit.
18 Made a payment of $500 on the equipment purchased on May 12.
27 Paid a utility bill of $140.

1. Identify the company's business transactions, and prepare journal entries to record them.

2. Post the transactions to the following T accounts: Cash; Accounts Receivable; Medical Supplies; Prepaid Rent; Equipment; Accounts Payable; J. Wright, Capital; Veterinary Fees Earned; and Utilities Expense.

3. Prepare a trial balance for the month of May.

Section 3: Business Applications

Can a business transaction benefit a business even though no cash is received when the transaction takes place? Take a look at the May 15 transaction.

SOLUTION

Section 1: Concepts

Recognition helps decide when the transaction should be recorded, *valuation* refers to the value that is assigned to the transaction, and *classification* shows how to categorize the transaction (as an asset, expense, revenue, etc.)

Section 2: Accounting Applications

1.

	A	B	C	D	E
1	May	1	Cash	20,000	
2			J. Wright, Capital		20,000
3			Issued $20,000 in cash		
4			to form Paws and Hoofs Clinic		
5		3	Prepaid Rent	600	
6			Cash		600
7			Paid two months' rent in advance		
8			for an office		
9		9	Medical Supplies	400	
10			Cash		400
11			Purchased medical supplies for cash		
12		12	Equipment	4,000	
13			Accounts Payable		3,000
14			Cash		1,000
15			Purchased equipment on credit,		
16			paying 25 percent down		
17		15	Accounts Receivable	350	
18			Veterinary Fees Earned		350
19			Fee on credit for delivery of a calf		
20		18	Accounts Payable	500	
21			Cash		500
22			Partial payment for equipment		
23			purchased May 12		
24		27	Utilities Expense	140	
25			Cash		140
26			Paid utility bill		
27					

Note: With regards to Paws and Hoofs' agreement to provide $6,000 in services over the next year to Quarter Horse Stables, making an agreement to provide services is an important economic event, but it is not recorded because it does not meet the recognition concept. No services have yet been performed and earned and thus, Paws and Hoofs is not yet entitled to payment.

2.

	A	B	C	D	E	F	G	H	I	J	K	L	M
1			Cash							Accounts Payable			
2	May	1	20,000	May	3	600		May	18	500	May	12	3,000
3					9	400					Bal.		2,500
4					12	1,000							
5					18	500				J. Wright, Capital			
6					27	140					May	1	20,000
7			20,000			2,640							
8	Bal.		17,360							Veterinary Fees Earned			
9											July	15	350
10			Accounts Receivable										
11	May	15	350							Utilities Expense			
12								May	27	140			
13			Medical Supplies										
14	May	9	400										
15													
16			Prepaid Rent										
17	May	3	600										
18													
19			Equipment										
20	May	12	4,000										
21													

3.

	A	B	C
1	Paws and Hoofs Clinic		
2	Trial Balance		
3	May 31, 2014		
4			
5	Cash	17,360	
6	Accounts Receivable	350	
7	Medical Supplies	400	
8	Prepaid Rent	600	
9	Equipment	4,000	
10	Accounts Payable		2,500
11	J. Wright, Capital		20,000
12	Veterinary Fees Earned		350
13	Utilities Expense	140	
14		22,850	22,850
15			

Section 3: Business Applications

A business transaction can benefit a business even though no cash is received at the time of the transaction. For example, on May 15, Jim Wright provided a service and thus earned a revenue and added an asset to accounts receivable, which will provide cash for the business when the client pays the bill. The revenue is recognized at May 15 although the cash payment will happen later.

Chapter Review

Explain how the concepts of recognition, valuation, and classification apply to business transactions. **LO 1**

To measure a business transaction, you must determine when the transaction occurred (recognition), what value to place on the transaction (valuation), and how the components of the transaction should be categorized (classification). In general, recognition occurs when title passes, and a transaction is valued at the exchange price—the fair value or cost at the time the transaction is recognized. Classification refers to assigning transactions to the appropriate accounts.

Explain the double-entry system and the usefulness of T accounts in analyzing business transactions. **LO 2**

In the double-entry system, each transaction must be recorded with at least one debit and one credit, and the total amount of the debits must equal the total amount of the credits. Each asset, liability, and component of owner's equity, including revenues and expenses, has a separate account, which is a device for storing transaction data. The chart of accounts is a list of account numbers and titles. It serves as a table of contents for the ledger. The T account is a useful tool for quickly analyzing the effects of transactions. It shows how increases and decreases in assets, liabilities, and owner's equity are recorded. The accounting cycle is a series of steps whose basic purpose is to produce financial statements for decision makers.

Demonstrate how the double-entry system is applied to common business transactions. **LO 3**

The double-entry system is applied by analyzing transactions to determine which accounts are affected and by using T accounts to show how the transactions affect the accounting equation. The transactions may be recorded in journal form with the date, debit account, and debit amount shown on one line, and the credit account (indented) and credit amount on the next line. The amounts are shown in their respective debit and credit columns.

Prepare a trial balance, and describe its value and limitations. **LO 4**

A trial balance is used to check that the debit and credit balances are equal. It is prepared by listing each account balance in the appropriate Debit or Credit column. The two columns are then added, and the totals are compared. The major limitation of a trial balance is that it does not guarantee that the transactions were analyzed correctly or recorded in the proper accounts.

Record transactions in the general journal, and post transactions to the ledger. **LO 5**

The general journal is a chronological record of all transactions. It contains the date of each transaction, the titles of the accounts involved, the amounts debited and credited, and an explanation of each entry. After transactions have been entered in the general journal, they are posted to the ledger. Posting transfers the amounts in the Debit and Credit columns of the general journal to the Debit and Credit columns of the corresponding account in the ledger. After each entry is posted, a new balance is entered in the appropriate Balance column.

Explain why ethical financial reporting depends on proper recording of business transactions. **LO 6**

GAAP provides guidance about the treatment of business transactions in terms of recognition, valuation, and classification. Failure to follow these guidelines is a major reason some companies issue fraudulent financial statements. Usually, a transaction should be recorded when title to merchandise passes from the supplier to the purchaser and creates an obligation to pay.

Show how the timing of transactions affects cash flows and liquidity. **LO 7**

Some transactions generate immediate cash. For those that do not, there is a holding period in either Accounts Receivable or Accounts Payable before the cash is received or paid. The timing of cash flows is critical to a company's ability to maintain adequate liquidity so that it can pay its bills on time.

Key Terms

account balance 44 (LO2)
accounting cycle 46 (LO2)
accounts 42 (LO2)
business transactions 40 (LO1)
chart of accounts 42 (LO2)
classification 41 (LO1)
compound entry 50 (LO3)
cost principle 41 (LO1)
credit 44 (LO2)

debit 44 (LO2)
double-entry system 42 (LO2)
fair value 40 (LO1)
footings 44 (LO2)
general journal 58 (LO5)
general ledger 42 (LO2)
journal 47 (LO3)
journal entry 47 (LO3)
journal form 48 (LO3)

ledger account form 59 (LO5)
normal balance 45 (LO2)
posting 59 (LO5)
recognition 40 (LO1)
recognition point 62 (LO6)
source documents 47 (LO3)
T account 44 (LO2)
trial balance 56 (LO4)
valuation 40 (LO1)

Chapter Assignments

DISCUSSION QUESTIONS

LO 1   **DQ1.** A company incurs a cost for a part that is needed to repair a piece of equipment. Is the cost an asset or an expense? Explain.

LO 1, 6   **DQ2. CONCEPT** ▷ Which is the most important issue in recording a transaction: recognition, valuation, or classification?

LO 2   **DQ3.** Which account would be most likely to have an account balance that is not normal?

LO 2   **DQ4.** How would the asset accounts in the chart of accounts for Blue Design Studio differ if it were a retail company that sold promotional products instead of a service company?

LO 2, 3   **DQ5.** How are assets and expenses related, and why are the debit and credit effects for asset accounts and expense accounts the same?

LO 2, 3   **DQ6.** In what way are unearned revenues the opposite of prepaid expenses?

LO 6   **DQ7. CONCEPT** ▷ What is an example of how a company could make false financial statements through a violation of the recognition concept?

LO 7   **DQ8. BUSINESS APPLICATION** ▷ If a company's cash flows for expenses temporarily exceed its cash flows from revenues, how might it make up the difference so that it can maintain liquidity?

SHORT EXERCISES

LO 1   **Classification of Accounts**

SE1. CONCEPT ▷ Tell whether each of the following accounts is an asset, a liability, a revenue, an expense, or none of these:

a. Accounts Payable
b. Supplies
c. Withdrawals
d. Fees Earned

e. Supplies Expense
f. Accounts Receivable
g. Unearned Revenue
h. Equipment

LO **1, 3, 6**

Recognition, Valuation, and Classification

SE2. CONCEPT ▶ Tell how the concepts of recognition, valuation, and classification apply to the transaction that follows.

Cash				Supplies			
Dr.		**Cr.**		**Dr.**		**Cr.**	
	June 1	1,000		June 1	1,000		

LO **1, 6**

Recognition

SE3. CONCEPT ▶ Which of the following events would be recognized and entered in Hallmark Company's accounting records? Why?

Jan. 10   Hallmark places an order for office supplies.
Feb. 15   Hallmark receives the office supplies and a bill for them.
Mar.   1   Hallmark pays for the office supplies.

LO **2**

Normal Balances

SE4. Tell whether the normal balance of each account in **SE1** is a debit or a credit.

LO **3**

Transaction Analysis

SE5. Shawn Michael started a computer programming business, Michael's Programming Service. For each transaction that follows, indicate which account is debited and which account is credited.

May   2   Shawn Michael invested $10,000.
       5   Purchased a computer for $5,000 in cash.
       7   Purchased supplies on credit for $600.
      19   Received cash for programming services performed, $1,000.
      22   Received cash for programming services to be performed, $1,200.
      25   Paid the rent for May, $1,300.
      31   Billed a customer for programming services performed, $500.

LO **3**

Recording Transactions in T Accounts

SE6. Set up T accounts and record each transaction in **SE5**. Determine the balance of each account.

LO **4**

Preparing a Trial Balance

SE7. From the T accounts created in **SE6**, prepare a trial balance dated May 31, 2014.

LO **5**

Recording Transactions in the General Journal

SE8. Prepare a general journal form like the one in Exhibit 8 and label it Page 4. Record the following transactions in the journal:

Sept.   6   Billed a customer for services performed, $3,800.
       16   Received partial payment from the customer billed on September 6, $1,800.

LO **5**

Posting to the Ledger Accounts

SE9. Prepare three ledger account forms like the one in Exhibit 9 for the following accounts: Cash (111), Accounts Receivable (113), and Service Revenue (411). Post the transactions that are recorded in **SE8** to the ledger accounts for 2014, at the same time making the proper posting references. Also prepare a trial balance.

LO **5**

Recording Transactions in the General Journal

SE10. Record the transactions in **SE5** in the general journal for 2014.

LO 6   **Identifying Ethical Transactions**

SE11. CONCEPT For each of the following ethical situations involving business transactions, indicate what accounting concept has been violated or whether there is no violation:

1. A sales transaction is recorded on the first day of the fiscal year when payment was received even though the service for the customer was completed in the year before.
2. A laser printer in excellent condition purchased at a garage sale has an estimated value of $150, but is recorded at the $50 paid for it.
3. A purchase of truck fuel is recorded as an expense (instead of as an asset) because it will be used in the current period.

LO 7   **Timing and Cash Flows**

SE12. BUSINESS APPLICATION ▶ Use the T account for Cash below to record the portion of each of the following transactions, if any, that affect cash. How do these transactions affect the company's liquidity?

Cash

Jan. 2   Provided services for cash, $2,400.
      4   Paid expenses in cash, $1,400.
      8   Provided services on credit, $2,200.
      9   Incurred expenses on credit, $1,600.

EXERCISES: SET A

LO 1, 6   **Recognition**

E1A. CONCEPT ▶ Which of the following events would be recognized and recorded in Abril Company's accounting records on the date indicated?

Jan. 15   Abril offers to purchase a tract of land for $280,000. There is a high likelihood that the offer will be accepted.
Feb.   2   Abril receives notice that its rent will increase from $1,000 to $1,200 per month effective March 1.
Mar. 29   Abril receives its utility bill for the month of March. The bill is not due until April 9.
June 10   Abril places an order for new office equipment costing $42,000.
July   6   The office equipment Abril ordered on June 10 arrives. Payment is not due until August 1.

LO 2   **T Accounts, Normal Balance, and the Accounting Equation**

E2A. You are given the following list of accounts with dollar amounts:

Rent Expense	$ 900
Cash	3,450
Service Revenue	1,500
T. Captain, Withdrawals	750
Accounts Payable	1,200
T. Captain, Capital	2,400

Insert each account name at the top of its corresponding T account and enter the dollar amount as a normal balance in the account. Then show that the accounting equation is in balance.

(Continued)

Owner's Equity

Assets = Liabilities + T. Captain, − T. Captain, + Revenues − Expenses
                            Capital   Withdrawals

LO **1, 2** **Classification of Accounts**

E3A. CONCEPT ▶ The following ledger accounts are for Afocentric Service Company:

a. Supplies
b. Utilities Expense
c. Accounts Receivable
d. D. Minimus, Capital
e. Land
f. Prepaid Rent
g. Accounts Payable
h. Investments in Securities
i. Service Revenue
j. Supplies Expense
k. Prepaid Insurance
l. Wages Expense

m. Fees Earned
n. D. Minimus, Withdrawals
o. Wages Payable
p. Unearned Revenue
q. Office Equipment
r. Rent Payable
s. Notes Receivable
t. Interest Expense
u. Notes Payable
v. Cash
w. Interest Receivable
x. Rent Expense

Complete the following table, using X's to indicate each account's classification and normal balance (whether a debit or a credit increases the account).

| | | | Type of Account | | | | Normal Balance | |
| | | | Owner's Equity | | | | (increases balance) | |
Item	Asset	Liability	D. Minimus, Capital	D. Minimus Withdrawals	Revenue	Expense	Debit	Credit
a.	X						X	

LO **3** **Transaction Analysis**

E4A. Analyze transactions **a–g**, using the example that follows.

a. Melissa Faubert invested $2,400 in cash to establish Faubert's Beauty Parlor.
b. Paid two months' rent in advance, $1,680.
c. Purchased supplies on credit, $120.
d. Received cash for salon services, $600.
e. Paid for supplies purchased in **c**.
f. Paid utility bill, $72.
g. Withdrew $100 in cash.

Example

a. The asset account Cash was increased. Increases in assets are recorded by debits. Debit Cash $2,400. A component of owner's equity, M. Faubert, Capital, was increased. Increases in owner's capital are recorded by credits. Credit M. Faubert, Capital $2,400.

LO **3** **Transaction Analysis**

E5A. The accounts that follow are applicable to Harold's Car Service, a company that repairs cars.

1. Cash
2. Accounts Receivable
3. Supplies
4. Equipment

5. Accounts Payable
6. Repair Services Revenue
7. Wages Expense
8. Rent Expense

Harold's completed the following transactions:

		Debit	Credit
a.	Paid for supplies purchased on credit last month.	5	1
b.	Received cash from customers billed last month.	___	___
c.	Made a payment on accounts payable.	___	___
d.	Purchased supplies on credit.	___	___
e.	Billed a client for repair services.	___	___
f.	Made a rent payment for the current month.	___	___
g.	Received cash from customers for repair services not yet billed.	___	___
h.	Paid employee wages.	___	___
i.	Ordered equipment.	___	___
j.	Received and paid for the equipment ordered in i.	___	___

Analyze each transaction and show the accounts affected by entering the corresponding numbers in the appropriate debit or credit columns as shown in transaction **a.** Indicate no entry, if appropriate.

LO 3   **Recording Transactions in T Accounts**

E6A. Open the following T accounts: Cash; Repair Supplies; Repair Equipment; Accounts Payable; C. Ferdinand, Capital; Withdrawals; Repair Fees Earned; Salaries Expense; and Rent Expense. Record the following transactions for the month of June directly in the T accounts; use the letters to identify the transactions in your T accounts. Determine the balance in each account.

a. Collin Ferdinand opened Ferdinand Repair Service by investing $8,600 in cash and $3,200 in repair equipment.
b. Paid $800 for the current month's rent.
c. Purchased repair supplies on credit, $1,000.
d. Purchased additional repair equipment for cash, $600.
e. Paid salary to an employee, $900.
f. Paid $400 of amount purchased on credit in **c.**
g. Accepted cash for repairs completed, $3,720.
h. Withdrew $1,200 in cash.

LO 3   **Analysis of Transactions**

E7A. Explain each transaction (**a–h**) entered in the following T accounts:

Cash				Accounts Receivable				Equipment			
a.	10,000	b.	3,750	c.	2,000	g.	375	b.	3,750	h.	225
g.	375	e.	900					d.	2,250		
h.	225	f.	1,125								

Accounts Payable				F. Mills, Capital				Service Revenue			
f.	1,125	d.	2,250			a.	10,000			c.	2,000

Wages Expense		
e.	900	

LO **3, 5**   **Analysis of Unfamiliar Transactions**

E8A. Managers and accountants often encounter transactions with which they are unfamiliar. Use your analytical skills to analyze and prepare journal entries for the following transactions, which have not yet been discussed in the text.

May 1   Purchased merchandise inventory on account, $1,200.
      2   Purchased marketable securities for cash, $2,800.
      3   Returned part of merchandise inventory purchased for full credit, $250.
      4   Sold merchandise inventory on account, $800 (record sale only).
      5   Purchased land and a building for $300,000. Payment is $60,000 cash, and there is a 30-year mortgage for the remainder. The purchase price is allocated as follows: $100,000 to the land and $200,000 to the building.
      6   Received an order for $12,000 in services to be provided. With the order was a deposit of $4,000.

LO **4**   **Trial Balance**

E9A. After recording the transactions in **E6A**, prepare a trial balance in proper sequence for Ferdinand Repair Service as of June 30, 2014.

LO **4**   **Preparing a Trial Balance**

E10A. The list that follows presents Shah Company's accounts (in alphabetical order) as of March 31, 2014. The list does not include the amount of Accounts Payable.

A. Shah, Capital	$18,870	Equipment	$ 7,200
Accounts Receivable	1,800	Land	3,120
Building	20,400	Notes Payable	12,000
Cash	5,400	Prepaid Insurance	660

Prepare a trial balance with the proper heading (see Exhibit 7) and with the accounts listed in the chart of accounts sequence (see Exhibit 2). Compute the balance of Accounts Payable.

LO **4**   **Effects of Errors on a Trial Balance**

E11A. ACCOUNTING CONNECTION ▶ Which of the following errors would cause a trial balance to have unequal totals? Explain your answers.

a. A payment to a creditor was recorded as a debit to Accounts Payable for $258 and as a credit to Cash for $204.
b. A payment of $300 to a creditor for an account payable was debited to Accounts Receivable and credited to Cash.
c. A purchase of office supplies of $840 was recorded as a debit to Office Supplies for $84 and as a credit to Cash for $84.
d. A purchase of equipment for $900 was recorded as a debit to Supplies for $900 and as a credit to Cash for $900.

LO **4**   **Correcting Errors in a Trial Balance**

E12A. Hasson Services' trial balance at the end of July 2014 follows. It does not balance because of a number of errors. Hasson's accountant compared the amounts in the trial balance with the ledger, recomputed the account balances, and compared the postings. He found the following errors:

a. The balance of Cash was understated by $400.
b. A cash payment of $210 was credited to Cash for $120.
c. A debit of $60 to Accounts Receivable was not posted.
d. Supplies purchased for $30 were posted as a credit to Supplies.
e. A debit of $90 to Prepaid Insurance was not posted.
f. The Accounts Payable account had debits of $2,660 and credits of $4,590.
g. The Notes Payable account, with a credit balance of $1,200, was not included on the trial balance.
h. The debit balance of N. Hasson, Withdrawals was listed in the trial balance as a credit.

i   A $100 debit to N. Hasson, Withdrawals was posted as a credit.
j. The actual balance of Utilities Expense, $130, was listed as $13 in the trial balance.

Hasson Services
Trial Balance
July 31, 2014

	Debits	Credits
Cash	1,720	
Accounts Receivable	2,830	
Supplies	60	
Prepaid Insurance	90	
Equipment	3,700	
Accounts Payable		2,270
N. Hasson, Capital		5,280
N. Hasson, Withdrawals		350
Revenues		2,960
Salaries Expense	1,300	
Rent Expense	300	
Advertising Expense	170	
Utilities Expense	13	
	10,183	10,860

Prepare a corrected trial balance.

LO 5   **Recording Transactions in the General Journal**

E13A. Record the transactions in **E6A** in the general journal.

LO 5   **Recording Transactions in the General Journal**
and Posting to the Ledger Accounts

E14A. Open a general journal form like the one in Exhibit 8, and label it Page 10. Then record the following transactions in the journal:

Dec. 14   Purchased equipment for $12,000, paying $4,000 as a cash down payment.
     28   Paid $6,000 of the amount owed on the equipment.

Prepare three ledger account forms like the one shown in Exhibit 9. Use the following account numbers: Cash, 111; Office Equipment, 146; and Accounts Payable, 212. Then post the two transactions from the general journal to the ledger accounts, being sure to make proper posting references. Assume that the Cash account has a debit balance of $16,000 on the day prior to the first transaction.

LO 6   **Application of Recognition Point**

E15A. BUSINESS APPLICATION ▶ Affordable Flower Shop uses a large amount of supplies in its business. The following table summarizes selected transaction data for supplies that Affordable purchased:

Order	Date Shipped	Date Received	Amount
a	June 26	July 5	$ 600
b	July 10	July 15	1,500
c	July 16	July 22	800
d	July 23	July 30	1,200
e	July 27	Aug. 1	1,500
f	Aug. 3	Aug. 7	1,000

Determine the total purchases of supplies for July alone under each of the following assumptions:

1. Affordable recognizes purchases when orders are shipped.
2. Affordable recognizes purchases when orders are received.

LO 7   **Cash Flow Analysis**

E16A. BUSINESS APPLICATION ▶ A company engaged in the following transactions:

Dec. 1   Performed services for cash, $1,500.
      1   Paid expenses in cash, $1,100.
      2   Performed services on credit, $1,800.
      3   Collected on account, $1,200.
      4   Incurred expenses on credit, $1,300.
      5   Paid on account, $700.

Enter the correct titles on the following T accounts and enter the above transactions in the accounts. Determine the cash balance after these transactions, the amount still to be received, and the amount still to be paid.

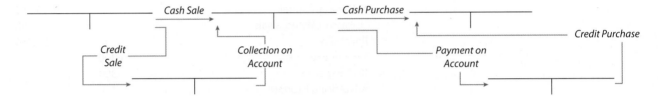

EXERCISES: SET B

Visit the textbook companion web site at www.cengagebrain.com to access Exercise Set B for this chapter.

PROBLEMS

LO 2   **T Accounts, Normal Balance, and The Accounting Equation**

✔ Total assets: $145,580

P1. Highland Design Company creates radio and television advertising for local businesses in the twin cities. The following alphabetical list shows Highland Design's account balances as of January 31, 2014:

Accounts Payable	$ 6,420	Rent Expense	$ 11,880
Accounts Receivable	78,000	R. Mehta, Capital	74,000
Cash	18,400	R. Mehta, Withdrawals	36,000
Design Revenue	210,000	Telephone Expense	960
Equipment	?	Unearned Revenue	18,000
Loans Payable	10,000	Wages Expense	124,000

REQUIRED

Insert the account title at the top of its corresponding T account and enter the dollar amount as a normal balance in the account. Determine the balance of Equipment and then show that the accounting equation is in balance.

			Owner's Equity				
Assets	=	Liabilities	+	R. Mehta, Capital	− R. Mehta, Withdrawals	+ Revenues	− Expenses

LO **3**   **Transaction Analysis**

P2. The following accounts are applicable to George's Warehouse Sweeps:

1. Cash	7. Accounts Payable
2. Accounts Receivable	8. R. Marcuson, Capital
3. Supplies	9. R. Marcuson, Withdrawals
4. Prepaid Insurance	10. Service Revenue
5. Equipment	11. Rent Expense
6. Notes Payable	12. Repair Expense

George's Warehouse Sweeps completed the following transactions:

	Debit	**Credit**
a. Paid for supplies purchased on credit last month.	7	1
b. Received a bill for repairs.	____	____
c. Paid the current month's rent.	____	____
d. Purchased supplies on credit.	____	____
e. Received cash from customers for services performed but not yet billed.	____	____
f. Purchased equipment on account.	____	____
g. Billed customers for services performed.	____	____
h. Returned part of the equipment purchased in **f** for a credit.	____	____
i. Received payments from customers previously billed.	____	____
j. Paid the bill received in **b**.	____	____
k. Received an order for services to be performed.	____	____
l. Paid for repairs with cash.	____	____
m. Made a payment to reduce the principal of the note payable.	____	____
n. Made a cash withdrawal.	____	____

REQUIRED

Analyze each transaction and show the accounts affected by entering the corresponding numbers in the appropriate debit or credit column as shown in transaction **a.** Indicate no entry, if appropriate.

LO **3, 4, 7**   **Transaction Analysis, T Accounts, and Trial Balance**

✔ 3: Trial balance: $16,200

P3. Jennifer Lopez opened a school for administrative skills called Lopez Office Training and completed the following transactions:

a. Contributed the following assets to the business:

Cash	$5,700
Computers	4,300
Office Equipment	3,600

b. Found a location for her business and paid the first month's rent, $260.
c. Paid for an advertisement announcing the opening of the school, $190.
d. Received applications from three students for a four-week secretarial program and two students for a ten-day keyboarding course. The students will be billed a total of $1,300.
e. Purchased supplies on credit, $330.
f. Billed the enrolled students, $1,740.
g. Purchased a second-hand computer, $480, and office equipment, $380, on credit.
h. Paid for the supplies purchased on credit in **e**, $330.
i. Paid cash to repair a broken computer, $40.
j. Received partial payment from students previously billed, $1,080.
k. Paid the utility bill for the current month, $90.
l. Paid an assistant one week's salary, $440.
m. Made a cash withdrawal of $300.

(Continued)

REQUIRED

1. Set up the following T accounts: Cash; Accounts Receivable; Supplies; Computers; Office Equipment; Accounts Payable; J. Lopez, Capital; J. Lopez, Withdrawals; Tuition Revenue; Salaries Expense; Utilities Expense; Rent Expense; Repair Expense; and Advertising Expense.

2. Record the transactions directly in the T accounts, using the transaction letter to identify each debit and credit.

3. Prepare a trial balance using today's date.

4. **BUSINESS APPLICATION** ▶ Examine transactions **f** and **j**. What were the revenues, and how much cash was received from the revenues? What business issues might you see arising from the differences in these numbers?

LO **1, 3, 4**

✔ 3: Trial balance: $21,080

Transaction Analysis, Journal Form, T Accounts, and Trial Balance

P4. Sid Patel bid for and won a concession to rent bicycles in the local park during the summer. During the month of April, Patel completed the following transactions for his bicycle rental business:

Apr.   2   Began business by placing $14,400 in a business checking account in the name of the company.

       3   Purchased supplies on account for $300.

       4   Purchased 10 bicycles for $5,000, paying $2,400 down and agreeing to pay the rest in 30 days.

       5   Paid $5,800 in cash for a small shed to store the bicycles and to use for other operations.

       8   Paid $800 in cash for shipping and installation costs (considered an addition to the cost of the shed) to place the shed at the park entrance.

       9   Hired a part-time assistant to help out on weekends at $14 per hour.

     10   Paid a maintenance person $150 to clean the grounds.

     13   Received $1,940 in cash for rentals.

     17   Paid $300 for the supplies purchased on April 3.

     18   Paid a $110 repair bill on bicycles.

     23   Billed a company $220 for bicycle rentals for an employee outing.

     25   Paid the $200 fee for April to the Park District for the right to operate the bicycle concession.

     27   Received $1,920 in cash for rentals.

     29   Paid the assistant $480.

     30   Made a cash withdrawal of $1,000.

REQUIRED

1. Prepare journal entries to record these transactions.

2. Set up the following T accounts and post all the journal entries: Cash; Accounts Receivable; Supplies; Shed; Bicycles; Accounts Payable; S. Patel, Capital; S. Patel, Withdrawals; Rental Revenue; Wages Expense; Maintenance Expense; Repair Expense; and Concession Fee Expense.

3. Prepare a trial balance for Patel Rentals as of April 30, 2014.

4. **CONCEPT** ▶ Compare and contrast how the issues of recognition, valuation, and classification are settled in the transactions of April 3 and 10.

LO **3, 4, 5, 7**

✔ 5: Trial balance: $30,900

Transaction Analysis, General Journal, Ledger Accounts, and Trial Balance

P5. Nordtown Company is a marketing firm. The company's trial balance on August 31, 2014, follows.

Nordtown Company
Trial Balance
August 31, 2014

Cash (111)	10,590	
Accounts Receivable (113)	5,500	
Office Supplies (116)	610	
Office Equipment (146)	4,200	
Accounts Payable (212)		2,600
D. Guetta, Capital (311)		18,300
	20,900	20,900

During the month of September, the company completed the following transactions:

Sept. 2 Paid rent for September, $650.
  3 Received cash from customers on account, $2,300.
  7 Ordered supplies, $380.
  10 Billed customers for services provided, $2,800.
  12 Made a payment on accounts payable, $1,300.
  14 Received the supplies ordered on September 7 and agreed to pay for them in 30 days, $380.
  17 Discovered some of the supplies were not as ordered and returned them for full credit, $80.
  19 Received cash from a customer for services provided, $4,800.
  24 Paid the utility bill for September, $250.
  26 Received a bill, to be paid in October, for advertisements placed in the local newspaper during the month of September to promote Nordstrom Company, $700.
  29 Billed a customer for services provided, $2,700.
  30 Paid salaries for September, $3,800.
  30 Made a cash withdrawal of $1,200.

REQUIRED

1. Open accounts in the ledger for the accounts in the trial balance plus the following accounts: D. Guetta, Withdrawals (313); Marketing Fees (411); Salaries Expense (511); Utilities Expense (512); Rent Expense (514); and Advertising Expense (516).
2. Enter the August 31, 2014, account balances from the trial balance.
3. Enter the September transactions in the general journal (page 22).
4. Post the journal entries to the ledger accounts. Be sure to make the appropriate posting references in the journal and ledger as you post.
5. Prepare a trial balance as of September 30, 2014.
6. **BUSINESS APPLICATION** ▶ Examine the transactions for September 3, 10, 19, and 29. What were the revenues, and how much cash was received from the revenues? What business issues might you see arising from the differences in these numbers?

ALTERNATE PROBLEMS

LO **2**   **T Accounts, Normal Balance, and the Accounting Equation**

✔ Total assets: $57,880

P6. Carlson Construction Company builds foundations for buildings and parking lots. The following alphabetical list shows Carlson's account balances as of April 30, 2014:

(Continued)

Accounts Payable	$ 3,900	Notes Payable	$20,000
Accounts Receivable	10,120	Revenue Earned	17,400
B. Carlson, Capital	40,000	Supplies	6,500
B. Carlson, Withdrawals	7,000	Supplies Expense	7,200
Cash	?	Utilities Expense	420
Equipment	27,500	Wages Expense	8,800

REQUIRED

Insert the account at the top of its corresponding T account, and enter the dollar amount as a normal balance in the account. Determine the balance of cash and then show that the accounting equation is in balance.

Owner's Equity

Assets = Liabilities + B. Carlson, − B. Carlson, + Revenues − Expenses
                            Capital   Withdrawals

LO 3   **Transaction Analysis**

P7. The following accounts are applicable to Raymond's Chimney Sweeps:

1. Cash	7. Accounts Payable
2. Accounts Receivable	8. R. Foth, Capital
3. Supplies	9. R. Foth, Withdrawals
4. Prepaid Insurance	10. Service Revenue
5. Equipment	11. Rent Expense
6. Notes Payable	12. Repair Expense

Raymond's Chimney Sweeps completed the following transactions:

	Debit	**Credit**
a. Paid for supplies purchased on credit last month.	7	1
b. Billed customers for services performed.	___	___
c. Paid the current month's rent.	___	___
d. Purchased supplies on credit.	___	___
e. Received cash from customers for services performed but not yet billed.	___	___
f. Purchased equipment on account.	___	___
g. Received a bill for repairs.	___	___
h. Returned part of the equipment purchased in **f** for a credit.	___	___
i. Received payments from customers previously billed.	___	___
j. Paid the bill received in **g**.	___	___
k. Received an order for services to be performed.	___	___
l. Paid for repairs with cash.	___	___
m. Made a payment to reduce the principal of the note payable.	___	___
n. Made a cash withdrawal.	___	___

REQUIRED

Analyze each transaction and show the accounts affected by entering the corresponding numbers in the appropriate debit or credit column as shown in transaction **a**. Indicate no entry, if appropriate.

LO **3, 4, 7**

✔ 3: Trial balance: $32,400

Transaction Analysis, T Accounts, and Trial Balance

P8. B. Turner opened a school for administrative skills called Blitz Secretarial Training.

a. Turner contributed the following assets to the business:

Cash	$11,400
Computers	8,600
Office Equipment	7,200

b. Found a location for his business and paid the first month's rent, $520.
c. Paid for an advertisement announcing the opening of the school, $380.
d. Received applications from three students for a four-week secretarial program and two students for a ten-day keyboarding course. The students will be billed a total of $2,600.
e. Purchased supplies on credit, $660.
f. Billed the enrolled students, $3,480.
g. Purchased a second-hand computer, $960, and office equipment, $760, on credit.
h. Paid for the supplies purchased on credit in **e**, $660.
i. Paid cash to repair a broken computer, $80.
j. Received partial payment from students previously billed, $2,160.
k. Paid the utility bill for the current month, $180.
l. Paid an assistant one week's salary, $880.
m. Made a cash withdrawal of $600.

REQUIRED

1. Set up the following T accounts: Cash; Accounts Receivable; Supplies; Computers; Office Equipment; Accounts Payable; B. Turner, Capital; B. Turner, Withdrawals; Tuition Revenue; Salaries Expense; Utilities Expense; Rent Expense; Repair Expense; and Advertising Expense.
2. Record the transactions directly in the T accounts, using the transaction letter to identify each debit and credit.
3. Prepare a trial balance using today's date.
4. **BUSINESS APPLICATION** ▶ Examine transactions **f** and **j**. What were the revenues and how much cash was received from the revenues? What business issues might you see arising from the differences in these numbers?

LO **1, 3, 4**

✔ 3: Trial balance: $37,600

Transaction Analysis, T Accounts, and Trial Balances

P9. David Roberts began an upholstery cleaning business on August 1 and engaged in the following transactions during the month:

Aug.
1   Began business by depositing $30,000 in a bank account in the name of the company.
2   Ordered cleaning supplies, $6,000.
3   Purchased cleaning equipment for cash, $5,600.
4   Made two months' van lease payment in advance, $2,400.
7   Received the cleaning supplies ordered on August 2 and agreed to pay half the amount in 10 days and the rest in 30 days.
9   Paid for repairs on the van with cash, $2,160.
12 Received cash for cleaning upholstery, $1,920.
17 Paid half the amount owed on supplies received on August 7, $3,000.
21 Billed customers for cleaning upholstery, $2,680.
24 Paid cash for additional repairs on the van, $160.
27 Received $1,200 from the customers billed on August 21.
31 Made a cash withdrawal of $1,400.

REQUIRED

1. Set up the following T accounts: Cash; Accounts Receivable; Cleaning Supplies; Prepaid Lease; Cleaning Equipment; Accounts Payable; D. Roberts, Capital; D. Roberts, Withdrawals; Cleaning Revenue; and Repair Expense.

(Continued)

2. Record transactions directly in the T accounts. Identify each entry by date.

3. Prepare a trial balance for Roberts Upholstery Cleaning as of August 31, 2014.

4. **CONCEPT** ▶ Compare and contrast how the issues of recognition, valuation, and classification are settled in the transactions of August 7 and 9.

LO **3, 4, 5, 7**

CASH FLOW

SPREADSHEET

GENERAL LEDGER

✔ 5: Trial balance: $23,805

Transaction Analysis, General Journal, Ledger Accounts, and Trial Balance

P10. Mount Prospect Nursery School Company provides baby-sitting and child-care programs. On January 31, 2014, the company had the following trial balance:

Mount Prospect Nursery School Company
Trial Balance
January 31, 2014

	Debits	Credits
Cash (111)	1,870	
Accounts Receivable (113)	1,700	
Equipment (141)	1,040	
Buses (143)	17,400	
Notes Payable (211)		15,000
Accounts Payable (212)		1,640
J. Ziden, Capital (311)		5,370
	22,010	22,010

During the month of February, the company completed the following transactions:

Feb. 2 Paid this month's rent, $270.

3 Received fees for this month's services, $650.

4 Purchased supplies on account, $85.

5 Reimbursed the bus driver for gas expenses, $40.

6 Ordered playground equipment, $1,000.

8 Made a payment on account, $170.

9 Received payments from customers on account, $1,200.

10 Billed customers who had not yet paid for this month's services, $700.

11 Paid for the supplies purchased on February 4.

13 Purchased and received playground equipment ordered on February 6 for cash, $1,000.

17 Purchased equipment on account, $290.

19 Paid this month's utility bill, $145.

22 Received payment for one month's services from customers previously billed, $500.

26 Paid part-time assistants for services, $460.

27 Purchased gas and oil for the bus on account, $325.

28 Made a cash withdrawal of $110.

REQUIRED

1. Open accounts in the ledger for the accounts in the trial balance plus the following ones: Supplies (115); J. Ziden, Withdrawals (313); Service Revenue (411); Rent Expense (511); Gas and Oil Expense (512); Wages Expense (513); and Utilities Expense (514).

2. Enter the January 31, 2014, account balances from the trial balance.

3. Enter the above transactions in the general journal (Pages 17 and 18).

4. Post the entries to the ledger accounts. Be sure to make the appropriate posting references in the journal and ledger as you post.

5. Prepare a trial balance as of February 28, 2014.

6. **BUSINESS APPLICATION** ▶ Examine the transactions for February 3, 9, 10, and 22. What were the revenues, and how much cash was received from the revenues? What business issue might you see arising from the differences in these numbers?

CASES

LO 1, 3

Conceptual Understanding: Valuation and Classification of Business Transactions

C1. CONCEPT ▶ Tower Garden Center purchased two pre-owned trucks at a cash-only auction for 15 percent below current market value. The owners have asked you to record this purchase at current market value. You don't think that is correct. Write the owners a brief business memorandum in good form based on your knowledge of Chapter 2. Explain how the purchase of the pre-owned trucks will affect the balance sheet, include the entry to record the transaction, and explain why the amount must be at the price paid for the trucks.

LO 1, 3, 6

Conceptual Understanding: Recording of Rebates

C2. CONCEPT ▶ Is it revenue or a reduction of an expense? That is the question companies that receive manufacturer's rebates for purchasing a large quantity of product must answer. Food companies like **Sara Lee**, **Kraft Foods**, and **Nestlé** give supermarkets special manufacturer's rebates of up to 45 percent, depending on the quantities purchased. Some firms recorded these rebates as revenue, and others recorded them as a reduction of the cost until the SEC said that only one way is correct. What, then, is the correct way for supermarkets to record these rebates? Does your answer change net income?

LO 1, 2, 3

Interpreting Financial Statements: Interpreting a Bank's Financial Statements

C3. Mellon Bank is a large bank holding company. Selected accounts from the company's 2011 annual report are as follows (in millions):[5]

Cash and Due from Banks	$ 4,175
Loans to Customers	43,585
Securities Available for Sale	78,467
Deposits by Customers	219,094

1. Indicate whether each of these accounts is an asset, a liability, or a component of stockholders' equity on Mellon Bank's balance sheet.
2. Assume that you are in a position to do business with Mellon. Show how Mellon Bank's accountants would prepare the entry in T account form to record each of the following transactions:
   a. You sell securities in the amount of $2,000 to the bank.
   b. You deposit in the bank the $2,000 received from selling the securities.
   c. You borrow $5,000 from the bank.

LO 7

Interpreting Financial Statements: Cash Flows

C4. BUSINESS APPLICATION ▶ Having been promoted recently, you now have access to your firm's monthly financial statements. You notice that revenues are increasing rapidly and that income is at an all-time high. The balance sheet shows growth in receivables, and accounts payable have declined. However, the chief financial officer is concerned because the firm's cash flows from operating activities are decreasing. What are some reasons why a company with a positive net income may fall short of cash from its operating activities? What could be done to improve this situation?

Annual Report Case: Recognition, Valuation, and Classification

C5. CONCEPT ▶ Refer to the Summary of Significant Accounting Policies in the notes to the financial statements in the **CVS** annual report in the Supplement to Chapter 16.

1. How does the concept of recognition apply to advertising costs?
2. How does the concept of valuation apply to inventories?
3. How does the concept of classification apply to cash and cash equivalents?

LO **1, 6**

Comparison Analysis: Revenue Recognition

C6. BUSINESS APPLICATION ▶ Refer to the financial statements of **CVS** and **Southwest Airlines Co.** in the Supplement to Chapter 16. What is the total revenue for CVS and Southwest on the respective income statements? How do you think the nature of each business will affect revenue recognition for prescriptions filled for CVS versus airline tickets for Southwest? When do you think cash is received and revenues are earned for each company?

LO **1, 6**

Ethical Dilemma: Recognition Point and Ethical Considerations

C7. BUSINESS APPLICATION ▶ Robert Shah, a sales representative for Quality Office Supplies Corporation, will receive a substantial bonus if he meets his annual sales goal. The company's recognition point for sales is the day of shipment. On December 31, Shah realizes he needs sales of $2,000 to reach his sales goal and receive the bonus. He calls a purchaser for a local insurance company, whom he knows well, and asks him to buy $2,000 worth of copier paper today. The purchaser says, "But Robert, that's more than a year's supply for us." Shah says, "Buy it today. If you decide it's too much, you can return however much you want for full credit next month." The purchaser says, "Okay, ship it." The paper is shipped on December 31 and recorded as a sale. On January 15, the purchaser returns $1,750 worth of paper for full credit (approved by Shah) against the bill. Should the shipment on December 31 be recorded as a sale? Discuss the ethics of Shah's action.

Continuing Case: Annual Report Project

C8. CONCEPT ▶ Using the most recent annual report of the company you have chosen to study and that you have accessed online at the company's website, identify in the first note to the financial statements (usually labeled: Significant Accounting Policies) an accounting policy that illustrates each of the following:

1. Recognition
2. Valuation
3. Classification

CHAPTER 3
Adjusting the Accounts

BUSINESS INSIGHT
Reliable Answering Service

Reliable Answering Service takes telephone messages for doctors, lawyers, and other professionals and relays them immediately when they involve an emergency. At the end of any accounting period, Reliable has many transactions that will affect future periods. Examples include *office supplies* and *prepaid expenses*, which will benefit future periods and, therefore, are recorded as assets. Another example is *unearned revenue*, which represents receipts for services the company will not perform and earn until a future period. If prepaid expenses and unearned revenue are not accounted for properly at the end of a period, the company's income will be misstated. Similar misstatements can occur when a company fails to record (accrue) expenses that it incurred or revenue that it has earned but not yet received. Knowing the answers to the following questions will help prevent such misstatements.

1. CONCEPT ▷ *Why are the concepts of continuity, periodicity, and accrual accounting necessary for Reliable to account for transactions that span accounting periods?*

2. ACCOUNTING APPLICATION ▷ *How does Reliable adjust its revenues and expenses so that its net income is properly measured?*

3. BUSINESS APPLICATION ▷ *Which accounts on Reliable's income statement are potentially affected by adjusting entries? Which account on Reliable's balance sheet is never affected by an adjusting entry?*

LEARNING OBJECTIVES

LO 1 Define *net income*, and explain the concepts underlying income measurement.

LO 2 Distinguish cash basis of accounting from accrual accounting, and explain how accrual accounting is accomplished.

LO 3 Identify four situations that require adjusting entries, and illustrate typical adjusting entries.

LO 4 Prepare financial statements from an adjusted trial balance.

LO 5 Explain the importance of ethical measurement of net income and the relation of net income to cash flows.

Jasmin Awad/iStockphoto

SECTION 1

CONCEPTS

LO 1 Concepts Underlying Income Measurement

For a business to succeed or even survive, it must earn a profit. Profit, however, means different things to different people. Accountants prefer to use the term **net income** because it can be precisely defined as the *net increase in owner's equity that results from a company's operations*. Exhibit 1 illustrates the concepts underlying the measurement of net income.

Exhibit 1
Concepts Underlying Net Income

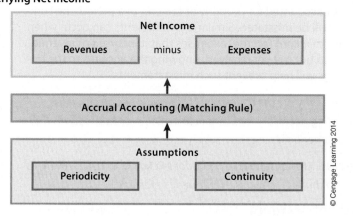

© Cengage Learning 2014

Net Income

Net income is accumulated in the Owner's Capital account and reported on the income statement. Management, owners, and others use it to assess a company's progress in meeting the goal of profitability. Readers of income statements need to understand net income and its strengths and weaknesses as an indicator of a company's performance.

In its simplest form, net income results when revenues exceed expenses:

$$\text{Net Income} = \text{Revenues} - \text{Expenses}$$

When expenses exceed revenues, a **net loss** occurs.

Revenues are *increases in owner's equity* resulting from selling goods, rendering services, or performing other business activities. When a business delivers a product or provides a service to a customer, it usually receives cash or a promise from customers to pay cash in the near future. In other words, revenue may be *earned* through the sale of goods or services, even though the cash may not be received until later. The promise to pay is recorded in either Accounts Receivable or Notes Receivable. The total of these accounts and the total cash received from customers in an accounting period are the company's revenues for that period.

Expenses are *decreases in owner's equity* resulting from the cost of selling goods or rendering services and the cost of the activities necessary to carry on a business, such as attracting and serving customers. Examples include salaries expense, rent expense, advertising expense, utilities expense, and depreciation (allocation of cost) of a building or office equipment. These expenses are often called the *cost of doing business* or *expired costs*. Note that the primary purpose of an expense is to generate revenue.

Not all increases in owner's equity arise from revenues, nor do all decreases in owner's equity arise from expenses. Owner's investments increase owner's equity but are not revenues, and withdrawals decrease owner's equity but are not expenses.

Income Measurement Assumptions

Users of financial reports should be aware that estimates and assumptions play a major role in the measurement of net income and other key indicators of performance. The major assumptions made in measuring business income are *continuity*, *periodicity*, and *accrual accounting* (the *matching rule*).

Continuity Certain expense and revenue transactions are allocated over several accounting periods. Choosing the number of accounting periods raises the issue of *continuity*. What is the expected life of the business? Many businesses last less than five years, and in any given year, thousands of businesses go bankrupt. The majority of companies present annual financial statements on the assumption that the business will continue to operate indefinitely—that is, that the company is a **going concern**. The **continuity** assumption is as follows.

> *Unless there is evidence to the contrary, the accountant assumes that the business is a going concern and will continue to operate indefinitely.*

The continuity assumption allows the cost of certain assets to be held on the balance sheet until a future accounting period, when the cost will become an expense. When a firm is facing bankruptcy, the accountant may prepare financial statements based on the assumption that the firm will go out of business and sell all of its assets.

Periodicity Not all transactions can be easily assigned to specific periods. For example, when a company purchases a building, it must estimate the number of years the building will be in use. The portion of the cost of the building that is assigned to each period depends on this estimate and requires an assumption about **periodicity**. The assumption is as follows.

> *Although the lifetime of a business is uncertain, it is nonetheless useful to estimate the business's net income in terms of accounting periods.*

STUDY NOTE: Accounting periods are of equal length so that one period can be compared with the next.

Financial statements may be prepared for any time period, but generally, to make comparisons easier, the periods are of equal length. A 12-month accounting period is called a **fiscal year**; accounting periods of less than a year are called **interim periods**. The fiscal year of many organizations is the calendar year, January 1 to December 31. However, retailers and other companies often end their fiscal years during a slack season, so that the fiscal year corresponds to the yearly cycle of business activity. For example, **Toys "R" Us**'s fiscal year ends in January and **Apple Computer**'s ends in September.

Accrual Accounting (Matching Rule) Under **accrual accounting** (often referred to as *the matching rule*) net income is measured by assigning:

- Revenues to the accounting period in which the goods are sold or the services performed.
- Expenses to the accounting period in which they are used to produce revenue.

A direct relationship between expenses and revenues is often difficult to identify. When there is no direct means of connecting expenses and revenues, costs are allocated among the accounting periods that benefit from the costs. For example, a building's cost is expensed over the building's expected useful life, and interest on investments is recorded as income even though it may not have been received.

APPLY IT!

Match the assumptions or actions with the concepts that follow.

1. Increases in owner's equity resulting from selling goods, rendering services, or performing other business activities.
2. Increase in owner's equity that results from a company's operations.
3. Decreases in owner's equity resulting from the cost of selling goods, rendering services, and other business activities.

a. Net income
b. Revenues
c. Expenses

SOLUTION

1. b; 2. a; 3. c

TRY IT! SE1, E1A, E1B

LO2 Concepts Underlying Accrual Accounting

The **cash basis of accounting** is the practice of accounting for revenues in the period in which cash is received and for expenses in the period in which cash is paid. With this method, taxable income is calculated as the difference between cash receipts from revenues and cash payments for expenses. Although this method works well for some small businesses and many individuals, it does not fit the needs of most businesses.

In contrast, as noted above, in *accrual accounting*, revenues and expenses are recorded when they are earned or incurred rather than when they are received or paid. Adjusting the accounts is a technique used to accomplish accrual accounting.

Recognizing Revenues

As you may recall, the process of determining when revenue should be recorded is called **revenue recognition**. The Securities and Exchange Commission requires that all the following conditions be met before revenue is recognized:[1]

- Persuasive evidence of an arrangement exists.
- A product or service has been delivered.
- The seller's price to the buyer is fixed or determinable.
- Collectibility is reasonably ensured.

For example, suppose Blue Design Studio has created a brochure for a customer and that the transaction meets the SEC's four criteria:

- The company and the customer agree that the customer owes for the service.
- The service has been rendered.
- Both parties understand the price.
- There is a reasonable expectation that the customer will pay the bill.

When Blue bills the customer, it records the transaction as revenue by debiting Accounts Receivable and crediting Design Revenue. Note that revenue can be recorded because there is a reasonable expectation that cash will be received.

International Perspective

IFRS Revenue Recognition: Principles Versus Rules

Revenue recognition highlights the differences between international and U.S. accounting standards. Although U.S. standards are referred to as generally accepted accounting *principles*, the FASB has issued extensive *rules* (specific guidance) for revenue recognition in various situations and industries. The IASB, on the other hand, generally has a few broad IFRS for revenue recognition and leaves it to companies and their auditors to determine how to apply the broad *principle* in specific situations. The FASB and IASB are currently working together to converge on a single standard for revenue recognition; but it is a challenge, given the very different approaches.

Recognizing Expenses

Expenses are recorded when all of the following conditions are met:

- There is an agreement to purchase goods or services.
- The goods have been delivered or the services rendered.
- A price has been established or can be determined.
- The goods or services have been used to produce revenue.

For example, when Blue Design Studio receives its utility bill, it recognizes the expense as having been incurred and as having helped produce revenue. Blue records this transaction by debiting Utilities Expense and crediting Accounts Payable. Until the bill is paid, Accounts Payable serves as a holding account. Note that recognition of the expense does not depend on the payment of cash.

APPLY IT!

Four conditions must be met before revenue can be recognized. Identify which of these conditions applies to the following actions:

a. Determines that the firm has a good credit rating.

b. Agrees to a price for services before it performs them.

c. Performs services.

d. Signs a contract to perform services.

SOLUTION

a. Collectibility is reasonably assured.

b. The seller's price to the buyer is fixed or determinable.

c. A product or service has been delivered.

d. Persuasive evidence of an arrangement exists.

TRY IT! E1A, E2A, E1B, E2B

SECTION 2

ACCOUNTING APPLICATIONS

ACCOUNTING APPLICATIONS

■ Prepare adjusting entries

■ Prepare financial
  statements from an
  adjusted trial balance

**RELEVANT
LEARNING OBJECTIVES**

LO 3 Identify four situations
that require adjusting
entries, and illustrate typical
adjusting entries.

LO 4 Prepare financial
statements from an
adjusted trial balance.

LO 3 The Adjustment Process

Accrual accounting also involves adjusting the accounts. Adjustments are necessary because the accounting period, by definition, ends on a particular day. The balance sheet must list all assets and liabilities as of the end of that day, and the income statement must contain all revenues and expenses applicable to the period ending on that day. Although operating a business is a continuous process, there must be a cutoff point for the periodic reports. Some transactions invariably span the cutoff point, and therefore, some accounts need adjustment.

In Exhibit 2, some of the accounts in Blue Design Studio's trial balance as of July 31 do not show the correct balances for preparing the financial statements. The trial balance lists prepaid rent of $3,200 for the months of July and August. So, on July 31, one-half of the $3,200 represents rent expense for July, and the remaining $1,600 represents an asset that will be used in August. An adjustment is needed to reflect the $1,600 balance in the Prepaid Rent account and the $1,600 rent expense. As you will see, several other accounts in Blue's trial balance do not reflect their correct balances. Like the Prepaid Rent account, they need to be adjusted.

Exhibit 2
Trial Balance for Blue Design Studio

Blue Design Studio		
Trial Balance		
July 31, 2014		
Cash	22,480	
Accounts Receivable	4,600	
Office Supplies	5,200	
Prepaid Rent	3,200	
Office Equipment	16,320	
Accounts Payable		6,280
Unearned Design Revenue		1,400
J. Blue, Capital		40,000
J. Blue, Withdrawals	2,800	
Design Revenue		12,400
Wages Expense	4,800	
Utilities Expense	680	
	60,080	60,080

When transactions span more than one accounting period, *accrual accounting* requires the use of **adjusting entries**. Exhibit 3 shows the four situations in which adjusting entries must be made. Each adjusting entry affects one balance sheet account and one income statement account. Note that adjusting entries provide information about past or future cash flows but never involve an entry to the Cash account.

Exhibit 3
The Four Types of Adjustments

The four types of adjusting entries are as follows.

- **Type 1. Allocating recorded costs between two or more accounting periods.** Examples of these costs are prepayments of rent, insurance, and supplies and the depreciation of plant and equipment. The adjusting entry involves an asset account and an expense account.
- **Type 2. Recognizing unrecorded expenses.** Examples of these expenses are wages and interest that have been incurred but are not recorded during an accounting period. The adjusting entry involves an expense account and a liability account.
- **Type 3. Allocating recorded, unearned revenues between two or more accounting periods.** Examples include payments received in advance and deposits made for goods or services to be delivered or provided in the future. The adjusting entry involves a liability account and a revenue account.
- **Type 4. Recognizing unrecorded, earned revenues.** An example is revenue that a company has earned for providing a service but for which it has not billed or collected a fee by the end of the accounting period. The adjusting entry involves an asset account and a revenue account.

Adjusting entries are either deferrals or accruals.

- A **deferral** is the postponement of the *recognition* of an expense already paid (Type 1 adjustment) or of revenue received in advance (Type 3 adjustment). The cash payment or receipt is recorded before the adjusting entry is made.
- An **accrual** is the *recognition* of expense (Type 2 adjustment) or a revenue (Type 4 adjustment) that has arisen but not been recorded during the accounting period. The cash payment or receipt occurs in a future accounting period, after the adjusting entry has been made.

Type 1 Adjustment: Allocating Recorded Costs (Deferred Expenses)

Companies often make expenditures that benefit more than one period. These costs are debited to an asset account. At the end of an accounting period, the amount of the asset that has been used is transferred from the asset account to an expense account. Two important adjustments of this type are for prepaid expenses and the depreciation of plant and equipment.

Prepaid Expenses Companies customarily pay some expenses, including those for rent, supplies, and insurance, in advance. These costs are called **prepaid expenses**. By the end of an accounting period, a portion or all of the prepaid services or goods will have been used. The required adjusting entry reduces the asset and increases the expense, as shown in Exhibit 4. The amount of the adjustment equals the cost of the goods or services used or expired.

STUDY NOTE: The expired portion of a prepayment is converted to an expense; the unexpired portion remains an asset.

Exhibit 4
Adjustment for Prepaid
(Deferred) Expenses

If adjusting entries for prepaid expenses are not made at the end of an accounting period, both the balance sheet and the income statement will present incorrect information. The company's assets will be overstated, and its expenses will be understated. Thus, owner's equity on the balance sheet and net income on the income statement will be overstated. Examples of adjusting entries for Blue Design Studio follow.

Adjustment for Prepaid Rent

Transaction Blue Design Studio paid two months' rent in advance at the beginning of July. The advance payment resulted in an asset—the right to occupy the office for two months. As each day in the month passed, part of the asset's cost expired and became an expense. By July 31, one-half of the asset's cost ($1,600) had expired.

Analysis The journal entry to record the expiration of prepaid rent

▼ *decreases* the asset account *Prepaid Rent* with a credit

▲ *increases* the expense account *Rent Expense* with a debit

Application of Double Entry

Comment The Prepaid Rent account now has a balance of $1,600, which represents one month's rent that will be expensed during August.

Think of accounting for supplies as using a storage cabinet in an office. Supplies are put in the cabinet when purchased (assets). Employees take some out and use them during the accounting period (expenses). At the end of the accounting period, the supplies left in the cabinet can be used in the next period (assets).

Adjustment for Supplies

Transaction Blue Design Studio purchased $5,200 of office supplies in early July. At the end of July, an inventory shows that office supplies costing $3,660 are still on hand. This means that of the $5,200 of supplies originally purchased, $1,540 worth were used (became an expense) by July 31.

Analysis The journal entry to record the consumption of office supplies

▼ *decreases* the asset account *Office Supplies* with a credit

▲ *increases* the expense account *Office Supplies Expense* with a debit

Application of Double Entry

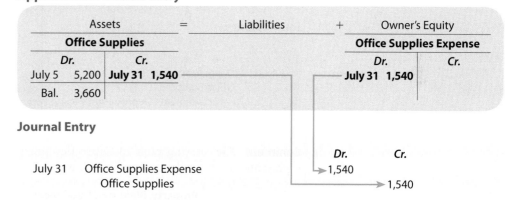

Journal Entry

July 31	Office Supplies Expense		Dr.	Cr.
			1,540	
	Office Supplies			1,540

Comment The asset account Office Supplies now reflects the correct balance of $3,660 of supplies yet to be consumed.

STUDY NOTE: *In accounting, depreciation refers only to the allocation of an asset's cost, not to any decline in the asset's value.*

STUDY NOTE: *The difficulty in estimating an asset's useful life is further evidence that the net income figure is, at best, an estimate.*

Depreciation of Plant and Equipment When a company buys a long-term asset—such as a building, truck, computer, or store fixture—it is, in effect, prepaying for the usefulness of that asset for as long as it benefits the company. Because a long-term asset is a deferral of an expense, the accountant must allocate the cost of the asset over its estimated useful life. The amount allocated to any one accounting period is called **depreciation** (or *depreciation expense*).

It is often impossible to tell exactly how long an asset will last or how much of the asset has been used in any one period. For this reason, depreciation must be estimated. Accountants have developed a number of methods for estimating depreciation.[2]

To maintain historical costs, separate accounts are used to accumulate the depreciation on each long-term asset. These **Accumulated Depreciation** accounts are called *contra accounts*. A **contra account** is paired with a related account—in our example, an asset account. The balance of a contra account is shown on a financial statement as a deduction from its related account. The net amount is called the **carrying value** (or *book value*) of the asset. As time passes, the accumulated depreciation grows, and the carrying value of the asset declines.

Adjustment for Plant and Equipment

Transaction On July 31, Blue Design Studio records $300 of depreciation of office equipment.

Analysis The journal entry to record depreciation

▲ *increases* the contra account *Accumulated Depreciation—Office Equipment* with a credit

▲ *increases* the expense account *Depreciation Expense—Office Equipment* with a debit

Application of Double Entry

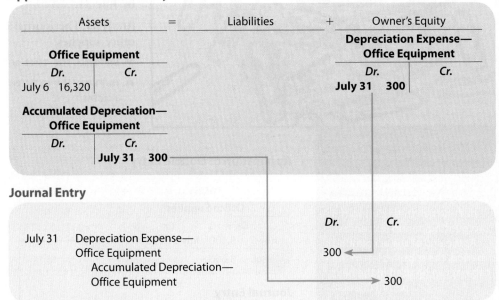

Comment The carrying value of Office Equipment is $16,020 ($16,320 − $300) and is presented on the balance sheet as follows.

Property, Plant, and Equipment		
Office equipment	$16,320	
Less accumulated depreciation	300	$16,020

Business Application **Netflix** has prepaid expenses and property and equipment similar to those in the examples we have presented. Among Netflix's prepaid expenses are payments to movie companies for rights to DVDs called Prepaid Content. By paying in advance, Netflix is able to negotiate lower prices. These fixed payments are debited to Prepaid Content. When the movies produce revenue, the prepaid amounts are transferred to expense through adjusting entries.[3]

Type 2 Adjustment: Recognizing Unrecorded Expenses (Accrued Expenses)

Usually, at the end of an accounting period, some expenses incurred during the period have not been recorded in the accounts. These expenses require adjusting entries. One such expense is interest on borrowed money. Each day, interest accumulates on the debt. As shown in Exhibit 5, an adjusting entry records the accumulated interest, which is an expense of the period, and the corresponding liability to pay the interest. Other common unrecorded expenses are wages and utilities. As the expense and the corresponding liability accumulate, they are said to *accrue*—hence the term **accrued expenses**.

Balance Sheet

Liability

2. Recognizing unrecorded expenses.

Liability Account	Expense Account
Adjusting Entry Credit	Adjusting Entry Debit

Amount equals cost of expense incurred.

Income Statement

Asset

Expense

1. Allocating recorded costs between two or more accounting periods.

4. Recognizing unrecorded, earned revenues.

3. Allocating recorded, unearned revenues between two or more accounting periods.

Revenue

© Cengage Learning 2014

Exhibit 5
Adjustment for Unrecorded (Accrued) Expenses

Adjustment for Unrecorded (Accrued) Wages

Transaction Suppose Blue Design Studio has two pay periods a month rather than one. In July, its pay periods end on the 12th and the 26th, as indicated in the calendar below.

July						
Sun	**M**	**T**	**W**	**Th**	**F**	**Sa**
	1	2	3	4	5	6
7	8	9	10	11	12	13
14	15	16	17	18	19	20
21	22	23	24	25	26	27
28	**29**	**30**	**31**			

By the end of business on July 31, Blue's assistant will have worked three days (Monday, Tuesday, and Wednesday) beyond the last pay period. The employee has earned the wages for those days but will not be paid until the first payday in August. The wages for these three days are rightfully an expense for July, and the liabilities should reflect that the company owes the assistant for those days. Because the assistant's wage rate is $2,400 every two weeks, or $240 per day ($2,400 ÷ 10 working days), the expense is $720 ($240 × 3 days). On July 31, Blue would record the $720 accrual of unrecorded wages.

Analysis The journal entry to record the accrual of wages

▲ *increases* the owner's equity account *Wages Expense* with a debit

▲ *increases* the liability account *Wages Payable* with a credit

Application of Double Entry

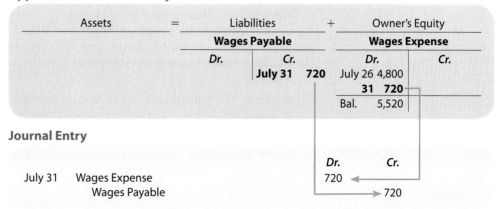

Assets	=	Liabilities	+	Owner's Equity
		Wages Payable		**Wages Expense**
Dr.		*Dr.*	*Cr.*	*Dr.*	*Cr.*
			July 31 720	July 26 4,800	
				31 720	
				Bal. 5,520	

Journal Entry

		Dr.	*Cr.*
July 31	Wages Expense	720	
	Wages Payable		720

Comment Note that the increase in Wages Expense will *decrease* owner's equity and that total wages for the month are $5,520, of which $720 will be paid next month.

Business Application In 2011, **Netflix** had accrued expenses of $63,693,000. If the expenses had not been accrued, Netflix's liabilities would be significantly understated, as would the corresponding expenses on Netflix's income statement. The end result would be an overstatement of the company's earnings.

Type 3 Adjustment: Allocating Recorded, Unearned Revenues (Deferred Revenues)

STUDY NOTE: *Unearned revenue is a liability because there is an obligation to deliver goods or perform a service, or to return the payment. Once the goods have been delivered or the service performed, the liability is transferred to revenue.*

When a company receives revenues in advance, it has an obligation to deliver goods or perform services. **Unearned revenues** are therefore shown in a liability account.

For example, publishing companies usually receive cash in advance for magazine subscriptions. These receipts are recorded in a liability account, Unearned Subscriptions. If the company fails to deliver the magazines, subscribers are entitled to their money back. As the company delivers each issue of the magazine, it earns a part of the advance receipts. This earned portion must be transferred from the Unearned Subscriptions account to the Subscription Revenue account, as shown in Exhibit 6.

Exhibit 6
Adjustment for Unearned (Deferred) Revenues

Balance Sheet

	Asset	Liability
Expense	1. Allocating recorded costs between two or more accounting periods.	2. Recognizing unrecorded expenses.
Revenue	4. Recognizing unrecorded, earned revenues.	3. Allocating recorded, unearned revenues between two or more accounting periods.

(left axis: Income Statement)

Liability Account

Adjusting Entry Debit

Revenue Account

Adjusting Entry Credit

Amount equals price of services performed or goods delivered.

© Cengage Learning 2014

Adjustment for Unearned Revenue

Transaction During July, Blue Design Studio received $1,400 from another firm as advance payment for a series of brochures. By the end of the month, it had completed $800 of work on the brochures, and the other firm had accepted the work. On July 31, Blue would record the performance of services for which $800 cash was received in advance.

Analysis The journal entry to record performing services for which cash was received in advance

▲ *increases* the owner's equity account *Design Revenue* with a credit

▼ *decreases* the liability account *Unearned Design Revenue* with a debit

Application of Double Entry

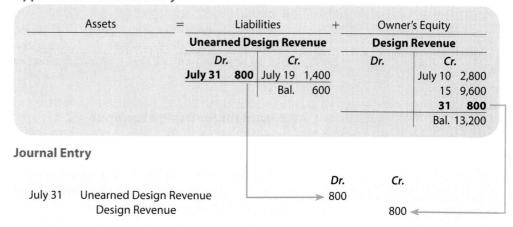

Assets	=	Liabilities	+	Owner's Equity

Unearned Design Revenue

Dr.		Cr.	
July 31	800	July 19	1,400
		Bal.	600

Design Revenue

Dr.		Cr.	
		July 10	2,800
		15	9,600
		31	**800**
		Bal.	13,200

Journal Entry

		Dr.	Cr.
July 31	Unearned Design Revenue	800	
	Design Revenue		800

Comment Unearned Design Revenue now reflects the amount of work still to be performed, $600.

Business Application **Netflix** has a current liability account called Deferred (Unearned) Revenue. Deferred revenue consists of subscriptions (monthly payments) billed in advance to customers. Subscription revenues are pro-rated over each subscriber's monthly subscription period. As time passes and customers use the service, the revenue is transferred from Netflix's Deferred Revenue account to its Subscription Revenue account.

Type 4 Adjustment: Recognizing Unrecorded, Earned Revenues (Accrued Revenues)

Accrued revenues are revenues that a company has earned by performing a service or delivering goods but for which no entry has been made in the accounting records. Any revenues earned but not recorded during an accounting period require an adjusting entry that debits an asset account and credits a revenue account, as shown in Exhibit 7. For example, the interest on a note receivable is earned day by day but may not be received until another accounting period. In this case, Interest Receivable should be

Exhibit 7
Adjustment for Unrecorded (Accrued) Revenues

debited and Interest Income should be credited for the interest accrued at the end of the current period.

When a company earns revenue by performing a service—such as designing a series of brochures—but will not receive the revenue until a future accounting period, it must make an adjusting entry. This type of adjusting entry involves an asset account and a revenue account.

Adjustment for Design Revenue

Transaction During July, Blue Design Studio agrees to create two advertisements for Maggio's Pizza Company and to finish the first advertisement by July 31. By the end of July, Blue has earned $400 for completing the first advertisement, but it will not bill Maggio's until the entire project has been completed. On July 31, Blue records the accrual of $400 of unrecorded revenue.

Analysis The journal entry to record the accrual of unrecorded revenue

▲ *increases* the owner's equity account *Design Revenue* with a credit

▲ *increases* the asset account *Accounts Receivable* with a debit

Application of Double Entry

Comment Design Revenue now reflects the total revenue earned during July, $13,600. On the balance sheet, revenues that have been earned but not recorded are usually combined with accounts receivable.

Business Application Since **Netflix**'s subscribers pay their subscriptions in advance by credit card, Netflix does not need to bill customers for services provided but not paid. The company is in the enviable position of having no accounts receivable and thus a high degree of liquidity.

A Note About Business Transactions

Thus far, we have presented a full analysis of each journal entry and showed you the thought process behind each entry. Because you should now be fully aware of the effects of transactions on the accounting equation and the rules of debit and credit, we present simplified journal entries in the rest of the book.

APPLY IT! ▶

On December 31, the end of the current fiscal year, the following information is available to assist Bora Company's accountants in making adjusting entries:

a. Bora's Supplies account shows a beginning balance of $6,000. Purchases during the year were $10,300. The end-of-year inventory reveals supplies on hand of $3,000.

b. On July 1, the company completed negotiations with a client and accepted an advance of $4,800 for services to be performed monthly for a year. The $4,800 was credited to Unearned Services Revenue.

c. Among the assets of the company is a note receivable in the amount of $100,000. On December 31, the accrued interest on this note amounted to $6,000.

d. On Saturday, January 3, the company, which is on a six-day workweek, will pay its regular employees their weekly wages of $9,000.

1. Identify each adjustment as a Type 1, 2, 3, or 4 adjusting entry.
2. Prepare adjusting entries for each item listed.

SOLUTION

1. a. Type 1; b. Type 3; c. Type 4; d. Type 2

2.

			Dr.	Cr.
a.	Dec. 31	Supplies Expense	13,300	
		Supplies		13,300
		To record supplies used ($6,000 + $10,300 − $3,000 = $13,300)		
b.	Dec. 31	Unearned Services Revenue	2,400	
		Services Revenue		2,400
		To record service revenue earned [($4,800/12 months) × 6 months = $2,400]		
c.	Dec. 31	Interest Receivable	6,000	
		Interest Income		6,000
		To record interest earned but not received		
d.	Dec. 31	Wages Expense	4,500	
		Wages Payable		4,500
		To record wages incurred but not paid [($9,000/6 days) × 3 days = $4,500]		

TRY IT! SE2, SE3, SE4, SE5, SE6, E1A, E3A, E4A, E5A, F6A, E7A, E8A, E9A, E1B, E3B, E4B, E5B, E6B, E7B, E8B, E9B

LO4 Using the Adjusted Trial Balance to Prepare Financial Statements

After adjusting entries have been recorded and posted, an **adjusted trial balance** is prepared by listing all accounts and their balances. If the adjusting entries have been posted to the accounts correctly, the adjusted trial balance will have equal debit and credit totals. Exhibit 8 shows the adjusted trial balance for Blue Design Studio and its relationship to the company's income statement, balance sheet, and statement of owner's equity. Some accounts in Exhibit 8, such as Cash and Accounts Payable, have the same balances as in the trial balance in Exhibit 2 because no adjusting entries affected them. The balances of other accounts, such as Office Supplies and Prepaid Rent, differ from those in the trial balance because adjusting entries did affect them. The adjusted trial balance also includes accounts that do not appear in the trial balance—for example, depreciation accounts and Wages Payable.

Exhibit 8
Relationship of the Adjusted Trial Balance to the Income
Statement, Statement of Owner's Equity, and Balance Sheet

Blue Design Studio
Adjusted Trial Balance
July 31, 2014

Cash	22,480	
Accounts Receivable	5,000	
Office Supplies	3,660	
Prepaid Rent	1,600	
Office Equipment	16,320	
Accumulated Depreciation— Office Equipment		300
Accounts Payable		6,280
Unearned Design Revenue		600
Wages Payable		720
J. Blue, Capital		40,000
J. Blue, Withdrawals	2,800	
Design Revenue		13,600
Wages Expense	5,520	
Utilities Expense	680	
Rent Expense	1,600	
Office Supplies Expense	1,540	
Depreciation Expense— Office Equipment	300	
	61,500	61,500

Blue Design Studio
Income Statement
For the Month Ended July 31, 2014

Revenues:		
Design revenue		$13,600
Expenses:		
Wages expense	$5,520	
Utilities expense	680	
Rent expense	1,600	
Office supplies expense	1,540	
Depreciation expense— office equipment	300	
Total expenses		9,640
Net income		$ 3,960

Blue Design Studio
Statement of Owner's Equity
For the Month Ended July 31, 2014

J. Blue, capital, July 1, 2014	$ 0
Investment by J. Blue	40,000
Net income	3,960
Subtotal	$43,960
Less withdrawals	2,800
J. Blue, capital, July 31, 2014	$41,160

Blue Design Studio
Balance Sheet
July 31, 2014

Assets

Cash		$22,480
Accounts receivable		5,000
Office supplies		3,660
Prepaid rent		1,600
Office equipment	$16,320	
Less accumulated depreciation	300	16,020
Total assets		$48,760

Liabilities

Accounts payable	$ 6,280
Unearned design revenue	600
Wages payable	720
Total liabilities	$ 7,600

Owner's Equity

J. Blue, capital	41,160
Total liabilities and owner's equity	$48,760

STUDY NOTE: *The net income figure from the income statement is needed to prepare the statement of owner's equity, and the bottom-line figure of that statement is needed to prepare the balance sheet. This dictates the order in which the statements are prepared.*

Exhibit 9

Effects of Adjusting Entries on the Financial Statements

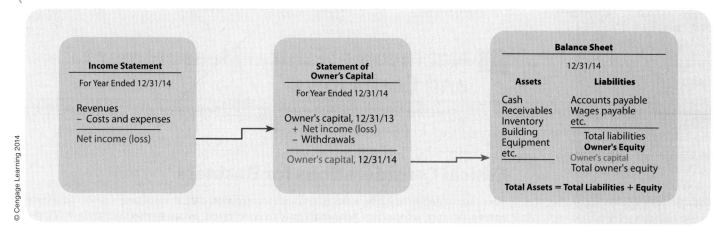

The adjusted trial balance facilitates the preparation of the income statement, the statement of owner's equity, and the balance sheet. As shown in Exhibit 8, the revenue and expense accounts are used to prepare the income statement, and the asset and liability accounts are used to prepare the balance sheet.

Notice that the net income from the income statement is combined with the Withdrawals account on the statement of owner's equity to give the net change in the J. Blue, Capital account. The balance of J. Blue, Capital at July 31 is used in preparing the balance sheet.

Adjusting Entries and the Financial Statements

Exhibit 9 shows that adjusting entries always affect at least one balance sheet account and one income statement account but not the statement of cash flows.

APPLY IT!

The adjusted trial balance for Carroll Company on December 31, 2014, contains the following accounts and balances: D. Carroll, Capital, $300 (as of December 1, 2014); D. Carroll, Withdrawals, $100; Service Revenue, $1,000; Rent Expense, $300; Wages Expense, $400; and Telephone Expense, $100. Compute net income and prepare a statement of owner's equity in proper form for the month of December.

SOLUTION

Net income = Service Revenue − Rent Expense − Wages Expense − Telephone Expense
= $1,000 − $300 − $400 − $100
= $1,000 − $800
= $200

Carroll Company
Statement of Owner's Equity
For the Month Ended December 31, 2014

D. Carroll, capital, December 1, 2014	$300
Net income	200
Subtotal	$500
Less withdrawals	100
D. Carroll, capital, December 31, 2014	$400

TRY IT! SE7, SE8, E10A, E10B

SECTION 3

BUSINESS APPLICATIONS

BUSINESS APPLICATIONS

■ Ethics
■ Cash flows
■ Liquidity

**RELEVANT
LEARNING OBJECTIVE**

LO 5 Explain the
importance of ethical
measurement of net income
and the relation of net
income to cash flows.

LO 5 Net Income: Ethical Measurement and Cash Flows

In this section, we consider the ethical measurement of net income and the relation of accrual-based net income to cash flows.

Ethical Considerations for Business

Account adjustments take time to calculate and enter in the records. Also, adjusting entries do not affect cash flows in the current period because they never involve the Cash account. You might ask, "Why go to all the trouble of making them? Why worry about them?" For one thing, the SEC has identified issues related to *accrual accounting* and adjustments as an area of utmost importance because of the potential for abuse and misrepresentation.[4]

All adjustments are important because of their effect on profitability and liquidity. Adjusting entries affect net income, and they affect profitability comparisons from one period to the next. They also affect assets and liabilities on the balance sheet and thus provide information about a company's *future* cash inflows and outflows. This information is needed to assess the need for cash to pay ongoing obligations. The potential for abuse arises because judgment underlies the adjusting entries. When this judgment is misused, performance measures can be misleading.

Applying *accrual accounting* involves making assumptions. It also involves exercising judgment. Consider the assumptions and judgment involved in estimating the useful life of a building. The estimate should be based on realistic assumptions, but management has latitude in making that estimate, and its judgment will affect the final net income that is reported.

The manipulation of revenues and expenses to achieve a specific outcome is called **earnings management**. Research has shown that companies that manage their earnings are much more likely to exceed projected earnings targets by a little than to fall short by a little. Management may want to manage earnings to keep them from falling short in order to:

■ Meet a previously announced goal and thus meet the expectations of the market.
■ Keep the company's stock price from dropping.
■ Meet a goal that will enable it to earn bonuses.
■ Avoid embarrassment.

Earnings management, though not the best practice, is not always illegal. However, when the estimates involved in earnings management begin moving outside a reasonable range, the financial statements become misleading. For instance, net income is misleading when revenue is overstated by a significant amount or when expenses are understated by a significant amount. As noted earlier in the text, the preparation of financial statements that are intentionally misleading constitutes fraudulent financial reporting. Evidence of fraudulent financial reporting is often evidenced by lack of sufficient cash flows as explained in the next section.

Business Perspective
Adjusting Entries and Fraudulent Financial Reporting

Improper adjusting entries often play an important role in companies that fraudulently prepare the financial statements. The reason is that adjustments may easily be falsely prepared or ignored. The most common fraud technique involved improper *revenue recognition*, followed by the overstatement of existing assets or capitalization of expenses. Revenue may be overstated by simply debiting Accounts Receivable and crediting Revenue. Expenses may be understated by recording expenses as assets or keeping on the balance sheet assets that have been used up. The SEC investigated 347 alleged cases of public company fraudulent financial reporting from 1998 to 2007. Consistent with the high-profile frauds at **Enron, WorldCom**, etc., the dollar magnitude of fraudulent financial reporting soared in the last decade, with an average of nearly $400 million per case.[5]

Using Accrual-Based Information to Make Management Decisions

Management has the short-range goal of ensuring that it has sufficient cash to ensure the company's liquidity. Ultimately, cash must flow from income-producing activities for a company to be successful. To plan payments to creditors and assess the need for short-term borrowing, managers must know how to use accrual-based information to analyze cash flows.

Almost every revenue or expense account on the income statement has one or more related accounts on the balance sheet. For instance, Supplies Expense is related to Supplies, Wages Expense is related to Wages Payable, and Design Revenue is related to Unearned Design Revenue. As we have shown, these accounts are related by making adjusting entries, the purpose of which is to apply *accrual accounting* to the measurement of net income.

A company's cash inflows and cash outflows can also be determined by analyzing these relationships. For example, suppose that after receiving the financial statements in Exhibit 8, management wants to know how much cash was expended for office supplies. On the income statement, Office Supplies Expense is $1,540, and on the balance sheet, Office Supplies is $3,660. Because July was the company's first month of operation, there was no prior balance of office supplies, so the amount of cash expended for office supplies during the month was $5,200 ($1,540 + $3,660 = $5,200). Thus, the cash flow used in purchasing office supplies—$5,200—was much greater than the amount expensed in determining income—$1,540. Management can anticipate that the cash needed may be less than the amount expensed because the company will probably not have to buy office supplies in August. Understanding these cash flow effects enables management to better predict the business's need for cash.

The general rule for determining the cash flow received from any revenue or paid for any expense (except depreciation, which is a special case) is to determine the potential cash payments or cash receipts and deduct the amount not paid or not received. As shown in Exhibit 10, the application of the general rule varies with the type of asset or liability account.

Business Perspective
Are Misstatements of Earnings Always Overstatements?

Not all misstatements of earnings are overstatements. For instance, privately held companies, which do not have to be concerned about the effect of their earnings announcements on owners or investors, may understate income to reduce or avoid income taxes. In an unusual case involving a public company, the SEC cited and fined **Microsoft** for understating its income. Microsoft, a very successful company, accomplished this by overstating its unearned revenue on the balance sheet. The company's motive in trying to appear less successful than it actually was may have been that it was facing government charges of being a monopoly.[6]

Type of Account	Potential Payment or Receipt Not Paid or Received				Result
Prepaid Expense	Ending Balance	+ Expense for the Period	− Beginning Balance	=	Cash Payments for Expenses
Unearned Revenue	Ending Balance	+ Revenue for the Period	− Beginning Balance	=	Cash Receipts from Revenues
Accrued Payable	Beginning Balance	+ Expense for the Period	− Ending Balance	=	Cash Payments for Expenses
Accrued Receivable	Beginning Balance	+ Revenue for the Period	− Ending Balance	=	Cash Receipts from Revenues

Exhibit 10
Determination of Cash Flows from Accrual-Based Information

For instance, suppose that on May 31, the balance of Prepaid Insurance was $480, and that on June 30, the balance was $670. If the insurance expense during June was $120, the amount of cash expended on insurance during June can be computed as follows.

Prepaid Insurance at June 30	$670
Insurance Expense during June	120
Potential cash payments for insurance	$790
Less Prepaid Insurance at May 31	480
Cash payments for insurance during June	$310

The beginning balance is deducted because it was paid in a prior period. Note that the cash payments equal the expense plus the increase in the balance of the Prepaid Insurance account [$120 + ($670 − $480) = $310]. In this case, the cash paid was almost three times the amount of insurance expense. In future months, cash payments are likely to be less than the expense.

APPLY IT!

Supplies had a balance of $400 at the end of May and $360 at the end of June. Supplies Expense was $550 for the month of June. How much cash was paid for supplies during June?

SOLUTION

Supplies at June 30	$360
Supplies Expense during June	550
Potential cash payments for supplies	$910
Less Supplies at May 31	400
Cash payments for supplies during June	$510

TRY IT! SE9, SE10, E11A, E12A, E11B, E12B

TriLevel Problem

The beginning of this chapter focused on Reliable Answering Service, a company that has many transactions that span accounting periods. Complete the following requirements in order to answer the questions posed at the beginning of the chapter.

Section 1: Concepts
As we learned in the chapter opener, Reliable has many transactions that will affect future periods like office supplies, prepaid expenses, and unearned revenue. *Why are the concepts of continuity, periodicity, and accrual accounting necessary for Reliable to account for transactions that span accounting periods?*

Section 2: Accounting Applications
How does Reliable adjust its revenues and expenses so that its net income is properly measured?

Jasmin Awad/iStockphoto

Reliable Answering Service

Reliable's trial balance follows.

	A	B	C	D	E
1			**Reliable Answering Service**		
2			**Trial Balance**		
3			**December 31, 2014**		
4					
5	Cash			2,160	
6	Accounts Receivable			1,250	
7	Office Supplies			180	
8	Prepaid Insurance			240	
9	Office Equipment			3,400	
10	Accumulated Depreciation—Office Equipment				600
11	Accounts Payable				700
12	Unearned Revenue				460
13	T. Ramos, Capital				4,870
14	T. Ramos, Withdrawals			400	
15	Answering Service Revenue				2,900
16	Wages Expense			1,500	
17	Rent Expense			400	
18				9,530	9,530
19					

The following information is also available for the company on December 31, 2014:

a. Insurance that expired during December amounted to $40.
b. Office supplies on hand on December 31 totaled $75.
c. Depreciation for December totaled $100.
d. Accrued wages on December 31 totaled $120.
e. Revenues earned for services performed in December but not billed by the end of the month totaled $300.
f. Revenues received in advance of services still to be performed totaled $300 at the end of the year.

Required
In order to understand how Reliable adjusts its revenues and expenses so that its net income is properly measured, complete the following:

1. Determine the required adjusting entries, and record them in the general journal.
2. Post the entries to the T accounts. Open new T accounts as needed.
3. Prepare an adjusted trial balance.
4. Prepare an income statement, a statement of owner's equity, and a balance sheet for the month ended December 31, 2014.

Section 3: Business Applications
Which accounts on Reliable's income statement are potentially affected by adjusting entries? Which account on Reliable's balance sheet is never affected by an adjusting entry?

SOLUTION   **Section 1: Concepts**
Reliable applies the concept of *continuity* when its accountants assume that it will continue to operate indefinitely. The company applies the concept of *periodicity* by estimating its net income in terms of accounting periods. Reliable uses *accrual accounting* to measure net income by *recognizing revenues* when they are earned, and *recognizing expenses* when they are incurred. This process may require adjustment of income statement and balance sheet accounts except Cash.

Section 2: Accounting Applications

1.

			Dr.	Cr.
a.	Dec. 31	Insurance Expense	40	
		Prepaid Insurance		40
		To record expired insurance		
b.	Dec. 31	Office Supplies Expense	105	
		Office Supplies		105
		To record office supplies used ($180 − $75 = $105)		
c.	Dec. 31	Depreciation Expense	100	
		Accumulated Depreciation—Office Equipment		100
		To record depreciation expense		
d.	Dec. 31	Wages Expense	120	
		Wages Payable		120
		To record wages incurred but not paid		
e.	Dec. 31	Accounts Receivable	300	
		Answering Service Revenue		300
		To record revenues earned but not received		
f.	Dec. 31	Unearned Revenues	160	
		Answering Service Revenue		160
		To record revenues earned by end of year ($460 − $300 = $160)		

2.

	A	B	C	D	E F	G	H	I	J K	L	M	N
1		**Cash**				**Accounts Receivable**				**Office Supplies**		
2	Bal.	2,160			Bal.	1,250			Bal.	180	(b)	105
3					(e)	300			Bal.	75		
4					Bal.	1,550						
5										**Accumulated Depreciation—**		
6		**Prepaid Insurance**				**Office Equipment**				**Office Equipment**		
7	Bal.	240	(a)	40	Bal.	3,400					Bal.	600
8	Bal.	200									(c)	100
9											Bal.	700
10												
11		**Accounts Payable**				**Unearned Revenue**				**Wages Payable**		
12			Bal.	700	(f)	160	Bal.	460			(d)	120
13							Bal.	300				
14										**Answering**		
15		**T. Ramos, Capital**				**T. Ramos, Withdrawals**				**Service Revenue**		
16			Bal.	4,870	Bal.	400					Bal.	2,900
17											(e)	300
18											(f)	160
19											Bal.	3,360
20												
21		**Wages Expense**				**Rent Expense**				**Insurance Expense**		
22	Bal.	1,500			Bal.	400			(a)	40		
23	(d)	120										
24	Bal.	1,620										
25						**Depreciation Expense—**						
26		**Office Supplies Expense**				**Office Equipment**						
27	(b)	105			(c)	100						
28												

3.

	A	B	C	D	E
1			**Reliable Answering Service**		
2			**Adjusted Trial Balance**		
3			**December 31, 2014**		
4					
5	Cash			2,160	
6	Accounts Receivable			1,550	
7	Office Supplies			75	
8	Prepaid Insurance			200	
9	Office Equipment			3,400	
10	Accumulated Depreciation—Office Equipment				700
11	Accounts Payable				700
12	Unearned Revenue				300
13	Wages Payable				120
14	T. Ramos, Capital				4,870
15	T. Ramos, Withdrawals			400	
16	Answering Service Revenue				3,360
17	Wages Expense			1,620	
18	Rent Expense			400	
19	Insurance Expense			40	
20	Office Supplies Expense			105	
21	Depreciation Expense—Office Equipment			100	
22				10,050	10,050
23					

4.

	A	B	C	D	E
1			**Reliable Answering Service**		
2			**Income Statement**		
3			**For the Month Ended December 31, 2014**		
4					
5	**Revenues**				
6			Answering service revenue		$3,360
7					
8	**Expenses**				
9			Wages expense	$1,620	
10			Rent expense	400	
11			Insurance expense	40	
12			Office supplies expense	105	
13			Depreciation expense—office equipment	100	
14			Total expenses		2,265
15	**Net income**				$1,095
16					

	A	B	C	D	E
1			**Reliable Answering Service**		
2			**Statement of Owner's Equity**		
3			**For the Month Ended December 31, 2014**		
4					
5			T. Ramos, capital, November 30, 2014		$4,870
6			Net income		1,095
7			Subtotal		$5,965
8			Less T. Ramos, withdrawals		400
9			T. Ramos, capital, December 31, 2014		$5,565
10					

	A	B	C	D	E
1			**Reliable Answering Service**		
2			**Balance Sheet**		
3			**December 31, 2014**		
4					
5			**Assets**		
6	Cash				$2,160
7	Accounts receivable				1,550
8	Office supplies				75
9	Prepaid insurance				200
10	Office equipment			$3,400	
11		Less accumulated depreciation		700	2,700
12	Total assets				$6,685
13					
14			**Liabilities**		
15	Accounts payable				$ 700
16	Unearned revenue				300
17	Wages payable				120
18	Total liabilities				$1,120
19					
20			**Owner's Equity**		
21	T. Ramos, capital, December 31, 2014				5,565
22	Total liabilities and owner's equity				$6,685
23					
24					

Section 3: Business Applications

All accounts on the income statement are potentially affected by adjusting entries. On the other hand, cash on the balance sheet is never affected by an adjusting entry.

Chapter Review

Define *net income*, and explain the concepts underlying income measurement. **LO 1**

Net income is the net increase in owner's equity that results from a company's operations. Net income equals revenues minus expenses; when expenses exceed revenues, a net loss results. Revenues equal the price of goods sold or services rendered during a specific period. Expenses are the costs of goods and services used in the process of producing revenues.

The continuity assumption recognizes that, without evidence to the contrary, accountants must assume that a business will continue to operate indefinitely. The periodicity assumption recognizes that it is useful to estimate the business's net income in terms of accounting periods. Accrual accounting holds that revenues must be assigned to the period in which the goods are sold or the services performed, and expenses must be assigned to the period in which they are used to produce revenue.

Distinguish cash basis of accounting from accrual accounting, and explain how accrual accounting is accomplished. **LO 2**

The cash basis of accounting is based on cash received and cash paid. In contrast, accrual accounting consists of all the techniques accountants use to measure net income, which include recognizing revenues when they are earned, expenses when they are incurred, and adjusting the accounts.

Identify four situations that require adjusting entries, and illustrate typical adjusting entries. **LO 3**

Adjusting entries are required when (1) recorded costs must be allocated between two or more accounting periods; (2) unrecorded expenses exist; (3) recorded, unearned revenues must be allocated between two or more periods, and (4) unrecorded, earned revenues exist. The preparation of adjusting entries is summarized as follows.

	Type of Account		
Type of Adjusting Entry	Debited	Credited	Examples of Balance Sheet Accounts
1. Allocating recorded costs (previously paid, expired)	Expense	Asset (or contra-asset)	Prepaid rent Prepaid insurance Office supplies Accumulated depreciation—office equipment
2. Accrued expenses (incurred, not paid)	Expense	Liability	Interest payable Wages payable
3. Allocating recorded, unearned revenues (previously received, earned)	Liability	Revenue	Unearned revenue
4. Accrued revenues (earned, not received)	Asset	Revenue	Accounts receivable Interest receivable

Prepare financial statements from an adjusted trial balance. **LO 4**

An adjusted trial balance is prepared after adjusting entries have been posted to the accounts. Its purpose is to test whether total debits equal total credits after the adjusting entries have been posted and before the financial statements are prepared. The balances in the revenue and expense accounts in the adjusted trial balance are used to prepare the income statement. The balances in the asset and liability accounts in the adjusted trial balance and in the statement of owner's equity are used to prepare the balance sheet.

Explain the importance of ethical measurement of net income and the relation of net income to cash flows. **LO 5**

Because applying accrual accounting involves making assumptions and exercising judgment, it can lead to earnings management, which is the manipulation of revenues and expenses to achieve a specific outcome. When the estimates involved in earnings management move outside a reasonable range, financial statements become misleading. Financial statements that are intentionally misleading constitute fraudulent financial reporting.

To ensure a company's liquidity, managers must know how to use accrual-based information to analyze cash flows. The general rule for determining the cash flow received from any revenue or paid for any expense (except depreciation) is to determine the potential cash payments or cash receipts and deduct the amount not received or not paid.

Key Terms

accrual 91 (LO3)
accrual accounting
  (matching rule) 87 (LO1)
accrued expenses 94 (LO3)
accrued revenues 97 (LO3)
Accumulated Depreciation 93 (LO3)
adjusted trial balance 99 (LO4)
adjusting entries 90 (LO3)
carrying value 93 (LO3)

cash basis of accounting 88 (LO2)
continuity 87 (LO1)
contra account 93 (LO3)
deferral 91 (LO3)
depreciation 93 (LO3)
earnings management 102 (LO5)
expenses 86 (LO1)
fiscal year 87 (LO1)
going concern 87 (LO1)

interim periods 87 (LO1)
net income 86 (LO1)
net loss 86 (LO1)
periodicity 87 (LO1)
prepaid expenses 91 (LO3)
revenue recognition 88 (LO2)
revenues 86 (LO1)
unearned revenues 96 (LO3)

Chapter Assignments

DISCUSSION QUESTIONS

LO 1   **DQ1.** When a company has net income, what happens to its assets and/or to its liabilities?

LO 3   **DQ2.** Will the carrying value of a long-term asset normally equal its market value?

LO 5   **DQ3.** If, at the end of the accounting period, you were looking at the T account for a prepaid expense like supplies, would you look for the amounts expended in cash on the debit or credit side? On which side would you find the amount expensed during the period?

LO 5   **DQ4. BUSINESS APPLICATION** ▶ Is accrual accounting more closely related to a company's goal of profitability or liquidity?

LO 5   **DQ5. BUSINESS APPLICATION** ▶ Would you expect net income to be a good measure of a company's liquidity? Why or why not?

LO 5   **DQ6. BUSINESS APPLICATION** ▶ Can you think of some situations when earnings management is acceptable?

SHORT EXERCISES

LO 1, 2   **Accrual Accounting Concepts**

SE1. CONCEPT ▶ Match the concepts of accrual accounting that follow with the appropriate assumptions or actions.

1. Assumes expenses should be assigned to the accounting period in which they are used to produce revenues
2. Assumes a business will last indefinitely
3. Assumes revenues are earned at a point in time
4. Assumes net income that is measured for a short period of time, such as one quarter

a. Periodicity
b. Continuity
c. Accrual accounting
d. Revenue recognition

LO 3   **Adjustment for Prepaid Insurance**

SE2. The Prepaid Insurance account began the year with a balance of $460. During the year, insurance in the amount of $1,040 was purchased. At the end of the year (December 31), the amount of insurance still unexpired was $700. Prepare the year-end journal entry to record the adjustment for insurance expense for the year.

LO 3   **Adjustment for Supplies**

SE3. The Supplies account began the year with a balance of $380. During the year, supplies in the amount of $980 were purchased. At the end of the year (December 31), the inventory of supplies on hand was $440. Prepare the year-end journal entry to record the adjustment for supplies expense for the year.

LO 3   **Adjustment for Depreciation**

SE4. The depreciation expense on office equipment for the month of March is $100. This is the third month that the office equipment, which cost $1,900, has been owned. Prepare the adjusting entry to record depreciation for March and show the balance sheet presentation for office equipment and related accounts after the March 31 adjustment.

LO 3   **Adjustment for Accrued Wages**

SE5. Wages are paid each Saturday for a six-day workweek. Wages are currently $1,380 per week. Prepare the adjusting entry required on June 30, assuming July 1 falls on a Tuesday.

LO 3   **Adjustment for Unearned Revenue**

SE6. During the month of August, deposits in the amount of $1,100 were received for services to be performed. By the end of the month, services in the amount of $760 had been performed. Prepare the necessary adjustment for Service Revenue at the end of the month.

LO 4   **Preparation of an Income Statement and Statement of Owner's Equity from an Adjusted Trial Balance**

SE7. Shah Company's adjusted trial balance on December 31, 2014, contains the following accounts and balances: A. Shah, Capital, $8,600; A. Shah, Withdrawals, $350; Service Revenue, $2,600; Rent Expense, $400; Wages Expense, $900; Utilities Expense, $200; and Telephone Expense, $50. Prepare an income statement and statement of owner's equity for the month of December.

LO 4   **Preparation of an Income Statement and Statement of Owner's Equity from an Adjusted Trial Balance**

SE8. Malesherbes Company's adjusted trial balance on June 30, 2014, contains the following accounts and balances: C. Fondren, Capital, $12,750; C. Fondren, Withdrawals, $580; Service Revenue, $6,300; Rent Expense, $900; Wages Expense, $1,050; Utilities Expense, $300; and Telephone Expense, $90. Prepare an income statement and statement of owner's equity for the month of June.

LO 5   **Determination of Cash Flows**

SE9. BUSINESS APPLICATION ▶ Unearned Revenue had a balance of $650 at the end of November and $450 at the end of December. Service Revenue was $2,550 for the month of December. How much cash was received for services provided during December?

LO 5   **Determination of Cash Flows**

SE10. BUSINESS APPLICATION ▶ Unearned Revenue had a balance of $1,120 at the end of November and $890 at the end of December. Service Revenue was $4,600 for the month of December. How much cash was received for services provided during December?

EXERCISES: SET A

LO **1, 2, 3**   **Applications of Accounting Concepts Related to Accrual Accounting**

E1A. CONCEPT ▶ Carlos Company's accountant makes the assumptions or performs the activities listed below. Tell which of the following concepts of accrual accounting most directly relates to each assumption or action: (a) periodicity, (b) continuity, (c) accrual accounting, (d) revenue recognition, (e) deferral, and (f) accrual.

1. Recognizes the usefulness of financial statements prepared on a monthly basis even though they are based on estimates.
2. Prepares an income statement that shows the revenues earned and the expenses incurred during the accounting period.
3. In estimating the life of a building, assumes that the business will last indefinitely.
4. Postpones the recognition of a one-year insurance policy as an expense by initially recording the expenditure as an asset.
5. Records a sale when the customer is billed.
6. Recognizes, by making an adjusting entry, wages expense that has been incurred but not yet recorded.

LO **2**   **Application of Conditions for Revenue Recognition**

E2A. CONCEPT ▶ Four conditions must be met before revenue should be recognized. In each of the following cases, tell which condition has *not* been met:

a. Company Alpha accepts a contract to perform services in the future for $4,000.
b. Company Beta ships products worth $6,000 to another company without an order from the other company but tells the company it can return the products if it does not sell them.
c. Company Centric performs $20,000 of services for a firm with financial problems.
d. Company Radiant agrees to work out a price later for services that it performs for another company.

LO **3**   **Adjusting Entry for Unearned Revenue**

E3A. Stardust publishes a monthly magazine featuring local restaurant reviews and upcoming social, cultural, and sporting events. Subscribers pay for subscriptions either one year or two years in advance. Cash received from subscribers is credited to an account called Magazine Subscriptions Received in Advance. On December 31, 2014, the end of the company's fiscal year, the balance of this account is $750,000. Expiration of subscriptions revenue is as follows.

During 2014	$150,000
During 2015	375,000
During 2016	225,000

Prepare the adjusting entry for December 31, 2014.

LO **3**   **Adjusting Entries for Prepaid Insurance**

E4A. An examination of the Prepaid Insurance account shows a balance of $10,280 at the end of an accounting period, before adjustment. Prepare journal entries to record the insurance expense for the period under the following independent assumptions:

1. An examination of the insurance policies shows unexpired insurance that cost $4,935 at the end of the period.
2. An examination of the insurance policies shows insurance that cost $1,735 has expired during the period.

LO 3 **Adjusting Entries for Supplies: Missing Data**

E5A. Each of the following columns represents a Supplies account:

	a	b	c	d
Supplies on hand at June 1	$264	$217	$196	$?
Supplies purchased during the month	52	?	174	1,928
Supplies consumed during the month	194	972	?	1,632
Supplies on hand at June 30	?	436	56	1,118

1. Determine the amounts indicated by the question marks.
2. Make the adjusting entry for column **a**, assuming supplies purchased are debited to an asset account.

LO 3 **Adjusting Entry for Accrued Salaries**

E6A. Kindle Company has a five-day workweek and pays salaries of $70,000 each Friday.

1. Prepare the adjusting entry required on May 31, assuming that June 1 falls on a Wednesday.
2. Prepare the journal entry to pay the salaries on June 3, including the amount of salaries payable from requirement **1**.

LO 3 **Revenue and Expense Recognition**

E7A. Lacoma Company produces computer software that Kozuch Company sells. Lacoma receives a royalty of 15 percent of sales. Kozuch pays royalties to Lacoma semi-annually—on May 1 for sales made in July through December of the previous year and on November 1 for sales made in January through June of the current year. Royalty expense for Kozuch and royalty income for Lacoma in the amount of $12,000 were accrued on December 31, 2013. Cash in the amounts of $12,000 and $20,000 was paid and received on May 1 and November 1, 2014, respectively. Software sales during the July to December 2014 period totaled $300,000.

1. Calculate the amount of royalty expense for Kozuch and royalty income for Lacoma during 2014.
2. Record the adjusting entry that each company made on December 31, 2014.

LO 3 **Accounting for Revenue Received in Advance**

E8A. Chris Gayle, a lawyer, received $72,000 on October 1 to represent a client in real estate negotiations over the next 12 months.

1. Prepare the journal entries required in Gayle's records on October 1 and at the end of the fiscal year, December 31.
2. **ACCOUNTING CONNECTION** ▶ How would this transaction be reflected on the income statement and balance sheet on December 31?

LO 3 **Adjusting Entries**

E9A. Prepare year-end adjusting entries for each of the following:

1. Office Supplies has a balance of $168 on January 1. Purchases debited to Office Supplies during the year amount to $830. A year-end inventory reveals supplies of $570 on hand.
2. Depreciation of office equipment is estimated to be $4,260 for the year.
3. Property taxes for six months, estimated at $1,750, have accrued but have not been recorded.
4. Unrecorded interest income on U.S. government bonds is $1,700.
5. Unearned Revenue has a balance of $1,800. Services for $600 received in advance have now been performed.
6. Services totaling $400 have been performed; the customer has not yet been billed.

Preparation of Financial Statements

E10A. Prepare the monthly income statement, monthly statement of owner's equity, and the balance sheet at August 31, 2014, for Krishna Cleaning Company from the data provided in the adjusted trial balance that follows. The owner made no investments during the period.

Krishna Cleaning Company
Adjusted Trial Balance
August 31, 2014

Cash	4,590	
Accounts Receivable	2,592	
Prepaid Insurance	380	
Prepaid Rent	200	
Cleaning Supplies	152	
Cleaning Equipment	3,200	
Accumulated Depreciation—Cleaning Equipment		320
Truck	7,200	
Accumulated Depreciation—Truck		720
Accounts Payable		420
Wages Payable		80
Unearned Janitorial Revenue		920
A. Ambrose, Capital		15,034
A. Ambrose, Withdrawals	2,000	
Janitorial Revenue		14,620
Wages Expense	5,680	
Rent Expense	1,200	
Gas, Oil, and Other Truck Expenses	580	
Insurance Expense	380	
Supplies Expense	2,920	
Depreciation Expense—Cleaning Equipment	320	
Depreciation Expense—Truck	720	
	32,114	32,114

Determination of Cash Flows

E11A. BUSINESS APPLICATION ▶ After adjusting entries had been made, Infosys Company's balance sheets showed the following asset and liability amounts at the end of 2013 and 2014:

	2014	2013
Prepaid insurance	$1,200	$1,450
Wages payable	600	1,100
Unearned fees	2,100	950

The following amounts were taken from the 2014 income statement:

Insurance expense	$1,900
Wages expense	9,750
Fees earned	4,450

Calculate the amount of cash paid for insurance and wages and the amount of cash received for fees during 2014.

LO 5 **Relationship of Expenses to Cash Paid**

E12A. BUSINESS APPLICATION ▶ Wipro Company's income statement included the following expenses for 2014:

Rent expense	$ 78,000
Interest expense	11,700
Salaries expense	124,500

The related balance sheet account balances at year end for last year and this year follow.

	Last Year	This Year
Prepaid rent	—	$ 1,350
Interest payable	$1,800	—
Salaries payable	7,500	18,000

1. Compute the cash paid for rent during the year.
2. Compute the cash paid for interest during the year.
3. Compute the cash paid for salaries during the year.

EXERCISES: SET B

Visit the textbook companion web site at www.cengagebrain.com to access Exercise Set B for this chapter.

PROBLEMS

LO 3 **Determining Adjustments**

✔ d: Revenue balance: $9,150

P1. At the end of the first three months of operation, Kubose Answering Service's trial balance appears as follows. Dhaval Bose, Kubose's owner, has hired an accountant to prepare financial statements to determine how well the company is doing after three months. Upon examining the accounting records, the accountant finds the following items of interest:

a. An inventory of office supplies reveals supplies on hand of $133.
b. The Prepaid Rent account includes the rent for the first three months plus a deposit for April's rent.
c. Depreciation on the equipment for the first three months is $208.
d. The balance of the Unearned Answering Service Revenue account represents a 12-month service contract paid in advance on February 1.
e. On March 31, accrued wages total $80.

Kubose Answering Service
Trial Balance
March 31, 2014

Cash	3,482	
Accounts Receivable	4,236	
Office Supplies	903	
Prepaid Rent	800	
Equipment	4,700	
Accounts Payable		2,673
Unearned Answering Service Revenue		888
D. Bose, Capital		5,933
D. Bose, Withdrawals	2,130	
Answering Service Revenue		9,002
Wages Expense	1,900	
Office Cleaning Expense	345	
	18,496	18,496

(Continued)

REQUIRED

All adjustments affect one balance sheet account and one income statement account. For each of these situations, show the accounts affected, the amount of the adjustment (using a + or − to indicate an increase or decrease), and the balance of the account after the adjustment in the following format:

Balance Sheet Account	Amount of Adjustment (+ or −)	Balance After Adjustment	Income Statement Account	Amount of Adjustment (+ or −)	Balance After Adjustment

LO **2, 3**

GENERAL LEDGER

✔ 1b: Debit to Insurance Expense: $6,874

Preparing Adjusting Entries

P2. On November 30, the end of the current fiscal year, the following information is available to assist Allerton Company's accountants in making adjusting entries:

a. Allerton's Supplies account shows a beginning balance of $2,350. Purchases during the year were $4,218. The end-of-year inventory reveals supplies on hand of $1,397.

b. The Prepaid Insurance account shows the following on November 30:

Beginning balance	$4,720
July 1	4,200
October 1	7,272

The beginning balance represents the unexpired portion of a one-year policy purchased in September of the previous year. The July 1 entry represents a new one-year policy, and the October 1 entry represents additional coverage in the form of a three-year policy.

c. The following table contains the cost and annual depreciation for buildings and equipment, all of which Allerton purchased before the current year:

Account	Cost	Annual Depreciation
Buildings	$298,000	$16,000
Equipment	374,000	40,000

d. On October 1, the company completed negotiations with a client and accepted an advance of $18,600 for services to be performed monthly for a year. The $18,600 was credited to Unearned Services Revenue.

e. The company calculated that, as of November 30, it had earned $7,000 on an $11,000 contract that would be completed and billed in January.

f. Among the liabilities of the company is a note payable in the amount of $300,000. On November 30, the accrued interest on this note amounted to $18,000.

g. On Saturday, December 2, the company, which is on a six-day workweek, will pay its regular employees their weekly wages of $15,000.

h. On November 29, the company completed negotiations and signed a contract to provide services to a new client at an annual rate of $23,000.

REQUIRED

1. Prepare adjusting entries for each item listed above.
2. **CONCEPT** ▶ Explain how the conditions for revenue recognition are applied to transactions **e** and **h**.

GENERAL LEDGER

LO **3, 4**

Determining Adjusting Entries, Posting to T Accounts, and Preparing an Adjusted Trial Balance

GENERAL LEDGER

✔ 3: Adjusted trial balance: $106,167

P3. Kinokawa Consultants Company's trial balance on December 31, 2014, follows.

Kinokawa Consultants Company
Trial Balance
December 31, 2014

Cash	12,786	
Accounts Receivable	24,840	
Office Supplies	991	
Prepaid Rent	1,400	
Office Equipment	6,700	
Accumulated Depreciation—Office Equipment		1,600
Accounts Payable		1,820
Notes Payable		10,000
Unearned Service Revenue		2,860
K. Wah, Capital		29,387
K. Wah, Withdrawals	15,000	
Service Revenue		58,500
Salaries Expense	33,000	
Utilities Expense	1,750	
Rent Expense	7,700	
	104,167	104,167

The following information is also available:

a. Ending inventory of office supplies, $86
b. Prepaid rent expired, $700
c. Depreciation of office equipment for the period, $600
d. Interest accrued on the note payable, $600
e. Salaries accrued at the end of the period, $200
f. Service revenue still unearned at the end of the period, $1,410
g. Service revenue earned but not billed, $600

REQUIRED

1. Open T accounts for the accounts in the trial balance plus the following: Interest Payable; Salaries Payable; Office Supplies Expense; Depreciation Expense—Office Equipment; and Interest Expense. Enter the account balances.
2. Determine the adjusting entries and post them directly to the T accounts.
3. Prepare an adjusted trial balance.
4. **ACCOUNTING CONNECTION** ▶ Which financial statements do each of the above adjustments affect? What financial statement is *not* affected by the adjustments?

LO **3, 4**

Determining Adjusting Entries and Tracing Their Effects to Financial Statements

✔ 4: Adjusted trial balance: $633,209

P4. Hertz Limo Service was organized to provide limousine service between the airport and various suburban locations. It has just completed its second year of business. Its trial balance follows.

Hertz Limo Service
Trial Balance
June 30, 2014

Cash (111)	9,812	
Accounts Receivable (113)	14,227	
Prepaid Rent (117)	12,000	
Prepaid Insurance (118)	4,900	
Prepaid Maintenance (119)	12,000	
Spare Parts (140)	11,310	
Limousines (148)	200,000	
Accumulated Depreciation—Limousines (149)		25,000
Notes Payable (211)		45,000
Unearned Passenger Service Revenue (212)		30,000
A. Phylum, Capital (311)		78,211
A. Phylum, Withdrawals (313)	20,000	
Passenger Service Revenue (411)		428,498
Gas and Oil Expense (510)	89,300	
Salaries Expense (511)	206,360	
Advertising Expense (513)	26,800	
	606,709	606,709

The following information is also available:

a. To obtain space at the airport, Hertz paid two years' rent in advance when it began the business.
b. An examination of insurance policies reveals that $2,800 expired during the year.
c. To provide regular maintenance for the vehicles, Hertz deposited $12,000 with a local garage. An examination of maintenance invoices reveals charges of $10,944 against the deposit.
d. An inventory of spare parts shows $1,902 on hand.
e. Hertz depreciates all of its limousines at the rate of 12.5 percent per year. No limousines were purchased during the year. (Round answer to the nearest dollar.)
f. A payment of $1,500 for one full year's interest on notes payable is now due.
g. Unearned Passenger Service Revenue on June 30 includes $17,815 for tickets that employers purchased for use by their executives but which have not yet been redeemed.

REQUIRED

1. Determine the adjusting entries and enter them in the general journal (Page 14).
2. Open ledger accounts for the accounts in the trial balance plus the following: Interest Payable (213); Rent Expense (514); Insurance Expense (515); Spare Parts Expense (516); Depreciation Expense—Limousines (517); Maintenance Expense (518); and Interest Expense (519). Record the balances shown in the trial balance.
3. Post the adjusting entries from the general journal to the ledger accounts, showing proper references.
4. Prepare an adjusted trial balance, an income statement, a statement of owner's equity, and a balance sheet. The owner made no investments during the period.
5. **ACCOUNTING CONNECTION ▶** What effect do the adjusting entries have on the income statement?

LO **3**

✔ e: Unearned Cleaning Revenue
balance: $1,200

Determining Adjustments

P5. At the end of its fiscal year, Berwyn Cleaners' trial balance is as follows.

Berwyn Cleaners
Trial Balance
September 30, 2014

Cash	11,788	
Accounts Receivable	26,494	
Prepaid Insurance	3,400	
Cleaning Supplies	7,374	
Land	18,000	
Building	185,000	
Accumulated Depreciation—Building		45,600
Accounts Payable		20,400
Unearned Cleaning Revenue		1,600
Mortgage Payable		110,000
F. Berwyn, Capital		56,560
F. Berwyn, Withdrawals	10,000	
Cleaning Revenue		157,634
Wages Expense	101,330	
Cleaning Equipment Rental Expense	6,000	
Delivery Truck Expense	4,374	
Interest Expense	11,000	
Other Expenses	7,034	
	391,794	391,794

The following information is also available:

a. A study of the company's insurance policies shows that $680 is unexpired at the end of the year.
b. An inventory of cleaning supplies shows $1,244 on hand.
c. Estimated depreciation on the building for the year is $12,800.
d. Accrued interest on the mortgage payable is $1,000.
e. On September 1, the company signed a contract, effective immediately, with Hope County Hospital to dry clean, for a fixed monthly charge of $400, the uniforms used by doctors in surgery. The hospital paid for four months' service in advance.
f. Sales and delivery wages are paid on Saturday. The weekly payroll is $2,520. September 30 falls on a Thursday, and the company has a six-day pay week.

REQUIRED

All adjustments affect one balance sheet account and one income statement account. For each of the above situations, show the accounts affected, the amount of the adjustment (using a + or − to indicate an increase or decrease), and the balance of the account after the adjustment in the following format:

Balance Sheet Account	Amount of Adjustment (+ or −)	Balance After Adjustment	Income Statement Account	Amount of Adjustment (+ or −)	Balance After Adjustment

LO **3, 4**

Determining Adjusting Entries, Posting to T Accounts, and Preparing an Adjusted Trial Balance

P6. Brave Advisors Service's trial balance on December 31, 2014, is as follows.

✔ 3: Adjusted trial balance:
$121,792

Brave Advisors Service
Trial Balance
December 31, 2014

Cash	16,500	
Accounts Receivable	8,250	
Office Supplies	2,662	
Prepaid Rent	1,320	
Office Equipment	9,240	
Accumulated Depreciation—Office Equipment		1,540
Accounts Payable		5,940
Notes Payable		11,000
Unearned Service Revenue		2,970
B. Cooper, Capital		24,002
B. Cooper, Withdrawals	22,000	
Service Revenue		72,600
Salaries Expense	49,400	
Rent Expense	4,400	
Utilities Expense	4,280	
	118,052	118,052

The following information is also available:

a. Ending inventory of office supplies, $264
b. Prepaid rent expired, $440
c. Depreciation of office equipment for the period, $660
d. Accrued interest expense at the end of the period, $550
e. Accrued salaries at the end of the period, $330
f. Service revenue still unearned at the end of the period, $1,166
g. Service revenue earned but unrecorded, $2,200

REQUIRED

1. Open T accounts for the accounts in the trial balance plus the following: Interest Payable; Salaries Payable; Office Supplies Expense; Depreciation Expense—Office Equipment; and Interest Expense. Enter the balances shown on the trial balance.
2. Determine the adjusting entries and post them directly to the T accounts.
3. Prepare an adjusted trial balance.
4. **ACCOUNTING CONNECTION** ▶ Which financial statements do each of the above adjustments affect? Which financial statement is not affected by the adjustments?

LO **2, 3**

Preparing Adjusting Entries

P7. On June 30, the end of the current fiscal year, the following information is available to BND Company's accountants for making adjusting entries:

✔ 1d: Debit to Supplies Expense:
$4,195

a. Among the liabilities of the company is a mortgage payable in the amount of $240,000. On June 30, the accrued interest on this mortgage amounted to $12,000.
b. On Friday, July 2, the company, which is on a five-day workweek and pays employees weekly, will pay its regular salaried employees $19,200.
c. On June 29, the company completed negotiations and signed a contract to provide monthly services to a new client at an annual rate of $3,600.
d. The Supplies account shows a beginning balance of $1,615 and purchases during the year of $3,766. The end-of-year inventory reveals supplies on hand of $1,186.

e. The Prepaid Insurance account shows the following entries on June 30:

Beginning balance	$1,530
January 1	2,900
May 1	3,366

The beginning balance represents the unexpired portion of a one-year policy purchased in April of the previous year. The January 1 entry represents a new one-year policy, and the May 1 entry represents the additional coverage of a three-year policy. (Round final answer to the nearest dollar.)

f. The following table contains the cost and annual depreciation for buildings and equipment, all of which were purchased before the current year:

Account	Cost	Annual Depreciation
Buildings	$185,000	$ 7,300
Equipment	218,000	21,800

g. On June 1, the company completed negotiations with another client and accepted an advance of $21,000 for services to be performed for a year. The $21,000 was credited to Unearned Service Revenue.

h. The company calculates that, as of June 30, it had earned $3,500 on a $7,500 contract that will be completed and billed in August.

REQUIRED

1. Prepare adjusting entries for each item listed above.
2. **CONCEPT** ▶ Explain how the conditions for revenue recognition are applied to transactions **c** and **h**.

LO **3, 4**

Determining Adjusting Entries and Tracing Their Effects to Financial Statements

P8. Kevin Steven opened a small tax-preparation service. Steven Tax Service's trial balance at the end of its second year of operation is as follows.

✔ 3: Adjusted trial balance: $29,778

Steven Tax Service
Trial Balance
December 31, 2014

Cash	2,268	
Accounts Receivable	1,031	
Prepaid Insurance	240	
Office Supplies	782	
Office Equipment	7,100	
Accumulated Depreciation—Office Equipment		770
Accounts Payable		635
Unearned Tax Fees		219
K. Steven, Capital		5,439
K. Steven, Withdrawals	6,000	
Tax Fees Revenue		21,926
Office Salaries Expense	8,300	
Advertising Expense	650	
Rent Expense	2,400	
Telephone Expense	218	
	28,989	28,989

(Continued)

The following information is also available:

a. Office supplies on hand, December 31, 2014, $227
b. Insurance still unexpired, $120
c. Estimated depreciation of office equipment, $770
d. Telephone expense for December, $19; the bill was received but not recorded.
e. The services for all unearned tax fees had been performed by the end of the year.

REQUIRED

1. Open T accounts for the accounts in the trial balance plus the following: Office Supplies Expense; Insurance Expense; and Depreciation Expense—Office Equipment. Record the balances shown in the trial balance.
2. Determine the adjusting entries and post them directly to the T accounts.
3. Prepare an adjusted trial balance, an income statement, a statement of owner's equity, and a balance sheet. The owner made no investments during the period.
4. **ACCOUNTING CONNECTION** ▶ Why is it not necessary to show the effects of the above transactions on the statement of cash flows?

ALTERNATE PROBLEMS

LO **3**

Determining Adjustments

✔ e: Wages Expense balance: $3,748

P9. At the end of the first three months of operation, Evergreen Repair's trial balance is as follows.

Evergreen Repair
Trial Balance
March 31, 2014

Cash	7,983	
Accounts Receivable	5,872	
Office Supplies	970	
Prepaid Rent	1,500	
Equipment	5,200	
Accounts Payable		2,629
Unearned Repair Revenue		1,146
J. Kita, Capital		11,314
J. Kita, Withdrawals	1,800	
Repair Revenue		12,236
Wages Expense	3,580	
Office Cleaning Expense	420	
	27,325	27,325

Jonah Kita, Evergreen's owner, has hired an accountant to prepare financial statements to determine how well the company is doing after three months. Upon examining the accounting records, the accountant finds the following items of interest:

a. An inventory of office supplies reveals supplies on hand of $469.
b. The Prepaid Rent account includes the rent for the first three months plus a deposit for April's rent.
c. Depreciation on the equipment for the first three months is $560.
d. The balance of the Unearned Repair Revenue account represents a 12-month service contract paid in advance on February 1.
e. On March 31, accrued wages total $168.

REQUIRED

All adjustments affect one balance sheet account and one income statement account. For each of these situations, show the accounts affected, the amount of the adjustment (using a + or − to indicate an increase or decrease), and the balance of the account after the adjustment in the following format:

Balance Sheet Account	Amount of Adjustment (+ or −)	Balance After Adjustment	Income Statement Account	Amount of Adjustment (+ or −)	Balance After Adjustment

LO **2, 3**

Preparing Adjusting Entries

GENERAL LEDGER

✔ 1d: Debit to Unearned Service Revenue: $10,667

P10. On March 31, the end of the current fiscal year, the following information is available to assist Zun Cleaning Company's accountants in making adjusting entries:

a. Zun's Supplies account shows a beginning balance of $5,962. Purchases during the year were $10,294. The end-of-year inventory reveals supplies on hand of $3,105.

b. The Prepaid Insurance account shows the following on March 31:

Beginning balance	$ 5,990
September 1	6,480
January 1	10,080

The beginning balance represents the unexpired portion of a one-year policy purchased in January of the previous year. The September 1 entry represents a new one-year policy, and the January 1 entry represents additional coverage in the form of a three-year policy.

c. The following table contains the cost and annual depreciation for buildings and equipment, all of which Zun purchased before the current year:

Account	Cost	Annual Depreciation
Buildings	$ 804,000	$34,000
Equipment	1,029,000	52,000

d. On December 1, the company completed negotiations with a client and accepted an advance of $32,000 for services to be performed monthly for a year. The $32,000 was credited to Unearned Services Revenue. (Round to the nearest dollar.)

e. The company calculated that, as of March 31, it had earned $9,200 on a $17,000 contract that would be completed and billed in January.

f. Among the liabilities of the company is a note payable in the amount of $600,000. On March 31, the accrued interest on this note amounted to $17,470.

g. On Saturday, April 3, the company, which is on a six-day workweek, will pay its regular employees their weekly wages of $22,000. (Round to the nearest dollar.)

h. On March 31, the company completed negotiations and signed a contract to provide services to a new client at an annual rate of $19,000, beginning April 1.

REQUIRED

1. Prepare adjusting entries for each item listed above.
2. **CONCEPT** ▶ Explain how the conditions for revenue recognition are applied to transactions **e** and **h**.

LO **3, 4**

Determining Adjusting Entries, Posting to T Accounts, and Preparing an Adjusted Trial Balance

✔ 3: Adjusted trial balance: $208,345

P11. Lee Technology Corporation's trial balance on December 31, 2014, is as follows.

Lee Technology Corporation
Trial Balance
December 31, 2014

Cash	35,572	
Accounts Receivable	59,680	
Office Supplies	2,443	
Prepaid Rent	2,400	
Office Equipment	14,300	
Accumulated Depreciation—Office Equipment		3,200
Accounts Payable		2,640
Notes Payable		15,000
Unearned Service Revenue		5,650
E. Lee, Capital		88,705
E. Lee, Withdrawals	15,000	
Service Revenue		89,000
Salaries Expense	58,000	
Utilities Expense	3,600	
Rent Expense	13,200	
	204,195	204,195

The following information is also available:

a. Ending inventory of office supplies, $538
b. Prepaid rent expired, $1,200
c. Depreciation of office equipment for the period, $800
d. Interest accrued on the note payable, $750
e. Salaries accrued at the end of the period, $800
f. Service revenue still unearned at the end of the period, $3,675
g. Service revenue earned but not billed, $1,800

REQUIRED

1. Open T accounts for the accounts in the trial balance plus the following: Interest Payable; Salaries Payable; Office Supplies Expense; Depreciation Expense—Office Equipment; and Interest Expense. Enter the account balances.
2. Determine the adjusting entries and post them directly to the T accounts.
3. Prepare an adjusted trial balance.
4. **ACCOUNTING CONNECTION** ▶ Which financial statements do each of the above adjustments affect? What financial statement is not affected by the adjustments?

LO **3, 4**

Determining Adjusting Entries and Tracing Their Effects to Financial Statements

 SPREADSHEET

GENERAL LEDGER

✔ 4: Adjusted trial balance: $749,468

P12. USA Car Rental Service was organized to provide car rental service at the airport. It has just completed its second year of business. Its trial balance follows.

USA Car Rental Service
Trial Balance
June 30, 2014

Cash (111)	15,708	
Accounts Receivable (113)	19,830	
Prepaid Rent (117)	18,000	
Prepaid Insurance (118)	6,400	
Prepaid Maintenance (119)	13,620	
Spare Parts (140)	12,200	
Cars (148)	270,000	
Accumulated Depreciation—Car (149)		35,000
Notes Payable (211)		78,000
Unearned Rental Service Revenue (212)		42,000
S. Navarro, Capital (311)		66,567
S. Navarro, Withdrawals (313)	30,000	
Rental Service Revenue (411)		492,151
Gas and Oil Expense (510)	104,900	
Salaries Expense (511)	206,360	
Advertising Expense (513)	16,700	
	713,718	713,718

The following information is also available:

a. To obtain space at the airport, USA paid two years' rent in advance when it began the business.
b. An examination of insurance policies reveals that $2,000 expired during the year.
c. To provide regular maintenance for the vehicles, USA deposited $13,620 with a local garage. An examination of maintenance invoices reveals charges of $7,890 against the deposit.
d. An inventory of spare parts shows $2,170 on hand.
e. USA depreciates all of its cars at the rate of 12.5 percent per year. No cars were purchased during the year.
f. A payment of $2,000 for one full year's interest on notes payable is now due.
g. Unearned Rental Service Revenue on June 30 includes $20,325 for cars that customers prepaid but have not yet been rented.

REQUIRED

1. Determine the adjusting entries and enter them in the general journal (Page 14).
2. Open ledger accounts for the accounts in the trial balance plus the following: Interest Payable (213); Rent Expense (514); Insurance Expense (515); Spare Parts Expense (516); Depreciation Expense—Cars (517); Maintenance Expense (518); and Interest Expense (519). Record the balances shown in the trial balance.
3. Post the adjusting entries from the general journal to the ledger accounts, showing proper references.
4. Prepare an adjusted trial balance, an income statement, a statement of owner's equity, and a balance sheet. The owner made no investments during the period.
5. **ACCOUNTING CONNECTION** ▶ What effect do the adjusting entries have on the income statement?

LO **2, 3**

✔ e: Upholstery Revenue
balance: $158,034

Determining Adjustments

P13. Gonzales Upholstery's trial balance at the end of its fiscal year follows.

Gonzales Upholstery
Trial Balance
September 30, 2014

Cash	16,288	
Accounts Receivable	16,494	
Prepaid Insurance	1,900	
Upholstery Supplies	4,370	
Land	18,000	
Building	125,000	
Accumulated Depreciation—Building		26,300
Accounts Payable		17,400
Unearned Upholstery Revenue		1,600
Mortgage Payable		90,000
C. Gonzales, Capital		7,756
C. Gonzales, Withdrawals	10,000	
Upholstery Revenue		157,634
Wages Expense	81,930	
Upholstery Equipment Rental Expense	6,000	
Delivery Truck Expense	4,374	
Interest Expense	9,300	
Other Expenses	7,034	
	300,690	300,690

The following information is also available:

a. A study of the company's insurance policies shows that $380 is unexpired at the end of the year.
b. An inventory of upholstery supplies shows $1,040 on hand.
c. Estimated depreciation on the building for the year is $9,800.
d. Accrued interest on the mortgage payable is $960.
e. On September 1, the company signed a contract, effective immediately, with County Community Bank to repair and reupholster office furniture, for a fixed monthly charge of $400. The bank paid for four months' service in advance.
f. Sales and delivery wages are paid on Saturday. The weekly payroll is $1,530. September 30 falls on a Thursday, and the company has a six-day pay week.

REQUIRED

All adjustments affect one balance sheet account and one income statement account. For each of the above situations, show the accounts affected, the amount of the adjustment (using a + or − to indicate an increase or decrease), and the balance of the account after the adjustment in the following format:

Balance Sheet Account	Amount of Adjustment (+ or −)	Balance After Adjustment	Income Statement Account	Amount of Adjustment (+ or −)	Balance After Adjustment

LO **3, 4**

Determining Adjusting Entries, Posting to T Accounts, and Preparing an Adjusted Trial Balance

✔ 3: Adjusted trial balance: $128,191

P14. Scoop Consulting Service's trial balance on December 31, 2014, is as follows.

Scoop Consulting Service
Trial Balance
December 31, 2014

Cash	19,250	
Accounts Receivable	7,360	
Office Supplies	2,861	
Prepaid Rent	1,820	
Office Equipment	9,240	
Accumulated Depreciation—Office Equipment		2,140
Accounts Payable		5,940
Notes Payable		11,000
Unearned Service Revenue		4,120
A. Chase, Capital		24,111
A. Chase, Withdrawals	22,000	
Service Revenue		76,200
Salaries Expense	51,300	
Rent Expense	5,400	
Utilities Expense	4,280	
	123,511	123,511

The following information is also available:

a. Ending inventory of office supplies, $564
b. Prepaid rent expired, $470
c. Depreciation of office equipment for the period, $820
d. Accrued interest expense at the end of the period, $730
e. Accrued salaries at the end of the period, $630
f. Service revenue still unearned at the end of the period, $2,722
g. Service revenue earned but unrecorded, $2,500

REQUIRED

1. Open T accounts for the accounts in the trial balance plus the following: Interest Payable; Salaries Payable; Office Supplies Expense; Depreciation Expense—Office Equipment; and Interest Expense. Enter the balances shown on the trial balance.
2. Determine the adjusting entries and post them directly to the T accounts.
3. Prepare an adjusted trial balance.
4. **ACCOUNTING CONNECTION** ▶ Which financial statements do each of the above adjustments affect? Which financial statement is not affected by the adjustments?

LO **2, 3**

Preparing Adjusting Entries

GENERAL LEDGER

✔ 1e: Debit to Insurance Expense: $2,781

P15. On June 30, the end of the current fiscal year, the following information is available to Axel Company's accountants for making adjusting entries:

a. Among the liabilities of the company is a mortgage payable in the amount of $280,000. On June 30, the accrued interest on this mortgage amounted to $14,000.
b. On Friday, July 2, the company, which is on a five-day workweek and pays employees weekly, will pay its regular salaried employees $23,100.
c. On June 29, the company completed negotiations and signed a contract to provide monthly services to a new client at an annual rate of $6,645.
d. The Supplies account shows a beginning balance of $1,975 and purchases during the year of $2,846. The end-of-year inventory reveals supplies on hand of $1,984.

(Continued)

e. The Prepaid Insurance account shows the following entries on June 30:

Beginning balance	$1,333
January 1	2,544
May 1	3,168

The beginning balance represents the unexpired portion of a one-year policy purchased in April of the previous year. The January 1 entry represents a new one-year policy, and the May 1 entry represents the additional coverage of a three-year policy.

f. The following table contains the cost and annual depreciation for buildings and equipment, all of which were purchased before the current year:

Account	Cost	Annual Depreciation
Buildings	$235,000	$ 6,301
Equipment	198,000	11,520

g. On June 1, the company completed negotiations with another client and accepted an advance of $31,080 for services to be performed for a year. The $31,080 was credited to Unearned Service Revenue.

h. The company calculates that, as of June 30, it had earned $3,600 on a $9,600 contract that will be completed and billed in August.

REQUIRED

1. Prepare adjusting entries for each item listed above.
2. **CONCEPT** ▶ Explain how the conditions for revenue recognition are applied to transactions **c** and **h**.

LO **3, 4**

Determining Adjusting Entries and Tracing Their Effects to Financial Statements

SPREADSHEET

✔ 3: Adjusted trial balance: $45,198

P16. Simone Jacobs opened a small tax-preparation service. At the end of its second year of operation, Jacobs Financial Advisors Service had the following trial balance.

Jacobs Financial Advisors Service
Trial Balance
December 31, 2014

Cash	11,265	
Accounts Receivable	2,191	
Prepaid Insurance	520	
Office Supplies	682	
Office Equipment	7,980	
Accumulated Depreciation—Office Equipment		790
Accounts Payable		437
Unearned Tax Fees		519
S. Jacobs, Capital		5,474
S. Jacobs, Withdrawals	7,500	
Tax Fees Revenue		36,926
Office Salaries Expense	9,700	
Advertising Expense	650	
Rent Expense	3,200	
Telephone Expense	458	
	44,146	44,146

The following information is also available:

a. Office supplies on hand, December 31, 2014, $319
b. Insurance still unexpired, $180
c. Estimated depreciation of office equipment, $870
d. Telephone expense for December, $182; the bill was received but not recorded.
e. The services for all unearned tax fees had been performed by the end of the year.

REQUIRED

1. Open T accounts for the accounts in the trial balance plus the following: Office Supplies Expense; Insurance Expense; and Depreciation Expense—Office Equipment. Record the balances shown in the trial balance.
2. Determine the adjusting entries and post them directly to the T accounts.
3. Prepare an adjusted trial balance, an income statement, a statement of owner's equity, and a balance sheet. The owner made no investments during the period.
4. **ACCOUNTING CONNECTION** ▶ Why is it not necessary to show the effects of the above transactions on the statement of cash flows?

CASES

LO **2, 3**   **Conceptual Understanding: Importance of Adjustments**

C1. Never Flake Company provided a rust-prevention coating for the underside of new automobiles. The company advertised widely and offered its services through new-car dealers. When a dealer sold a new car, the salesperson attempted to sell the rust-prevention coating as an option. A key selling point was Never Flake's warranty, which stated that it would repair any damage due to rust at no charge for as long as the buyer owned the car.

For several years, Never Flake had been very successful, but in 2013, the company suddenly declared bankruptcy. Company officials said that the firm had only $5.5 million in assets against liabilities of $32.9 million. Most of the liabilities represented potential claims under the company's lifetime warranty. It seemed that owners were keeping their cars longer than they had previously. Therefore, more damage was being attributed to rust.

Discuss what accounting decisions could have helped Never Flake to survive under these circumstances.

LO **2, 3, 5**   **Conceptual Understanding: Earnings Management and Fraudulent Financial Reporting**

C2. BUSINESS APPLICATION ▶ In recent years, the Securities and Exchange Commission (SEC) has been waging a public campaign against corporate accounting practices that manage or manipulate earnings to meet the expectations of Wall Street analysts. Corporations engage in such practices in the hope of avoiding shortfalls that might cause serious declines in their stock price.

For each of the following cases that the Securities and Exchange Commission challenged, explain why each was a violation of the accrual accounting:

a. **Lucent Technologies** sold telecommunications equipment to companies from which there was no reasonable expectation of payment because of the companies' poor financial condition.
b. **America Online (AOL)** recorded advertising as an asset rather than as an expense.
c. **Eclipsys** recorded software contracts as revenue even though it had not yet rendered the services.
d. **Xerox Corporation** recorded revenue from lease agreements at the time the leases were signed rather than over the lease term.
e. **KnowledgeWare** recorded revenue from sales of software even though it told customers they did not have to pay until they had the software.

LO **2, 3**   **Interpreting Financial Reports: Application of Accrual Accounting**

C3. The **Lyric Opera of Chicago** is one of the largest and best-managed opera companies in the United States. Managing opera productions requires advance planning, including the development of scenery, costumes, and stage properties and the sale of tickets. To measure how well the company is operating in any given year, management must apply accrual accounting to these and other transactions. At year-end, April 30, 2011, Lyric Opera's balance sheet showed deferred production costs and other assets of

$1,978,322 and deferred ticket and other revenue of $12,710,639.[7] What accounting policies and adjusting entries are applicable to these accounts? Why are they important to Lyric Opera's management?

LO **2, 3**

Interpreting Financial Reports: Analysis of an Asset Account

C4. The Walt Disney Company is engaged in the financing, production, and distribution of motion pictures and television programming. In Disney's 2011 annual report, the balance sheet contains an asset called "film and television costs." Film and television costs, which consist of the costs associated with producing films and television programs less the amount expensed, were $4,357 million. The notes reveal that the amount of film and television costs expensed (amortized) during the year was $3,521 million. The amount spent for new film productions was $3,184 million.[8]

1. **CONCEPT** ▶ What are film and television costs, and why would they be classified as an asset?
2. Prepare T accounts to record the amount the company spent on new film and television production during the year (assume all expenditures are paid for in cash).
3. Prepare an adjusting entry in T account form to record the expense for film and television productions.
4. **CONCEPT** ▶ Suggest a method by which The Walt Disney Company might have determined the amount of the expense in **3** in accordance with accrual accounting.

LO **3**

Annual Report Case: Analysis of Balance Sheet and Adjusting Entries

C5. In the **CVS** annual report in the Supplement to Chapter 16, refer to the balance sheet and the Summary of Significant Accounting Policies in the notes to the financial statements.

1. Examine the accounts in the current assets, property and equipment, and current liabilities sections of CVS's balance sheet. Which are most likely to have had year-end adjusting entries? Describe the nature of the adjusting entries. For more information about the property and equipment section, refer to the notes to the financial statements.
2. Where is depreciation (and amortization) expense disclosed in CVS's financial statements?
3. CVS has a statement on the "Use of Estimates" in its Summary of Significant Accounting Policies. Read this statement, and tell how important estimates are in determining depreciation expense. What assumptions do accountants use in estimating depreciation?

LO **5**

Ethical Dilemma: Importance of Adjustments

C6. BUSINESS APPLICATION ▶ Central Appliance Service Co., Inc., has achieved fast growth by selling service contracts on large appliances, such as washers, dryers, and refrigerators. For a fee, the company agrees to provide all parts and labor on an appliance after the regular warranty runs out. For example, by paying a fee of $200, a person who buys a dishwasher can add two years to the regular one-year warranty on the appliance. In 2014, the company sold service contracts in the amount of $1.8 million, all of which applied to future years. Management wanted all the sales recorded as revenues in 2014, contending that the amount of the contracts could be determined and the cash had been received. Do you agree with this logic? How would you record the cash receipts? What assumptions do you think Central Appliance should make? Would you consider it unethical to follow management's recommendation? Who might be hurt or helped by this action?

Continuing Case: Annual Report Project

C7. Using the most recent annual report of the company you have chosen to study and that you have accessed online at the company's website, examine the current assets and current liabilities of your company. Identify accounts that would likely fall into one of the following two categories:

1. Deferral
2. Accrual

CHAPTER 4
Completing the Accounting Cycle

Speedy Movers provides moving and storage services for the local college and its students and employees. Speedy's busiest times are generally in the late spring and early fall. Thus, to keep an eye on fluctuations in earnings and cash flows, Speedy prepares financial statements each quarter.

As you know from Chapter 3, before a company prepares financial statements, it must make adjusting entries to the income statement and owner's equity accounts. After those entries have been made, an adjusted trial balance is prepared. Accounts from the adjusted trial balance are then used to prepare the financial statements. For example, in preparing its income statement, Speedy would use the revenue and expense accounts from its adjusted trial balance.

In addition, Speedy, like all other companies, must prepare its accounts for the next accounting period by making closing entries. Doing all this takes time and effort, but the results benefit both management and external users of the company's financial statements. To accomplish these tasks, Speedy needs to be able to answer the following questions.

1. **CONCEPT** ▶ *Why are the concepts of permanent and temporary accounts important to making closing entries?*

2. **ACCOUNTING APPLICATION** ▶ *What steps must a company follow to prepare its accounts for the next accounting period?*

3. **BUSINESS APPLICATION** ▶ *Why are closing entries important to good financial reporting in the current accounting period and the next accounting period?*

LEARNING OBJECTIVES

LO 1 Describe the role of closing entries in the preparation of financial statements.

LO 2 Prepare closing entries.

LO 3 Prepare reversing entries.

LO 4 Prepare a work sheet.

LO 5 Explain the importance of the work sheet and closing entries when managing a business.

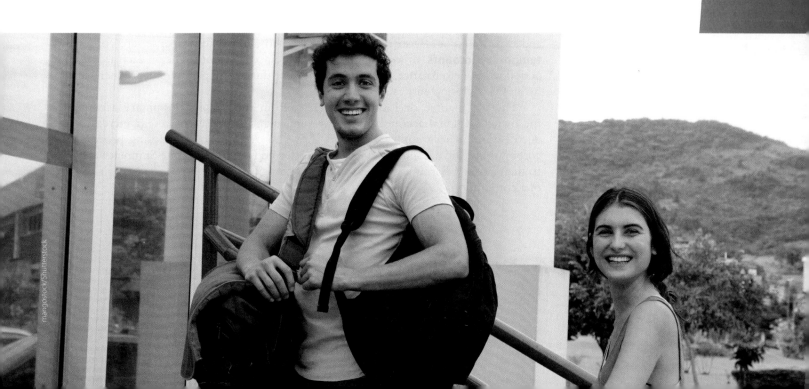

SECTION 1

CONCEPTS

CONCEPTS
- Periodicity
- Accrual accounting

RELEVANT LEARNING OBJECTIVE

LO 1 Describe the role of closing entries in the preparation of financial statements.

LO 1 Concepts Underlying Closing Entries

All companies prepare financial statements annually, but interim reports prepared quarterly or even monthly give management an ongoing view of a company's financial performance. Up this point, you have studied the first five steps of the accounting cycle. In this chapter, the final step, preparation of closing entries and the post-closing trial balance, is covered.

Closing Entries

Closing entries are journal entries made at the end of an accounting period. They have two purposes:

- **Setting the stage for the next accounting period:** Since the income statement reports net income (or loss) for a single accounting period and shows revenues and expenses for only that period, it is necessary to clear revenue and expense accounts and the withdrawals accounts of their balances. This step enables them to start over with a zero balance in the next accounting period.
- **Summarizing a period's revenues and expenses:** The **Income Summary account** is a temporary account that summarizes all revenues and expenses for the period. It is used only in the closing process, and its balance equals the net income or loss.

The preparation of closing entries is an important step in achieving two important concepts introduced in Chapter 3. Closing entries assist in achieving both *periodicity* and *accrual accounting* by being the process by which the life of the business is divided into equal time periods. Further, they summarize the effects of each accounting period on owner's equity and set the stage for the next accounting period.

To accomplish the closing process, it is important to understand the concepts of *permanent* and *temporary accounts*. Balance sheet accounts, such as Cash and Accounts Payable, are considered **permanent accounts** (or *real accounts*) because they carry their end-of-period balances into the next accounting period. In contrast, revenue and expense accounts, such as Revenues Earned and Wages Expense, are considered **temporary accounts** (or *nominal accounts*). Temporary accounts begin each accounting period with a zero balance, accumulate a balance during the period, and are then cleared by means of closing entries.

The net income or loss is transferred from the Income Summary account to the owner's Capital account because revenues and expenses represent increases and decreases in owner's equity. Exhibit 1 shows an overview of the closing process. For corporations, the net income or loss is transferred from the Income Summary account to the Retained Earnings account, which is part of the stockholders' (owner's) equity of a corporation.

Exhibit 1
Overview of the Closing Process

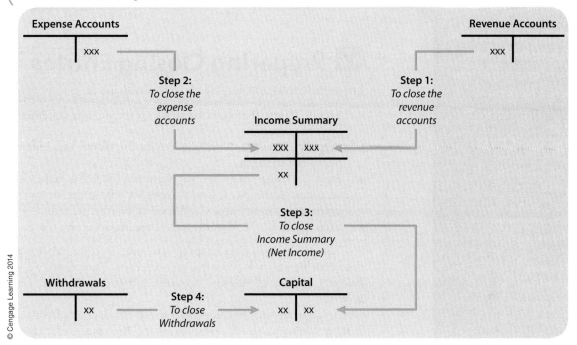

© Cengage Learning 2014

APPLY IT!

Match the concepts that follow to the related statements.

_____ 1. Important in assuring that owner's equity is affected properly by revenues and expenses.

_____ 2. Usually begin the accounting period with a balance.

_____ 3. Begin each period with a zero balance.

_____ 4. Divides the life of the business into equal time periods.

a. periodicity
b. accrual accounting
c. permanent accounts
d. temporary accounts

SOLUTION

1. b; 2. c; 3. d; 4. a

TRY IT! SE1

LO 2 Preparing Closing Entries

The steps involved in making closing entries are as follows.

■ **Step 1.** Close the credit balances on the income statement accounts to the Income Summary account.
■ **Step 2.** Close the debit balances on the income statement accounts to the Income Summary account.
■ **Step 3.** Close the Income Summary account balance to the owner's Capital account. (Although it is not necessary to use the Income Summary account when preparing closing entries, it does simplify the procedure.)
■ **Step 4.** Close the Withdrawals account balance to the owner's Capital account.

You will learn in later chapters that not all credit balance accounts are revenues and not all debit balance accounts are expenses. Therefore, we often use the term *credit balances* instead of *revenue accounts* and the term *debit balances* instead of *expense accounts*.

An adjusted trial balance provides all the data needed to record the closing entries. Exhibit 2 shows the relationships of the four kinds of closing entries to Blue Design Studio's adjusted trial balance.

Exhibit 2
Preparing Closing Entries from the Adjusted Trial Balance

Blue Design Studio Adjusted Trial Balance July 31, 2014		
Cash	22,480	
Accounts Receivable	5,000	
Office Supplies	3,660	
Prepaid Rent	1,600	
Office Equipment	16,320	
Accumulated Depreciation—Office Equipment		300
Accounts Payable		6,280
Unearned Design Revenue		600
Wages Payable		720
J. Blue, Capital		40,000
J. Blue, Withdrawals	2,800	
Design Revenue		13,600
Wages Expense	5,520	
Utilities Expense	680	
Rent Expense	1,600	
Office Supplies Expense	1,540	
Depreciation Expense—Office Equipment	300	
	61,500	61,500

Exhibit 2
Preparing Closing Entries from the Adjusted Trial Balance
(*Continued*)

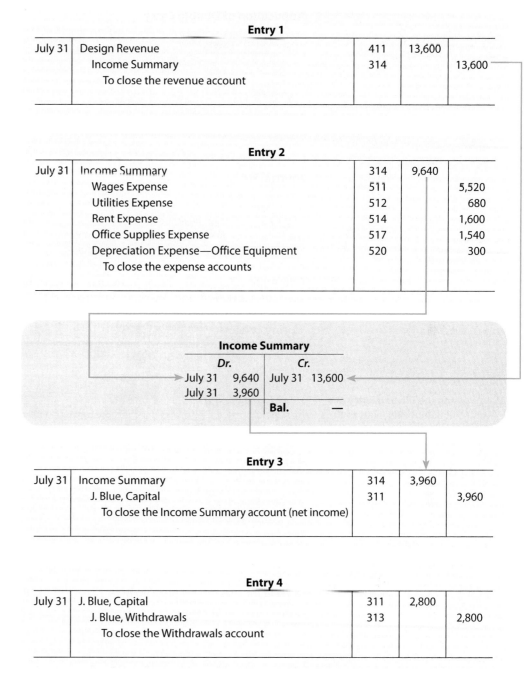

Entry 1

July 31	Design Revenue	411	13,600	
	Income Summary	314		13,600
	To close the revenue account			

Entry 2

July 31	Income Summary	314	9,640	
	Wages Expense	511		5,520
	Utilities Expense	512		680
	Rent Expense	514		1,600
	Office Supplies Expense	517		1,540
	Depreciation Expense—Office Equipment	520		300
	To close the expense accounts			

Income Summary

	Dr.		Cr.	
July 31	9,640	July 31	13,600	
July 31	3,960			
		Bal.	—	

Entry 3

July 31	Income Summary	314	3,960	
	J. Blue, Capital	311		3,960
	To close the Income Summary account (net income)			

Entry 4

July 31	J. Blue, Capital	311	2,800	
	J. Blue, Withdrawals	313		2,800
	To close the Withdrawals account			

Step 1: Closing the Credit Balances

In the adjusted trial balance in Exhibit 2, Design Revenue shows a credit balance of $13,600 and is closed by debiting it for $13,600 and crediting the Income Summary account for the same amount.

Closing the Revenue Account

Accounts On July 31, Design Revenue of $13,600 credit balance is closed to Income Summary.

Analysis The journal entry to close Revenue

▼ *decreases* the owner's equity account *Design Revenue* with a debit

▲ *increases* the owner's equity account *Income Summary* with a credit

Application of Double Entry

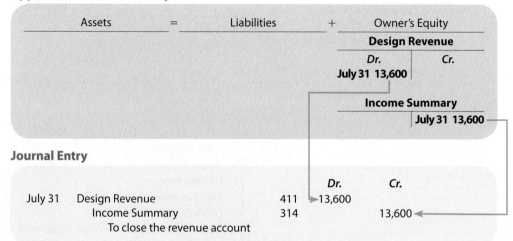

Journal Entry

			Dr.	Cr.
July 31	Design Revenue	411	13,600	
	Income Summary	314		13,600
	To close the revenue account			

Comment Design Revenue now has a zero balance in preparation for the next accounting period and Income Summary reflects revenue for the period. Exhibit 3 shows Design Revenue and Income Summary ledger accounts at this point in the closing process.

Design Revenue   Account No. 411

Date		Item	Post. Ref.	Debit	Credit	Balance Debit	Balance Credit
July	10		J1		2,800		2,800
	15		J1		9,600		12,400
	31	Adj.	J3		800		13,200
	31	Adj.	J3		400		13,600
	31	Closing	J4	13,600			—

Income Summary   Account No. 314

Date		Item	Post. Ref.	Debit	Credit	Balance Debit	Balance Credit
July	31	Closing	J4		13,600		13,600

Step 2: Closing the Debit Balances

Several expense accounts show balances in the adjusted trial balance in Exhibit 2. A compound entry is needed to credit each of these expense accounts for its balance and to debit the Income Summary account for the total, as follows.

Closing the Expense Accounts

Accounts On July 31, expenses accounts shown in the trial balance in Exhibit 2 are closed to Income Summary.

Analysis The journal entry to close the expense accounts

▼ *decreases* the owner's equity account *Income Summary* with a debit

▼ *decreases* the owner's equity expense accounts with a credit

Application of Double Entry

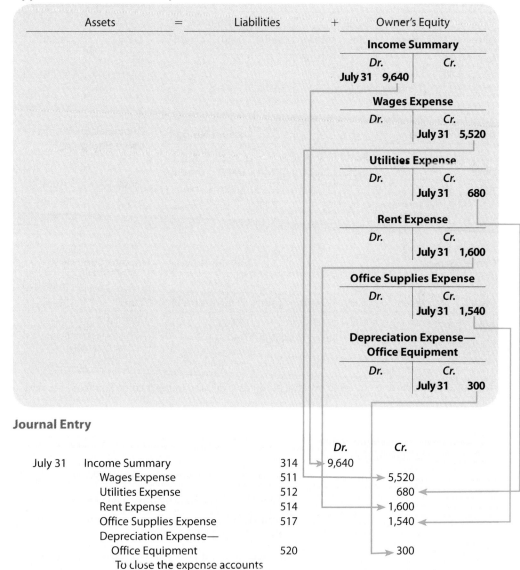

Assets	=	Liabilities	+	Owner's Equity

Income Summary

Dr.	Cr.
July 31 9,640	

Wages Expense

Dr.	Cr.
	July 31 5,520

Utilities Expense

Dr.	Cr.
	July 31 680

Rent Expense

Dr.	Cr.
	July 31 1,600

Office Supplies Expense

Dr.	Cr.
	July 31 1,540

Depreciation Expense— Office Equipment

Dr.	Cr.
	July 31 300

Journal Entry

STUDY NOTE: *The Income Summary account now reflects the account balance of the Design Revenue account before it was closed.*

			Dr.	Cr.
July 31	Income Summary	314	9,640	
	Wages Expense	511		5,520
	Utilities Expense	512		680
	Rent Expense	514		1,600
	Office Supplies Expense	517		1,540
	Depreciation Expense—			
	Office Equipment	520		300
	To close the expense accounts			

Closing entries bring the temporary account balances to zero, allowing a fresh start for the next accounting period.

Comment All expense accounts now have zero balances in preparation for the next accounting period and Income Summary reflects revenue and expenses for the period. Exhibit 4 shows all expense ledger accounts and the Income Summary ledger account at this point in the accounting cycle.

Wages Expense   Account No. 511

Date		Item	Post. Ref.	Debit	Credit	Balance Debit	Balance Credit
July	26		J1	4,800		4,800	
	31	Adj.	J3	720		5,520	
	31	Closing	J4		5,520	—	

Office Supplies Expense   Account No. 517

Date		Item	Post. Ref.	Debit	Credit	Balance Debit	Balance Credit
July	31	Adj.	J3	1,540		1,540	
	31	Closing	J4		1,540	—	

Utilities Expense   Account No. 512

Date		Item	Post. Ref.	Debit	Credit	Balance Debit	Balance Credit
July	30		J2	680		680	
	31	Closing	J4		680	—	

Depreciation Expense— Office Equipment   Account No. 520

Date		Item	Post. Ref.	Debit	Credit	Balance Debit	Balance Credit
July	31	Adj.	J3	300		300	
	31	Closing	J4		300	—	

Rent Expense   Account No. 514

Date		Item	Post. Ref.	Debit	Credit	Balance Debit	Balance Credit
July	31	Adj.	J3	1,600		1,600	
	31	Closing	J4		1,600	—	

Income Summary   Account No. 314

Date		Item	Post. Ref.	Debit	Credit	Balance Debit	Balance Credit
July	31	Closing	J4		13,600		13,600
	31	Closing	J4	9,640*			3,960

*Total of all credit closing entries to expense accounts is debited to the Income Summary account.

Exhibit 4
Posting the Closing Entry of Debit Balance Accounts to the Income Summary Account

Step 3: Closing the Income Summary Account Balance

A credit balance in the Income Summary account represents a net income (i.e., revenues exceed expenses), and a debit balance represents a net loss (i.e., expenses exceed revenues). The balance, whatever its nature, is closed to the owner's Capital account, as follows.

Closing the Income Summary Account

Accounts On July 31, Income Summary account balance of $3,960 credit is closed to J. Blue, Capital.

Analysis The journal entry to close Income Summary

▼ *decreases* the owner's equity account *Income Summary* with a debit

▲ *increases* the owner's equity account *J. Blue, Capital* with a credit

Application of Double Entry

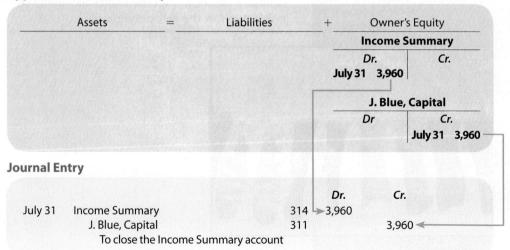

Journal Entry

			Dr.	Cr.
July 31	Income Summary	314	3,960	
	J. Blue, Capital	311		3,960
	To close the Income Summary account			

STUDY NOTE: *At this point, the credit balance of the Income Summary account ($3,960) represents net income—the key measure of performance. When a net loss occurs, debit the owner's Capital account (to reduce it) and credit the Income Summary account (to close it).*

Comment Income Summary now has a zero balance in preparation for the next accounting period and J. Blue, Capital reflects the income for the period. Exhibit 5 shows Income Summary and J. Blue, Capital ledger accounts at this point in the closing process.

Exhibit 5

Posting the Closing Entry of the Income Summary Account Balance to the Owner's Equity Account

Income Summary   Account No. 314

Date		Item	Post. Ref.	Debit	Credit	Balance Debit	Balance Credit
July	31	Closing	J4		13,600		13,600
	31	Closing	J4	9,640			3,960
	31	Closing	J4	3,960			—

J. Blue, Capital   Account No. 311

Date		Item	Post. Ref.	Debit	Credit	Balance Debit	Balance Credit
July	1		J1		40,000		40,000
	31	Closing	J4		3,960		43,960

Step 4: Closing the Withdrawals Account Balance

The Withdrawals account shows the amount by which owner's Capital decreased during an accounting period. The debit balance of the Withdrawals account is closed to the owner's Capital account, as follows.

Closing the Withdrawals Account

Account On July 31, Withdrawals in the amount of $2,800 debit is closed to J. Blue, Capital.

Analysis The journal entry to close Withdrawals

▼ *decreases* the owner's equity account *J. Blue, Capital* with a debit

▼ *decreases* the owner's equity account *Withdrawals* with a credit

Application of Double Entry

STUDY NOTE: *In a corporation, payments to owners are called dividends, and they are closed to the Retained Earnings account.*

Assets	=	Liabilities	+	Owner's Equity

J. Blue Capital

Dr.	Cr.
July 31 2,800	

Withdrawals

	Cr.
	July 31 2,800

Journal Entry

July 31	J. Blue, Capital	311	Dr. 2,800	Cr.
	Withdrawals	313		2,800
	To close the Withdrawals account			

STUDY NOTE: *Note that the Withdrawals account is closed to the owner's Capital account, not to the Income Summary account.*

Comment Withdrawals now has a zero balance in preparation for the next accounting period and J. Blue, Capital reflects the income minus the withdrawals for the period. Exhibit 6 shows Income Summary and J. Blue, Capital ledger accounts at this point in the closing process.

© Cengage Learning 2014

Exhibit 6

Posting the Closing Entry of the Withdrawals Account Balance to the Owner's Capital Account

J. Blue, Withdrawals   **Account No. 313**

Date		Item	Post. Ref.	Debit	Credit	Balance Debit	Balance Credit
July	31		J2	2,800		2,800	
	31	Closing	J4		2,800	—	

J. Blue, Capital   **Account No. 311**

Date		Item	Post. Ref.	Debit	Credit	Balance Debit	Balance Credit
July	1		J1		40,000		40,000
	31	Closing	J4		3,960		43,960
	31	Closing	J4	2,800			41,160

The Accounts After Closing

After all the steps in the closing process have been completed and all closing entries have been posted, everything is ready for the next accounting period. The revenue, expense, and withdrawals accounts (temporary accounts) have zero balances. The owner's Capital account has been increased or decreased to reflect net income or net loss (net income in our example) and has been decreased for withdrawals. The balance sheet accounts (permanent accounts) show the correct balances, which are carried forward to the next period, as shown in the **post-closing trial balance** in Exhibit 7.

Exhibit 7

Post-Closing Trial Balance

Blue Design Studio
Post-Closing Trial Balance
July 31, 2014

Cash	22,480	
Accounts Receivable	5,000	
Office Supplies	3,660	
Prepaid Rent	1,600	
Office Equipment	16,320	
Accumulated Depreciation—Office Equipment		300
Accounts Payable		6,280
Unearned Design Revenue		600
Wages Payable		720
J. Blue, Capital		41,160
	49,060	49,060

© Cengage Learning 2014

Business Perspective
Closing Process in the Internet Age

Just a few years ago, it took companies eleven to fourteen days to close the accounts at the end of the year, but today the average is five to eight days. In fact, Cisco Systems, the big software company, is able to close its books in just one day. The company's CEO says this enables his managers to "spot problems and opportunities at any time" and that it has an important impact on a company's future success. The key to the success is for financial systems to work together seamlessly over the Internet so that companies have real-time transactions with real-time reporting.[1]

APPLY IT!

Refer to the following partial adjusted trial balance for Fountas Recreational Park. (Except for K. Fountas, Capital, balance sheet accounts have been omitted.)

Fountas Recreational Park
Partial Adjusted Trial Balance
June 30, 2014

K. Fountas, Capital	93,070
K. Fountas, Withdrawals	36,000
Campsite Rentals	88,200
Wages Expense	23,850
Insurance Expense	3,784
Utilities Expense	1,800
Supplies Expense	1,320
Depreciation Expense—Building	6,000

1. Prepare the necessary closing entries.
2. Compute the ending balance of the owner's Capital account.

SOLUTION

1.

June 30	Campsite Rentals		88,200	
	Income Summary			88,200
	To close the credit balance account			
30	Income Summary		36,754	
	Wages Expense			23,850
	Insurance Expense			3,784
	Utilities Expense			1,800
	Supplies Expense			1,320
	Depreciation Expense—Building			6,000
	To close the debit balance accounts			
30	Income Summary		51,446	
	K. Fountas, Capital			51,446
	To close the Income Summary account			
	$88,200 − $36,754 = $51,446			
30	K. Fountas, Capital		36,000	
	K. Fountas, Withdrawals			36,000
	To close the Withdrawals account			

2.

K. Fountas, Capital

Dr.		Cr.	
June 30	36,000	Beg. Bal.	93,070
		June 30	51,446
		End. Bal.	108,516

TRY IT! SE3, SE4, SE5, SE6, SE10, E1A, E3A, E1B, E3B

LO3 Reversing Entries: An Optional First Step

A **reversing entry** is an optional journal entry made on the first day of an accounting period. It has the opposite effect of an adjusting entry made at the end of the previous period—that is, it debits the credits and credits the debits of an earlier adjusting entry. The sole purpose of reversing entries is to simplify routine bookkeeping procedures, and they apply only to certain adjusting entries. As used in this text, reversing entries apply only to accruals (accrued revenues and expenses).

To see how reversing entries can be helpful, consider this adjusting entry to accrue wages expense made in Blue Design Studio's records.

Application of Double Entry

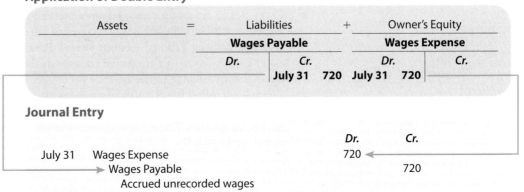

Assets	=	Liabilities	+	Owner's Equity	
		Wages Payable		**Wages Expense**	
		Dr.	Cr.	Dr.	Cr.
			July 31 720	July 31 720	

Journal Entry

			Dr.	Cr.
July 31	Wages Expense		720	
	Wages Payable			720
	Accrued unrecorded wages			

When the company pays its assistant on the next regular payday, its accountant would make the journal entry that follows.

Application of Double Entry

Journal Entry

			Dr.	Cr.
Aug. 9	Wages Payable		720	
	Wages Expense		1,680	
	Cash			2,400
	Paid two weeks wages to assistant, $720 of			
	which accrued in the previous period			

If no reversing entry is made at the time of payment, the accountant would have to find out how much of the $2,400 applies to the current accounting period and how much applies to the previous period. That may seem easy in our example, but think how difficult and time-consuming it would be if a company had hundreds of employees working on different schedules. A reversing entry helps solve the problem of applying revenues and expenses to the correct accounting period.

For example, consider the following sequence of entries and their effects on the Wages Expense account:

1. Adjusting Entry

		Dr.	Cr.
July 31	Wages Expense	720	
	Wages Payable		720

2. Closing Entry

July 31	Income Summary	5,520	
	Wages Expense		5,520

3. Reversing Entry

Aug. 1	Wages Payable	720	
	Wages Expense		720

4. Payment Entry

Aug. 9	Wages Expense	2,400	
	Cash		2,400

Wages Expense   **Account No. 511**

Date		Post. Ref.	Debit	Credit	Balance Debit	Balance Credit
July	26	J1	4,800		4,800	
	31	J3	720		5,520	
	31	J4		5,520	—	
Aug.	1	J5		720		720
	9	J6	2,400		1,680	

Here, you can see that

- Entry 1 adjusted Wages Expense to accrue $720 in the July accounting period.
- Entry 2 closed the $5,520 in Wages Expense for July to Income Summary, leaving a zero balance.
- Entry 3, the reversing entry, set up a credit balance of $720 on August 1 in Wages Expense, which is the expense recognized through the adjusting entry in July (and also reduced the liability account Wages Payable to a zero balance). The reversing entry always sets up an abnormal balance in the income statement account and produces a zero balance in the balance sheet account.
- Entry 4 recorded the $2,400 payment of wages as a debit to Wages Expense, automatically leaving a balance of $1,680, which represents the correct wages expense to date in August. The reversing entry simplified the process of making the payment entry on August 9.

Reversing entries apply to any accrued expenses or revenues. Blue Design Studio's only accrued expense was wages expense. An adjusting entry for the company's accrued revenue (Design Revenue) would require the reversing entry that follows.

		Dr.	*Cr.*
Aug. 1	Design Revenue	400	
	Accounts Receivable		400
	Reversed the adjusting entry for accrued revenue earned		

APPLY IT!

Which of the following accounts, after adjustment, will most likely require reversing entries?

a. Salaries Payable
b. Accumulated Depreciation
c. Interest Payable

d. Supplies
e. Taxes Payable

SOLUTION

a., c., and e.

TRY IT! SE8, SE9, E2A, E6A, E2B, E6B

LO4 The Work Sheet: An Accountant's Tool

To organize data and important information, accountants use **working papers**. Because working papers provide evidence of past work, they also enable accountants to retrace their steps when they need to verify information in the financial statements.

A **work sheet** is a special kind of working paper. It serves as a preliminary step in preparing financial statements. Using a work sheet lessens the possibility of omitting an adjustment and helps the accountant check the arithmetical accuracy of the accounts. The work sheet is never published and is rarely seen by management.

Because preparing a work sheet is a mechanical process, many accountants use a computer for this purpose. Some accountants use a spreadsheet program to prepare the work sheet. Others use a general ledger system to prepare financial statements from the adjusted trial balance.

Preparing the Work Sheet

A common form of work sheet has one column for account names and multiple columns with headings like the ones shown in Exhibit 8. A heading that includes the name of the company and the period of time covered (as on the income statement) identifies the work sheet. As Exhibit 8 shows, preparation of a work sheet involves five steps.

Step 1. Enter and Total the Account Balances in the Trial Balance Columns The debit and credit balances of the accounts on the last day of an accounting period are copied from the ledger into the Trial Balance columns (the green columns in Exhibit 8). When accountants use a work sheet, they do not have to prepare a separate trial balance.

Step 2. Enter and Total the Adjustments in the Adjustments Columns The required adjustments are entered in the Adjustments columns of the work sheet (the purple columns in Exhibit 8). As each adjustment is entered, a letter is used to identify its debit and credit parts. For example, in Exhibit 8, the letter (a) identifies the adjustment made for the rent that Blue Design Studio prepaid on July 3, which results in a debit to Rent Expense and a credit to Prepaid Rent. These identifying letters may be used to reference supporting computations or documentation for the related adjusting entries.

Blue Design Studio
Work Sheet
For the Month Ended July 31, 2014

Account Name	Trial Balance Debit	Trial Balance Credit	Adjustments Debit	Adjustments Credit	Adjusted Trial Balance Debit	Adjusted Trial Balance Credit	Income Statement Debit	Income Statement Credit	Balance Sheet Debit	Balance Sheet Credit
Cash	22,480				22,480				22,480	
Accounts Receivable	4,600		(f) 400		5,000				5,000	
Office Supplies	5,200			(b) 1,540	3,660				3,660	
Prepaid Rent	3,200			(a) 1,600	1,600				1,600	
Office Equipment	16,320				16,320				16,320	
Accumulated Depreciation—Office Equipment				(c) 300		300				300
Accounts Payable		6,280				6,280				6,280
Unearned Design Revenue		1,400	(e) 800			600				600
J. Blue, Capital		40,000				40,000				40,000
J. Blue, Withdrawals	2,800				2,800				2,800	
Design Revenue		12,400		(e) 800		13,600		13,600		
				(f) 400						
Wages Expense	4,800		(d) 720		5,520		5,520			
Utilities Expense	680				680		680			
	60,080	60,080								
Rent Expense			(a) 1,600		1,600		1,600			
Office Supplies Expense			(b) 1,540		1,540		1,540			
Depreciation Expense— Office Equipment			(c) 300		300		300			
Wages Payable				(d) 720		720				720
			5,360	5,360	61,500	61,500	9,640	13,600	51,860	47,900
Net Income							3,960			3,960
							13,600	13,600	51,860	51,860

Note: The columns of the work sheet are prepared in the following order. (1) Trial Balance, (2) Adjustments, (3) Adjusted Trial Balance, and (4) Income Statement and Balance Sheet columns. In the fifth step, the Income Statement and Balance Sheet columns are totaled.

Exhibit 8
The Work Sheet

A trial balance includes only accounts that have balances. If an adjustment involves an account that does not appear in the trial balance, the new account is added below the accounts listed on the work sheet. For example, Rent Expense has been added to Exhibit 8. Accumulated depreciation accounts, which have a zero balance only in the initial period of operation, are the sole exception to this rule. They are listed immediately after their associated asset accounts.

When all the adjustments have been made, the two Adjustments columns must be totaled. This procedure proves that the debits and credits of the adjustments are equal, and it generally reduces errors in the work sheet.

Step 3. Enter and Total the Adjusted Account Balances in the Adjusted Trial Balance Columns The adjusted trial balance in the work sheet is prepared by combining the amount of each account in the Trial Balance columns with the corresponding amount in the Adjustments columns and entering each result in the Adjusted Trial Balance columns (the beige columns in Exhibit 8).

Exhibit 8 contains examples of **crossfooting**, or adding and subtracting a group of numbers horizontally.

- The first line shows Cash with a debit balance of $22,480. Because there are no adjustments to the Cash account, $22,480 is entered in the debit column of the Adjusted Trial Balance columns.
- On the second line, Accounts Receivable shows a debit of $4,600 in the Trial Balance columns. Because there is a debit of $400 in the Adjustments columns, it is added to the $4,600 and carried over to the debit column of the Adjusted Trial Balance columns at $5,000.
- On the next line, Office Supplies shows a debit of $5,200 in the Trial Balance columns and a credit of $1,540 in the Adjustments columns. Subtracting $1,540 from $5,200 results in a $3,660 debit balance in the Adjusted Trial Balance columns.

This process is followed for all the accounts, including those added below the trial balance totals. The Adjusted Trial Balance columns are then *footed* (totaled) to check the accuracy of the crossfooting.

Step 4. Extend the Account Balances from the Adjusted Trial Balance Columns to the Income Statement or Balance Sheet Columns Each account in the adjusted trial balance is extended to its proper place as a debit or credit in either the Income Statement columns or the Balance Sheet columns (the blue columns in Exhibit 8). As shown in Exhibit 8, revenue and expense accounts are extended to the Income Statement columns, and asset, liability, Capital, and Withdrawals accounts are extended to the Balance Sheet columns.

To avoid overlooking an account, the accounts are extended line by line, beginning with the first line (Cash). For instance, the Cash debit balance of $22,480 is extended to the debit column of the Balance Sheet columns; then, the Accounts Receivable debit balance of $5,000 is extended to the debit column of the Balance Sheet columns; and so forth.

Step 5. Total the Income Statement Columns and the Balance Sheet Columns. Enter the Net Income or Net Loss in Both Pairs of Columns as a Balancing Figure, and Recompute the Column Totals. This last step, shown in the orange columns at the bottom of Exhibit 8, is necessary to compute net income or net loss and to prove the arithmetical accuracy of the work sheet.

Net income (or net loss) is equal to the difference between the total debits and credits of the Income Statement columns.

Revenues (Income Statement credit column total)	$13,600
Expenses (Income Statement debit column total)	(9,640)
Net Income	$ 3,960

In this case, revenues (credit column) exceed expenses (debit column). Thus, Blue Design Studio has a net income of $3,960. The same difference occurs between the total debits and credits of the Balance Sheet columns.

The $3,960 is entered in the debit side of the Income Statement columns and in the credit side of the Balance Sheet columns to balance the columns. Remember that the excess of revenues over expenses (net income) increases owner's equity and that increases in owner's equity are recorded by credits.

When a net loss occurs, the opposite rule applies. The excess of expenses over revenues—net loss—is placed in the credit side of the Income Statement columns as a balancing figure. It is then placed in the debit side of the Balance Sheet columns because a net loss decreases owner's equity, and decreases in owner's equity are recorded by debits.

As a final check, the four columns are totaled again. If the Income Statement columns and the Balance Sheet columns do not balance, an account may have been extended or sorted to the wrong column, or an error may have been made in adding the columns. Of course, equal totals in the two pairs of columns are not absolute proof of accuracy. If an asset has been carried to the Income Statement debit column (or an expense has been carried to the Balance Sheet debit column) or a similar error with revenues or liabilities has been made, the work sheet will balance, but the net income figure will be wrong.

Exhibit 9
Adjustments from the Work Sheet Entered in the General Journal

General Journal			Post. Ref.	Debit	Credit
Date		**Description**			
2014					
(a) July	31	Rent Expense	514	1,600	
		Prepaid Rent	117		1,600
		To recognize expiration of one month's rent			
(b)	31	Office Supplies Expense	517	1,540	
		Office Supplies	116		1,540
		To recognize office supplies used during the month			
(c)	31	Depreciation Expense—Office Equipment	520	300	
		Accumulated Depreciation—Office Equipment	147		300
		To record depreciation of office equipment for a month			
(d)	31	Wages Expense	511	720	
		Wages Payable	214		720
		To accrue unrecorded wages			
(e)	31	Unearned Design Revenue	213	800	
		Design Revenue	411		800
		To recognize payment for services not yet performed			
(f)	31	Accounts Receivable	113	400	
		Design Revenue	411		400
		To accrue design fees earned but unrecorded			

Page 2

Closing Entries and the Financial Statements

Closing entries set the accounts on the income statement to zero and transfer the resulting balance of net income or loss to the owner's Capital account on the balance sheet as depicted in Exhibit 10. Closing entries do not affect cash flows.

Exhibit 10

The Effect of Closing Entries on the Financial Statements

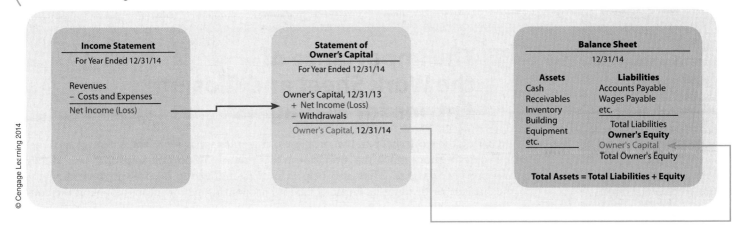

© Cengage Learning 2014

APPLY IT!

Place the following columns of a work sheet in the proper order:

a. Balance Sheet columns
b. Trial Balance columns
c. Income Statement columns
d. Adjusted Trial Balance columns
e. Adjustments columns

SOLUTION

b., e., d., c., a.

TRY IT! SE11, E4A, E6A, E7A, E8A, E4B, E6B, E7B, E8B

SECTION 3   **BUSINESS APPLICATIONS**

BUSINESS APPLICATION
■ Using a work sheet

RELEVANT LEARNING OBJECTIVE

LO 5   Explain the importance of the work sheet and closing entries when managing a business.

LO 5 The Importance of the Work Sheet and Closing Entries for Managers

Preparing the work sheet and recording closing entries may seem like technical accounting topics without much function, but in fact they are important steps that save money and prevent mistakes. They also help in understanding the business by providing the mechanism for dividing its financial life into accounting periods; thus, applying the concept of *periodicity*.

Using the Work Sheet

Accountants use the completed work sheet in performing three principal tasks. These tasks are as follows.

■ **Recording the adjusting entries in the general journal:** Because the information needed to record the adjusting entries can be copied from the work sheet, entering the adjustments in the journal is an easy step, as shown in Exhibit 9. The adjusting entries are then posted to the general ledger.

■ **Recording the closing entries in the general journal:** The Income Statement columns of the work sheet show all the accounts that need to be closed, except for the Withdrawals account. Exhibits 2 through 6 show how the closing entries are entered in the journal and posted to the ledger.

■ **Preparing the financial statements:** Once the work sheet has been completed, preparing the financial statements is simple because the account balances have been sorted into the Income Statement and Balance Sheet columns.

Closing entries are important to managing a business for the following reasons:

■ The owners of the business expect periodic reports of the progress of the business.

■ In planning a business' future operations, management needs to prepare budgets for future time periods.

■ For management to evaluate a company's process in achieving its profitability goals, it is necessary to divide the life of the business into relatively short time periods.

International Perspective

IFRS) Why Are IFRS Important to Multinational Companies?

Many U.S. companies, both private and public, operate in different countries. If these companies were able to use IFRS for all their operations throughout the world (including in the United States), it would simplify the process of preparing combined or consolidated financial statements. Currently, these companies face a difficult task every time they need to prepare financial statements for combined or consolidated operations because the accounting records of the foreign divisions often follow the accounting standards of their respective countries or IFRS. In either case, their financial statements must be converted to U.S. GAAP before they can be combined with the accounts of the U.S. company. The use of IFRS for the entire company would save money and enable the company to report more timely results. This is one reason many U.S. multinational companies favor the adoption of IFRS in the United States.

© Cengage Learning 2014

APPLY IT!

Indicate whether each of the following items is associated with a purpose of (a) the work sheet or (b) closing entries:

1. Preparing the financial statements.
2. Financial statements that are up to date for measuring financial progress.
3. Recording adjusting entries.
4. Recording closing entries.
5. Preparing budgets.

SOLUTION

1. a; 2. b; 3. a; 4. a; 5. b

TRY IT! SE11, E5A, E6A, E7A, E8A, E5B, E6B, E7B, E8B

TriLevel Problem

Speedy Movers

The beginning of this chapter focused on Speedy Movers. At the end of an accounting period, Speedy Movers, like all other companies, must prepare its accounts for the next accounting period. Complete the following requirements in order to answer the questions posed at the beginning of the chapter.

Section 1: Concepts
Why are the concepts of permanent and temporary accounts important to making closing entries?

Section 2: Accounting Applications
What steps must a company follow to prepare its accounts for the next accounting period? Refer to Speedy Movers' partial adjusted trial balance below.

	A	B	C
1	Speedy Movers		
2	Partial Adjusted Trial Balance		
3	June 30, 2014		
4			
5	J. Thomas, Capital		24,740
6	J. Thomas, Withdrawals	18,000	
7	Moving Services Revenue		185,400
8	Driver Wages Expense	88,900	
9	Fuel Expense	19,000	
10	Other Wages Expense	14,400	
11	Packing Supplies Expense	6,200	
12	Office Equipment Rental Expense	3,000	
13	Utilities Expense	4,450	
14	Insurance Expense	4,200	
15	Interest Expense	5,100	
16	Depreciation Expense	10,040	
17			

1. Prepare the necessary closing entries. (Note that this adjusted trial balance is "partial" in that it omits all balance sheet accounts except the owner's equity accounts.)

2. Compute the ending balance of the owner's Capital account.

Section 3: Business Applications
Why are closing entries important to good financial reporting in the current accounting period and the next accounting period?

SOLUTION

Section 1: Concepts

Permanent accounts and temporary accounts are used in the process of achieving *periodicity* and *accrual accounting*. Permanent accounts (or real accounts) are accounts that carry forward their balances into the next accounting period. They are the balance sheet accounts. On the other hand, temporary accounts (or nominal accounts) are accounts that begin each accounting period with a zero balance, accumulate a balance during the period, and are then cleared by means of closing entries. Thus, temporary accounts show a company's revenues and expenses for a particular period of time. They are the income statement accounts and the owner's withdrawal accounts.

Section 2: Accounting Applications

1.

	A	B	C	D	E
1	June	30	Moving Serivces Revenue	185,400	
2			Income Summary		185,400
3			To close the credit balance account		
4		30	Income Summary	155,290	
5			Driver Wages Expense		88,900
6			Fuel Expense		19,000
7			Other Wages Expense		14,400
8			Packing Supplies Expense		6,200
9			Office Equipment Rental Expense		3,000
10			Utilities Expense		4,450
11			Insurance Expense		4,200
12			Interest Expense		5,100
13			Depreciation Expense		10,040
14			To close the debit balance accounts		
15		30	Income Summary	30,110	
16			J. Thomas, Capital		30,110
17			To close the Income Summary account		
18			$185,400 - $155,290 = $30,110		
19		30	J. Thomas, Capital	18,000	
20			J. Thomas, Withdrawals		18,000
21			To close the Withdrawals account		
22					

2.

	A	B	C	D	E	F
1			**J. Thomas, Capital**			
2	June	30	18,000	Beg. Bal.		24,740
3				June	30	30,110
4				End. Bal.		36,850

Section 3: Business Applications

Closing entries are helpful for business owners who expect periodic reports of the progress of the business. These entries also help management to prepare budgets for future time periods in planning a business' future operation. Finally, closing entries help divide the life of the business into relatively short time periods so that management can evaluate a company's progress in achieving its profitability goals.

Chapter Review

Describe the role of closing entries in the preparation of financial statements.

Closing entries have two purposes: (1) They clear the balances of all temporary accounts (revenue, expense, and Withdrawals accounts) so that they have zero balances at the beginning of the next accounting period, and (2) they summarize a period's revenues and expenses in the Income Summary account so that the net income or loss for the period can be transferred as a total to owner's Capital.

Prepare closing entries.

The first two steps in preparing closing entries are to transfer the balances of the revenue and expense accounts to the Income Summary account. The balance of the Income Summary account is then transferred to the owner's Capital account. Finally, the balance of the Withdrawals account is transferred to owner's Capital. After the closing entries have been posted to the ledger accounts, a post-closing trial balance is prepared as a final check on the balance of the ledger and to ensure that all temporary (nominal) accounts have been closed.

Prepare reversing entries.

Reversing entries are optional journal entries made on the first day of an accounting period. Reversing entries have the opposite effect of adjusting entries made at the end of the previous period—that is, a reversing entry debits the credits and credits the debits of an earlier adjusting entry. The sole purpose of reversing entries is to simplify routine bookkeeping procedures, and they apply only to accruals.

Prepare a work sheet.

The five steps in preparing a work sheet are (1) enter and total the account balances in the Trial Balance columns; (2) enter and total the adjustments in the Adjustments columns; (3) enter and total the adjusted account balances in the Adjusted Trial Balance columns; (4) extend the account balances from the Adjusted Trial Balance columns to the Income Statement or Balance Sheet columns; and (5) total the Income Statement and Balance Sheet columns, enter the net income or net loss in both pairs of columns as a balancing figure, and recompute the column totals.

Explain the importance of the work sheet and closing entries when managing a business.

A work sheet is useful in recording both adjusting and closing entries and in preparing the financial statements. The income statement and balance sheet can be prepared directly from the Income Statement and Balance Sheet columns of the completed work sheet. The statement of owner's equity is prepared using owner's Withdrawals, net income, additional investments, and the beginning balance of the owner's Capital account.

The work sheet assists in preparing adjusting and closing entries as well as the financial statements. Closing entries are useful for (1) owners of the business who expect periodic reports of the progress of the business, (2) management to prepare budgets for future time periods in planning a business' future operations, and (3) management to evaluate a company's progress in achieving its profitability goals.

Key Terms

closing entries 132 (LO1)
crossfooting 145 (LO4)
Income Summary account 132 (LO1)

permanent accounts 132 (LO1)
post-closing trial balance 140 (LO2)
reversing entry 141 (LO3)
temporary accounts 132 (LO1)

work sheet 143 (LO4)
working papers 143 (LO4)

Chapter Assignments

DISCUSSION QUESTIONS

LO 1   **DQ1.** Why is the accounting cycle called a "cycle"?

LO 2   **DQ2.** Could closing entries be made without using the Income Summary account?

LO 2   **DQ3.** Why does the post-closing trial balance contain only balance sheet accounts?

LO 3   **DQ4.** Why are reversing entries helpful?

LO 4   **DQ5.** Under what circumstances would the Income Statement and Balance Sheet columns on a work sheet balance when they are initially totaled?

SHORT EXERCISES

LO 1   **Concepts Underlying Closing Entries**

SE1. CONCEPT ▶ Match the following concepts to the related statements:

a. periodicity
b. accrual accounting
c. permanent accounts
d. temporary accounts

1. Encompasses all the techniques that determine income for an accounting period.
2. Accumulate from zero each accounting period.
3. Concept that embodies assumption that life of business can be divided into accounting periods.
4. Have a balance that carries forwarded from one accounting period to another.

LO 1   **Accounting Cycle**

SE2. Resequence the following activities to indicate the usual order of the accounting cycle:

a. Close the accounts.
b. Analyze the transactions.
c. Post the entries to the ledger.
d. Prepare the financial statements.
e. Adjust the accounts.
f. Record the transactions in the journal.
g. Prepare the post-closing trial balance.
h. Prepare the initial trial balance.
i. Prepare the adjusted trial balance.

LO 2   **Closing Revenue Accounts**

SE3. Assume that at the end of the accounting period there are credit balances of $3,400 in Patient Services Revenues and $1,800 in Laboratory Fees Revenues. Prepare the required closing entry. The accounting period ends December 31.

LO 2   **Closing Expense Accounts**

SE4. Assume that debit balances at the end of the accounting period are $1,400 in Rent Expense, $1,100 in Wages Expense, and $500 in Other Expenses. Prepare the required closing entry. The accounting period ends December 31.

LO 2   **Closing the Income Summary Account**

SE5. Assuming that total revenues were $5,200 and total expenses were $3,000, prepare the journal entry to close the Income Summary account to the P. Mehta, Capital account. The accounting period ends December 31.

LO 2   **Closing the Withdrawals Account**

SE6. Assuming that withdrawals during the accounting period were $800, prepare the journal entry to close the P. Mehta, Withdrawals account to the P. Mehta, Capital account. The accounting period ends December 31.

LO **2**   **Posting Closing Entries**

SE7. Show the effects of the transactions in **SE3**, **SE4**, **SE5**, and **SE6** by entering beginning balances in appropriate T accounts and recording the transactions. Assume that the P. Mehta, Capital account had a beginning balance of $1,300.

LO **3**   **Preparation of Reversing Entries**

SE8. Below, indicated by letters, are the adjusting entries at the end of March.

Account Name	Debit	Credit
Prepaid Insurance		(a) 180
Accumulated Depreciation—Office Equipment		(b)1,050
Salaries Expense	(c) 360	
Insurance Expense	(a) 180	
Depreciation Expense—Office Equipment	(b)1,050	
Salaries Payable		(c) 360
	1,590	1,590

Prepare the required reversing entry or entries.

LO **3**   **Effects of Reversing Entries**

SE9. Assume that prior to the adjustments in **SE8**, Salaries Expense had a debit balance of $1,800 and Salaries Payable had a zero balance. Prepare a T account for each of these accounts. Enter the beginning balance. Post the adjustment for accrued salaries, the appropriate closing entry, and the reversing entry. Then, enter the transaction in the T accounts for a payment of $480 for salaries on April 3.

LO **2**   **Preparation of Closing Entries**

SE10. Katsu Company's adjusted trial balance on December 31, 2014, contains the following accounts and balances: F. Katsu, Capital, $8,600; F. Katsu, Withdrawals, $350; Service Revenue, $2,600; Rent Expense, $400; Wages Expense, $900; Utilities Expense, $200; and Telephone Expense, $50. Prepare the closing entries.

LO **2, 4, 5**   **Preparation of Closing Entries from a Work Sheet**

SE11. Prepare the required closing journal entries for the year ended December 31, using the items from the Income Statement columns of a work sheet that follow and assuming that withdrawals by the owner, A. Riley, were $7,000.

Account Name	Debit	Credit
Repair Revenue		35,860
Wages Expense	13,260	
Rent Expense	2,800	
Supplies Expense	6,390	
Insurance Expense	1,370	
Depreciation Expense—Repair Equipment	3,020	
	26,840	35,860
Net Income	9,020	
	35,860	35,860

EXERCISES: SET A

LO 2   **Preparation of Closing Entries**

E1A. Hamilton Realty Company's income statement accounts at the end of its fiscal year, December 31, follow. Prepare the required closing entries. Lewis Hamilton is the owner.

Account Name	Debit	Credit
Commission Revenue		$25,620
Wages Expense	$8,110	
Rent Expense	1,200	
Supplies Expense	4,260	
Insurance Expense	915	
Depreciation Expense—Office Equipment	1,345	
Total Expenses		15,830
Net Income		$ 9,790

LO 3   **Reversing Entries**

E2A. Selected September T accounts for Kalgan Company follow.

Supplies					Supplies Expense				
Dr.		**Cr.**			**Dr.**		**Cr.**		
9/1 Bal.	1,720	9/30 Adj.	2,560		9/30 Adj.	2,560	9/30 Closing	2,560	
Sept. purchases	1,880								
Bal.	**1,040**				**Bal.**	—			

Wages Payable					Wages Expense				
Dr.		**Cr.**			**Dr.**		**Cr.**		
		9/30 Adj.	1,280		Sept. wages	7,880	9/30 Closing	9,160	
					9/30 Adj.	1,280			
		Bal.	**1,280**		**Bal.**	—			

1. **ACCOUNTING CONNECTION** ▶ In which of the accounts would a reversing entry be helpful? Why?
2. Prepare the appropriate reversing entry.
3. Prepare the journal entry to record a payment on October 25 for wages totaling $6,280. How much of this amount represents wages expense for October?

LO 2   **Preparation of a Trial Balance**

E3A. An alphabetical list presenting the accounts and balances for Ken's Cleaners on June 30, 2014, follows. All the accounts have normal balances.

Accounts Payable	$ 30,840
Accounts Receivable	15,300
Accumulated Depreciation—Office Equipment	2,700
Advertising Expense	3,600
Cash	15,270
Office Equipment	31,020
Prepaid Insurance	3,360
Rent Expense	14,400
Revenue from Cleaning	115,800
I. Bell, Capital	61,260
I. Bell, Withdrawals	54,000
Supplies	1,650
Wages Expense	72,000

Prepare the trial balance by listing the accounts in the correct order, with the balances in the appropriate debit or credit column.

LO 4 **Completion of a Work Sheet**

E4A. A highly simplified alphabetical list of trial balance accounts and their normal balances for the month ended March 31, 2014, follows.

Accounts Payable	8
Accounts Receivable	14
Accumulated Depreciation—Office Equipment	2
Cash	8
K. Pollard, Capital	24
K. Pollard, Withdrawals	12
Office Equipment	16
Prepaid Insurance	4
Service Revenue	46
Supplies	8
Unearned Revenues	6
Utilities Expense	4
Wages Expense	20

1. Prepare a work sheet, entering the trial balance accounts in the order in which they would normally appear and entering the balances in the correct debit or credit column.
2. Complete the work sheet using the following information: expired insurance, $2; estimated depreciation on office equipment, $2; accrued wages, $2; and unused supplies on hand, $2. In addition, $4 of the unearned revenues balance had been earned by the end of the month.

LO 5 **Preparation of Statement of Owner's Equity**

E5A. The Capital, Withdrawals, and Income Summary accounts for Strauss's Hair Salon are shown in the T accounts that follow. The closing entries have been recorded for the year ended December 31, 2014.

B. Strauss, Capital

Dr.		Cr.	
12/31/14	9,000	12/31/13	26,000
		12/31/14	19,000
		Bal.	**36,000**

Income Summary

Dr.		Cr.	
12/31/14	43,000	12/31/14	62,000
12/31/14	19,000		
Bal.	—		

B. Strauss, Withdrawals

Dr.		Cr.	
4/1/14	3,000	12/31/14	9,000
7/1/14	3,000		
10/1/14	3,000		
Bal.	—		

Prepare a statement of owner's equity for Strauss's Hair Salon.

LO 3, 4, 5 **Preparation of Adjusting and Reversing Entries from Work Sheet Columns**

E6A. The items that follow are from the Adjustments columns of a work sheet dated June 30, 2014.

| | Adjustments | |
Account Name	Debit	Credit
Prepaid Insurance		(a) 480
Office Supplies		(b) 1,260
Accumulated Depreciation—Office Equipment		(c) 2,800
Accumulated Depreciation—Store Equipment		(d) 4,400
Office Salaries Expense	(e) 480	
Store Salaries Expense	(e) 960	
Insurance Expense	(a) 480	
Office Supplies Expense	(b) 1,260	
Depreciation Expense—Office Equipment	(c) 2,800	
Depreciation Expense—Store Equipment	(d) 4,400	
Salaries Payable		(e) 1,440
	10,380	10,380

1. Prepare the adjusting entries.
2. Where required, prepare appropriate reversing entries.

LO 2, 4, 5 **Preparation of Closing Entries from the Work Sheet**

E7A. The items that follow are from the Income Statement columns of Winter's Repair Shop's work sheet for the year ended December 31, 2014. Prepare journal entries to close the revenue, expense, Income Summary, and Withdrawals accounts. The owner, A. Winter, withdrew $2,500 during the year.

| | Income Statement | |
Account Name	Debit	Credit
Repair Revenue		12,810
Wages Expense	4,055	
Rent Expense	600	
Supplies Expense	2,130	
Insurance Expense	458	
Depreciation Expense—Repair Equipment	672	
	7,915	12,810
Net Income	4,895	
	12,810	12,810

LO 4, 5 **Adjusting Entries and Preparation of a Balance Sheet**

E8A. In the partial work sheet for K. Joe Company that follows, the Trial Balance and Income Statement columns have been completed. All amounts are in dollars.

| | Trial Balance | | Income Statement | |
Account Name	Debit	Credit	Debit	Credit
Cash	28			
Accounts Receivable	48			
Supplies	44			
Prepaid Insurance	32			
Building	100			
Accumulated Depreciation—Building		32		
Accounts Payable		16		
Unearned Revenues		8		
K. Joe, Capital		128		
Revenues		176		184
Wages Expense	108		120	
	360	360		

Account Name	Trial Balance		Income Statement	
	Debit	Credit	Debit	Credit
Insurance Expense			16	
Supplies Expense			32	
Depreciation Expense—Building			8	
Wages Payable				
			176	184
Net Income			8	
			184	184

1. Show the adjusting entries without giving an explanation.
2. Prepare a balance sheet for December 31, 2014.

EXERCISES: SET B

Visit the textbook companion web site at www.cengagebrain.com to access Exercise Set B for this chapter.

PROBLEMS

LO **1, 2** **Preparation of Closing Entries**

P1. Salinas Trailer Rental rents small trailers by the day for local moving jobs. Its adjusted trial balance at the end of the current fiscal year follows.

Salinas Trailer Rental
Adjusted Trial Balance
June 30, 2014

Cash	1,384	
Accounts Receivable	1,944	
Supplies	238	
Prepaid Insurance	720	
Trailers	24,000	
Accumulated Depreciation—Trailers		14,400
Accounts Payable		542
Wages Payable		400
D. Anatole, Capital		11,388
D. Anatole, Withdrawals	14,400	
Trailer Rentals Revenue		91,092
Wages Expense	46,800	
Insurance Expense	1,440	
Supplies Expense	532	
Depreciation Expense—Trailers	4,800	
Other Expenses	21,564	
	117,822	117,822

REQUIRED

1. From the information given, record closing entries.
2. **CONCEPT** ▶ If closing entries were not prepared at the end of the accounting period, what problems would result in the next accounting period?

Closing Entries Using T Accounts and Preparation of Financial Statements

P2. Carlton Tennis Club's adjusted trial balance at the end of its fiscal year follows.

Carlton Tennis Club
Adjusted Trial Balance
June 30, 2014

Cash	26,200	
Prepaid Advertising	9,600	
Supplies	1,200	
Land	100,000	
Building	645,200	
Accumulated Depreciation—Building		260,000
Equipment	156,000	
Accumulated Depreciation—Equipment		50,400
Accounts Payable		73,000
Wages Payable		9,000
Property Taxes Payable		22,500
Unearned Revenue—Locker Fees		3,000
J. Kojas, Capital		471,150
J. Kojas, Withdrawals	54,000	
Revenue from Court Fees		678,100
Revenue from Locker Fees		9,600
Wages Expense	351,000	
Maintenance Expense	51,600	
Advertising Expense	39,750	
Utilities Expense	64,800	
Supplies Expense	6,000	
Depreciation Expense—Building	30,000	
Depreciation Expense—Equipment	12,000	
Property Taxes Expense	22,500	
Miscellaneous Expense	6,900	
	1,576,750	1,576,750

REQUIRED

1. Prepare T accounts and enter the balances for J. Kojas, Capital; J. Kojas, Withdrawals; Income Summary, and all revenue and expense accounts.
2. Enter the four required closing entries in the T accounts, labeling the components *a* (credit balances), *b* (debit balances), *c* (Income Summary), and *d* (withdrawals), as appropriate.
3. Prepare an income statement, a statement of owner's equity, and a balance sheet for Carlton Tennis Club.
4. **CONCEPT** ▶ Explain why it is necessary to make closing entries at the end of an accounting period.

LO **2**   **Preparation of Closing Entries**

P3. Primorsk is a global specialized staffing firm. Information adapted from the statement of earnings (in thousands, without earnings per share information) in its annual report for the year ended December 31, 2014, follows. The firm reported distributing cash (dividends) in the amount of $95,562,000 to the owners in 2014.

Revenues	
Service revenues	$6,676,878
Interest income	21,896
Total revenues	$6,698,774
Expenses	
Employee compensation and benefits	$3,930,780
Selling, general, and administrative expenses	1,983,646
Income taxes	308,608
Total expenses	$6,223,034
Net income	$ 475,740

REQUIRED

1. Prepare the closing entries Primorsk would have made on December 31, 2014. Treat income taxes as an expense and cash distributions to owners as withdrawals.

2. **ACCOUNTING CONNECTION ▶** Based on your handling of requirement 1 and the effect of expenses and cash distributions on owner's capital, what theoretical reason can you give for not including expenses and cash distributions in the same closing entry?

LO **2, 3, 4, 5**

Preparation of a Work Sheet, Financial Statements, and Adjusting, Closing, and Reversing Entries

SPREADSHEET

P4. At the end of the fiscal year, Siglo Delivery Service's trial balance appeared as follows.

✔ 2: Net income: $62,392
✔ 2: Total assets: $247,148

Siglo Delivery Service
Trial Balance
August 31, 2014

Cash	10,072	
Accounts Receivable	29,314	
Prepaid Insurance	5,340	
Delivery Supplies	14,700	
Office Supplies	2,460	
Land	15,000	
Building	196,000	
Accumulated Depreciation—Building		53,400
Trucks	103,800	
Accumulated Depreciation—Trucks		30,900
Office Equipment	15,900	
Accumulated Depreciation—Office Equipment		10,800
Accounts Payable		9,396
Unearned Lockbox Fees		8,340
Mortgage Payable		72,000
R. Siglo, Capital		128,730
R. Siglo, Withdrawals	30,000	
Delivery Service Revenue		283,470
Lockbox Fees Earned		28,800
Truck Drivers' Wages Expense	120,600	
Office Salaries Expense	44,400	
Gas, Oil, and Truck Repairs Expense	31,050	
Interest Expense	7,200	
	625,836	625,836

(Continued)

REQUIRED

1. Enter the trial balance amounts in the Trial Balance columns of a work sheet and complete the work sheet using the information that follows.
   a. Expired insurance, $3060
   b. Inventory of unused delivery supplies, $1,430
   c. Inventory of unused office supplies, $186
   d. Estimated depreciation on the building, $14,400
   e. Estimated depreciation on the trucks, $15,450
   f. Estimated depreciation on the office equipment, $2,700
   g. The company credits the lockbox fees of customers who pay in advance to the Unearned Lockbox Fees account. Of the amount credited to this account during the year, $5,630 had been earned by August 31.
   h. Lockbox fees earned but unrecorded and uncollected at the end of the accounting period, $816
   i. Accrued but unpaid truck drivers' wages at the end of the year, $1,920

2. Prepare an income statement, a statement of owner's equity, and a balance sheet for the company. Assume the owner, Raul Siglo, made no additional investments.
3. Prepare adjusting, closing, and, when necessary, reversing entries from the work sheet.
4. **BUSINESS APPLICATION** ▶ Can the work sheet be used as a substitute for the financial statements? Explain your answer.

LO **1, 2**

The Complete Accounting Cycle Without a Work Sheet: Two Months (*second month optional*)

P5. On May 1, 2014, Leon Stoker opened Stoker's Repair Service. During the month, he completed the following transactions for the company:

✔5: May 31, 2014, net income: $962
✔5: May 31, 2014, total assets: $18,048
✔11: June 30, 2014, net income: $1,034
✔11: June 30, 2014, total assets: $18,408

May	1	Began business by depositing $10,000 in a bank account in the name of the company.
	1	Paid the rent for the store for current month, $850.
	1	Paid the premium on a one-year insurance policy, $960.
	2	Purchased repair equipment from Latin Company, $8,400. Terms were $1,200 down and $600 per month for one year. First payment is due June 1.
	5	Purchased repair supplies from Tanaka Company on credit, $936.
	8	Paid cash for an advertisement in a local newspaper, $120.
	15	Received cash repair revenue for the first half of the month, $800.
	21	Paid Tanaka Company on account, $450.
	31	Received cash repair revenue for the last half of May, $1,950.
	31	Made a withdrawal, $600.

REQUIRED FOR MAY

1. Prepare journal entries to record the May transactions. Include the Post. Ref. column and fill in using the account numbers listed in requirement 2.
2. Open the following accounts: Cash (111); Prepaid Insurance (117); Repair Supplies (119); Repair Equipment (144); Accumulated Depreciation—Repair Equipment (145); Accounts Payable (212); L. Stoker, Capital (311); L. Stoker, Withdrawals (313); Income Summary (314); Repair Revenue (411); Store Rent Expense (511); Advertising Expense (512); Insurance Expense (513); Repair Supplies Expense (514); and Depreciation Expense—Repair Equipment (515). Post the May journal entries to the ledger accounts.
3. Using the following information, record adjusting entries in the general journal and post to the ledger accounts:
   a. One month's insurance has expired.
   b. The remaining inventory of unused repair supplies is $338.
   c. The estimated depreciation on repair equipment is $140.
4. From the accounts in the ledger, prepare an adjusted trial balance.
   (*Note:* Normally, a trial balance is prepared before adjustments but is omitted here to save time.)

5. From the adjusted trial balance, prepare an income statement, a statement of owner's equity, and a balance sheet for May.
6. Prepare and post closing entries.
7. Prepare a post-closing trial balance.
   (Optional)
   During June, Leon Stoker completed these transactions for Stoker's Repair Service.

   June   1   Paid the monthly rent, $850.
           1   Made the monthly payment to Latin Company, $600.
           6   Purchased additional repair supplies on credit from Tanaka Company, $1,726.
         15   Received cash repair revenue for the first half of the month, $1,828.
         20   Paid cash for an advertisement in the local newspaper, $120.
         23   Paid Tanaka Company on account, $1,200.
         30   Received cash repair revenue for the last half of the month, $1,634.
         30   Recorded a withdrawal by owner, $600.
8. Prepare and post journal entries to record the June transactions.
9. Using the following information, record adjusting entries in the general journal and post to the ledger accounts.

   a. One month's insurance has expired.
   b. The inventory of unused repair supplies is $826.
   c. The estimated depreciation on repair equipment is $140.

10. From the accounts in the ledger, prepare an adjusted trial balance.
11. From the adjusted trial balance, prepare the June income statement, statement of owner's equity, and balance sheet.
12. Prepare and post closing entries.
13. Prepare a post-closing trial balance.

ALTERNATE PROBLEMS

LO **1, 2**   **Preparation of Closing Entries**

P6. Villa Consultant Company's adjusted trial balance at the end of its fiscal year follows.

Villa Consultant Company
Adjusted Trial Balance
December 31, 2014

Cash	14,550	
Accounts Receivable	4,650	
Prepaid Insurance	1,170	
Office Supplies	880	
Office Equipment	12,600	
Accumulated Depreciation—Office Equipment		1,530
Automobile	13,500	
Accumulated Depreciation—Automobile		1,500
Accounts Payable		3,400
Unearned Consulting Fees		3,000
J. Villa, Capital		29,070
J. Villa, Withdrawals	14,000	
Consulting Fees Earned		66,430
Office Salaries Expense	27,000	
Advertising Expense	5,050	
Rent Expense	5,300	
Telephone Expense	3,200	
Depreciation Expense—Office Equipment	1,530	
Depreciation Expense—Automobile	1,500	
	104,930	104,930

(Continued)

REQUIRED

1. Prepare the required closing entries.
2. **CONCEPT** ▶ Explain why closing entries are necessary at the end of the accounting period.

LO **1, 2**

✔ 3: Net income: $206,300
✔ 3: Total assets: $1,255,600

Closing Entries Using T Accounts and Preparation of Financial Statements

P7. Kilda Recreational Club's adjusted trial balance at the end of its fiscal year follows.

Kilda Recreational Club
Adjusted Trial Balance
June 30, 2014

Cash	52,400	
Prepaid Advertising	19,200	
Supplies	2,400	
Land	200,000	
Building	1,290,400	
Accumulated Depreciation—Building		520,000
Equipment	312,000	
Accumulated Depreciation—Equipment		100,800
Accounts Payable		146,000
Wages Payable		18,000
Property Taxes Payable		45,000
Unearned Revenue—Locker Fees		6,000
M. Kilda, Capital		942,300
M. Kilda, Withdrawals	108,000	
Revenue from Court Fees		1,356,200
Revenue from Locker Fees		19,200
Wages Expense	702,000	
Maintenance Expense	103,200	
Advertising Expense	79,500	
Utilities Expense	129,600	
Supplies Expense	12,000	
Depreciation Expense—Building	60,000	
Depreciation Expense—Equipment	24,000	
Property Taxes Expense	45,000	
Miscellaneous Expense	13,800	
	3,153,500	3,153,500

REQUIRED

1. Prepare T accounts and enter the balances for M. Kilda, Capital; M. Kilda, Withdrawals; Income Summary, and all revenue and expense accounts.
2. Enter the four required closing entries in the T accounts, labeling the components *a* (credit balances), *b* (debit balances), *c* (Income Summary), and *d* (withdrawals), as appropriate.

3. Prepare an income statement, a statement of owner's equity, and a balance sheet for Kilda Recreational Club.

4. **CONCEPT** ▶ Explain why it is necessary to make closing entries at the end of an accounting period.

LO **2**   **Preparation of Closing Entries**

P8. Change Painting Company's adjusted trial balance at December 31, 2014, follows. The owner made no investments during the period.

Change Painting Company
Adjusted Trial Balance
December 31, 2014

Cash	9,500	
Accounts Receivable	5,184	
Prepaid Insurance	760	
Prepaid Rent	400	
Painting Supplies	304	
Painting Equipment	7,750	
Accumulated Depreciation—Painting Equipment		640
Truck	14,400	
Accumulated Depreciation—Truck		1,440
Accounts Payable		840
Wages Payable		590
Unearned Painting Revenue		3,380
G. Ranke, Capital		30,068
G. Ranke, Withdrawals	4,000	
Painting Revenue		29,240
Wages Expense	11,360	
Rent Expense	2,700	
Gas, Oil, and Other Truck Expenses	1,160	
Insurance Expense	760	
Supplies Expense	5,840	
Depreciation Expense—Painting Equipment	640	
Depreciation Expense—Truck	1,440	
	66,198	66,198

REQUIRED

Prepare the required closing entries.

LO **2, 3, 4, 5**

SPREADSHEET

GENERAL LEDGER

✔ 2: June 30, 2014, net income: $197,244
✔ 2: June 30, 2014, total assets: $1,403,472

Preparation of a Work Sheet, Financial Statements, and Adjusting, Closing, and Reversing Entries

P9. Julio Theater Company's trial balance at the end of its current fiscal year follows.

Julio Theater Company
Trial Balance
June 30, 2014

Cash	63,600	
Accounts Receivable	37,088	
Prepaid Insurance	39,200	
Office Supplies	1,560	
Cleaning Supplies	7,180	
Land	40,000	
Building	800,000	
Accumulated Depreciation—Building		78,800
Theater Furnishings	740,000	
Accumulated Depreciation—Theater Furnishings		130,000
Office Equipment	63,200	
Accumulated Depreciation—Office Equipment		31,120
Accounts Payable		91,012
Gift Books Liability		83,800
Mortgage Payable		600,000
P. Julio, Capital		625,296
P. Julio, Withdrawals	120,000	
Ticket Sales Revenue		822,800
Theater Rental Revenue		90,400
Usher Wages Expense	314,000	
Office Wages E...	48,000	
	225,400	
	54,000	
	2,553,228	2,553,228

...nce amounts in the Trial Balance columns of a work
...heet using the following information:

...upplies, $488.
...g supplies, $936.
...e building, $28,000.
...e theater furnishings, $72,000.
...e office equipment, $6,320.
...ooks sold during the year to the Gift Books Liability
...klet of ticket coupons that is purchased in advance
...s the coupons at some point in the future. On June
...00 worth of the gift books had been redeemed.
...ges at the end of the accounting period, $1,720.

...statement of owner's equity, and a balance sheet.
...s by the owner, P. Julio.
...en necessary, reversing entries from the work sheet.
...he work sheet be used as a substitute for the finan-
...er.

LO **1, 2**

The Complete Accounting Cycle Without a Work Sheet: Two Months (*second month optional*)

SPREADSHEET

GENERAL LEDGER

✔ 5: June 30, 2014, net income: $1,924
✔ 5: June 30, 2014, total assets: $36,096
✔ 10: July 31, 2014, net income: $2,068
✔ 10: July 31, 2014, total assets: $36,816

P10. On June 1, 2014, Bob Lutz opened Lutz Repair Service. During the month, he completed the following transactions for the company:

June	1	Began business by depositing $20,000 in a bank account in the name of the company.
	1	Paid the rent for the store for current month, $1,700.
	1	Paid the premium on a one-year insurance policy, $1,920.
	2	Purchased repair equipment from Bilbao Company, $16,800. Terms were $2,400 down and $1,200 per month for one year. First payment is due June 1.
	5	Purchased repair supplies from Rusin Company on credit, $1,872.
	8	Paid cash for an advertisement in a local newspaper, $240.
	15	Received cash repair revenue for the first half of the month, $1,600.
	21	Paid Rusin Company on account, $900.
	30	Received cash repair revenue for the last half of May, $3,900.
	30	Made a withdrawal, $1,200.

REQUIRED FOR JUNE

1. Prepare journal entries to record the June transactions. Include the Post. Ref. column and fill in using the account numbers listed in requirement 2.
2. Open the following accounts: Cash (111); Prepaid Insurance (117); Repair Supplies (119); Repair Equipment (144); Accumulated Depreciation—Repair Equipment (145); Accounts Payable (212); B. Lutz, Capital (311); B. Lutz, Withdrawals (313); Income Summary (314); Repair Revenue (411); Store Rent Expense (511); Advertising Expense (512); Insurance Expense (513); Repair Supplies Expense (514); and Depreciation Expense—Repair Equipment (515). Post the May journal entries to the ledger accounts.
3. Using the following information, record adjusting entries in the general journal and post to the ledger accounts:

   d. One month's insurance has expired.
   e. The remaining inventory of unused repair supplies is $676.
   f. The estimated depreciation on repair equipment is $280.

4. From the accounts in the ledger, prepare an adjusted trial balance.
   (*Note:* Normally, a trial balance is prepared before adjustments but is omitted here to save time.)
5. From the adjusted trial balance, prepare an income statement, a statement of owner's equity, and a balance sheet for June.
6. Prepare and post closing entries.
7. Prepare a post-closing trial balance.
   (*Optional*)
   During July, Bob Lutz completed these transactions for Lutz Repair Service:

July	1	Paid the monthly rent, $1,700.
	1	Made the monthly payment to Bilbao Company, $1,200.
	6	Purchased additional repair supplies on credit from Rusin Company, $3,452.
	15	Received cash repair revenue for the first half of the month, $3,656.
	20	Paid cash for an advertisement in the local newspaper, $240.
	23	Paid Rusin Company on account, $2,400.
	30	Received cash repair revenue for the last half of the month, $3,268.
	30	Recorded a withdrawal by owner, $1,200.

(Continued)

8. Prepare and post journal entries to record the July transactions.
9. Using the following information, record adjusting entries in the general journal and post to the ledger accounts.

    d. One month's insurance has expired.
    e. The inventory of unused repair supplies is $1,652.
    f. The estimated depreciation on repair equipment is $280.

10. From the accounts in the ledger, prepare an adjusted trial balance.
11. From the adjusted trial balance, prepare the July income statement, statement of owner's equity, and balance sheet.
12. Prepare and post closing entries.
13. Prepare a post-closing trial balance.

CASES

LO 1   **Conceptual Understanding: Interim Financial Statements**

C1. Gulf Coast Drilling Company provides services for drilling operations off the coast of Louisiana. The company has a significant amount of debt to National Bank of New Orleans. The bank requires the company to provide it with quarterly financial statements. Explain what is involved in preparing financial statements every quarter.

LO 1   **Conceptual Understanding: Purpose of Closing Entries**

C2. Pamela Turnbow, owner of Turnbow Fashions Company, notices the amount of time it takes the company's accountant to prepare closing entries. She suggests that the company could save time and money by not doing closing entries. She argues that only adjusting entries are needed to determine the company's earnings. Explain the purposes of closing entries and why they are worth doing.

LO 1   **Conceptual Understanding: Accounting Efficiency**

C3. Turner Cabinets Company manufactures storage cabinets used in industry. It sells its cabinets to some customers on credit with generous terms specifying payment six months after purchase and an interest rate based on current bank rates. Because the interest on the loans accrues a little every day but is not paid until the note's due date, an adjusting entry must be made at the end of each accounting period to debit Interest Receivable and credit Interest Income for the amount of the interest accrued but not received to date. The company prepares financial statements every month. Keeping track of what has been accrued in the past is time-consuming because the notes carry different dates and interest rates.

Form in-class groups to determine what the accountant can do to simplify the process of making the adjusting entry for accrued interest each month. Compare the groups' solutions in a class discussion.

LO 1   **Ethical Dilemma: Ethics and Time Pressure**

C4. Thomas Odzer, an accountant for Mennix Company, has made adjusting entries and is preparing the adjusted trial balance for the first six months of the year. Financial statements must be delivered to the bank by 5 P.M. to support a critical loan agreement. By noon, Odzer has been unable to balance the adjusted trial balance. The figures are off by $1,320, so he increases the balance of the owner's Capital account by $1,320. He closes the accounts, prepares the statements, and sends them to the bank on time. He hopes that no one will notice the problem and believes that he can find the error and correct it by the end of next month. Are Odzer's actions ethical? Why or why not? Did he have other alternatives?

LO 1   **Annual Report Case: Fiscal Year, Closing Process, and Interim Reports**

C5. Refer to the notes to the financial statements in the **CVS** annual report in the Supplement to Chapter 16. When does CVS end its fiscal year? For what reasons might it have chosen this date? From the standpoint of completing the accounting cycle, what advantage does this date have? Does CVS prepare interim financial statements? What are the implications of interim financial statements for the accounting cycle?

LO 1   **Comparison Analysis: Interim Financial Reporting and Seasonality**

C6. Both **CVS** and **Southwest Airlines** provide quarterly financial information in their financial statements. Quarterly financial reports provide important information about the "seasonality" of a company's operations. *Seasonality* refers to how dependent a company is on sales during different seasons of the year, and how that affects a company's need to plan for cash flows and inventory. From the quarterly financial information for CVS in the Supplement to Chapter 16, determine the effects of seasons on CVS's net revenues and net earnings by calculating for the most recent year the percentage of quarterly net sales and net earnings to annual net sales and net earnings. Discuss the results. How do you think the effect of seasons might differ for Southwest's operating revenues and income?

Continuing Case: Annual Report Project

C7. Using the most recent annual report of the company you have chosen to study and that you have accessed online at the company's website, examine all four of the financial statements. Identify the accounts in these statements that would be affected by closing entries. Describe how they would be affected.

CHAPTER 5
Foundations of Financial Reporting and the Classified Balance Sheet

Surf-With-Park Company is a retailer of casual beach wear for college students. It has two stores, and the owner, Alan Park, now wants to open a third. To obtain a loan, he will have to present a balance sheet to his bank. In the past, he has simply provided a list of the post-closing account balances at the end of the year and not prepared a balance sheet. In other words, he is looking for answers to the questions that appear below.

1. CONCEPT ▶ *Why are relevance and faithful representation as well as enhancing qualitative characteristics important to understanding financial statements?*

2. ACCOUNTING APPLICATION ▶ *How should the balance sheet be organized to provide the best information?*

3. BUSINESS APPLICATION ▶ *What key measures best capture a company's financial performance?*

LEARNING OBJECTIVES

LO 1 Describe the objective of financial reporting, and identify the conceptual framework underlying accounting information.

LO 2 Identify and define the basic components of financial reporting, and prepare a classified balance sheet.

LO 3 Use classified financial statements to evaluate liquidity and profitability.

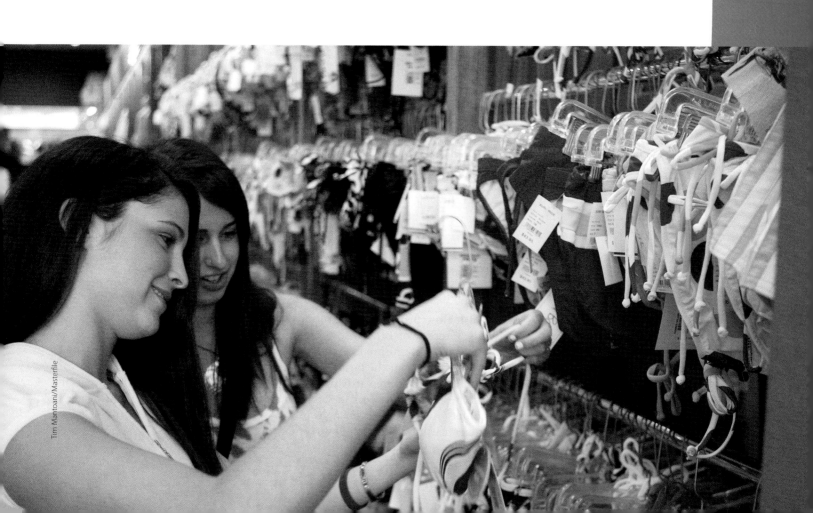

Tim Mantoani/Masterfile

CONCEPTS

LO 1 Concepts Underlying Financial Reporting

The FASB and the IASB are working toward convergence of U.S. generally accepted accounting principles (GAAP) with international financial reporting standards (IFRS). Their goal is "to increase the international comparability and the quality of standards used in the United States [which] is consistent with the FASB's obligation to its domestic constituents, who benefit from comparability across national borders."[1] An important part of this convergence project is agreement on the objective of financial reporting and conceptual framework underlying it. Exhibit 1 illustrates these factors, which we discuss in this section.

Exhibit 1
Concepts Underlying Financial Reporting

© Cengage Learning 2014

Objective of Financial Reporting

The Financial Accounting Standards Board (FASB) emphasizes the needs of current and potential investors (owners) and creditors while recognizing the needs of other users when it defines the objective of financial reporting as follows.[2]

> To provide financial information about the reporting entity that is useful to present and potential equity investors, lenders, and other creditors in making decisions in their capacity as capital providers. Information that is decision-useful to capital providers may also be useful to other users of financial reporting who are not capital providers.

To be useful for decision making, financial reporting must enable the user to:

- ■ **Assess cash flow prospects.** The ultimate value of a business and its ability to pay dividends, interest, or otherwise provide returns to capital providers depends on its ability to generate future cash flows. Capital providers and other users therefore need information about the business's ability to generate cash flows.
- ■ **Assess management's stewardship.** Capital providers and others need information about the business's resources (assets), claims against them (liabilities and owner's [stockholders'] equity), and changes in these resources and claims resulting from transactions (earnings and cash flows) and other economic events.

Financial reporting includes the financial statements (balance sheet, income statement, statement of owner's equity, and statement of cash flows) that are periodically presented to parties outside the business. Management's underlying assumptions and methods and estimates used in the financial statements are also important components of financial reporting. Because of a potential conflict of interest between managers, who must prepare the statements, and investors or creditors, who invest in or lend money to the business, financial statements usually are audited by outside accountants.

Qualitative Characteristics of Accounting Information

Introductory textbooks simplify basic accounting concepts to help students. All the problems can be solved, and all the numbers add up. In practice, however, accounting information is neither simple nor precise. The FASB emphasizes this fact in the following statement:

> *The information provided by financial reporting often results from approximate, rather than exact, measures. The measures commonly involve numerous estimates, classifications, summarizations, judgments, and allocations. The outcome of economic activity in a dynamic economy is uncertain and results from combinations of many factors. Thus, despite the aura of precision that may seem to surround financial reporting in general and financial statements in particular, with few exceptions the measures are approximations, which may be based on rules and conventions, rather than exact amounts.*[3]

The goal of generating accounting information is to provide data that different users need to make informed decisions for their unique situations. How this goal is achieved provides much of the interest and controversy in accounting. To facilitate interpretation of accounting information, the FASB has established standards, or **qualitative characteristics**, by which to judge the information.[4] The most fundamental of these characteristics are *relevance* and *faithful representation*. *Comparability, verifiability, timeliness,* and *understandability* are enhancing characteristics that assist in interpreting accounting information.

Relevance **Relevance** means that the information has a direct bearing on a decision. In other words, if the information were not available, a different decision would be made. To be relevant, information must have *predictive value, confirmative value,* or both. Further, it is subject to *materiality.*

- **Predictive value:** Information has **predictive value** if it helps capital providers make decisions about future actions. For example, the statement of cash flows can provide information as to whether the company has sufficient funds to expand or if it will need to raise funds from capital providers.
- **Confirmative value:** Information has **confirmative value** if it confirms or changes previous evaluations. For example, the income statement provides information as to whether or not a company met earnings expectations.
- **Materiality:** Information is **material** if its omission or misstatement could influence the user's economic decisions taken on the basis of the specific entity's financial statements. **Materiality** is related to both the nature of an item and its size or misstatement. Immaterial items are not relevant to the economic decision. The materiality of an item normally is determined by relating its dollar value to an element of the financial statements, such as net income or total assets. As a rule, when an item is worth 5 percent or more of net income, accountants treat it as material. However, materiality depends not only on the value of an item but also on its nature. For example, in a multimillion-dollar company, a mistake of $5,000 in recording an item may not be important, but the discovery of even a small bribe or theft can be very important. Moreover, many small errors can add up to a material amount.

The financial statements may provide information that is both predictive and confirmative. For example, the statement of cash flows not only helps to project future cash flows but also confirms expectations about various prior actions.

Business Perspective
How Much Is Material?

The materiality issue was long a pet peeve of the SEC, which contended that companies were increasingly abusing the convention to protect their stocks from taking a pounding when earnings did not reach their targets. Thus, the SEC issued a rule that includes both quantitative and qualitative guides. The traditional rule of thumb of 5 percent or more of net income is acceptable as an initial screening. However, companies cannot decline to book items in the interest of meeting earnings estimates, preserving a growing earnings trend, converting a loss to a profit, increasing management compensation, or hiding an illegal transaction, such as a bribe.[5]

Faithful Representation **Faithful representation** means that the financial information is *complete*, *neutral*, and *free from material error*.

- Completeness: **Complete information** provides all information necessary for a reliable decision.
- Neutrality: **Neutral information** is free from bias intended to achieve a certain result or to bring about a particular behavior.
- Free from material error: To be **free from material error** means information meets a minimum level of accuracy so it does not distort what is being reported. Free from material error does not mean that information is absolutely accurate because most financial information is based on estimates and judgments.

If major uncertainties about faithful representation exist, they should be *disclosed* in a note to the financial statements.

Enhancing Qualitative Characteristics Other qualitative characteristics that the FASB has established for interpreting accounting information include:

- Comparability: **Comparability** is the quality that enables users to identify similarities and differences between two sets of financial data.
- Verifiability: **Verifiability** is the quality that different knowledgeable and independent observers could reach consensus, although not necessarily complete agreement, that a particular depiction is a faithful representation.
- Timeliness: **Timeliness** is the quality that enables users to receive information in time to influence their decisions.
- Understandability: **Understandability** is the quality that enables users to comprehend the meaning of the information.

STUDY NOTE: Theoretically, a $10 stapler is a long-term asset and should therefore be capitalized and depreciated over its useful life. However, the concepts of materiality and cost constraint allow the stapler to be expensed entirely in the year of purchase.

These enhancing characteristics are subject to the **cost constraint** (or **cost-benefit**), which holds that the benefits to be gained from providing accounting information should be greater than the costs of providing it. Of course, minimum levels of relevance and faithful representation must be reached if accounting information is to be useful. Beyond the minimum levels, however, it is up to the FASB and the SEC, which stipulate the information that must be reported, and the accountant, who provides the information, to judge the costs and benefits in each case.

Accounting Conventions

For accounting information to be understandable, accountants must prepare financial statements in accordance with accepted practices, which include some concepts that are not formally part of the agreed-upon conceptual framework and which may conflict with it at times. Familiarity with the **accounting conventions**, or *constraints*, used in preparing financial statements enables the user to better understand accounting information. Among these accounting conventions are *consistency*, *full disclosure*, and *conservatism*.

Consistency **Consistency** requires that once a company has adopted an accounting procedure, it must use it from one period to the next unless a note to the financial statements informs users of a change. Generally accepted accounting principles specify what the note must contain:

The nature of and justification for a change in accounting principle and its effect on income should be disclosed in the financial statements of the period in which the change is made. The justification for the change should explain clearly why the newly adopted accounting principle is preferable.[6]

For example, in the notes to its financial statements, **Goodyear Tire & Rubber Company** disclosed that it had changed its method of accounting for inventories because management felt it improved the matching of revenues and costs. Without such an acknowledgment, users of financial statements can assume that the treatment of a particular transaction, account, or item has not changed since the last period.

Full Disclosure (Transparency) **Full disclosure** (or **transparency**) requires that financial statements present all the information relevant to users' understanding of the statements. The statements must include any explanation needed to keep them from being misleading. For instance, the notes should disclose any change that a company has made in its accounting procedures.

A company must also disclose significant events arising after the balance sheet date. For example, suppose that a firm has purchased a piece of land for a future subdivision. Shortly after the end of its fiscal year, the firm is ordered to halt construction because the Environmental Protection Agency asserts that the land was once a toxic waste dump. This information, which obviously affects the users of the financial statements, must be disclosed in the statements for the fiscal year just ended.

Additional disclosures required by the FASB and other official bodies include the accounting procedures used in preparing the financial statements and important terms of a company's debt and commitments. Beyond the required disclosures, the application of the full-disclosure convention is based on the judgment of management and of the accountants who prepare the financial statements.

In recent years, independent auditors, the stock exchanges, and the SEC have made more demands for disclosure by publicly owned companies. As a result, more and better information about corporations is now available to investors and creditors than ever before.

Conservatism When accountants are uncertain about the judgments or estimates they must make, they look to the convention of **conservatism**. This convention holds that, when faced with choosing between two equally acceptable procedures or estimates, accountants should choose the one that is least likely to overstate assets and income. One of the most common applications of conservatism is the use of the *lower-of-cost-or-market method* in accounting for inventories. Under this method, if an item's market value is greater than its original cost, the more conservative cost figure is used. If the market value is below the original cost, the more conservative market value is used. The latter situation often occurs in the computer industry.

Conservatism can be a useful tool, but if abused, it can lead to incorrect and misleading financial statements. For example, there is no uncertainty about how a long-term asset of material cost should be treated. As explained in Chapter 3, the cost of such

STUDY NOTE: *The purpose of conservatism is not to produce the lowest net income and lowest asset value. It is a guideline for choosing among GAAP alternatives, and it should be used with care.*

Business Perspective
When Is "Full Disclosure" Too Much?

Ernst & Young, a large accounting firm, reported that over a 20-year period, the total number of pages in the annual reports of 25 large, well-known companies increased an average of 84 percent, and the number of pages of notes increased 325 percent—from 4 to 17 pages. Management's discussion and analysis increased 300 percent, from 3 pages to 12.[7] Because some people feel that "these documents are so daunting that people don't read them at all," the SEC allows companies to issue to the public "summary reports" in which the bulk of the notes can be reduced.

Summary reports are controversial because many analysts feel that the notes provide the detailed information necessary to understand complex business operations. One analyst remarked, "To banish the notes for fear they will turn off readers would be like eliminating fractions from math books on the theory that the average student prefers to work with whole numbers."[8] Detailed reports still must be filed with the SEC, but more and more companies are providing summary reports to the public.

an asset should be spread over the asset's useful life. When conservatism is used to justify expensing a long-term asset in the period of purchase, income and assets for the current period will be understated, and income in future periods will be overstated. Accountants therefore apply the conservatism convention only when they are uncertain about which accounting procedure or estimate to use.

Ethical Financial Reporting

As noted earlier, under the Sarbanes-Oxley Act, chief executive officers and chief financial officers of all publicly traded companies must certify that, to their knowledge, their quarterly and annual statements are accurate and complete. After this legislation passed, an investigation by the audit committee of **Dell**'s board of directors and management disclosed weaknesses in the company's controls and led to restatements of the financial statements for the prior four years. After extensive improvements in control and the restatements, the company's chief executive officer, Michael S. Dell, made the following certifying statement in the company's annual report to the SEC:

> *Based on my knowledge, the financial statements, and other financial information included in this report, fairly present in all material respects the financial condition, results of operations and cash flows . . . for the periods represented in this report.*[9]

Fraudulent financial reporting can have high costs for investors, lenders, employees, and customers. It can also have high costs for the people who condone, authorize, or prepare misleading reports—even those at the highest corporate levels. In March 2005, Bernard J. Ebbers, former CEO of **WorldCom**, was convicted of seven counts of filing false reports with the SEC and one count each of securities fraud and conspiracy.[10] In 2006, both Kenneth Lay, **Enron Corporation**'s former chairman, and Jeffrey Skilling, Enron's former CEO, were convicted on charges similar to the ones of which Ebbers was convicted.

International Perspective
IFRS What Is the Future of the Conservatism Convention?

Conservatism, which has been the bedrock of U.S. accounting practice for many decades, clearly conflicts with the agreed upon concept of *neutrality* in the conceptual framework. The practice under IFRS, for example, of writing up the value of an asset, such as inventory or equipment, that has increased in fair value and recording the increase as income violates the conservatism convention under U.S. GAAP. Thus, the convergence of IFRS with GAAP may well influence the way accountants in the United States prepare financial statements, but it will likely take a generation for this to change.

APPLY IT!

Match each concept that follows with the category in which it belongs.

a. Objective of accounting information
b. Underlies relevant financial information
c. Underlies faithful representation
d. Enhancing qualitative characteristics
e. Accounting convention

1. Consistency
2. Verifiability
3. Predictive value
4. Timeliness
5. Neutrality
6. Conservatism
7. Comparability
8. Completeness
9. Materiality
10. Confirmative value
11. Understandability
12. Furnishing information that is useful to capital providers

SOLUTION

1. e;   2. d;   3. b;   4. d;   5. c;   6. e;   7. d;   8. c;
9. b;   10. b;   11. d;   12. a

TRY IT! SE1, SE2, E1A, E2A, E1B, E2B

ACCOUNTING APPLICATIONS

**ACCOUNTING
APPLICATIONS**

- ■ Identify components of a classified balance sheet
- ■ Prepare a classified balance sheet

**RELEVANT
LEARNING OBJECTIVE**

LO 2 Identify and define the basic components of financial reporting, and prepare a classified balance sheet.

LO 2 Classified Balance Sheet

As you know, a balance sheet presents a company's financial position at a particular time. The balance sheets presented thus far categorize accounts as assets, liabilities, and owner's equity. Because even a fairly small company can have hundreds of accounts, subcategories within the major categories can make financial statements much more useful. General-purpose external financial statements that are divided into subcategories are called **classified financial statements**. Exhibit 2 depicts the subcategories into which the principal elements of assets, liabilities, and owner's equity are broken down. This format enables owners and creditors to study and evaluate relationships among the subcategories.

Exhibit 2
Classified Balance Sheet

© Cengage Learning 2014

The subcategories of Bonali Company's classified balance sheet, shown in Exhibit 3, are those used by most U.S. corporations. The subcategories under owner's equity would, of course, be different if Bonali were a corporation or partnership rather than a sole proprietorship.

Assets

As shown in Exhibit 3, the classified balance sheet of a U.S. company typically divides assets into four categories: current assets; investments; property, plant, and equipment; and intangible assets. These categories are listed in the order of how easily they can be converted into cash. For example, current assets are usually more easily converted to cash than are property, plant, and equipment. For simplicity, some companies group investments, intangible assets, and other miscellaneous assets into a category called **other assets**.

Current Assets **Current assets** include cash and other assets that a company can reasonably expect to convert to cash, sell, or consume within one year or its normal operating cycle, whichever is longer. A company's **normal operating cycle** is the average time it needs to go from spending cash to receiving cash. For example, suppose a company uses cash to buy inventory and sells the inventory to a customer on credit. To classify the resulting receivable as a current asset, there must be a reasonable expectation that it will be collected in cash before the normal operating cycle ends.

As discussed, cash is a current asset. Short-term investments, notes and accounts receivable, and inventory that a company expects to convert to cash (by selling it) within

Bonali Company
Balance Sheet
December 31, 2014

Assets

Current assets:

Cash	$ 41,440	
Short-term investments	28,000	
Notes receivable	32,000	
Accounts receivable	141,200	
Merchandise inventory	191,600	
Prepaid insurance	26,400	
Supplies	6,784	
Total current assets		$467,424

Investments:

Land held for future use		50,000

Property, plant, and equipment:

Land		$ 18,000	
Building	$ 82,600		
Less accumulated depreciation	34,560	48,040	
Equipment	$108,000		
Less accumulated depreciation	57,800	50,200	
Total property, plant, and equipment			116,240

Intangible assets:

Trademark		2,000
Total assets		$635,664

Liabilities

Current liabilities:

Notes payable	$ 60,000	
Accounts payable	102,732	
Salaries payable	8,000	
Total current liabilities		$170,732

Long-term liabilities:

Mortgage payable		71,200
Total liabilities		$241,932

Owner's Equity

J. Bonali, capital	$393,732	
Total owner's equity		393,732
Total liabilities and owner's equity		$635,664

© Cengage Learning 2014

Business Perspective
Normal Operating Cycles Can Be Long

The normal operating cycle for most companies is less than one year, but there are exceptions. For example, because of the length of time it takes **The Boeing Company** to build aircraft, its normal operating cycle exceeds one year. The inventory used in building the planes is nonetheless considered a current asset because the planes will be sold within the normal operating cycle. Another example is a company that sells on an installment basis. The payments for a television set or a refrigerator can extend over 24 or 36 months, but these receivables are still considered current assets.

the next year or the normal operating cycle are also current assets. On the balance sheet, they are listed in order of how easily they can be converted to cash.

Prepaid expenses, such as rent and insurance paid in advance, and supplies bought for use rather than for sale should be classified as current assets. These assets are current in the sense that if they had not been paid for earlier, they would require a current outlay of cash.

Investments **Investments** include assets, usually long-term, that are not used in normal business operations and that management does not plan to convert to cash within the next year. Examples of items in this category include the following:

- Securities held for long-term investment
- Long-term notes receivable
- Land held for future use
- Plant or equipment not used in the business
- Special funds established to pay off a debt or buy a building
- Large permanent investments (those a company does not intend to sell) made in another company for the purpose of controlling that company

Property, Plant, and Equipment **Property, plant, and equipment** (also called *operating assets, fixed assets, tangible assets, long-lived assets,* or *plant assets*) include tangible long-term assets used in a business's day-to-day operations. They represent a place to operate (land and buildings) and the equipment used to produce, sell, and deliver goods or services. Through depreciation, the costs of these assets (except the cost of land) are spread over the periods they benefit. Past depreciation is recorded in the Accumulated Depreciation accounts and deducted from their related asset accounts on the balance sheet.

To reduce clutter on the balance sheet, property, plant, and equipment accounts and related accumulated depreciation accounts are often combined—for example:

Property, plant, and equipment (net) $116,240

The company provides the details in a note to the financial statements.

The property, plant, and equipment category also includes natural resources owned by the company, such as forest lands, oil and gas properties, and coal mines, if they are used in the regular course of business. If they are not, they are listed in the investments category.

Intangible Assets **Intangible assets** are long-term assets with no physical substance. Their value stems from the rights or privileges accruing to their owners. Examples include patents, copyrights, franchises, and trademarks. These assets are recorded at cost, which is spread over the expected life of the right or privilege. **Goodwill**, which arises in an acquisition of another company, is another intangible asset that is recorded at cost, but the cost is not allocated (amortized) over future periods. Goodwill is reviewed each year for possible loss of value, or impairment.

Intangible assets can be worth an enormous amount for some companies. Consider the value of Coca-Cola's trademark, which over the years has become a familiar and easily recognizable symbol worldwide.

STR/AFP/GETTY IMAGES/Newscom

Liabilities

Liabilities are divided into two categories: current liabilities and long-term liabilities.

Current Liabilities **Current liabilities** are obligations that must be satisfied within one year or within the company's normal operating cycle, whichever is longer. These liabilities are typically paid out of current assets or by incurring new short-term liabilities. Examples include:

- Notes payable
- Accounts payable
- The current portion of long-term debt
- Salaries and wages payable
- Customer advances (unearned revenues)

STUDY NOTE: *The portion of a mortgage due during the next year or the current operating cycle is classified as a current liability. The portion due after the next year or the current operating cycle is classified as a long-term liability.*

Long-Term Liabilities **Long-term liabilities** are debts that fall due more than one year in the future or beyond the normal operating cycle and thus will be paid out of noncurrent assets. Examples include:

- Mortgages payable
- Long-term notes
- Bonds payable
- Employee pension obligations
- Long-term lease liabilities

Owner's Equity

The terms *owner's equity, proprietorship, owner's capital,* and *net worth* are used to refer to the owner's interest, or equity, in a company. However, the first three terms are preferred to *net worth* because many assets are recorded at their original cost rather than at their current value.

Although the form of business organization does not usually affect the accounting treatment of assets and liabilities, the equity section of the balance sheet differs depending on whether the business is a sole proprietorship, a partnership, or a corporation.

Sole Proprietorship The owner's equity section of a sole proprietorship would be similar to the one shown for Bonali Company in Exhibit 3:

Owner's Equity

J. Bonali, capital $393,732

STUDY NOTE: *Equity in a sole proprietorship and a partnership differs only in the number of Capital accounts.*

Partnership The equity section of a partnership's balance sheet is called **partners' equity**. It is much like that in a sole proprietorship's balance sheet. It might appear as follows.

Partners' Equity

R. Hay, capital	$168,750	
J. Bonali, capital	224,982	
Total partners' equity		$393,732

Corporation Corporations are by law separate, legal entities that are owned by their stockholders. The equity section of a balance sheet for a corporation is called **stockholders' equity** (or *shareholders' equity*) and has two parts: *contributed capital* and *retained earnings*. It might appear as follows.

Stockholders' Equity

Contributed capital:		
Common stock, $10 par value, 20,000 shares authorized, issued, and outstanding	$200,000	
Additional paid-in capital	40,000	
Total contributed capital	$240,000	
Retained earnings	153,732	
Total stockholders' equity		$393,732

Remember that owner's equity accounts show the sources of and claims on assets. These claims are not on any particular asset but on the assets as a whole. It follows, then, that a corporation's contributed and earned capital accounts measure its stockholders' claims on assets and also indicate the sources of the assets. The **Contributed Capital** (or *Paid-in Capital*) accounts reflect the amounts of assets invested by stockholders. Generally, contributed capital is shown on corporate balance sheets by two amounts: (1) the face, or par, value of issued stock and (2) the amounts paid in, or contributed, in excess

Business Perspective
Terminology In Financial Statements Is Not Consistent

Although balance sheets generally resemble the one shown in Exhibit 3 for Bonali Company, no two companies have financial statements that are exactly alike. **CVS**'s balance sheet is a good example of some of the variations. As shown in the Supplement to Chapter 16, it provides data for two years (three years for the income statement) so that users can evaluate changes from one year to the next. Note that its major classifications are similar but not identical to those of Bonali. For instance, Bonali has asset categories for investments, and CVS has an asset category called "other assets," which is a small amount of its total assets. Also note that CVS has various accounts listed in the liabilities under "Total Current Liabilities." Because these accounts are listed after current liabilities, they represent longer-term liabilities, due more than one year after the balance sheet date.

of the par value per share. In the previous illustration, stockholders invested amounts equal to the par value of the outstanding stock of $200,000 plus $40,000 in additional paid-in capital for a total of $240,000.

The **Retained Earnings** account is sometimes called *Earned Capital* because it represents the stockholders' claim to the assets that are earned from operations and reinvested in corporate operations. Distributions of assets to shareholders, which are called **dividends**, reduce the Retained Earnings account just as withdrawals of assets by the owner of a business reduce the Capital account. Thus, the Retained Earnings balance represents the earnings of the corporation less dividends paid to stockholders over the life of the business.

Overview of Classified Balance Sheet Accounts

Like accounts on the balance sheet and income statement can be grouped, as shown in Exhibit 4. Such groupings aid in analysis of the statements.

Exhibit 4
Classified Balance Sheet Groups Accounts into Useful Categories

Balance Sheet
December 31, 2014

Assets	Liabilities
Current assets	Current liabilities
Investments	Long-term liabilities
Property, plant, and equipment	Total liabilities
Intangible assets	
	Owner's Equity
	Owner's capital
	Total owner's equity

Total Assets   =   Total Liabilities + Owner's Equity

© Cengage Learning 2014

APPLY IT!

Match each account title that follows with the category that appears on a balance sheet or indicate that it does not appear on the balance sheet.

a. Current assets
b. Investments
c. Property, plant, and equipment
d. Intangible assets
e. Current liabilities
f. Long-term liabilities
g. Owner's capital
h. Not on balance sheet

1. Trademark
2. Supplies

3. Land Held for Future Use
4. Property Taxes Payable
5. Note Payable in Five Years
6. Investment by Owner
7. Land Used in Operations
8. Accumulated Depreciation
9. Accounts Receivable
10. Interest Expense
11. Unearned Revenue
12. Prepaid Rent

SOLUTION

1. d;   2. a;   3. b;   4. e;   5. f;   6. g;
7. c;   8. c;   9. a;   10. h;   11. e;   12. a

TRY IT! SE3, SE4, E3A, E4A, E3B, E4B

BUSINESS APPLICATIONS

LO 3 Using Classified Financial Statements

Owners and creditors base decisions largely on their assessments of a firm's potential liquidity and profitability, often relying on ratios. Ratios use the components of classified financial statements to reflect how well a firm has performed in terms of maintaining liquidity and achieving profitability. Accounts must be classified correctly before the ratios are computed. Otherwise, the ratios will be incorrect.

Evaluation of Liquidity

Liquidity means having enough money on hand to pay bills when they are due and to take care of unexpected needs for cash. Two measures of liquidity are working capital and current ratio.

Working Capital **Working capital**, which uses two elements of the classified balance sheet, is the amount by which current assets exceed current liabilities. It is an important measure of liquidity because current liabilities must be satisfied within one year or one operating cycle, whichever is longer, and current assets are used to pay the current liabilities. Thus, the working capital is what is on hand to continue business operations.

For Bonali Company, working capital is computed as follows.

Current assets	$467,424
Less current liabilities	170,732
Working capital	$296,692

Working capital can be used to buy inventory, obtain credit, and finance expanded sales. Lack of working capital can lead to a company's failure.

Current Ratio The current ratio is closely related to working capital. Many bankers and other creditors believe it is a good indicator of a company's ability to pay its debts on time. The **current ratio** is the ratio of current assets to current liabilities. For Bonali Company, it is computed as follows.

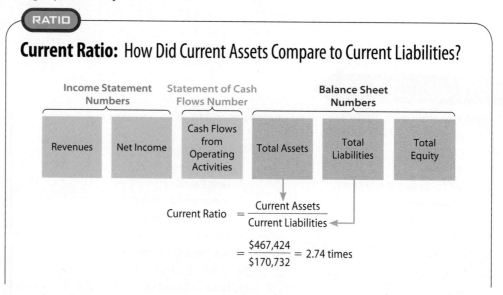

RATIO

Current Ratio: How Did Current Assets Compare to Current Liabilities?

$$\text{Current Ratio} = \frac{\text{Current Assets}}{\text{Current Liabilities}}$$

$$= \frac{\$467,424}{\$170,732} = 2.74 \text{ times}$$

Based on Bizmin Industry Financial Report, December 2011.

Thus, Bonali has $2.74 of current assets for each $1.00 of current liabilities. Is this good or bad? The answer requires a comparison of this year's current ratio with ratios for earlier years and with similar measures for companies in the same industry, which for Bonali is clothing. The average current ratio varies from industry to industry. For the advertising industry, which has large receivables, the current ratio is 1.10. The industrial machinery manufacturing industry, in which companies carry large merchandise inventories, has an average current ratio of 2.00. The current ratio for Bonali, 2.74, exceeds the average for its industry, 1.80.

A very low current ratio can be unfavorable, indicating that a company will not be able to pay its debts on time. But that is not always the case. For example, **McDonald's** and various other successful companies have low current ratios because they carefully plan their cash flows. A very high current ratio may indicate that a company is not using its assets to the best advantage. In other words, it could probably use its excess funds more effectively to increase its overall profit.

Evaluation of Profitability

Just as important as paying bills on time is **profitability**—the ability to earn a satisfactory income. As a goal, profitability competes with liquidity for attention because liquid assets are not the best profit-producing resources. Cash means purchasing power; but a satisfactory profit can be made only if purchasing power is used to buy profit-producing (and less liquid) assets, such as inventory and long-term assets.

To evaluate a company's profitability, you must relate its current performance to its past performance and prospects for the future, as well as to the averages of other companies in the same industry. The following are the ratios commonly used to evaluate a company's ability to earn income:

- Profit margin
- Asset turnover
- Return on assets
- Debt to equity ratio
- Return on equity

Profit Margin The **profit margin** shows the percentage of each sales dollar that results in net income. It is an indication of how well a company is controlling its costs: the lower its costs, the higher its profit margin. The profit margin uses two elements of the income statements: net income and revenues (often called *net sales* or *net revenues*). If Bonali Company had $71,524 of net income and $1,248,624 of revenues, its profit margin would be computed as follows.

Profit Margin: How Much Income Does Each Dollar of Sales Generate?

Thus, on each dollar of revenue, Bonali makes 5.7 cents. Is this a satisfactory profit? The answer requires a comparison with the profit margin ratios of other companies in the clothing industry, which is 4.2. A difference of 1 or 2 percent in a company's profit margin can be the difference between a fair year and a very profitable one.

Asset Turnover   The **asset turnover** ratio measures how efficiently assets are used to produce sales. In other words, how much revenue is generated by each dollar of assets? A company with a high asset turnover uses its assets more productively than one with a low asset turnover.

The asset turnover ratio uses revenues from the income statement and total assets from the balance sheet. It is computed by dividing revenues by average total assets. Since revenues take place over the year, they are compared with average total assets, which is intended to represent the usual level of assets over the year. Average total assets are the sum of assets at the beginning and end of the period divided by 2. If Bonali Company had $1,248,624 of revenues, and $594,480 of assets at the beginning of the year, its asset turnover would be computed as follows.

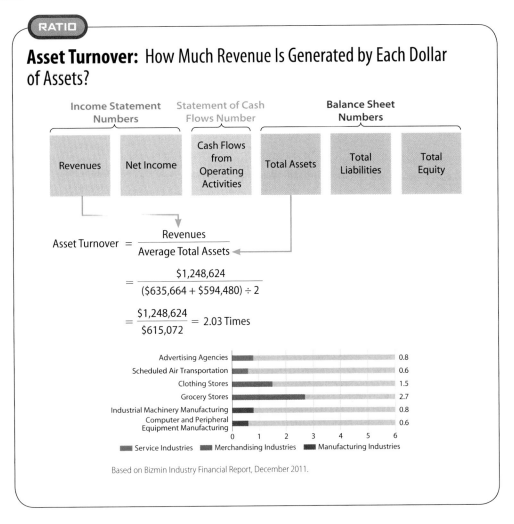

RATIO

Asset Turnover: How Much Revenue Is Generated by Each Dollar of Assets?

$$\text{Asset Turnover} = \frac{\text{Revenues}}{\text{Average Total Assets}}$$

$$= \frac{\$1,248,624}{(\$635,664 + \$594,480) \div 2}$$

$$= \frac{\$1,248,624}{\$615,072} = 2.03 \text{ Times}$$

Industry	Value
Advertising Agencies	0.8
Scheduled Air Transportation	0.6
Clothing Stores	1.5
Grocery Stores	2.7
Industrial Machinery Manufacturing	0.8
Computer and Peripheral Equipment Manufacturing	0.6

Service Industries   Merchandising Industries   Manufacturing Industries

Based on Bizmin Industry Financial Report, December 2011.

Thus, Bonali produces $2.03 in sales for each dollar invested in assets. Its asset turnover of 2.03 times is greater than the industry average of 1.5 times. In other words, the company is more productive in producing revenue than other companies in the clothing industry.

Return on Assets The profit margin and asset turnover ratios are important measures, but they have limitations. For example, the profit margin ratio does not consider the assets necessary to produce income, and the asset turnover ratio does not take into account the amount of income produced. The **return on assets** ratio overcomes these deficiencies by relating net income to average total assets. If Bonali Company had $71,524 of net income, its return on assets would be computed as follows.

STUDY NOTE: *Return on assets is a widely used measure of profitability. It is a combination of the profit margin and the asset turnover.*

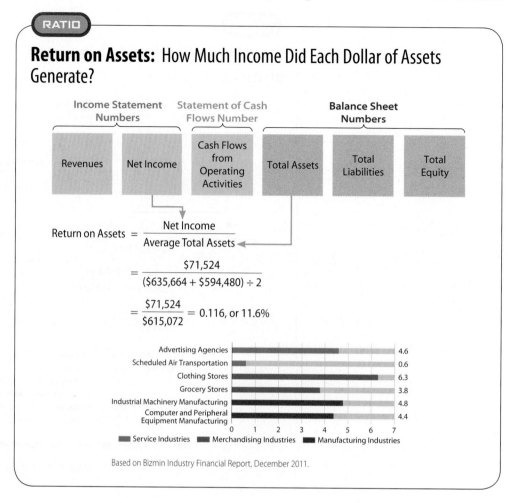

RATIO

Return on Assets: How Much Income Did Each Dollar of Assets Generate?

Income Statement Numbers | Statement of Cash Flows Number | Balance Sheet Numbers

Revenues | Net Income | Cash Flows from Operating Activities | Total Assets | Total Liabilities | Total Equity

$$\text{Return on Assets} = \frac{\text{Net Income}}{\text{Average Total Assets}}$$

$$= \frac{\$71,524}{(\$635,664 + \$594,480) \div 2}$$

$$= \frac{\$71,524}{\$615,072} = 0.116, \text{ or } 11.6\%$$

Industry	Value
Advertising Agencies	4.6
Scheduled Air Transportation	0.6
Clothing Stores	6.3
Grocery Stores	3.8
Industrial Machinery Manufacturing	4.8
Computer and Peripheral Equipment Manufacturing	4.4

0 1 2 3 4 5 6 7

■ Service Industries   ■ Merchandising Industries   ■ Manufacturing Industries

Based on Bizmin Industry Financial Report, December 2011.

For each dollar of invested assets, Bonali earned 11.6 cents of net income. This ratio combines the firm's income-generating strength (profit margin) and its revenue-generating effectiveness (asset turnover):

$$\frac{\text{Net Income}}{\text{Net Sales}} \times \frac{\text{Net Sales}}{\text{Average Total Assets}} = \frac{\text{Net Income}}{\text{Average Total Assets}}$$

Profit Margin $\times$ Asset Turnover $=$ Return on Assets

5.7% $\times$ 2.03 Times $=$ 11.6%

A company's management can improve overall profitability by increasing the profit margin, the asset turnover, or both. A financial statement user must consider how these two ratios interact to produce return on assets.

Bonali's profit margin of 5.7 percent is above the clothing industry's average of 4.2 percent. Its asset turnover of 2.03 times is greater than the industry average of 1.5 percent. Bonali is able to achieve a higher profit margin than the industry norm without sacrificing asset turnover. Clearly, its strategy is working because the company's return on assets of 11.6 percent is also greater than the industry average of 6.3 percent.

You can see the different ways in which various industries combine profit margin and asset turnover to produce return on assets. For instance, by comparing the return on assets for grocery stores and computer companies, you can see how they achieve that return in very different ways. The grocery store industry has a profit margin of 1.4 percent, which when multiplied by an asset turnover of 2.7 times gives a return on assets of 3.8 percent. The computer industry has a higher profit margin, 7.4 percent, and a lower asset turnover, 0.6 time, and produces a return on assets of 4.4 percent.

Business Perspective
What Performance Measures Do Top Companies Use to Compensate Executives?

The boards of directors of public companies often use financial ratios to judge the performance of their top executives and to determine annual bonuses. Public companies must disclose the ratios or performance measures they use in creating these compensation plans. Studies show that the most successful companies use earnings goals combined with sales growth 61 percent of the time compared to 43 percent for less successful companies. Among the most common earnings goals are return on assets and return on equity. Clearly, successful companies set objectives that will provide management with performance incentives.[11]

Debt to Equity Ratio The **debt to equity ratio** reflects a company's strategy for financing its operations. It shows the proportion of a company's assets financed by creditors and the proportion financed by the owner. It is thus a measure of financial risk; the more debt a company has in relation to its owner's equity, the greater its financial risk. Creditors and interest on debt must be paid on time regardless of how well or poorly a company is performing. Owner's equity, on the other hand, does not have to be repaid, and withdrawals can be deferred when a company's performance is poor.

The debt to equity ratio uses two elements of the balance sheet: total liabilities and total equity. Since the balance sheets of most companies do not show total liabilities, a short way of determining them is to deduct the total owner's equity from total assets. For Bonali Company, it is computed as follows.

RATIO

Debt to Equity Ratio: What Is the Company's Level of Financial Risk?

$$\text{Debt to Equity Ratio} = \frac{\text{Total Liabilities}}{\text{Total Equity}}$$

$$= \frac{\$241{,}932}{\$393{,}732}$$

$$= 0.614, \text{ or } 61.4\%$$

Based on Bizmin Industry Financial Report, December 2011.

A debt to equity ratio of 1.0 means that equal amounts of liabilities and owner's equity are used to finance a company's assets. A ratio of 0.5 means that if a company has 50 cents of liabilities for every dollar of equity, one-third of a company's total assets are financed by creditors. Bonali's debt to equity ratio of 61.4 percent means that Bonali relied more on owners than on creditors to finance its assets.

The debt to equity ratio does not fit neatly into either the liquidity or profitability category. It is clearly very important to liquidity analysis because it relates to debt and its repayment. It is also relevant to profitability for two reasons:

■ Creditors are interested in the proportion of the business that is debt-financed because the more debt a company has, the more profit it must earn to ensure the payment of interest to creditors.

■ Owners are interested in the proportion of the business that is debt-financed because the amount of interest paid on debt affects the amount of profit left to provide a return on the owner's investment.

The debt to equity ratio also shows how much expansion is possible through borrowing additional long-term funds.

Return on Equity **Return on equity** is the ratio of net income to average owner's equity. It indicates whether a company has earned a favorable return for the owner. Return on equity will always be greater than return on assets because total equity will always be less than total assets. While greater return on assets is an advantage, the more debt a company has, the greater its financial risk. A company must, therefore, carefully balance the amount of financial risk it assumes with its desire to increase its return to the owner.

Using the ending owner's equity from Bonali Company's balance sheet and assuming that the beginning owner's equity was $402,212, and that the company had net income of $71,524, Bonali's return on equity is computed as follows.

RATIO

Return on Equity: How Much Net Income Does a Company Make for Each Dollar Invested by the Owner?

$$\text{Return on Equity} = \frac{\text{Net Income}}{\text{Average Owner's Equity}}$$

$$= \frac{\$71,524}{(\$393,732 + \$402,212) \div 2}$$

$$= \frac{\$71,524}{\$397,972} = 0.180, \text{ or } 18.0\%$$

Advertising Agencies	10.0
Scheduled Air Transportation	8.6
Clothing Stores	14.4
Grocery Stores	10.0
Industrial Machinery Manufacturing	8.6
Computer and Peripheral Equipment Manufacturing	9.2

■ Service Industries ■ Merchandising Industries ■ Manufacturing Industries

Based on Bizmin Industry Financial Report, December 2011.

International Perspective

IFRS **How Has the Goal of Convergence of U.S. GAAP and IFRS Made Financial Analysis More Difficult?**

Although the SEC believes that the ideal outcome of an international standard-setting process would be worldwide use of a single set of accounting standards for both domestic and international financial reporting, the reality is that such consistency does not now exist and will be a challenge to implement.[12] For a period of time, financial statement users will have difficulty comparing companies' performance. Profitability measures of foreign firms that file in the United States using IFRS will not be comparable to profitability measures of companies that file using U.S. GAAP. For instance, consider the reporting earnings of the following European companies under both standards in a recent year (earnings in millions of euros):

	IFRS Earnings	GAAP Earnings	% Diff.
Bayer AG	1,695	269	530.1%
Reed Elsevier	625	399	56.6
Benetton Group	125	100	25.0

Given that assets and equity for these companies are also likely to differ as well as the use of fair value in valuing assets and liabilities, all profitability ratios—profit margin, asset turnover, return on assets, debt to equity ratio, and return on equity—will be affected.

Bonali earned 18.0 cents for every dollar invested by the owner. Is this is an acceptable return? Bonali's average return on equity of 18.0 percent is better than the average of 14.4 percent for the clothing industry. Although the air transportation industry's return on equity of 8.6 percent is one of the lowest of the selected industries, it also has the highest debt to equity ratio (880 percent).

APPLY IT!

Roth Company is considering applying for a bank loan. Various data from Roth's classified financial statements follows.

	2014	2013			2014	2013
Current assets	$200,000	$170,000		Owner's equity	$ 640,000	$ 610,000
Total assets	880,000	710,000		Sales	1,200,000	1,050,000
Current liabilities	90,000	50,000		Net income	60,000	80,000
Long-term liabilities	150,000	50,000				

Its total assets and owner's equity at the beginning of 2013 were $690,000 and $590,000, respectively.

1. Use (a) liquidity analysis and (b) profitability analysis to document Roth's financial position.
2. Discuss Roth's profitability and liquidity. Do you think it will qualify for a bank loan?

SOLUTION

1. (a) Liquidity analysis

	Current Assets	Current Liabilities	Working Capital	Current Ratio
2013	$170,000	$50,000	$120,000	3.40
2014	200,000	90,000	110,000	2.22
Decrease in working capital			$ 10,000	
Decrease in current ratio				1.18

(b) Profitability analysis

	Net Income	Sales	Profit Margin	Average Total Assets	Assets Turnover	Return on Assets	Average Owner's Equity	Return on Equity
2013	$80,000	$1,050,000	7.6%	$700,000[a]	1.50	11.4%	$600,000[c]	13.3%
2014	60,000	1,200,000	5.0%	795,000[b]	1.51	7.5%	625,000[d]	9.6%
Increase (decrease)	($20,000)	$ 150,000	(2.6)%	$ 95,000	0.01	(3.9)%	$ 25,000	(3.7)%

[a]($710,000 + $690,000) ÷ 2
[b]($880,000 + $710,000) ÷ 2
[c]($610,000 + $590,000) ÷ 2
[d]($640,000 + $610,000) ÷ 2

2. Both working capital and the current ratio declined between 2013 and 2014 because the $40,000 increase in current liabilities ($90,000 − $50,000) was greater than the $30,000 increase in current assets.

Net income decreased by $20,000 despite an increase in sales of $150,000 and an increase in average total assets of $95,000. Thus, the profit margin fell from 7.6 percent to 5.0 percent, and return on assets fell from 11.4 percent to 7.5 percent. Asset turnover showed almost no change and so did not contribute to the decline in profitability. The decrease in return on equity, from 13.3 percent to 9.6 percent, was not as great as the decrease in return on assets because the growth in total assets was financed mainly by debt, as shown in the capital structure analysis below.

	Total Liabilities	Owner's Equity	Debt to Equity Ratio
2013	$100,000	$610,000	16.4%
2014	240,000	640,000	37.5%
Increase	$140,000	$ 30,000	21.1%

Total liabilities increased by $140,000, while owner's equity increased by $30,000. Thus, the amount of the business financed by debt increased between 2013 and 2014.

Both liquidity and profitability have declined. Roth will probably have to focus on improving current operations before expanding or getting a bank loan.

TRY IT! SE5, SE6, SE7, E5A, E6A, E7A, E8A, E5B, E6B, E7B, E8B

TriLevel Problem

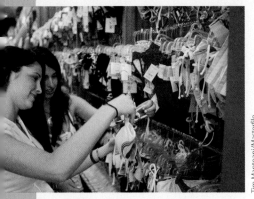

Tim Mantoani/Masterfile

Surf-With-Park Company

The beginning of this chapter focused on Alan Park, who was considering expanding Surf-With-Park Company. Complete the following requirements in order to answer the questions posed at the beginning of the chapter.

Section 1: Concepts
Why are relevance and faithful representation as well as enhancing qualitative characteristics important to understanding financial statements?

Section 2: Accounting Applications
How should the balance sheet be organized to provide the best information? From the information provided, prepare a classified balance sheet for Surf-With-Park Company.

	A	B	C
1	**Surf-With-Park Company**		
2	**Post-Closing Trial Balance**		
3	**December 31, 2014**		
4	**Account Name**	**Debit**	**Credit**
5	Cash	16,000	
6	Short-Term Investments	16,500	
7	Notes Receivable	5,000	
8	Accounts Receivable	138,000	
9	Merchandise Inventory	72,500	
10	Prepaid Rent	800	
11	Prepaid Insurance	2,400	
12	Sales Supplies	640	
13	Office Supplies	220	
14	Deposit for Future Advertising	1,840	
15	Building, Not in Use	24,800	
16	Land	11,700	
17	Delivery Equipment	20,600	
18	Accumulated Depreciation—Delivery Equipment		14,200
19	Trademark	2,000	
20	Accounts Payable		57,300
21	Salaries Payable		2,600
22	Interest Payable		420
23	Long-Term Notes Payable		40,000
24	A. Park, Capital		198,480
25		313,000	313,000
26			

Section 3: Business Applications

What key measures best capture a company's financial performance? To answer this question, complete the following requirements:

1. Compute Surf-With-Park's: (a) current ratio, and (b) debt to equity ratio.
2. As a user of the classified balance sheet, why would you want to know the current ratio or the debt to equity ratio?

SOLUTION

Section 1: Concepts

Understanding of the conceptual framework helps accountants prepare financial statements that users can understand and use to make decisions. *Relevance* means that the information has a direct bearing on a decision and includes the concepts of *predictive value* and *confirmative value*, and *materiality*, subject to the *cost constraint*. *Faithful representation* means that the financial information is *complete*, *neutral*, and *free from material error*. Enhancing qualitative characteristics include *comparability* to enable users to identify similarities and differences between two sets of financial data, *verifiability* to assure users that information as presented can be substantiated, *timeliness* to enable users to receive information in time to influence their decisions, and *understandability* to enable users to comprehend the meaning of the information. Further, the benefits of information must exceed the costs of providing it. The accounting conventions of *consistency*, *full disclosure*, and *conservatism* help accountants to decide what information to present when uncertainties exist.

Section 2: Accounting Applications

	A	B	C	D	E
1	Surf-With-Park Company				
2	Balance Sheet				
3	June 30, 2014				
4	Assets				
5	Current assets:				
6	Cash		$ 16,000		
7	Short-term investments		16,500		
8	Notes receivable		5,000		
9	Accounts receivable		138,000		
10	Merchandise inventory		72,500		
11	Prepaid rent		800		
12	Prepaid insurance		2,400		
13	Sales supplies		640		
14	Office supplies		220		
15	Deposit for future advertising		1,840		
16	Total current assets			$253,900	
17	Investments:				
18	Building, not in use			24,800	
19	Property, plant, and equipment:				
20	Land		$ 11,700		
21	Delivery equipment	$ 20,600			
22	Less accumulated depreciation	14,200	6,400		
23	Total property, plant, and equipment			18,100	
24	Intangible assets:				
25	Trademark			2,000	
26	**Total assets**			$298,800	
27	Liabilities				
28	**Current liabilities:**				
29	Accounts payable		$ 57,300		
30	Salaries payable		2,600		
31	Interest payable		420		
32	Total current liabilities			$ 60,320	
33	**Long-term liabilities:**				
34	Long-term notes payable			40,000	
35	**Total liabilities**			$100,320	
36	Owner's Equity				
37	A. Park, capital		$198,480		
38	Total owner's equity			198,480	
39	Total liabilities and owner's equity			$298,800	

Section 3: Business Applications

1. a.   Current Ratio $= \dfrac{\text{Current Assets}}{\text{Current Liabilities}}$

$$= \dfrac{\$253,900}{\$60,320} = 4.2$$

   b.   Debit to Equity Ratio $= \dfrac{\text{Total Liabilities}}{\text{Owner's Equity}}$

$$= \dfrac{\$100,320}{\$198,480} = 50.5\%$$

2. A user of the classified balance sheet would want to know the current ratio because it is a good indicator of a company's ability to pay its bills and to repay outstanding loans. The other measure, the debt to equity ratio, shows the proportion of the company financed by creditors in comparison with that financed by owners. That measure is very important to liquidity analysis because it is related to debt and its repayment. It is also relevant to profitability analysis because the amount of debt affects the amount of interest expense and the owner's return on investment.

Chapter Review

Describe the objective of financial reporting, and identify the conceptual framework underlying accounting information. **LO 1**

The objective of financial reporting is to provide financial information about the reporting entity to present and potential equity investors, lenders, and other creditors in their capacity as capital providers. Financial information must enable the reader to assess cash flow prospects and management's stewardship. Financial information must exhibit the concepts of relevance and faithful representation. To be relevant, it must have predictive value, confirmative value, or both, subject to materiality. To be faithfully represented, it must be complete, neutral, and free from error. Enhancing qualitative characteristics are comparability, verifiability, timeliness, and understandability, all subject to the cost constraint. Because accountants' measurements are not exact, certain conventions are applied to help users interpret financial statements. Consistency requires the use of the same accounting procedures from period to period and enhances the comparability of financial statements. Full disclosure means including all relevant information in the financial statements. Conservatism entails using the procedure that is least likely to overstate assets and income. Since the passage of the Sarbanes-Oxley Act, CEOs and CFOs have been required to certify that their companies' financial statements are accurate and complete.

Identify and define the basic components of financial reporting, and prepare a classified balance sheet. **LO 2**

The basic components of a classified balance sheet are as follows.

Assets	Liabilities	Owner's Equity
Current assets	Current liabilities	Owner's capital
Investments	Long-term liabilities	
Property, plant, and equipment		
Intangible assets		

Current assets are cash and other assets that a firm can reasonably expect to convert to cash or use up during the next year or the normal operating cycle, whichever is longer. Investments are assets, usually long-term, that are not used in the normal operation of a business. Property, plant, and equipment are tangible long-term assets used in day-to-day operations. Intangible assets are long-term assets with no physical substance whose value stems from the rights or privileges they are accruing to their owners.

A current liability is an obligation that must be satisfied within the next year or the normal operating cycle, whichever is longer. Long-term liabilities are debts that fall due more than one year in the future or beyond the normal operating cycle.

The equity section of a sole proprietorship's balance sheet differs from the equity section of a partnership's or corporation's balance sheet in that it does not have subcategories for contributed capital (the assets invested by stockholders) and retained earnings (stockholders' claim to assets earned from operations and reinvested in operations).

Use classified financial statements to evaluate liquidity and profitability. **LO 3**

In evaluating a company's performance, investors (owners) and creditors rely on the data provided in financial statements. Two measures of liquidity are working capital and the current ratio. Five measures of profitability are profit margin, asset turnover, return on assets, debt to equity ratio, and return on equity. Data from multiple years and industry averages are useful in interpreting these ratios.

Key Terms and Ratios

accounting conventions 172 (LO1)
classified financial
   statements 175 (LO2)
comparability 172 (LO1)
complete information 172 (LO1)
confirmative value 171 (LO1)
conservatism 173 (LO1)
consistency 172 (LO1)
Contributed Capital 178 (LO2)
cost-benefit 172 (LO1)
cost constraint 172 (LO1)
current assets 175 (LO2)
current liabilities 177 (LO2)
dividends 179 (LO2)
faithful representation 172 (LO1)
free from material error 172 (LO1)
full disclosure 173 (LO1)

goodwill 177 (LO2)
intangible assets 177 (LO2)
investments 177 (LO2)
liquidity 180 (LO3)
long-term liabilities 178 (LO2)
material 171 (LO1)
materiality 171 (LO1)
neutral information 172 (LO1)
normal operating cycle 175 (LO2)
other assets 175 (LO2)
partners' equity 178 (LO2)
predictive value 171 (LO1)
profitability 181 (LO3)
property, plant, and
   equipment 177 (LO2)
qualitative characteristics 171 (LO1)
relevance 171 (LO1)

Retained Earnings 179 (LO2)
stockholders' equity 178 (LO2)
timeliness 172 (LO1)
transparency 173 (LO1)
understandability 172 (LO1)
verifiability 172 (LO1)

RATIOS
asset turnover 182 (LO3)
current ratio 180 (LO3)
debt to equity ratio 185 (LO3)
profit margin 181 (LO3)
return on assets 183 (LO3)
return on equity 186 (LO3)
working capital 180 (LO3)

Chapter Assignments

DISCUSSION QUESTIONS

LO 1   **DQ1. CONCEPT** ▶ How do the four basic financial statements meet the stewardship objective of financial reporting?

LO 1   **DQ2. CONCEPT** ▶ What are some areas that require estimates to record transactions under the matching rule?

LO 1   **DQ3. CONCEPT** ▶ How can financial information be consistent but not comparable?

LO 1   **DQ4. CONCEPT** ▶ When might an amount be material to management but not to the CPA auditing the financial statements?

LO 2   **DQ5.** Why is it that land held for future use and equipment not currently used in the business are classified as investments rather than as property, plant, and equipment?

LO 3   **DQ6. BUSINESS APPLICATION** ▶ Why is it important to compare a company's financial performance with industry standards?

LO 3   **DQ7. BUSINESS APPLICATION** ▶ Is the statement "Return on assets is a better measure of profitability than profit margin" true or false and why?

SHORT EXERCISES

LO 1 **Objectives and Qualitative Characteristics**

SE1. CONCEPT ▶ Identify each of the following statements as related to either an objective (O) of financial information or as a qualitative (Q) characteristic of accounting information:

a. Information about business resources, claims to those resources, and changes in them should be provided.
b. Decision makers must be able to interpret accounting information.
c. Information that is useful in making investment and credit decisions should be furnished.
d. Accounting information must exhibit relevance and faithful representation.
e. Information useful in assessing cash flow prospects should be provided.

LO 1 **Enhancing Qualitative Characteristics and Accounting Conventions**

SE2. CONCEPT ▶ State which of these selected enhancing qualitative characteristics and accounting conventions—comparability, verifiability, timeliness, cost constraint, consistency, full disclosure, materiality, or conservatism—is being followed in each case that follows.

1. Management provides detailed information about the company's long-term debt in the notes to the financial statements.
2. A company does not account separately for discounts received for prompt payment of accounts payable because few of these transactions occur and the total amount of the discounts is small.
3. Management eliminates a weekly report on property, plant, and equipment acquisitions and disposals because no one finds it useful.
4. A company follows the policy of recognizing a loss on inventory when the market value of an item falls below its cost but does nothing if the market value rises.
5. When several accounting methods are acceptable, management chooses a single method and follows that method from year to year.
6. The internal audit department comes up with similar estimates to management's determination of fair value of investments.
7. The company makes every effort to complete its financial statements within one week after the end of the accounting period.

LO 2 **Classification of Accounts: Balance Sheet**

SE3. Tell whether each of the following accounts is a current asset; an investment; property, plant, and equipment; an intangible asset; a current liability; a long-term liability; owner's equity; or not on the balance sheet:

1. Delivery Trucks
2. Accounts Payable
3. Note Payable (due in 90 days)
4. Delivery Expense
5. Owner's Capital
6. Prepaid Insurance
7. Trademark
8. Investment to Be Held Six Months
9. Factory Not Used in Business

LO 2 **Classified Balance Sheet**

SE4. Using the following accounts, prepare a classified balance sheet at year end, May 31, 2014: Accounts Payable, $1,600; Accounts Receivable, $2,200; Accumulated Depreciation—Equipment, $1,400; Cash, $400; Owner's Investment, $2,000; Equipment, $6,000; Franchise, $400; Investments (long-term), $1,000; Merchandise Inventory, $1,200; Notes Payable (long-term), $800; Owner's Capital, $?; Wages Payable, $200. Assume that this is the company's first year of operations.

LO 3

Liquidity Ratios

SE5. BUSINESS APPLICATION ▶ Using the following accounts and balances taken from a year-end balance sheet, compute working capital and the current ratio:

Accounts Payable	$3,500	Merchandise Inventory	$ 6,000
Accounts Receivable	5,000	Notes Payable in Three Years	6,500
Cash	2,000	Owner's Capital	24,000
Marketable Securities	1,000	Property, Plant, and Equipment	20,000

LO 3

Profitability Ratios

SE6. BUSINESS APPLICATION ▶ Using the following information from a balance sheet and an income statement, compute the (1) profit margin, (2) asset turnover, (3) return on assets, (4) debt to equity ratio, and (5) return on equity. The previous year's total assets were $200,000, and owner's equity was $140,000. (Round to one decimal place.)

Total Assets	$240,000	Net Sales	$260,000
Total Liabilities	60,000	Cost of Goods Sold	140,000
Total Owner's Equity	180,000	Operating Expenses	80,000

LO 3

Profitability Ratios

SE7. BUSINESS APPLICATION ▶ Assume that a company has a profit margin of 12.0 percent, an asset turnover of 6.4 times, and a debt to equity ratio of 50 percent. What are the company's return on assets and return on equity? (Round to one decimal place.)

EXERCISES: SET A

LO 1

Financial Accounting Concepts

E1A. CONCEPT ▶ The lettered items that follow represent a classification scheme for the concepts of financial accounting. Match each numbered term in the list that follows with the letter of the category in which it belongs.

a. Qualitative characteristics
b. Financial statements
c. Objective of accounting information
d. Accounting measurement considerations
e. Accounting processing considerations
f. Decision makers (users of accounting information)
g. Accounting conventions
h. Business activities or entities relevant to accounting measurement

7. Cost-benefit
8. Predictive value
9. Business transactions
10. Consistency
11. Full disclosure
12. Furnishing information that is useful to investors and creditors
13. Specific business entities
14. Classification
15. Management
16. Neutrality
17. Internal accounting control
18. Valuation
19. Investors
20. Completeness
21. Relevance
22. Furnishing information that is useful in assessing cash flow prospects

1. Conservatism
2. Verifiability
3. Statement of cash flows
4. Materiality
5. Faithful representation
6. Recognition

LO **1**

Qualitative Characteristics and Accounting Conventions

E2A. CONCEPT ▶ Each of the statements that follow violates one or more accounting concepts. State which of these selected qualitative characteristics and accounting conventions—relevance, faithful representation, comparability, verifiability, timeliness, understandability, cost constraint, consistency, materiality, conservatism, or full disclosure—is (are) violated.

1. A company changes its method of accounting for depreciation.
2. The asset account for a pickup truck still used in the business is written down to what the truck could be sold for, even though the carrying value under conventional depreciation methods is higher.
3. A series of reports that are time-consuming and expensive to prepare are presented to the owner each month, even though they are never used.
4. The company in 1 does not indicate in the financial statements that the method of depreciation was changed, nor does it specify the effect of the change on net income.
5. A company's new office building, which is built next to the company's existing factory, is debited to the factory account because it represents a fairly small dollar amount in relation to the factory.
6. Information is presented in a way that is not useful to users.
7. A transaction is recorded that does not represent the substance of the economic event.
8. Information is presented in a way that is confusing to users.
9. Similar transactions are recorded using different accounting principles.
10. Information is reported long after the economic events they represent.
11. Various experts come up with widely different estimates of an amount.

LO **2**

Classification of Accounts: Balance Sheet

E3A. The lettered items that follow represent a classification scheme for a balance sheet, and the numbered items in the list are account titles. Match each account with the letter of the category in which it belongs.

a. Current liabilities
b. Owner's equity
c. Current assets
d. Intangible assets
e. Property, plant, and equipment
f. Investments
g. Long-term liabilities
h. Not on balance sheet

5. Note Payable in Five Years
6. Building Used in Operations
7. Fund Held to Pay Off Long-Term Debt
8. Inventory
9. Prepaid Insurance
10. Depreciation Expense
11. Accounts Receivable
12. Interest Expense

1. Patent
2. Building Held for Sale
3. Prepaid Rent
4. Wages Payable

13. Unearned Revenue
14. Short-Term Investments
15. Accumulated Depreciation
16. Owner's Capital

LO **2**

Classified Balance Sheet Preparation

E4A. The following data pertain to Wagoner Company: Accounts Payable, $20,400; Accounts Receivable, $15,200; Accumulated Depreciation—Building, $5,600; Accumulated Depreciation—Equipment, $6,800; Bonds Payable, $24,000; Building, $28,000; Cash, $12,480; Copyright, $2,480; Equipment, $60,800; Inventory, $16,000; Investment in Corporate Securities (long-term), $8,000; Investment in Six-Month Government Securities, $6,560; Y. Wagoner, Capital, $95,280; Land, $3,200; Prepaid Rent, $480; and Revenue Received in Advance, $1,120. Prepare a classified balance sheet at December 31, 2014. Assume that this is Wagoner's first year of operations.

LO **3**   ### Liquidity Ratios

E5A. BUSINESS APPLICATION ▶ The accounts and balances that follow are from Kellman Company's general ledger. Compute the (1) working capital and (2) current ratio. (Round to one decimal place.)

Accounts Payable	$13,280
Accounts Receivable	8,160
Cash	1,200
Current Portion of Long-Term Debt	8,000
K. Kellman, Capital	22,640
Long-Term Investments	8,320
Marketable Securities	10,080
Merchandise Inventory	20,320
Notes Payable (90 days)	12,000
Notes Payable (2 years)	16,000
Notes Receivable (90 days)	20,800
Notes Receivable (2 years)	8,000
Prepaid Insurance	320
Property, Plant, and Equipment	48,000
Property Taxes Payable	1,000
Salaries Payable	680
Supplies	280
Unearned Revenue	600

LO **3**   ### Profitability Ratios

E6A. BUSINESS APPLICATION ▶ The following amounts are from Shimura Company's financial statements at the end of the current year: total assets, $426,000; total liabilities, $172,000; owner's equity, $254,000; net sales, $782,000; cost of goods sold, $486,000; operating expenses, $178,000; and withdrawals, $40,000. During the current year, total assets increased by $75,000. Total owner's equity was affected only by net income and withdrawals. Compute the (1) profit margin, (2) asset turnover, (3) return on assets, (4) debt to equity ratio, and (5) return on equity. (Round to one decimal place.)

LO **3**   ### Liquidity and Profitability Ratios

E7A. BUSINESS APPLICATION ▶ A company's simplified balance sheet and income statement follow.

Balance Sheet
December 31, 2014

Assets		Liabilities	
Current assets	$ 50,000	Current liabilities	$ 20,000
Investments	10,000	Long-term liabilities	30,000
Property, plant, and equipment	146,500	Total liabilities	$ 50,000
Intangible assets	13,500	**Owner's Equity**	
		Owner's capital	170,000
Total assets	$220,000	Total liabilities and owner's equity	$220,000

Income Statement
For the Year Ended December 31, 2014

Net sales	$410,000
Cost of goods sold	250,000
Gross margin	$160,000
Operating expenses	135,000
Net income	$ 25,000

Total assets and owner's equity at the beginning of 2014 were $180,000 and $140,000, respectively. The owner made no investments or withdrawals during the year.

1. Compute the following liquidity measures: (a) working capital and (b) current ratio. (Round to one decimal place.)
2. Compute the following profitability measures: (a) profit margin, (b) asset turnover, (c) return on assets, (d) debt to equity ratio, and (e) return on equity. (Round to one decimal place.)

LO 3 **Liquidity and Profitability Ratios**

E8A. BUSINESS APPLICATION ▶ Villegas Company is considering applying for a bank loan. Various data from Villegas's classified financial statements follow.

	2014	2013
Current assets	$100,000	$ 85,000
Total assets	440,000	355,000
Current liabilities	45,000	25,000
Long-term liabilities	75,000	25,000
Owner's equity	320,000	305,000
Sales	600,000	525,000
Net income	30,000	40,000

Its total assets and owner's equity at the beginning of 2013 were $345,000 and $295,000, respectively.

1. Use (a) liquidity analysis and (b) profitability analysis to document Villegas's financial position. (Round to two decimal places.)
2. Discuss Villegas's profitability and liquidity. Do you think it will qualify for a bank loan?

EXERCISES: SET B

Visit the textbook companion website at www.cengagebrain.com to access Exercise Set B for this chapter.

PROBLEMS

LO 1 **Qualitative Characteristics and Accounting Conventions**

P1. CONCEPT ▶ In each case that follows, qualitative characteristics and accounting conventions may have been violated.

1. After careful study, Schuss Company, which has offices in 40 states, has determined that its method of depreciating office furniture should be changed. The new method is adopted for the current year, and the change is noted in the financial statements.
2. In the past, Waldemar Company has recorded operating expenses in general accounts (e.g., Salaries Expense and Utilities Expense). Management has determined that despite the additional recordkeeping costs, the company's income statement should break down each operating expense into its components of selling expense and administrative expense.
3. Leon Company's auditor discovered that a company official had authorized the payment of a $1,200 bribe to a local official. Management argued that because the item was so small in relation to the size of the company ($1,700,000 in sales), the illegal payment should not be disclosed.
4. J&J Bookstore built a small addition to its main building to house a new computer games section. Because no one could be sure that the computer games section would succeed, the accountant took a conservative approach and recorded the addition as an expense.

(Continued)

5. Since it began operations ten years ago, Reed Company has used the same generally accepted inventory method. The company does not disclose in its financial statements what inventory method it uses.

6. Go-Fast Gas has a number of aged service stations around the local community. The company has not included the buildings at these locations on its financial statements because it does not plan on selling them.

7. Social Internet Company is planning to ask the bank for a loan. It asks its accountants to make its financial prospects look as attractive as possible.

8. Acre Company's auditors are having difficulty reproducing estimates in Acre's financial statements due to estimates that cannot be substantiated.

REQUIRED

In each of these cases, identify the qualitative characteristic or accounting convention that applies, state whether or not the treatment is in accord with the accounting concept and generally accepted accounting principles, and briefly explain why.

LO **2, 3**

SPREADSHEET

✔ 1: Total assets: $597,600

Classified Balance Sheet

P2. The information that follows is from Jason's Hardware Company's June 30, 2014, post-closing trial balance.

Account Name	Debit	Credit
Cash	32,000	
Short-Term Investments	33,000	
Notes Receivable	10,000	
Accounts Receivable	276,000	
Merchandise Inventory	145,000	
Prepaid Rent	1,600	
Prepaid Insurance	4,800	
Sales Supplies	1,280	
Office Supplies	440	
Deposit for Future Advertising	3,680	
Building, Not in Use	49,600	
Land	23,400	
Delivery Equipment	41,200	
Accumulated Depreciation—Delivery Equipment		28,400
Trademark	4,000	
Accounts Payable		114,600
Salaries Payable		5,200
Interest Payable		840
Long-Term Notes Payable		80,000
J. Smith, Capital		396,960
	626,000	626,000

REQUIRED

1. Prepare a classified balance sheet for Jason's Hardware Company.
2. **BUSINESS APPLICATION** ▶ Compute Jason's Hardware's current ratio and debt to equity ratio. (Round to one decimal place.)
3. **BUSINESS APPLICATION** ▶ As a user of the classified balance sheet, why would you want to know the current ratio or the debt to equity ratio?

LO **3**

Liquidity and Profitability Ratios

P3. BUSINESS APPLICATION ▶ Julio Company has had poor operating results for the past two years. As Julio's accountant, you have the following information available to you:

✔ 1b: 2014 current ratio: 2.3
✔ 2e: 2014 return on equity: 15.6%

	2014	2013
Current assets	$ 45,000	$ 35,000
Total assets	145,000	110,000
Current liabilities	20,000	10,000
Long-term liabilities	20,000	—
Owner's equity	105,000	100,000
Net sales	262,000	200,000
Net income	16,000	11,000

Total assets and owner's equity at the beginning of 2013 were $90,000 and $80,000, respectively. The owner made no investments in 2013 or 2014.

REQUIRED

1. Compute the following measures of liquidity for 2013 and 2014: (a) working capital and (b) current ratio. Comment on the differences between the years. (Round to one decimal place.)
2. Compute the following measures of profitability for 2013 and 2014: (a) profit margin, (b) asset turnover, (c) return on assets, (d) debt to equity ratio, and (e) return on equity. Comment on the change in performance from 2013 to 2014. (Round to one decimal place.)

LO **2, 3**   **Classified Balance Sheet**

✔ 1: Total assets: $625,800

P4. The information that follows is from Cullen's Hardware Company's June 30, 2014, post-closing trial balance.

Account Name	Debit	Credit
Cash	42,800	
Short-Term Investments	34,300	
Sales Supplies	1,280	
Merchandise Inventory	145,000	
Prepaid Rent	2,100	
Prepaid Insurance	4,800	
Accounts Receivable	287,000	
Office Supplies	440	
E. Cullen, Capital		412,660
Notes Receivable	10,000	
Land	31,400	
Delivery Equipment	43,200	
Accumulated Depreciation—Delivery Equipment		28,400
Trademark	4,000	
Accounts Payable		124,600
Salaries Payable		7,700
Deposit for Future Advertising	3,680	
Interest Payable		840
Long-Term Notes Payable		80,000
Building, Not in Use	44,200	
	654,200	654,200

REQUIRED

1. Prepare a classified balance sheet for Cullen's Hardware Company.
2. **BUSINESS APPLICATION** ▶ Compute Cullen's Hardware's current ratio and debt to equity ratio. (Round to one decimal place.)
3. **BUSINESS APPLICATION** ▶ As a user of the classified balance sheet, why would you want to know the current ratio or the debt to equity ratio?

ALTERNATE PROBLEMS

LO **1**   **Accounting Conventions**

P5. CONCEPT ▶ In each case that follows, qualitative characteristics and accounting conventions may have been violated.

1. Elite Manufacturing Company uses the cost method for computing the balance sheet amount of inventory unless the market value of the inventory is less than the cost, in which case the market value is used. At the end of the current year, the market value is $302,000 and the cost is $324,000. The company uses the $302,000 figure to compute the value of inventory because management believes it is the more cautious approach.

2. Livery Service Company has annual sales of $20,000,000. It follows the practice of recording any items costing less than $500 as expenses in the year purchased. During the current year, it purchased several chairs for the executive conference room at $490 each, including freight. Although the chairs were expected to last for at least ten years, they were recorded as an expense in accordance with company policy.

3. Stardust Company closed its books on October 31, 2013, before preparing its annual report. On November 3, 2013, a fire destroyed one of the company's two factories. Although the company had fire insurance and would not suffer a loss on the building, it seemed likely that it would suffer a significant decrease in sales in 2014 because of the fire. It did not report the fire damage in its 2013 financial statements because the fire had not affected its operations during that year.

4. Primal Drug Company spends a substantial portion of its profits on research and development. The company had been reporting its $12,000,000 expenditure for research and development as a lump sum, but management recently decided to begin classifying the expenditures by project, even though its recordkeeping costs will increase.

5. During the current year, Ziegler Company changed from one generally accepted method of accounting for inventories to another method, without disclosing the change.

6. Due to pressing business issues, Judson Products is consistently behind schedule in preparing its financial statements.

7. Thomas Electronics is a complex global business whose financial statements use many technical terms not known by the typical investor.

8. Siro Company produces financial statements that are not helpful in assessing the company's prospects in the future.

REQUIRED

For each of these cases, identify the accounting concept that applies, state whether or not the treatment is in accord with the concept, and briefly explain why.

LO **2, 3**   **Classified Balance Sheet**

✔ 1: Total assets: $595,600

P6. The information that follows is from Matt's Hardware Company's April 30, 2014, post-closing trial balance.

Account Name	Debit	Credit
Cash	31,000	
Short-Term Investments	33,000	
Notes Receivable	10,000	
Accounts Receivable	276,000	
Merchandise Inventory	145,000	
Prepaid Rent	1,600	
Prepaid Insurance	4,800	

Sales Supplies	1,280	
Office Supplies	440	
Deposit for Future Advertising	3,680	
Building, Not in Use	49,600	
Land	22,400	
Delivery Equipment	41,200	
Accumulated Depreciation—Delivery Equipment		28,400
Trademark	4,000	
Accounts Payable		114,600
Salaries Payable		5,200
Interest Payable		840
Long-Term Notes Payable		80,000
M. Shah, Capital		394,960

REQUIRED

1. Prepare a classified balance sheet for Matt's Hardware.
2. **BUSINESS APPLICATION** ▶ Compute Matt's Hardware's current ratio and debt to equity ratio. (Round to one decimal place.)
3. **BUSINESS APPLICATION** ▶ As a user of the classified balance sheet, why would you want to know the current ratio or the debt to equity ratio?

LO **3**

RATIO

SPREADSHEET

✔ 1b: 2014 current ratio: 2.0
✔ 2c: 2014 return on assets: 14.8%

Liquidity and Profitability Ratios

P7. BUSINESS APPLICATION ▶ A summary of data from Pinder Construction Supply Company's income statements and balance sheets for 2014 and 2013 follows.

	2014	2013
Current assets	$ 366,000	$ 310,000
Total assets	2,320,000	1,740,000
Current liabilities	180,000	120,000
Long-term liabilities	800,000	580,000
Owner's equity	1,340,000	1,040,000
Net sales	4,600,000	3,480,000
Net income	300,000	204,000

Total assets and owner's equity at the beginning of 2013 were $1,360,000 and $840,000, respectively.

REQUIRED

1. Compute the following liquidity measures for 2013 and 2014: (a) working capital and (b) current ratio. Comment on the differences between the years. (Round to one decimal place.)
2. Compute the following measures of profitability for 2013 and 2014: (a) profit margin, (b) asset turnover, (c) return on assets, (d) debt to equity ratio, and (e) return on equity. Comment on the change in performance from 2013 to 2014. (Round to one decimal place.)

LO **2, 3**

RATIO

✔ 1: Total assets: $571,470

Classified Balance Sheet

P8. The information that follows is from Rodriguez's Tools Company's April 30, 2014, post-closing trial balance.

(*Continued*)

Account Name	Debit	Credit
Cash	31,000	
Short-Term Investments	43,500	
Accounts Receivable	239,000	
Merchandise Inventory	113,000	
Notes Receivable	10,000	
Interest Payable		930
Sales Supplies	1,280	
Office Supplies	540	
Deposit for Future Advertising	3,120	
Long-Term Notes Payable		99,000
Land	34,700	
Delivery Equipment	42,230	
Accumulated Depreciation—Delivery Equipment		28,400
Building, Not in Use	72,100	
Accounts Payable		129,600
Salaries Payable		4,600
Prepaid Rent	1,800	
Prepaid Insurance	3,600	
C. Rodriguez, Capital		337,340
Trademark	4,000	

REQUIRED

1. Prepare a classified balance sheet for Rodriguez's Tools.
2. **BUSINESS APPLICATION** ▶ Compute Rodriguez's Tools' current ratio and debt to equity ratio. (Round to one decimal place.)
3. **BUSINESS APPLICATION** ▶ As a user of the classified balance sheet, why would you want to know the current ratio or the debt to equity ratio?

CASES

LO 1

Conceptual Understanding: Consistency, Full Disclosure, and Materiality

C1. CONCEPT ▶ Metro Parking, which operates a seven-story parking building, has a calendar year-end. It serves daily and hourly parkers, as well as monthly parkers who pay a fixed monthly rate in advance. The company traditionally has recorded all cash receipts as revenues when received. Most monthly parkers pay in full during the month prior to that in which they have the right to park. The company's auditors have said that beginning in 2014, the company should consider recording the cash receipts from monthly parking on an accrual basis, crediting Unearned Revenues. Total cash receipts for 2014 were $1,250,000, and the cash receipts received in 2014 and applicable to January 2015 were $62,500. Discuss the relevance of the accounting concepts of consistency, full disclosure, and materiality to the decision to record the monthly parking revenues on an accrual basis.

LO 1

Conceptual Understanding: Materiality

C2. CONCEPT ▶ Laskowski, Inc., operates a chain of consumer electronics stores. This year, the company achieved annual sales of $75 million, on which it earned a net income of $3 million. At the beginning of the year, management implemented a new inventory system that enabled it to track all purchases and sales. At the end of the year, a physical inventory revealed that the actual inventory was $120,000 below what the new system indicated it should be. The inventory loss, which probably resulted from shoplifting, was reflected in a higher cost of goods sold. The problem concerns management but seems to be less important to the company's auditors. What is materiality? Why might the inventory loss concern management more than it does the auditors? Do you think the amount of inventory loss is material?

LO **3**   **Interpreting Financial Reports: Comparison of Profitability**

C3. BUSINESS APPLICATION ▶ Two of the largest chains of clothing stores in the United States are **The Gap, Inc.** and **Abercrombie & Fitch Co.** In fiscal 2011, Gap had net income of $833 million, and Abercrombie & Fitch had net income of $128 million. It is difficult to judge from these figures alone which company is more profitable because they do not take into account the relative sales, sizes, and investments of the companies. Data (in millions) needed for a complete financial analysis of the two companies follow:

	Gap	Abercrombie & Fitch*
Net sales	$14,549	$4,158
Beginning total assets	7,065	2,941
Ending total assets	7,422	3,048
Beginning total liabilities	2,985	1,051
Ending total liabilities	4,667	1,186
Beginning stockholders' equity	4,080	1,891
Ending stockholders' equity	2,755	1,862

*Abercrombie & Fitch's data is rounded to the nearest dollar.

1. Determine which company was more profitable by computing profit margin, asset turnover, the debt to equity ratio, return on assets, and return on equity for the two companies. Comment on the relative profitability of the two companies. (Round to one decimal place or the nearest tenth of a percent.)
2. What do the ratios tell you about the factors that go into achieving an adequate return on assets in the clothing retail industry? For industry data, refer to the graphs in the ratio boxes throughout the chapter.
3. How would you characterize the use of debt financing in the clothing retail industry and the use of debt by these two companies?

LO **2, 3**   **Annual Report Case: Classified Balance Sheet**

C4. BUSINESS APPLICATION ▶ Refer to the **CVS** annual report in the Supplement to Chapter 16 to answer the following questions.

1. Does CVS use a classified balance sheet?
2. Did CVS's debt to equity ratio change from 2010 to 2011? (Round to the nearest tenth of a percent.)
3. What is the contributed capital for 2011? How does contributed capital compare with retained earnings?

LO **3**   **Comparison Case: Financial Performance**

C5. BUSINESS APPLICATION ▶ Compare the financial performance of **CVS** and **Southwest Airlines Co.** on the basis of profitability in 2011 and 2010. Use the following ratios: profit margin, asset turnover, return on assets, and return on equity. (Round to one decimal place or to the nearest tenth of a percent.) In 2009, total assets, total stockholders' equity, and cash flows from operating activities for CVS were $61,141 million, $35,768 million, and $4,035 million, respectively. Southwest's total assets were $14,269 million in 2009, and its total stockholders' equity and cash flow from operating activities were $5,454 million and $985 million, respectively. Comment on the relative performance of the two companies. In general, how does Southwest's performance compare to CVS's with respect to profitability? What distinguishes Southwest's profitability performance from that of CVS?

LO **1**   **Ethical Dilemma: Ethics and Financial Reporting**

C6. Beacon Systems develops computer software and licenses it to financial institutions. The firm records revenues from the software it has developed on a percentage of com-

(*Continued*)

pletion basis. For example, if a project is 50 percent complete, then 50 percent of the contracted revenue is recognized. Preliminary estimates for a $7 million project now in development are that the project is 75 percent complete. Estimates of completion are a matter of judgment, and management therefore feels justified in asking for a new report showing that the project is 90 percent complete. The change will enable senior managers to meet their financial goals for the year and thus receive substantial year-end bonuses. Do you think management's action is ethical? If you were the company controller and were asked to prepare the new report, would you do it? What action would you take?

Continuing Case: Annual Report Project

 C7. BUSINESS APPLICATION ▶ Using the most recent annual report of the company you have chosen to study and that you have accessed online at the company's website, use the classified balance sheet together with the income statement to compute the following ratios for the last two years and indicate whether each has improved. (Round to one decimal place or to the nearest tenth of a percent.)

a. Current ratio
b. Profit margin
c. Asset turnover
d. Return on assets
e. Debt to equity ratio
f. Return on equity

CHAPTER 6
Accounting for Merchandising Operations

Mink Company is a fast-growing, discount merchandising company that specializes in selling stylish, low-priced fashions to young people. Like all other merchandisers, Mink has two key decisions to make: the price at which it will sell goods and the level of service it will provide. A department store may set the price of its merchandise at a relatively high level and provide a great deal of service. A discount store, on the other hand, may price its merchandise at a relatively low level and provide limited service.

1. **CONCEPT** ▶ *How do faithful representation and classification apply to merchandise operations?*

2. **ACCOUNTING APPLICATION** ▶ *How can merchandising transactions be recorded to reflect the company's performance?*

3. **BUSINESS APPLICATION** ▶ *How can Mink manage its operating cycle so that it has adequate cash to maintain liquidity?*

LEARNING OBJECTIVES

LO 1 Define *merchandising accounting*, and differentiate perpetual from periodic inventory systems.

LO 2 Describe the features of multistep and single-step classified income statements.

LO 3 Describe the terms of sale related to merchandising transactions.

LO 4 Prepare an income statement, and record merchandising transactions under the perpetual inventory system.

LO 5 Prepare an income statement, and record merchandising transactions under the periodic inventory system.

LO 6 Explain the role of the operating cycle and foreign business transactions in evaluating the liquidity of a merchandising company.

101images/Shutterstock

CONCEPTS

CONCEPTS
- Faithful representation
- Classification

**RELEVANT
LEARNING OBJECTIVE**

LO 1 Define *merchandising accounting* and differentiate perpetual from periodic inventory systems.

LO 1 Concepts Underlying Merchandising Accounting

A merchandising company earns income by buying and selling goods, which are called **merchandise inventory**. Whether a merchandiser is a wholesaler or a retailer, it uses the same basic accounting methods as a service company. However, the buying and selling of goods adds to the complexity of the accounting process. One complexity is the *classification* of items on the merchandising income statement so that the statement *faithfully represents* the operations of the company. Further, merchandise inventory is an important component on the **operating cycle**, which is the cycle of buying and holding merchandise until it is sold and then collecting payment for the sales.

To *faithfully represent* accounting for merchandising inventories, two basic systems of accounting for merchandise inventory are used: the *perpetual inventory system* and the *periodic inventory system*.

- Under the **perpetual inventory system**, continuous records are kept of the quantity and, usually, the cost of individual items as they are bought and sold. The cost of each item is recorded in the Merchandise Inventory account when it is purchased. As merchandise is sold, its cost is transferred from the Merchandise Inventory account to the Cost of Goods Sold account. Thus, at all times the balance of the Merchandise Inventory account equals the cost of goods on hand, and the balance in Cost of Goods Sold equals the cost of merchandise sold to customers.

- Under the **periodic inventory system**, the inventory not yet sold is counted periodically. This physical count is called **physical inventory**, which is usually taken at the end of the accounting period. No detailed records of the inventory are maintained during the accounting period. The figure for inventory is accurate only on the balance sheet date. (Note that the value of ending inventory on the balance sheet is determined by multiplying the quantity of each inventory item by its unit cost.) As soon as any purchases or sales are made in the new accounting period, the inventory figure becomes a historical amount, and it remains so until the new ending inventory amount is entered at the end of this accounting period.

Note that the perpetual inventory system does not eliminate the need for a physical count of the inventory. One should be taken periodically to ensure that the actual number of goods on hand matches the quantity indicated by the computer records.

Each system has advantages. Managers use the detailed data from the perpetual inventory system to respond to customers' inquiries about product availability, to order inventory more effectively in order to avoid running out of stock, and to control the costs associated with investments in inventory. Managers may choose the periodic inventory system because it reduces the amount of clerical work. If a business is fairly small, management can maintain control over its inventory simply through observation or by use of an offline system of cards or computer records. However, for larger companies, the lack of detailed records may lead to lost sales or high operating costs.

Business Perspective
How Have Bar Codes Influenced the Choice of Inventory Systems?

Most grocery stores, which traditionally used the periodic inventory system, now employ bar coding to update the physical inventory as items are sold. At the checkout counter, the cashier scans into the cash register the electronic marking, called a *bar code* or *universal product code* (*UPC*), that appears on each product. The cash register is linked to a computer that records the sale. Bar coding has become common in all types of retail companies, manufacturing firms, and hospitals. It has also become a major factor in the increased use of the perpetual inventory system. Interestingly, some retail businesses now use the perpetual inventory system for keeping track of the physical flow of inventory and the periodic inventory system for preparing their financial statements.

Because of the difficulty and expense of accounting for the purchase and sale of each item, companies that sell items of low value in high volume have traditionally used the periodic inventory system. Examples of such companies include small retailers, drugstores, and grocery stores. In contrast, companies that sell items that have a high unit value, such as appliances, have tended to use the perpetual inventory system. The distinction between high and low unit value for inventory systems has blurred considerably in recent years. Although the periodic inventory system is still widely used, computerization has led to an increase in the use of the perpetual inventory system.

APPLY IT!

Indicate whether each of the statements that follow is more applicable to (a) perpetual inventory system, (b) periodic inventory system, or (c) both systems.

1. Requires a physical count of inventory at end of period.
2. No detailed records of the inventory are maintained during the accounting period.
3. Continuous records are kept of the quantity.
4. Inventory figure is accurate only on the balance sheet date.
5. The balance in Cost of Goods Sold equals the cost of merchandise sold to customers at all times.
6. Helps to manage inventory more effectively and thus avoid running out of stock.
7. Is less costly to maintain but may lead to lost sales.

SOLUTION

1. c; 2. b; 3. a; 4. b; 5. a; 6. a; 7. b

TRY IT! SE1, E1A, E1B

ACCOUNTING APPLICATIONS

LO 2 Forms of the Income Statement

In the income statements we have presented thus far, expenses have been deducted from revenue in a single step to arrive at net income. Here, we look at a multistep income statement and a more complex single-step format.

Multistep Income Statement

A **multistep income statement** goes through a series of steps, or subtotals, to arrive at net income. In a service company's multistep income statement, the operating expenses are deducted from revenues in a single step to arrive at income from operations. In contrast, because manufacturing and merchandising companies make or buy goods for sale, their income statements include an additional step of calculating gross margin by subtracting the cost of goods from net sales. Exhibit 1 compares the multistep income statement of a service company (which provides services as opposed to products) with that of a **merchandising company** (which buys and sells products) and a **manufacturing company** (which makes and sells products).

Exhibit 1

A Comparison of the Components of Multistep Income Statements for Service and Merchandising or Manufacturing Companies

© Cengage Learning 2014

We will use Davila Company, a merchandising company, to illustrate the multistep income statement. Davila's multistep income statement is presented in Exhibit 2. Like balance sheets, income statements vary among companies. You will rarely, if ever, find an income statement exactly like the one presented for Davila Company. Companies use different terms and different structures.

Exhibit 2
Multistep Income Statement for Davila Company

Davila Company
Income Statement
For the Year Ended December 31, 2014

	Gross sales		$1,300,924	
	Less Sales returns and allowances		52,300	
Step 1	Net sales			$1,248,624
	Cost of goods sold			815,040
	Gross margin			$ 433,584
	Operating expenses:			
	Selling expenses		$ 219,120	
Step 2	General and administrative expenses		138,016	
	Total operating expenses			357,136
	Income from operations			$ 76,448
	Other revenues and expenses:			
Step 3	Interest income		$ 5,600	
	Less interest expense		10,524	
	Excess of other expenses over other revenues			4,924
Step 4	Net income			$ 71,524

© Cengage Learning 2014

Net Sales (or Net Revenue) Net sales (or *net revenue*) is computed as follows.

Net Sales = Gross Sales − Sales Returns and Allowances

- **Gross sales** consist of the total revenue from cash and credit sales during a period. Under the revenue recognition concept, even when cash from a credit sale is not received during the current period, it is recorded if title to the merchandise has passed to the buyer.
- **Sales returns and allowances** include cash refunds and credits on account. They also include any discounts from selling prices made to customers who have returned defective products or products that are otherwise unsatisfactory. If other types of discounts are given to customers, they also should be deducted from gross sales.

For Davila, net sales is computed as follows.

$1,300,924 − $52,300 = $1,248,624

Cost of Goods Sold (or Cost of Sales) **Cost of goods sold** (or *cost of sales* or *cost of revenue*) is the amount a merchandiser paid for the merchandise it sold during a period. For a manufacturer, it is the cost of making the products it sold during a period. Davila's cost of goods sold is $815,040.

Gross Margin (or Gross Profit) **Gross margin** (or *gross profit*) is computed as follows.

Gross Margin = Net Sales − Cost of Goods Sold

International Perspective

IFRS Income Statements Under IFRS May Not Show Cost of Goods Sold

Under U.S. GAAP, the Cost of Goods Sold account is needed because the income statement requires listing costs and expense by function, such as cost of goods sold, selling expenses, and general and administrative expenses. IFRS, on the other hand, give companies the option of listing by function, like U.S. GAAP, or by nature, such as materials costs, labor costs, and so forth. Most European companies choose the latter option, thus not showing any cost of goods sold, gross margin, or operating income on their income statements.

STUDY NOTE: *Gross margin measures profitability. When it is less than operating expenses, the company suffers a net loss from operations.*

A company's gross margin must be sufficient to cover operating expenses and provide an adequate net income. Davila's gross margin is computed as follows (as shown in Step 1 in Exhibit 2).

$$\$1,248,624 - \$815,040 = \$433,584$$

Managers and owners are interested in both the amount and **percentage of gross margin**. The percentage is computed as follows.

$$\text{Percentage of Gross Margin} = \text{Gross Margin} \div \text{Net Sales}$$

For Davila, percentage of gross margin is computed as follows.

$$\$433,584 \div \$1,248,624 = 34.7^* \%$$

*Rounded

Business Application Gross margin information is useful in planning business operations.

- For instance, management may try to increase total sales of a product by reducing the selling price. Although this strategy reduces the percentage of gross margin, it will work if the number of items sold increases enough to raise the absolute amount of gross margin. Discount warehouse stores like **Sam's Club** and **Costco Wholesale Corporation** follow this strategy.
- On the other hand, management may decide to keep a high gross margin from sales and try to increase sales and the amount of gross margin by increasing operating expenses, such as advertising. Upscale specialty stores like **Neiman Marcus** and **Tiffany & Co.** use this strategy.

Other strategies to increase gross margin include using better purchasing methods to reduce the cost of goods sold.

Operating Expenses Operating expenses are the expenses, other than the cost of goods sold, that are incurred in running a business. They are often grouped into the categories of selling expenses and general and administrative expenses and computed as follows.

$$\text{Operating Expenses} = \text{Selling Expenses} + \text{General and Administrative Expenses}$$

- **Selling expenses** include the costs of storing goods and preparing them for sale; preparing displays, advertising, and otherwise promoting sales; and delivering goods to a buyer if the seller has agreed to pay the cost of delivery.
- **General and administrative expenses** include expenses for accounting, personnel, credit checking, collections, and any other expenses that apply to overall operations. Although occupancy expenses, such as expenses of rent, insurance, and utilities, are often classified as general and administrative expenses, they can also be allocated between selling expenses and general and administrative expenses.

For Davila, operating expenses are computed as follows.

$$\$219,120 + \$138,016 = \$357,136$$

Business Application Careful planning and control of operating expenses can improve a company's profitability.

Income from Operations (or Operating Income) Income from operations (or *operating income*) is the income from a company's main business and is computed as follows.

$$\text{Income from Operations} = \text{Gross Margin} - \text{Operating Expenses}$$

For Davila, income from operations is computed as follows (as shown in Step 2 in Exhibit 2).

$$\$433,584 - \$357,136 = \$76,448$$

Business Application Income from operations is often used to compare the profitability of two or more companies or divisions within a company.

Other Revenues and Expenses (or Nonoperating Revenues and Expenses)
Other revenues and expenses (or *nonoperating revenues and expenses*) are not related to a company's operating activities. Among the items included in this section are revenues from investments (such as dividends and interest on stocks, bonds, and savings accounts) and interest expense and other expenses that result from borrowing money. Davila's other revenues and expenses appear in Step 3 of Exhibit 2.

Net Income (or Net Earnings) **Net income** (or *net earnings*) is the final figure, or "bottom line," of an income statement and is computed as follows.

$$\text{Net Income} = \text{Gross Margin} - \text{Operating Expenses} +/- \text{Other Revenues and Expenses}$$

For Davila, net income is computed as follows (as shown in Step 4 of Exhibit 2).

$$\$433,584 - \$357,136 - \$4,924 = \$71,524$$

Net income is an important performance measure because it represents the amount of earnings that accrue to owners. It is the amount transferred to owner's capital from all the income that business operations have generated during a period.

Single-Step Income Statement

Exhibit 3 shows a **single-step income statement** for Davila Company. In this statement, net income is derived in a single step by putting the major categories of revenues in the first part of the statement and the major categories of costs and expenses in the second part. Both the multistep form and the single-step form have advantages: the multistep form shows the components used in deriving net income, and the single-step form has the advantage of simplicity.

Exhibit 3
Single-Step Income Statement for Davila Company

Davila Company Income Statement For the Year Ended December 31, 2014		
Revenues:		
Net sales		$1,248,624
Interest income		5,600
Total revenues		$1,254,224
Costs and expenses:		
Cost of goods sold	$815,040	
Selling expenses	219,120	
General and administrative expenses	138,016	
Interest expense	10,524	
Total costs and expenses		1,182,700
Net income		$ 71,524

APPLY IT!

A single-step income statement follows. Present the information in a multistep income statement, and indicate what insights can be obtained from the multistep form as opposed to the single-step form.

Diviney Company
Income Statement
For the Year Ended December 31, 2014

Revenues:		
Net sales		$500,000
Interest income		50,000
Total revenues		$550,000
Costs and expenses:		
Cost of goods sold	$300,000	
Selling expenses	100,000	
General and administrative expenses	75,000	
Interest expense	25,000	
Total costs and expenses		500,000
Net income		$ 50,000

SOLUTION

Diviney Company
Income Statement
For the Year Ended December 31, 2014

Net sales		$500,000
Cost of goods sold		300,000
Gross margin		$200,000
Operating expenses:		
Selling expenses	$100,000	
General and administrative expenses	75,000	
Total operating expenses		175,000
Income from operations		$ 25,000
Other revenues and expenses:		
Interest income	$ 50,000	
Less interest expense	25,000	
Excess of other revenues over other expenses		25,000
Net income		$ 50,000

TRY IT! SE2, SE3, E1A, E2A, E3A, E4A, E1B, E2B, E3B, E4B

LO3 Terms of Sale

When goods are sold on credit, both parties should understand the amount and timing of payment as well as other terms of the purchase. Sellers quote prices in different ways. Many merchants quote the price at which they expect to sell their goods. Others, particularly manufacturers and wholesalers, quote prices as a percentage (usually 30 percent or more) off their list or catalogue prices. Such a reduction is called a **trade discount.**

For example, if an article is listed at $1,000 with a trade discount of 40 percent, or $400, the seller records the sale at $600, and the buyer records the purchase at $600. The seller may raise or lower the trade discount depending on the quantity purchased. The list price and related trade discount are used only to arrive at an agreed-upon price. They do not appear in the accounting records.

Sales and Purchases Discounts

The terms of sale are usually printed on the sales invoice and are part of the sales agreement. Terms differ from industry to industry. In some industries, payment is expected in a short period of time. In these cases, the invoice is marked "n/10" ("net 10") or "n/30" ("net 30"), meaning that the amount of the invoice is due either 10 days or 30 days after the invoice date. If the invoice is due 10 days after the end of the month, it is marked "n/10 eom."

STUDY NOTE: *A trade discount applies to the list or catalogue price. A sales discount applies to the sales price.*

Sales Discount In some industries, it is customary to give a **sales discount** for early payment. An invoice that offers a sales discount might be labeled "2/10, n/30," which means that the buyer either can pay within 10 days of the invoice date and take a 2 percent discount or can wait 30 days and pay the full amount. It is often advantageous for a buyer to take the discount because the saving of 2 percent over a period of 20 days (from the 11th day to the 30th day) represents an effective annual rate of 36.5 percent

(365 days ÷ 20 days × 2% = 36.5%). Most companies would be better off borrowing money from a lender so that they can take advantage of the discount from the supplier.

Because it is not possible to know at the time of a sale whether the customer will take advantage of a sales discount, the discounts are recorded by the seller only at the time the customer pays. For example, suppose Kawar Motor Company sells merchandise to a customer on September 20 for $600 on terms of 2/10, n/30. Kawar records the sale on September 20 for the full amount of $600. If the customer pays on or before September 30, Kawar will receive $588 in cash and will reduce its accounts receivable by $600. The difference of $12 ($600 × 0.02) will be debited to an account called *Sales Discounts*. Sales Discounts is a contra-revenue account with a normal debit balance that is deducted from sales on the income statement.

Although sales discounts were intended to increase the seller's liquidity by reducing the amount of money tied up in accounts receivable, the practice of giving sales discounts has been declining. Sales discounts are costly to the seller, and from the buyer's viewpoint, the amount of the discount is usually very small in relation to the price of the purchase.

Purchase Discounts **Purchase discounts** are discounts that a buyer takes for the early payment of merchandise. For example, the buyer that purchased the merchandise from Kawar Motor Company will record the purchase on September 20 at $600. If the buyer pays on or before September 30, it will record cash paid of $588 and reduce its Accounts Payable by $600. The difference of $12 is recorded as a credit to an account called *Purchases Discounts*. The Purchases Discounts account reduces the Cost of Goods Sold account or the Purchases account, depending on the inventory method used. As a result of the decline in the use of sales discounts, the use of purchase discounts is also declining.

Transportation Costs

In some industries, the seller usually pays transportation costs and charges a price that includes those costs. In other industries, it is customary for the purchaser to pay transportation charges. The following special terms designate whether the seller or the purchaser pays the freight charges.

- **FOB shipping point** means that the seller places the merchandise "free on board" at the point of origin and the buyer bears the shipping costs. The title to the merchandise passes to the buyer at that point. For example, when the sales agreement for the purchase of a car says "FOB factory," the buyer must pay the freight from the factory where the car was made to wherever he or she is located, and the buyer owns the car from the time it leaves the factory.
- **FOB destination** means that the seller bears the transportation costs to the delivery point. The seller retains title until the merchandise reaches its destination and usually prepays the shipping costs, in which case the buyer makes no accounting entry for freight.

The effects of these special shipping terms are summarized as follows.

Shipping Term	Where Title Passes	Who Pays the Cost of Transportation
FOB shipping point	At origin	Buyer
FOB destination	At destination	Seller

When the buyer pays the transportation charge, it is called **freight-in**, and it is added to the cost of merchandise purchased. Thus, freight-in increases the buyer's cost of inventory, as well as the cost of goods sold after they are sold. When freight-in is a relatively small amount, most companies include the cost in the cost of goods sold on the income statement rather than allocating part of it to merchandise inventory.

Pierre-Yves Babelon/Shutterstock

Shipping terms affect the financial statements. FOB shipping point means the buyer pays the freight charges. When relatively small, these charges are usually included in the cost of goods sold on the buyer's income statement. FOB destination means the seller pays the freight charges. They are included in selling expenses on the seller's income statement.

When the seller pays the transportation charge, it is called **delivery expense** (or *freight-out*). Because the seller incurs this cost to facilitate the sale of its product, the cost is included in selling expenses on the income statement.

Terms of Debit and Credit Card Sales

Many retailers allow customers to use debit or credit cards to charge their purchases. Debit cards deduct directly from a person's bank account, whereas a credit card allows for payment later. Three of the most widely used credit cards are **American Express**, **MasterCard**, and **Visa**. The customer establishes credit with the lender (the credit card issuer) and receives a card to use in making purchases. If a seller accepts the card, the customer signs an invoice at the time of the sale. The sale is communicated to the seller's bank, resulting in a cash deposit in the seller's bank account. Thus, the seller does not have to establish the customer's credit, collect from the customer, or tie up money in accounts receivable. The lender takes a discount, which is a selling expense for the merchandiser. For example, if a restaurant makes sales of $1,000 on Visa credit cards and Visa takes a 4 percent discount on the sales, the restaurant would record Cash in the amount of $960 and Credit Card Expense in the amount of $40.

© Alija / iStockphoto.com

Business Perspective
Are We Becoming a Cashless Society?

Are checks and cash obsolete? Do you "swipe it"? Most Americans do. About 71 percent of Americans (including 41 percent of college students) use credit or debit cards rather than checks. Consumers who have cards like the convenience and have on average 3.5 cards. Retailers, like **McDonald's** and **Starbucks**, like the cards, even though there are fees, because the use of cards usually increases the amount of sales.[1]

APPLY IT!

A local appliance dealer sells refrigerators that it buys from the manufacturer.

1. The manufacturer sets a list or catalogue price of $1,200 for a refrigerator. The manufacturer offers its dealers a 40 percent trade discount.

2. Assume the same terms as **1**, except the manufacturer sells the machine under terms of FOB shipping point. The cost of shipping is $120.

3. Assume the same terms as **2**, except the manufacturer offers a sales discount of 2/10, n/30. Sales discounts do not apply to shipping costs.

What is the net cost of the refrigerator to the dealer, assuming payment is made within 10 days of purchase?

SOLUTION

1. $1,200 − ($1,200 × 0.40) = $720
2. $720 + $120 = $840
3. $840 − ($720 × 0.02) = $825.60

TRY IT! SE4, SE5, E5A, E5B

LO 4 Perpetual Inventory System

We will use Kawar Motor Company to illustrate merchandising transactions under the perpetual inventory system. Kawar's income statement is presented in Exhibit 4. The focal point of the statement is cost of goods sold, which is deducted from net sales to arrive at gross margin. Under the perpetual inventory system, the Merchandise Inventory and Cost of Goods Sold accounts are continually updated during the accounting period as purchases, sales, and other inventory transactions occur.

Exhibit 4

Income Statement Under the Perpetual Inventory System

STUDY NOTE: *On the income statement, freight-in is included as part of cost of goods sold, and delivery expense (freight-out) is included as an operating (selling) expense.*

Kawar Motor Company	
Income Statement	
For the Year Ended December 31, 2014	
Net sales	$957,300
Cost of goods sold*	525,440
Gross margin	$431,860
Operating expenses	313,936
Net income	$117,924

*Freight-in has been included in cost of goods sold.

© Cengage Learning 2014

Purchases of Merchandise

Exhibit 5 shows how transactions involving purchases of merchandise are recorded under the perpetual inventory system. The focus of these journal entries is Accounts Payable. In this section, we present a summary of the entries made for merchandise purchases.[2]

Exhibit 5

Recording Purchase Transactions Under the Perpetual Inventory System

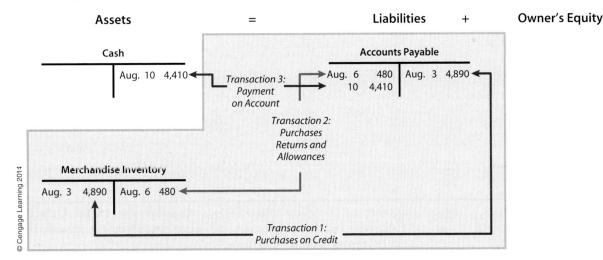

© Cengage Learning 2014

The examples that follow show how Kawar Motor Company would record purchase transactions under the perpetual inventory system.

Purchase on Credit

Transaction 1 On August 3, Kawar received merchandise purchased on credit, invoice dated August 1, terms n/10, $4,890.

Analysis Under the perpetual inventory system, the cost of merchandise is recorded in the Merchandise Inventory account at the time of purchase, which

▲ *increases* the *Merchandise Inventory* account

▲ *increases* the *Accounts Payable* account

Application of Double Entry

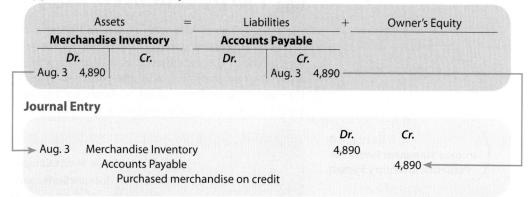

Journal Entry

Comment In this transaction, payment is due ten days from the invoice date. If an invoice includes a charge for shipping or if shipping is billed separately, it should be *recognized* as a debit to Freight-In.

Purchases Returns and Allowances

Transaction 2 On August 6, Kawar returned part of merchandise received on August 3 for credit, $480.

Analysis Under the perpetual inventory system, when a buyer is allowed to return all or part of a purchase or is given an allowance, accounts payable is reduced and merchandise inventory is decreased for the cost of the merchandise returned. This journal entry

▼ *decreases* the *Accounts Payable* account

▼ *decreases* the *Merchandise Inventory* account

Application of Double Entry

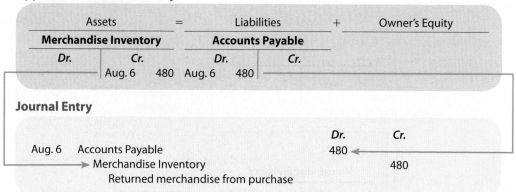

Journal Entry

Comment Note that under the perpetual inventory method, the Purchase Returns and Allowances account is not used and does not appear as a separate item on a merchandising company income statement.

Payments on Account

Transaction 3 On August 10, Kawar paid amount in full due for the purchase of August 3, part of which was returned on August 6, $4,410.

Analysis The journal entry to record the payment for the net amount due of $4,410 ($4,890 − $480)

▼ *decreases* the *Accounts Payable* account

▼ *decreases* the *Cash* account

Application of Double Entry

Journal Entry

		Dr.	Cr.
Aug. 10	Accounts Payable	4,410	
	Cash		4,410
	Made payment on account		

Comment Kawar pays the purchase price less the price of merchandise returned. After the payment, the balance of accounts payable for the purchase recorded on August 3 is zero.

Sales of Merchandise

Exhibit 6 shows how transactions involving sales of merchandise are recorded under the perpetual inventory system. These transactions involve several accounts, including Cash, Accounts Receivable, Merchandise Inventory, Sales Returns and Allowances, and Cost of Goods Sold. The following sections present a summary of the entries made for sales of merchandise.

Exhibit 6
Recording Sales Transactions Under the Perpetual Inventory System

Sales on Credit

Transaction 4 On August 7, Kawar sold merchandise on credit, terms n/30, FOB shipping point, $1,200. The cost of the merchandise was $720.

Analysis Under the perpetual inventory system, sales always require two entries, as shown in Exhibit 6. First, the sale is recorded, which

▲ *increases* the *Accounts Receivable* account

▲ *increases* the *Sales* account

Second, Cost of Goods Sold is updated by a transfer from Merchandise Inventory, which

▲ *increases* the *Cost of Goods Sold* account

▼ *decreases* the *Merchandise Inventory* account

Application of Double Entry

Application of Double Entry

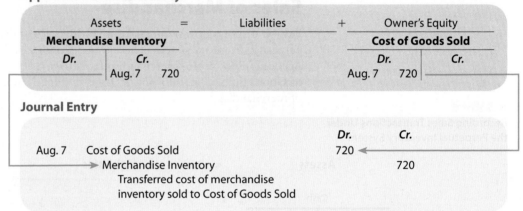

Comment In the case of cash sales, Cash is debited for the amount of the sale. If the seller pays for the shipping, it should be *recognized* as a debit to Delivery Expense.

Sales Returns and Allowances

Transaction 5 On August 9, Kawar accepted, for full credit, a return of part of merchandise sold on August 7, and returned it to merchandise inventory, $300. The cost of the merchandise was $180.

Analysis Under the perpetual inventory system, when a seller allows the buyer to return all or part of a sale or gives an allowance, two journal entries are necessary. First, the original sale is reversed using a contra-revenue account, which

▲ *increases* the *Sales Returns and Allowances* account

▼ *decreases* the *Accounts Receivable* account

The **Sales Returns and Allowances account** gives management a readily available measure of unsatisfactory products and dissatisfied customers. This account is a contra-revenue account with a normal debit balance, and it is deducted from sales on the income statement.

Second, the cost of the merchandise must also be transferred from the Cost of Goods Sold account back into the Merchandise Inventory account, which

▲ *increases* the *Merchandise Inventory* account

▼ *decreases* the *Cost of Goods Sold* account

STUDY NOTE: *Because the Sales account is established with a credit, its contra account, Sales Returns and Allowances, is established with a debit.*

Application of Double Entry

Journal Entry

		Dr.	Cr.
Aug. 9	Sales Returns and Allowances	300	
	Accounts Receivable		300
	Accepted returns of merchandise		

Application of Double Entry

Journal Entry

		Dr.	Cr.
Aug. 9	Merchandise Inventory	180	
	Cost of Goods Sold		180
	Transferred cost of merchandise returned		
	to Merchandise Inventory		

Comment If the company makes an allowance instead of accepting a return, or if the merchandise cannot be returned to inventory and resold, this second entry transferring into Merchandise Inventory and reducing Cost of Goods Sold is not made.

Receipts on Account

Transaction 6 On September 5, Kawar collected in full for sale of merchandise on August 7, less the return on August 9, $900.

Analysis The journal entry to record the collection for the net amount due of $900 ($1,200 − $300)

▲ *increases* the *Cash* account

▼ *decreases* the *Accounts Receivable* account

Application of Double Entry

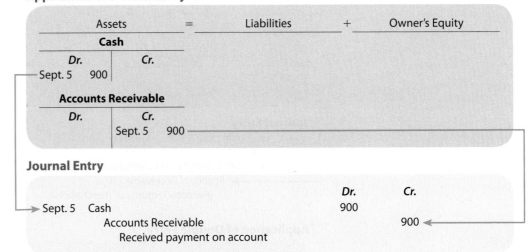

Assets	=	Liabilities	+	Owner's Equity

Cash

Dr.	Cr.
Sept. 5 900	

Accounts Receivable

Dr.	Cr.
	Sept. 5 900

Journal Entry

	Dr.	Cr.
Sept. 5 Cash	900	
Accounts Receivable		900
Received payment on account		

Comment After the payment on the account, the balance in accounts receivable for the August 7 transaction is zero.

Business Perspective
How Are Web Sales Doing?

In spite of the demise of many Internet retailers, merchandise sales over the Internet continue to thrive. U.S. Internet sales are expected to reach almost $300 billion in 2014.[3] The companies that have been most successful in using the Internet are established mail-order retailers like **Lands' End** and **L.L. Bean**. Other retailers have also used the Internet to enhance their operations. For example, **Office Depot**, which focuses primarily on business-to-business Internet sales, has set up customized webpages for tens of thousands of corporate clients. These webpages allow customers to make online purchases and check store inventories. Although Internet transactions are recorded in the same way as on-site transactions, the technology adds a level of complexity to the transactions.

APPLY IT! ▶

For each lettered transaction that follows, indicate which numbered accounts are debited or credited by placing the account numbers in the appropriate columns, assuming the use of a perpetual inventory system. (*Note*: Some may require more than one transaction.)

1. Cash
2. Accounts Receivable
3. Merchandise Inventory
4. Accounts Payable

5. Sales
6. Sales Returns and Allowances
7. Cost of Goods Sold

	Account Debited	Account Credited
a. Purchase on credit	——	——
b. Purchase return for credit	——	——
c. Purchase for cash	——	——
d. Sale on credit	——	——
e. Sale for cash	——	——
f. Sales return for credit	——	——
g. Payment on account	——	——
h. Receipt on account	——	——

SOLUTION

	Account Debited	Account Credited
a. Purchase on credit	3	4
b. Purchase return for credit	4	3
c. Purchase for cash	3	1
d. Sale on credit	2, 7	3, 5
e. Sale for cash	1, 7	3, 5
f. Sales return for credit	3, 6	2, 7
g. Payment on account	4	1
h. Receipt on account	1	2

TRY IT! SE6, E6A, E8A, E9A, E10A, E6B, E8B, E9B, E10B

LO5 Periodic Inventory System

To illustrate merchandising transactions under the periodic inventory system, we will continue with the Kawar Motor Company example. Kawar's income statement appears in Exhibit 7. A major feature of this statement is the computation of cost of goods sold. The cost of goods sold must be computed on the income statement because it is not updated for purchases, sales, and other transactions during the accounting period, as it is under the perpetual inventory system.

Exhibit 7
Income Statement Under the Periodic Inventory System

STUDY NOTE: *Most published financial statements are condensed, eliminating the detail shown here under cost of goods sold.*

Kawar Motor Company			
Income Statement			
For the Year Ended December 31, 2014			
Net sales			$957,300
Cost of goods sold:			
Merchandise inventory, December 31, 2013		$211,200	
Purchases	$505,600		
Less purchases returns and allowances	31,104		
Net purchases	$474,496		
Freight-in	32,944		
Net cost of purchases		507,440	
Cost of goods available for sale		$718,640	
Less merchandise inventory, December 31, 2014		193,200	
Cost of goods sold			525,440
Gross margin			$431,860
Operating expenses			313,936
Net income			$117,924

© Cengage Learning 2014

It is important to distinguish between the cost of goods available for sale and the cost of goods sold. The **cost of goods available for sale** is the total cost of merchandise that *could* be sold in the accounting period. The *cost of goods sold* is the cost of merchandise *actually* sold. The difference between the two numbers is the amount *not* sold, or the ending merchandise inventory. The cost of goods available for sale is the sum of the following two factors.

- The amount of merchandise on hand at the beginning of the period.
- The net cost of purchases during the period. (**Net cost of purchases** consist of total purchases plus freight-in less any deductions such as purchases returns and allowances and discounts from suppliers for early payment.)

In Exhibit 7, Kawar has cost of goods available for sale of $718,640 ($211,200 + $507,440). The ending inventory of $193,200 is deducted from this figure to determine the cost of goods sold of $525,440 ($718,640 − $193,200). Exhibit 8 illustrates these relationships.

Exhibit 8
The Components of Cost of Goods Sold

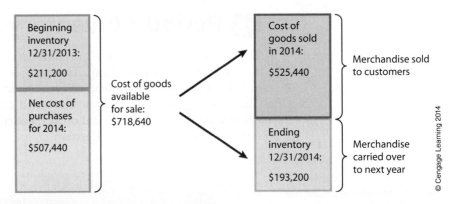

Purchases of Merchandise

Exhibit 9 shows how purchases of merchandise are recorded under the periodic inventory system. In the perpetual inventory system, the Merchandise Inventory account is adjusted each time a purchase, a sale, or another inventory transaction occurs. In the periodic inventory system, the Merchandise Inventory account stays at its beginning balance until the physical inventory is recorded at the end of the period. The periodic system uses a Purchases account to accumulate purchases and a Purchases Returns and Allowances account to accumulate returns of and allowances on purchases.

STUDY NOTE: *Purchases and Purchases Returns and Allowances accounts are used only in a periodic inventory system.*

Exhibit 9
Recording Purchase Transactions Under the Periodic Inventory System

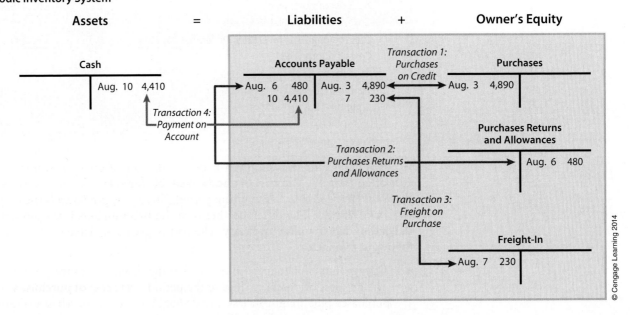

The examples that follow show how Kawar Motor Company would record purchase transactions under the periodic inventory system.

Purchases on Credit

Transaction 1 On August 3, Kawar received merchandise purchased on credit, invoice dated August 1, terms n/10, $4,890.

Analysis Under the periodic inventory system, the cost of merchandise is recorded in the **Purchases account** at the time of purchase. The Purchases account does not indicate whether merchandise has been sold or is still on hand. The journal entry to record purchases made by a company

▲ *increases* the *Purchases* account

▲ *increases* the *Accounts Payable* account

Application of Double Entry

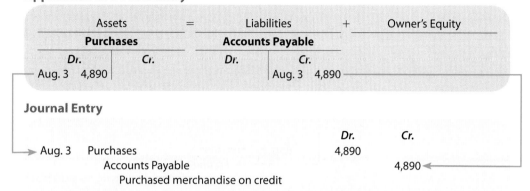

Journal Entry

		Dr.	Cr.
Aug. 3	Purchases	4,890	
	Accounts Payable		4,890
	Purchased merchandise on credit		

Comment Under the periodic inventory system, purchased merchandise is temporarily *classified* as Purchases. Its sole purpose is to accumulate the total cost of merchandise purchased for resale during a period. (Purchases of other assets, such as equipment, are recorded and *classified* in the appropriate asset account, not in the Purchases account.)

Purchases Returns and Allowances

Transaction 2 On August 6, Kawar returned part of merchandise received on August 3 for credit, $480.

Analysis Purchases Returns and Allowances is a contra-purchases account with a normal credit balance, and it is deducted from purchases on the income statement to arrive at net purchases, which

▼ *decreases* the *Accounts Payable* account

▲ *increases* the *Purchases Returns and Allowances* account

Application of Double Entry

Journal Entry

		Dr.	Cr.
Aug. 6	Accounts Payable	480	
	Purchases Returns and Allowances		480
	Returned merchandise from purchase		

STUDY NOTE: Because debits establish the Purchases account, credits create its contra account, Purchases Returns and Allowances.

Comment The **Purchases Returns and Allowances account** is used in a periodic inventory system.

Freight-In

Transaction 3 On August 7, Kawar received a bill for freight costs of the purchases on August 3, $230.

Analysis The journal entry to record freight costs on purchases

▲ *increases* the *Freight-In* account

▲ *increases* the *Accounts Payable* account

Application of Double Entry

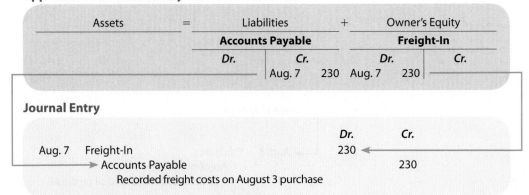

Journal Entry

		Dr.	Cr.
Aug. 7	Freight-In	230	
	Accounts Payable		230
	Recorded freight costs on August 3 purchase		

Comment Freight-in is added on the income statement to net purchases to arrive at the net cost of purchases under the periodic method.

Payments on Account

Transaction 4 On August 10, Kawar paid amount in full due for the purchase of August 3, part of which was returned on August 6, $4,410.

Analysis The journal entry to record payment for the net amount due of $4,410 ($4,890 – $480)

▼ *decreases* the *Accounts Payable* account

▼ *decreases* the *Cash* account

Application of Double Entry

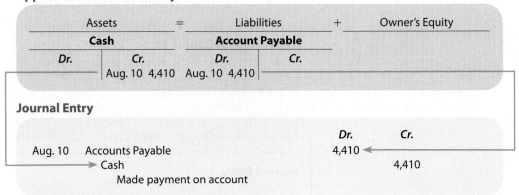

Journal Entry

		Dr.	Cr.
Aug. 10	Accounts Payable	4,410	
	Cash		4,410
	Made payment on account		

Comment Kawar pays the purchase price less the price of merchandise returned. After the payment, the balance of accounts payable with the supplier is zero.

Sales of Merchandise

Exhibit 10 shows how transactions involving sales of merchandise are recorded under the periodic inventory system.

Exhibit 10
Recording Sales Transactions Under the Periodic Inventory System

Sales on Credit

Transaction 5 On August 7, Kawar sold merchandise on credit, terms n/30, FOB destination, $1,200. The cost of the merchandise was $720.

Analysis As shown in Exhibit 10, under the periodic inventory system, credit sales require only one entry, which

▲ *increases* the *Accounts Receivable* account

▲ *increases* the *Sales* account

Application of Double Entry

Journal Entry

		Dr.	Cr.
Aug. 7	Account Receivable	1,200	
	Sales		1,200
	Sold merchandise on credit		

Comment In the case of cash sales, Cash is debited for the amount of the sale. If the seller pays for the shipping, the amount should be debited to Delivery Expense.

Sales Returns and Allowances

Transaction 6 On August 9, Kawar accepted return of part of merchandise sold on August 7 for full credit and returned it to merchandise inventory, $300. The cost of the merchandise was $180.

Analysis Under the periodic inventory system, when a seller allows the buyer to return all or part of a sale or gives an allowance, only one journal entry is needed, which

▲ *increases* the *Sales Returns and Allowances* account

▼ *decreases* the *Accounts Receivable* account

Application of Double Entry

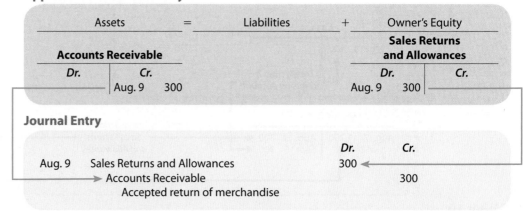

Comment The Sales Returns and Allowances account is a contra-revenue account with a normal debit balance and is deducted from sales on the income statement.

Receipts on Account

Transaction 7 On September 5, Kawar collected in full for sale of merchandise on August 7, less the return on August 9, $900.

Analysis The journal entry to record collection for the net amount due of $900 ($1,200 – $300)

▲ *increases* the *Cash* account

▼ *decreases* the *Accounts Receivable* account

Application of Double Entry

Comment After the payment on the account, the balance in accounts receivable for that transaction is zero.

Business Perspective
Are Sales Returns Worth Accounting For?

Some industries routinely have a high percentage of sales returns. More than 6 percent of all nonfood items sold in stores are eventually returned to vendors. This amounts to over $100 billion a year, or more than the gross national product of two-thirds of the world's nations.[4] Book publishers like **Simon & Schuster** often have returns as high as 30 to 50 percent because to gain the attention of potential buyers, they must distribute large numbers of copies to many outlets. Magazine publishers like **AOL Time Warner** expect to sell no more than 35 to 38 percent of the magazines they send to newsstands and other outlets.[5] In all these businesses, it pays management to scrutinize the Sales Returns and Allowances account for ways to reduce returns and increase profitability.

Merchandising Transactions and the Financial Statements

Merchandising transactions can affect all the financial statements as shown in Exhibit 11.

Exhibit 11
Merchandising Income Statement Groups Accounts in Useful Categories

© Cengage Learning 2014

Income Statement
For the Year Ended December 31, 2014

Net sales
Cost of goods sold
   Gross margin
Operating expenses
   Income from operations
Other revenues and expenses
   Net income

APPLY IT!

For each lettered transaction that follows, indicate which numbered accounts are debited or credited by placing the account numbers in the appropriate columns, assuming the use of a periodic inventory system.

1. Cash
2. Accounts Receivable
3. Merchandise Inventory
4. Accounts Payable
5. Sales
6. Sales Returns and Allowances
7. Purchases
8. Purchases Returns and Allowances

	Account Debited	Account Credited
a. Purchase on credit	___	___
b. Purchase return for credit	___	___
c. Purchase for cash	___	___
d. Sale on credit	___	___
e. Sale for cash	___	___
f. Sales return for credit	___	___
g. Payment on account	___	___
h. Receipt on account	___	___

SOLUTION

	Account Debited	Account Credited
a. Purchase on credit	7	4
b. Purchase return for credit	4	8
c. Purchase for cash	7	1
d. Sale on credit	2	5
e. Sale for cash	1	5
f. Sales return for credit	6	2
g. Payment on account	4	1
h. Receipt on account	1	2

TRY IT! SE7, SE8, SE9, E7A, E11A, E12A, E13A, E14A, E7B, E11B, E12B, E13B, E14B

SECTION 3 ▶ BUSINESS APPLICATIONS

RELEVANT LEARNING OBJECTIVE

LO 6 Explain the role of the operating cycle and the effect of foreign business transactions in evaluating the liquidity of a merchandising company.

LO 6 The Operating Cycle and Foreign Business Transactions

Maintaining adequate liquidity in the operating cycle is important to managing a merchandising company.

CASH FLOW ## Operating Cycle

Merchandising businesses engage in a series of transactions to buy, sell, and collect for merchandise inventory called the *operating cycle*. Exhibit 12 shows these transactions. Some companies buy merchandise for cash and sell it for cash, but these companies are usually small companies, such as a produce market or a hot dog stand. Most companies buy merchandise on credit and sell it on credit, thereby engaging in the following four transactions:

1. Purchase of merchandise inventory for cash or on credit
2. Sales of merchandise inventory for cash or on credit
3. Collection of cash from credit sales
4. Payment for purchases made on credit

The first three transactions represent the time it takes to purchase inventory, sell it, and collect for it. Merchandisers must be able to do without the cash for this period of time either by relying on cash flows from other sources within the company or by borrowing. If they lack the cash to pay bills when they come due, they can be forced out of business. Thus, managing cash flow is a critical concern.

Exhibit 12
Cash Flows in the Operating Cycle

© Cengage Learning 2014

The suppliers that sell the company the merchandise usually also sell on credit, thus helping alleviate the cash flow problem by providing financing for a period of time before they require payment (transaction 4). However, this period is rarely as long as the operating cycle. The period between the time the supplier must be paid and the end of the operating cycle is called the *financing period* (or *cash gap*).

The **financing period**, illustrated in Exhibit 13, is the amount of time from the purchase of inventory until it is sold and payment is collected, less the amount of time

Exhibit 13
The Financing Period

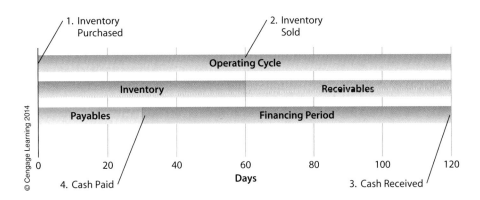

© Cengage Learning 2014

STUDY NOTE: *A company must provide financing for the average days' inventory plus the average number of days to collect credit sales less the average number of days it is allowed to pay its suppliers.*

creditors give the company to pay for the inventory. Thus, if it takes 60 days to sell the inventory, 60 days to collect for the sale, and creditors' payment terms are 30 days, the financing period is 90 days [(60 + 60) – 30]. During the financing period, the company will be without cash from this series of transactions and will need either to have funds available internally or to borrow from a bank.

The way in which a merchandising company manages its inventories, receivables, and payables will affect its financing period. For example, compare **Costco**'s financing period with that of a traditional discount store chain, **Target Corporation**:

	Target	Costco	Difference
Days' inventory	58 days	29 days	(29) days
Days' receivables	35	4	(31)
Less days' payable	(60)	(31)	29
Financing period	33 days	2 days	(31) days

Costco has an advantage over Target because it sells inventory and collects receivables much faster. Its very short financing period is one of the reasons Costco can charge such low prices.[6]

By reducing its financing period, a company can improve its cash flow. Many merchandisers, including Costco, do this by selling as much as possible for cash. Cash sales include sales made on bank *credit cards,* such as Visa or MasterCard, and on *debit cards,* which draw directly on the purchaser's bank account. They are considered cash sales because funds from them are available to the merchandiser immediately. Small retail stores may have mostly cash sales and very few credit sales, whereas large wholesale concerns may have almost all credit sales.

Foreign Business Transactions

Most large merchandising and manufacturing firms and even many small ones transact some of their business overseas. For example, a U.S. manufacturer may expand by selling its product to foreign customers, or it may lower its product cost by buying a less expensive part from a source in another country. Such sales and purchase transactions may take place in Japanese yen, British pounds, or some other foreign currency.

While all transactions involve money measures, an international transaction is measured in two different currencies, and one currency has to be translated into another by using an *exchange rate.* As noted earlier, the values of other currencies in relation to the dollar rise and fall daily according to supply and demand. Thus, if there is a delay between the date of sale or purchase and the date of payment, the amount of cash involved in an international transaction may differ from the originally agreed-upon amount.

If the billing of an international sale and the payment for it are both in the domestic currency, no accounting problem arises. For example, if a U.S. maker of precision tools sells $160,000 worth of its products to a British company and bills the British company in dollars, the U.S. company will receive $160,000 when it collects payment. However, if the U.S. company bills the British company in pounds and accepts payment in pounds, it will incur an **exchange gain or loss** if the exchange rate between dollars and pounds changes between the date of sale and the date of payment, as shown in the following examples.

- **Sale in foreign currency**: Assume that a U.S. company billed a sale of $200,000 at £100,000, reflecting an exchange rate of 2.00 (that is, $2.00 per pound) on the sale date. Now assume that by the date of payment, the exchange rate has fallen to 1.90. When the U.S. company receives its £100,000, it will be worth only $190,000 (£100,000 × $1.90 = $190,000). It will have incurred an exchange loss of $10,000 because it agreed to accept a fixed number of British pounds in payment for its products, and the value of each pound dropped before the payment was made. Had the value of the pound in relation to the dollar increased, the company would have made an exchange gain.

- **Purchase in foreign currency**: The same logic applies to purchases as to sales. Assume that a U.S company purchases products from a British company for $200,000. If the payment is to be made in U.S. dollars, no accounting problem arises. However, if the British company expects to be paid in pounds, the U.S. company will have an exchange gain of $10,000 because it agreed to pay a fixed £100,000, and between the dates of purchase and payment, the exchange value of the pound decreased from $2.00 to $1.90. To make the £100,000 payment, the U.S. company has to expend only $190,000.

Exchange gains and losses are reported on the income statement. Because of their bearing on financial performance, they are of interest to managers and investors.

APPLY IT! ▶

Rola Company's management made the following decisions. Indicate whether each decision pertains primarily to (a) cash flow management, (b) choice of inventory system, or (c) foreign transactions.

1. Decided to decrease the credit terms offered to customers from 30 days to 20 days to speed up collection of accounts.
2. Decided to purchase goods made by a supplier in India.
3. Decided that sales would increase if salespeople knew how much inventory was on hand at any one time.
4. Decided to try to negotiate a longer time to pay suppliers than had been previously granted.

SOLUTION

1. a; 2. c; 3. b; 4. a

TRY IT! SE10, SE11, E1A, E15A, E1B, E15B

TriLevel Problem

Mink Company

The beginning of this chapter focused on Mink Company, a merchandiser. Complete the following requirements in order to answer the questions posed at the beginning of the chapter.

Section 1: Concepts
How do faithful representation and classification apply to merchandise operations?

Section 2: Accounting Applications
How can merchandising transactions be recorded to reflect the company's performance?

To answer this question, prepare journal entries to record the transactions that follow, assuming that Mink uses (1) the perpetual inventory system and (2) the periodic inventory system.

July	1	Sold merchandise to Eric Ortega on credit, terms n/30, FOB shipping point, $2,100 (cost, $1,260).
	2	Purchased merchandise on credit from Debra Company, terms n/30, FOB shipping point, $3,800.
	2	Paid Custom Freight $290 for freight charges on merchandise received.
	9	Purchased merchandise on credit from RBT Company, terms n/30, FOB shipping point, $3,600, including $200 freight costs paid by RBT Company.
	11	Accepted from Eric Ortega a return of merchandise, which was returned to inventory, $300 (cost, $180).
	14	Returned for credit $600 of merchandise purchased on July 2.
	16	Sold merchandise for cash, $1,000 (cost, $600).
	22	Paid Debra Company for purchase of July 2 less return on July 14.
	23	Received full payment from Eric Ortega for his July 1 purchase, less return on July 11.

Section 3: Business Applications
How can Mink manage its operating cycle so that it has adequate cash to maintain liquidity?

SOLUTION

Section 1: Concepts
Classification of items on the merchandising company financial statements is important because how the amount of goods available for sale is split between ending inventory and cost of goods sold impacts both the income statement and the balance sheet. Thus, a merchandising company needs to classify its accounts properly so that the statements *faithfully represent* the operations of the company. In order to faithfully represent accounting for merchandising inventories, a company can choose between the perpetual inventory system and the periodic inventory system. The perpetual inventory system is a system in which continuous records are kept of the quantity and the cost of individual items as they are bought and sold. The periodic inventory system is a system in which continuous records are not kept but the inventory not yet sold is counted periodically.

Section 2: Accounting Applications

(1) and (2). (*Note:* Accounts that differ under the two systems are in bold type.)

	A	B	C	D	E	F	G	H	I	J	K	L	M	N
1						**1. Perpetual Inventory System**						**2. Periodic Inventory System**		
2	July	1				Accounts Receivable	2,100					Accounts Receivable	2,100	
3						Sales		2,100				Sales		2,100
4						Sold merchandise on						Sold merchandise on		
5						account to Eric Ortega,						account to Eric Ortega,		
6						terms n/30, FOB shipping						terms n/30, FOB shipping		
7						point						point		
8		1				**Cost of Goods Sold**	1,260							
9						**Merchandise Inventory**		1,260						
10						Transferred cost of								
11						merchandise sold to Cost								
12						of Goods Sold account								
13		2				**Merchandise Inventory**	3,800					**Purchases**	3,800	
14						Accounts Payable		3,800				Accounts Payable		3,800
15						Purchased merchandise						Purchased merchandise		
16						on account from Debra						on account from Debra		
17						Company, terms n/30, FOB						Company, terms n/30, FOB		
18						shipping point						shipping point		
19		2				Freight-In	290					Freight-In	290	
20						Cash		290				Cash		290
21						Paid freight on July 2						Paid freight on July 2		
22						purchase						purchase		
23		9				**Merchandise Inventory**	3,400					**Purchases**	3,400	
24						Freight-In	200					Freight-In	200	
25						Accounts Payable		3,600				Accounts Payable		3,600
26						Purchased merchandise on						Purchased merchandise on		
27						account from RBT Company,						account from RBT Company,		
28						terms n/30, FOB shipping						terms n/30, FOB shipping		
29						point, freight paid by supplier						point, freight paid by supplier		
30		11				Sales Returns and Allowances	300					Sales Returns and Allowances	300	
31						Accounts Receivable		300				Accounts Receivable		300
32						Accepted return of						Accepted return of		
33						merchandise from Eric						merchandise from Eric		
34						Ortega						Ortega		

	A	B	C	D	E	F	G	H	I	J	K	L	M	N
1						**1. Perpetual Inventory System**						**2. Periodic Inventory System**		
2	July	11				**Merchandise Inventory**	180							
3						**Cost of Goods Sold**		180						
4						Transferred cost of								
5						merchandise returned to								
6						Merchandise Inventory								
7						account								
8		14				Accounts Payable	600					Accounts Payable	600	
9						**Merchandise Inventory**		600				**Purchases Returns and Allowances**		600
10						Returned portion of						Returned portion of		
11						merchandise purchased						merchandise purchased		
12						from Debra Company						from Debra Company		
13		16				Cash	1,000					Cash	1,000	
14						Sales		1,000				Sales		1,000
15						Sold merchandise for cash						Sold merchandise for cash		
16		16				**Cost of Goods Sold**	600							
17						**Merchandise Inventory**		600						
18						Transferred cost of								
19						merchandise sold to Cost of								
20						Goods Sold account								
21		22				Accounts Payable	3,200					Accounts Payable	3,200	
22						Cash		3,200				Cash		3,200
23						Made payment on account to						Made payment on account to		
24						Debra Company						Debra Company		
25						$3,800 − $600 = $3,200						$3,800 − $600 = $3,200		
26		23				Cash	1,800					Cash	1,800	
27						Accounts Receivable		1,800				Accounts Receivable		1,800
28						Received payment on						Received payment on		
29						account from Eric Ortega						account from Eric Ortega		
30						$2,100 − $300 = $1,800						$2,100 − $300 = $1,800		

Section 3: Business Applications

Mink engages in all parts of the merchandising cycle. It buys goods on credit, which gives it time to carry the goods in inventory until customers buy them. It sells the goods both for cash and on credit. When it sells on credit, it must wait to collect payment. Thus, the company must arrange for short-term financing to ensure that it has enough cash on hand to maintain liquidity.

Chapter Review

Define *merchandising accounting*, and differentiate perpetual from periodic inventory systems. **LO 1**

Merchandising companies differ from service companies in that they earn income by buying and selling goods. The buying and selling of goods adds to the complexity of the business and requires choosing whether to use the perpetual or the periodic inventory system. Using these systems and use of the multistep income statement, properly classified, results in faithful representation of the company's operations.

Describe the features of multistep and single-step classified income statements. **LO 2**

Classified income statements for external reporting can be in multistep or single-step form. The multistep form arrives at net income through a series of steps, usually with a separate section for other revenues and expenses; the single-step form arrives at net income in a single step.

Describe the terms of sale related to merchandising transactions. **LO 3**

A trade discount is a reduction from the list or catalogue price of a product. A sales discount is a discount given for early payment of a sale on credit. Terms of 2/10, n/30 mean that the buyer can take a 2 percent discount if the invoice is paid within 10 days of the invoice date. Otherwise, the buyer is obligated to pay the full amount in 30 days. Discounts on sales are recorded in the Sales Discounts account, and discounts on purchases are recorded in the Purchases Discounts account. FOB shipping point means that the buyer bears the cost of transportation and that title to the goods passes to the buyer at the shipping origin. FOB destination means that the seller bears the cost of transportation and that title does not pass to the buyer until the goods reach their destination. Debit and credit card sales are considered cash sales and involve a fee paid by the seller for convenience.

Prepare an income statement, and record merchandising transactions under the perpetual inventory system. **LO 4**

Under the perpetual inventory system, the Merchandise Inventory account is continuously adjusted by entering purchases, sales, and other inventory transactions as they occur. Purchases increase the Merchandise Inventory account, and purchases returns decrease it. As goods are sold, their cost is transferred from the Merchandise Inventory account to the Cost of Goods Sold account.

Prepare an income statement, and record merchandising transactions under the periodic inventory system. **LO 5**

When the periodic inventory system is used, the cost of goods sold section of the income statement must include the following elements.

Purchases − Purchases Returns and Allowances + Freight-In = Net Cost of Purchases

Beginning Merchandise Inventory + Net Cost of Purchases = Cost of Goods Available for Sale

Cost of Goods Available for Sale − Ending Merchandise Inventory = Cost of Goods Sold

Under the periodic inventory system, the Merchandise Inventory account stays at the beginning level until the physical inventory is recorded at the end of the period. A Purchases account is used to accumulate purchases of merchandise during the period, and a Purchases Returns and Allowances account is used to accumulate returns of purchases and allowances on purchases.

Explain the role of the operating cycle and foreign business transactions in evaluating the liquidity of a merchandising company. **LO 6**

The series of transactions (the operating cycle) of a merchandising company requires careful cash flow management. Also, if a company has international transactions, it must deal with changing exchange rates.

Key Terms

cost of goods available for
   sale 221 (LO5)
cost of goods sold 209 (LO2)
delivery expense 214 (LO3)
exchange gain or loss 230 (LO6)
financing period 228 (LO6)
FOB destination 213 (LO3)
FOB shipping point 213 (LO3)
freight-in 213 (LO3)
general and administrative
   expenses 210 (LO2)
gross margin 209 (LO2)
gross sales 209 (LO2)
income from operations 211 (LO2)
manufacturing company 208 (LO2)
merchandise inventory 206 (LO1)

merchandising company 208 (LO1)
multistep income
   statement 208 (LO2)
net cost of purchases 221 (LO5)
net income 211 (LO2)
net sales 209 (LO2)
operating cycle 206 (LO1)
operating expenses 210 (LO2)
other revenues and
   expenses 211 (LO2)
percentage of gross
   margin 210 (LO2)
periodic inventory system 206 (LO1)
perpetual inventory
   system 206 (LO1)
physical inventory 206 (LO1)

purchase discounts 213 (LO3)
Purchases account 222 (LO5)
Purchases Returns and Allowances
   account 223 (LO5)
sales discount 212 (LO3)
sales returns and
   allowances 209 (LO2)
Sales Returns and Allowances
   account 218 (LO4)
selling expenses 210 (LO2)
single-step income
   statement 211 (LO2)
trade discount 212 (LO3)

Chapter Assignments

DISCUSSION QUESTIONS

LO 1   **DQ1. CONCEPT** ▶ In what ways does having merchandise inventory impact faithful representation and classification?

LO 1   **DQ2.** Why is a physical inventory needed under both the periodic and perpetual inventory systems?

LO 2   **DQ3.** Which is the better measure of a company's performance—income from operations or net income?

LO 3   **DQ4.** Assume a large shipment of uninsured merchandise to your company is destroyed when the delivery truck has an accident and burns. Would you want the terms to be FOB shipping point or FOB destination?

LO 4   **DQ5.** Under the perpetual inventory system, the Merchandise Inventory account is constantly updated. What would cause it to have the wrong balance?

LO 6   **DQ6. BUSINESS APPLICATION** ▶ Can a company have a "negative" financing period?

LO 6   **DQ7. BUSINESS APPLICATION** ▶ Suppose you sold goods to a company in Europe at a time when the exchange rate for the dollar was declining in relation to the euro. Would you want the European company to pay you in dollars or euros?

SHORT EXERCISES

LO 1   **Characteristics of Inventory Systems**

SE1. Indicate whether each of the statements that follow is more applicable to a perpetual inventory system, periodic inventory system, or both.

1. Inventory figure is not accurate until the balance sheet date.
2. Requires a physical count of inventory at end of period.

(Continued)

3. No detailed records of the inventory are maintained during the accounting period.
4. Continuous records are kept of the quantity of inventory on hand.
5. Cost of Goods Sold is calculated only at the end of the accounting period.
6. Effective system for managing inventory and thus avoiding running out of stock.
7. Is more costly to maintain but may lead to increased sales.

LO 2 **Single-Step Income Statement**

SE2. Using the following accounts, prepare a single-step income statement at year end, May 31, 2014: Cost of Goods Sold, $1,680; General Expenses, $900; Interest Expense, $420; Interest Income, $180; Net Sales, $4,800; Selling Expenses, $1,110.

LO 2 **Multistep Income Statement**

SE3. Using the accounts presented in **SE2**, prepare a multistep income statement.

LO 3 **Terms of Sale**

SE4. A dealer buys tooling machines from a manufacturer and resells them to its customers.

a. The manufacturer sets a list or catalogue price of $6,000 for a machine. The manufacturer offers its dealers a 20 percent trade discount.
b. The manufacturer sells the machine under terms of FOB shipping point. The cost of shipping is $350.
c. The manufacturer offers a sales discount of 2/10, n/30. The sales discount does not apply to shipping costs.

What is the net cost of the machine to the dealer, assuming it is paid for within 10 days of purchase?

LO 3 **Sales and Sales Returns**

SE5. On April 15, Sanborn Company sold merchandise to Barr Company for $3,000 on terms of 2/10, n/30. Assume a return of merchandise on April 20 of $600 and collection in full on April 25. What is the amount collected by Sanborn on April 25?

LO 4 **Purchases of Merchandise: Perpetual Inventory System**

SE6. Record each of the following transactions using T accounts, assuming the perpetual inventory system is used:

Aug. 2   Purchased merchandise on credit from Vera Company, invoice dated August 1, terms n/10, FOB shipping point, $1,150.
      3   Received bill from Strauss Shipping Company for transportation costs on August 2 shipment, invoice dated August 1, terms n/30, $105.
      7   Returned damaged merchandise received from Vera on August 2 for credit, $180.
      10 Paid in full the amount due to Vera for the purchase of August 2, part of which was returned on August 7.

LO 5 **Purchases of Merchandise: Periodic Inventory System**

SE7. Record the transactions in **SE6** using T accounts, assuming the periodic inventory system is used.

LO 5 **Cost of Goods Sold: Periodic Inventory System**

SE8. Using the data that follows and assuming cost of goods sold is $273,700, prepare the cost of goods sold section of a merchandising income statement (periodic inventory system). Include the amount of purchases for the month of October.

Freight-in	$13,800
Merchandise inventory, Sept. 30, 2014	37,950
Merchandise inventory, Oct. 31, 2014	50,600
Purchases	?
Purchases returns and allowances	10,350

LO **5**   **Sales of Merchandise: Periodic Inventory System**

SE9. Record the following transactions using T accounts, assuming the periodic inventory system is used:

Aug.   4   Sold merchandise on credit to Rock Company, terms n/30, FOB destination, $2,520.

      5   Paid transportation costs for sale of August 4, $231.

      9   Part of the merchandise sold on August 4 was accepted back from Rock for full credit and returned to merchandise inventory, $735.

Sept.   3   Collected in full the amount due from Rock for merchandise sold on August 4, less the return on August 9.

LO **6**   **Operating Cycle**

SE10. BUSINESS APPLICATION ▶ On average, Obras Company holds its inventory 40 days before it is sold, waits 25 days for customers' payments, and takes 33 days to pay suppliers. For how many days must it provide financing in its operating cycle?

LO **1, 6**   **Identification of Management Issues**

SE11. BUSINESS APPLICATION ▶ Identify each of the following decisions as most directly related to (a) cash flow management, (b) choice of inventory system, or (c) foreign merchandising transactions:

1. Determination of the amount of time from the purchase of inventory until it is sold and the amount due is collected.
2. Determination of the effects of changes in exchange rates.
3. Determination of policies governing sales of merchandise on credit.
4. Determination of whether to use the periodic or the perpetual inventory system.

EXERCISES: SET A

LO **1, 2**   **Concept Identification**

E1A. CONCEPT ▶ Sutton Hills Company's management made the decisions that follow. Indicate which of the decisions relates primarily to (a) classification, (b) merchandising inventory, (c) periodic inventory system, or (d) operating cycle.

1. Decided to purchase and sell goods.
2. Decided to use a form of income statement that would show gross margin separately from operating income.
3. Decided to reduce the credit terms offered to customers from 30 days to 20 days to speed up collection of accounts.
4. Decided that the benefits of keeping track of each item of inventory as it is bought and sold would exceed the costs of such a system.

LO **2**   **Classification of Accounts: Income Statement**

E2A. Using the classification scheme below for a multistep income statement, match each account with the letter of the category in which it belongs.

a. Other revenues and expenses
b. Cost of sales
c. General and administrative expenses
d. Selling expenses
e. Net sales
f. Not on income statement

1. Sales Discounts
2. Cost of Goods Sold
3. Dividend Income
4. Advertising Expense
5. Office Salaries Expense
6. Freight Out Expense
7. Prepaid Insurance
8. Utilities Expense
9. Sales Salaries Expense
10. Rent Expense
11. Depreciation Expense—Delivery Equipment
12. Interest Expense

LO 2   **Preparation of Income Statements**

E3A. A company has the following data: net sales, $405,000; cost of goods sold, $220,000; selling expenses, $90,000; general and administrative expenses, $60,000; interest expense, $4,000; and interest income, $3,000.

1. Prepare a single-step income statement.
2. Prepare a multistep income statement.

LO 2   **Multistep Income Statement**

E4A. ACCOUNTING CONNECTION ▶ A single-step income statement follows. Present the information in a multistep income statement, and indicate what insights can be obtained from the multistep form as opposed to the single-step form.

Nomar Parra Company
Income Statement
For the Year Ended December 31, 2014

Revenues:		
Net sales		$1,197,132
Interest income		5,720
Total revenues		$1,202,852
Costs and expenses:		
Cost of goods sold	$777,080	
Selling expenses	203,740	
General and administrative expenses	100,688	
Interest expense	13,560	
Total costs and expenses		1,095,068
Net income		$ 107,784

LO 3   **Terms of Sale**

E5A. A household appliance dealer buys microwave ovens from a manufacturer and resells them to its customers.

a. The manufacturer sets a list or catalogue price of $1,500 for a microwave. The manufacturer offers its dealers a 30 percent trade discount.
b. The manufacturer sells the machine under terms of FOB destination. The cost of shipping is $150.
c. The manufacturer offers a sales discount of 2/10, n/30. Sales discounts do not apply to shipping costs.

What is the net cost of the microwave to the dealer, assuming it is paid for within 10 days of purchase?

LO 3, 4   **Purchases Involving Discounts: Perpetual Inventory System**

E6A. Linear Company engaged in the following transactions:

July   2   Purchased merchandise on credit from Green Company, terms 2/10, n/30, FOB destination, invoice dated July 1, $2,000.
          6   Returned some merchandise to Green for full credit, $250.
         11   Paid Green for purchase of July 2 less return and discount.
         14   Purchased merchandise on credit from Green, terms 2/10, n/30, FOB destination, invoice dated July 12, $2,250.
         31   Paid amount owed Green for purchase of July 14.

Prepare journal entries and, assuming the perpetual inventory system, determine the total amount paid to Green.

LO 3, 5 **Sales Involving Discounts: Periodic Inventory System**

E7A. Given the following transactions engaged in by Fournier Company, prepare journal entries and, assuming the periodic inventory system, determine the total amount received from Brook Company:

Dec.   1   Sold merchandise on credit to Brook Company, terms 2/10, n/30, FOB shipping point, $500.
       3   Accepted a return from Brook for full credit, $200.
      10   Collected amount due from Brook for the sale, less the return and discount.
      11   Sold merchandise on credit to Brook, terms 2/10, n/30, FOB shipping point, $800.
      31   Collected amount due from Brook for the sale of December 11.

LO 4 **Preparation of the Income Statement: Perpetual Inventory System**

F8A. Selected account balances at December 31, 2014, for Infosys Company follow. Prepare a multistep income statement for the year ended December 31, 2014. Show detail of net sales. The company uses the perpetual inventory system, and Freight-In has not been included in Cost of Goods Sold.

Account Name	Debit	Credit
Sales		$475,000
Sales Returns and Allowances	$ 23,500	
Cost of Goods Sold	280,000	
Freight-In	13,500	
Selling Expenses	43,000	
General and Administrative Expenses	87,000	

LO 4 **Recording Purchases: Perpetual Inventory System**

E9A. The transactions that follow took place under the perpetual inventory system. Record each transaction using T accounts.

a. Purchased merchandise on credit, terms n/30, FOB shipping point, $5,000.
b. Paid freight on the shipment in transaction **a**, $270.
c. Purchased merchandise on credit, terms n/30, FOB destination, $2,800.
d. Purchased merchandise on credit, terms n/30, FOB shipping point, $5,200, which includes freight paid by the supplier of $400.
e. Returned part of the merchandise purchased in transaction **c**, $1,000.
f. Paid the amount owed on the purchase in transaction **a**.
g. Paid the amount owed on the purchase in transaction **d**.
h. Paid the amount owed on the purchase in transaction **c** less the return in **e**.

LO 4 **Recording Sales: Perpetual Inventory System**

E10A. On November 15, TCS Company sold merchandise for $2,600 on terms of n/30 to Quaker Company. On November 20, Quaker returned some of the merchandise for a credit of $600, and on November 25, Quaker paid the balance owed. Use T accounts to record the sale, return, and receipt of cash under the perpetual inventory system for TCS. The cost of the merchandise sold on November 15 was $1,500, and the cost of the merchandise returned to inventory on November 20 was $350.

LO 5 **Preparation of the Income Statement: Periodic Inventory System**

E11A. Using the selected year-end account balances at December 31, 2014, for Proof General Store that follow, prepare a 2014 multistep income statement. Show detail of net sales. The company uses the periodic inventory system. Beginning merchandise inventory was $26,000; ending merchandise inventory is $22,000.

(Continued)

Account Name	Debit	Credit
Sales		$297,000
Sales Returns and Allowances	$ 15,200	
Purchases	114,800	
Purchases Returns and Allowances		4,000
Freight-In	5,600	
Selling Expenses	48,500	
General and Administrative Expenses	37,200	

LO 5   **Merchandising Income Statement: Missing Data, Multiple Years**

E12A. Determine the missing data for each letter in the following three income statements for Fulco Company (in thousands):

	2014	2013	2012
Sales	$ p	$ h	$1,144
Sales returns and allowances	96	76	a
Net sales	q	1,268	b
Merchandise inventory, beginning	r	i	152
Purchases	768	676	c
Purchases returns and allowances	124	j	68
Freight-in	s	116	88
Net cost of purchases	756	k	d
Cost of goods available for sale	888	848	728
Merchandise inventory, ending	156	l	168
Cost of goods sold	t	716	e
Gross margin	568	m	504
Selling expenses	u	312	f
General and administrative expenses	156	n	132
Total operating expenses	520	512	g
Net income	v	o	108

LO 5   **Recording Purchases: Periodic Inventory System**

E13A. Using the data in **E9A**, use T accounts to record each of the transactions under the periodic inventory system.

LO 5   **Recording Sales: Periodic Inventory System**

E14A. Using the relevant data in **E10A**, use T accounts to record each of the transactions under the periodic inventory system.

LO 6   **Foreign Merchandising Transactions**

E15A. BUSINESS APPLICATION ▶ Winter Treats Company purchased a special-purpose machine from Blanco Company, a French firm, on credit for €50,000. At the date of purchase, the exchange rate was $1.00 per euro. On the date of the payment, which was made in euros, the value of the euro was $1.25. Did Winter Treats incur an exchange gain or loss? How much was it?

EXERCISES: SET B

Visit the textbook companion website at www.cengagebrain.com to access Exercise Set B for this chapter.

PROBLEMS

LO **2**

Forms of the Income Statement

✔1: Income from operations 2014: $66,426
✔ 1: Income from operations 2013:
$110,628

P1. Matuska Tools Corporation's income statements follow.

Matuska Tools Corporation
Income Statements
For the Years Ended July 31, 2014 and 2013

	2014	2013
Revenues:		
Net sales	$525,932	$475,264
Interest income	800	700
Total revenues	$526,732	$475,964
Costs and expenses:		
Cost of goods sold	$234,948	$171,850
Selling expenses	161,692	150,700
General and administrative expenses	62,866	42,086
Interest expense	3,600	850
Total costs and expenses	$463,106	$365,486
Net income	$ 63,626	$110,478

REQUIRED

1. Prepare a multistep income statement for 2013 and 2014 showing percentages of net sales for each component (e.g., cost of goods sold divided by net sales). (Round percentages to one decimal place.)

2. **ACCOUNTING CONNECTION** ▶ Did income from operations increase or decrease between 2013 and 2014? Write a short explanation of why this change occurred.

LO **2, 4, 6**

Merchandising Income Statement: Perpetual Inventory System

✔ 1: Net income: $15,435

P2. Selected accounts from Murray's Furniture Store's adjusted trial balance as of June 30, 2014, the end of the fiscal year, follow.

Murray's Furniture Store
Partial Adjusted Trial Balance
June 30, 2014

Sales		162,000
Sales Returns and Allowances	2,000	
Cost of Goods Sold	61,400	
Freight-In	2,300	
Store Salaries Expense	32,625	
Office Salaries Expense	12,875	
Advertising Expense	24,300	
Rent Expense	2,400	
Insurance Expense	1,200	
Utilities Expense	1,560	
Store Supplies Expense	2,880	
Office Supplies Expense	1,175	
Depreciation Expense—Store Equipment	1,050	
Depreciation Expense—Office Equipment	800	

REQUIRED

1. Prepare a multistep income statement for Murray's. Freight-In should be combined with Cost of Goods Sold. Store Salaries Expense, Advertising Expense, Store Supplies Expense, and Depreciation Expense—Store Equipment are selling expenses. The other expenses are general and administrative expenses. The company uses the perpetual inventory system. Show details of net sales and operating expenses.

2. **BUSINESS APPLICATION** ▶ Based on your knowledge at this point in the course, how would you use Murray's income statement to evaluate the company's profitability? What other financial statement should you consider and why?

LO **4**

Merchandising Transactions: Perpetual Inventory System

P3. Fulco Company engaged in the following transactions in March 2014:

Mar. 7   Sold merchandise on credit to James William, terms n/30, FOB shipping point, $3,000 (cost, $1,800).

8   Purchased merchandise on credit from Leverage Company, terms n/30, FOB shipping point, $6,000.

9   Paid Leverage Company for shipping charges on merchandise purchased on March 8, $254.

10   Purchased merchandise on credit from Rourke Company, terms n/30, FOB shipping point, $9,600, including $600 freight costs paid by Rourke.

14   Sold merchandise on credit to Deepak Soni, terms n/30, FOB shipping point, $2,400 (cost, $1,440).

14   Returned damaged merchandise received from Leverage Company on March 8 for credit, $600.

17   Received check from James William for his purchase of March 7.

19   Sold merchandise for cash, $1,800 (cost, $1,080).

20   Paid Rourke Company for purchase of March 10.

21   Paid Leverage Company the balance from the transactions of March 8 and March 14.

24   Accepted from Deepak Soni a return of merchandise, which was put back in inventory, $200 (cost, $120).

REQUIRED

1. Prepare journal entries to record the transactions, assuming use of the perpetual inventory system. (*Hint:* Refer to the TriLevel Problem feature.)

2. **ACCOUNTING CONNECTION ▶** Receiving cash rebates from suppliers based on the past year's purchases is a common practice in some industries. If, at the end of the year, Fulco receives rebates in cash from a supplier, should these cash rebates be reported as revenue? Why or why not?

LO **2, 5, 6**

✔ 1: Net income: $23,941

Merchandising Income Statement: Periodic Inventory System

P4. Selected accounts from Dence's Gourmet Shop's adjusted trial balance as of March 31, 2014, the end of the current fiscal year, follow. The merchandise inventory for Dence's was $81,222 at the beginning of the year and $76,664 at the end of the year.

Dence's Gourmet Shop
Partial Adjusted Trial Balance
March 31, 2014

Sales		433,912
Sales Returns and Allowances	11,250	
Purchases	221,185	
Purchases Returns and Allowances		30,238
Freight-In	10,078	
Store Salaries Expense	107,550	
Office Salaries Expense	26,500	
Advertising Expense	18,200	
Rent Expense	14,400	
Insurance Expense	2,800	
Utilities Expense	18,760	
Store Supplies Expense	464	
Office Supplies Expense	814	
Depreciation Expense—Store Equipment	1,800	
Depreciation Expense—Office Equipment	1,850	

REQUIRED

1. Prepare a multistep income statement for Dence's. Store Salaries Expense, Advertising Expense, Store Supplies Expense, and Depreciation Expense—Store Equipment are selling expenses. The other expenses are general and administrative expenses. The company uses the periodic inventory system. Show details of net sales and operating expenses.

2. **BUSINESS APPLICATION** ▶ Based on your knowledge at this point in the course, how would you use Dence's income statement to evaluate the company's profitability? What other financial statements should you consider, and why?

LO 5   **Merchandising Transactions: Periodic Inventory System**

P5. Refer to the data in **P3**.

REQUIRED

1. Prepare journal entries to record the transactions, assuming use of the periodic inventory system. (*Hint:* Refer to the TriLevel Problem feature.)

2. **ACCOUNTING CONNECTION** ▶ Most companies call the first line of the income statement *net sales*. Other companies call it *sales*. Do you think these terms are equivalent and comparable? What would be the content of net sales? Why might a company use *sales* instead of *net sales*?

LO 4   **Merchandising Transactions: Perpetual Inventory System**

GENERAL LEDGER

P6. Teague Company engaged in the following transactions in October 2014:

Oct. 7   Sold merchandise on credit to Mel Forde, terms n/30, FOB shipping point, $12,000 (cost, $7,200).

     8   Purchased merchandise on credit from Surf Company, terms n/30, FOB shipping point, $24,000.

     9   Paid Surf Company for shipping charges on merchandise purchased on October 8, $1,016.

     10   Purchased merchandise on credit from Tata Company, terms n/30, FOB shipping point, $38,400, including $2,400 freight costs paid by Tata.

     14   Sold merchandise on credit to David Johnson, terms n/30, FOB shipping point, $9,600 (cost, $5,760).

     14   Returned damaged merchandise received from Surf Company on October 8 for credit, $2,400.

     17   Received check from Mel Forde for her purchase of October 7.

     19   Sold merchandise for cash, $7,200 (cost, $4,320).

     20   Paid Tata Company for purchase of October 10.

     21   Paid Surf Company the balance from the transactions of October 8 and October 14.

     24   Accepted from David Johnson a return of merchandise, which was put back in inventory, $800 (cost, $480).

REQUIRED

1. Prepare journal entries to record the transactions, assuming use of the perpetual inventory system. (*Hint:* Refer to the TriLevel Problem feature.)

2. **ACCOUNTING CONNECTION** ▶ Receiving cash rebates from suppliers based on the past year's purchases is a common practice in some industries. If, at the end of the year, Teague receives rebates in cash from a supplier, should these cash rebates be reported as revenue? Why or why not?

ALTERNATE PROBLEMS

LO **2**

Forms of the Income Statement

✔ 1: Income from operations 2014: $132,852
✔ 1: Income from operations 2013: $221,256

P7. Sigma Company's single-step income statements for 2014 and 2013 follow.

Sigma Company
Income Statements
For the Years Ended April 30, 2014 and 2013

	2014	2013
Revenues:		
Net sales	$1,051,864	$950,528
Interest income	3,600	1,700
Total revenues	$1,055,464	$952,228
Costs and expenses:		
Cost of goods sold	$ 469,896	$343,700
Selling expenses	323,384	301,400
General and administrative expenses	125,732	84,172
Interest expense	7,200	3,400
Total costs and expenses	$ 926,212	$732,672
Net income	$ 129,252	$219,556

REQUIRED

1. Prepare multistep income statements for 2013 and 2014 showing percentages of net sales for each component (e.g., cost of goods sold divided by net sales). (Round percentages to one decimal place.)
2. **ACCOUNTING CONNECTION** ▶ Did income from operations increase or decrease from 2013 to 2014? Write a short explanation of why this change occurred.

LO **2, 4, 6**

Merchandising Income Statement: Perpetual Inventory System

✔ 1: Net income: $10,522

P8. Selected accounts from Keystone Furniture's adjusted trial balance as of August 31, 2014, the end of the fiscal year, follow.

Keystone Furniture
Partial Adjusted Trial Balance
August 31, 2014

Sales		867,824
Sales Returns and Allowances	22,500	
Cost of Goods Sold	442,370	
Freight-In	20,156	
Store Salaries Expense	215,100	
Office Salaries Expense	53,000	
Advertising Expense	36,400	
Rent Expense	28,800	
Insurance Expense	5,600	
Utilities Expense	17,520	
Store Supplies Expense	4,928	
Office Supplies Expense	3,628	
Depreciation Expense—Store Equipment	3,600	
Depreciation Expense—Office Equipment	3,700	

REQUIRED

1. Prepare a multistep income statement for Keystone. Store Salaries Expense, Advertising Expense, Store Supplies Expense, and Depreciation Expense—Store Equipment are selling expenses. The other expenses are general and administrative expenses. The company uses the perpetual inventory system. Show details of net sales and operating expenses.

2. **BUSINESS APPLICATION ▶** Based on your knowledge at this point in the course, how would you use the income statement for Keystone to evaluate the company's profitability? What other financial statement should be considered, and why?

LO 4

Merchandising Transactions: Perpetual Inventory System

P9. Naib Company engaged in the following transactions in July 2014:

July	1	Sold merchandise to Lina Lopez on credit, terms n/30, FOB shipping point, $4,200 (cost, $2,520).
	3	Purchased merchandise on credit from Ruff Company, terms n/30, FOB shipping point, $7,600.
	5	Paid Craft Freight for freight charges on merchandise received, $580.
	8	Purchased merchandise on credit from Kansas Supply Company, terms n/30, FOB shipping point, $7,200, which includes $400 freight costs paid by Kansas Supply.
	12	Returned some of the merchandise purchased on July 3 for credit, $1,200.
	15	Sold merchandise on credit to Peter Watts, terms n/30, FOB shipping point, $2,400 (cost, $1,440).
	17	Sold merchandise for cash, $2,000 (cost, $1,200).
	18	Accepted for full credit a return from Lina Lopez and returned merchandise to inventory, $400 (cost, $240).
	24	Paid Ruff Company for purchase of July 3 less return of July 12.
	25	Received check from Lina Lopez for July 1 purchase less the return on July 18.

REQUIRED

1. Prepare journal entries to record the transactions, assuming use of the perpetual inventory system. (*Hint:* Refer to the TriLevel Problem feature.)
2. **ACCOUNTING CONNECTION ▶** Most companies call the first line of the income statement *net sales*. Other companies call it *sales*. Do you think these terms are equivalent and comparable? What would be the content of net sales? Why might a company use *sales* instead of *net sales?*

LO 5

Merchandising Transactions: Periodic Inventory System

P10. Refer to the data in **P9**.

REQUIRED

1. Prepare journal entries to record the transactions, assuming use of the periodic inventory system. (*Hint:* Refer to the TriLevel Problem feature.)
2. **ACCOUNTING CONNECTION ▶** Receiving cash rebates from suppliers based on the past year's purchases is common in some industries. If at the end of the year, Naib receives rebates in cash from a supplier, should these cash rebates be reported as revenue? Why or why not?

LO 2, 5, 6

SPREADSHEET

✔ 1: Net income: $3,435

Merchandising Income Statement: Periodic Inventory System

P11. Selected accounts from Will's Sports Equipment's adjusted trial balance on September 30, 2014, the fiscal year end, follow. The company's beginning merchandise inventory was $38,200 and ending merchandise inventory is $29,400 for the period.

(Continued)

Will's Sports Equipment
Partial Adjusted Trial Balance
September 30, 2014

Sales		165,000
Sales Returns and Allowances	2,000	
Purchases	70,200	
Purchases Returns and Allowances		2,600
Freight-In	2,300	
Store Salaries Expense	32,625	
Office Salaries Expense	12,875	
Advertising Expense	24,300	
Rent Expense	2,400	
Insurance Expense	1,200	
Utilities Expense	1,560	
Store Supplies Expense	2,880	
Office Supplies Expense	1,175	
Depreciation Expense—Store Equipment	1,050	
Depreciation Expense—Office Equipment	800	

REQUIRED

1. Prepare a multistep income statement for Will's. Store Salaries Expense, Advertising Expense, Store Supplies Expense, and Depreciation Expense—Store Equipment are selling expenses. The other expenses are general and administrative expenses. The company uses the periodic inventory system. Show details of net sales and operating expenses.

2. **BUSINESS APPLICATION** ▶ Based on your knowledge at this point in the course, how would you use Will's income statement to evaluate the company's profitability? What other financial statements should you consider and why?

LO 5   **Merchandising Transactions: Periodic Inventory System**

P12. Refer to the data in **P6**.

REQUIRED

Prepare journal entries to record the transactions, assuming use of the periodic inventory system. (*Hint:* Refer to the TriLevel Problem feature.)

CASES

LO 1   **Conceptual Understanding: Periodic versus Perpetual Inventory Systems**

C1. Books Unlimited is a well-established chain of 20 bookstores in western Ohio. In recent years, the company has grown rapidly, adding five new stores in regional malls. Each store's manager selects stock based on the market in his or her region. Managers select books from a master list of titles that the central office provides. Every six months, a physical inventory is taken, and financial statements are prepared using the periodic inventory system. At that time, books that have not sold well are placed on sale or, whenever possible, returned to the publisher.

Management has found that when selecting books, managers of the new stores are not judging the market as well as the managers of the older, more established stores. Management is therefore thinking of implementing a perpetual inventory system and carefully monitoring sales from the central office. Do you think Books Unlimited should switch to the perpetual inventory system or stay with the periodic inventory system it has used in the past? Discuss the advantages and disadvantages of each system.

LO **6**

Conceptual Understanding: Effects of a Weak Dollar

C2. BUSINESS APPLICATION ▶ **McDonald's** reports that its sales in Europe exceed its sales in the United States. This performance, while reflective of the company's phenomenal success in Europe, was also attributed to the weak dollar in relation to the euro. McDonald's reports its sales wherever they take place in U.S. dollars. Explain why a weak dollar relative to the euro would lead to an increase in McDonald's reported European sales. Why is a weak dollar not relevant to a discussion of McDonald's sales in the United States?

LO **6**

Conceptual Understanding: Cash Flow Management

C3. BUSINESS APPLICATION ▶ Amazing Sound Source, Inc., has been in business for 30 years. It carries a large inventory so that it can offer customers a wide selection of merchandise and deliver purchases quickly. It accepts credit cards and checks but also provides 90 days' credit to reliable customers who have made purchases in the past. It maintains good relations with suppliers by paying invoices quickly.

To pay bills during the past year, the company has had to borrow from its bank. An analysis of the company's financial statements reveals that, on average, inventory is on hand for 70 days before being sold and that receivables are held for 90 days before being paid. Accounts payable are, on average, paid in 20 days.

What are the operating cycle and financing period? How long are Amazing Sound Source's operating cycle and financing period? Describe three ways in which this company can improve its cash flow management.

LO **6**

Annual Report Case: The Operating Cycle and Financing Period

C4. BUSINESS APPLICATION ▶ Write a brief memorandum to your instructor describing **CVS**'s operating cycle and financing period. To do this, refer to the CVS annual report in the Supplement to Chapter 16 and to Exhibits 5 and 8. Your memorandum should identify the most common transactions in the operating cycle as they apply to CVS. It should also refer to the importance of accounts receivable, accounts payable, and merchandise inventory in CVS's financial statements. Recall from previous chapters that CVS had inventory days on hand of about 44 days, days' receivable of 19 days, and days payable of 21 days. Complete the memorandum by explaining why CVS's operating cycle and financing period are favorable to the company.

LO **2**

Comparison Analysis: Income Statement Analysis

C5. Refer to the **CVS** annual report in the Supplement to Chapter 16 and to the following data (in millions) for **Walgreens** in 2011: net sales, $72,184; cost of sales, $51,692; total operating expenses, $16,561; and inventories, $8,044. Determine which company—CVS or Walgreens—had more profitable merchandising operations in 2011 by preparing a schedule that compares the companies based on net sales, cost of sales, gross margin, total operating expenses, and income from operations as a percentage of sales. (*Hint:* You should put the income statements in comparable formats.) In addition, for each company, compute inventories as a percentage of the cost of sales. Which company has the highest prices in relation to costs of sales? Which company is more efficient in its operating expenses? Which company manages its inventories better? Overall, on the basis of the income statement, which company is more profitable? Explain your answers.

LO **1, 2, 4, 5**

Decision Analysis: Analysis of a Merchandising Income Statement

C6. In 2013, Lisa Perry opened Lisa's Jeans Company, a small store that sold designer jeans in a suburban mall. Perry worked 14 hours a day and controlled all aspects of the operation. The company was such a success that in 2014, Perry opened a second store in another mall. Because the new shop needed her attention, she hired a manager for the original store.

During 2014, the new store was successful, but the original store's performance did not match its performance in 2013. Concerned about this, Perry compared the two years' results for the original store. Her analysis showed the following:

(Continued)

	2014	2013
Net sales	$325,000	$350,000
Cost of goods sold	225,000	225,000
Gross margin	$100,000	$125,000
Operating expenses	75,000	50,000
Income before income taxes	$ 25,000	$ 75,000

Perry's analysis also revealed that the cost and the selling price of the jeans were roughly the same in both years, as was the level of operating expenses, except for the new manager's $25,000 salary. The amount of sales returns and allowances was insignificant in both years.

Studying the situation further, Perry discovered the following about the cost of goods sold.

	2014	2013
Purchases	$200,000	$271,000
Total purchases allowances	15,000	20,000
Freight-in	19,000	27,000
Physical inventory, end of year	32,000	53,000

Still not satisfied, Perry went through all the individual sales and purchase records for 2014. She found that they were correct, but given the unit purchases and sales during the year, the 2014 ending inventory should have been $57,000. After puzzling over all this information, Perry has come to you for accounting help.

1. Using Perry's new information, compute the cost of goods sold for 2013 and 2014 and account for the difference in income before income taxes between 2013 and 2014.
2. Suggest at least two reasons for the discrepancy in the 2014 ending inventory. How might Perry improve the management of the original store?

Continuing Case: Annual Report Project

C7. Using the most recent annual report of the company you have chosen to study and that you have accessed online at the company's website, examine the income statement of your company. Answer the following questions.

1. Does your company use a multistep income statement?
2. For the most recent year, what is the company's gross margin, operating income, and net income? Briefly explain why these numbers are different.

Special-purpose journals promote efficiency, economy, and control. Although manual special-purpose journals are used by some companies, the concepts also underlie computerized general ledger accounting systems.

Most business transactions—90 to 95 percent—fall into one of four categories. Each kind of transaction can be recorded in a special-purpose journal.

Transaction	Special-Purpose Journal	Posting Abbreviation
Sale of merchandise on credit	Sales journal	S
Purchase on credit	Purchases journal	P
Receipt of cash	Cash receipts journal	CR
Disbursement of cash	Cash payments journal	CP

The general journal is used to record transactions, like purchase returns, sales returns, and adjusting and closing entries, that do not fall into any of these special categories. (When transactions are posted from the general journal to the ledger accounts, the posting abbreviation used is *J*.)

Using special-purpose journals greatly reduces the work involved in entering and posting transactions in the general ledger. For example, in most cases, instead of posting every debit and credit for each transaction, only the total amounts of the transactions are posted. In addition, labor can be divided by assigning each journal to a different employee. This division of labor is important in establishing good internal control.

Sales Journal

STUDY NOTE: A cash sale is entered into the cash receipts journal, not into the sales journal.

The **sales journal** is designed to handle all credit sales. Cash sales are recorded in the cash receipts journal. Exhibit 1 illustrates a page from a typical sales journal and related ledger accounts. Six sales transactions involving five customers are recorded.

Notice how the sales journal saves time:

- Only one line is needed to record each transaction. Each entry consists of a debit to a customer in Accounts Receivable. The corresponding credit to Sales is understood.
- The account names do not have to be written out because each entry automatically is debited to Accounts Receivable and credited to Sales.
- No explanations are necessary because the function of the sales journal is to record only credit sales.
- Only one amount—the total credit sales for the month—has to be posted. It is posted twice: once as a debit to Accounts Receivable and once as a credit to Sales. Imagine the time saved when there are hundreds of sales transactions.

Controlling Accounts and Subsidiary Ledgers Controlling accounts and subsidiary ledgers contain important details about the figures in special-purpose journals and the general journal. A **controlling account** (or *control account*) is an account in the general ledger that maintains the total of the individual account balances in a subsidiary ledger. A **subsidiary ledger** is a ledger separate from the general ledger that contains a group of related accounts, such as a list of customers. The total of the balances in the subsidiary ledger accounts equals the balance in the corresponding controlling account.

Up to this point, we've used a single Accounts Receivable account. However, a single entry in Accounts Receivable does not tell us how much each customer has bought and how much each customer has paid or still owes. In practice, almost all companies that sell to customers on credit keep an individual accounts receivable record for each customer. If the company has 6,000 credit customers, there are 6,000 accounts receivable.

Exhibit 1
Sales Journal and Related Ledger Accounts

Sales Journal						Page 1
Date		**Account Debited**	**Invoice Number**	**Terms**	**Post. Ref.**	**Amount (Debit/ Credit Accounts Receivable/Sales)**
July	1	Peter Clark	721	2/10, n/30	√	750
	5	Georgetta Jones	722	2/10, n/30	√	500
	8	Eugene Cumberland	723	2/10, n/30	√	335
	12	Maxwell Gertz	724	2/10, n/30	√	1,165
	18	Peter Clark	725	1/10, n/30	√	1,225
	25	Michael Powers	726	2/10, n/30	√	975
						4,950
						(114/411)

STUDY NOTE: The check marks indicate daily postings to the subsidiary ledger accounts, which normally are listed in alphabetical or numerical order. Also, the column totals are posted to the appropriate general ledger accounts at the end of the month.

Post total at end of month.

Accounts Receivable					114
		Post.			Balance
Date		**Ref.**	**Debit**	**Credit**	**Debit**	**Credit**
July	31	S1	4,950		4,950	

Sales					411
		Post.			Balance
Date		**Ref.**	**Debit**	**Credit**	**Debit**	**Credit**
July	31	S1		4,950		4,950

© Cengage Learning 2014

To include all these accounts in the general ledger with the other asset, liability, and owner's equity accounts would make it very bulky. Consequently, most companies place individual customers' accounts in a separate, subsidiary ledger. In the accounts receivable subsidiary ledger, customers' accounts are filed either alphabetically or numerically (if account numbers are used).

When a company uses an accounts receivable subsidiary ledger, it still must maintain an Accounts Receivable account in the general ledger. This account controls in the sense that its balance must equal the total of the individual account balances in the subsidiary ledger. Transactions that involve accounts receivable, such as credit sales, must be posted to the individual customers' accounts daily. Postings to the controlling account in the general ledger are made at least once a month. When the amounts in the subsidiary ledger and the controlling account do not match, the accountant must find the error and correct it.

Most companies use an accounts payable subsidiary ledger as well. It is possible to use a subsidiary ledger for almost any account in the general ledger, such as Notes Receivable or Equipment, when management wants specific information on individual items.

Summary of the Sales Journal Procedure Using a sales journal involves the following steps, as shown in Exhibit 2:

- **Step 1:** Enter each sales invoice in the sales journal on a single line. Record the date, the customer's name, the invoice number, and the amount. No column is needed for the terms if the terms on all sales are the same.
- **Step 2:** At the end of each day, post each individual sale to the customer's account in the accounts receivable subsidiary ledger. As each sale is posted, place a check mark (or customer account number, if used) in the Post. Ref. (posting reference) column of the sales journal to indicate that it has been posted. In the Post. Ref.

column of each customer's account, place an *S* and the sales journal page number (*S1* means Sales Journal—Page 1) to indicate the source of the entry.

- **Step 3:** At the end of the month, sum the Amount column in the sales journal to determine the total credit sales, and post the total to the general ledger accounts (debit Accounts Receivable and credit Sales). Place the numbers of the accounts debited and credited beneath the total in the sales journal to indicate that this step has been completed. In the general ledger, indicate the source of the entry in the Post. Ref. column of each account.
- **Step 4:** Verify the accuracy of the posting by adding the account balances of the accounts receivable subsidiary ledger and comparing the total with the balance of the Accounts Receivable controlling account in the general ledger. You can do this by listing the accounts in a schedule of accounts receivable, like the one in Exhibit 3, in the order in which the accounts are maintained. This step is performed after posting collections on account in the *cash receipts journal*, which we explain later.

STUDY NOTE: In theory, the sum of the account balances from the subsidiary accounts must equal the balance in the related general ledger controlling account at any point in time. In practice, however, the equality is verified only at the end of the month, when the general ledger is posted.

Exhibit 2
Relationship of Sales Journal, General Ledger, and Accounts Receivable Subsidiary Ledger and the Posting Procedure

Sales Journal   Page 1

Date		Account Debited	Invoice Number	Terms	Post. Ref.	Amount (Debit/Credit Accounts Receivable/Sales)
July	1	Peter Clark	721	2/10, n/30	√	750
	5	Georgetta Jones	722	2/10, n/30	√	500
	8	Eugene Cumberland	723	2/10, n/30	√	335
	12	Maxwell Gertz	724	2/10, n/30	√	1,165
	18	Peter Clark	725	1/10, n/30	√	1,225
	25	Michael Powers	726	2/10, n/30	√	975
						4,950
						(114/411)

Post individual amounts daily to subsidiary ledger accounts.

Post total at end of month to general ledger accounts.

STUDY NOTE: Accounts in the subsidiary ledger are maintained in alphabetical order. If account numbers are used to identify customers, the accounts would be listed in account number order.

General Ledger

Accounts Receivable   114

Date	Post. Ref.	Debit	Credit	Balance Debit	Balance Credit
July 31	S1	4,950		4,950	

STUDY NOTE: Subsidiary accounts are posted daily to prevent customers from exceeding their credit limits and to have up-to-date balances for customers wishing to pay their accounts.

Sales   411

Date	Post. Ref.	Debit	Credit	Balance Debit	Balance Credit
July 31	S1		4,950		4,950

Accounts Receivable Sub. Ledger

Peter Clark

Date		Post. Ref.	Debit	Credit	Balance
July	1	S1	750		750
	18	S1	1,225		1,975

Eugene Cumberland

Date		Post. Ref.	Debit	Credit	Balance
July	8	S1	335		335

Continue posting to Maxwell Gertz, Georgetta Jones, and Michael Powers.

© Cengage Learning 2014

© Cengage Learning 2014

Exhibit 3
Schedule of Accounts Receivable

Mitchell's Used Car Sales
Schedule of Accounts Receivable
July 31, 2011

Peter Clark	$1,975
Eugene Cumberland	335
Maxwell Gertz	1,165
Georgetta Jones	500
Michael Powers	975
Total Accounts Receivable	$4,950

STUDY NOTE: *Columns can be added to a special-purpose journal for accounts that are commonly used.*

Sales Taxes Many cities and states require retailers to collect a sales tax from their customers and periodically remit the total collected to the city or state. In this case, an additional column is needed in the sales journal to record the credit to Sales Taxes Payable on credit sales, as shown in Exhibit 4.

Exhibit 4
Section of a Sales Journal with a Column for Sales Taxes

						Debit	Credits	
							Sales	
		Invoice			Post.	Accounts	Tax	
Date		Account Debited	Number	Terms	Ref.	Receivable	Payable	Sales
Sept.	1	Ralph P. Hake	727	2/10, n/30	√	206	6	200

Sales Journal — Page 7

© Cengage Learning 2014

Purchases Journal

STUDY NOTE: *A cash purchase is entered into the cash payments journal, not into the purchases journal.*

The **purchases journal** is used to record purchases on credit. It can take the form of either a single-column journal or a multicolumn journal. In the single-column journal (shown in Exhibit 5), only credit purchases of merchandise for resale to customers are recorded. This kind of transaction is recorded with a debit to Purchases and a credit to Accounts Payable. When the single-column purchases journal is used, credit purchases of items other than merchandise are recorded in the general journal. Cash purchases are recorded in the *cash payments journal*, which we explain later.

Like the Accounts Receivable account, the Accounts Payable account in the general ledger is generally used as a controlling account. So that the company knows how much it owes each supplier, it keeps a separate account for each supplier in an accounts payable subsidiary ledger.

The procedure for using the purchases journal is much like that for using the sales journal.

- **Step 1:** Enter each purchase invoice in the purchases journal on a single line. Record the date, the supplier's name, the invoice date, the terms (if given), and the amount. It is not necessary to record the shipping terms in the terms column because they do not affect the payment date.

■ **Step 2:** At the end of each day, post each individual purchase to the supplier's account in the accounts payable subsidiary ledger. As each purchase is posted, place a check mark in the Post. Ref. column of the purchases journal to show that it has been posted. Also place a *P* and the page number of the purchases journal (*P1* stands for Purchases Journal—Page 1) in the Post. Ref. column of each supplier's account to show the source of the entry.

■ **Step 3:** At the end of the month, sum the Amount column in the purchases journal, and post the total to the general ledger as a debit to Purchases and a credit to Accounts Payable. Place the numbers of the accounts debited and credited beneath the totals in the purchases journal to show that this step has been carried out. In the general ledger, indicate the source of the entry in the Post. Ref. column of each account.

■ **Step 4:** Check the accuracy of the posting by adding the account balances of the accounts payable subsidiary ledger and comparing the total with the balance of the Accounts Payable controlling account in the general ledger. This step can be done by preparing a schedule of accounts payable from the subsidiary ledger.

Exhibit 5 illustrates the procedure for using a purchases journal.

Exhibit 5
Relationship of Single-Column Purchases Journal to the General Ledger and the Accounts Payable Subsidiary Ledger

Purchases Journal — Page 1

Date		Account Credited	Date of Invoice	Terms	Post. Ref.	Amount (Debit/Credit Purchases/ Accounts Payable)
July	1	Jones Chevrolet	7/1	2/10, n/30	√	2,500
	2	Marshall Ford	7/2	2/15, n/30	√	300
	3	Dealer Sales	7/3	n/30	√	700
	12	Thomas Auto	7/11	n/30	√	1,400
	17	Dealer Sales	7/17	2/10, n/30	√	3,200
	19	Thomas Auto	7/17	n/30	√	1,100
						9,200
						(511/212)

Post total at end of month.   Post individual amounts daily.

General Ledger

Accounts Payable — 212

Date	Post. Ref.	Debit	Credit	Balance Debit	Balance Credit
July 31	P1		9,200		9,200

Purchases — 511

Date	Post. Ref.	Debit	Credit	Balance Debit	Balance Credit
July 31	P1	9,200		9,200	

Accounts Payable Sub. Ledger

Dealer Sales

Date		Post. Ref.	Debit	Credit	Balance
July	3	P1		700	700
	17	P1		3,200	3,900

Jones Chevrolet

Date		Post. Ref.	Debit	Credit	Balance
July	1	P1		2,500	2,500

Continue posting to Marshall Ford and Thomas Auto.

© Cengage Learning 2014

The single-column purchases journal can be expanded to record credit purchases of items other than merchandise by adding separate debit columns for other accounts that are used often. For example, the multicolumn purchases journal in Exhibit 6 has columns for Freight In, Store Supplies, Office Supplies, and Other Accounts. In Exhibit 6, the total credits to Accounts Payable ($9,637) equal the total debits to Purchases, Freight In, Store Supplies, Office Supplies, and Parts ($9,200 + $50 + $145 + $42 + $200). Again, the individual transactions in the Accounts Payable column are posted daily to the accounts payable subsidiary ledger, and the totals of each column in the purchases journal are posted monthly to the corresponding general ledger accounts. Entries in the Other Accounts column are posted individually to the named accounts, and the column total is not posted.

Exhibit 6
A Multicolumn Purchases Journal

Purchases Journal											Page 1
					Credit	**Debits**					
										Other Accounts	
Date	**Account Credited**	**Date of Invoice**	**Terms**	**Post. Ref.**	**Accounts Payable**	**Purchases**	**Freight In**	**Store Supplies**	**Office Supplies**	**Account** / **Post. Ref.**	**Amount**
July 1	Jones Chevrolet	7/1	2/10, n/30	√	2,500	2,500					
2	Marshall Ford	7/2	2/15, n/30	√	300	300					
2	Shelby Car Delivery	7/2	n/30	√	50		50				
3	Dealer Sales	7/3	n/30	√	700	700					
12	Thomas Auto	7/11	n/30	√	1,400	1,400					
17	Dealer Sales	7/17	2/10, n/30	√	3,200	3,200					
19	Thomas Auto	7/17	n/30	√	1,100	1,100					
25	Osborne Supply	7/21	n/10	√	187			145	42		
28	Auto Supply	7/28	n/10	√	200					Parts / 120	200
					9,637	9,200	50	145	42		200
					(212)	(511)	(514)	(132)	(133)		(√)

Cash Receipts Journal

All transactions involving receipts of cash are recorded in the **cash receipts journal**. Examples of these transactions are cash from cash sales and cash from credit customers in payment of their accounts. Although all cash receipts require a debit to Cash, they differ in that they require a variety of credit entries. Thus, the cash receipts journal must have several columns. The Other Accounts column is used to record credits to accounts not specifically represented by a column. The account numbers are entered in the Post. Ref. column, and the amounts are posted daily to the appropriate account in the general ledger. The Other Accounts column totals, therefore, are not posted at the end of the month. Only at the end of the month are the control account balances meaningful or correct.

The cash receipts journal presented in Exhibit 7 has the following debit and credit columns:

- Debit columns
    - **Cash:** Each entry must have an amount in this column because each transaction involves a receipt of cash.
    - **Sales Discounts:** This company allows a 2 percent discount for prompt payment. Therefore, it is useful to have a column for sales discounts. Notice that in the transactions of July 8 and 28, the debits to Cash and Sales Discounts equal the credits to Accounts Receivable.
    - **Other Accounts:** The Other Accounts column (sometimes called *Sundry Accounts*) is used for transactions that involve both a debit to Cash and a debit to some account other than Sales Discounts.
- Credit columns
    - **Accounts Receivable:** This column is used to record collections on account from customers. The name of the customer is written in the Account Debited/Credited column so that the payment can be entered in the corresponding account in the accounts receivable subsidiary ledger. Posting to the individual accounts receivable accounts is usually done daily so that each customer's balance is up-to-date.
    - **Sales:** This column is used to record all cash sales. Retail firms that use cash registers would make an entry at the end of each day for the total sales from each cash register. The debit, of course, is in the Cash debit column.
    - **Other Accounts:** This column is used for the credit portion of any entry that is neither a cash collection from accounts receivable nor a cash sale. The name of the account to be credited is indicated in the Account Debited/Credited column. For example, the transactions of July 1, 20, and 24 involve credits to accounts other than Accounts Receivable or Sales. These individual postings should be done daily (or weekly if there are just a few of them). If a company finds that it consistently is crediting a certain account in the Other Accounts column, it can add another credit column to the cash receipts journal for that particular account.

The procedure for posting the cash receipts journal follows.

- **Step 1:** Post the transactions in the Accounts Receivable column daily to the individual accounts in the accounts receivable subsidiary ledger. The amount credited to the customer's account is the same as that credited to Accounts Receivable. A check mark in the Post. Ref column of the cash receipts journal indicates that the amount has been posted, and a *CR1* (Cash Receipts Journal—Page 1) in the Post. Ref. column of each subsidiary ledger account indicates the source of the entry.
- **Step 2:** Post the debits/credits in the Other Accounts columns daily, or at intervals during the month, to the general ledger accounts. Write the account number in the Post. Ref. column of the cash receipts journal as the individual items are posted to indicate that the posting has been done, and write *CR1* in the Post. Ref. column of the general ledger account to indicate the source of the entry.
- **Step 3:** At the end of the month, total the columns in the cash receipts journal, as shown below. The sum of the Debits column totals must equal the sum of the Credits column totals:

Debits Column Totals		Credits Column Totals	
Cash	$32,528	Accounts Receivable	$ 1,850
Sales Discounts	22	Sales	5,200
Other Accounts	0	Other Accounts	25,500
Total Debits	$32,550	Total Credits	$32,550

This step is called *crossfooting*.

Exhibit 7

Relationship of the Cash Receipts Journal to the General Ledger and the Accounts Receivable Subsidiary Ledger

Cash Receipts Journal   Page 1

			Debits			Credits		
Date	Account Debited/Credited	Post. Ref.	Cash	Sales Discounts	Other Accounts	Accounts Receivable	Sales	Other Accounts
July 1	Henry Mitchell, Capital	311	20,000					20,000
5	Sales		1,200				1,200	
8	Georgetta Jones	√	490	10		500		
13	Sales		1,400				1,400	
16	Peter Clark	√	750			750		
19	Sales		1,000				1,000	
20	Store Supplies	132	500					500
24	Notes Payable	213	5,000					5,000
26	Sales		1,600				1,600	
28	Peter Clark	√	588	12		600		
			32,528	22		1,850	5,200	25,500
			(111)	(412)		(114)	(411)	(√)

Post individual amounts in Accounts Receivable ledger columns daily.

Post totals at end of month.

Total not posted.

Post individual amounts in Other Accounts column daily.

General Ledger

Cash   111

Date	Post. Ref.	Debit	Credit	Balance Debit	Balance Credit
July 31	CR1	32,528		32,528	

Accounts Receivable   114

Date	Post. Ref.	Debit	Credit	Balance Debit	Balance Credit
July 31	S1	4,950		4,950	
31	CR1		1,850	3,100	

Store Supplies   132

Date	Post. Ref.	Debit	Credit	Balance Debit	Balance Credit
Bal.				500	
July 20	CR1		500	—	

Accounts Receivable Subsidiary Ledger

Peter Clark

Date	Post. Ref.	Debit	Credit	Balance
July 1	S1	750		750
16	CR1		750	—
18	S1	1,225		1,225
28	CR1		600	625

Georgetta Jones

Date	Post. Ref.	Debit	Credit	Balance
July 5	S1	500		500
8	CR1		500	—

Continue posting to Notes Payable and Henry Mitchell, Capital.

Continue posting to Sales and Sales Discounts.

- **Step 4:** Post the Debits column totals as follows.
  a. **Cash:** Posted as a debit to the Cash account.
  b. **Sales Discounts:** Posted as a debit to the Sales Discounts account.
- **Step 5:** Post the Credits column totals as follows.
  a. **Accounts Receivable:** Posted as a credit to the Accounts Receivable controlling account.
  b. **Sales:** Posted as a credit to the Sales account.
- **Step 6:** Write the account numbers below each column in the cash receipts journal as they are posted to indicate that these steps have been completed. *CR1* is written in the Post. Ref. column of each account in the general ledger to indicate the source of the entry.
- **Step 7:** Notice that the total of the Other Accounts column is not posted because each entry was posted separately when the transaction occurred. The individual accounts were posted in Step 2. Place a check mark at the bottom of the column to show that postings in that column have been made and that the total is not posted.

Cash Payments Journal

STUDY NOTE: *The cash payments journal can accommodate all cash payments. It functions like the cash receipts journal, although it uses some different general ledger accounts.*

All transactions involving payments of cash are recorded in the **cash payments journal** (or *cash disbursements journal*). Examples of these transactions are cash purchases and payments of obligations resulting from earlier purchases on credit. The form of the cash payments journal is much like that of the cash receipts journal.

The cash payments journal presented in Exhibit 8 includes the following credit and debit columns:

- Credit columns
  - **Cash:** Each entry must have an amount in this column because each transaction involves a payment of cash.
  - **Purchases Discounts:** When purchases discounts are taken, they are recorded in this column.
  - **Other Accounts:** This column is used to record credits to accounts other than Cash or Purchases Discounts. Notice that the July 31 transaction shows a purchase of Land for $15,000, with a check for $5,000 and a note payable for $10,000.
- Debit columns
  - **Accounts Payable:** This column is used to record payments to suppliers that have extended credit to the company. Each supplier's name is written in the Payee column so that the payment can be entered in the supplier's account in the accounts payable subsidiary ledger.
  - **Salary Expense, Advertising Expense, and Rent Expense:** Continue posting the column total for any column that has an account title at the top. These are accounts for which there are usually multiple expenditures in a month. Placing the account number at the bottom of the column indicates the total has been posted to its respective account.
  - **Other Accounts:** Cash can be expended for many reasons. Therefore, an Other Accounts or Sundry Accounts column is needed in the cash payments journal. The title of the account to be debited is written in the Account Credited/Debited column, and the amount is entered in the Other Accounts debit column. If a company finds that a particular account appears often in the Other Accounts column, it can add another debit column to the cash payments journal.

The procedure for posting the cash payments journal, shown in Exhibit 8, follows.

- **Step 1:** Post the transactions in the Accounts Payable columns daily to the individual accounts in the accounts payable subsidiary ledger. Place a check mark in the

Exhibit 8

Relationship of the Cash Payments Journal to the General Ledger and the Accounts Payable Subsidiary Ledger

Cash Payments Journal — Page 1

						Credits		Debits				
Date	Ck. No.	Payee	Account Credited/ Debited	Post. Ref.	Cash	Purchases Discounts	Other Accounts	Accounts Payable	Salary Expense	Advertising Expense	Rent Expense	Other Accounts
July 2	101	Sondra Tidmore	Purchases	511	400							400
6	102	Daily Journal			100					100		
8	103	Siviglia Agency			250						250	
11	104	Jones Chevrolet		√	2,450	50		2,500				
16	105	Charles Kuntz			600				600			
17	106	Marshall Ford		√	294	6		300				
24	107	Grabow & Company	Prepaid Insurance	119	480							480
27	108	Dealer Sales		√	3,136	64		3,200				
		Daily Journal			100					100		
30	109	A&B Equipment Company	Office Equipment	144	900							400
			Service Equipment	146								500
31	110	Burns Real Estate	Notes Payable	213	5,000		10,000					
			Land	141								15,000
					13,710	120	10,000	6,000	600	200	250	16,780
					(111)	(512)	(√)	(212)	(611)	(612)	(613)	(√)

Post individual amounts in Other Accounts column daily.

Post totals at end of month.

Post individual amounts in Accounts Payable column daily.

Totals not posted.

General Ledger

Cash   111

Date	Post. Ref.	Debit	Credit	Balance Debit	Balance Credit
July 31	CR1	32,528		32,528	
31	CP1		13,710	18,818	

Prepaid Insurance   119

Date	Post. Ref.	Debit	Credit	Balance Debit	Balance Credit
July 24	CP1	480		480	

Continue posting to Land, Office Equipment, Service Equipment, Notes Payable, and Purchases.

Continue posting to Purchases Discounts and Accounts Payable, Salary Expense, Advertising Expense, and Rent Expense.

Accounts Payable Subsidiary Ledger

Dealer Sales

Date	Post. Ref.	Debit	Credit	Balance
July 3	P1		700	700
17	P1		3,200	3,900
27	CP1	3,200		700

Jones Chevrolet

Date	Post. Ref.	Debit	Credit	Balance
July 1	P1		2,500	2,500
11	CP1	2,500		—

Marshall Ford

Date	Post. Ref.	Debit	Credit	Balance
July 2	P1		300	300
17	CP1	300		—

Post. Ref. column of the cash payments journal to indicate that the posting has been made.

- **Step 2:** Post the debits/credits in the Other Accounts debit/credit columns to the general ledger daily or at intervals during the month. Write the account number in the Post. Ref. column of the cash payments journal as the individual items are posted to indicate that the posting has been completed and *CP1* (Cash Payments Journal-Page 1) in the Post. Ref. column of each general ledger account.
- **Step 3:** At the end of the month, the columns are footed and crossfooted. That is, the sum of the Credits column totals must equal the sum of the Debits column totals, as follows.

Credit Column Totals		Debit Column Totals	
Cash	$13,710	Accounts Payable	$ 6,000
Purchases Discounts	120	Salary Expense	600
Other Accounts	10,000	Advertising Expense	200
		Rent Expense	250
		Other Accounts	16,780
Total Credits	$23,830	Total Debits	$23,830

- **Step 4:** At the end of the month, post the column totals for Cash, Purchases Discounts, Accounts Payable, Salary Expense, Advertising Expense, and Rent Expense to their respective accounts in the general ledger. Write the account number below each column in the cash payments journal as it is posted to indicate that this step has been completed and *CP1* in the Post. Ref. column of each general ledger account. Place a check mark under the total of each Other Accounts column in the cash payments journal to indicate that the postings in the column have been made and that the total is not posted.

General Journal

Adjusting and closing entries are recorded in the general journal. Transactions that do not involve sales, purchases, cash receipts, or cash payments should also be recorded in the general journal. Usually, there are only a few of these transactions. Two examples of entries that do not fit in a special-purpose journal are a return of merchandise bought on account and an allowance from a supplier for credit. These entries are shown in Exhibit 9.

Exhibit 9
Transactions Recorded in the General Journal

STUDY NOTE: *The general journal is used only to record transactions that cannot be accommodated by the special-purpose journals. Whenever a controlling account is recorded, it must be "double posted" to the general ledger and the subsidiary accounts. All general journal entries are posted daily; column totals are neither obtained nor posted.*

© Cengage Learning 2014

	General Journal				Page 1
Date		**Description**	**Post. Ref.**	**Debit**	**Credit**
July	25	Accounts Payable, Thomas Auto	212/√	700	
		Purchases Returns and			
		Allowances	513		700
		Returned used car for			
		credit; invoice date 7/11			
	26	Sales Returns and Allowances	413	35	
		Accounts Receivable, Maxwell			
		Gertz	114/√		35
		Allowance for faulty tire			

Notice that the entries include a debit or a credit to a controlling account (Accounts Payable or Accounts Receivable). The name of the customer or supplier also is given here. When this kind of debit or credit is made to a controlling account in the general ledger, the entry must be posted twice: once to the controlling account and once to the individual account in the subsidiary ledger. This procedure keeps the subsidiary ledger equal to the controlling account. Notice that the July 26 transaction is posted by a debit to Sales Returns and Allowances in the general ledger (shown by the account number 413), a credit to the Accounts Receivable controlling account in the general ledger (account number 114), and a credit to the Maxwell Gertz account in the accounts receivable subsidiary ledger (check mark).

Key Terms

cash payments journal 257
cash receipts journal 254
controlling account 249

purchases journal 252
sales journal 249
special-purpose journals 249

subsidiary ledger 249

Chapter Assignments

GENERAL LEDGER

✔ 1: Total cash receipts: $23,340
✔ 1: Total cash payments: $17,012

PROBLEMS

Cash Receipt and Cash Payments Journals

P1. Kimball Company is a small retail business that uses a manual data processing system similar to the one described in the chapter. Among its special-purpose journals are multicolumn cash receipts and cash payments journals. The cash transactions for Kimball Company during the month of November follow.

Nov. 1 Paid November rent to R. Carello, $1,000, with check no. 782.
     3 Paid Stavos Wholesale on account, $2,300 less a 2 percent discount, check no. 783.
     4 Received payment on account of $1,000, within the 2 percent discount period, from J. Walker.
     5 Cash sales, $2,632.
     8 Paid Moving Freight on account, $598, with check no. 784.
     9 The owner, Fred Kimball, invested an additional $10,000 in cash and a truck valued at $14,000 in the business.
   11 Paid Escobedo Supply on account, $284, with check no. 785.
   14 Cash sales, $2,834.
   15 Paid Moving Freight $310 for the freight on a shipment of merchandise received today, with check no. 786.
   16 Paid Ludman Company on account, $1,600 less a 2 percent discount, with check no. 787.
   17 Received payment on account from P. Sivula, $120.
   18 Cash sales, $1,974.
   19 Received payment on a note receivable, $1,800 plus $36 interest.
   20 Purchased office supplies from Escobedo Supply, $108, with check no. 788.

Nov. 21   Paid a note payable in full to Kenington Bank, $4,100 including $100 interest, with check no. 789.

24   Cash sales, $2,964.

25   Paid $500 less a 2 percent discount to Stavos Wholesale, with check no. 790.

26   Paid sales clerk Tracy Dye $1,100 for her monthly salary, with check no. 791.

27   Purchased equipment from Standard Corporation for $16,000, paying $4,000 with check no. 792 and signing a note payable for the difference.

30   Fred Kimball withdrew $1,200 from the business, using check no. 793.

REQUIRED

1. Enter these transactions in the cash receipts and cash payments journals.
2. Foot and crossfoot the journals.
3. **ACCOUNTING CONNECTION** ▶ If a manager wanted to know the total sales for the accounting period, where else would the manager need to refer to obtain the data needed?

Purchases and General Journals

P2. Meloon Lawn Supply Company uses a multicolumn purchases journal and a general journal similar to those illustrated in the text. The company also maintains an accounts payable subsidiary ledger. The items that follow represent the company's credit transactions for the month of July.

July 2   Purchased merchandise from Diego Fertilizer Company, $2,640.

3   Purchased office supplies of $166 and store supplies of $208 from Laronne Supply, Inc.

5   Purchased cleaning equipment from Whitman Company, $1,856.

7   Purchased display equipment from Laronne Supply, Inc., $4,700.

10   Purchased lawn mowers from Brandon Lawn Equipment Company, for resale, $8,400 (which included transportation charges of $350).

14   Purchased merchandise from Diego Fertilizer Company, $3,444.

18   Purchased a lawn mower from Brandon Lawn Equipment Company to be used in the business, $950 (which included transportation charges of $70).

23   Purchased store supplies from Laronne Supply, Inc., $54.

27   Returned a defective lawn mower purchased on July 10 for full credit, $750.

REQUIRED

1. Enter the preceding transactions in the purchases journal and the general journal. Assume that all terms are n/30 and that invoice dates are the same as the transaction dates. Use Page 1 for all references.
2. Foot and crossfoot the purchases journal.
3. Open the following general ledger accounts: Store Supplies (116), Office Supplies (117), Lawn Equipment (142), Display Equipment (144), Cleaning Equipment (146), Accounts Payable (211), Purchases (611), Purchases Returns and Allowances (612), and Freight In (613). Open accounts payable subsidiary ledger accounts as needed. Post from the journals to the ledger accounts.

Comprehensive Use of Special-Purpose Journals

P3. Ye Olde Book Store opened its doors for business on May 1. During May, the following transactions took place:

May 1   Linda Berrill began the business by depositing $42,000 in the new company's bank account.

3   Issued check no. C001 to Remax Rentals for one month's rent, $1,000.

4   Received a shipment of books from Chassman Books, Inc., invoice dated May 3, terms 5/10, n/60, FOB shipping point, $15,680.

SPREADSHEET

GENERAL LEDGER

✔ 2: Total accounts payable in purchases journal: $22,418

SPREADSHEET

GENERAL LEDGER

✔ 5: Total sales in sales journal: $3,652
✔ 5: Total accounts payable in purchases journal: $34,748
✔ 5: Total cash receipts: $75,428
✔ 5: Total cash disbursements: $34,882
✔ 7: Total debits in trial balance: $91,616

(Continued)

May 5   Received a bill for freight from Menden Shippers for the previous day's shipment, terms n/30, $790.

6   Received a shipment from Lakeside Books, invoice dated May 6, terms 2/10, n/30, FOB shipping point, $11,300.

7   Issued check no. C002 to Pappanopoulos Freight for transportation charges on the previous day's shipment, $574.

8   Issued check no. C003 to Yun Chao Equipment Company for store equipment, $10,400.

9   Sold books to Midtown Center, terms 5/10, n/30, invoice no. 1001, $1,564.

10   Returned books to Chassman Books, Inc., for credit, $760.

11   Issued check no. C004 to WCAM for radio commercials, $235.

12   Issued check no. C005 to Chassman Books, Inc., for balance of amount owed less discount.

13   Cash sales for the first two weeks, $4,018. (For this problem, cash sales are recorded every two weeks, not daily as they are in actual practice.)

14   Issued check no. C006 to Lakeside Books, $6,000 less discount.

15   Signed a 90-day, 10 percent note for a bank loan and received $20,000 in cash.

15   Sold books to Steve Oahani, terms n/30, invoice no. 1002, $260.

16   Issued a credit memorandum to Midtown Center for returned books, $124.

17   Received full payment from Midtown Center of balance owed less discount.

18   Sold books to Missy Porter, terms n/30, invoice no. 1003, $194.

19   Received a shipment from Perspectives Publishing Company, invoice dated May 18, terms 5/10, n/60, $4,604.

20   Returned additional books purchased on May 4 to Chassman Books, Inc., for credit at gross price, $1,436.

21   Sold books to Midtown Center, terms 5/10, n/30, invoice no. 1004, $1,634.

23   Received a shipment from Chassman Books, Inc., invoice dated May 19, terms 5/10, n/60, FOB shipping point, $2,374.

24   Issued check no. C007 to Menden Shippers for balance owed on account plus shipping charges of $194 on previous day's shipment.

27   Cash sales for the second two weeks, $7,488.

29   Issued check no. C008 to Payroll for salaries for first four weeks of the month, $1,400.

30   Issued check no. C009 to WXAM for radio commercials, $235.

31   Cash sales for the last four days of the month, $554.

REQUIRED

1. Prepare a sales journal, a multicolumn purchases journal, a cash receipts journal, a cash payments journal, and a general journal. Use Page 1 for all journal references.

2. Open the following general ledger accounts: Cash (111), Accounts Receivable (112), Store Equipment (141), Accounts Payable (211), Notes Payable (212), Linda Berrill, Capital (311), Sales (411), Sales Discounts (412), Sales Returns and Allowances (413), Purchases (511), Purchases Discounts (512), Purchases Returns and Allowances (513), Freight In (514), Salaries Expense (611), Advertising Expense (612), and Rent Expense (613).

3. Open accounts receivable subsidiary ledger accounts for Midtown Center, Steve Oahani, and Missy Porter.

4. Open accounts payable subsidiary ledger accounts for Chassman Books, Inc.; Lakeside Books; Menden Shippers; and Perspectives Publishing Company.

5. Enter the transactions in the journals and post as appropriate.

6. Foot and crossfoot the journals, and make the end-of-month postings.

7. Prepare a trial balance of the general ledger and prove the control balances of Accounts Receivable and Accounts Payable by preparing schedules of accounts receivable and accounts payable.

CHAPTER 7
Inventories

Grabs Company is a new store that sells a variety of stylish leather boots and bags. Because Grabs is a merchandising company, inventory is an important component of its total assets. The decisions that Darcy Ming, the company's owner, makes about how to account for inventory can have a significant impact on its operating results. Darcy has several decisions to make, including which inventory system and costing method to use, how to value inventory, and how much inventory to keep in stock.

1. CONCEPT ▶ *Why is the relationship between accrual accounting and valuation important for inventory accounting?*

2. ACCOUNTING APPLICATION ▶ *How would Grabs account for merchandising inventory using (a) the average-cost method, (b) the FIFO method, and (c) the LIFO method under periodic and perpetual inventory systems?*

3. BUSINESS APPLICATION ▶ *How do decisions about inventory valuation and inventory levels affect operating results?*

LEARNING OBJECTIVES

LO 1 Explain the concepts underlying inventory accounting.

LO 2 Calculate inventory cost under the periodic inventory system using various costing methods.

LO 3 Explain the effects of inventory costing methods on income determination and income taxes.

LO 4 Calculate inventory cost under the perpetual inventory system using various costing methods.

LO 5 Use the retail method and gross profit method to estimate the cost of ending inventory.

LO 6 Evaluate inventory level, and demonstrate the effects of inventory misstatements on income measurement.

CONCEPTS
- Accrual accounting (matching rule)
- Valuation
- Conservatism
- Disclosure

RELEVANT LEARNING OBJECTIVE

LO 1 Explain the concepts underlying inventory accounting.

LO 1 Concepts Underlying Inventory Accounting

For any company that makes or sells merchandise, inventory is an extremely important asset. Managing this asset requires not only protecting goods from theft or loss, but also ensuring that operations are highly efficient. Further, as you will see in this chapter, proper accounting for inventory is essential because misstatements will affect net income in at least two years.

Inventory is considered a current asset because a company normally sells it within a year or within its operating cycle. For a merchandising company like **CVS** or **Walgreens**, inventory consists of all goods owned and held for sale in the regular course of business. Because manufacturing companies like **Toyota** are engaged in making products, they have three kinds of inventory:

- Raw materials (goods used in making products)
- Work in process (partially completed products)
- Finished goods ready for sale

In a note to its financial statements, Toyota showed the following breakdown of its inventories (figures are in millions):[1]

Inventories	2011	2010
Raw materials (includes supplies)	$ 4,457	$ 3,634
Work in process	2,626	2,142
Finished goods	8,602	9,512
Total inventories	$15,685	$15,288

The work in process and the finished goods inventories have three cost components:

- Cost of the raw materials that go into the product
- Cost of the labor used to convert the raw materials to finished goods
- Overhead costs that support the production process

Overhead costs include the costs of indirect materials (such as packing materials), indirect labor (such as the salaries of supervisors), factory rent, depreciation of plant assets, utilities, and insurance.

Accrual Accounting and Valuation of Inventories

The primary objective of **inventory accounting** is to apply *accrual accounting* to the determination of cost of inventory sold during the accounting period. *Valuation* of inventories is usually at cost. **Inventory cost** includes the following:

- Invoice price less purchases discounts
- Freight-in, including insurance in transit
- Applicable taxes and tariffs

Other costs—for ordering, receiving, and storing—should, in principle, be included in inventory cost. In practice, however, it is so difficult to allocate such costs to specific inventory items that they are usually considered expenses of the period.

Inventory *valuation* depends on the prices of goods, which usually vary during the year. A company may have purchased identical lots of merchandise at different prices. Also, for identical items, it is often impossible to tell which have been sold and which are still in inventory. Thus, it is necessary to make an assumption about the order in which items have been sold. Because the assumed order of sale may or may not be the same as the actual order of sale, the assumption is really about the *flow of costs* rather than the *flow of physical inventory*.

Goods Flows and Cost Flows

STUDY NOTE: *The assumed flow of inventory costs does not have to correspond to the physical flow of goods.*

Goods flow refers to the actual physical movement of goods in the operations of a company. **Cost flow** refers to the association of costs with their *assumed* flow. The assumed cost flow may or may not be the same as the actual goods flow. A difference arises because several choices of assumed cost flow are available under generally accepted accounting principles. In fact, it is sometimes preferable to use an assumed cost flow that bears no relationship to goods flow because it results in a better estimate of income, which is the main goal of inventory accounting.

Merchandise in Transit Because merchandise inventory includes all items that a company owns and holds for sale, the status of any merchandise in transit, whether the company is selling it or buying it, must be evaluated to see if the merchandise should be included in the inventory count. Neither the seller nor the buyer has *physical* possession of merchandise in transit. As Exhibit 1 shows, ownership is determined by the terms of the shipping agreement, which indicate when title passes. Outgoing goods shipped FOB (free on board) destination are included in the seller's merchandise inventory, whereas those shipped FOB shipping point are not. Conversely, incoming goods shipped FOB shipping point are included in the buyer's merchandise inventory, but those shipped FOB destination are not.

Exhibit 1
Merchandise in Transit

Goods in Transit

Shipping point

Seller's Warehouse

BOUTIQUE

Destination

Customer's Store

© Cengage Learning 2014

Terms
FOB shipping point: buyer owns inventory in transit.
FOB destination: seller owns inventory in transit.

Merchandise Not Included in Inventory At the time a company takes a physical inventory, it may have merchandise to which it does not hold title. For example, it may have sold goods but not yet delivered them to the buyer, but because the sale has been completed, title has passed to the buyer. Thus, the merchandise should be included in the buyer's inventory, not the seller's. Goods held on consignment also fall into this category. A **consignment** is merchandise that its owner (the consignor) places on the premises of another company (the consignee) with the understanding that payment is expected only when the merchandise is sold and that unsold items may be returned to the consignor. Title to consigned goods remains with the consignor until the consignee sells the goods. Consigned goods should not be included in the consignee's physical inventory.

Conservatism and the Lower-of-Cost-or-Market (LCM) Rule

Although cost is usually the most appropriate *valuation* basis, inventory may at times be properly shown in the financial statements at less than its historical, or original, cost. If

International Perspective
IFRS Is "Market" the Same as Fair Value Under IFRS?

When the lower-of-cost-or-market rule is used, what does "market" mean? Under international financial reporting standards (IFRS), market is considered fair value, which is defined as the amount at which an asset can be sold. However, in valuing inventory under U.S. standards, market is normally considered the replacement cost, or the amount at which an identical asset can be purchased. The two "market" values, selling price and purchasing price, can often be quite different for the same asset. This is an issue that will have to be addressed if the U.S. and international standards are to achieve convergence.

STUDY NOTE: *Cost must be determined by one of the inventory costing methods before it can be compared with the market value.*

the market value of inventory falls below its historical cost because of physical deterioration, obsolescence, or decline in price level, a loss has occurred. This loss is recognized by writing the inventory down to **market**—that is, to its current replacement cost. For a merchandising company, market is the amount that it would pay at the present time for the same goods, purchased from the usual suppliers and in the usual quantities.

When the replacement cost of inventory falls below its historical cost (as determined by an inventory costing method), the **lower-of-cost-or-market (LCM) rule** requires that the inventory be written down to the lower value and that a loss be recorded. This rule is an example of the *conservatism* concept because the loss is recognized before an actual transaction takes place. It is also an application of conservatism because, if the replacement cost rises, no gain is recognized and the inventory remains at cost until it is sold. According to an AICPA survey, approximately 80 percent of large companies apply the LCM rule to their inventories for financial reporting.[2]

Disclosure of Inventory Methods

The *disclosure* concept requires that companies disclose their inventory methods, including the use of LCM, in the notes to their financial statements. For example, **Toyota** discloses its use of the lower-of-cost-or-market method in this note to its financial statements:

> *Inventories are valued at cost, not in excess of market, cost being determined on the "average cost" basis....*[3]

Summary of Inventory Decisions

STUDY NOTE: *Management considers the behavior of inventory costs over time when selecting inventory costing methods.*

As you can see in Exhibit 2, in accounting for inventory, management must choose among different processing systems, costing methods, and *valuation* methods. These different systems and methods usually result in different amounts of reported net income. Thus, management's choices affect investors' and creditors' evaluations of a company, as well as the internal performance reviews on which bonuses and executive compensation are based.

The *consistency* concept requires that once a company has decided on the accounting systems and methods it will use for inventory, it must use them from one period to the next. When a change is justifiable, the *full disclosure convention* requires that the company clearly describes the change and its effects in the notes to the financial statements.

Because the *valuation* of inventory affects income, it can have a large impact on the income taxes a company pays—and the taxes it pays can impact its cash flows. Federal income tax regulations are specific about the valuation methods a company may use. As a result, management is sometimes faced with the dilemma of how to apply GAAP to income determination and still minimize income taxes.

Exhibit 2
Management Choices in Accounting for Inventories

© Cengage Learning 2014

APPLY IT!

Match each lettered item or convention that follows with its related numbered item.

a. An inventory cost
b. An assumption used in the valuation of inventory
c. Full disclosure convention
d. Conservatism convention
e. Consistency convention
f. Not an inventory cost or assumed flow

1. Cost of consigned goods
2. A note to the financial statements explaining inventory policies
3. Application of the LCM rule
4. Goods flow
5. Transportation charge for merchandise shipped FOB shipping point
6. Cost flow
7. Choosing a method and sticking with it
8. Transportation charge for merchandise shipped FOB destination

SOLUTION

1. f; 2. c; 3. d; 4. b; 5. a;
6. b; 7. e; 8. f

TRY IT! SE1, E1A, E1B

ACCOUNTING APPLICATIONS

LO 2 Inventory Cost Under the Periodic Inventory System

The value assigned to the ending inventory is the result of two measurements: quantity and cost. Under the periodic inventory system, quantity is determined by taking a physical inventory. Cost is determined by using one of the following methods, each based on an assumption of cost flow:

■ Specific identification method
■ Average-cost method
■ First-in, first-out (FIFO) method
■ Last-in, first-out (LIFO) method

If the prices of merchandise purchased never changed, inventory methods would be unnecessary. However, because prices do change, assumptions must be made about the order in which goods are sold. The choice of method depends on the nature of the business, the financial effects, and the cost of implementation.

To illustrate how each method is used under the periodic inventory system, we use Boilen Company. The following data for April, a month in which prices were rising, are available:

April	1	Inventory	160 units @ $10.00	$ 1,600
	6	Purchase	440 units @ $12.50	5,500
	25	Purchase	400 units @ $14.00	5,600
Goods available for sale			1,000 units	$12,700
Sales			560 units	
On hand April 30			440 units	

The problem of inventory costing is to divide the cost of the goods available for sale ($12,700) between the 560 units sold and the 440 units on hand.

Specific Identification Method

The **specific identification method** identifies the cost of each item in the ending inventory. It can be used only when it is possible to identify the units as coming from specific purchases. For instance, if Boilen's April 30 inventory consisted of 100 units from the April 1 inventory, 200 units from the April 6 purchase, and 140 units from the April 25 purchase, the specific identification method would assign the costs as follows.

Periodic Inventory System—Specific Identification Method			
100 units @ $10.00	$1,000	Cost of goods available for sale	$12,700
200 units @ $12.50	2,500		
140 units @ $14.00	1,960	Less April 30 inventory	5,460
440 units at a cost of	$5,460	Cost of goods sold	$ 7,240

Although the specific identification method may appear logical, most companies do not use it for the following reasons:

■ It is usually impractical, if not impossible, to keep track of the purchase and sale of individual items.
■ When a company deals in items that are identical but bought at different prices, deciding which items were sold becomes arbitrary. If the company were to use the

specific identification method, it could raise or lower income by choosing the lower- or higher-priced items.

Average-Cost Method

Under the **average-cost method** (or *weighted average method*), inventory is priced at the average cost of the goods available for sale during the period. Average cost is computed as follows.

$$\text{Average Cost} = \frac{\text{Total Cost of Goods Available for Sale}}{\text{Total Units Available for Sale}}$$

This gives an average unit cost that is applied to the units in the ending inventory. For Boilen, the ending inventory would be $5,588, or $12.70 per unit, determined as follows.

Periodic Inventory System—Average-Cost Method

Cost of Goods Available for Sale ÷ Units Available for Sale = Average Unit Cost
$12,700 ÷ 1,000 units = $12.70

Ending inventory: 440 units @ $12.70 =	$ 5,588
Cost of goods available for sale	$12,700
Less April 30 inventory	5,588
Cost of goods sold	$ 7,112

The average-cost method tends to level out the effects of cost increases and decreases because the cost of the ending inventory is influenced by all the prices paid during the year and by the cost of the beginning inventory. Some analysts, however, believe that recent costs are more relevant for income measurement and decision making.

First-In, First-Out (FIFO) Method

STUDY NOTE: *Because of their perishable nature, some products, such as milk, require a physical flow of first-in, first-out. However, the inventory method used to account for them can be based on an assumed cost flow that differs from FIFO, such as average-cost or LIFO.*

The **first-in, first-out (FIFO) method** assumes that the costs of the first items acquired should be assigned to the first items sold. The costs of the goods on hand at the end of a period are assumed to be from the most recent purchases, and the costs assigned to goods that have been sold are assumed to be from the earliest purchases. Any business, regardless of its goods flow, can use the FIFO method because the assumption underlying it is based on the flow of costs, not the flow of goods. For Boilen, the FIFO method would result in an ending inventory of $6,100, computed as follows.

Periodic Inventory System—FIFO Method

400 units @ $14.00 from purchase of April 25	$ 5,600
40 units @ $12.50 from purchase of April 6	500
440 units at a cost of	$ 6,100
Cost of goods available for sale	$12,700
Less April 30 inventory	6,100
Cost of goods sold	$ 6,600

Thus, the FIFO method values the ending inventory at the most recent costs and includes earlier costs in the cost of goods sold.

▲ During periods of rising prices, FIFO yields the highest possible amount of net income because the cost of goods sold shows the earliest costs incurred, which are lower during periods of inflation. Another reason for this is that businesses tend to raise selling prices as costs increase, even when they purchased the goods before the cost increase.

▼ In periods of declining prices, FIFO tends to charge the older and higher prices against revenues, thus reducing income. Consequently, a major criticism of FIFO is that it magnifies the effects of the business cycle on income.

Last-In, First-Out (LIFO) Method

The **last-in, first-out (LIFO) method** of costing inventories assumes that the costs of the last items purchased should be assigned to the first items sold and that the cost of the ending inventory should reflect the cost of the goods purchased earliest. Under LIFO, Boilen's April 30 inventory would be $5,100, computed as follows.

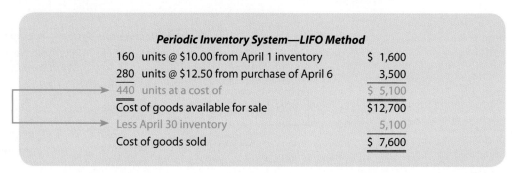

Periodic Inventory System—LIFO Method	
160 units @ $10.00 from April 1 inventory	$ 1,600
280 units @ $12.50 from purchase of April 6	3,500
440 units at a cost of	$ 5,100
Cost of goods available for sale	$12,700
Less April 30 inventory	5,100
Cost of goods sold	$ 7,600

The effect of LIFO is to value inventory at the earliest prices and to include the cost of the most recently purchased goods in the cost of goods sold. The logical argument for LIFO is that a certain size of inventory is necessary in a going concern. When inventory is sold, it must be replaced with more goods. The supporters of LIFO reason that the fairest determination of income occurs if the current costs of merchandise are matched against current sales prices, regardless of which physical units of merchandise are sold. When prices are moving either up or down, the cost of goods sold will, under LIFO, show costs closer to the price level at the time the goods are sold. Thus, the LIFO method tends to show a smaller net income during inflationary times and a larger net income during deflationary times than other methods of inventory *valuation*. The peaks and valleys of the business cycle tend to be smoothed out.

An argument can also be made against LIFO. Because the inventory *valuation* on the balance sheet reflects earlier prices, it often gives an unrealistic picture of the inventory's current value. Balance sheet measures like working capital and current ratio may be distorted and must be interpreted carefully.

STUDY NOTE: *Physical flow under LIFO can be likened to the changes in a gravel pile as the gravel is sold. As the gravel on top leaves the pile, more is purchased and added to the top. The gravel on the bottom may never be sold.*

STUDY NOTE: *In inventory valuation, the flow of costs—and hence income determination—is more important than the physical movement of goods and balance sheet valuation.*

International Perspective

IFRS Achieving Convergence of Inventory Methods Will Be Difficult

Achieving convergence in inventory methods between U.S. and international accounting standards will be very difficult. While, LIFO is the second most popular inventory method in the United States, outside the United States, very few companies use LIFO because it is not allowed under international financial reporting standards (IFRS). Furthermore, U.S. companies may use different inventory methods for different portions of their inventory as long as there is proper *disclosure*; but international standards only allow this practice in very limited cases. Also, as noted earlier in the chapter, U.S. and international standards have different ways of measuring the "market" value of inventories. Because these differences are so significant, the FASB and IASB have decided not to pursue convergence with regard to inventories at this time.[4]

Summary of Inventory Costing Methods

Exhibit 3 summarizes how the four inventory costing methods affect the cost of goods sold and inventory when a company uses the periodic inventory system. In periods of rising prices, FIFO yields the highest inventory *valuation*, the lowest cost of goods sold, and hence a higher net income. LIFO yields the lowest inventory valuation, the highest cost of goods sold, and thus a lower net income.

Exhibit 3

The Impact of Costing Methods on the Income Statement and Balance Sheet Under the Periodic Inventory System

© Cengage Learning 2014

Cost of Goods Available for Sale
$12,700

	Income Statement—Cost of Goods Sold	Balance Sheet—Inventory
Specific Identification	$7,240	$5,460
Average-Cost	$7,112	$5,588
FIFO	$6,600	$6,100
LIFO	$7,600	$5,100

▨ Income Statement—Cost of Goods Sold

▨ Balance Sheet—Inventory

APPLY IT!

Using the data that follows and the periodic inventory system, determine the cost of goods sold associated with the sale on May 6 under the following methods: (a) average-cost, (b) FIFO, and (c) LIFO.

Inventory Data—April 30

May	1	Inventory	100 units @ $4.00
	5	Purchase	200 units @ $5.00
		Sales in May	250 units

SOLUTION

a. Average-cost method:

100 units × $4	$ 400
200 units × $5	1,000
300 units	$1,400

$1,400 ÷ 300 = $4.67* per unit

Cost of goods sold = 250 units × $4.67* = **$1,168***

*Rounded

b. FIFO method:

100 units × $4	$ 400
150 units × $5	750
Cost of goods sold	$1,150

c. LIFO method:

200 units × $5	$1,000
50 units × $4	200
Cost of goods sold	$1,200

TRY IT! SE2, SE3, SE4, SE5, E2A, E3A, E2B, E3B

LO3 Impact of Inventory Decisions

Continuing with the Boilen Company example and assuming Boilen had April sales of $10,000, Exhibit 4 shows how the specific identification, average-cost, FIFO, and LIFO methods of pricing inventory affect gross margin. Differences in gross margin will affect net income to the same extent.

Exhibit 4
Effects of Inventory Costing Methods on Gross Margin

	Specific Identification Method	Average-Cost Method	FIFO Method	LIFO Method
Sales	$10,000	$10,000	$10,000	$10,000
Cost of goods sold				
Beginning inventory	$ 1,600	$ 1,600	$ 1,600	$ 1,600
Purchases	11,100	11,100	11,100	11,100
Cost of goods available for sale	$12,700	$12,700	$12,700	$12,700
Less ending inventory	5,460	5,588	6,100	5,100
Cost of goods sold	$ 7,240	$ 7,112	$ 6,600	$ 7,600
Gross margin	$ 2,760	$ 2,888	$ 3,400	$ 2,400

© Cengage Learning 2014

Keeping in mind that April was a period of rising prices, Exhibit 4 shows that LIFO, which charges the most recent—and, for Boilen, the highest—prices to the cost of goods sold, resulted in the lowest gross margin. Conversely, FIFO, which charges the earliest—and, in this case, the lowest—prices to the cost of goods sold, produced the highest gross margin. The gross margin under the average-cost method falls between the gross margins produced by LIFO and FIFO. During a period of declining prices, the LIFO method would produce a higher gross margin than the FIFO method because the cost of goods sold would be lower, thus the higher gross margin. Both methods have the greatest impact on gross margin during prolonged periods of price changes, whether up or down.

Effects on the Financial Statements

As Exhibit 5 shows, the FIFO, LIFO, and average-cost methods are widely used. Each method has its advantages and disadvantages. Among the factors managers should consider in choosing an inventory costing method are the trend of prices and the effects of each method on financial statements, income taxes, and cash flows.

Exhibit 5
Inventory Costing Methods Used by 500 Large Companies

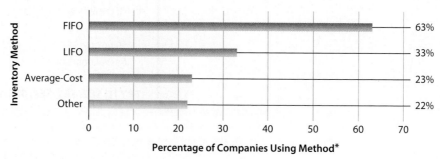

*Totals more than 100% due to use of more than one method.

Source: "Industry Costing Methods Used by 500 Large Companies." Copyright © 2011 by AICPA. Reproduced with permission.

As noted, inventory costing methods have different effects on the income statement and balance sheet. The LIFO method is best suited for the income statement because it *matches* revenues and the cost of goods sold. But it is not the best method for *valuing* inventory on the balance sheet, particularly during a prolonged period of price increases or decreases. FIFO, on the other hand, is well suited to the balance sheet because the ending inventory is closest to current values, thus giving a more realistic view of a company's current assets.

Effects on Income Taxes

The Internal Revenue Service governs how inventories must be valued for federal income tax purposes. IRS regulations give companies a wide choice of inventory costing methods, including specific identification, average-cost, FIFO, and LIFO. Except when companies use the LIFO method, they may use the lower-of-cost-or-market rule. However, if a company wants to change the *valuation* method it uses for income tax purposes, it must have advance approval from the IRS.* This requirement conforms to the *consistency convention*. A company should change its inventory method only if there is a good reason to do so. The company must show the nature and effect of the change in its financial statements.

Many accountants believe that using the FIFO and average-cost methods in periods of rising prices causes businesses to overstate their profit, resulting in excess income tax. Profit is overstated because the cost of goods sold is understated relative to current prices. Thus, the company must buy replacement inventory at higher prices, and at the same time pay income taxes. During periods of rapid inflation, billions of dollars reported as profits and paid in income taxes were believed to be the result of the poor matching of current costs and revenues under the FIFO and average-cost methods. Consequently, many companies, believing that prices would continue to rise, switched to the LIFO inventory method. When a company uses the LIFO method for tax purposes, the IRS requires that it use the same method in its accounting records.

Over a period of rising prices, a business that uses the LIFO method may find that its inventory is valued at a figure far below what it currently pays for the same items. Management must monitor such a situation carefully. If it lets the inventory quantity at year end fall below the level at the beginning of the year, the company will pay higher income taxes. Higher income before taxes results because the company expenses the historical costs of inventory, which are below current costs.

When sales have reduced inventories below the levels set in prior years, it is called a **LIFO liquidation**—that is, units sold exceed units purchased for the period. Managers can prevent a LIFO liquidation by making enough purchases before the end of the year to restore the desired inventory level. Sometimes, however, a LIFO liquidation cannot be avoided because products are discontinued or supplies are interrupted, as in the case of a strike. In a recent year, 28 out of 500 large companies reported a LIFO liquidation in which their net income increased due to the matching of historical costs with present sales dollars.[5]

Effects on Cash Flows

Generally speaking, a company's choice of average cost, FIFO, or LIFO does not affect cash flows. However, the choice of inventory method will affect the amount of income tax paid. Therefore, choosing a method that results in lower income will result in lower income taxes. In most other cases where there is a choice of accounting method, a company may choose different methods for income tax computations and financial reporting.

STUDY NOTE: In periods of rising prices, LIFO results in lower net income and lower taxes.

---

*A single exception to this rule is that when companies change to LIFO from another method, they do not need advance approval from IRS.

APPLY IT! ▶

Match the following inventory costing methods with the related statements:
(a) Average cost, (b) FIFO, or (c) LIFO

1. In periods of rising prices, this method results in the highest cost of goods sold.

2. In periods of rising prices, this method results in the highest income.

3. In periods of rising prices, this method results in the lowest ending inventory cost.

4. In periods of rising prices, this method results in the lowest income tax.

5. In periods of decreasing prices, this method results in neither the highest inventory cost nor the lowest income.

6. In periods of decreasing prices, this method results in the lowest income.

7. In periods of decreasing prices, this method results in the highest cost of goods sold.

8. In periods of decreasing prices, this method results in the lowest income tax.

SOLUTION
1. c; 2. b; 3. c; 4. c; 5. a; 6. b; 7. b; 8. b

TRY IT! SE6, E4A, E5A, E4B, E5B

LO 4 Inventory Cost Under the Perpetual Inventory System

Under the perpetual inventory system, inventory is updated as purchases and sales take place. The cost of goods sold is accumulated as sales are made and costs are transferred from the Inventory account to the Cost of Goods Sold account. The cost of the ending inventory is the balance of the Inventory account. Goods are valued using one of the following inventory costing methods: specific identification, average-cost, first-in, first-out (FIFO), or last-in, first-out (LIFO). To illustrate costing methods under the perpetual inventory system, we continue with the Boilen Company example. The following data for April, a month in which prices were rising, are available:

Inventory Data—April 30

April	1	Inventory	160 units @ $10.00
	6	Purchase	440 units @ $12.50
	10	Sale	560 units
	25	Purchase	400 units @ $14.00
	30	Inventory	440 units

Specific Identification Method

STUDY NOTE: *The specific identification method produces the same inventory cost and cost of goods sold under the perpetual system as under the periodic system because the cost of goods sold and the ending inventory are based on the cost of the identified items sold and on hand.*

The detailed records of purchases and sales maintained under the perpetual system facilitate the use of the specific identification method. For instance, if Boilen's April 30 inventory consisted of 100 units from the April 1 inventory, 200 units from the April 6 purchase, and 140 units from the April 25 purchase, the specific identification method would assign the costs as follows.

Perpetual Inventory System—Specific Identification Method

100 units @ $10.00	$1,000	Cost of goods available for sale	$12,700
200 units @ $12.50	2,500		
140 units @ $14.00	1,960	Less April 30 inventory	5,460
440 units at a cost of	$5,460	Cost of goods sold	$ 7,240

Average-Cost Method

Under the perpetual system, an average is computed after each purchase or series of purchases, as follows.

Perpetual Inventory System—Average-Cost Method

April	1	Inventory	160 units @ $10.00	$1,600
	6	Purchase	440 units @ $12.50	5,500
	6	Balance	600 units @ $11.83*	$7,100
				(new average computed)
	10	Sale	560 units @ $11.83*	→ (6,625)
	10	Balance	40 units @ $11.83*	$ 475
	25	Purchase	400 units @ $14.00	5,600
	30	Inventory	440 units @ $13.81*	$6,075
				(new average computed)
		Cost of goods sold		→ $6,625

*Rounded

The costs applied to sales become the cost of goods sold, $6,625. The ending inventory is the balance, $6,075.

FIFO Method

When costing inventory with the FIFO and LIFO methods, it is necessary to keep track of the components of inventory because, as sales are made, the costs must be assigned in the proper order. The FIFO method is applied as follows.

Perpetual Inventory System—FIFO Method

April	1	Inventory	160 units @ $10.00		$1,600
	6	Purchase	440 units @ $12.50		5,500
	10	Sale	160 units @ $10.00	$(1,600)	
			400 units @ $12.50	(5,000)	(6,600)
	10	Balance	40 units @ $12.50		$ 500
	25	Purchase	400 units @ $14.00		5,600
	30	Inventory	40 units @ $12.50	$ 500	
			400 units @ $14.00	5,600	$6,100
		Cost of goods sold			$6,600

STUDY NOTE: *The average-cost method produces different results under the perpetual and periodic systems. Under the periodic system, the average cost is computed for all goods available for sale during the period.*

STUDY NOTE: *Under the FIFO perpetual inventory system, Boilen's ending inventory of $6,100 and the cost of goods sold of $6,600 are the same as under the periodic inventory system. This will always occur because the ending inventory under both systems consists of the last items purchased—in this case, the entire purchase of April 25 and 40 units from the purchase of April 6.*

Business Perspective
More Companies Enjoy LIFO!

The availability of better technology may partially account for the increasing use of LIFO in the United States. Using the LIFO method under the perpetual inventory system has always been a tedious process, especially if done manually. The development of faster and less expensive computer systems has made it easier for companies that use the perpetual inventory system to switch to LIFO and enjoy its economic benefits.

LIFO Method

The LIFO method is applied as follows.

		Perpetual Inventory System—LIFO Method			
April	1	Inventory	160 units @ $10.00		$ 1,600
	6	Purchase	440 units @ $12.50		5,500
	10	Sale	440 units @ $12.50	$(5,500)	
			120 units @ $10.00	(1,200)	(6,700)
	10	Balance	40 units @ $10.00		$ 400
	25	Purchase	400 units @ $14.00		5,600
	30	Inventory	40 units @ $10.00	$ 400	
			400 units @ $14.00	5,600	$6,000
		Cost of goods sold			$ 6,700

The ending inventory of $6,000 includes 40 units from the beginning inventory and 400 units from the April 25 purchase.

Summary of Inventory Costing Methods

Exhibit 6 compares the specific identification, average-cost, FIFO, and LIFO methods under the perpetual inventory system for Boilen. In this period of rising prices, FIFO produces the highest inventory value and lowest cost of goods sold, and LIFO produces the lowest inventory cost and highest cost of goods sold. The average-cost method is in between. Specific identification is the same as under the periodic inventory system.

Exhibit 6
The Impact of Costing Methods on the Income Statement and Balance Sheet Under the Perpetual Inventory System

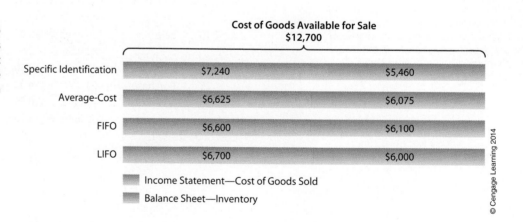

Cost of Goods Available for Sale
$12,700

	Income Statement—Cost of Goods Sold	Balance Sheet—Inventory
Specific Identification	$7,240	$5,460
Average-Cost	$6,625	$6,075
FIFO	$6,600	$6,100
LIFO	$6,700	$6,000

Income Statement—Cost of Goods Sold
Balance Sheet—Inventory

© Cengage Learning 2014

APPLY IT! ▶

Using the data that follows and the perpetual inventory system, determine the cost of goods sold associated with the sale on May 6 under the following methods: (a) average-cost, (b) FIFO, and (c) LIFO.

Inventory Data—April 30

May	1	Inventory	120 units @ $8.00
	5	Purchase	200 units @ $10.00
	6	Sale	220 units

SOLUTION

a. Average-cost method:

120 units × $8	$ 960
200 units × $10	2,000
320 units	$2,960

$2,960 ÷ 320 = $9.25 per unit

Cost of goods sold = 220 units × $9.25 = $2,035

b. FIFO method:

120 units × $8	$ 960
100 units × $10	1,000
Cost of goods sold	$1,960

c. LIFO method:

200 units × $10	$2,000
20 units × $8	160
Cost of goods sold	$2,160

TRY IT! SE7, SE8, SE9, E6A, E7A, E6B, E7B

LO5 Valuing Inventory by Estimation

It is sometimes necessary or desirable to estimate the value of the ending inventory. The retail method and gross profit method are most commonly used for this purpose.

Retail Method

The **retail method** estimates the cost of the ending inventory by using the ratio of cost to retail price. Retail merchandising businesses use this method for two main reasons:

■ To prepare financial statements for each period, the retail method can be used to estimate the cost without taking the time or going to the expense of determining the cost of each item in the inventory.

■ Because items in a retail store normally have a price tag or a universal product code, it is common practice to take the physical inventory "at retail" from these price tags or codes and to reduce the total value to cost by using the retail method. *At retail* means the amount of the inventory at the marked selling prices of the items.

STUDY NOTE: When estimating inventory by the retail method, the inventory need not be counted.

When the retail method is used, the records must show the beginning inventory at cost and at retail. They must also show the amount of goods purchased during the period at cost and at retail. The net sales at retail is the balance of the Sales account less returns and allowances. A simple example of the retail method is shown in Exhibit 7.

As shown in Exhibit 7, goods available for sale is determined at cost and at retail by listing the beginning inventory and net purchases for the period at cost and at their expected selling price, adding freight-in to the Cost column, and totaling. The ratio of these two amounts (cost to retail price) provides an estimate of the cost of each dollar of retail sales value. The estimated ending inventory at retail is then determined, as shown in Exhibit 7, by deducting sales for the period from the retail price of the goods that were available for sale during the period. The inventory at retail is then converted to cost on the basis of the ratio of cost to retail.

The cost of the ending inventory can also be estimated by applying the ratio of cost to retail price to the total retail value of the physical count of the ending inventory.

Exhibit 7
Retail Method of
Inventory Estimation

	Cost	Retail
Beginning inventory	$ 80,000	$110,000
Net purchases for the period (excluding freight-in)	214,000	290,000
Freight-in	6,000	
Goods available for sale	$300,000	$400,000
Ratio of cost to retail price: $\dfrac{\$300,000}{\$400,000} = 75\%$		
Net sales during the period		320,000
Estimated ending inventory at retail		$ 80,000
Ratio of cost to retail	75%	
Estimated cost of ending inventory	$ 60,000	

© Cengage Learning 2014

STUDY NOTE: *Freight-in does not appear in the Retail column because retailers automatically price their goods high enough to cover freight charges.*

Applying the retail method in practice is often more difficult than this simple example because of such complications as changes in retail price during the period, different markups on different types of merchandise, and varying volumes of sales for different types of merchandise.

Gross Profit Method

The **gross profit method** (or *gross margin method*) assumes that the ratio of gross margin for a business remains relatively stable from year to year. The gross profit method is used in place of the retail method when records of the retail prices of the beginning inventory and purchases are not available. It is a useful way of estimating the amount of inventory lost or destroyed by theft, fire, or other hazards. Insurance companies often use it to verify loss claims. The gross profit method is acceptable for estimating the cost of inventory for interim reports, but it is not acceptable for valuing inventory in the annual financial statements.

As Exhibit 8 shows, the gross profit method involves the following steps:

- **Step 1.** Calculate the cost of goods available for sale in the usual way (add purchases to beginning inventory).
- **Step 2.** Estimate the cost of goods sold by deducting the estimated gross margin of 30 percent from sales.
- **Step 3.** Deduct the estimated cost of goods sold from the goods available for sale to arrive at the estimated cost of the ending inventory.

Exhibit 8
Gross Profit Method of
Inventory Estimation

Step 1. Beginning inventory at cost		$100,000
Purchases at cost (including freight-in)		580,000
Cost of goods available for sale		$680,000
Step 2. Less estimated cost of goods sold		
Sales at selling price	$800,000	
Less estimated gross margin		
($800,000 × 30%)	240,000	
Estimated cost of goods sold		560,000
Step 3. Estimated cost of ending inventory		$120,000

© Cengage Learning 2014

Inventory and the Financial Statements

Cost of goods sold is created by the transfer from the balance sheet the cost of the inventories sold to the income statement during the period. The amount of the transfer depends on the *valuation* of inventories using one of the methods illustrated in this chapter. The transfer is depicted in Exhibit 9.

Exhibit 9

**Valuation of Inventory on the Balance Sheet Impacts
Cost of Goods Sold on the Income Statement**

APPLY IT!

Tommy's Vintage Shop had net retail sales of $195,000 during the current year. The following additional information was obtained from the company's accounting records:

	At Cost	At Retail
Beginning inventory	$ 40,000	$ 60,000
Net purchases (excluding freight-in)	130,000	210,000
Freight-in	5,500	

Using the retail method, estimate the company's ending inventory at cost. Assuming that a physical count taken at year-end revealed an inventory of $66,000 at retail value, what is the estimated amount of inventory shrinkage (loss due to theft, damage, etc.) at cost using the retail method?

SOLUTION

	Cost	Retail
Beginning inventory	$ 40,000	$ 60,000
Net purchases for the period (excluding freight-in)	130,000	210,000
Freight-in	5,500	
Goods available for sale	$175,500	$270,000

Ratio of cost to retail price: $\dfrac{\$175,500}{\$270,000} = 65\%$

Net sales during the period		195,000
Estimated ending inventory at retail		$ 75,000
Ratio of cost to retail	65%	
Estimated cost of ending inventory	$ 48,750	

Estimated Inventory Loss = Estimated Cost – (Retail Inventory Count × 65%)

= $48,750 – ($66,000 × 65%) = $48,750 – $42,900

= $5,850

TRY IT! SE10, E8A, E9A, E8B, E9B

BUSINESS APPLICATIONS

LO 6 Management Issues Related to Inventory

The ability to control inventory levels is a critical skill in managing a business. Further, misstatements in *valuing* inventory will have significant effects on reported net income and income taxes.

Evaluating the Level of Inventory

The level of inventory a company maintains has important economic consequences, and it involves conflicting goals. One goal is to have a great variety and quantity of goods on hand so that customers have a choice and do not have to wait for an item to be restocked. But this goal conflicts with the goal of controlling costs, which favors keeping the level of inventory low. Handling and storage costs and the interest cost of the funds needed to maintain high inventory levels are usually substantial. Some of the costs of carrying inventory are insurance, property tax, and storage costs. Other costs may result from spoilage and theft. However, low inventory levels can result in disgruntled customers and lost sales. Managers control inventory by closely observing two ratios: inventory turnover and days' inventory on hand.

Inventory Turnover **Inventory turnover** is the average number of times a company sells an amount equal to its average level of inventory during a period. For example, using **Nike**'s annual report, we can compute the company's inventory turnover for 2011 as follows (figures are in millions).

RATIO

Inventory Turnover: How Many Times Did the Company Sell Its Inventory During an Accounting Period?

$$\text{Inventory Turnover} = \frac{\text{Cost of Goods Sold}}{\text{Average Inventory}}$$

$$\text{Nike Inventory Turnover} = \frac{\$11,354}{(\$2,715 + \$2,041) \div 2}$$

$$= \frac{\$11,354}{\$2,378} = 4.8 \text{ times}$$

Based on Bizmin Industry Financial Report, December 2011.

Days' Inventory on Hand **Days' inventory on hand** is the average number of days it takes a company to sell an amount equal to its average inventory. It is computed using the inventory turnover. For **Nike**, it is computed as follows.

STUDY NOTE: *Inventory turnover will be systematically higher if year-end levels are low. For example, many merchandisers' year-end is in January when inventories are lower than at any other time of the year.*

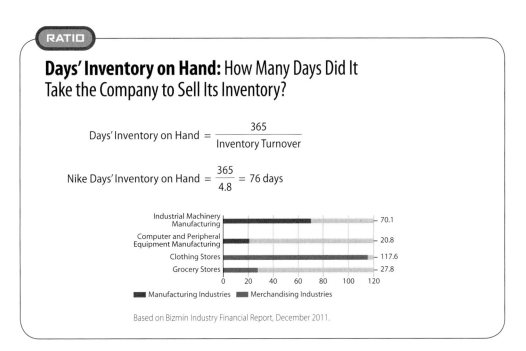

RATIO

Days' Inventory on Hand: How Many Days Did It Take the Company to Sell Its Inventory?

$$\text{Days' Inventory on Hand} = \frac{365}{\text{Inventory Turnover}}$$

$$\text{Nike Days' Inventory on Hand} = \frac{365}{4.8} = 76 \text{ days}$$

Industrial Machinery Manufacturing	70.1
Computer and Peripheral Equipment Manufacturing	20.8
Clothing Stores	117.6
Grocery Stores	27.8

■■■ Manufacturing Industries ■■■ Merchandising Industries

Based on Bizmin Industry Financial Report, December 2011.

Harley-Davidson uses a just-in-time operating environment when producing its legendary motorcycles—often with only 8 to 10 hours of inventory on hand. A lack of supply can therefore shut down assembly lines, so the company is careful when considering where to source parts because of the longer lead times and customs delays that can occur.

Hupeng/Dreamstime

Nike turned its inventory over 4.8 times in 2011 or, on average, about every 76 days. Thus, on average, products are held in inventory for almost three months before being sold. Until the products are sold, Nike either has to tie up its own money or obtain outside financing.

Inventory Management

To reduce their levels of inventory, many merchandisers and manufacturers use supply-chain management in conjunction with a just-in-time operating environment. With **supply-chain management**, a company uses the Internet to order and track goods that it needs immediately. A **just-in-time (JIT) operating environment** is one in which goods arrive just at the time they are needed.

Nike uses supply-chain management to increase inventory turnover. It manages its inventory purchases through business-to-business transactions that it conducts over the Internet. It also uses a JIT operating environment in which it works closely with suppliers to coordinate and schedule shipments. Thus, Nike has less money tied up in inventory and its cost of carrying inventory is reduced.

Business Perspective
A Whirlwind Inventory Turnover—How Does Dell Do It?

Dell Computer Corporation turns its inventory over every 10 days. How can it do this when other computer companies have inventory on hand for 60 days or even longer? Technology and good inventory management are a big part of the answer.

Dell's speed from order to delivery sets the standard for the computer industry. Consider that a computer ordered by 9 A.M. can be delivered the next day by 9 P.M. How can Dell do this when it does not start ordering components and assembling computers until a customer places an order? First, Dell's suppliers keep components warehoused just minutes from Dell's factories, making efficient, just-in-time operations possible. Dell also saves time by sending an e-mail message for some finished products to a shipper, such as **United Parcel Service**, and the shipper picks up the product from a supplier and schedules it to arrive with the PC. In addition to contributing to a high inventory turnover, this practice saves Dell in freight costs. Dell is showing the world how to run a business in the cyber age by selling more than $39 million worth of computers a day on its website.[6]

Effects of Inventory Misstatements on Income Measurement

The reason inventory accounting is so important to income measurement is the way income is measured. Recall that gross margin is the difference between net sales and the cost of goods sold, and that the cost of goods sold depends on the portion of the cost of goods available for sale assigned to the ending inventory. These relationships lead to the following conclusions:

- The higher the value of the ending inventory, the lower the cost of goods sold and the higher the gross margin.
- Conversely, the lower the value of the ending inventory, the higher the cost of goods sold and the lower the gross margin.

Because the amount of gross margin has a direct effect on net income, the value assigned to the ending inventory also affects net income. In effect, the value of the ending inventory determines what portion of the cost of goods available for sale is assigned to the cost of goods sold and what portion is assigned to inventory.

The basic issue in separating goods sold and goods not sold is to assign a value to the goods not sold, the ending inventory. The goods not assigned to the ending inventory are used to determine the cost of goods sold. Because the figures for the ending inventory and the cost of goods sold are related, a misstatement in the inventory figure at the end of a period will cause an equal misstatement in gross margin and income before income taxes. The amount of assets and owner's equity will be misstated by the same amount.

Inventory Misstatements and Fraud   Inventory is particularly susceptible to fraudulent financial reporting. For example, it is easy to overstate or understate inventory by including end-of-the-year purchase and sales transactions in the wrong fiscal year or by simply misstating inventory by mistake. A misstatement can also occur because of deliberate manipulation of operating results motivated by a desire to enhance the market's perception of the company, obtain bank financing, or achieve compensation incentives.

In one case, **Rite Aid Corporation**, the large drugstore chain, falsified income by manipulating its computerized inventory system to cover losses from shoplifting, employee theft, and spoilage.[7] In another case, bookkeepers at **Rent-Way, Inc.**, which rents furniture to apartment dwellers, boosted income artificially over several years by overstating inventory in small increments.[8]

Inventory Misstatements Illustrated   Whatever the causes of an overstatement or understatement of inventory, the three examples that follow illustrate the effects. In each case, the beginning inventory, the net cost of purchases, and the cost of goods available for sale are stated correctly. In Example 1, the ending inventory is correctly stated; in Example 2, it is overstated by $3,000; and in Example 3, it is understated by $3,000.

Example 1. Ending Inventory Correctly Stated at $5,000

Cost of Goods Sold for the Year		Income Statement for the Year	
Beginning inventory	$ 6,000	Net sales	$50,000
Net cost of purchases	29,000	Cost of goods sold	30,000
Cost of goods available for sale	$35,000	Gross margin	$20,000
Ending inventory	5,000	Operating expenses	16,000
Cost of goods sold	$30,000	Income before income taxes	$ 4,000

Example 2. Ending Inventory Overstated by $3,000

Cost of Goods Sold for the Year		Income Statement for the Year	
Beginning inventory	$ 6,000	Net sales	$50,000
Net cost of purchases	29,000	Cost of goods sold	27,000
Cost of goods available for sale	$35,000	Gross margin	$23,000
Ending inventory	8,000	Operating expenses	16,000
Cost of goods sold	$27,000	Income before income taxes	$ 7,000

Example 3. Ending Inventory Understated by $3,000

Cost of Goods Sold for the Year		Income Statement for the Year	
Beginning inventory	$ 6,000	Net sales	$50,000
Net cost of purchases	29,000	Cost of goods sold	33,000
Cost of goods available for sale	$35,000	Gross margin	$17,000
Ending inventory	2,000	Operating expenses	16,000
Cost of goods sold	$33,000	Income before income taxes	$ 1,000

STUDY NOTE: *A misstatement of inventory has the opposite effect in two successive accounting periods.*

In all three examples, the cost of goods available for sale was $35,000. The difference in income before income taxes resulted from how this $35,000 was divided between the ending inventory and the cost of goods sold.

Because the ending inventory in one period becomes the beginning inventory in the following period, a misstatement in inventory *valuation* affects both the current period and the following period. Over two periods, the errors in income before income taxes will offset, or counterbalance, each other. For instance, in Example 2, the overstatement of the ending inventory will cause a $3,000 overstatement of the beginning inventory in the following year, which will result in a $3,000 understatement of income. Because the total income before income taxes for the two periods is the same, it may appear that one need not worry about inventory misstatements. However, the misstatements violate the *accrual accounting*. In addition, management, creditors, and investors base many decisions on the accountant's determination of net income. The accountant has an obligation to make the net income figure for each period as useful as possible.

The effects of inventory misstatements on income before income taxes are as follows.

Year 1	Year 2
Ending inventory overstated	**Beginning inventory overstated**
Cost of goods sold understated	Cost of goods sold overstated
Income before income taxes overstated	Income before income taxes understated
Ending inventory understated	**Beginning inventory understated**
Cost of goods sold overstated	Cost of goods sold understated
Income before income taxes understated	Income before income taxes overstated

APPLY IT! ➤

During 2014, Tom's Sporting Goods had beginning inventory of $500,000, ending inventory of $700,000, and cost of goods sold of $2,100,000. Compute the inventory turnover and days' inventory on hand.

SOLUTION

$$\text{Inventory Turnover} = \frac{\text{Cost of Goods Sold}}{\text{Average Inventory}}$$

$$= \frac{\$2,100,000}{(\$700,000 + \$500,000)/2} = \frac{\$2,100,000}{\$600,000}$$

$$= 3.5 \text{ times}$$

$$\text{Day's Inventory on Hand} = \frac{365}{\text{Inventory Turnover}}$$

$$= \frac{365}{3.5} = 104.3^* \text{ days}$$

*Rounded

TRY IT! SE11, SE12, E10A, E11A, E12A, E10B, E11B, E12B

TriLevel Problem

Blue Jean Images/Alamy Limited

Grabs Company

The beginning of this chapter focused on Grabs Company, a merchandising company facing decisions about which inventory system and costing method to use, how to value inventory, and how much inventory to keep in stock. Complete the following requirements in order to answer the questions posed at the beginning of the chapter.

Section 1: Concepts
Why is the relationship between accrual accounting and valuation important for inventory accounting?

Section 2: Accounting Applications
How would Grabs Company account for merchandising inventory using (a) the average-cost method, (b) the FIFO method, and (c) the LIFO method under periodic and perpetual inventory systems?

The following data about Grabs' inventory and purchases from May are available:

	A	B	C	D	E	F	G
1				**Beginning Inventory and Purchases**			
2	**Date**			**Units**	**Cost**	**Total**	**Sales Units**
3	May	1	Inventory	2,800	$20	$ 56,000	
4		8	Purchase	1,200	22	26,400	
5		10	Sale				3,200
6		24	Purchase	1,600	24	38,400	
7							
8	Totals			5,600		$120,800	3,200
9							

1. Assuming that Grabs uses the periodic inventory system, compute the cost that should be assigned to the ending inventory and to the cost of goods sold, using (a) the average-cost method, (b) the FIFO method, and (c) the LIFO method.

2. Assuming that Grabs uses the perpetual inventory system, compute the cost that should be assigned to the ending inventory and to the cost of goods sold, using (a) the average-cost method, (b) the FIFO method, and (c) the LIFO method.

Section 3: Business Applications
How do decisions about inventory valuation and inventory levels affect operating results?

To better understand the situation, compute Grab's inventory turnover and days' inventory on hand under each of the inventory cost flow assumptions in Accounting Applications requirement **1**. What conclusion can you draw from this comparison?

SOLUTION

Section 1: Concepts
Accrual accounting requires that costs associated with goods that are sold be transferred from the balance sheet to cost of goods sold on the income statement. To determine what dollar amount will be transferred, one of various acceptable *valuation* methods must be chosen.

Section 2: Accounting Applications

	Units	Amount
Beginning inventory	2,800	$ 56,000
Purchases	2,800	64,800
Available for sale	5,600	$120,800
Sales	3,200	
Ending inventory	2,400	

1. Periodic inventory system:

   a. Average-cost method

Cost of goods available for sale	$120,800
Less ending inventory consisting of 2,400 units at $21.57*	51,768
Cost of goods sold	$ 69,032

   *$120,800 ÷ 5,600 units = $21.57 (rounded)

   b. FIFO method

Cost of goods available for sale		$120,800
Less ending inventory consisting of		
May 24 purchase (1,600 × $24)	$38,400	
May 8 purchase (800 × $22)	17,600	56,000
Cost of goods sold		$ 64,800

   c. LIFO method

Cost of goods available for sale	$120,800
Less ending inventory consisting of beginning inventory (2,400 × $20)	48,000
Cost of goods sold	$ 72,800

2. Perpetual inventory system:

a. Average-cost method

Date			Units	Cost	Amount
May	1	Inventory	2,800	$20.00	$ 56,000
	8	Purchase	1,200	22.00	26,400
	8	Balance	4,000	20.60	$ 82,400
	10	Sale	(3,200)	20.60	(65,920)
	10	Balance	800	20.60	$ 16,480
	24	Purchase	1,600	24.00	38,400
	31	Inventory	2,400	22.87*	$ 54,880
Cost of goods sold					$ 65,920

*Rounded

b. FIFO method

Date			Units	Cost	Amount
May	1	Inventory	2,800	$20	$ 56,000
	8	Purchase	1,200	22	26,400
	8	Balance	2,800	20	
			1,200	22	$ 82,400
	10	Sale	(2,800)	20	
			(400)	22	(64,800)
	10	Balance	800	22	$ 17,600
	24	Purchase	1,600	24	38,400
	31	Inventory	800	22	
			1,600	24	$ 56,000
Cost of goods sold					$ 64,800

c. LIFO method

Date			Units	Cost	Amount
May	1	Inventory	2,800	$20	$ 56,000
	8	Purchase	1,200	22	26,400
	8	Balance	2,800	20	
			1,200	22	$ 82,400
	10	Sale	(1,200)	22	
			(2,000)	20	(66,400)
	10	Balance	800	20	$ 16,000
	24	Purchase	1,600	24	38,400
	31	Inventory	800	20	
			1,600	24	$ 54,400
Cost of goods sold					$ 66,400

Section 3: Business Applications

The decisions that Darcy Ming or any other manager makes about the evaluation of inventory affect a company's net income, the amount of taxes it pays, and its cash flows. Decisions about inventory levels also have important economic consequences: too low a level can result in disgruntled customers and too high a level can result in substantial storage, handling, and interest costs.

	Average-Cost	FIFO	LIFO
Cost of Goods Sold / Average Inventory	$\dfrac{\$69{,}032}{(\$51{,}768 + \$56{,}000)/2} =$	$\dfrac{\$64{,}800}{(\$56{,}000 + \$56{,}000)/2} =$	$\dfrac{\$72{,}800}{(\$48{,}000 + \$56{,}000)/2} =$
	$\dfrac{\$69{,}032}{\$53{,}884} = 1.3$	$\dfrac{\$64{,}800}{\$56{,}000} = 1.2$	$\dfrac{\$72{,}800}{\$52{,}000} = 1.4$
Inventory Turnover:	1.3 times	1.2 times	1.4 times
Days' Inventory on Hand:	(365 days ÷ 1.3 times)	(365 days ÷ 1.2 times)	(365 days ÷ 1.4 times)
	280.8 days*	304.2 days*	260.7 days*

*Rounded

In periods of rising prices, the LIFO method will always result in a higher inventory turnover and lower days' inventory on hand than the other costing methods. When comparing inventory ratios for two or more companies, their inventory methods should be considered.

Chapter Review

Explain the concepts underlying inventory accounting. **LO 1**

Inventory cost includes the invoice price less purchases discounts; freight-in, including insurance in transit; and applicable taxes. Goods flow refers to the actual physical flow of merchandise in a business, whereas cost flow refers to the assumed flow of costs. The lower-of-cost-or-market rule states that if the replacement cost (market cost) of the inventory is lower than the original cost, the lower figure should be used.

The objective of inventory accounting is the proper determination of income through the matching of costs and revenues. Management must choose the type of processing system, costing method, and valuation method the company will use. Because the value of inventory affects a company's net income, management's choices will affect not only external and internal evaluations of the company but also the amount of income taxes the company pays and its cash flows.

Calculate inventory cost under the periodic inventory system using various costing methods. **LO 2**

The value assigned to the ending inventory is the result of two measurements: quantity and cost. Under the periodic inventory system, quantity is determined by taking a physical inventory. Cost is determined by using one of four inventory methods, each based on a different assumption of cost flow. The specific identification method identifies the actual cost of each item in inventory. The average-cost method assumes that the cost of inventory is the average cost of goods available for sale during the period. The first-in, first-out (FIFO) method assumes that the costs of the first items acquired should be assigned to the first items sold. The last-in, first-out (LIFO) method assumes that the costs of the last items acquired should be assigned to the first items sold.

Explain the effects of inventory costing methods on income determination and income taxes. **LO 3**

During periods of rising prices, the LIFO method will show the lowest gross margin and thus net income; FIFO, the highest; and average-cost, in between. LIFO and FIFO have the opposite effects in periods of falling prices. The Internal Revenue Service requires a company that uses LIFO for tax purposes to use LIFO in its accounting records. It also does not allow a company that uses LIFO to apply the lower-of-cost-or-market rule.

Calculate inventory cost under the perpetual inventory system using various costing methods. **LO 4**

Under the perpetual inventory system, the cost of goods sold is accumulated as sales are made and costs are transferred from the Inventory account to the Cost of Goods Sold account. The cost of the ending inventory is the balance of the Inventory account. The specific identification method and the FIFO method produce the same results under both the perpetual and periodic inventory systems. The results differ for the average-cost method because an average is calculated after each sale rather than at the end of the accounting period. Results also differ for the LIFO method because the cost components of inventory change constantly as goods are bought and sold.

Use the retail method and gross profit method to estimate the cost of ending inventory. **LO 5**

Two methods of estimating the value of inventory are the retail method and the gross profit method. Under the retail method, inventory is determined at retail prices and is then reduced to estimated cost by applying a ratio of cost to retail price. Under the gross profit method, the cost of goods sold is estimated by reducing sales by the estimated gross margin. The estimated cost of goods sold is then deducted from the cost of goods available for sale to estimate the cost of the ending inventory.

Evaluate inventory level, and demonstrate the effects of inventory misstatements on income measurement. **LO 6**

The level of inventory has important economic consequences. To evaluate inventory levels, managers commonly use inventory turnover and its related measure, days' inventory on hand. Supply-chain management and a just-in-time operating environment are a means of increasing inventory turnover and reducing inventory carrying costs.

If the value of the ending inventory is understated or overstated, a corresponding error—dollar for dollar—will be made in income before income taxes. Furthermore, because the ending inventory of one period is the beginning inventory of the next, the misstatement affects two accounting periods, although the effects are opposite.

Key Terms and Ratios

average-cost method 269 (LO2)
consignment 265 (LO1)
cost flow 265 (LO1)
first-in, first-out (FIFO) method 269 (LO2)
goods flow 265 (LO1)
gross profit method 278 (LO5)
inventory accounting 264 (LO1)
inventory cost 264 (LO1)

just-in-time (JIT) operating environment 281 (LO6)
LIFO liquidation 273 (LO3)
last-in, first-out (LIFO) method 270 (LO2)
lower-of-cost-or-market (LCM) rule 266 (LO1)
market 266 (LO1)
retail method 277 (LO5)

specific identification method 268 (LO2)
supply-chain management 281 (LO6)

RATIOS
days' inventory on hand 281 (LO6)
inventory turnover 280 (LO6)

Chapter Assignments

DISCUSSION QUESTIONS

LO 1 **DQ1. CONCEPT** ▶ Which is more important from the standpoint of inventory costing: accrual accounting or valuation?

LO 2, 4 **DQ2.** Which of the following methods do not require a physical inventory: periodic inventory system, perpetual inventory method, retail method, or gross profit method?

LO 1, 6 **DQ3. CONCEPT** ▶ Given that the LCM rule is an application of the conservatism convention in the current accounting period, is the effect of this application also conservative in the next period?

LO 2, 3, 4 **DQ4.** Under what condition would all four methods of inventory pricing produce exactly the same results?

LO 4 **DQ5.** Under the perpetual inventory system, why is the cost of goods sold not determined by deducting the ending inventory from goods available for sale, as it is under the periodic method?

LO 6 **DQ6. BUSINESS APPLICATION** ▶ Is it good or bad for a retail store to have a large inventory?

LO 6 **DQ7. BUSINESS APPLICATION** ▶ Why is misstatement of inventory one of the most common means of financial statement fraud?

SHORT EXERCISES

LO 1   **Inventory Concepts**

SE1. CONCEPT ▶ Match the items that follow with their related statements.

a. Inventory accounting
b. Goods flow
c. Cost flow
d. Lower-of-cost-or-market (LCM) rule
e. Valuation
f. Conservatism

1. Refers to the association of costs with their assumed flow.
2. Has the objective of matching costs of the period against revenues for the period.
3. Requires that the inventory be written down to the lower value and that a loss be recorded.
4. Refers to the actual physical movement of goods in the operations of a company.
5. Related to the lower-of-cost-or-market (LCM) rule.
6. Can vary depending on the assumptions about the flow of costs.

LO 2   **Specific Identification Method**

SE2. Assume the following data with regard to inventory for Vegan Company:

Aug.	1	Inventory	40 units @ $10 per unit	$ 400
	8	Purchase	50 units @ $11 per unit	550
	22	Purchase	35 units @ $12 per unit	420
Goods available for sale			125 units	$1,370
Aug.	15	Sale	45 units	
	28	Sale	25 units	
Inventory, Aug. 31			55 units	

Assuming that the inventory consists of 30 units from the August 8 purchase and 25 units from the purchase of August 22, calculate the cost of ending inventory and cost of goods sold.

LO 2   **Average-Cost Method: Periodic Inventory System**

SE3. Using the data in **SE2**, calculate the cost of ending inventory and cost of goods sold according to the average-cost method under the periodic inventory system. (Round final answer to the nearest dollar.)

LO 2   **FIFO Method: Periodic Inventory System**

SE4. Using the data in **SE2**, calculate the cost of ending inventory and cost of goods sold according to the FIFO method under the periodic inventory system.

LO 2   **LIFO Method: Periodic Inventory System**

SE5. Using the data in **SE2**, calculate the cost of ending inventory and cost of goods sold according to the LIFO method under the periodic inventory system.

LO 3   **Effects of Inventory Costing Methods and Changing Prices**

SE6. Prepare a table with four columns that shows the ending inventory and cost of goods sold for each of the results from your calculations in **SE2** through **SE5**, including the effects of the different prices at which the merchandise was purchased. Which method(s) would result in the lowest income taxes?

LO 4   **Average-Cost Method: Perpetual Inventory System**

SE7. Using the data in **SE2**, calculate the cost of ending inventory and cost of goods sold according to the average-cost method under the perpetual inventory system. (Round to the nearest dollar.)

LO 4   **FIFO Method: Perpetual Inventory System**

SE8. Using the data in **SE2**, calculate the cost of ending inventory and cost of goods sold according to the FIFO method under the perpetual inventory system.

LO 4   **LIFO Method: Perpetual Inventory System**

SE9. Using the data in **SE2**, calculate the cost of ending inventory and cost of goods sold according to the LIFO method under the perpetual inventory system.

LO 5   **Retail Inventory Method**

SE10. Blue Jeans Shop had net retail sales of $390,000 during the current year. The following additional information was obtained from the company's accounting records:

	At Cost	At Retail
Beginning inventory	$ 80,000	$120,000
Net purchases (excluding freight-in)	260,000	420,000
Freight-in	16,400	

Using the retail method, estimate the company's ending inventory at cost. Assuming that a physical count taken at year-end revealed an inventory of $132,000 at retail value, what is the estimated amount of inventory shrinkage (loss due to theft, damage, etc.) at cost using the retail method?

LO 6   **Management Issues**

SE11. BUSINESS APPLICATION ▶ Indicate whether each of the following items is associated with (a) allocating the cost of inventories in accordance with the accrual accounting, (b) assessing the impact of inventory decisions, (c) evaluating the level of inventory, or (d) engaging in an unethical practice:

1. Calculating days' inventory on hand.
2. Ordering a supply of inventory to satisfy customer needs.
3. Valuing inventory at an amount to achieve a specific profit objective.
4. Calculating the income tax effect of an inventory method.
5. Deciding the cost to place on ending inventory.

LO 6   **Inventory Turnover and Days' Inventory on Hand**

SE12. BUSINESS APPLICATION ▶ During 2014, Victoria's Fashion had beginning inventory of $480,000, ending inventory of $560,000, and cost of goods sold of $2,200,000. Compute the inventory turnover and days' inventory on hand. (Round to one decimal place.)

EXERCISES: SET A

LO 1, 2, 3   **Accounting Conventions and Inventory Valuation**

E1A. CONCEPT ▶ Dynamic Company, a telecommunications equipment company, has used the LIFO method adjusted for lower of cost or market for a number of years. Due to falling prices of its equipment, it has had to adjust (reduce) the cost of inventory to market each year for two years. The company is considering changing its method to FIFO adjusted for lower of cost or market in the future. Explain how the accounting conventions of consistency, full disclosure, and conservatism apply to this decision. If the change were made, why would management expect fewer adjustments to market in the future?

LO 2   **Periodic Inventory System and Inventory Costing Methods**

E2A. Portia's Parts Shop recorded the following purchases and sales during the past year:

Jan.	1	Beginning inventory	125 cases @ $23	$ 2,875
Feb.	25	Purchase	100 cases @ $26	2,600
June	15	Purchase	200 cases @ $28	5,600
Oct.	15	Purchase	150 cases @ $28	4,200
Dec.	15	Purchase	100 cases @ $30	3,000
Goods available for sale			675	$18,275
Total sales			500 cases	
Dec.	31	Ending inventory	175 cases	

Assume that the company sold all of the June 15 purchase and 100 cases each from the January 1 beginning inventory, the October 15 purchase, and the December 15 purchase.

Determine the costs that should be assigned to ending inventory and cost of goods sold according to the periodic inventory method under each of the assumptions that follow. (Round to the nearest dollar and assume the periodic inventory system.)

1. Costs are assigned by the specific identification method.
2. Costs are assigned by the average-cost method.
3. Costs are assigned by the FIFO method.
4. Costs are assigned by the LIFO method.
5. **ACCOUNTING CONNECTION ▶** What conclusions can be drawn about the effect of each method on the income statement and the balance sheet of Portia's Parts Shop?

LO **2** **Periodic Inventory System and Inventory Costing Methods**

E3A. During its first year of operation, Lux Company purchased 5,600 units of a product at $42 per unit. During the second year, it purchased 6,000 units of the same product at $48 per unit. During the third year, it purchased 5,000 units at $60 per unit. Lux managed to have an ending inventory each year of 1,000 units. The company uses the periodic inventory system.

Prepare cost of goods sold statements that compare the value of ending inventory and the cost of goods sold for each of the three years using

1. the FIFO inventory costing method.
2. the LIFO method.
3. **ACCOUNTING CONNECTION ▶** From the resulting data, what conclusions can you draw about the relationships between the changes in unit price and the changes in the value of ending inventory?

LO **2, 3** **Periodic Inventory System and Inventory Costing Methods**

E4A. In chronological order, the inventory, purchases, and sales of a single product for a recent month are as follows.

			Units	Amount per Unit
June	1	Beginning inventory	150	$30
	4	Purchase	400	33
	12	Purchase	800	36
	16	Sale	1,300	60
	24	Purchase	300	39

1. Using the periodic inventory system, compute the cost of ending inventory, cost of goods sold, and gross margin. Use the average-cost, FIFO, and LIFO inventory costing methods. (Round unit costs to cents and totals to dollars.)
2. **ACCOUNTING CONNECTION ▶** Explain the differences in gross margin produced by the three methods.

LO 3   **Effects of Inventory Costing Methods on Cash Flows**

E5A. ACCOUNTING CONNECTION ▶ Mills, Inc., sold 120,000 cases of glue at $20 per case during 2014. Its beginning inventory consisted of 20,000 cases at a cost of $12 per case. During 2014, it purchased 60,000 cases at $14 per case and, later, 50,000 cases at $15 per case. Operating expenses were $550,000, and the applicable income tax rate was 30 percent.

1. Using the periodic inventory system, compute net income using the FIFO method and the LIFO method for costing inventory. Which alternative produces the larger cash flow?

2. The company is considering a purchase of 10,000 cases at $15 per case just before the year end. What effect on net income and on cash flow will this proposed purchase have under each method? (*Hint:* What are the income tax consequences?)

LO 4   **Perpetual Inventory System and Inventory Costing Methods**

E6A. Refer to the data provided in **E4A.**

1. Using the perpetual inventory system, compute the cost of ending inventory, cost of goods sold, and gross margin. Use the average-cost, FIFO, and LIFO inventory costing methods. (Round unit costs to the nearest cent.)

2. **ACCOUNTING CONNECTION** ▶ Explain the reasons for the differences in gross margin produced by the three methods.

LO 2, 4   **Periodic and Perpetual Systems and Inventory Costing Methods**

E7A. During July 2014, Micanopy, Inc., sold 500 units of its product Empire for $8,000. The following units were available:

	Units	Cost
Beginning inventory	200	$ 2
Purchase 1	80	4
Purchase 2	120	6
Purchase 3	300	9
Purchase 4	180	12

A sale of 500 units was made after purchase 3. Of the units sold, 200 came from beginning inventory and 300 came from purchase 3.

Determine cost of goods available for sale and ending inventory in units. Then determine the costs that should be assigned to cost of goods sold and ending inventory under each of the following assumptions. (For each alternative, show the gross margin. Round unit costs to cents and totals to dollars.)

1. Costs are assigned under the periodic inventory system using (a) the specific identification method, (b) the average-cost method, (c) the FIFO method, and (d) the LIFO method.

2. Costs are assigned under the perpetual inventory system using (a) the average-cost method, (b) the FIFO method, and (c) the LIFO method.

LO 5   **Retail Method**

E8A. Warmer's Dress Shop had net retail sales of $250,000 during the current year. The following additional information was obtained from the company's accounting records:

	At Cost	At Retail
Beginning inventory	$ 40,000	$ 60,000
Net purchases (excluding freight-in)	140,000	220,000
Freight-in	10,400	

1. Using the retail method, estimate the company's ending inventory at cost.
2. Assume that a physical inventory taken at year end revealed an inventory on hand of $18,000 at retail value. What is the estimated amount of inventory shrinkage (loss due to theft, damage, etc.) at cost using the retail method?

LO 5   **Gross Profit Method**

E9A. David Patel was at home when he received a call from the fire department telling him his store had burned. His business was a total loss. The insurance company asked him to prove his inventory loss. For the year, until the date of the fire, Patel's company had sales of $450,000 and purchases of $280,000. Freight-in amounted to $13,700, and beginning inventory was $45,000. Patel always priced his goods to achieve a gross margin of 40 percent. Compute Patel's estimated inventory loss.

LO 6   **Management Issues**

E10A. BUSINESS APPLICATION ▶ Indicate whether each of the following items is associated with (a) allocating the cost of inventories in accordance with the accrual accounting, (b) assessing the impact of inventory decisions, (c) evaluating the level of inventory, or (d) engaging in an unethical action.

1. Application of the just-in-time operating environment.
2. Determining the effects of inventory methods on income taxes.
3. Computing inventory turnover.
4. Valuing inventory at an amount to meet management's targeted net income.
5. Determining the effects of inventory decisions on cash flows.
6. Apportioning the cost of goods available for sale to ending inventory and cost of goods sold.
7. Determining the assumption about the flow of costs into and out of the company.

LO 6   **Inventory Ratios**

E11A. BUSINESS APPLICATION ▶ Big Sale Stores is assessing its levels of inventory for 2013 and 2014 and has gathered the following data:

	2014	2013	2012
Ending inventory	$192,000	$162,000	$138,000
Cost of goods sold	960,000	900,000	

Compute the inventory turnover and days' inventory on hand for 2013 and 2014 (round to one decimal place), and comment on the results.

LO 6   **Effects of Inventory Errors**

E12A. BUSINESS APPLICATION ▶ Necessary Toys Company's condensed income statements for two years follow.

	2014	2013
Sales	$252,000	$210,000
Cost of goods sold	150,000	108,000
Gross margin	$102,000	$102,000
Operating expenses	60,000	60,000
Income before income taxes	$ 42,000	$ 42,000

After the end of 2014, the company discovered that an error had resulted in an $18,000 understatement of the 2013 ending inventory.

Compute the corrected operating income for 2013 and 2014. What effect will the error have on operating income and owner's equity for 2015?

EXERCISES: SET B

Visit the textbook companion website at www.cengagebrain.com to access Exercise Set B for this chapter.

PROBLEMS

LO **2, 6**

SPREADSHEET

✔ 1: Cost of goods available
for sale: $10,560,000
✔ 2c: Income before income taxes
using LIFO: $740,000

Periodic Inventory System and Inventory Costing Methods

P1. Midori Company merchandises a single product called Gloss. The following data represent beginning inventory and purchases of Gloss during the past year: January 1 inventory, 68,000 units at $11.00; February purchases, 80,000 units at $12.00; March purchases, 160,000 units at $12.40; May purchases, 120,000 units at $12.60; July purchases, 200,000 units at $12.80; September purchases, 160,000 units at $12.60; and November purchases, 60,000 units at $13.00. Sales of Gloss totaled 786,000 units at $20.00 per unit. Selling and administrative expenses totaled $5,102,000 for the year. Midori uses the periodic inventory system.

REQUIRED

1. Prepare a schedule to compute the cost of goods available for sale.
2. Compute income before income taxes under each of the following inventory cost flow assumptions: (a) the average-cost method, (b) the FIFO method, and (c) the LIFO method. (Round cost to the nearest cent.)
3. **BUSINESS APPLICATION** ▶ Compute inventory turnover and days' inventory on hand under each of the inventory cost flow assumptions listed in requirement **2**. (Round to one decimal place.) What conclusion can you draw?

LO **2, 3**

CASH FLOW

SPREADSHEET

✔ 1: Cost of goods sold for average-cost
method for April: $19,320
✔ 1: Cost of goods sold for average-cost
method for May: $44,237

Periodic Inventory System and Inventory Costing Methods

P2. The inventory of Wood4Fun and data on purchases and sales for a two-month period follow. The company closes its books at the end of each month. It uses the periodic inventory system.

Apr.	1	Beginning inventory	50 units @ $204
	10	Purchase	100 units @ $220
	17	Sale	90 units
	30	Ending inventory	60 units
May	2	Purchase	100 units @ $216
	14	Purchase	50 units @ $224
	22	Purchase	60 units @ $234
	30	Sale	200 units
	31	Ending inventory	70 units

REQUIRED

1. Compute the cost of ending inventory of Wood4Fun on April 30 and May 31 using the average-cost method. In addition, determine cost of goods sold for April and May. (Round unit costs to the nearest cent.)
2. Compute the cost of the ending inventory on April 30 and May 31 using the FIFO method. In addition, determine cost of goods sold for April and May.
3. Compute the cost of the ending inventory on April 30 and May 31 using the LIFO method. In addition, determine cost of goods sold for April and May.
4. **ACCOUNTING CONNECTION** ▶ Do the cash flows from operations for April and May differ depending on which inventory costing method is used—average-cost, FIFO, or LIFO? Explain.

LO **3, 4, 6**

Perpetual Inventory System and Inventory Costing Methods

P3. Use the data provided in **P2**, but assume that the company uses the perpetual inventory system. (*Hint:* In preparing the solutions, it is helpful to determine the balance of

✔ 3: Cost of goods sold for LIFO
method for April: $19,800
✔ 3: Cost of goods sold for LIFO
method for May: $44,680

inventory after each transaction, as shown in the Business Insight: Concepts and Applications feature in this chapter.)

REQUIRED

1. Determine the cost of ending inventory and cost of goods sold for April and May using the average-cost method. (Round unit costs to the nearest cent.)
2. Determine the cost of ending inventory and cost of goods sold for April and May using the FIFO method.
3. Determine the cost of ending inventory and cost of goods sold for April and May using the LIFO method.
4. **BUSINESS APPLICATION** ▶ Assume that this company grows for many years in a long period of rising prices. How realistic do you think the balance sheet value for inventory would be and what effect would it have on the inventory turnover ratio?

LO **5**   **Retail Method**

✔ 3: Estimated inventory shortage
at cost: $24,208
✔ 3: Estimated inventory shortage at
retail: $35,600

P4. Quester Company operates a large discount store and uses the retail method to estimate the cost of ending inventory. Management suspects that in recent weeks there have been unusually heavy losses from shoplifting or employee pilferage. To estimate the amount of the loss, the company has taken a physical inventory and will compare the results with the estimated cost of inventory. Data from Quester's accounting records follow.

	At Cost	At Retail
August 1 beginning inventory	$205,952	$297,200
Purchases	286,932	434,000
Purchases returns and allowances	(8,172)	(12,800)
Freight-in	3,800	
Sales		436,732
Sales returns and allowances		(3,732)
August 31 physical inventory at retail		249,800

REQUIRED

1. Using the retail method, prepare a schedule to estimate the dollar amount of the store's month-end inventory at cost.
2. Use the store's cost to retail ratio to reduce the retail value of the physical inventory to cost.
3. Calculate the estimated amount of inventory shortage at cost and at retail.
4. **ACCOUNTING CONNECTION** ▶ Many retail chains use the retail method because it is efficient. Why do you think using this method is an efficient way for these companies to operate?

LO **5**   **Gross Profit Method**

✔ 1: Estimated loss of inventory in
fire: $326,513.50

P5. Groh Brothers is a large retail furniture company that operates in two adjacent warehouses. One warehouse is a showroom, and the other is used to store merchandise. On the night of June 22, 2014, a fire broke out in the storage warehouse and destroyed the merchandise stored there. Fortunately, the fire did not reach the showroom, so all the merchandise on display was saved.

Although the company maintained a perpetual inventory system, its records were rather haphazard, and the last reliable physical inventory had been taken on December 31. In addition, there was no control of the flow of goods between the showroom and the warehouse. Thus, it was impossible to tell what goods should have been in either place. As a result, the insurance company required an independent estimate of the amount of loss. The insurance company examiners were satisfied when they received the following information:

(Continued)

Merchandise inventory on December 31, 2013	$363,700.00
Purchases, January 1 to June 22, 2014	603,050.00
Purchases returns, January 1 to June 22, 2014	(2,676.50)
Freight-in, January 1 to June 22, 2014	13,275.00
Sales, January 1 to June 22, 2014	989,762.50
Sales returns, January 1 to June 22, 2014	(7,450.00)
Merchandise inventory in showroom on June 22, 2014	100,740.00
Average gross margin	44%

REQUIRED

1. Prepare a schedule that estimates the amount of the inventory lost in the fire.
2. **ACCOUNTING CONNECTION** ▶ What are some other reasons management might need to estimate the amount of inventory?

ALTERNATE PROBLEMS

Periodic Inventory System and Inventory Costing Methods

LO **2, 6**

RATIO

SPREADSHEET

✔ 1: Cost of goods available for sale: $157,980
✔ 1c: Income before income taxes using LIFO: $101,850

P6. Aberdeen Company sold 2,200 cabinets during 2014 at $160 per cabinet. Its beginning inventory on January 1 was 130 cabinets at $56. Purchases made during the year were as follows.

February	225 cabinets @ $62.00
April	350 cabinets @ $65.00
June	700 cabinets @ $70.00
August	300 cabinets @ $66.00
October	400 cabinets @ $68.00
November	250 cabinets @ $72.00

The company's selling and administrative expenses for the year were $101,000. The company uses the periodic inventory system.

REQUIRED

1. Prepare a schedule to compute the cost of goods available for sale.
2. Compute income before income taxes under each of the following inventory cost flow assumptions: (a) the average-cost method, (b) the FIFO method, and (c) the LIFO method. (Round unit cost to the nearest cent, and total costs to the nearest dollar.)
3. **BUSINESS APPLICATION** ▶ Compute inventory turnover and days' inventory on hand under each of the inventory cost flow assumptions in requirement **2**. (Round to one decimal place.) What conclusion can you draw from this comparison?

Periodic Inventory System and Inventory Costing Methods

LO **2, 3**

CASH FLOW

SPREADSHEET

✔ 1: Cost of goods sold for average-cost method for March: $4,578
✔ 1: Cost of goods sold for average-cost method for April: $10,660

P7. DiPaolo's inventory, purchases, and sales for March and April follow. The company closes its books at the end of each month. It uses the periodic inventory system.

Mar.	1	Beginning inventory	60 units @ $49
	10	Purchase	100 units @ $52
	19	Sale	90 units
	31	Ending inventory	70 units
Apr.	4	Purchase	120 units @ $53
	15	Purchase	50 units @ $54
	23	Sale	200 units
	25	Purchase	100 units @ $55
	30	Ending inventory	140 units

REQUIRED

1. Compute the cost of the ending inventory on March 31 and April 30 using the average-cost method. In addition, determine cost of goods sold for March and April. (Round unit costs to the nearest cent.)
2. Compute the cost of the ending inventory on March 31 and April 30 using the FIFO method. Also determine cost of goods sold for March and April.
3. Compute the cost of the ending inventory on March 31 and April 30 using the LIFO method. Also determine cost of goods sold for March and April.
4. **ACCOUNTING CONNECTION** ▶ Do the cash flows from operations for March and April differ depending on which inventory costing method is used—average-cost, FIFO, or LIFO? Explain.

LO **3, 4, 6**

✔ 3: Cost of goods sold for LIFO method for March: $4,680
✔ 3: Cost of goods sold for LIFO method for April: $10,560

Perpetual Inventory System and Inventory Costing Methods

P8. Use the data provided in **P7**, but assume that the company uses the perpetual inventory system. (*Hint*: In preparing the solutions, it is helpful to determine the balance of inventory after each transaction, as shown in the Business Insight: Concepts and Applications feature in this chapter.)

REQUIRED

1. Determine the cost of ending inventory and cost of goods sold for March and April using the average-cost method. (Round unit costs to the nearest cent.)
2. Determine the cost of ending inventory and cost of goods sold for March and April using the FIFO method.
3. Determine the cost of ending inventory and cost of goods sold for March and April using the LIFO method.
4. **BUSINESS APPLICATION** ▶ Assume that this company grows for many years in a long period of rising prices. How realistic do you think the balance sheet value for inventory would be and what effect would it have on the inventory turnover ratio?

LO **5**

✔ 3: Estimated inventory shortage at cost: $3,456
✔ 3: Estimated inventory shortage at retail: $4,800

Retail Method

P9. Alberta Company operates a large discount store and uses the retail method to estimate the cost of ending inventory. Management suspects that in recent weeks there have been unusually heavy losses from shoplifting or employee pilferage. To estimate the amount of the loss, the company has taken a physical inventory and will compare the results with the estimated cost of inventory. Data from Alberta's accounting records follow.

	At Cost	At Retail
October 1 beginning inventory	$184,000	$239,200
Purchases	261,500	383,300
Purchases returns and allowances	(7,360)	(10,500)
Freight-in	2,500	
Sales		514,300
Sales returns and allowances		(2,700)
October 31 physical inventory at retail		95,600

REQUIRED

1. Using the retail method, prepare a schedule to estimate the dollar amount of the store's month-end inventory at cost.
2. Use the store's cost to retail ratio to reduce the retail value of the physical inventory to cost.
3. Calculate the estimated amount of inventory shortage at cost and at retail.
4. **ACCOUNTING CONNECTION** ▶ Many retail chains use the retail method because it is efficient. Why do you think using this method is an efficient way for these companies to operate?

LO 5

✔ 1: Estimated loss of inventory
in fire: $1,306,054

Gross Profit Method

P10. Zubac Company is a large retail furniture company that operates in two adjacent warehouses. One warehouse is a showroom, and the other is used to store merchandise. On the night of April 22, 2014, a fire broke out in the storage warehouse and destroyed the merchandise stored there. Fortunately, the fire did not reach the showroom, so all the merchandise on display was saved.

Although the company maintained a perpetual inventory system, its records were rather haphazard, and the last reliable physical inventory had been taken on December 31. In addition, there was no control of the flow of goods between the showroom and the warehouse. Thus, it was impossible to tell what goods should have been in either place. As a result, the insurance company required an independent estimate of the amount of loss. The insurance company examiners were satisfied when they received the following information:

Merchandise inventory on December 31, 2013	$1,454,800
Purchases, January 1 to April 22, 2014	2,412,200
Purchases returns, January 1 to April 22, 2014	(10,706)
Freight-in, January 1 to April 22, 2014	53,100
Sales, January 1 to April 22, 2014	3,959,050
Sales returns, January 1 to April 22, 2014	(29,800)
Merchandise inventory in showroom on April 22, 2014	402,960
Average gross margin	44%

REQUIRED

1. Prepare a schedule that estimates the amount of the inventory lost in the fire.
2. **ACCOUNTING CONNECTION** ▶ What are some other reasons management might need to estimate the amount of inventory?

CASES

LO 2, 3

CASH FLOW

Conceptual Understanding: LIFO Inventory Method

C1. Sixty-eight percent of chemical companies use the LIFO inventory method for the costing of inventories, whereas only 13 percent of computer equipment companies use LIFO.[9]

Describe the LIFO inventory method. What effects does it have on reported income, cash flows, and income taxes during periods of price changes? Why do you think so many chemical companies use LIFO and most companies in the computer industry do not?

LO 1

Interpreting Financial Reports: LCM and Conservatism

C2. CONCEPT ▶ **ExxonMobil Corporation**, the world's second-largest company, uses the LIFO inventory method for most of its inventories. Its inventory costs are heavily dependent on the cost of oil. When the price of oil was down, ExxonMobil, following the lower-of-cost-or-market (LCM) rule, wrote down its inventory by $325 million. In the next year, when the price of oil recovered, the company reported that market price exceeded the LIFO carrying values by $6.8 billion.[10] Explain why the LCM rule resulted in a write-down in the first year. What is the inconsistency between the first- and second-year treatments of the change in the price of oil? How does the accounting convention of conservatism explain the inconsistency? If the price of oil declined substantially in a third year, what would be the likely consequence?

LO 2, 3

Interpreting Financial Reports: FIFO and LIFO

C3. ExxonMobil Corporation had net income of $41.0 billion in 2011. Inventories under the LIFO method used by the company were $11.7 billion in 2011. Inventory would have been $25.6 billion higher if the company had used FIFO.[11] Why do you suppose ExxonMobil's management chooses to use the LIFO inventory method? On what economic conditions, if any, do those reasons depend?

LO 1, 3, 5, 6

Annual Report Case: Inventory Costing Methods and Ratios

C4. BUSINESS APPLICATION ▶ Refer to the note related to inventories in the **CVS** annual report in the Supplement to Chapter 16 to answer the following questions: What inventory method(s) does CVS use? Do you think many of the company's inventories are valued at market? Why or why not? Few companies use the retail method, so why do you think CVS uses it? Compute and compare the inventory turnover and days' inventory on hand for CVS for 2011 and 2010. Ending inventories in 2009 were $10,343 million. (Round to one decimal place.)

LO 6

Comparison Analysis: Inventory Efficiency

C5. BUSINESS APPLICATION ▶ Refer to **CVS**'s annual report in the Supplement to Chapter 16 and to the following data (in millions) for **Walgreens**: cost of goods sold, $51,692 and $48,444 for 2011 and 2010, respectively; inventories, $8,044, $7,378, and $6,789 for 2011, 2010, and 2009, respectively.[12] Ending inventories for 2009 for CVS were $10,343 million.

Calculate inventory turnover and days' inventory on hand for 2010 and 2011. (Round to one decimal place.) If you did **C4**, refer to your answer there for CVS. Has either company improved its performance in these areas over the past two years? If so, what advantage does this give the company? Which company appears to make the most efficient use of inventories? Explain your answers.

LO 6

Evaluation of Inventory Levels

C6. BUSINESS APPLICATION ▶ **JCPenney**, a large retail company with many stores, has an inventory turnover of about 3.8 times. **Dell Computer Corporation**, an Internet mail-order company, has an inventory turnover of about 36.0. Dell achieves its high turnover through supply-chain management in a just-in-time operating environment. Why is inventory turnover important to companies like JCPenney and Dell? Why are comparisons among companies important? Are JCPenney and Dell a good match for comparison? Describe supply-chain management and a just-in-time operating environment. Why are they important to achieving a favorable inventory turnover?

LO 3, 6

Ethical Dilemma: Inventories, Income Determination, and Ethics

C7. Lady, Inc., whose fiscal year ends on December 31, designs and sells fashions for young professional women. Margaret Lutz, president of the company, fears that the forecasted profitability goals for 2014 will not be reached. She is pleased when Lady, Inc., receives a large order on December 30, 2014, from The Executive Woman, a retail chain of upscale stores for businesswomen. Lutz immediately directs the controller to record the sale, which represents 13 percent of Lady's annual sales. At the same time, she directs the inventory control department not to separate the goods for shipment until after January 1, 2015. Separated goods are not included in inventory because they have been sold.

On December 31, 2014, the company's auditors arrive to observe the year-end taking of the physical inventory under the periodic inventory system. How will Lutz's actions affect Lady's profitability in 2014? How will they affect Lady's profitability in 2015? Were Lutz's actions ethical? Why or why not?

Continuing Case: Annual Report Project

C8. Using the most recent annual report of the company you have chosen to study and that you have accessed online at the company's website, examine inventory(ies) on the balance sheet and accompanying note on inventory(ies) of your company. Answer the following questions:

(Continued)

1. What percentage is inventory(ies) to total current assets? Do you think this percentage represents the importance of inventory(ies) to the company's operations?

2. Find the note about inventory(ies) in the notes to the financial statements. Does the company have more than one type of inventory? If so, what are they? What method(s) are used to value inventory(ies)? What other facts, if any, are disclosed about inventory(ies) in the note?

3. **BUSINESS APPLICATION** ▶ Calculate inventory turnover and days' inventory on hand for the most recent two years. (Round to one decimal place.) Has the company improved its performance in these areas over the past two years?

CHAPTER 8
Cash and Internal Control

Sung's Grill is a popular neighborhood restaurant. Its business has increased substantially over the past year, and Emma Sung, the restaurant's owner, has had to hire more cashiers, waiters, and kitchen help. She has become concerned about possible theft of cash and food inventory, and she is looking for ways to prevent it. She is also concerned about whether the restaurant's sales and other transactions are being recorded properly. She is particularly concerned about the accuracy of the restaurant's financial statements, because she is considering applying for a bank loan so that she can open a second restaurant. To obtain a loan, she will have to present Sung's Grill's financial statements to the bank.

1. **CONCEPT** ▷ *Why is each of the five components of internal control important to the faithful representation of a company's operations in its financial statements?*

2. **ACCOUNTING APPLICATION** ▷ *How can Sung's Grill maintain control over its cash?*

3. **BUSINESS APPLICATION** ▷ *How can Sung's Grill's bank and other users of its financial statements be confident that the restaurant has an adequate system of internal control?*

LEARNING OBJECTIVES

LO 1 Describe the components of internal control, control activities, and limitations on internal control.

LO 2 Apply internal control activities to common merchandising transactions.

LO 3 Define *cash equivalents*, and explain methods of controlling cash, including bank reconciliations.

LO 4 Demonstrate the use of a simple imprest (petty cash) system.

LO 5 Identify the internal control roles of management and the auditor.

SECTION 1

CONCEPTS

CONCEPT

■ Faithful
representation

**RELEVANT
LEARNING OBJECTIVE**

LO 1 Describe the
components of
internal control, control
activities, and limitations on
internal control.

LO 1 Concepts Underlying Internal Control

It is important that a company's financial statements *faithfully represent* the company's operations. This means, for instance, that the financial statements are *free from material error*. **Internal control** is a process that achieves this goal by establishing the *reliability* of the accounting records and financial statements and ensures that the company's assets are protected.[1]

The Need for Internal Controls

Buying and selling, the principal transactions of merchandising businesses, involve assets—cash, accounts receivable, and merchandise inventory—that are vulnerable to theft and embezzlement. This potential for embezzlement exists because the large number of transactions that are usually involved in a merchandising business (e.g., cash receipts, receipts on account, payments for purchases, and receipts and shipments of inventory) makes monitoring the accounting records difficult. If a merchandising company does not take steps to protect its assets, it can suffer high losses of both cash and inventory. Management's responsibility is to establish an environment, accounting systems, and internal control procedures that will protect the assets.

A company's merchandise inventory includes the following:

■ all goods intended for sale regardless of where they are located—on shelves, in storerooms, in warehouses, or in trucks between warehouses and stores
■ goods in transit from suppliers if title to the goods has passed to the merchandiser

Ending inventory does not include the following:

■ merchandise that a company has sold but not yet delivered to customers
■ goods that it cannot sell because they are damaged or obsolete

Taking a **physical inventory** facilitates control over merchandise inventory. This process involves an actual count of all merchandise on hand. A physical inventory must be taken under both the periodic and the perpetual inventory systems. Merchandisers usually take a physical inventory after the close of business on the last day of their fiscal year. To facilitate the process, they often end the fiscal year in a slow season, when inventories are at relatively low levels. For example, many department stores end their fiscal year in January or February. After hours—at night, on a weekend, or when the store closes for taking inventory—employees count all items and record the results on numbered inventory tickets or sheets, following procedures to ensure that no items will be missed. Using bar coding to take inventory electronically has greatly facilitated the process in many companies.

Most companies experience losses of merchandise inventory from spoilage, shoplifting, and theft. Inventory shortages can also result from honest mistakes, such as accidentally tagging inventory with the wrong number. The periodic inventory system provides no means of identifying these losses because the costs are automatically included in the cost of goods sold. For example, suppose a company has lost $1,250 in stolen merchandise during a period. When the physical inventory is taken, the missing items are not in stock, so they cannot be counted. Because the ending inventory does not contain these items, the amount subtracted from the cost of goods available for sale is less than it would be if the goods were in stock. The cost of goods sold, then, is overstated by $1,250.

H. Mark Weidman Photography/Alamy

Merchandise inventory includes all goods intended for sale wherever they are located—on store shelves, in warehouses, on car lots, or in transit from suppliers if title to the goods has passed to the merchandiser. To prevent loss of inventory, a merchandiser must have an effective system of internal control.

STUDY NOTE: An adjustment to the Merchandise Inventory account will be needed if the physical inventory reveals a difference between the actual inventory and the amount in the records.

The perpetual inventory system makes it easier to identify such losses. Because the Merchandise Inventory account is continuously updated for sales, purchases, and returns, the loss will show up as the difference between the inventory records and the physical inventory taken at the end of the accounting period. Once the amount of the loss has been identified, the ending inventory is updated by crediting the Merchandise Inventory account. The offsetting debit is usually an increase in Cost of Goods Sold because the loss is considered a cost that reduces the company's gross margin.

Components of Internal Control

An effective system of internal control has five interrelated components.[2]

Control Environment The **control environment** is created by management's overall attitude, awareness, and actions. It encompasses the following:

- a company's ethics, philosophy and operating style
- organizational structure
- method of assigning authority and responsibility
- personnel policies and practices

Personnel should be qualified to handle responsibilities, which means that they must be trained and informed about what is expected of them. For example, the manager of a retail store should train employees to follow prescribed procedures for handling cash sales, credit card sales, and returns and refunds.

Risk Assessment **Risk assessment** involves identifying areas in which risks of loss of assets or inaccuracies in accounting records are high so that adequate controls can be implemented. Among the greater risks in a retail store are that employees or customers may steal cash or goods.

Control Activities The policies and procedures management puts in place to see that its directives are carried out are called **control activities**.

Information and Communication **Information and communication** pertains to the way the accounting system gathers and treats information about the company's transactions and to how it communicates individual responsibilities within the system.

Monitoring Management's regular assessment of the quality of internal control, including periodic review of compliance with all policies and procedure, is part of **monitoring**. Large companies often have a staff of internal auditors who review the system of internal control to determine if it is working properly and if procedures are being followed. In smaller businesses, owners and managers conduct these reviews.

Control Activities

The goal of control activities is to safeguard a company's assets and ensure the reliability of its accounting records. Some standard control activities follow.

Authorization **Authorization** is the approval of certain transactions and activities. In a retail store, for example, cashiers customarily authorize cash sales; but other transactions, such as issuing a refund, may require a manager's approval.

Recording Transactions To establish accountability for assets, all transactions should be recorded. For example, if a retail store uses a cash register that records sales, refunds, and other transactions on a paper tape or computer disk, the cashier can be held accountable for the cash received and the merchandise removed during his or her shift.

Business Perspective
Shoplifters: Beware!

With theft from shoplifting approaching $30 billion per year, retailers are increasing their use of physical controls beyond the usual electronic warning if a customer tries to walk out without paying. Companies, such as **Macy's** and **Babies 'R' Us**, have installed more than 6 million video cameras in stores across the country. Advanced surveillance software can compare a shopper's movements between video images and recognize unusual activity. For instance, removing 10 items from a shelf or opening a drawer that normally is closed would trigger the system to alert a security guard.[3]

Documents and Records Well-designed documents help ensure that transactions are properly recorded. For example, using prenumbered invoices and other documents is a way of ensuring that all transactions are recorded.

Physical Controls **Physical controls** limit access to assets. For example, in a retail store, only the person responsible for the cash register should have access to it. Other employees should not be able to open the cash drawer when the cashier is not present. Similarly, only authorized personnel should have access to warehouses and storerooms. Access to accounting records, including those stored in company computers, should also be controlled.

Periodic Independent Verification **Periodic independent verification** means that someone other than the people responsible for the accounting records and assets should periodically check the records against the assets. For example, at the end of each shift or day in a retail store, the owner or manager should count the cash in the cash drawer and compare the amount with the amount recorded on the tape or computer disk in the cash register. Other examples of independent verification are periodic counts of physical inventory and reconciliations of monthly bank statements.

Separation of Duties **Separation of duties** means that no one person should authorize transactions, handle assets, and keep records of assets. For example, in a well-managed electronics store, each employee oversees only a single part of a transaction. A sales employee takes the order and creates an invoice. Another employee receives the customer's cash or credit card payment and issues a receipt. Once the customer has a receipt, and only then, a third employee obtains the item from the warehouse and gives it to the customer. A person in the accounting department subsequently compares all sales recorded in the cash register with the sales invoices and updates the inventory in the accounting records. The separation of duties means that a mistake, careless or not, cannot be made without being seen by at least one other person.

Sound Personnel Practices: Personnel practices that promote internal control include the following:

- adequate supervision
- rotation of key people among different jobs
- insistence that employees take vacations
- bonding of personnel who handle cash or inventory

Bonding is the process of carefully checking an employee's background and insuring the company against theft by that person. Bonding does not guarantee against theft, but it does prevent or reduce loss if theft occurs. Prudent personnel practices help ensure that employees know their jobs, are honest, and will find it difficult to carry out and conceal embezzlement over time.

Internal Control and Achieving Control Objectives

A system of internal control applied effectively to merchandising transactions can achieve important management objectives. As noted, it can prevent losses of cash and inventory due to theft or fraud, and it can ensure that records of transactions and account balances are accurate. It can also help managers achieve the following broader objectives:

- Keep enough inventory on hand to sell to customers without overstocking merchandise.
- Keep sufficient cash on hand to pay for purchases in time to receive discounts.
- Keep credit losses as low as possible by making credit sales only to customers who are likely to pay on time.

Limitations on Internal Control

STUDY NOTE: *While no control procedure can guarantee the prevention of theft, the more that are in place, the less likely it is that theft will occur.*

No system of internal control is without weaknesses. As long as people perform control procedures, an internal control system will be vulnerable to human error. Errors can arise from misunderstandings, mistakes in judgment, carelessness, distraction, or fatigue. Separation of duties can be defeated through collusion by employees who secretly agree to deceive a company. In addition, established procedures may be ineffective against employees' errors or dishonesty, and controls that were initially effective may become ineffective when conditions change.

In some cases, the costs of establishing and maintaining elaborate control systems may exceed the benefits. In a small business, for example, active involvement by the owner can be a practical substitute for the separation of some duties.

Business Perspective
Which Frauds Are Most Common in Retail?

The frauds commonly facing retailers are credit card, check fraud, false invoices and phantom vendors, and expense account abuse. The most common reasons for the occurrences of these frauds are poor internal controls over cashiers, management override of internal controls, and collusion. The most common methods of detecting them are good control procedures over cash receipts at the cash register, internal auditor review, notification by a customer, and accidental discovery. Companies that are successful in preventing fraud have a good system of internal control, a formal code of ethics, and a program to monitor compliance that includes a system for reporting incidents of fraud. These companies routinely communicate the existence of the program to their employees.[4]

APPLY IT!

Match the internal control components with the related statements that follow.

a. Control environment
b. Risk assessment
c. Control activities
d. Information and communication
e. Monitoring

1. Establishes separation of duties.
2. Communicates appropriate information to employees.
3. Has an internal audit department.
4. Periodic independent verification of employees' work.
5. Assesses the possibility of losses.
6. Instructs and trains employees.
7. Has well-designed documents and records.
8. Limits physical access to authorized personnel.

SOLUTION

1. c; 2. d; 3. e; 4. c; 5. b; 6. a; 7. c; 8. c

TRY IT! SE1, SE2, SE3, SE4, E1A, E2A, E3A, E1B, E2B, E3B

SECTION 2

ACCOUNTING APPLICATIONS

- ■ Account for merchandising transactions
- ■ Implement control of cash
- ■ Prepare a bank reconciliation
- ■ Use petty cash

RELEVANT LEARNING OBJECTIVES

LO 2 Apply internal control activities to common merchandising transactions.

LO 3 Define *cash equivalents*, and explain methods of controlling cash, including bank reconciliations.

LO 4 Demonstrate the use of a simple imprest (petty cash) system.

ACCOUNTING APPLICATIONS

LO 2 Internal Control over Merchandising Transactions

It's clear that sound internal control activities are needed when assets are involved. We now turn our attention to how merchandising companies apply internal control activities to business transactions. Maintaining internal control is especially difficult for a merchandiser because management must not only establish controls for cash sales, receipts, purchases, and cash payments, but also protect its inventory. Service and manufacturing businesses use similar procedures.

One control that managers use is the cash budget, which projects future cash receipts and disbursements. By maintaining adequate cash balances, a company is able to take advantage of discounts on purchases, prepared to borrow money when necessary, and able to avoid the damaging effects of being unable to pay bills when they are due. By investing excess cash, the company can earn interest until the cash is needed.

A more specific control is the separation of duties that involve the handling of cash. Such separation makes theft without detection extremely unlikely unless two or more employees conspire. The separation of duties is easier in large businesses than in small ones, where one person may have to carry out several duties. The effectiveness of internal control over cash varies, based on the size and nature of the company. Most firms, however, should use the following procedures:

- ■ Separate the functions of authorization, recordkeeping, and custodianship of cash.
- ■ Limit the number of people who have access to cash, and designate who those people are.
- ■ Bond all employees who have access to cash.
- ■ Keep the amount of cash on hand to a minimum by using banking facilities as much as possible.
- ■ Physically protect cash on hand by using cash registers, cashiers' cages, and safes.
- ■ Record and deposit all cash receipts promptly, and make payments by check rather than by currency.
- ■ Have a person who does not handle or record cash make unannounced audits of the cash on hand.
- ■ Have a person who does not authorize, handle, or record cash transactions reconcile the Cash account each month.

Each of these procedures helps safeguard cash by making it more difficult for any one individual to steal or misuse it without being detected.

Business Perspective
Are Money Market Funds Always a Safe Bet?

When companies have more cash than they need for current operations, they often earn interest on their excess cash by investing it in money market funds. Investments in money market funds have traditionally been considered safe because these funds have usually invested in very safe securities. However, in recent years, in an attempt to earn a slightly higher interest rate, a few money market funds invested in batches of subprime mortgages. This turned out to be a very poor decision. **Bank of America**, for instance, had to shut down its $34 billion money market fund—called Columbia Strategic Cash Portfolio—when investors pulled out $21 billion because the fund was losing a great deal of money due to its investment in subprime loans.[5]

Control of Cash Receipts

Cash payments for sales of goods and services can be received by mail or over the counter in the form of checks, credit or debit cards, or currency. Whatever the source of the cash, it should be recorded immediately in a cash receipts journal. Such a journal establishes a written record that should prevent errors and make theft more difficult.

Control of Cash Received by Mail Cash received by mail is vulnerable to theft by the employees who handle it. For that reason, companies that deal in mail-order sales generally ask customers to pay by credit card, check, or money order instead of with currency.

When cash is received in the mail, two or more employees should handle it. The employee who opens the mail should make a list in triplicate of the money received. The list should contain each customer's name, the purpose for which the money was sent, and the amount. One copy goes with the cash to the cashier, who deposits the money. The second copy goes to the accounting department for recording. The person who opens the mail keeps the third copy. Errors can be easily caught because the amount deposited by the cashier must agree with the amount received and the amount recorded in the cash receipts journal.

Control of Cash Received Over the Counter Cash registers and prenumbered sales tickets are common tools for controlling cash received over the counter. The amount of a cash sale is rung up on the cash register at the time of the sale. The register should be placed so that the customer can see the amount recorded. Each cash register should have a locked-in tape on which it prints the day's transactions. At the end of the day, the cashier counts the cash in the register and turns it in to the cashier's office. Another employee takes the tape out of the cash register and records the cash receipts for the day in the cash receipts journal. The amount of cash turned in and the amount recorded on the tape should agree; if not, any differences must be explained.

Large retail chains like **Costco** commonly monitor cash receipts by having each cash register tied directly into a computer that records each transaction. Whether the elements are performed manually or with a computer, separating responsibility for cash receipts, cash deposits, and recordkeeping is necessary to ensure good internal control.

In some stores, internal control is further strengthened by the use of prenumbered sales tickets and a central cash register or cashier's office, where all sales are rung up and collected by a person who does not participate in the sale. The salesperson completes a prenumbered sales ticket at the time of the sale, giving one copy to the customer and keeping a copy. At the end of the day, all sales tickets must be accounted for, and the sales total computed from the sales tickets must equal the total sales recorded on the cash register.

Control of Purchases and Cash Disbursements

Cash disbursements are particularly vulnerable to fraud and embezzlement. In one case, the treasurer of one of the nation's largest jewelry retailers was charged with stealing

Business Perspective
How Do Computers Promote Internal Control?

Building good internal controls into accounting programs is a difficult challenge for computer programmers. These programs must include controls that prevent unintentional errors, as well as unauthorized access and tampering. They prevent errors through reasonableness checks (such as not allowing any transactions over a specified amount), mathematical checks that verify the arithmetic of transactions, and sequence checks that require documents and transactions to be in proper order. They typically use passwords and questions about randomly selected personal data to prevent unauthorized access to computer records. They may also use *firewalls*, which are strong electronic barriers to unauthorized access, and *data encryption*, which is a way of coding data so that if they are stolen, they are useless to the thief.

over $500,000 by systematically overpaying the company's federal income taxes and keeping the refund checks.

To avoid this type of theft, cash payments should be made only after they have been specifically authorized and supported by documents that establish the validity and amount of the claims. A company should also separate the duties involved in purchasing goods and services and the duties involved in paying for them. The degree of separation that is possible varies, depending on the size of the business.

Exhibit 1 shows how a large company can maximize the separation of duties. Five internal units (the requesting department, the purchasing department, the accounting department, the receiving department, and the treasurer) and two firms outside the company (the vendor and the bank) play a role in this control plan. Notice that business documents are crucial components of the plan.

Exhibit 1

Internal Controls in a Large Company: Separation of Duties and Documentation

STUDY NOTE: *Every business document must have a number for purposes of reference.*

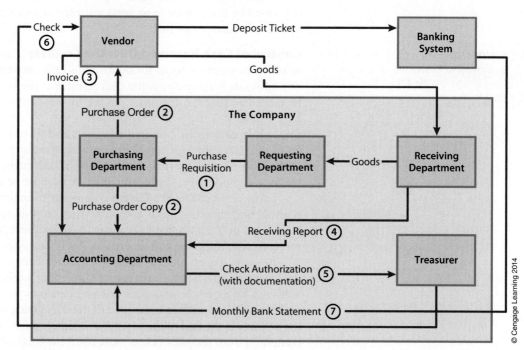

Note: Circled numbers refer to documents in Exhibit 2.

© Cengage Learning 2014

Exhibit 2 illustrates the typical sequence in which documents are used in a company's internal control plan for purchases and cash disbursements.

Exhibit 2
Internal Control Plan for Purchases and Cash Disbursements

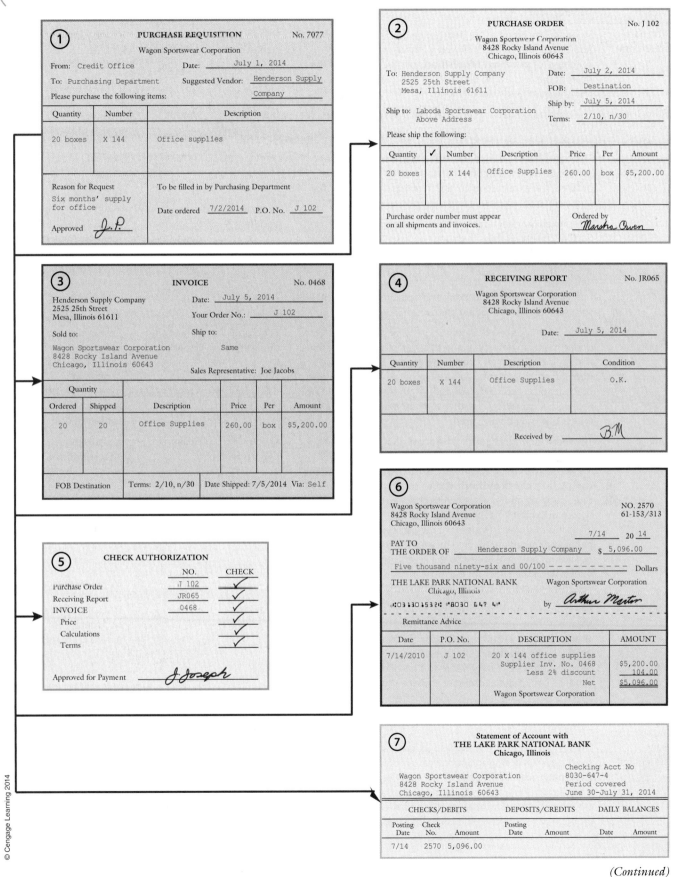

Business Document	Description	Prepared by	Sent to	Verification and Related Procedures
① Purchase requisition	To begin, the credit office (requesting department) of Wagon Sportswear Corporation fills out a formal request for a purchase, or **purchase requisition**, for office supplies. The head of the requesting department approves it and forwards it to the purchasing department.	Requesting department	Purchasing department	Purchasing verifies authorization.
② Purchase order	The purchasing department prepares a **purchase order**. The purchase order indicates that Wagon Sportswear will not pay any bill that does not include a purchase order number. The purchase order is addressed to the vendor (seller) and contains a description of the quantity and type of items ordered, the expected price, the shipping date and terms, and other instructions.	Purchasing department	Vendor	Vendor sends goods or services in accordance with purchase order.
③ Invoice	After receiving the purchase order, the vendor, Henderson Supply Company, ships the goods and sends an **invoice** to Wagon Sportswear. The invoice shows the quantity of goods delivered, describes what they are, and lists the price and terms of payment. If all the goods cannot be shipped immediately, the invoice indicates the estimated date of shipment for the remaining goods.	Vendor	Accounting department	Accounting receives invoice from vendor.
④ Receiving report	When the goods reach Wagon Sportswear's receiving department, an employee notes the quantity, type of goods, and their condition on a **receiving report**. The receiving department does not receive a copy of the purchase order or the invoice, so its employees don't know what should be received or its value. Thus, they are not tempted to steal any excess that may be delivered.	Receiving department	Accounting department	Accounting compares invoice, purchase order, and receiving report. Accounting verifies prices.
⑤ Check authorization	The receiving report goes to the accounting department, where it is compared to the purchase order and the invoice. If everything is correct, the accounting department completes a **check authorization** and attaches it to the three supporting documents. The check authorization form shown in Exhibit 2 has a space for each item to be checked off as it is examined. Notice that the accounting department has all the documentary evidence for the transaction, but it does not have access to the assets purchased, nor does it write the check for payment. Thus, the accounting department cannot conceal fraud by falsifying documents.	Accounting department	Treasurer	Accounting attaches check authorization to invoice, purchase order, and receiving report.
⑥ Check	The treasurer examines all the documents. If the treasurer approves them, he or she signs or authorizes an electronic **check**, which is an authorization for the bank to pay the vendor in the amount of the invoice less any applicable discount. The check is then sent to the vendor or the vendor's bank, with a remittance advice showing what the check is for. A vendor that is not paid the proper amount will complain, thus providing a form of outside control over the payment.	Treasurer	Vendor	Treasurer verifies all documents before preparing check.
⑦ Bank statement	The vendor deposits the check in its bank, and the canceled check appears in Wagon Sportswear's monthly **bank statement**, which may be in either paper or electronic form. If the treasurer has made the check out for the wrong amount (or altered an amount that was already filled in), the problem will show up in the company's bank reconciliation.	Buyer's bank	Accounting department	Accounting compares amount and payee's name on returned check with check authorization.

Note: Circled numbers refer to documents on the previous page.

APPLY IT!

Items **a–e** below are a company's departments. Items **f** and **g** are firms with which the company has transactions.

Use the letter of the department or firm to indicate which one prepares and sends the business documents that follow.

a. Requesting department
b. Purchasing department
c. Receiving department
d. Accounting department

e. Treasurer
f. Vendor
g. Bank

	Prepared by	Received by
1. Receiving report	____	____
2. Purchase order	____	____
3. Purchase requisition	____	____
4. Check	____	____
5. Invoice	____	____
6. Check authorization	____	____
7. Bank statement	____	____

SOLUTION

	Prepared by	Received by
1. Receiving report	c	d
2. Purchase order	b	f
3. Purchase requisition	a	b
4. Check	d, e	f
5. Invoice	f	d
6. Check authorization	d	e
7. Bank statement	g	d

TRY IT! SE4, SE5, SE6, SE7, E2A, E3A, E4A, E5A, E2B, E3B, E4B, E5B

LO3 Cash Equivalents and Cash Control

Cash Equivalents

STUDY NOTE: *The statement of cash flows explains the change in the balance of cash and cash equivalents from one period to the next.*

At times, a company may have more cash than it needs to pay its debts. Excess cash should not remain idle, especially during periods of high interest rates. Management may decide to invest the excess cash in short-term interest-bearing accounts or certificates of deposit (CDs) at banks and other financial institutions, in government securities (such as U.S. Treasury notes), or in other securities. If these investments have a term of 90 days or less when they are purchased, they are called **cash equivalents** because the funds revert to cash so quickly they are treated as cash on the balance sheet.

Nike describes its treatment of cash and cash equivalents as follows.

> *Cash and equivalents represent cash and short-term, highly liquid investments with maturities of three months or less at date of purchase. The carrying amounts reflected in the consolidated balance sheet for cash and equivalents approximate fair value.*[6]

Like Nike, most companies record cash equivalents at their approximate fair value, that is, their market value.

According to a survey of large U.S. corporations, 2.5 percent use the term *cash* as the balance sheet caption, and 96 percent use either *cash and cash equivalents* or *cash and equivalents*. The rest either combine cash with marketable securities or have no cash.[7]

Cash Control Methods

Earlier in the chapter, we discussed the concept of internal control and how it applies to cash transactions. Here, we address additional ways of controlling cash.

Imprest Systems Most companies need to keep some currency and coins on hand. Currency and coins are needed for cash registers, for paying expenses that are impractical to pay by check, and for situations that require cash advances—for example, when sales representatives need cash for travel expenses. One way to control a cash fund and cash advances is by using an **imprest system**. A common form of imprest system is a *petty cash fund*, which is discussed in more depth later in the chapter.

Banking Services Banks provide safe depositories for cash, negotiable instruments, and other valuable business documents such as stocks and bonds. The checking accounts that they provide improve control by minimizing the amount of currency a company needs to keep on hand and by supplying permanent records of all cash payments. Banks also serve as agents in a variety of transactions, such as the collection and payment of certain kinds of debts and the exchange of foreign currencies.

    Electronic funds transfer (EFT) is a method of conducting business transactions that does not involve the actual transfer of cash. With EFT, a company electronically transfers cash from its bank to another company's bank. For the banks, the electronic transfer is simply a bookkeeping entry. Companies today rely heavily on this method of payment. **Wal-Mart**, for example, makes 75 percent of its payments to suppliers through EFT.

    Automated teller machines (ATMs) allow bank customers to make deposits, withdraw cash, transfer funds among accounts, and pay bills. Large consumer banks like **Citibank**, **Chase**, and **Bank of America** process hundreds of thousands of ATM transactions each week. Many banks also give customers the option of paying bills online or over the telephone with debit cards. In 2011, debit cards accounted for more than $1.5 trillion in transactions.[8] When a customer makes a retail purchase using a debit card, the amount of the purchase is deducted directly from the buyer's bank account. The bank usually documents debit card transactions for the retailer, but the retailer must develop new internal controls to ensure that the transactions are recorded properly and that unauthorized transfers do not occur.

STUDY NOTE: *Bank reconciliations are an important factor in internal control. If carried out by someone who cannot access the company's bank account, they provide an independent check on people who do have access.*

Bank Reconciliations Rarely does the balance of a company's Cash account exactly equal the cash balance on its bank statement. The bank may not yet have recorded certain transactions that appear in the company's records, and the company may not yet have recorded certain bank transactions. A **bank reconciliation** is the process of accounting for the difference between the balance on a company's bank statement and the balance in its Cash account.

    The following transactions commonly appear in a company's records but not on its bank statement:

- **Outstanding checks:** Checks that a company has issued and recorded but that do not yet appear on its bank statement.
- **Deposits in transit:** Deposits a company has sent to its bank but that the bank did not receive in time to enter on the bank statement.

Transactions that may appear on the bank statement but not in the company's records include the following:

- **Service charges (SC):** Banks often charge a fee for the use of a checking account. Many banks base this service charge on a number of factors, such as the average balance of the account during the month or the number of checks drawn.
- **NSF (nonsufficient funds) checks:** An NSF check is a check that a company has deposited but that is not paid when the bank presents it to the issuer's bank. The bank charges the company's account and returns the check so that the company can try to collect the amount due. If the bank has deducted the NSF check on the bank statement but the company has not deducted it from its book balance, an adjustment

must be made in the bank reconciliation. The company usually reclassifies the NSF check from Cash to Accounts Receivable because it must now collect from the person or company that wrote the check.

- **Miscellaneous debits and credits:** Banks also charge for other services, such as stopping payment on checks and printing checks. The bank notifies the depositor of each deduction by including a debit memorandum with the monthly statement. A bank also sometimes serves as an agent in collecting on promissory notes for the depositor. When it does, it includes a credit memorandum in the bank statement, along with a debit memorandum for the service charge.
- **Interest income:** Banks commonly pay interest on a company's average balance. Accounts that pay interest are sometimes called NOW or money market accounts.

An error by either the bank or the depositor will require immediate correction.

To illustrate the preparation of a bank reconciliation, suppose that Kalita Services Company's bank statement for August shows a balance of $1,735.53 on August 31 and that on the same date, the company's records show a cash balance of $1,207.95. Exhibit 3 shows Kalita Services' bank reconciliation for August.

Exhibit 3
Bank Reconciliation

Kalita Services Company
Bank Reconciliation
August 31, 2014

Balance per bank, August 31		$ 1,735.53
① Add deposit of August 31 in transit		138.00
		$ 1,873.53
② Less outstanding checks:		
No. 551, issued on July 14	$ 75.00	
No. 576, issued on Aug. 30	20.34	
No. 578, issued on Aug. 31	250.00	
No. 579, issued on Aug. 31	185.00	
No. 580, issued on Aug. 31	65.25	595.59
Adjusted bank balance, August 31		**$1,277.94**
Balance per books, August 31		$ 1,207.95
Add:		
④ Note receivable collected by bank	$140.00	
④ Interest income on note	10.00	
⑦ Interest income	7.81	157.81
		$ 1,365.76
Less:		
③ Overstatement of deposit of August 6	$ 15.00	
④ Collection fee	2.50	
⑤ NSF check of Austin Chase	64.07	
⑥ Service charge	6.25	87.82
Adjusted book balance, August 31		**$1,277.94**

Note: Circled numbers refer to documents In Exhibit 2.

The circled numbers in the exhibit refer to the following:

1. The bank has not recorded a deposit in the amount of $138.00 that the company mailed to the bank on August 31.
2. The bank has not paid the five checks that the company issued in July and August. Even though the July 14 check was deducted in the July 30 reconciliation, it must be deducted again in each subsequent month in which it remains outstanding.
3. The company incorrectly recorded a $150.00 deposit from cash sales as $165.00. On August 6, the bank received the deposit and correctly recorded the amount.
4. Among the returned checks was a credit memorandum showing that the bank had collected a promissory note from K. Diaz in the amount of $140.00, plus

$10.00 in interest on the note. A debit memorandum was also enclosed for the $2.50 collection fee. The company had not entered these amounts in its records.

5. Also returned with the bank statement was an NSF check for $64.07 that the company had received from a customer named Austin Chase. The NSF check was not reflected in the company's records.

6. A debit memorandum was enclosed for the regular monthly service charge of $6.25. The company had not yet recorded this charge.

7. Interest earned on the company's average balance was $7.81.

In Exhibit 3, starting from their separate balances, both the bank and book amounts are adjusted to the amount of $1,277.94. This adjusted balance is the amount of cash the company owns on August 31 and thus is the amount that should appear on its August 31 balance sheet.

When outstanding checks are presented to the bank for payment and the bank receives and records the deposit in transit, the bank balance will automatically become correct. However, the company must update its book balance by recording all the items reported by the bank. Thus, Kalita Services would record an increase (debit) in Cash with the following items:

▼ *Decrease* (credit) in *Notes Receivable*, $140.00

▲ *Increase* (credit) in *Interest Income*, $10.00 (interest on note)

▲ *Increase* (credit) in *Interest Income*, $7.81 (interest on average bank balance)

The company would record a reduction (credit) in Cash with the following items:

▼ *Decrease* (debit) in *Sales*, $15.00 (error in recording deposit)

▲ *Increase* (debit) in *Accounts Receivable*, $64.07 (return of NSF check)

▲ *Increase* (debit) in *Bank Service Charges*, $8.75 ($6.25 + $2.50)

APPLY IT! ▶

At year end, Binsu Company had currency and coins in cash registers of $1,100, money orders from customers of $2,000, deposits in checking accounts of $12,000, U.S. Treasury bills due in 80 days of $50,000, certificates of deposit at the bank that mature in six months of $200,000, and U.S. Treasury bonds due in one year of $100,000. Calculate the amount of cash and cash equivalents that will be shown on the company's year-end balance sheet.

SOLUTION

Currency and coins	$ 1,100
Money orders	2,000
Checking accounts	12,000
U.S. Treasury bills (due in 80 days)	50,000
Cash and cash equivalents	$65,100

The certificates of deposit and U.S. Treasury Bonds mature in more than 90 days and thus are not cash equivalents.

TRY IT! SE8, SE9, E6A, E7A, E6B, E7B

LO 4 Petty Cash Funds

It is not always practical to use checks. For example, it is sometimes necessary to make small payments of cash for postage stamps, shipping charges due, or minor purchases of pens, paper, and other office supplies. For situations in which it is inconvenient to pay by check, most companies set up a **petty cash fund**. One of the best ways to control a petty cash fund is through an imprest system, in which the fund is established for a fixed amount. A voucher documents each cash payment made from the fund. The fund is periodically reimbursed, based on the vouchers, by the exact amount necessary to restore its original cash balance.

Establishing the Petty Cash Fund

Some companies have a regular cashier or other employee who administers the petty cash fund.

Establishing the Petty Cash Fund

Transaction On October 14, Davis Company establishes the petty cash fund by issuing a check for $100 intended to cover two to four weeks of small expenditures. The check is cashed and the money placed in the petty cash box, drawer, or envelope.

Analysis The journal entry to establish the petty cash fund

▲ *increases* the *Petty Cash* account

▼ *decreases* the *Cash* account

Application of Double Entry

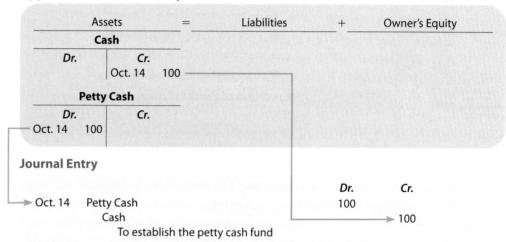

Journal Entry

		Dr.	Cr.
Oct. 14	Petty Cash	100	
	Cash		100
	To establish the petty cash fund		

Comment The only entry required when the fund is established is to record the check.

Making Disbursements from the Petty Cash Fund

The custodian of the petty cash fund should prepare a **petty cash voucher**, or written authorization, for each expenditure, as shown in Exhibit 4. On each petty cash voucher, the custodian enters the date, amount, and purpose of the expenditure. The person who receives the payment signs the voucher.

Exhibit 4
Petty Cash Voucher

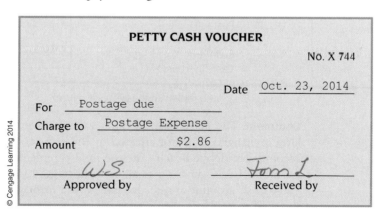

The custodian should be informed that unannounced audits of the fund will be made occasionally. The cash in the fund plus the sum of the petty cash vouchers should at all times equal the amount shown in the Petty Cash account.

Reimbursing the Petty Cash Fund

At specified intervals, when the fund becomes low, and at the end of a period, the petty cash fund is replenished by a check issued to the custodian for the exact amount of the

STUDY NOTE: *Even though withdrawals from petty cash are generally small, the cumulative total over time can represent a substantial amount. Accordingly, an effective system of internal control must be established for the fund.*

expenditures. From time to time, there may be minor discrepancies in the amount of cash left in the fund at the time of reimbursement. In those cases, the amount of the discrepancy is recorded in a Cash Short or Over account—as a debit if short or as a credit if over.

Reimbursing the Petty Cash Fund

Transaction On October 28 (after two weeks), Davis Company replenishes its petty cash fund, established earlier, which has a cash balance of $14.27 and petty cash vouchers as follows: postage, $25.00; supplies, $30.55; and freight-in, $30.00.

Analysis The journal entry to replenish the fund

▲ *increases* the *Postage Expense* account

▲ *increases* the *Supplies Expense* account

▲ *increases* the *Freight-In* account

▲ *increases* the *Cash Short or Over* account

▼ *decreases* the *Cash* account

Application of Double Entry

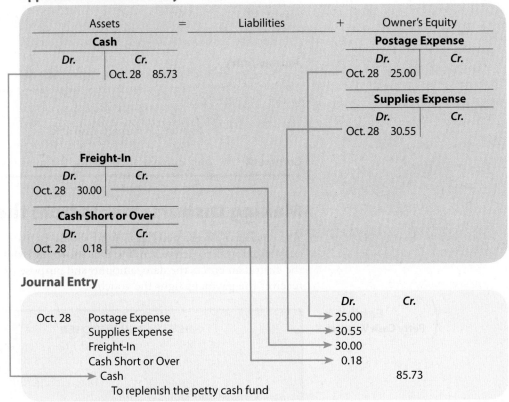

Comment The Petty Cash account is debited when the fund is established or the fund level is changed. It is not affected by the entry to replenish the fund. Expense or asset accounts are debited each time the fund is replenished, including in this case $0.18 to Cash Short or Over for a small cash shortage. In most cases, no further entries to the Petty Cash account are needed unless the firm wants to change the fixed amount of the fund.

The petty cash fund should be replenished at the end of a period to bring it up to its fixed amount and ensure that changes in the other accounts involved are reflected in the current period's financial statements. If the petty cash fund is not replenished at the end of the period, expenditures are shown through an adjusting entry debiting the expense accounts and crediting Petty Cash. The result is a reduction in the petty cash fund and the Petty Cash account by the amount of the adjusting entry. In the financial statements, the balance of the Petty Cash account is usually combined with other cash accounts.

Internal Control and the Financial Statements

Internal control applies to all transactions and ensures the fair presentation of the financial statements as shown in Exhibit 5.

Exhibit 5

Internal Control and the Income Statement and Balance Sheet

Income Statement
For the Year Ended April 30, 2014

Net sales
Cost of goods sold
  Gross margin
Operating expenses
  Operating income
Other revenues and expenses
  Interest income
  Net income

Balance Sheet
April 30, 2014

Assets
Cash and cash equivalents
Accounts receivable, net
Merchandise inventory
Notes receivable
Property, plant, and equipment

Liabilities
Current liabilities
Long-term liabilities
  Total liabilities

Owner's Equity
Owner's capital
  Total owner's equity

Total Assets = Total Liabilities + Owner's Equity

© Cengage Learning 2014

APPLY IT!

A petty cash fund is established at $150 on July 1. At the end of July, the fund has a cash balance of $59 and petty cash vouchers for postage, $37, and office supplies, $52. Prepare the journal entry to establish the fund on July 1 and the entry on July 31 to replenish the fund.

SOLUTION

July 1	Petty Cash	150	
	Cash		150
	To establish petty cash fund		
July 31	Postage Expense	37	
	Office Supplies Expense	52	
	Cash Over or Short	2	
	Cash		91
	To replenish petty cash fund		

TRY IT! SE10, E8A, E9A, E8B, E9B

SECTION 3

BUSINESS APPLICATIONS
- Management's responsibility
- Independent auditor's audit

RELEVANT LEARNING OBJECTIVE

LO 5 Identify the internal control roles of management and the auditor.

BUSINESS APPLICATIONS

LO 5 Management Issues Related to Internal Control

A company's management and its auditor have important responsibilities for the internal control of a company.

Management's Responsibility for Internal Control

Management is responsible for establishing a satisfactory system of internal controls. In other words, management must safeguard the firm's assets, ensure the reliability of its accounting records, and see that its employees comply with all legal requirements and operate the firm to the best advantage of its owners.

Section 404 of the Sarbanes-Oxley Act requires that the chief executive officer, the chief financial officer, and the auditors of a public company fully document and certify the company's system of internal controls. For example, in its annual report, **Costco**'s management acknowledges its responsibility for internal control as follows.

> *Our management is responsible for establishing and maintaining adequate internal control over financial reporting.*[9]

Independent Accountant's Audit of Internal Control

Although privately owned companies usually are not required to have an independent certified public accountant audit their financial statements, many companies choose to do so. These companies are also not required to have their internal control systems audited. Public companies like **Costco**, on the other hand, are required to not only have an independent audit of their financial statements, they must also have an audit of their internal control. For instance, Costco's auditors state:

> *In our opinion, the Company maintained, in all material respects, effective internal control over financial reporting...*[10]

Business Perspective
Will Sarbanes-Oxley Stop Fraud?

Although the Sarbanes-Oxley Act has heightened awareness of internal control and has required increased diligence, it will never stop fraud from occurring. For instance, a recent study of 350 alleged accounting fraud cases investigated by the SEC found that fraud affects companies of all sizes. The average fraud was $12.1 million, and more than 30 cases involved fraud over $500 million. Additional guidance with regard to internal controls are expected to be issued.[11]

APPLY IT!

Match the items with the related statements that follow.

a. Internal control
b. A need of internal control
c. Management's responsibility
d. Independent accountant's audit

1. Provides reasonable assurance to outside parties that management maintains internal control over financial reporting.
2. Established by management to ensure the reliability of accounting records and financial statements in accordance with GAAP.
3. Human error can cause errors in the financial statements.
4. To assure the establishment of a system of internal control and assess its effectiveness.

SOLUTION

1. d; 2. a; 3. b; 4. c

TRY IT! SE1, E10A, E10B

TriLevel Problem

Sung's Grill

The beginning of this chapter focused on Emma Sung, the owner of Sung's Grill, who was looking for ways to ensure that the restaurant's assets were protected and that all its transactions were recorded properly. Complete the following requirements in order to answer the questions posed at the beginning of the chapter.

Section 1: Concepts

Why is each of the five components of internal control important to the faithful representation of a company's operations in its financial statements?

Section 2: Accounting Applications

How can Sung's Grill maintain control over its cash?

In order to have better control over cash, Emma Sung has established several rules for cashiers. Match each of the internal controls with the control activities that follow. (*Hint:* Some may have more than one answer.)

a. Authorization
b. Recording transactions
c. Documents and records
d. Physical controls
e. Periodic independent verification
f. Separation of duties
g. Sound personnel practices

1. Emma Sung hires experienced cashiers who are bonded and checks the references of all new employees.
2. New cashiers are trained in all procedures before being allowed to handle cash.
3. All food bills are prenumbered sequentially.
4. When a customer finishes a meal, the waiter writes up a bill that describes the food items purchased, including the total price.
5. The waiters are not allowed to access the cash register.
6. If the sale is by credit card, the cashier runs the credit card through a scanner that verifies the customer's credit. The scanner prints out a receipt and a slip for the customer to sign. The signed slip is put in the cash register, and the customer is given the receipt and a copy of the sales invoice.
7. All sales, whether cash or credit, are rung up on the cash register.
8. The cash register must be locked when the cashier is not present. The cashier is the only person other than Emma Sung who has a key.
9. Refunds or discounts are made only with Emma Sung's approval.
10. At the end of each day, Emma counts the cash and checks in the cash register and compares the total with the amount recorded on the tape inside the register. She totals all the signed credit card slips and ensures that the total equals the amount recorded by the scanner.

Section 3: Business Applications
How can Sung's Grill's bank and other users of its financial statements be confident that the restaurant has an adequate system of internal control?

SOLUTION

Section 1: Concepts

An effective system of internal control contributes to the *faithful representation* of a company's operations through five interrelated components: control environment, risk assessment, control activities, information and communication, and monitoring. Since internal control is a process, all of these components need to be present if the company wants to have an effective internal control system; for example, management needs to create an environment that encourages compliance with laws, regulations, and standards. Management has to also identify and asses possible risks and implement control activities that will ensure safeguard of its assets and reliability of its accounting records. Information and communication is also crucial because it encompasses the accounting system and how information and data are communicated within the company and to the external parties. Finally, an effective system of internal control requires continuous monitoring, which means that management reviews compliance with required laws and regulations to make sure everything works as planned and takes necessary actions when problems arise.

Section 2: Accounting Applications

1. g
2. g
3. c
4. a, c
5. d, f
6. b, c
7. b, d
8. d
9. a, f
10. e

Section 3: Business Applications

As the owner of Sung's Grill, Emma Sung is responsible for establishing an effective system of internal control which is essential for reliable financial reporting. Emma, as the top executive, certifies the restaurant's system of internal control. However, the best way for any business to assure users of the integrity of its financial statements is to have an independent auditor assess the reliability of its internal control system. Thus, Emma can hire independent auditors to audit its financial statements and to audit its system of internal control. The auditor's report will be a credible source of information for banks and any other users of Sung's Grill's financial statements.

Chapter Review

Describe the components of internal control, control activities, and limitations on internal control. **LO 1**

Internal control establishes the reliability of the accounting records and financial statements in accordance with generally accepted accounting principles (GAAP) and ensures that the company's assets are protected. Internal control consists of all the policies and procedures a company uses to ensure the reliability of financial reporting, compliance with laws and regulations, and the effectiveness and efficiency of operations. Internal control has five components: the control environment, risk assessment, control activities, information and communication, and monitoring. Control activities include having managers authorize certain transactions, recording all transactions to establish accountability for assets, using well-designed documents to ensure proper recording of transactions, instituting physical controls, periodically checking records and assets, separating duties, and using sound personnel practices. A system of internal control relies on the people who implement it. Human error, collusion, and failure to recognize changed conditions can contribute to a system's failure.

Apply internal control activities to common merchandising transactions. **LO 2**

To implement internal control over cash sales, receipts, purchases, and disbursements, the functions of authorization, recordkeeping, and custodianship of cash should be kept separate. The people who have access to cash should be specifically designated and their number limited. Employees who have access to cash should be bonded. The control system should also provide for the use of banking services, physical protection of assets, prompt recording and deposit of cash receipts, and payment by check. A person who does not authorize, handle, or record cash transactions should make unannounced audits of the cash on hand, and the Cash account should be reconciled each month.

Define *cash equivalents*, and explain methods of controlling cash, including bank reconciliations. **LO 3**

Cash equivalents are investments that have a term of 90 days or less. Most companies record cash equivalents at their approximate fair value. Methods of controlling cash include imprest systems; banking services, including electronic funds transfer; and bank reconciliations. A bank reconciliation accounts for the difference between the balance on a company's bank statement and the balance in its Cash account. It involves adjusting for outstanding checks, deposits in transit, service charges, NSF checks, miscellaneous debits and credits, and interest income.

Demonstrate the use of a simple imprest (petty cash) system. **LO 4**

An imprest system is a method of controlling small cash expenditures by setting up a fund at a fixed amount and periodically reimbursing the fund to restore the original balance. A petty cash fund, one example of an imprest system, is established by a debit to Petty Cash and a credit to Cash. It is replenished by debits to various expense or asset accounts and a credit to Cash. Each expenditure should be supported by a petty cash voucher.

Identify the internal control roles of management and the auditor. **LO 5**

Management's responsibility is to establish an environment, accounting systems, and internal control procedures that will protect the assets. Public companies must engage an independent CPA to verify that management is indeed meeting these goals.

Key Terms

authorization 303 (LO1)
bank reconciliation 312 (LO3)
bank statement 310 (LO2)
bonding 304 (LO1)
cash equivalents 311 (LO3)
check 310 (LO2)
check authorization 310 (LO2)
control activities 303 (LO1)
control environment 303 (LO1)
deposits in transit 312 (LO3)
electronic funds transfer
   (EFT) 312 (LO3)

imprest system 312 (LO3)
information and
   communication 303 (LO1)
internal control 302 (LO1)
invoice 310 (LO2)
monitoring 303 (LO1)
NSF (nonsufficient funds)
   checks 312 (LO3)
outstanding checks 312 (LO3)
periodic independent
   verification 304 (LO1)
petty cash fund 314 (LO4)

petty cash voucher 315 (LO4)
physical controls 304 (LO1)
physical inventory 302 (LO1)
purchase order 310 (LO2)
purchase requisition 310 (LO2)
receiving report 310 (LO2)
risk assessment 303 (LO1)
separation of duties 304 (LO1)

Chapter Assignments

DISCUSSION QUESTIONS

LO 1   **DQ1.** Why is a system of internal control not able to overcome collusion by employees?

LO 1   **DQ2. CONCEPT** ▶ In what way does internal control contribute to faithful representation in its financial statements?

LO 2   **DQ3.** Which of the following accounts would be assigned a higher level of risk: Building or Merchandising Inventory?

LO 2   **DQ4.** Why is it important to record the amount of cash received through the mail or over the counter?

LO 3   **DQ5.** What role does a bank reconciliation play in internal control over cash?

LO 3   **DQ6.** Name some businesses whose needs for cash fluctuate during the year. Name some whose needs for cash are relatively stable over the year.

LO 5   **DQ7. BUSINESS APPLICATION** ▶ Why is it important for public companies to have an audit of management's assessment of internal control?

SHORT EXERCISES

LO 1, 5   **Internal Control**

SE1. Match the items with the related statements that follow.

a. Internal control
b. A need of internal control
c. Management's responsibility
d. Independent accountant's audit

1. Evaluates management's assessment of internal control over financial reporting.
2. A process that establishes reliability of accounting records and financial statements in accordance with GAAP.
3. Many assets such as cash and inventories are at risk of loss.
4. Establishes a system of internal control and assesses its effectiveness

LO 1, 2   **Components of Internal Control**

SE2. Match the items with the related statements that follow.

a. Control environment
b. Risk assessment
c. Control activities
d. Information and communication
e. Monitoring

1. Policies and procedures management puts in place to see that its directives are carried out.
2. Identifying areas where losses may occur.
3. Regular assessment of the quality of internal controls.
4. Management's overall attitude, awareness, and actions.
5. Pertains to the accounting system.

LO 1   **Limitations of Internal Control**

SE3. Internal control is subject to several inherent limitations. Indicate whether each of the following situations is an example of (a) human error, (b) collusion among employees, (c) changed conditions, or (d) cost-benefit considerations:

1. Effective separation of duties in a restaurant is impractical because the business is too small.
2. The cashier and the manager of a retail shoe store work together to avoid the internal controls for the purpose of embezzling funds.
3. The cashier in a pizza shop does not understand the procedures for operating the cash register and thus fails to ring up all the sales and count the cash at the end of the day.
4. At a law firm, computer supplies are mistakenly delivered to the reception area instead of the receiving area because the supplier began using a different system of shipment. As a result, the receipt of supplies is not recorded.

LO **1, 2**   **Separation of Duties**

SE4. Match the functions for collecting cash by Sonja Cleaners with the statements that follow.

a. Authorization
b. Custody
c. Recordkeeping

1. The cashier is responsible for funds in the cash register.
2. All sales are recorded on prenumbered invoices and rung up on the cash register.
3. All refunds must be approved by the manager.

LO **2**   **Physical Controls**

SE5. Match the assets of a small retail store with the related physical controls that follow.

a. Cash
b. Merchandise inventory
c. Supplies
d. Computers

1. An alarm that signals if unsold items leave the store.
2. Cash register.
3. A locked cabinet in the supplies closet.
4. A cable with a lock.
5. A locked showcase.

LO **1, 2**   **Internal Control Activities**

SE6. Match the check-writing policies for a small business to the control activities that follow.

a. Authorization
b. Recording transactions
c. Documents and records
d. Physical controls
e. Periodic independent verification
f. Separation of duties
g. Sound personnel practices

1. The person who writes the checks to pay bills is different from the people who authorize the payments and keep records of the payments.
2. The checks are kept in a locked drawer. The only person who has the key is the person who writes the checks.
3. The person who writes the checks is bonded.
4. Once each month the owner compares and reconciles the amount of money shown in the accounting records with the amount in the bank account.
5. The owner of the business approves each check before it is mailed.
6. Information pertaining to each check is recorded on the check stub.
7. Every day, all checks are recorded in the accounting records, using the information on the check stubs.

LO **2**   **Business Documents**

SE7. Arrange the following business documents in the normal order in which they would be prepared:

1. Invoice
2. Purchase order
3. Check
4. Receiving report
5. Bank statement
6. Purchase requisition
7. Check authorization

LO 3   **Cash and Cash Equivalents**

SE8. Compute the amount of cash and cash equivalents on Steen Wash Company's balance sheet if, on the balance sheet date, it has currency and coins on hand of $250, deposits in checking accounts of $1,500, U.S. Treasury bills due in 80 days of $15,000, and U.S. Treasury bonds due in 200 days of $25,000.

LO 3   **Bank Reconciliation**

SE9. Prepare a bank reconciliation from the following information:

a. Balance per bank statement as of June 30, $4,862.77
b. Balance per books as of June 30, $2,479.48
c. Deposits in transit, $654.24
d. Outstanding checks, $3,028.89
e. Interest on average balance, $8.64

LO 4   **Petty Cash Fund**

SE10. A petty cash fund is established at $100. At the end of May, the fund has a cash balance of $36 and petty cash vouchers for postage, $29, and office supplies, $34. Prepare the journal entry on May 31, 2014, to replenish the fund.

EXERCISES: SET A

LO 1   **Components of Internal Control**

E1A. Match the items with the related statements that follow.

a. Control environment
b. Risk assessment
c. Control activities
d. Information and communication
e. Monitoring

1. Management encourages employees to follow the rules.
2. The company has an internal audit department.
3. Management regularly considers what losses the company might face.
4. The company gathers appropriate information and communicates it to employees.
5. Management puts separation of duties in place.
6. Personnel are well trained and instructed in their duties.
7. The company employs good physical controls.
8. The company has a good accounting system.
9. Managers are observant and review how procedures by those who report to them are carried out.

LO 1, 2   **Control Procedures**

E2A. Some conditions for internal control follow.

a. Transactions are executed in accordance with management's general or specific authorization.
b. Transactions are recorded as necessary to permit preparation of financial statements and maintain accountability for assets.
c. Access to assets is permitted only as allowed by management.
d. At reasonable intervals, the records of assets are compared with the existing assets.

Marika Jonssen, who operates a small grocery store, has established the following policies with regard to the checkout cashiers:

1. Cashiers may accept checks for purchases under $100 with proper identification. For checks over $100, they must receive approval from Jonssen.
2. Each cashier has his or her own cash drawer, to which no one else has access.
3. Every sale must be rung up on the cash register and a receipt given to the customer. Each sale is recorded on a tape inside the cash register.

4. At the end of each day, Jonssen counts the cash in the drawer and compares it with the amount on the tape inside the cash register.

Match the conditions for internal control to each of the policies listed.

LO **1, 2**   **Internal Control Procedures**

E3A. A list of control procedures follows.

a. Authorization
b. Recording transactions
c. Documents and records
d. Physical controls

e. Periodic independent verification
f. Separation of duties
g. Sound personnel practices

Real Video Store maintains the following policies with regard to purchases of new DVDs at each of its branch stores:

1. Once each month a person from the home office visits each branch store to examine the receiving records and to compare the inventory of DVDs with the accounting records.
2. Employees are required to take vacations, and the duties of employees are rotated periodically.
3. Purchases of new DVDs must be authorized by purchase order in the home office and paid for by the treasurer in the home office. Receiving reports are prepared in each branch and sent to the home office.
4. All new personnel receive one hour of training in how to receive and catalogue new DVDs.
5. The company maintains a perpetual inventory system that keeps track of all DVDs purchased, sold, and on hand.

Match the control procedures to each of the policies listed. (*Hint:* Some may have more than one answer.)

LO **2**   **Business Documents**

E4A. Items **a–e** below are a company's departments. Items **f** and **g** are firms with which the company has transactions.

a. Requesting department
b. Purchasing department
c. Receiving department
d. Accounting department

e. Treasurer
f. Vendor
g. Bank

Use the letter of the department or firm to indicate which one prepares and sends the following business documents:

	Prepared by	Received by
1. Purchase requisition	____	____
2. Bank statement	____	____
3. Purchase order	____	____
4. Check authorization	____	____
5. Invoice	____	____
6. Check	____	____
7. Receiving report	____	____

LO **2**   **Use of Accounting Records in Internal Control**

E5A. ACCOUNTING CONNECTION ▶ Careful scrutiny of accounting records and financial statements can lead to the discovery of fraud or embezzlement. Each of the situations that follow may indicate a breakdown in internal control. Indicate the nature of the possible fraud or embezzlement in each of these situations.

1. Wages expense for a branch office was 15 percent higher in 2014 than in 2013, even though the office was authorized to employ only the same four employees and raises were only 2.5 percent in 2014.

(Continued)

2. Sales returns and allowances increased from 2.5 percent to 10 percent of sales in the first two months of 2014, after record sales in 2013 resulted in large bonuses for the sales staff.

3. Gross margin decreased from 20 percent of net sales in 2013 to 10 percent in 2014, even though there was no change in pricing. Ending inventory was 25 percent less at the end of 2014 than it was at the beginning of the year. There is no immediate explanation for the decrease in inventory.

4. A review of daily records of cash register receipts shows that one cashier consistently accepts more discount coupons for purchases than do the other cashiers.

LO 3 **Cash and Cash Equivalents**

E6A. At year end, Bottle Water Company had currency and coins in cash registers of $5,600, money orders from customers of $10,000, deposits in checking accounts of $64,000, U.S. Treasury bills due in 80 days of $180,000, certificates of deposit at the bank that mature in six months of $200,000, and U.S. Treasury bonds due in one year of $100,000. Calculate the amount of cash and cash equivalents that will be shown on the company's year-end balance sheet.

LO 3 **Bank Reconciliation**

E7A. Prepare a bank reconciliation from the following information:

a. Balance per bank statement as of May 31, $16,655.44
b. Balance per books as of May 31, $12,091.94
c. Deposits in transit, $2,234.81
d. Outstanding checks, $6,808.16
e. Bank service charge, $9.85

LO 4 **Imprest System**

E8A. ACCOUNTING CONNECTION ▶ Developing a convenient means of providing sales representatives with cash for their incidental expenses, such as entertaining a client at lunch, is a problem many companies face. Under one company's plan, the sales representatives receive advances in cash from the petty cash fund. Each advance is supported by an authorization from the sales manager. The representative returns the receipt for the expenditure and any unused cash, which is replaced in the petty cash fund. The cashier of the petty cash fund is responsible for seeing that the receipt and the cash returned equal the advance. When the petty cash fund is reimbursed, the amount of the representative's expenditure is debited to Direct Sales Expense.

What is the weak point in this system? What fundamental principle of internal control is being ignored? What improvement in the procedure can you suggest?

LO 4 **Petty Cash Transactions**

E9A. A small company maintains a petty cash fund for minor expenditures. In February and March 2014, the following transactions took place:

a. The fund was established in the amount of $200.00 on Feb. 1 from the proceeds of check no. 2717.

b. On Feb. 28, the petty cash fund had cash of $30.92 and the following receipts on hand: postage, $80.00; supplies, $49.88; delivery service, $24.80; and rubber stamp, $14.40. Check no. 2748 was drawn to replenish the fund.

c. On March 31, the petty cash fund had cash of $44.12 and these receipts on hand: postage, $68.40; supplies, $65.68; and delivery service, $12.80. The petty cash custodian could not account for the shortage. Check no. 2897 was drawn to replenish the fund.

Prepare the journal entries necessary to record each transaction.

LO 5 **Management and Auditor Responsibility for Internal Control**

E10A. BUSINESS APPLICATION ▶ Match the items with the related statements that follow.

a. Management's responsibility
b. Section 404 of Sarbanes-Oxley Act
c. Independent accountant's responsibility
d. Internal control

1. Provides reasonable assurance to outside parties that management maintains internal control over financial reporting.
2. Established by management to ensure the reliability of accounting records and financial statements in accordance with GAAP.
3. Requires that the chief executive officer, the chief financial officer, and the auditors of a public company fully document and certify the company's system of internal controls.
4. To assure the establishment of a system of internal control and assess its effectiveness.

EXERCISES: SET B

Visit the textbook companion website at www.cengagebrain.com to access Exercise Set B for this chapter.

PROBLEMS

LO 1 **Internal Control Components**

P1. Arcadia Company, a small retail bookstore, has experienced losses of inventory over the past year. Jason Arcadia, the owner, on the advice of his accountant, has adopted a set of internal controls in an effort to stop the losses. Arcadia has taken the following steps:

1. He regularly considers ways in which inventory losses might occur.
2. He had his accountant set up an accounting system over inventory.
3. He requires all new and existing employees to attend a training session in which they are instructed in their duties.
4. He makes sure that different employees perform the duties of authorization, custody, and recordkeeping.
5. He spends time "on the floor" encouraging employees to follow the procedures.
6. He periodically gathers appropriate information about inventory situations and communicates his findings to employees.
7. He had all items in inventory marked with an electronic bar code that signals an alarm if someone tries to take an item out of the store without paying for it.
8. He observes and reviews how internal control procedures are carried out.
9. He hires his accountant to periodically conduct internal audit work

REQUIRED

1. Show that Arcadia's new system engages all the components of internal control by matching each of the steps with the internal control components that follow. (*Hint:* Some may have more than one answer.)
   a. Control environment
   b. Risk assessment
   c. Control activities
   d. Information and communication
   e. Monitoring
2. **BUSINESS APPLICATION** ▶ As the owner of a small company, why is it important that Jason Arcadia take an active part in the management of the internal control system?

LO 1, 2 **Internal Control Procedures**

P2. Transco Printers makes printers for personal computers and maintains a factory outlet showroom through which it sells its products to the public. The company's management has set up a system of internal controls over the inventory of printers to prevent theft and to ensure the accuracy of the accounting records.

(Continued)

All printers in inventory at the factory outlet are kept in a secured warehouse behind the showroom, except for the sample printers on display. Only authorized personnel may enter the warehouse. When a customer buys a printer, a sales invoice is written in triplicate by the cashier and is marked "paid." The sales invoices are sequentially numbered, and all must be accounted for. The cashier sends the pink copy of the completed invoice to the warehouse, gives the blue copy to the customer, and keeps the green copy. The customer drives around to the warehouse entrance. The warehouse attendant takes the blue copy of the invoice from the customer and gives the customer the printer and the pink copy of the invoice.

The company maintains a perpetual inventory system for the printers at the outlet. The warehouse attendant at the outlet signs an inventory transfer sheet for each printer received. An accountant at the factory is assigned responsibility for maintaining the inventory records based on copies of the inventory transfer sheets and the sales invoices. The records are updated daily and may be accessed by computer but not modified by the sales personnel and the warehouse attendant. The accountant also sees that all pre-numbered inventory transfer sheets are accounted for and compares copies of them with the ones signed by the warehouse attendant. Once every three months, the company's internal auditor takes a physical count of the printer inventory and compares the results with the perpetual inventory records.

All new employees are required to read a sales and inventory manual and attend a two-hour training session about the internal controls. They must demonstrate that they can perform the functions required of them.

REQUIRED

1. Give an example of how each of the following control activities is applied to internal control over inventory at Transco Printers:

a. Authorization	e. Periodic independent verification
b. Recording transactions	f. Separation of duties
c. Documents and records	g. Sound personnel practices
d. Physical controls	

2. **ACCOUNTING CONNECTION** ▶ Can the described system protect against an employee who picks up a printer and carries it off when leaving work?

LO **1, 2** **Internal Control Activities**

P3. East-West Sports Shop is a small neighborhood sporting goods store. The shop's owner, Sunny Hazel, has set up a system of internal control over sales to prevent theft and to ensure the accuracy of the accounting records.

When a customer buys a product, the cashier writes up a sales invoice that describes the purchase, including the total price. All sales invoices are pre-numbered sequentially.

If the sale is by credit card, the cashier runs the credit card through a scanner that verifies the customer's credit. The scanner prints out a receipt and a slip for the customer to sign. The signed slip is put in the cash register, and the customer is given the receipt and a copy of the sales invoice.

If the sale is by cash or check, the cashier rings it up on the cash register and gives change, if appropriate. Checks must be written for the exact amount of the purchase and must be accompanied by identification. The sale is recorded on a tape inside the cash register that cannot be accessed by the cashier. The cash register may be locked with a key. The cashier is the only person other than Hazel who has a key. The cash register must be locked when the cashier is not present. Refunds are made only with Hazel's approval, are recorded on pre-numbered credit memorandum forms, and are rung up on the cash register.

At the end of each day, Hazel counts the cash and checks in the cash register and compares the total with the amount recorded on the tape inside the register. Hazel totals all the signed credit card slips and ensures that the total equals the amount recorded by the scanner. Hazel also makes sure that all sales invoices and credit memoranda are accounted for. Hazel prepares a bank deposit ticket for the cash, checks, and signed credit card slips, less $40 in change to be put in the cash register the next day, and removes the record of the day's credit card sales from the scanner. All the records are placed in an envelope that is sealed and sent to the company's accountant for verification and recording in the company records. On the way home, Hazel places the bank deposit in the night deposit box.

The company hires experienced cashiers who are bonded. Hazel spends the first half-day with new cashiers, showing them the procedures and overlooking their work.

REQUIRED

1. Give an example of how each of the following control activities is applied to internal control over sales and cash at East-West Sports Shop: (Do not address controls over inventory.)

   a. Authorization
   b. Recording transactions
   c. Documents and records
   d. Physical controls
   e. Periodic independent verification
   f. Separation of duties
   g. Sound personnel practices

2. **ACCOUNTING CONNECTION** ▶ Can the system as described protect against a cashier who accepts cash for a sale but does not ring up the sale and pockets the cash? If so, how does it prevent this action?

LO 3

Bank Reconciliation

GENERAL LEDGER

SPREADSHEET

✔ 1: Adjusted book balance,
May 31: $54,485.60

P4. The following information is available for Sedona, Inc., as of May 31, 2014:

a. Cash on the books as of May 31 amounted to $42,754.16. Cash on the bank statement for the same date was $52,351.46.
b. A deposit of $5,220.94, representing cash receipts of May 31, did not appear on the bank statement.
c. Outstanding checks totaled $3,936.80.
d. A check for $1,920.00 returned with the statement was recorded incorrectly in the check register as $1,380.00. The check was for a cash purchase of merchandise.
e. The bank service charge for May amounted to $25.
f. The bank collected $12,360.00 for Sedona, on a note. The face value of the note was $12,000.00.
g. An NSF check for $183.56 from a customer, Eva Mendez, was returned with the statement.
h. The bank mistakenly charged to the company account a check for $850.00 drawn by another company.
i. The bank reported that it had credited the account for $120.00 in interest on the average balance for May.

REQUIRED

1. Prepare a bank reconciliation for Sedona as of May 31, 2014.
2. Prepare the journal entries necessary to adjust the accounts.
3. What amount of cash should appear on Sedona's balance sheet as of May 31?
4. **ACCOUNTING CONNECTION** ▶ Why is a bank reconciliation considered an important control over cash?

LO 4

Imprest (Petty Cash) Transaction

SPREADSHEET

✔ 1: June 30 credit to Cash: $507.24

P5. A small company maintains a petty cash fund for minor expenditures. The following transactions occurred in June and July 2014:

a. The fund was established in the amount of $600.00 on June 1 from the proceeds of check no. 30.
b. On June 30, the petty cash fund had cash of $92.76 and the following receipts on hand: postage, $240.00; supplies, $149.64; delivery service, $74.40; and rubber stamp, $43.20. Check no. 1577 was drawn to replenish the fund.
c. On July 31, the petty cash fund had cash of $132.36 and the following receipts on hand: postage, $205.20; supplies, $197.04; and delivery service, $38.40. The petty

(Continued)

cash custodian could not account for the shortage. Check no. 1628 was written to replenish the fund.

REQUIRED

1. Prepare the journal entries necessary to record each of these transactions.
2. **ACCOUNTING CONNECTION** ▶ A charity reimburses volunteers for small out-of-pocket expenses such as parking and gasoline when the volunteers are carrying out the business of the charity. How might an imprest (petty cash) fund be helpful in controlling these expenditures?

ALTERNATE PROBLEMS

LO 1 **Internal Control Components**

P6. Faubert Company, a small electronics distributor, has experienced losses of inventory over the past year. Melissa Faubert, the owner, on the advice of her accountant, has adopted a set of internal controls in an effort to stop the losses. Faubert has taken the following steps:

1. She encourages employees to follow the rules.
2. She regularly considers ways in which inventory losses might occur.
3. She puts separation of duties in place.
4. She gathers appropriate information and communicates it to employees.
5. She sees that new and existing employees are well trained and instructed in their duties.
6. She makes sure inventories are physically protected with locked storage and electronic monitors.
7. She observes and reviews how procedures by those who report to her are carried out.
8. She had her accountant install a better accounting system over inventory.
9. She trains new employees in how to properly carry out control procedures.

REQUIRED

1. Show that Faubert's new system engages all the components of internal control by matching each of the steps with the internal control components that follow. (*Hint:* Some may have more than one answer.)
   a. Control environment   d. Control activities
   b. Risk assessment   e. Monitoring
   c. Information and communication
2. **BUSINESS APPLICATION** ▶ As the owner of a small company, why is it important that Melissa take an active part in the management of the internal control system?

LO 1, 2 **Control Activities**

P7. Midori Cabinet Company provides maintenance services to factories in and around Boca-Raton, Florida. The company, which buys a large amount of cleaning supplies, consistently has been over budget in its expenditures for these items. In the past, supplies were left out in the open in the warehouse to be taken each evening as needed by the onsite supervisors. A clerk in the accounting department periodically ordered additional supplies from a long-time supplier. No records were maintained other than to record purchases. Once a year, an inventory of supplies was made for the preparation of the financial statements.

To solve the budgetary problem, management decides to implement a new system for purchasing and controlling supplies. The following actions take place:

1. Management places a supplies clerk in charge of a secured storeroom for cleaning supplies.
2. Supervisors use a purchase requisition to request supplies for the jobs they oversee.
3. Each job receives a predetermined amount of supplies based on a study of each job's needs.

4. In the storeroom, the supplies clerk notes the levels of supplies and completes the purchase requisition when new supplies are needed.
5. The purchase requisition goes to the purchasing clerk, a new position. The purchasing clerk is solely responsible for authorizing purchases and preparing the purchase orders.
6. Supplier prices are monitored constantly by the purchasing clerk to ensure that the lowest price is obtained.
7. When supplies are received, the supplies clerk checks them in and prepares a receiving report. The supplies clerk sends the receiving report to accounting, where each payment to a supplier is documented by the purchase requisition, the purchase order, and the receiving report.
8. The accounting department also maintains a record of supplies inventory, supplies requisitioned by supervisors, and supplies received.
9. Once each month, the warehouse manager takes a physical inventory of cleaning supplies in the storeroom and compares it against the supplies inventory records that the accounting department maintains.

REQUIRED

1. Indicate which of the control activities that follow applies to each of the improvements in the internal control system. (*Hint:* More than one may apply.)
   a. Authorization
   b. Recording transactions
   c. Documents and records
   d. Physical controls
   e. Periodic independent verification
   f. Separation of duties
   g. Sound personnel practices
2. **ACCOUNTING CONNECTION** ▶ Explain why each new control activity (a through g) is an improvement over the activities of the old system.

LO **1, 2**   **Internal Control Activities**

P8. ACCOUNTING CONNECTION ▶ Fuentes is a retail store with several departments. Its internal control procedures for cash sales and purchases are as follows.

Cash sales. The sales clerk in each department rings up every cash sale on the department's cash register. The cash register produces a sales slip, which the clerk gives to the customer along with the merchandise. A continuous tape locked inside the cash register makes a carbon copy of the sales ticket. At the end of each day, the sales clerk presses a "total" key on the register, and it prints the total sales for the day on the continuous tape. The sales clerk then unlocks the tape, reads the total sales figure, and makes the entry in the accounting records for the day's cash sales. Next, she counts the cash in the drawer, places the $200 change fund back in the drawer, and gives the cash received to the cashier. Finally, she files the cash register tape and is ready for the next day's business.

Purchases. At the request of the various department heads, the purchasing agent orders all goods. When the goods arrive, the receiving clerk prepares a receiving report in triplicate. The receiving clerk keeps one copy; the other two copies go to the purchasing agent and the department head. Invoices are forwarded immediately to the accounting department to ensure payment before the discount period elapses. After payment, the invoice is forwarded to the purchasing agent for comparison with the purchase order and the receiving report and is then returned to the accounting office for filing.

REQUIRED

1. Identify the significant internal control weaknesses in each of the above situations.
2. In each case identified in requirement 1, recommend changes that would improve the system.

LO **3**

SPREADSHEET

✔ 1: Adjusted book balance,
April 30: $149,473.28

Bank Reconciliation

P9. The following information is available for Delta Company as of April 30, 2014:

a. Cash on the books as of April 30 amounted to $114,175.28. Cash on the bank statement for the same date was $141,717.08.

b. A deposit of $14,249.84, representing cash receipts of April 30, did not appear on the bank statement.

c. Outstanding checks totaled $7,293.64.

d. A check for $2,420.00 returned with the statement was recorded as $2,024.00. The check was for advertising.

e. The bank service charge for April amounted to $26.00.

f. The bank collected $36,400.00 for Delta Company on a note. The face value of the note was $36,000.00.

g. An NSF check for $1,140.00 from a customer, Hasan Ali, was returned with the statement.

h. The bank mistakenly deducted a check for $800.00 that was drawn by Alpha Corporation.

i. The bank reported a credit of $460.00 for interest on the average balance.

REQUIRED

1. Prepare a bank reconciliation for Delta as of April 30, 2014.
2. Prepare the necessary journal entries from the reconciliation.
3. State the amount of cash that should appear on Delta's balance sheet as of April 30.
4. **ACCOUNTING CONNECTION** ▶ Why is a bank reconciliation a necessary internal control?

LO **4**

✔ July 31 credit to Cash: $737.16

Imprest (Petty Cash) Fund Transactions

P10. On July 1, 2014, Acting Company established an imprest (petty cash) fund in the amount of $800.00 in cash from a check drawn for the purpose of establishing the fund. On July 31, the petty cash fund has cash of $62.84 and the following receipts on hand: for merchandise received, $408.60; freight-in, $131.48; laundry service, $168.00; and miscellaneous expense, $29.08. A check was drawn to replenish the fund.

On Aug. 31, the petty cash fund has cash of $110.00 and the following receipts on hand: merchandise, $393.68; freight-in, $152.60; laundry service, $168.00; and miscellaneous expense, $15.72. The petty cash custodian is not able to account for the excess cash in the fund. A check is drawn to replenish the fund.

REQUIRED

1. Prepare the journal entries necessary to record each of these transactions. The company uses the periodic inventory system.
2. **ACCOUNTING CONNECTION** ▶ What are two examples of why a local semiprofessional baseball team might have need for an imprest (petty cash) system?

CASES

LO **1, 2**

Conceptual Understanding: Control Systems

C1. In the spring of each year, Steinbrook College's theater department puts on a contemporary play. Before the performance, the theater manager instructs student volunteers in their duties as cashier, ticket taker, and usher.

The cashier, who is located in a box office at the entrance to the auditorium, receives cash from customers and enters the number of tickets and the amount paid into a computer, which prints out serially numbered tickets. The cashier puts the cash in a locked cash drawer and gives the tickets to the customer.

Customers give their tickets to the ticket taker. The ticket taker tears each ticket in half, gives one half to the customer, and puts the other half in a locked box.

When customers present their ticket stubs to an usher, the usher shows them to their seats.

1. Describe how each of the control activities discussed in this chapter (authorization, recording transactions, documents and records, physical controls, periodic independent verification, separation of duties, and sound personnel practices) apply to the to the control system that includes the cashier, ticket taker, and usher.
2. Could the cashier issue a ticket to a friend without taking in cash? Could the ticket taker allow friends to enter without a ticket? If so, how might they be caught?

LO 1, 2 **Interpreting Financial Reports: Internal Control Lapse**

C2. Starbucks Corporation accused an employee and her husband of embezzling $3.7 million by billing the company for services from a fictitious consulting firm. The couple created a phony company called RAD Services Inc. and charged Starbucks for work they never provided. The employee worked in Starbucks' Information Technology Department.[12] RAD Services charged Starbucks as much as $492,800 for consulting services in a single week. For such a fraud to have taken place, certain control activities were likely not implemented. Identify and describe these activities.

LO 1, 2 **Conceptual Understanding: Internal Controls**

C3. Go to a local retail business, such as a bookstore, clothing shop, gift shop, grocery store, hardware store, or car dealership. Ask to speak to someone who is knowledgeable about the store's methods of internal control. After you and other members of the class have completed this step individually, your instructor will divide the class into groups. Group members will compare their findings and develop answers to the questions that follow. A member of each group will then present the group's answers to the class.

1. How does the company protect itself against inventory theft and loss?
2. What control activities, including authorization, recording transactions, documents and records, physical controls, periodic independent verification, separation of duties, and sound personnel practices, does the company use?
3. Can you see these control procedures in use?

LO 1, 5 **Annual Report Case: Internal Control Responsibilities**

C4. BUSINESS APPLICATION ▶ To answer the questions that follow, refer to "Management's Report on Internal Control Over Financial Reporting" and the "Report of Independent Registered Public Accounting Firm" in **CVS**'s annual report in the Supplement to Chapter 16.

1. What is management's responsibility with regard to internal control over financial reporting?
2. What is management's conclusion regarding its assessment of internal control over financial reporting?
3. Does CVS's auditor agree with management's assessment?
4. What does the auditor say about the limitations or risks associated with internal control?

LO 1 **Comparison Analysis: Contrasting Internal Control Needs**

C5. BUSINESS APPLICATION ▶ In a typical **CVS** store, customers wheel carts down aisles to select items for purchase and take them to a checkout counter where they pay with cash or credit card. The company is concerned that customers might leave the store with merchandise that they have not paid for. Typically, customers of **Southwest Airlines** have already paid for their tickets when they arrive at the gate. The company is concerned that customers who do not have tickets might be allowed on the plane. (Southwest does not have assigned seating.) Compare the risks for each company in the situations just described and the internal control process.

LO **1, 2**   **Ethical Dilemma: Personal Responsibility for Mistakes**

C6. Suppose you have a part-time sales position over the winter break in a small clothing store that is part of a national chain. The store's one full-time employee, with whom you have become friendly, hired you. Explain what you would do in the situations described below, and identify two internal control problems that exist in each situation.

1. You arrive at the store at 6 p.m. to take over the evening shift from the full-time employee who hired you. You notice that this person takes a coat from a rack, puts it on, and leaves by the back door. You are not sure if the coat is one that was for sale or if it belonged to the employee.

2. You are the only person in the store on a busy evening. At closing time, you total the cash register and the receipts and discover that the cash register is $20 short of cash. You consider replacing the $20 out of your pocket because you think you may have made a mistake and are afraid you might lose your job if the company thinks you took the money.

Continuing Case: Annual Report Project

C7. Using the most recent annual report of the company you have chosen to study and that you have accessed online at the company's website, examine the balance sheet and accompanying notes of your company. Answer the following questions:

1. What percentage is cash to total current assets? Do you think this percentage represents the importance of cash to the company's operations?

2. Find the note about cash in the notes to the financial statements. What is included in cash?

3. Given the industry your company is in, what do you think are some of its most important internal control issues?

CHAPTER 9
Receivables

Smart Computer Company sells computer products for cash or on credit. The company's peak sales occur in August and September, when students are shopping for computers and computer-related supplies, and during the pre-holiday season in November and December. It is now January, and Jimmy Smart, the company's owner, has been reviewing the company's performance over the past two years. He has determined that in those years, approximately 1.5 percent of net sales have been uncollectible. He is concerned that, this year, the company may not have enough cash to cover operations before sales begin to increase again in late summer. In this chapter, we discuss concepts and techniques that would help Smart maintain its liquidity and manage its receivables.

1. CONCEPT ▶ *How do companies like Smart Computer apply accrual accounting to their receivables, and how do they properly disclose the value of their receivables?*

2. ACCOUNTING APPLICATION ▶ *How can Smart Computer estimate the value of its receivables?*

3. BUSINESS APPLICATION ▶ *How can the company evaluate the effectiveness of its credit policies and the level of its accounts receivable?*

LEARNING OBJECTIVES

LO 1 Define receivables, and explain the allowance method for valuation of receivables as an application of accrual accounting.

LO 2 Apply the allowance method of accounting for uncollectible accounts.

LO 3 Make common calculations for notes receivable.

LO 4 Show how to evaluate the level of receivables, and identify alternative means of financing receivables.

Aldo Murillo/iStockphoto.com

SECTION 1

CONCEPTS

LO 1 Concepts Underlying Notes and Accounts Receivable

The most common receivables are accounts receivable and notes receivable. The *allowance method* is used to apply *accrual accounting* to the *valuation* of accounts receivable. Proper *disclosure* in the financial statements and the notes to them is important for users of the statements to interpret them.

Accounts Receivable

Accounts receivable are short-term financial assets that arise from sales on credit and are often called **trade credit**. Terms of trade credit usually range from 5 to 60 days, depending on industry practice, and may allow customers to pay in installments. Credit sales or loans not made in the ordinary course of business, such as those made to employees, officers, or owners, should appear separately under asset titles like Receivables from Employees. Exhibit 1 shows the level of accounts receivable in selected industries.

Exhibit 1
Accounts Receivable as a Percentage of Total Assets for Selected Industries

Based on Bizmin Industry Financial Report, December 2011.

Companies that sell on credit do so to be competitive and to increase sales. In setting credit terms, a company must keep in mind the credit terms of its competitors and the needs of its customers. Obviously, any company that sells on credit wants customers who will pay their bills on time. To increase the likelihood of selling only to customers who will pay on time, most companies develop control procedures and maintain a credit department. The credit department's responsibilities include examining each person or company that applies for credit and approving or rejecting a credit sale to that customer. Typically, the credit department asks for information about the customer's financial resources and debts. It may also check personal references and credit bureaus for further information. Based on the information it has gathered, it decides whether to extend credit to the customer.

Companies that are too lenient in granting credit can run into difficulties when customers don't pay. For example, **Sprint**, one of the weaker companies in the competitive cell phone industry, targeted customers with poor credit histories. It attracted so many who failed to pay their bills that its stock dropped by 50 percent, to $2.50, because of the losses that resulted.[1]

You may already be familiar with promissory notes if you have taken out student loans or car loans. When you take out these loans, you sign a contract with a lender promising to repay the loan under certain terms.

STUDY NOTE: *Accounts receivable and accounts payable are distinguished from notes receivable and notes payable because the former were not created by a formal promissory note.*

Companies that extend credit to customers know that some of these customers cannot or will not pay. The accounts of such customers are called **uncollectible accounts** (or *bad debts*), and they are expenses of selling on credit. In accordance with *accrual accounting*, to match these expenses to the revenues they help generate, they should be recognized at the time credit sales are made.

Some companies recognize a loss when they determine that an account is uncollectible by reducing Accounts Receivable and increasing Uncollectible Accounts Expense. Federal regulations require companies to use this method—called the **direct charge-off method**—in computing taxable income. However, because a direct charge-off is usually recorded in a different period from the one in which the sale takes place, this method is not in accord with *accrual accounting*. Generally accepted accounting principles, therefore, require the use of the allowance method of accounting for uncollectible accounts.

Notes Receivable

Notes receivable are short-term financial assets supported by written agreements called promissory notes. A **promissory note** is an unconditional promise to pay a definite sum of money on demand or at a future date. The person or company that signs the note and, thereby, promises to pay is the *maker* of the note. The entity to whom payment is to be made is the *payee*. The promissory note shown in Exhibit 2 is an unconditional promise by the maker, Samuel Mason, to pay a definite sum—or principal ($1,000)—to the payee, Cook County Bank & Trust, on August 18, 2014. The note is dated May 20, 2014, and bears an interest rate of 8 percent. This interest accrues by a small amount each day the note is outstanding, increasing the payee's interest receivable and interest income.

Exhibit 2
A Promissory Note

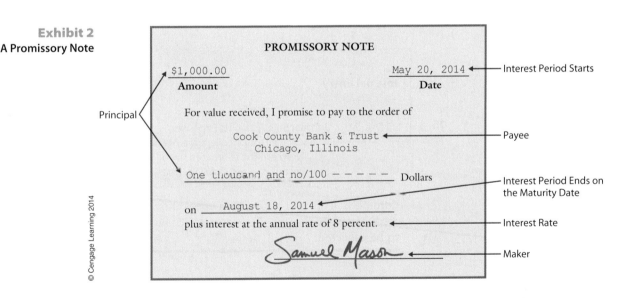

PROMISSORY NOTE

$1,000.00   May 20, 2014 — Interest Period Starts
Amount   **Date**

Principal

For value received, I promise to pay to the order of

Cook County Bank & Trust — Payee
Chicago, Illinois

One thousand and no/100 — — — — — Dollars — Interest Period Ends on the Maturity Date

on   August 18, 2014 — Interest Period Ends
plus interest at the annual rate of 8 percent. — Interest Rate

Samuel Mason — Maker

© Cengage Learning 2014

The nature of a company's business generally determines how frequently it receives promissory notes from customers. Firms that sell durable goods of high value, such as farm machinery and automobiles, often accept promissory notes. Among the advantages of these notes are that they produce interest income and represent a stronger legal claim against a debtor than accounts receivable do. In addition, selling—or discounting—promissory notes to banks is a common financing method. Almost all companies occasionally accept promissory notes, and many companies obtain them in settlement of past-due accounts receivable.

The Allowance Method: Using Accrual Accounting to Value Receivables

The **allowance method** is an application of *accrual accounting*, which requires estimated losses from bad debts to be matched with the revenues they help to produce. Further, they serve to *value* accounts receivable on the balance sheet. As mentioned earlier, when management extends credit to increase sales, it knows it will incur some losses from uncollectible accounts. Losses from credit sales should be recognized when the sales are made. Of course, at that time, management cannot identify which customers will not pay their debts, nor can it predict the exact amount of money the company will lose. Therefore, to follow accrual accounting (*the matching principle*), losses from uncollectible accounts must be estimated, and the estimate becomes an expense in the period in which the sales are made.

Uncollectible Accounts: The Allowance Method

Transaction Mandy Sales Company made most of its sales on credit during its first year of operation, 2014. At the end of the year, accounts receivable amounted to $200,000. On December 31, 2014, management reviewed the collectible status of the accounts receivable. Approximately $12,000 of the $200,000 of accounts receivable were estimated to be uncollectible.

Analysis The adjusting entry to record estimated uncollectible accounts

  ▲ *increases* the *Uncollectible Accounts Expense* account

  ▲ *increases* the *Allowance for Uncollectible Accounts* account

Application of Double Entry

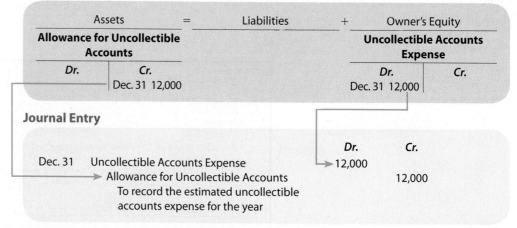

A = L + OE
−12,000   −12,000

Comment This transaction is an application of *accrual accounting* in that uncollectible accounts expense and is used to *value* accounts receivable at the amount that is expected to be collected.

International Perspective
(IFRS) Can Users Depend on the Allowance for Uncollectible Accounts?

Financial statements contain many estimates, one of which is the allowance for uncollectible accounts. In their effort to converge U.S. GAAP and IFRS, the FASB and the IASB have agreed that estimates must be a faithful representation of what they purport to represent and that they be verifiable. Under their agreement, faithful information is unbiased and contains no errors or omissions. Further, verifiability means that two independent experts could reach agreement as to the estimate.[2] In other words, users can be assured that net accounts receivable (accounts receivable less the allowance) represent the best estimate of the future cash receipts from the receivables.

Disclosure of Receivables

A payee includes all the promissory notes it holds that are due in less than one year as *notes receivable* in the current assets section of its balance sheet. Any interest accrued on these notes is also included in the current assets section—as **interest receivable**. Because notes are financial instruments, companies may voluntarily *disclose* their fair value. In most cases, fair value approximates the amount in the account records.

Uncollectible Accounts Expense appears on the income statement as an operating expense. **Allowance for Uncollectible Accounts** appears on the balance sheet as a contra account, deducted from accounts receivable in the current assets section. It reduces the accounts receivable to the amount expected to be collectible (net realizable value), as follows.

STUDY NOTE: *The allowance account often has other titles, such as* Allowance for Doubtful Accounts *and* Allowance for Bad Debts. Bad Debts Expense *is a title often used for* Uncollectible Accounts Expense.

Current assets:		
Cash		$ 20,000
Short-term investments		30,000
Notes receivable		15,000
Accounts receivable	$200,000	
Less allowance for uncollectible accounts	12,000	188,000
Interest receivable		1,000
Inventory		112,000
Total current assets		$366,000

A variation of the *disclosure* of accounts receivable on the balance sheet follows.

Accounts receivable (net of allowance for uncollectible accounts of $12,000) $188,000

Accounts receivable may also be shown at "net," with the amount of the allowance for uncollectible accounts identified in a note to the financial statements. For most companies, the "net" amount of accounts receivable approximates fair value. Fair value disclosures are not required for accounts receivable, but 59 percent of large companies made this disclosure voluntarily. Of those, 85 percent indicated that the net accounts receivable approximated fair value.[3]

APPLY IT! ▶

Match the concepts that follow to the related statements.

1. Preparing an adjusting entry to record the estimated uncollectible accounts expense.
2. Subtracting the allowance for uncollectible accounts from accounts receivable.
3. Preparing an adjusting entry to record interest earned on notes receivable.
4. Reporting the net realizable value of receivables on the balance sheet.
5. Separating accounts receivable from receivables from employees.

a. valuation
b. accrual accounting
c. periodicity
d. disclosure

SOLUTION

1. b; 2. a; 3. b; 4. d; 5. d

ACCOUNTING APPLICATIONS

LO 2 Uncollectible Accounts

The allowance account is necessary because the specific uncollectible accounts will not be identified until later. It is not like another contra account, Accumulated Depreciation, whose purpose is to show how much of the plant and equipment cost has been allocated as an expense to previous periods.

If management takes an optimistic view and projects a small loss from uncollectible accounts, the resulting net accounts receivable will be larger than if management takes a pessimistic view. The net income will also be larger under the optimistic view because the estimated expense will be smaller. The company's accountant makes an estimate based on past experience and current economic conditions. For example, losses from uncollectible accounts are normally expected to be greater in a recession than during a period of economic growth. The final decision on the amount of the expense will depend on objective information, such as the accountant's analyses, and on certain qualitative factors, such as how investors, bankers, creditors, and others view the performance of the debtor company. Regardless of the qualitative considerations, the estimated losses from uncollectible accounts should be realistic.

Two common methods of estimating uncollectible accounts expense are the percentage of net sales method and the accounts receivable aging method.

Percentage of Net Sales Method

The basis for the **percentage of net sales method** is the amount of this year's *net sales* that will not be collected. The answer determines the amount of uncollectible accounts expense for the year.

Uncollectible Accounts: The Percentage of Net Sales Method

Transaction The following balances represent Varta Company's ending figures for 2014:

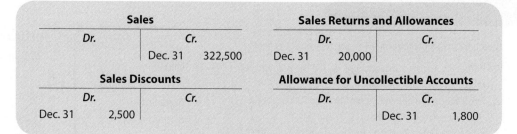

Sales				Sales Returns and Allowances		
Dr.		Cr.		Dr.		Cr.
		Dec. 31	322,500	Dec. 31	20,000	

Sales Discounts				Allowance for Uncollectible Accounts		
Dr.		Cr.		Dr.		Cr.
Dec. 31	2,500				Dec. 31	1,800

Business Perspective
Cash Collections Can Be Hard to Estimate

Companies must not only sell goods and services but also must generate cash flows by collecting on those sales. When there are changes in the economy, some companies make big mistakes in estimating the amount of accounts they will collect. For example, when the dot-com bubble burst in the early 2000s, companies like **Nortel Networks**, **Cisco Systems**, and **Lucent Technologies** increased their estimates of allowances for uncollectible accounts—actions that eliminated previously reported earnings and caused the companies' stock prices to fall.[4] However, it turned out that these companies had overestimated how bad the losses would be. In later years, they reduced their allowances for credit losses, thereby increasing their reported earnings.[5]

The following are Varta's actual losses from uncollectible accounts for the past three years:

Year	Net Sales	Losses from Uncollectible Accounts	Percentage
2011	$260,000	$ 5,100	1.96
2012	297,500	6,950	2.34
2013	292,500	4,950	1.69
Total	$850,000	$17,000	2.00

Varta's management believes that its uncollectible accounts will continue to average about 2 percent of net sales. The uncollectible accounts expense for the year 2014 is therefore estimated as follows.

$$0.02 \times (\$322,500 - \$20,000 - \$2,500) = 0.02 \times \$300,000 = \$6,000$$

Analysis The journal entry to record the estimated uncollectible accounts

▲ *increases* the *Uncollectible Accounts Expense* account

▲ *increases* the *Allowance for Uncollectible Accounts* account

Application of Double Entry

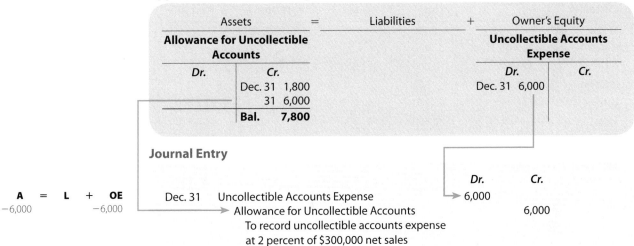

Comment This application of *accrual accounting* leaves the Allowance for Uncollectible Accounts with a balance of $7,800. The balance consists of the $6,000 estimated uncollectible accounts receivable from 2014 sales and the $1,800 estimated uncollectible accounts receivable from previous years.

Accounts Receivable Aging Method

The basis for the **accounts receivable aging method** is the amount of the *ending balance of accounts receivable* that will not be collected. With this method, the ending balance of Allowance for Uncollectible Accounts is determined directly through an analysis of accounts receivable. The difference between the amount determined to be uncollectible and the actual balance of Allowance for Uncollectible Accounts is the expense for the period. In theory, this method should produce the same result as the percentage of net sales method, but in practice it rarely does.

The **aging of accounts receivable** is the process of listing each customer's receivable account according to the due date of the account. If the customer's account is

STUDY NOTE: An aging of accounts receivable is an important tool in cash management because it helps to determine what amounts are likely to be collected in the months ahead.

past due, there is a possibility that the account will not be paid. And that possibility increases as the account extends further beyond the due date. The aging of accounts receivable helps management evaluate its credit and collection policies and alerts it to possible problems.

To illustrate the accounts receivable aging method, we will use Radko Company. Exhibit 3 illustrates the aging of accounts receivable for Radko. Each account receivable is classified as being not yet due or as being 1–30 days, 31–60 days, 61–90 days, or over 90 days past due. Based on past experience, the estimated percentage for each category is determined and multiplied by the amount in each category to determine the estimated, or target, balance of Allowance for Uncollectible Accounts. In total, it is estimated that $4,918 of the $88,800 in accounts receivable will not be collected.

Exhibit 3
Analysis of Accounts Receivable by Age

Radko Company
Analysis of Accounts Receivable by Age
December 31, 2014

Customer	Total	Not Yet Due	1–30 Days Past Due	31–60 Days Past Due	61–90 Days Past Due	Over 90 Days Past Due
K. Lee	$ 300		$ 300			
F. Moll	800			$ 800		
T. Orr	2,000	$ 1,800	200			
P. Govin	500				$ 500	
Others	85,200	42,000	28,000	7,600	4,400	$3,200
Totals	$88,800	$43,800	$28,500	$8,400	$4,900	$3,200
Estimated percentage uncollectible		1.0	2.0	10.0	30.0	50.0
Allowance for Uncollectible Accounts	$ 4,918	$ 438	$ 570	$ 840	$1,470	$1,600

Once the target balance for Allowance for Uncollectible Accounts has been determined, the amount of the adjustment depends on the current balance of the allowance account. We will assume two cases for the balance of Radko's Allowance for Uncollectible Accounts on December 31: (1) a credit balance of $1,600 and (2) a debit balance of $1,600.

Adjusting the Allowance Account: Credit Balance

Transaction In the first case, an adjustment of $3,318 is needed to bring the balance of the allowance account to a $4,918 credit balance.

Targeted balance for allowance for uncollectible accounts	$4,918
Less current credit balance of allowance for uncollectible accounts	1,600
Uncollectible accounts expense	$3,318

Analysis The journal entry to record the estimated uncollectible accounts

▲ *increases* the *Uncollectible Accounts Expense* account

▲ *increases* the *Allowance for Uncollectible Accounts* account

Application of Double Entry

Journal Entry

A = L + OE
−3,318   3,318

		Dr.	Cr.
Dec. 31	Uncollectible Accounts Expense	3,318	
	Allowance for Uncollectible Accounts		3,318
	To bring the allowance for uncollectible accounts to the level of estimated losses		

Comment This application of *accrual accounting* results in a balance of Allowance for Uncollectible Accounts of $4,918.

Adjusting the Allowance Account: Debit Balance

Transaction In the second case, because Allowance for Uncollectible Accounts has a debit balance of $1,600, the estimated uncollectible accounts expense for the year will have to be $6,518 to reach the targeted balance of $4,918, calculated as follows.

Targeted balance for allowance for uncollectible accounts	$4,918
Plus current debit balance of allowance for uncollectible accounts	1,600
Uncollectible accounts expense	$6,518

Analysis The journal entry to record the estimated uncollectible accounts

▲ *increases* the *Uncollectible Accounts Expense* account

▲ *increases* the *Allowance for Uncollectible Accounts* account

Application of Double Entry

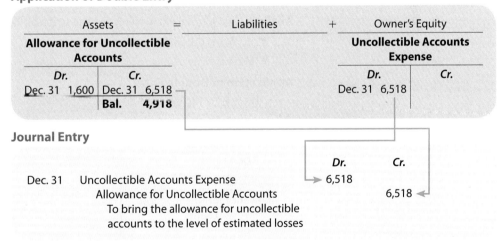

Journal Entry

A = L + OE
−6,518   −6,518

		Dr.	Cr.
Dec. 31	Uncollectible Accounts Expense	6,518	
	Allowance for Uncollectible Accounts		6,518
	To bring the allowance for uncollectible accounts to the level of estimated losses		

Comment After this entry applying *accrual accounting*, Allowance for Uncollectible Accounts has a credit balance *valuation* of $4,918, which represents the amount of losses expected in the future.

Comparison of the Two Methods

Both the percentage of net sales method and the accounts receivable aging method estimate the uncollectible accounts expense in accordance with *accrual accounting*, but as shown in

Exhibit 4, they do so in different ways. The percentage of net sales method is an income statement approach. It assumes that a certain proportion of sales will not be collected, and this proportion is the *amount of Uncollectible Accounts Expense* for the period. The accounts receivable aging method is a balance sheet approach. It assumes that a certain proportion of accounts receivable outstanding will not be collected. This amount is the *targeted balance of the Allowance for Uncollectible Accounts account.* The expense for the period is the difference between the targeted balance and the current balance of the allowance account.

Exhibit 4
Two Methods of Estimating Uncollectible Accounts

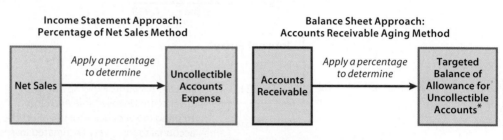

*Add current debit balance or subtract current credit balance to determine uncollectible accounts expense.

© Cengage Learning 2014

Writing Off Uncollectible Accounts

Regardless of the method used to estimate uncollectible accounts, the total of accounts receivable written off in a period will rarely equal the estimated uncollectible amount. The allowance account will show a credit balance when the total written off is less than the estimated uncollectible amount. It will show a debit balance when the total written off is greater than the estimated uncollectible amount.

When it becomes clear that a specific account receivable will not be collected, the amount should be written off to Allowance for Uncollectible Accounts. Remember that the uncollectible amount was already accounted for as an expense when the allowance was established.

Writing Off Uncollectible Accounts

Transaction On January 15, 2015, P. Govin, who owes Radko Company $500, is declared bankrupt by a federal court.

Analysis The journal entry to record the write-off of an account receivable as uncollectible

▼ *decreases* the *Accounts Receivable* account

▼ *decreases* the *Allowance for Uncollectible Accounts* account

Application of Double Entry

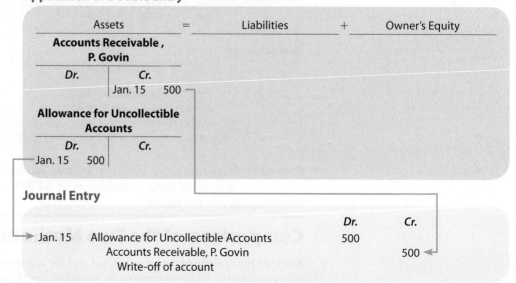

$$A = L + OE$$
$$+500$$
$$-500$$

Comment The application of *accrual accounting* recognized the failure to collect this account through the estimate of uncollectible accounts occurred in a prior period. In the earlier period, it was not possible to identify which accounts would not be received.

Although the write-off removes the uncollectible amount from Accounts Receivable, it does not affect the estimated net realizable value of accounts receivable. It simply reduces P. Govin's account to zero and reduces Allowance for Uncollectible Accounts by $500, as shown below.

	Balances Before Write-Off	Balances After Write-Off
Accounts receivable	$88,800	$88,300
Less allowance for uncollectible accounts	4,918	4,418
Estimated net realizable value of accounts receivable	$83,882	$83,882

Occasionally, a customer whose account has been written off as uncollectible will later be able to pay some or all of the amount owed. When that happens, two entries must be made: one to reverse the earlier write-off (which is now incorrect) and another to show the collection of the account.

APPLY IT!

Drums Instruments Co. sells its merchandise on credit. In the company's last fiscal year, which ended July 31, it had net sales of $7,000,000. At the end of the fiscal year, it had Accounts Receivable of $1,800,000 and a credit balance of $11,200 in Allowance for Uncollectible Accounts. In the past, the company has been unable to collect on approximately 1 percent of its net sales. An aging analysis of accounts receivable has indicated that $80,000 of current receivables are estimated to be uncollectible.

1. Calculate the amount of uncollectible accounts expense, and use T accounts to determine the resulting balance of Allowance for Uncollectible Accounts under the percentage of net sales method and the accounts receivable aging method.

2. How would your answers change if Allowance for Uncollectible Accounts had a debit balance of $11,200 instead of a credit balance?

SOLUTION

1. Percentage of net sales method:

Allowance for Uncollectible Accounts

Dr.		Cr.	
	July 31		11,200
	31 UA Exp.		70,000*
	July 31 Bal.		**81,200**

*Uncollectible Accounts Expense = $7,000,000 × 0.01

Aging Method:

Allowance for Uncollectible Accounts

Dr.		Cr.	
	July 31		11,200
	31 UA Exp.		68,800*
	July 31 Bal.		**80,000**

*Uncollectible Accounts Expense = $80,000 − $11,200

2. Under the percentage of net sales method, the amount of the expense is the same. However, if the allowance account (before adjustment) has a debit balance, its ending balance will be $58,800 ($70,000 − $11,200). Under the accounts receivable aging method, the ending balance in the allowance account is the same. However, if the allowance account (before adjustment) has a debit balance, the amount of the expense will be $91,200 ($80,000 + $11,200).

TRY IT! SE3, SE4, SE5, E2A, E3A, E4A, E5A, E6A, E7A, E2B, E3B, E4B, E5B, E6B, E7B

LO3 Common Calculations for Notes Receivable

As defined previously, notes are promises to pay a definite amount at a definite future date. Such notes typically state a rate of interest that must also be paid at that future date. These features are the basis for several calculations that are common to promissory notes:

- Maturity date
- Duration of a note
- Interest
- Maturity value
- Accrued interest

Maturity Date

The **maturity date** is the date on which a promissory note must be paid. This date must be stated on the note or be determinable from the facts stated on the note. The following are among the most common statements of maturity date:

- A specific date, such as "November 14, 2014"
- A specific number of months after the date of the note, such as "three months after November 14, 2014"
- A specific number of days after the date of the note, such as "60 days after November 14, 2014"

The maturity date is obvious when a specific date is stated. When the maturity date is a number of months from the date of the note, one simply uses the same day in the appropriate future month. For example, a note dated January 20 that is due in two months would be due on March 20.

When the maturity date is a specific number of days from the date of the note, however, the exact maturity date must be determined. In computing this date, it is important to exclude the date of the note. For example, a note dated May 20 and due in 90 days would be due on August 18, determined as follows.

Days remaining in May (31 − 20)	11
Days in June	30
Days in July	31
Days in August	18
Total days	90

Duration of a Note

The **duration of a note** is the time between a promissory note's issue date and its maturity date. Interest is calculated on the basis of the duration of a note. Identifying the duration is easy when the maturity date is a specific number of days from the date of the note. However, when the maturity date is stated as a specific date, the exact number of days must be determined. Assume that a note issued on May 10 matures on August 10. The duration of the note is 92 days.

Days remaining in May (31 − 10)	21
Days in June	30
Days in July	31
Days in August	10
Total days	92

Interest

Interest is the cost of borrowing money or the return on lending money, depending on whether one is the borrower or the lender. The amount of interest is based on three factors:

- Principal (the amount of money borrowed or lent)
- Rate of interest
- Length of the loan

The formula used in computing interest follows.

$$\text{Principal} \times \text{Rate of Interest} \times \text{Time} = \text{Interest}$$

Interest rates are usually stated on an annual basis. For example, the interest on a one-year, 8 percent, $1,000 note would be:

$$\text{Principal} \times \text{Rate of Interest} \times \text{Time} = \text{Interest}$$
$$\$1,000 \times 8/100 \times 1 = \$80$$

If the term of the note is three months instead of a year, the interest charge would be calculated as follows.

$$\$1,000 \times 8/100 \times 3/12 = \$20$$

When the term of a note is expressed in days, the exact number of days must be used in computing the interest. Thus, if the term of the note described was 45 days, the interest would be $9.86, computed as follows.

$$\$1,000 \times 8/100 \times 45/365 = \$9.86^*$$

*Rounded

Maturity Value

The **maturity value** is the total proceeds of a promissory note—face value plus interest—at the maturity date. The maturity value of a 90-day, 8 percent, $1,000 note is computed as follows.

$$\text{Maturity Value} = \text{Principal} + \text{Interest}$$
$$= \$1,000 + (\$1,000 \times 8/100 \times 90/365)$$
$$= \$1,000 + \$19.73^*$$
$$= \$1,019.73$$

*Rounded

Some notes, called *non-interest-bearing notes*, do not specify an interest rate. The maturity value of these notes is the face value, or principal amount. The principal includes an implied interest cost.

Accrued Interest

Accrued interest must be apportioned to the periods in which it belongs. For example, assume that the $1,000, 90-day, 8 percent note discussed previously was received on August 31 and that the fiscal year ended on September 30. In this case, interest for 30 days, or $6.58, is calculated as follows.

$$\text{Principal} \times \text{Rate of Interest} \times \text{Time} = \text{Interest}$$
$$\$1,000 \times 8/100 \times 30/365 = \$6.58^*$$

*Rounded

The $6.58 of interest would be earned in the fiscal year that ends on September 30. The remainder of the interest income, $13.15, would be calculated as follows.

$$\$1,000 \times 8/100 \times 60/365 = \$13.15^*$$

*Rounded

This amount would be recorded as income, and the interest receivable ($6.58) would be shown as received when the note is paid. Note that all the cash for the interest is received when the note is paid, but the interest income is apportioned to two fiscal years.

Dishonored Note

A note not paid at maturity is called a **dishonored note**. The holder, or payee, of a dishonored note should transfer the total amount due (including interest income) from Notes Receivable to an individual account receivable for the debtor. This transfer accomplishes two things:

- It leaves only notes that are presumably collectible in the Notes Receivable account.
- It establishes a record showing that the customer has dishonored a note receivable, which may be helpful in deciding whether to extend credit to that customer in the future.

Receivables and the Financial Statements

Exhibit 5 shows that accounts receivable on the balance sheet is closely related to sales on the income statement. The estimation of uncollectible credit sales affects the amount of net accounts receivable and operating expenses. Interest income on notes receivable affects the amount of assets and revenues.

Exhibit 5
Valuation of Accounts Receivable on the Balance
Sheet Impacts Net Sales on the Income Statement

© Cengage Learning 2014

APPLY IT!

Assume that on December 1, 2014, a company receives a 90-day, 8 percent, $5,000 note and that the company prepares financial statements monthly.

1. What is the maturity date of the note?

2. How much interest will be earned on the note if it is paid when due?

3. What is the maturity value of the note?

4. If the company's fiscal year ends on December 31, describe the adjusting entry that would be made, including the amount.

5. How much interest will be earned on this note in 2015?

SOLUTION

1. Maturity date is March 1, 2015, determined as follows.

Days remaining in December (31 – 1)	30
Days in January	31
Days in February	28
Days in March	1
Total days	90

2. Interest: $5,000 \times 8/100 \times 90/365 = \$98.63*$

3. Maturity value: $5,000 + \$98.63 = \$5,098.63$

4. An adjusting entry to accrue 30 days of interest income in the amount of $32.88* ($5,000 \times 8/100 \times 30/365$) would be needed.

5. Interest earned in 2015: $65.75 ($98.63 − $32.88)

    * Rounded

TRY IT! SE6, SE7, SE8, E8A, E9A, E10A, E11A, E8B, E9B, E10B, E11B

BUSINESS APPLICATIONS

RELEVANT LEARNING OBJECTIVE

LO 4 Show how to evaluate the level of receivables, and identify alternative means of financing receivables.

LO 4 Evaluating the Level of Accounts Receivable and Ethical Ramifications

Receivables are an important asset for any company that sells on credit. For them, it is critical to manage the level of receivables. Two common measures of the effect of a company's credit policies are *receivables turnover* and *days' sales uncollected*. Further, many companies manage their receivables by using various means to finance them. Finally, the judgments in estimating uncollectible accounts are a temptation for unethical behavior.

Receivables Turnover

The **receivables turnover** shows how many times, on average, a company turned its receivables into cash during a period. It reflects the relative size of a company's accounts receivable and the success of its credit and collection policies. It may also be affected by external factors, such as seasonal conditions and interest rates.

The receivables turnover is computed by dividing net sales by the average accounts receivable (net of allowances). Theoretically, the numerator should be net credit sales; but since the amount of net credit sales is rarely available in public reports, investors use total net sales. Using data from **Nike**'s annual report, we can compute the company's receivables turnover in 2011 as follows (dollar amounts are in millions).

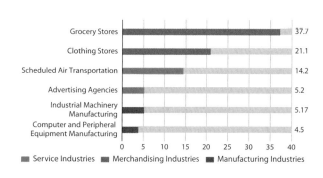

RATIO

Receivables Turnover: How Many Times Did the Company Collect Its Accounts Receivable During an Accounting Period?

$$\text{Receivables Turnover} = \frac{\text{Net Sales}}{\text{Average Accounts Receivable}}$$

$$\frac{\$20,962}{(\$3,138 + \$2,650)/2} = \frac{\$20,962}{\$2,894} = 7.2 \text{ times*}$$

* Rounded

Grocery Stores	37.7
Clothing Stores	21.1
Scheduled Air Transportation	14.2
Advertising Agencies	5.2
Industrial Machinery Manufacturing	5.17
Computer and Peripheral Equipment Manufacturing	4.5

0 5 10 15 20 25 30 35 40

■ Service Industries ■ Merchandising Industries ■ Manufacturing Industries

Based on Bizmin Industry Financial Report, December 2011.

To interpret a company's ratios, you must take into consideration the norms of the industry in which it operates. As shown, the receivables turnover ratio varies substantially from industry to industry. Because grocery stores have few receivables, they have a very high turnover (37.7). The turnover in the industrial machinery manufacturing industry is much lower (5.2) because that industry tends to have longer credit terms.

Days' Sales Uncollected

Days' sales uncollected shows, on average, how long it takes to collect accounts receivable. To determine the days' sales uncollected, the number of days in a year is divided by the receivables turnover. For **Nike**, it is computed as follows.

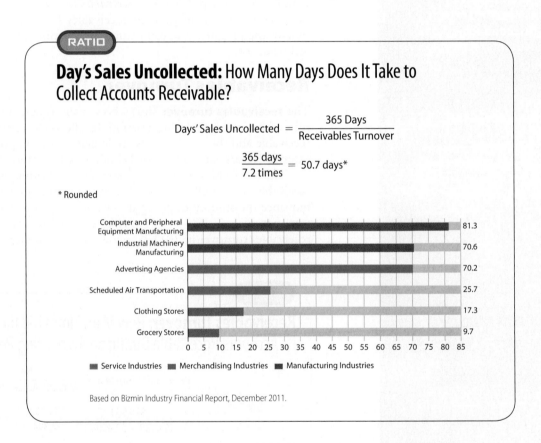

RATIO

Day's Sales Uncollected: How Many Days Does It Take to Collect Accounts Receivable?

$$\text{Days' Sales Uncollected} = \frac{365 \text{ Days}}{\text{Receivables Turnover}}$$

$$\frac{365 \text{ days}}{7.2 \text{ times}} = 50.7 \text{ days*}$$

* Rounded

Industry	Days
Computer and Peripheral Equipment Manufacturing	81.3
Industrial Machinery Manufacturing	70.6
Advertising Agencies	70.2
Scheduled Air Transportation	25.7
Clothing Stores	17.3
Grocery Stores	9.7

■ Service Industries ■ Merchandising Industries ■ Manufacturing Industries

Based on Bizmin Industry Financial Report, December 2011.

*STUDY NOTE: For many businesses with seasonal sales activity, such as **Nordstrom**, **Dillard's**, and **Macy's**, receivables are highest at the balance sheet date, resulting in an artificially low receivables turnover and a high days' sales uncollected.*

As you can see, grocery stores have the lowest days' sales uncollected (9.7 days), and they therefore require the least amount of receivables financing. The industrial machinery manufacturing industry, on the other hand, has more days' sales uncollected (70.6).

Financing Receivables

Companies that have significant amounts of assets tied up in accounts receivable may be unwilling or unable to wait until they collect cash from their receivables. Many corporations have set up finance companies to help their customers pay for the purchase of their products. For example, **Ford** has set up Ford Motor Credit Company (FMCC) and **Sears** has set up Sears Roebuck Acceptance Corporation (SRAC). Other companies borrow funds by pledging their accounts receivable as collateral. If a company does not pay back its loan, the creditor can take the collateral (in this case, the accounts receivable) and convert it to cash to satisfy the loan.

Companies can also finance their receivables by selling or transferring accounts receivable to another entity. Three methods of financing receivables in this way are factoring, securitization, and discounting.

Factoring As illustrated in Exhibit 6, **factoring** is the sale or transfer of accounts receivable to an entity, called a **factor**. Factoring can be done with or without recourse. *With recourse* means that the seller of the receivables is liable to the factor (i.e., the purchaser) if a receivable cannot be collected. *Without recourse* means that the factor bears any losses from unpaid accounts. A company's acceptance of credit cards like **Visa**, **MasterCard**, or **American Express** is an example of factoring without recourse because the issuers of the cards accept the risk of nonpayment.

Exhibit 6
How Factoring Works

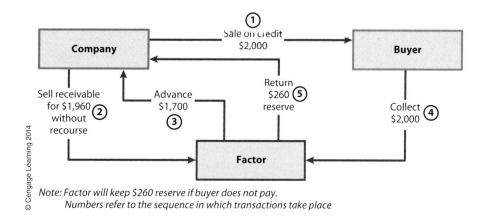

Note: Factor will keep $260 reserve if buyer does not pay.
Numbers refer to the sequence in which transactions take place

The factor's fee for sales with recourse is usually about 2 percent of the accounts receivable. The fee is higher for sales without recourse because the factor's risk is greater. In accounting terminology, a seller of receivables with recourse is said to be contingently liable. A **contingent liability** is a potential liability that can develop into a real liability if a particular event occurs. In this case, the event would be a customer's nonpayment of a receivable. A contingent liability generally requires *disclosure* in the notes to the financial statements.

Securitization **Securitization** is a process in which a company groups its receivables in batches and sells them at a discount to other companies or investors. When the receivables are paid, the buyers get the full amount. Their profit depends on the amount of the discount. **Circuit City** tried to avoid bankruptcy by selling all its receivables without recourse and, therefore, have no further liability. If Circuit City had sold its receivables with recourse and a customer did not pay, it would have had to make good on the debt.[6] However, by selling without recourse, it had to accept a lower price for its receivables, and it still went bankrupt.

Business Perspective
Why Are Subprime Loans Bad?

Although subprime loans (home loans to individuals with poor credit ratings and low incomes) represent only a small portion of the mortgage loan market, they have caused huge problems in the real estate market. These loans are a form of securitization in that they are batched together and sold in units as safe investments, when in fact they are quite risky. When people were unable to keep up with their mortgage payments, the investments were marked down to their fair value. This loss of value led to the demise of such venerable firms as **Lehman Brothers**, the sale of **Merrill Lynch**, and ultimately a massive government bailout of several well-known financial institutions.[7]

Discounting **Discounting** is a method of financing receivables by selling promissory notes held as notes receivable to a financial lender, usually a bank. The bank derives its profit by deducting the interest from the maturity value of the note. The holder of the note (usually the payee) endorses the note and turns it over to the bank. The bank expects to collect the maturity value of the note (principal plus interest) on the maturity date, but it also has recourse against the note's endorser.

For example, if Company X holds a $20,000 note from Company Z and the note will pay $1,200 in interest, a bank may be willing to buy the note for $19,200. If Company Z pays, the bank will receive $21,200 at maturity and realize a $2,000 profit. If it fails to pay, Company X is liable to the bank for payment. In the meantime, Company X has a contingent liability in the amount of the discounted note plus interest that it must *disclose* in the notes to its financial statements.

Ethics and Estimates in Accounting for Receivables

As noted, companies extend credit to customers because they want to increase their sales and earnings. However, they know they will always have some credit customers who cannot or will not pay. Of course, at the time a company makes credit sales, it cannot identify which customers will not pay their bills, nor can it predict the exact amount of money it will lose. Therefore, to adhere to *accrual accounting*, it must estimate losses from uncollectible accounts. As shown earlier in the chapter, the estimate becomes an expense in the fiscal year in which the sales are made.

Because the amount of uncollectible accounts can only be estimated and the exact amount will not be known until later, a company's earnings can be easily manipulated. Earnings can be overstated by underestimating the amount of losses from uncollectible accounts and understated by overestimating the amount of the losses. Misstatements of earnings can occur simply because of a bad estimate. But, as we have noted elsewhere, they can be deliberately made to meet analysts' estimates of earnings, reduce income taxes, or meet benchmarks for bonuses.

Examples of unethical or questionable practices in dealing with uncollectible accounts include the following cases investigated by the SEC:

- The policy of **Household International**, a large personal finance company, seems to be flexible about when to declare loans delinquent. As a result, the company can vary its estimates of uncollectible accounts from year to year.[8]
- By making large allowances for estimated uncollectible accounts and then gradually reducing them, **Bank One** improved its earnings over several years.[9]
- **HealthSouth** manipulated its income by varying its estimates of the difference between what it charged patients and what it could collect from insurance companies.[10]

Companies with high ethical standards try to be accurate in their estimates of uncollectible accounts, and they *disclose* the basis of their estimates. For example, **Nike**'s management describes, in the statement that follows, the basis for its estimates of uncollectible accounts.

> *We make ongoing estimates relating to the ability to collect our accounts receivable and maintain an allowance for estimated losses resulting from the inability of our customers to make required payments. In determining the amount of the allowance, we consider our historical level of credit losses and make judgments about the creditworthiness of significant customers based on ongoing credit evaluations. Since we cannot predict future changes in the financial stability of our customers, actual future losses from uncollectible accounts may differ from our estimates.*[11]

APPLY IT!

Toni Company has net accounts receivable of $60,000 and net sales of $500,000. Last year's net accounts receivable were $40,000. Compute Toni's receivables turnover and days' sales uncollected.

SOLUTION

$$\text{Receivables Turnover} = \frac{\text{Net Sales}}{\text{Average Accounts Receivable}}$$

$$= \frac{\$500,000}{(\$60,000 + \$40,000) \div 2}$$

$$= \frac{\$500,000}{\$50,000} = 10.0 \text{ times}$$

$$\text{Days' Sales Uncollected} = \frac{365 \text{ days}}{\text{Receivables Turnover}} = \frac{365 \text{ days}}{10.0 \text{ times}} = 36.5 \text{ days}$$

TRY IT! SE9, SE10, E12A, E13A, E12B, E13B

TriLevel Problem

Smart Computer Company

The beginning of this chapter focused on Smart Computer Company. The following data (in thousands) are from the company's records for year end of 2014, before adjustments:

	2014
Cash	$ 100
Accounts receivable	800
Allowance for doubtful accounts	(42)
Net sales	2,400

Complete the following requirements in order to answer the questions posed at the beginning of the chapter.

Section 1: Concepts
How do companies like Smart Computer Company apply accrual accounting to their receivables, and how do they properly disclose the value of their receivables?

Section 2: Accounting Applications
How can Smart Computer Company estimate the value of its receivables?

In order to estimate the value of Smart's receivables, compute Uncollectible Accounts Expense for 2014, and determine the ending balance of Allowance for Uncollectible Accounts and Accounts Receivable, Net, under (a) the percentage of net sales method assuming 1.5 percent of net sales to be uncollectible and (b) the accounts receivable aging method, assuming year-end uncollectible accounts to be $76,000.

Section 3: Business Applications
How can the company evaluate the effectiveness of its credit policies and the level of its accounts receivable?

To answer this question, management can compare the current year's receivables turnover and days' sales uncollected with those ratios in previous years.

1. Compute the receivables turnover and days' sales uncollected for 2014, using the data from the accounts receivable aging method calculated in the Accounting Applications above and assuming that the prior year's net accounts receivable were $620,000.
2. Why do the two methods of calculating Uncollectible Accounts Expense produce different results?
3. What are the implications of the receivables turnover and days' sales uncollected results for Smart?

SOLUTION

Section 1: Concepts

Companies make credit sales now but collect money on those sales in the future. Some of the customers who purchased a product or service on credit will not pay their bills. Due to the uncertainty in regards to the *value* of receivables, companies need to estimate how much of their receivables will not be collected. U.S. GAAP requires companies to use the allowance method to estimate the level of uncollectible accounts. The allowance method follows *accrual accounting* and results in the proper *valuation* of accounts receivable because it deducts the amount of estimated uncollectible accounts from accounts receivable on the balance sheet. It also *matches* the expense of uncollectible accounts with the revenues generated by the receivables. Accounts receivable are *disclosed* on the balance sheet at their net of allowance amount and notes to the financial statements disclose pertinent information about accounts receivable and notes receivable.

Section 2: Accounting Applications

a. Percentage of net sales method:

Uncollectible Accounts Expense = 1.5 percent × $2,400,000 = $36,000

Allowance for Uncollectible Accounts = $36,000 + $42,000 = $78,000

Accounts Receivable, Net = $800,000 − $78,000 = $722,000

b. Accounts receivable aging method:

Uncollectible Accounts Expense = $76,000 − $42,000 = $34,000

Allowance for Uncollectible Accounts = $76,000

Accounts Receivable, Net = $800,000 − $76,000 = $724,000

Section 3: Business Applications

1. $$\text{Receivables Turnover} = \frac{\text{Net Sales}}{\text{Average Accounts Receivable}} = \frac{\$2,400,000}{(\$724,000 + \$620,000) \div 2}$$

$$= \frac{\$2,400,000}{\$672,000}$$

$$= \underline{\underline{3.6 \text{ times*}}}$$

$$\text{Day's Sales Uncollected} = \frac{365 \text{ days}}{\text{Receivables Turnover}} = \frac{365 \text{ days}}{3.6 \text{ times}} = \underline{\underline{101.4 \text{ days*}}}$$

   * Rounded

2. Both methods of computing Uncollectible Accounts Expense are estimates and thus are likely to give different results. Ideally, the results are similar.

3. It takes Smart 101.4 days on average to collect its sales. This is almost four months, which means the company must manage its cash and borrowings carefully or revise its credit terms.

Chapter Review

Define receivables, and explain the allowance method for valuation of receivables as an application of accrual accounting. **LO 1**

Accounts receivable are short-term financial assets that arise from sales on credit. Notes receivable consists of promissory notes. A promissory note is an unconditional promise to pay a definite sum of money on demand or at a future date. The allowance method matches estimated losses from bad debts with the revenues they help to generate. It also aids in valuing the accounts receivable on the balance sheet. Notes receivable that are due in less than one year may be shown at their fair value in the current assets section of the balance sheet. Accounts receivable are also shown in the current assets section at their net realizable value; i.e., reduced by the allowance for uncollectible accounts. Interest receivable is also included in the current assets section. The uncollectible accounts expense is deducted from revenues on the income statement.

Apply the allowance method of accounting for uncollectible accounts. **LO 2**

Uncollectible accounts expense is estimated by using either the percentage of net sales method or the accounts receivable aging method. Under the first method, bad debts are judged to be a certain percentage of sales. Under the second method, certain percentages are applied to groups of accounts receivable that have been arranged by due dates.

The estimate of uncollectible accounts is debited to Uncollectible Accounts Expense and credited to the allowance account. When an individual account is determined to be uncollectible, it is removed from Accounts Receivable by debiting the allowance account and crediting Accounts Receivable. If the written-off account is later collected, the earlier entry is reversed and the collection is recorded in the normal way.

Make common calculations for notes receivable. **LO 3**

In accounting for promissory notes, common calculations include the maturity date, the duration of a note, the interest and interest rate, and the maturity value.

Show how to evaluate the level of receivables, and identify alternative means of financing receivables. **LO 4**

The management of receivables is critical to maintaining adequate liquidity. Management must (1) consider the need for short-term investing and borrowing as cash fluctuates during seasonal cycles, (2) establish credit policies that balance the need for sales with the ability to collect, (3) evaluate the level of receivables using receivables turnover and days' sales uncollected, (4) assess the need to increase cash flows through alternative means of the financing of receivables, and (5) understand the importance of ethics in estimating credit losses.

Key Terms and Ratios

accounts receivable 336 (LO1)
accounts receivable aging method 341 (LO2)
aging of accounts receivable 341 (LO2)
Allowance for Uncollectible Accounts 339 (LO1)
allowance method 338 (LO1)
contingent liability 351 (LO4)
direct charge-off method 337 (LO1)
discounting 352 (LO4)

dishonored note 347 (LO3)
duration of a note 346 (LO3)
factor 351 (LO4)
factoring 351 (LO4)
interest 346 (LO3)
interest receivable 339 (LO1)
maturity date 346 (LO3)
maturity value 347 (LO3)
notes receivable 337 (LO1)
percentage of net sales method 340 (LO2)

promissory note 337 (LO1)
securitization 351 (LO4)
trade credit 336 (LO1)
uncollectible accounts 337 (LO1)

RATIOS
days' sales uncollected 350 (LO4)
receivables turnover 349 (LO4)

Chapter Assignments

DISCUSSION QUESTIONS

LO 1   **DQ1. CONCEPT** ▶ What accounting concepts are violated by the direct charge-off method of recognizing uncollectible accounts? Why?

LO 1, 2   **DQ2.** In what ways is Allowance for Uncollectible Accounts similar to Accumulated Depreciation? In what ways is it different?

LO 3   **DQ3.** Under what circumstances would an accrual of interest income on an interest-bearing note receivable not be required at the end of an accounting period?

LO 4   **DQ4. BUSINESS APPLICATION** ▶ Why is it advantageous for a company to finance its receivables?

LO 4   **DQ5. BUSINESS APPLICATION** ▶ To increase its sales, a company decides to increase its credit terms from 15 to 30 days. What effect will this change in policy have on receivables turnover and days' sales uncollected?

LO 4   **DQ6. BUSINESS APPLICATION** ▶ How might the receivables turnover and days' sales uncollected reveal that management is consistently underestimating the amount of losses from uncollectible accounts? Is this action ethical?

SHORT EXERCISES

LO 1   ### Accounts Receivable and Notes Receivable

SE1. Indicate which of the following is more closely associated with (a) accounts receivable or (b) notes receivable:

1. Backed by a written promissory note.
2. Appears separate from receivables from employees.
3. Requires an estimate of uncollectible accounts.
4. Banks often have this type of receivable.
5. Often referred to as trade credit.

LO 1   ### Evaluating the Level of Accounts Receivable

SE2. During its first year of operation in 2014, Browne Sales Corporation made most of its sales on credit. At the end of the year, accounts receivable amounted to $199,000. On December 31, 2014, management reviewed the collectible status of the accounts receivable. Approximately $16,500 of the $199,000 of accounts receivable were estimated to be uncollectible. What adjusting entry would be made December 31, 2014?

LO 2   ### Percentage of Net Sales Method

SE3. At the end of October, Santa Fe Company's management estimates the uncollectible accounts expense to be 1 percent of net sales of $1,385,000. Prepare the journal entry to record the uncollectible accounts expense, assuming the Allowance for Uncollectible Accounts has a debit balance of $7,000.

LO 2   ### Accounts Receivable Aging Method

SE4. An aging analysis on June 30 of the accounts receivable of U-Z Door Corporation indicates that uncollectible accounts amount to $86,000. Prepare the journal entry to record uncollectible accounts expense under each of the following independent assumptions:

a. Allowance for Uncollectible Accounts has a credit balance of $18,000 before adjustment.
b. Allowance for Uncollectible Accounts has a debit balance of $14,000 before adjustment.

LO 2 **Write-off of Accounts Receivable**

SE5. Chicago Corporation, which uses the allowance method, has accounts receivable of $25,400 and an allowance for uncollectible accounts of $4,900. An account receivable from Tom Novak of $2,200 is deemed to be uncollectible and is written off. What is the amount of net accounts receivable before and after the write-off?

LO 3 **Interest Computations**

SE6. Determine the interest on the following notes. (Round to the nearest cent.)

a. $58,940 at 6 percent for 60 days.
b. $14,280 at 9 percent for 30 days.
c. $30,600 at 12 percent for 60 days.
d. $21,070 at 10 percent for 90 days.
e. $46,360 at 15 percent for 120 days.

LO 3 **Notes Receivable Calculations**

SE7. Determine the maturity date, interest at maturity, and maturity value for a 120-day, 8 percent, $34,000 note from Archer Corporation dated July 7. (Round to the nearest cent.)

LO 3 **Notes Receivable Calculations**

SE8. On August 25, Intercontinental Company received a 90-day, 9 percent note in settlement of an account receivable in the amount of $20,000. Determine the maturity date, amount of interest on the note, and maturity value. (Round to the nearest cent.)

LO 4 **Management Issues**

SE9. BUSINESS APPLICATION ▶ Indicate whether each of the following actions is related to (a) managing cash needs, (b) setting credit policies, (c) financing receivables, or (d) ethically reporting receivables:

1. Selling accounts receivable to a factor.
2. Borrowing funds for short-term needs during slow periods.
3. Conducting thorough checks of new customers' ability to pay.
4. Making every effort to reflect possible future losses accurately.

LO 4 **Short-Term Liquidity Ratios**

 SE10. BUSINESS APPLICATION ▶ Wellman Company has cash of $80,000, net accounts receivable of $180,000, and net sales of $1,440,000. Last year's net accounts receivable were $140,000. Compute the following ratios: (a) receivables turnover and (b) days' sales uncollected. (Round to the nearest whole day.)

EXERCISES: SET A

LO 1 **Evaluating the Level of Accounts Receivable**

E1A. During its first year of operation in 2014, Jameson Sales Corporation made most of its sales on credit. At the end of the year, accounts receivable amounted to $175,000. On December 31, 2014, management reviewed the collectible status of the accounts receivable. Approximately 7.5% of the $175,000 of accounts receivable were estimated to be uncollectible. What adjusting entry would be made December 31, 2014?

LO 2 **Percentage of Net Sales Method**

E2A. At the end of the year, Bertha Enterprises estimates the uncollectible accounts expense to be 0.7 percent of net sales of $15,150,000. The current credit balance of Allowance for Uncollectible Accounts is $25,800. Prepare the entry to record the uncollectible accounts expense. What is the balance of Allowance for Uncollectible Accounts after this adjustment?

LO 2 **Accounts Receivable Aging Method**

E3A. Security Service Company's Accounts Receivable account shows a debit balance of $104,000 at the end of the year. An aging analysis of the individual accounts indicates estimated uncollectible accounts to be $6,700.

Prepare the journal entry to record the uncollectible accounts expense under each of the following independent assumptions: (a) Allowance for Uncollectible Accounts has a credit balance of $800 before adjustment, and (b) Allowance for Uncollectible Accounts has a debit balance of $800 before adjustment. What is the balance of Allowance for Uncollectible Accounts after each of these adjustments?

LO 2 **Aging Method and Net Sales Method Contrasted**

E4A. At the beginning of 2014, the balances for Accounts Receivable and Allowance for Uncollectible Accounts were $215,000 and $15,700 (credit), respectively. During the year, credit sales were $1,600,000 and collections on account were $1,475,000. In addition, $17,500 in uncollectible accounts was written off.

Using T accounts, determine the year-end balances of Accounts Receivable and Allowance for Uncollectible Accounts. Then prepare the year-end adjusting entry to record the uncollectible accounts expense under each of the following conditions. Also show the year-end balance sheet presentation of accounts receivable and allowance for uncollectible accounts.

a. Management estimates the percentage of uncollectible credit sales to be 1.2 percent of total credit sales.
b. Based on an aging of accounts receivable, management estimates the end-of-year uncollectible accounts receivable to be $19,350.

Post the results of each of the entries to the T account for Allowance for Uncollectible Accounts.

LO 2 **Aging Method and Net Sales Method Contrasted**

E5A. ACCOUNTING CONNECTION ▶ During 2014, DeLuca Company had net sales of $5,700,000. Most of the sales were on credit. At the end of 2014, the balance of Accounts Receivable was $700,000 and Allowance for Uncollectible Accounts had a debit balance of $24,000. DeLuca's management uses two methods of estimating uncollectible accounts expense: the percentage of net sales method and the accounts receivable aging method. The percentage of uncollectible sales is 1.5 percent of net sales, and based on an aging of accounts receivable, the end-of-year uncollectible accounts total $70,000.

Prepare the year-end adjusting entry to record the uncollectible accounts expense under each method. What will the balance of Allowance for Uncollectible Accounts be after each adjustment? Why are the results different? Which method is likely to be more reliable? Why?

LO 2 **Aging Method and Net Sales Method Contrasted**

E6A. ACCOUNTING CONNECTION ▶ Dapper Hat Makers Company sells merchandise on credit. During the fiscal year ended July 31, the company had net sales of $2,300,000. At the end of the year, it had Accounts Receivable of $600,000 and a debit balance in Allowance for Uncollectible Accounts of $3,400. In the past, approximately 1.4 percent of net sales have proved to be uncollectible. Also, an aging analysis of accounts receivable reveals that $30,000 of the receivables appears to be uncollectible.

Prepare journal entries to record uncollectible accounts expense using (a) the percentage of net sales method and (b) the accounts receivable aging method. What is the resulting balance of Allowance for Uncollectible Accounts under each method? How would your answers under each method change if Allowance for Uncollectible Accounts had a credit balance of $3,400 instead of a debit balance? Why do the methods result in different balances?

LO 2   **Write-off of Accounts Receivable**

E7A. Norcia Company, which uses the allowance method, began the year with Accounts Receivable of $32,500 and an allowance for uncollectible accounts of $3,200 (credit). The company sold merchandise to Bruce Willis for $3,600 and later received $1,200 from Willis. The rest of the amount due from Willis had to be written off as uncollectible. Using T accounts, show the beginning balances and the effects of the Willis transactions on Accounts Receivable and Allowance for Uncollectible Accounts. What is the amount of net accounts receivable before and after the write-off?

LO 3   **Interest Computations**

E8A. Determine the interest on the following notes. (Round to the nearest cent.)

a. $38,760 at 10 percent for 90 days.
b. $27,200 at 12 percent for 60 days.
c. $30,600 at 9 percent for 30 days.
d. $51,000 at 15 percent for 120 days.
e. $18,360 at 6 percent for 60 days.

LO 3   **Notes Receivable Calculations**

E9A. Determine the maturity date, interest at maturity, and maturity value for a 90-day, 10 percent, $18,000 note from Archer Corporation dated February 15. (Round to the nearest cent.)

LO 3   **Notes Receivable Calculations**

E10A. Determine the maturity date, interest in 2013 and 2014, and maturity value for a 90-day, 12 percent, $15,000 note from a customer dated December 1, 2013, assuming a December 31 year end. (Round to the nearest cent.)

LO 3   **Notes Receivable Calculations**

E11A. Determine the maturity date, interest at maturity, and maturity value for each of the following notes. (Round to the nearest cent.)

a. A 60-day, 10 percent, $2,400 note dated January 5 received from S. William for granting a time extension on a past-due account.
b. A 60-day, 12 percent, $1,500 note dated March 9 received from E. Watson for granting a time extension on a past-due account.

LO 4   **Management Issues**

E12A. BUSINESS APPLICATION ▶ Indicate whether each of the following actions is primarily related to (a) managing cash needs, (b) setting credit policies, (c) financing receivables, or (d) ethically reporting accounts receivable:

1. Selling notes receivable to a financing company.
2. Changing the terms for credit sales in an effort to reduce the days' sales uncollected.
3. Buying a U.S. Treasury bill with cash that is not needed for a few months.
4. Comparing receivable turnovers for two years.
5. Setting a policy that allows customers to buy on credit.
6. Making careful estimates of losses from uncollectible accounts.
7. Establishing a department whose responsibility is to approve customers' credit.
8. Borrowing funds for short-term needs in a period when sales are low.
9. Revising estimated credit losses in a timely manner when conditions change.

LO **4**

Short-Term Liquidity Ratios

E13A. BUSINESS APPLICATION ▶ Using the following data from Moontrust Corporation's financial statements, compute the receivables turnover and the days' sales uncollected. (Round to one decimal place or to the nearest whole day.)

Current assets:	
Cash	$ 70,000
Short-term investments	170,000
Notes receivable	240,000
Accounts receivable, net	400,000
Inventory	500,000
Prepaid assets	50,000
Total current assets	$1,430,000
Current liabilities:	
Notes payable	$ 600,000
Accounts payable	150,000
Accrued liabilities	20,000
Total current liabilities	$ 770,000
Net sales	$3,200,000
Last year's accounts receivable, net	$ 360,000

EXERCISES: SET B

Visit the textbook companion website at www.cengagebrain.com to access Exercise Set B for this chapter.

PROBLEMS

LO **2, 4**

Methods of Estimating Uncollectible Accounts and Receivables Analysis

P1. McLennon Company had an Accounts Receivable balance of $320,000 and a credit balance in Allowance for Uncollectible Accounts of $16,700 at January 1, 2014. During the year, the company recorded the following transactions:

a. Sales on account, $1,052,000.
b. Sales returns and allowances by credit customers, $53,400.
c. Collections from customers, $993,000.
d. Worthless accounts written off, $19,800.

✔ 2a: Uncollectible accounts expense, percentage of net sales method: $24,965
✔ 2b: Accounts receivable aging method: $27,100

The company's past history indicates that 2.5 percent of its net credit sales will not be collected.

REQUIRED

1. Prepare T accounts for Accounts Receivable and Allowance for Uncollectible Accounts. Enter the beginning balances, and show the effects on these accounts of the items listed above, summarizing the year's activity. Determine the ending balance of each account.

2. Compute Uncollectible Accounts Expense, determine the ending balance of Allowance for Uncollectible Accounts and net Accounts Receivable under (a) the percentage of net sales method and (b) the accounts receivable aging method, assuming an aging of the accounts receivable shows that $24,000 may be uncollectible.

3. Compute the receivables turnover and days' sales uncollected, using the data from the accounts receivable aging method in requirement **2**. (Round to one decimal place or to the nearest whole day.)

4. **ACCOUNTING CONNECTION** ▶ How do you explain that the two methods used in requirement **2** result in different amounts for Uncollectible Accounts Expense? What rationale underlies each method?

LO **2**

✔ 3: Amount of uncollectible
accounts expense: $72,714

Accounts Receivable Aging Method

P2. Techno Designs Store uses the accounts receivable aging method to estimate uncollectible accounts. On February 1, 2014, the balance of the Accounts Receivable account was a debit of $442,341, and the balance of Allowance for Uncollectible Accounts was a credit of $43,700. During the year, the store had sales on account of $3,722,000, sales returns and allowances of $60,000, worthless accounts written off of $44,300, and collections from customers of $3,211,000. As part of the end-of-year (January 31, 2015) procedures, an aging analysis of accounts receivable is prepared. The analysis, which is partially complete, follows.

Customer Account	Total	Not Yet Due	1–30 Days Past Due	31–60 Days Past Due	61–90 Days Past Due	Over 90 Days Past Due
Balance Forward	$793,791	$438,933	$149,614	$106,400	$57,442	$41,402

To finish the analysis, the following accounts need to be classified:

Account	Amount	Due Date
J. Curtis	$11,077	Jan. 15
T. Dawson	9,314	Feb. 15 (next fiscal year)
L. Zapata	8,664	Dec. 20
R. Copa	780	Oct. 1
E. Land	14,710	Jan. 4
S. Qadri	6,316	Nov. 15
A. Rosenthal	4,389	Mar. 1 (next fiscal year)
	$55,250	

From past experience, the company has found that the following rates are realistic for estimating uncollectible accounts:

Time	Percentage Considered Uncollectible
Not yet due	2
1–30 days past due	5
31–60 days past due	15
61–90 days past due	25
Over 90 days past due	50

REQUIRED

1. Complete the aging analysis of accounts receivable.
2. Compute the end-of-year balances (before adjustments) of Accounts Receivable and Allowance for Uncollectible Accounts.
3. Prepare an analysis computing the estimated uncollectible accounts. (Round to the nearest whole dollar.)
4. How much is Techno Designs Store's estimated uncollectible accounts expense for the year? (Round the adjustment to the nearest whole dollar.)
5. **ACCOUNTING CONNECTION** ▶ What role do estimates play in applying the aging analysis? What factors might affect these estimates?

LO **4**

Notes Receivable Calculations

✔ 2: Total accrued interest income
as of June 30: $3,856.44

P3. West Palm Company engaged in the following transactions involving promissory notes:

May   3   Sold engines to Mittal Company for $120,000 in exchange for a 90-day, 12 percent promissory note.

      16   Sold engines to Tata Company for $64,000 in exchange for a 60-day, 13 percent note.

      31   Sold engines to Arsenal Company for $60,000 in exchange for a 90-day, 11 percent note.

(Continued)

REQUIRED

1. For each of the notes, determine the (a) maturity date, (b) interest on the note, and (c) maturity value. (Round to the nearest cent.)
2. Assume that the fiscal year for West Palm ends on June 30. How much interest income should be recorded on that date? (Round to the nearest cent.)
3. **ACCOUNTING CONNECTION** ▶ What are the effects of the transactions in May on cash flows for the year ended June 30?

LO **3**

✔ 5: Interest in 2015: $425.34

Notes Receivable Calculations

P4. Assume that on December 16, 2014, Harris Company receives a 90-day, 9 percent, $23,000 note, payable in full with interest at maturity, and that the company prepares monthly financial statements.

REQUIRED

1. What is the maturity date of the note?
2. How much interest will be earned on the note if it is paid when due? (Round to the nearest cent.)
3. What is the maturity value of the note?
4. If the company's fiscal year ends on December 31, 2014, calculate the amount of the adjusting entry that would be made for interest.
5. How much interest will be earned on this note in 2015? (Round to the nearest cent.)
6. **ACCOUNTING CONNECTION** ▶ How much cash will be received for interest in 2014? Why does the amount of cash received for interest differ from the amount of interest earned?

ALTERNATE PROBLEMS

LO **2, 4**

Methods of Estimating Uncollectible Accounts and Receivables Analysis

RATIO

SPREADSHEET

GENERAL LEDGER

✔ 2a: Uncollectible accounts expense, percentage of net sales method: $17,952
✔ 2b: Accounts receivable aging method: $15,700

P5. On December 31 of last year, Target System Company's balance sheet had Accounts Receivable of $298,000 and a credit balance in Allowance for Uncollectible Accounts of $20,300. During the current year, Target System's records included the following selected activities: (a) sales on account, $1,195,000; (b) sales returns and allowances, $73,000; (c) collections from customers, $1,150,000; and (d) accounts written off as worthless, $16,000. In the past, 1.6 percent of Target System's net sales have been uncollectible.

REQUIRED

1. Prepare T accounts for Accounts Receivable and Allowance for Uncollectible Accounts. Enter the beginning balances, and show the effects on these accounts of the items listed above, summarizing the year's activity. Determine the ending balance of each account.
2. Compute Uncollectible Accounts Expense, determine the ending balance of Allowance for Uncollectible Accounts and net Accounts Receivable under (a) the percentage of net sales method and (b) the accounts receivable aging method. Assume that an aging of the accounts receivable shows that $20,000 may be uncollectible.
3. Compute the receivables turnover and days' sales uncollected, using the data from the accounts receivable aging method in requirement **2**. (Round to one decimal place or to the nearest whole day.)
4. **ACCOUNTING CONNECTION** ▶ How do you explain that the two methods used in requirement **2** result in different amounts for Uncollectible Accounts Expense? What rationale underlies each method?

LO **2**

✔ 4: Amount of uncollectible
accounts expense: $9,110

Accounts Receivable Aging Method

P6. Flossmoor Company uses the accounts receivable aging method to estimate uncollectible accounts. At the beginning of the year, the balance of the Accounts Receivable account was a debit of $88,430, and the balance of Allowance for Uncollectible Accounts was a credit of $7,200. During the year, the company had sales on account of $473,000, sales returns and allowances of $4,200, worthless accounts written off of $7,900, and collections from customers of $450,730. At the end of year (December 31, 2014), a junior accountant for Flossmoor was preparing an aging analysis of accounts receivable. At the top of page 6 of the report, the following totals appeared:

Customer Account	Total	Not Yet Due	1–30 Days Past Due	31–60 Days Past Due	61–90 Days Past Due	Over 90 Days Past Due
Balance Forward	$89,640	$49,030	$24,110	$9,210	$3,990	$3,300

To finish the analysis, the following accounts need to be classified:

Account	Amount	Due Date
B. Singh	$ 930	Jan. 14 (next year)
L. Wells	620	Dec. 24
A. Rocky	1,955	Sept. 28
T. Cila	2,100	Aug. 16
M. Mix	375	Dec. 14
S. Prince	2,685	Jan. 23 (next year)
J. Wendt	295	Nov. 5
	$8,960	

From past experience, the company has found that the following rates are realistic for estimating uncollectible accounts:

Time	Percentage Considered Uncollectible
Not yet due	2
1–30 days past due	5
31–60 days past due	15
61–90 days past due	25
Over 90 days past due	50

REQUIRED

1. Complete the aging analysis of accounts receivable.
2. Compute the end-of-year balances (before adjustments) of Accounts Receivable and Allowance for Uncollectible Accounts.
3. Prepare an analysis computing the estimated uncollectible accounts. (Round to the nearest dollar.)
4. Calculate Flossmoor's estimated uncollectible accounts expense for the year. (Round to the nearest whole dollar).
5. **ACCOUNTING CONNECTION** ▶ What role do estimates play in applying the aging analysis? What factors might affect these estimates?

LO **3**

✔ 2: Total accrued interest income as
of August 31: $6,025.64

Notes Receivable Calculations

P7. Vision Importing Company engaged in the following transactions involving promissory notes:

July 2 Sold engines to Morgan Company for $180,000 in exchange for a 90-day, 12 percent promissory note.

   15 Sold engines to Level Company for $96,000 in exchange for a 60-day, 13 percent note.

   30 Sold engines to Level Company for $90,000 in exchange for a 90-day, 11 percent note.

(Continued)

REQUIRED

1. For each of the notes, determine the (a) maturity date, (b) interest on the note, and (c) maturity value. (Round to the nearest cent.)
2. Assume that the fiscal year for Vision Importing ends on August 31. How much interest income should be recorded on that date? (Round to the nearest cent.)
3. **ACCOUNTING CONNECTION** ▶ What are the effects of the transactions in July on cash flows for the year ended August 31?

LO **3**

Notes Receivable Calculations

✔ 5: Interest in 2015: $3.92

P8. Assume that on November 3, 2014, Harris Company receives a 60-day, 6.5 percent, $11,000 note, payable in full with interest at maturity, and that the company prepares monthly financial statements.

REQUIRED

1. What is the maturity date of the note?
2. How much interest will be earned on the note if it is paid when due? (Round to the nearest cent.)
3. What is the maturity value of the note?
4. If the company's fiscal year ends on December 31, calculate the amount of the adjusting entry that would be made.
5. How much interest will be earned on this note in 2015? (Round to the nearest cent.)
6. **ACCOUNTING CONNECTION** ▶ How much cash will be received for interest in 2014? Why does the amount of cash received for interest differ from the amount of interest earned?

CASES

LO **1**

Conceptual Understanding: Role of Credit Sales

C1. CONCEPT ▶ **Mitsubishi Corp.**, a broadly diversified Japanese company, instituted a credit plan called Three Diamonds for customers who buy its major electronic products, such as large-screen televisions, from specified retail dealers.[12] Under the plan, approved customers who make purchases in July of one year do not have to make any payments until September of the next year. Nor do they have to pay interest during the intervening months. Mitsubishi pays the dealer the full amount less a small fee, sends the customer a Mitsubishi credit card, and collects from the customer at the specified time. What was Mitsubishi's motivation for establishing such generous credit terms? What costs are involved? What are the accounting implications?

LO **1, 2**

Conceptual Understanding: Role of Estimates in Accounting for Receivables

C2. CONCEPT ▶ **CompuCredit** is a credit card issuer in Atlanta. It prides itself on making credit cards available to almost anyone in a matter of seconds over the Internet. The cost to the consumer is an interest rate of 28 percent, about double that of companies that provide cards only to customers with good credit. Despite its high interest rate, CompuCredit was successful for many years. To calculate its income, the company estimated that 10 percent of its $1.3 billion in accounts receivable would not be paid; the industry average is 7 percent. Some analysts were critical of CompuCredit for being too optimistic in its projections of losses.[13] In fact, during the recent recession, CompuCredit losses from uncollectible accounts increased and exceeded its interest income and the company reported large operating losses.[14] Why are estimates necessary in accounting for receivables? If CompuCredit were to use the same estimate of losses as other companies in its industry, would it have been better or worse off? How would one determine if CompuCredit's estimate of losses is reasonable?

LO 4

Conceptual Understanding: Receivables Financing

C3. Gerard Appliances, Inc., is a small manufacturer of washing machines and dryers. It sells its products to large, established discount retailers that market the appliances under their own names. Gerard generally sells the appliances on trade credit terms of n/60, but if a customer wants a longer term, it will accept a note with a term of up to nine months. At present, the company is having cash flow troubles and needs $10 million immediately. Its Cash balance is $400,000, its Accounts Receivable balance is $4.6 million, and its Notes Receivable balance is $7.4 million. How might Gerard Appliances use its accounts receivable and notes receivable to raise the cash it needs? What are its prospects for raising the needed cash?

LO 1, 4

Interpreting Financial Reports: Accounting for Accounts Receivable

C4. BUSINESS APPLICATION ▶ Robinson Products Co., a major consumer goods company, sells more than 3,000 products in 135 countries. Its report to the Securities and Exchange Commission in 2014 presented the following data:

	2014	2013	2012
Net sales	$9,820,000	$9,730,000	$9,888,000
Accounts receivable	1,046,000	1,048,000	1,008,000
Allowance for uncollectible accounts	37,200	42,400	49,000
Uncollectible accounts expense	30,000	33,400	31,600
Uncollectible accounts written off	38,600	40,200	35,400
Recoveries of accounts previously written off	3,400	200	2,000

1. Compute the ratio of uncollectible accounts expense to net sales and to accounts receivable and the ratio of allowance for uncollectible accounts to accounts receivable for 2012, 2013, and 2014. (Round to two decimal places for net sales and one decimal place for accounts receivable.)
2. Compute the receivables turnover and days' sales uncollected for each year assuming that net accounts receivable in 2011 were $930,000. (Round to one decimal place or to the nearest whole day.)
3. What is your interpretation of the ratios? Describe management's attitude toward the collectability of accounts receivable over the three-year period.

LO 1, 2, 4

Annual Report Case: Cash and Receivables

C5. Refer to the **CVS** annual report in the Supplement to Chapter 16 to answer the following questions:

1. Which customers represent the main source of CVS's accounts receivable, and how much is CVS's allowance for uncollectible accounts?
2. What do you think CVS's seasonal needs for cash are? Where in CVS's financial statements is the seasonality of sales discussed?

LO 1, 4

Comparison Analysis: Accounts Receivable Analysis

C6. BUSINESS APPLICATION ▶ Refer to the **CVS** annual report in the Supplement to Chapter 16 and to the following data (in millions) for **Walgreens**: net sales, $72,184 and $67,420 for 2011 and 2010, respectively; accounts receivable, net, $2,497 and $2,450 for 2011 and 2010, respectively.[15]

1. Compute receivables turnover and days' sales uncollected for 2011 and 2010 for CVS and Walgreens. Accounts receivable in 2009 were $5,457 million for CVS and $2,496 million for Walgreens. (Round to one decimal place.)
2. Do you discern any differences in the two companies' credit policies? Explain your answer.

LO **1, 4**   **Ethical Dilemma: Uncollectible Accounts**

C7. BUSINESS APPLICATION ▶ Mullin Interiors, a successful retailer of high-quality furniture, is located in an affluent suburb where a large insurance company has just announced that it will lay off 4,000 employees. Because most of Mullin Interiors' sales are made on credit, accounts receivable is one of its major assets. Although the company's annual losses from uncollectible accounts are not out of line, they represent a sizable amount. The company depends on bank loans for its financing. Sales and net income have declined in the past year, and some customers are falling behind in paying their accounts.

Veronica Mullin, the owner, knows that the bank's loan officer likes to see a steady performance. She has therefore instructed the company's controller to underestimate the uncollectible accounts this year to show a small growth in earnings. Mullin believes this action is justified because earnings in future years will average out the losses. Since the company has a history of success, she believes the adjustments are meaningless accounting measures anyway.

Are Mullin's actions ethical? Would any parties be harmed by her actions? How important is it to try to be accurate in estimating losses from uncollectible accounts?

Continuing Case: Annual Report Project

C8. Using the most recent annual report of the company you have chosen to study and that you have accessed online at the company's website, examine the balance sheet and accompanying notes of your company. Answer the following questions:

1. What percentage of total current assets is accounts receivable? Is this figure the total accounts receivable or net accounts receivable? Why or why not?

2. Find the disclosures about accounts receivable in the notes to the financial statements. What is the amount of the allowance account and what percentage of total accounts receivable is it?

3. Does the company have notes receivable on the balance sheet? If so, read the note to the financial statements on notes receivable. What do you learn from it about the business?

4. **BUSINESS APPLICATION** ▶ Compute receivables turnover and days' sales uncollected for the most recent year.

CHAPTER 10
Long-Term Assets

BUSINESS INSIGHT
Neighborhood Carriers

An issue involved in accounting for long-term assets is how to allocate their costs over their expected useful lives. For instance, suppose that on January 2, 2014, Neighborhood Carriers pays $29,000 for a small van that it will use in making deliveries to its customers. The company expects that the van will be driven a total of 150,000 miles over a 5-year period and that, at the end of that time, it will be worth $2,000. Based on the mileage shown in the following table, Neighborhood Carriers can allocate the cost of the van over the 5 years. However, the company can choose other ways of allocating this cost.

Years	Miles
2014	30,000
2015	52,500
2016	45,000
2017	15,000
2018	7,500
Total	150,000

1. **CONCEPT** ▶ *What is the classification of long-term assets, how are the assets valued, and what is the distinction in recognizing capital and revenue expenditures?*

2. **ACCOUNTING APPLICATION** ▶ *In what ways are the costs of long-term assets, such as a delivery van, allocated to the periods they benefit?*

3. **BUSINESS APPLICATION** ▶ *How does management decide to acquire, finance, and evaluate long-term assets?*

LEARNING OBJECTIVES

LO 1 Identify the classifications of long-term assets, and describe how they are valued by allocating their costs to the periods that they benefit.

LO 2 Account for the acquisition costs of property, plant, and equipment.

LO 3 Compute depreciation under the straight-line, production, and declining-balance methods.

LO 4 Account for the disposal of depreciable assets.

LO 5 Identify the issues related to accounting for natural resources, and compute depletion.

LO 6 Identify the issues related to accounting for intangible assets, including research and development costs and goodwill.

LO 7 Describe the disclosure of acquiring and financing long-term assets, and calculate free cash flow.

CONCEPTS

CONCEPTS
- Valuation
- Classification
- Accrual Accounting (matching rule)
- Disclosure
- Recognition

RELEVANT LEARNING OBJECTIVE

LO 1 Identify the classifications of long-term assets, and describe how they are valued by allocating their costs to the periods that they benefit.

LO 1 Concepts Underlying Long-Term Assets

Long-term assets (or *fixed assets*) have the following characteristics:

- **They have a useful life of more than one year.** This distinguishes them from current assets, which a company expects to use up or convert to cash within 1 year or during its operating cycle, whichever is longer. The most common criterion for the useful life of a long-term asset is that it be capable of repeated use for more than a year.
- **They are used in the operation of a business.** For an asset to be *classified* as property, plant, and equipment, it must be "put in use," which means it is available for its intended purpose. An emergency generator is "put in use" when it is available for emergencies, even if it is never used. Assets not used in the normal course of business, such as land held for speculative reasons or buildings no longer used in ordinary operations, should be *classified* as investments.
- **They are not intended for resale to customers.** An asset that a company intends to resell to customers should be *classified* as inventory, no matter how durable it is. For example, a computer that a company uses in an office is a long-term plant asset. An identical computer that a company sells to customers is inventory.

Exhibit 1 shows the relative importance of long-term assets in various industries.

Exhibit 1
Long-Term Assets as a Percentage of Total Assets for Selected Industries

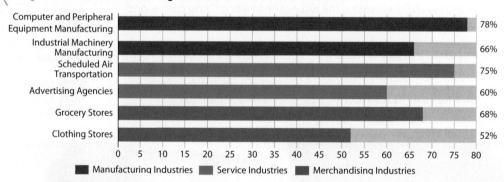

Based on Bizmin Industry Financial Report, December 2011.

Classification, Accrual Accounting, and Disclosure of Long-Term Assets

Long-terms assets are *classified* as property, plant, and equipment; natural resources; and intangible assets. **Property, plant, and equipment** is land and other long-term assets that have physical substance. **Natural resources** are assets purchased for the economic value that can be extracted from them, such as oil and gas. **Intangible assets** are long-term assets that have no physical substance, such as copyrights and patents. Under *accrual accounting* the cost of these assets, with the exception of land and some intangible assets, is allocated to the periods they benefit, as follows.

- The periodic allocation of the costs of plant and equipment over their estimated useful lives is called **depreciation**. Although land is property, it is not depreciated because it has an unlimited life.
- The allocation of the costs of natural resources is called **depletion**.
- The allocation of the costs of most long-term intangible assets, which represent a legal right or advantage, is called **amortization**. Some intangible assets not subject to amortization.

The methods used to determine depreciation, depletion, and amortization are *disclosed* in the notes to the financial statements. Exhibit 2 shows how long-term assets are *classified* and defines the *accrual accounting* methods of allocating their cost of their use to the income statement.

Exhibit 2
Classification of Long-Term Assets and Methods of Accounting for Them

Balance Sheet Long-Term Assets	Income Statement Expenses

Property, Plant, and Equipment: long-term assets with physical substance used in business operations

- Land
- Plant Assets
  - Plant
  - Buildings
  - Equipment

Land is not expensed because it has an unlimited life.

Depreciation: periodic allocation of the cost of a tangible long-lived asset (other than land and natural resources) over its estimated useful life

Natural Resources: long-term assets purchased for the economic value that can be taken from the land and used up, as with ore, lumber, oil, and gas or other resources contained in the land

- Mines
- Timberland
- Oil and Gas Fields

Depletion: exhaustion of a natural resource through mining, cutting, pumping, or other extraction and the way in which the cost is allocated

Intangible Assets: long-term assets that have no physical substance but have a value based on rights or advantages accruing to the owner

Subject to Amortization and Impairment Test

- Copyrights
- Customer lists
- Franchises
- Licenses
- Leaseholds
- Noncompete covenants
- Patents
- Software

Subject Only to Annual Impairment Test

- Brand names
- Goodwill
- Trademarks

Amortization: periodic allocation of the cost of an intangible asset to the periods it benefits

Impairment: occurs when the fair value of the asset falls below the carrying value; all long-term assets are subject to an annual test for impairment

© Cengage Learning 2014

Valuation and Disclosure of Long-Term Assets

Long-term assets are generally reported and *valued* at carrying value. **Carrying value** (or *book value*) is the unexpired part of an asset's cost, computed as shown in Exhibit 3. If a long-term asset loses some or all of its potential to generate revenue before the end of its useful life, it is *impaired*, and its carrying value is reduced.

Asset impairment occurs when the carrying value of a long-term asset exceeds its fair value.[1] *Fair value* is the amount for which the asset could be bought or sold in a current transaction. For example, if the sum of the expected cash flows from an asset is less than its carrying value, the asset would be impaired, and a loss would be recorded. When the market prices used to establish fair value are not available, the amount of an impairment must be estimated from the best available information.

Exhibit 3
Carrying Value of Long-Term Assets on the Balance Sheet

Building	$200,000	Mines	$100,000	Patents	$20,000
Less Accumulated Depreciation	30,000	Less Accumulated Depletion	40,000	Less Accumulated Amortization	5,000
Total Plant Assets	$170,000	Total Natural Resources	$ 60,000	Total Intangible Assets	$15,000

© Cengage Learning 2014

Business Perspective

Impairments reflect valuations at a point in time. For example, in 2004, **Apple Computer** recognized losses of $5.5 million in asset impairments. With the huge success of the iPhone and iPad in subsequent years, the company had no occasion to recognize impairments in subsequent years. Taking a large write-down in a bad year is often called "taking a big bath" because it "cleans" future years of the bad year's costs and thus can help a company return to a profitable status. In other words, by taking the largest possible loss in a bad year, companies hope to reduce the costs of depreciation or amortization on the asset in subsequent years.[2]

Recognition of the Acquisition Cost of Long-Term Assets

An **expenditure** is a payment or an obligation to make a future payment for an asset or a service. Expenditures are *classified* as capital expenditures or revenue expenditures.

- A **capital expenditure** is for the purchase or expansion of a long-term asset. Capital expenditures are recorded in asset accounts because they benefit more than the current period.
- A **revenue expenditure** is for the ordinary repairs and maintenance needed to keep a long-term asset in good operating condition. For example, trucks, machines, and other equipment require periodic tune-ups and routine repairs. Expenditures of this type are recorded in expense accounts because their benefits are realized in the current period.

Capital expenditures include outlays for plant assets, natural resources, and intangible assets. They also include the following:

- **Additions** are enlargements to the physical layout of a plant asset. For example, if a new wing is added to a building, the benefits from the expenditure will be received over several years, and the amount paid should be debited to an asset account.
- **Betterments** are improvements to a plant asset but not an addition to the plant's physical layout. Installation of an air-conditioning system is an example. Because betterments provide benefits over a period of years, their costs should be debited to an asset account.
- **Extraordinary repairs** are repairs that significantly enhance a plant asset's estimated useful life or residual value. For example, the overhaul of a building's heating and cooling system may extend the system's useful life by five years. Extraordinary repairs are typically recorded by reducing the Accumulated Depreciation account. The effect is to increase the asset's carrying value by the cost of the extraordinary repair. The new carrying value should be depreciated over the asset's new estimated useful life.

International Perspective
IFRS Asset Impairment Under IFRS

The IFRS method of evaluating asset impairment does not consider the sum of the expected cash flows as is done under U. S. GAAP. Instead, it compares the carrying value with the recoverable amount. The recoverable amount is the greater of either the *net selling price* (the market value of the asset less disposal costs) or the *value in use*, which is based on the cash generating ability of the asset adjusted for interest rates. This is called *present value*, which will be explained in a later chapter.

Because the recoverable value is usually less than the sum of the expected cash flows, the IFRS method is much more likely than the GAAP method to result in write-offs due to impairment. The IFRS method also allows reversals of impairment write-offs if the value later increases because of revaluation, whereas the GAAP method prohibits future impairment reversals. One exception under IFRS is that goodwill impairments cannot be reversed.

The distinction between capital and revenue expenditures is important in applying *accrual accounting*, as illustrated in the examples that follow.

	Asset Incorrectly Recorded as Revenue Expenditure	**Revenue Expenditure Incorrectly Recorded as Asset**
Example	The purchase of a machine that will benefit a company for several years is mistakenly recorded as a revenue expenditure.	A revenue expenditure, such as the routine overhaul of a piece of machinery, is charged to an asset account.
Result	The total cost of the machine becomes an expense on the income statement in the current period.	▼ The expense of the current period will be *understated*.
	▼ Current net income will be reported at a lower amount *(understated)*.	▲ Current net income will be *overstated* by the same amount.
	▲ In future periods, net income will be reported at a higher amount *(overstated)*.	▼ The net income of future periods will be *understated*.

APPLY IT!

Match each term that follows with the corresponding action.

1. Addition
2. Betterment
3. Extraordinary repair
4. Revenue expenditure
5. Impairment

a. Repainting of an existing building.
b. Installation of a new roof that extends an existing building's useful life.
c. Erection of a new storage facility at the back of an existing building.
d. Decrease in value of intangible asset below carrying value.
e. Installation of a new heating system in an existing building.

SOLUTION

1. c;   2. e;   3. b;   4. a;   5. d

TRY IT! E1A, E1B

ACCOUNTING APPLICATIONS

LO 2 Acquisition Cost of Property, Plant, and Equipment

The acquisition cost of property, plant, and equipment includes all expenditures reasonable and necessary to get an asset in place and ready for use. For example, the cost of installing and testing a machine is a legitimate cost of acquiring the machine. However, if the machine is damaged during installation, the cost of repairs is an operating expense.

The cost of an asset is equal to its purchase price plus other costs:

Cost of Asset = Purchase Price + Additional Expenditures (freight, installation, etc.)

Thus, expenditures for freight, insurance while in transit, and installation are included in the cost of the asset because they are necessary for the asset to function. In accordance with *accrual accounting*, these expenditures are allocated over the asset's useful life.

Any interest charges incurred in purchasing an asset are not a cost of the asset. They are a cost of borrowing the money to buy the asset and are, therefore, an operating expense. An exception to this rule is that interest costs incurred during the construction of an asset are properly included as a cost of the asset.[3]

Many companies establish policies that define when an expenditure should be recorded as an expense or as an asset. For example, small expenditures for items that qualify as long-term assets may be treated as expenses because the amounts involved are not *material*. Thus, although a wastebasket may last for years, it would be recorded as an expense rather than as a depreciable asset.

Specific Applications of Determining the Acquisition Cost of Property, Plant, and Equipment

The sections that follow discuss some of the problems of determining the cost of long-term plant assets.

Land The purchase price of land should be debited to the Land account. Other expenditures that should be debited to Land include:

- Commissions to real estate agents
- Lawyers' fees
- Accrued taxes paid by the purchaser
- Costs of preparing the land to build on, such as the costs of tearing down old buildings and grading the land
- Assessments for local improvements, such as putting in streets and sewage systems
- Landscaping

Land is not depreciated because it has an unlimited useful life.

Assume that a company pays $340,000 for land, $16,000 in brokerage and legal fees, $20,000 to have an old building on the site torn down, and $2,000 to have the site graded. It receives $8,000 in salvage from the old building. The cost of the land is $370,000, calculated as follows.

Net purchase price		$340,000
Brokerage and legal fees		16,000
Tearing down old building	$20,000	
Less salvage	8,000	12,000
Grading		2,000
Total cost		$370,000

Like other costs involved in preparing land for use, the cost of implosion is debited to Land. Other expenditures debited to Land include the purchase price of the land, brokerage and legal fees involved in the purchase, taxes paid by the purchaser, and landscaping.

Land Improvements Some improvements to real estate, such as driveways, parking lots, and fences, have a limited life and, thus, are subject to depreciation. They should be recorded in an account called Land Improvements.

Buildings When a company buys a building, the cost includes the purchase price and all expenditures required to put the building in usable condition. When a company uses a contractor to construct a building, the cost includes the net contract price plus other expenditures necessary to put the building in usable condition. When a company constructs its own building, the cost includes:

- Costs of materials, labor, overhead and other indirect costs
- Architects' fees and lawyers' fees
- Insurance during construction
- Interest on construction loans during the period of construction
- Building permits

Because buildings have a limited useful life, they are subject to depreciation.

Leasehold Improvements Improvements to leased property on the books of the lessee that become the property of the lessor (the owner of the property) at the end of the lease are called **leasehold improvements**. For example, a tenant's installation of light fixtures, carpets, or walls would be considered a leasehold improvement. These improvements are usually classified in the property, plant, and equipment section of the balance sheet.[4] The cost of a leasehold improvement is depreciated over the remaining term of the lease or the useful life of the improvement, whichever is shorter.

A study of large companies showed that 26 percent report leasehold improvements. The percentage is likely to be much higher for small businesses because they generally operate in leased premises.[5]

Equipment The cost of equipment includes all expenditures connected with purchasing the equipment and preparing it for use. These expenditures include:

- Invoice price less cash discounts
- Freight, including insurance
- Excise taxes and tariffs
- Buying expenses
- Installation costs
- Test runs to ready the equipment for operation

Equipment is subject to depreciation.

Group Purchases Companies sometimes purchase land and other assets for a lump sum. The lump-sum purchase price must be apportioned between the land and the other assets. For example, suppose that a company buys a building and land for $170,000. The company can determine what it would have paid for the building and for the land if it had purchased them separately and apply the appropriate percentages to the lump-sum price. If appraisals yield estimates of $20,000 for the land and $180,000 for the building, the lump-sum price would be allocated as follows.

	Appraisal	Percentage	Apportionment
Land	$ 20,000	10% ($ 20,000 ÷ $200,000)	$ 17,000 ($170,000 × 10%)
Building	180,000	90% ($180,000 ÷ $200,000)	153,000 ($170,000 × 90%)
Totals	$200,000	100%	$170,000

APPLY IT!

Match each term that follows with the corresponding action.

1. Land
2. Land improvement
3. Leasehold improvement
4. Buildings
5. Equipment

a. Purchase of a computer.
b. Purchase of a lighting system for a parking lot.
c. Construction of a foundation for a new building.
d. Installation of partitions and shelves in a leased space.
e. Clearing of land in preparation for construction of a new building.

SOLUTION

1. e;   2. b;   3. d;   4. c;   5. a

TRY IT! SE1, SE2, E2A, E3A, E4A, E2B, E3B, E4B

LO3 Depreciation

As noted earlier, depreciation is the periodic allocation of the cost of property, plant, and equipment (other than land) over the asset's estimated useful life. In accounting for depreciation, it is important to keep the following points in mind:

- All plant assets, except land, have a limited useful life, and the costs of these assets must be distributed as expenses over the years they benefit.
- Depreciation refers to the allocation of the cost of a plant asset to the periods it benefits, not to the asset's physical deterioration or its decrease in market value. The term *depreciation* describes the gradual conversion of the cost of the asset into an expense.
- Depreciation is not a process of *valuation*. Accounting records are not indicators of changing price levels. They are kept in accordance with the *cost principle*. Because of an advantageous purchase price and market conditions, the value of a building may increase. Nevertheless, because depreciation is a process of allocation, not valuation, depreciation on the building must continue to be recorded.

Physical deterioration and obsolescence are the major factors in limiting a depreciable asset's useful life.

- **Physical deterioration:** The result of use or exposure to the elements, such as wind and sun. Periodic repairs and a sound maintenance policy may keep buildings and equipment in good operating order, but every machine or building must, at some point, be discarded.
- **Obsolescence:** The process of going out of date. Because of fast-changing technology and demands, machinery and even buildings often become obsolete before they wear out.

Accountants do not distinguish between physical deterioration and obsolescence because they are interested in the length of an asset's useful life, not in what limits its useful life.

STUDY NOTE: *Depreciation is the allocation of the acquisition cost of a plant asset. Any similarity between carrying value and current market value is pure coincidence.*

STUDY NOTE: *A computer may function just as well as it did when purchased four years ago, but because much faster and more efficient computers are now available, it is obsolete.*

Business Perspective
How Long Is the Useful Life of an Airplane?

Most airlines depreciate their planes over an estimated useful life of 10 to 20 years. But how long will a properly maintained plane really last? **Western Airlines** paid $3.3 million for a new Boeing 737 in July 1968. More than 78,000 flights and 30 years later, this aircraft was still flying for **Vanguard Airlines**, a no-frills airline. Among the other airlines that have owned this plane are **Piedmont**, **Delta**, and **US Airways**. Virtually every part of the plane has been replaced over the years. **Boeing** believes the plane could theoretically make double the number of flights before it is retired.

The useful lives of many types of assets can be extended indefinitely if the assets are correctly maintained. However, each airline that owned the plane would have depreciated it over a "reasonable" useful life.

Factors in Computing Depreciation

Four factors affect the computation of depreciation:

- **Cost** is the net purchase price of an asset plus all reasonable and necessary expenditures to get it in place and ready for use.
- **Residual value** (or *salvage value, disposal value,* and *trade-in value*) is the portion of an asset's acquisition cost that a company expects to recover when it disposes of the asset.

STUDY NOTE: *Depreciable cost, not acquisition cost, is allocated over a plant asset's useful life.*

- **Depreciable cost** is an asset's cost less its residual value. For example, a truck that cost $24,000 and that has a residual value of $6,000 would have a depreciable cost of $18,000. Depreciable cost must be allocated over the estimated useful life of the asset.
- **Estimated useful life** is the total number of service units expected from a long-term asset. Service units may be measured in terms of the years an asset is expected to be used, the units it is expected to produce, the miles it is expected to be driven, or similar measures. In computing an asset's estimated useful life, an accountant should consider all relevant information, including past experience with similar assets, the asset's present condition, the company's repair and maintenance policy, and current technological and industry trends.

At the end of a period, depreciation is recorded with an adjusting entry that takes the following form:

A	=	L	+	OE
− XXX				− XXX

Depreciation Expense—Asset Name	XXX	
Accumulated Depreciation—Asset Name		XXX
To record depreciation for the period		

Methods of Computing Depreciation

Many methods are used to allocate the cost of plant assets to accounting periods. The most common methods are the straight-line method, the production method, and the declining-balance method (an accelerated method).

Straight-Line Method

Method When the **straight-line method** is used, the asset's depreciable cost is spread evenly over the estimated useful life of the asset. The straight-line method is based on the assumption that depreciation depends only on the passage of time.

STUDY NOTE: *Estimates of residual value and useful life are, at best, educated guesses.*

Formula The depreciation expense for each period is computed by dividing the depreciable cost (cost less estimated residual value) by the number of accounting periods in the asset's estimated useful life:

$$\text{Depreciation Expense} = (\text{Cost} - \text{Residual Value}) \div \text{Estimated Useful Life}$$

International Perspective
IFRS Depreciation of Buildings Under IFRS

Under GAAP, the costs of a building and its components, such as a heating and air conditioning system, are usually lumped together as one asset and are depreciated over the life of the building. Under IFRS, however, a building and its components are depreciated on an individual basis. In other words, each component of a building—each property, plant. and equipment asset—is considered to have its own useful life and fair value and is depreciated on that basis. Because many of a building's assets often have shorter useful lives than the building itself, IFRS tend to increase depreciation expense. These standards also require more precise record keeping.

Example A delivery truck cost $20,000 and has an estimated residual value of $2,000 at the end of its estimated useful life of five years. Under the straight-line method, the annual depreciation would be $3,600, calculated as follows.

$$\text{Depreciation Expense} = \frac{\text{Cost} - \text{Residual Value}}{\text{Estimated Useful Life}} = \frac{\$20,000 - \$2,000}{5 \text{ Years}} = \$3,600 \text{ per Year}$$

Exhibit 4 shows the depreciation schedule for the five years. Note that in addition to annual depreciation being the same each year, the accumulated depreciation increases uniformly and the carrying value decreases uniformly until it reaches the estimated residual value.

Exhibit 4
Depreciation Schedule, Straight-Line Method

	Cost	Annual Depreciation	Accumulated Depreciation	Carrying Value
Date of purchase	$20,000	—	—	$20,000
End of first year	20,000	$3,600	$ 3,600	16,400
End of second year	20,000	3,600	7,200	12,800
End of third year	20,000	3,600	10,800	9,200
End of fourth year	20,000	3,600	14,400	5,600
End of fifth year	20,000	3,600	18,000	2,000

© Cengage Learning 2014

Production Method

Method The **production method** (or *units of production method*) is based on the assumption that depreciation is solely the result of use and that the passage of time plays no role in the process. The production method is appropriate when a company has widely fluctuating rates of production. For example, carpet mills often close during the first two weeks in July but may run double shifts in September. With the production method, depreciation would be in direct relation to a mill's units of output.

Formula Under the production method, depreciation is calculated as follows.

$$\text{Depreciation Expense} = \frac{\text{Cost} - \text{Residual Value}}{\text{Estimated Units of Useful Life}}$$

Example Assume that the delivery truck in the previous example has an estimated useful life of 90,000 miles. The depreciation cost per mile would be determined as follows.

$$\frac{\text{Depreciation}}{\text{Expense}} = \frac{\text{Cost} - \text{Residual Value}}{\text{Estimated Units of Useful Life}} = \frac{\$20,000 - \$2,000}{90,000} = \$0.20 \text{ per Mile}$$

If the truck were driven 20,000 miles in the first year, 30,000 miles in the second, 10,000 miles in the third, 20,000 miles in the fourth, and 10,000 miles in the fifth, the depreciation schedule for the truck would be as shown in Exhibit 5. As you can see, the amount of depreciation each year is directly related to the units of use. The carrying value decreases each year until it reaches the estimated residual value.

Exhibit 5
Depreciation Schedule, Production Method

	Cost	Miles	Annual Depreciation	Accumulated Depreciation	Carrying Value
Date of purchase	$20,000	—	—	—	$20,000
End of first year	20,000	20,000	$4,000	$ 4,000	16,000
End of second year	20,000	30,000	6,000	10,000	10,000
End of third year	20,000	10,000	2,000	12,000	8,000
End of fourth year	20,000	20,000	4,000	16,000	4,000
End of fifth year	20,000	10,000	2,000	18,000	2,000

© Cengage Learning 2014

In considering whether to use the production method, it is important to keep the following points in mind:

- It must be possible to estimate with reasonable accuracy the output of an asset over its useful life.
- The unit used to measure the estimated useful life of an asset must be appropriate for the asset.

Declining-Balance Method An **accelerated method** of depreciation results in relatively large amounts of depreciation in the early years of an asset's life and smaller amounts in later years. This type of method is based on the assumption that many plant assets are most efficient when new and so provide the greatest benefits in their first years.

Under an accelerated method, depreciation charges will be highest in years when revenue generation from the asset is highest. Fast-changing technologies often cause equipment to become obsolete and lose service value rapidly. In addition, repair expense is likely to increase as an asset ages. In such cases, using an accelerated method is appropriate. Thus, the total of repair plus depreciation expense will remain fairly constant over the years.

Declining-Balance Method

Method The **declining-balance method** is the most common accelerated method of depreciation. With this method, depreciation is computed by applying a fixed rate to the declining carrying value of a long-term asset. It therefore results in higher depreciation charges in the early years of the asset's life. Though any fixed rate can be used, the most common rate is a percentage equal to twice the straight-line depreciation percentage. When this rate is used, the method is usually called the **double-declining-balance method**.

Example In our example of the straight-line method, the delivery truck had an estimated useful life of five years, and the annual depreciation rate for the truck was therefore 20 percent:

$$\text{Annual Depreciation Rate} = \frac{\text{Percent of Useful Life}}{\text{Estimated Useful Life}}$$

$$= \frac{100\%}{5 \text{ Years}}$$

$$= 20\%$$

Declining-Balance Depreciation Rate = 2 × 20% = 40%

STUDY NOTE: *The double-declining-balance method is the only method presented here in which the residual value is not deducted before calculating depreciation.*

Under the double-declining-balance method, the fixed rate would be 40 percent, or "double" the straight-line rate.

This rate is applied to the carrying value at the end of the previous year. With this method, the depreciation schedule would be as shown in Exhibit 6.

Exhibit 6
Depreciation Schedule, Double-Declining-Balance Method

	Cost	Annual Depreciation	Accumulated Depreciation	Carrying Value
Date of purchase	$20,000	—	—	$20,000
End of first year	20,000	(40% × $20,000) = $8,000	$ 8,000	12,000
End of second year	20,000	(40% × $12,000) = 4,800	12,800	7,200
End of third year	20,000	(40% × $ 7,200) = 2,880	15,680	4,320
End of fourth year	20,000	(40% × $ 4,320) = 1,728	17,408	2,592
End of fifth year	20,000	592*	18,000	2,000

*Depreciation is limited to the amount necessary to reduce carrying value to residual value: $2,592 (previous carrying value) − $2,000 (residual value) = $592.

© Cengage Learning 2014

Comparison of the Three Methods Exhibit 7 compares yearly depreciation and carrying value under the three methods. The graph on the left shows yearly depreciation.

- Straight-line depreciation is uniform at $3,600 per year over the 5-year period.
- The double-declining-balance method begins at $8,000 and decreases each year to amounts that are less than straight-line (ultimately, $592).
- The production method does not generate a regular pattern because of the random fluctuation of the depreciation from year to year.

The graph on the right side of Exhibit 7 shows the carrying value under the three methods. Each method starts in the same place (cost of $20,000) and ends at the same place (residual value of $2,000). However, the patterns of carrying value during the asset's useful life differ. For instance, the carrying value under the straight-line method is always greater than under the double-declining-balance method, except at the beginning and end of the asset's useful life.

Exhibit 7

Graphic Comparison of Three Methods of Determining Depreciation

Methods

— Straight-line   — Production   — Double-declining-balance

© Cengage Learning 2014

Business Perspective
Accelerated Methods Save Money!

As shown in the graph below, an AICPA study of 500 large companies found that the overwhelming majority used the straight-line method of depreciation for financial reporting. Only about 5 percent used some type of accelerated method, and 3 percent used the production method. However, these figures tend to be misleading about the importance of accelerated depreciation methods. Federal income tax laws allow either the straight-line method or an accelerated method, and, for tax purposes, about 75 percent of the 500 companies studied preferred an accelerated method. The straight-line method can be advantageous for financial reporting because it can produce the highest net income, and an accelerated method can be beneficial for tax purposes because it can result in lower income taxes.

Note: Calculation more than 100% due to companies using more than one method.

Source: "Depreciation Methods Used by 600 Large Companies for Financial Reporting." Copyright © 2011 by AICPA. Reproduced with permission.

© Alija / iStockphoto.com

Special Issues in Determining Depreciation

Other issues in depreciating assets include group depreciation, depreciation for partial years, revision of depreciation rates, and accelerated cost recovery for tax purposes.

Group Depreciation The estimated useful life of an asset is the average length of time assets of the same type are expected to last. For example, the average useful life of a particular type of machine may be six years. However, some machines in this category may last only two or three years, while others may last eight or nine years or longer. For this reason, and for convenience, large companies group similar assets, such as machines, to calculate depreciation. A survey of large businesses indicated that 67 percent used this method, called **group depreciation**, for all or part of their plant assets.[6]

Depreciation for Partial Years To simplify our examples of depreciation, we have assumed that plant assets were purchased at the beginning or end of a period. However, the time of year is normally not a factor in the decision to buy or sell assets. Thus, it is often necessary to calculate depreciation for partial years. Some companies compute depreciation to the nearest month. Others use the half-year convention, in which one-half year of depreciation is taken in the year the asset is purchased and one-half year is taken in the last year of the asset's life.

Revision of Depreciation Rates The periodic depreciation charge is seldom precise. Sometimes, the estimate of useful life is revised, so that the periodic depreciation expense increases or decreases over the asset's remaining useful life. For example, suppose a delivery truck cost $14,000 and has a residual value of $2,000. The truck was expected to last six years, and it was depreciated on the straight-line basis. However, after two years of intensive use, it is determined that the truck will last only two more years, but its residual value at the end of the two years will still be $2,000. At the end of the second year, the asset account and its related accumulated depreciation account would be as follows.

Delivery Truck				Accumulated Depreciation—Delivery Truck		
	Dr.		Cr.		Dr.	Cr.
Cost	14,000					Depreciation, Year 1 2,000
						Depreciation, Year 2 2,000

The remaining depreciable cost is computed as follows.

Cost − Depreciation Already Taken − Residual Value = Depreciable Cost

$$\$14{,}000 - \$4{,}000 - \$2{,}000 = \$8{,}000$$

The new annual periodic depreciation charge is computed by dividing the remaining depreciable cost of $8,000 by the remaining useful life of two years. Therefore, the new periodic depreciation charge is $4,000.[7]

Special Rules for Tax Purposes Over the years, Congress has revised the federal income tax law to encourage businesses to invest in new plant and equipment. For instance, the tax law allows rapid write-offs of plant assets, which differs considerably from the depreciation methods most companies use for financial reporting. Tax methods of depreciation are usually not acceptable for financial reporting because the periods over which deductions may be taken are often shorter than the assets' estimated useful lives. A change in the federal income tax law—the result of the **Economic Stimulus Act of 2008**—allows a small company to expense the first $250,000 of equipment expenditures rather than record them as assets and depreciate them over their useful lives. Also, for assets that are subject to depreciation, there is a bonus first-year deduction.

APPLY IT! ▶

On January 13, 2014, Miko Company purchased a company car for $47,500. Miko expects the car to last five years or 120,000 miles, with an estimated residual value of $7,500. During 2015, the car is driven 27,000 miles. Miko's year-end is December 31. Compute the depreciation for 2015 under each of the following methods: (1) straight-line, (2) production, and (3) double-declining-balance. Using the amount computed in (3), prepare the journal entry to record depreciation expense for the second year and compute carrying value of the company car as it would appear on the balance sheet.

SOLUTION

Depreciation computed:

1. Straight-line method: ($47,500 − $7,500) ÷ 5 years = $8,000
2. Production method: ($47,500 − $7,500) ÷ 120,000 miles = $0.3333 per mile

$$27,000 \text{ miles} \times \$0.3333 = \$9,000*$$

3. Double-declining-balance method: (1 ÷ 5) × 2 = 0.40

   2014: $47,500 × 0.40 = $19,000

   2015: ($47,500 − $19,000) × 0.40 = $11,400
   * Rounded

Journal entry:

Depreciation Expense	11,400	
Accumulated Depreciation		11,400
To record depreciation of car: ($47,500 − $19,000) × 0.40		

Balance sheet carrying value:

Company car	$47,500	
Less accumulated depreciation	30,400	$17,100

TRY IT! SE3, SE4, SE5, E4A, E5A, E6A, E7A, E4B, E5B, E6B, E7B

LO 4 Disposal of Depreciable Assets

When plant assets, like buildings and equipment, are no longer useful because they have physically deteriorated or become obsolete, a company can:

- Discard them
- Sell them
- Trade them in on the purchase of a new asset

Regardless of how a company disposes of a plant asset, it must record depreciation expense for the partial year up to the date of disposal. This step is required because the company used the asset until that date and, under accrual accounting, the accounting period should receive the proper allocation of depreciation expense.

To illustrate how a company records each type of disposal, we will use BTL Company.

> **STUDY NOTE:** *When a company disposes of an asset, it must bring the depreciation up to date and remove all evidence of ownership of the asset, including the contra account Accumulated Depreciation.*

Discarded Plant Assets

If an asset remains in use beyond the end of its estimated life, its cost and accumulated depreciation remain in the ledger accounts. Thus, proper records will be available for maintaining control over plant assets. If the residual value is zero, the carrying value of a fully depreciated asset is zero. When the asset is discarded, no gain or loss results. For assets with a carrying value, however, a loss equal to the carrying value should be recorded.

Discarding Assets with a Carrying Value

Transaction BTL purchases a machine on January 2, 2014, for $13,000 and plans to depreciate it on a straight-line basis over an estimated useful life of eight years. The machine's residual value at the end of eight years is estimated to be $600. On December 31, 2019, the balances of the relevant accounts are as shown below. On January 2, 2020, management disposes of the asset.

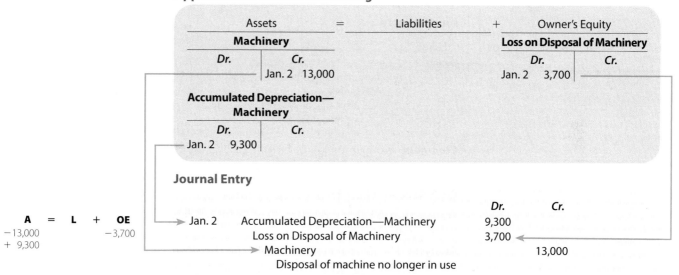

Machinery			Accumulated Depreciation— Machinery		
Dr.		Cr.	Dr.		Cr.
13,000					9,300

The discarded equipment has a carrying value of $3,700 at the time of its disposal ($13,000 less accumulated depreciation of $9,300).

Analysis A loss equal to the carrying value should be recorded. This journal entry

▼ *decreases* the asset *Machinery* with a credit

▼ *decreases* Machinery's related *Accumulated Depreciation* with a debit

▲ *increases* the *Loss on Disposal of Machinery* account with a debit

Application of Accrual Accounting

Assets		= Liabilities +	Owner's Equity	
Machinery			**Loss on Disposal of Machinery**	
Dr.	Cr.		Dr.	Cr.
	Jan. 2 13,000		Jan. 2 3,700	
Accumulated Depreciation— Machinery				
Dr.	Cr.			
Jan. 2 9,300				

Journal Entry

		Dr.	Cr.
A = L + OE	Jan. 2 Accumulated Depreciation—Machinery	9,300	
−13,000 −3,700	Loss on Disposal of Machinery	3,700	
+ 9,300	Machinery		13,000
	Disposal of machine no longer in use		

Comment *Recognized* gains and losses on disposals of plant assets are *classified* as other revenues and expenses on the income statement.

Plant Assets Sold for Cash

The entry to record a plant asset sold for cash is similar to the one just illustrated, except that the receipt of cash should also be recorded. The following entries show how to record the sale of a machine at three different selling prices.

Cash Received Equal to Carrying Value

Transaction $3,700 cash is received and is exactly equal to the $3,700 carrying value of the machine.

Analysis The journal entry to record the sale of an asset at carrying value

▼ *decreases* the *Machinery* account and the *Accumulated Depreciation* account

▲ *increases* the *Cash* account

Application of Double Entry

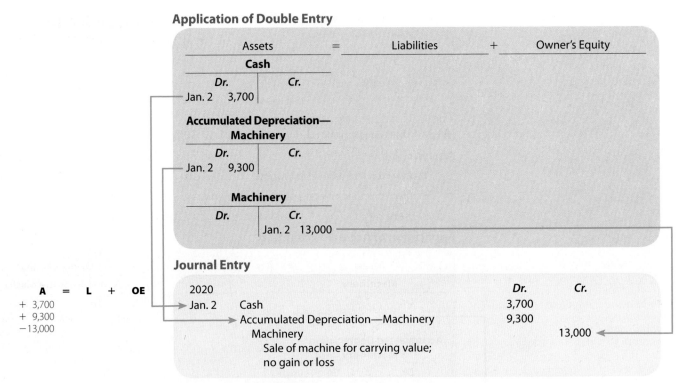

Journal Entry

A = L + OE
+ 3,700
+ 9,300
− 13,000

2020		Dr.	Cr.
Jan. 2	Cash	3,700	
	Accumulated Depreciation—Machinery	9,300	
	Machinery		13,000
	Sale of machine for carrying value; no gain or loss		

Comment No gain or loss is *recognized* because the amount of cash is exactly equal to the carrying value of the machinery being sold.

Cash Received Less Than Carrying Value

Transaction $2,000 cash is received, which is less than the carrying value of $3,700, resulting in a loss of $1,700.

Analysis The journal entry to record the sale of an asset at less than carrying amount

▼ *decreases* the *Machinery* account and the *Accumulated Depreciation* account

▲ *increases* the *Cash* account

▲ *increases* the *Loss on Sale of Machinery* account for the difference

Application of Double Entry

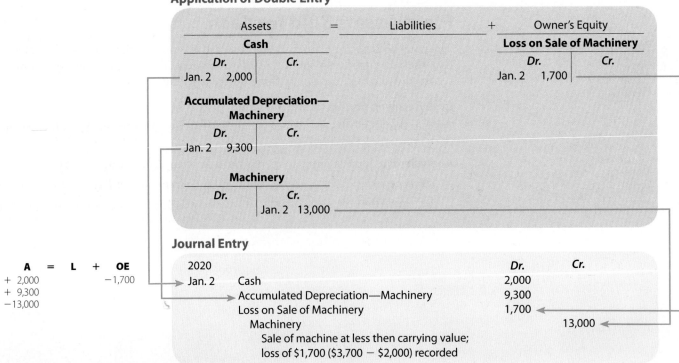

Journal Entry

A = L + OE
+ 2,000   − 1,700
+ 9,300
− 13,000

2020		Dr.	Cr.
Jan. 2	Cash	2,000	
	Accumulated Depreciation—Machinery	9,300	
	Loss on Sale of Machinery	1,700	
	Machinery		13,000
	Sale of machine at less then carrying value; loss of $1,700 ($3,700 − $2,000) recorded		

Comment A loss is *recognized* because the amount of cash is less than the carrying value of the machinery being sold.

Cash Received More Than Carrying Value

Transaction $4,000 cash is received, which exceeds the carrying value of $3,700, resulting in a gain of $300.

Analysis The journal entry to record the sale of an asset at less than carrying amount

▼ *decreases* the *Machinery* account and the *Accumulated Depreciation* account

▲ *increases* the *Cash* account

▲ *increases* the *Gain on Sale of Machinery* account for the difference

Application of Double Entry

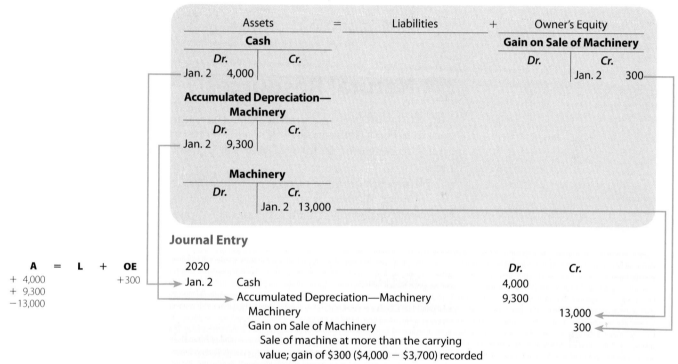

Journal Entry

A	=	L	+	OE
+ 4,000				+300
+ 9,300				
− 13,000				

2020		Dr.	Cr.
Jan. 2	Cash	4,000	
	Accumulated Depreciation—Machinery	9,300	
	Machinery		13,000
	Gain on Sale of Machinery		300
	Sale of machine at more than the carrying value; gain of $300 ($4,000 − $3,700) recorded		

Comment A gain is *recognized* because the amount of cash is more than the carrying value of the machinery being sold.

Exchanges of Plant Assets

Exchanges may involve similar assets, such as an old machine traded in on a newer model, or dissimilar assets, such as a cement mixer traded in on a truck. In either case, the purchase price is reduced by the amount of the trade-in allowance.

Basically, accounting for exchanges of plant assets is similar to accounting for sales of plant assets.

▲ If the trade-in allowance is greater than the asset's carrying value, the company realizes a gain.

▼ If the allowance is less, it suffers a loss.[8]

APPLY IT!

On January 2, the first day of business of the current year, Kamila Company sold a car that cost $47,500 and on which $30,400 of accumulated depreciation had been recorded. For each of the following assumptions, prepare the journal entry (without explanation) for the disposal: (1) The car was sold for $17,100 cash. (2) The car was sold for $15,000 cash. (3) The car was sold for $20,000 cash.

SOLUTION

	Dr.	Cr.
1. Cash	17,100	
Accumulated Depreciation—Automobile	30,400	
Automobile		47,500
2. Cash	15,000	
Accumulated Depreciation—Automobile	30,400	
Loss on Sale of Automobile	2,100	
Automobile		47,500
3. Cash	20,000	
Accumulated Depreciation—Automobile	30,400	
Automobile		47,500
Gain on Sale of Automobile		2,900

TRY IT! SE6, E8A, E9A, E8B, E9B

LO 5 Natural Resources

Natural resources are long-term assets that appear on a balance sheet with descriptive titles like "Timberlands," "Oil and gas reserves," and "Mineral deposits." These assets are converted to inventory by cutting, pumping, mining, or other extraction methods.

Natural resources are recorded at acquisition cost, which may include some costs of development. As these resources are converted to inventory, their asset accounts must be proportionally reduced. For example, the carrying value of oil reserves on the balance sheet is reduced by the proportional cost of the barrels pumped during the period. The original cost of the oil reserves is thus gradually reduced, and depletion is recognized.

Depletion

Depletion refers not only to the exhaustion of a natural resource but also to the proportional allocation of the cost of a natural resource to the units extracted. The way in which the cost of a natural resource is allocated closely resembles the production method of calculating depreciation. When a natural resource is purchased or developed, the total units that will be available, such as tons of coal, must be estimated. The depletion cost per unit is computed as follows.

$$\text{Depletion Cost per Unit} = \frac{\text{Cost} - \text{Residual Value}}{\text{Estimated Number of Units}}$$

Depletion of a Natural Resource

Transaction A mine was purchased for $3,600,000. It has an estimated residual value of $600,000, and it contains an estimated 3,000,000 tons of coal. The depletion charge per ton of coal is $1, calculated as follows.

$$\text{Depletion Cost per Unit} = \frac{\text{Cost} - \text{Residual Value}}{\text{Estimated Number of Units}}$$

$$\frac{\$3,600,000 - \$600,000}{3,000,000 \text{ Tons}} = \$1 \text{ per Ton}$$

The amount of the depletion cost for each accounting period is then computed by multiplying the depletion cost per unit by the number of units extracted and sold. Thus, if 230,000 tons of coal are mined and sold during the first year, the depletion charge for the year is $230,000.

Analysis The journal entry to record the depletion of a natural resource

▲ *increases* the *Depletion Expense* account

▲ *increases* the *Accumulated Depletion* account

Application of Double Entry

	Assets	=	Liabilities	+	Owner's Equity	
	Accumulated Depletion—Coal Deposits				**Depletion Expense—Coal Deposits**	
Dr.	Cr.				Dr.	Cr.
	Dec. 31 230,000				Dec. 31 230,000	

Journal Entry

			Dr.	Cr.
Dec. 31	Depletion Expense—Coal Deposits		230,000	
	Accumulated Depletion—Coal Deposits			230,000
	To record depletion of coal mine:			
	$1 per ton for 230,000 tons mined and sold			

A = L + OE
−230,000   −230,000

On the balance sheet, data for the mine would be presented as follows.

Coal deposits	$3,600,000	
Less accumulated depletion	230,000	$3,370,000

Comment If a natural resource is not sold in the year it is extracted, it is reported as inventory. It would be *recorded* as a depletion *expense* in the year it is *sold*.

Depreciation of Plant Assets Related to Natural Resources

The extraction of natural resources generally requires special on-site buildings and equipment (e.g., conveyors, drills, and pumps). The useful life of these plant assets may be longer than the estimated time it will take to deplete the resources. However, a company may plan to abandon these assets after all the resources have been extracted because they no longer serve a useful purpose. In this case, they should be depreciated on the same basis as the depletion.

For example, suppose machinery with a useful life of ten years is installed on an oil field that is expected to be depleted in eight years. The machinery should be depreciated over the eight-year period, using the production method. That way, each year's depreciation will be proportional to the year's depletion.[9]

Development and Exploration Costs in the Oil and Gas Industry

The costs of exploring and developing oil and gas resources can be accounted for under one of two methods: successful efforts or full costing. The Financial Accounting Standards Board permits the use of either method.[10]

Successful Efforts Accounting Under **successful efforts accounting**, the cost of successful exploration—for example, an exploration that produces an oil well—is a cost of the resource. It should be recorded as an asset and depleted over the resource's estimated life. The cost of an unsuccessful exploration—such as one that produces a dry well—is written off immediately as a loss. Because of these immediate write-offs, successful efforts accounting is considered the more conservative method and is used by most large oil companies.

Business Perspective
How Do You Measure What's Underground? With a Good Guess.

Accounting standards require publicly traded energy companies to *disclose* in their annual reports their production activities, estimates of their proven oil and gas reserves, and estimates of the future cash flows those reserves are expected to generate. Since the reserves are often miles underground or beneath deep water, these figures are considered "supplementary" and not reliable enough to be audited independently. As a result, some companies have overestimated their reserves and, thus, overestimated their future prospects. Apparently, some managers at **Royal Dutch/Shell Group** were receiving bonuses based on the amount of new reserves added to the annual report. When the company announced that it was reducing its reported reserves by 20 percent, the price of its stock dropped.[11]

Full-Costing Method Small, independent oil companies argue that the cost of dry wells is part of the overall cost of the systematic development of an oil field and is, thus, a part of the cost of producing wells. Under the **full-costing method**, all costs, including the cost of dry wells, are recorded as assets and depleted over the estimated life of the resources. This method tends to improve a company's earnings performance in its early years.

APPLY IT!

Sharp Mining Company paid $8,800,000 for land containing an estimated 40 million tons of ore. The land without the ore is estimated to be worth $2,000,000. The company spent $1,380,000 to erect buildings on the site and $2,400,000 on equipment installed on site. The buildings have an estimated useful life of 30 years, and the equipment has an estimated useful life of 10 years. Neither the buildings nor the equipment has a residual value. The company expects to mine all the usable ore in 10 years. During its first year of operation, it mined and sold 2,800,000 tons of ore.

1. Compute the depletion charge per ton.
2. Compute the depletion expense that Sharp Mining should record for its first year of operation.
3. Determine the depreciation expense for the year for the buildings, making it proportional to the depletion.
4. Determine the depreciation expense for the year for the equipment, using two alternatives:
   (a) making the expense proportional to the depletion, and
   (b) using the straight-line method.

SOLUTION

1. $\dfrac{\$8,800,000 - \$2,000,000}{40,000,000 \text{ tons}} = \$0.17 \text{ per ton}$

2. $2,800,000 \text{ tons} \times \$0.17 \text{ per ton} = \$476,000$

3. $\dfrac{2,800,000 \text{ tons}}{40,000,000 \text{ tons}} \times \$1,380,000 = \$96,600$

4. a. $\dfrac{2,800,000 \text{ tons}}{40,000,000 \text{ tons}} \times \$2,400,000 = \$168,000$

   b. $\dfrac{\$2,400,000}{10 \text{ years}} \times 1 \text{ year} = \$240,000$

TRY IT! SE7, E10A, E10B

LO 6 Intangible Assets

An intangible asset is both long-term and nonphysical. Its value comes from the long-term rights it affords its owner. Exhibit 8 describes the following most common types of intangible assets and their accounting treatment. Like intangible assets, some current assets—for example, accounts receivable and certain prepaid expenses—have no physical substance; but because they are short-term, they are not classified as intangible assets.

© Alija / iStockphoto.com

Exhibit 8
Accounting for Intangible Assets

Type	Description	Usual Accounting Treatment
Subject to Amortization and Annual Impairment Test		
Copyright	An exclusive right granted by the federal government to reproduce and sell literary, musical, and other artistic materials and computer programs for a period of the author's life plus 70 years.	Record at acquisition cost, and amortize over the asset's useful life, which is often much shorter than its legal life. For example, the cost of paperback rights to a popular novel would typically be amortized over a useful life of 2 to 4 years.
Patent	An exclusive right granted by the federal government for a period of 20 years to make a particular product or use a specific process. A design may be granted a patent for 14 years.	The cost of successfully defending a patent in a patent infringement suit is added to the acquisition cost of the patent. Amortize over the asset's useful life, which may be less than its legal life.
Leasehold	A right to occupy land or buildings under a long-term rental contract. For example, if Company A sells or subleases its right to use a retail location to Company B for 10 years in return for one or more rental payments, Company B has purchased a leasehold.	The lessor (Company A) debits Leasehold for the amount of the rental payment and amortizes it over the remaining life of the lease. The lessee (Company B) debits payments to Lease Expense.
Software	Capitalized costs of computer programs developed for sale, lease, or internal use.	Record the amount of capitalizable production costs, and amortize over the estimated economic life of the product.
Noncompete covenant	A contract limiting the rights of others to compete in a specific industry or line of business for a specified period.	Record at acquisition cost, and amortize over the contract period.
Franchise, License	A right to an exclusive territory or market or the right to use a formula, technique, process, or design.	Debit Franchise or License for the acquisition cost, and amortize it over a reasonable life.
Customer list	A list of customers or subscribers.	Debit Customer List for amount paid, and amortize over the asset's expected life.
Subject to Annual Impairment Test Only		
Goodwill	The excess of the amount paid for a business over the fair market value of the business's net assets.	Debit Goodwill for the acquisition cost, and review impairment annually.
Trademark, Brand name	A registered symbol or name that can be used only by its owner to identify a product or service.	Debit Trademark or Brand Name for the acquisition cost, and review impairment annually.

Exhibit 9 shows the percentage of companies (out of those surveyed) that report various intangible assets. For some companies, intangible assets make up a substantial portion of total assets. For example, **Apple**'s goodwill and other acquired intangible assets amounted to $4.4 billion in 2011. How these assets are accounted for has a major effect on Apple's performance. For example, acquired intangible assets are amortized over six years, and amortization expenses for these costs amounted to $192 million in 2011.

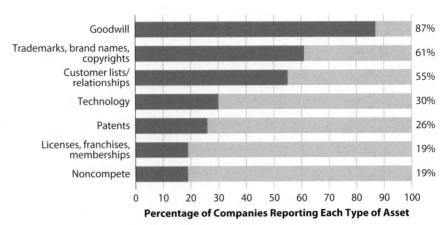

Exhibit 9
Assets Reported by
Large Companies

Goodwill	87%
Trademarks, brand names, copyrights	61%
Customer lists/relationships	55%
Technology	30%
Patents	26%
Licenses, franchises, memberships	19%
Noncompete	19%

0   10   20   30   40   50   60   70   80   90   100

Percentage of Companies Reporting Each Type of Asset

Source: Data from American Institute of Certified Public Accountants, *Accounting Trends & Techniques* (New York: AICPA, 2011).

The purchase of an intangible asset is a special kind of capital expenditure. Such assets are accounted for at the amount that a company paid for them. Some intangible assets, such as goodwill and trademarks, may be acquired at little or no cost. Even though these assets may have great value and may be needed for profitable operations, a company should include them on its balance sheet only if it purchased them from another party at a price established in the marketplace. When a company develops its own intangible assets, it should record the costs of development as expenses. An exception is the cost of internally developed computer software after a working prototype of the software has been developed.

Purchased intangible assets are recorded at cost or at fair value when purchased as part of a group of assets. The useful life of an intangible asset is the period over which the asset is expected to contribute to the company's future cash flows. The useful life may be definite or indefinite.[12]

■ **Definite useful life:** A definite useful life is subject to a legal limit or can be reasonably estimated. Examples include patents, copyrights, and leaseholds. The estimated useful lives of these assets are often less than their legal limits. The cost of an intangible asset with a definite useful life should be allocated to expense through periodic amortization.

■ **Indefinite useful life:** An indefinite useful life is not limited by legal, regulatory, contractual, competitive, economic, or other factors. This definition does not imply that these assets last forever. Examples can include trademarks and brands, which can last for as short or as long as the company is successful in using them. The costs of intangible assets with an indefinite life are not amortized as long as circumstances continue to support an indefinite life.

All intangible assets, whether definite or indefinite, are subject to an annual impairment test to determine if the assets justify their value on the balance sheet. If they have lost some or all of their value in producing future cash flows, they should be written down to their fair value or to zero if they have no fair value. The amount of the write-down is

Business Perspective
Who's Number One in Brands?

Brands are intangible assets that often do not appear on a company's balance sheet because, rather than purchasing them, the company has developed them over time. According to one report, the 10 most valuable brands were:[13]

Apple	Coca-Cola
Google	AT&T
IBM	Marlboro
McDonald's	China Mobile
Microsoft	GE

Apple's brand was valued at almost $153 billion, whereas GE's brand was valued at $50 billion.

shown on the income statement as an impairment charge (deduction) in determining income from operations.

To illustrate accounting for intangible assets with limited useful lives, suppose Soda Bottling Company purchases a patent on a unique bottle cap for $36,000. The purchase would be recorded with an entry of $36,000 in the asset Patents.[14] Although the patent for the bottle cap will last for 20 years, Soda determines that it will sell the product that uses the cap for only six years. Thus, the annual amortization expense is $6,000 ($36,000 ÷ 6 years). When the expense is recorded, the Patents account is reduced directly by the amount of the amortization expense (in contrast to the treatment of other long-term assets, for which depreciation or depletion is accumulated in separate contra accounts). The journal entry would be as follows.

A	**=**	**L**	**+**	**OE**					
−6,000				−6,000	Dec. 31	Amortization Expense—Patents		6,000	
						Patents			6,000
						To record amortization of patient			

Research and Development Costs

Most successful companies carry out research and development (R&D) activities, often within a separate department. Among these activities are development of new products, testing of existing and proposed products, and pure research. The costs of these activities are substantial for many companies. In a recent year, **General Motors** spent $8.1 billion, or about 5.4 percent of its revenues, on R&D.[15] R&D costs can be even greater in high-tech fields like pharmaceuticals. For example, **Abbott Laboratories** recently spent $4.1 billion, or 10.6 percent of its revenues, on R&D.[16]

The Financial Accounting Standards Board requires that all R&D costs be charged to expense in the period in which they are incurred.[17] The reasoning is that it is too hard to trace specific costs to specific profitable developments. Also, the costs of research and development are continuous and necessary for the success of a business and so should be treated as current expenses.

Computer Software Costs

The costs that companies incur in developing computer software for sale or lease or for their own internal use are considered research and development costs until the product has proved feasible. Thus, costs incurred before that point should be charged to expense as they are incurred. A product is deemed feasible when a detailed working program has been designed. Once that occurs, all software production costs are recorded as assets and are amortized over the software's estimated economic life, using the straight-line method. If at any time a company cannot expect to realize the amount of the unamortized software costs, the asset should be written down to the amount expected to be realized.[18]

International Perspective
IFRS R&D Costs Under IFRS

In contrast to GAAP, under which all research and development costs are expensed, IFRS require that research costs be expensed and that development costs be capitalized and amortized. This requires a judgment about what constitutes research and what constitutes development. These differences in accounting treatments—immediate expensing versus amortization over time—can have considerable impact on reported income over many years.

Goodwill

Goodwill generally refers to a company's good reputation. From an accounting standpoint, goodwill exists when a purchaser pays more for a business than the fair market value of the business's net assets. In other words, the purchaser would pay less if it bought the assets separately. Most businesses are worth more as going concerns than as collections of assets.

Goodwill reflects all the factors that allow a company to earn a higher-than-market rate of return on its assets, including:

- Customer satisfaction
- Good management
- Manufacturing efficiency
- The advantages of having a monopoly
- Good locations
- Good employee relations

The FASB requires that purchased goodwill be reported as a separate line item on the balance sheet and that it be reviewed annually for impairment. If the fair value of goodwill is less than its carrying value, it is considered impaired. In that case, it is reduced to its fair value, and the impairment charge is reported on the income statement.[19]

A company should record goodwill only when it acquires a controlling interest in another business. The amount to be recorded as goodwill can be determined by writing the identifiable net assets up to their fair market values at the time of purchase and subtracting the total from the purchase price. For example, suppose a company pays $11,400,000 to purchase another business.

- If the net assets of the business (total assets − total liabilities) are *fairly valued* at $10,000,000, the amount of the goodwill is $1,400,000 ($11,400,000 − $10,000,000).
- If the fair market value of the net assets is more or less than $10,000,000, an entry is made in the accounting records to adjust the assets to the fair market value. The goodwill would then represent the difference between the adjusted net assets and the purchase price of $11,400,000.

Long-Term Assets and the Financial Statements

Exhibit 10 shows that purchase, use, and disposal of long-term assets affect all financial statements. As you can see, the acquisition cost of long-term assets increases by the amount of capital expenditures and accumulated depreciation increases by the amount of depreciation expense.

Business Perspective

Wake up! Goodwill Is Growing!

Eighty-nine percent of 500 large companies separately report goodwill as an asset.[20] Because much of the growth of these companies has come through purchasing other companies, goodwill as a percentage of total assets has also grown. As shown right, the amount of goodwill can be material.[21]

	Goodwill (in billions)	Percentage of Total Assets
General Mills	$ 8,205	38%
Heinz	$ 3,298	32%
Cisco Systems	$16,823	19%

Exhibit 10
Relationship of Long-Term Assets
to the Financial Statements

APPLY IT!

For each of the following intangible assets, indicate (a) if the asset is to be amortized over its useful life or (b) if the asset is not amortized but only subject to annual impairment test:

1. Goodwill
2. Copyright
3. Brand name
4. Patent
5. Trademark

SOLUTION

1. b;   2. a;   3. b;   4. a;   5. b

TRY IT! SE8, E11A, E12A, E11B, E12B

BUSINESS APPLICATIONS

RELEVANT LEARNING OBJECTIVE

LO 7 Describe the disclosure of acquiring and financing long-term assets, and calculate free cash flow.

LO 7 Management Decisions Relating to Long-Term Assets

The decision to acquire and finance a long-term asset is a complex process. Although some companies are profitable enough to pay for long-term assets out of cash flows from operations, for major long-term acquisitions of long-term assets, a company may need to finance them with the issue of stock, long-term notes, or bonds.

CASH FLOW **Acquiring and Financing Long-Term Assets**

A good place to study a company's investing and financing activities is its statement of cash flows and in the *disclosures* in the notes to the financial statements. For example, **Apple**'s decision to establish retail stores required very careful analysis. Evaluating data to make sound decisions about acquiring long-term assets is part of the capital budgeting process, a topic covered in detail in managerial accounting texts. However, information about acquisitions of long-term assets appears in the investing activities section of the statement of cash flows. The investing section of Apple's statement of cash flows in its 2011 annual report shows acquisition of property, plant, and equipment to be $4.3 billion in 2011. Apple's management reveals the portion of this amount spent on retail stores in 2011 and it's plans for 2012 in the notes, as follows:

> *The Company's actual cash payments for capital expenditures during 2011 were $4.3 billion, of which $612 million relates to retail store facilities. . . . The Company anticipates utilizing approximately $8.0 billion for capital expenditures during 2012, including approximately $900 million for retail store facilities and approximately $7.1 billion for product tooling and manufacturing process equipment, and corporate facilities and infrastructure, including information systems hardware, software and enhancements.*

The financing section of Apple's statement of cash flows reveals that the company raised $813 million through the issuance of common stock in 2011. Since this is much less than the $4.3 billion in acquisitions, the company must have used funds it already had from its operations. A measure of the company's success in funding these acquisitions is free cash flow, discussed in the next section.

Free Cash Flow Although not a financial ratio, **free cash flow** is an important measure of a company's ability to finance long-term assets. It is the amount of cash that remains after deducting the funds a company must commit to continue operating at its planned level. These commitments include:

■ Current or continuing operations
■ Interest
■ Income taxes
■ Dividends
■ Net capital expenditures (purchases of plant assets minus sales of plant assets)

If a company fails to pay for current or continuing operations, interest, and income taxes, its creditors or the government can take legal action. Although the payment of dividends is not required, dividends represent a commitment to stockholders. If they are reduced or eliminated, stockholders may be unhappy, which will cause the price of the company's stock to fall.

A positive free cash flow means that a company has met all its cash commitments and has cash available to reduce debt or to expand operations. A negative free cash flow means that it will have to sell investments, borrow money, or issue stock to continue at its planned level. If its free cash flow remains negative for several years, a company may not be able to raise cash by issuing stock or bonds.

Using data from **Apple**'s statement of cash flows in its 2011 annual report, we can compute the company's free cash flow as follows (in millions).

$$\text{Free Cash Flow} = \text{Net Cash Flows from Operating Activities} - \text{Dividends}$$
$$- \text{Purchases of Plant Assets} + \text{Sales of Plant Assets}$$
$$= \$37,529 - \$0 - \$4,260 + \$0$$
$$= \$33,269$$

This analysis confirms Apple's strong financial position. Its cash flow from operating activities far exceeded its net capital expenditures of $4,260 million. A factor in its positive free cash flow of $33,269 million is that the company pays no dividends. In addition, the financing activities section of Apple's statement of cash flows indicates that the company, rather than incurring debt for expansion, actually made net investments of $32,464 million.

Ethics in Acquiring and Financing Long-Term Assets

When a company records a long-term asset, it defers some of the asset's cost to later periods. Thus, the current period's profitability looks better than it would have if the asset's total cost had been expensed immediately. Management has considerable latitude in making the judgments and estimates necessary to account for long-term assets, and this latitude has sometimes been used unethically. For example, in the **WorldCom** accounting fraud, management ordered that expenditures that should have been recorded as operating expenses be recorded as long-term assets and written off over several years. The result was an overstatement of income by about $10 billion, which ultimately led to one of the largest bankruptcies in the history of U.S. business.

To avoid fraudulent reporting of long-term assets, a company's management must apply accrual accounting in resolving properly two important issues:

■ The amount of the total cost of a long-term asset to allocate to expense in the current period.
■ The amount to retain on the balance sheet as an asset.

To resolve these issues, management must answer four important questions about the acquisition, use, and disposal of each long-term asset. These questions are illustrated in Exhibit 11.

Exhibit 11
Issues in Accounting for Long-Term Assets

© Cengage Learning 2014

1. How is the cost of the long-term asset determined?
2. How should the expired portion of the cost of the long-term asset be allocated against revenues over time?
3. How should subsequent expenditures, such as repairs and additions, be treated?
4. How should disposal of the long-term asset be recorded?

Management's answers to these questions can be found in the company's annual report under management's discussion and analysis and in the notes to the financial statements.

APPLY IT!

In the past year, Bivak Company had net cash flows of $133,000 from operating activities. It expended $61,000 for property, plant, and equipment; sold property, plant, and equipment for $14,000; and paid dividends of $20,000. Calculate the company's free cash flow. What does the result tell you about the company?

SOLUTION

Net cash flows from operating activities	$133,000
Purchases of property, plant, and equipment	(61,000)
Sales of property, plant, and equipment	14,000
Dividends	(20,000)
Free cash flow	$ 66,000

Bivak's operations provide sufficient cash flows to fund its current expansion and its payment of dividends without raising additional capital.

TRY IT! SE9, SE10, E13A, E14A, E13B, E14B

TriLevel Problem

Neighborhood Carriers

The beginning of this chapter focused on Neighborhood Carriers, a company that had a choice to make about which depreciation method it would use in allocating the cost of its delivery van over a 5-year period. In addition to its delivery van, Neighborhood Carriers' plant assets might include land, buildings, and equipment, as well as leasehold improvements if it operates out of a rented space. All these assets would be depreciated. Neighborhood Carriers might also have intangible assets, such as a trademark, which would be amortized. In accounting for its delivery van, Neighborhood Carriers would have to determine the purchase price, useful life, residual value, and costs of repairs, maintenance, and other expenses. The company could use any one of the three common methods of calculating depreciation. Complete the following requirements in order to answer the questions posed at the beginning of the chapter.

Section 1: Concepts
What is the classification of long-term assets, how are the assets valued, and what is the distinction in recognizing capital and revenue expenditures?

Section 2: Accounting Applications
In what ways are the costs of long-term assets, such as a delivery van, allocated to the periods they benefit? Complete the following to answer this question:

1. Compute the depreciation expense and carrying value of the delivery van for 2014 to 2018 using the following methods: (a) straight-line, (b) production, and (c) double-declining-balance. The cost of the delivery van was $29,000, and its expected salvage value is $2,000. The expected production over the life of the delivery van is 150,000 units (30,000 in 2014; 52,500 in 2015; 45,000 in 2016; 15,000 in 2017; and 7,500 in 2018).

2. Assuming the straight-line method is used and that the delivery van is sold for $5,000 on December 31, 2018, show the entry to record the sale.

3. What conclusions can you draw from the patterns of yearly depreciation?

Section 3: Business Applications
How does management decide to acquire, finance, and evaluate long-term assets?

SOLUTION

Section 1: Concepts

Long-term assets are *classified* as property, plant, and equipment, natural resources, or intangible assets. Tangible assets have physical substance and, except for land, are subject to depreciation. Natural resources are assets extracted from the land and purchased for their economic value, which is subject to depletion. Finally, intangible assets have no physical substance and have a value that is based on legal rights or advantages accruing to their owners. Most intangible assets are subject to amortization. Depreciation, depletion, and amortization serve to *value* the assets on the balance sheet and apply *accrual accounting* to expenses on the income statement. Some intangible assets, including goodwill, are not amortized but are subject to an annual impairment test to determine if their fair value is below their carrying value.

Expenditures related to long-term assets are *recognized* either as capital expenditures or revenue expenditures. A capital expenditure is for the purchase or expansion of a long-term asset and is recorded in asset accounts because it benefits several future accounting periods. On the other hand, a revenue expenditure is for the ordinary repairs and maintenance needed to keep a long-term asset in good operating condition.

Section 2: Accounting Applications

1.

	A	B	C	D	E	F	G	H
1		**Depreciation**						**Carrying**
2		**Method**	**Year**	**Computation**			**Depreciation**	**Value**
3	a.	Straight-line	2014	$27,000	÷	5	$5,400	$23,600
4			2015	27,000	÷	5	5,400	18,200
5			2016	27,000	÷	5	5,400	12,800
6			2017	27,000	÷	5	5,400	7,400
7			2018	27,000	÷	5	5,400	2,000
8								
9-10	b.	Production	2014	$27,000	×	$\dfrac{30,000}{150,000}$	$5,400	$23,600
11								
12-13			2015	27,000	×	$\dfrac{52,500}{150,000}$	9,450	14,150
14								
15-16			2016	27,000	×	$\dfrac{45,000}{150,000}$	8,100	6,050
17								
18-19			2017	27,000	×	$\dfrac{15,000}{150,000}$	2,700	3,350
20								
21-22			2018	27,000	×	$\dfrac{7,500}{150,000}$	1,350	2,000
23								
24	c.	Double-	2014	$29,000	×	0.40	$11,600	$17,400
25		declining-	2015	17,400	×	0.40	6,960	10,440
26		balance	2016	10,440	×	0.40	4,176	6,264
27			2017	6,264	×	0.40	2,506*	3,758
28			2018	3,758	−	$2,000	1,758**	2,000
29		* Rounded						
30		** Remaining depreciation to reduce carrying value to residual value						
31		($3,758 − $2,000)						
32								

2. Dec. 31 Cash 5,000
          Accumulated Depreciation—Delivery Van 27,000
            Delivery Van 29,000
            Gain on Sale of Delivery Van 3,000
              To record the sale of delivery van

3. In the earlier years, the amount of depreciation under the double-declining-balance method is significantly greater than the amount under the straight-line method. In the later years, the opposite is true. The carrying value under the straight-line method is greater than under the double-declining-balance method at the end of all years except the fifth year. Depreciation under the production method differs from depreciation under the other methods in that it follows no regular pattern. It varies with the amount of use. Consequently, depreciation is greatest in 2015 and 2016, which are the years of greatest use.

Section 3: Business Applications

The decision to acquire a long-term asset involves determining if the company has sufficient funds to make the purchase and, if not, to obtain appropriate financing. A company can finance a long-term asset purchase with cash or by issuing stocks, long-term notes, or bonds. Management needs to analyze the company's statement of cash flows and calculate free cash flow as follows.

$$\text{Free Cash Flow} = \text{Net Cash Flows from Operating Activities} - \text{Dividends} - \text{Purchases of Plant Assets} + \text{Sales of Plant Assets}$$

Finally, when acquiring and recording long-term assets, the company needs to apply accrual accounting in deciding how to allocate the total cost of the asset to expense in the current period and over time (whether the purchase is a capital or revenue expenditure and choosing a deprecation method), how to treat subsequent expenditures (repair and maintenance, betterments, etc.), and how to record the disposal of the asset. These decisions will impact the long-term asset's value presented on the balance sheet as well as the net income amount in current and future periods.

Chapter Review

Identify the classifications of long-term assets, and describe how they are valued by allocating their costs to the periods that they benefit. | LO 1

Long-term assets have a useful life of more than one year, are used in the operation of a business, and are not intended for resale. They are classified as property, plant, and equipment; natural resources; or intangible assets. In the latter category are patents, trademarks, franchises, and other rights, as well as goodwill. Accrual accounting and valuation of long-term asset are applied through depreciation, depletion, amortization, or impairment tests, depending on the classification of the asset.

Capital expenditures are classifed as assets, whereas revenue expenditures are classified as expenses of the current period. Capital expenditures include not only outlays for plant assets, natural resources, and intangible assets, but also expenditures for additions, betterments, and extraordinary repairs that increase an asset's residual value or extend its useful life. Revenue expenditures are made for ordinary repairs and maintenance. The error of classifying a capital expenditure as a revenue expenditure, or vice versa, has an important effect on net income.

Account for the acquisition costs of property, plant, and equipment. **LO 2**

The acquisition cost of property, plant, and equipment includes all expenditures reasonable and necessary to get the asset in place and ready for use. Among these expenditures are the purchase price, installation cost, freight charges, and insurance during transit. The acquisition cost of a plant asset is allocated over the asset's useful life.

Compute depreciation under the straight-line, production, and declining-balance methods. **LO 3**

Depreciation—the periodic allocation of the cost of a plant asset over its estimated useful life—is commonly computed by using the straight-line method, the production method, or an accelerated method. The straight-line method is related directly to the passage of time, whereas the production method is related directly to use or output. An accelerated method, which results in relatively large amounts of depreciation in earlier years and reduced amounts in later years, is based on the assumption that plant assets provide greater economic benefits in their earlier years than in later ones. The most common accelerated method is the declining-balance method.

Account for the disposal of depreciable assets. **LO 4**

A company can dispose of a long-term plant asset by discarding or selling it or exchanging it for another asset. An asset being disposed of must have depreciation recorded up to the date of disposal. To record the disposal, the carrying value must be removed from the asset account and the depreciation to date must be removed from the accumulated depreciation account. When a company sells a depreciable long-term asset at a price that differs from its carrying value, it should report the gain or loss on its income statement. In recording exchanges of similar plant assets, a gain or loss may arise.

Identify the issues related to accounting for natural resources, and compute depletion. **LO 5**

Natural resources are depletable assets that are converted to inventory by cutting, pumping, mining, or other forms of extraction. They are recorded at cost as long-term assets. As natural resources are sold, their costs are allocated as expenses through depletion charges. The depletion charge is based on the ratio of the resource extracted to the total estimated resource. A major issue related to this subject is accounting for oil and gas reserves.

Identify the issues related to accounting for intangible assets, including research and development costs and goodwill. **LO 6**

The purchase of an intangible asset should be treated as a capital expenditure and recorded at acquisition cost. All intangible assets are subject to annual tests for impairment of value. Intangible assets with a definite life are also amortized annually. The FASB requires that research and development costs be expensed. Software costs are treated as research and development costs and expensed until a feasible working program is developed, after which time the costs may be capitalized and amortized over a reasonable estimated life. Goodwill is the excess of the amount paid for a business over the fair market value of the net assets and is usually related to the business's superior earning potential. It should be recorded only when a company purchases an entire business, and it should be reviewed annually for possible impairment.

Describe the disclosure of acquiring and financing long-term assets, and calculate free cash flow. **LO 7**

Information about the acquisition and financing of long-term assets is found in the statement of cash flows and in the disclosures in the notes to the financial statements. Free cash flow is the amount of cash that remains after deducting the funds a company must commit to continue operating at its planned level.

Key Terms

accelerated method 377 (LO3)
additions 370 (LO1)
amortization 368 (LO1)
asset impairment 369 (LO1)
betterments 370 (LO1)

brand name 387 (LO6)
capital expenditure 370 (LO1)
carrying value 369 (LO1)
copyright 387 (LO6)
cost 375 (LO3)

customer list 387 (LO6)
declining-balance method 377 (LO3)
depletion 368 (LO1)
depreciable cost 375 (LO3)
depreciation 368 (LO1)

Chapter Assignments

DISCUSSION QUESTIONS

LO 1 **DQ1. CONCEPT** ▶ Is carrying value ever the same as market value?

LO 2 **DQ2.** What incentive does a company have to allocate more of a group purchase price to land than to building?

LO 3 **DQ3.** Which depreciation method would best reflect the risk of obsolescence from rapid technological changes?

LO 4 **DQ4.** When would the disposal of a long-term asset result in no gain or loss?

LO 5 **DQ5.** When would annual depletion not equal depletion expense?

LO 6 **DQ6.** Why would a firm amortize a patent over fewer years than the patent's life?

LO 6 **DQ7.** Why would a company spend millions of dollars on goodwill?

LO 7 **DQ8. BUSINESS APPLICATION** ▶ What major advantage does a company that has positive free cash flow have over a company that has negative free cash flow?

SHORT EXERCISES

LO 2 **Classifying Cost of Long-Term Assets**

SE1. CONCEPT ▶ Gallon Auto purchased a neighboring lot for a new building and parking lot. Indicate whether each of the following expenditures is properly charged to (a) Land, (b) Land Improvements, or (c) Buildings:

1. Paving costs
2. Architects' fee for building design
3. Cost of clearing the property
4. Cost of the property

5. Building construction costs
6. Lights around the property
7. Building permit
8. Interest on the construction loan

LO 2 **Group Purchase**

SE2. Pattia Company purchased property with a warehouse and parking lot for $1,500,000. An appraiser valued the components of the property if purchased separately as follows.

Land	$ 400,000
Land improvements	200,000
Building	1,000,000
Total	$1,600,000

Determine the cost to be assigned to each component.

LO 3 **Straight-Line Method**

SE3. Sunburn Fitness Center purchased a new step machine for $8,250. The apparatus is expected to last four years and have a residual value of $750. What will the depreciation expense be for each year under the straight-line method?

LO 3 **Production Method**

SE4. Assume that the step machine in **SE3** has an estimated useful life of 8,000 hours and was used for 2,400 hours in year 1; 2,000 hours in year 2; 2,200 hours in year 3; and 1,400 hours in year 4. How much would depreciation expense be in each year? (Round to the nearest dollar.)

LO 3 **Double-Declining-Balance Method**

SE5. Assume that the step machine in **SE3** is depreciated using the double-declining-balance method. How much would depreciation expense be in each year? (Round to two decimal places.)

LO 4 **Disposal of Plant Assets: No Trade-In**

SE6. Times Printing owned a piece of equipment that cost $32,400 and on which it had recorded $18,000 of accumulated depreciation. The company disposed of the equipment on January 2, the first day of business of the current year.

1. Calculate the carrying value of the equipment.
2. Calculate the gain or loss on the disposal under each of the following assumptions:
   a. The equipment was discarded as having no value.
   b. The equipment was sold for $6,000 cash.
   c. The equipment was sold for $16,000 cash.

LO 5 **Natural Resources**

SE7. Walden Green Company purchased land containing an estimated 4,000,000 tons of ore for $16,000,000. The land will be worth $2,400,000 without the ore after 8 years of active mining. Although the equipment needed for the mining will have a useful life of 20 years, it is not expected to be usable and will have no value after the mining on this site is complete. Compute the depletion charge per ton and the amount of depletion expense for the first year of operation, assuming that 600,000 tons of ore are mined and sold. Also, compute the first-year depreciation on the mining equipment using the production method, assuming a cost of $19,200,000 with no residual value.

LO 6 **Intangible Assets: Computer Software**

SE8. Satyam Company has created a new software application for PCs. Its costs during research and development were $500,000. Its costs after the working program was developed were $350,000. Although the company's copyright may be amortized over 40 years, management believes that the product will be viable for only 5 years. How should the costs be accounted for? At what value will the software appear on the balance sheet after 1 year?

LO 7 **Management Issues**

SE9. BUSINESS APPLICATION ▶ Indicate whether each of the following actions is primarily related to (a) acquisition of long-term assets, (b) evaluating the adequacy of financing of long-term assets, or (c) applying accrual accounting to long-term assets:

1. Deciding between common stock and long-term notes for the raising of funds.
2. Relating the acquisition cost of a long-term asset to the cash flows generated by the asset.
3. Determining how long an asset will benefit the company.
4. Deciding to use cash flows from operations to purchase long-term assets.
5. Determining how much an asset will sell for when it is no longer useful to the company.
6. Calculating free cash flow.

LO 7   **Free Cash Flow**

SE10. BUSINESS APPLICATION ▶ Maki Corporation had cash flows from operating activities during the past year of $194,000. During the year, the company expended $25,000 for dividends; expended $158,000 for property, plant, and equipment; and sold property, plant, and equipment for $12,000. Calculate the company's free cash flow. What does the result tell you about the company?

EXERCISES: SET A

LO 1   **Recognition and Classification of Capital Expenditures**

E1A. CONCEPT ▶ Tell whether each of the following transactions related to an office building is a revenue expenditure (RE) or a capital expenditure (CE). In addition, indicate whether each transaction is an ordinary repair (OR), an extraordinary repair (ER), an addition (A), a betterment (B), or none of these (N).

1. The hallways and ceilings in the building are repainted at a cost of $4,150.
2. The hallways, which have tile floors, are carpeted at a cost of $14,000.
3. A new wing is added to the building at a cost of $87,500.
4. Furniture is purchased for the entrance to the building at a cost of $8,250.
5. The air-conditioning system is overhauled at a cost of $14,250. The overhaul extends the useful life of the air-conditioning system by 10 years.
6. A cleaning firm is paid $100 per week to clean the newly installed carpets.

LO 2   **Recognizing and Classifying the Cost of Long-Term Assets**

E2A. CONCEPT ▶ Fraser Manufacturing purchased land next to its factory to be used as a parking lot. The following expenditures were incurred by the company: purchase price, $300,000; broker's fees, $24,000; title search and other fees, $2,200; demolition of a cottage on the property, $8,000; general grading of property, $4,200; paving parking lots, $40,000; lighting for parking lots, $32,000; and signs for parking lots, $6,400. Determine the amounts that should be debited to the Land account and the Land Improvements account.

LO 2   **Group Purchase**

E3A. Sea Scout purchased a car wash for $240,000. If purchased separately, the land would have cost $60,000, the building $135,000, and the equipment $105,000. Determine the amount that should be recorded in the new business's records for land, building, and equipment.

LO 2, 3   **Cost of Long-Term Asset and Depreciation**

E4A. Melissa Mertz purchased a used tractor for $17,500. Before the tractor could be used, it required new tires, which cost $1,100, and an overhaul, which cost $1,400. Its first tank of fuel cost $75. The tractor is expected to last six years and have a residual value of $2,000. Determine the cost and depreciable cost of the tractor and calculate the first year's depreciation under the straight-line method.

LO 3   **Depreciation Methods**

E5A. On January 13, 2013, Precision Oil Company purchased a drilling truck for $90,000. Precision expects the truck to last five years or 200,000 miles, with an estimated residual value of $15,000 at the end of that time. During 2014, the truck is driven 48,000 miles. Precision's year end is December 31. Compute the depreciation for 2014 under each of the following methods: (1) straight-line, (2) production, and (3) double-declining-balance. Using the amount computed in **(3)**, prepare the journal entry to record depreciation expense for the second year, and show how the Drilling Truck account would appear on the balance sheet.

LO 3 **Double-Declining-Balance Method**

E6A. Crescendo Company purchased a computer for $1,120. It has an estimated useful life of four years and an estimated residual value of $120. Compute the depreciation charge for each of the four years using the double-declining-balance method.

LO 3 **Revision of Depreciation Rates**

E7A. NewLife Hospital purchased a special X-ray machine. The machine, which cost $623,120, was expected to last ten years, with an estimated residual value of $63,120. After two years of operation (and depreciation charges using the straight-line method), it became evident that the X-ray machine would last a total of only seven years. The estimated residual value, however, would remain the same. Given this information, determine the new depreciation charge for the third year on the basis of the revised estimated useful life.

LO 4 **Disposal of Plant Assets**

E8A. A piece of equipment that cost $64,800 and on which $36,000 of accumulated depreciation had been recorded was disposed of on January 2, the first day of business of the current year. For each of the following assumptions, compute the gain or loss on the disposal:

1. The equipment was discarded as having no value.
2. The equipment was sold for $12,000 cash.
3. The equipment was sold for $36,000 cash.

LO 4 **Disposal of Plant Assets**

E9A. Star Company purchased a computer on January 2, 2012, at a cost of $2,500. The computer is expected to have a useful life of five years and a residual value of $250. Assume that the computer is disposed of on July 1, 2015. Using the straight line method, record the depreciation expense for half a year and the disposal under each of the following assumptions:

1. The computer is discarded.
2. The computer is sold for $400.
3. The computer is sold for $1,100.

LO 5 **Natural Resource Depletion and Depreciation of Related Plant Assets**

E10A. Mertz Company purchased land containing an estimated 5 million tons of ore for a cost of $8,800,000. The land without the ore is estimated to be worth $500,000. During its first year of operation, the company mined and sold 750,000 tons of ore. Compute the depletion charge per ton. (Round to two decimal places.) Compute the depletion expense that Mertz should record for the year.

LO 6 **Amortization of Copyrights and Trademarks**

E11A. Complete the following requirements regarding amortizing copyrights and trademarks:

1. Argyle Publishing Company purchased the copyright to a basic computer textbook for $40,000. The usual life of a textbook is about four years. However, the copyright will remain in effect for another 50 years. Calculate the annual amortization of the copyright.
2. **ACCOUNTING CONNECTION** ▶ Scion Company purchased a trademark from a well-known supermarket for $320,000. The company's management argued that the trademark's useful life was indefinite. Explain how the cost should be accounted for.

LO 6 **Accounting for a Patent**

E12A. At the beginning of the fiscal year, David Company purchased for $1,030,000 a patent that applies to the manufacture of a unique tamper-proof lid for medicine bottles. David incurred legal costs of $450,000 in successfully defending use of the lid by a competitor. David estimated that the patent would be valuable for at least ten years.

(Continued)

During the first two years of operations, David successfully marketed the lid. At the beginning of the third year, a study appeared in a consumer magazine showing that children could in fact remove the lid. As a result, all orders for the lids were canceled, and the patent was rendered worthless.

Prepare journal entries to record the following: (a) purchase of the patent, (b) successful defense of the patent, (c) amortization expense for the first year, and (d) write-off of the patent as worthless.

LO 7

Management Issues

E13A. BUSINESS APPLICATION ▶ Indicate whether each of the following actions is primarily related to (a) acquisition of long-term assets, (b) evaluating the financing of long-term assets, or (c) applying accrual accounting to long-term assets:

1. Deciding whether to rent or buy a piece of equipment.
2. Allocating costs on a group purchase.
3. Deciding to use the production method of depreciation.
4. Determining the total units a machine will produce.
5. Deciding to borrow funds to purchase equipment.
6. Estimating the savings a new machine will produce and comparing that amount to cost.
7. Examining the trend of free cash flow over several years.

LO 7

Free Cash Flow

E14A. BUSINESS APPLICATION ▶ Zee Corporation had net cash flows from operating activities during the past year of $432,000. During the year, the company expended $924,000 for property, plant, and equipment; sold property, plant, and equipment for $108,000; and paid dividends of $100,000. Calculate the company's free cash flow. What does the result tell you about the company?

EXERCISES: SET B

Visit the textbook companion website at www.cengagebrain.com to access Exercise Set B for this chapter.

PROBLEMS

LO 1

Identification of Long-Term Assets Terminology

P1. Common terms associated with long-term assets follow.

a. Tangible assets	g. Depreciation
b. Natural resources	h. Depletion
c. Intangible assets	i. Amortization
d. Additions	j. Revenue expenditure
e. Betterments	
f. Extraordinary repair	

REQUIRED

1. For each of the statements that follow, identify the term with which it is associated. (If two terms apply, choose the one that is most closely associated.)
   1. Periodic cost associated with intangible assets.
   2. Cost of constructing a new wing on a building.
   3. A group of assets encompassing property, plant, and equipment.
   4. Cost associated with enhancing a building but not expanding it.
   5. Periodic cost associated with tangible assets.
   6. A group of assets that gain their value from contracts or rights.
   7. Cost of normal repairs to a building.

8. Assets whose value derives from what can be extracted from them.

9. Periodic cost associated with natural resources.

10. Cost of a repair that extends the useful life of a building.

2. **ACCOUNTING CONNECTION** ▶ Assuming the company uses cash for all its expenditures, which of the terms listed above would you expect to see on the income statement? Which ones would not result in an outlay of cash?

LO **2**

Determining Cost of Assets

✔ 1: Land: $723,900
✔ 1: Land Improvements: $142,000
✔ 1: Buildings: $1,383,600
✔ 1: Equipment: $210,800

P2. Cergo Computers constructed a new training center in 2014, which you have been hired to manage. A review of the accounting records shows the following expenditures debited to an asset account called Training Center:

Attorney's fee, land acquisition	$ 34,900
Cost of land	598,000
Architect's fee, building design	102,000
Building	1,020,000
Parking lot and sidewalk	135,600
Electrical wiring, building	164,000
Landscaping	55,000
Cost of surveying land	9,200
Training equipment, tables, and chairs	136,400
Installation of training equipment	68,000
Cost of grading the land	14,000
Cost of changes in building to soundproof rooms	59,200
Total account balance	$2,396,300

During the center's construction, an employee of Cergo worked full-time overseeing the project. He spent two months on the purchase and preparation of the site, six months on the construction, one month on land improvements, and one month on equipment installation and training-room furniture purchase and setup. His salary of $64,000 during this ten-month period was charged to Administrative Expense. The training center was placed in operation on November 1.

REQUIRED

1. Prepare a schedule with the following four column (account) headings: Land, Land Improvements, Building, and Equipment. Place each of the above expenditures in the appropriate column. Total the columns.

2. **CONCEPT** ▶ What impact does the classification of the items among several accounts have on evaluating the profitability performance of the company?

LO **3, 4**

Comparison of Depreciation Methods

✔ 1a: Depreciation, year 3: $165,000
✔ 1b: Depreciation, year 3: $132,000
✔ 1c: Depreciation, year 3: $90,000

P3. Zeigler Manufacturing Company purchased a robot for $720,000 at the beginning of year 1. The robot has an estimated useful life of four years and an estimated residual value of $60,000. The robot, which should last 20,000 hours, was operated 6,000 hours in year 1; 8,000 hours in year 2; 4,000 hours in year 3; and 2,000 hours in year 4.

REQUIRED

1. Compute the annual depreciation and carrying value for the robot for each year assuming the following depreciation methods: (a) straight-line, (b) production, and (c) double-declining-balance.

2. If the robot is sold for $750,000 after year 2, what would be the amount of gain or loss under each method?

3. **ACCOUNTING CONNECTION** ▶ What conclusions can you draw from the patterns of yearly depreciation and carrying value in requirement **1**? Do the three methods differ in their effect on the company's profitability? Do they differ in their effect on the company's operating cash flows? Explain.

LO **3, 4**

CASH FLOW

SPREADSHEET

✔ 1a: Depreciation, year 3: $54,250
✔ 1b: Depreciation, year 3: $81,375
✔ 1c: Depreciation, year 3: $53,407

Comparison of Depreciation Methods

P4. Italian Construction Company purchased a new crane for $360,500 at the beginning of year 1. The crane has an estimated residual value of $35,000 and an estimated useful life of six years. The crane is expected to last 10,000 hours. It was used 1,800 hours in year 1; 2,000 hours in year 2; 2,500 hours in year 3; 1,500 hours in year 4; 1,200 hours in year 5; and 1,000 hours in year 6.

REQUIRED

1. Compute the annual depreciation and carrying value for the new crane for each of the six years under each of the following methods: (a) straight-line, (b) production, and (c) double-declining-balance (round percentage to two decimal places.)
2. If the crane is sold for $250,000 after year 3, what would be the amount of gain or loss under each method?
3. **ACCOUNTING CONNECTION** ▶ Do the three methods differ in their effect on the company's profitability? Do they differ in their effect on the company's operating cash flows? Explain.

LO **5**

SPREADSHEET

✔ 2: Depletion expense: $121,500

Natural Resource Depletion and Depreciation of Related Plant Assets

P5. Bychowski Company purchased land containing an estimated 10 million tons of ore for a cost of $3,300,000. The land without the ore is estimated to be worth $600,000. The company expects that all the usable ore can be mined in 10 years. Buildings costing $300,000 with an estimated useful life of 20 years were erected on the site. Equipment costing $360,000 with an estimated useful life of 10 years was installed. Because of the remote location, neither the buildings nor the equipment has an estimated residual value. During its first year of operation, the company mined and sold 450,000 tons of ore.

REQUIRED

1. Compute the depletion charge per ton.
2. Compute the depletion expense that Bychowski should record for the year.
3. Determine the depreciation expense for the year for the buildings, making it proportional to the depletion.
4. Determine the depreciation expense for the year for the equipment under two alternatives: (a) making the expense proportional to the depletion and (b) using the straight-line method.
5. **ACCOUNTING CONNECTION** ▶ Suppose the company mined and sold 250,000 tons of ore (instead of 450,000) during the first year. Would the change in the results in requirements **2** or **3** affect earnings or cash flows? Explain.

ALTERNATE PROBLEMS

LO **2**

✔ 1: Land: $426,212
✔ 1: Land Improvements: $166,560
✔ 1: Buildings: $833,940
✔ 1: Machinery: $1,262,640
✔ 1: Expense: $18,120

Determining Cost of Assets

P6. Krall Company was formed on January 1, 2014, and began constructing a new plant. At the end of 2014, its auditor discovered that all expenditures involving long-term assets had been debited to an account called Fixed Assets. An analysis of the Fixed Assets account, which had a year-end balance of $2,644,972, disclosed that it contained the following items:

Cost of land	$ 316,600
Surveying costs	4,100
Transfer of title and other fees required by the county	920
Broker's fees for land	21,144
Attorney's fees associated with land acquisition	7,048
Cost of removing timber from land	50,400
Cost of grading land	4,200
Cost of digging building foundation	34,600
Architect's fee for building and land improvements (80 percent building)	64,800
Cost of building construction	710,000
Cost of sidewalks	11,400
Cost of parking lots	54,400
Cost of lighting for grounds	80,300
Cost of landscaping	11,800
Cost of machinery	989,000
Shipping cost on machinery	55,300
Cost of installing machinery	176,200
Cost of testing machinery	22,100
Cost of changes in building to comply with safety regulations pertaining to machinery	12,540
Cost of repairing building that was damaged in the installation of machinery	8,900
Cost of medical bill for injury received by employee while installing machinery	2,400
Cost of water damage to building during heavy rains prior to opening the plant for operation	6,820
Account balance	$2,644,972

Krall sold the timber it cleared from the land to a firewood dealer for $5,000. This amount was credited to Miscellaneous Income. During the construction period, two of Krall's supervisors devoted full time to the construction project. Their annual salaries were $48,000 and $42,000, respectively. They spent two months on the purchase and preparation of the land, six months on the construction of the building (approximately one-sixth of which was devoted to improvements on the grounds), and one month on machinery installation. When the plant began operation on October 1, the supervisors returned to their regular duties. Their salaries were debited to Factory Salaries Expense.

REQUIRED

1. Prepare a schedule with the following column headings: Land, Land Improvements, Buildings, Machinery, and Expense. Place each of the above expenditures in the appropriate column. Negative amounts should be shown in parentheses. Total the columns.
2. **CONCEPT** ▶ What impact does the classification of the items among several accounts have on evaluating the profitability performance of the company?

LO **3, 4**

Comparison of Depreciation Methods

CASH FLOW

✔ 1a: Depreciation, year 3: $5,000
✔ 1b: Depreciation, year 3: $8,000
✔ 1c: Depreciation, year 3: $2,813

P7. Bao Wao Designs Inc. purchased a computerized blueprint printer that will assist in the design and display of plans for factory layouts. The cost of the printer was $22,500, and its expected useful life is four years. The company can probably sell the printer for $2,500 at the end of four years. The printer is expected to last 6,000 hours. It was used 1,200 hours in year 1; 1,800 hours in year 2; 2,400 hours in year 3; and 600 hours in year 4.

REQUIRED

1. Compute the annual depreciation and carrying value for the new blueprint printer for each of the four years (round to the nearest dollar where necessary) under each of the following methods: (a) straight-line, (b) production, and (c) double-declining-balance.

(Continued)

2. If the printer is sold for $12,000 after year 2, what would be the gain or loss under each method?

3. **ACCOUNTING CONNECTION** ▶ What conclusions can you draw from the patterns of yearly depreciation and carrying value in requirement **1**? Do the three methods differ in their impact on profitability? Do they differ in their effect on the company's operating cash flows? Explain.

LO **3, 4**

✔ 1a: Depreciation, year 3: $51,667
✔ 1b: Depreciation, year 3: $77,500
✔ 1c: Depreciation, year 3: $51,852

Comparison of Depreciation Methods

P8. Niles Construction Company purchased a new crane for $350,000 at the beginning of year 1. The crane has an estimated residual value of $40,000 and an estimated useful life of six years. The crane is expected to last 10,000 hours. It was used 1,800 hours in year 1; 2,000 hours in year 2; 2,500 hours in year 3; 1,500 hours in year 4; 1,200 hours in year 5; and 1,000 hours in year 6.

REQUIRED

1. Compute the annual depreciation and carrying value for the new crane for each of the six years (round to the nearest dollar where necessary) under each of the following methods: (a) straight-line, (b) production, and (c) double-declining-balance (round percentage to two decimal places).

2. If the crane is sold for $500,000 after year 3, what would be the amount of gain or loss under each method?

3. **ACCOUNTING CONNECTION** ▶ Do the three methods differ in their effect on the company's profitability? Do they differ in their effect on the company's operating cash flows? Explain.

LO **5**

✔ 2: Depletion expense: $288,000

Natural Resource Depletion and Depreciation of Related Plant Assets

P9. Crystler Mining Company purchased land containing an estimated 10 million tons of ore for a cost of $4,400,000. The land without the ore is estimated to be worth $800,000. The company expects that all the usable ore can be mined in 10 years. Buildings costing $400,000 with an estimated useful life of 30 years were erected on the site. Equipment costing $480,000 with an estimated useful life of 10 years was installed. Because of the remote location, neither the buildings nor the equipment has an estimated residual value. During its first year of operation, the company mined and sold 800,000 tons of ore.

REQUIRED

1. Compute the depletion charge per ton.
2. Compute the depletion expense that Crystler Mining should record for the year.
3. Determine the depreciation expense for the year for the buildings, making it proportional to the depletion.
4. Determine the depreciation expense for the year for the equipment under two alternatives: (a) making the expense proportional to the depletion and (b) using the straight-line method.
5. **ACCOUNTING CONNECTION** ▶ Suppose the company mined and sold 1,000,000 tons of ore (instead of 800,000) during the first year. Would the change in the results in requirements **2** or **3** affect earnings or cash flows? Explain.

CASES

LO **7**

Conceptual Understanding: Effect of Change in Estimates

C1. The airline industry was hit particularly hard after the 9/11 attacks on the World Trade Center in 2001. In 2002, **Southwest Airlines**, one of the healthier airline companies, decided to lengthen the useful lives of its aircraft from 22 to 27 years. Shortly thereafter, following Southwest's lead, other airlines made the same move.[22] What advantage, if any, did the airlines gain by making this change in estimate? Would it have changed earnings or cash flows, and if it did, would the change have been favorable or negative?

Some people argue that the useful lives and depreciation of airplanes are irrelevant. They claim that because of the extensive maintenance and testing that airline companies are required by law to perform, the planes theoretically can be in service for an indefinite future period. What is wrong with this argument?

LO 1 **Conceptual Understanding: Impairment Test**

C2. BUSINESS APPLICATION ▶ An annual report of **Costco Wholesale Corporation**, the large discount company, contained the following statement:

> *The Company periodically evaluates long-lived assets for impairment when … circumstances occur that may indicate the carrying amount of the asset group … may not be fully recoverable.*[23]

What does the concept of impairment mean in accounting? What effect does impairment have on profitability and cash flows? Why would the concept of impairment be referred to as a conservative accounting approach?

LO 3 **Conceptual Understanding: Accounting Estimates**

C3. IBM, the large computer equipment and services company, stated in one of its annual reports that "Property, plant and equipment are carried at cost and depreciated over their estimated useful lives using the straight-line method."[24] What estimates are necessary to carry out this policy? What factors should be considered in making each of the estimates?

LO 6 **Interpreting Financial Reports: Brands**

C4. CONCEPT ▶ **Starwood Hotels & Resorts Worldwide, Inc.**, and **Marriott International** provide hospitality services. Starwood Hotels' well-known brands include St. Regis, The Luxury Collection, W Hotels, Westin Hotels & Resorts, Le Meridien, Sheraton Hotels & Resorts, Four Points by Sheraton, Aloft by W Hotels, and Element by Westin. Marriott also owns or manages properties with recognizable brand names, such as Marriott Hotels & Resorts, Ritz-Carlton Hotel Company and Destination Club, Bulgari Hotels & Resorts, Marriott ExecuStay, Marriott Executive Apartments, Marriott Vacation Club, Grand Residences by Marriott, Spring Hill Suites by Marriott, Renaissance Hotels & Resorts, AC Hotels by Marriott, JW Marriott Hotels & Resorts, EDITION Hotels, Autograph Collection, Courtyard by Marriott, Residence Inn by Marriott, Fairfield Inn & Suites by Marriott, TownePlace Suites by Marriott, and Marriott Conference Centers.

On its balance sheet, Starwood Hotels & Resorts includes brands of $313 million (see note 7), or 3.3 percent of total assets. Marriott International, however, does not list brands among its intangible assets.[25] What principles of accounting for intangibles require Starwood to record brands as an asset while Marriott does not? How do these differences in accounting for brands generally affect the net income and return on assets of these two competitors?

LO 1, 2, 3 **Annual Report Case: Long-Term Assets**

C5. To answer the following questions, refer to the **CVS** annual report in the Supplement to Chapter 16. Examine the balance sheets, as well as the summary of significant accounting policies on property and equipment in the notes to the financial statements.

1. What percentage of total assets in 2011 was property and equipment, net? Identify the major categories of CVS's property and equipment. Which types of property and equipment are most significant? What are leasehold improvements? How significant are these items, and what are their effects on CVS's earnings?
2. What method of depreciation does CVS use? How long does management estimate its buildings will last as compared with furniture and equipment? What does this say about the company's need to remodel its stores?
3. How does the company determine if it has impaired assets?

Comparison Analysis: Long-Term Assets and Free Cash Flows

C6. To complete the assignments listed below, refer to the **CVS** annual report and the financial statements of **Southwest Airlines Co.** in the Supplement to Chapter 16.

1. Prepare a table that shows the net amount each company spent on property and equipment (from the statement of cash flows), the net amount of its property and equipment (from the balance sheet), and the percentage of net amount spent to the net amount of property and equipment for each of the past two years. (Round percentages to one decimal place.) In which company did the amount of property and equipment grow more rapidly?

2. **BUSINESS APPLICATION** ▶ Calculate free cash flow for both companies for the past two years. What conclusions can you draw about each company's need to raise funds from debt and equity and its ability to grow?

Ethical Dilemma: Ethics and Allocation of Acquisition Costs

C7. BUSINESS APPLICATION ▶ Hamlin Company has purchased land and a warehouse for $18,000,000. The warehouse is expected to last 20 years and to have a residual value equal to 10 percent of its cost. The chief financial officer (CFO) and the controller are discussing the allocation of the purchase price. The CFO believes that the largest amount possible should be assigned to the land because that would improve reported net income in the future. Depreciation expense would be lower because land is not depreciated. He suggests allocating one-third, or $6,000,000, of the cost to the land. This would result in depreciation expense each year of $540,000 [($12,000,000 − $1,200,000) ÷ 20 years].

The controller disagrees. She argues that the smallest amount possible, say one-fifth of the purchase price, should be allocated to the land because the depreciation of the warehouse, which is tax-deductible, would be greater and thus reduce income taxes. Under this plan, annual depreciation would be $648,000 [($14,400,000 − $1,440,000) ÷ 20 years]. The annual tax savings at a 30 percent tax rate is $32,400 [($648,000 − $540,000) × 0.30].

How would each decision affect the company's cash flows? Ethically, how should the purchase cost be allocated? Who would be affected by the decision?

Continuing Case: Annual Report Project

C8. Using the most recent annual report of the company you have chosen to study and that you have accessed online at the company's website, examine the balance sheet and the statement of cash flows and accompanying notes of your company. Answer the following questions:

1. **CONCEPT** ▶ What percentage of total assets is property, plant, and equipment? What items are classified in this category?
2. **CONCEPT** ▶ What percentage of total assets are intangible assets? What items are classified in this category?
3. How much did the company invest in property, plant, and equipment during the year?
4. **BUSINESS APPLICATION** ▶ Compute free cash flow for the most recent year.
5. Find the disclosures about property, plant, and equipment in the notes to the financial statements. What depreciation methods does the company use?
6. Find the disclosures about intangible assets in the notes to the financial statements. What intangible assets are amortized and which are not? Has the company recognized any impairments of intangible assets?

CHAPTER 11
Current Liabilities and Fair Value Accounting

In January 2014, Teresa Madej started a business called Teresa's Fitness Center. In addition to offering exercise classes, the center sells nutritional supplements. Teresa has limited experience in running a business, but she knows that it is important for a company to manage its liabilities so that it has enough cash on hand to pay debts when they come due.

Teresa is also well aware that incurring liabilities is a necessary part of doing business. When she started her business, Teresa signed a promissory note to her bank for $16,000. To help operate the business, she hired two exercise instructors to whom she pays monthly salaries, and she has incurred debt in maintaining an inventory of nutritional supplements. Other liabilities include taxes owed to both the federal and state governments, as well as $3,600 in annual property taxes that the business owes the city government.

As the company approaches the end of its second fiscal year, Teresa is anxious to assess its liquidity.

1. CONCEPT ▶ *How do the concepts of recognition, valuation, classification, and disclosure apply to current liabilities?*

2. ACCOUNTING APPLICATION ▶ *What are the company's current liabilities and their total amount?*

3. BUSINESS APPLICATION ▶ *Why is it important for Teresa Madej to identify and account for all her company's current liabilities?*

LEARNING OBJECTIVES

LO 1 Define *current liabilities*, and identify the concepts underlying them.

LO 2 Identify, compute, and record definitely determinable and estimated current liabilities.

LO 3 Distinguish contingent liabilities from commitments.

LO 4 Identify the valuation approaches to fair value accounting, define *time value of money* and *interest*, and apply them to present values.

LO 5 Apply the present value concept to simple valuation situations.

LO 6 Use ratio analysis to manage the impact of current liabilities' impact on liquidity.

CONCEPTS

LO 1 Concepts Underlying Current Liabilities

Current liabilities are debts and obligations that a company expects to satisfy within one year or within its normal operating cycle, whichever is longer. They require not only careful management of liquidity and cash flows but also close monitoring. Managers must understand how current liabilities should be *recognized*, *valued*, *classified*, and *disclosed*.

Recognition

Timing is important in the *recognition* of liabilities. Failure to record a liability often goes along with failure to record an expense. The two errors lead to an understatement of expense and an overstatement of income.

Generally accepted accounting principles require that a liability be recorded when an obligation occurs, as when goods are bought on credit. However, some current liabilities are not the result of direct transactions. One reason for making adjusting entries is to *recognize* unrecorded liabilities that accrue during the period. Accrued liabilities include salaries payable and interest payable. Other liabilities that can only be estimated, such as taxes payable, must also be recognized through adjusting entries.

Agreements for future transactions do not have to be *recognized*. For instance, **Microsoft** might agree to pay an executive $250,000 a year for a period of three years, or it might agree to buy an unspecified amount of advertising at a certain price over the next five years. Such contracts, though they are definite commitments, are not considered liabilities because they are for future—not past—transactions. Because there is no current obligation, no liability is recognized. However, if the amounts involved are material, these commitments would be mentioned in the notes to the financial statements.

Valuation

On the balance sheet, a liability is generally *valued* at the amount of money needed to pay the debt or reported at the fair market value of the goods or services to be delivered. For most liabilities, at least one of these amounts is definitely known. For example, **Amazon.com** sells a large number of gift certificates that are redeemable in the future. The amount of the liability (unearned revenue) is known, but the exact timing is not known.

Some companies, however, must estimate future liabilities. For example, if an automobile dealer sells a car with a one-year warranty on parts and service, the obligation is definite because the sale has occurred; but the amount of the obligation can only be estimated.

Classification

As discussed earlier, current liabilities are due in the next year or within the normal operating cycle, whichever is longer, and are normally paid out of current assets or with cash generated by operations. They contrast with **long-term liabilities**, which are liabilities due beyond one year or beyond the normal operating cycle. For example, Teresa's Fitness Center may incur long-term liabilities to finance its expansion to a larger location. The distinction between current and long-term liabilities affects the evaluation of a company's liquidity.

Disclosure

STUDY NOTE: Disclosure of the fair value and the bases for estimating the fair value of short-term notes payable, loans payable, and other short-term debt are required unless it is not practical to estimate the value.

In addition to reporting current liabilities in the balance sheet, a company may need to include additional explanation in the notes to its financial statements. For example, if a company's Notes Payable account is large, it should *disclose* the balances, maturity dates, interest rates, and other features of the debts in an explanatory note. Any special credit arrangements should also be disclosed. For example, in this note to its 2011 financial statements, **Hershey Foods Corporation** discloses the nature of its credit arrangements:

Short-Term Debt

As a source of short-term financing, . . . we entered into a new five-year agreement establishing an unsecured revolving [letter of credit] to borrow up to $1.1 billion, with an option to increase borrowings by an additional $400 million with the consent of the lenders.[1]

A **line of credit** with a bank allows a company to borrow funds when they are needed to finance current operations. Unused lines of credit allow a company to borrow on short notice up to the credit limit, with little or no negotiation. Thus, the type of *disclosure* in Hershey's note is helpful in assessing whether a company has additional borrowing power.

APPLY IT!

Indicate whether each of the following actions relates to (a) recognition of liabilities, (b) valuation of liabilities, (c) classification of liabilities, or (d) disclosure of liabilities:

1. Determining whether a liability is current or long-term.
2. Determining the dollar amount of a liability.
3. Determining what information should be reported about a liability.
4. Determining that a liability exists.

SOLUTION

1. c;   2. b;   3. d;   4. a

TRY IT! SE1, E1A, E1B

ACCOUNTING APPLICATIONS

LO 2 Common Types of Current Liabilities

As noted earlier, a company incurs current liabilities to meet its needs for cash during the operating cycle. These liabilities fall into two major groups: definitely determinable liabilities and estimated liabilities.

Definitely Determinable Liabilities

Current liabilities that are set by contract or statute and that can be measured exactly are called **definitely determinable liabilities**. The objectives in accounting for these liabilities are to:

- determine their existence and amount
- record them properly

The most common definitely determinable liabilities are described in the sections that follow.

Accounts Payable Accounts payable (or *trade accounts payable*) are short-term obligations to suppliers for goods and services. The amount in the Accounts Payable control account is supported by an accounts payable subsidiary ledger. This separate ledger contains an individual account for each person or company to whom money is owed.

Notes Payable Short-term notes payable are represented by **promissory notes**, which are written agreements to pay according to certain terms. A company may sign promissory notes to obtain bank loans, pay suppliers for goods and services, or secure credit from other sources. The interest rate is usually stated separately on the face of the note, as shown in Exhibit 1.

Exhibit 1
Promissory Note

> Chicago, Illinois   January 1, 2013
>
> <u>Sixty days</u> after date I promise to pay First Federal Bank the sum of <u>$16,000</u> with interest at the rate of 3% per annum.
>
> *Teresa Madej*
> Teresa's Fitness Center

© Cengage Learning 2014

Issuance of Note Payable

Transaction Borrowed $16,000 from bank and signed 60-day, 3% promissory note.

Analysis The journal entry to record the issuance of the note payable

- ▲ *increases* the *Cash* account
- ▲ *increases* the *Notes Payable* account

Application of Double Entry

Journal Entry

A = L + OE
+16,000 +16,000

		Dr.	Cr.
Jan. 1	Cash	16,000	
	Notes Payable		16,000
	Issued 60-day, 3% promissory note		

Comment The transaction is *recognized* by an increase in assets and liabilities.

Payment of Note with Interest

Transaction On March 1, Teresa repays the $16,000 plus interest.

Analysis The journal entry to record the payment of the note with interest after 60 days

▲ *increases* the *Interest Expense* account

▼ *decreases* the *Notes Payable* account

▼ *decreases* the *Cash* account

Application of Double Entry

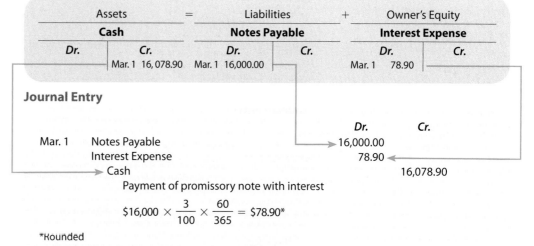

Journal Entry

A = L + OE
−16,078.90 −16,000.00 −78.90

		Dr.	Cr.
Mar. 1	Notes Payable	16,000.00	
	Interest Expense	78.90	
	Cash		16,078.90
	Payment of promissory note with interest		

$$\$16{,}000 \times \frac{3}{100} \times \frac{60}{365} = \$78.90^*$$

*Rounded

Comment The transaction is *recognized* by a decrease in assets and liabilities and an increase in interest expense.

Bank Loans and Commercial Paper Although a company signs a promissory note for the full amount of a line of credit, it has great flexibility in using the available funds. It can increase its borrowing up to the limit when it needs cash and reduce the amount borrowed when it generates enough cash of its own. Both the amount borrowed and the interest rate charged by the bank may change daily. The bank may require the company to meet certain financial goals (such as maintaining specific profit margins, current ratios, or debt to equity ratios) to retain its line of credit.

Companies with excellent credit ratings can borrow short-term funds by issuing commercial paper. **Commercial paper** refers to unsecured loans (i.e., loans not backed up by any specific assets) that are sold to the public, usually investment firms. Companies can quickly lose access to commercial paper if their credit rating drops. Because of disappointing operating results in recent years, well-known companies like **Chrysler**, **Lucent Technologies**, and **Motorola** have lost some or all of their ability to issue commercial paper.

The portion of a line of credit currently used and the amount of commercial paper issued are usually combined with notes payable in the current liabilities section of the balance sheet. Details are disclosed in a note to the financial statements.

Accrued Liabilities As noted earlier, a key reason for making adjusting entries is to *recognize* liabilities that are not already in the accounting records. **Accrued liabilities** (or *accrued expenses)* can include estimated liabilities.

Interest payable, a definitely determinable liability, is an accrued liability. Interest accrues daily on interest-bearing notes. An adjusting entry is made at the end of each period to record the interest obligation up to that point.

Recognizing Accrual Interest Expense

Transaction The accounting period of Teresa's note in Exhibit 1 ends on January 31, or 30 days after the issuance of the 60-day note.

Analysis The adjusting entry to record the payment of the note with interest after 30 days

▲ *increases* the *Interest Expense* account

▲ *increases* the *Interest Payable* account

Application of Double Entry

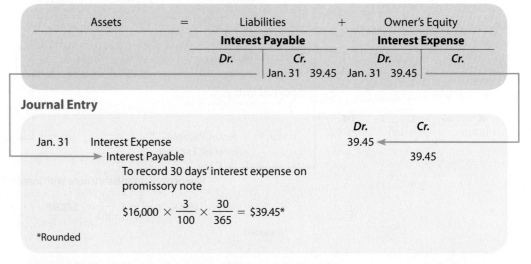

Assets	=	Liabilities	+	Owner's Equity
		Interest Payable		**Interest Expense**
		Dr.	*Cr.*	*Dr.*	*Cr.*
			Jan. 31 39.45	Jan. 31 39.45	

A	=	L	+	OE
		+39.45		−39.45

Journal Entry

			Dr.	Cr.
Jan. 31	Interest Expense		39.45	
	Interest Payable			39.45
	To record 30 days' interest expense on promissory note			

$$\$16{,}000 \times \frac{3}{100} \times \frac{30}{365} = \$39.45^*$$

*Rounded

Comment The accrued interest is *recognized* by an increase in expense and liabilities.

Dividends Payable **Cash dividends** are a distribution of earnings to a corporation's stockholders, and a corporation's board of directors has the sole authority to declare them. The corporation has no liability for dividends until the date of declaration. During the brief time between that date and the date of payment, the dividends declared are considered current liabilities of the corporation.

Sales and Excise Taxes Payable Most states and many cities levy a sales tax on retail transactions, and the federal government imposes an excise tax on some products, such as gasoline. A merchant that sells goods subject to these taxes must collect the taxes and forward them periodically to the appropriate government agency. Until the merchant remits the amount it has collected to the government, that amount represents a current liability.

Recording Sales and Excise Taxes

Transaction On June 1, Teresa's Fitness Center makes a $200 sale of nutritional supplements that is subject to a 5 percent sales tax and a 10 percent excise tax.

Analysis The journal entry to record the sale

▲ *increases* the *Cash* account

▲ *increases* the *Sales* account

▲ *increases* the *Sales Tax Payable* account

▲ *increases* the *Excise Tax Payable* account

Application of Double Entry

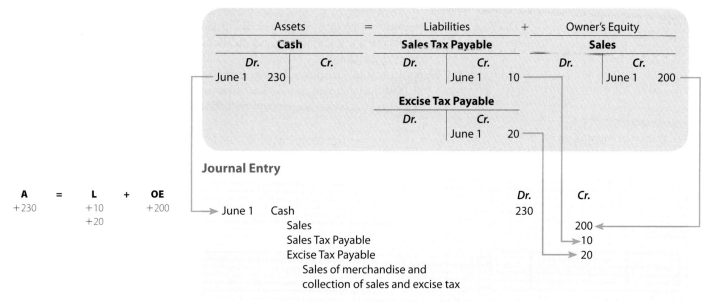

A	=	L	+	OE
+230		+10		+200
		+20		

Journal Entry

			Dr.	Cr.
June 1	Cash		230	
	Sales			200
	Sales Tax Payable			10
	Excise Tax Payable			20
	Sales of merchandise and collection of sales and excise tax			

Comment The sale is properly *recognized* at $200, and the taxes collected, which are not revenues, are *classified* as liabilities to be remitted to the appropriate government agencies.

Companies that have a physical presence in many cities and states require a complex accounting system for sales taxes because the rates vary from state to state and city to city. For Internet companies, the sales tax situation is simpler. For example, **Amazon.com** is an Internet company without a physical presence in most states. Thus, it does not always have to collect sales tax from its customers. This situation may change in the future, but so far Congress has exempted most Internet sales from sales tax.

Current Portion of Long-Term Debt The portion of long-term debt that is due within the next year and is to be paid from current assets is *classified* as a current liability. No journal entry is necessary when this is the case. The total debt is simply reclassified as short-term and long-term when the company prepares its balance sheet and other financial statements.

Payroll Liabilities In the banking and airlines industries, payroll costs represent more than half of all operating costs. Payroll accounting is important because complex laws and significant liabilities are involved. The employer is liable to employees for wages and salaries and to various agencies for amounts withheld from wages and salaries and for related taxes. **Wages** are compensation of employees at an hourly rate; **salaries** are compensation of employees at a monthly or yearly rate.

Because payroll accounting applies only to an organization's employees, it is important to distinguish between employees and independent contractors, as follows.

- An **employee** is paid a wage or salary by the organization and is under its direct supervision and control.
- An **independent contractor** offers services for a fee but is not under the organization's direct control or supervision. Certified public accountants, advertising agencies, and lawyers, for example, often act as independent contractors.

Exhibit 2 shows how payroll liabilities relate to employee earnings and employer taxes and other costs. When accounting for payroll liabilities, it is important to keep the following in mind:

- The amount payable to employees is less than the amount of their earnings. This occurs because employers are required by law or are requested by employees to withhold certain amounts from wages and send them directly to government agencies or other organizations.
- An employer's total liabilities exceed employees' earnings because the employer must pay additional taxes and make other contributions (e.g., for pensions and medical care) that increase the payroll costs and liabilities.

Exhibit 2
Illustration of Payroll Costs

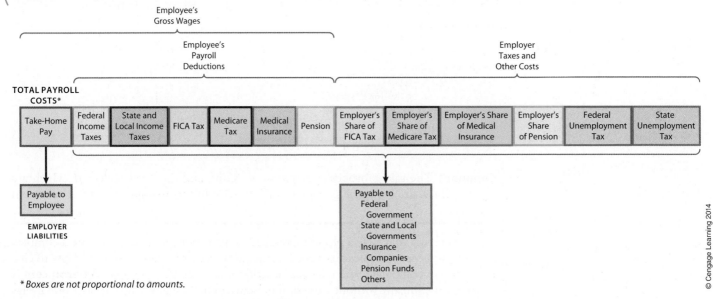

Boxes are not proportional to amounts.

© Cengage Learning 2014

STUDY NOTE: *Vacation pay, sick pay, personal days, health insurance, life insurance, and pensions are additional costs that may be negotiated between employers and employees.*

The most common withholdings, taxes, and other payroll costs are described below.

- **Federal income taxes:** Employers are required to withhold federal income taxes from employees' paychecks and pay them to the U. S. Treasury. These taxes are collected each time an employee is paid.
- **State and local income taxes:** Most states and some local governments levy income taxes. In most cases, the procedures for withholding are similar to those for federal income taxes.
- **Social security (FICA) tax:** The social security program (the Federal Insurance Contribution Act) provides retirement and disability benefits and survivor's benefits. The 2012 Social Security tax rate of 6.2 percent was paid by both employee and employer on the first $110,100 earned by an employee during the calendar year.* Both the rate and the base to which it applies are subject to change in future years.

*A temporary reduction in the employee social security contribution to 4.2 percent was enacted in 2011 and continued in 2012; but since it is not possible to predict if it will continue, the full 6.2 percent rate is used in the examples in this text.

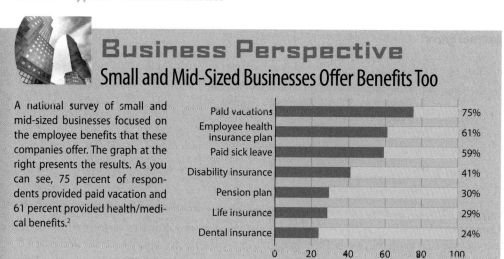

Business Perspective
Small and Mid-Sized Businesses Offer Benefits Too

A national survey of small and mid-sized businesses focused on the employee benefits that these companies offer. The graph at the right presents the results. As you can see, 75 percent of respondents provided paid vacation and 61 percent provided health/medical benefits.[2]

Benefit	Percent
Paid vacations	75%
Employee health insurance plan	61%
Paid sick leave	59%
Disability insurance	41%
Pension plan	30%
Life insurance	29%
Dental insurance	24%

- **Medicare tax:** A major extension of the social security program is Medicare, which provides hospitalization and medical insurance for persons over age 65. In 2012, the Medicare tax rate was 1.45 percent of gross income, with no limit, paid by *both* employee and employer.
- **Medical insurance:** Many organizations provide medical benefits to employees. Often, the employee contributes a portion of the cost through withholdings from income and the employer pays the rest—usually a greater amount—to the insurance company.
- **Pension contributions:** Many organizations also provide pension benefits to employees. A portion of the pension contribution is withheld from the employee's income, and the organization pays the rest of the amount into the pension fund.
- **Federal unemployment insurance (FUTA) tax:** This tax pays for programs for unemployed workers. It is paid *only* by employers and recently was 6.2 percent of the first $7,000 earned by each employee. (This rate may vary from state to state.) The employer is allowed a credit for unemployment taxes it pays to the state. The maximum credit is 5.4 percent of the first $7,000 earned by each employee. Most states set their rate at this maximum. Thus, the FUTA tax most often paid is 0.8 percent (6.2 percent – 5.4 percent) of the taxable wages.
- **State unemployment insurance tax:** State unemployment programs provide compensation to eligible unemployed workers. The compensation is paid out of the fund provided by the 5.4 percent of the first $7,000 (or the amount the state sets) earned by each employee. In some states, employers with favorable employment records may be entitled to pay less than 5.4 percent.

STUDY NOTE: *The employee pays all federal, state, and local taxes on income. The employer and employee share FICA and Medicare taxes. The employer bears FUTA and state unemployment taxes.*

Recording Payroll and Related Withholdings

Transaction On February 15, Teresa's Fitness Center's wages for employees total $65,000, and withholdings for employees are as follows.

- $10,800 for federal income taxes
- $2,400 for state income taxes
- $4,030 for social security tax
- $942 for Medicare tax
- $1,800 for medical insurance
- $2,600 for pension contributions

Analysis The journal entry to record payroll and related withholdings

▲ *increases* the *Wages Expense* account

▲ *increases* a *Payable* account for each type of withholding

▲ *increases* the *Wages Payable* account

Journal Entry

A	=	L	+	OE
		+10,800		−65,000
		+2,400		
		+4,030		
		+942		
		+1,800		
		+2,600		
		+42,428		

Feb. 15	Wages Expense	65,000	
	Employees' Federal Income Taxes Payable		10,800
	Employees' State Income Taxes Payable		2,400
	Social Security Tax Payable		4,030
	Medicare Tax Payable		942
	Medical Insurance Premiums Payable		1,800
	Pension Contributions Payable		2,600
	Wages Payable		42,428
	To record the payroll		

Comment Wages Expense is recorded for the gross wages, but the various withholding are *recognized* as liabilities before net amount payable to employees is determined. Although the employees earned at total of $65,000, their take-home pay total was only $42,428.

Recording Employer Payroll Taxes and Health Insurance Cost and Pension Benefits

Transaction On February 15, Teresa records the fitness center's share of payroll taxes (50 percent), the health insurance premiums (80 percent) and the pension contributions (50 percent).

Analysis The journal entry to record employer payroll taxes, health insurance costs, and pension benefits

▲ *increases* the *Payroll Taxes and Benefits Expense* account

▲ *increases* each *Tax Payable* account

▲ *increases* the *Medical Insurance Premiums Payable* account

▲ *increases* the *Pension Contributions Payable* account

Journal Entry

A	=	L	+	OE
		+4,030		−18,802
		+942		
		+7,200		
		+2,600		
		+520		
		+3,510		

Feb. 15	Payroll Taxes and Benefits Expense	18,802	
	Social Security Tax Payable		4,030
	Medicare Tax Payable		942
	Medical Insurance Premiums Payable		7,200*
	Pension Contributions Payable		2,600
	Federal Unemployment Tax Payable		520
	State Unemployment Tax Payable		3,510
	To record payroll taxes and other costs		

*The employees' share of premiums is 20%. Thus, the employer's share is: ($1,800 ÷ 0.20) − $1,800 = $7,200

Comment Note that the payroll taxes and benefits expense increases the total cost of the payroll to $83,802 ($18,802 + $65,000), which exceeds the amount earned by the employees by almost 29 percent.

Unearned Revenues Unearned revenues are advance payments for goods or services that a company must provide in a future period. The company *recognizes* the revenue over that period.

Recording Unearned Revenues

Transaction On June 1, Teresa's Fitness Center receives cash from a customer in advance for a one-year membership in the fitness center in the amount of $360.

Analysis The journal entry to record unearned revenues

> ▲ *increases* the *Cash* account
>
> ▲ *increases* the *Unearned Revenue* account

Application of Double Entry

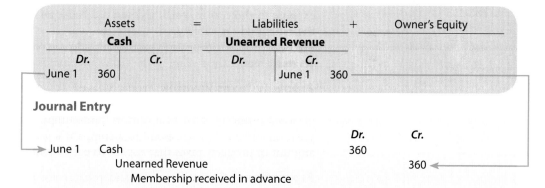

Journal Entry

A	=	L	+	OE
+360		+360		

		Dr.	Cr.
June 1	Cash	360	
	Unearned Revenue		360
	Membership received in advance		

Comment Teresa's Fitness Center has a liability of $360 that will slowly be reduced over the year as it provides the service.

Recognizing Unearned Revenues That Are Now Earned

Transaction On June 30, Teresa needs to record the amount of revenues earned at the end of the first month.

Analysis The journal entry to record unearned revenues that have been earned

> ▲ *increases* the *Revenue* account
>
> ▼ *decreases* the *Unearned Revenue* account

Application of Double Entry

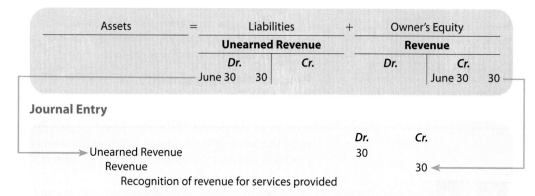

Journal Entry

A	=	L	+	OE
		−30		+30

	Dr.	Cr.
Unearned Revenue	30	
Revenue		30
Recognition of revenue for services provided		

Comment Many businesses, including special-order firms, repair companies, and construction companies, ask for a deposit. Until they deliver the goods or services, these deposits are *classified* as current liabilities.

Estimated Liabilities

Estimated liabilities are definite debts or obligations whose exact dollar amount cannot be known until a later date. The primary accounting problem is to estimate and record the amount of the liability. The following are examples of estimated liabilities.

Income Taxes Payable The federal government, most state governments, and some cities and towns levy a tax on a corporation's income. The amount of the liability depends on the results of a corporation's operations, which are often not known until after the end of the corporation's fiscal year. However, because income taxes are an expense in the year in which income is earned, an adjusting entry is necessary to record the estimated tax liability.

Sole proprietorships and partnerships do *not* pay income taxes. However, their owners must report their share of the firm's income on their individual tax returns.

Property Taxes Payable Property taxes are a main source of revenue for local governments. They are levied annually on real property, such as land and buildings, and on personal property, such as inventory and equipment. Because the fiscal years of local governments rarely correspond to a company's fiscal year, it is necessary to estimate the amount of property taxes that applies to each month of the year.

Promotional Costs Coupons and rebates are part of many companies' marketing programs. Because of frequent flyer programs, for example, U.S. airline companies today have more than 10 trillion "free miles" outstanding. What are the accounting implications of these promotional programs? Companies usually record the costs as a reduction in sales (a contra-sales account) rather than as an expense with a corresponding current liability.

Hershey Foods Corporation accrues almost $1 billion in promotional costs each year. In its annual report, Hershey acknowledged the difficulty of estimating the accrued liability for promotional programs:

> *Accrued liabilities requiring the most difficult or subjective judgments include liabilities associated with marketing promotion programs.. . . We determine the amount of the accrued liability by analysis of programs offered, historical trends, expectations regarding customer and consumer participation, sales and payment trends; and experience with payment patterns associated with similar, previously offered programs. The estimated costs of these programs are reasonably likely to change in the future due to changes in trends with regard to customer and consumer participation, particularly for new programs and for programs related to the introduction of new products.[3]*

Product Warranty Liability When a firm sells a product or service with a warranty, it has a liability for the length of the warranty. The warranty is a feature of the product and is included in the selling price. Its cost should therefore be debited to an expense account in the period of the sale. Based on past experience, it should be possible to estimate the amount the warranty will cost the company in the future. Warranties on some products will cost the company very little; others may cost a lot.

Business Perspective
What Is the Cost of Frequent Flyer Miles?

In the early 1980s, **American Airlines** developed a frequent flyer program that awards free trips and other bonuses to customers based on the number of miles they fly on the airline. It is estimated that 180 million people now participate in similar programs. Estimated liabilities for these tickets have become an important consideration in evaluating an airline's financial position. Complicating the estimate is that almost half the miles have been earned through purchases from hotels, car rental and telephone companies, Internet service providers like **AOL**, and bank credit cards.[4]

Recording Product Liability

Transaction A muffler company like **Midas** guarantees that it will replace free of charge any muffler it sells that fails during the time the buyer owns the car. The company charges a small service fee for replacing the muffler. In the past, 6 percent of the mufflers sold have been returned for replacement under the warranty. The average cost of a muffler is $50. On July 31, Midas must record the accrued liability and related expense. The company sold 700 mufflers during the month.

Analysis The journal entry to record the accrued liability and related expense

- ▲ *increases* the *Product Warranty Expense* account
- ▲ *increases* the *Estimated Product Warranty Liability* account

Application of Double Entry

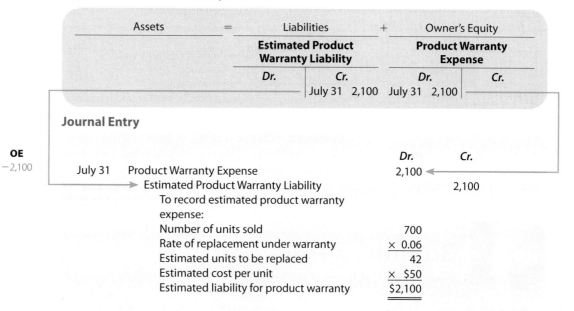

Assets	=	Liabilities	+	Owner's Equity
		Estimated Product Warranty Liability		**Product Warranty Expense**
		Dr.	Cr.	Dr.	Cr.
			July 31 2,100	July 31 2,100	

Journal Entry

A = L + OE
   +2,100   −2,100

		Dr.	Cr.
July 31	Product Warranty Expense	2,100	
	Estimated Product Warranty Liability		2,100
	To record estimated product warranty expense:		
	Number of units sold	700	
	Rate of replacement under warranty	× 0.06	
	Estimated units to be replaced	42	
	Estimated cost per unit	× $50	
	Estimated liability for product warranty	$2,100	

Comment The expense and liability for the estimated warranty are *recognized* at the time of sale of the product.

Recording Product Liability and Service

Transaction On December 5, a customer returns with a defective muffler, which cost $60, and pays a $30 service fee to have it replaced.

Analysis The journal entry to record this liability and service

- ▲ *increases* the *Cash* account
- ▲ *increases* the *Service Revenue* account
- ▼ *decreases* the *Merchandise Inventory* account
- ▼ *decreases* the *Estimated Product Warranty Liability* account

Application of Double Entry

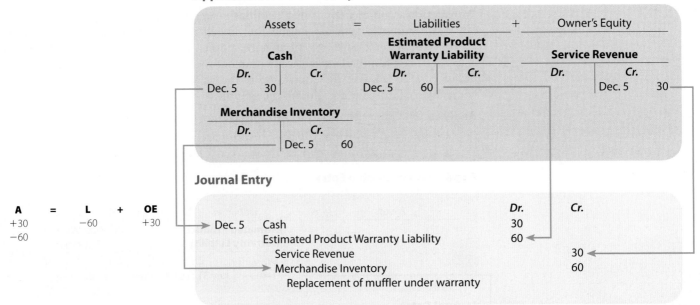

A	=	L	+	OE
+30		−60		+30
−60				

Journal Entry

		Dr.	Cr.
Dec. 5	Cash	30	
	Estimated Product Warranty Liability	60	
	Service Revenue		30
	Merchandise Inventory		60
	Replacement of muffler under warranty		

Comment When a muffler is returned for replacement under the warranty, the cost of the muffler reduces the Merchandise Inventory account and the Estimated Product Warranty Liability account. This is an example of an entry for a transaction with two components: providing a service (revenue) and fulfilling an obligation (liability).

Business Perspective
Those Little Coupons Can Add Up

Many companies promote their products by issuing coupons that offer "cents off" or other enticements. Because four out of five shoppers use coupons, companies are forced by competition to distribute them. The total value of unredeemed coupons, each of which represents a potential liability for the issuing company, is staggering. In 2011, marketers distributed approximately 305 billion coupons, of which less than 1% of all coupons were digital coupons. In total, the coupons were worth about $470 billion, but consumers redeemed only $4.6 billion in savings.[5] Thus, a big advertiser can issue millions of coupons and expect less than 1 percent to be redeemed.

Vacation Pay Liability In most companies, employees accrue paid vacation as they work during the year. For example, an employee may earn 52 weeks' salary for 50 weeks' work. The cost of the two weeks' vacation should be allocated as an expense over the year so that month-to-month costs will not be distorted. The vacation pay represents 4 percent (two weeks' vacation divided by 50 weeks) of an employee's pay.

Recording Vacation Pay Expense

Transaction Diviney Company has a vacation policy of two weeks of paid vacation for each 50 weeks of work, has a payroll of $42,000, and paid $2,000 of that amount to employees on vacation for the week ended April 20. Because of past experience with employee turnover, the company assumes that only 75 percent of the employees will ultimately collect vacation pay. The computation of vacation pay expense based on the payroll of employees not on vacation ($42,000 − $2,000) is as follows.

$$\$40,000 \times 4 \text{ percent} \times 75 \text{ percent} = \$1,200$$

Diviney must record vacation pay expense for the week ended April 20.

Analysis The journal entry to record vacation pay expense

▲ *increases* the *Vacation Pay Expense* account

▲ *increases* the *Estimated Liability for Vacation Pay* account

Application of Double Entry

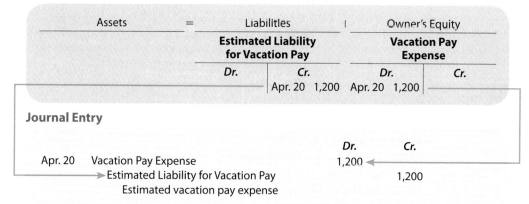

Assets	=	Liabilities		Owner's Equity	
		Estimated Liability for Vacation Pay		**Vacation Pay Expense**	
		Dr.	Cr.	Dr.	Cr.
			Apr. 20 1,200	Apr. 20 1,200	

Journal Entry

A = L + OE
+1,200   −1,200

		Dr.	Cr.
Apr. 20	Vacation Pay Expense	1,200	
	Estimated Liability for Vacation Pay		1,200
	Estimated vacation pay expense		

Just as employees earn paid vacation days and holidays when working, employers incur expenses and liabilities for those paid days off.

Comment Vacation Pay Expense and corresponding liability are *recognized* on this date because the employee earned the vacation pay in the week working rather than when the vacation is taken.

YanLev/Shutterstock.com

Recording Payment When Vacation is Taken

Transaction On August 31, Diviney Company needs to record the $2,000 paid to employees on vacation during August.

Analysis The journal entry for a company to record payment for employees on vacation

▼ *decreases* the *Estimated Liability for Vacation Pay* account

▼ *decreases* the *Cash* account

Application of Double Entry

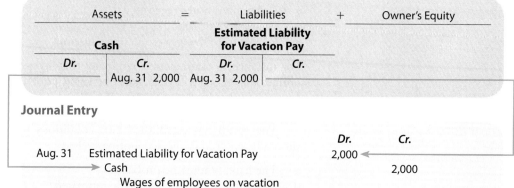

Assets	=	Liabilities	+	Owner's Equity
Cash		**Estimated Liability for Vacation Pay**		
Dr.	Cr.	Dr.	Cr.	
	Aug. 31 2,000	Aug. 31 2,000		

Journal Entry

A* = L + OE
−2,000   −2,000

*Assumes Cash paid.

		Dr.	Cr.
Aug. 31	Estimated Liability for Vacation Pay	2,000	
	Cash		2,000
	Wages of employees on vacation		

Comment The treatment of vacation pay presented here can also be applied to other payroll costs, such as bonus plans and contributions to pension plans.

APPLY IT!

Tellex Corp. manufactures and sells clocks. Each clock costs $30 to produce and sells for $60. In addition, each clock carries a warranty that provides for free replacement if it fails during the two years following the sale. In the past, 2 percent of the clocks sold have had to be replaced under the warranty. During May, Tellex sold 20,000 clocks, and 350 clocks were replaced under the warranty. Prepare journal entries to record the estimated liability for product warranties during the month and the clocks replaced under warranty during the month (use May 31).

SOLUTION

May 31	Product Warranty Expense	12,000	
	Estimated Product Warranty Liability		12,000
	To record estimated product warranty expense:		
	Number of units sold	20,000	
	Rate of replacement under warranty	× 0.02	
	Estimated units to be replaced	400	
	Estimated cost per unit	× $30	
	Estimated liability for product warranty	$12,000	
May 31	Estimated Product Warranty Liability	10,500	
	Merchandise Inventory		10,500
	Replacement of clocks under warranty		
	350 clocks × $30 = $10,500		

TRY IT! SE2, SE3, SE4, E2A, E3A, E4A, E5A, E6A, E2B, E3B, E4B, E5B, E6B

LO 3 Contingent Liabilities and Commitments

The FASB requires companies to *disclose* in a note to their financial statements any contingent liabilities and commitments. A **contingent liability** is a *potential* liability because it depends on a future event arising out of a past transaction. Contingent liabilities often involve the following:

- Lawsuits
- Income tax disputes
- Discounted notes receivable
- Guarantees of debt
- Failure to follow government regulations

For instance, a construction company that signed a contract with a state to build a bridge may be sued by the state for using poor materials. The past transaction is the contract for building the bridge. The future event is the outcome of the lawsuit, which is not yet known.

The FASB has established two conditions for determining when a contingency should be entered in the accounting records:

- The liability must be probable.
- The liability can be reasonably estimated.[6]

STUDY NOTE: Contingencies are recorded when they are probable and can be reasonably estimated.

Estimated liabilities like those for income taxes, warranties, and vacation pay that we described earlier meet those conditions. They are, therefore, accrued in the accounting records.

International Perspective

IFRS Balance Sheet Liabilities Are Often Greater Under IFRS

U.S. GAAP do not record commitments, such as purchase agreements, as liabilities even though they are a *legal* obligation, since they do not meet the technical definition of a liability. *Disclosure* in a note to the financial statements is required. Under IFRS, however, these agreements are *recognized* when an entity has a demonstrable commitment.

In a survey of large companies, lawsuits involving many different issues and environmental concerns, including toxic waste cleanup, were among the most common types of contingencies reported.[7] In a note to its 2011 financial statements, **Microsoft** described its contingent liabilities as lawsuits involving infringement of European competition law, antitrust and overcharge actions, and patent and intellectual property claims, among other matters. Microsoft's management stated:

> We also are subject to a variety of other claims and suits . . . While we intend to vigorously defend these matters, there exists the possibility of adverse outcomes that we estimate could reach approximately $800 million in aggregate beyond recorded amounts. Were unfavorable final outcomes to occur, there exists the possibility of a material adverse impact on our financial statements for the period in which the effects become reasonably estimable.[8]

A **commitment** is a legal obligation that does not meet the technical requirements for *recognition* as a liability and so is not recorded. Common examples are purchase agreements, construction or acquisition of long-term assets, and leases.[9] For example, **Microsoft** also reported in its notes to its financial statements that it had construction commitments of $263 million and purchase commitments of $5.6 billion.[10] Knowledge of these amounts is very important for planning cash flows in the coming years.

APPLY IT!

Indicate whether each of the following is (a) a contingent liability or (b) a commitment:

1. A tax dispute with the IRS
2. A long-term lease agreement
3. An agreement to purchase goods in the future
4. A potential lawsuit over a defective product

SOLUTION

1. a;   2. b;   3. b;   4. a

TRY IT! SE5, E7A, E7B

LO4 Valuation Approaches to Fair Value Accounting

Recall that *fair value* is the price for which an asset or liability could be sold, or exit the company, as opposed to the price for which the company could buy the asset or liability. As pointed out previously, the concept of fair value applies to some financial assets, such as cash equivalents and investments, and to some liabilities, such as notes payable. Fair value is also applicable to determining whether tangible assets such as inventories and long-term assets have sustained a permanent decline in value below their cost. The FASB identifies three approaches to measurement of fair value:[11]

- **Market approach:** External market transactions are ideal for *valuing* investments and liabilities for which there is an active market and quoted prices are available

International Perspective

IFRS Do the FASB and IASB Agree on Fair Value Measurement?

As part of their effort to converge U.S. GAAP with IFRS, the FASB and the IASB agreed in 2011, after almost ten years of effort, to issue a converged fair value measurement standard ASU 2011-04 (Topic 820) by the FASB and IFRS 13 by the IASB. In this standard, they agree on a common definition of fair value, including concepts and assumptions as well as *disclosures*. This is a major step forward in the effort to bring U.S. GAAP closer to global accounting standards.[12]

for the specific asset or liability. However, an active market or a quoted price is not always available. For example, there may not be a market for special-purpose equipment. In these cases, it may be possible to observe quoted prices for comparable types of equipment.

- **Income (or cash flow) approach:** The income approach, as defined by the FASB, converts future cash flows to a single present value. This approach is used when the market approach cannot be used because there are no identical or comparable quoted prices available. It is based on management's best determination of the future cash amounts generated by an asset or payments that will be made for a liability. It is based on internally generated information, which should be reasonable for the circumstances. For instance, management may estimate the cash flows or cost savings expected to be generated by the special-purpose equipment.

- **Cost approach:** The cost approach is based on the amount that currently would be required to replace an asset with the same or a comparable asset. For example, inventory is usually *valued* at lower of cost or market, where market is the replacement cost. For plant assets like special-purpose equipment, the replacement cost of a new asset must be adjusted to take into account the asset's age, condition, depreciation, and obsolescence.

The following sections, which focus on the income or cash flow approach, require knowledge of interest and the time value of money and present value techniques.

Interest, the Time Value of Money, and Future Value

The concept of the **time value of money** refers to the costs or benefits of holding or not holding money over time. **Interest** is the cost of using money for a specific period. For example, if you have $100 and hold that amount for one year without putting it in a savings account, you have forgone the interest that the money would have earned. However, if you put the $100 in an interest-bearing checking account, you will have the $100 plus the interest at the end of the year.

The amount of principal plus interest after one or more periods is known as **future value**. Future value may be computed using either simple interest or compound interest.

- **Simple interest** is the interest cost for one or more periods when the principal sum—the amount on which interest is computed—stays the same from period to period.

- **Compound interest** is the interest cost for two or more periods when, after each period, the interest earned in that period is added to the amount on which interest is computed in future periods. In other words, the principal sum is increased at the end of each period by the interest earned in that period.

STUDY NOTE: *Compound interest is useful in business because it helps decision makers choose among alternative courses of action.*

The examples that follow illustrate these concepts.

Future Value Using Simple Interest

Measure *Simple interest* is the interest cost for one or more periods when the principal sum stays the same from period to period.

Example Willy Wang accepts an 8 percent, $15,000 note due in 90 days. How much will he receive at that time? The interest is calculated as follows.

$$\text{Interest} = \text{Principal} \times \text{Rate} \times \text{Time}$$
$$= \$15,000.00 \times 8/100 \times 90/365$$
$$= \$295.89$$

Therefore, the future value that Wang will receive is $15,295.89, calculated as follows.

$$\text{Total} = \text{Principal} + \text{Interest}$$
$$- \$15,000.00 + \$295.89$$
$$= \$15,295.89$$

Future Value Using Compound Interest

Measure *Compound interest* is the interest cost for two or more periods when, after each period, the interest earned in that period is added to the amount on which interest is computed in future periods.

Example Terry Soma deposits $10,000 in an account that pays 6 percent interest. She expects to leave the principal and accumulated interest in the account for three years. If the interest is paid at the end of each year and is then added to the principal and this amount in turn earns interest, how much will Soma's account total at the end of three years? The amount is computed as follows.

Year	Principal Amount at Beginning of Year	Annual Amount of Interest (Principal at Beginning of Year × 6%)	Accumulated Amount at End of Year (Principal at Beginning of Year + Annual Amount of Interest)
1	$10,000.00	$600.00	$10,600.00
2	10,600.00	636.00	11,236.00
3	11,236.00	674.16	11,910.16

Soma will have $11,910.16 in her account at the end of three years. Note that the amount of interest increases each year by the interest rate times the interest of the previous year. For example, between year 1 and year 2, the interest increased by $36, which equals 6 percent times $600.

Present Value

Suppose you had the choice of receiving $100 today or one year from today. No doubt you would choose to receive it today. Why? If you have the money today, you can put it in a savings account to earn interest so you will have more than $100 a year from today. In other words, because the amount today (present value) does not include any interest, it is less than the amount in the future (future value). **Present value** is the amount that must be invested today at a given rate of interest to produce a given future value. Thus, present value and future value are closely related.

Present Value

Measure *Present value* is the amount that must be invested today at a given rate of interest to produce a given future value.

Example Lucia Fontaine needs $10,000 one year from now. How much does she have to invest today to achieve that goal if the interest rate is 5 percent? From earlier examples, we can establish the following equation:

Present Value × (1.0 + Interest Rate) = Future Value
Present Value × 1.05   = $10,000.00
Present Value   = $10,000.00 ÷ 1.05
Present Value   = $9,523.81*

*Rounded

To achieve a future value of $10,000, Fontaine must invest a present value of $9,523.81. Interest of 5 percent on $9,523.81 for one year equals $476.19, and these two amounts added together equal $10,000.

Present Value of a Single Sum Due in the Future

Measure The present value of a single amount of cash is the amount to be received at a specified date in the future.

Example Ron Moore wants to be sure of having $8,000 at the end of three years. How much must he invest today in a 5 percent savings account to achieve this goal?

Manual Computation We can compute the present value of $8,000 at compound interest of 5 percent for three years by adapting the above equation:

Year	Amount at End of Year	Divide by		Present Value at Beginning of Year
3	$8,000.00	÷ 1.05	=	$7,619.05*
2	7,619.05	÷ 1.05	=	7,256.24*
1	7,256.24	÷ 1.05	=	6,910.70*

*Rounded

Moore must invest $6,910.70 today to achieve a value of $8,000 in three years.

Table Computation We can simplify the calculation by using a table of present values. Refer to Table 1 in Appendix B. The point at which the 5 percent column and the row for period 3 intersect shows a factor of 0.864, as shown in Exhibit 3. This factor, when multiplied by $1, gives the present value of $1 to be received three years from now at 5 percent interest. Thus, we solve the problem as follows.

Future Value: $8,000

Year 1   Year 2   Year 3

Present Value: $6,912

Future Value × Factor = Present Value
$8,000   × 0.864 = $6,912

Except for a rounding difference of $1.30, this result is the same as our earlier one.

Exhibit 3
Present Value of $1 to Be Received at the End of a Given Number of Periods

Period	1%	2%	3%	4%	5%	6%	7%	8%	9%	10%
1	0.990	0.980	0.971	0.962	0.952	0.943	0.935	0.926	0.917	0.909
2	0.980	0.961	0.943	0.925	0.907	0.890	0.873	0.857	0.842	0.826
3	0.971	0.942	0.915	0.889	**0.864**	0.840	0.816	0.794	0.772	0.751

© Cengage Learning 2014

Present Value of an Ordinary Annuity

It is often necessary to compute the present value of a series of receipts or payments equally spaced over time, with compound interest—in other words, the present value of an **ordinary annuity**.

Present Value of an Ordinary Annuity

Measure An *ordinary annuity* is a series of equal payments or receipts that will begin one time period from the current date.

Example Vickie Long has sold a piece of property and is to receive $18,000 in three equal annual payments of $6,000 beginning one year from today. What is the present value of this sale if the current interest rate is 5 percent?

Manual Computation Using Table 1 in Appendix B, we can compute the present value by calculating a separate value for each of the three payments and summing the results, as follows.

Future Receipts (Annuity)				Present Value Factor at 5 Percent (from Exhibit 3)		Present Value
Year 1	Year 2	Year 3				
$6,000			×	0.952	=	$ 5,712
	$6,000		×	0.907	=	5,442
		$6,000	×	0.864	=	5,184
Total Present Value						$16,338

The present value of the sale is $16,338. Thus, there is an implied interest cost (given the 5 percent rate) of $1,662 ($18,000 − $16,338) associated with the payment plan.

Table Computation We can make this calculation more easily by using Table 2 in Appendix B. The point at which the 5 percent column intersects the row for period 3 shows a factor of 2.723 (as shown in Exhibit 4), which is the sum of the three present value factors in the table above (0.952 + 0.907 + 0.864 = 2.723). When multiplied by $1, this factor gives the present value of a series of three $1 payments (spaced one year apart) at compound interest of 5 percent. Thus, we solve the problem as follows.

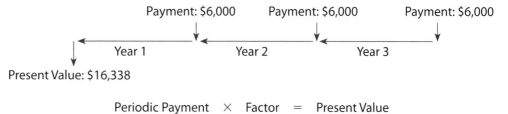

Periodic Payment	×	Factor	=	Present Value
$6,000	×	2.723	=	$16,338

This result is the same as the one we computed earlier.

Exhibit 4
Present Value of an Ordinary $1 Annuity Received in Each Period for a Given Number of Periods

© Cengage Learning 2014

Period	1%	2%	3%	4%	5%	6%	7%	8%	9%	10%
1	0.990	0.980	0.971	0.962	0.952	0.943	0.935	0.926	0.917	0.909
2	1.970	1.942	1.913	1.886	1.859	1.833	1.808	1.783	1.759	1.736
3	2.941	2.884	2.829	2.775	**2.723**	2.673	2.624	2.577	2.531	2.487

Time Periods As in all our examples, the compounding period is in most cases one year, and the interest rate is stated on an annual basis. However, in Tables 1 and 2 in Appendix B, the far left columns refer not to years but to periods. This wording accommodates compounding periods of less than one year. Savings accounts that record interest quarterly and bonds that pay interest semiannually are cases in which the compounding period is less than one year. To use the tables in these cases, you must divide the annual interest rate by the number of periods in the year and multiply the number of periods in one year by the number of years.

Present Value When Compounding Period Is Less than One Year

Measure The present value is the amount of interest calculated or compounded more than once per year.

Example Compute the present value of a $6,000 payment that is to be made in two years. The annual interest rate of 8 percent, and the compounding period is semiannual.

Manual Computation Before using present value tables in this computation, we must compute the interest rate that applies to each compounding period and the total number of compounding periods.

- The interest rate to use is 4 percent (8% annual rate ÷ 2 periods per year).
- The total number of compounding periods is 4 (2 periods per year × 2 years).

Table Computation We can then use Table 1 in Appendix B to compute the present value of the payment, $5,130, as follows.

$$\text{Principal} \times \text{Factor} = \text{Present Value}$$
$$\$6{,}000 \times 0.855 = \$5{,}130$$

This procedure is used whenever the corresponding period is less than one year. For example, a monthly compounding requires dividing the annual interest rate by 12 and multiplying the number of years by 12 to use the tables. This method can be used with the present value tables in Appendix B.

APPLY IT!

Use Tables 1 and 2 in Appendix B to determine the present value of the following:

1. A single payment of $10,000 at 5 percent for 10 years
2. 10 annual payments of $1,000 at 5 percent
3. A single payment of $10,000 at 7 percent for 5 years
4. 10 annual payments of $1,000 at 9 percent

SOLUTION

1. From Table 1: $10,000 × 0.614 = $6,140
2. From Table 2: $1,000 × 7.722 = $7,722
3. From Table 1: $10,000 × 0.713 = $7,130
4. From Table 2: $1,000 × 6.418 = $6,418

TRY IT! SE6, SE7, SE8, E8A, E9A, E10A, E11A, E12A, E13A, E8B, E9B, E10B, E11B, E12B, E13B

LO5 Applications Using Present Value

The concept of present value is widely used in business decision making and financial reporting. For example, the *value* of a long-term note receivable or payable can be determined by calculating the present value of the future interest payments. As mentioned earlier, the FASB has made present value an important component of its approach in determining the fair value of assets and liabilities when a market price is not available.

The SEC has issued guidance on how to apply fair value accounting.[13] For instance, it states that management's internal assumptions about expected cash flows may be used to measure fair value and that market quotes may be used when they are from an orderly, active market. Thus, **Microsoft** may determine the expected present value of the future cash flows of an investment by using its internal cash flow projections and a market rate of interest. By comparing the result to the current value of the investment, Microsoft can determine if an adjustment needs to be made to record a gain or loss.

In the sections that follow, we illustrate two useful applications of present value. These applications will be helpful in understanding the uses of present value that we discuss in later chapters.

Valuing an Asset at Present Value

As already discussed, an asset is something that will provide future benefits to the company that owns it. Usually, the purchase price of an asset represents the present value of those future benefits. It is possible to evaluate a proposed purchase price by comparing it with the present value of the asset to the company.

The Present Value of an Asset

Measure The present value of an asset is based on the saving it will generate over its useful life.

Example Mike Yeboah is thinking of buying a new machine that will reduce his annual labor cost by $1,400 per year. The machine will last eight years. The interest rate that Yeboah assumes for making equipment purchases is 10 percent. What is the maximum amount (present value) that Yeboah should pay for the machine?

Table Computation The present value of the machine is equal to the present value of an ordinary annuity of $1,400 per year for eight years at compound interest of 10 percent. Using the present value factor from Appendix B, we compute the present value as follows.

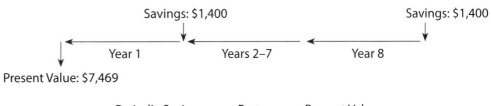

Periodic Savings	×	Factor	=	Present Value
$1,400	×	5.335	=	$7,469

Yeboah should not pay more than $7,469 for the machine because this amount equals the present value of the benefits he would receive from owning it.

Present Value of a Deferred Payment

To encourage buyers to make a purchase, sellers sometimes agree to defer payment for a sale. This practice is common among companies that sell agricultural equipment to farmers who need new equipment in the spring but cannot pay for it until they sell their crops in the fall.

Present Value of a Deferred Payment

Measure The present value is the amount of a payment to be received later.

Example Field Helpers Corporation sells a tractor to Sasha Ptak for $100,000 on February 1 and agrees to take payment ten months later, on December 1. With such an agreement, the future payment includes not only the selling price but also an implied (imputed) interest cost.

Table Computation If the prevailing annual interest rate for such transactions is 12 percent compounded monthly, the actual price of the tractor would be the present value of the future payment, computed using the factor from Appendix B [10 periods, 1 percent (12 percent ÷ 12 months)], as follows.

Future Payment	×	Factor	=	Present Value
$100,000	×	0.905	=	$90,500

Ptak records the present value, $90,500, in his purchase records, and Field Helpers Corporation records it in its sales records. The balance consists of interest expense or interest income.

Other Applications

Other applications of present value in accounting include the following:

- Computing imputed interest on non-interest-bearing notes
- Accounting for installment notes
- Valuing a bond
- Recording lease obligations
- Pension obligations
- Valuing debt
- Depreciating property, plant, and equipment
- Making capital expenditure decisions
- Accounting for any item in which time is a factor

Current Liabilities and the Financial Statements

As presented in Exhibit 5, the application of *accrual accounting* to unearned revenues and accrued expenses impacts the amount of current liabilities on the balance sheet and revenues and expenses on the income statement.

Exhibit 5
Accrued Expenses and Related Accrued Liabilities

© Cengage Learning 2014

Jerry owns a restaurant and has the opportunity to buy a high-quality espresso coffee machine for $5,000. After carefully studying expected costs and revenues, Jerry estimates that the machine will produce a net cash inflow of $1,600 annually and will last for five years. He determines that an interest rate of 10 percent is an adequate return on his investment.

Calculate the present value of the machine to Jerry. Based on your calculation, do you think Jerry would be wise to purchase the machine? Explain your answer.

SOLUTION

Calculation of the present value:

Annual cash inflow	$ 1,600.00
Factor from Table 2, Appendix B (5 years at 10%)	× 3.791
Present value of net cash flows	$ 6,065.60
Less purchase price	−5,000.00
Net present value	$ 1,065.60

The present value of the net cash flows from the machine exceeds the purchase price. Thus, the investment will return more than 10 percent to Jerry's business. A decision to purchase the machine would, therefore, be wise.

TRY IT! SE8, E11A, E12A, E13A, E11B, E12B, E13B

SECTION 3

BUSINESS
APPLICATIONS
■ Liquidity
■ Cash flows

RELEVANT
LEARNING OBJECTIVE

LO 6 Use ratio analysis to manage the impact of current liabilities' impact on liquidity.

BUSINESS APPLICATIONS

LO 6 Business Issues Related to Current Liabilities

The primary reason a company incurs current liabilities is to meet its needs for cash during the operating cycle. Failure to manage the cash flows related to current liabilities can have serious consequences for a business. For instance, if suppliers are not paid on time, they may withhold vital shipments. Continued failure to pay current liabilities can lead to bankruptcy.

Working Capital and the Current Ratio

As explained in Chapter 6, the *operating cycle* is the length of time it takes to purchase inventory, sell the inventory, and collect the resulting receivable. Most current liabilities arise from purchases of inventory, accrued expenses arise from operating costs, and unearned revenues arise from customers' advance payments. Companies incur short-term debt to raise cash during periods of inventory buildup or while waiting for the collection of receivables. They use the cash to pay the portion of long-term debt that is currently due and to pay liabilities arising from operations.

To evaluate a company's ability to pay its current liabilities, analysts often use two measures of liquidity, both of which we defined in an earlier chapter:

■   Working Capital = Current Assets − Current Liabilities
■   Current Ratio = Current Assets ÷ Current Liabilities

As shown below (in millions), **Nike**'s short-term liquidity as measured by working capital and the current ratio was positive in 2010 but decreased in 2011.

	Current Assets	−	Current Liabilities	=	Working Capital	Current Ratio*
2010	$10,959	−	$3,364	=	$7,595	3.26**
2011	$11,297	−	$3,958	=	$7,339	2.85**

*Current Assets ÷ Current Liabilities
**Rounded

The decrease in Nike's working capital and current ratio was caused primarily by a large decrease in cash and equivalents and an increase in all current liabilities. Overall, Nike is in a strong current situation.

Evaluating Accounts Payable

Another consideration in managing liquidity and cash flows is the time suppliers give a company to pay for purchases. Measurements commonly used to assess a company's ability to pay within a certain time frame are payables turnover and days' payable.

Payables Turnover **Payables turnover** is the number of times, on average, that a company pays its accounts payable in an accounting period. This measure reflects the relative size of accounts payable, the credit terms offered by suppliers, and a company's diligence in paying its suppliers.

To measure payables turnover for **Nike**, we must first calculate purchases by adjusting the cost of goods sold for the change in inventory.

▲ An *increase* in inventory means purchases were more than the cost of goods sold.

▼ A *decrease* means purchases were less than the cost of goods sold.

Nike's cost of goods sold in 2011 was $20,862 million, and its inventory increased by $674 million. Using these data, we can compute Nike's payables turnover as follows (in millions).

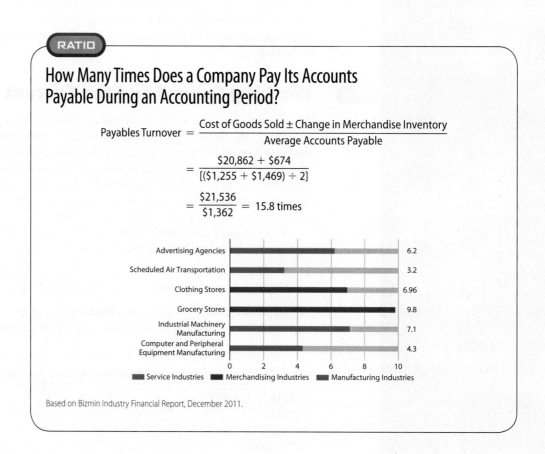

As you can see, Nike's payables turnover is greater than the industries illustrated. This indicates that Nike pays its suppliers very quickly.

Days' Payable **Days' payable** shows how long, on average, a company takes to pay its accounts payable. For **Nike**, it is computed as follows.

RATID

How Many Days Did It Take to Pay Accounts Payable?

$$\text{Days' Payable} = \frac{365 \text{ days}}{\text{Payables Turnover}} = \frac{365 \text{ days}}{15.8 \text{ times}} = 23.1 \text{ days}$$

Industry	Value
Advertising Agencies	58.9
Scheduled Air Transportation	120
Clothing Stores	52.4
Grocery Stores	37.3
Industrial Machinery Manufacturing	51.4
Computer and Peripheral Equipment Manufacturing	85.6

Service Industries   Merchandising Industries   Manufacturing Industries

Based on Bizmin Industry Financial Report, December 2011.

As shown, Nike's days' payable of 23.1 days, like its payables turnover of 15.8 times, indicates that Nike is prompt in paying its suppliers.

APPLY IT!

Jackie's Cookie Company has current assets of $30,000 and current liabilities of $20,000, of which accounts payable are $15,000. Jackie's cost of goods sold is $125,000, its merchandise inventory increased by $5,000, and accounts payable were $11,000 the prior year. Calculate Jackie's working capital, payables turnover, and days' payable.

SOLUTION

Working Capital $= $ Current Assets $-$ Current Liabilities

$= $30,000 - $20,000$

$= $10,000$

$$\text{Payables Turnover} = \frac{\text{Cost of Goods Sold} \pm \text{Change in Inventory}}{\text{Average Accounts Payable}}$$

$$= \frac{\$125,000 + \$5,000}{(\$15,000 + \$11,000) \div 2} = \frac{\$130,000}{\$13,000}$$

$= 10 \text{ Times}$

Days' Payable $= 365$ days $\div$ Payables Turnover

$$= \frac{365 \text{ days}}{10 \text{ times}} = 36.5 \text{ days}$$

TRY IT! SE9, E15A, E15B

TriLevel Problem

Teresa's Fitness Center

Identification and Evaluation of Current Liabilities, Contingencies, and Commitments

The beginning of this chapter focused on Teresa Madej, the owner of Teresa's Fitness Center, who was anxious to assess her company's status at the end of the first year of operations. Complete the following requirements in order to answer the questions posed at the beginning of the chapter.

Section 1: Concepts

How do the concepts of recognition, valuation, classification, and disclosure apply to current liabilities?

Section 2: Accounting Applications

Madej has not yet filed any tax reports for her business and, therefore, owes taxes. Because she has limited experience in running a business, she has brought you all her business records—a checkbook, canceled checks, deposit slips, suppliers' invoices, a notice of annual property taxes of $3,600 due to the city, and a promissory note to her bank for $16,000. She wants you to determine what her business owes the government and other parties.

You analyzed all her records and determined the following as of December 31, 2014:

Unpaid invoices for nutritional supplements	$12,000
Sales of nutritional supplements (excluding sales tax)	57,000
Cost of supplements sold	33,600
Exercise instructors' salaries	22,800
Exercise revenues	81,400
Current assets	40,000
Supplements inventory, December 31, 2014	27,000
Supplements inventory, December 31, 2013	21,000

You learned that the company sold gift certificates in the amount of $700 that have not been redeemed and that it deducted $1,374 from its two employees' salaries for federal income taxes owed to the government. The current social security tax is 6.2 percent on maximum earnings of $110,100 for each employee, and the current Medicare tax is 1.45 percent (no maximum earnings). The FUTA tax is 5.4 percent to the state and 0.8 percent to the federal government on the first $7,000 earned by each employee; both employees earned more than $7,000. Madej has not filed a sales tax report to the state (6 percent of supplements sales).

What are the company's current liabilities and their total amount? (Ignore tax on company income.)

Section 3: Business Applications

Why is it important for Teresa Madej to identify and account for all her company's current liabilities? To answer this question, evaluate the company's liquidity by calculating working capital, payables turnover, and days' payable. Comment on the results. (*Note:* Assume average accounts payable were the same as year-end accounts payable.)

SOLUTION

Section 1: Concepts

First of all, generally accepted accounting principles require that a liability be recorded when an obligation occurs, which refers to the *recognition* of liabilities. In addition, liabilities must be properly *valued*, which refers to knowing or properly estimating the amount of money needed to pay the debt. Furthermore, because of the impact that *classification* can have on a company's reported liquidity, it is very important to distinguish between current and long-term liabilities. Finally, to allow financial statement users to more clearly understand how a company uses some liability accounts, any special arrangements or additional explanation should be *disclosed* in the notes to the financial statements.

Section 2: Accounting Applications

	A	B	C	D	E	F	G
1	Accounts payable						$12,000.00
2	Notes payable						16,000.00
3	Property taxes payable						3,600.00
4	Sales tax payable		($57,000	×	0.06	)	3,420.00
5	Social security tax payable		($22,800	×	0.062	) × 2	2,827.20
6	Medicare tax payable		($22,800	×	0.0145	) × 2	661.20
7	State unemployment tax payable		($ 7,000	×	0.054	) × 2	756.00
8	Federal unemployment tax payable		($ 7,000	×	0.008	) × 2	112.00
9	Employees' federal income taxes payable						1,374.00
10	Unearned revenues						700.00
11	Total current liabilities						$41,450.40
12							

Note: The company may have current liabilities for which you have not seen any documentary evidence. For instance, invoices for accounts payable could be missing. In addition, the company may have accrued liabilities, such as vacation pay for its two employees, which would require establishing an estimated liability. If the promissory note to Madej's bank is interest-bearing, it also would require an adjustment to accrue interest payable, and the company could have other loans outstanding for which you have not seen documentary evidence. Moreover, the company may have to pay penalties and interest to the federal and state governments because of its failure to remit tax payments on a timely basis. City and state income tax withholdings for the employees could be other overlooked liabilities.

Section 3: Business Applications

	A	B	C	D	E	F
1	Working Capital	=	Current Assets	–	Current Liabilities	
2		=	$40,000.00	–	$41,450.40	
3		=	($1,450.40)			
4						
5	Payables Turnover	=	Cost of Goods Sold +/– Change in Merchandise Inventory			
6			Accounts Payable			
7						
8		=	$33,600	+	$6,000	
9			$12,000			
10						
11		=	$39,600			
12			$12,000			
13						
14		=	3.3 times			
15						
16	Days' Payable	=	365 days			
17			Payables Turnover			
18						
19		=	365 days			
20			3.3 times			
21						
22		=	110.6* days			
23	*Rounded					

It is important for Teresa Madej to identify and account for all her current liabilities because these amounts are taken into consideration when evaluating her company's liquidity. Working capital shows a company's ability to pay its current liabilities. Payables turnover shows the relative size of accounts payable, the credit terms offered by suppliers, and a company's diligence in paying its suppliers, and days' payable shows how long, on average, a company takes to pay its accounts payables.

Teresa's Fitness Center has a negative working capital of $1,495.40, its payables turnover is only 3.3 times, and it takes an average of 110.6 days to pay its accounts payable. Its liquidity is, therefore, highly questionable. Many of its current assets are inventory, which it must sell to generate cash, and it must pay most of its current liabilities sooner than the 110.6 days would indicate.

Chapter Review

Define *current liabilities*, and identify the concepts underlying them. LO 1

Liabilities result from past transactions and should be recognized at the time a transaction obligates a company to make future payments. They are valued at the amount of money necessary to satisfy the obligation or at the fair value of the goods or services to be delivered. Liabilities are classified as current or long-term. Companies are required to provide supplemental disclosure when the nature or details of the obligations would help in understanding the liability.

Identify, compute, and record definitely determinable and estimated current liabilities. LO 2

The two major categories of current liabilities are definitely determinable liabilities and estimated liabilities. Definitely determinable liabilities include accounts payable, bank loans and commercial paper, notes payable, accrued liabilities, dividends payable, sales and excise taxes payable, the current portion of long-term debt, payroll liabilities, and unearned revenues. Estimated liabilities definitely exist, but their amounts are uncertain and must be estimated. They include liabilities for income taxes, property taxes, promotional costs, product warranties, and vacation pay.

Distinguish contingent liabilities from commitments. LO 3

A contingent liability is a potential liability that arises from a past transaction and is dependent on a future event. Contingent liabilities often involve lawsuits, income tax disputes, discounted notes receivable, guarantees of debt, and failure to follow government regulations. A commitment is a legal obligation, such as a purchase agreement, that is not recorded as a liability.

Identify the valuation approaches to fair value accounting, define *time value of money* and *interest*, and apply them to present values. LO 4

The FASB identifies three approaches to measuring fair value. The market approach is useful when there is an active market in which quoted prices are available for the specific asset or liability. The income (or cash flow) approach converts future cash flows to a single present value. The cost approach is based on the amount that currently would be required to replace an asset with a comparable one.

The time value of money refers to the costs or benefits derived from holding or not holding money over time. Interest is the cost of using money for a specific period. The amount on which simple interest is computed stays the same from period to period. In the computation of compound interest, the interest for a period is added to the principal amount before the interest for the next period is computed.

Future value is the amount an investment will be worth at a future date if invested at compound interest. Present value is the amount that must be invested today at a given rate of interest to produce a given future value. An ordinary annuity is a series of equal payments made at the end of equal intervals of time, with compound interest on the payments. The present value of an ordinary annuity is the present value of a series of payments. Calculations of present values are simplified by using the appropriate tables, which appear in an appendix to this book.

Apply the present value concept to simple valuation situations. **LO 5**

Present value is commonly used in determining fair value and may be used in determining the value of an asset, in computing the present value of deferred payments, and in establishing a fund for loan repayment. Present value can also be applied to numerous other accounting situations in which time is a factor.

Use ratio analysis to manage the impact of current liabilities' impact on liquidity. **LO 6**

Current liabilities are an important consideration in managing a company's liquidity and cash flows. Key measures of liquidity are working capital, payables turnover, and days' payable.

Key Terms and Ratios

accounts payable 412 (LO2)
accrued liabilities 414 (LO2)
cash dividends 414 (LO2)
commercial paper 413 (LO2)
commitment 425 (LO3)
compound interest 426 (LO4)
contingent liability 424 (LO3)
current liabilities 410 (LO1)
definitely determinable liabilities 412 (LO2)

employee 416 (LO2)
estimated liabilities 420 (LO2)
future value 426 (LO4)
independent contractor 416 (LO2)
interest 426 (LO4)
line of credit 411 (LO1)
long-term liabilities 410 (LO1)
ordinary annuity 429 (LO4)
present value 427 (LO4)
promissory notes 412 (LO2)

salaries 415 (LO2)
short-term notes payable 412 (LO2)
simple interest 426 (LO4)
time value of money 426 (LO4)
unearned revenues 418 (LO2)
wages 415 (LO2)

RATIOS
days' payable 434 (LO6)
payables turnover 433 (LO6)

Chapter Assignments

DISCUSSION QUESTIONS

LO **1, 2** **DQ1. CONCEPT** ▶ James Williams, a star college basketball player, received a contract from the Midwest Blazers to play professional basketball. The contract calls for a salary of $420,000 a year for four years, dependent on his making the team in each of those years. Should this contract be considered a liability and recorded on the books of the basketball team? Why or why not?

LO **1, 3** **DQ2. CONCEPT** ▶ When would a commitment be recognized in the accounting records?

LO **2** **DQ3.** Do adjusting entries involving estimated liabilities and accruals ever affect cash flows?

LO **4** **DQ4.** Is a friend who borrows money from you for three years and agrees to pay you interest after each year paying you simple or compound interest?

LO **4** **DQ5.** Ordinary annuities assume that the first payment is made at the end of each year. In a transaction, who is better off in this arrangement, the payer or the receiver? Why?

LO **4, 5** **DQ6.** Why is present value one of the most useful concepts in making business decisions?

LO **6** **DQ7. BUSINESS APPLICATION** ▶ Is increasing payables turnover good or bad for a company? Why or why not?

SHORT EXERCISES

LO 1, 6
Issues in Accounting for Liabilities

SE1. CONCEPT ▶ Indicate whether each of the following actions relates to (a) managing liquidity and cash flow, (b) recognition of liabilities, (c) valuation of liabilities, (d) classification of liabilities, or (e) disclosure of liabilities:

1. Determining that a liability will be paid in less than one year.
2. Estimating the amount of a liability.
3. Providing information about when liabilities are due and their interest rates.
4. Determining when a liability arises.
5. Assessing working capital and payables turnover.

LO 2
Interest Expense on Note Payable

SE2. On the last day of August, Broadway Company borrowed $120,000 on a bank note for 60 days at 10 percent interest. Assume that interest is stated separately. Prepare the following journal entries: (1) August 31, recording of note; and (2) October 30, payment of note plus interest. (Round to the nearest cent.)

LO 2
Payroll Expenses

SE3. The following payroll totals for the month of April are from the payroll register of Myth Corporation: salaries, $446,000; federal income taxes withheld, $62,880; Social Security tax withheld, $27,652; Medicare tax withheld, $6,467; medical insurance deductions, $13,160; and salaries subject to unemployment taxes, $313,200.

Determine the total and components of (1) the monthly payroll and (2) employer payroll expenses, assuming Social Security and Medicare taxes equal to the amounts for employees, a federal unemployment insurance tax of 0.8 percent, a state unemployment tax of 5.4 percent, and medical insurance premiums for which the employer pays 80 percent of the cost.

LO 2
Product Warranty Liability

SE4. Maiden Corp. manufactures and sells travel clocks. Each clock costs $12.50 to produce and sells for $25. In addition, each clock carries a warranty that provides for free replacement if it fails during the two years following the sale. In the past, 5 percent of the clocks sold have had to be replaced under the warranty. During October, Maiden sold 52,000 clocks, and 2,800 clocks were replaced under the warranty. Prepare journal entries to record the estimated liability for product warranties during the month and the clocks replaced under warranty during the month.

LO 2, 3
Types of Liabilities

SE5. Indicate whether each of the following is (a) a definitely determinable liability, (b) an estimated liability, (c) a commitment, or (d) a contingent liability:

1. Dividends payable
2. Pending litigation
3. Income taxes payable
4. Current portion of long-term debt
5. Vacation pay liability
6. Guaranteed loans of another company
7. Purchase agreement

LO 4
Simple and Compound Interest

SE6. Maruti Motors, Inc., receives a one-year note that carries a 12 percent annual interest rate on $3,000 for the sale of a used car. Compute the maturity value under each of the following assumptions: (1) Simple interest is charged. (2) The interest is compounded semiannually. (3) The interest is compounded quarterly. (Round to the nearest cent.)

LO **4**   **Present Value Calculations**

SE7. Find the present value of (1) a single payment of $24,000 at 6 percent for 12 years, (2) 12 annual payments of $2,000 at 6 percent, (3) a single payment of $5,000 at 9 percent for five years, and (4) five annual payments of $5,000 at 9 percent. (*Hint:* Use Tables 1 and 2 in Appendix B.)

LO **4, 5**   **Valuing an Asset for the Purpose of Making a Purchasing Decision**

SE8. ACCOUNTING CONNECTION Luke Ricci owns a machine shop and has the opportunity to purchase a new machine for $60,000. After carefully studying projected costs and revenues, Ricci estimates that the new machine will produce a net cash flow of $14,400 annually and will last for eight years. Ricci believes that an interest rate of 10 percent is adequate for his business.

Calculate the present value of the machine to Ricci. Does the purchase appear to be a smart business decision? Why? (*Hint:* Use Table 2 in Appendix B.)

LO **6**   **Measuring Short-Term Liquidity**

RATIO

SE9. BUSINESS APPLICATION Luster Company has current assets of $130,000 and current liabilities of $80,000, of which accounts payable are $70,000. Luster's cost of goods sold is $460,000, its merchandise inventory increased by $20,000, and accounts payable were $50,000 the prior year. Calculate Luster's working capital, payables turnover, and days' payable. (Round to one decimal place.)

EXERCISES: SET A

LO **1, 6**   **Issues in Accounting for Liabilities**

CASH FLOW

E1A. CONCEPT ▶ Indicate whether each of the following actions relates to (a) managing liquidity and cash flows, (b) recognition of liabilities, (c) valuation of liabilities, (d) classification of liabilities, or (e) disclosure of liabilities:

1. Providing information about financial instruments on the balance sheet.
2. Measuring working capital.
3. Setting a liability at the fair market value of goods to be delivered.
4. Relating the payment date of a liability to the length of the operating cycle.
5. Recording a liability in accordance with the accrual accounting.
6. Estimating the amount of "cents-off" coupons that will be redeemed.
7. Categorizing a liability as long-term debt.
8. Comparing days' payable with last year.

LO **2**   **Interest Expense on Note Payable**

E2A. On the last day of October, Lake Company borrows $60,000 on a bank note for 60 days at 12 percent interest. Interest is not included in the face amount. Prepare the following journal entries: (1) October 31, recording of note; (2) November 30, accrual of interest expense (round to the nearest cent); and (3) December 30, payment of note plus interest.

LO **2**   **Sales and Excise Taxes**

E3A. Lindstrom Design Services billed its customers a total of $245,100 for the month of August, including 9 percent federal excise tax and 5 percent sales tax.

1. Determine the proper amount of service revenue to report for the month.
2. Prepare a journal entry to record the revenue and related liabilities for the month.

LO **2**   **Payroll Expenses**

E4A. At the end of October, the payroll register for Noir Tool Corporation contained the following totals: wages, $371,000; federal income taxes withheld, $94,884; state income taxes withheld, $15,636; Social Security tax withheld, $23,002; Medicare tax

(Continued)

withheld, $5,379.50; medical insurance deductions, $12,870; and wages subject to unemployment taxes, $57,240.

Determine the total and components of the (1) monthly payroll and (2) employer payroll expenses, assuming Social Security and Medicare taxes equal to the amount for employees, a federal unemployment insurance tax of 0.8 percent, a state unemployment tax of 5.4 percent, and medical insurance premiums for which the employer pays 80 percent of the cost.

LO 2   **Product Warranty Liability**

E5A. Boulware Company manufactures and sells electronic games. Each game costs $25 to produce, sells for $45, and carries a warranty that provides for free replacement if it fails during the two years following the sale. In the past, 7 percent of the games sold had to be replaced under the warranty. During July, Boulware sold 13,000 games, and 1,400 games were replaced under the warranty.

1. Prepare a journal entry to record the estimated liability for product warranties during the month.
2. Prepare a journal entry to record the games replaced under warranty during the month.

LO 2   **Vacation Pay Liability**

E6A. Funz Corporation gives three weeks' paid vacation to each employee who has worked at the company for one year. Based on studies of employee turnover and previous experience, management estimates that 65 percent of the employees will qualify for vacation pay this year.

1. Assume that Funz's July payroll is $300,000, of which $20,000 is paid to employees on vacation. Figure the estimated employee vacation benefit for the month. (Round to the nearest thousandth.)
2. Prepare a journal entry to record the employee benefit for July.
3. Prepare a journal entry to record the pay to employees on vacation.

LO 3   **Contingencies and Commitments**

E7A. Indicate whether each of the following related to an airline company relates to (a) contingency or (b) commitment:

1. The company has agreed to purchase 10 new airplanes over the next three years.
2. The company has a lawsuit pending against it.

LO 4   **Determining an Advance Payment**

E8A. Katie Davis is contemplating paying five years' rent in advance. Her annual rent is $12,600. Calculate the single sum that would have to be paid now for the advance rent. Assume compound interest of 8 percent. (*Hint:* Use Table 2 in Appendix B.)

LO 4   **Present Value Calculations**

E9A. Find the present value of (1) a single payment of $12,000 at 6 percent for 12 years, (2) 12 annual payments of $1,000 at 6 percent, (3) a single payment of $2,500 at 9 percent for five years, and (4) 5 annual payments of $2,500 at 9 percent. (*Hint:* Use Tables 1 and 2 in Appendix B.)

LO 4   **Present Value of a Lump-Sum Contract**

E10A. A contract calls for a lump-sum payment of $30,000. Find the present value of the contract, assuming that (1) the payment is due in five years and the current interest rate is 9 percent; (2) the payment is due in ten years and the current interest rate is 9 percent; (3) the payment is due in five years and the current interest rate is 5 percent; and (4) the payment is due in ten years and the current interest rate is 5 percent. (*Hint:* Use Table 1 in Appendix B.)

LO **4, 5**   **Present Value of an Annuity Contract**

E11A. A contract calls for annual payments of $2,400. Find the present value of the contract, assuming that (1) the number of payments is 7 and the current interest rate is 6 percent; (2) the number of payments is 14 and the current interest rate is 6 percent; (3) the number of payments is 7 and the current interest rate is 8 percent; and (4) the number of payments is 14 and the current interest rate is 8 percent. (*Hint:* Use Table 2 in Appendix B.)

LO **4, 5**   **Valuing an Asset for the Purpose of Making a Purchasing Decision**

E12A. ACCOUNTING CONNECTION ▶ Sid Patel owns a service station and has the opportunity to purchase a car-wash machine for $15,000. After carefully studying projected costs and revenues, Patel estimates that the car-wash machine will produce a net cash flow of $2,600 annually and will last for eight years. He determines that an interest rate of 14 percent is adequate for his business. Calculate the present value of the machine to Patel. (*Hint:* Use Table 2 in Appendix B.) Does the purchase appear to be a smart business decision? Why?

LO **4, 5**   **Deferred Payment**

E13A. Alligood Equipment Corporation sold a precision tool machine with computer controls to Kaui Corporation for $400,000 on January 2 and agreed to take payment nine months later on October 2. Assuming that the prevailing annual interest rate for such a transaction is 16 percent compounded quarterly, what is the actual sale (purchase) price of the machine tool? (*Hint:* Use Table 1 in Appendix B.)

LO **4, 5**   **Negotiating the Sale of a Business**

E14A. Helen Knight is attempting to sell her business to Chris Bosh. The company has assets of $1,800,000, liabilities of $1,600,000, and owner's equity of $200,000. Both parties agree that the proper rate of return to expect is 12 percent; however, they differ on other assumptions. Knight believes that the business will generate at least $200,000 per year of cash flows for 20 years. Bosh thinks that $160,000 in cash flows per year is more reasonable and that only 10 years in the future should be considered. Determine the range for negotiation by computing the present value of Knight's offer to sell and of Bosh's offer to buy. (*Hint:* Use Table 2 in Appendix B.)

LO **6**   **Measuring Short-Term Liquidity**

E15A. BUSINESS APPLICATION ▶ In 2013, Copia Company had current assets of $155,000 and current liabilities of $100,000, of which accounts payable were $65,000. Cost of goods sold was $425,000, merchandise inventory increased by $40,000, and accounts payable were $55,000 in the prior year. In 2014, Copia had current assets of $210,000 and current liabilities of $160,000, of which accounts payable were $75,000. Cost of goods sold was $475,000, and merchandise inventory decreased by $15,000. Calculate Copia's working capital, payables turnover, and days' payable for 2013 and 2014. Assess Copia's liquidity and cash flows in relation to the change in payables turnover from 2013 to 2014. (Round to one decimal place.)

EXERCISES: SET B

Visit the textbook companion website at www.cengagebrain.com to access Exercise Set B for this chapter.

PROBLEMS

LO **1, 2, 3**

Identification of Current Liabilities, Contingencies, and Commitments

P1. Common types of current liabilities, contingencies, and commitments follow.

a. Accounts payable
b. Bank loans and commercial paper
c. Notes payable
d. Dividends payable
e. Sales and excise taxes payable
f. Current portion of long-term debt
g. Payroll liabilities
h. Unearned revenues

i. Income taxes payable
j. Property taxes payable
k. Promotional costs
l. Product warranty liability
m. Vacation pay liability
n. Contingent liability
o. Commitment

REQUIRED

1. For each of the following statements, identify the type of current liability, contingency, or commitment to which it gives rise or with which it is most closely associated:

   1. A company agrees to replace parts of a product if they fail.
   2. An employee earns one day off for each month worked.
   3. A company signs a contract to lease a building for five years.
   4. A company puts discount coupons in the newspaper.
   5. A company agrees to pay insurance costs for employees.
   6. A portion of a mortgage on a building is due this year.
   7. The board of directors declares a dividend.
   8. A company has trade payables.
   9. A company has a pending lawsuit against it.
   10. A company arranges for a line of credit.
   11. A company signs a note due in 60 days.
   12. A company operates in a state that has a sales tax.
   13. A company earns a profit that is taxable.
   14. A company owns buildings that are subject to property taxes.

2. **ACCOUNTING CONNECTION** ▶ Of the items listed from **a** to **o**, which ones would you not expect to see listed on the balance sheet with a dollar amount? Of those items that would be listed on the balance sheet with a dollar amount, which ones would you consider to involve the most judgment or discretion on the part of management?

LO **2**

Notes Payable and Wages Payable

✔ 1: Part A: December 31 Interest Expense: $426.08
✔ 2: Part B: October 31 Payroll Taxes and Benefits Expense: $23,444.88

P2. Part A: Blue Blaze Company, whose fiscal year ends December 31, completed the following transactions involving notes payable:

2013
Nov. 25 Purchased a new loading cart by issuing a 60-day 10 percent note for $43,200.
Dec. 31 Made the end-of-year adjusting entry to accrue interest expense. (Round to the nearest cent.)

2014
Jan. 24 Paid off the loading cart note. (Round to the nearest cent.)

REQUIRED

1. Prepare journal entries for Blue Blaze's notes payable transactions.
2. **ACCOUNTING CONNECTION** ▶ When notes payable appears on the balance sheet, what other current liability would you look for to be associated with the notes? What would it mean if this other current liability did not appear?

Part B: At the end of October, the payroll register for Blue Blaze Company contained the following totals: wages, $92,750; federal income taxes withheld, $23,721; state income taxes withheld, $3,909; Social Security tax withheld, $5,751; Medicare tax withheld, $1,345; medical insurance deductions, $3,200; and wages subject to unemployment taxes, $57,240.

REQUIRED

Prepare journal entries to record the (1) monthly payroll and (2) employer payroll expenses, assuming Social Security and Medicare taxes equal to the amount for employees, a federal unemployment insurance tax of 0.8 percent, a state unemployment tax of 5.4 percent, and medical insurance premiums for which the employer pays 80 percent of the cost.

LO **2**

GENERAL LEDGER

✔ 2: End of month estimated product warranty liability: $168,160

Product Warranty Liability

P3. Reliance Company manufactures and sells wireless video cell phones, which it guarantees for five years. If a cell phone fails, it is replaced free, but the customer is charged a service fee for handling. In the past, management has found that only 3 percent of the cell phones sold required replacement under the warranty. The average cell phone costs the company $240. At the beginning of September, the account for estimated liability for product warranties had a credit balance of $208,000. During September, 250 cell phones were returned under the warranty. The company collected $9,860 of service fees for handling. During the month, the company sold 2,800 cell phones.

REQUIRED

1. Prepare journal entries to record (a) the cost of cell phones replaced under warranty and (b) the estimated liability for product warranties for cell phones sold during the month.
2. Compute the balance of the Estimated Product Warranty Liability account at the end of the month.
3. **ACCOUNTING CONNECTION** ▶ If the company's product warranty liability is underestimated, what are the effects on current and future years' income?

LO **2, 6**

RATIO

✔ 1: Total current liabilities: $20,152.10

Identification and Evaluation of Current Liabilities

P4. Stan Styka opened a small dryer repair shop, Styka Repair Shop, on January 2, 2014. The shop also sells a limited number of dryer parts. In January 2015, Styka realized he had never filed any tax reports for his business and therefore probably owes a considerable amount of taxes. Since he has limited experience in running a business, he has brought you all his business records, including a checkbook, canceled checks, deposit slips, suppliers' invoices, a notice of annual property taxes of $2,310 due to the city, and a promissory note to his father-in-law for $2,500. He wants you to determine what his business owes the government and other parties (but not employees).

You analyze all his records and determine the following as of December 31, 2014:

Unpaid invoices for dryer parts	$ 9,000
Parts sales (excluding sales tax)	44,270
Cost of parts sold	31,125
Workers' salaries	18,200
Repair revenues	60,300
Current assets	16,300
Dryer parts inventory	11,750

You learn that the company has deducted $476 from the two employees' salaries for federal income taxes owed to the government. The current Social Security tax is 6.2 percent on maximum earnings of $110,100 for each employee, and the current Medicare tax is 1.45 percent (no maximum earnings). The FUTA tax is 5.4 percent to the state and .8 percent to the federal government on the first $7,000 earned by each employee, and each employee earned more than $7,000. Styka has not filed a sales tax report to the state (5 percent of sales).

(Continued)

REQUIRED

1. Determine Styka Repair Shop's current liabilities as of December 31, 2014.
2. **ACCOUNTING CONNECTION** ▶ What additional information would you want from Styka to satisfy yourself that all current liabilities have been identified?
3. **BUSINESS APPLICATION** ▶ Evaluate Styka's liquidity by calculating working capital, payables turnover, and days' payable. (Round to one decimal place.) Comment on the results. (Assume average accounts payable were the same as year-end accounts payable.)

<table>
<tr><td>LO **4, 5**</td></tr>
</table>

Applications of Present Value

SPREADSHEET

✔ 1a: Present value of liability: $187,750
✔ 1b: Cost of buyout: $79,250

P5. Austin Corporation's management took the following actions, which went into effect on January 2, 2014. Each action involved an application of present value.

a. Austin Corporation enters into a purchase agreement that calls for a payment of $250,000 three years from now.
b. Bought out the contract of a member of top management for a payment of $25,000 per year for four years beginning January 2, 2015.

REQUIRED

1. Assuming an annual interest rate of 10 percent and using Tables 1 and 2 in Appendix B, answer the following questions:
   a. In action **a**, what is the present value of the liability for the purchase agreement?
   b. In action **b**, what is the cost (present value) of the buyout?
2. **ACCOUNTING CONNECTION** ▶ Many businesses analyze present value extensively when making decisions about investing in long-term assets. Why is this type of analysis particularly appropriate for such decisions?

ALTERNATE PROBLEMS

LO **1, 2, 3**

Identification of Current Liabilities, Contingencies, and Commitments

P6. Common types of current liabilities, contingencies, and commitments follow.

a. Accounts payable
b. Bank loans and commercial paper
c. Notes payable
d. Dividends payable
e. Sales and excise taxes payable
f. Current portion of long-term debt
g. Payroll liabilities
h. Unearned revenues

i. Income taxes payable
j. Property taxes payable
k. Promotional costs
l. Product warranty liability
m. Vacation pay liability
n. Contingent liability
o. Commitment

REQUIRED

1. For each of the following statements, identify the type of current liability, contingency, or commitment to which it gives rise or with which it is most closely associated:

   1. The board of directors declares a dividend.
   2. A company signs a note due in 60 days.
   3. A company has a pending lawsuit against it.
   4. A company signs a contract to lease a building for five years.
   5. A company arranges for a line of credit.
   6. A company agrees to pay insurance costs for employees.
   7. A portion of a mortgage on a building is due this year.
   8. A company agrees to replace parts of a product if they fail.
   9. A company has trade payables.
   10. A company operates in a state that has a sales tax.
   11. A company puts discount coupons in the newspaper.
   12. A company earns a profit that is taxable.

13. A company owns buildings that are subject to property taxes.
14. An employee earns one day off for each month worked.

2. **ACCOUNTING CONNECTION** ▶ Of the items listed from **a** to **o**, which ones would you not expect to see listed on the balance sheet with a dollar amount? Of those items that would be listed on the balance sheet with a dollar amount, which ones would you consider to involve the most judgment or discretion on the part of management?

LO **2**

SPREADSHEET

GENERAL LEDGER

✔ 1: Part A: June 30 Interest
Expense: $552.33
✔ 2: Part B: July 31 Payroll Taxes and
Benefits Expense: $70,334.64

Notes Payable and Wages Payable

P7. Part A: Candlelight Corporation, whose fiscal year ended June 30, 2014, completed the following transactions involving notes payable:

May 21 Obtained a 60-day extension on an $36,000 trade account payable owed to a supplier by signing a 60-day $36,000 note. Interest is in addition to the face value, at the rate of 14 percent.

June 30 Made the end-of-year adjusting entry to accrue interest expense. (Round to the nearest cent.)

July 20 Paid off the note plus interest due the supplier. (Round to the nearest cent.)

REQUIRED

1. Prepare journal entries for the notes payable transactions.
2. **ACCOUNTING CONNECTION** ▶ When notes payable appears on the balance sheet, what other current liability would you look for to be associated with the notes? What would it mean if this other current liability did not appear?

Part B: The payroll register for Candlelight Corporation contained the following totals at the end of July: wages, $278,250; federal income taxes withheld, $71,163; state income taxes withheld, $11,727; Social Security tax withheld, $17,253; Medicare tax withheld, $4,035; medical insurance deductions, $9,600; and wages subject to unemployment taxes, $171,720.

REQUIRED

Prepare journal entries to record the (1) monthly payroll and (2) employer payroll expenses, assuming Social Security and Medicare taxes equal to the amount for employees, a federal unemployment insurance tax of 0.8 percent, a state unemployment tax of 5.4 percent, and medical insurance premiums for which the employer pays 80 percent of the cost.

LO **2**

GENERAL LEDGER

✔ 2: End of the month
estimated product warranty
liability: $21,870

Product Warranty Liability

P8. Treetech Company is engaged in the retail sale of high-definition televisions (HDTVs). Each HDTV has a 24-month warranty on parts. If a repair under warranty is required, a charge for the labor is made. Management has found that 20 percent of the HDTVs sold require some work before the warranty expires. Furthermore, the average cost of replacement parts has been $120 per repair. At the beginning of January, the account for the estimated liability for product warranties had a credit balance of $28,600. During January, 112 HDTVs were returned under the warranty. The cost of the parts used in repairing the HDTVs was $17,530, and $18,884 was collected as service revenue for the labor involved. During January, the month before the Super Bowl, Treetech sold 450 new HDTVs.

REQUIRED

1. Prepare journal entries to record each of the following: (a) the warranty work completed during the month, including related revenue; (b) the estimated liability for product warranties for HDTVs sold during the month.
2. Compute the balance of the Estimated Product Warranty Liability account at the end of the month.
3. **ACCOUNTING CONNECTION** ▶ If the company's product warranty liability is overestimated, what are the effects on current and future years' income?

Identification and Evaluation of Current Liabilities

P9. Daisy Luna opened a small motorcycle repair shop, Luna Cycle Repair, on January 2, 2014. The shop also sells a limited number of motorcycle parts. In January 2015, Luna realized she had never filed any tax reports for her business and therefore probably owes a considerable amount of taxes. Since she has limited experience in running a business, she has brought you all her business records, including a checkbook, canceled checks, deposit slips, suppliers' invoices, a notice of annual property taxes of $4,620 due to the city, and a promissory note to her father-in-law for $5,000. She wants you to determine what her business owes the government and other parties (but not employees).

You analyze all her records and determine the following as of December 31, 2014:

Unpaid invoices for motorcycle parts	$ 18,000
Parts sales (excluding sales tax)	88,540
Cost of parts sold	62,250
Workers' salaries	20,400
Repair revenues	120,600
Current assets	32,600
Motorcycle parts inventory	23,500

You learn that the company has deducted $952 from the two employees' salaries for federal income taxes owed to the government. The current Social Security tax is 6.2 percent on maximum earnings of $110,100 for each employee, and the current Medicare tax is 1.45 percent (no maximum earnings). The FUTA tax is 5.4 percent to the state and 0.8 percent to the federal government on the first $7,000 earned by each employee, and each employee earned more than $7,000. Luna has not filed a sales tax report to the state (5 percent of sales).

REQUIRED

1. Determine Luna Cycle Repair's current liabilities as of December 31, 2014.
2. **ACCOUNTING CONNECTION** ▶ What additional information would you want from Luna to satisfy yourself that all current liabilities have been identified?
3. **BUSINESS APPLICATION** ▶ Evaluate Luna's liquidity by calculating working capital, payables turnover, and days' payable. (Round to one decimal place.) Comment on the results. (Assume average accounts payable were the same as year-end accounts payable.)

Applications of Present Value

P10. Lisette, Inc.'s management took the following actions that went into effect on January 2, 2014. Each action involved an application of present value.

a. Asked for another fund to be established by a single payment to accumulate to $150,000 in four years.
b. Approved the purchase of a parcel of land for future plant expansion. Payments are to start January 2, 2014, at $100,000 per year for five years.

REQUIRED

1. Assuming an annual interest rate of 8 percent and using Tables 1 and 2 in Appendix B, answer the following questions:
   a. In action **a**, how much will need to be deposited initially to accumulate the desired amount?
   b. In action **b**, what is the purchase price (present value) of the land?
2. **ACCOUNTING CONNECTION** ▶ What is the fundamental reason present value analysis is a useful tool in making business decisions?

CASES

LO 2   **Conceptual Understanding: Frequent Flyer Plan**

C1. CONCEPT ▶ JetFly Airways instituted a frequent flyer program in which passengers accumulate points toward a free flight based on the number of miles they fly on the airline. One point was awarded for each mile flown, and a minimum of 750 miles was awarded for any one flight. Because of competition in 2014, the company began a bonus plan in which passengers receive triple the normal mileage points. In the past, about 1.5 percent of passenger miles were flown by passengers who had converted points to free flights; with the triple mileage program, JetFly expects that the rate will increase to 2.5 percent.

During 2014, the company had passenger revenues of $966.3 million and passenger transportation operating expenses of $802.8 million before depreciation and amortization. Operating income was $86.1 million. What is the appropriate rate to use to estimate free miles? What effect would the estimated liability for free travel by frequent flyers have on 2014 net income? Describe several ways to estimate the amount of this liability. Be prepared to discuss the arguments for and against recognizing this liability.

LO 3   **Conceptual Understanding: Lawsuits and Contingent Liabilities**

C2. CONCEPT ▶ When faced with lawsuits, many companies recognize a loss and therefore credit a liability or reserve account for any future losses that may result. For instance, in the famous **WorldCom** case, **Citibank**, one of the world's largest financial services firms, announced it was setting up reserves or liabilities of $5.6 billion because of pending lawsuits due to its relationship with WorldCom.[14] Were these pending lawsuits contingent liabilities? According to the FASB, what conditions must exist before a liability related to a pending lawsuit can be entered in the accounting records?

LO 4, 5   **Conceptual Understanding: Present Value**

C3. In its "Year-End Countdown Sale," a local **Cadillac** car dealer advertised "0% interest for 60 months!"[15] What role does the time value of money play in this promotion? Assuming that the car dealer is able to borrow funds at 8 percent interest, what is the cost to the dealer of every customer who takes advantage of this offer? If you could borrow money to buy a car from this dealer, which rate would be more relevant in determining how much you might offer for the car: the rate at which you borrow money, or the rate at which the dealer borrows money?

LO 6   **Interpreting Financial Reports: Comparison of Two**

    Companies' Ratios with Industry Ratios

C4. BUSINESS APPLICATION ▶ Both **Oracle Corporation** and **Cisco Systems** are in the computer industry. The data that follows (in millions) are from the end of their fiscal years 2011.[16]

	Oracle	Cisco
Accounts payable	$ 701	$ 876
Cost of goods sold	8,398	16,682
Increase (decrease) in inventory	(28)	(147)

Compare the payables turnover and days' payable for both companies. How are cash flows affected by days' payable? How do **Oracle**'s and **Cisco Systems**' ratios compare with the computer industry ratios shown in the chapter? (Use year-end amounts for ratios and round to one decimal place.)

LO 1, 3   **Annual Report Case: Commitments and Contingencies**

C5. CONCEPT ▶ Read **CVS**'s note on commitments and contingencies in the Supplement to Chapter 16. What commitments and contingencies does the company have? Why is it important to consider this information when analyzing accounts payable? What

(Continued)

two conditions have to be met to record commitments and contingencies as liabilities on the balance sheet?

LO **6**   **Comparison Case: Payables Analysis**

 C6. BUSINESS APPLICATION ▶ Refer to **CVS**'s financial statements in the Supplement to Chapter 16 and to the following data for **Walgreens** (amounts in millions):

	2011	**2010**	**2009**
Cost of goods sold	$51,692	$48,444	$45,722
Accounts payable	4,810	4,585	4,308
Increase (decrease) in merchandise inventory	(592)	(307)	533

Compute the payables turnover and days' payable for CVS and Walgreens in 2010 and 2011. (Round to one decimal place.) In 2009, CVS had accounts payable of $3,560 million, and in 2010, its merchandise inventory decreased by $352. Which company do you think made the most use of financing from creditors during the operating cycle? Did the trend change?

LO **2**   **Ethical Dilemma: Known Legal Violations**

C7. Surf and Turf is a large restaurant in the suburbs of Chicago. Ronald Swift, an accounting student at a nearby college, recently secured a full-time accounting job there. He felt fortunate to have a good job that accommodated his class schedule. After a few weeks on the job, Swift realized that his boss, the owner of the business, was paying the kitchen workers in cash and not withholding federal and state income taxes or social security and Medicare taxes. Swift knows that federal and state laws require these taxes to be withheld and paid to the appropriate agency in a timely manner. He also realizes that if he raises this issue, he could lose his job. What alternatives are available to Swift? What action would you take if you were in his position? Why did you make this choice?

LO **4, 5**   **Business Communication: Baseball Contract**

C8. Devon Turner, who has been playing shortstop for the St. Louis Titans for five years, made the All-Star team in 2014. He has three years left on a contract that pays him $2.4 million a year. He wants to renegotiate his contract because other players with records similar to his are receiving as much as $10.5 million per year for five years.

Titans' management has a policy of never renegotiating a current contract but is willing to consider extending Turner's contract to additional years. In fact, the Titans have offered Turner an additional three years at $6.0 million, $9.0 million, and $12.0 million, respectively. They have also added an option year at $15.0 million. Management points out that this package is worth $42.0 million, or $10.5 million per year on average. Turner is considering this offer and is also thinking of asking for a bonus if and when he signs the contract.

Write a memorandum to Turner that comments on management's position and evaluates the offer, assuming a current interest rate of 10 percent. (*Hint*: Use present values.) Propose a range for the signing bonus. Finally, include other considerations that may affect the value of the offer.

Continuing Case: Annual Report Project

C9. BUSINESS APPLICATION ▶ Using the most recent annual report of the company you have chosen to study and that you have accessed online at the company's website, identify on the balance sheet the current liabilities that are definitely determinable and those that are probably estimates. Also, calculate the following for the most recent two years:

1. Working capital
2. Payables turnover
3. Days' payable

CHAPTER 12
Accounting for Partnerships

Patrick Ankin and Eric Kent reached an agreement in 2014 to pool their resources and form a partnership to manufacture and sell university T-shirts. Patrick contributed $100,000 and Eric contributed $150,000 to the partnership. Before they prepared their partnership agreement, they had to decide how they would share the income or losses of the business and how they would handle both the admission of new partners and the withdrawal of partners. Later on, they consider the need to bring in another partner, Adele Matiz.

1. CONCEPT ▶ *How does the separate entity concept apply to partners' interest in a partnership?*

2. ACCOUNTING APPLICATION ▶ *How would Patrick Ankin and Eric Kent share the income or losses of their business, and how would they handle any changes in ownership that might occur?*

3. BUSINESS APPLICATION ▶ *As the partnership grows, what alternate forms of partnership-like entities might the partners consider?*

LEARNING OBJECTIVES

LO 1 Define the *partnership* form of business, and identify its principal characteristics.

LO 2 Record partners' investments of cash and other assets when a partnership is formed.

LO 3 Compute and record the income or losses that partners share, based on stated ratios, capital balance ratios, and partners' salaries and interest.

LO 4 Record a person's admission to or withdrawal from a partnership.

LO 5 Compute and record the distribution of assets to partners when they liquidate their partnership.

LO 6 Identify alternate forms of partnership-type entities.

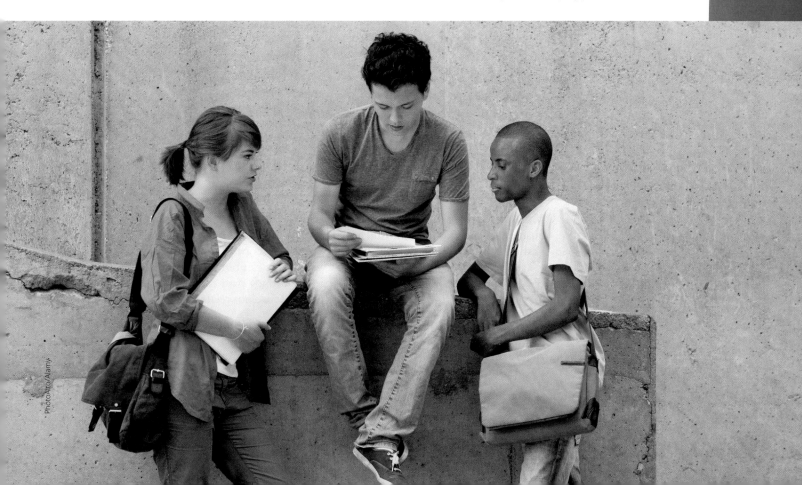

SECTION 1

CONCEPTS

CONCEPT
■ Separate entity

**RELEVANT
LEARNING OBJECTIVE**

LO 1 Define the *partnership* form of business, and identify its principal characteristics.

LO 1 Concepts Underlying Partnerships

The Uniform Partnership Act, which has been adopted by most states, defines a **partnership** as "an association of two or more persons to carry on as co-owners of a business for profit." Normally, partnerships are formed when owners of small businesses wish to combine capital or managerial talents for some common business purpose. Partnerships are treated as *separate entities,* with their own accounting records and financial statements. However, legally there is no economic separation between a partnership and its owners. Note that corporations are legal entities (whereas partnerships and sole proprietorships are not), but all three are considered separate accounting entities.

Characteristics of Partnerships

Some of the important characteristics of partnerships follow.

Voluntary Association A partnership is a voluntary association of individuals. Therefore, a partner is responsible under the law for his or her partners' actions within the scope of the business. Therefore, a partner must be allowed to choose the people who join the partnership.

Partnership Agreement To form a partnership, two or more people simply agree to partner in a business enterprise. Their **partnership agreement** does not have to be in writing. However, it is good business practice to have a written document that clearly states the details of the partnership, including:

■ Name, location, and purpose of the business
■ Names of the partners and their respective duties
■ Investments of each partner
■ Method of distributing income and losses
■ Procedures for the admission and withdrawal of partners, the withdrawal of assets allowed each partner, and the liquidation (termination) of the business

Limited Life Because a partnership is formed by an agreement, it has a **limited life**. It may be dissolved when (a) a new partner is admitted; (b) when a partner withdraws, goes bankrupt, is incapacitated (to the point that he or she cannot perform as obligated), retires, or dies; or (c) when the terms of the partnership agreement are met (e.g., when the project for which the partnership was formed is completed). The partnership agreement can be written to cover each of these situations, thus allowing the partnership to continue legally.

Mutual Agency Each partner is an agent of the partnership within the scope of the business. Because of this **mutual agency**, any partner can bind the partnership to a business agreement as long as he or she acts within the scope of the company's normal operations. For example, a partner in a used-car business can bind the partnership through the purchase or sale of used cars. But this partner cannot bind the partnership to a contract for buying men's clothing or any other goods that are not related to the used-car business.

Unlimited Liability Each partner has personal **unlimited liability** for all the debts of the partnership. If a partnership cannot pay its debts, creditors must first satisfy their claims from the assets of the business. If these assets are not enough to pay all debts, the creditors can seek payment from the personal assets of each partner. If a partner's personal assets are used up before the debts are paid, the creditors can claim additional assets from the remaining partners who are able to pay. Each partner, then, can be required by law to pay all the debts of the partnership.

Andresr/Shutterstock.com

Unlimited liability means that potential responsibility for debts is not limited by one's investment, as it is in a corporation. Each person is personally liable for all debts of the partnership, including those arising from contingent liabilities such as lawsuits. Liability can be avoided only by filing for personal bankruptcy.

STUDY NOTE: *There is no federal income tax on partnerships. Partners are taxed at their personal rates. However, partnerships must file an informational return with the IRS, and some state and local governments levy a tax on them. An example of this is the Michigan Single Business Tax.*

Co-Ownership of Partnership Property When individuals invest property in a partnership, they give up the right to their separate use of the property. The property becomes an asset of the partnership and is owned jointly by the partners.

Participation in Partnership Income Each partner has the right to share in the company's income and the responsibility to share in its losses. The partnership agreement should state the method of distributing income and losses to each partner. If the agreement describes how income should be shared but does not mention losses, losses are distributed in the same way as income. If the agreement does not describe the method of income and loss distribution, the partners must share income and losses equally.

Advantages and Disadvantages of Partnerships Summarized

In sum, partnerships have both advantages and disadvantages.

Advantages of Partnerships

Partnership has the following advantages:

- It can be easy to form, change, and dissolve.
- It facilitates the pooling of capital resources and individual talents.
- It has no corporate tax burden. Because a partnership is not a legal entity for tax purposes, it does not have to pay a federal income tax, as do corporations, but must file an informational return.
- It gives the partners a certain amount of freedom and flexibility.

Disadvantages of Partnerships

On the other hand, partnership has the following disadvantages:

- The life of a partnership is limited.
- One partner can bind the partnership to a contract (mutual agency).
- The partners have unlimited personal liability.
- It is more difficult for a partnership to raise large amounts of capital and to transfer ownership interests than it is for a corporation.

APPLY IT!

Indicate whether each statement that follows is a reflection of (a) voluntary association, (b) a partnership agreement, (c) limited life, (d) mutual agency, (e) unlimited liability, or (f) separate entity.

1. A partner may be required to pay the debts of the partnership out of personal assets.
2. A partnership must be dissolved when a partner is admitted, withdraws, retires, or dies.
3. Any partner can bind the partnership to a business agreement.
4. A partner does not have to remain a partner if he or she does not want to.
5. From an accounting standpoint, the affairs of partnerships are distinct and apart from those of their partners.
6. Details of the arrangements among partners are specified in a written contract.

SOLUTION

1. e; 2. c; 3. d; 4. a; 5. f; 6. b

TRY IT! SE1, E1A, E1B

ACCOUNTING APPLICATIONS

LO 2 Accounting for Partners' Equity

Although accounting for a partnership is very similar to accounting for a sole proprietorship, there are differences. One is that the owner's equity in a partnership is called **partners' equity**. In accounting for partners' equity, it is necessary to maintain separate Capital and Withdrawals accounts for each partner and to divide the income and losses of the company among the partners.

The differences in the Capital accounts of a sole proprietorship and a partnership are as follows.

Sole Proprietorship			Partnership					
Largo, Capital			**Sand, Capital**			**Kira, Capital**		
Dr.	Cr.		Dr.	Cr.		Dr.	Cr.	
	50,000			30,000			40,000	
Largo, Withdrawals			**Sand, Withdrawals**			**Kira, Withdrawals**		
Dr.	Cr.		Dr.	Cr.		Dr.	Cr.	
12,000			5,000			6,000		

In the partners' equity section of the balance sheet, the balance of each partner's Capital account is listed separately:

Liabilities and Partners' Equity

	Dr.	Cr.
Total liabilities		$28,000
Partners' equity:		
Sand, capital	$25,000	
Kira, capital	34,000	
Total partners' equity		59,000
Total liabilities and partners' equity		$87,000

Each partner invests cash or other assets or both in the partnership, according to the partnership agreement. Noncash assets should be *valued* at their fair market value on the date they are transferred to the partnership. The assets invested by a partner are debited to the proper account, and the total amount is credited to the partner's Capital account.

To illustrate, we will use Lori Mind and Rose Padilla, who have agreed to combine their capital and equipment in a partnership to operate a jewelry store.

Recording Partners' Investments

Transaction According to their partnership agreement, Mind will invest $28,000 in cash and $37,000 worth of furniture and displays, and Padilla will invest $40,000 in cash and $30,000 worth of equipment. Related to the equipment is a note payable for $10,000, which the partnership assumes.

Analysis The journal entry to record Mind and Padilla's initial investments

▲ *increases Cash* and other assets with debits for their value

▲ *increases* each partner's capital with a credit for the amount of the partner's contribution to the partnership

Journal Entries

A	=	L	+	OE
+28,000				+65,000
+37,000				

2014		Dr.	Cr.
July 1	Cash	28,000	
	Furniture and Displays	37,000	
	Lori Mind, Capital		65,000
	Initial investment of Lori Mind		
	in Mind and Padilla		

A	=	L	+	OE
+30,000		+10,000		+60,000
+40,000				

		Dr.	Cr.
1	Cash	40,000	
	Equipment	30,000	
	Notes Payable		10,000
	Rose Padilla, Capital		60,000
	Initial investment of Rose Padilla		
	in Mind and Padilla		

STUDY NOTE: *Padilla's noncash contribution is equal to the fair market value of the equipment less the amount owed on the equipment because the partnership assumed the liability.*

Comment The *values* assigned to the assets would be included in the partnership agreement. These values can differ from those carried on the partners' personal books. For example, the equipment that Rose Padilla contributed had a value of only $22,000 on her books, but its market value had increased considerably after she purchased it. The book value of Padilla's equipment is not important. The fair market value of the equipment at the time of transfer *is* important, however, because it represents the amount of money Padilla has invested in the partnership. Later investments are recorded in the same way.

APPLY IT!

On June 1, Daisy and Malcolm form a partnership to operate a fitness center. Daisy contributes cash of $24,000, and Malcolm contributes exercise equipment that cost $20,000 but is valued at $16,000. Prepare the journal entry to record the partners' initial investments.

SOLUTION

		Dr.	Cr.
June 1	Cash	24,000	
	Exercise Equipment	16,000	
	Daisy, Capital		24,000
	Malcolm, Capital		16,000
	Formation of partnership		

TRY IT! SE2, E2A, E2B

LO 3 Distribution of Partnership Income and Losses

A partnership's income and losses can be distributed according to whatever method the partners specify in the partnership agreement. If the agreement says nothing about the distribution of income and losses, the partners share them equally. Income in this form of business normally has three components:

- Return to the partners for the use of their capital (called *interest on partners' capital*)
- Compensation for services the partners have rendered (partners' salaries)
- Other income for any special contributions individual partners may make to the partnership or for risks they may take

The breakdown of total income into its three components helps clarify how much each partner has contributed to the firm.

If all partners contribute equal capital, have similar talents, and spend the same amount of time in the business, then an equal distribution of income and losses would be fair. However, if one partner works full-time in the firm and another devotes only a fourth of his or her time, then the distribution of income or losses should reflect that difference.

Distributing income and losses among partners can be accomplished by using stated ratios or capital balance ratios or by paying the partners' salaries and interest on their capital and sharing the remaining income according to stated ratios. Salaries and interest here are not salaries expense or interest expense in the ordinary sense of the terms. They do not affect the amount of reported net income. Instead, they refer to ways of determining each partner's share of net income or net loss on the basis of time the partner spends and the money he or she invests in the partnership. The computations of each partner's share of net income are relevant to the closing entries in which the Income Summary account is closed to the partners' Capital accounts.

Stated Ratios

One method of distributing income and losses is to give each partner a stated ratio of the total income or loss. If each partner is making an equal contribution to the firm, each can assume the same share of income and losses. It is important to understand that an equal contribution to the firm does not necessarily mean an equal capital investment in the firm. One partner may be devoting more time and talent to the firm, whereas another may have made a larger capital investment. If the partners contribute unequally to the firm, unequal stated ratios can be appropriate.

Distributing Income Using Stated Ratios

Transaction Mind and Padilla had a net income last year of $140,000. The stated ratio is 60 percent for Mind and 40 percent for Padilla.

Computation The computation of each partner's share of the income is computed as follows.

Mind ($140,000 × 0.60)	$ 84,000
Padilla ($140,000 × 0.40)	56,000
Net income	$140,000

Analysis The journal entry to record each partner's share of the income

- ■ *closes Income Summary* with a debit for the amount of net income
- ▲ *increases* each partner's capital account with a credit for their share of net income

Journal Entry

A	=	L	+	OE
				−140,000
				+84,000
				+56,000

2015		Dr.	Cr.
July 30	Income Summary	140,000	
	Lori Mind, Capital		84,000
	Rose Padilla, Capital		56,000
	Distribution of income for the year to the		
	partners' Capital accounts		

Comment This entry illustrates the *separate entity* concept that the partners as individuals are separate from the partnership entity.

Capital Balance Ratios

Income and losses may be distributed according to capital balances. The ratio used may be based on each partner's capital balance at the beginning of the year or on the average capital balance of each partner during the year.

Ratios Based on Beginning Capital Balances At the start of the fiscal year, July 1, 2014, Lori Mind's Capital account showed a $65,000 balance and Rose Padilla's Capital account showed a $60,000 balance. In this example, these balances reflect the partners' initial investment. The total partners' equity in the firm was $125,000.

Each partner's capital balance at the beginning of the year divided by the total partners' equity at the beginning of the year is that partner's beginning capital balance ratio:

	Beginning Capital Balance	**Beginning Capital Balance Ratio**
Lori Mind	$ 65,000	$65,000 ÷ $125,000 = 0.52 = 52%
Rose Padilla	60,000	$60,000 ÷ $125,000 = 0.48 = 48%
	$125,000	

The income that each partner should receive is determined by multiplying the total income by each partner's capital ratio. If income for the year was $140,000, Lori Mind's share of that income was $72,800, and Rose Padilla's share was $67,200.

Lori Mind	$140,000 × 0.52 =	$ 72,800
Rose Padilla	$140,000 × 0.48 =	67,200
		$140,000

Ratios Based on Average Capital Balances If Mind and Padilla use beginning capital balance ratios to determine the distribution of income, they do not consider any investments or withdrawals made during the year. If the partners believe their capital balances will change dramatically during the year, they can choose average capital balance ratios as a fairer means of distributing income and losses.

To compute each partner's average capital balance, it's necessary to examine the changes that have occurred during the year in each partner's Capital account as a result of investments and withdrawals.

■ **Step 1:** The partner's beginning capital is multiplied by the number of months the balance remains unchanged:

Capital Balance × Months Unchanged = Total

■ **Step 2:** After the balance changes, the new balance is multiplied by the number of months it remains unchanged. The process continues until the end of the year.

■ **Step 3:** The totals of these computations are added, and then they are divided by 12 to determine the average capital balances:

Total ÷ 12 months = Average Capital Balance

■ **Step 4:** Once the average capital balances are determined, the method of figuring capital balance ratios for sharing income and losses is the same as the method used for beginning capital balances.

The following T accounts show the activity over the year in Mind and Padilla's partners' Capital and Withdrawals accounts:

Lori Mind, Capital				**Lori Mind, Withdrawals**			
Dr.		Cr.		Dr.		Cr.	
		7/1/2014	65,000	1/1/2015	10,000		

Rose Padilla, Capital				**Rose Padilla, Withdrawals**			
Dr.		Cr.		Dr.		Cr.	
		7/1/2014	60,000	11/1/2014	10,000		
		2/1/2015	8,000				

Lori Mind withdrew $10,000 on January 1, 2015, and Rose Padilla withdrew $10,000 on November 1, 2014, and invested an additional $8,000 of equipment on February 1, 2015. Again, the income for the year's operations (July 1, 2014, to June 30, 2015) was $140,000. The calculations for the average capital balances and the distribution of income follow.

Average Capital Balances

Partner	Date	Capital Balance	×	Months Unchanged	=	Total		Average Capital Balance
Mind	July–Dec.	$65,000	×	6	=	$390,000		
	Jan.–June	$55,000	×	6	=	330,000		
				12		$720,000	÷ 12 =	$ 60,000
Padilla	July–Oct.	$60,000	×	4	=	$240,000		
	Nov.–Jan.	$50,000	×	3	=	150,000		
	Feb.–June	$58,000	×	5	=	290,000		
				12		$680,000	÷ 12 =	56,667*
						Total average capital		$116,667

*Rounded

Average Capital Balance Ratios

$$\text{Mind} = \frac{\text{Mind's Average Capital Balance}}{\text{Total Average Capital}} = \frac{\$60,000}{\$116,667} = 0.514^* = 51.4\%$$

$$\text{Padilla} = \frac{\text{Padilla's Average Capital Balance}}{\text{Total Average Capital}} = \frac{\$56,667}{\$116,667} = 0.486^* = 48.6\%$$

*Rounded

Distribution of Income

Partner	Income	×	Ratio	=	Share of Income
Mind	$140,000	×	0.514	=	$ 71,960
Padilla	$140,000	×	0.486	=	68,040
			Total income		$140,000

Salaries, Interest, and Stated Ratios

Partners generally do not contribute equally to a firm. To make up for unequal contributions, a partnership agreement can allow for partners' salaries, interest on partners' capital balances, or both in the distribution of income. Again, salaries and interest of this kind are not deducted as expenses before the partnership income is determined.

To illustrate an allowance for partners' salaries, assume that Mind and Padilla agree to annual salaries of $8,000 and $7,000, respectively, and to divide any remaining income equally between them. Each salary is charged to the appropriate partner's Withdrawals account when paid. Assuming the same $140,000 income for the first year, the calculations for Mind and Padilla follow.

	Income of Partner		Income Distributed
	Mind	**Padilla**	
Total income for distribution			$ 140,000
Distribution of salaries:			
Mind	$ 8,000		
Padilla		$ 7,000	(15,000)
Remaining income after salaries			$ 125,000
Equal distribution of remaining income:			
Mind ($125,000 × 0.50)	62,500		
Padilla ($125,000 × 0.50)		62,500	(125,000)
Remaining income			—
Income of partners	$70,500	$69,500	$ 140,000

Salaries allow for differences in the services that partners provide the business. However, they do not take into account the differences in invested capital. To allow for capital differences, each partner can receive, in addition to salary, a stated interest on his or her invested capital. Suppose that Lori Mind and Rose Padilla agree to annual salaries of $8,000 and $7,000, respectively, as well as 10 percent interest on their beginning capital balances. They also agreed to share any remaining income equally. The calculations for Mind and Padilla, assuming income of $140,000, follow.

	Income of Partner		Income Distributed
	Mind	**Padilla**	
Total income for distribution			$ 140,000
Distribution of salaries:			
Mind	$ 8,000		
Padilla		$ 7,000	(15,000)
Remaining income after salaries			$ 125,000
Distribution of interest:			
Mind ($65,000 × 0.10)	6,500		
Padilla ($60,000 × 0.10)		6,000	(12,500)
Remaining income after salaries and interest			$ 112,500
Equal distribution of remaining income:			
Mind ($112,500 × 0.50)	56,250		
Padilla ($112,500 × 0.50)		56,250	(112,500)
Remaining income			—
Income of partners	$70,750	$69,250	$ 140,000

If the partnership agreement allows for the distribution of salaries or interest or both, the amounts must be allocated to the partners, even if profits are not enough to cover the salaries and interest. In fact, even if the company has a loss, these allocations must nonetheless be made. After the allocation of salaries and interest, the negative balance, or loss, must be distributed according to the stated ratio in the partnership agreement or equally if the agreement does not mention a ratio.

For example, assume that Mind and Padilla agreed to the following conditions, with much higher annual salaries, for the distribution of income and losses:

	Salaries	**Interest**	**Beginning Capital Balance**
Mind	$70,000	10 percent of beginning capital balance	$65,000
Padilla	$60,000	10 percent of beginning capital balance	$60,000

The computations for the distribution of the income and losses, again assuming income of $140,000, follows.

| | Income of Partner | | Income |
	Mind	Padilla	Distributed
Total income for distribution			$ 140,000
Distribution of salaries:			
Mind	$70,000		
Padilla		$60,000	(130,000)
Remaining income after salaries			$ 10,000
Distribution of interest:			
Mind ($65,000 × 0.10)	6,500		
Padilla ($60,000 × 0.10)		6,000	(12,500)
Negative balance after salaries and interest			$ (2,500)
Equal distribution of negative balance:*			
Mind ($2,500 × 0.50)	(1,250)		
Padilla ($2,500 × 0.50)		(1,250)	2,500
Remaining income			—
Income of partners	$75,250	$64,750	$ 140,000

*Notice that the negative balance is distributed equally because the agreement does not indicate how income and losses should be distributed after salaries and interest are paid.

On the partnership income statement, the distribution of income or losses is presented below the net income figure, as shown in Exhibit 1.

Exhibit 1
Partial Income Statement for Mind and Padilla

Mind and Padilla
Partial Income Statement
For the Year Ended June 30, 2015

Net income		$140,000
Distribution to the partners:		
Mind:		
Salary distribution	$70,000	
Interest on beginning capital balance	6,500	
Total	$76,500	
One-half of remaining negative amount	(1,250)	
Share of net income		$ 75,250
Padilla:		
Salary distribution	$60,000	
Interest on beginning capital balance	6,000	
Total	$66,000	
One-half of remaining negative amount	(1,250)	
Share of net income		64,750
Net income distributed		$140,000

Meg and Raphael share income in their partnership in a 1:4 ratio. Meg and Raphael receive salaries of $16,000 and $10,000, respectively. How would they share a net income of $22,000 (before salaries are distributed)?

SOLUTION

	Income of Partner		Income
	Meg	Raphael	Distributed
Total income for distribution			$ 22,000
Distribution of salaries:			
Meg	$16,000		
Raphael		$ 10,000	(26,000)
Negative balance after salaries			$ (4,000)
Distribution of negative balance:			
Meg ($4,000 × 0.20)	(800)		
Raphael ($4,000 × 0.80)		(3,200)	4,000
Remaining income			—
Income of partners	$15,200	$ 6,800	$ 22,000

TRY IT! SE3, SE4, SE5, E3A, E4A, E5A, E3B, E4B, E5B

LO 4　Dissolution of a Partnership

Dissolution of a partnership occurs whenever there is a change in the original association of partners. When a partnership is dissolved, the partners lose their authority to continue the business as a *going concern*. This does not mean that the business operation necessarily is ended or interrupted. However, from a legal and accounting standpoint, the *separate entity* ceases to exist. The remaining partners can act for the partnership in finishing the affairs of the business or in forming a new partnership that will be a new accounting entity. The dissolution of a partnership takes place through, among other events, the admission of a new partner, the withdrawal of a partner, or the death of a partner.

Admission of a New Partner

The admission of a new partner dissolves the old partnership because a new association has been formed. Dissolving the old partnership and creating a new one requires the consent of all the original partners and the ratification of a new agreement.

An individual can be admitted to a partnership in one of two ways:

■ Purchasing an interest in the partnership from one or more of the original partners
■ Investing assets in the partnership

Purchasing an Interest from a Partner When a person purchases an interest in a partnership from an original partner, the transaction is personal between these two people. However, the interest purchased must be transferred from the Capital account of the selling partner to the Capital account of the new partner.

Purchasing All Interest from a Partner

Transaction Lori Mind decides to sell her interest of $70,000 in Mind and Padilla to Adam Novak for $100,000 on August 31, 2016. Rose Padilla agrees to the sale.

Analysis The journal entry to record this sale

▼ *decreases Lori Mind, Capital* with a debit
▲ *increases Adam Novak, Capital* with a credit

Journal Entry

A = L + OE
−70,000
+70,000

2016		Dr.	Cr.
Aug. 31	Lori Mind, Capital	70,000	
	Adam Novak, Capital		70,000
	Transfer of Lori Mind's equity to Adam Novak		

Comment Notice that the entry records the book value of the equity, not the amount Novak pays. The amount Novak pays is a personal matter between Novak and Mind. Because the amount paid does not affect the assets or liabilities of the firm, it is not entered in the records.

Purchasing Partial Interest from Partners

Transaction Adam Novak purchases half of Lori Mind's $70,000 interest in the partnership and half of Rose Padilla's $80,000 interest by paying a total of $100,000 to the two partners on August 31, 2016. The assets of the firm are valued correctly.

Analysis The journal entry to record this sale

▼ *decreases Lori Mind, Capital* and *Rose Padilla, Capital* with debits

▲ *increases Adam Novak, Capital* with a credit

Journal Entry

A = L + OE
−35,000
−40,000
+75,000

2012		Dr.	Cr.
Aug. 31	Lori Mind, Capital	35,000	
	Rose Padilla, Capital	40,000	
	Adam Novak, Capital		75,000
	Transfer of half of Lori Mind's and Rose		
	Padilla's equity to Adam Novak		

Comment If the asset accounts did not reflect their current values, the asset accounts (and Capital accounts) would need to be adjusted before admitting the new partner. A new partnership *entity separate* from its partners has now been formed with three partners instead of two.

Investing Assets in a Partnership When a new partner is admitted through an investment in the partnership, both the assets and the partners' equity in the firm increase. This is because the assets the new partner invests become partnership assets, and as partnership assets increase, partners' equity increases.

New Partner Investing Assets in a Partnership

Transaction Adam Novak wants to invest $75,000 for a one-third interest in the partnership of Mind and Padilla. The Capital accounts of Lori Mind and Rose Padilla are $70,000 and $80,000, respectively. The assets of the firm are valued correctly. The partners agree to admit Novak.

Computation Novak's $75,000 investment equals a one-third interest after it is added to the previously existing capital of the partnership:

Lori Mind, Capital	$ 70,000
Rose Padilla, Capital	80,000
Novak's investment	75,000
Total capital after Novak's investment	$225,000
One-third interest = $225,000 ÷ 3 =	$ 75,000

Analysis The journal entry to record the admission of a new partner

▲ *increases Cash* with a debit

▲ *increases Adam Novak, Capital* with a credit

Journal Entry

2016		Dr.	Cr.
Aug. 31	Cash	75,000	
	Adam Novak, Capital		75,000
	Admission of Adam Novak for a one-third interest in the company		

A	=	L	+	OE
+75,000				+75,000

Comment A new partnership *entity separate* from its partners has now been formed. The cash from the new partner, Adam Novak, goes to the partnership and not to the partners. The partnership assets and partnership equity have grown by $75,000.

Bonus to the Old Partners A partnership is sometimes so profitable or otherwise advantageous that a new investor is willing to pay more than the actual dollar interest he or she receives in the partnership. For instance, suppose an individual pays $100,000 for an $80,000 interest in a partnership. The $20,000 excess of the payment over the interest purchased is a **bonus** to the original partners. The bonus must be distributed to the original partners according to the partnership agreement. When the agreement does not cover the distribution of bonuses, it should be distributed to the original partners in accordance with the method for distributing income and losses.

STUDY NOTE: The original partners receive a bonus because the entity is worth more as a going concern than the fair market value of the net assets would otherwise indicate. That is, the new partner is paying for unrecorded partnership value.

Bonus to the Old Partners

Transaction Assume that Mind and Padilla's firm has operated for several years and that the partners' capital balances and the stated ratios for distribution of income and loss are as follows.

Partners	Capital Balances	Stated Ratios
Mind	$160,000	55%
Padilla	140,000	45
	$300,000	100%

Adam Novak wants to join the firm. He offers to invest $100,000 on December 1 for a one-fifth interest in the business and income. The original partners agree to the offer.

Computation The computation of the bonus to the original partners follows.

Partners' equity in the original partnership		$300,000
Cash investment by Adam Novak		100,000
Partners' equity in the new partnership		$400,000
Partners' equity assigned to Adam Novak ($400,000 × ⅕)		$ 80,000
Bonus to the original partners:		
Investment by Adam Novak	$100,000	
Less equity assigned to Adam Novak	80,000	$ 20,000
Distribution of bonus to original partners:		
Lori Mind ($20,000 × 0.55)	$ 11,000	
Rose Padilla ($20,000 × 0.45)	9,000	$ 20,000

Analysis The journal entry to record the bonus for the existing partners

▲ *increases Cash* by $100,000 with a debit

▲ *increases* each partner's capital account with a credit

Journal Entry

	A	=	L	+	OE
	+100,000				+11,000
					+9,000
					+80,000

2016			Dr.	Cr.
Dec. 1	Cash		100,000	
	Lori Mind, Capital			11,000
	Rose Padilla, Capital			9,000
	Adam Novak, Capital			80,000
	Investment by Adam Novak for a one-fifth			
	interest in the firm, and the bonus distributed			
	to the original partners			

Comment A new partnership *entity separate* from its partners has now been formed. The partners, Lori Mind and Rose Padilla, receive an increase in their capital accounts for part of Adam Novak's contribution to the partnership. Novak's desire to join the partnership makes him willing to accept less than the share would have been if he had not paid a bonus to the other partners.

Bonus to the New Partner A partnership might want a new partner for several reasons. A partnership in financial trouble might need additional cash, or the partners might want to expand the firm's markets and need more capital. Also, the partners might know a person who would bring a unique talent to the firm. Under these conditions, a new partner may be admitted to the partnership with the understanding that part of the original partners' capital will be transferred (credited) to the new partner's Capital account as a bonus.

Bonus to the New Partner

Transaction Suppose that Lori Mind and Rose Padilla have invited Adam Novak to join the firm. Novak is going to invest $60,000 on December 1 for a one-fourth interest in the company. The stated ratios for distribution of income or loss for Mind and Padilla are 55 percent and 45 percent, respectively. If Novak is to receive a one-fourth interest in the firm, the interest of the original partners represents a three-fourths interest in the business.

Computation The computation of Novak's bonus follows.

Total equity in partnership:		
Lori Mind, Capital		$160,000
Rose Padilla, Capital		140,000
Investment by Adam Novak		60,000
Partners' equity in the new partnership		$360,000
Partners' equity assigned to Adam Novak ($360,000 × ¼)		$ 90,000
Bonus to new partner:		
Equity assigned to Adam Novak	$90,000	
Less cash investment by Adam Novak	60,000	$ 30,000
Distribution of bonus from original partners:		
Lori Mind ($30,000 × 0.55)	$16,500	
Rose Padilla ($30,000 × 0.45)	13,500	$ 30,000

Analysis The journal entry to record the bonus to the new partner

    ▲ *increases Cash* with a debit

    ▼ *decreases Lori Mind, Capital* and *Rose Padilla, Capital* with debits

    ▲ *increases Adam Novak, Capital* with a credit

Journal Entry

	A	=	L	+	OE
	+60,000				
					−16,500
					−13,500
					+90,000

2016		Dr.	Cr.
Dec. 1	Cash	60,000	
	Lori Mind, Capital	16,500	
	Rose Padilla, Capital	13,500	
	Adam Novak, Capital		90,000
	To record the investment by Adam Novak of cash and a bonus from Mind and Padilla		

Comment A new partnership *entity separate* from its partners has now been formed. The partners, Lori Mind and Rose Padilla, were willing to accept a decrease in their capital accounts to get Adam Novak to join the new partnership.

Withdrawal of a Partner

STUDY NOTE: *There is no impact on the income statement when a partner withdraws. The only change is on the balance sheet.*

Generally, a partner has the right to withdraw from a partnership in accord with legal requirements. However, to avoid disputes when a partner does decide to withdraw or retire from the firm, the partnership agreement should describe the procedures to be followed. The agreement should specify:

- Whether an audit will be performed
- How the assets will be reappraised
- How a bonus will be determined
- By what method the withdrawing partner will be paid

A partner who wants to withdraw from a partnership can do so in one of several ways. The partner can sell his or her interest to another partner or to an outsider, with the consent of the remaining partners, or the partner can withdraw assets equal to his or her capital balance, less than his or her capital balance (with a bonus to the remaining partners), or greater than his or her capital balance (with a bonus to the withdrawing partner). These alternatives are illustrated in Exhibit 2.

Exhibit 2
Alternative Ways for a Partner to Withdraw

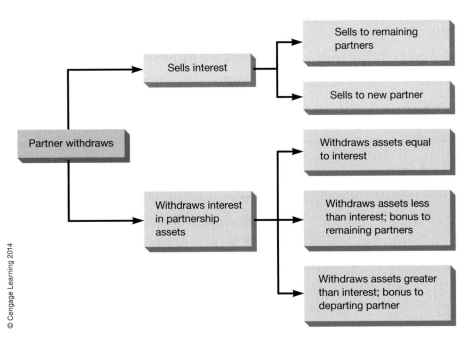

© Cengage Learning 2014

Withdrawal by Selling Interest When a partner sells his or her interest to another partner or to an outsider, with the consent of the other partners, the transaction is personal. It does not change the partnership assets or the partners' equity.

Withdrawal by Selling Interest

Transaction The capital balances of Mind, Padilla, and Novak are $140,000, $100,000, and $60,000, respectively, for a total of $300,000. Padilla wants to withdraw from the partnership and is reviewing two offers for her interest. The offers are (1) to sell her interest to Novak for $110,000 or (2) to sell her interest to Mary Smith for $120,000. The remaining partners have agreed to either potential transaction. Because Novak and Smith would pay for Padilla's interest from their personal assets, the partnership accounting records would show only the transfer of Padilla's interest to Novak or Smith.

Analysis In either case, the journal entry to record the partner's withdrawal by selling her interest

▼ *decreases Rose Padilla, Capital* with a debit

▲ *increases Adam Novak, Capital* or *Mary Smith, Capital* with a credit

Journal Entries

1. If Padilla's interest is purchased by Novak:			
Rose Padilla, Capital		100,000	
Adam Novak, Capital			100,000
Sale of Padilla's partnership interest to Novak			
2. If Padilla's interest is purchased by Smith:			
Rose Padilla, Capital		100,000	
Mary Smith, Capital			100,000
Sale of Padilla's partnership interest to Smith			

Comment Selling a partnership interest does not affect the assets and liabilities of the partnership. Therefore, total equity remains unchanged. The only effect of a partner's selling his or her interest to the existing partners or to a new partner is that a new *separate entity* is formed with a change of names in the partners' equity section of the balance sheet.

Withdrawal by Removing Assets

Withdrawal by Removing Assets A partnership agreement can allow a withdrawing partner to remove assets from the firm equal to his or her capital balance.

Withdrawal by Removing Assets

Transaction Adam Novak decides to withdraw from Mind, Padilla, and Novak on January 21, 2016. Novak's capital balance is $60,000. The partnership agreement states that he can withdraw cash from the firm equal to his capital balance. If there is not enough cash, he must accept a promissory note from the new partnership for the balance. The remaining partners ask that Novak take only $50,000 because of a cash shortage at the time of his withdrawal, and he agrees to this request.

Analysis The journal entry to record Novak's withdrawal

▼ *decreases Adam Novak, Capital* with a debit

▼ *decreases Cash* with a credit

▲ *increases Notes Payable, Adam Novak* with a credit

Journal Entry

2016		Dr.	Cr.
Jan. 21	Adam Novak, Capital	60,000	
	Cash		50,000
	Notes Payable, Adam Novak		10,000
	Withdrawal of Adam Novak from the partnership		

Comment Since Adam Novak is no longer a partner, the partnership entity had changed again. The *separate entity* now consists of the two remaining partners.

The preceding example showed the case when the partner withdraws taking an amount equal to his or her capital. It is not always the case that the withdrawal is equal to the capital account.

- When a withdrawing partner removes assets that represent less than his or her capital balance, the equity that the partner leaves in the business is divided among the remaining partners according to their stated ratios. This distribution is considered a bonus to the remaining partners.
- When a withdrawing partner takes out assets that are greater than his or her capital balance, the excess is treated as a bonus to the withdrawing partner. The remaining partners absorb the bonus by reducing their capital accounts according to their stated ratios. Alternative arrangements can be spelled out in the partnership agreement.

Death of a Partner

When a partner dies, the partnership is dissolved because the original association has changed. The partnership agreement should state the actions to be taken. Normally, the books are closed, and financial statements are prepared. These actions are necessary to determine the capital balance of each partner on the date of the death. The agreement may also indicate whether an audit should be conducted, assets appraised, and a bonus recorded, as well as what procedures have been established for settling with the deceased partner's heirs. The remaining partners may purchase the deceased's equity, sell it to outsiders, or deliver certain business assets to the estate. If the firm intends to continue, a new partnership must be formed.

APPLY IT!

Alpha and Beta each own a $50,000 interest in a partnership. They agree to admit Gamma as a partner by selling her a one-third interest for $80,000. How large a bonus will be distributed to Alpha and Beta?

SOLUTION

Partners' equity in the original partnership		$100,000
Cash investment by Gamma		80,000
Partners' equity in the new partnership		$180,000
Partners' equity assigned to Gamma ($180,000 × ⅓)		$ 60,000
Bonus to the original partners:		
Investment by Gamma	$80,000	
Less equity assigned to Gamma	60,000	$ 20,000
Distribution of bonus to original partners:		
Alpha ($20,000 × 0.50)	$10,000	
Beta ($20,000 × 0.50)	10,000	$ 20,000

TRY IT! SE6, SE7, SE8, SE9, E6A, E7A, E6B, E7B

LO 5 Liquidation of a Partnership

The **liquidation** of a partnership is the process of selling enough assets to pay the partnership's liabilities and distributing any remaining assets among the partners. Liquidation is a special form of dissolution. When a partnership is liquidated, the business will not continue. As the assets of the business are sold, any gain or losses should be distributed to the partners according to the stated ratios. As cash becomes available, it must be applied first to outside creditors, then to loans from partners, and finally to the partners' capital balances.

The process of liquidation can have a variety of financial outcomes. We look at two: (1) assets sold for a gain and (2) assets sold for a loss. To illustrate both alternatives, assume that the books have been closed for Mind, Padilla, and Novak, and that the following balance sheet exists before liquidation:

Mind, Padilla, and Novak
Balance Sheet
February 2, 2017

Assets		Liabilities	
Cash	$ 60,000	Accounts payable	$120,000
Accounts receivable	40,000		
Merchandise inventory	100,000		
Plant assets (net)	200,000	**Partners' Equity**	
		Mind, capital	$ 85,000
		Padilla, capital	95,000
		Novak, capital	100,000
		Total partners' equity	$280,000
Total assets	$400,000	Total liabilities and partners' equity	$400,000

The stated ratios of Mind, Padilla, and Novak are 3:3:4, or 30, 30, and 40 percent, respectively.

Gain on Sale of Assets

The following transactions took place in the liquidation of Mind, Padilla, and Novak:

1. On February 13, the accounts receivable were collected for $35,000.
2. On February 14, the inventory was sold for $110,000.
3. On February 15, the plant assets were sold for $200,000.
4. On February 16, the accounts payable of $120,000 were paid.
5. On February 20, the net gain of $5,000 from the realization of the assets was distributed according to the partners' stated ratios.
6. On February 20, the partners received cash equal to the balances of their Capital accounts.

These transactions are summarized in the statement of liquidation in Exhibit 3. The entries with their assumed transaction dates follow.

Journal Entries

Explanation on Statement of Liquidation

2017		Dr.	Cr.	
Feb. 13	Cash	35,000		
	Gain or Loss from Realization	5,000		1.
	Accounts Receivable		40,000	
	Collection of accounts receivable			
14	Cash	110,000		2.
	Merchandise Inventory		100,000	
	Gain or Loss from Realization		10,000	
	Sale of inventory			

A = L + OE
+35,000
−40,000   −5,000

A = L + OE
+110,000
−100,000   +10,000

Journal Entries

Explanation on Statement of Liquidation

								Dr.	Cr.	

A = **L** + **OE**
+200,000
−200,000

Feb. 15 Cash — 200,000 — 3.
    Plant Assets — 200,000
    Sale of plant assets

A = **L** + **OE**
−120,000   −120,000

16 Accounts Payable — 120,000 — 4.
    Cash — 120,000
    Payment of accounts payable

A = **L** + **OE**
−5,000
+1,500
+1,500
+2,000

20 Gain or Loss from Realization — 5,000 — 5.
    Lori Mind, Capital — 1,500
    Rose Padilla, Capital — 1,500
    Adam Novak, Capital — 2,000
    Distribution of the net gain on assets ($10,000 gain minus $5,000 loss) to the partners

A = **L** + **OE**
−285,000
−86,500
−96,500
−102,000

20 Lori Mind, Capital — 86,500 — 6.
    Rose Padilla, Capital — 96,500
    Adam Novak, Capital — 102,000
    Cash — 285,000
    Distribution of cash to the partners

Exhibit 3
Statement of Liquidation Showing Gain on Sale of Assets

Mind, Padilla, and Novak
Statement of Liquidation
February 2–20, 2017

Explanation	Cash	Other Assets	Accounts Payable	Mind, Capital (30%)	Padilla, Capital (30%)	Novak, Capital (40%)	Gain (or Loss) from Realization
Balance 2/2/17	$ 60,000	$ 340,000	$ 120,000	$ 85,000	$ 95,000	$ 100,000	
1. Collection of Accounts Receivable	35,000	(40,000)					$ (5,000)
	$ 95,000	$ 300,000	$ 120,000	$ 85,000	$ 95,000	$ 100,000	$ (5,000)
2. Sale of Inventory	110,000	(100,000)					10,000
	$ 205,000	$ 200,000	$ 120,000	$ 85,000	$ 95,000	$ 100,000	$ 5,000
3. Sale of Plant Assets	200,000	(200,000)					
	$ 405,000	—	$ 120,000	$ 85,000	$ 95,000	$ 100,000	$ 5,000
4. Payment of Liabilities	(120,000)		(120,000)				
	$ 285,000		—	$ 85,000	$ 95,000	$ 100,000	$ 5,000
5. Distribution of Gain (or Loss) from Realization				1,500	1,500	2,000	(5,000)
	$ 285,000			$ 86,500	$ 96,500	$ 102,000	—
6. Distribution of Cash to Partners	(285,000)			(86,500)	(96,500)	(102,000)	
	—			—	—	—	

Notice that the cash distributed to the partners is the balance in their respective Capital accounts. Cash is not distributed according to the partners' stated ratios.

Loss on Sale of Assets

When a firm's assets are sold at a loss, the partners share the loss on liquidation according to their stated ratios. For example, assume that during the liquidation of Mind, Padilla, and Novak, the total cash received from the collection of accounts receivable and the sale of inventory and plant assets was $140,000. The statement of liquidation appears in Exhibit 4.

Exhibit 4
Statement of Liquidation Showing Loss on Sale of Assets

				Mind, Padilla, and Novak Statement of Liquidation February 2–20, 2017			
Explanation	**Cash**	**Other Assets**	**Accounts Payable**	**Mind, Capital (30%)**	**Padilla, Capital (30%)**	**Novak, Capital (40%)**	**Gain (or Loss) from Realization**
Balance 2/2/17	$ 60,000	$ 340,000	$ 120,000	$ 85,000	$ 95,000	$100,000	
1. Collection of Accounts Receivable and Sale of Inventory and Plant Assets	140,000	(340,000)					$(200,000)
	$200,000	—	$ 120,000	$ 85,000	$ 95,000	$100,000	$(200,000)
2. Payment of Liabilities	(120,000)		(120,000)				
	$ 80,000		—	$ 85,000	$ 95,000	$100,000	$(200,000)
3. Distribution of Gain (or Loss) from Realization				(60,000)	(60,000)	(80,000)	200,000
	$ 80,000			$ 25,000	$ 35,000	$ 20,000	—
4. Distribution of Cash to Partners	(80,000)			(25,000)	(35,000)	(20,000)	
	—			—	—	—	

© Cengage Learning 2014

The entries for the transactions summarized in the statement of liquidation in Exhibit 4 are as follows.

Journal Entries

			Explanation on Statement of Liquidation
	2017	Dr.	Cr.
A = L + OE	Feb. 15 Cash	140,000	1.
+140,000	Gain or Loss from Realization	200,000	
−40,000 −200,000	Accounts Receivable		40,000
−100,000	Merchandise Inventory		100,000
−200,000	Plant Assets		200,000
	Collection of accounts receivable and the sale of inventory and plant assets.		
A = L + OE	16 Accounts Payable	120,000	2.
−120,000 −120,000	Cash		120,000
	Payment of accounts payable		

Journal Entries

Explanation on Statement of Liquidation ⌐

				Dr.	Cr.	
2017						
Feb. 20	Lori Mind, Capital			60,000		4.
	Rose Padilla, Capital			60,000		
	Adam Novak, Capital			80,000		
		Gain or Loss from Realization			200,000	
		Distribution of the loss on assets to the partners				
20	Lori Mind, Capital			25,000		5.
	Rose Padilla, Capital			35,000		
	Adam Novak, Capital			20,000		
		Cash			80,000	
		Distribution of cash to the partners				

A	=	L	+	OE
				−60,000
				−60,000
				−80,000
				+200,000

A	=	L	+	OE
−80,000				−25,000
				−35,000
				−20,000

In some liquidations, a partner's share of the loss is greater than his or her capital balance. In such a situation, because partners are subject to unlimited liability, the partner must make up the deficit in his or her Capital account from personal assets.

Liquidations Where Loss Is Greater than a Partners' Capital Balance

Transaction After the sale of assets and the payment of liabilities, the remaining assets and partners' equity of Mind, Padilla, and Novak look like this:

Assets:		
Cash		$30,000
Partners' equity:		
Mind, capital	$25,000	
Padilla, capital	20,000	
Novak, capital	(15,000)	$30,000

Adam Novak must pay $15,000 into the partnership from personal funds to cover his deficit.

Analysis Two journal entries are required. First, the journal entry to record Novak's $15,000 payment

  ▲ *increases Cash* increased with a debit
  ▲ *increases Adam Novak, Capital* with a credit

Journal Entry

		Dr.	Cr.
2017			
Feb. 20	Cash	15,000	
	Adam Novak, Capital		15,000
	Additional investment of Adam Novak to cover the negative balance in his Capital account		

A	=	L	+	OE
+15,000				+15,000

After Novak pays $15,000, there is enough cash to pay Mind and Padilla their capital balances and, thus, to complete the liquidation. This journal entry

  ▼ *decreases Lori Mind, Capital* and *Rose Padilla, Capital* with debits
  ▼ *decreases Cash* with a credit

Journal Entry

		Dr.	Cr.
2017			
Feb. 20	Lori Mind, Capital	25,000	
	Rose Padilla, Capital	20,000	
	Cash		45,000
	Distribution of cash to the partners		

A	=	L	+	OE
−45,000				−25,000
				−20,000

Comment The *separate partnership entity* is now ended and the partners have received their share of the cash.

If a partner does not have the cash to cover his or her obligations to the partnership, the remaining partners share the loss according to their established stated ratios. Remember that all partners have unlimited liability.

Liquidations Where Partners Share the Loss

Transaction If Adam Novak cannot pay the $15,000 deficit in his Capital account, Mind and Padilla must share the deficit according to their stated ratios. Each has a 30 percent stated ratio, so each must bear 50 percent of the deficit that Novak cannot pay.

Computation The new stated ratios are computed as follows.

	Old Ratios	New Ratios
Mind	30%	$30 \div 60 = 0.50 = 50\%$
Padilla	30	$30 \div 60 = 0.50 = 50$
	60%	100%

Analysis The journal entry to record the partners' payment of the $15,000 deficit

▼ *decreases Lori Mind, Capital* and *Rose Padilla, Capital* with debits

▲ *increases Adam Novak, Capital* with a credit

THEN,

▼ *decreases Lori Mind, Capital* and *Rose Padilla, Capital* with debits

▼ *decreases Cash* with a credit

Journal Entries

A	=	L	+	OE	2017			Dr.	Cr.
				−7,500	Feb. 20	Lori Mind, Capital		7,500	
				−7,500		Rose Padilla, Capital		7,500	
				+15,000		Adam Novak, Capital			15,000
						Transfer of Novak's deficit to Mind and Padilla			
A	**=**	**L**	**+**	**OE**	20	Lori Mind, Capital		17,500	
−30,000				−17,500		Rose Padilla, Capital		12,500	
				−12,500		Cash			30,000
						Distribution of cash to the partners			

Comment Novak's inability to meet his obligations at the time of liquidation does not relieve him of his liabilities to Mind and Padilla. If he is able to pay his liabilities at some time in the future, Mind and Padilla can collect the amount of Novak's deficit that they absorbed.

The Balance Sheet and Partner's Equity

Exhibit 5 shows how the assets, liabilities, and each partner's equity are reported on a balance sheet for a partnership.

Exhibit 5
Partnership Balance Sheet

© Cengage Learning 2014

Balance Sheet

December 31, 2014

Assets	**Liabilities**
Current assets	Current liabilities
Investments	Long-term liabilities
Property, plant, and equipment	Total liabilities
Intangible assets	
	Partner's Equity
	Partner 1, capital
	Partner 2, capital
	Total partner's capital

Total Assets = Total Liabilities + Partner's Equity

APPLY IT!

After the partnership between Tim and John has been operating for a year, their Capital accounts are $30,000 and $20,000, respectively. The firm has cash of $24,000 and inventory of $26,000. The partners decide to liquidate the partnership. The inventory is liquidated for only $8,000. Assuming the partners share income and losses in the ratio of one-third to Tim and two-thirds to John, how much cash will be distributed to each partner in liquidation?

SOLUTION

Loss on inventory computed:
$26,000 − $8,000 = $18,000

	Tim	John
Distribution of cash to partners:		
Capital balances	$30,000	$ 20,000
Distribution of loss:		
Tim ($18,000 × ⅓)	(6,000)	
John ($18,000 × ⅔)		(12,000)
Cash to partners	$24,000	$ 8,000

TRY IT! SE10, E8A, E9A, E8B, E9B

BUSINESS APPLICATION

■ Identify alternate forms of partnership-type entities

RELEVANT LEARNING OBJECTIVE

LO 6 Identify alternate forms of partnership-type entities.

LO 6 Alternate Forms of Partnership-Type Entities

Limited Partnerships and Joint Ventures

Other common forms of association that are a type of partnership or similar to a partnership are limited partnerships, joint ventures, and companies with some partnership-like characteristics.

Limited Partnerships

A **limited partnership (LP)** is a special type of partnership that, like corporations, confines the limited partner's potential loss to the amount of his or her investment. Under this type of partnership, the unlimited liability disadvantage of a partnership can be overcome. Usually, the limited partnership has a general partner who has unlimited liability but allows other partners to limit their potential loss. The potential loss of all partners in an ordinary partnership is limited only by personal bankruptcy laws.

Limited partnerships resemble corporations in that the liability of the partners is restricted to the amount of their investment in the business. Because limited partnerships curtail an investor's risk, they are sometimes used in place of corporations to raise funds from the public to finance large projects, such as the exploration and drilling of oil and gas wells, the manufacture of airplanes, and the development of real estate (including shopping centers, office buildings, and apartment complexes). For example, **Alliance Capital Management Limited Partnership**, a large investment advisor, manages more than \$90 billion in assets for corporate and individual investors in various projects. The company's partnership units, or shares of ownership, sell on the New York Stock Exchange and can be purchased by the individual investor.

Joint Ventures

In today's global environment, more companies are looking to form joint ventures with other companies. These alliances are similar to partnerships. A **joint venture** is an association of two or more entities for the purpose of achieving a specific goal, such as the manufacture of a product in a new market. Many joint ventures have an agreed-upon limited life. The entities forming joint ventures usually involve companies but sometimes involve governments, especially in emerging economies. A joint venture brings together the resources, technical skills, political ties, and other assets of each of the parties for a common goal. Profits and losses are shared on an agreed-upon basis.

When U.S. companies make investments abroad, they often find it wise to partner with a local company. Because many countries require that local investors own a substantial percentage of a newly formed business, partnering with a local company is often a necessary step. One way of accomplishing this is to form a joint venture, which matches a country's need for outside capital and operational know-how with the investors' interest in business expansion and profitability. Joint ventures frequently take the form of partnerships among two or more corporations and other investors. Any income or losses from operations are divided among the participants according to a predetermined agreement.

Business Perspective
What Are the Risks of Being a Partner in an Accounting Firm?

Partners in large accounting firms can make over $250,000 per year, with top partners drawing over $800,000. However, consideration of those incomes should take into account the risks that partners take and the fact that the incomes of partners in small accounting firms are often much lower.

Partners are not compensated in the same way as managers in corporations. Partners' income is not guaranteed; rather, it is based on the performance of the partnership. Also, each partner is required to make a substantial investment of capital in the partnership. This capital remains at risk for as long as the partner chooses to stay in the partnership. For instance, in one notable case, when a large firm was convicted of destroying evidence in the **Enron** case, the partners lost their total investments as well as their income when their firm was subjected to lawsuits and other losses. The firm was eventually liquidated.

© Cengage Learning 2014

STUDY NOTE: Many types of organizations have been created by law. They include S corporations and limited partnerships. Each provides legal (especially tax) advantages and disadvantages.

Companies That Look Like Partnerships

Some types of business organizations mimic the characteristics of partnerships:

■ **S corporations: S corporations** are corporations that U.S. tax laws treat as partnerships. Unlike normal corporations, S corporations do not pay federal income taxes. They have a limited number of stockholders, who report the income or losses on their investments in the business on their personal tax returns. This avoids the problem of double taxation.

■ **Limited liability company (LLC):** In a **limited liability company (LLC)**, the members are partners, and their liability is limited to their investment in the business. LLCs are used frequently by accounting and consultancy firms.

■ **Special-purpose entities (SPEs): Special-purpose entities (SPEs)**, which gained notoriety because of the **Enron** case, are firms with limited lives that a company creates to achieve a specific objective, such as raising money by selling receivables. By meeting certain conditions, a company that sets up an SPE can legitimately avoid including the debt of the SPE on its balance sheet. Enron used SPEs extensively and fraudulently to hide debt and other commitments.

APPLY IT!

Identify each of the following statements as either (a) limited partnership, (b) joint venture, (c) S corporation, (d) limited liability company, or (e) special-purpose entity:

1. Entities with limited lives that a company creates to achieve a specific objective.
2. An association of two or more entities for the purpose of achieving a specific goal.
3. Corporations that U.S. tax laws treat as partnerships, and they do not pay income taxes.
4. An entity in which members are partners, and their liability is limited to their investment in the business.
5. A special type of partnership that confines the limited partner's potential loss to the amount of his or her investment.

SOLUTION

1. e; 2. b; 3. c; 4. d; 5. a

TRY IT! SE11, E10A, E10B

TriLevel Problem

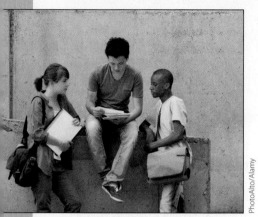

Ankin and Kent Partnership

Distribution of Income and Admission of a Partner

The beginning of this chapter focused on Patrick Ankin and Eric Kent, who were forming their partnership in 2014. They were faced with a number of important decisions. Complete the following requirements in order to answer the questions posed at the beginning of the chapter.

Section 1: Concepts

How does the separate entity concept apply to partners' interest in a partnership?

Section 2: Accounting Applications

How would Patrick Ankin and Eric Kent share the income or losses of their business, and how would they handle any changes in ownership that might occur?

Patrick and Eric drafted a written partnership agreement that clearly stated the details of the arrangement, including the name, location, and purpose of the business; their names and respective duties; the investments each of them had made; the method of distributing income and losses; and the procedures for the admission and withdrawal of partners, the withdrawal of assets allowed each partner, and the liquidation (termination) of the business. They decided that Patrick, who had contributed $100,000 to the partnership, was to receive an annual salary of $6,000 and that Eric was to receive 3 percent interest annually on his original investment of $150,000. They were to share income and losses after salary and interest in a 2:3 ratio.

1. In 2014, the partnership had an income of $27,000, and in 2015, it had a loss of $2,000 (before salaries and interest). Compute Patrick Ankin and Eric William's share of the income and loss for the two years, and prepare the required journal entries.

2. On January 1, 2016, Adele Matiz offers Patrick and Eric $60,000 for a 15 percent interest in the partnership. They agree to Matiz's offer because they need her resources to expand the business. On January 1, 2016, the balance in Patrick's Capital account is $113,600, and the balance in Eric's Capital account is $161,400. Record the admission of Adele Matiz to the partnership, assuming that her investment represents a 15 percent interest in the total partners' capital and that a bonus will be distributed to Patrick and Eric in the ratio of 2:3.

Section 3: Business Applications

As the partnership grows, what alternate forms of partnership-like entities might the partners consider?

SOLUTION

Section 1: Concepts

A partnership is an association of two or more persons to carry on as co-owners of a business for profit. A partnership is treated in the accounting records and financial statements as a *separate entity* apart from the partners who have an interest in the partnership.

Section 2: Accounting Applications

1.

	A	B	C	D
		Income(Loss) of Partner		Income
		Ankin	Kent	Distributed
1				
2				
3	**2014**			
4	Total income for distribution			$ 27,000
5	Distribution of salary:			
6	Ankin	$ 6,000		(6,000)
7	Remaining income after salary			$ 21,000
8	Distribution of interest:			
9	Kent ($150,000 × 0.03)		$ 4,500	(4,500)
10	Remaining income after salary and			
11	interest			$ 16,500
12	Distribution of remaining income:			
13	Ankin ($16,500 × 2/5)	6,600		
14	Kent ($16,500 × 3/5)		9,900	(16,500)
15	Remaining income			—
16	Income of partners	$12,600	$14,400	$ 27,000
17				
18				
19	**2015**			
20	Total loss for distribution			$ (2,000)
21	Distribution of salary:			
22	Ankin	$ 6,000		(6,000)
23	Negative balance after salary			$ (8,000)
24	Distribution of interest:			
25	Kent ($150,000 × 0.03)		$ 4,500	(4,500)
26	Negative balance after salary			$(12,500)
27	and interest			
28	Distribution of remaining income:			
29	Ankin ($12,500 × 2/5)	(5,000)		
30	Kent ($12,500 × 3/5)		(7,500)	12,500
31	Remaining income			—
32	Income and loss of partners	$ 1,000	$(3,000)	$ (2,000)
33				

Journal Entry:

2014	Dr.	Cr.
Income Summary	27,000	
Patrick Ankin, Capital		12,600
Eric Kent, Capital		14,400
Distribution of income for the year to the partners' Capital accounts		

Journal Entry:

2015	Dr.	Cr.
Eric Kent, Capital	3,000	
Income Summary		2,000
Patrick Ankin, Capital		1,000
Distribution of the loss for the year to the partners' Capital accounts		

2.

Capital Balance and Bonus Computation

Matiz, Capital = (Original Partners' Capital + New Partner's Investment) × 15%

= ($113,600 + $161,400 + $60,000) × 0.15 = $50,250

Bonus = New Partner's Investment − Matiz, Capital

= $60,000 − $50,250

= $9,750

Distribution of Bonus

Ankin = $9,750 × $^2/_5$ = $3,900

Kent = $9,750 × $^3/_5$ = 5,850

Total bonus $9,750

Journal Entry:

2016		Dr.	Cr.
Jan. 1	Cash	60,000	
	Patrick Ankin, Capital		3,900
	Eric Kent, Capital		5,850
	Adele Matiz, Capital		50,250
	Sale of a 15 percent interest in the partnership to Adele Matiz and the bonus paid to the original partners		

Section 3: Business Applications

As the partnership business grows, the partners may want to consider changing the form of organization to a limited partnership, joint venture, or limited liability company. This change would help overcome some of the disadvantages of partnerships, such as the unlimited liability of partners and limited life of the partnership.

Chapter Review

Define the *partnership* form of business, and identify its principal characteristics. **LO 1**

A partnership is a voluntary association of two or more people who combine their talents and resources to carry on a business. Legally, the partnership is not separate from its partners. Their joint effort should be supported by a partnership agreement that spells out the venture's operating procedures. A partnership is dissolved by a partner's admission, withdrawal, or death and therefore has a limited life. Each partner acts as an agent of the partnership within the scope of normal operations and is personally liable for the partnership's debts. Property invested in the partnership becomes an asset of the partnership, owned jointly by all the partners. Each partner has the right to share in the company's income and the responsibility to share in its losses. For accounting purposes, however, the partnership is treated as a separate entity with its own accounting records and financial statements.

Record partners' investments of cash and other assets when a partnership is formed. **LO 2**

A partnership is formed when the partners contribute cash, other assets, or a combination of both to the business. The details are stated in the partnership agreement. Initial investments are recorded with a debit to Cash or another asset account and a credit to the investing partner's Capital account. The recorded amount of the other assets should be their fair market value on the date of transfer to the partnership. In addition, a partnership can assume an investing partner's liabilities. When this occurs, the partner's Capital account is credited with the difference between the assets invested and the liabilities assumed.

Compute and record the income or losses that partners share, based on stated ratios, capital balance ratios, and partners' salaries and interest. **LO 3**

The partners must share income and losses in accordance with the partnership agreement. If the agreement says nothing about the distribution of income and losses, the partners share them equally. Common methods used for distributing income and losses include stated ratios, capital balance ratios, and salaries and interest on capital investments.

Stated ratios usually are based on the partners' relative contributions to the partnership. When capital balance ratios are used, income or losses are divided strictly on the basis of each partner's capital balance. The use of salaries and interest on capital investment takes into account both efforts (salary) and capital investment (interest) in dividing income or losses among the partners.

Record a person's admission to or withdrawal from a partnership. **LO 4**

An individual is admitted to a partnership by purchasing a partner's interest or by contributing additional assets. When an interest is purchased, the withdrawing partner's capital is transferred to the new partner. When the new partner contributes assets to the partnership, it may be necessary to recognize a bonus shared or borne by the original partners or by the new partner.

A person can withdraw from a partnership by selling his or her interest in the business to the remaining partners or a new partner or by withdrawing company assets. When assets are withdrawn, the amount can be equal to, less than, or greater than the partner's capital interest. When assets that have a value less than or greater than the partner's interest are withdrawn, a bonus is recognized and distributed among the remaining partners or to the departing partner.

Compute and record the distribution of assets to partners when they liquidate their partnership. **LO 5**

The liquidation of a partnership entails selling the assets necessary to pay the company's liabilities and then distributing any remaining assets to the partners. Any gain or loss on the sale of the assets is shared by the partners according to their stated ratios. When a partner has a deficit balance in a Capital account, that partner must contribute personal assets equal to the deficit. When a partner does not have personal assets to cover a capital deficit, the deficit must be absorbed by the solvent partners according to their stated ratios.

Identify alternate forms of partnership-type entities. **LO 6**

Common alternate forms of association similar to a regular partnership are limited partnerships, joint ventures, and limited liability companies. Each of these forms of business overcomes certain disadvantages of partners.

Key Terms

bonus 463 (LO4)
dissolution 461 (LO4)
joint venture 474 (LO6)
limited liability company (LLC) 475 (LO6)
limited life 452 (LO1)

limited partnership (LP) 474 (LO6)
liquidation 467 (LO5)
mutual agency 452 (LO1)
partners' equity 454 (LO2)
partnership 452 (LO1)
partnership agreement 452 (LO1)

S corporations 475 (LO6)
special-purpose entities (SPEs) 475 (LO6)
unlimited liability 452 (LO1)

Chapter Assignments

DISCUSSION QUESTIONS

LO 1   **DQ1. CONCEPT** ▶ Even though, from accounting standpoint, partnerships are separate entities from the partners, why is it important for people to form partnerships with people they can trust?

LO 2   **DQ2.** When accounts receivable are transferred into a partnership, at what amount should they be recorded?

LO 3   **DQ3.** What is a disadvantage of receiving a large salary as part of a partner's distribution?

LO 4   **DQ4.** If the value of a partnership is worth far more than the book value of the assets on the balance sheet, would a new partner entering the partnership be more likely to pay a bonus to the old partners or receive a bonus from the old partners?

LO 5   **DQ5.** When a partnership is dissolved, what is an alternate approach to selling all the assets and distributing the proceeds, and what decisions will have to be made if this approach is taken?

SHORT EXERCISES

LO 1   **Partnership Characteristics**

SE1. Indicate whether each statement below is a reflection of (a) voluntary association, (b) a partnership agreement, (c) limited life, (d) mutual agency, or (e) unlimited liability.

1. A written contract among partners.
2. Any partner can sign a contract obligating the partnership.
3. A partner may be liable for the debts of the partnership.
4. A partnership ends when a partner is admitted, withdraws, retires, or dies.
5. A partner may leave a partnership if he or she wants to.

LO 2   **Partnership Formation**

SE2. Martin contributes cash of $24,000, and Steven contributes office equipment that cost $20,000 but is valued at $16,000 to the formation of a new partnership. Prepare the journal entry to form the partnership.

LO 3   **Distribution of Partnership Income**

SE3. During the first year, the Martin and Steven partnership in **SE2** earned an income of $10,000. Assume the partners agreed to share income and losses in the ratio of the beginning balances of their capital accounts. How much income should be transferred to each Capital account?

LO 3   **Distribution of Partnership Income**

SE4. During the first year, the Martin and Steven partnership in **SE2** earned an income of $10,000. Assume the partners agreed to share income and losses by figuring interest on the beginning capital balances at 10 percent and dividing the remainder equally. How much income should be transferred to each Capital account?

LO 3   **Distribution of Partnership Income**

SE5. During the first year, the Martin and Steven partnership in **SE2** earned an income of $10,000. Assume the partners agreed to share income and losses by figuring interest on the beginning capital balances at 10 percent, allowing a salary of $12,000 to Martin, and dividing the remainder equally. How much income (or loss) should be transferred to each Capital account?

LO 4 **Withdrawal of a Partner**

SE6. After the partnership has been operating for a year, the Capital accounts of Martin and Steven are $15,000 and $10,000, respectively. Steven withdraws from the partnership by selling his interest in the business to Sania for $8,000. What will be the Capital account balances of the partners in the new Martin and Sania partnership? Prepare the journal entry to record the transfer of ownership on the partnership books.

LO 4 **Admission of a New Partner**

SE7. After the partnership has been operating for a year, the Capital accounts of Martin and Steven are $30,000 and $20,000, respectively. Sania buys a one-sixth interest in the partnership by investing cash of $22,000. What will be the Capital account balances of the partners in the new Martin, Steven, and Sania partnership, assuming a bonus to the old partners, who share income and losses equally? Prepare the journal entry to record the transfer of ownership on the partnership books.

LO 4 **Admission of a New Partner**

SE8. After the partnership has been operating for a year, the Capital accounts of Martin and Steven are $15,000 and $10,000, respectively. Sania buys a one-fourth interest in the partnership by investing cash of $5,000. What will be the Capital account balances of the partners in the new Martin, Steven, and Sania partnership, assuming that the new partner receives a bonus and that Martin and Steven share income and losses equally? Prepare the journal entry to record the transfer of ownership on the partnership books.

LO 4 **Withdrawal of a Partner**

SE9. After the partnership has been operating for several years, the Capital accounts of Martin, Steven, and Sania are $50,000, $32,000, and $18,000, respectively. Sania decides to leave the partnership and is allowed to withdraw $18,000 in cash. Prepare the journal entry to record the withdrawal on the partnership books.

LO 5 **Liquidation of a Partnership**

SE10. After the partnership has been operating for a year, the Capital accounts of Martin and Steven are $15,000 and $10,000, respectively. The firm has cash of $12,000 and office equipment of $13,000. The partners decide to liquidate the partnership. The office equipment is sold for only $4,000. Assuming the partners share income and losses in the ratio of one-third to Martin and two-thirds to Steven, how much cash will be distributed to each partner in liquidation?

LO 6 **Types of Partnerships**

SE11. BUSINESS APPLICATION ▶ Indicate whether each statement that follows is a reflection of (a) normal partnership (b) limited partnership, (c) joint venture, or (d) S corporation.

1. A special type of partnership that, like corporations, confines the limited partner's potential loss to the amount of his or her investment.
2. A form of organization that has the disadvantage of unlimited liability.
3. An association formed by two or more entities for the purpose of achieving a specific goal.
4. A form of organization that makes it difficult to raise large amounts of capital.
5. A form of corporation that is treated as a partnership and pays no federal income taxes.

EXERCISES: SET A

LO 1

Partnership Characteristics

E1A. Indicate whether each action that follows is a reflection of (a) voluntary association, (b) a partnership agreement, (c) limited life, (d) mutual agency, or (e) unlimited liability.

1. A partner signs an contract obligating the partnership.
2. A partner leaves a partnership for personal reasons.
3. A partner has to pay some of the debts of the partnership.
4. The partners write a contract among themselves.
5. A partner leaves the partnership ending the partnership.

LO 1

Partnership Advantages and Disadvantages

E2A. Indicate whether each statement below is a reflection of an (a) advantage or a (b) disadvantage of the partnership form of business.

1. It is easy to form, change, and dissolve.
2. The life of a partnership is limited.
3. It gives the partners a certain amount of freedom and flexibility.
4. It is more difficult for a partnership to raise large amounts of capital and to transfer ownership interests than it is for a corporation.

LO 2

Partnership Formation

E3A. Hanna Hark and Jamie Rice are watch repairmen who want to form a partnership and open a jewelry store. An attorney prepares their partnership agreement, which indicates that assets invested in the partnership will be recorded at their fair market value and that liabilities will be assumed at book value.

The assets contributed by each partner and the liabilities assumed by the partnership follow.

Assets	Hanna Hark	Jamie Rice	Total
Cash	$ 80,000	$60,000	$140,000
Accounts receivable	104,000	40,000	144,000
Allowance for uncollectible accounts	8,000	6,000	14,000
Supplies	2,000	1,000	3,000
Equipment	40,000	20,000	60,000
Liabilities			
Accounts payable	64,000	18,000	82,000

Prepare the journal entries necessary to record the original investments of Hark and Rice in the partnership.

LO 3

Distribution of Income

E4A. Isha Shah and Brian Ruben agreed to form a partnership. Shah contributed $400,000 in cash, and Ruben contributed assets with a fair market value of $800,000. The partnership, in its initial year, reported net income of $240,000. Calculate the distribution of the first year's income to the partners under each of the following conditions:

1. Shah and Ruben failed to include stated ratios in the partnership agreement.
2. Shah and Ruben agreed to share income and losses in a 3:2 ratio.
3. Shah and Ruben agreed to share income and losses in the ratio of their original investments.
4. Shah and Ruben agreed to share income and losses by allowing 10 percent interest on original investments and sharing any remainder equally.

LO 3

Distribution of Income or Losses: Salaries and Interest

E5A. Assume that the partnership agreement of Shah and Ruben in **E4A** states that Shah and Ruben are to receive salaries of $40,000 and $48,000, respectively; that Shah is to receive 6 percent interest on his capital balance at the beginning of the year; and that the remainder of income and losses are to be shared equally. Calculate the distribution of the income or losses under the following conditions:

1. Income totaled $240,000 before deductions for salaries and interest.
2. Income totaled $96,000 before deductions for salaries and interest.
3. There was a loss of $4,000.
4. There was a loss of $80,000.

LO 3 **Distribution of Income: Average Capital Balance**

E6A. Amine and Ankit operate a furniture rental business. Their capital balances on January 1, 2014, were $320,000 and $480,000, respectively. Amine withdrew cash of $64,000 from the business on April 1, 2014. Ankit withdrew $120,000 cash on October 1, 2014. Amine and Ankit distribute partnership income based on their average capital balances each year. Income for 2014 was $320,000. Compute the income to be distributed to Amine and Ankit using their average capital balances in 2014. (Round percentages to the nearest tenth of a percent.)

LO 4 **Admission of a New Partner: Recording a Bonus**

E7A. Gamine, Ronald, and Fenny have equity in a partnership of $80,000, $80,000, and $120,000, respectively, and they share income and losses in a ratio of 1:1:3. The partners have agreed to admit Amit to the partnership. Prepare journal entries to record the admission of Amit to the partnership under the following conditions:

1. Amit invests $120,000 for a 20 percent interest in the partnership, and a bonus is recorded for the original partners.
2. Amit invests $120,000 for a 40 percent interest in the partnership, and a bonus is recorded for Amit.

LO 4 **Withdrawal of a Partner**

E8A. Sam, Richard, and Tom are partners. They share income and losses in the ratio of 3:2:1. Tom's Capital account has a $240,000 balance. Sam and Richard have agreed to let Tom take $320,000 of the company's cash when he retires from the business. What journal entry must be made on the partnership's books when Tom retires, assuming that a bonus to Tom is recognized and absorbed by the remaining partners?

LO 5 **Partnership Liquidation**

E9A. Assume the following assets, liabilities, and partners' equity in the Winner and Perry partnership on December 31, 2014:

Assets	=	Liabilities	+	Winner, Capital	+	Perry, Capital
$320,000	=	$20,000	+	$180,000	+	$120,000

The partnership has no cash. When the partners agree to liquidate the business, the assets are sold for $240,000, and the liabilities are paid. Winner and Perry share income and losses in a ratio of 3:1.

1. Prepare a statement of liquidation.
2. Prepare journal entries for the sale of assets, payment of liabilities, distribution of loss from realization, and final distribution of cash to Winner and Perry.

LO 5 **Partnership Liquidation**

E10A. BUSINESS APPLICATION ▶ Abby, Anna, and Anita are partners in a tanning salon. The assets, liabilities, and capital balances as of July 1, 2014, follow.

Assets	$960,000
Liabilities	320,000
Abby, Capital	280,000
Anna, Capital	80,000
Anita, Capital	280,000

(Continued)

Because competition is strong, business is declining, and the partnership has no cash, the partners have decided to sell the business. Abby, Anna, and Anita share income and losses in a ratio of 3:1:1, respectively. The assets were sold for $520,000, and the liabilities were paid. Anna has no other assets and will not be able to cover any deficits in her Capital account. Prepare a statement of liquidation to show how the ending cash balance will be distributed to the partners.

EXERCISES: SET B

Visit the textbook companion website at www.cengagebrain.com to access Exercise Set B for this chapter.

PROBLEMS

LO **2, 3**

✔ 2c: Thomas 2013 income: $67,200;
Thomas 2014 income: $32,000
✔ 2d: Thomas 2013 income: $72,000;
Thomas 2014 income: $28,000
✔ 2f: Thomas 2013 income: $85,200;
Thomas 2014 income: $41,200

Partnership Formation and Distribution of Income

P1. In January 2013, Edi Thomas and George Lopez agreed to produce and sell chocolate candies. Thomas contributed $480,000 in cash to the business. Lopez contributed the building and equipment, valued at $440,000 and $280,000, respectively. The partnership had an income of $168,000 during 2013 but was less successful during 2014, when income was only $80,000.

REQUIRED

1. Prepare the journal entry to record the investment of both partners in the partnership.
2. Determine the share of income for each partner in 2013 and 2014 under each of the following conditions:
   a. The partners agreed to share income equally.
   b. The partners failed to agree on an income-sharing arrangement.
   c. The partners agreed to share income according to the ratio of their original investments.
   d. The partners agreed to share income by allowing interest of 10 percent on their original investments and dividing the remainder equally.
   e. The partners agreed to share income by allowing salaries of $80,000 for Thomas and $56,000 for Lopez, and dividing the remainder equally.
   f. The partners agreed to share income by paying salaries of $80,000 to Thomas and $56,000 to Lopez, allowing interest of 9 percent on their original investments, and dividing the remainder equally.
3. **ACCOUNTING CONNECTION** ▶ What are some of the factors that need to be considered in choosing the plan of partners' income sharing among the options shown in requirement 2?

LO **3**

SPREADSHEET

✔ 1: Chevron income: $58,400
✔ 3: Wilkes income: $32,160

Distribution of Income: Salaries and Interest

P2. Wilkes and Chevron are partners in a tennis shop. They have agreed that Wilkes will operate the store and receive a salary of $104,000 per year. Chevron will receive 10 percent interest on his average capital balance during the year of $500,000. The remaining income or losses are to be shared by Wilkes and Chevron in a 2:3 ratio.

REQUIRED

Determine each partner's share of income and losses under each of the following conditions. In each case, the income or loss is stated before the distribution of salary and interest.

1. Income was $168,000.
2. Income was $88,000.
3. The loss was $25,600.

LO **4**

Admission and Withdrawal of a Partner

✔ 1c: credit Mason, Capital: $6,000
✔ 1d: credit Frank, Capital: $96,000
✔ 1f: debit Mason, Capital: $90,000

P3. Mason, Jiri, and James are partners in Woodware Company. Their capital balances as of July 31, 2014, are as follows.

Mason, Capital		Jiri, Capital		James, Capital	
Dr.	*Cr.*	*Dr.*	*Cr.*	*Dr.*	*Cr.*
	90,000		30,000		60,000

Each partner has agreed to admit Frank to the partnership.

REQUIRED

1. Prepare the journal entries to record Frank's admission to or Mason's withdrawal from the partnership under each of the following conditions:
   a. Frank pays Mason $25,000 for 20 percent of Mason's interest in the partnership.
   b. Frank invests $40,000 cash in the partnership and receives an interest equal to her investment.
   c. Frank invests $60,000 cash in the partnership for a 20 percent interest in the business. A bonus is to be recorded for the original partners on the basis of their capital balances.
   d. Frank invests $60,000 cash in the partnership for a 40 percent interest in the business. The original partners give Frank a bonus according to the ratio of their capital balances on July 31, 2014.
   e. Mason withdraws from the partnership, taking $105,000. The excess of withdrawn assets over Mason's partnership interest is distributed according to the balances of the Capital accounts.
   f. Mason withdraws by selling her interest directly to Frank for $120,000.

2. **ACCOUNTING CONNECTION** ▶ When a new partner enters a partnership, why would the new partner pay a bonus to the old partners, or why would the old partners pay a bonus to the new partner?

LO **5**

Partnership Liquidation

✔ 1: Cash distributed to Josh: $336,000

P4. Josh, John, and Hassan are partners in a retail lighting store. They share income and losses in the ratio of 2:2:1, respectively. The partners have agreed to liquidate the partnership. The partnership balance sheet before the liquidation follows.

Josh, John, and Hassan
Partnership Balance Sheet
August 31, 2014

Assets		Liabilities	
Cash	$ 280,000	Accounts payable	$ 360,000
Other assets	880,000		
		Partners' Equity	
		Josh, capital	$ 400,000
		John, capital	240,000
		Hassan, capital	160,000
		Total partners' equity	$ 800,000
Total assets	$1,160,000	Total liabilities and partners' equity	$1,160,000

The other assets were sold on September 1, 2014, for $720,000. Accounts payable were paid on September 4, 2014. The remaining cash was distributed to the partners on September 11, 2014.

(Continued)

REQUIRED

1. Prepare a statement of liquidation.
2. Prepare the following journal entries:
   a. The sale of the other assets.
   b. Payment of the accounts payable.
   c. The distribution of the loss from realization.
   d. The distribution to the partners of the remaining cash.

ALTERNATE PROBLEMS

LO 3

SPREADSHEET

✔ 2: Jan income: $60,400; Pat income: $178,640; Misa income: $72,160
✔ 3: Jan loss: $152,000; Pat income: $51,200; Misa loss: $12,800

Distribution of Income: Salaries and Interest

P5. Jan, Pat, and Misa are partners in South Central Company. The partnership agreement states that Jan is to receive 8 percent interest on his capital balance at the beginning of the year, Pat is to receive a salary of $200,000 a year, and Misa will be paid interest of 6 percent on his average capital balance during the year. Jan, Pat, and Misa will share any income or loss after salary and interest in a 5:3:2 ratio. Jan's capital balance at the beginning of the year was $1,200,000, and Misa's average capital balance for the year was $1,440,000.

REQUIRED

Determine each partner's share of income and losses under the following conditions. In each case, the income or loss is stated before the distribution of salary and interest.

1. Income was $1,090,400.
2. Income was $311,200.
3. The loss was $113,600.

LO 4

✔ 1c: credit Sasha, Capital: $16,000
✔ 1d: credit Rob, Capital: $188,000
✔ 1f: debit Sasha, Capital: $100,000

Admission and Withdrawal of a Partner

P6. Sasha, Serge, and Sander are partners in the Image Gallery. As of November 30, 2014, the balance in Sasha's Capital account was $100,000, the balance in Serge's was $120,000, and the balance in Sander's was $180,000. Sasha, Serge, and Sander share income and losses in a ratio of 2:3:5.

REQUIRED

1. Prepare journal entries for each of the following independent conditions:
   a. Rob pays Sander $200,000 for four-fifths of Sander's interest.
   b. Rob is to be admitted to the partnership with a one-third interest for a $200,000 cash investment.
   c. Rob is to be admitted to the partnership with a one-third interest for a $320,000 cash investment. A bonus, based on the partners' ratio for income and losses, is to be distributed to the original partners when Rob is admitted.
   d. Rob is to be admitted to the partnership with a one-third interest for an $164,000 cash investment. A bonus is to be given to Rob on admission.
   e. Sasha withdraws from the partnership, taking $132,000 in cash.
   f. Sasha withdraws from the partnership by selling his interest directly to Rob for $140,000.
2. **ACCOUNTING CONNECTION** ▶ In general, when a new partner enters a partnership, why would the new partner pay a bonus to the old partners, or why would the old partners pay a bonus to the new partner?

LO **5**

SPREADSHEET

✔ 1: Cash distributed to
Tailor: $208,800

Partnership Liquidation

P7. Leverage Partnership's balance sheet as of July 31, 2014, follows.

Leverage Partnership
Balance Sheet
July 31, 2014

Assets		Liabilities	
Cash	$ 12,000	Accounts payable	$ 960,000
Accounts receivable	240,000		
Inventory	528,000	**Partners' Equity**	
Equipment (net)	924,000	Gauri, capital	$ 144,000
		Tailor, capital	360,000
		Pavel, capital	240,000
		Total partners' equity	$ 744,000
Total assets	$1,704,000	Total liabilities and partners' equity	$1,704,000

The partners—Gauri, Tailor, and Pavel—share income and losses in the ratio of 5:3:2. Because of a mutual disagreement, Gauri, Tailor, and Pavel have decided to liquidate the business.

Assume that Gauri cannot contribute any additional personal assets to the company during liquidation and that the following transactions occurred during liquidation: (a) Accounts receivable were sold for 60 percent of their book value. (b) Inventory was sold for $552,000. (c) Equipment was sold for $600,000. (d) Accounts payable were paid in full. (e) Gain or loss from realization was distributed to the partners' Capital accounts. (f) Gauri's deficit was transferred to the remaining partners in their new income and loss ratio. (g) The remaining cash was distributed to Tailor and Pavel.

REQUIRED

1. Prepare a statement of liquidation.
2. Prepare journal entries to liquidate the partnership and distribute any remaining cash.

LO **2, 3, 4, 5**

✔ December 31, 2013 income
to Slater: $88,000
✔ January 1, 2014 debit to Slater,
Capital: $54,000
✔ December 31, 2014 loss to
Zadoney: $13,920
✔ Cash distributed to Nissan: $509,600

Comprehensive Partnership Transactions

P8. The events that follow pertain to a partnership formed by Mercian Zadoney and Michael Slater to operate a floor-cleaning company.

2013

Feb. 14   The partnership was formed. Zadoney transferred to the partnership $160,000 cash, land worth $160,000, a building worth $960,000, and a mortgage on the building of $480,000. Slater transferred to the partnership $80,000 cash and equipment worth $320,000.

Dec. 31   During 2013, the partnership earned income of just $168,000. The partnership agreement specifies that income and losses are to be divided by paying salaries of $80,000 to Zadoney and $120,000 to Slater, allowing 8 percent interest on beginning capital investments, and dividing any remainder equally.

2014

Jan.   1   To improve the prospects for the company, the partners decided to take in a new partner, George Nissan, who had experience in the floor-cleaning business. Nissan invested $312,000 for a 25 percent interest in the business. A bonus was transferred in equal amounts from the original partners' Capital accounts to Nissan's Capital account.

Dec. 31   During 2014, the company earned income of $174,400. The new partnership agreement specified that income and losses would be divided by paying salaries of $120,000 to Slater and $160,000 to Nissan (no salary to Zadoney), allowing 8 percent interest on beginning capital balances after Nissan's admission, and dividing the remainder equally.

(Continued)

2015

Jan. 1 Because it appeared that the business could not support the three partners, the partners decided to liquidate the partnership. The asset and liability accounts of the partnership were as follows: Cash, $814,400; Accounts Receivable (net), $136,000; Land, $160,000; Building (net), $896,000; Equipment (net), $472,000; Accounts Payable, $176,000; and Mortgage Payable, $448,000. The equipment was sold for $400,000. The accounts payable were paid. The loss was distributed equally to the partners' Capital accounts. A statement of liquidation was prepared, and the remaining assets and liabilities were distributed. Zadoney agreed to accept cash plus the land and building at book value and the mortgage payable as payment for his share. Slater accepted cash and the accounts receivable for his share. Nissan was paid in cash.

REQUIRED

Prepare journal entries to record all of the facts above. Support your computations with schedules, and prepare a statement of liquidation in connection with the January 1, 2015, entries.

CASES

LO 3

Conceptual Understanding: Distribution of Partnership Income and Losses

C1. Landow, Donovan, and Hansa, who are forming a partnership to operate an antiques gallery, are discussing how income and losses should be distributed. Among the facts they are considering are the following:

a. Landow will contribute cash for operations of $100,000, Donovan will contribute a collection of antiques that is valued at $300,000, and Hansa will not contribute any assets.
b. Landow and Hansa will handle day-to-day business operations. Hansa will work full-time, and Landow will devote about half-time to the partnership. Donovan will not devote time to day-to-day operations. A full-time clerk in a retail store would make about $20,000 in a year, and a full-time manager would receive about $30,000.
c. The current interest rate on long-term bonds is 8 percent.

Landow, Donovan, and Hansa have just hired you as the partnership's accountant. Write a memorandum describing an equitable plan for distributing income and losses. Outline the reasons why you believe this plan is equitable. According to your plan, which partner will gain the most if the partnership is very profitable, and which will lose the most if the partnership has large losses?

LO 1, 2, 3

Conceptual Understanding: Partnership Agreement

C2. Form a partnership with one or two of your classmates. Assume that the two or three of you are forming a small service business. For example, you might form a company that hires college students to paint houses during the summer or to provide landscaping services.

Working together, draft a partnership agreement for your business. The agreement can be a simple one, with just a sentence or two for each provision. However, it should include the name, location, and purpose of the business; the names of the partners and their respective duties; the investments of each partner; methods for distributing profits and losses; and procedures for dealing with the admission or withdrawal of partners, the withdrawal of assets, the death of a partner, and liquidation of the business. Include a title, date, and signature lines.

LO **1, 3**   **Interpreting Financial Reports: Effects of a Lawsuit on Partnership**

C3. The Springfield Clinic is owned and operated by ten local doctors as a partnership. Recently, a paralyzed patient sued the clinic for malpractice, for a total of $20 million. The clinic carries malpractice liability insurance in the amount of $10 million. There is no provision for the possible loss from this type of lawsuit in the partnership's financial statements. The condensed balance sheet for 2014 follows.

Springfield Clinic
Condensed Balance Sheet
December 31, 2014

Assets		
Current assets	$246,000	
Property, plant, and equipment (net)	750,000	
Total assets		$996,000
Liabilities and Partners' Equity		
Current liabilities	$180,000	
Long-term debt	675,000	
Total liabilities		$855,000
Partners' equity		141,000
Total liabilities and partners' equity		$996,000

1. How should information about the lawsuit be disclosed in the December 31, 2014, financial statements of the partnership?
2. Assume that the clinic and its insurance company settle out of court by agreeing to pay a total of $10.1 million, of which $100,000 must be paid by the partnership. What effect will the payment have on the clinic's December 31, 2014, financial statements? Discuss the effect of the settlement on the Springfield Clinic doctors' personal financial situations.

LO **6**   **Conceptual Understanding: International Joint Ventures**

C4. BUSINESS APPLICATION ▶ **Nokia**, the Finnish telecommunications company, has formed an equally owned joint venture with Capital Corporation, a state-owned Chinese company, to develop a center for the manufacture and development of telecommunications equipment in China, the world's fastest-growing market for this kind of equipment. The main aim of the development is to persuade Nokia's suppliers to move close to the company's main plant. The Chinese government looks favorably on companies that involve local suppliers.[1] What advantages does a joint venture have over a single company in entering a new market in another country? What are the potential disadvantages? Divide into groups. One-half of the groups will make a strong argument for the joint venture. The other half will make a strong case against the joint venture. Engage in a class debate over the joint venture.

LO **5, 6**   **Ethical Dilemma: Death of a Partner**

C5. South Shore Realty was started 20 years ago when T. S. Tyler, R. C. Strong, and A. J. Hibbert established a partnership to sell real estate near Galveston, Texas. The partnership has been extremely successful. In 2014, Tyler, the senior partner, who in recent years had not been very active in the partnership, died. Unfortunately, the partnership agreement is vague about how the partnership interest of a partner who dies should be valued. It simply states that "the estate of a deceased partner shall receive compensation for his or her interest in the partnership in a reasonable time after death." The attorney for Tyler's family believes that the estate should receive one-third of the assets of the partnership based on the fair market value of the net assets (total assets less total liabilities). The total assets of the partnership are $10 million in the accounting records, but the assets are worth at least $20 million. Because the firm's total liabilities

(Continued)

are $4 million, the attorney is asking for $5.3 million (one-third of $16 million). Strong and Hibbert do not agree, but all parties want to avoid a protracted, expensive lawsuit. They have decided to put the question to an arbitrator, who will make a determination of the settlement.

Here are some other facts that may or may not be relevant. The current balances in the partners' Capital accounts are $1.5 million for Tyler, $2.5 million for Strong, and $2.0 million for Hibbert. Net income in 2014 is to be distributed to the Capital accounts in the ratio of 1:4:3. Before Tyler's semiretirement, the distribution ratio was 3:3:2. Assume you or your group is the arbitrator, and develop what you would consider a fair distribution of assets to Tyler's estate. Defend your solution.

LO **1, 6**

Conceptual Understanding: Comparison of Career Opportunities in Partnerships and Corporations

C6. Accounting firms are among the world's largest partnerships and provide a wide range of attractive careers for business and accounting majors. You can explore careers in public accounting by linking to the website of one of the Big Four accounting firms: **Deloitte & Touche, Ernst & Young, KPMG International**, and **PricewaterhouseCoopers**. Each firm's home page has a career opportunity section. For the firm you choose, compile a list of facts about the firm—size, locations, services, and career opportunities. Do you have the interest and background for a career in public accounting? Why or why not? How do you think working for a large partnership would differ from or be the same as working for a large corporation? Be prepared to discuss your findings in class.

CHAPTER 13
Accounting for Corporations

In 2014, a group of investors in Wisconsin formed a corporation called Vietecha, Inc. The corporation's state charter authorized it to issue 2 million shares of $1 par value common stock and 50,000 shares of 4 percent, $20 par value cumulative and convertible preferred stock. Vietecha's **initial public offering (IPO)** (i.e., its first sale of stock to the public) occurred on February 1, 2014, when it issued 200,000 shares of common stock for $250,000 and, thereby, realized its first influx of contributed capital.

During its first year of operations, Vietecha engaged in a number of other transactions involving common stock, as well as transactions involving preferred stock, treasury stock, and dividends. In this chapter, you will learn how to account for these transactions. You will also learn why corporations are the dominant form of business in the U.S. economy and how a corporation's owners—its stockholders—can evaluate the return on their investments.

1. CONCEPT ▷ *How does the separate entity concept apply to the stockholders in a corporation?*

2. ACCOUNTING APPLICATION ▷ *How should a corporation account for its stock transactions and dividends?*

3. BUSINESS APPLICATION ▷ *What measures should stockholders use to evaluate the return on their investments?*

LEARNING OBJECTIVES

LO 1 Define the *corporate* form of business and its characteristics.

LO 2 Identify the components of stockholders' equity and their characteristics.

LO 3 Account for the issuance of stock for cash and other assets.

LO 4 Account for treasury stock.

LO 5 Account for cash dividends.

LO 6 Account for stock dividends and stock splits.

LO 7 Describe the statement of stockholders' equity, and compute book value per share.

LO 8 Calculate dividend yield and return on equity, and define stock options.

Dmitriy Shironosov/Alamy Limited

SECTION 1

CONCEPTS

CONCEPT
■ Separate entity

RELEVANT LEARNING OBJECTIVE

LO1 Define the *corporate form of business* and its characteristics.

LO1 Concepts Underlying the Corporate Form of Business

In Chapter 1, we defined a *corporation* as a *separate entity* chartered by the state and *legally separate* from its owners—that is, its stockholders. **Contributed capital**, which refers to stockholders' investments in a corporation, is a major means of financing a corporation. Managing contributed capital requires an understanding of the advantages and disadvantages of the corporate form of business and of the issues involved in equity financing. It also requires familiarity with dividend policies, with how to use return on equity to evaluate performance, and with stock option plans.

The Corporate Form of Business

The corporate form of business is well suited to today's trends toward large organizations, international trade, and professional management. Although fewer in number than sole proprietorships and partnerships, corporations dominate the U.S. economy, in part because of their ability to raise large amounts of capital. In 2007, the peak market year, the amount of new capital that corporations raised was $2.7 trillion. Even though the following years were not the best for markets, the amount of new capital raised by corporations was $1.4 trillion.[1]

To form a corporation, most states require individuals, called *incorporators*, to sign an application and file it with the proper state official. This application contains the **articles of incorporation**. If approved by the state, these articles, which form the company charter, become a contract between the state and the incorporators. The company is then authorized to do business as a corporation.

The authority to manage a corporation is delegated by its stockholders to a board of directors and by the board of directors to the corporation's officers. That is, the stockholders elect a board of directors, which sets corporate policies and chooses the corporation's officers, who in turn carry out the corporate policies in their management of the business, as shown in Exhibit 1.

Exhibit 1
The Corporate Organization

Stockholders	Board of Directors	Management
Invest in shares of capital stock and elect board of directors	Determines corporate policy, declares dividends, and appoints management	Executes policy and carries out day-to-day operations

© Cengage Learning 2014

Stockholders A unit of ownership in a corporation is called a **share of stock**. The articles of incorporation state the maximum number of shares that a corporation is authorized to issue. The number of shares held by stockholders is the outstanding stock, which may be less than the number authorized in the articles of incorporation. To invest in a corporation, a stockholder transfers cash or other resources to the corporation. In return, the stockholder receives shares of stock representing a proportionate share of ownership.

Board of Directors A corporation's **board of directors** decides on major business policies. Among the board's specific duties are authorizing contracts, setting executive salaries, and arranging major loans with banks. The declaration of dividends is another important function of the board of directors. **Dividends** are distributions, among the stockholders, of the assets that a corporation's earnings have generated. Only the board of directors has the authority to declare dividends.

The composition of the board of directors varies from company to company, but generally it includes several officers of the corporation and several outsiders. The outsiders are called *independent directors* because they do not directly participate in managing the business.

Management Management, appointed by the board of directors to carry out corporate polices and run day-to-day operations, consists of the operating officers—generally the president, or chief executive officer; vice presidents; chief financial officer; and chief operating officer. Besides being responsible for running the business, management has the duty of reporting the financial results of its administration to the board of directors and the stockholders. Though management must, at a minimum, make a comprehensive annual report, it generally reports more often. The annual reports of public corporations are available to the public.

Advantages and Disadvantages of Incorporation

As noted, managers of a corporation must be familiar with the advantages and disadvantages of this form of business.

Advantages of Incorporation Some of the advantages of the corporate form of business follow.

- **Separate legal entity:** As a *separate legal entity*, a corporation can buy and sell property, sue other parties, enter into contracts, hire and fire employees, and be taxed.
- **Limited liability:** Because a corporation is a *legal entity, separate* from its owners, its creditors can satisfy their claims only against the assets of the corporation, not against the personal property of the corporation's owners. Because the owners are not responsible for the corporation's debts, their liability is limited to the amount of their investment. In contrast, the personal property of sole proprietors and partners generally is available to creditors.
- **Ease of capital generation:** It is fairly easy for a corporation to raise capital because shares of ownership in the business are available to a great number of potential investors for a small amount of money. As a result, a single corporation can have many owners.
- **Ease of transfer of ownership:** A stockholder can normally buy and sell shares of stock without affecting the corporation's activities or needing the approval of other owners.
- **Lack of mutual agency:** If a stockholder tries to enter into a contract for a corporation, the corporation is not bound by the contract. In a partnership, because of what is called *mutual agency*, all the partners can be bound by one partner's actions.
- **Continuous existence:** Because a corporation is a *separate legal entity*, an owner's death, incapacity, or withdrawal does not affect the life of the corporation. A corporation's life is set by its charter and regulated by state laws.
- **Centralized authority and responsibility:** The board of directors represents the stockholders and delegates the responsibility and authority for day-to-day operation to a single person, usually the president. Operating power is centralized rather than divided among the multiple owners of the business. The president may delegate authority over certain segments of the business to others, but he or she is held accountable to the board of directors. If the board is dissatisfied with the performance of the president, it can replace that person.
- **Professional management:** Large corporations have many owners, most of whom are not able to make timely decisions about business operations. Thus, management and ownership are usually separate. This allows management to hire the best talent available to run the business.

Disadvantages of Incorporation Some of the disadvantages of corporations follow.

- **Government regulation:** As "creatures of the state," corporations are subject to greater control and regulation than are other forms of business. They must file many reports with the state in which they are chartered. Publicly held corporations must also file reports with the Securities and Exchange Commission and with the stock exchanges on which they are listed. They must also maintain internal controls and have audits conducted in compliance with regulations set by the Public Company Accounting Oversight Board (PCAOB). Meeting these requirements is very costly.

- **Double taxation:** A major disadvantage of the corporate form of business is **double taxation**. Because a corporation is a *separate legal entity*, its earnings are subject to federal and state income taxes, which may be as much as 35 percent of corporate earnings. If any of a corporation's after-tax earnings are paid out as dividends, the earnings are taxed again as income to the stockholders. In contrast, the earnings of sole proprietorships and partnerships are taxed only once, as income to the owners.

- **Limited liability:** Limited liability restricts the ability of a small corporation to borrow money. Because creditors can lay claim only to the assets of a corporation, they may limit their loans to the level secured by those assets or require stockholders to guarantee the loans personally.

- **Separation of ownership and control:** Just as limited liability can be a drawback of incorporation, so can the separation of ownership and control. Management sometimes makes decisions that are not good for the corporation. Poor communication can also make it hard for stockholders to exercise control over the corporation or even to recognize that management's decisions are harmful.

Equity Financing

Equity financing is accomplished by issuing stock to investors in exchange for assets, usually cash. Once the stock has been issued to them, the stockholders can transfer their ownership at will. Large corporations can have millions of shares of stock, thousands of which change ownership every day. They, therefore, often appoint independent **registrars** and **transfer agents** (usually banks and trust companies) to help perform the transfer duties. The outside agents are responsible for transferring the corporation's stock, maintaining stockholders' records, preparing a list of stockholders for stockholders' meetings, and paying dividends.

Two important terms in equity financing are par value and legal capital:

- **Par value** is an arbitrary amount assigned to each share of stock. It must be recorded in the capital stock accounts. Par value usually bears little, if any, relationship to the market value of the shares. For example, although **Google**'s stock initially sold for $85 per share and the market value is now much higher, its par value per share is only $0.001.

- **Legal capital** is the number of shares issued multiplied by the par value. It is the minimum amount that a corporation can report as contributed capital. For example, even though the total market value of **Google**'s shares now exceeds $200 billion, Google's legal capital is only about $325,140 (325.14 million shares × $0.001).

To help with its initial public offering (IPO), a corporation often uses an **underwriter**—an intermediary between the corporation and the investing public. For a fee—usually less than 1 percent of the selling price—the underwriter guarantees the sale of the stock. The corporation records the amount of the net proceeds of the offering in its Capital Stock and Additional Paid-in Capital accounts. The net proceeds are what the public paid less the underwriter's fees, legal expenses, and any other direct costs of the offering.

The costs of forming a corporation are called **start-up and organization costs**. These costs include:

- State incorporation fees
- Attorneys' fees for drawing up the articles of incorporation
- The cost of printing stock certificates
- Accountants' fees for registering the firm's initial stock
- Other expenditures necessary for the formation of the corporation

STUDY NOTE: Start-up and organization costs are expensed as they are incurred.

Theoretically, start-up and organization costs benefit the entire life of a corporation. For that reason, a case can be made for recording them as intangible assets and amortizing them over the life of the corporation. However, a corporation's life normally is not known, so accountants expense start-up and organization costs as they are incurred.

Advantages of Equity Financing Financing a business by issuing common stock has several advantages.

- **Decreased financial risk:** Issuing common stock is less risky than financing with long-term debt because a company does not pay dividends on common stock unless the board of directors decides to pay them. In contrast, if a company does not pay interest on long-term debt, it can be forced into bankruptcy.
- **Increased cash for operations:** When a company does not pay a cash dividend, it can shift the cash generated by profitable operations back into the company's operations. **Google**, for instance, does not currently pay any dividends, and its issuance of common stock provides it with funds for expansion.
- **Better debt to equity ratio:** A company can use the proceeds of a common stock issue to maintain or improve its debt to equity ratio.

Disadvantages of Equity Financing Issuing common stock also has certain disadvantages.

- **Increased tax liability:** Whereas the interest on debt is tax-deductible, the dividends paid on stock are not tax-deductible.
- **Decreased stockholder control:** When a corporation issues more stock, it dilutes its ownership. Thus, the current stockholders must yield some control to the new stockholders.

APPLY IT!

Match each item that follows with the topic to which it pertains.

a. Advantage of the corporate form of business
b. Disadvantage of the corporate form of business
c. Dividend policies

1. U.S. tax policies
2. Separate legal entity
3. Ease of ownership transfer
4. Distributing cash to stockholders
5. Need to deal with government regulation

SOLUTION
1. b; 2. a; 3. a; 4. c; 5. b

TRY IT! SE1, SE2, E1A, E1B

SECTION 2   **ACCOUNTING APPLICATIONS**

ACCOUNTING APPLICATIONS

- Prepare the statement of stockholders' equity
- Record the issuance of stock for cash and other assets
- Record the purchase, sale, and retirement of treasury stock
- Account for cash dividends
- Account for stock dividends and stock splits

RELEVANT LEARNING OBJECTIVES

LO 2 Identify the components of stockholders' equity and their characteristics.

LO 3 Account for the issuance of stock for cash and other assets.

LO 4 Account for treasury stock.

LO 5 Account for cash dividends.

LO 6 Account for stock dividends and stock splits.

LO 7 Describe the statement of stockholders' equity, and compute book value per share.

LO 2 Components of Stockholders' Equity

In a corporation's balance sheet, the owners' claims to the business are called **stockholders' equity**. As shown in Exhibit 2, this section of a corporate balance sheet usually has at least three components.

- **Contributed capital:** The stockholders' investments in the corporation.
- **Retained earnings:** The earnings of the corporation since its inception, less any losses, dividends, or transfers to contributed capital. **Retained earnings** are reinvested in the business. They are not a pool of funds to be distributed to the stockholders; instead, they represent the stockholders' claim to assets resulting from profitable operations.
- **Treasury stock:** Shares of the corporation's own stock that it has bought back on the open market are called **treasury stock**. The cost of these shares is treated as a reduction in stockholders' equity. By buying back the shares, the corporation reduces the ownership of the business.

Exhibit 2
Stockholders' Equity Section of a Balance Sheet

Stockholders' Equity		
Contributed capital:		
Preferred stock, $50 par value, 2,000 shares authorized, issued, and outstanding		$100,000
Common stock, $5 par value, 60,000 shares authorized, 40,000 shares issued, 36,000 shares outstanding	$200,000	
Additional paid-in capital	100,000	300,000
Total contributed capital		$400,000
Retained earnings		120,000
Total contributed capital and retained earnings		$520,000
Less: Treasury stock, common (4,000 shares at cost)		40,000
Total stockholders' equity		$480,000

© Cengage Learning 2014

In keeping with the convention of *full disclosure*, the stockholders' equity section of a balance sheet gives a great deal of information about the corporation's stock. Under contributed capital, it lists the kinds of stock, their par values, and the number of shares authorized, issued, and outstanding. Corporations may disclose more detail in a **statement of stockholders' equity** (or *statement of changes in stockholders' equity*). This

International Perspective
IFRS How Does a Stock Become a Debt Under IFRS?

A significant difference between International Financial Reporting Standards (IFRS) and U.S. GAAP is the issue of what constitutes stockholders' equity. This issue is important because it affects financial ratios such as return on assets, requirements under loan agreements, and the capital requirements of banks. Under U.S. GAAP, most preferred stocks are *classified* as stockholders' equity. In contrast, under IFRS, most preferred stocks are *classified* as liabilities because they resemble debt in that they have fixed dividends rates and are often cumulative.

The FASB is considering a proposal that would require these special preferred stocks to be classified as a liability on the balance sheet, which would be more in line with IFRS.[2]

© loops7 / iStockphoto.com

statement summarizes changes in the components of the stockholders' equity section of the balance sheet.

A corporation can issue two types of stock:

- **Common stock** is the basic form of stock. If a corporation issues only one type of stock, it is common stock. Because shares of common stock carry voting rights, they generally provide their owners with the means of controlling the corporation. Common stock is also called *residual equity*, which means that if the corporation is liquidated, the claims of all creditors and usually those of preferred stockholders rank ahead of the claims of common stockholders.

- **Preferred stock** is stock that a corporation may issue to attract investors whose goals differ from those of common stockholders. Preferred stock gives its owners preference over common stockholders, usually in terms of receiving dividends and in terms of claims to assets if the corporation is liquidated.

In addition to identifying the kind of stock and its par value, the description of contributed capital in Exhibit 2 specifies the number of shares authorized, issued, and outstanding.

- **Authorized shares** are the maximum number of shares that a corporation's state charter allows it to issue. Most corporations are authorized to issue more shares than they need to issue at the time they are formed. Thus, they are able to raise more capital in the future by issuing additional shares. When a corporation issues all of its authorized shares, it cannot issue more without a change in its state charter.

- **Issued shares** are those that a corporation sells or otherwise transfers to stockholders. The owners of a corporation's issued shares own 100 percent of the business. Unissued shares have no rights or privileges until they are issued.

- **Outstanding shares** are shares that a corporation has issued and that are still in circulation. Treasury stock is not outstanding because it consists of shares that a corporation has issued but has bought back and thereby put out of circulation. Thus, a corporation can have more shares issued than are currently outstanding.

Exhibit 3 shows the relationship of authorized shares to issued, unissued, outstanding, and treasury shares. For example, **Google** has 9 billion authorized shares of stock and only about 325 million shares issued. With its excess of authorized shares, Google has plenty of flexibility for future stock transactions.

Business Perspective
Are You a First-Class or Second-Class Stockholder?

When companies go public, the founders of the company or top management often get first-class shares with extra votes, while outsiders get second-class shares with fewer votes. The class A and class B shares of **Adolph Coors Company**, the large brewing firm, are an extreme example. The company's class B shares, owned by the public, have no votes except in the case of a merger. Its class A shares, held by the Coors family trust, have all the votes on all other issues.

Google also has two classes of identical common shares, except that each class B share is entitled to ten votes and each class A share is entitled to only one vote. Class A shares are the ones that Google offered to the public in its IPO. As a result, Class B holders control 70 percent of the company.[3]

Shareholder advocates maintain that this practice gives a privileged few shareholders all or most of the control of a company and that it denies other shareholders voting power consistent with the risk they are taking. Defenders of the practice argue that it shields top executives from the market's obsession with short-term results and allows them to make better long-term decisions. They also point out that many investors don't care about voting rights as long as the stock performs well.

Unissued Shares	Outstanding Shares	Treasury Shares

Issued Shares

Authorized Shares

Exhibit 3
Relationship of
Authorized Shares
to Unissued, Issued,
Outstanding, and
Treasury Shares

© Cengage Learning 2014

STUDY NOTE: *Preferred stock has many different characteristics. They are rarely exactly the same from company to company.*

Characteristics of Preferred Stock

Most preferred stock has one or more of the following characteristics: preference as to dividends, preference as to assets if a corporation is liquidated, convertibility, and a callable option. A corporation may offer several different classes of preferred stock, each with distinctive characteristics to attract different investors.

Preference as to Dividends Preferred stockholders ordinarily must receive a certain amount of dividends before common stockholders receive anything. The amount that preferred stockholders must be paid before common stockholders can be paid is usually stated in dollars per share or as a percentage of the par value of the preferred shares. For example, a company might pay an annual dividend of $4 per share on preferred stock, or it might issue preferred stock at $50 par value and pay an annual dividend of 8 percent of par value, which would also be $4 per share.

Preferred stockholders have no guarantee of receiving dividends. A company's board of directors must declare dividends on preferred stock before any liability arises. The consequences of not granting an annual dividend on preferred stock vary according to whether the stock is noncumulative or cumulative.

■ If the stock is **noncumulative preferred stock** and the board of directors fails to declare a dividend on it in any given year, the company is under no obligation to make up the missed dividend in future years.

■ If the stock is **cumulative preferred stock**, the dividend amount per share accumulates from year to year, and the company must pay the whole amount before it pays any dividends on common stock.

Dividends not paid in the year they are due are called **dividends in arrears**. If a corporation has dividends in arrears, it should report the amount either in the body of its financial statements or in a note to its financial statements. The following note is typical of one that might appear in a corporation's annual report:

> *On December 31, 2014, the company was in arrears by $37,851,000 ($1.25 per share) on dividends to its preferred stockholders. The company must pay all dividends in arrears to preferred stockholders before paying any dividends to common stockholders.*

Business Perspective
How Does a Stock Become a Debt?

Some companies have used the flexibility of preferred stocks to create a type of stock that is similar to debt. Usually, stocks do not have maturity dates, and companies do not buy them back except at the option of management. However, **CMS Energy**, **Time Warner**, **Xerox**, and other companies have issued preferred stock that is "mandatorily redeemable." This means that the issuing companies are required to buy back the stock at fixed future dates or under predetermined conditions. Thus, these special preferred stocks are similar to long-term debt in that they have a fixed maturity date. In addition, in much the same way as long-term debt requires periodic interest payments at a fixed rate, these stocks require an annual dividend payment, also at a fixed rate. Even though companies list these stocks in the stockholders' equity section of their balance sheets, the astute analyst will treat them as debt when calculating a company's debt to equity ratio.[4]

© Aija / iStockphoto.com

Dividends in Arrears

Transaction Harbach Corporation has 20,000 outstanding shares of $10 par value, 6 percent cumulative preferred stock. Operations in 2015 produced income of only $8,000. However, the board of directors declared a $6,000 cash dividend to the preferred stockholders.

Computation Dividends in arrears are calculated as follows.

2015 dividends due preferred stockholders [(20,000 × $10) × 0.06]	$12,000
Less 2015 dividends declared to preferred stockholders	6,000
2015 preferred stock dividends in arrears	$ 6,000

Comment Before the corporation can pay a dividend in 2016 to common stockholders, it must pay the preferred stockholders the $6,000 in arrears from 2015, plus $12,000 for 2016 for a total of $18,000.

Dividend Distribution

Transaction In 2016, Harbach Corporation earns income of $60,000 and wants to pay dividends to both preferred and common stockholders. The board of directors declares a $24,000 dividend.

Computation The dividend would be distributed as follows.

2016 declaration of dividends	$24,000
Less 2015 preferred stock dividends in arrears	6,000
Amount available for 2016 dividends	$18,000
Less 2016 dividends due preferred stockholders [(20,000 × $10) × 0.06]	12,000
Remainder available to common stockholders	$ 6,000

Preference as to Assets Preferred stockholders often have preference in terms of their claims to a corporation's assets if the corporation goes out of business. If a corporation is liquidated, these preferred stockholders have a right to receive the par value of their stock or a larger stated liquidation value per share before the common stockholders receive any share of the assets. This preference can also extend to any dividends in arrears owed to the preferred stockholders.

Convertible Preferred Stock Owners of **convertible preferred stock** can exchange their shares of preferred stock for shares of common stock at a ratio stated in the preferred stock contract. If the market value of the common stock increases, the conversion feature allows these stockholders to share in the increase by converting their stock to common stock.

Suppose that a company issues 1,000 shares of 8 percent, $100 par value convertible preferred stock for $100 per share. Each share of stock can be converted to five shares of the company's common stock at any time. The market value of the common stock when the company issues the convertible preferred stock is $15 per share. The owner of one share of preferred stock purchased for $100, therefore, has an investment if converted into common stock with a market value of about $75. The investor would not convert at this point, preferring to receive the 8 percent dividend.

Now suppose that in the next few years, the market value of a share of the common stock increases from $15 to $30. By converting each of their shares to five common shares, preferred stockholders can realize $150 (5 shares × $30 per share) or a gain of $50 above the $100 they paid per share of preferred stock.

Callable Preferred Stock Most preferred stock is **callable preferred stock**—that is, the issuing corporation can redeem it at a price stated in the preferred stock contract. An owner of callable preferred stock that is not convertible must surrender it to the issuing corporation when asked to do so. If the preferred stock is convertible, the stockholder can either surrender the stock to the corporation or convert it to common stock when the corporation calls the stock. The *call price*, or *redemption price*, is usually higher than the stock's par value. For example, preferred stock that has a $100 par value might be callable at $103 per share.

When preferred stock is called and surrendered, the stockholder is entitled to the following:

- The par value of the stock
- The call premium
- Any dividends in arrears
- The current period's dividend prorated by the proportion of the year to the call date

A corporation may decide to call its preferred stock for any of the following reasons:

- It may want to force conversion of the preferred stock to common stock because the dividend that it pays on preferred shares is higher than the dividend that it pays on the equivalent number of common shares.
- It may be able to replace the outstanding preferred stock with a preferred stock at a lower dividend rate or with long-term debt, which can have a lower after-tax cost.
- It may simply be profitable enough to retire the preferred stock.

APPLY IT!

Romeo Corporation has 2,000 shares of $100 par value, 7 percent cumulative preferred stock outstanding and 200,000 shares of $1 par value common stock outstanding. In the corporation's first three years of operation, its board of directors declared cash dividends as follows:

    2014: None
    2015: $20,000
    2016: $30,000

Determine the total cash dividends paid to the preferred and common stockholders during each of the three years.

SOLUTION

2014:	None	
2015:	Preferred dividends in arrears (2,000 shares × $100 × 0.07)	$14,000
	Current year remainder to preferred ($20,000 − $14,000)	6,000
	Total to preferred stockholders	$20,000
2016:	Preferred dividends in arrears ($14,000 − $6,000)	$ 8,000
	Current year to preferred (2,000 shares × $100 × 0.07)	14,000
	Total to preferred stockholders	$22,000
	Total to common stockholders ($30,000 − $22,000)	8,000
	Total dividends in 2016	$30,000

TRY IT! SE4, SE5, E2A, E3A, E4A, E5A, E2B, E3B, E4B, E5B

LO 3 Issuance of Common Stock

A share of capital stock may be either par or no-par. The value of par stock is stated in the corporate charter and on each stock certificate. It can be $0.01, $1, $5, $100, or any other amount established by the organizers of the corporation. The par values of common stocks tend to be lower than those of preferred stocks.

A corporation cannot declare a dividend that would cause stockholders' equity to fall below the legal capital. Par value is thus a minimum cushion of capital that protects a corporation's creditors.

No-par stock does not have a par value. A corporation may issue stock without a par value for several reasons. For one thing, rather than recognizing par value as an arbitrary figure, investors may confuse it with the stock's market value. For another, most states do not allow a stock issue below par value, and this limits a corporation's flexibility in obtaining capital.

To illustrate accounting for the issuance of stock, we will use Rexio Corporation.

Accounting for Par Value Stock

When a corporation issues par value stock, the appropriate Capital Stock account (usually Common Stock or Preferred Stock) is credited for the par value regardless of whether the proceeds are more or less than the par value. When a corporation issues stock at a price greater than par value, as is usually the case, the proceeds in excess of par are credited to an account called Additional Paid-in Capital.

Issuing Stock Above Par Value

Transaction Rexio Corporation is authorized to issue 10,000 shares of $10 par value common stock. On January 1, 2014, it issues 5,000 shares at $12 each.

Analysis The journal entry to record the issuance of the stock above par value

- ▲ *increases Cash* with a debit for the proceeds of $60,000 (5,000 shares × $12)
- ▲ *increases Common Stock* with a credit for the total par value of $50,000 (5,000 shares × $10)
- ▲ *increases Additional Paid-in Capital* with a credit for the difference of $10,000 (5,000 shares × $2)

Application of Double Entry

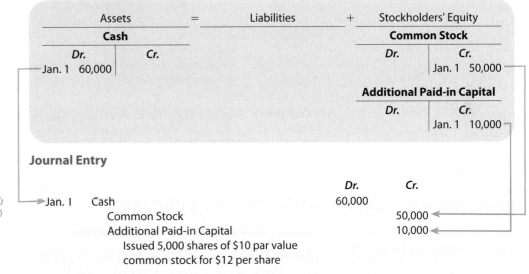

Journal Entry

		Dr.	Cr.
Jan. 1	Cash	60,000	
	Common Stock		50,000
	Additional Paid-in Capital		10,000
	Issued 5,000 shares of $10 par value common stock for $12 per share		

A = L + SE
+60,000   +50,000
          +10,000

STUDY NOTE: *If a corporation issues stock for less than par value, an account called Discount on Capital Stock is debited for the difference. The issuance of stock at a discount rarely occurs. It is illegal in many states.*

Comment The amount in excess of par value is part of Rexio's contributed capital and will be included in the stockholders' equity section of its balance sheet. Immediately after the stock issue, this section of Rexio's balance sheet would appear as follows.

Contributed capital:	
Common stock, $10 par value, 10,000 shares authorized, 5,000 shares issued and outstanding	$50,000
Additional paid-in capital	10,000
Total contributed capital	$60,000
Retained earnings	—
Total stockholders' equity	$60,000

No-Par Stock

Most states require that all or part of the proceeds from a corporation's issuance of no-par stock be designated as legal capital, which cannot be used unless the corporation is liquidated. The purpose of this requirement is to protect the corporation's assets for creditors. State laws often require corporations to place a **stated value** on each share of stock that they issue, but even when this is not required, a corporation's board of directors may do so as a matter of convenience. The stated value can be any value set by the board unless the state specifies a minimum amount, which is sometimes the case. The stated value can be set before or after the shares are issued if the state law is not specific.

Issuing No-Par Stock with No Stated Value

Transaction On January 1, 2014, Rexio issues 5,000 shares of no-par common stock at $15 per share.

Analysis The journal entry to record this no-par stock with no stated value

▲ *increases Cash* with a debit of $75,000 (5,000 shares × $15)

▲ *increases Common Stock* with a credit of $75,000

Application of Double Entry

A	=	L	+	SE
+75,000				+75,000

Journal Entry

		Dr.	Cr.
Jan. 1	Cash	75,000	
	Common Stock		75,000
	Issued 5,000 shares of no-par common stock for $15 per share		

Comment Because the stock does not have a stated or par value, all proceeds ($75,000) of the issue are *credited* to Common Stock and are part of the company's legal capital.

As noted earlier, state laws may require corporations to put a stated value on each share of stock that they issue.

Issuing No-Par Stock with a Stated Value

Event Assume the same facts as were provided previously, except that Rexio puts a $10 stated value on each share of its no-par stock.

Analysis The journal entry to record this no-par stock with a stated value

▲ *increases Cash* with a debit of $75,000 (5,000 shares × $15)

▲ *increases Common Stock* with a credit of $50,000 (the stated value decided by Rexio's board of directors)

▲ *increases Additional Paid-in Capital* with a credit of $25,000, which is the difference between the proceeds ($75,000) and the total stated value ($50,000)

Application of Double Entry

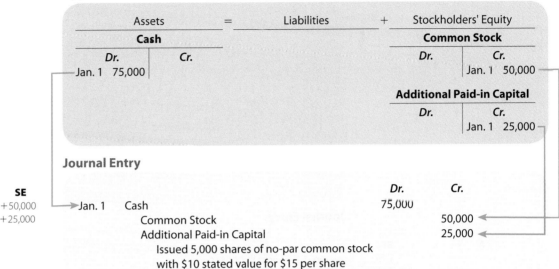

	Assets	=	Liabilities	+	Stockholders' Equity	

Cash

Dr.	Cr.
Jan. 1 75,000	

Common Stock

Dr.	Cr.
	Jan. 1 50,000

Additional Paid-in Capital

Dr.	Cr.
	Jan. 1 25,000

Journal Entry

A	=	L	+	SE
+75,000				+50,000
				+25,000

		Dr.	Cr.
Jan. 1	Cash	75,000	
	Common Stock		50,000
	Additional Paid-in Capital		25,000
	Issued 5,000 shares of no-par common stock with $10 stated value for $15 per share		

Comment In this case, the company's legal capital is $50,000 because the no-par common stock has a stated value.

Start-up companies commonly exchange services or intellectual property for stock in the company because they have very little money and need people with a wealth of expertise in specific areas. For example, Mark Zuckerberg and Adam D'Angelo, the founders of Facebook, essentially traded the intellectual property involved in creating programming language and their time investment for stock in the company.

Ian Dagnall/Alamy

Issuance of Stock for Noncash Assets

A corporation may issue stock in return for assets or services other than cash. Transactions of this kind usually involve a corporation's exchange of stock for land or buildings or for the services of attorneys and others who help organize the corporation. Generally, this kind of transaction is recorded at the *fair market value* of the stock given up by the corporation. If the stock's fair market value cannot be determined, the fair market value of the assets or services received can be used.

Issuing Stock for Noncash Assets When No Market Value for the Stock Exists

Transaction When Rexio was formed on January 1, 2014, its attorney agreed to accept 200 shares of its $10 par value common stock for services rendered. At that time, the market value of the stock could not be determined. However, for similar services, the attorney would have charged Rexio $3,000.

Analysis The journal entry to record stock exchanged for noncash assets when no market value for the stock exists

▲ *increases Legal Expenses* with a debit of $3,000 (estimated cost for attorney services)

▲ *increases Common Stock* with a credit for the total par value of $2,000 (200 shares × $10)

▲ *increases Additional Paid-in Capital* with a credit for the difference of the proceeds ($3,000) and the total stated value ($2,000)

Application of Double Entry

Journal Entry

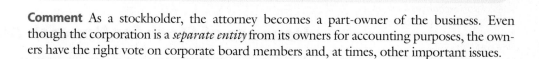

			Dr.	Cr.
Jan. 1	Legal Expenses		3,000	
	Common Stock			2,000
	Additional Paid-in Capital			1,000
	Issued 200 shares of $10 par value common stock for attorney's services			

Comment As a stockholder, the attorney becomes a part-owner of the business. Even though the corporation is a *separate entity* from its owners for accounting purposes, the owners have the right vote on corporate board members and, at times, other important issues.

Issuance of Stock for Noncash Assets When Market Value for the Stock Exists

Transaction Two years later, Rexio exchanged 500 shares of its $10 par value common stock for a piece of land. At the time of the exchange, Rexio's stock was selling on the market for $16 per share.

Analysis In this case, the market value of the land is irrelevant because the value of the stock is known. The journal entry to record stock exchanged for noncash assets when a market value for the stock exists

- ▲ *increases Land* with a debit of $8,000 (500 shares × $16)
- ▲ *increases Common Stock* with a credit of $5,000 (500 shares × $10)
- ▲ *increases Additional Paid-in Capital* with a credit for $3,000 ($8,000 − $5,000)

Application of Double Entry

Journal Entry

Norma Company is authorized to issue 10,000 shares of common stock. The company sold 1,000 shares at $10 per share. Prepare the journal entries to record the sale of stock for cash under each of the following independent alternatives: (1) The stock has a par value of $2, and (2) the stock has no par value but a stated value of $1 per share.

SOLUTION

1.

	Dr.	Cr.
Cash	10,000	
Common Stock		2,000
Additional Paid-in Capital		8,000
Issued 1,000 shares of $2 par value common stock at $10 per share		

2.

Cash	10,000	
Common Stock		1,000
Additional Paid-in Capital		9,000
Issued 1,000 shares of no-par value common stock with a stated value of $1 at $10 per share		

TRY IT! SE6, SE7, E6A, E7A, E8A, E6B, E7B, E8B

LO4 Accounting for Treasury Stock

As noted earlier, treasury stock is stock that the issuing company has reacquired, usually by purchasing shares on the open market. Although repurchasing its own stock can be a drain on a corporation's cash, it is common practice. In a recent year, 323, or 65 percent, of 500 large companies held treasury stock.[5]

A company may want to buy back its own stock for any of the following reasons:

- To distribute to employees through stock option plans.
- To maintain a favorable market for its stock.
- To increase its earnings per share or stock price per share.
- To have additional shares of stock available for purchasing other companies.
- To prevent a hostile takeover.

Treasury stock is not considered a purchase of assets but is a reduction in stockholders' equity. A company can hold treasury shares for an indefinite period or reissue or retire them. Treasury shares have no rights until they are reissued. Like unissued shares, they do not have voting rights, rights to dividends, or rights to assets during liquidation of the company. However, there is one major difference between unissued shares and treasury shares. A share of stock issued at par value or greater and that was reacquired as treasury stock can be reissued at less than par value.

Purchase of Treasury Stock

When a firm purchases treasury stock, it is recorded at cost. The par value, stated value, or original issue price of the stock is ignored. To illustrate accounting for treasury stock, we will use Kobak Corporation.

STUDY NOTE: *Treasury stock is not the same as unissued stock. Treasury stock represents shares that have been issued but are no longer outstanding. Unissued shares, on the other hand, have never been in circulation.*

Purchase of Treasury Stock

Transaction On September 15, Kobak Corporation purchases 2,000 shares of its common stock on the market at a price of $50 per share.

Analysis The entry to record this purchase of treasury stock

    ▲ *increases Treasury Stock, Common* with a debit of $100,000 (2,000 shares × $50)

    ▼ *decreases Cash* with a credit of $100,000 (2,000 shares × $50)

Application of Double Entry

$$A = L + SE$$
$$-100{,}000 \qquad -100{,}000$$

Journal Entry

		Dr.	Cr.
Sept. 15	Treasury Stock, Common	100,000	
	Cash		100,000
	Acquired 2,000 shares of the company's common stock for $50 per share		

Comment In the stockholders' equity section of Kobak's balance sheet, $100,000 would be deducted from total contributed capital and retained earnings, as shown below.

Contributed capital:	
Common stock, $5 par value, 200,000 shares authorized, 60,000 shares issued, 58,000 shares outstanding	$ 300,000
Additional paid-in capital	60,000
Total contributed capital	$ 360,000
Retained earnings	1,800,000
Total contributed capital and retained earnings	$2,160,000
Less: Treasury stock, common (2,000 shares at cost)	100,000
Total stockholders' equity	$2,060,000

Note that the number of shares issued, and therefore the legal capital, has not changed. However, the number of shares outstanding has *decreased* as a result of the transaction.

Sale of Treasury Stock

Treasury shares can be sold at cost, above cost, or below cost.

Sale of Treasury Shares at Cost

Transaction On November 15, Kobak sold 2,000 shares of its $5 par value common stock on the market at a price of $50 per share.

Analysis When treasury shares are sold at cost, the entry is the reverse of the previous transaction for the purchase of the shares. The journal entry to record this sale of treasury stock at cost

    ▲ *increases Cash* with a debit for the sales amount

    ▼ *decreases Treasury Stock, Common* with a credit for the same amount

Application of Double Entry

Journal Entry

A = L + SE
+100,000   +100,000

	Dr.	Cr.
Nov. 15 Cash	100,000	
Treasury Stock, Common		100,000
Reissued 2,000 shares of treasury stock for		
$50 per share		

Sale of Treasury Shares Above Cost

Transaction On November 15, Kobak sold for $60 per share 1,000 of the treasury shares that it repurchased at $50 per share.

Analysis Even though the treasury stock was sold above cost, no gain is recorded. The journal entry to record this sale of treasury stock above cost

- ▲ *increases Cash* with a debit of $60,000 (1,000 shares × $60)
- ▼ *decreases Treasury Stock, Common* with a credit of $50,000 (1,000 shares × $50)
- ▲ *increases Paid-in Capital, Treasury Stock* with a credit of $10,000 ($60,000 − $50,000)

Application of Double Entry

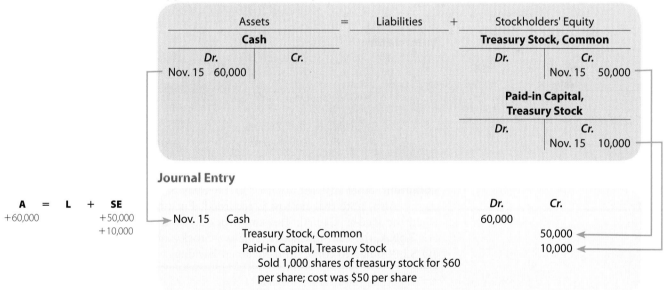

Journal Entry

A = L + SE
+60,000   +50,000
        +10,000

	Dr.	Cr.
Nov. 15 Cash	60,000	
Treasury Stock, Common		50,000
Paid-in Capital, Treasury Stock		10,000
Sold 1,000 shares of treasury stock for $60		
per share; cost was $50 per share		

Comment When treasury shares are sold for an amount greater than their cost, the excess of the sales price over the cost is not considered a gain but is credited to Paid-in Capital, Treasury Stock.

Sale of Treasury Shares Below Cost

Transaction On December 15, Kobak sells its remaining 1,000 treasury shares for $38 per share.

Analysis When treasury shares are sold below their cost, the difference is deducted from Paid-in Capital, Treasury Stock. If this account does not exist or if its balance is insufficient to cover the excess of cost over the reissue price, Retained Earnings absorbs the excess. The journal entry to record the sale of treasury stock below cost

▲ *increases Cash* with a debit of $38,000 (1,000 shares × $38)

▼ *decreases Paid-in Capital, Treasury Stock* with a debit of $10,000

▼ *decreases Retained Earnings* with a debit for the remaining $2,000 by which the shares were sold below their cost ($50,000 − $38,000 − $10,000)

▼ *decreases Treasury Stock, Common* with a credit of $50,000 ($38,000 + $10,000 + $2,000)

Application of Double Entry

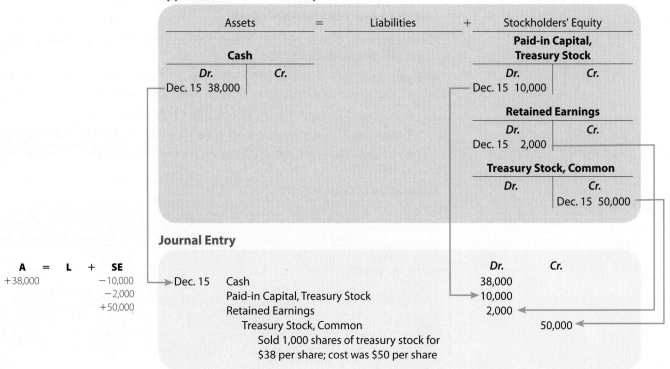

Comment Note that the *decrease* in Treasury Stock, Common *increases* stockholders' equity. Also, note that no loss is recorded. Further, Retained Earnings is debited only when the Paid-in Capital, Treasury Stock account does not exist or has been depleted. For Kobak, the Paid-in Capital, Treasury Stock had a balance of $10,000 so the remaining $2,000 had to come from Retained Earnings.

Retirement of Treasury Stock

If a company decides not to reissue treasury stock, it can retire the stock. All items related to those shares are then removed from the associated capital accounts. If the cost of buying back the treasury stock is less than the company received when it issued the stock, the difference is recorded in Paid-in Capital, Retirement of Stock. If the cost is more than was received when the stock was first issued, the difference is a reduction in stockholders' equity and is debited to Retained Earnings.

Retiring Treasury Stock

Transaction On November 15, Kobak decides to retire the 2,000 shares of stock that it bought back for $100,000.

Analysis If the $5 par value common stock was originally issued at $6 per share, the journal entry to record this retirement of treasury stock

▼ *decreases Common Stock* with a debit of $10,000 (2,000 shares × $5)

▼ *decreases Additional Paid-in Capital* with a debit of $2,000 [2,000 shares × ($6 − $5)]

▼ *decreases Retained Earnings* with a debit of $88,000 ($100,000 − $10,000 − $2,000)

▼ *decreases Treasury Stock, Common* with a credit of $100,000 (2,000 shares × $50)

Application of Double Entry

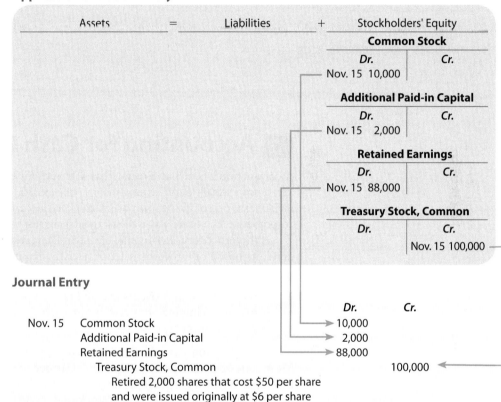

Journal Entry

			Dr.	Cr.
A = L + SE	Nov. 15	Common Stock	10,000	
−10,000		Additional Paid-in Capital	2,000	
−2,000		Retained Earnings	88,000	
−88,000		Treasury Stock, Common		100,000
+100,000		Retired 2,000 shares that cost $50 per share		
		and were issued originally at $6 per share		

Comment The Additional Paid-in Capital was reduced by $2,000 because this is how much was in that account since the stock had a $5 par value and was sold at $6 share [2,000 shares × ($6 − $5)]. Note that this transaction does not change the total stockholders' equity because all accounts are in stockholders' equity.

APPLY IT!

Prepare journal entries to record the following stock transactions for Junior Company during 2015:

May 1 Purchased 5,000 shares of its own $1 par value common stock for $10 per share, the current market price.

17 Sold 1,000 shares of treasury stock purchased on May 1 for $11 per share.

SOLUTION

	Dr.	Cr.
May 1		
Treasury Stock, Common	50,000	
Cash		50,000
Purchased 5,000 shares of Junior Company's common stock at $10 per share		
May 17		
Cash	11,000	
Treasury Stock, Common		10,000
Paid-in Capital, Treasury Stock		1,000
Sold 1,000 shares of treasury stock for $11 per share		

TRY IT! SE8, SE9, E9A, E10A, E9B, E10B

LO 5 Accounting for Cash Dividends

A corporation's board of directors has sole authority to declare dividends; but senior managers, who usually serve as members of the board, influence dividend policies. Receiving dividends is one of two ways in which stockholders can earn a return on their investment in a corporation. The other way is to sell their shares for more than they paid for them.

Although a corporation may have sufficient cash and retained earnings to pay a dividend, its board of directors may not declare dividends for several reasons:

- The corporation may need the cash for expansion.
- It may want to improve its overall financial position by liquidating debt.
- It may be facing major uncertainties, such as a pending lawsuit, strike, or a projected decline in the economy.

A corporation pays dividends quarterly, semiannually, annually, or at other times. Most states do not allow a corporation to declare a dividend that exceeds its retained earnings. When a corporation does declare a dividend that exceeds retained earnings, it is, in essence, returning to the stockholders part of their contributed capital. This is called a **liquidating dividend**. A corporation usually pays a liquidating dividend only when it is going out of business or reducing its operations.

Having sufficient retained earnings in itself does not justify the declaration of a dividend. If a corporation does not have cash or other assets readily available for distribution, it might have to borrow money to pay the dividend—an action most boards of directors want to avoid.

Companies usually pay dividends only when they have had profitable operations. For example, **Apple** began paying dividends in 1987, but it stopped those payments in 1996 to conserve cash after it suffered large operating losses in 1995. Factors other than earnings also affect the decision to pay dividends. Among them are the following:

- **Industry policies:** A company may change its dividend policy to bring it into line with the prevailing policy in its industry. For example, despite positive earnings, **AT&T Corporation** slashed its dividends by 83 percent in 2002. This action put AT&T's policy more in line with the policies of its peers in the telecommunications industry, most of which do not pay dividends.
- **Volatility of earnings:** If a company has years of good earnings followed by years of poor earnings, it may want to keep dividends low to avoid giving a false impression of sustained high earnings. For example, for many years, **General Motors** paid a fairly low but stable dividend but declared a bonus dividend in especially good years.

■ **Effect on cash flows:** A company may not pay dividends because its operations do not generate enough cash to do so or because it wants to invest cash in future operations. **Abbott Laboratories** increases its dividends per share each year to reward its stockholders but also keeps back a portion of its earnings to spend for other purposes, such as researching and developing new drugs. In a recent year, for example, the company with earnings per share of $3.03 paid a $1.92 per share dividend.[6]

In recent years, because of a 15 percent reduction in the tax rate on dividends, attitudes toward dividends have changed. Many firms have either increased their dividends or started to pay dividends for the first time.

Dividend Dates Three important dates are associated with dividends: the declaration date, the record date, and the payment date.

■ The **declaration date** is the date on which the board of directors formally declares that the corporation is going to pay a dividend. Because the legal obligation to pay the dividend arises at this time, a liability for Dividends Payable is recorded and the Dividends account is debited. In the accounting process, Retained Earnings will be reduced by the total dividends declared.

■ The **record date** is the date on which ownership of stock, and therefore the right to receive a dividend, is determined. Persons who own the stock on the record date will receive the dividend. No entry is made on this date. Between the record date and the date of payment, the stock is said to be **ex-dividend**. If the owner on the date of record sells the shares of stock before the date of payment, the right to the dividend remains with that person; it does not transfer with the shares to the second owner.

■ The **payment date** is the date on which the dividend is paid to the stockholders of record. On this date, the Dividends Payable account is eliminated, and the Cash account is reduced.

Dividend Transactions Assume a board of directors declares a cash dividend of $28,000 on December 21. The record date is December 31, which is also the end of the company's accounting period. The dividend payment date is January 11.

Declaration Date

Transaction On December 21, the company declared a cash dividend of $28,000.

Analysis The journal entry to record the dividend on the declaration date (December 21)

▲ *increases* the equity account *Dividends* with a debit on the declaration date

▲ *increases* the liability account *Dividends Payable* with a credit in the amount of the total dividends declared

Journal Entry

		Dr.	Cr.
Dec. 21	Dividends	28,000	
	Dividends Payable		28,000
	Declaration of dividends		

Comment The Dividends account reduces equity by appearing as a deduction from retained earnings on the statement of stockholders' equity, and Dividends Payable appears as a liability on the balance sheet.

Record Date

Event December 31, the record date for the dividends declared on December 21.

Analysis As noted, no journal entry is made on the record date (December 31).

Comment Journal entries for dividends are made only on the declaration date and the payment date.

Payment Date

Transaction On January 11, the company made the dividend payment.

Analysis The journal entry to record the dividend on the payment date (January 11)

▼ *decreases* the liability account *Dividends Payable* with a debit in the amount of the total dividends declared

▼ *decreases* the asset account *Cash* with a credit

Journal Entry

A	=	L	+	SE
−28,000		−28,000		

		Dr.	Cr.
Jan. 11	Dividends Payable	28,000	
	Cash		28,000
	Payment of dividends		

Comment When the date of declaration and the payment date occur in the same period, the amount of dividends shown on the statement of stockholders' equity and on the statement of cash flows will be equal. In this example, however, the accounting period ended between the dates of declaration and payment. Thus, dividends declared during the period ending December 31 exceed the amount paid for dividends. As a result,

- The statement of stockholders' equity for the accounting period will show a *decrease* of $28,000 in the amount of the dividends declared.
- The statement of cash flows will not show the dividends because the cash has not yet been paid out.

APPLY IT!

Jask Corporation has authorized 100,000 shares of $1 par value common stock, of which 80,000 are issued and 70,000 are outstanding. On March 15, the board of directors declared a cash dividend of $0.10 per share, payable on April 15 to stockholders of record on May 1. Prepare the journal entries, as necessary, for each of the three dates.

SOLUTION

Journal Entry:

Mar. 15	Dividends	7,000	
	Dividends Payable		7,000
	Declaration of dividends		

April 15: no entry

Journal Entry:

May 1	Dividends Payable	7,000	
	Cash		7,000
	Payment of dividends		

TRY IT! SE10, E11A, E12A, E11B, E12B

🖈6 Stock Dividends and Stock Splits

Two transactions that commonly modify the content of stockholders' equity are stock dividends and stock splits.

Stock Dividends

A **stock dividend** is a proportional distribution of shares among a corporation's stockholders. Unlike a cash dividend, a stock dividend involves no distribution of assets, and so it has no effect on assets or liabilities. A board of directors may declare a stock dividend for the following reasons:

▪ To give stockholders some evidence of the company's success without affecting working capital (which would be the case if it paid a cash dividend)

▪ To reduce the stock's market price by increasing the number of shares outstanding (a goal, however, more often met by a stock split).

▪ To make a nontaxable distribution to stockholders (because stock dividends that meet certain conditions are not considered income and are thus not taxed).

▪ To increase the company's permanent capital by transferring an amount from retained earnings to contributed capital.

> **STUDY NOTE:** The declaration of a stock dividend results in a reshuffling of stockholders' equity—that is, a portion of retained earnings is converted to contributed capital (by closing the Stock Dividends account). Total stockholders' equity is not affected.

A stock dividend does not affect total stockholders' equity. Basically, it transfers a dollar amount from retained earnings to contributed capital. The amount transferred is the fair market value (usually, the market price) of the additional shares. When stock distributions are small—less than 20 to 25 percent of a company's outstanding common stock—generally accepted accounting principles require that the market price be used to account for the stock dividends.[7]

Stock Dividend Transactions To illustrate accounting for stock dividends, we will use Wing Corporation. Stockholders' equity in Wing is as follows.

Contributed capital:	
Common stock, $5 par value, 50,000 shares authorized,	
15,000 shares issued and outstanding	$ 75,000
Additional paid-in capital	15,000
Total contributed capital	$ 90,000
Retained earnings	450,000
Total stockholders' equity	$540,000

Declaration Date

Transaction On February 24, when the market price of Wing's $5 par value common stock is $20 per share, the board of directors declares a 10 percent stock dividend to be distributed on March 31 to stockholders of record on March 15.

Analysis The journal entry to record this stock dividend on the declaration date (February 24)

> **STUDY NOTE:** For a small stock dividend, the portion of retained earnings transferred is determined by multiplying the number of shares to be distributed by the stock's market price on the declaration date.

▲ *increases* the *Stock Dividends* account with a debit of $30,000 (0.10 × 15,000 shares × $20), the total market value of the stock dividend

▲ *increases Common Stock Distributable* (a temporary account until the 1,500 shares are distributed on March 31) with a credit at total par value of $7,500 (1,500 shares × $5)

▲ *increases Additional Paid-in Capital* with a credit of $22,500 ($30,000 − $7,500), the amount by which the total market value of the stock to be issued exceeds its total par value

Journal Entry

A	=	L	+	SE
				−30,000
				+7,500
				+22,500

			Dr.	Cr.
Feb. 24	Stock Dividends		30,000	
	Common Stock Distributable			7,500
	Additional Paid-in Capital			22,500
	Declared a 10 percent stock dividend on			
	common stock, distributable on March 31 to			
	stockholders of record on March 15:			
	15,000 shares × 0.10 = 1,500 shares			
	1,500 shares × $20 per share = $30,000			
	1,500 shares × $5 per share = $7,500			

Comment Because Common Stock Distributable represents an obligation to distribute additional shares of capital stock, it is a stockholders' equity account, not a liability account, as Cash Dividends Payable is. Also, the Stock Dividends account appears as a deduction from retained earnings on the statement of stockholders' equity.

Record Date

Analysis No entry is needed on the date of record (March 15).

Payment Date

Analysis The journal entry to record the stock dividend on the distribution, or payment, date (March 31)

▼ *decreases Common Stock Distributable* to zero with debit of $7,500 (1,500 shares × $5)

▲ *increases Common Stock* with a credit of $7,500 (1,500 shares × $5)

Journal Entry

A	=	L	+	SE
				−7,500
				+7,500

			Dr.	Cr.
Mar. 31	Common Stock Distributable		7,500	
	Common Stock			7,500
	Distributed a stock dividend of 1,500 shares			
	of common stock			

Effect of a Stock Dividend on Stockholders' Equity If financial statements are prepared between the declaration date and the date of distribution, Common Stock Distributable should be reported as part of contributed capital.

Contributed capital:	
Common stock, $5 par value, 50,000 shares	
authorized, 15,000 shares issued and outstanding	$ 75,000
Common stock distributable, 1,500 shares	7,500
Additional paid-in capital	37,500
Total contributed capital	$120,000
Retained earnings	420,000
Total stockholders' equity	$540,000

Note that after the stock dividend has been distributed:

▪ Total stockholders' equity is the same before and after the stock dividend.
▪ The assets of the corporation are not reduced, as they would be by a cash dividend.
▪ The proportionate ownership in the corporation of any individual stockholder is the same before and after the stock dividend.

Large Stock Dividends All stock dividends have some effect on the market price of a company's stock, but some are so large that they have a material effect. For example, a 50 percent stock dividend would cause the market price of a stock to drop about 33 percent because the increase would be one-third of the shares outstanding. The AICPA has ruled that large stock dividends—those greater than 20 to 25 percent—should be accounted for by transferring the par or stated value of the stock on the declaration date from retained earnings to contributed capital.[8]

Stock Splits

A **stock split** occurs when a corporation increases the number of shares of stock issued and outstanding and reduces the par or stated value proportionally. A company may plan a stock split for the following reasons:

- To lower its stock's market price per share and, thereby, increase the demand and volume of trading for its stock at this lower price.
- To signal to the market its success in achieving its operating goals.

Business Application **Nike** achieved these strategic objectives in 2007 by increasing its cash dividend and declaring a 2-for-1 stock split.[9] After the stock split, the number of the company's outstanding shares doubled, thereby cutting the share price from about $80 per share to $40 per share. The stock split left each stockholder's total wealth unchanged but increased the income stockholders received from dividends. Although there is no fundamental reason why a stock should go up because of a stock split, the stock split was a sign that Nike has continued to do well. In fact, Nike's stock continued to rise during the difficult years for the economy that followed to over $100 per share in 2012.[10]

Stock Split

Transaction Wing has 15,000 shares of $5 par value stock outstanding and the market value is $70 per share. The corporation plans a 2-for-1 split.

Analysis The journal entry to record this split

▼ *decreases* the par value to $2.50 per share ($5.00 ÷ 2)

▲ *increases* the number of shares outstanding to 30,000 (15,000 shares × 2)

After the split, a stockholder who previously owned 200 shares of the $5 par value stock will own:

- 400 shares of the $2.50 par value stock in outstanding shares of stock
- the same proportionate share of the company as before the split
- approximately the same total market value of stock because the 2-for-1 stock split will cause the price of the stock to drop by approximately 50 percent, to about $35

Journal Entry A stock split does not increase the number of shares authorized, nor does it change the balances in the stockholders' equity section of the balance sheet. It simply changes the par value and the number of shares issued for both shares outstanding and treasury stock. Thus, a journal entry is unnecessary. However, it is appropriate to document the change with a memorandum entry in the general journal.

Business Perspective
Do Stock Splits Help Increase a Company's Market Price?

When **General Mills**, the cereal company, completed a 2-for-1 split in May 2010, its stock dropped from about $70 per share to about $35 per share. Since then, the price has trended upward.[11]

| July 15 | The 15,000 shares of $5 par value common stock issued and outstanding were split 2 for 1, resulting in 30,000 shares of $2.50 par value common stock issued and outstanding. |

The stockholders' equity before and after the stock split follows.

Before Stock Split		After Stock Split	
Contributed capital:		Contributed capital:	
Common stock, $5 par value, 50,000 shares authorized; 15,000 shares issued and outstanding	$ 75,000	Common stock, $2.50 par value, 50,000 shares authorized, 30,000 shares issued and outstanding	$ 75,000
Additional paid-in capital	15,000	Additional paid-in capital	15,000
Total contributed capital	$ 90,000	Total contributed capital	$ 90,000
Retained earnings	450,000	Retained earnings	450,000
Total stockholders' equity	$540,000	Total stockholders' equity	$540,000

Comment The balances of all accounts remain the same. Only the par value and number of shares issued and outstanding change. If the number of split shares exceeds the number of authorized shares, the corporation's board of directors must secure state and stockholders' approval before it can issue the additional shares.

APPLY IT!

Kelly Corporation's board of directors declared a 2 percent stock dividend applicable to the outstanding shares of its $10 par value common stock, of which 1,000,000 shares are authorized, 300,000 are issued, and 100,000 are held in the treasury. Then, the board declared a 2-for-1 stock split on issued shares. How many authorized, issued, and treasury shares existed after each of these transactions? What is the par value per share?

SOLUTION

Stock dividend applies to outstanding shares:
   (300,000 shares − 100,000 shares) × 0.02 = 4,000 shares

Stock split applies to all issued shares:
   304,000 shares × 2 = 608,000 shares

Authorized shares are unchanged (1,000,000, but par value is now $5 per share); issued shares are 608,000; and outstanding shares are 408,000 (608,000 − 200,000 treasury shares).

TRY IT! SE11, SE12, SE13, E13A, E14A, E15A, E13B, E14B, E15B

LO 7 The Statement of Stockholders' Equity and Book Value per Share

The following sections describe the statement of stockholders' equity and show how to calculate book value per share.

Statement of Stockholders' Equity

STUDY NOTE: *The statement of stockholders' equity is a labeled calculation of the change in each stockholder's equity account over an accounting period.*

The statement of stockholders' equity (or *statement of changes in stockholders' equity*) summarizes changes in the components of the stockholders' equity section of the balance sheet. Most companies use this statement in place of the statement of retained earnings because it reveals much more about the stockholders' equity transactions that took place during the period. For example, in the statement of stockholders' equity in Exhibit 4, the first line shows the beginning balance of each account in the stockholders' equity section of Snow Corporation's balance sheet. Each subsequent line *discloses* the effects of transactions on those accounts.

Exhibit 4
Statement of Stockholders' Equity

Snow Corporation
Statement of Stockholders' Equity
For the Year Ended December 31, 2015

	Preferred Stock $100 Par Value 8% Convertible	Common Stock $10 Par Value	Additional Paid-in Capital	Retained Earnings	Treasury Stock	Total
Balance, December 31, 2014	$ 800,000	$600,000	$ 600,000	$1,200,000		$3,200,000
Net income				540,000		540,000
Issuance of 10,000 shares of common stock		100,000	400,000			500,000
Conversion of 2,000 shares of preferred stock to 6,000 shares of common stock	(200,000)	60,000	140,000			—
10 percent stock dividend on common stock, 7,600 shares		76,000	304,000	(380,000)		—
Purchase of 1,000 shares of treasury stock					$(48,000)	(48,000)
Cash dividends:						
Preferred stock				(48,000)		(48,000)
Common stock				(95,200)		(95,200)
Balance, December 31, 2015	$ 600,000	$836,000	$1,444,000	$1,216,800	$(48,000)	$4,048,800

© Cengage Learning 2014

As shown in Exhibit 4, Snow had the following:

- Net income of $540,000
- 10,000 shares of common stock issued for $500,000
- Conversion of $200,000 of preferred stock to common stock
- A 10 percent stock dividend on common stock
- Treasury stock purchases of $48,000
- Cash dividends on both preferred and common stock

STUDY NOTE: *The ending balances on the statement of stockholders' equity appear in the stockholders' equity section of the balance sheet.*

The ending balances of the accounts appear at the bottom of the statement. Those accounts and balances make up the stockholders' equity section of Snow's balance sheet on December 31, 2015, as shown in Exhibit 5.

Exhibit 5
Stockholders' Equity
Section of a Balance Sheet

Snow Corporation
Balance Sheet
December 31, 2015

Stockholders' Equity

Contributed capital:		
Preferred stock, $100 par value, 8 percent convertible, 20,000 shares authorized. 6,000 shares issued and outstanding		$ 600,000
Common stock, $10 par value, 200,000 shares authorized, 83,600 shares issued. 82,600 shares outstanding	$ 836,000	
Additional paid-in capital	1,444,000	2,280,000
Total contributed capital		$2,880,000
Retained earnings		1,216,800
Total contributed capital and retained earnings		$4,096,800
Less: Treasury stock, common (1,000 shares, at cost)		48,000
Total stockholders' equity		$4,048,800

© Cengage Learning 2014

Book Value per Share

The word *value* is associated with shares of stock in several ways. Par value or stated value is set when the stock is authorized, and it establishes a company's legal capital. Neither par value nor stated value has any relationship to a stock's book value or market value. The **book value** of stock represents a company's total assets less its liabilities. It is simply the stockholders' equity in a company or, to put it another way, it represents a company's net assets. The **book value per share** is, therefore, the equity of the owner of one share of stock in the net assets of a company. That value generally does not equal the amount a stockholder receives if the company is sold or liquidated because, in most cases, assets are recorded at historical cost, not at their current market value.

Book Value per Share of Common Stock If a company has only common stock outstanding, book value per share is calculated as follows.

Stockholders' Equity ÷ Common Shares Outstanding = Book Value per Share

Common stock distributable is included in the number of shares outstanding, but treasury stock is not. For example, if a firm has total stockholders' equity of $2,060,000 and 58,000 shares outstanding, the book value per share of its common stock would be $35.52 ($2,060,000 ÷ 58,000 shares, rounded).

Book Value for Common and Preferred Stock If a company has both preferred and common stock, determining the book value per share is not so simple. Generally, the preferred stock's call value (or par value, if a call value is not specified) and any dividends in arrears are subtracted from stockholders' equity to determine the equity pertaining to common stock. Refer to the stockholders' equity section of Snow's balance sheet in Exhibit 5. If Snow has no dividends in arrears and its preferred stock is callable at $105, the equity pertaining to its common stock would be calculated as follows.

Total stockholders' equity	$4,048,800
Less equity allocated to preferred stockholders (6,000 shares × $105)	630,000
Equity pertaining to common stockholders	$3,418,800

As indicated in Exhibit 5, Snow has 82,600 shares of common stock outstanding (83,600 shares issued less 1,000 shares of treasury stock). Its book values per share are computed as follows.

Preferred stock: $630,000 ÷ 6,000 shares = $105 per share
Common stock: $3,418,800 ÷ 82,600 shares = $41.39 per share (rounded)

Book Value for Dividends in Arrears Assume the same facts except that Snow's preferred stock is 8 percent cumulative and that one year of dividends is in arrears. The stockholders' equity would be allocated as follows.

Total stockholders' equity		$4,048,800
Less call value of outstanding preferred shares	$630,000	
Dividends in arrears ($600,000 × 0.08)	48,000	
Equity allocated to preferred stockholders		678,000
Equity pertaining to common stockholders		$3,370,800

The book values per share would then be as follows.

Preferred stock: $678,000 ÷ 6,000 shares = $113 per share
Common stock: $3,370,800 ÷ 82,600 shares = $40.81 per share (rounded)

Stockholders' Equity and the Financial Statements

The stockholders' equity of a corporation, as shown on the balance sheet in Exhibit 6, is separated into contributed capital, retained earnings, and treasury stock.

Exhibit 6
Stockholders' Equity
on the Balance Sheet

© Cengage Learning 2014

Balance Sheet

December 31, 2014

Assets	**Liabilities**
Current assets	Current liabilities
Investments	Long-term liabilities
Property, plant, and equipment	Total liabilities
Intangible assets	

Stockholders' Equity

Preferred stock, par value
Common stock, par value
Paid in capital in excess of par value, common
Paid in capital in excess of par value, treasury
    Total contributed capital
Retained earnings
Less treasury stock
    Total stockholders' equity

Total Assets = Total Liabilities + Stockholders' Equity

APPLY IT!

Using the data from the stockholders' equity section of Puskin Corporation's balance sheet that follows, compute the book value per share for both the preferred and common stock.

Contributed capital:

Preferred stock, $100 par value, 6 percent cumulative, 20,000 shares authorized, 2,000 shares issued and outstanding*	$ 200,000
Common stock, $5 par value, 200,000 shares authorized. 100,000 shares issued and outstanding	500,000
Additional paid-in capital	300,000
Total contributed capital	$1,000,000
Retained earnings	500,000
Total stockholders' equity	$1,500,000

*The preferred stock is callable at $104 per share, and one year's dividends are in arrears.

SOLUTION

Total stockholders' equity		$1,500,000
Less call value of outstanding preferred shares	$208,000	
Dividends in arrears ($200,000 × 0.06)	12,000	
Equity allocated to preferred stockholders		220,000
Equity pertaining to common stockholders		$1,280,000

Preferred stock book value per share: $220,000 ÷ 2,000 shares = $110, or $104 + $6 = $110 per share
Common stock book value per share: ($1,500,000 − $220,000) ÷ 100,000 common shares = $12.80 per share

TRY IT! SE14, SE15, E16A, E17A, E16B, E17B

BUSINESS APPLICATIONS

RELEVANT
LEARNING OBJECTIVE

LO 8   Calculate dividend
yield and return on
equity, and define stock
options.

LO 8 Evaluating Dividend Policies, Company Performance, and Stock Options

Investors use the dividend yield ratio to evaluate the amount of dividends they receive. In addition to evaluating dividends, investors will also want to evaluate a firm's past and future performance, using return on equity, the price-earnings ratio, and cash flow information. Both employees and investors evaluate stock options to determine their effects on compensation (employees) and the financial performance of the company (investors).

Dividend Yield

Dividend yield is computed by dividing the dividends per share by the market price per share. To illustrate, **Microsoft** built up a large cash balance through its years of profitable operations, with no dividends paid. In 2005, it paid a large dividend of $3.40 per share and began paying regular dividends thereafter ($0.35 per share in 2006). By 2011, Microsoft's annual dividend increased to $5.4 billion ($0.64 per share).[12] Microsoft's dividend yield is computed as follows.

> **RATIO**
>
> ### Dividend Yield: What Is the Return from Dividends on Each Share of Stock?
>
> $$\text{Dividend Yield} = \frac{\text{Dividends per Share}}{\text{Market Price per Share}} = \frac{\$0.64}{\$26} = 2.5\%^*$$
>
> *Rounded

Because the yield is relatively low, Microsoft shareholders must expect some of their return to come from increases in the price of the shares.

Return on Equity

Return on equity is the most important ratio associated with stockholders' equity. It is also a common measure of management's performance. For instance, when *Business Week* and *Forbes* rate companies on their success, return on equity is the major basis of their evaluations. In addition, the compensation of top executives is often tied to return on equity benchmarks. Return on equity is the ratio of net income to average total stockholders' equity. **Microsoft**'s return on equity in 2011 is computed as follows.

> **RATIO**
>
> ### Return on Equity: How Much Does the Company Earn on the Stockholders' Investment in the Company?

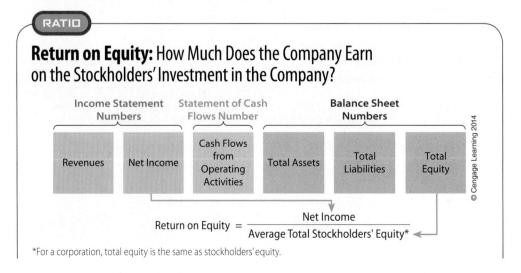

*For a corporation, total equity is the same as stockholders' equity.

© Cengage Learning 2014

$$= \frac{\$23{,}150}{(\$57{,}083 + \$46{,}175) \div 2}$$

$$= \frac{\$23{,}150}{\$51{,}629}$$

$$= 44.8\%^{**}$$

**Rounded

Microsoft's healthy 44.8 percent return on equity depends, of course, on the amount of net income the company earns. However, it also depends on the level of stockholders' equity, which in turn depends on management decisions about the amount of stock the company sells to the public. As a company sells more shares,

▲ stockholders' equity *increases*

▼ return on equity *decreases*

Management can keep stockholders' equity at a minimum, thereby increasing return on equity, by financing the business with cash flows from operations and by issuing long-term debt instead of stock. However, issuing long-term debt increases a company's financial risk because the interest and principal of the debt must be paid in a timely manner.

Management can also reduce stockholders' equity, thereby increasing return on equity, by buying back the company's shares on the open market. The cost of treasury stock has the following effect:

▼ Stockholders' equity *decreases*

▲ Return on equity *increases*

Many companies buy back their own stock instead of paying or increasing dividends. Their reason for doing so is that it puts money into the hands of stockholders in the form of market price appreciation without creating a commitment to higher dividends in the future. For instance, in 2011, **Microsoft** purchased $11.6 billion of its common stock on the open market.[13] Microsoft's stock repurchases will improve the company's return on equity, increase its earnings per share, and lower its price/earnings ratio.

Price-Earnings Ratio

The **price/earnings (P/E) ratio** is a measure of investors' confidence in a company's future. It is calculated by dividing the market price per share by the earnings per share. The price/earnings ratio will vary as market price per share fluctuates daily and the amount of earnings per share changes. Using the annual earnings per share from **Microsoft**'s 2011 income statement, its P/E ratio can be calculated as follows.

> **RATIO**
>
> ### Price/Earnings Ratio: What Value Does the Market Place on the Company's Earnings?
>
> $$\text{Price/Earnings (P/E) Ratio} = \frac{\text{Market Price per Share}}{\text{Earnings per Share}} = \frac{\$26}{\$2.69} = 9.7 \text{ times}^*$$
>
> *Rounded

Because the market price is 9.7 times earnings, investors are paying a moderately high price in relation to earnings. They do so expecting that Microsoft will continue to be successful.

Cash Flow Information

The best source of information concerning cash flows related to stock transactions and dividends is the financing activities section of the statement of cash flows. For instance, **Microsoft**'s cash flows from these activities are clearly revealed in this partial section of the company's statement of cash flows (in millions):

	2011	2010
Financing Activities		
Common stock issued	$ 2,422	$ 2,311
Common stock repurchased	(11,555)	(11,269)
Common stock cash dividend	**(5,180)**	**(4,578)**

Note the increasing amounts of common stock repurchased (treasury stock) and the small amount of new common stock issued in 2011. Both actions are a reflection of the company's success.

Stock Options as Compensation

More than 98 percent of public companies encourage employees to invest in their common stock through **stock option plans**.[14] Most such plans give employees the right to purchase stock in the future at a fixed price. Investors evaluate these plans to determine their effect on current and future financial statements and the value of their investment.

Some companies offer stock option plans only to management personnel, but others, including **Google**, make them available to all employees. Because the market value of a company's stock is tied to a company's performance, these plans are a means of both motivating and compensating employees. As the market value of the stock goes up, the difference between the option price and the market price grows, which increases the amount of compensation. Another key benefit of stock option plans is that compensation expense is tax-deductible.

In one example of how firms value stock options, **Google** recognized $1.97 billion of stock-based compensation expense in 2011. This amount represented about 7.6 percent of the company's total expenses and 20.3 percent of the net income.[15]

Business Perspective
Politics and Accounting Don't Mix

The FASB has long held that stock options should be treated as an expense, because they are a form of compensation. However, technology industry leaders have maintained that expensing stock options would hurt their companies' profits and growth. The U.S. Congress pressured the FASB to back down, using the companies' reasoning that stock options essentially have no value and, thus, are not an expense on the income statement, although they should be mentioned in a note to the financial statements. Many stock options were being granted, and the companies granting them were very loose in how they accounted for them. Many of the stock transactions were back-dated so that the exercise price would be most advantageous to the executives who were benefiting. By 2010, the SEC had settled more than 60 criminal investigations related to stock options, usually resulting in settlements and significant fines.[16]

APPLY IT! ▶

In 2014, Chalet Corporation earned $2.20 per share and paid a dividend of $0.88 per share. At year-end, the price of its stock was $44 per share. Calculate the dividend yield and the price/earnings ratio.

SOLUTION

$$\text{Dividend Yield} = \frac{\text{Dividends per Share}}{\text{Market Price per Share}}$$

$$= \frac{\$0.88}{\$44.00} = 2.0\%$$

$$\text{Price/Earnings (P/E) Ratio} = \frac{\text{Market Price per Share}}{\text{Earnings per Share}}$$

$$= \frac{\$44.00}{\$2.20} = 20.0 \text{ times}$$

TRY IT! SE3, SE16, E18A, E18B

TriLevel Problem

Vietecha, Inc.

The beginning of this chapter focused on Vietecha, Inc., a company that had engaged in several transactions involving stock, including the initial public offering of common stock, the issuance of preferred stock, as well as treasury stock and dividends. Complete the following requirements in order to answer the questions posed at the beginning of the chapter.

Section 1: Concepts
How does the separate entity concept apply to the stockholders in a corporation?

Section 2: Accounting Applications
How should a corporation account for its stock transactions and dividends?

As noted earlier, Vietecha's state charter authorized it to issue 2 million shares of $1 par value common stock and 50,000 shares of 4 percent, $20 par value cumulative and convertible preferred stock. Vietecha engaged in the following transactions involving stock and dividends during 2014:

Feb.   1   Issued 200,000 shares of common stock for $250,000.
    15   Issued 6,000 shares of common stock for accounting and legal services. The bills for these services totaled $7,200.
Mar.   15   Issued 240,000 shares of common stock to Jesus Miko in exchange for a building and land appraised at $200,000 and $50,000, respectively.
Apr.   2   Purchased 40,000 shares of its own common stock at $1.25 per share from a person who changed her mind about investing in the company.
July   1   Issued 50,000 shares of preferred stock for $1,000,000.
Sept. 30   Sold 20,000 of the shares in the treasury for $1.50 per share.
Dec.   31   Vietecha's board of directors declared dividends of $49,820 payable on January 15, 2015, to stockholders of record on January 7. Dividends included preferred dividends of $20,000 for one-half year.

For the period ended December 31, 2014, Vietecha reported net income of $80,000 and earnings per common share of $0.14. At December 31, the market price per common share was $1.60.

1. Record Vietecha's stock transactions using T accounts.
2. Prepare the stockholders' equity section of Vietecha's balance sheet as of December 31, 2014. (*Hint:* Use net income and dividends to calculate retained earnings.)

Section 3: Business Applications

What measures should stockholders use to evaluate the return on their investments?

To better answer this question, calculate Vietecha's dividend yield on common stock, price/earnings ratio, and return on equity.

SOLUTION

Section 1: Concepts

A corporation is an *entity*, chartered by the state, that is *separate* from its owners both legally and from an accounting standpoint. Vietecha's founders chose the corporate form of business rather than a partnership because it is relatively easy for a corporation to raise capital by issuing stock. Moreover, this approach to financing does not burden a company with debt and interest payments. Among the several other advantages that corporations have over partnerships are limited liability, ease of transfer of ownership, and continuous existence.

Section 2: Accounting Applications

1.

	Assets				=		Liabilities			+		Stockholders' Equity		
	Cash						**Dividends Payable**					**Preferred Stock**		
Feb. 1	250,000	Apr. 2	50,000					Dec. 31	49,820				July 1	1,000,000
July 1	1,000,000													
Sept. 30	30,000											**Common Stock**		
Bal.	1,230,000												Feb. 1	200,000
	Building												15	6,000
Mar. 15	200,000												Mar. 15	240,000
													Bal.	446,000
	Land													
Mar. 15	50,000											**Additional Paid-in Capital**		
													Feb. 1	50,000
													15	1,200
													Mar. 15	10,000
													Bal.	61,200
												Paid-in Capital, Treasury Stock		
													Sept. 30	5,000
	Assets				=		Liabilities			+		Stockholders' Equity		
												Dividends		
											Dec. 31	49,820		
												Treasury Stock		
											Apr. 2	50,000	Sept. 30	25,000
											Bal.	25,000		
												Start-up and Organization Costs		
											Feb. 15	7,200		

2.

	A	B	C	
1	Vietecha, Inc.			
2	Balance Sheet			
3	December 31, 2014			
4				
5	Stockholders' Equity			
6				
7	Contributed capital:			
8	Preferred stock, 4 percent cumulative convertible, $20 par value, 50,000 shares authorized, issued, and outstanding			$1,000,000
9	Common stock $1 par value, 2,000,000 shares authorized, 446,000 shares issued, and 426,000 shares outstanding			446,000
10	Additional paid-in capital		$61,200	
11	Paid-in capital, treasury stock		5,000	66,200
12	Total contributed capital			$1,512,200
13	Retained earnings			30,180*
14	Total contributed capital and retained earnings			$1,542,380
15	Less treasury stock (20,000 shares, at cost)			25,000
16	Total stockholders' equity			$1,517,380
17				
18	*Retained Earnings = Net Income – Cash Dividends Declared Retained Earnings = $80,000 – $49,820 = $30,180			

Section 3: Business Applications

Dividend yield on common stock, price/earnings ratio, and return on equity:

$$\text{Dividends per Share} = \frac{\text{Common Stock Dividend}}{\text{Common Shares Outstanding}} = \frac{\$29,820}{426,000} = \$0.07^*$$

$$\text{Dividends Yield} = \frac{\text{Dividends per Share}}{\text{Market Price per Share}} = \frac{\$0.07}{\$1.60} = 4.4\%^*$$

$$\text{Price/Earnings Ratio} = \frac{\text{Market Price per Share}}{\text{Earnings per Share}} = \frac{\$1.60}{\$0.14} = 11.4 \text{ times}^*$$

*Rounded

The opening balance of stockholders' equity on February 1, 2014, was $250,000.

$$\text{Return on Equity} = \frac{\text{Net Income}}{\text{Average Stockholders' Equity}}$$

$$= \frac{\$80,000}{(\$1,517,380 + \$250,000) \div 2}$$

$$= \frac{\$80,000}{\$883,690}$$

$$= 9.1\%^*$$

*Rounded

Chapter Review

Define the *corporate* form of business and its characteristics. **LO 1** The corporate form of business has definite advantages over sole proprietorships and partnerships, such as limited liability and the ability to raise large amounts of capital, but choosing a corporate form of business requires a careful weighing of the advantages and disadvantages as well as the issues involved in using equity financing.

Most states require corporations to issue stock at a minimum value called legal capital. Legal capital is represented by the stock's par or stated value.

Identify the components of stockholders' equity and their characteristics. **LO 2**

The stockholders' equity section of a corporate balance sheet usually has at least three components: contributed capital, retained earnings, and treasury stock. Contributed capital consists of money raised through stock issues. A corporation can issue two types of stock: common stock and preferred stock. Common stockholders have voting rights; they also share in the earnings of the corporation. Preferred stockholders usually have preference over common stockholders in one or more areas. Retained earnings are reinvested in the corporation. They represent stockholders' claims to assets resulting from profitable operations. Treasury stock is stock that the issuing corporation has reacquired. It is treated as a deduction from stockholders' equity.

Preferred stock generally gives its owners first right to dividend payments. Only after these stockholders have been paid can common stockholders receive any portion of a dividend. If the preferred stock is cumulative and dividends are in arrears, a corporation must pay the amount in arrears to preferred stockholders before it pays any dividends to common stockholders. Preferred stockholders also usually have preference over common stockholders in terms of their claims to assets if the corporation is liquidated. In addition, preferred stock may be convertible to common stock, and it is often callable at the option of the corporation.

Account for the issuance of stock for cash and other assets. **LO 3**

Corporations normally issue their stock in exchange for cash or other assets. When stock is issued for cash at par or stated value, Cash is debited and Common Stock or Preferred Stock is credited. When stock is sold at an amount greater than par or stated value, the excess is recorded in Additional Paid-in Capital.

When stock is issued for noncash assets, the general rule is to record the stock at its market value. If this value cannot be determined, the fair market value of the asset received is used to record the transaction.

Account for treasury stock. **LO 4**

Treasury stock is stock that the issuing company has reacquired. A company may buy back its own stock for several reasons, including a desire to create stock option plans, maintain a favorable market for the stock, increase earnings per share, or purchase other companies. The purchase of treasury stock is recorded at cost and is deducted from stockholders' equity. Treasury stock can be reissued or retired. It is similar to unissued stock in that it does not have rights until it is reissued.

Account for cash dividends. **LO 5**

The liability for payment of dividends arises on the date the board of directors declares a dividend. The declaration is recorded with a debit to Dividends and a credit to Dividends Payable. The record date—the date on which ownership of the stock, and thus of the right to receive a dividend, is determined—requires no entry. On the payment date, the Dividends Payable account is eliminated, and the Cash account is reduced.

Account for stock dividends and stock splits. **LO 6**

A stock dividend is a proportional distribution of shares among a corporation's stockholders. The following is a summary of the key dates and accounting treatments of stock dividends:

Key Date	Stock Dividend
Declaration date	Debit Stock Dividends for the market value of the stock to be distributed (if the stock dividend is small) and credit Common Stock Distributable for the stock's par value and Additional Paid-in Capital for the excess of the market value over the stock's par value.
Record date	No entry is needed.
Date of distribution	Debit Common Stock Distributable and credit Common Stock for the par value of the stock

A company usually declares a stock split to reduce the market value of its stock and thereby increase the demand for the stock. Because the par value of the stock normally decreases in proportion to the number of additional shares issued, a stock split has no effect on the dollar amount in stockholders' equity. A stock split does not require a journal entry, but a memorandum entry in the general journal is appropriate.

Describe the statement of **LO 7** **stockholders' equity, and compute book value per share.**

The statement of stockholders' equity summarizes changes during a period in each component of the stockholders' equity section of the balance sheet.

Book value per share is calculated by dividing stockholders' equity by the number of common shares outstanding. If a company has both preferred and common stock, the call or par value of the preferred stock and any dividends in arrears are deducted from stockholders' equity before dividing by the common shares outstanding.

Calculate dividend yield **LO 8** **and return on equity, and define stock options.**

Investors evaluate dividend policies and company performance by determining the dividend yield, return on equity, and the price/earnings ratio. Another issue involved in managing contributed capital is using stock options as compensation.

Key Terms and Ratios

articles of incorporation 492 (LO1)
authorized shares 497 (LO2)
board of directors 492 (LO1)
book value 518 (LO7)
book value per share 518 (LO7)
callable preferred stock 499 (LO2)
common stock 497 (LO2)
contributed capital 492 (LO1)
convertible preferred
  stock 499 (LO2)
cumulative preferred
  stock 498 (LO2)
declaration date 511 (LO5)
dividends 493 (LO1)
dividends in arrears 498 (LO2)
double taxation 494 (LO1)

ex-dividend 511 (LO5)
initial public offering (IPO) 491
issued shares 497 (LO2)
legal capital 494 (LO1)
liquidating dividend 510 (LO5)
noncumulative preferred
  stock 498 (LO2)
no-par stock 501 (LO3)
outstanding shares 497 (LO2)
par value 494 (LO1)
payment date 511 (LO5)
preferred stock 497 (LO2)
record date 511 (LO5)
registrars 494 (LO1)
retained earnings 496 (LO2)
share of stock 492 (LO1)

start-up and organization
  costs 495 (LO1)
statement of stockholders'
  equity 496 (LO2)
stock dividend 513 (LO6)
stock option plans 522 (LO8)
stock split 515 (LO6)
stockholders' equity 496 (LO2)
transfer agents 494 (LO1)
treasury stock 496 (LO2)
underwriter 494 (LO1)

RATIOS
dividend yield 520 (LO8)
price/earnings (P/E) ratio 521 (LO8)
return on equity 520 (LO8)

Chapter Assignments

DISCUSSION QUESTIONS

LO 1 **DQ1.** Why are most large companies established as corporations rather than as partnerships?

LO 2 **DQ2.** Why does a company usually not want to issue all its authorized shares?

LO 2 **DQ3.** Why would a company want to issue callable preferred stock?

LO 2 **DQ4.** What arguments can you give for treating preferred stock as debt rather than equity when carrying out financial analysis?

LO 4 **DQ5.** Why is treasury stock not considered an investment or an asset?

LO 5 **DQ6.** If an investor sells shares after the declaration date but before the date of record, does the seller still receive the dividend?

LO 6   **DQ7.** Upon receiving shares of stock from a stock dividend, why should the stockholder not consider the value of the stock as income?

LO 6, 7   **DQ8.** What is the effect of a stock dividend or a stock split on book value per share?

LO 8   **DQ9. BUSINESS APPLICATION** ▶ Why do many companies like to give stock options as compensation?

LO 8   **DQ10. BUSINESS APPLICATION** ▶ What relevance does par value or stated value have to a financial ratio, such as return on equity or debt to equity?

SHORT EXERCISES

LO 1   ### Advantages and Disadvantages of a Corporation

SE1. CONCEPT ▶ Identify whether each of the following characteristics is an advantage or a disadvantage of the corporate form of business:

1. Ease of transfer of ownership
2. Taxation
3. Separate legal entity
4. Lack of mutual agency
5. Government regulation
6. Continuous existence

LO 1   ### Effect of Start-up and Organization Costs

SE2. At the beginning of 2014, Salinas Company incurred the following start-up and organization costs: (1) attorneys' fees with a market value of $10,000, paid with 6,000 shares of $1 par value common stock, and (2) incorporation fees of $6,000 cash. Calculate total start-up and organization costs. What will be the effect of these costs on the income statement and balance sheet?

LO 1, 5, 8   ### Management Issues

SE3. BUSINESS APPLICATION ▶ Indicate whether each of the following actions is related to (a) managing under the corporate form of business, (b) using equity financing, (c) determining dividend policies, (d) evaluating performance using return on equity, or (e) issuing stock options:

1. Considering whether to make a distribution to stockholders.
2. Controlling day-to-day operations.
3. Determining whether to issue preferred or common stock.
4. Compensating management based on the company's meeting or exceeding the targeted return on equity.
5. Compensating employees by giving them the right to purchase shares at a given price.
6. Transferring shares without the approval of other owners.

LO 2   ### Stockholders' Equity

SE4. Prepare the stockholders' equity section of Waldemar Corporation's balance sheet from the following accounts and balances on December 31, 2014:

Common Stock, $10 par value, 30,000 shares authorized, 20,000 shares issued, and 19,500 shares outstanding	$200,000
Additional Paid-in Capital	100,000
Retained Earnings	15,000
Treasury Stock, Common (500 shares, at cost)	7,500

LO 2 | **Preferred Stock Dividends with Dividends in Arrears**

SE5. Mazurka Corporation has 2,000 shares of $100, 8 percent cumulative preferred stock outstanding and 40,000 shares of $1 par value common stock outstanding. In the company's first three years of operation, its board of directors paid the following cash dividends: 2013, none; 2014, $40,000; and 2015, $80,000. Determine the total cash dividends and dividends per share paid to the preferred and common stockholders during each of the three years.

LO 3 | **Issuance of Stock**

SE6. Sigma Company is authorized to issue 100,000 shares of common stock. The company sold 5,000 shares at $12 per share. Prepare journal entries to record the sale of stock for cash under each of the following independent alternatives: (1) The stock has a par value of $5, and (2) the stock has no par value but a stated value of $1 per share.

LO 3 | **Issuance of Stock for Noncash Assets**

SE7. Tulip Corporation issued 16,000 shares of its $1 par value common stock in exchange for land that had a fair market value of $100,000. Prepare the journal entries necessary to record the issuance of the stock for the land under each of these conditions: (1) The stock was selling for $7 per share on the day of the transaction; (2) management attempted to place a value on the common stock but could not do so.

LO 4 | **Treasury Stock Transactions**

SE8. Prepare the journal entries necessary to record Dao Company's following stock transactions during 2014:

Oct. 1   Purchased 2,000 shares of its own $2 par value common stock for $20 per share, the current market price.
   17   Sold 500 shares of treasury stock purchased on October 1 for $25 per share.
   21   Sold 800 shares of treasury stock purchased on October 1 for $18 per share.

LO 4 | **Retirement of Treasury Stock**

SE9. Refer to the information for Dao Company in **SE8**. On October 28, 2014, Dao retired the remaining 700 shares of treasury stock. The shares were originally issued at $5 per share. Prepare the necessary journal entry.

LO 5 | **Cash Dividends**

SE10. Leon Corporation has authorized 400,000 shares of $1 par value common stock, of which 320,000 are issued and 280,000 are outstanding. On May 15, the board of directors declared a cash dividend of $0.20 per share, payable on June 15 to stockholders of record on June 1. Prepare the entries using T accounts, as necessary, for each of the three dates.

LO 6 | **Stock Dividends**

SE11. On February 15, Mite Corporation's board of directors declared a 2 percent stock dividend applicable to the outstanding shares of its $10 par value common stock, of which 400,000 shares are authorized, 260,000 are issued, and 40,000 are held in the treasury. The stock dividend was distributed on March 15 to stockholders of record on March 1. On February 15, the market value of the common stock was $15 per share. On March 30, the board of directors declared a $0.50 per share cash dividend. No other stock transactions have occurred. Prepare journal entries to record, as necessary, the transactions of February 15, March 1, March 15, and March 30.

LO 6   **Stock Split**

SE12. On August 10, 2014, Geller, Inc.'s board of directors declared a 3-for-1 stock split of its $9 par value common stock, of which 400,000 shares were authorized and 125,000 were issued and outstanding. The market value on that date was $60 per share. On the same date, the balance of additional paid-in capital was $3,000,000, and the balance of retained earnings was $3,250,000. Prepare the stockholders' equity section of the company's balance sheet after the stock split. What entry, if any, is needed to record the stock split?

LO 6, 7   **Effects of Stockholders' Equity Actions**

SE13. Tell whether each of the following actions will increase, decrease, or have no effect on total assets, total liabilities, and total stockholders' equity:

1. Declaration of a stock dividend
2. Declaration of a cash dividend
3. Stock split
4. Purchase of treasury stock

LO 7   **Statement of Stockholders' Equity**

SE14. Refer to Snow Corporation's statement of stockholders' equity in Exhibit 4 to answer the following questions: (1) At what price per share were the 10,000 shares of common stock sold? (2) What was the conversion price per share of the common stock? (Round to the nearest cent.) (3) At what price was the common stock selling on the date of the stock dividend? (4) At what price per share was the treasury stock purchased?

LO 7   **Book Value for Preferred and Common Stock**

SE15. Using data from the stockholders' equity section of Tramot Corporation's balance sheet that follows, and assuming one year's dividend in arrears, compute the book value per share for both the preferred and the common stock. (Round to the nearest cent.)

Contributed capital:	
Preferred stock, $100 par value, 8 percent cumulative, 20,000 shares authorized, 1,000 shares issued and outstanding	$ 100,000
Common stock, $10 par value, 200,000 shares authorized, 80,000 shares issued and outstanding	800,000
Additional paid-in capital	1,032,000
Total contributed capital	$1,932,000
Retained earnings	550,000
Total stockholders' equity	$2,482,000

LO 8   **Dividend Yield and Price/Earnings Ratio**

SE16. BUSINESS APPLICATION ▶ In 2014, Konstan Corporation earned $3.30 per share and paid a dividend of $1.65 per share. At year-end, the price of its stock was $33 per share. Calculate the dividend yield and the price/earnings ratio.

EXERCISES: SET A

LO 1   **Advantages and Disadvantages of a Corporation**

E1A. CONCEPT ▶ Identify whether each of the following characteristics is an advantage (A) or a disadvantage (D) of the corporate form of business:

1. Continuous existence
2. Government regulation
3. Separate legal entity
4. Double taxation
5. Professional management

LO 2

Stockholders' Equity

E2A. The accounts and balances that follow are from Hastings Corporation's records on December 31, 2014.

Preferred Stock, $100 par value, 9 percent cumulative, 10,000 shares authorized, 6,000 shares issued and outstanding	$600,000
Common Stock, $12 par value, 45,000 shares authorized, 30,000 shares issued, and 28,500 shares outstanding	360,000
Additional Paid-in Capital	194,000
Retained Earnings	23,000
Treasury Stock, Common (1,500 shares, at cost)	30,000

Prepare the stockholders' equity section of Hastings' balance sheet as of December 31, 2014.

LO 2

Characteristics of Common and Preferred Stock

E3A. Indicate whether each of the following characteristics is more closely associated with common stock (C) or preferred stock (P):

1. Can be callable
2. Generally receives dividends before other classes of stock
3. Often receives dividends at a set rate
4. Is considered the residual equity of a company
5. Can be convertible
6. More likely to have dividends that vary in amount from year to year
7. Can be entitled to receive dividends not paid in past years
8. Likely to have full voting rights
9. Receives assets first in liquidation

LO 2

Cash Dividends with Dividends in Arrears

E4A. Rutherford Corporation has 20,000 shares of its $100 par value, 7 percent cumulative preferred stock outstanding and 100,000 shares of its $1 par value common stock outstanding. In Rutherford's first four years of operation, its board of directors paid the following cash dividends: 2011, none; 2012, $240,000; 2013, $280,000; 2014, $280,000. Determine the dividends per share and total cash dividends paid to the preferred and common stockholders during each of the four years.

LO 2

Cash Dividends on Preferred and Common Stock

E5A. Ex-Act Corporation pays dividends at the end of each year. The dividends that it paid for 2012, 2013, and 2014 were $160,000, $120,000, and $360,000, respectively. Calculate the total amount of dividends Ex-Act paid in each of these years to its common and preferred stockholders under both of the following capital structures: (1) 40,000 shares of $100 par, 6 percent noncumulative preferred stock and 120,000 shares of $10 par common stock; (2) 20,000 shares of $100 par, 7 percent cumulative preferred stock and 120,000 shares of $10 par common stock. Ex-Act had no dividends in arrears at the beginning of 2012.

LO 2, 3

Stock Entries Using T Accounts; Stockholders' Equity

E6A. Gormanus Corporation was organized in 2014. It was authorized to issue 400,000 shares of no-par common stock with a stated value of $5 per share, and 80,000 shares of $100 par value, 6 percent noncumulative preferred stock. On March 1, the company issued 120,000 shares of its common stock for $15 per share and 16,000 shares of its preferred stock for $100 per share.

1. Record the issuance of the stock using T accounts.
2. Prepare the stockholders' equity section of Gormanus' balance sheet as it would appear immediately after the company issued the common and preferred stock.

LO 3   **Issuance of Stock**

E7A. Sussex Company is authorized to issue 100,000 shares of common stock. On August 1, the company issued 5,000 shares at $25 per share. Prepare journal entries to record the issuance of stock for cash under each of the following alternatives: (1) the stock has a par value of $25; (2) the stock has a par value of $10; (3) the stock has no par value; and (4) the stock has a stated value of $1 per share.

LO 3   **Issuance of Stock for Noncash Assets**

E8A. On July 1, 2014, Jones Corporation, a new corporation, issued 40,000 shares of its common stock to finance a corporate headquarters building. The building has a fair market value of $1,200,000 and a book value of $800,000. Because Jones is a new corporation, it is not possible to establish a market value for its common stock. Prepare journal entries to record the issuance of stock for the building, assuming the following conditions: (1) the par value of the stock is $10 per share; (2) the stock is no-par stock; and (3) the stock has a stated value of $4 per share.

LO 4   **Treasury Stock Transactions**

E9A. Record DeMeo Corporation's following stock transactions, which represent all the company's treasury stock transactions during 2014, using T accounts:

May   5   Purchased 800 shares of its own $2 par value common stock for $20 per share, the current market price.
       17   Sold 300 shares of treasury stock purchased on May 5 for $22 per share.
       21   Sold 200 shares of treasury stock purchased on May 5 for $20 per share.
       28   Sold the remaining 300 shares of treasury stock purchased on May 5 for $19 per share.

LO 4   **Treasury Stock Transactions Including Retirement**

E10A. Record Carmel Corporation's following stock transactions, which represent all its treasury stock transactions for the year, using T accounts:

June   1   Purchased 1,000 shares of its own $30 par value common stock for $70 per share, the current market price.
       10   Sold 250 shares of treasury stock purchased on June 1 for $80 per share.
       20   Sold 350 shares of treasury stock purchased on June 1 for $58 per share.
       30   Retired the remaining shares purchased on June 1. The original issue price was $42 per share.

LO 5   **Cash Dividends**

E11A. Nogel Corporation secured authorization from the state for 200,000 shares of $10 par value common stock. It has 80,000 shares issued and 70,000 shares outstanding. On June 5, the board of directors declared a $0.25 per share cash dividend to be paid on June 25 to stockholders of record on June 15. Record these events using T accounts.

LO 5   **Cash Dividends**

E12A. Bennett Corporation has 500,000 authorized shares of $1 par value common stock, of which 200,000 are issued, including 20,000 shares of treasury stock. On October 15, the corporation's board of directors declared a cash dividend of $0.50 per share payable on November 15 to stockholders of record on November 1. Record these events using T accounts.

LO **6**

Journal Entries: Stock Dividends

E13A. Panza Corporation has 60,000 shares of its $1 par value common stock outstanding. Prepare journal entries to record the following transactions as they relate to the company's common stock:

July 17 Declared a 10 percent stock dividend on common stock to be distributed on August 10 to stockholders of record on July 31. Market value of the stock was $5 per share on this date.

31 Date of record.

Aug. 10 Distributed the stock dividend declared on July 17.

Sept. 1 Declared a $0.50 per share cash dividend on common stock to be paid on September 16 to stockholders of record on September 10.

LO **6**

Stock Split

E14A. Charles Corporation currently has 250,000 shares of $1 par value common stock authorized with 100,000 shares outstanding. The board of directors declared a 2-for-1 split on May 15, 2014, when the market value of the common stock was $2.50 per share. The retained earnings balance on May 15 was $350,000. Additional paid-in capital on this date was $10,000. Prepare the stockholders' equity section of the company's balance sheet before and after the stock split. What entry, if any, would be necessary to record the stock split?

LO **6**

Stock Split

E15A. On January 15, 2014, Agard International's board of directors declared a 3-for-1 stock split of its $12 per value common stock, of which 1,600,000 shares were authorized and 400,000 were issued and outstanding. The market value on that date was $45 per share. On the same date, the balance of additional paid-in capital was $8,000,000, and the balance of retained earnings was $16,000,000. Prepare the stockholders' equity section of Agard's balance sheet before and after the stock split. What entry, if any, is needed to record the stock split?

LO **7**

Statement of Stockholders' Equity

E16A. The stockholders' equity section of Manco Corporation's balance sheet on December 31, 2014, follows.

Contributed capital:	
Common stock, $2 par value, 250,000 shares authorized, 200,000 shares issued and outstanding	$ 400,000
Additional paid-in capital	600,000
Total contributed capital	$1,000,000
Retained earnings	2,100,000
Total stockholders' equity	$3,100,000

Prepare a statement of stockholders' equity for the year ended December 31, 2015, assuming these transactions occurred in sequence in 2015:

a. Issued 5,000 shares of $100 par value, 9 percent cumulative preferred stock at par after obtaining authorization from the state.

b. Issued 20,000 shares of common stock in connection with the conversion of bonds having a carrying value of $300,000.

c. Declared and issued a 2 percent common stock dividend. The market value on the date of declaration was $14 per share.

d. Purchased 5,000 shares of common stock for the treasury at a cost of $16 per share.

e. Earned net income of $230,000.

f. Declared and paid the full-year's dividend on preferred stock and a dividend of $0.40 per share on common stock outstanding at the end of the year.

LO **7**   **Book Value for Preferred and Common Stock**

E17A. The stockholders' equity section of Plaka Corporation's balance sheet follows. Assuming one year's dividend in arrears, determine the book value per share for both the preferred and the common stock. (Round to the nearest cent.)

Contributed capital:	
Preferred stock, $100 par value, callable at $105 per share, 6 percent cumulative, 5,000 shares authorized, 100 shares issued and outstanding	$10,000
Common stock, $5 par value, 50,000 shares authorized, 5,000 shares issued, 4,500 shares outstanding	25,000
Additional paid-in capital	14,000
Total contributed capital	$49,000
Retained earnings	47,500
Total contributed capital and retained earnings	$96,500
Less treasury stock, common (500 shares at cost)	7,500
Total stockholders' equity	$89,000

LO **8**   **Dividend Yield and Price/Earnings Ratio**

E18A. BUSINESS APPLICATION ▶ In 2014, Konstan Corporation earned $4.40 per share and paid a dividend of $2.00 per share. At year-end, the price of its stock was $66 per share. Calculate the dividend yield and the price/earnings ratio. (Round the dividend yield to the nearest tenth of a percent.)

EXERCISES: SET B

Visit the textbook companion website at www.cengagebrain.com to access Exercise Set B for this chapter.

PROBLEMS

LO **1, 2, 3, 4, 5**   **Common Stock Transactions and Stockholders' Equity**

✔ 2: Total stockholders' equity: $302,400

P1. On March 1, 2014, Kissell Corporation began operations with a charter from the state that authorized 100,000 shares of $4 par value common stock. Over the next quarter, the company engaged in the transactions that follow.

Mar.	1	Issued 30,000 shares of common stock, $200,000.
	2	Paid fees associated with obtaining the charter and starting up and organizing the corporation, $24,000.
Apr.	10	Issued 13,000 shares of common stock, $130,000.
	15	Purchased 5,000 shares of common stock, $50,000
May	31	The board of directors declared a $0.20 per share cash dividend to be paid on June 15 to shareholders of record on June 10.

REQUIRED

1. Record the above transactions using T accounts.
2. Prepare the stockholders' equity section of Kissell's balance sheet on May 31, 2014. Net income earned during the first quarter was $30,000.
3. **ACCOUNTING CONNECTION** ▶ What effect, if any, will the cash dividend declaration on May 31 have on Kissell's net income, retained earnings, and cash flows?

LO **2, 8**   **Preferred and Common Stock Dividends and Dividend Yield**

✔ 1: Total dividends in 2014: preferred, $40,000; common, $90,000

P2. Avaya Corporation had the following stock outstanding from 2011 through 2014:
Preferred stock: $100 par value, 8 percent cumulative, 5,000 shares authorized, issued, and outstanding
Common stock: $10 par value, 100,000 shares authorized, issued, and outstanding

The company paid $30,000, $30,000, $94,000, and $130,000 in dividends during 2011, 2012, 2013, and 2014, respectively. The market price per common share was $7.25 and $8.00 per share at the end of years 2013 and 2014, respectively.

REQUIRED

1. Determine the dividends per share and the total dividends paid to common stockholders and preferred stockholders in 2011, 2012, 2013, and 2014.
2. Perform the same computations, with the assumption that the preferred stock was noncumulative.
3. **BUSINESS APPLICATION** ▶ Calculate the 2013 and 2014 dividend yield for common stock, using the dividends per share computed in requirement **2**. (Round to the nearest tenth of a percent.)
4. **ACCOUNTING CONNECTION** ▶ How are cumulative preferred stock and noncumulative preferred stock similar to long-term bonds? How do they differ from long-term bonds?

LO **1, 2, 3, 4, 5**

Comprehensive Stockholders' Equity Transactions

P3. In January 2014, Vanowski Corporation was organized and authorized to issue 2,000,000 shares of no-par common stock and 50,000 shares of 5 percent, $50 par value, noncumulative preferred stock. The stock-related transactions for the first year's operations follow.

			Account			
			Debited		Credited	
			Account Number	Dollar Amount	Account Number	Dollar Amount
Jan.	19	Sold 15,000 shares of common stock for $31,500. State law requires a minimum of $1 stated value per share.	110	$31,500	310 312	$15,000 $16,500
	21	Issued 5,000 shares of common stock to attorneys and accountants for services valued at $11,000 and provided during the organization of the corporation.	—	—	—	—
Feb.	7	Issued 30,000 shares of common stock for a building that had an appraised value of $78,000.	—	—	—	—
Mar.	22	Purchased 10,000 shares of its common stock at $3 per share.	—	—	—	—
July	15	Issued 5,000 shares of common stock to employees under a stock option plan that allows any employee to buy shares at the current market price, which is now $3 per share.	—	—	—	—
Aug.	1	Sold 2,500 shares of treasury stock for $4 per share.	—	—	—	—
Sept.	1	Declared a cash dividend of $0.15 per common share to be paid on September 25 to stockholders of record on September 15.	—	—	—	—

(*Continued*)

Sept.	15	Date of record for cash dividends.	—	—	—	—
	25	Paid cash dividends to stockholders of record on September 15.	—	—	—	—
Oct.	30	Issued 4,000 shares of common stock for a piece of land. The stock was selling for $3 per share, and the land had a fair market value of $12,000.	—	—	—	—
Dec.	15	Issued 2,200 shares of preferred stock for $50 per share.	—	—	—	—

REQUIRED

1. For each of these transactions, indicate the account numbers and dollar amounts (as shown in the example) for the account(s) debited and credited, using the account numbers that follow.

110 Cash	312 Additional Paid-in Capital
120 Land	313 Paid-in Capital, Treasury Stock
121 Building	340 Retained Earnings
220 Dividends Payable	341 Dividends
305 Preferred Stock	350 Treasury Stock, Common
310 Common Stock	510 Start-up and Organization Costs

2. **BUSINESS APPLICATION** ▶ Why is the stockholders' equity section of the balance sheet an important consideration in analyzing the performance of a company?

LO **2, 3, 4, 5, 8**

✔ 2: Total stockholders' equity: $236,520

Comprehensive Stockholders' Equity Transactions and Stockholders' Equity

P4. Kraft Unlimited, Inc., was organized and authorized to issue 5,000 shares of $100 par value, 9 percent preferred stock and 50,000 shares of no par, $5 stated value common stock on July 1, 2014. Stock-related transactions for Kraft Unlimited follow.

July	1	Issued 10,000 shares of common stock at $11 per share.
	1	Issued 500 shares of common stock at $11 per share for services rendered in connection with the organization of the company.
	2	Issued 1,000 shares of preferred stock at par value for cash.
	10	Issued 2,500 shares of common stock for land on which the asking price was $35,000. Market value of the stock was $12. Management wishes to record the land at the market value of the stock.
Aug.	2	Purchased 1,500 shares of its common stock at $13 per share.
	10	Declared a cash dividend for one month on the outstanding preferred stock and $0.02 per share on common stock outstanding, payable on August 22 to stockholders of record on August 12.
	12	Date of record for cash dividends.
	22	Paid cash dividends.

REQUIRED

1. Prepare journal entries to record these transactions.
2. Prepare the stockholders' equity section of Kraft's balance sheet as it would appear on August 31, 2014. Net income for July was zero and August was $11,500.
3. **BUSINESS APPLICATION** ▶ Calculate dividend yield, price/earnings ratio, and return on equity. Assume earnings per common share are $1.00 and market price per common share is $20. For beginning stockholders' equity, use the balance after the July transactions. (Round to the nearest tenth of a percent.)

4. **BUSINESS APPLICATION** ▶ Discuss the results in requirement **3**, including the effect on investors' returns and the company's profitability as it relates to stockholders' equity.

LO **4**

Treasury Stock

P5. Rolex Company was involved in the following treasury stock transactions during 2014:

a. Purchased 80,000 shares of its $1 par value common stock on the market for $2.50 per share.
b. Purchased 16,000 shares of its $1 par value common stock on the market for $2.80 per share.
c. Sold 44,000 shares purchased in (**a**) for $131,000.
d. Sold the other 36,000 shares purchased in (**a**) for $72,000.
e. Sold 6,000 of the remaining shares of treasury stock for $1.60 per share.
f. Retired all the remaining shares of treasury stock. All shares originally were issued at $1.50 per share.

✔ 1: Balance in Retained Earnings: $17,200 debit

REQUIRED

1. Record the treasury stock transactions using T accounts.
2. **ACCOUNTING CONNECTION** ▶ What is the reasoning behind treating the purchase of treasury stock as a reduction in stockholders' equity as opposed to treating it as an investment asset?

LO **6, 7**

Dividends, Stock Splits, and Stockholders' Equity

P6. The stockholders' equity section of Minh, Inc.'s balance sheet as of December 31, 2013, follows.

Contributed capital:	
Common stock, $3 par value, 1,000,000 shares authorized, 80,000 shares issued and outstanding	$240,000
Additional paid-in capital	75,000
Total contributed capital	$315,000
Retained earnings	240,000
Total stockholders' equity	$555,000

✔ 2: Total retained earnings: $423,200
✔ 2: Total stockholders' equity: $1,049,000

A review of Minh's stockholders' equity records disclosed the following transactions during 2014:

Mar. 25   The board of directors declared a 5 percent stock dividend to stockholders of record on April 20 to be distributed on May 1. The market value of the common stock was $21 per share.

Apr. 20   Date of record for stock dividend.

May 1   Issued stock dividend.

Sept. 10   Declared a 3-for-1 stock split.

Dec. 15   Declared a 10 percent stock dividend to stockholders of record on January 15 to be distributed on February 15. The market price on this date is $9 per share.

REQUIRED

1. Record the stockholders' equity components of these transactions using T accounts.
2. Prepare the stockholders' equity section of Minh's balance sheet as of December 31, 2014. Assume net income for 2014 is $494,000.
3. **ACCOUNTING CONNECTION** ▶ If you owned 2,000 shares of Minh stock on March 1, 2014, how many shares would you own on February 15, 2015? Would your proportionate share of the ownership of the company be different on the latter date from what it was on the former date? Explain your answer.

LO **3, 4, 5, 6, 7**

GENERAL LEDGER

✔ 2: Total stockholders' equity: $5,605,600

Comprehensive Stockholders' Equity Transactions

P7. On December 31, 2014, the stockholders' equity section of Delux Corporation's balance sheet appeared as follows:

Contributed capital:	
Common stock, $8 par value, 400,000 shares authorized, 120,000 shares issued and outstanding	$ 960,000
Additional paid-in capital	2,560,000
Total contributed capital	$3,520,000
Retained earnings	1,648,000
Total stockholders' equity	$5,168,000

Selected transactions involving stockholders' equity in 2015 follow.

Jan. 4 The board of directors obtained authorization for 40,000 shares of $40 par value noncumulative preferred stock that carried an indicated dividend rate of $4 per share and was callable at $42 per share.

14 The company sold 24,000 shares of the preferred stock at $40 per share and issued another 4,000 in exchange for a building valued at $160,000.

Mar. 8 The board of directors declared a 2-for-1 stock split on the common stock.

Apr. 20 After the stock split, the company purchased 6,000 shares of common stock for the treasury at a price of $12 per share.

May 4 The company sold 2,000 of the shares purchased on April 20, at an average price of $16 per share.

July 15 The board of directors declared a cash dividend of $4 per share on the preferred stock and $0.40 per share on the common stock.

25 Date of record.

Aug. 15 Paid the cash dividend.

Nov. 28 The board of directors declared a 15 percent stock dividend when the common stock was selling for $20 per share to be distributed on January 5 to stockholders of record on December 15.

Dec. 15 Date of record for the stock dividend.

REQUIRED

1. Prepare journal entries to record these transactions.
2. Prepare the stockholders' equity section of Delux's balance sheet as of December 31, 2015. Net loss for 2015 was $436,000. (*Hint:* Use T accounts to keep track of transactions.)
3. **ACCOUNTING CONNECTION** ▶ Compute the book value per share for preferred and common stock (including common stock distributable) on December 31, 2014 and 2015, using end-of-year shares outstanding. (Round to the nearest cent.) What effect would you expect the change in book value to have on the market price per share of the company's stock?

ALTERNATE PROBLEMS

LO **1, 2, 3, 4, 5**

GENERAL LEDGER

✔ 2: Total retained earnings: $32,000
✔ 2: Total stockholders' equity: $1,342,000

Common Stock Transactions and Stockholders' Equity

P8. Canterbury Corporation began operations on September 1, 2014. The corporation's charter authorized 300,000 shares of $8 par value common stock. Canterbury engaged in the transactions that follow during its first quarter.

Sept. 1 Issued 50,000 shares of common stock, $500,000.

1 Paid an attorney $32,000 to help start up and organize the corporation and obtain a corporate charter from the state.

Oct. 2 Issued 80,000 shares of common stock, $960,000.

15 Purchased 10,000 shares of common stock for $150,000.

Nov. 30 Declared a cash dividend of $0.40 per share to be paid on December 15 to stockholders of record on December 10.

REQUIRED

1. Prepare entries using T accounts to record the above transactions.
2. Prepare the stockholders' equity section of Canterbury's balance sheet on November 30, 2014. Net income for the quarter was $80,000.
3. **ACCOUNTING CONNECTION** ▶ What effect, if any, will the cash dividend declaration on November 30 have on net income, retained earnings, and cash flows?

LO **2, 8**

✔ 1: Total dividends in 2014: preferred, $280,000; common, $820,000

Preferred and Common Stock Dividends and Dividend Yield

P9. Rhinehart Corporation had both common stock and preferred stock outstanding from 2012 through 2014. Information about each stock for the three years follows.

Type	Par Value	Shares Outstanding	Other
Preferred	$100	40,000	7% cumulative
Common	20	600,000	

The company paid $140,000, $800,000, and $1,100,000 in dividends for 2012 through 2014, respectively. The market price per common share was $15 and $17 per share at the end of years 2013 and 2014, respectively.

REQUIRED

1. Determine the dividends per share and total dividends paid to the common and preferred stockholders each year. (Round to the nearest cent.)
2. Assuming that the preferred stock was noncumulative, repeat the computations performed in requirement **1**. (Round to the nearest cent.)
3. **BUSINESS APPLICATION** ▶ Calculate the 2013 and 2014 dividend yield for common stock using dividends per share computed in requirement **2**. (Round to the nearest tenth of a percent.)
4. **ACCOUNTING CONNECTION** ▶ How are cumulative preferred stock and noncumulative preferred stock similar to long-term bonds? How do they differ from long-term bonds?

LO **2, 3, 4, 5, 8**

✔ 2: Total stockholders' equity: $1,765,900

Comprehensive Stockholders' Equity Transactions and Financial Ratios

P10. Gorlin Corporation was chartered in the Commonwealth of Massachusetts. The company was authorized to issue 20,000 shares of $100 par value, 6 percent preferred stock and 100,000 shares of no-par common stock. The common stock has a $2 stated value. The stock-related transactions for the quarter ended October 31, 2014, follow.

Aug. 3 Issued 20,000 shares of common stock at $22 per share.

15 Issued 16,000 shares of common stock for land. Asking price for the land was $200,000. Common stock's market value was $12 per share. Management wishes to record the land at the market value of the stock.

22 Issued 10,000 shares of preferred stock for $1,000,000.

Oct. 4 Issued 10,000 shares of common stock for $120,000.

10 Purchased 5,000 shares of common stock for the treasury for $13,000.

15 Declared a quarterly cash dividend on the outstanding preferred stock and $0.10 per share on common stock outstanding, payable on October 31 to stockholders of record on October 25.

25 Date of record for cash dividends.

31 Paid the cash dividends declared on October 15.

(*Continued*)

REQUIRED

1. Record transactions for the quarter ended October 31, 2014, using T accounts.
2. Prepare the stockholders' equity section of Gorlin's balance sheet as of October 31, 2014. Net income for the quarter was $46,000.
3. **BUSINESS APPLICATION** ▶ Calculate dividend yield, price/earnings ratio, and return on equity. (Round the dividend yield and return on equity to the nearest tenth of a percent. Round the price/earnings ratio to the nearest tenth.) Assume earnings per common share are $1.97 and market price per common share is $25. For beginning stockholders' equity, use the balance after the August transactions.
4. **BUSINESS APPLICATION** ▶ Discuss the results in requirement **3**, including the effect on investors' returns and the firm's profitability as it relates to stockholders' equity.

LO **1, 2, 3, 4, 5**

Comprehensive Stockholders' Equity Transactions

P11. In January 2014, Imperial Corporation was organized and authorized to issue 4,000,000 shares of no-par common stock and 100,000 shares of 5 percent, $50 par value, noncumulative preferred stock. The stock-related transactions for the first year's operations follow.

			Account			
			Debited		Credited	
			Account Number	Dollar Amount	Account Number	Dollar Amount
Jan.	19	Sold 30,000 shares of common stock for $63,000. State law requires a minimum of $1 stated value per share.	110	$63,000	310 312	$30,000 $33,000
	21	Issued 10,000 shares of common stock to attorneys and accountants for services valued at $22,000 and provided during the organization of the corporation.	—	—	—	—
Feb.	7	Issued 60,000 shares of common stock for a building that had an appraised value of $156,000.	—	—	—	—
Mar.	22	Purchased 20,000 shares of its common stock at $3 per share.	—	—	—	—
July	15	Issued 10,000 shares of common stock to employees under a stock option plan that allows any employee to buy shares at the current market price, which is now $3 per share.	—	—	—	—
Aug.	1	Sold 5,000 shares of treasury stock for $4 per share.	—	—	—	—
Sept.	1	Declared a cash dividend of $0.15 per common share to be paid on September 25 to stockholders of record on September 15.	—	—	—	—
	15	Date of record for cash dividends.	—	—	—	—

Sept.	25	Paid cash dividends to stockholders of record on September 15.	—	—	—	—
Oct.	30	Issued 8,000 shares of common stock for a piece of land. The stock was selling for $3 per share, and the land had a fair market value of $24,000.	—	—	—	—
Dec.	15	Issued 4,400 shares of preferred stock for $50 per share.	—	—	—	—

REQUIRED

1. For each of these transactions, provided the account numbers and dollar amounts (as shown in the example) for the account(s) debited and credited using the account numbers that follow.

110 Cash	312 Additional Paid-in Capital
120 Land	313 Paid-in Capital, Treasury Stock
121 Building	340 Retained Earnings
220 Dividends Payable	341 Dividends
305 Preferred Stock	350 Treasury Stock, Common
310 Common Stock	510 Start-up and Organization Costs

2. **BUSINESS APPLICATION** ▶ Why is the stockholders' equity section of the balance sheet an important consideration in analyzing the performance of a company?

LO **4**

✔ 1: Balance in Retained Earnings: $34,400 debit

Treasury Stock

P12. Khandi Company was involved in the following treasury stock transactions during 2014:

a. Purchased 160,000 shares of its $1 par value common stock on the market for $2.50 per share.
b. Purchased 32,000 shares of its $1 par value common stock on the market for $2.80 per share.
c. Sold 88,000 shares purchased in (**a**) for $262,000.
d. Sold the other 72,000 shares purchased in (**a**) for $144,000.
e. Sold 12,000 of the remaining shares of treasury stock for $1.60 per share.
f. Retired all the remaining shares of treasury stock. All shares originally were issued at $1.50 per share.

REQUIRED

1. Record the treasury stock transactions using T accounts.
2. **ACCOUNTING CONNECTION** ▶ What is the reasoning behind treating the purchase of treasury stock as a reduction in stockholders' equity as opposed to treating it as an investment asset?

LO **6, 7**

✔ 2. Total retained earnings: $798,100;
2. Total stockholders' equity: $2,964,000

Dividends, Stock Splits, and Stockholders' Equity

P13. The stockholders' equity section of Villa Corporation's balance sheet as of December 31, 2013, follows.

Contributed capital:	
Common stock, $4 par value, 500,000 shares authorized, 200,000 shares issued and outstanding	$ 800,000
Additional paid-in capital	1,000,000
Total contributed capital	$1,800,000
Retained earnings	1,200,000
Total stockholders' equity	$3,000,000

(*Continued*)

Villa had the following transactions in 2014:

Feb. 28 The board of directors declared a 10 percent stock dividend to stockholders of record on March 25 to be distributed on April 5. The market value on this date is $16.

Mar. 25 Date of record for stock dividend.

Apr. 5 Issued stock dividend.

Aug. 3 Declared a 2-for-1 stock split.

Nov. 20 Purchased 18,000 shares of the company's common stock at $8 per share for the treasury.

Dec. 31 Declared a 5 percent stock dividend to stockholders of record on January 25 to be distributed on February 5. The market value per share was $9.

REQUIRED

1. Record the stockholders' equity components of these transactions using T accounts.
2. Prepare the stockholders' equity section of Villa's balance sheet as of December 31, 2014. Assume net income for 2014 is $108,000.
3. **ACCOUNTING CONNECTION** ▶ If you owned 1,000 shares of Villa stock on February 1, 2014, how many shares would you own on February 5, 2015? Would your proportionate share of the ownership of the company be different on the latter date from what it was on the former date? Explain your answer.

LO **3, 4, 5, 6, 7**

✔ 2. Total stockholders' equity:
$11,211,200

Comprehensive Stockholders' Equity Transactions

P14. On December 31, 2014, the stockholders' equity section of Torez Corporation's balance sheet appeared as follows.

Contributed capital:

Common stock, $8 par value, 800,000 shares authorized, 240,000 shares issued and outstanding	$ 1,920,000
Additional paid-in capital	5,120,000
Total contributed capital	$ 7,040,000
Retained earnings	3,296,000
Total stockholders' equity	$10,336,000

The following are selected transactions involving stockholders' equity in 2015. On January 4, the board of directors obtained authorization for 80,000 shares of $40 par value noncumulative preferred stock that carried an indicated dividend rate of $4 per share and was callable at $42 per share. On January 14, the company sold 48,000 shares of the preferred stock at $40 per share and issued another 8,000 in exchange for a building valued at $320,000. On March 8, the board of directors declared a 2-for-1 stock split on the common stock. On April 20, after the stock split, the company purchased 12,000 shares of common stock for the treasury at a price of $12 per share; 4,000 of these shares subsequently were sold on May 4 at an average price of $16 per share. On July 15, the board of directors declared a cash dividend of $4 per share on the preferred stock and $0.40 per share on the common stock. The date of record was July 25. The dividends were paid on August 15. The board of directors declared a 15 percent stock dividend on November 28, when the common stock was selling for $20. The date of record for the stock dividend was December 15, and the dividend was to be distributed on January 5.

REQUIRED

1. Prepare journal entries to record these transactions.
2. Prepare the stockholders' equity section of Torez's balance sheet as of December 31, 2015. Net loss for 2015 was $872,000. (*Hint:* Use T accounts to keep track of transactions.)

3. **BUSINESS APPLICATION** ▶ Compute the book value per share for preferred and common stock (including common stock distributable) on December 31, 2014 and 2015, using end-of-year shares outstanding. (Round to the nearest cent.) What effect would you expect the change in book value to have on the market price per share of the company's stock?

CASES

LO 1 ## Conceptual Understanding: Reasons for Issuing Common Stock

C1. DreamWorks Animation, led by billionaire **Microsoft** founder Paul Allen, went public in a recent year with its class A common stock at $28 per share, raising $650 million. By the end of the first day, it was up 27 percent to $38 per share, giving the company a value of almost $1 billion. This initial enthusiasm did not last. By the end of 2007, the price was only around $25 per share.[17] As a growing company that has produced such animated hits as Shrek, DreamWorks could have borrowed significant funds by issuing long-term debt. What are some advantages of issuing common stock as opposed to long-term debt? What are some disadvantages?

LO 4 ## Conceptual Understanding: Purposes of Treasury Stock

C2. BUSINESS APPLICATION ▶ Many companies in recent years have bought back their common stock. For example, **IBM**, with large cash holdings, spent almost $35 billion over three years repurchasing its stock.[18] What are the reasons companies buy back their own shares? What is the effect of common stock buybacks on earnings per share, return on equity, return on assets, debt to equity, and the current ratio?

LO 2, 3 ## Interpreting Financial Reports: Effect of Stock Issue

C3. When **Google, Inc.** went public with an IPO, it used an auction system that allowed everyone to participate rather than allocating shares of stock to a few insiders. The company's IPO drew widespread attention. Announcements of the IPO would have been similar to the following:

22,500,000 Shares

GOOGLE, INC.

$0.001 Par Value Common Stock

Price $85 a share

The gross proceeds of the IPO before issue costs were $1.9 billion.

A portion of the stockholders' equity section of the balance sheet adapted from Google's annual report, which was issued prior to this stock offering, follows.

Stockholders' Equity
(Dollar amounts in thousands)

Common stock, $0.001 par value, 700,000,000 shares authorized; 161,000,000 shares issued and outstanding	$ 161
Additional paid-in capital	725,219
Retained earnings	191,352

1. Assume that the net proceeds to Google after issue costs were $1.8 billion. Prepare the journal entry to record the stock issuance on Google's accounting.
2. Prepare the stockholders' equity section portion of Google's balance sheet shown above after the issue of the common stock, based on the information given. (Round all answers to the nearest thousand.)
3. Based on your answer in **2**, did Google have to increase its authorized shares to undertake this stock issue?
4. What amount per share did Google receive and how much did Google's underwriters receive to help in issuing the stock? What do underwriters do to earn their fee?

LO 6   **Conceptual Understanding: Stock Split**

C4. When **Crocs**, the shoe company, reported in early 2007 that its first-quarter earnings had increased from the previous year, its stock price jumped to over $80 per share. At the same time, the company announced a 2-for-1 stock split.[19] What is a stock split and what effect does it have on the company's stockholders' equity? What effect will it likely have on the market value of the company's stock? In light of your answers, do you think the stock split is positive for the company and for its stockholders?

LO 2, 8   **Interpreting Financial Reports: Stockholders' Equity**

C5. Refer to the **CVS Corporation** annual report in the Supplement to Chapter 16 to answer the following questions:

1. What type of capital stock does CVS have? What is the par value? How many shares were authorized, issued, and outstanding at the end of fiscal 2011?
2. **BUSINESS APPLICATION** ▶ What is the dividend yield (use average price of stock in last quarter) for CVS and its relationship to the investors' total return? (Round the average price to the nearest cent; round the dividend yield to the nearest tenth of a percent.) Does the company rely mostly on stock or on earnings for its stockholders' equity? (CVS's fourth quarter of 2011 high and low market prices were $41.35 and $32.28, respectively.)
3. **BUSINESS APPLICATION** ▶ Does the company have a stock option plan? To whom do the stock options apply? Do employees have significant stock options? Given the market price of the stock shown in the report, do these options represent significant value to the employees?

LO 3, 4, 5, 8   **Interpreting Financial Reports: Return on Equity, Treasury Stock, and Dividends Policy**

C6. Refer to the annual report of **CVS Corporation** and the financial statements of **Southwest Airlines Co.** in the Supplement to Chapter 16.

1. **BUSINESS APPLICATION** ▶ Compute the return on equity for both companies for fiscal 2011 and 2010. Total stockholders' equity for CVS and Southwest in 2009 was $35,768 million and $5,454 million, respectively.
2. **BUSINESS APPLICATION** ▶ Did either company purchase treasury stock during these years? How will the purchase of treasury stock affect return on equity and earnings per share?
3. Did either company issue stock during these years? What are the details?
4. Compare the dividend policy of the two companies.

Continuing Case: Annual Report Project

C7. Using the most recent annual report of the company you have chosen to study and that you have accessed online at the company's website, examine the balance sheet and accompanying notes of your company. Answer the following questions:

1. What percentage of total liabilities and stockholders' equity is stockholders' equity? What kinds of stock does the company have?
2. Is retained earnings a significant component of stockholders' equity?
3. Does the company have treasury stock? What effect does it have on total stockholders' equity?
4. **BUSINESS APPLICATION** ▶ Compute return on equity for your company.

CHAPTER 14
Long-Term Liabilities

Swan Manufacturing Company wants to expand its metal window division, but it does not have enough long-term capital to finance the project. As indicated in the data from Swan's balance sheets that follow, the company has, until now, been able to rely on the issuance of capital stock to take care of its financing needs. (Note the increase in stockholders' equity between 2013 and 2014.) Not included in the balance sheets are annual payments of $100,000 that Swan makes on long-term leases of various properties.

	2014	2013
Total current liabilities	$1,000,000	$ 800,000
Long-term debt	0	0
Total stockholders' equity	3,200,000	3,000,000
Total liabilities and stockholders' equity	$4,200,000	$3,800,000

Swan's management is now considering several options, including the issuance of long-term bonds, for financing expansion of the metal window division. In making its decision, management will have to assess how much debt the company should carry and how much risk it is undertaking by assuming long-term debt.

1. CONCEPT ▶ *How do the concepts of recognition, valuation, classification, and disclosure apply to long-term liabilities?*

2. ACCOUNTING APPLICATION ▶ *How are long-term bonds accounted for in Swan's records?*

3. BUSINESS APPLICATION ▶ *What should Swan consider in deciding to issue long-term debt?*

LEARNING OBJECTIVES

LO 1 Explain the concepts underlying long-term liabilities, and identify the types of long-term liabilities.

LO 2 Describe the features of a bond issue and the major characteristics of bonds.

LO 3 Record bonds issued at face value and at a discount or premium.

LO 4 Use present values to determine the value of bonds.

LO 5 Amortize bond discounts and bond premiums using the straight-line and effective interest methods.

LO 6 Account for the retirement of bonds and the conversion of bonds into stock.

LO 7 Record bonds issued between interest dates, and record year-end adjustments.

LO 8 Explain and demonstrate the accounting issues related to leases and pensions.

LO 9 Evaluate the decision to issue long-term debt, including analyzing long-term debt.

CONCEPTS

RELEVANT LEARNING OBJECTIVE

LO 1 Explain the concepts underlying long-term liabilities, and identify the types of long-term liabilities.

LO 1 Concepts Underlying Long-Term Liabilities

Profitable operations and short-term credit seldom provide sufficient funds for a growing business. Growth usually requires investments in long-term assets, research and development, and other activities to expand the business. To finance these assets and activities, the company needs funds that will be available for longer periods. Contributed capital by owners is one source of long-term funds. Long-term liabilities are another source. **Long-term liabilities** are debts and obligations that a company expects to satisfy in more than one year or beyond its normal operating cycle, whichever is longer. Managers must understand how long-term liabilities should be *recognized, valued, classified,* and *disclosed*.

Recognition

Generally accepted accounting principles require that long-term liabilities be *recognized* and recorded when an obligation occurs even though the obligation may not be due for many years. Some long-term liabilities, such as a note payable due in five years, are easy to identify, but others, such as promises to pay employees pensions after they retire, are more difficult. Nevertheless, recognition of long-term liabilities is important because managers and stockholders need to know how much a company is obligated to pay in the future.

Valuation

On the balance sheet, long-term liabilities are generally *valued* at the amount of money needed to pay the debt or at the fair market value of the goods or services to be delivered. The amount of most liabilities is definitely known (as with notes payable). Other long-term liabilities require judgment and estimates about conditions in the future (as with pension obligations).

Classification

In contrast to current liabilities, a liability is *classified* as long-term when it is due beyond one year or beyond the normal operating cycle. The distinction between current and long-term liabilities affects the evaluation of a company's liquidity. For example, when a portion of a long-term liability becomes due in the next year and will be paid out of current assets, it should be classified as a current liability. The investor or creditor can then see what current obligations will need to be paid soon.

Disclosure

Because of the complex nature of many long-term liabilities, extensive *disclosures* in the notes to the financial statements are often required. For example, the disclosures for long-term notes should include the balances, maturity dates, interest rates, and other features of the debts. Any special credit arrangements should also be disclosed. When estimates and judgments are involved, as with pension liabilities, these should also be disclosed.

Types of Long-Term Debt

To structure long-term financing to the best advantage of their companies, managers must know the characteristics of the various types of long-term debt. Long-term debt includes bonds payable, notes payable, mortgages, and other more complex obligations.

Bonds Payable Long-term **bonds payable** are the most common type of long-term debt. They can have many different characteristics, including the amount of interest, whether the company can elect to repay them before their maturity date, and whether they can be converted to common stock. We cover bonds in detail in later sections of this chapter.

Notes Payable Long-term **notes payable**, those that come due in more than one year, are also very common. They differ from bonds mainly in the way the contract with the creditor is structured. A long-term note is a promissory note that represents a loan from a bank or other creditor, whereas a bond is a more complex financial instrument that usually involves debt to many creditors. Analysts often do not distinguish between long-term notes and bonds because they have similar effects on the financial statements.

Mortgages Payable A **mortgage** is a long-term debt secured by real property. It is usually paid in equal monthly installments. Each monthly payment includes interest on the debt and a reduction in the debt. Exhibit 1 shows the first three monthly payments on a $100,000, 9 percent mortgage.

Exhibit 1
Monthly Payment Schedule on a $100,000, 9 Percent Mortgage

	A	B	C	D	E
Payment Date	Unpaid Balance at Beginning of Period	Monthly Payment	Interest for 1 Month at ¾% on Unpaid Balance* (¾% × A)	Reduction in Debt (B − C)	Unpaid Balance at End of Period (A − D)
June 1					$100,000
July 1	$100,000	$1,200	$750	$450	99,550
August 1	99,550	1,200	747	453	99,097
September 1	99,097	1,200	743	457	98,640
*Rounded					

© Cengage Learning 2014

Mortgages Payable

Transaction The mortgage was obtained on June 1, and the monthly payments are $1,200.

Analysis The journal entry to record the July 1 mortgage payment

▼ *decreases* the *Mortgage Payable* account with a debit of $450

▲ *increases* the *Mortgage Interest Expense* account with a debit of $750

▼ *decreases* the *Cash* account with a credit of $1,200

Application of Double Entry

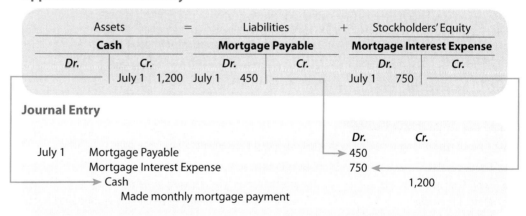

A	=	L	+	SE
−1,200		−450		−750

Journal Entry

		Dr.	Cr.
July 1	Mortgage Payable	450	
	Mortgage Interest Expense	750	
	Cash		1,200
	Made monthly mortgage payment		

Comment Notice from the entry and from Exhibit 1 that the July 1 payment represents the following:

- Interest expense: $100,000 × 0.09 × 1/12 = $750
- Reduction in debt: $1,200 − $750 = $450

Therefore, the July payment reduces the unpaid balance to $99,550. August's interest expense is slightly less than July's because of the decrease in the debt.

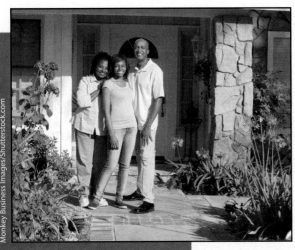

A mortgage is a type of long-term debt that is secured by real property. Most mortgages are paid in equal monthly installments.

Other Long-Term Obligations Other common long-term obligations consist of the following:

- **Long-term leases:** When a long-term lease has a term that corresponds closely to the life of the asset and, thus, is more like a purchase of an asset than a shorter-term lease, it is called a **capital lease**. In this case, a long-term asset with a corresponding long-term liability is *recognized* on the balance sheet. Long-term leases are covered in more detail later in the chapter.

- **Pension liabilities:** A liability arises from a contract that requires a company to make payments to its employees after they retire. Pension obligations are covered in more detail later in the chapter.

- **Other post-retirement benefits:** A liability arises from a contract that requires a company to provide medical and other benefits to its employees after they retire. *Recognition* and *valuation* of the liability requires estimates and assumptions about retirement age, mortality, and, most significantly, future trends in health care benefits.

- **Deferred income taxes:** A common long-term liability on the balance sheets of many companies, **deferred income taxes** are the result of using different accounting methods to calculate income taxes on the income statement and income tax liability on the income tax return. For instance, companies often use straight-line depreciation for financial reporting and an accelerated method to calculate income tax liability. Because straight-line depreciation is less than accelerated depreciation in the early years of an asset's life, the assumption is that the income taxes will eventually have to be paid. Thus, the difference is listed as deferred income taxes. Because companies try to manage their affairs to minimize income taxes paid, deferred income taxes can become quite large. For example, **Southwest Airlines** has deferred income taxes of about $2.6 billion or almost 23 percent of its total liabilities.[1]

Business Perspective
Post-Retirement Liabilities Affect Everyone

The rule requiring *recognition* of unfunded pension plans as liabilities impacts even government entities. Most government entities have defined benefit pension plans and provide post-retirement medical benefits. As a result, states, school districts, and municipalities are all encountering previously ignored pension and health care liabilities. For example, the state of New Jersey actually stopped setting aside funds to pay for health care in order to give a tax cut. No one added up the cost until the new accounting rule required it. The estimated cost to provide the health care promised to New Jersey's current and future retirees was $58 billion, or twice the state's annual budget.[2] These cases, while extreme, are not unusual, especially in light of the decrease in government tax collections during the recent recession. Citizens across the country will face tax increases to pay for these liabilities.

APPLY IT!

Match each type of long-term liability that follows with the statement to which it applies.

a. Bonds payable	1. Cost of health care after employees' retirement
b. Long-term notes payable	2. The most common type of long-term debt
c. Mortgage payable	3. The result of differences between accounting income and taxable income
d. Long-term lease	4. Debt that is secured by real estate
e. Pension liabilities	5. Promissory note that is due in more than one year
f. Other post-retirement benefits	6. Company requirement to make payments to its employees after they retire
g. Deferred income taxes	7. Often similar in form to purchasing a long-term asset

SOLUTION

1. f, 2. a, 3. g, 4. c, 5. b, 6. e, 7. d

TRY IT! SE1, SE2, E1A, E1B

ACCOUNTING APPLICATIONS

LO 2 The Nature of Bonds

A **bond** is a security, usually long term, representing money that a corporation borrows from the investing public. (The federal, state, and local governments also issue bonds to raise money, as do foreign countries.) A bond entails a promise to repay the amount borrowed, called the *principal,* on a specified date and to pay interest at a specified rate at specified times—usually semiannually. In contrast to stockholders, who are the owners of a corporation, bondholders are a corporation's creditors.

When a public corporation decides to issue bonds, it must submit the appropriate legal documents to the Securities and Exchange Commission (SEC) for permission to borrow the funds. The SEC reviews the corporation's financial health and the specific terms of the **bond indenture**, which is a contract that defines the rights, privileges, and limitations of the bondholders. The bond indenture generally describes such things as:

- the maturity date of the bonds
- interest payment dates
- the interest rate

It may also cover repayment plans and restrictions.

Once the bond issue is approved, the corporation has a limited time in which to issue the authorized bonds. As evidence of its debt to the bondholders, the corporation provides each of them with a **bond certificate**.

Bond Issue: Prices and Interest Rates

A **bond issue** is the total value of bonds issued at one time. For example, a $1,000,000 bond issue could consist of one thousand $1,000 bonds. The prices of bonds are stated in terms of a percentage of the face value, or principal, of the bonds. A bond issue quoted at 103½ means that a $1,000 bond costs $1,035 ($1,000 × 1.035). When a bond sells at exactly 100, it is said to sell at **face value** (or *par value*). When it sells below 100, it is said to sell at a *discount*; above 100, at a *premium*. For instance, a $1,000 bond quoted at 87.62 would be selling at a discount and would cost the buyer $876.20.

Face Interest Rate and Market Interest Rate Two interest rates relevant to bond prices are the face interest rate and the market interest rate.

- The **face interest rate** is the fixed rate of interest paid to bondholders based on the face value of the bonds. To allow time to file with the SEC, publicize the bond issue, and print the bond certificates, a company must decide in advance what the face interest rate will be. Most companies try to set the face interest rate as close as possible to the market interest rate.
- The **market interest rate** (or *effective interest rate*) is the rate of interest paid in the market on bonds of similar risk.* The market interest rate fluctuates daily. Because a company has no control over it, the market interest rate often differs from the face interest rate on the issue date.

Discounts and Premiums If the market interest rate fluctuates from the face interest rate before the issue date, the issue price will not equal the bonds' face value.

---

* At the time this chapter was written, the market interest rates on corporate bonds were volatile. Therefore, we use a variety of interest rates in our examples.

STUDY NOTE: *A bond sells at face value when the face interest rate of the bond is identical to the market interest rate for similar bonds on the date of issue. When the face interest and the market interest rates are different, a discount or premium arises.*

This fluctuation in market interest rate causes the bonds to sell at either a discount or a premium.

- A **discount** equals the excess of the face value over the issue price. The issue price will be less than the face value when the market interest rate is higher than the face interest rate.
- A **premium** equals the excess of the issue price over the face value. The issue price will be more than the face value when the market interest rate is lower than the face interest rate.

Discounts or premiums are contra-accounts that are subtracted from or added to bonds payable on the balance sheet.

Characteristics of Bonds

A bond indenture can be written to fit an organization's financing needs. As a result, the bonds issued in today's financial markets have many different features. We describe several of the more important features in the following paragraphs.

Unsecured and Secured Bonds   Bonds can be either unsecured or secured.

STUDY NOTE: *Do not confuse the terms* indenture *and* debenture. *An indenture is a bond contract, whereas a debenture is an unsecured bond. A debenture bond of a stable company actually might be a less risky investment than a secured bond of an unstable company.*

- **Unsecured bonds** (or *debenture bonds*) are issued on the basis of a corporation's general credit.
- **Secured bonds** carry a pledge of certain corporate assets as a guarantee of repayment. A pledged asset may be a specific asset, such as a truck, or a general category of asset, such as property, plant, and equipment.

Term and Serial Bonds   When all the bonds of an issue mature at the same time, they are called **term bonds**. For instance, a company may decide to issue $1,000,000 worth of bonds, all due 20 years from the date of issue.

When the bonds of an issue mature on different dates, they are called **serial bonds**. For example, suppose that a $1,000,000 bond issue calls for paying $200,000 of the principal every five years. This arrangement means that after the issuing company makes the first $200,000 payment, $800,000 of the bonds would remain outstanding for the next five years, $600,000 for the next five years, and so on. A company may issue serial bonds to ease the task of paying off what it owes on the bonds.

STUDY NOTE: *An advantage of issuing serial bonds is that the organization retires the bonds over a period of years, rather than all at once.*

Callable and Convertible Bonds   When bonds are callable and convertible, a company may be able to retire them before their maturity dates. When a company does retire a bond issue before its maturity date, it is called **early extinguishment of debt**. Doing so can be to a company's advantage.

Callable bonds give the issuer the right to buy back and retire the bonds before maturity at a specified **call price**, which is usually above face value. Callable bonds give a company flexibility in financing its operations. For example, if bond interest rates drop, the company can call the bonds and reissue debt at a lower interest rate. A company might also call its bonds if it has earned enough to pay off the debt, if the reason for having the debt no longer exists, or if it wants to restructure its debt to equity ratio. The bond indenture states the time period and the prices at which the bonds can be redeemed.

Convertible bonds allow the bondholder to exchange a bond for a specified number of shares of common stock. The face value of a convertible bond when issued is greater than the market value of the shares to which it can be converted. However, if the market price of the common stock rises above a certain level, the value of the bond rises in relation to the value of the common stock. Even if the stock price does not rise, the investor still holds the bond and receives both the periodic interest payments and the face value at the maturity date.

One advantage of issuing convertible bonds is that the interest rate is usually lower because investors are willing to give up some current interest in the hope that the value of the stock will increase and the value of the bonds will, therefore, also increase. In addition, if the bonds are both callable and convertible and the market value of the stock rises to a level at which the bond is worth more than face value, management can avoid repaying the bonds by calling them for redemption, thereby forcing the bondholders to convert their bonds into common stock. The bondholders will agree to convert because no gain or loss results from the transaction.

Registered and Coupon Bonds **Registered bonds** are issued in the names of the bondholders. The issuing organization keeps a record of the bondholders' names and addresses and pays them interest by check. Most bonds today are registered.

 Coupon bonds are not registered with the organization. Instead, they bear coupons stating the amount of interest due and the payment date. The bondholder removes the coupons from the bonds on the interest payment dates and presents them at a bank for collection.

APPLY IT!

Match each term that follows with the term that could be an alternate (or sometimes opposite) term.

a. Face interest rate	1. Secured
b. Discount	2. Coupon
c. Unsecured	3. Convertible
d. Term	4. Premium
e. Registered	5. Market interest rate
f. Callable	6. Serial

SOLUTION

1. c, 2. e, 3. f, 4. b, 5. a, 6. d

TRY IT! SE3, E2A, E2B

LO3 Accounting for the Issuance of Bonds

When the board of directors decides to issue bonds, it is not necessary to make an entry to record the SEC's authorization of the bond issue. However, most companies *disclose* the authorization in the notes to their financial statements. The note lists the number and *value* of bonds authorized, the interest rate, the interest payment dates, and the life of the bonds.

 If the face interest rate on the bonds issued equals the market interest rate, the bonds will sell at their face value. If the face rate is less than the market rate, the bonds will sell at a discount. If the face rate is greater than the market rate, the bonds will sell at a premium.

Bonds Issued at Face Value

Transaction Carrot Corporation issues $200,000 of 7 percent, five-year bonds on January 1, 2014, and sells them on the same date for their face value. The bond indenture states that interest is to be paid on January 1 and July 1 of each year.

Analysis The journal entry to record the issuance of the bonds at face value

▲ *increases* the *Cash* account with a debit

▲ *increases* the *Bonds Payable* account with a credit

Application of Double Entry

STUDY NOTE: *When calculating semiannual interest, multiply the annual rate by one-half year.*

Interest Expense Carrot pays interest on January 1 and July 1 of each year. Thus, Carrot would owe the bondholders $7,000 interest on July 1, 2014:

$$\text{Interest} = \text{Principal} \times \text{Rate} \times \text{Time}$$
$$= \$200,000 \times \frac{7}{100} \times 6/12 \text{ year}$$
$$= \$7,000$$

Analysis The journal entry to record the interest paid to the bondholders on each semiannual interest payment date (January 1 or July 1)

▲ *increases* the *Bond Interest Expense* account with a debit

▼ ▲ *decreases* the *Cash* account with a credit (or *increases* the *Interest Payable* account with a credit)

Application of Double Entry

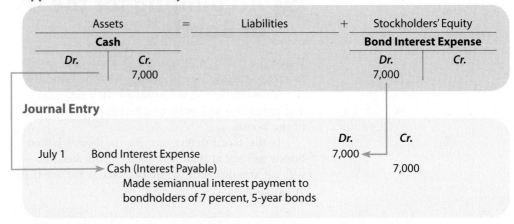

A* = **L** + **SE**
−7,000   −7,000
*Assumes cash paid.

Comment It is common for bond interest to be paid twice per year.

Bonds Issued at a Discount

Transaction Carrot issues $200,000 of 7 percent, five-year bonds at 95.9445 on January 1, 2014, when the market interest rate is 8 percent. In this case, the bonds are being issued at a discount because the market interest rate exceeds the face interest rate.

Analysis The entry to record the issuance of the bonds at a discount

▲ *increases* the *Cash* account with a debit for the amount of the bond issue less the discount

▲ *increases* the *Unamortized Bond Discount* account with a debit for the amount of discount

▲ *increases* the *Bonds Payable* account with a credit for the amount of the bond issued

Application of Double Entry

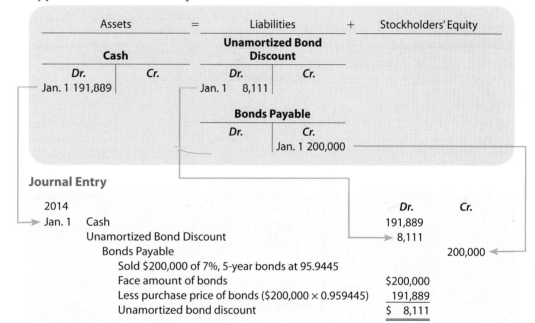

Assets	=	Liabilities	+	Stockholders' Equity

Cash

Dr.	Cr.
Jan. 1 191,889	

Unamortized Bond Discount

Dr.	Cr.
Jan. 1 8,111	

Bonds Payable

Dr.	Cr.
	Jan. 1 200,000

Journal Entry

A	=	L	+	SE
+191,889		−8,111		
		+200,000		

2014		Dr.	Cr.
Jan. 1	Cash	191,889	
	Unamortized Bond Discount	8,111	
	Bonds Payable		200,000

Sold $200,000 of 7%, 5-year bonds at 95.9445

Face amount of bonds	$200,000
Less purchase price of bonds ($200,000 × 0.959445)	191,889
Unamortized bond discount	$ 8,111

Comment If a balance sheet is prepared immediately after the bonds are issued at a discount, the liability for bonds payable is reported as follows.

Long-term liabilities

7% bonds payable, due 1/1/2019	$200,000	
Less unamortized bond discount	8,111	$191,889

Unamortized Bond Discount is a contra-liability account. Its balance is deducted from the face amount of the bonds to arrive at the carrying value, or present value, of the bonds. The bond discount is described as unamortized because it will be amortized (written off) over the life of the bonds.

Business Perspective
100-Year Bonds Are Not for Everyone

With interest rates on long-term debt at historically low levels, some companies attempt to lock in those low costs for long periods. In 1993, in a classic example, **The Walt Disney Company** aggressively issued $150 million of 100-year bonds at a yield of only 7.5 percent. Among the others that followed Walt Disney's lead by issuing 100-year bonds were the **Coca-Cola Company, Columbia HCA Healthcare, Bell South, IBM**, and even the People's Republic of China. Some analysts wondered if even Mickey Mouse could survive 100 years. In fact, in 2012, interest rates had dropped so far that Disney is now paying more than the market rate of only 5.7 percent. Investors who purchased the bonds have had a gain because the bonds are now selling at a premium at $132.[3]

Bonds Issued at a Premium

Transaction Carrot issues $200,000 of 7 percent, five-year bonds for $208,530 on January 1, 2014, when the market interest rate is 6 percent. This means that investors will purchase the bonds at 104.265 percent of their face value. In this case, the bonds are being issued at a premium because the face interest rate exceeds the market rate for similar investments.

Analysis The journal entry to record the bond issuance at a premium

▲ *increases* the *Cash* account for the amount of the bond issue plus the premium

▲ *increases* the *Unamortized Bond Premium* account for the amount of the premium

▲ *increases* the *Bonds Payable* account for the amount of the bond issue

Application of Double Entry

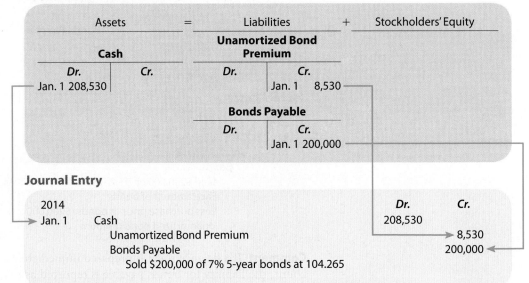

A	=	L	+	SE
+208,530		+8,530		
		+200,000		

Journal Entry

2014		Dr.	Cr.
Jan. 1	Cash	208,530	
	Unamortized Bond Premium		8,530
	Bonds Payable		200,000
	Sold $200,000 of 7% 5-year bonds at 104.265		

Comment Immediately after this entry is made, bonds payable would be presented on the balance sheet as follows.

Long-term liabilities

7% bonds payable, due 1/1/2019	$200,000	
Plus unamortized bond premium	8,530	$208,530

STUDY NOTE: *The carrying amount is always the face value of the bonds less the unamortized discount or plus the unamortized premium.*

Here, the carrying value of the bonds payable is $208,530, which equals the face value of the bonds plus the unamortized bond premium. This means that the purchasers were willing to pay a premium of $8,530 to buy these bonds because their face interest rate was higher than the market interest rate.

Bond Issue Costs

The costs of issuing bonds can amount to as much as 5 percent of a bond issue. These costs often include the fees of underwriters, whom corporations hire to take care of the details of marketing a bond issue. Because the issue costs benefit the whole life of a bond issue, they are spread over that period. It is generally accepted practice to establish a separate account for these costs and to amortize them over the life of the bonds.

Because issue costs decrease the amount of money a company receives from a bond issue, they have the effect of raising the discount or lowering the premium on the issue. Thus, bond issue costs can be spread over the life of the bonds through the amortization of a discount or premium. This method simplifies recordkeeping. In the rest of our discussion, we assume that all bond issue costs increase the discounts or decrease the premiums on bond issues.

APPLY IT!

Nico Foods is planning to issue $1,000,000 in long-term bonds. Depending on market conditions, Nico's CPA advises that the bonds could be issued at (a) 99, (b) 100, or (b) 101. Calculate the amount that Nico would receive under each alternative. Indicate whether it is at face value, a discount or a premium, and the amount of discount or premium of each.

SOLUTION

(a) $1,000,000 \times 0.99 = \$990,000$; a discount of $10,000

(b) $1,000,000 \times 1.00 = \$1,000,000$; at face value; no discount or premium

(c) $1,000,000 \times 1.01 = \$1,010,000$; a premium of $10,000

TRY IT! SE5, E6A, E6B

LO 4 Using Present Value to Value a Bond

A bond's value is determined by summing the following two present value amounts, based on concepts presented previously in Chapter 11:

- a series of fixed interest payments
- a single payment at maturity

As noted, the amount of interest a bond pays is fixed over its life. The market interest rate, on the other hand, varies from day to day and is the rate used to determine the bond's present value. Thus, the amount investors are willing to pay for a bond varies because the bond's present value changes as the market interest rate changes. In the next sections, we show how to calculate the present value of a bond when the market rate is above the face value and when it is below the face value. Exhibit 2 illustrates both examples.

Exhibit 2
Using Present Value to Value a
$20,000, 9 Percent, Five-Year Bond

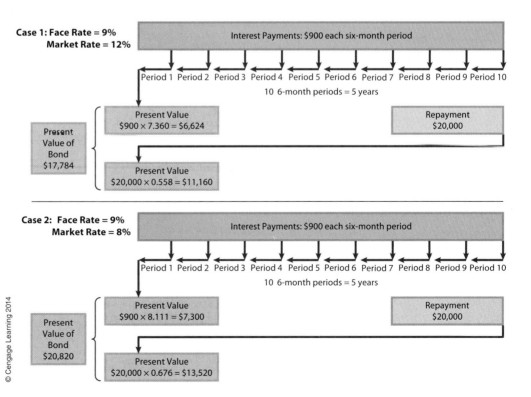

© Cengage Learning 2014

Market Rate Above Face Rate

Measure Calculate the present value of a bond when the market rate is above the face value.

Example A bond has a face value of $20,000 and pays fixed interest of $900 every six months (a 9 percent annual rate). The bond is due in five years. If the market interest rate today is 12 percent, what is the present value of the bond?

Table Computation Use Table 2 in Appendix B to calculate the present value of the periodic interest payments of $900, and use Table 1 in the same appendix to calculate the present value of the single payment of $20,000 at maturity. Because interest payments are made every six months, the compounding period is half a year. Thus, we have to convert the annual rate to a semiannual rate of 6 percent ($12\% \div 2$ six-month periods per year) and use ten periods (5 years $\times$ 2 six-month periods per year). The present value of the bond is therefore computed as follows.

Present value of 10 periodic payments at 6%: $900 $\times$ 7.360	
(from Table 2 Appendix B)	$ 6,624
Present value of a single payment at the end of 10 periods at 6%:	
$20,000 $\times$ 0.558 (from Table 1 in Appendix B)	11,160
Present value of $20,000 bond	$17,784

The market interest rate has increased so much since the bond was issued—from 9 percent to 12 percent—that the value of the bond today is only $17,784. That amount is all investors would be willing to pay at this time for a bond that provides income of $900 every six months and a return of the $20,000 principal in five years.

Market Rate Below Face Rate

Measure Calculate the present value of a bond when the market rate is below the face value.

Example Suppose the market interest rate on the bond described above falls to 8 percent (4 percent semiannually). The present value of the bond will be greater than the face value of $20,000.

Table Computation

Present value of 10 periodic payments at 4%: $900 $\times$ 8.111	
(from Table 2 in Appendix B)	$ 7,300
Present value of a single payment at the end of 10 periods at 4%:	
$20,000 $\times$ 0.676 (from Table 2 in Appendix B)	13,520
Present value of $20,000 bond	$20,820

APPLY IT!

Romero Company's $500,000 bond issue pays semiannual interest of $16,000 and is due in 20 years. The market interest rate is 6 percent. Calculate the present value of the bond issue.

SOLUTION

Present value of 40 periodic payments of 3% (from Table 2 in Appendix B):

$16,000 $\times$ 23.115 = $369,840

Present value of a single payment at the end of 20 years (40 periods) at 3% (from Table 1 in Appendix B):

$500,000 $\times$ 0.307 = 153,500

Total value of the bond issue = $523,340

TRY IT! SE4, E3A, E4A, E3B, E4B

LO 5 Amortization of Bond Discounts and Premiums

To record interest expense properly and ensure that the carrying value of bonds payable at maturity equals face value, it is necessary to systematically reduce the bond discount or premium—that is, to *amortize* them—over the life of the bonds. This can be accomplished by using either the straight-line method or the effective interest method.

Amortizing a Bond Discount

In one of our earlier examples, Carrot Corporation issued $200,000 of five-year bonds at a time when the market interest rate of 8 percent exceeded the face interest rate of 7 percent. The bonds sold for $191,889, resulting in an unamortized bond discount of $8,111.

Because it affects interest expense each year, the bond discount should be amortized over the life of the bond issue. In this way, the unamortized bond discount will decrease gradually over time, and the carrying value of the bond issue (face value less unamortized discount) will increase gradually. By the maturity date, the carrying value of the bond issue will equal its face value, and the unamortized bond discount will be zero.

Calculating Total Interest Expense When a corporation issues bonds at a discount, the market (or effective) interest rate that it pays is greater than the face interest rate on the bonds. The reason is that the interest expense is the stated interest payments *plus* the amount of the bond discount. That is, although the company does not receive the full face value of the bonds on issue, it still must pay back the full face value at maturity. The difference between the issue price and the face value must be added to the total interest payments to arrive at the actual interest expense.

Interest Expense for Bond Issued at a Discount

To have each year's interest expense reflect the market interest rate, the discount must be allocated over the remaining life of the bonds as an increase in the interest expense each period. Thus, interest expense for each period will exceed the actual payment of interest by the amount of the bond discount amortized over the period. This process of allocation is called *amortization of the bond discount.*

The total expense to Carrot of issuing its $200,000 bonds at a discount is as follows.

Cash to be paid to bondholders	
Face value at maturity	$200,000
Interest payments ($200,000 × 0.07 × 5 years)	70,000
Total cash paid to bondholders	$270,000
Less cash received from bondholders	191,889
Total interest cost	$ 78,111

Or, alternatively:

Interest payments ($200,000 × 0.07 × 5 years)	$ 70,000
Bond discount	8,111
Total interest cost	$ 78,111

The total interest cost of $78,111 is made up of $70,000 in interest payments and the $8,111 bond discount. Thus, the bond discount *increases* the interest paid on the bonds from the face interest rate to the market interest rate. The market (or effective) interest rate is the real interest cost of the bond over its life.

Some bonds do not require periodic interest payments. These bonds, called **zero coupon bonds**, are simply a promise to pay a fixed amount at the maturity date. They are issued at a large discount because the only interest that the buyer earns or the issuer pays is the discount. For example, a five-year, $200,000 zero coupon bond issued when the market rate is 10 percent, compounded semiannually, would sell for only $122,800. That amount is the present value of a single payment of $200,000 at the end of five years. The discount of $77,200 ($200,000 − $122,800) is the total interest expense, which is amortized over the life of the bond.

Straight-Line Method The **straight-line method** equalizes amortization of a bond discount for each interest period in the life of the bonds.

Amortizing a Bond Discount Using the Straight-Line Method

Transaction Using the Carrot Corporation example, the interest payment dates of the bond issue are January 1 and July 1 of each year, and the bonds mature in five years.

Bond Discount Amortized and Interest Expense With the straight-line method, the amount of the bond discount amortized and the interest expense for each semiannual period are calculated in four steps.

Step 1: Determine the total number of interest payments.

$$\text{Total Interest Payments} = \text{Interest Payments per Year} \times \text{Life of Bonds}$$
$$= 2 \times 5 = 10$$

Step 2: Determine the amount of bond discount amortization per period.

$$\text{Amortization of Bond Discount per Interest Period} = \frac{\text{Bond Discount}}{\text{Total Interest Payments}}$$

$$= \frac{\$8,111}{10}$$

$$= \$811^*$$

* Rounded

Step 3: Determine the cash interest payment.

$$\text{Cash Interest Payment} = \text{Face Value} \times \text{Face Interest Rate} \times \text{Time}$$
$$= \$200,000 \times 0.07 \times 6/12 = \$7,000$$

Step 4: Determine the interest expense per period.

$$\text{Interest Expense per Interest Period} = \text{Interest Payment} + \text{Amortization of Bond Discount}$$
$$= \$7,000 + \$811 = \$7,811$$

Analysis The journal entry to record the bond discount amortized and interest expense

▲ *increases* the *Bond Interest Expense* account with a debit for the amount calculated in Step 4,

▼ *decreases* the *Unamortized Bond Discount* account with a credit for the amount calculated in Step 2, and

▼▲ *decreases* the *Cash* account (or *increases* the *Interest Payable* account with a credit) for the amount in Step 3.

Application of Double Entry

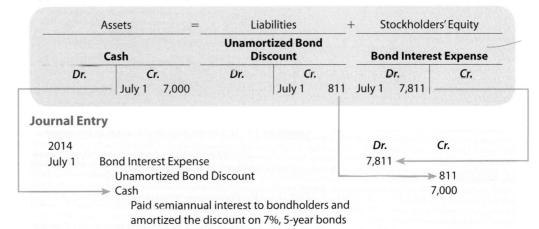

	Assets		=	Liabilities		+	Stockholders' Equity	
	Cash			**Unamortized Bond Discount**			**Bond Interest Expense**	
	Dr.	*Cr.*		*Dr.*	*Cr.*		*Dr.*	*Cr.*
		July 1 7,000			July 1 811		July 1 7,811	

Journal Entry

A*	=	L	+	SE
−7,000		+811		−7,811

*Assumes cash paid.

2014			*Dr.*	*Cr.*
July 1	Bond Interest Expense		7,811	
	Unamortized Bond Discount			811
	Cash			7,000
	Paid semiannual interest to bondholders and amortized the discount on 7%, 5-year bonds			

Comment Notice that the bond interest expense is $7,811, but the amount paid to the bondholders is the $7,000 face interest payment. The difference of $811 is the credit to Unamortized Bond Discount. This lowers the debit balance of Unamortized Bond Discount and raises the carrying value of the bonds payable by $811 each interest period. If no changes occur in the bond issue, this entry will be made every six months during the life of the bonds. When the bond issue matures, the Unamortized Bond Discount account will have a zero balance, and the carrying value of the bonds will be $200,000—exactly equal to the amount due the bondholders.

Although the straight-line method has long been used, it has a certain weakness. When it is used to amortize a discount, the carrying value goes up each period, but the bond interest expense stays the same; thus, the rate of interest falls over time. Conversely, when this method is used to amortize a premium, the rate of interest rises over time. The Accounting Principles Board, therefore, holds that the straight-line method should be used only when it does not lead to a material difference from the effective interest method.[4] A *material difference* is one that affects the evaluation of a company.

Effective Interest Method When the **effective interest method** is used to compute the interest and amortization of a bond discount, a constant interest rate is applied to the carrying value of the bonds at the beginning of each interest period. This constant rate is the market rate (i.e., the effective rate) at the time the bonds were issued. The amount amortized each period is the difference between the interest computed by using the market rate and the actual interest paid to bondholders.

Amortizing a Bond Discount Using the Effective Interest Method

Transaction Use the same facts for Carrot that we used earlier—a $200,000 bond issue at 7 percent, with a five-year maturity and interest to be paid twice a year. The market rate at the time the bonds were issued was 8 percent, so the bonds sold for $191,889, a discount of $8,111. Exhibit 3 shows the interest and amortization of the bond discount.

Carrying Value, Interest Expense, Discount Amortized, and Discount Unamortized The amounts in Exhibit 3 for period 1 were computed as follows. (Amounts are rounded to the nearest dollar.)

Column A The carrying value of the bonds is computed as:

$$\text{Face Value} - \text{Unamortized Discount} = \text{Carrying Value}$$

$$\$200,000 - \$8,111 = \$191,889$$

Column B The interest expense to be recorded is the effective interest, computed as:

$$\text{Carrying Value} \times \text{Market Interest Rate} \times \text{Interest Time Period} = \text{Interest Expense}$$
$$\$191,889 \times 0.08 \times 6/12 = \$7,676$$

Column C The interest paid in the period is a constant amount, computed as:

$$\text{Face Value} \times \text{Face Interest Rate} \times \text{Interest Time Period} = \text{Interest Payments}$$
$$\$200,000 \times 0.07 \times 6/12 = \$7,000$$

Column D The discount amortized is computed as:

$$\text{Interest Expense} - \text{Interest Payment} = \text{Amortized Discount}$$
$$\$7,676 - \$7,000 = \$676$$

Column E The unamortized bond discount is computed as:

$$\frac{\text{Discount at the Beginning}}{\text{of the Period}} - \frac{\text{Current Period}}{\text{Amortization}} = \frac{\text{Unamortized}}{\text{Discount}}$$
$$\$8,111 - \$676 = \$7,435$$

The unamortized discount decreases in each interest payment period because it is amortized as a portion of interest expense.

Column F The carrying value of the bonds at the end of the period is computed as:

$$\frac{\text{Carrying Value at}}{\text{Beginning of Period}} + \frac{\text{Amortization}}{\text{During Period}} = \frac{\text{Carrying Value at}}{\text{End of Period}}$$
$$\$191,889 + \$676 = \$192,565$$

Notice that the sum of the carrying value and the unamortized discount (column F + column E) always equals the face value of the bonds (for example, $192,565 + $7,435 = $200,000).

Analysis The journal entry to record the bond discount amortized and interest expense is exactly like the one when the straight-line method is used. However, the amounts debited and credited to the various accounts are different. This journal entry

▲ *increases* the *Bond Interest Expense* account with a debit for the amount calculated in column B

▼ *decreases* the *Unamortized Bond Discount* account with a credit for the amount calculated in column D

▼▲ *decreases* the *Cash* account (or *increases* the *Interest Payable* account) with a credit for the amount in column C

Application of Double Entry

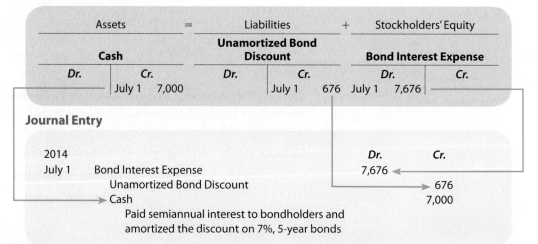

A*	=	L	+	SE
−7,000		+676		−7,676

*Assumes cash paid.

Journal Entry

2014		Dr.	Cr.
July 1	Bond Interest Expense	7,676	
	Unamortized Bond Discount		676
	Cash		7,000
	Paid semiannual interest to bondholders and amortized the discount on 7%, 5-year bonds		

Comment Although an interest and amortization table is useful because it can be prepared in advance for all periods, it is not necessary to have one to determine the amortization of a discount for any one interest payment period. It is necessary only to multiply the carrying value by the effective interest rate and subtract the interest payment from the result. For example, the amount of discount to be amortized in the seventh interest payment period is $855, calculated as:

$$(\text{Carrying Value} \times \text{Interest Rate}) - \text{Interest Payment} = \text{Amortized Discount}$$

$$(\$196,370 \times 0.04) - \$7,000 = \$855$$

Exhibit 3
Interest and Amortization Table of a Bond Discount: Effective Interest Method

	A	B	C	D	E	F
Semiannual Interest Period	Carrying Value at Beginning of Period	Semiannual Interest Expense at 8% to Be Recorded* (4% × A)	Semiannual Interest Payment to Bondholders (3½% × $200,000)	Amortization of Bond Discount (B − C)	Unamortized Bond Discount at End of Period (E − D)	Carrying Value at End of Period (A + D)
0					$8,111	$191,889
1	$191,889	$7,676	$7,000	$676	7,435	192,565
2	192,565	7,703	7,000	703	6,732	193,268
3	193,268	7,731	7,000	731	6,001	193,999
4	193,999	7,760	7,000	760	5,241	194,759
5	194,759	7,790	7,000	790	4,451	195,549
6	195,549	7,822	7,000	822	3,629	196,371
7	196,371	7,855	7,000	855	2,774	197,226
8	197,226	7,889	7,000	889	1,885	198,115
9	198,115	7,925	7,000	925	960	199,040
10	199,040	7,960**	7,000	960	—	200,000

* Rounded

** Last period's interest expense equals $7,960 ($7,000 + $960). It does not equal $7,962 ($199,040 × 0.04) because of the cumulative effect of rounding.

© Cengage Learning 2014

STUDY NOTE: *The bond interest increases each period because the carrying value of the bonds (the principal on which the interest is calculated) increases each period.*

Exhibit 4, which is based on the data in Exhibit 3, shows how the effective interest method affects the amortization of a bond discount. Notice that the carrying value at the beginning of Period 1 (the issue price) is initially less than the face value but that it gradually increases toward the face value over the life of the bond issue. Notice also that interest expense exceeds interest payments by the amount of the bond discount amortized. Interest expense increases gradually over the life of the bond because it is based on the gradually increasing carrying value (multiplied by the market interest rate).

Exhibit 4
Carrying Value and Interest Expense—Bonds Issued at a Discount

© Cengage Learning 2014

Amortizing a Bond Premium

Like a discount, a bond premium must be amortized over the life of the bonds so that it can be matched to its effects on interest expense during that period. In the following sections, we calculate Carrot's total interest expense and amortize its bond premium using the straight-line and effective interest methods.

Calculation of Total Interest Expense When bondholders pay more than face value for the bonds, the premium represents an amount that they will not receive at maturity. The premium is in effect a reduction, in advance, of the total interest paid on the bonds over the life of the bond issue. The total interest expense over the issue's life needs to be determined.

Interest Expense for a Bond Issued at a Premium

In our earlier example of bonds issued at a premium, Carrot issued $200,000 of five-year bonds when the market interest rate was 6 percent and the face interest rate was 7 percent. The bonds sold for $208,530, which resulted in an unamortized bond premium of $8,530 ($208,530 − $200,000).

The total interest expense over the bond issue's life is computed as follows.

Cash to be paid to bondholders	
Face value at maturity	$200,000
Interest payments ($200,000 × 0.07 × 5 years)	70,000
Total cash paid to bondholders	$270,000
Less cash received from bondholders	208,530
Total interest expense	$ 61,470

Alternatively, the total interest expense can be computed as follows:

Interest payments ($200,000 × 0.07 × 5 years)	$ 70,000
Less bond premium	8,530
Total interest expense	$ 61,470

Notice that the total interest payments of $70,000 exceed the total interest expense of $61,470 by $8,530, the amount of the bond premium.

Straight-Line Method Under the straight-line method, the bond premium is spread evenly over the life of the bond issue.

Amortizing a Bond Premium Using the Straight-Line Method

Transaction When bonds are issued at a premium, interest expense will be less than the interest rate on the bonds due to the amortization of the premium.

Bond Premium Amortized and Interest Expense As with bond discounts, the amount of the bond premium amortized and the interest expense for each semiannual period are computed in four steps.

Step 1: Determine the number of interest payments.

Total Interest Payments = Interest Payments per Year × Life of Bonds
$$= 2 \times 5 = 10$$

Step 2: Determine the amount of bond premium amortization per period.

$$\text{Amortization of Bond Premium per Interest Period} = \frac{\text{Bond Premium}}{\text{Total Interest Payments}}$$

$$= \frac{\$8,530}{10}$$

$$= \$853$$

Step 3: Determine the cash interest payment.

Cash Interest Payment = Face Value × Face Interest Rate × Time
$$= \$200,000 \times 0.07 \times 6/12 = \$7,000$$

Step 4: Determine the interest expense per period.

Interest Expense per Interest Period = Interest Payment − Amortization of Bond Premium
$$= \$7,000 - \$853 = \$6,147$$

Analysis The journal entry to record the bond premium amortized and interest expense

- ▲ *increases* the *Bond Interest Expense* account with a debit for the amount calculated in Step 4
- ▼ *decreases* the *Unamortized Bond Premium* account with a debit for the amount calculated in Step 2
- ▼▲ *decreases* the *Cash* account (or *increases* the *Interest Payable* account) with a credit for the amount in Step 3

Application of Double Entry

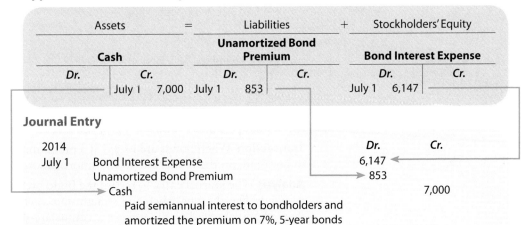

		A	=	L	+	SE
		−7,000		−853		−6,147

Journal Entry

		Dr.	Cr.
2014			
July 1	Bond Interest Expense	6,147	
	Unamortized Bond Premium	853	
	Cash		7,000
	Paid semiannual interest to bondholders and amortized the premium on 7%, 5-year bonds		

Comment Note that the bond interest expense is $6,147, but the amount that bondholders receive is the $7,000 face interest payment. The difference of $853 is the debit to Unamortized Bond Premium. This lowers the credit balance of the Unamortized Bond Premium account and the carrying value of the bonds payable by $853 each interest period. If the bond issue remains unchanged, the same entry will be made on every semiannual interest date over the life of the bond issue. When the bond issue matures, the balance in the Unamortized Bond Premium account will be zero, and the carrying value of the bonds payable will be $200,000—exactly equal to the amount due the bondholders.

Effective Interest Method Under the straight-line method, the effective interest rate changes constantly, because it is determined by comparing the fixed interest expense with a carrying value that changes as a result of amortizing the discount or premium. To apply a fixed interest rate over the life of the bonds based on the actual market rate at the time of the bond issue, one must use the effective interest method. With this method, the interest expense decreases slightly each period (see Exhibit 5, column B) because the amount of the bond premium amortized increases slightly (column D). This occurs because a fixed rate is applied each period to the gradually decreasing carrying value (column A).

Exhibit 5
Interest and Amortization Table of a Bond Premium: Effective Interest Method

	A	B	C	D	E	F
Semiannual Interest Period	Carrying Value at Beginning of Period	Semiannual Interest Expense at 6% to Be Recorded* (3% × A)	Semiannual Interest Payment to Bondholders (3½% × $200,000)	Amortization of Bond Premium (C – B)	Unamortized Bond Premium at End of Period (E – D)	Carrying Value at End of Period (A – D)
0					$8,530	$208,530
1	$208,530	$6,256	$7,000	$744	7,786	207,786
2	207,786	6,234	7,000	766	7,020	207,020
3	207,020	6,211	7,000	789	6,231	206,231
4	206,231	6,187	7,000	813	5,418	205,418
5	205,418	6,163	7,000	837	4,581	204,581
6	204,581	6,137	7,000	863	3,718	203,718
7	203,718	6,112	7,000	888	2,830	202,830
8	202,830	6,085	7,000	915	1,915	201,915
9	201,915	6,057	7,000	943	972	200,972
10	200,972	6,028**	7,000	972	—	200,000

* Rounded

** Last period's interest expense equals $6,028 ($7,000 – $972); it is actually equal to $6,029 ($200,972 × 0.03) but the difference is because of the cumulative effect of rounding.

Amortizing a Bond Premium Using the Effective Interest Method

Transaction When bonds are issued at a premium, interest expense will be less than the interest rate on the bonds due to the amortization of the premium.

Analysis The journal entry to record the bond premium amortized and interest expense is exactly like the one when the straight-line method is used. However, the amounts debited and credited to the various accounts are different. The journal entry to record the bond premium amortized and interest expense using the effective interest method

▲ *increases* the *Bond Interest Expense* account with a debit for the amount calculated in column B

▼ *decreases* the *Unamortized Bond Premium* account with a debit for the amount calculated in column D

▼▲ *decreases* the *Cash* account (or *increases* the *Interest Payable* account) with a credit for the amount in column C

Application of Double Entry

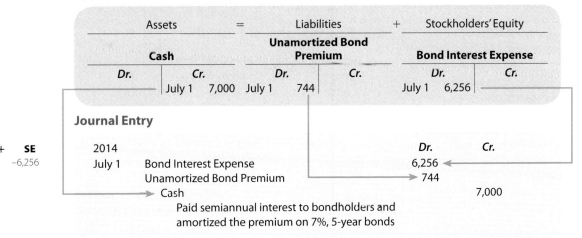

| | Assets | = | Liabilities | + | Stockholders' Equity |

Comment Note that the unamortized bond premium (column E) decreases gradually to zero as the carrying value decreases to the face value (column F). To find the amount of premium amortized in any one interest payment period, subtract the effective interest expense (the carrying value times the effective interest rate, column B) from the interest payment (column C). In semiannual interest period 5, for example, the amortization of premium is $837, which is calculated as follows.

Interest Payment − (Carrying Value × Interest Rate) = Amortized Premium

$$\$7{,}000 - (\$205{,}418 \times 0.03) = \$837$$

Exhibit 6, which is based on the data in Exhibit 5, shows how the effective interest method affects the amortization of a bond premium. Note that the carrying value at the beginning of Period 1 (issue price) is initially greater than the face value, but that it gradually decreases toward the face value over the bond issue's life. Also, the interest payments exceed interest expense by the amount of the premium amortized. Interest expense decreases gradually over the life of the bond because it is based on the gradually decreasing carrying value (multiplied by the market interest rate).

Exhibit 6
Carrying Value and Interest Expense—Bonds Issued at a Premium

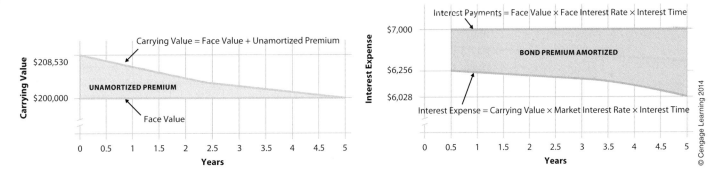

APPLY IT!

On June 1, Scott Corporation issues $4,000,000 of 8 percent, 20-year bonds at 97. Interest is payable semiannually, on May 31 and November 30. Scott's fiscal year ends on November 30.

1. Using the straight-line method of amortization, prepare journal entries for June 1 and November 30.

2. Using the effective interest method and assuming the same facts as above except that the market rate of interest is 9 percent, prepare the journal entry for November 30.

SOLUTION

1.

		Dr.	Cr.
June 1	Cash	3,880,000	
	Unamortized Bond Discount	120,000	
	Bonds Payable		4,000,000
	Issue of $4,000,000 of 8%,		
	20-year bonds at 97		
	$4,000,000 \times 0.97 = \$3,880,000$		
Nov. 30	Bond Interest Expense	163,000	
	Unamortized Bond Discount		3,000
	Cash		160,000
	Paid bondholders semiannual interest and		
	amortized the discount on 8%, 20-year bonds		
	$120,000 \div 40$ periods $= \$3,000$		
	$4,000,000 \times 0.04 = \$160,000$		

2.

		Dr.	Cr.
Nov. 30	Bond Interest Expense	174,600	
	Unamortized Bond Discount		14,600
	Cash		160,000
	Paid bondholders semiannual interest and		
	amortized the discount on 8%, 20-year bonds		
	$3,880,000 \times 0.045 = \$174,600$		
	$4,000,000 \times 0.04 = \$160,000$		

TRY IT! SE5, SE6, SE7, E6A, E7A, E8A, E9A, E12A, E16A, E6B, E7B, E8B, E9B, E12B, E16B

LO 6 Retirement and Conversion of Bonds

Two ways in which a company can reduce its bond debt are by:

- retiring the bonds or
- converting the bonds into common stock.

Retirement of Bonds

Usually, companies repay bonds when they are due—on the maturity date. However, as noted when discussing callable and convertible bonds, retiring a bond issue before its maturity date can be to a company's advantage. For example, when interest rates drop, many companies refinance their bonds at the lower rate. Although companies usually pay a premium for early extinguishment of bond debt, what they save on interest can make the refinancing cost-effective. Bonds may be retired either by calling the bonds or by buying them back from the bondholders on the open market. In either case, the transaction analysis is the same.

Retirement of Bonds

Transaction Suppose Carrot Corporation can call, or retire, at 105 the $200,000 of bonds it issued at a premium (104.265) on January 1, 2014, and that it decides to do so on July 1, 2017. The retirement thus takes place on the seventh interest payment date. Assume that the entry for the required interest payment and the amortization of the premium has been made.

Analysis The journal entry to record the retirement of the bonds

▼ *decreases* the *Bonds Payable* account with a debit for the face amount to remove the bonds from the balance sheet

▼ *decreases* the *Unamortized Bond Premium* account with a debit (or the Unamortized Bond Discount account with a credit) to remove the related premium (or discount) with a credit from the records

▼ *decreases* the *Cash* account for the amount required to call the bonds

▲ *increases* the *Loss on Retirement of Bonds* account with a debit (or *increases* the *Gain on Retirement of Bonds* account with a credit) for the net amount

Application of Double Entry

Journal Entry

A	=	L	+	SE	
−210,000		−200,000		−7,170	
		−2,830			

2017		Dr.	Cr.
July 1	Bonds Payable	200,000	
	Unamortized Bond Premium	2,830	
	Loss on Retirement of Bonds	7,170	
	Cash		210,000
	Retired 7% bonds at 105		

Comment In this entry, the cash paid is the face value times the call price ($200,000 × 1.05 = $210,000). The unamortized bond premium can be found in column E of Exhibit 5 on the seventh period line. The loss on retirement of bonds occurs because the call price of the bonds is greater than the carrying value ($210,000 − $202,830 = $7,170). Sometimes, a rise in the market interest rate can cause the market value of bonds to fall considerably below their face value. If it has the cash to do so, the company may find it advantageous to purchase the bonds on the open market and retire them. For example, if Carrot were able to purchase the above bonds on the open market at 85, a gain would be *recognized* for the difference between the purchase price of the bonds and the carrying value of the retired bonds.

Conversion of Bonds

When a bondholder converts bonds to common stock, the company records the common stock at the carrying value of the bonds. The bond liability and the unamortized discount or premium are written off the books. For this reason, no gain or loss on the transaction is recorded.

Conversion of Bonds to Common Stock

Transaction Suppose that Carrot Corporation does not call its bonds on July 1, 2017. Instead, the corporation's bondholders decide to convert all their bonds to $8 par value common stock under a convertible provision of 40 shares of common stock for each $1,000 bond.

Analysis The journal entry to record the conversion of bonds to common stock

▼ *decreases* the *Bonds Payable* account with a debit for the face amount to remove the bonds from the balance sheet

▼ *decreases* the *Unamortized Bond Premium* account with a debit (or the *Unamortized Bond Discount* account with a credit) to remove the related premium (or discount) from the records

▲ *increases* the *Common Stock* account for the par value of the shares

▲ *increases* the *Additional Paid-in Capital* account for the amount required to balance the entry

Application of Double Entry

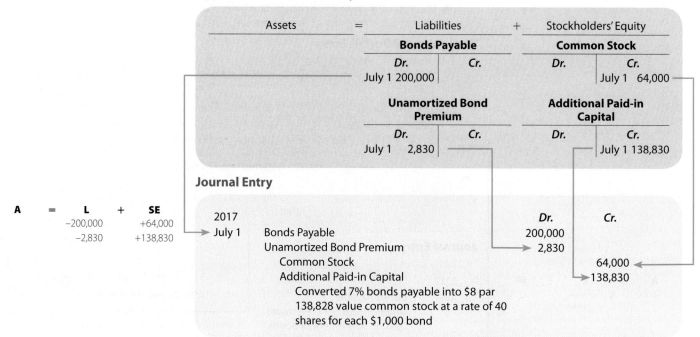

Comment The unamortized bond premium is found in column E of Exhibit 5 on the seventh period line. At a rate of 40 shares for each $1,000 bond, 8,000 shares will be issued, with a total par value of $64,000 (8,000 × $8). The Common Stock account is credited for the amount of the par value of the stock issued. In addition, Additional Paid-in Capital is credited for the difference between the carrying value of the bonds and the par value of the stock issued ($202,830 − $64,000 = $138,830). No gain or loss is recorded.

APPLY IT!

Assume that in the Carrot example of retirement in this section the company is able to buy the $200,000 in bonds on the open market at 95 and retire them. The Unamortized Bond Premium remains at $2,830. Prepare the journal entry to record the purchase and retirement on July 1, 2017.

SOLUTION

2017		Dr.	Cr.
July 1	Bonds Payable	200,000	
	Unamortized Bond Premium	2,830	
	Gain on Retirement of Bonds		12,830
	Cash		190,000
	Retired 7% bonds at 95		

TRY IT! SE8, SE9, E10A, E11A, E13A, E10B, E11B, E13B

LO7 Other Bonds Payable Issues

Among the other issues involved in accounting for bonds payable are the sale of bonds between interest payment dates and the year-end accrual of bond interest expense.

Sale of Bonds Between Interest Dates

Although corporations may issue bonds on an interest payment date, as in the previous examples, they often issue them between interest payment dates. When that is the case, they generally collect from the investors the interest that would have accrued for the partial period preceding the issue date. At the end of the first interest period, they pay the interest for the entire period. In other words, the interest collected when bonds are sold is returned to investors on the next interest payment date.

There are two reasons for following this procedure:

■ From a practical standpoint, if a company issued bonds on several different days and did not collect the accrued interest, records would have to be maintained for each bondholder and date of purchase. The interest due each bondholder would, therefore, have to be computed for a different time period. Clearly, this procedure would involve large bookkeeping costs. On the other hand, if accrued interest is collected when the bonds are sold, the corporation can pay the interest due for the entire period on the interest payment date, thereby eliminating the extra computations and costs.

■ When accrued interest is collected in advance, the amount is subtracted from the full interest paid on the interest payment date. Thus, the resulting interest expense represents the amount for the time the money was borrowed.

Bonds Issued Between Interest Payment Dates

Transaction Suppose Carrot Corporation sold $200,000 of 7 percent, five-year bonds for face value on May 1, 2014, rather than on January 1, 2014. Carrot pays interest on January 1 and July 1 of each year.

Analysis The journal entry to record bonds sold between interest dates

▲ *increases* the *Cash* account for the amount the bond issue plus the accrued interest

▼ *decreases* the *Bond Interest Expense* account for the amount of the accrued interest

▲ *increases* the *Bonds Payable* account for the amount of the bond issue

Application of Double Entry

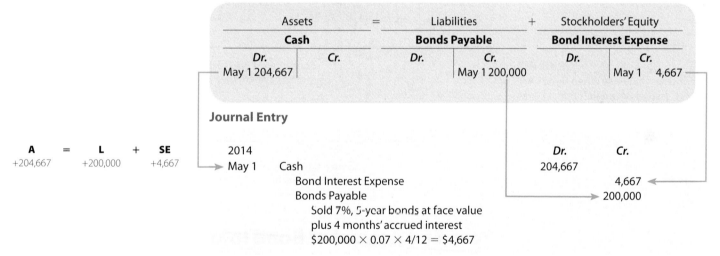

Comment Cash is debited for the amount received, $204,667 (the face value of $200,000 plus four months' accrued interest of $4,667). Bond Interest Expense is credited for the $4,667 of accrued interest, and Bonds Payable is credited for the face value of $200,000.

Interest Payment for Bonds Issued Between Interest Payment Dates

Transaction On July 1, the first semiannual interest payment is made.

Analysis The journal entry to record the first semiannual interest payment

▲ *increases* the *Bond Interest Expense* account for the amount of interest paid

▼ *decreases* the *Cash* account for the amount of cash paid

Application of Double Entry

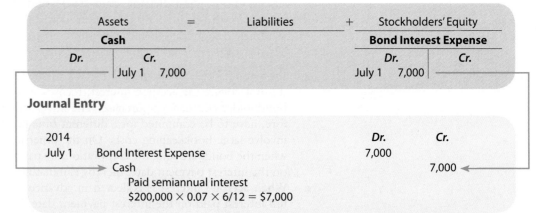

A = **L** + **SE**
−7,000   −7,000

Comment Notice that the entire half-year interest is debited to Bond Interest Expense and credited to Cash because Carrot pays bond interest every six months, in full six-month amounts. Exhibit 7 illustrates this process. The actual interest expense for the two months that the bonds were outstanding is $2,333. This amount is the net balance of the $7,000 debit to Bond Interest Expense on July 1 less the $4,667 credit to Bond Interest Expense on May 1. The following T account clearly shows these steps:

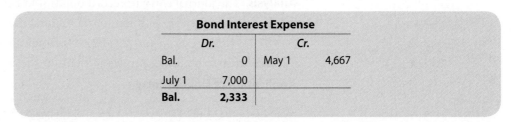

Exhibit 7
Interest Expense When Bonds Are Issued Between Interest Dates

© Cengage Learning 2014

Year-End Accrual of Bond Interest Expense

Bond interest payment dates rarely correspond with a company's fiscal year. Therefore, an adjustment must be made to accrue the interest expense on the bonds from the last interest payment date to the end of the fiscal year. In addition, any discount or premium on the bonds must be amortized for the partial period.

Year-End Accrual of Bond Interest Expense When Year-End Falls Between Bond Interest Dates

Transaction In the example of bonds issued at a premium, Carrot Corporation issued $200,000 of bonds on January 1, 2014, at 104.265 percent of face value. Suppose Carrot's fiscal year ends on September 30, 2014. In the period since the interest payment and amortization of the premium on July 1, three months' worth of interest has accrued.

Analysis Under the effective interest method, the adjusting entry

▲ *increases* the *Bond Interest Expense* account

▼ *decreases* the *Unamortized Bond Premium* account

▲ *increases* the *Bond Interest Payable* account

Application of Double Entry

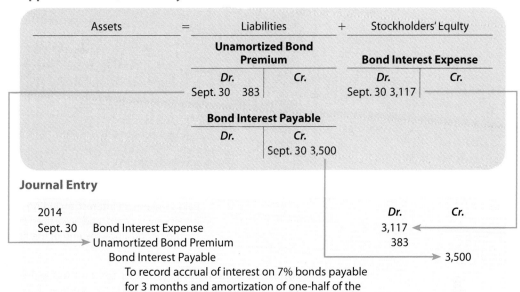

Assets	=	Liabilities	+	Stockholders' Equity

Unamortized Bond Premium

Dr.	Cr.
Sept. 30 383	

Bond Interest Expense

Dr.	Cr.
Sept. 30 3,117	

Bond Interest Payable

Dr.	Cr.
	Sept. 30 3,500

Journal Entry

A = L + SE
    −383   −3,117
   +3,500

2014		Dr.	Cr.
Sept. 30	Bond Interest Expense	3,117	
	Unamortized Bond Premium	383	
	Bond Interest Payable		3,500
	To record accrual of interest on 7% bonds payable for 3 months and amortization of one-half of the premium for the second interest payment period		

Comment This entry covers one-half of the second interest period. Unamortized Bond Premium is debited for $383, which is one-half of $766, the amortization of the premium for the second period from Exhibit 5. Bond Interest Payable is credited for $3,500, which is three months' interest on the face value of the bonds ($200,000 × 0.07 × 3/12). Bond Interest Expense is debited for $3,117 ($3,500 − $383), which is the bond interest expense for the three-month period (or one-half of $6,234).

Payment of Interest When the Interest Payment Date Falls After Year-End Accrual

Transaction On the interest payment date of January 1, 2015, Carrot Corporation makes the entry to pay the bondholders and amortize the premium.

Analysis The journal entry to pay the bondholders and amortize the premium

▲ *increases* the *Bond Interest Expense* account

▼ *decreases* the *Bond Interest Payable* account

▼ *decreases* the *Unamortized Bond Premium* account

▼ *decreases* the *Cash* account

Application of Double Entry

Comment One-half ($3,500) of the amount paid ($7,000) was accrued on September 30. Unamortized Bond Premium is debited for $383, the remaining amount to be amortized for the period ($766 − $383). The resulting bond interest expense is the amount that applies to the three-month period from October 1 to December 31.

Bond discounts are recorded at year-end in the same way as bond premiums. The difference is that the amortization of a bond discount increases interest expense instead of decreasing it.

APPLY IT!

Flis Associates sold $1,000,000 in bonds on April 1. The bonds carry a face interest rate of 8 percent, which is to be paid on January 1 and July 1. Prepare journal entries for (a) the issue of the bonds on April 1 at 100 and (b) the interest payment on July 1. (c) How much was the total interest expense for the first six months of the year?

SOLUTION

(a) Apr. 1	Cash	1,020,000	
	Bonds Payable		1,000,000
	Bond Interest Expense		20,000
	Issuance of 8 percent bonds		
(b) July 1	Bond Interest Expense	40,000	
	Cash		40,000
	Interest payment		

(c) Total interest expense: $40,000 − $20,000 = $20,000

TRY IT! SE7, SE10, E12A, E14A, E15A, E16A, E12B, E14B, E15B, E16B

LO 8 Long-Term Leases

A company can obtain an operating asset in the following ways:

- **By borrowing money and buying the asset:** When a company uses this method, it records the asset and liability at the amount paid, and the asset is subject to periodic depreciation.
- **By renting the asset on a short-term lease:** When a company uses this method, the risks of ownership of the asset remain with the lessor (the owner), and the lease

is shorter than the asset's useful life. This type of agreement is called an **operating lease**. Payments on operating leases are properly treated as rent expense.

- **By obtaining the asset on a long-term lease:** This is one of the fastest-growing ways of financing plant assets in the United States today. A long-term lease on a plant asset has several advantages. It requires no immediate cash payment, the rental payment is deducted in full for tax purposes, and it costs less than a short-term lease. Acquiring the use of plant assets under long-term leases does create several accounting challenges, however.

Capital Leases Long-term leases may be carefully structured, as they are by companies like **CVS**, so that they can be accounted for as operating leases. However, accounting standards require that a long-term lease be treated as a capital lease when it meets *all* of the following conditions:

- It cannot be canceled.
- Its duration is about the same as the useful life of the asset.
- It stipulates that the lessee has the option to buy the asset at a nominal price at the end of the lease.

STUDY NOTE: *A capital lease is, in substance, an installment purchase, and the leased asset and related liability must be recognized at their present value.*

A capital lease is, thus, more like a purchase or sale on installment than a rental. The lessee in a capital lease should record an asset, depreciation on the asset, and a long-term liability equal to the present value of the total lease payments during the lease term.[5] Much like a mortgage payment, each lease payment consists partly of interest expense and partly of repayment of debt.

To illustrate capital leases, we will use Urban Manufacturing Company, which enters into a long-term lease for a machine. The lease terms call for an annual payment of $8,000 for six years, which approximates the useful life of the machine. At the end of the lease period, the title to the machine passes to Urban. This lease is clearly a capital lease and should be recorded as an asset and a liability. Present value techniques can be used to place a value on the asset and on the corresponding liability in a capital lease. An example of a payment schedule for a capital lease is presented in Exhibit 8.

Exhibit 8

Payment Schedule on an 8 Percent Capital Lease

	A	B	C	D
Year	Lease Payment	Interest (8%) on Unpaid Obligation* (D × 8%)	Reduction of Lease Obligation (A – B)	Balance of Lease Obligation (D – C)
Beginning				$36,984
1	$ 8,000	$ 2,959	$ 5,041	31,943
2	8,000	2,555	5,445	26,498
3	8,000	2,120	5,880	20,618
4	8,000	1,649	6,351	14,267
5	8,000	1,141	6,859	7,408
6	8,000	592**	7,408	—
	$48,000	$11,016	$36,984	

* Rounded

** The last year's interest equals $592 ($8,000 − $7,408). It does not exactly equal $593 ($7,408 × $\frac{8}{100}$ × 1) because of the cumulative effect of rounding.

© Cengage Learning 2014

Capital Lease Recognition

Transaction Urban's interest cost on the unpaid part of its obligation is 8 percent. Using the factor for 8 percent and six periods in Table 2 in Appendix B, the present value of the lease payments can be computed as follows.

Periodic Payment × Factor = Present Value
$8,000 × 4.623 = $36,984

Analysis The journal entry to record the lease

▲ *increases* the *Capital Lease Equipment* account with a debit

▲ *increases* the *Capital Lease Obligations* account with a credit

Application of Double Entry

A = L + SE
+36,984   +36,984

Comment Capital Lease Equipment is *classified* as a long-term asset. Capital Lease Obligations is *classified* as a long-term liability.

Depreciation Recorded

Transaction Each year, Urban must record depreciation on the leased asset. Assume straight-line depreciation, a six-year life, and no residual value.

Analysis The journal entry to record depreciation

▲ *increases* the *Depreciation Expense—Capital Lease Equipment* account with a debit

▲ *increases* the contra-asset account *Accumulated Depreciation—Capital Lease Equipment* with a credit

Application of Double Entry

A = L + SE
−6,164   −6,164

Comment The depreciation expense is computed by dividing the present value of the capital lease by the term of the lease ($36,984 ÷ 6 = $6,164).

Lease Payment

Transaction Refer to the data in Exhibit 8. Urban makes the first payment on its capital lease.

Analysis The journal entry to record the first lease payment

- ▲ *increases* the *Interest Expense* account with a debit
- ▼ *decreases* the *Capital Lease Obligations* account with credit
- ▼ *decreases* the *Cash* account with a credit

Application of Double Entry

Assets	=	Liabilities	+	Stockholders' Equity
Cash		**Capital Lease Obligations**		**Interest Expense**
Dr. / Cr.		Dr. / Cr.		Dr. / Cr.
8,000 (Cr.)		5,041 (Dr.)		2,959 (Dr.)

Journal Entry

A	=	L	+	SE
–8,000		–5,041		–2,959

	Dr.	Cr.
Interest Expense (column B)	2,959	
Capital Lease Obligations (column C)	5,041	
Cash (column A)		8,000
Made payment on capital lease		

Comment The interest expense for each year is computed by multiplying the interest rate (8 percent) by the amount of the remaining lease obligation. Exhibit 8 shows these calculations. This example suggests why companies are motivated to engage in off-balance-sheet financing for leases. By structuring long-term leases so that they can be accounted for as operating leases, companies avoid recording them on the balance sheet as long-term assets and liabilities. This practice, which is legal, not only improves the debt to equity ratio by showing less debt on the balance sheet, but also improves the return on assets by reducing the total assets.

International Perspective

IFRS Recording Liabilities and Assets Will Not Look the Same Under IFRS

Under U.S. GAAP, most leases are accounted for as operating expenses. Current lease payments are generally recorded as operating expenses, and future lease obligations appear as described in the footnotes to the financial statements. Under International Financial Reporting Standards (IFRS), lease obligations are recorded at fair value as a liability, and the related debt is recorded as an asset. Fair value is usually measured at the discounted present value of the future lease payments. The result is that more assets and liabilities will appear to be greater under IFRS than under GAAP.

Pension Liabilities

Most employees of medium-sized and large companies are covered by a **pension plan**, a contract that requires a company to pay benefits to its employees after they retire. Some companies pay the full cost of the pension plan; but in many companies, employees share the cost by contributing part of their salaries or wages. The contributions from employer and employees are usually paid into a **pension fund**, which is invested on behalf of the employees. Pension benefits typically consist of monthly payments to retired employees and other payments upon disability or death.

Employers whose pension plans do not have sufficient assets to cover the present value of their pension obligations must record the amount of the shortfall as a liability. If a pension plan has sufficient assets to cover its obligations, no balance sheet reporting is required or permitted.

There are two kinds of pension plans:

- **Defined contribution plan:** The employer makes a fixed annual contribution, usually a percentage of the employee's gross pay. The amount of the contribution is specified in an agreement between the company and the employees. Retirement payments vary depending on how much the employee's retirement account earns. Employees usually control their own investment accounts, can make additional contributions of their own, and can transfer the funds if they leave the company. Examples of defined contribution plans include 401(k) plans, profit-sharing plans, and employee stock ownership plans (ESOPs). Companies prefer defined contribution plans because the employees assume the risk that their pension assets will earn a sufficient return to meet their retirement needs.

- **Defined benefit plan:** The employer contributes an amount annually to fund estimated future pension liability. The exact amount of the liability will not be known until the retirement or death of the current employees. Although the amount of future benefits is fixed, the annual contributions vary depending on assumptions about how much the pension fund will earn.

Annual pension expense under a defined contribution plan is simple and predictable. Pension expense equals the fixed amount of the annual contribution. In contrast, annual expense under a defined benefit plan is one of the most complex topics in accounting. The intricacies are reserved for advanced courses, but in concept, the procedure is simple. Computation of the annual expense takes into account the estimation of such factors as the average remaining service life of active employees, the long-run return on pension plan assets, and future salary increases. An accounting standard requires companies and other entities with defined benefit plans not backed by a fund sufficient to pay them to record the unfunded portion as a liability.[6] For many companies this can amount to millions or even billions of dollars.

Because pension expense under a defined benefit plan is not predictable and can vary from year to year, many companies are adopting the more predictable defined contribution plans.

Long-Term Liabilities and the Financial Statements

As presented in Exhibit 9, long-term liabilities arise from a variety of financing and obligations. Long-term liabilities are amounts to be paid more than one year after the balance sheet date.

Exhibit 9
Long-Term Liabilities on the Balance Sheet

Balance Sheet
December 31, 2014

Assets	Liabilities
Current assets	Current liabilities
Investments	Long-term liabilities:
Property, plant, and equipment	Bonds payable
Intangible assets	Notes payable
	Mortgage payable
	Capital lease obligation
	Pension and post-retirement liabilities
	Deferred income taxes
	Total long-term liabilities
	Total liabilities
	Stockholders' Equity
	Contributed capital
	Retained earnings
	Total stockholders' equity

Total Assets = Total Liabilities + Stockholders' Equity

© Cengage Learning 2014

APPLY IT!

Eureka Corporation has leased a machine that has a useful life of 10 years. The terms of the lease are payments of $60,000 per year for 10 years. Eureka currently is able to borrow money at a long-term interest rate of 12 percent. Calculate (a) the present value of the lease and (b) prepare the journal entry to record the lease agreement.

SOLUTION

(a) Present value of the lease is equal to periodic payment × factor (Table 2 in Appendix B: 12%, 10 periods)

$60,000 × 5.650 = $339,000

(b) The journal entry to record the lease is:

Capital Lease Machine	339,000	
Capital Lease Obligations		339,000
To record the lease contract		

TRY IT! SE11, E17A, E17B

SECTION 3

BUSINESS APPLICATIONS
- Evaluate a company's level of debt
  - Debt to equity ratio
  - Interest coverage ratio

RELEVANT LEARNING OBJECTIVE

LO 9 Evaluate the decision to issue long-term debt, including analyzing long-term debt.

BUSINESS APPLICATIONS

LO 9 Management Issues Related to Long-Term Debt Financing

A key decision for management is whether to rely solely on stockholders' equity for long-term funds or to rely partially on long-term debt. Some companies, such as **Microsoft** and **Apple**, do not issue long-term debt; but like **CVS** and **Southwest Airlines**, most companies find it useful to do so. To make a decision, it is important to know the advantages and disadvantages of issuing long-term debt and to analyze the risks of the issue of the company's finances. Further, it is also important to understand the long-term effects of more complex obligations such as leases and pensions.

Evaluating the Decision to Issue Long-Term Debt

Because long-term debt must be paid at maturity and usually requires periodic payments of interest, issuing common stock has two advantages over issuing long-term debt:

- **Permanent financing:** Common stock does not have to be paid back.
- **Dividend payment optional:** Dividends on common stock are normally paid only if the company earns sufficient income.

Issuing long-term debt, however, has the following advantages over issuing common stock:

- **Stockholder control:** When a corporation issues long-term debt, common stockholders do not relinquish any of their control over the company because bondholders and other creditors do not have voting rights. In contrast, when a corporation issues additional shares of common stock, the votes of the new stockholders may force current stockholders and management to give up some control.
- **Tax advantage:** The interest on debt is tax-deductible, whereas dividends on common stock are not. For example, if a corporation pays $100,000 in interest and its income tax rate is 30 percent, its net cost will be $70,000 because it will save $30,000 on income taxes. To pay $100,000 in dividends on common stock, the corporation would have to earn $142,857 before income taxes [$100,000 \div (1 - 0.30)].
- **Financial leverage:** If a corporation earns more from the funds it raises by incurring long-term debt than it pays in interest on the debt, the excess will increase its earnings for the stockholders. This concept is called **financial leverage** (or *trading on equity*). For example, if a company earns 10 percent on a $1,000,000 investment financed by long-term 8 percent notes, it will earn $20,000 before income taxes ($100,000 – $80,000). The debt to equity ratio, which we will discuss later in this chapter, is considered an overall measure of a company's financial leverage.

Despite these advantages, debt financing is not always in a company's best interest. It may entail the following:

- **Financial risk:** A high level of debt exposes a company to financial risk. A company whose plans for earnings do not pan out, whose operations are subject to the ups and downs of the economy, or whose cash flow is weak may be unable to pay the principal amount of its debt at the maturity date or even to make periodic interest payments. Creditors can then force the company into bankruptcy. **TWA**, **Continental Airlines**, and **United Airlines** filed for bankruptcy protection because they could not make payments on their long-term debt and other liabilities. (While in bankruptcy, they restructured their debt and interest payments: TWA sold off its assets; Continental and United subsequently came out of bankruptcy. The latter two airlines have since merged.)

Business Perspective
How Does Debt Affect a Company's Ability to Borrow?

Credit ratings by agencies like **Standard & Poor's (S&P)** reflect the fact that the greater a company's debt, the greater its financial risk. S&P rates companies from AAA (best) to CCC (worst) based on various factors, including a company's debt to equity ratio, as shown below.

Rating	AAA	AA	A	BBB	BB	B	CCC
Debt to Equity Ratio*	4.5	34.1	42.9	47.9	59.8	76.0	75.7

*Averages of companies with similar ratings. Ratings also take into effect other factors, such as the companies' profitability, interest coverage, and stability.

These ratings affect not only how much a company can borrow but also what the interest will cost. The lower its rating, the more a company must pay in interest, and vice versa.

For a company in a heavily debt-laden industry such as the auto industry, a change in credit rating can mean millions of dollars. For instance, when S&P lowered **General Motors'** credit ratings to "junk status" (i.e., BB), it meant that GM had to pay 1 or more percentage points in additional interest. On GM's $291 billion debt, this amounted to about $2–$3 billion.[7] S&P proved to be correct in its downgrade, as GM subsequently went bankrupt and had to be bailed out by the federal government.

■ **Negative financial leverage:** Financial leverage can work against a company if the earnings from its investments do not exceed its interest payments. For example, many small retail companies failed in recent years because they relied too heavily on debt financing before developing sufficient resources to ensure their survival.

Evaluating Long-Term Debt

Financial leverage is advantageous as long as a company is able to make timely interest payments and repay the debt at maturity. Because failure to do so can force a company into bankruptcy, a company must assess the financial risk involved. Financial risk is measured by the debt to equity ratio and the interest coverage ratio.

Debt to Equity Ratio To assess how much debt to carry, managers compute the **debt to equity ratio**, which shows the amount of debt a company carries in relation to its stockholders' equity. The higher this ratio, the greater the company's financial risk. Using data from Swan Manufacturing Company presented in the chapter opener, we can compute its debt to equity ratio in 2014 as follows (in thousands).

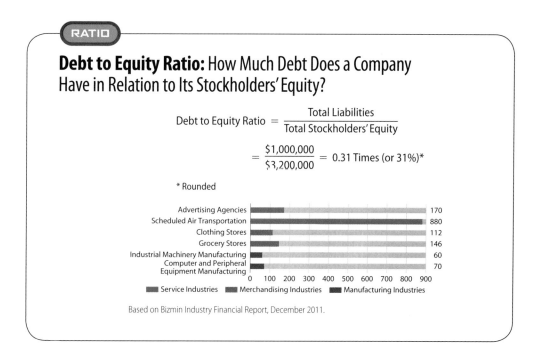

RATIO

Debt to Equity Ratio: How Much Debt Does a Company Have in Relation to Its Stockholders' Equity?

$$\text{Debt to Equity Ratio} = \frac{\text{Total Liabilities}}{\text{Total Stockholders' Equity}}$$

$$= \frac{\$1,000,000}{\$3,200,000} = 0.31 \text{ Times (or 31\%)*}$$

* Rounded

Advertising Agencies	170
Scheduled Air Transportation	880
Clothing Stores	112
Grocery Stores	146
Industrial Machinery Manufacturing	60
Computer and Peripheral Equipment Manufacturing	70

0 100 200 300 400 500 600 700 800 900

■ Service Industries ■ Merchandising Industries ■ Manufacturing Industries

Based on Bizmin Industry Financial Report, December 2011.

As illustrated, a debt to equity ratio of 0.31 times (or 31%) is relatively low, but it does not tell the whole story. As noted in the chapter opener, Swan also has long-term leases on various properties, which require annual payments of $100,000. Swan structures these leases in such a way that they do not appear as liabilities on the balance sheet. This practice is called **off-balance-sheet financing** and, as used by Swan, is entirely legal. The leases are, however, long-term commitments of cash payments and so have the effect of long-term liabilities.

Interest Coverage Ratio

The **interest coverage ratio** measures the degree of protection a company has from default on interest payments. The lower this ratio, the greater the financial risk.

Most analysts want to see an interest coverage ratio of at least 3 or 4 times. Lower interest coverage would mean the company is at risk from a downturn in the economy. Swan's 2014 income statement shows that the company had income before income taxes of $250,000 and interest expense of $50,000. Using these figures, we can compute Swan's interest coverage ratio as follows.

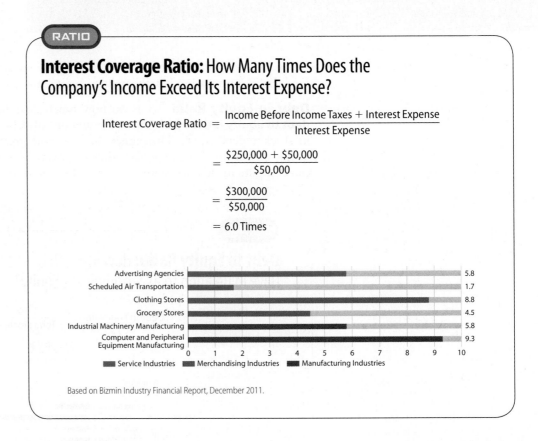

RATIO

Interest Coverage Ratio: How Many Times Does the Company's Income Exceed Its Interest Expense?

$$\text{Interest Coverage Ratio} = \frac{\text{Income Before Income Taxes} + \text{Interest Expense}}{\text{Interest Expense}}$$

$$= \frac{\$250,000 + \$50,000}{\$50,000}$$

$$= \frac{\$300,000}{\$50,000}$$

$$= 6.0 \text{ Times}$$

Advertising Agencies	5.8
Scheduled Air Transportation	1.7
Clothing Stores	8.8
Grocery Stores	4.5
Industrial Machinery Manufacturing	5.8
Computer and Peripheral Equipment Manufacturing	9.3

■ Service Industries ■ Merchandising Industries ■ Manufacturing Industries

Based on Bizmin Industry Financial Report, December 2011.

In comparison, Swan's strong interest coverage ratio of 6.0 times shows that it is in no danger of being unable to make interest payments. However, in computing this ratio, management will add the company's off-balance-sheet rent expense of $100,000 to its interest expense. This procedure decreases the interest coverage ratio to about 2.7 times. Although still adequate to cover interest payments, the adjusted coverage ratio is far less robust, which demonstrates the significant effect that off-balance-sheet financing for leases can have on a company's financial situation.

Cash Flow Information

The best source of information concerning cash flows about short-term and long-term debt is the financing activities section of the statement of cash flows. For instance, **McDonald's** cash flows are clearly revealed in this excerpt from its 2011 statement of cash flows (in millions):[8]

Financing Activities	2011	2010	2009
Net short-term borrowings	$ 260.6	$ 3.1	$ (285.4)
Long-term financing issuances	1,367.3	1,931.8	1,169.3
Long-term financing repayments	(624.0)	(1,147.5)	(664.6)

Note that McDonald's has little short-term borrowing and that the company's cash inflows for long-term borrowing for the three years exceeded cash outflows for long-term borrowing by $2,032.3 million.

APPLY IT!

Compute the interest coverage ratios for 2013 and 2014 from Travis Corporation's partial income statements that follow.

	2014	2013
Income from operations	$27,500	$34,000
Interest expense	5,000	4,000
Income before income taxes	$22,500	$30,000
Income taxes	8,250	10,200
Net income	$14,250	$19,800

SOLUTION

2013

$$\frac{\$30,000 + \$4,000}{\$4,000} = \frac{\$34,000}{\$4,000} = 8.5\ \text{Times}$$

2014

$$\frac{\$22,500 + \$5,000}{\$5,000} = \frac{\$27,500}{\$5,000} = 5.5\ \text{Times}$$

TRY IT! SE12, E18A, E18B

TriLevel Problem

Swan Manufacturing Company

The beginning of this chapter focused on Swan Manufacturing Company, whose management was considering how to finance the expansion of its metal window division. Ultimately, however, it decided to raise capital by issuing long-term bonds. Complete the following requirements in order to answer the questions posed at the beginning of the chapter.

Section 1: Concepts
How do the concepts of recognition, valuation, classification, and disclosure apply to long-term liabilities?

Section 2: Accounting Applications
How are long-term bonds accounted for in Swan's records?

Swan's bond indenture stated that the company would issue $2,500,000 of 8 percent, five-year bonds on January 1, 2015, and would pay interest semiannually on June 30 and December 31 in each of the five years. It also stated that the bonds would be callable at 104 and that each $1,000 bond would be convertible to 30 shares of $10 par value common stock.

Swan sold the bonds on January 1, 2015, at 96 because the market rate of interest for similar investments was 9 percent. It decided to amortize the bond discount by using the effective interest method. On July 1, 2017, management called and retired half the bonds, and investors converted the other half to common stock.

1. Prepare an interest and amortization schedule for the first five interest periods.

2. Prepare journal entries to record the sale of the bonds, the first two interest payments, the bond retirement, and the bond conversion.

Section 3: Business Applications

What should Swan consider in deciding to issue long-term debt?

Using the figures presented for Swan in the chapter opener and recalling that the company had income before income taxes of $250,000 and interest expense of $50,000, compute its debt to equity ratio and interest coverage ratio in the first year of the bond issue. What is your assessment of Swan's level of debt?

SOLUTION

Section 1: Concepts

Generally accepted accounting principles require that long-term liabilities be *recognized* and recorded when an obligation occurs even though the obligation may not be due for many years. On the balance sheet, long-term liabilities are generally *valued* at the amount of money needed to pay the debt or at the fair market value of the goods or services to be delivered. A liability is *classified* as a long-term liability when it is due beyond one year or beyond the normal operating cycle. Because of the complex nature of many long-term liabilities, extensive *disclosures* in the notes to the financial statements are often required.

Section 2: Accounting Applications

1.

	A	B	C	D	E	F	G
1			Interest and Amortization of Bond Discount				
2	Semiannual Interest Payment Date	Carrying Value at Beginning of Period	Semiannual Interest Expense* (9% × 1/2)	Semiannual Interest Paid (8% × 1/2)	Amortization of Discount	Unamortized Bond Discount at End of Period	Carrying Value at End of Period
3	Jan. 1, 2015					$100,000	$2,400,000
4	June 30, 2015	$2,400,000	$108,000	$100,000	$8,000	92,000	2,408,000
5	Dec. 31, 2015	2,408,000	108,360	100,000	8,360	83,640	2,416,360
6	June 30, 2016	2,416,360	108,736	100,000	8,736	74,904	2,425,096
7	Dec. 31, 2016	2,425,096	109,129	100,000	9,129	65,775	2,434,225
8	June 30, 2017	2,434,225	109,540	100,000	9,540	56,235	2,443,765
9							

*Rounded

2.

	A	B	C	D	E
1	2015				
2	Jan.	1	Cash	2,400,000	
3			Unamortized Bond Discount	100,000	
4			Bonds Payable		2,500,000
5			Sold $2,500,000 of 8%, 5-year bonds at 96		
6	June	30	Bond Interest Expense	108,000	
7			Unamortized Bond Discount		8,000
8			Cash		100,000
9			Paid semiannual interest and amortized		
10			the discount on 8%, 5-year bonds		
11	Dec.	31	Bond Interest Expense	108,360	
12			Unamortized Bond Discount		8,360
13			Cash		100,000
14			Paid semiannual interest and amortized		
15			the discount on 8%, 5-year bonds		
16	2017				
17	July	1	Bonds Payable	1,250,000	
18			Loss on Retirement of Bonds	78,118	
19			Unamortized Bond Discount		28,118
20			Cash		1,300,000
21			Called $1,250,000 of 8% bonds and retired		
22			them at 104 ($56,235 × 1/2 = $28,118*)		
23			Bonds Payable	1,250,000	
24			Unamortized Bond Discount		28,117
25			Common Stock		375,000
26			Additional Paid-in Capital		846,883
27			Converted $1,250,000 of 8% bonds into		
28			common stock		
29			1,250 × 30 shares = 37,500 shares		
30			37,500 shares × $10 = $375,000		
31			$56,235 − $28,118 = $28,117		
32			$1,250,000 − ($28,117 + $375,000) = $846,883		
33					

Section 3: Business Applications

Swan's management should consider how much debt the company should carry and how much risk is posed by the assumption of long-term debt by computing the company's debt to equity ratio and interest coverage ratio. It should also consider the effect of off-balance-sheet financing of a long-term lease.

$$\text{Debit to Equity Ratio} = \frac{(\text{Total Liabilities} + \text{Bond Issue less Discount})}{\text{Stockholders' Equity}}$$

$$= \frac{\$1,000,000 + \$2,400,000}{\$3,200,000}$$

$$= \frac{\$3,400,000}{\$3,200,000}$$

$$= 1.06 \text{ Times*}$$

* Rounded

$$\text{Interest Coverage} = \frac{\text{Income Before Income Taxes} + \text{Interest Expense} + \text{Bond Interest Expense}}{\text{Interest Expense} + \text{Bond Interest Expense}}$$

$$= \frac{\$250,000 + \$50,000 + \$216,360}{\$50,000 + \$216,360}$$

$$= \frac{\$516,360}{\$266,360}$$

$$= 1.94 \text{ Times*}$$

* Rounded

The increased debt will represent more risk, especially since Swan has long-term lease obligations.

Chapter Review

Explain the concepts underlying long-term liabilities, and identify the types of long-term liabilities. **LO 1**

Long-term debt is used to finance assets and business activities, such as research and development, that will produce income in future years. The management issues related to long-term debt are whether to take on long-term debt, how much debt to carry, and what types of debt to incur. Common types of long-term debt are bonds, notes, mortgages, long-term leases, pension liabilities, other post-retirement benefits, and deferred income taxes.

Describe the features of a bond issue and the major characteristics of bonds. **LO 2**

A bond is a security that represents money borrowed from the investing public. When a corporation issues bonds, it enters into a contract, called a bond indenture, with the bondholders. The bond indenture defines the terms of the bond issue. A bond issue is the total value of bonds issued at one time. The prices of bonds are stated in terms of a percentage of the face value, or principal, of the bonds. The face interest rate is the fixed rate of interest paid to bondholders based on the face value. The market interest rate is the rate of interest paid in the market on bonds of similar risk. If the market rate fluctuates from the face interest rate before the bond issue date, the bonds will sell at either a discount or a premium.

A corporation can issue several types of bonds, each having different characteristics. For example, a bond issue may or may not require security (secured versus unsecured bonds). It may be payable at a single time (term bonds) or at several times (serial bonds). And the holder may receive interest automatically (registered bonds) or may have to return coupons to receive interest payable (coupon bonds). Bonds may also be callable and convertible.

Record bonds issued at face value and at a discount or premium. **LO 3**

Bondholders pay face value for bonds when the interest rate on the bonds approximates the market rate for similar investments. The issuing corporation records the bond issue at face value as a long-term liability in the Bonds Payable account. Bonds are issued at a discount when their face interest rate is lower than the market rate for similar investments. The difference between the face value and the issue price is debited to Unamortized Bond Discount. Bonds are issued at a premium when their face interest rate is greater than the market interest rate on similar investments. The difference between the issue price and the face value is credited to Unamortized Bond Premium.

Use present values to determine the value of bonds. **LO 4**

The value of a bond is determined by summing the present values of (1) the series of fixed interest payments of the bond issue and (2) the single payment of the face value at maturity. Tables 1 and 2 in the appendix on present value tables should be used in making these computations.

Amortize bond discounts and bond premiums using the straight-line and effective interest methods. **LO 5**

The straight-line method allocates a fixed portion of a bond discount or premium each interest period to adjust the interest payment to interest expense. The effective interest method, which is used when the effects of amortization are material, applies a constant rate of interest to the carrying value of the bonds. To find interest and the amortization of discounts or premiums, the effective interest rate is applied to the carrying value of the bonds (face value minus the discount or plus the premium) at the beginning of the interest period. The amount of the discount or premium to be amortized is the difference between the interest figured by using the effective rate and that obtained by using the face rate. The results of using the effective interest method on bonds issued at a discount or a premium are summarized below and compared with issuance at face value:

	Bonds Issued at		
	Face Value	**Discount**	**Premium**
Trend in carrying value over bond term	Constant	Increasing	Decreasing
Trend in interest expense over bond term	Constant	Increasing	Decreasing
Interest expense versus interest payments	Interest expense = interest payments	Interest expense > interest payments	Interest expense < interest payments
Classification of bond discount or premium	Not applicable	Contra-liability (deducted from Bonds Payable)	Adjunct-liability (added to Bonds Payable)

Account for the retirement of bonds and the conversion of bonds into stock. **LO 6**

Callable bonds can be retired before maturity at the option of the issuing corporation. The call price is usually an amount greater than the face value of the bonds, in which case the corporation recognizes a loss on the retirement of the bonds. Sometimes, a rise in the market interest rate causes the market value of the bonds to fall below face value. If a company purchases its bonds on the open market at a price below carrying value, it recognizes a gain on the transaction.

Convertible bonds allow the bondholder to convert bonds to the issuing corporation's common stock. When bondholders exercise this option, the common stock issued is recorded at the carrying value of the bonds being converted. No gain or loss is recognized.

Record bonds issued between interest dates, and record year-end adjustments. **LO 7**

When bonds are sold between the interest payment dates, the issuing corporation collects from investors the interest that has accrued since the last interest payment date. When the next interest payment date arrives, the corporation pays the bondholders interest for the entire interest period.

When the end of a corporation's fiscal year does not fall on an interest payment date, the corporation must accrue bond interest expense from the last interest payment date to the end of its fiscal year. This accrual results in the inclusion of the interest expense in the year it is incurred.

Explain and demonstrate the accounting issues related to leases and pensions. **LO 8**

An operating lease is a contract under which a company rents an asset. Payments on operating leases are properly treated as rent expense. On the other hand, a capital lease is a lease that cannot be canceled, has duration about the same as the useful life of the asset, or stipulates that the lessee has the option to buy the asset at a nominal price at the end of the lease. A capital lease is like a purchase or sale on installment. The lessee in a capital lease records an asset, depreciation on the asset, and a long-term liability equal to the present value of the total lease payments during the lease term.

A pension plan is a contract that requires a company to pay benefits to its employees after they retire. The two types of pension plans are defined contribution plans and defined benefit plans.

Evaluate the decision **LO 9** to issue long-term debt, including analyzing long-term debt.

Management needs to decide between issuing long-term debt and issuing common stock or a combination of these two options. The advantages of issuing long-term debt are that common stockholders do not relinquish any control, interest on debt is tax-deductible, and financial leverage can increase earnings. The disadvantages are that interest and principal must be paid on time and financial leverage can work against a company if an investment is not successful. The level of debt can be evaluated using the debt to equity ratio and the interest coverage ratio.

Key Terms and Ratios

bond 549 (LO2)
bond certificate 549 (LO2)
bond indenture 549 (LO2)
bond issue 549 (LO2)
bonds payable 546 (LO1)
call price 550 (LO2)
callable bonds 550 (LO2)
capital lease 548 (LO1)
convertible bonds 550 (LO2)
coupon bonds 551 (LO2)
deferred income taxes 548 (LO1)
defined benefit plan 576 (LO8)
defined contribution plan 576 (LO8)
discount 550 (LO2)

early extinguishment of debt 550 (LO2)
effective interest method 559 (LO5)
face interest rate 549 (LO2)
face value 549 (LO2)
financial leverage 578 (LO9)
long-term liabilities 546 (LO1)
market interest rate 549 (LO2)
mortgage 547 (LO1)
notes payable 547 (LO1)
off-balance-sheet financing 580 (LO9)
operating lease 573 (LO8)
pension fund 576 (LO8)

pension plan 576 (LO8)
premium 550 (LO2)
registered bonds 551 (LO2)
secured bonds 550 (LO2)
serial bonds 550 (LO2)
straight-line method 558 (LO5)
term bonds 550 (LO2)
unsecured bonds 550 (LO2)
zero coupon bonds 558 (LO5)

RATIOS

debt to equity ratio 579 (LO9)
interest coverage ratio 580 (LO9)

Chapter Assignments

DISCUSSION QUESTIONS

LO 2, 9
RATIO
DQ1. BUSINESS APPLICATION ▶ If a company with a high debt to equity ratio wants to increase its debt when the economy is weak, what kind of bond might it issue?

LO 3   **DQ2.** What determines whether bonds are issued at a discount, premium, or face value?

LO 4   **DQ3.** Why does the market price of a bond vary over time?

LO 5   **DQ4.** When is it acceptable to use the straight-line method to amortize a bond discount or premium?

LO 6   **DQ5.** Why are callable and convertible bonds considered to add to management's future flexibility in financing a business?

LO 7   **DQ6. CONCEPT** ▶ Why must the accrual of bond interest be recorded at the end of an accounting period?

LO 9   **DQ7. BUSINESS APPLICATION** ▶ How does a lender assess the risk that a borrower may default—that is, not pay interest and principal when due?

LO 8   **DQ8. BUSINESS APPLICATION** ▶ Why might a company lease a long-term asset rather than buy it and issue long-term bonds?

SHORT EXERCISES

LO 1   Types of Long-Term Liabilities

SE1. Match the liabilities that follow with the statement to which it applies.

1. Bonds payable	a. May result in a capital lease
2. Long-term notes payable	b. Differences in income taxes on accounting income
3. Mortgage payable	and taxable income
4. Long-term lease	c. The most popular form of long-term financing
5. Pension liabilities	d. Often used to purchase land and buildings
6. Other post-retirement benefits	e. Often used interchangeably with bonds payable
7. Deferred income taxes	f. Future health care costs are a major component
	g. May include 401(k), ESOPs, or profit-sharing

LO 1   Mortgage Payable

SE2. Hagler Corporation purchased a building by signing a $150,000 long-term mortgage with monthly payments of $1,200. The mortgage carries an interest rate of 8 percent per year. Prepare a monthly payment schedule showing the monthly payment, the interest for the month, the reduction in debt, and the unpaid balance for the first three months. (Round to the nearest dollar.)

LO 2   Bond Characteristics

SE3. Match each term that follows with the related term.

1. Discount	a. Convertible
2. Callable	b. Secured
3. Face interest rate	c. Coupon
4. Unsecured	d. Market interest rate
5. Registered	e. Serial
6. Term	f. Premium

LO 4   Valuing Bonds Using Present Value

SE4. Sanchez, Inc., is considering the sale of two bond issues. Choice A is a $1,200,000 bond issue that pays semiannual interest of $64,000 and is due in 20 years. Choice B is a $1,200,000 bond issue that pays semiannual interest of $60,000 and is due in 15 years. Assume that the market interest rate for each bond is 12 percent. Calculate the amount that Sanchez will receive if both bond issues occur. (*Hint:* Calculate the present value of each bond issue and sum.)

LO 3, 5   Straight-Line Method

SE5. On April 1, 2014, Angel Corporation issued $8,000,000 in 8.5 percent, five-year bonds at 98. The semiannual interest payment dates are April 1 and October 1. Prepare journal entries to record the issue of the bonds by Angel on April 1, 2014, and the first two interest payments on October 1, 2014, and April 1, 2015. Use the straight-line method and ignore year-end accruals.

LO 3, 5   Effective Interest Method

SE6. On March 1, 2014, Smart Way Freight Company sold $200,000 of its 9.5 percent, 20-year bonds at 106. The semiannual interest payment dates are March 1 and September 1. The market interest rate is 8.9 percent. The firm's fiscal year ends August 31. Prepare journal entries to record the sale of the bonds on March 1, the accrual of interest and amortization of premium on August 31, and the first interest payment on September 1. Use the effective interest method to amortize the premium.

LO 3, 5, 7   Year-End Accrual of Bond Interest

SE7. On October 1, 2014, Tender Corporation issued $250,000 of 9 percent bonds at 96. The bonds are dated October 1 and pay interest semiannually. The market rate of

(Continued)

interest is 10 percent, and the company's year-end is December 31. Prepare the journal entries to record the issuance of the bonds, the accrual of the interest on December 31, 2014, and the payment of the first semiannual interest on April 1, 2015. Assume the company uses the effective interest method to amortize the bond discount.

LO 6   **Bond Retirement**

SE8. Noble Corporation has outstanding $400,000 of 8 percent bonds callable at 104. On December 1, immediately after the payment of the semiannual interest and the amortization of the bond discount were recorded, the unamortized bond discount equaled $10,500. On that date, $240,000 of the bonds were called and retired. Prepare the journal entry to record the retirement of the bonds on December 1.

LO 6   **Bond Conversion**

SE9. Evergreen Corporation has $2,000,000 of 6 percent bonds outstanding. There is $40,000 of unamortized discount remaining on the bonds after the March 1, 2014, semiannual interest payment. The bonds are convertible at the rate of 20 shares of $10 par value common stock for each $1,000 bond. On March 1, 2014, bondholders presented $1,200,000 of the bonds for conversion. Prepare the journal entry to record the conversion of the bonds.

LO 7   **Bond Issue Between Interest Dates**

SE10. Dawn Corporation sold $400,000 of 9 percent, 10-year bonds for face value on September 1, 2014. The issue date of the bonds was May 1, 2014. The company's fiscal year ends on December 31, and this is its only bond issue. Prepare the journal entry to record the sale of the bonds on September 1 and the first semiannual interest payment on November 1, 2014. What is the bond interest expense for the year ended December 31, 2014?

LO 8   **Leases and Pensions Definitions**

SE11. Match each term that follows with the appropriate definition.

1. Defined benefit plan
2. Capital lease
3. Pension plan
4. Operating lease
5. Defined contribution plan

a. A contract that requires a company to pay benefits to its employees after they retire.
b. A short-term lease used for renting assets where ownership of the asset remain with the lessor, and the lease is shorter than the asset's useful life.
c. A plan in which the employer makes a fixed specified annual contribution, usually a percentage of the employee's gross pay.
d. A long-term lease that cannot be canceled, has duration about the same as the useful life of the asset, and stipulates that the lessee has the option to buy the asset at a nominal price at the end of the lease.
e. A plan in which the employer contributes an amount annually to fund estimated future pension liability.

LO 9   **Bond Versus Common Stock Financing**

SE12. BUSINESS APPLICATION ▶ Indicate whether each of the following is an advantage or a disadvantage of using long-term bond financing rather than issuing common stock:

1. Interest paid on bonds is tax-deductible.
2. Investments are sometimes not as successful as planned.
3. Financial leverage can have a negative effect when investments do not earn as much as the interest payments on the related debt.
4. Bondholders do not have voting rights in a corporation.
5. Positive financial leverage may be achieved.

EXERCISES: SET A

LO 1 **Mortgage Payable**

E1A. Pittman Corporation purchased a building by signing a $75,000 long-term mortgage with monthly payments of $1,000. The mortgage carries an interest rate of 12 percent.

1. Prepare a monthly payment schedule showing the monthly payment, the interest for the month, the reduction in debt, and the unpaid balance for the first three months. (Round to the nearest dollar.)
2. Prepare the journal entries to record the purchase and the first two monthly payments.

LO 2 **Bond Issue Features and Bond Characteristics**

E2A. Match each term that follows with the appropriate definition.

1. Face interest rate	a. A contract that defines the rights, privileges, and limitations of the bondholders.
2. Bond indenture	
3. Secured bonds	b. Bonds that allow the bondholder to exchange a bond for a specified number of shares of common stock.
4. Bond issue	
5. Coupon bonds	c. The fixed rate of interest paid to bondholders based on the face value of the bonds.
6. Callable bonds	
7. Market interest rate	d. Bonds that give the issuer the right to buy back and retire the bonds before maturity at a specified price, which is usually above face value.
8. Convertible bonds	
9. Registered bonds	

e. The rate of interest paid in the market on bonds of similar risk.

f. The total value of bonds issued at one time.

g. Bonds issued in the names of the bondholders.

h. Bonds that carry a pledge of certain corporate assets as a guarantee of repayment.

i. Bonds not registered with the organization but bearing coupons stating the amount of interest due and the payment date.

LO 4 **Valuing Bonds Using Present Value**

E3A. Tsang, Inc., is considering the sale of two bond issues. Choice A is a $1,600,000 bond issue that pays semiannual interest of $128,000 and is due in 20 years. Choice B is a $1,600,000 bond issue that pays semiannual interest of $120,000 and is due in 15 years. Assume that the market interest rate for each bond is 12 percent. Calculate the amount that Tsang will receive if both bond issues are made. (*Hint:* Calculate the present value of each bond issue and sum.)

LO 4 **Valuing Bonds Using Present Value**

E4A. Use the present value tables in Appendix B to calculate the issue price of a $600,000 bond issue in each of the following independent cases. Assume interest is paid semiannually.

a. A 10-year, 8 percent bond issue; the market interest rate is 10 percent.

b. A 10-year, 8 percent bond issue; the market interest rate is 6 percent.

c. A 10-year, 10 percent bond issue; the market interest rate is 8 percent.

d. A 20-year, 10 percent bond issue; the market interest rate is 12 percent.

e. A 20-year, 10 percent bond issue; the market interest rate is 6 percent.

LO 4 **Zero Coupon Bonds**

E5A. The state of Idaho needs to raise $50,000,000 for highway repairs. Officials are considering issuing zero coupon bonds, which do not require periodic interest payments. The current market interest rate for the bonds is 10 percent. What face value of

(Continued)

bonds must be issued to raise the needed funds, assuming the bonds will be due in 30 years and compounded annually? How would your answer change if the bonds were due in 50 years? How would both answers change if the market interest rate were 8 percent instead of 10 percent?

LO **3, 5** **Straight-Line Method**

E6A. Norris Corporation issued $2,000,000 in 10.5 percent, 10-year bonds on February 1, 2014, at 104. Semiannual interest payment dates are January 31 and July 31. Use the straight-line method and ignore year-end accruals.

1. With regard to the bond issue on February 1, 2014:
   a. How much cash is received?
   b. How much is Bonds Payable?
   c. What is the difference between **a** and **b** called and how much is it?

2. With regard to the bond interest payment on July 31, 2014:
   a. How much cash is paid in interest?
   b. How much is the amortization?
   c. How much is interest expense?

3. With regard to the bond interest payment on January 31, 2015:
   a. How much cash is paid in interest?
   b. How much is the amortization?
   c. How much is interest expense?

LO **3, 5** **Straight-Line Method**

E7A. Waterbury Corporation issued $16,000,000 in 8.5 percent, five-year bonds on March 1, 2014, at 96. The semiannual interest payment dates are September 1 and March 1. Prepare the journal entries to record the issue of the bonds by Waterbury on March 1, 2014, and the first two interest payments on September 1, 2014, and March 1, 2015. Use the straight-line method and ignore year-end accruals.

LO **3, 5** **Effective Interest Method**

E8A. Linz Company sold $250,000 of 9.5 percent, 20-year bonds on April 1, 2014, at 106. The semiannual interest payment dates are March 31 and September 30. The market interest rate is 8.9 percent. The company's fiscal year ends September 30. Use the effective interest method to calculate the amortization. (Round to the nearest cent.)

1. With regard to the bond issue on April 1, 2014:
   a. How much cash is received?
   b. How much is Bonds Payable?
   c. What is the difference between **a** and **b** called and how much is it?

2. With regard to the bond interest payment on September 30, 2014:
   a. How much cash is paid in interest?
   b. How much is the amortization?
   c. How much is interest expense?

3. With regard to the bond interest payment on March 31, 2015:
   a. How much cash is paid in interest?
   b. How much is the amortization?
   c. How much is interest expense?

LO **3, 5** **Effective Interest Method**

E9A. On March 1, 2014, Minnow Corporation issued $600,000 of 10 percent, five-year bonds. The semiannual interest payment dates are February 28 and August 31. Because the market rate for similar investments was 11 percent, the bonds had to be issued at a discount. The discount on the issuance of the bonds was $24,335. The company's fiscal year ends February 28. Prepare the journal entries to record the bond issue on March 1, 2014, the payment of interest, and the amortization of the discount on August 31, 2014 and on February 28, 2015. Use the effective interest method. (Round to the nearest dollar.)

LO 6   **Bond Retirement**

E10A. Freed Corporation has outstanding $800,000 of 8 percent bonds callable at 104. On September 1, immediately after recording the payment of the semiannual interest and the amortization of the discount, the unamortized bond discount equaled $21,000. On that date, $480,000 of the bonds was called and retired.

1. How much cash must be paid to retire the bonds?
2. Is there a gain or loss on retirement, and if so, how much is it?

LO 6   **Bond Conversion**

E11A. Marisol Corporation has $800,000 of 6 percent bonds outstanding. There is $40,000 of unamortized discount remaining on these bonds after the July 1, 2014, semiannual interest payment. The bonds are convertible at the rate of 40 shares of $5 par value common stock for each $1,000 bond. On July 1, 2014, bondholders presented $600,000 of the bonds for conversion.

1. Is there a gain or loss on conversion, and if so, how much is it?
2. How many shares of common stock are issued in exchange for the bonds?
3. In dollar amounts, how does this transaction affect the total liabilities and the total stockholders' equity of the company? In your answer, show the effects on four accounts.

LO 5, 7   **Effective Interest Method and Interest Accrual**

E12A. The long-term debt section of Karidis Corporation's balance sheet at the end of its fiscal year, December 31, 2013, follows.

Long-term liabilities
    Bonds payable—8%, interest payable

1/1 and 7/1, due 12/31/16	$500,000	
Less unamortized bond discount	40,000	$460,000

Using the effective interest method, prepare the journal entries relevant to the interest payments on July 1, 2014, December 31, 2014, and January 1, 2015. Assume a market interest rate of 10 percent.

LO 4, 6   **Time Value of Money and Early Extinguishment of Debt**

E13A. Flanders, Inc., has a $700,000, 8 percent bond issue that was issued a number of years ago at face value. There are now 10 years left on the bond issue, and the market interest rate is 16 percent. Interest is paid semiannually. The company purchases the bonds on the open market at the calculated current market value and retires the bonds.

1. Using present value tables, calculate the current market value of the bond issue.
2. Is there a gain or loss on retirement of the bonds, and if so, how much is it?

LO 3, 7   **Bond Issue on and Between Interest Dates**

E14A. O'Brien, Inc., is authorized to issue $3,600,000 in bonds on June 1. The bonds carry a face interest rate of 9 percent, which is to be paid on June 1 and December 1. Prepare journal entries to record the issue of the bonds by O'Brien under the assumptions that (a) the bonds are issued on September 1 at 100 and (b) the bonds are issued on June 1 at 105.

LO 7   **Bond Issue Between Interest Dates**

E15A. Fleetwood Corporation sold $800,000 of 12 percent, 10-year bonds at face value on September 1, 2014. The issue date of the bonds was May 1, 2014.

1. Prepare the journal entries to record the sale of the bonds on September 1 and the first semiannual interest payment on November 1, 2014.
2. The company's fiscal year ends on December 31, and this is its only bond issue. What is the bond interest expense for the year ended December 31, 2014?

LO 3, 5, 7   **Year-End Accrual of Bond Interest**

E16A. Rapid Tech Corporation issued $2,000,000 of 9 percent bonds on October 1, 2014, at 96. The bonds are dated October 1 and pay interest semiannually. The market interest rate is 10 percent, and Rapid Tech's fiscal year ends on December 31. Prepare the journal entries to record the issuance of the bonds, the accrual of the interest on December 31, 2014, and the first semiannual interest payment on April 1, 2015. Assume the company uses the effective interest method to amortize the bond discount.

LO 8   **Recording Lease Obligations**

E17A. BUSINESS APPLICATION ▶ Rigby Corporation has leased a piece of equipment that has a useful life of 12 years. This capital lease requires payments of $86,000 per year for 12 years. Rigby currently is able to borrow money at a long-term interest rate of 15 percent. (Round to the nearest dollar.)

1. Calculate the present value of the lease.
2. Prepare the journal entry to record the lease agreement.
3. Prepare the journal entry to record depreciation of the equipment for the first year using the straight-line method.
4. Prepare the journal entries to record the lease payments for the first two years.

LO 9   **Interest Coverage Ratio**

E18A. BUSINESS APPLICATION ▶ Compute the interest coverage ratios for 2013 and 2014 from Dasbol Corporation's partial income statements that follow. (Round to one decimal place.) State whether the ratio improved or worsened over time.

	2014	2013
Income from operations	$47,780	$36,920
Interest expense	11,600	6,600
Income before income taxes	$36,180	$30,320
Income taxes	10,800	9,000
Net income	$25,380	$21,320

EXERCISES: SET B

Visit the textbook companion website at www.cengagebrain.com to access Exercise Set B for this chapter.

PROBLEMS

LO 1, 2   **Bond Terminology**

P1. Some common terms associated with bonds follow.

a. Bond certificate   g. Term bonds   m. Face interest rate
b. Bond issue   h. Serial bonds   n. Market interest rate
c. Bond indenture   i. Registered bonds   o. Effective interest rate
d. Unsecured bonds   j. Coupon bonds   p. Bond premium
e. Debenture bonds   k. Callable bonds   q. Bond discount
f. Secured bonds   l. Convertible bonds

REQUIRED

1. For each of the statements that follow, identify the category above with which it is associated. (If two statements apply, choose the category with which it is most closely associated.)

   1. Occurs when bonds are sold at more than face value
   2. Rate of interest that will vary depending on economic conditions
   3. Bonds that may be exchanged for common stock
   4. Bonds that are not registered
   5. A bond issue in which all bonds are due on the same date
   6. Occurs when bonds are sold at less than face value
   7. Rate of interest that will be paid regardless of market conditions
   8. Bonds that may be retired at management's option
   9. A document that is evidence of a company's debt
  10. Same as market rate of interest
  11. Bonds for which the company knows who owns them
  12. A bond issue for which bonds are due at different dates
  13. The total value of bonds issued at one time
  14. Bonds whose payment involves a pledge of certain assets
  15. Same as debenture bonds
  16. Contains the terms of the bond issue
  17. Bonds issued on the general credit of the company

2. **ACCOUNTING CONNECTION** ▶ What effect will a decrease in interest rates below the face interest rate and before a bond is issued have on the cash received from the bond issue? What effect will the decrease have on interest expense? What effect will the decrease have on the amount of cash paid for interest?

LO **3, 5, 6, 9**

SPREADSHEET

✔ 1d(3): Interest expense: $374,400
✔ 2d(3): Interest expense: $385,600

Bond Basics—Straight-Line Method, Retirement, and Conversion

P2. Sasina Corporation has $8,000,000 of 9.5 percent, 25-year bonds dated May 1, 2014, with interest payable on April 30 and October 31. The company's fiscal year ends on December 31, and it uses the straight-line method to amortize bond premiums or discounts. The bonds are callable after 10 years at 103, or each $1,000 bond is convertible into 40 shares of $10 par value common stock.

REQUIRED

1. Assume the bonds are issued at 103.5 on May 1, 2014.
  a. How much cash is received?
  b. How much is Bonds Payable?
  c. What is the difference between **a** and **b** called, and how much is it?
  d. With regard to the bond interest payment on October 31, 2014:
    (1) How much cash is paid in interest?
    (2) How much is the amortization?
    (3) How much is interest expense?

2. Assume the bonds are issued at 96.5 on May 1, 2014.
  a. How much cash is received?
  b. How much is Bonds Payable?
  c. What is the difference between **a** and **b** called, and how much is it?
  d. With regard to the bond interest payment on October 31, 2014:
    (1) How much cash is paid in interest?
    (2) How much is the amortization?
    (3) How much is interest expense?

3. Assume the issue price in requirement **1** and that the bonds are called and retired 10 years later.
  a. How much cash will have to be paid to retire the bonds?
  b. Is there a gain or loss on the retirement, and if so, how much is it?

(Continued)

4. Assume the issue price in requirement **2** and that the bonds are converted to common stock 10 years later.
   a. Is there a gain or loss on conversion, and if so, how much is it?
   b. How many shares of common stock are issued in exchange for the bonds?
   c. In dollar amounts, how does this transaction affect the total liabilities and the total stockholders' equity of the company? In your answer, show the effects on four accounts.

5. **BUSINESS APPLICATION** ▶Assume that after 10 years market interest rates have dropped significantly and that the price of the company's common stock has risen significantly. Also assume that management wants to improve its credit rating by reducing its debt to equity ratio and that it needs what cash it currently has for expansion. Would management prefer the approach and result in requirement **3** or **4**? Explain your answer. What would be a disadvantage of the approach you chose?

LO **3, 5**

GENERAL LEDGER

✔ 1: Bond Interest Expense, May 31: $439,184
✔ 2: Bond Interest Expense, May 31: $457,350

Bond Transactions—Effective Interest Method

P3. Zapala Corporation has $10,000,000 of 9 percent, 20-year bonds dated June 1, 2014, with interest payment dates of May 31 and November 30. The company's fiscal year ends November 30. It uses the effective interest method to amortize bond premiums or discounts.

REQUIRED

1. Assume the bonds are issued at 109.9 on June 1 to yield an effective interest rate of 8 percent. Prepare the journal entries for June 1, 2014, November 30, 2014, and May 31, 2015. (Round to the nearest dollar.)
2. Assume the bonds are issued at 91.4 on June 1 to yield an effective interest rate of 10 percent. Prepare the journal entries for June 1, 2014, November 30, 2014, and May 31, 2015. (Round to the nearest dollar.)
3. **ACCOUNTING CONNECTION** ▶ Explain the role that market interest rates play in causing a premium in requirement **1** and a discount in requirement **2**.

LO **3, 5, 7**

SPREADSHEET

✔ 2a: Total interest expense in 2014: $474,200
✔ 2b: Total cash paid for interest in 2014: $380,000

Bonds Issued at a Discount and a Premium—Effective Interest Method

P4. Yacuma Corporation issued bonds twice during 2014. The transactions follow.

2014

Jan. 1   Issued $2,000,000 of 9.2 percent, 10-year bonds dated January 1, 2014, with interest payable on June 30 and December 31. The bonds were sold at 98.1, resulting in an effective interest rate of 9.5 percent.

Apr. 1   Issued $4,000,000 of 9.8 percent, 10-year bonds dated April 1, 2014, with interest payable on March 31 and September 30. The bonds were sold at 101, resulting in an effective interest rate of 9.5 percent.

June 30   Paid semiannual interest on the January 1 issue and amortized the discount, using the effective interest method.

Sept. 30   Paid semiannual interest on the April 1 issue and amortized the premium, using the effective interest method.

Dec. 31   Paid semiannual interest on the January 1 issue and amortized the discount, using the effective interest method.

      31   Made an end-of-year adjusting entry to accrue interest on the April 1 issue and to amortize half the premium applicable to the second interest period.

2015

Mar. 31   Paid semiannual interest on the April 1 issue and amortized the premium applicable to the second half of the second interest period.

REQUIRED

1. Prepare the journal entries to record the bond transactions. (Round to the nearest dollar.)

2. **ACCOUNTING CONNECTION** ▶ Describe the effect of the above transactions on profitability and liquidity by answering the following questions:
   a. What is the total interest expense in 2014 for each of the bond issues?
   b. What is the total cash paid in 2014 for each of the bond issues?
   c. What differences, if any, do you observe, and how do you explain them?

LO 8

SPREADSHEET

✔ 1a: Present value of lease: $171,864
✔ 2a: Unpaid balance at the end of third month: $157,582

Lease Versus Purchase

P5. Wooster Corporation can either lease or buy a small garage next to its business that will provide parking for its customers. The company can lease the building for a period of 12 years, which approximates the useful life of the facility and thus qualifies as a capital lease. The terms of the lease are payments of $24,000 per year for 12 years. Wooster currently is able to borrow money at a long-term interest rate of 9 percent. The company can purchase the building by signing an $160,000 long-term mortgage with monthly payments of $2,000. The mortgage also carries an interest rate of 9 percent.

REQUIRED

1. With regard to the lease option:
   a. Calculate the present value of the lease. (Round to the nearest dollar.)
   b. Prepare the journal entry to record the lease agreement.
   c. Prepare the journal entry to record depreciation of the building for the first year using the straight-line method.
   d. Prepare the journal entries to record the lease payments for the first two years.

2. With regard to the purchase option:
   a. Prepare a monthly payment schedule showing the monthly payment, the interest for the month, the reduction in debt, and the unpaid balance for the first three months. (Round to the nearest dollar.)
   b. Prepare the journal entries to record the purchase and the first two monthly payments.

3. **BUSINESS APPLICATION** ▶Based on your calculations, which option seems to be best? Aside from cost, name an advantage and a disadvantage of each option.

ALTERNATE PROBLEMS

LO **3, 5, 6, 9**

✔ 1d(3): Interest expense: $517,500
✔ 2d(3): Interest expense: $532,500

Bond Basics—Straight-Line Method, Retirement, and Conversion

P6. Cozumel Corporation has $10,000,000 of 10.5 percent, 20-year bonds dated June 1, 2014, with interest payment dates of May 31 and November 30. After 10 years, the bonds are callable at 104, and each $1,000 bond is convertible into 25 shares of $20 par value common stock. The company's fiscal year ends on December 31. It uses the straight-line method to amortize bond premiums or discounts.

REQUIRED

1. Assume the bonds are issued at 103 on June 1, 2014.
   a. How much cash is received?
   b. How much is Bonds Payable?
   c. What is the difference between **a** and **b** called, and how much is it?
   d. With regard to the bond interest payment on November 30, 2014:
      (1) How much cash is paid in interest?
      (2) How much is the amortization?
      (3) How much is interest expense?

2. Assume the bonds are issued at 97 on June 1, 2014.
   a. How much cash is received?
   b. How much is Bonds Payable?

(Continued)

c. What is the difference between **a** and **b** called, and how much is it?

d. With regard to the bond interest payment on November 30, 2014:

   (1) How much cash is paid in interest?

   (2) How much is the amortization?

   (3) How much is interest expense?

3. Assume the issue price in requirement **1** and that the bonds are called and retired 10 years later.

   a. How much cash will have to be paid to retire the bonds?

   b. Is there a gain or loss on the retirement, and if so, how much is it?

4. Assume the issue price in requirement **2** and that the bonds are converted to common stock 10 years later.

   a. Is there a gain or loss on the conversion, and if so, how much is it?

   b. How many shares of common stock are issued in exchange for the bonds?

   c. In dollar amounts, how does this transaction affect the total liabilities and the total stockholders' equity of the company? In your answer, show the effects on four accounts.

5. **BUSINESS APPLICATION** ▶Assume that after 10 years, market interest rates have dropped significantly and that the price on the company's common stock has risen significantly. Also assume that management wants to improve its credit rating by reducing its debt to equity ratio and that it needs what cash it has for expansion. Which approach would management prefer—the approach and result in requirement **3** or **4**? Explain your answer. What would be a disadvantage of the approach you chose?

LO **3, 5**

GENERAL LEDGER

✔ 1: Bond Interest Expense, Feb. 28: $377,071
✔ 2: Bond Interest Expense, Feb. 28: $382,308

Bond Transactions—Effective Interest Method

P7. Krabna Corporation has $8,000,000 of 9.5 percent, 25-year bonds dated March 1, 2014, with interest payable on February 28 and August 31. The company's fiscal year end is February 28. It uses the effective interest method to amortize bond premiums or discounts. (Round to the nearest dollar.)

REQUIRED

1. Assume the bonds are issued at 102.5 on March 1, 2014, to yield an effective interest rate of 9.2 percent. Prepare the journal entries for March 1, 2014, August 31, 2014, and February 28, 2015.

2. Assume the bonds are issued at 97.5 on March 1, 2014, to yield an effective interest rate of 9.8 percent. Prepare the journal entries for March 1, 2014, August 31, 2014, and February 28, 2015.

3. **ACCOUNTING CONNECTION** ▶ Explain the role that market interest rates play in causing a premium in requirement **1** and a discount in requirement **2**.

LO **3, 5, 7**

SPREADSHEET

✔ 2a: Total interest expense in 2014: $889,352
✔ 2b: Total cash paid for interest in 2014: $778,000

Bonds Issued at a Discount and a Premium—Effective Interest Method

P8. Hart Corporation issued bonds twice during 2014. A summary of the transactions involving the bonds follows.

2014

Jan. 1   Issued $6,000,000 of 9.9 percent, 10-year bonds dated January 1, 2014, with interest payable on June 30 and December 31. The bonds were sold at 102.6, resulting in an effective interest rate of 9.4 percent.

Mar. 1   Issued $4,000,000 of 9.2 percent, 10-year bonds dated March 1, 2014, with interest payable March 1 and September 1. The bonds were sold at 98.2, resulting in an effective interest rate of 9.5 percent.

June 30   Paid semiannual interest on the January 1 issue and amortized the premium, using the effective interest method.

Sept. 1   Paid semiannual interest on the March 1 issue and amortized the discount, using the effective interest method.

Dec. 31 Paid semiannual interest on the January 1 issue and amortized the premium, using the effective interest method.

31 Made an end-of-year adjusting entry to accrue interest on the March 1 issue and to amortize two-thirds of the discount applicable to the second interest period.

2015

Mar. 1 Paid semiannual interest on the March 1 issue and amortized the remainder of the discount applicable to the second interest period.

REQUIRED

1. Prepare journal entries to record the bond transactions. (Round to the nearest dollar.)
2. **ACCOUNTING CONNECTION** ▶ Describe the effect on profitability and liquidity by answering the following questions:
   a. What is the total interest expense in 2014 for each of the bond issues?
   b. What is the total cash paid in 2014 for each of the bond issues?
   c. What differences, if any, do you observe and how do you explain them?

LO 8

Lease Versus Purchase

✔ 1a: Present value of lease: $343,728
✔ 2a: Unpaid balance at the end of third month: $315,164

P9. Martha Corporation can either lease or buy a small garage next to its business that will provide parking for its customers. The company can lease the building for a period of 12 years, which approximates the useful life of the facility and thus qualifies as a capital lease. The terms of the lease are payments of $48,000 per year for 12 years. Martha currently is able to borrow money at a long-term interest rate of 9 percent. The company can purchase the building by signing a $320,000 long-term mortgage with monthly payments of $4,000. The mortgage also carries an interest rate of 9 percent.

REQUIRED

1. With regard to the lease option:
   a. Calculate the present value of the lease. (Round to the nearest dollar.)
   b. Prepare the journal entry to record the lease agreement.
   c. Prepare the journal entry to record depreciation of the building for the first year using the straight-line method.
   d. Prepare the journal entries to record the lease payments for the first two years.

2. With regard to the purchase option:
   a. Prepare a monthly payment schedule showing the monthly payment, the interest for the month, the reduction in debt, and the unpaid balance for the first three months. (Round to the nearest dollar.)
   b. Prepare the journal entries to record the purchase and the first two monthly payments.

3. **BUSINESS APPLICATION** ▶ Based on your calculations, which option seems to be best? Aside from cost, name an advantage and a disadvantage of each option.

CASES

LO 1, 2, 6

Conceptual Understanding: Bond Issue

C1. Eastman Kodak, the more than 100-year-old photography company, recently declared bankruptcy after struggling for many years. One of its efforts to survive was a $1 billion bond issue several years ago. Even though the company's credit rating was low at the time, the bond issue was well received by the investment community because the company offered attractive terms. The offering comprised $500 million of 10-year unsecured notes and $500 million of 30-year convertible bonds. The convertibles were callable after seven years and would be convertible into common stock about 40 to 45 percent higher than the current price.[9]

(Continued)

What are unsecured notes? Why would they carry a relatively high interest rate? What are convertible securities? Why are they good for the investor and for the company? Why would they carry a relatively low interest rate? What does *callable* mean? What advantage does this feature give the company?

LO 2, 3

Conceptual Understanding: Bond Interest Rates and Market Prices

C2. Dow Chemical is one of the largest chemical companies in the world. Among its long-term liabilities was a bond due in 2011 that carried a face interest rate of 6.125 percent.[10] This bond sold on the New York Stock Exchange at 104 5/8. Did this bond sell at a discount or a premium? Assuming the bond was originally issued at face value, did interest rates rise or decline after the date of issue? Would you have expected the market rate of interest on this bond to be more or less than 6.125 percent? Did the current market price affect either the amount that the company paid in semiannual interest or the amount of interest expense for the same period? Explain your answers.

LO 6, 9

Conceptual Understanding: Characteristics of Convertible Debt

C3. Intel Corporation designs and manufactures advanced integrated digital technology platforms. The company has never earned a profit. In 2009, Intel issued $2,000,000,000 of junior subordinated convertible notes at 3.25 percent due in 2039 at face value. The notes are convertible into common stock at a price of $22.45 per share, which at the time of issue was above the market price. The market value of Intel's common stock ranged from $19.16 to $25.66 in 2011.[11] What reasons can you suggest for Intel's management choosing notes that are convertible into common stock rather than simply issuing nonconvertible notes or issuing common stock directly? Are there any disadvantages to this approach? If the price of the company's common stock goes to $17 per share, what would be the total theoretical value of the notes? If the holders of the notes were to elect to convert the notes into common stock, what would be the effect on the company's debt to equity ratio, and what would be the effect on the percentage ownership of the company by other stockholders?

LO 8, 9

Conceptual Understanding: Effect of Long-Term Leases

C4. BUSINESS APPLICATION ▶ Many companies use long-term leases to finance long-term assets. Although these leases are similar to mortgage payments, they are structured in such a way that they qualify as operating leases. As a result, the lease commitments do not appear on the companies' balance sheets.

In a recent year, **Continental Airlines** had almost $15 billion in total operating lease commitments, of which $1.5 billion was due in the current year. Further, the airline had total assets of $12.686 billion and total liabilities of $12.581 billion. Because of heavy losses in previous years, its stockholders' equity was only $0.105 billion.

What effect do these types of leases have on the balance sheet? Why would the use of these long-term leases make a company's debt to equity ratio, interest coverage ratio, and free cash flow look better than they really are? What is a capital lease? How does the application of capital lease accounting provide insight into a company's financial health?

LO 1, 8

Interpreting Financial Reports: Long-Term Debt, Leases, and Pensions

C5. BUSINESS APPLICATION ▶ To answer the following questions, refer to the financial statements and the notes to the financial statements in **CVS Corporation**'s annual report in the Supplement to Chapter 16:

1. Is it the practice of CVS to own or lease most of its buildings?
2. Does CVS lease property predominantly under capital leases or under operating leases? How much was rental expense for operating leases in 2011?
3. Does CVS have a defined benefit pension plan? Does it offer post-retirement benefits?

Interpreting Financial Reports: Use of Debt Financing

C6. BUSINESS APPLICATION ▶ Refer to the annual report of **CVS Corporation** and the financial statements of **Southwest Airlines Co.** in the Supplement to Chapter 16. Calculate the debt to equity ratio and the interest coverage ratio for both companies' two most recent years. (Round to one decimal place.) Find the note to the financial statements that contains information on leases and lease commitments by CVS. Southwest's lease expenses were $847 million and $631 million in 2011 and 2010, respectively, and total lease commitments for future years were $5,583 million. What effect do the total lease commitments and lease expense have on your assessment of the ratios you calculated? Evaluate and comment on the relative performance of the two companies with regard to debt financing. Which company has more risk of not being able to meet its interest obligations? How does leasing affect the analysis? Explain.

Continuing Case: Annual Report Project

C7. Using the most recent annual report of the company you have chosen to study and that you have accessed online at the company's website, examine the balance sheet and accompanying notes of your company. Answer the following questions:

1. What percentage of total liabilities and stockholders' equity is long-term liabilities? Does the company have long-term notes or bonds and deferred income taxes? How do these liabilities differ from each other?
2. Find the disclosures about these leases in the notes to the financial statements. What are the total lease obligations of the company?
3. Find the disclosures about pensions in the notes to the financial statements. What kind of pension plan does the company have? Does it offer post-retirement benefits?

CHAPTER 15
The Statement of Cash Flows

Deliga Corporation is a distributor of accessories for cell phones, iPods, iPhones, and other small electronic devices. Deliga's managers have just finished preparing the company's financial statements for 2015. Although they are satisfied with net sales for the year—$825,000— they are concerned because cash flows from operating activities are less than net income ($58,300 vs. $82,200) and because cash and cash equivalents decreased by $8,000 during the year. The company has recently been having difficulty paying its bills on time.

Strong cash flows are critical to achieving and maintaining liquidity. If cash flows exceed the amount a company needs for operations and expansion, it will not have to borrow additional funds. It can use excess cash to reduce debt, thereby lowering its debt to equity ratio and improving its financial position. That, in turn, can increase the market value of its stock.

Deliga's statement of cash flows provides the company's managers, as well as its stockholders and potential investors, with information that is essential to evaluating the strength of the company's cash flows and liquidity.

1. CONCEPT ▶ *How do relevance and classification apply to the statement of cash flows?*

2. ACCOUNTING APPLICATION ▶ *How is the statement of cash flows prepared using the indirect method?*

3. BUSINESS APPLICATION ▶ *What measures may be used to explain the apparent cause of Deliga's operating cash flow problem and the decline in its cash and cash equivalents?*

LEARNING OBJECTIVES

LO 1 Describe the principal purposes and concepts underlying the statement of cash flows, and identify its components and format.

LO 2 Use the indirect method to determine cash flows from operating activities.

LO 3 Determine cash flows from investing activities.

LO 4 Determine cash flows from financing activities.

LO 5 Analyze the statement of cash flows.

Robert Kneschke/Shutterstock.com

SECTION 1

CONCEPTS

**RELEVANT
LEARNING OBJECTIVE**

LO 1 Describe the principal
purposes and
concepts underlying the
statement of cash flows, and
identify its components and
format.

LO 1 Concepts Underlying the Statement of Cash Flows

Cash flows enable a company to pay expenses, debts, employees' wages, and taxes and to invest in the assets it needs for its operations. Without sufficient cash flows, a company cannot grow and prosper. Because of the importance of cash flows, one must be alert to the possibility that items may be incorrectly *classified* in a statement of cash flows and that the statement may not fully *disclose* all pertinent information. This chapter identifies the classifications used in a statement of cash flows and explains how to analyze the statement.

The **statement of cash flows** shows how a company's operating, investing, and financing activities have affected cash during a period. It explains the net increase (or decrease) in cash during the period. For purposes of this statement, **cash** is defined as including both cash and cash equivalents. **Cash equivalents** are investments that can be quickly converted to cash. They have a maturity of 90 days or less when they are purchased, and they include the following:

- Money market accounts
- Commercial paper (short-term corporate notes)
- U.S. Treasury bills

A company invests in cash equivalents to earn interest on cash that would otherwise be temporarily idle. Suppose, for example, that a company has $1,000,000 that it will not need for 30 days. To earn a return on this amount, the company could place the cash in an account that earns interest (such as a money market account), lend the cash to another corporation by purchasing that corporation's short-term notes (commercial paper), or purchase a short-term obligation of the U.S. government (a Treasury bill).

Cash equivalents should not be confused with short-term investments, also called **marketable securities**. Marketable securities have a maturity of more than 90 days but are intended to be held only until cash is needed for current operations. Purchases of marketable securities are treated as cash outflows, and sales of marketable securities are treated as cash inflows. Conversely, transfers between the Cash account and cash equivalents are not treated as cash inflows or cash outflows.

Relevance of the Statement of Cash Flows

The statement of cash flows provides information about a company's cash receipts and cash payments during a period, as well as about a company's operating, investing, and financing activities. Some information about those activities may be inferred from other financial statements, but the statement of cash flows summarizes *all* transactions that affect cash.

International Perspective
IFRS How Universal Is the Statement of Cash Flows?

Despite the importance of the statement of cash flows in assessing the liquidity of companies in the United States, there has been considerable variation in its use and format in other countries. For example, in many countries, the statement shows the change in working capital rather than the change in cash and cash equivalents. Although the European Union's principal directives for financial reporting do not address the statement of cash flows, international accounting standards require it, and international financial markets expect it to be presented. As a result, most multinational companies include the statement in their financial reports. Most European countries adopted the statement of cash flows when the European Union adopted international accounting standards.

© loops7 / iStockphoto.com

The information provided by the statement of cash flows is relevant to management in operating the business, as well as to investors and creditors in making investment and lending decisions. Management uses the statement of cash flows to:

- assess liquidity (e.g., to determine whether short-term financing is needed to pay current liabilities).
- determine dividend policy.
- evaluate the effects of major policy decisions involving investments and financing needs.

Investors and creditors use the statement of cash flows to assess a company's ability to:

- manage cash flows.
- generate positive future cash flows.
- pay its liabilities.
- pay dividends and interest.
- anticipate the need for additional financing.

Classification of Cash Flows

Amazon.com is the largest online retailer in the world and one of the 500 largest companies in the United States. Exhibit 1 shows the company's consolidated statements of cash flows for 2011, 2010, and 2009. As you can see, this statement has three major classifications: operating, investing, and financing activities.

The *classifications* of operating, investing, and financing activities are illustrated in Exhibit 2 and summarized next.

Operating Activities The first section of the statement of cash flows is cash flow from operating activities. **Operating activities** involve the cash inflows and outflows from activities that enter into the determination of net income. Cash inflows in this category include cash receipts from the sale of goods and services and from the sale of trading securities. **Trading securities** are a type of marketable security that a company buys and sells for making a profit in the near term as opposed to holding them indefinitely for investment purposes. Cash inflows from operating activities also include interest received on loans and dividends received on investments. Cash outflows from operating activities include cash payments for wages, inventory, expenses, interest, taxes, and the purchase of trading securities.

Investing Activities The second section of the statement of cash flows is cash flows from investing activities. **Investing activities** involve the acquisition and sale of property, plant, and equipment and other long-term assets, including long-term investments. They also involve the acquisition and sale of short-term marketable securities, other than trading securities, and the making and collecting of loans. Cash flows provided by investing activities include the cash received from selling marketable securities and long-term assets and from collecting on loans. Cash flows used by investing activities include the cash expended on purchasing these securities and assets and the cash lent to borrowers. Cash outflows for property, plant, and equipment, or capital expenditures, are usually shown separately from cash inflows from sales of these assets, as they are in **Amazon.com**'s statement in Exhibit 1. However, when the inflows are not material, some companies combine these two lines to show the net amount of outflow.

Financing Activities The third section of the statement of cash flows is cash flows from financing activities. **Financing activities** involve obtaining resources from stockholders and creditors. Cash inflows include the proceeds from stock issues and from short- and long-term borrowing. Cash outflows include the repayments of loans (excluding interest) and payments to owners, including cash dividends. Treasury stock transactions are also considered financing activities. Repayments of accounts payable or accrued liabilities are not considered repayments of loans. They are classified as cash outflows under operating activities.

STUDY NOTE: *Operating activities involve the day-to-day sale of goods and services, investing activities involve long-term assets and investments, and financing activities deal with stockholders' equity accounts and debt (borrowing).*

Cash Balances A reconciliation of the beginning and ending balances of cash appears at the bottom of the statement. These cash balances will tie into the cash balances on the balance sheet.

Exhibit 1
Consolidated Statement of Cash Flows

Amazon.com, Inc.
Consolidated Statements of Cash Flows

(In millions)	For the Years Ended		
	2011	**2010**	**2009**
Operating Activities:			
Net income	$ 631	$ 1,152	$ 902
Adjustments to reconcile net income to net cash from operating activities:			
Depreciation and amortization	1,083	568	378
Stock-based compensation	557	424	341
Other operating expense (income), net	154	106	103
Losses (gains) on sales of marketable securities, net	(4)	(2)	(4)
Other expense (income), net	(56)	(79)	(15)
Deferred income taxes	136	4	81
Excess tax benefits from stock-based compensation	(62)	(259)	(105)
Changes in operating assets and liabilities:			
Inventories	(1,777)	(1,019)	(531)
Accounts receivable, net and other	(866)	(295)	(481)
Accounts payable	2,997	2,373	1,859
Accrued expenses and other	1,067	740	300
Additions to unearned revenue	1,064	687	1,054
Amortization of previously unearned revenue	(1,021)	(905)	(589)
Net cash provided by operating activities	$ 3,903	$ 3,495	$ 3,293
Investing Activities:			
Purchases of fixed assets, including internal-use software and website development	(1,811)	(979)	(373)
Acquisitions, net of cash received and other	(705)	(352)	(40)
Sales and maturities of marketable securities and other investments	6,843	4,250	1,966
Purchases of marketable securities and other investments	(6,257)	(6,279)	(3,890)
Net cash provided by (used in) investing activities	$(1,930)	$(3,360)	$(2,337)
Financing Activities:			
Excess tax benefits from exercises of stock options	62	259	105
Common stock repurchased (treasury stock)	(277)	—	—
Proceeds from long-term debt and other	177	143	87
Repayments of long-term debt and capital lease obligations	(444)	(221)	(472)
Net cash provided by (used in) financing activities	$ (482)	$ 181	$ (280)
Foreign-currency effect on cash and cash equivalents	1	17	(1)
Net (decrease) increase in cash and cash equivalents	$ 1,492	$ 333	$ 675
Cash and cash equivalents, beginning of year	3,777	3,444	2,769
Cash and cash equivalents, end of year	$ 5,269	$ 3,777	$ 3,444

Source: Amazon.com, Inc., *Annual Report*, 2011 (adapted).

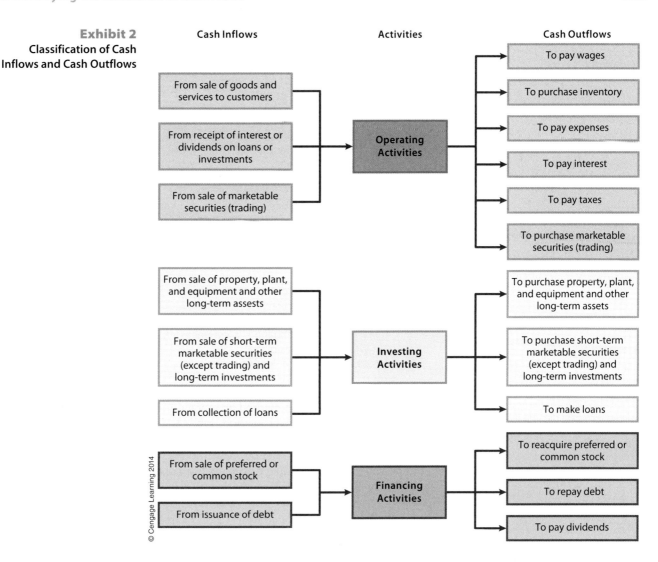

Exhibit 2
Classification of Cash Inflows and Cash Outflows

© Cengage Learning 2014

Required Disclosure of Noncash Investing and Financing Transactions

Companies occasionally engage in significant **noncash investing and financing transactions**. These transactions involve *only* long-term assets, long-term liabilities, or stockholders' equity. For instance, a company might exchange a long-term asset for a long-term liability, settle a debt by issuing capital stock, or take out a long-term mortgage to purchase real estate. Although noncash transactions represent significant investing and financing activities, they are not reflected in the body of the statement of cash flows because they do not affect current cash inflows or outflows. They will, however, affect future cash flows. For this reason, they must be *disclosed* in a separate schedule, usually following the statement of cash flows.

Alternate Presentations of Operating Activities

There are two ways of presenting operating activities on the statement of cash flows.

■ The **direct method** converts each item on the income statement from the accrual basis to the cash basis. The operating activities section of the statement of cash flows under the direct method follows in simplified format.

Cash Flows from Operating Activities

Cash receipts from:		
Sales	xxx	
Interest	xxx	xxx
Less cash payments for:		
Purchases	xxx	
Operating expenses	xxx	
Interest payments	xxx	
Income taxes	xxx	xxx
Cash flows from operating activities		xxx

■   The **indirect method** does not require the conversion of each item on the income statement. It lists only the items necessary to convert net income to cash flows from operations in the following format:

Cash Flows from Operating Activities

Net income		xxx
Adjustments to reconcile net income to net cash flows		
from operating activities:		
Plus non-cash expenses	xxx	
Plus or minus changes in current assets		
and current liabilities	xxx	
Cash flows from operating activities		xxx

STUDY NOTE: *The direct and indirect methods relate only to the operating activities section of the statement of cash flows. They are both acceptable for financial reporting purposes.*

The direct and indirect methods always produce the same amount of cash flows from operating activities. The direct method presentation of operating cash flows is more straightforward than that of the indirect method, but it is more difficult to implement in practice. Few accounting systems provide the data easily to make the calculations necessary for the direct method. Further, when the direct method is presented, preparation and *disclosure* of the indirect method of presenting cash flows from operating activities is also required.

Analysts prefer the indirect method to the direct method because it begins with net income and derives cash flows from operations. Analysts can readily identify the factors that cause cash flows from operations to differ from net income. Companies prefer the indirect method because it is easier and less expensive to prepare. As a result, the indirect method is the overwhelming choice of most companies and accountants. A survey of large companies shows that 98 percent use this method.[1]

International Perspective

IFRS The Direct Method May Become More Important Under IFRS

In the interest of converging U.S. GAAP with international financial reporting standards (IFRS), the IASB is promoting the use of the direct method, even though it is more costly for companies to prepare. IFRS will continue to require a reconciliation of net income and net cash flows from operating activities similar to what is now done in the indirect method. **CVS**'s statement of cash flows, as shown in the Supplement to Chapter 16, is one of the few U.S. companies to use the direct method with a reconciliation. Thus, its approach is very similar to what all companies may do if the U.S. adopts IFRS.

APPLY IT!

Mango Corporation engaged in the transactions that follow. Identify each transaction as (a) an operating activity, (b) an investing activity, (c) a financing activity, (d) a noncash transaction, or (e) not on the statement of cash flows.

1. Purchased office equipment, a long-term investment.
2. Decreased accounts receivable.
3. Sold land at cost.
4. Issued long-term bonds for plant assets.
5. Increased inventory.
6. Issued common stock.
7. Repurchased common stock.
8. Issued notes payable.
9. Increased income taxes payable.
10. Purchased a 60-day Treasury bill.
11. Purchased a long-term investment.
12. Declared and paid a cash dividend.

SOLUTION

1. b; 2. a; 3. b; 4. d; 5. a; 6. c; 7. c; 8. c; 9. a; 10. e (cash equivalent); 11. b; 12. c

TRY IT! SE1, SE6, E1A, E1B

SECTION 2 — ACCOUNTING APPLICATIONS

LO 2 — CASH FLOW — Step One: Determining Cash Flows from Operating Activities

As shown in Exhibit 3, preparing a statement of cash flows involves four steps:

■ **Step 1:** Determine cash flows from operating activities.
■ **Step 2:** Determine cash flows from investing activities.
■ **Step 3:** Determine cash flows from financing activities.
■ **Step 4:** Prepare the statement of cash flows.

In this section, we begin with determining cash flows from operating activities.

Exhibit 3
Preparation of the Statement of Cash Flows

© Cengage Learning 2014

To demonstrate the preparation of the statement of cash flows, we will use data for Eureka Corporation. Eureka's income statement for 2014 is presented in Exhibit 4, and its balance sheets for December 31, 2014 and 2013 appear in Exhibit 5. Exhibit 5 also shows the balance sheet accounts that we use for analysis and whether the change in each account is an increase or a decrease.

Exhibit 4
Income Statement

Eureka Corporation Income Statement For the Year Ended December 31, 2014		
Sales		$698,000
Cost of goods sold		520,000
Gross margin		$178,000
Operating expenses (including depreciation expense of $37,000)		147,000
Operating income		$ 31,000
Other income (expenses):		
Interest expense	$(23,000)	
Interest income	6,000	
Gain on sale of investments	12,000	
Loss on sale of plant assets	(3,000)	(8,000)
Income before income taxes		$ 23,000
Income taxes expense		7,000
Net income		$ 16,000

© Cengage Learning 2014

Exhibit 5
Comparative Balance Sheets Showing Changes in Accounts

Eureka Corporation
Comparative Balance Sheets
December 31, 2014 and 2013

	2014	2013	Change	Increase or Decrease
Assets				
Current assets:				
Cash	$ 47,000	$ 15,000	$ 32,000	Increase
Accounts receivable (net)	47,000	55,000	(8,000)	Decrease
Inventory	144,000	110,000	34,000	Increase
Prepaid expenses	1,000	5,000	(4,000)	Decrease
Total current assets	$ 239,000	$185,000	$ 54,000	
Investments	$ 115,000	$127,000	$ (12,000)	Decrease
Plant assets	$ 715,000	$505,000	$210,000	Increase
Less accumulated depreciation	(103,000)	(68,000)	(35,000)	Increase
Total plant assets	$ 612,000	$437,000	$175,000	
Total assets	$ 966,000	$749,000	$217,000	
Liabilities				
Current liabilities:				
Accounts payable	$ 50,000	$ 43,000	$ 7,000	Increase
Accrued liabilities	12,000	9,000	3,000	Increase
Income taxes payable	3,000	5,000	(2,000)	Decrease
Total current liabilities	$ 65,000	$ 57,000	$ 8,000	
Long-term liabilities:				
Bonds payable	295,000	245,000	50,000	Increase
Total liabilities	$ 360,000	$302,000	$ 58,000	
Stockholders' Equity				
Common stock, $5 par value	$ 276,000	$200,000	$ 76,000	Increase
Additional paid-in capital	214,000	115,000	99,000	Increase
Retained earnings	141,000	132,000	9,000	Increase
Treasury stock	(25,000)	0	(25,000)	Increase
Total stockholders' equity	$ 606,000	$447,000	$159,000	
Total liabilities and stockholders' equity	$ 966,000	$749,000	$217,000	

The income statement indicates how successful a company has been in earning an income from its operating activities. However, because that statement is prepared on an accrual basis, it does not reflect the inflow and outflow of cash related to operating activities. Revenues are recorded even though the company may not yet have received the cash, and expenses are recorded even though the company may not yet have expended the cash. Thus, to ascertain cash flows from operations in step 1 in preparing the statement of cash flows, the figures on the income statement must be converted from an accrual basis to a cash basis.

As Exhibit 6 shows, the indirect method focuses on adjusting items on the income statement to reconcile net income to net cash flows from operating activities. These items include the following:

- Depreciation, amortization, and depletion
- Gains and losses
- Changes in the balances of current asset and current liability accounts.

Exhibit 6
Indirect Method of
Determining Net
Cash Flows from
Operating Activities

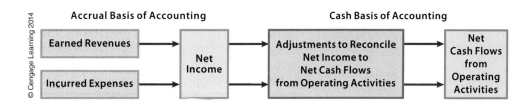

These adjusting items can be seen in the schedule in Exhibit 7, which shows the reconciliation of Eureka's net income to net cash flows from operating activities. Each adjusting item requires a different type of analysis as illustrated in the sections that follow.

Exhibit 7
Schedule of Cash
Flows from
Operating Activities:
Indirect Method

Eureka Corporation
Schedule of Cash Flows from Operating Activities
For the Year Ended December 31, 2014

Cash flows from operating activities:		
Net income		$16,000
Adjustments to reconcile net income to net cash flows from operating activities:		
Depreciation	$ 37,000	
Gain on sale of investments	(12,000)	
Loss on sale of plant assets	3,000	
Changes in current assets and current liabilities:		
Decrease in accounts receivable	8,000	
Increase in inventory	(34,000)	
Decrease in prepaid expenses	4,000	
Increase in accounts payable	7,000	
Increase in accrued liabilities	3,000	
Decrease in income taxes payable	(2,000)	14,000
Net cash flows from operating activities		$30,000

© Cengage Learning 2014

Depreciation, Amortization, and Depletion

Although the cash payments made for plant assets, intangible assets, and natural resources appear in the investing activities section of the statement of cash flows, the depreciation expense, amortization expense, and depletion expense associated with these assets appear in the operating activities section. The amount of these expenses can usually be found in the income statement or in a note to the financial statements.

STUDY NOTE: *Operating expenses on the income statement include depreciation expense, which does not require a cash outlay.*

Depreciation

Financial Statement Information Eureka's income statement (Exhibit 4) shows $37,000 of depreciation expense.

Journal Entry

	Dr.	Cr.
Depreciation Expense	37,000	
Accumulated Depreciation		37,000
To record annual depreciation on plant assets		

A	=	L	+	SE
−37,000				−37,000

Cash Flow Analysis

Depreciation	$37,000

When depreciation expense is recorded, the Cash account is not affected. Thus, net income needs to be adjusted upward by the amount of depreciation, or $37,000, because depreciation expense involves no current outlay of cash even though it appears on the income statement. Amortization and depletion expenses are handled in exactly the same way as depreciation expense.

Gains and Losses

Like depreciation expense, gains and losses that appear on the income statement do not affect cash flows from operating activities and need to be subtracted from or added to net income. The actual cash flows from these transactions are reflected in the investing and financing activities sections of the statement of cash flows.

Gain—Sale of Investments

Financial Statement Information Eureka's income statement (Exhibit 4) shows a $12,000 gain on the sale of investments.

Cash Flow Analysis

Gain on sale of investments	($12,000)

This amount is subtracted from net income to reconcile net income to net cash flows from operating activities. The reason for doing this is that the $12,000 is included in the investing activities section of the statement of cash flows as part of the cash from the sale of the investment. Because the gain has already been included in the calculation of net income, the $12,000 gain must be subtracted to prevent double counting.

Loss—Sale of Plant Assets

Financial Statement Information Eureka's income statement shows a $3,000 loss on the sale of plant assets.

Cash Flow Analysis

Loss on sale of plant assets	$3,000

As was the case with depreciation expense, a loss on the sale of assets is added to net income to reconcile net income to net cash flows from operating activities. The cash received associated with the transaction that resulted in this loss is reflected in the investing activities section of the statement of cash flows.

Changes in Current Assets

As explained in this section and the next, changes in current assets and current liabilities require a different approach to reconcile net income to cash flows from operating activities.

Decreases in current assets other than cash have positive effects on cash flows, and increases in current assets have negative effects on cash flows:

▼ A *decrease* in a current asset frees up invested cash, thereby increasing cash flow.

▲ An *increase* in a current asset consumes cash, thereby decreasing cash flow.

Decrease in Current Assets—Accounts Receivable

Financial Statement Information Eureka's balance sheet (Exhibit 5) shows an $8,000 decrease in accounts receivable. We can conclude that collections were $8,000 more than sales recorded for the year.

Cash Flow Analysis

Decrease in account receivable	$8,000

Because net sales in 2014 were $698,000, the total cash received from sales can be calculated as follows.

$$\text{Net Sales + Additional Cash Collections = Total Cash Collections Received}$$
$$\$698,000 + \$8,000 = \$706,000$$

The effect on Accounts Receivable can be illustrated as follows.

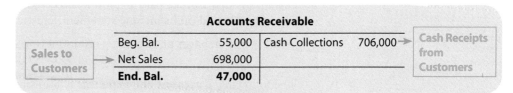

To reconcile net income to net cash flows from operating activities, the $8,000 decrease in accounts receivable is added to net income.

Increase in Current Assets—Inventory

Financial Statement Information Eureka's balance sheet (Exhibit 5) shows a $34,000 increase in inventory.

Cash Flow Analysis

Increase in inventory	($34,000)

Because the cost of goods sold in 2014 was $520,000, the total cash paid for inventory can be calculated as follows, as was done with accounts receivable.

$$\text{Cost of Goods Sold + Additional Purchases = Total Purchases}$$
$$\$520,000 + \$34,000 = \$554,000$$

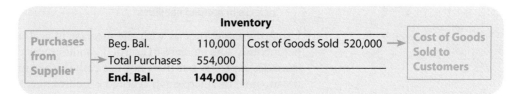

Thus, Eureka expended $34,000 more in cash for purchases than it included in the cost of goods sold on its income statement. Because of this expenditure, net income is higher than net cash flows from operating activities, so $34,000 must be deducted from net income.

Decrease in Current Assets—Prepaid Expenses

Financial Statement Information Continuing with current assets, Eureka's balance sheet (Exhibit 5) shows a $4,000 decrease in prepaid expenses.

Cash Flow Analysis

Decrease in prepaid expenses	$4,000

Using the same logic, the decrease shown on the balance sheet is added to net income because Eureka expended less cash on prepaid expenses than was included on the income statement.

Changes in Current Liabilities

The effect that changes in current liabilities have on cash flows is the opposite of the effect of changes in current assets:

▲ An *increase* in a current liability represents a postponement of a cash payment, which frees up cash and increases cash flow in the current period; thus, it is added to net income.

▼ A *decrease* in a current liability consumes cash, which decreases cash flow; thus, it is deducted from net income.

Increase in Current Liabilities—Accounts Payable

Financial Statement Information Eureka's balance sheet (Exhibit 5) shows a $7,000 increase in accounts payable.

Cash Flow Analysis

Increase in accounts payable $7,000

This means that Eureka paid $7,000 less to creditors than the amount indicated in the cost of goods sold on its income statement, illustrated as follows.

Purchases on Account* − Amount Unpaid = Total Cash Payments
$554,000 − $7,000 = $547,000

The following T account illustrates this relationship:

Cash Payments to Suppliers	**Accounts Payable**			
→ Payments on Account 547,000	Beg. Bal.	43,000	
	Purchases on Account	554,000* →	Purchases
	End. Bal.	**50,000**	

*Purchases = Cost of Goods Sold ($520,000) + Increase in Inventory ($34,000)

Thus, $7,000 must be added to net income to reconcile net income to net cash flows from operating activities.

Increase in Current Liabilities—Accrued Liabilities

Financial Statement Information Eureka's balance sheet (Exhibit 5) shows a $3,000 increase in accrued liabilities.

Cash Flow Analysis

Increase in accrued liabilities $3,000

Using the same logic as with the increase in accounts payable, this amount is added to net income. The increase in accrued liabilities was created by an adjusting entry that also increases expenses but does not use cash in the current period. Since expenses decrease net income, the increase in accrued expenses needs to be added to net income.

Decrease in Current Liabilities—Income Taxes Payable

Financial Statement Information Eureka's balance sheet (Exhibit 5) shows a $2,000 decrease in income taxes payable.

Cash Flow Analysis

Decrease in income taxes payable   ($2,000)

This amount is deducted from net income because the decrease in income taxes payable means the company paid this year's taxes plus an amount from the prior year, as follows.

Income Taxes Expense + Additional Payment = Total Income Taxes Payments
$7,000 + $2,000 = $9,000

Cash Paid for Income Taxes	**Income Taxes Payable**			
→ Income Taxes Payments 9,000	Beg. Bal.	5,000	
	Income Taxes Expense	7,000 →	Income Taxes Expense for the Year
	End. Bal.	**3,000**	

Schedule of Cash Flows from Operating Activities

In summary, Exhibit 7 shows that by using the indirect method, net income of $16,000 has been adjusted by reconciling items totaling $14,000 to arrive at net cash flows from operating activities of $30,000:

Net Income +/− Reconciling Items = Cash Flows from Operating Activities
$16,000 + $14,000 = $30,000

Although Eureka's net income was $16,000, the company actually had net cash flows of $30,000 from operating activities to use for purchasing assets, reducing debts, and paying dividends. The rules for reconciling items from the income statement that do not affect cash flows can be summarized as follows.

	Add to or Deduct from Net Income
Depreciation expense	✚ Add
Amortization expense	✚ Add
Depletion expense	✚ Add
Losses	✚ Add
Gains	━ Deduct

The following summarizes the adjustments from the balance sheet for increases and decreases in current assets and current liabilities:

	Add to Net Income ✚	*Deduct from Net Income* ━
Current assets:		
Accounts receivable (net)	▼ Decrease	▲ Increase
Inventory	▼ Decrease	▲ Increase
Prepaid expenses	▼ Decrease	▲ Increase
Current liabilities:		
Accounts payable	▲ Increase	▼ Decrease
Accrued liabilities	▲ Increase	▼ Decrease
Income taxes payable	▲ Increase	▼ Decrease

Business Perspective
What Is EBITDA, and Is It Any Good?

Some companies and analysts like to use EBITDA (an acronym for Earnings Before Interest, Taxes, Depreciation, and Amortization) as a shortcut measure of cash flows from operations. But experiences of the past decade have caused many analysts to reconsider this measure of performance. For instance, when **WorldCom** transferred $3.8 billion from expenses to capital expenditures in one year, it touted its EBITDA. At the time, the firm was, in fact, nearly bankrupt. The demise of **Vivendi**, the big French company that imploded when it did not have enough cash to pay its debts and that also touted its EBITDA, is another reason that analysts have had second thoughts about relying on this measure of performance.

Some analysts are now saying that EBITDA is "to a great extent misleading" and that it "is a confusing metric.... Some take it for a proxy for profits and some take it for a proxy for cash flow, and it's neither."[2] Cash flows from operations and free cash flow, both of which take into account interest, taxes, and depreciation, are better and more comprehensive measures of a company's ability to generate sufficient cash flows.

APPLY IT!

For the year ended June 30, 2015, RAK Corporation's net income was $7,400. Its depreciation expense was $2,000. During the year, its accounts receivable increased by $4,400, inventories increased by $7,000, prepaid rent decreased by $1,400, accounts payable increased by $14,000, salaries payable increased by $1,000, and income taxes payable decreased by $600. The company also had an $1,800 gain on the sale of investments. Use the indirect method to prepare a schedule of cash flows from operating activities.

SOLUTION

RAK Corporation
Schedule of Cash Flows from Operating Activities
For the Year Ended June 30, 2015

Cash flows from operating activities:		
Net income		$ 7,400
Adjustments to reconcile net income to net cash flows from operating activities:		
Depreciation	$ 2,000	
Gain on sale of investments	(1,800)	
Changes in current assets and current liabilities:		
Increase in accounts receivable	(4,400)	
Increase in inventories	(7,000)	
Decrease in prepaid rent	1,400	
Increase in accounts payable	14,000	
Increase in salaries payable	1,000	
Decrease in income taxes payable	(600)	4,600
Net cash flows from operating activities		$12,000

TRY IT! SE2, SE3, SE6, E2A, E3A, E4A, E8A, E2B, E3B, E4B, E8B

LO 3 Step Two: Determining Cash Flows from Investing Activities

Determining cash flows from investing activities is step 2 in preparing the statement of cash flows. In this step, accounts involving cash receipts and cash payments from investing activities are examined individually. The objective is to explain the change in each account balance from one period to the next.

Although investing activities relate mainly to the long-term assets shown on the balance sheet, they also include any short-term investments shown under current assets on the balance sheet and any investment gains and losses on the income statement. The balance sheets in Exhibit 5 show that Eureka had no short-term investments and that its long-term assets consisted of investments and plant assets. The income statement in Exhibit 4 shows that Eureka had a gain on the sale of investments and a loss on the sale of plant assets.

The following transactions pertain to Eureka's investing activities in 2014:

1. Purchased investments in the amount of $78,000.
2. Sold for $102,000 investments that cost $90,000.
3. Purchased plant assets in the amount of $120,000.
4. Sold for $5,000 plant assets that cost $10,000 and that had accumulated depreciation of $2,000.
5. Issued $100,000 of bonds at face value in a noncash exchange for plant assets.

In the sections that follow, we explain the effects of these transactions on Eureka's cash flows by analyzing their impact on the accounts related to investing activities.

Investments

Financial Statement Information Eureka's balance sheet (Exhibit 5) shows a $12,000 decrease in investments. To explain this decrease and its effects on the statement of cash flows, we will analyze the increases and decreases in Eureka's Investments account.

Purchase of Investments

Transaction 1 Purchased investments in the amount of $78,000.

Journal Entry

	Dr.	Cr.
Investments	78,000	
Cash		78,000
Purchase of investments		

Cash Flow Analysis

Purchase of investments	($78,000)

Sale of Investments

Transaction 2 Sold for $102,000 investments that cost $90,000.

Journal Entry

A = L + SE
+102,000   +12,000
−90,000

	Dr.	Cr.
Cash	102,000	
Investments		90,000
Gain on Sale of Investments		12,000
Sale of Investments for a gain		

Cash Flow Analysis

Sale of investments	$102,000

Note that the gain on the sale is included in the $102,000. This is the reason we excluded it in computing cash flows from operations. If it had not been excluded in that section, it would have been counted twice.

Reconciliation We have now explained the $12,000 decrease in the Investments account during 2014, as illustrated in the following T account:

Investments				
Dr.			**Cr.**	
Beg. Bal.	127,000	Sales		90,000
Purchases	78,000			
End. Bal.	**115,000**			

Purchases and sales are listed separately as cash outflows and inflows to give analysts a complete view of investing activities. However, some companies prefer to list them as a single net amount. If Eureka Corporation had short-term investments or marketable securities, the analysis of cash flows would be the same.

Plant Assets

Financial Statement Information Eureka's balance sheet shows the following:

- $210,000 increase in plant assets
- $35,000 increase in accumulated depreciation

Purchase of Plant Assets

Transaction 3 Purchased plant assets in the amount of $120,000.

Journal Entry

A = L + SE
+120,000
−120,000

	Dr.	Cr.
Plant Assets	120,000	
Cash		120,000

Cash Flow Analysis

Purchase of plant assets	($120,000)

Comment Cash outflows and cash inflows related to plant assets are listed separately, but companies sometimes combine them into a single net amount, called *capital expenditures*, when the cash inflows from sales are immaterial.

Sale of Plant Assets

Transaction 4 Sold for $5,000 plant assets that cost $10,000 and that had accumulated depreciation of $2,000.

Journal Entry

A = L + SE
+5,000   +3,000
+2,000
−10,000

	Dr.	Cr.
Cash	5,000	
Accumulated Depreciation	2,000	
Loss on Sale of Plant Assets	3,000	
Plant Assets		10,000
Sale of plant assets at a loss		

Cash Flow Analysis

Sale of plant assets	$5,000

STUDY NOTE: *The amount of a loss or gain on the sale of an asset is determined by the amount of cash received and does not represent a cash outflow or inflow.*

Note that this transaction results in a positive cash flow of $5,000, even though the plant assets were sold at a loss of $3,000. As noted in our analysis of operating activities, the loss on the sale of plant assets is added back to net income. This action avoids counting the loss in two sections of the statement of cash flows.

Issued Bonds in Exchange for Plant Assets

Transaction 5 Issued $100,000 of bonds at face value in a noncash exchange for plant assets.

Journal Entry

A = L + SE
+100,000   +100,000

	Dr.	Cr.
Plant Assets	100,000	
Bonds Payable		100,000
Issued bonds at face value for plant assets		

Cash Flow Analysis

Schedule of Noncash Investing and Financing Transactions	
Issue of bonds payable for plant assets	$100,000

Although this transaction does not involve an inflow or outflow of cash, it is a significant transaction involving both an investing activity (the purchase of plant assets) and a financing activity (the issue of bonds payable). Because one purpose of the statement of cash flows is to show important investing and financing activities, the transaction is *disclosed* at the bottom of the statement of cash flows or in a separate schedule.

Reconciliation We have now explained all the changes related to Eureka's Plant Assets account. The following T accounts summarize these changes:

Plant Assets

Dr.		Cr.	
Beg. Bal.	505,000	Sales	10,000
Cash Purchase	120,000		
Noncash Purchase	100,000		
End. Bal.	**715,000**		

Accumulated Depreciation

Dr.		Cr.	
Sale	2,000	Beg. Bal.	68,000
		Depreciation Expense	37,000
		End. Bal.	**103,000**

Had the balance sheet included specific plant asset accounts (e.g., Equipment and the related accumulated depreciation account) or other long-term asset accounts (e.g., Intangibles), the analysis would have been the same.

APPLY IT!

The following T accounts show Andre Company's plant assets and accumulated depreciation at the end of 2015:

Plant Assets

Dr.		Cr.	
Beg. Bal.	65,000	Disposals	23,000
Purchases	33,600		
End. Bal.	**75,600**		

Accumulated Depreciation

Dr.		Cr.	
Disposals	14,700	Beg. Bal.	34,500
		Depreciation	10,200
		End. Bal.	**30,000**

Andre's income statement shows a $4,400 gain on the sale of plant assets. Compute the amounts that should be shown as cash flows from investing activities and show how they should appear on Andre's 2015 statement of cash flows.

SOLUTION

Cash flows from investing activities:

Purchase of plant assets	$(33,600)
Sale of plant assets	12,700

The T accounts show total purchases of plant assets of $33,600, which is an outflow of cash, and the disposal of plant assets that cost $23,000 and that had accumulated depreciation of $14,700. The cash inflow from the disposal was as follows.

Plant assets	$23,000
Less accumulated depreciation	14,700
Book value	$ 8,300
Add gain on sale	4,400
Cash inflow from sale of plant assets	$12,700

Because the gain on the sale is included in the $12,700 in the investing activities section of the statement of cash flows, it should be deducted from net income in the operating activities section.

TRY IT! SE4, SE6, E5A, E6A, E8A, E5B, E6B, E8B

LO 4 Step Three: Determining Cash Flows from Financing Activities

Determining cash flows from financing activities is step 3 in preparing the statement of cash flows. It is very similar to determining cash flows from investing activities, but the accounts analyzed relate to short-term borrowings, long-term liabilities, and stockholders' equity. Because Eureka Corporation does not have short-term borrowings, we deal only with long-term liabilities and stockholders' equity accounts.

The following transactions pertain to Eureka's financing activities in 2014:

1. Issued $100,000 of bonds at face value in a noncash exchange for plant assets.
2. Repaid $50,000 of bonds at face value at maturity.
3. Issued 15,200 shares of $5 par value common stock for $175,000.
4. Paid cash dividends in the amount of $7,000.
5. Purchased treasury stock for $25,000.

Bonds Payable

Financial Statement Information Eureka's balance sheet (Exhibit 5) shows a $50,000 increase in Bonds Payable.

Issued Bonds

Transaction 1 Issued $100,000 of bonds at face value in a noncash exchange for plant assets. We have already analyzed Transaction 1 in connection with plant assets, but we also need to account for the change in the Bonds Payable account. As noted, this transaction is reported on the schedule of noncash investing and financing transactions.

Redeemed Bonds

Transaction 2 Repaid $50,000 of bonds at face value at maturity.

Journal Entry

		Dr.	Cr.
Bonds Payable		50,000	
Cash			50,000
Repayment of bonds at face value at maturity			

A = L + SE
−50,000 −50,000

Cash Flow Analysis

Repayment of bonds	($50,000)

Reconciliation The following T account explains the change in Bonds Payable:

Bonds Payable			
Dr.		**Cr.**	
Repayment	50,000	Beg. Bal.	245,000
		Noncash Issue	100,000
		End. Bal.	**295,000**

If Eureka Corporation had any notes payable, the analysis would be the same.

Common Stock

Increase in Common Stock and Additional Paid-in Capital

Financial Statement Information Eureka's balance sheet (Exhibit 5) shows a $76,000 increase in common stock and a $99,000 increase in additional paid-in capital.

Transaction 3 Issued 15,200 shares of $5 par value common stock for $175,000.

Journal Entry

A = L + SE
+175,000   +76,000
            +99,000

	Dr.	Cr.
Cash	175,000	
Common Stock		76,000
Additional Paid-In Capital		99,000
Issued 15,200 shares of $5 par value common stock		

Cash Flow Analysis

Issuance of common stock $175,000

Reconciliation The following analysis of this transaction is all that is needed to explain the changes in the two accounts during 2014:

Common Stock			Additional Paid-in Capital		
Dr.	Cr.		Dr.	Cr.	
	Beg. Bal.	200,000		Beg. Bal.	115,000
	Issue	76,000		Issue	99,000
	End. Bal.	**276,000**		**End. Bal.**	**214,000**

Retained Earnings

Increase in Retained Earnings

Financial Statement Information Eureka's balance sheet (Exhibit 5) shows a $9,000 increase in retained earnings.

Transaction 4 Paid cash dividends in the amount of $7,000.

Journal Entry

A = L + SE
   −7,000
   +7,000

	Dr.	Cr.
Retained Earnings	7,000	
Cash Dividends		7,000
To close the Cash Dividends account		

Cash Flow Analysis

Payment of dividends   ($7,000)

Reconciliation Recall that dividends will reduce Retained Earnings and that net income appears in the operating activities section of the statement of cash flows. Thus, we have now explained all the changes related to Eureka's Retained Earnings account. This T account shows the change in the Retained Earnings account:

Retained Earnings			
Dr.		Cr.	
Cash Dividends	7,000	Beg. Bal.	132,000
		Net Income	16,000
		End. Bal.	**141,000**

Treasury Stock

Increase in Treasury Stock

Financial Statement Information Eureka's balance sheet (Exhibit 5) shows a $25,000 increase in treasury stock.

STUDY NOTE: *Dividends paid, not dividends declared, appear on the statement of cash flows.*

High-tech companies with large amounts of intangible assets can lose up to 80 percent of their value in times of financial stress. As a hedge against economic downturns, these companies need to build cash reserves and may therefore choose to hoard cash rather than pay dividends.

Patryk Kosmider/Shutterstock.com

Transaction 5 Purchased treasury stock for $25,000.

Journal Entry

A	=	L	+	SE
−25,000				−25,000

	Dr.	Cr.
Treasury Stock	25,000	
Cash		25,000
Purchased treasury stock		

Cash Flow Analysis

Purchase of treasury stock	($25,000)

STUDY NOTE: *The purchase of treasury stock qualifies as a financing activity, but it is also a cash outflow.*

Reconciliation The following T account explains the change in Treasury Stock:

Treasury Stock

Dr.		Cr.
Purchase	25,000	

Step 4: Preparing the Statement of Cash Flows

We have now analyzed all of Eureka Corporation's income statement items, explained all balance sheet changes, and taken all additional information into account. Exhibit 8 shows how these data are assembled in Eureka's statement of cash flows.

Exhibit 8
Statement of Cash Flows: Indirect Method

Eureka Corporation
Statement of Cash Flows
For the Year Ended December 31, 2014

Cash flows from operating activities:		
Net income		$ 16,000
Adjustments to reconcile net income to net cash flows from operating activities:		
Depreciation	$ 37,000	
Gain on sale of investments	(12,000)	
Loss on sale of plant assets	3,000	
Changes in current assets and current liabilities:		
Decrease in accounts receivable	8,000	
Increase in inventory	(34,000)	
Decrease in prepaid expenses	4,000	
Increase in accounts payable	7,000	
Increase in accrued liabilities	3,000	
Decrease in income taxes payable	(2,000)	14,000
Net cash flows from operating activities		$ 30,000
Cash flows from investing activities:		
Purchase of investments	$ (78,000)	
Sale of investments	102,000	
Purchase of plant assets	(120,000)	
Sale of plant assets	5,000	
Net cash flows from investing activities		(91,000)
Cash flows from financing activities:		
Repayment of bonds	$ (50,000)	
Issuance of common stock	175,000	
Payment of dividends	(7,000)	
Purchase of treasury stock	(25,000)	
Net cash flows from financing activities		93,000
Net increase in cash		$ 32,000
Cash at beginning of year		15,000
Cash at end of year		$ 47,000
Schedule of Noncash Investing and Financing Transactions		
Issue of bonds payable for plant assets		$100,000

Cash Flows and the Financial Statements

As shown in Exhibit 9, the statement of cash flows explains the changes in cash on the balance sheet and reconciles the change in Cash (reported on the Balance Sheet) from one period to the next.

Exhibit 9
Relationship of the Statement of
Cash Flows to the Balance Sheet

© Cengage Learning 2014

APPLY IT!

During 2015, Brown Company issued $1,000,000 in long-term bonds at par, repaid $200,000 of notes payable at face value, issued notes payable of $40,000 for equipment, paid interest of $40,000, paid dividends of $25,000, and repurchased common stock in the amount of $50,000. Prepare the cash flows from financing activities section of the statement of cash flows.

SOLUTION

Cash flows from financing activities:	
Issuance of long-term bonds	$1,000,000
Repayment of notes payable	(200,000)
Payment of dividends	(25,000)
Purchase of treasury stock	(50,000)
Net cash flows from financing activities	$ 725,000

Note: Interest is an operating activity. The exchange of the notes payable for equipment is a noncash investing and financing transaction.

TRY IT! SE5, SE6, E7A, E8A, E7B, E8B

BUSINESS APPLICATIONS

 LO 5 Analyzing Cash Flows

An analysis of the statement of cash flows can reveal significant relationships. One area on which analysts focus is the cash inflows and outflows from operating activities, the first section on the statement of cash flows. Analysts use the information in this section to compute cash flow yield, cash flows to sales, cash flows to assets, and free cash flow.

Cash Flow Ratios

Cash flows from operating activities represent the cash generated from current or continuing operations. They are a measure of the ability to pay bills on time and to meet unexpected needs for cash, as well as how management spends the company's cash.

While the level of cash at the bottom of the statement of cash flows is certainly an important consideration, such information can be obtained from the balance sheet. The focal point of cash flow analysis is on cash inflows and outflows from operating activities. These cash flows are used in ratios that measure **cash-generating efficiency**, which is a company's ability to generate cash from its current or continuing operations. The ratios that analysts use to compute cash-generating efficiency are cash flow yield, cash flows to sales, and cash flows to assets.

In this section, we compute these ratios for **Amazon.com** in 2011 using data for net income and net cash flows from Exhibit 1 and the following information from Amazon. com's 2011 annual report (all dollar amounts are in millions):

	2011	**2010**
Net sales	$48,077	$34,204
Total assets	25,278	18,797

Cash Flow Yield **Cash flow yield** is the ratio of net cash flows from operating activities to net income. For **Amazon.com**, it is calculated as follows.

 Business Perspective
Can a Company Have Too Much Cash?

Having a surplus of cash on hand can be a benefit or a risk. Many companies put their excess cash to good use by investing in productive assets, conducting research and development, paying off debt, buying back stock, or paying dividends. Of course, companies must also keep enough cash on hand for emergencies; but when companies like **ExxonMobil**, **Microsoft**, and **Cisco Systems** accumulated large amounts of cash before the market crash in 2008, some commentators argued that this was poor management. They pointed out that shareholders suffer when executives are too conservative and keep the money in low-paying money market accounts or make unwise acquisitions.[3] However, these companies and others, like **Ford** and **Google**, that had cash reserves not only survived the down years, but also were prospering by 2010.[4] For financial statement users, it is important to look closely at the components of the statement of cash flows.

© Aija / iStockphoto.com

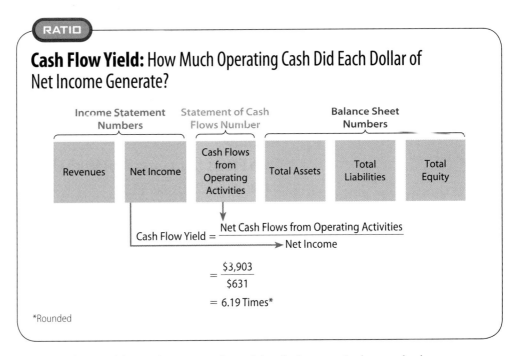

Cash flow yield is an important financial ratio because it shows whether a company is generating sufficient cash flow in relation to its net income or profitability. For most companies, the cash flow yield should exceed 1.0. Amazon.com's cash flow yield in 2011 was much better than that. With a cash flow yield of 6.19 times, Amazon.com was generating about $6.19 of cash for every dollar of net income.

The cash flow yield needs to be examined carefully. For instance, a firm with significant depreciable assets should have a cash flow yield greater than 1.0 because depreciation expense is added back to net income to arrive at cash flows from operating activities. If special items, such as discontinued operations, appear on the income statement and are material, income from continuing operations (from the income statement) should be used as the denominator. Also, an artificially high cash flow yield may result because a firm has very low net income, which is the denominator in the ratio.

Cash Flows to Sales **Cash flows to sales** is the ratio of net cash flows from operating activities to net sales. For **Amazon.com**, it is calculated as follows.

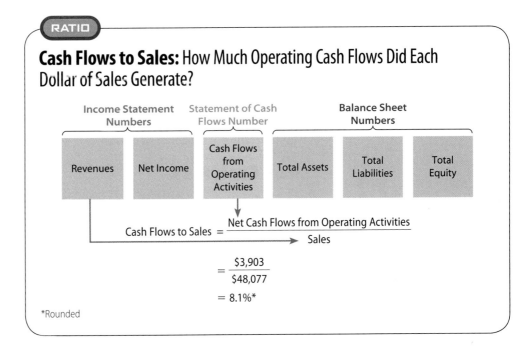

Amazon.com generated positive cash flows to sales of 8.1 percent. Another way to state this result is that every dollar of sales generated 8.1 cents in cash.

Cash Flows to Assets **Cash flows to assets** is the ratio of net cash flows from operating activities to average total assets. **Amazon.com**'s ratio is calculated as follows.

At 17.7 percent, Amazon.com's cash flows to assets ratio indicates that for every dollar of assets, the company generated almost 18 cents. This excellent result is higher than its cash flows to sales ratio because of its good asset turnover ratio:

$$\text{Asset Turnover} = \text{Sales} \div \text{Average Total Assets}$$
$$2.2 \text{ Times*} = \$48{,}077 \div \$22{,}038$$
$$\text{or}$$
$$\text{Asset Turnover} = \text{Cash Flows to Assets} \div \text{Cash Flows to Sales}$$
$$2.2 \text{ Times*} = 17.7\% \div 8.1\%$$

* Rounded

Cash flows to sales and cash flows to assets are closely related to the profitability measures of profit margin and return on assets. They exceed those measures by the amount of the cash flow yield ratio because cash flow yield is the ratio of net cash flows from operating activities to net income.

Free Cash Flow

As noted in an earlier chapter, **free cash flow** is the amount of cash that remains after deducting the funds a company must commit to continue operating at its planned level. Free cash flow is a very useful analytic tool. A study of 100 different measures showed it to be the best predictor of future increases in stock price.[5]

Free cash flow can be positive or negative:

- *Positive free cash flow* means that the company has met all of its planned cash commitments and has cash available to reduce debt or to expand.
- *Negative free cash flow* means that the company will have to sell investments, borrow money, or issue stock in the short term to continue at its planned level. If a company's free cash flow remains negative for several years, it may not be able to raise cash by issuing stocks or bonds. On the statement of cash flows, cash commitments for current and continuing operations, interest, and income taxes are incorporated in cash flows from current operations.

Amazon.com has a stated primary financial objective of "long-term sustainable growth in free cash flow."[6] The company definitely achieved this objective in 2011, as shown in the computation (in millions) that follows.

STUDY NOTE: The computation for free cash flow sometimes uses net capital expenditures in place of purchases plus sales of plant assets.

$$\text{Free Cash Flow} = \frac{\text{Net Cash Flows from}}{\text{Operating Activities}} - \text{Dividends} - \frac{\text{Purchases of}}{\text{Plant Assets}} + \frac{\text{Sales of}}{\text{Plant Assets}}$$

$$= \$3{,}903 - \$0 - \$1{,}811 + \$0$$

$$= \$2{,}092$$

Purchases of plant assets (capital expenditures) and sales (dispositions) of plant assets, if any, appear in the investing activities section of the statement of cash flows. Dividends, if any, appear in the financing activities section. Amazon.com is a growing company and does not have material sales of plant assets and does not pay dividends. The company's positive free cash flow of $2,092 million was due primarily to its strong operating cash flow of $3,903 million. Consequently, the company does not have to borrow money to expand.

Asking the Right Questions About the Statement of Cash Flows

Most readers of financial statements are accustomed to looking at the "bottom line" to get an overview of a company's financial status. They look at total assets on the balance sheet and net income on the income statement. However, the statement of cash flows requires a different approach because changes in the components of the statement during the year are far more revealing.

In interpreting a statement of cash flows, it pays to know the right questions to ask. To illustrate, we will use **Amazon.com** as an example.

Cash Flows and Net Income *What are the primary reasons that Amazon.com's cash flows from operating activities differed from net income in 2011?*

For Amazon.com, the largest positive items in 2011 were accounts payable and depreciation. They are added to net income for different reasons. Accounts payable represents

Business Perspective
What Do You Mean, "Free Cash Flow"?

Because the statement of cash flows has been around for less than 25 years, no generally accepted analyses have yet been developed. For example, the term *free cash flow* is commonly used in the business press, but there is no agreement on its definition. An article in *Forbes* defines *free cash flow* as "cash available after paying out capital expenditures and dividends, but *before taxes and interest*" [emphasis added].[7] An article in *The Wall Street Journal* defines it as "operating income less maintenance-level capital expenditures."[8] The definition with which we are most in agreement is the one used in *BusinessWeek:* free cash flow is net cash flows from operating activities less net capital expenditures and dividends. This "measures truly discretionary funds—company money that an owner could pocket without harming the business."[9]

an increase in the amount owed to creditors, whereas depreciation represents a noncash expense that is deducted in arriving at net income. Amazon.com's two largest negative items were increases in inventories and amortization of unearned revenue. As a growing company, Amazon.com was managing its operating cycle by generating cash from creditors to pay for increases in inventories.

Investing Activities *What were Amazon.com's most important investing activities other than capital expenditures?*

Amazon.com was actively buying and selling investments. However, sales of marketable securities and other investments were not sufficient to offset the purchase of marketable securities and other investments and the purchase of various assets.

Financing Activities *How did Amazon.com manage its financing activities during 2011?*

Excess tax benefits from stock-based compensation and proceeds from long-term debt provided some funds to buy back treasury stock and pay off some long-term debt, but the inflows were less than the outflows. Because of its good cash flow from operations, Amazon.com did not need long-term financing.

Cash Flow Trends *What has been the trend of cash flows for Amazon.com?*

Because cash flows can vary from year to year, analysts should look at trends in cash flow measures over several years. For example, Amazon.com's management states:

> Because of our model we are able to turn our inventory quickly and have a cash-generating operating cycle. On average our high inventory velocity means we generally collect from consumers before our payments to suppliers come due. Inventory turnover was 10, 11, and 12 for 2011, 2010, and 2009. We expect variability in inventory turnover over time since it is affected by several factors, including our product mix, the mix of sales by us and by other sellers, our continuing focus on in-stock inventory availability, our investment in new geographies and product lines, and the extent to which we choose to utilize outsource fulfillment providers. Accounts payable days were 74, 72, and 68 for 2011, 2010, and 2009. We expect some variability in accounts payable days over time since they are affected by several factors, including the mix of product sales, the mix of sales by other sellers, the mix of suppliers, seasonality, and changes in payment terms over time, including the effect of balancing pricing and timing of payment terms with suppliers.[10]

Ethical Considerations in Analyzing the Statement of Cash Flows

Although cash inflows and outflows are not as subject to manipulation as earnings are, managers are acutely aware of users' emphasis on cash flows from operations as an important measure of performance. Thus, an incentive exists to overstate these cash flows.

In earlier chapters, we cited an egregious example of earnings management. As you may recall, by treating operating expenses of about $10 billion over several years as purchases of equipment, **WorldCom** reduced reported expenses and improved reported earnings. In addition, by classifying payments of operating expenses as investments on the statement of cash flows, it was able to show an improvement in cash flows from operations. The inclusion of the expenditures in the investing activities section did not draw special attention because the company normally had large capital expenditures.

Another way a company can show an apparent improvement in its performance is through lack of transparency, or lack of full disclosure, in its financial statements. For instance, securitization—the sale of batches of accounts receivable—is clearly a means of financing, and the proceeds from it should be shown in the financing activities section of the statement of cash flows. However, because the accounting standards are somewhat vague about where these proceeds should go, some companies net the proceeds against the accounts receivable in the operating activities section of the statement and bury the explanation in the notes to the financial statements. By doing so, they make collections of receivables look better than they actually were. It is not illegal to do this; but from an ethical standpoint, it obscures the company's true performance.

APPLY IT!

In 2015, Benson Corporation had year-end assets of $2,400,000, sales of $2,000,000, net income of $400,000, net cash flows from operating activities of $360,000, dividends of $100,000, purchases of plant assets of $200,000, and sales of plant assets of $40,000. In 2014, year-end assets were $2,200,000. Calculate cash flow yield, cash flows to sales, cash flows to assets, and free cash flow.

SOLUTION

$$\text{Cash Flow Yield} = \frac{\$360,000}{\$400,000} = 0.9 \text{ Time}$$

$$\text{Cash Flows to Sales} = \frac{\$360,000}{\$2,000,000} = 0.18, \text{ or } 18\%$$

$$\text{Cash Flows to Assets} = \frac{\$360,000}{(\$2,400,000 + \$2,200,000) \div 2} = 0.16, \text{ or } 16\% \text{ (rounded)}$$

$$\text{Free Cash Flow} = \$360,000 - \$100,000 - \$200,000 + \$40,000 = \$100,000$$

TRY IT! SE7, SE8, E9A, E9B

TriLevel Problem

Deliga Corporation

The beginning of this chapter focused on Deliga Corporation, whose managers were concerned because in 2015, cash flows from operating activities were less than net income, cash and cash equivalents declined during the year, and the company was having trouble paying its bills on time. Complete the following requirements in order to answer the questions posed at the beginning of the chapter.

Section 1: Concepts
How do relevance and classification apply to the statement of cash flows?

Section 2: Accounting Applications
How is the statement of cash flows prepared using the indirect method?

Prepare a statement of cash flows using Deliga Corporation's income statement for 2015 and comparative balance sheets for 2015 and 2014 that follow.

	A	B	C	D	E
1			**Deliga Corporation**		
2			**Income Statement**		
3			**For the Year Ended December 31, 2015**		
4					
5	Net sales				$825,000
6	Cost of goods sold				460,000
7	Gross margin				$365,000
8	Operating expenses (including depreciation expense of $6,000				
9	on buildings and $11,550 on equipment and amortization				
10	expense of $2,400)				235,000
11	Operating income				$130,000
12	Other income:				
13			Interest expense	$(27,500)	
14			Dividend income	1,700	
15			Gain on sale of investments	6,250	
16			Loss on disposal of equipment	(1,150)	(20,700)
17	Income before income taxes				$109,300
18	Income taxes expense				26,100
19	Net income				$ 83,200

	A	B	C	D	E	F
1			**Deliga Corporation**			
2			**Comparative Balance Sheets**			
3			**December 31, 2015 and 2014**			
4						**Increase or**
5				**2015**	**2014**	**Change**	**Decrease**
6			**Assets**			
7		Cash		$ 52,925	$ 60,925	$ (8,000)	Decrease
8		Accounts receivable (net)		148,000	157,250	(9,250)	Decrease
9		Inventory		161,000	150,500	10,500	Increase
10		Prepaid expenses		3,900	2,900	1,000	Increase
11		Long-term investments		18,000	43,000	(25,000)	Decrease
12		Land		75,000	62,500	12,500	Increase
13		Buildings		231,000	231,000	—	—
14		Accumulated depreciation—buildings		(45,500)	(39,500)	(6,000)	Increase
15		Equipment		79,865	83,615	(3,750)	Decrease
16		Accumulated depreciation—equipment		(21,700)	(22,800)	1,100	Decrease
17		Intangible assets		9,600	12,000	(2,400)	Decrease
18		Total assets		$712,090	$741,390	$(29,300)	
19						
20		**Liabilities and Stockholders' Equity**				
21		Accounts payable		$ 66,875	$116,875	$(50,000)	Decrease
22		Notes payable (current)		37,850	72,850	(35,000)	Decrease
23		Accrued liabilities		2,500	—	2,500	Increase
24		Income taxes payable		10,000	—	10,000	Increase
25		Bonds payable		105,000	155,000	(50,000)	Decrease
26		Mortgage payable		165,000	175,000	(10,000)	Decrease
27		Common stock, $10 par value		200,000	170,000	30,000	Increase
28		Additional paid-in capital		45,000	25,000	20,000	Increase
29		Retained earnings		104,865	46,665	58,200	Increase
30		Treasury stock		(25,000)	(20,000)	(5,000)	Increase
31		Total liabilities and stockholders' equity		$712,090	$741,390	$(29,300)	

The company's records for 2015 provide this additional information:

a. Sold long-term investments that cost $35,000 for a gain of $6,250; made other long-term investments in the amount of $10,000.
b. Purchased five acres of land to build a parking lot for $12,500.
c. Sold equipment that cost $18,750 and that had accumulated depreciation of $12,650 at a loss of $1,150; purchased new equipment for $15,000.
d. Repaid notes payable in the amount of $50,000; borrowed $15,000 by signing new notes payable.
e. Converted $50,000 of bonds payable into 3,000 shares of common stock.
f. Reduced the Mortgage Payable account by $10,000.
g. Declared and paid cash dividends of $25,000.
h. Purchased treasury stock for $5,000.

Section 3: Business Applications

What measures may be used to explain the apparent cause of Deliga's operating cash flow problem and the decline in its cash and cash equivalents?

Compute the company's cash flow yield, cash flows to sales, cash flows to assets, and free cash flow for 2015. (Round ratios to the nearest decimal point.) What do your results indicate about the company's cash-generating efficiency? What do they indicate about Deliga's need to sell investments, issue stock, or borrow money to maintain current operations or finance future growth?

SOLUTION

Section 1: Concepts

The statement of cash flows is *relevant* to management, investors, and creditors for assessing the current and future liquidity of a company, its dividend policy, and its financing needs. Operating activities *classify* inflows and outflows from operating activities and include among other things cash inflows from the sales of goods and services, sale of trading securities, as well as interest and dividends on loans and investments while cash outflows include cash spent for wages, inventory, expenses, interest, taxes, and purchase of trading securities. Investing activities *classify* the acquisition and sale of short-term marketable securities, long-term investments, and property, plant, and equipment and the making and collecting of loans. Financing activities *classify* obtaining resources from stockholders and creditors and show proceeds from stock issues and from short- and long-term borrowings and deductions for repayment of loans, payment of dividends, and purchase of treasury stock. Finally, noncash investing and financing activities are *disclosed* in a separate schedule.

Section 2: Accounting Applications

	A	B	C	D	E
1			**Deliga Corporation**		
2			**Statement of Cash Flows**		
3			**For the Year Ended December 31, 2015**		
4					
5	Cash flows from operating activities:				
6	Net income				$83,200
7	Adjustments to reconcile net income to net cash flows				
8	from operating activities:				
9			Depreciation expense—buildings	$ 6,000	
10			Depreciation expense—equipment	11,550	
11			Amortization expense—intangible assets	2,400	
12			Gain on sale of investments	(6,250)	
13			Loss on disposal of equipment	1,150	
14			Changes in current assets and current liabilities:		
15			Decrease in accounts receivable	9,250	
16			Increase in inventory	(10,500)	
17			Increase in prepaid expenses	(1,000)	
18			Decrease in accounts payable	(50,000)	
19			Increase in accrued liabilities	2,500	
20			Increase in income taxes payable	10,000	(24,900)
21	Net cash flows from operating activities				$58,300
22	Cash flows from investing activities:				
23	Sale of long-term investments			$ 41,250[a]	
24	Purchase of long-term investments			(10,000)	
25	Purchase of land			(12,500)	
26	Sale of equipment			4,950[b]	
27	Purchase of equipment			(15,000)	
28	Net cash flows from investing activities				8,700
29	Cash flows from financing activities:				
30	Repayment of notes payable			$(50,000)	
31	Issuance of notes payable			15,000	
32	Reduction in mortgage			(10,000)	
33	Dividends paid			(25,000)	
34	Purchase of treasury stock			(5,000)	
35	Net cash flows from financing activities				(75,000)
36	Net (decrease) in cash				$ (8,000)
37	Cash at beginning of year				60,925
38	Cash at end of year				$52,925
39					
40			**Schedule of Noncash Investing and Financing Transactions**		
41	Conversion of bonds payable into common stock				$50,000
42					
43	[a]$35,000 + $6,250 (gain) = $41,250				
44	[b]$18,750 − $12,650 = $6,100 (book value) − $1,150 (loss) = $4,950				

Section 3: Business Applications

$$\text{Cash Flow Yield} = \frac{\$58,300}{\$83,200} = 0.7 \text{ Time*}$$

$$\text{Cash Flows to Sales} = \frac{\$58,300}{\$825,000} = 7.1\%^*$$

$$\text{Cash Flows to Assets} = \frac{\$58,300}{(\$712,090 + \$741,390) \div 2} = 8.0\%^*$$

$$\text{Free Cash Flow} = \$58,300 - \$25,000 - \$12,500 - \$15,000 + \$4,950 = \$10,750$$

*Rounded

Deliga should generate at least $1 of net cash flows from operations for each $1 of net income. However, its cash flow yield shows that it generated only 70 cents for each $1 of net income. Judging from this result alone, Deliga's cash-generating efficiency is weak, and it seems likely that the company will have to sell investments, borrow money, or issue stock to maintain current operations or finance future growth.

The operating activities section of Deliga's statement of cash flows shows that the company reduced its accounts payable by $50,000. This one item more than offset the effects of all the other items and accounts for Deliga's operating cash flow problem and the decline in its cash and cash equivalents. Either Deliga unnecessarily paid its creditors a large amount, or its creditors have changed their terms. In the aftermath of the recession of the last few years, it has not been unusual for creditors to give less favorable terms as credit from banks has tightened.

Chapter Review

Describe the principal purposes and concepts underlying the statement of cash flows, and identify its components and format. **LO 1**

The statement of cash flows is relevant to investors and creditors by providing information about a company's cash receipts and cash payments during a period in order to assess the company's cash-generating ability. It is relevant to management to assess liquidity, determine dividend policy, and plan investing and financing activities. Investors and creditors use it to assess the company's cash-generating ability.

The statement of cash flows has three major classifications: (1) operating activities, which involve the cash effects of transactions and other events that enter into the determination of net income; (2) investing activities, which involve the acquisition and sale of marketable securities and long-term assets and the making and collecting of loans; and (3) financing activities, which involve obtaining resources from stockholders and creditors. Noncash investing and financing transactions are also important because they affect future cash flows.

Use the indirect method to determine cash flows from operating activities. **LO 2**

The indirect method adjusts net income for all items in the income statement that do not have cash flow effects (such as depreciation, amortization, and gains and losses on sales of assets) and for changes in assets and liabilities that affect operating cash flows. Generally, increases in current assets have a negative effect on cash flows, and decreases have a positive effect. Conversely, increases in current liabilities have a positive effect on cash flows, and decreases have a negative effect.

Determine cash flows from investing activities. **LO 3**

Investing activities involve the acquisition and sale of property, plant, and equipment and other long-term assets, including long-term investments. They also involve the acquisition and sale of short-term marketable securities, other than trading securities, and the making and collecting of loans. Cash flows from investing activities are determined by analyzing the cash flow effects of changes in each account related to investing activities. The effects of gains and losses reported on the income statement must also be considered.

Determine cash flows
from financing activities.

Determining cash flows from financing activities is almost identical to determining cash flows from investing activities. The difference is that the accounts analyzed relate to short-term borrowings, long-term liabilities, and stockholders' equity. After the changes in the balance sheet accounts from one accounting period to the next have been explained, all the cash flow effects should have been identified, and the statement of cash flows can be prepared.

Analyze the statement
of cash flows.

Analysts tend to focus on a firm's degree of liquidity, which is determined by cash inflows and outflows. The ratios used to measure a firm's ability to generate sufficient cash are cash flow yield, cash flows to sales, and cash flows to assets. Free cash flow—the cash that remains after deducting the funds a firm must commit to continue operating at its planned level—is another important measure of the adequacy of cash flow.

Key Terms and Ratios

cash 602 (LO1)
cash equivalents 602 (LO1)
direct method 605 (LO1)
financing activities 603 (LO1)
indirect method 606 (LO1)
investing activities 603 (LO1)

marketable securities 602 (LO1)
noncash investing and
  financing transactions 605 (LO1)
operating activities 603 (LO1)
statement of cash flows 602 (LO1)
trading securities 603 (LO1)

RATIOS
cash flow yield 622 (LO5)
cash flows to assets 624 (LO5)
cash flows to sales 623 (LO5)
cash-generating
  efficiency 622 (LO5)
free cash flow 624 (LO5)

Chapter Assignments

DISCUSSION QUESTIONS

LO 1　**DQ1.** Which statement is more useful—the income statement or the statement of cash flows?

LO 2　**DQ2.** If a company has positive earnings, can cash flows from operating activities ever be negative?

LO 2, 3　**DQ3.** Which adjustments to net income in the operating activities section of the statement of cash flows are directly related to cash flows in other sections?

LO 5　**DQ4.** How would you respond to someone who says that the most important item on the statement of cash flows is the change in the cash balance for the year?

LO 5　**DQ5. BUSINESS APPLICATION** ▶ If a company's cash flow yield is less than 1.0, would its cash flows to sales and cash flows to assets be greater or less than profit margin and return on assets, respectively?

LO 5　**DQ6. BUSINESS APPLICATION** ▶ In computing free cash flow, what is an argument for treating the purchases of treasury stock like dividend payments?

SHORT EXERCISES

LO 1　**Classification of Cash Flow Transactions**

SE1. CONCEPT ▶ The list that follows itemizes Alpha Pro Corporation's transactions. Identify each as (a) an operating activity, (b) an investing activity, (c) a financing activity, (d) a noncash transaction, or (e) none of the above.

　1. Sold land.
　2. Declared and paid a cash dividend.

3. Paid interest.
4. Issued common stock for plant assets.
5. Issued preferred stock.
6. Borrowed cash on a bank loan.

LO 2   **Computing Cash Flows from Operating Activities: Indirect Method**

SE2. Stewart Construction Corporation had a net income of $16,500 during 2014. In that year, the company had depreciation expense of $7,000. Accounts Receivable increased by $5,500, and Accounts Payable increased by $2,500. Those were the company's only current assets and current liabilities. Use the indirect method to determine net cash flows from operating activities.

LO 2   **Computing Cash Flows from Operating Activities: Indirect Method**

SE3. During 2014, Cupello Corporation had a net income of $144,000. Included on its income statement were depreciation expense of $16,000 and amortization expense of $1,800. During the year, Accounts Receivable decreased by $8,200, Inventories increased by $5,400, Prepaid Expenses decreased by $1,000, Accounts Payable decreased by $14,000, and Accrued Liabilities decreased by $1,700. Use the indirect method to determine net cash flows from operating activities.

LO 3   **Cash Flows from Investing Activities and Noncash Transactions**

SE4. During 2014, Fargo Company purchased land for $375,000. It paid $125,000 in cash and signed a $250,000 mortgage for the rest. The company also sold for $95,000 cash a building that originally cost $90,000, on which it had $70,000 of accumulated depreciation, making a gain of $75,000. Prepare the cash flows from investing activities section and the schedule of noncash investing and financing transactions of the statement of cash flows.

LO 4   **Cash Flows from Financing Activities**

SE5. During 2014, North Dakota Company issued $1,000,000 in long-term bonds at 96, repaid $150,000 of bonds at face value, paid interest of $80,000, and paid dividends of $50,000. Prepare the cash flows from the financing activities section of the statement of cash flows.

LO 1, 2, 3, 4   **Identifying Components of the Statement of Cash Flows**

SE6. CONCEPT ▶ Assuming the indirect method is used to prepare the statement of cash flows, tell whether each of the following items would be reported (a) in cash flows from operating activities, (b) in cash flows from investing activities, (c) in cash flows from financing activities, (d) in the schedule of noncash investing and financing transactions, or (e) not on the statement of cash flows at all:

1. Dividends paid
2. Cash receipts from sales
3. Decrease in accounts receivable
4. Sale of plant assets
5. Gain on sale of investments
6. Issue of stock for plant assets
7. Issue of common stock
8. Net income

LO 5   **Cash-Generating Efficiency Ratios and Free Cash Flow**

SE7. BUSINESS APPLICATION ▶ In 2014, Melvin Corporation had year-end assets of $1,100,000, sales of $1,580,000, net income of $180,000, net cash flows from operating activities of $360,000, purchases of plant assets of $240,000, and sales of plant assets of $40,000, and it paid dividends of $80,000. In 2013, year-end assets were $1,000,000. Calculate the cash-generating efficiency ratios of cash flow yield, cash flows to sales, and cash flows to assets. Also calculate free cash flow. (Round to the nearest tenth of a percent.)

LO 5

Cash-Generating Efficiency Ratios and Free Cash Flow

SE8. BUSINESS APPLICATION ▶ Examine the cash flow measures in requirement **3** of the TriLevel Problem at the end of this chapter. Discuss the meaning of these ratios.

EXERCISES: SET A

LO 1

Classification of Cash Flow Transactions

E1A. CONCEPT ▶ VIP Corporation engaged in the transactions that follow. Identify each transaction as (a) an operating activity, (b) an investing activity, (c) a financing activity, (d) a noncash transaction, or (e) not on the statement of cash flows. Assume the indirect method is used. (*Hint:* More than one answer may apply.)

1. Paid interest.
2. Increased dividends receivable.
3. Declared and paid a cash dividend.
4. Purchased a long-term investment.
5. Increased accounts receivable.
6. Sold equipment at a loss.
7. Issued long-term bonds for plant assets.
8. Issued common stock.
9. Declared and issued a stock dividend.
10. Decreased wages payable.
11. Purchased a 60-day Treasury bill.
12. Repaid notes payable.
13. Purchased land.

LO 2

Cash Flows from Operating Activities: Indirect Method

E2A. The condensed single-step income statement for the year ended December 31, 2014, of Conti Chemical Company, a distributor of farm fertilizers and herbicides, follows.

Sales		$26,000,000
Less: Cost of goods sold	$15,200,000	
Operating expenses (including depreciation of $1,640,000)	7,600,000	
Income taxes expense	800,000	23,600,000
Net income		$ 2,400,000

Selected accounts from Conti Chemical's balance sheets for 2014 and 2013 follow.

	2014	2013
Accounts receivable	$4,800,000	$3,400,000
Inventory	1,680,000	2,040,000
Prepaid expenses	520,000	360,000
Accounts payable	1,920,000	1,440,000
Accrued liabilities	120,000	200,000
Income taxes payable	280,000	240,000

Prepare a schedule of cash flows from operating activities using the indirect method.

LO 2

Computing Cash Flows from Operating Activities: Indirect Method

E3A. During 2014, Ortega Corporation had net income of $82,000. Included on its income statement were depreciation expense of $4,600 and amortization expense of $600. During the year, Accounts Receivable increased by $6,800, Inventories decreased by $3,800, Prepaid Expenses decreased by $400, Accounts Payable increased by $10,000, and Accrued Liabilities decreased by $900. Determine net cash flows from operating activities using the indirect method.

LO **2**   **Preparing a Schedule of Cash Flows from
Operating Activities: Indirect Method**

E4A. For the year ended June 30, 2014, net income for Flake Corporation was $14,800. Depreciation expense was $4,000. During the year, Accounts Receivable increased by $8,800, Inventories increased by $14,000, Prepaid Rent decreased by $2,800, Accounts Payable increased by $28,000, Salaries Payable increased by $2,000, and Income Taxes Payable decreased by $1,200. Use the indirect method to prepare a schedule of cash flows from operating activities.

LO **3**   **Computing Cash Flows from Investing Activities: Investments**

E5A. Wilma Company's T account for long-term available-for-sale investments at the end of 2014 follows.

Investments

Dr.		Cr.	
Beg. Bal.	76,000	Sales of Investments	78,000
Purchases of Investments	116,000		
End. Bal.	**114,000**		

In addition, Wilma's income statement shows a loss on the sale of investments of $13,000. Compute the amounts to be shown as cash flows from investing activities, and show how they appear in the statement of cash flows.

LO **3**   **Computing Cash Flows from Investing Activities: Plant Assets**

E6A. The T accounts for plant assets and accumulated depreciation for Street Company at the end of 2014 follow.

Plant Assets				Accumulated Depreciation			
Dr.		Cr.		Dr.		Cr.	
Beg. Bal.	130,000	Disposals	46,000	Disposals	29,400	Beg. Bal.	69,000
Purchases	67,200					Depreciation	20,400
End. Bal.	**151,200**					**End. Bal.**	**60,000**

In addition, Street's income statement shows a gain on sale of plant assets of $8,800. Compute the amounts to be shown as cash flows from investing activities, and show how they appear on the statement of cash flows.

LO **4**   **Determining Cash Flows from Financing Activities: Notes Payable**

E7A. All transactions involving Notes Payable and related accounts of Sally Company during 2014 follow.

	Dr.	Cr.
Cash	36,000	
Notes Payable		36,000
Bank loan		

	Dr.	Cr.
Patent	60,000	
Notes Payable		60,000
Purchase of patent by issuing note payable		

	Dr.	Cr.
Notes Payable	10,000	
Interest Expense	1,000	
Cash		11,000
Repayment of note payable at maturity		

Determine the amounts of the transactions affecting financing activities and show how they appear on the statement of cash flows for 2014.

LO **2, 3, 4**   **Preparing the Statement of Cash Flows: Indirect Method**

E8A. Keeper Corporation's income statement for the year ended June 30, 2014, and its comparative balance sheets for June 30, 2014 and 2013 follow.

Keeper Corporation
Income Statement
For the Year Ended June 30, 2014

Sales	$234,000
Cost of goods sold	156,000
Gross margin	$ 78,000
Operating expenses	45,000
Operating income	$ 33,000
Interest expense	2,800
Income before income taxes	$ 30,200
Income taxes expense	12,300
Net income	$ 17,900

Keeper Corporation
Comparative Balance Sheets
June 30, 2014 and 2013

	2014	2013
Assets		
Cash	$ 69,900	$ 12,500
Accounts receivable (net)	21,000	26,000
Inventory	43,400	48,400
Prepaid expenses	3,200	2,600
Furniture	55,000	60,000
Accumulated depreciation—furniture	(9,000)	(5,000)
Total assets	$183,500	$144,500
Liabilities and Stockholders' Equity		
Accounts payable	$ 13,000	$ 14,000
Income taxes payable	1,200	1,800
Notes payable (long-term)	37,000	35,000
Common stock, $10 par value	115,000	90,000
Retained earnings	17,300	3,700
Total liabilities and stockholders' equity	$183,500	$144,500

Keeper issued a $22,000 note payable for purchase of furniture; sold at carrying value furniture that cost $27,000 with accumulated depreciation of $15,300; recorded depreciation on the furniture for the year, $19,300; repaid a note in the amount of $20,000; issued $25,000 of common stock at par value; and paid dividends of $4,300. Prepare Keeper's statement of cash flows for the year 2014 using the indirect method.

LO **5**   **Cash-Generating Efficiency Ratios and Free Cash Flow**

E9A. BUSINESS APPLICATION ▶ In 2014, Andy's Corporation had year-end assets of $2,400,000, sales of $3,300,000, net income of $280,000, net cash flows from operating activities of $390,000, dividends of $120,000, purchases of plant assets of $500,000, and sales of plant assets of $90,000. In 2013, year-end assets were $2,100,000. Calculate free cash flow and the cash-generating efficiency ratios of cash flow yield, cash flows to sales, and cash flows to assets. (Round to one decimal point or the nearest tenth of a percent.)

EXERCISES: SET B

Visit the textbook companion website at www.cengagebrain.com to access Exercise Set B for this chapter.

PROBLEMS

LO 1   **Classification of Cash Flow Transactions**

P1. CONCEPT ▶ Analyze each transaction listed in the table that follows and place X's in the appropriate columns to indicate the transaction's classification and its effect on cash flows using the indirect method.

	Cash Flow Classification				Effect on Cash Flows		
Transaction	Operating Activity	Investing Activity	Financing Activity	Noncash Transaction	Increase	Decrease	No Effect
1. Paid a cash dividend.							
2. Decreased accounts receivable.							
3. Increased inventory.							
4. Incurred a net loss.							
5. Declared and issued a stock dividend.							
6. Retired long-term debt with cash.							
7. Sold available-for-sale securities at a loss.							
8. Issued stock for equipment.							
9. Decreased prepaid insurance.							
10. Purchased treasury stock with cash.							
11. Retired a fully depreciated truck (no gain or loss).							
12. Increased interest payable.							
13. Decreased dividends receivable on investment.							
14. Sold treasury stock.							
15. Increased income taxes payable.							
16. Transferred cash to money market account.							
17. Purchased land and building with a mortgage.							

LO **1, 5**   **Interpreting and Analyzing the Statement of Cash Flows**

✔ 2: Free cash flow, 2013: ($183,114)
✔ 2: Free cash flow, 2014: $290,316

P2. The comparative statements of cash flows for Wung Corporation, a manufacturer of high-quality suits for men, follow. To expand its markets and familiarity with its brand, the company attempted a new strategic diversification in 2013 by acquiring a chain of retail men's stores in outlet malls. Its plan was to expand in malls around the country, but department stores viewed the action as infringing on their territory.

Wung Corporation
Statement of Cash Flows
For the Years Ended December 31, 2014 and 2013

(In thousands)	2014	2013
Cash flows from operating activities:		
Net income (loss)	$ (43,090)	$ 76,030
Adjustments to reconcile net income to net cash flows from operating activities:		
Depreciation	$ 70,438	$ 50,036
Loss on closure of retail outlets	70,000	
Changes in current assets and current liabilities:		
Decrease (increase) in accounts receivable	100,000	(89,606)
Decrease (increase) in inventory	120,814	(102,290)
Decrease (increase) in prepaid expenses	2,734	4,492
Increase (decrease) in accounts payable	61,158	2,532
Increase (decrease) in accrued liabilities	3,000	(5,576)
Increase (decrease) in income taxes payable	(16,600)	(12,562)
	$ 411,544	$(152,974)

(*Continued*)

Net cash flows from operating activities	$ 368,454	$ (76,944)
Cash flows from investing activities:		
Capital expenditures, net	$ (32,290)	$ (66,224)
Purchase of Retail Division, cash portion	—	(402,000)
Net cash flows from investing activities	$ (32,290)	$(468,224)
Cash flows from financing activities:		
Increase (decrease) in notes payable to banks	$ (247,000)	$ 456,800
Reduction in long-term debt	(18,476)	(21,622)
Payment of dividends	(45,848)	(39,946)
Purchase of treasury stock	—	(25,000)
Net cash flows from financing activities	$ (311,324)	$ 370,232
Net increase (decrease) in cash	$ 24,840	$(174,936)
Cash at beginning of year	32,064	207,000
Cash at end of year	$ 56,904	$ 32,064

Schedule of Noncash Investing and Financing Transactions

Issue of bonds payable for retail acquisition		$ 100,000

REQUIRED

Evaluate the success of the company's strategy by answering the questions that follow.

1. **ACCOUNTING CONNECTION** ▶ What are the primary reasons cash flows from operating activities differ from net income in 2013 and in 2014? What is the effect of the acquisition in 2013? What conclusions can you draw from the changes in 2014?
2. **BUSINESS APPLICATION** ▶ Compute free cash flow for both years. What was the total cost of the acquisition? Was the company able to finance expansion in 2013 by generating internal cash flow? What was the situation in 2013?
3. **ACCOUNTING CONNECTION** ▶ What are the most significant financing activities in 2013? How did the company finance the acquisition? Do you think this is a good strategy? What other issues might you question in financing activities?
4. **ACCOUNTING CONNECTION** ▶ Based on results in 2014, what actions was the company forced to take and what is your overall assessment of the company's diversification strategy?

LO **2, 3, 4, 5**

✔ 1: Net cash flows from operating activities: $23,400
✔ 1: Net cash flows from investing activities: ($7,200)
✔ 1: Net cash flows from financing activities: $51,000

Statement of Cash Flows: Indirect Method

P3. Chaplin Arts, Inc.'s comparative balance sheets for December 31, 2014 and 2013 follow.

Chaplin Arts, Inc.		
Comparative Balance Sheets		
December 31, 2014 and 2013		
	2014	**2013**
Assets		
Cash	$ 94,560	$ 27,360
Accounts receivable (net)	102,430	75,430
Inventory	112,890	137,890
Prepaid expenses	—	20,000
Land	25,000	—
Building	137,000	—
Accumulated depreciation—building	(15,000)	—
Equipment	33,000	34,000
Accumulated depreciation—equipment	(14,500)	(24,000)
Patents	4,000	6,000
Total assets	$479,380	$276,680

Liabilities and Stockholders' Equity

Accounts payable	$ 10,750	$ 36,750
Notes payable (current)	10,000	—
Accrued liabilities	—	12,300
Mortgage payable	162,000	—
Common stock, $10 par value	180,000	150,000
Additional paid-in capital	57,200	37,200
Retained earnings	59,430	40,430
Total liabilities and stockholders' equity	$479,380	$276,680

The following additional information about Chaplin Arts's operations during 2013 is available: (a) net income, $28,000; (b) building and equipment depreciation expense amounts, $15,000 and $3,000, respectively; (c) equipment that cost $13,500 with accumulated depreciation of $12,500 sold at a gain of $5,300; (d) equipment purchases, $12,500; (e) patent amortization, $3,000; purchase of patent, $1,000; (f) funds borrowed by issuing notes payable, $25,000; notes payable repaid, $15,000; (g) land and building purchased for $162,000 by signing a mortgage for the total cost; (h) 1,500 shares of $20 par value common stock issued for a total of $50,000; and (i) paid cash dividends, $9,000.

REQUIRED

1. Using the indirect method, prepare a statement of cash flows for Chaplin Arts.
2. **ACCOUNTING CONNECTION** ▶ Why did Chaplin Arts have an increase in cash of $67,200 when it recorded net income of only $28,000? Discuss and interpret.
3. **BUSINESS APPLICATION** ▶ Compute and assess cash flow yield and free cash flow for 2014. (Round to one decimal place.) What is your assessment of Chaplin Arts' cash-generating ability?

LO **2, 3, 4, 5**

✔ 1: Net cash flows from operating activities: ($106,000)
✔ 1: Net cash flows from investing activities: $34,000
✔ 1: Net cash flows from financing activities: $24,000

Statement of Cash Flows: Indirect Method

P4. Ben Tools, Inc.'s comparative balance sheets for December 31, 2014 and 2013, follow.

Ben Tools, Inc.
Comparative Balance Sheets
December 31, 2014 and 2013

	2014	2013
Assets		
Cash	$ 257,600	$ 305,600
Accounts receivable (net)	738,800	758,800
Inventory	960,000	800,000
Prepaid expenses	14,800	26,800
Long-term investments	440,000	440,000
Land	361,200	321,200
Building	1,200,000	920,000
Accumulated depreciation—building	(240,000)	(160,000)
Equipment	480,000	480,000
Accumulated depreciation—equipment	(116,000)	(56,000)
Intangible assets	20,000	40,000
Total assets	$4,116,400	$3,876,400
Liabilities and Stockholders' Equity		
Accounts payable	$ 470,800	$ 660,800
Notes payable (current)	40,000	160,000
Accrued liabilities	10,800	20,800
Mortgage payable	1,080,000	800,000
Bonds payable	1,000,000	760,000
Common stock	1,300,000	1,300,000
Additional paid-in capital	80,000	80,000
Retained earnings	254,800	194,800
Treasury stock	(120,000)	(100,000)
Total liabilities and stockholders' equity	$4,116,400	$3,876,400

(Continued)

During 2014, the company had net income of $96,000 and building and equipment depreciation expenses of $80,000 and $60,000, respectively. It amortized intangible assets in the amount of $20,000; purchased investments for $116,000; sold investments for $150,000, on which it recorded a gain of $34,000; issued $240,000 of long-term bonds at face value; purchased land and a warehouse through a $320,000 mortgage; paid $40,000 to reduce the mortgage; borrowed $60,000 by issuing notes payable; repaid notes payable in the amount of $180,000; declared and paid cash dividends in the amount of $36,000; and purchased treasury stock in the amount of $20,000.

REQUIRED

1. Using the indirect method, prepare a statement of cash flows for Ben Tools.
2. **ACCOUNTING CONNECTION** ▶ Why did Ben Tools experience a decrease in cash in a year in which it had a net income of $96,000? Discuss and interpret.
3. **BUSINESS APPLICATION** ▶ Compute and assess cash flow yield and free cash flow for 2014. Why is each of these measures important in assessing cash-generating ability?

LO **2, 3, 4, 5**

RATIO

SPREADSHEET

✔ 1: Net cash flows from operating activities: $126,600
✔ 1: Net cash flows from investing activities: ($25,800)
✔ 1: Net cash flows from financing activities: $14,000

Statement of Cash Flows: Indirect Method

P5. Yong Company's income statement for the year ended December 31, 2014, and its comparative balance sheets as of December 31, 2014 and 2013, follow.

Yong Company
Income Statement
For the Year Ended December 31, 2014

Sales		$1,609,000
Cost of goods sold		1,127,800
Gross margin		$ 481,200
Operating expenses (including depreciation expense of $46,800)		449,400
Income from operations		$ 31,800
Other income (expenses):		
Gain on sale of furniture and fixtures	$ 7,000	
Interest expense	(23,200)	(16,200)
Income before income taxes		$ 15,600
Income taxes expense		4,600
Net income		$ 11,000

Yong Company
Comparative Balance Sheets
December 31, 2014 and 2013

	2014	2013
Assets		
Cash	$164,800	$ 50,000
Accounts receivable (net)	165,200	200,000
Merchandise inventory	350,000	450,000
Prepaid rent	2,000	3,000
Furniture and fixtures	148,000	144,000
Accumulated depreciation—furniture and fixtures	(42,000)	(24,000)
Total assets	$788,000	$823,000
Liabilities and Stockholders' Equity		
Accounts payable	$143,400	$200,400
Income taxes payable	1,400	4,400
Notes payable (long-term)	40,000	20,000
Bonds payable	100,000	200,000
Common stock, $20 par value	240,000	200,000
Additional paid-in capital	181,440	121,440
Retained earnings	81,760	76,760
Total liabilities and stockholders' equity	$788,000	$823,000

During 2014, the company engaged in these transactions:

a. Sold at a gain of $7,000 furniture and fixtures that cost $35,600, on which it had accumulated depreciation of $28,800.
b. Purchased furniture and fixtures in the amount of $39,600.
c. Paid a $20,000 note payable and borrowed $40,000 on a new note.
d. Converted bonds payable in the amount of $100,000 into 4,000 shares of common stock.
e. Declared and paid $6,000 in cash dividends.

REQUIRED

1. Using the indirect method, prepare a statement of cash flows for Yong. Include a supporting schedule of noncash investing transactions and financing transactions.
2. **ACCOUNTING CONNECTION** ▶ What are the primary reasons for Yong's large increase in cash from 2013 to 2014, despite its low net income?
3. **BUSINESS APPLICATION** ▶ Compute and assess cash flow yield and free cash flow for 2014. (Round to one decimal place.) Compare and contrast what these two performance measures tell you about Yong's cash-generating ability.

ALTERNATE PROBLEMS

LO 1 **Classification of Cash Flow Transactions**

P6. CONCEPT ▶ Analyze each transaction listed in the table that follows and place X's in the appropriate columns to indicate the transaction's classification and its effect on cash flows using the indirect method.

| Transaction | Cash Flow Classification | | | | Effect on Cash Flows | | |
	Operating Activity	Investing Activity	Financing Activity	Noncash Transaction	Increase	Decrease	No Effect
1. Increased accounts payable.							
2. Decreased inventory.							
3. Increased prepaid insurance.							
4. Earned a net income.							
5. Declared and paid a cash dividend.							
6. Issued stock for cash.							
7. Retired long-term debt by issuing stock.							
8. Purchased a long-term investment with cash.							
9. Sold trading securities at a gain.							
10. Sold a machine at a loss.							
11. Retired fully depreciated equipment.							
12. Decreased interest payable.							
13. Purchased available-for-sale securities (long-term).							
14. Decreased dividends receivable.							
15. Decreased accounts receivable.							
16. Converted bonds to common stock.							
17. Purchased 90-day Treasury bill.							

Statement of Cash Flows: Indirect Method

P7. Reed Corporation's income statement for the year ended June 30, 2014, and its comparative balance sheets as of June 30, 2014 and 2013, follow.

Reed Corporation
Income Statement
For the Year Ended June 30, 2014

Sales		$8,081,800
Cost of goods sold		7,312,600
Gross margin		$ 769,200
Operating expenses (including depreciation expense of $120,000)		378,400
Income from operations		$ 390,800
Other income (expenses)		
Loss on sale of equipment	$ (8,000)	
Interest expense	(75,200)	(83,200)
Income before income taxes		$ 307,600
Income taxes expense		68,400
Net income		$ 239,200

Reed Corporation
Comparative Balance Sheets
June 30, 2014 and 2013

	2014	2013
Assets		
Cash	$ 334,000	$ 40,000
Accounts receivable (net)	200,000	240,000
Inventory	360,000	440,000
Prepaid expenses	1,200	2,000
Property, plant, and equipment	1,256,000	1,104,000
Accumulated depreciation—property, plant, and equipment	(366,000)	(280,000)
Total assets	$1,785,200	$1,546,000
Liabilities and Stockholders' Equity		
Accounts payable	$ 128,000	$ 84,000
Notes payable (due in 90 days)	60,000	160,000
Income taxes payable	52,000	36,000
Mortgage payable	720,000	560,000
Common stock, $5 par value	400,000	400,000
Retained earnings	425,200	306,000
Total liabilities and stockholders' equity	$1,785,200	$1,546,000

During 2014, the corporation sold at a loss of $8,000 equipment that cost $48,000, on which it had accumulated depreciation of $34,000. It also purchased land and a building for $200,000 through an increase of $200,000 in Mortgage Payable; made a $40,000 payment on the mortgage; repaid $160,000 in notes but borrowed an additional $60,000 through the issuance of a new note payable; and declared and paid a $120,000 cash dividend.

REQUIRED

1. Using the indirect method, prepare a statement of cash flows. Include a supporting schedule of noncash investing and financing transactions.
2. **ACCOUNTING CONNECTION** ▶ What are the primary reasons for Reed's large increase in cash from 2013 to 2014?
3. **BUSINESS APPLICATION** ▶ Compute and assess cash flow yield and free cash flow for 2014. (Round to one decimal place.) How would you assess the corporation's cash-generating ability?

LO **2, 3, 4, 5**

✔ 1: Net cash flows from operating
activities: $93,600
✔ 1: Net cash flows from investing
activities: ($28,800)
✔ 1: Net cash flows from financing
activities: $204,000

Statement of Cash Flows: Indirect Method

P8. Shah Fabrics, Inc.'s comparative balance sheets for December 31, 2014 and 2013, follow.

Shah Fabrics, Inc.
Comparative Balance Sheets
December 31, 2014 and 2013

	2014	2013
Assets		
Cash	$ 378,240	$ 109,440
Accounts receivable (net)	409,720	301,720
Inventory	451,560	551,560
Prepaid expenses	—	80,000
Land	100,000	—
Building	548,000	—
Accumulated depreciation—building	(60,000)	—
Equipment	132,000	136,000
Accumulated depreciation—equipment	(58,000)	(96,000)
Patents	16,000	24,000
Total assets	$1,917,520	$1,106,720
Liabilities and Stockholders' Equity		
Accounts payable	$ 43,000	$ 147,000
Notes payable (current)	40,000	—
Accrued liabilities	—	49,200
Mortgage payable	648,000	—
Common stock, $10 par value	720,000	600,000
Additional paid-in capital	228,800	148,800
Retained earnings	237,720	161,720
Total liabilities and stockholders' equity	$1,917,520	$1,106,720

Additional information about Shah Fabrics' operations during 2014 is as follows: (a) net income, $112,000; (b) building and equipment depreciation expense amounts, $60,000 and $12,000, respectively; (c) equipment that cost $54,000 with accumulated depreciation of $50,000 sold at a gain of $21,200; (d) equipment purchases, $50,000; (e) patent amortization, $12,000; purchase of patent, $4,000; (f) funds borrowed by issuing notes payable, $100,000; notes payable repaid, $60,000; (g) land and building purchased for $648,000 by signing a mortgage for the total cost; (h) 6,000 shares of $40 par value common stock issued for a total of $200,000; and (i) paid cash dividend, $36,000.

REQUIRED

1. Using the indirect method, prepare a statement of cash flows for Shah Fabrics.
2. **ACCOUNTING CONNECTION** ▶ Why did Shah Fabrics have an increase in cash of $268,800 when it recorded net income of only $112,000? Discuss and interpret.
3. **BUSINESS APPLICATION** ▶ Compute and assess cash flow yield and free cash flow for 2014. (Round to one decimal place.) What is your assessment of Shah Fabrics' cash-generating ability?

LO **2, 3, 4, 5**

✔ 1: Net cash flows from operating
activities: ($212,000)
✔ 1: Net cash flows from investing
activities: $68,000
✔ 1: Net cash flows from financing
activities: $48,000

Statement of Cash Flows: Indirect Method

P9. Kohl Ceramics, Inc.'s comparative balance sheets, for December 31, 2014 and 2013, follow.

Kohl Ceramics, Inc.
Comparative Balance Sheets
December 31, 2014 and 2013

	2014	2013
Assets		
Cash	$ 515,200	$ 611,200
Accounts receivable (net)	1,477,600	1,517,600
Inventory	1,920,000	1,600,000
Prepaid expenses	29,600	53,600
Long-term investments	880,000	880,000
Land	722,400	642,400
Building	2,400,000	1,840,000
Accumulated depreciation—building	(480,000)	(320,000)
Equipment	960,000	960,000
Accumulated depreciation—equipment	(232,000)	(112,000)
Intangible assets	40,000	80,000
Total assets	$8,232,800	$7,752,800
Liabilities and Stockholders' Equity		
Accounts payable	$ 941,600	$1,321,600
Notes payable (current)	80,000	320,000
Accrued liabilities	21,600	41,600
Mortgage payable	2,160,000	1,600,000
Bonds payable	2,000,000	1,520,000
Common stock	2,600,000	2,600,000
Additional paid-in capital	160,000	160,000
Retained earnings	509,600	389,600
Treasury stock	(240,000)	(200,000)
Total liabilities and stockholders' equity	$8,232,800	$7,752,800

During 2014, the company had net income of $192,000 and building and equipment depreciation expenses of $160,000 and $120,000, respectively. It amortized intangible assets in the amount of $40,000; purchased investments for $232,000; sold investments for $300,000, on which it recorded a gain of $68,000; issued $480,000 of long-term bonds at face value; purchased land and a warehouse through a $640,000 mortgage; paid $80,000 to reduce the mortgage; borrowed $120,000 by issuing notes payable; repaid notes payable in the amount of $360,000; declared and paid cash dividends in the amount of $72,000; and purchased treasury stock in the amount of $40,000.

REQUIRED

1. Using the indirect method, prepare a statement of cash flows for Kohl Ceramics.
2. **ACCOUNTING CONNECTION** ▶ Why did Kohl Ceramics experience a decrease in cash in a year in which it had a net income of $192,000? Discuss and interpret.
3. **BUSINESS APPLICATION** ▶ Compute and assess cash flow yield and free cash flow for 2014. Why is each of these measures important in assessing cash-generating ability?

LO **2, 3, 4, 5**

✔ 1: Net cash flows from operating
activities: $126,600
✔ 1: Net cash flows from investing
activities: ($25,800)
✔ 1: Net cash flows from financing
activities: $14,000
✔ 3: Free cash flow, 2014: $94,800

Statement of Cash Flows: Indirect Method

P10. William Corporation's income statement for the year ended December 31, 2014, and its comparative balance sheets as of December 31, 2014 and 2013, follow.

William Corporation
Income Statement
For the Year Ended December 31, 2014

Sales		$1,609,000
Cost of goods sold		1,127,800
Gross margin		$ 481,200
Operating expenses (including depreciation expense of $46,800)		449,400
Income from operations		$ 31,800
Other income (expenses)		
Gain on sale of furniture and fixtures	$ 7,000	
Interest expense	(23,200)	(16,200)
Income before income taxes		$ 15,600
Income taxes expense		4,600
Net income		$ 11,000

William Corporation
Comparative Balance Sheets
December 31, 2014 and 2013

	2014	2013
Assets		
Cash	$164,800	$ 50,000
Accounts receivable (net)	165,200	200,000
Merchandise inventory	350,000	450,000
Prepaid rent	2,000	3,000
Furniture and fixtures	148,000	144,000
Accumulated depreciation—furniture and fixtures	(42,000)	(24,000)
Total assets	$788,000	$823,000
Liabilities and Stockholders' Equity		
Accounts payable	$143,400	$200,400
Income taxes payable	1,400	4,400
Notes payable (long-term)	40,000	20,000
Bonds payable	100,000	200,000
Common stock, $20 par value	240,000	200,000
Additional paid-in capital	181,440	121,440
Retained earnings	81,760	76,760
Total liabilities and stockholders' equity	$788,000	$823,000

During 2014, William engaged in these transactions:

a. Sold at a gain of $7,000 furniture and fixtures that cost $35,600, on which it had accumulated depreciation of $28,800.
b. Purchased furniture and fixtures in the amount of $39,600.
c. Paid a $20,000 note payable and borrowed $40,000 on a new note.
d. Converted bonds payable in the amount of $100,000 into 4,000 shares of common stock.
e. Declared and paid $6,000 in cash dividends.

REQUIRED

1. Using the indirect method, prepare a statement of cash flows for William. Include a supporting schedule of noncash investing transactions and financing transactions.
2. **ACCOUNTING CONNECTION** ▶ What are the primary reasons for William's large increase in cash from 2013 to 2014, despite its low net income?
3. **BUSINESS APPLICATION** ▶ Compute and assess cash flow yield and free cash flow for 2014. (Round to one decimal place.) Compare and contrast what these two performance measures tell you about William's cash-generating ability.

CASES

LO 1, 2 **Conceptual Understanding: EBITDA and the Statement of Cash Flows**

C1. When **Fleetwood Enterprises, Inc.**, a large producer of recreational vehicles and manufactured housing, warned that it might not be able to generate enough cash to satisfy debt requirements and could be in default of a loan agreement, its cash flow, defined in the financial press as "EBITDA" (earnings before interest, taxes, depreciation, and amortization), was a negative $2.7 million. The company would have had to generate $17.7 million in the next accounting period to comply with the loan terms.[11] To what section of the statement of cash flows does EBITDA most closely relate? Is EBITDA a good approximation for this section of the statement of cash flows? Explain your answer, which should include an identification of the major differences between EBITDA and the section of the statement of cash flows you chose.

LO 5 **Interpreting Financial Reports: Classic Case—Anatomy of a Disaster**

C2. On October 16, 2001, Kenneth Lay, chairman and CEO of **Enron Corporation**, announced the company's earnings for the first nine months of 2001 as follows:

> *Our 26 percent increase in recurring earnings per diluted share shows the very strong results of our core wholesale and retail energy businesses and our natural gas pipelines. The continued excellent prospects in these businesses and Enron's leading market position make us very confident in our strong earnings outlook.*[12]

Less than six months later, the company filed for the biggest bankruptcy in U.S. history. Its stock dropped to less than $1 per share, and a major financial scandal was underway. Enron's statement of cash flows for the first nine months of 2001 and 2000 (restated to correct the previous accounting errors) follow. Assume you report to an investment analyst, who has asked you to analyze this statement for clues as to why the company went under.

Enron Corporation
Statement of Cash Flows
For the Nine Months Ended September 30, 2001 and 2000

(In millions)	2001	2000
Cash Flows from Operating Activities:		
Reconciliation of net income to net		
cash provided by operating activities:		
Net income	$ 225	$ 797
Cumulative effect of accounting changes, net of tax	(19)	—
Depreciation, depletion and amortization	746	617
Deferred income taxes	(134)	8
Gains on sales of non-trading assets	(49)	(135)
Investment losses	768	0
Changes in components of working capital:		
Receivables	987	(3,363)
Inventories	1	339
Payables	(1,764)	2,899
Other	464	(455)
Trading investments		
Net margin deposit activity	(2,349)	541
Other trading activities	173	(555)
Other, net	198	(566)
Net Cash Provided by (Used in) Operating Activities	$ (753)	$ 127

Cash Flows from Investing Activities:		
Capital expenditures	$(1,584)	$(1,539)
Equity investments	(1,172)	(858)
Proceeds from sales of non-trading investments	1,711	222
Acquisition of subsidiary stock	0	(485)
Business acquisitions, net of cash acquired	(82)	(773)
Other investing activities	(239)	(147)
Net Cash Used in Investing Activities	$(1,366)	$(3,580)
Cash Flows from Financing Activities:		
Issuance of long-term debt	$ 4,060	$ 2,725
Repayment of long-term debt	(3,903)	(579)
Net increase in short-term borrowings	2,365	1,694
Issuance of common stock	199	182
Net redemption of company-obligated preferred securities of subsidiaries	0	(95)
Dividends paid	(394)	(396)
Net (acquisition) disposition of treasury stock	(398)	354
Other financing activities	(49)	(12)
Net Cash Provided by Financing Activities	$ 1,880	$ 3,873
Increase (Decrease) in Cash and Cash Equivalents	$ (239)	$ 420
Cash and Cash Equivalents, Beginning of Period	1,240	333
Cash and Cash Equivalents, End of Period	$ 1,001	$ 753

1. **BUSINESS APPLICATION** ▶ For the two time periods shown, compute the cash-generating efficiency ratios of cash flow yield, cash flows to sales (Enron's revenues were $133,762 million in 2001 and $55,494 million in 2000), and cash flows to assets (use total assets of $61,783 million for 2001 and $64,926 million for 2000). Also compute free cash flows for the two years. (Round to one decimal place or the nearest tenth of a percent.)

2. Prepare a memorandum to the investment analyst that assesses Enron's cash generating efficiency in light of the chairman's remarks and that evaluates its available free cash flow, taking into account its financing activities. Identify significant changes in Enron's operating items and any special operating items that should be considered. Include your computations as an attachment.

LO 5   **Ethical Dilemma: Ethics and Cash Flow Classifications**

C3. BUSINESS APPLICATION ▶ Precise Metals, Inc., a fast-growing company that makes metals for equipment manufacturers, has an $800,000 line of credit at its bank. One section in the credit agreement says that the ratio of cash flows from operations to interest expense must exceed 3.0. If this ratio falls below 3.0, the company must reduce the balance outstanding on its line of credit to one-half the total line if the funds borrowed against the line of credit exceed one-half of the total line.

After the end of the fiscal year, the company's controller informs the president: "We will not meet the ratio requirements on our line of credit in 2010 because interest expense was $1.2 million and cash flows from operations were $3.2 million. Also, we have borrowed 100 percent of our line of credit. We do not have the cash to reduce the credit line by $400,000."

The president says, "This is a serious situation. To pay our ongoing bills, we need our bank to increase our line of credit, not decrease it. What can we do?" "Do you recall the $500,000 two-year note payable for equipment?" replied the controller. "It is now classified as 'Proceeds from Notes Payable' in cash flows provided from financing activities in the statement of cash flows. If we move it to cash flows from operations and call it 'Increase in Payables,' it would increase cash flows from operations to $3.7 million and put us over the limit." "Well, do it," ordered the president. "It surely doesn't make any

(Continued)

difference where it is on the statement. It is an increase in both places. It would be much worse for our company in the long term if we failed to meet this ratio requirement."

What is your opinion of the controller and president's reasoning? Is the president's order ethical? Who benefits and who is harmed if the controller follows the president's order? What are management's alternatives? What would you do?

LO **1, 5**   **Conceptual Understanding: Alternative Uses of Cash**

C4. Perhaps because of hard times in their start-up years, companies in the high tech sector of American industry seem more prone than those in other sectors to building up cash reserves. For example, companies like **Cisco Systems**, **Intel**, **Dell**, and **Oracle** have amassed large cash balances.

Assume you work for a company in the high-tech industry that has built up a substantial amount of cash. The company is still growing through development of new products, has some debt, and has never paid a dividend or bought treasury stock. The company is doing better than most companies in the current financial crisis but the company's stock price is lagging. Outline at least four strategies for using the company's cash to improve the company's financial outlook.

LO **1**   **Interpreting Financial Reports: Analysis of the Statement of Cash Flows**

C5. Refer to the statement of cash flows in the **CVS Corporation** annual report in the Supplement to Chapter 16 to answer the following questions:

1. Does CVS use the indirect method of reporting cash flows from operating activities? Other than net earnings, what are the most important factors affecting the company's cash flows from operating activities? Explain the trend of each of these factors.
2. Based on the cash flows from investing activities, in 2010 and 2011, would you say that CVS is a contracting or an expanding company? Explain.
3. Has CVS used external financing during 2010 and 2011? If so, where did it come from?

LO **1, 5**   **Interpreting Financial Reports: Cash Flows Analysis**

C6. BUSINESS APPLICATION ▶ Refer to the annual report of **CVS Corporation** and the financial statements of **Southwest Airlines** in the Supplement to Chapter 16. Calculate for 2011 and 2010 each company's cash flow yield, cash flows to sales, cash flows to assets, and free cash flow. (Round to one decimal place or to the nearest tenth of a percent.) At the end of 2009, Southwest's total assets were $14,269 million and CVS's total assets were $61,641 million.

Discuss and compare the trends of the cash-generating ability of CVS and Southwest. Comment on each company's change in cash and cash equivalents over the two-year period.

Continuing Case: Annual Report Project

C7. Using the most recent annual report of the company you have chosen to study and that you have accessed online at the company's website, examine the statement of cash flows and accompanying notes of your company. Answer the following questions:

1. Does the company use the direct or indirect method for computing cash flows from operating activities? What effect does depreciation have on cash flows? Have receivables, inventories, and payables had positive or negative effects on cash flows from operating activities?
2. What are the most important investing activities for the company in the most recent year?
3. What are the most important financing activities for the company in the most recent year?
4. **BUSINESS APPLICATION** ▶ Calculate cash flow yield, cash flows to sales, cash flows to assets, and free cash flow for the most recent year.

SUPPLEMENT TO CHAPTER 15
The Direct Method of Preparing the Statement of Cash Flows

To this point, the indirect method of preparing the statement of cash flows has been used. In this section, the direct method is presented.

Determining Cash Flows from Operating Activities

The principal difference between the indirect and the direct methods appears in the cash flows from operating activities section of the statement of cash flows.

- The indirect method starts with net income from the income statement and converts it to net cash flows from operating activities by adding or subtracting items that do not affect net cash flows.
- The direct method converts each item on the income statement to its cash equivalent, as illustrated in Exhibit 1. For instance, sales are converted to cash receipts from sales and purchases are converted to cash payments for purchases.

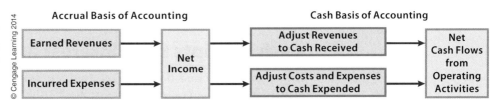

Exhibit 1
Direct Method of Determining Net Cash Flows from Operating Activities

To illustrate how to determine cash flows from operating activities under the direct method, we will use Eureka Corporation. Eureka's schedule of cash flows from operating activities is presented in Exhibit 2.

Exhibit 2
Schedule of Cash Flows from Operating Activities: Direct Method

Eureka Corporation
Schedule of Cash Flows from Operating Activities
For the Year Ended December 31, 2014

Cash receipts from:		
Sales	$706,000	
Interest received	6,000	$712,000
Cash payments for:		
Purchases	$547,000	
Operating expenses	103,000	
Interest	23,000	
Income taxes	9,000	682,000
Net cash flows from operating activities		$ 30,000

Cash Receipts from Sales

Sales result in a positive cash flow for a company. Cash sales are direct cash inflows. Credit sales are not direct cash inflows because some receivables may be uncollectible. For example, you cannot assume that credit sales are automatically inflows of cash, because the collections of accounts receivable in any one accounting period are not likely to equal credit sales. Some receivables may be uncollectible, sales from a prior period may be collected in the current period, or sales from the current period may be collected in the next period.

> ▲ If accounts receivables *increase* from one accounting period to the next, cash receipts from sales will not be as great as sales.

> ▼ If accounts receivable *decrease* from one accounting period to the next, cash receipts from sales will exceed sales.

The relationships among sales, changes in the accounts receivable, and cash receipts from sales are reflected in the formula that follows.

$$\text{Sales} \begin{cases} + \text{Decrease in Accounts Receivable} \\ \qquad\qquad\text{or} \\ - \text{Increase in Accounts Receivable} \end{cases} = \begin{array}{l} \text{Cash Receipts} \\ \text{from Sales} \end{array}$$

Refer to the balance sheets and the income statement for Eureka Corporation in Exhibits 4 and 5 in Chapter 15. Note that sales were $698,000 in 2014 and that accounts receivable decreased by $8,000. Thus, cash received from sales is $706,000:

$$\$698{,}000 + \$8{,}000 = \$706{,}000$$

Collections were $8,000 more than sales recorded for the year.

Cash Receipts from Interest and Dividends

Although interest and dividends received are most closely associated with investment activity and are often called *investment income*, the FASB *classifies* the cash received from these items as operating activities. To simplify the examples in this text, it is assumed that interest income equals interest received and that dividend income equals dividends received. Thus, based on Exhibit 4 in Chapter 15, interest received by Eureka Corporation is assumed to equal $6,000, which is the amount of interest income.

Cash Payments for Purchases

The cost of goods sold (from the income statement) must be adjusted for changes in two balance sheet accounts to arrive at cash payments for purchases. First, the cost of goods sold must be adjusted for changes in inventory to arrive at net purchases. Then, net purchases must be adjusted for the change in accounts payable to arrive at cash payments for purchases.

> ▲ If inventory has *increased* from one accounting period to another, net purchases will be greater than the cost of goods sold because net purchases during the period have exceeded the dollar amount of the items sold during the period.

> ▼ If inventory has *decreased*, net purchases will be less than the cost of goods sold.

> ▲ If accounts payable have *increased*, cash payments for purchases will be less than net purchases.

> ▼ If accounts payable have *decreased*, cash payments for purchases will be greater than net purchases.

These relationships may be stated in equation form as follows.

$$\text{Cost of Goods Sold} \begin{Bmatrix} + \text{ Increase in Inventory} \\ \text{or} \\ - \text{ Decrease in Inventory} \end{Bmatrix} \begin{Bmatrix} + \text{ Decrease in Accounts Payable} \\ \text{or} \\ - \text{ Increase in Accounts Payable} \end{Bmatrix} = \text{Cash Payments for Purchases}$$

From Exhibits 4 and 5 in Chapter 15, cost of goods sold is $520,000, inventory increased by $34,000, and accounts payable increased by $7,000. Thus, cash payments for purchases for Eureka are computed as follows.

$$\$520,000 + \$34,000 - \$7,000 = \$547,000$$

Eureka purchased $34,000 more inventory than it sold and paid out $7,000 less in cash than it made in purchases. The net result is that cash payments for purchases exceeded the cost of goods sold by $27,000 ($547,000 − $520,000).

Cash Payments for Operating Expenses

Just as the cost of goods sold does not represent the amount of cash paid for purchases during an accounting period, operating expenses do not match the amount of cash paid to employees, suppliers, and others for goods and services. Three adjustments must be made to operating expenses to arrive at the cash outflows. The first adjustment is for changes in prepaid expenses, such as prepaid insurance or prepaid rent.

▲ If prepaid assets *increase* during the accounting period, more cash will have been paid out than appears on the income statement as expenses.

▼ If prepaid assets *decrease*, the expenses shown on the income statement will exceed the cash spent.

The second adjustment is for changes in liabilities resulting from accrued expenses, such as wages payable and payroll taxes payable.

▲ If accrued liabilities *increase* during the accounting period, operating expenses on the income statement will exceed the cash spent.

▼ If accrued liabilities *decrease*, operating expenses will fall short of cash spent.

The third adjustment is made because certain expenses do not require a current outlay of cash; those expenses must be subtracted from operating expense to arrive at cash payments for operating expenses. The most common expenses in this category are depreciation expense, amortization expense, and depletion expense. For example, in 2014, Eureka recorded depreciation expense of $37,000. No cash payment was made in this transaction. Therefore, to the extent that operating expenses include depreciation and similar items, an adjustment is needed to reduce operating expenses to the amount of cash expended.

The three adjustments to operating expenses are summarized in the equations that follow.

$$\text{Operating Expenses} \begin{Bmatrix} + \text{ Increase in Prepaid Expenses} \\ \text{or} \\ - \text{ Decrease in Prepaid Expenses} \end{Bmatrix} \begin{Bmatrix} + \text{ Decrease in Accrued Liabilities} \\ \text{or} \\ - \text{ Increase in Accrued Liabilities} \end{Bmatrix} \begin{Bmatrix} - \text{ Depreciation and Other Noncash Expenses} \end{Bmatrix} = \text{Cash Payments for Operating Expenses}$$

According to Exhibits 4 and 5 in Chapter 15, Eureka's operating expenses (including depreciation of $37,000) were $147,000, prepaid expenses decreased by $4,000, and accrued liabilities increased by $3,000. As a result, Eureka's cash payments for operating expenses are computed as follows.

$$\$147,000 - \$4,000 - \$3,000 - \$37,000 = \$103,000$$

If there are prepaid expenses and accrued liabilities that are *not* related to specific operating expenses, they are not included in these computations. One example is income taxes payable, which is the accrued liability related to income taxes expense. The cash payment for income taxes will be discussed shortly.

Cash Payments for Interest

The FASB classifies cash payments for interest as operating activities. For the sake of simplicity, all examples in this text assume that interest payments are equal to interest expense on the income statement. Thus, based on Exhibit 4 in Chapter 15, Eureka's interest payments are assumed to be $23,000 in 2014.

Cash Payments for Income Taxes

The amount of income taxes expense that appears on the income statement rarely equals the amount of income taxes actually paid during the year. To determine cash payments for income taxes, income taxes are adjusted by the change in Income Taxes Payable.

▲ If Income Taxes Payable *increased* during the accounting period, cash payments for taxes will be less than the expense shown on the income statement.

▼ If Income Taxes Payable *decreased*, cash payments for taxes will exceed income taxes on the income statement.

In other words, the following equation is applicable:

$$\text{Income Taxes} \begin{cases} + \text{ Decrease in Income Taxes Payable} \\ \quad\quad\quad\quad\text{ or} \\ - \text{ Increase in Income Taxes Payable} \end{cases} = \begin{array}{l} \text{Cash Payments} \\ \text{for Income Taxes} \end{array}$$

In 2014, Eureka reported income taxes of $7,000 on its income statement and a decrease of $2,000 in Income Taxes Payable on its balance sheets (see Exhibits 4 and 5 in Chapter 15). As a result, cash payments for income taxes for Eureka during 2014 are calculated as follows.

$$\$7,000 + \$2,000 = \$9,000$$

Compiling the Statement of Cash Flows

Eureka's statement of cash flows under the direct method is presented in Exhibit 3. The only differences between that statement of cash flows and the one based on the indirect method shown in Exhibit 8 in Chapter 15 occur in the first and last sections. The middle sections, which present cash flows from investing activities and financing activities, net increases or decreases in cash, and the schedule of non-cash investing and financing activities, are the same under both methods.

The first section of the statement in Exhibit 3 shows the net cash flows from operating activities on a direct basis, as presented in Exhibit 2. The last section is the same as the cash flows from operating activities section of the statement of cash flows under the indirect method (see Exhibit 8 in Chapter 15). The FASB believes that when the direct method is used, a schedule must be provided that reconciles net income to net cash flows from operating activities. Thus, the statement of cash flows under the direct method includes a section that accommodates the main difference between it and the indirect method.

Exhibit 3
Statement of Cash
Flows: Direct Method

Eureka Corporation
Statement of Cash Flows
For the Year Ended December 31, 2014

Cash flows from operating activities:		
Cash receipts from:		
Sales	$ 706,000	
Interest received	6,000	$712,000
Cash payments for:		
Purchases	$ 547,000	
Operating expenses	103,000	
Interest	23,000	
Income taxes	9,000	682,000
Net cash flows from operating activities		$ 30,000
Cash flows from investing activities:		
Purchase of investments	$ (78,000)	
Sale of investments	102,000	
Purchase of plant assets	(120,000)	
Sale of plant assets	5,000	
Net cash flows from investing activities		(91,000)
Cash flows from financing activities:		
Repayment of bonds	$ (50,000)	
Issue of common stock	150,000	
Dividends paid	(7,000)	
Net cash flows from financing activities		93,000
Net increase in cash		$ 32,000
Cash at beginning of year		15,000
Cash at end of year		$ 47,000

Schedule of Noncash Investing and Financing Transactions

Issue of bonds payable for plant assets		$100,000
Reconciliation of net income to net cash flows from operating activities:		
Net income		$ 16,000
Adjustments to reconcile net income to net cash flows from operating activities:		
Depreciation	$ 37,000	
Gain on sale of investments	(12,000)	
Loss on sale of plant assets	3,000	
Changes in current assets and current liabilities:		
Decrease in accounts receivable	8,000	
Increase in inventory	(34,000)	
Decrease in prepaid expenses	4,000	
Increase in accounts payable	7,000	
Increase in accrued liabilities	3,000	
Decrease in income taxes payable	(2,000)	14,000
Net cash flows from operating activities		$ 30,000
Cash flows from investing activities:		
Purchase of investments	$ (78,000)	
Sale of investments	102,000	
Purchase of plant assets	(120,000)	
Sale of plant assets	5,000	
Net cash flows from investing activities		(91,000)
Cash flows from financing activities:		
Repayment of bonds	$ (50,000)	
Issuance of common stock	175,000	
Payment of dividends	(7,000)	
Purchase of treasury stock	(25,000)	
Net cash flows from financing activities		93,000
Net increase in cash		$ 32,000
Cash at beginning of year		15,000
Cash at end of year		$ 47,000

Assignments

SHORT EXERCISES

SE1. Cash Receipts from Sales and Cash Payments for Purchases: Direct Method

During 2014, Nebraska Wheat Company, a maker of whole-grain products, had sales of $426,500. The ending balance of accounts receivable was $127,400 in 2013 and $96,200 in 2014. Also, during 2014, Nebraska Wheat had cost of goods sold of $294,200. The ending balance of inventory was $36,400 in 2013 and $44,800 in 2014. The ending balance of accounts payable was $28,100 in 2013 and $25,900 in 2014. Using the direct method, calculate cash receipts from sales and cash payments for purchases in 2014.

SE2. Cash Payments for Operating Expenses and Income Taxes: Direct Method

During 2014, Nebraska Wheat Company had operating expenses of $79,000 and income tax expense of $12,500. Depreciation expense of $20,000 for 2014 was included in operating expenses. The ending balance of prepaid expenses was $3,600 in 2013 and $2,300 in 2014. The ending balance of accrued liabilities (excluding income taxes payable) was $3,000 in 2013 and $2,000 in 2014. The ending balance of income taxes payable was $4,100 in 2013 and $3,500 in 2014. Calculate cash payments for operating expenses and income taxes in 2014 using the direct method.

EXERCISES

E1. Computing Cash Flows from Operating Activities: Direct Method

Vlieg Corporation engaged in the transactions that follow in 2014. Using the direct method, compute the various cash flows from operating activities as required.

a. During 2014, Vlieg had cash sales of $41,300 and sales on credit of $123,000. During the same year, accounts receivable decreased by $18,000. Determine the cash receipts from sales during 2014.

b. During 2014, Vlieg's cost of goods sold was $119,000. During the same year, merchandise inventory increased by $12,500 and accounts payable decreased by $4,300. Determine the cash payments for purchases during 2014.

c. During 2014, Vlieg had operating expenses of $45,000, including depreciation of $15,600. Also during 2014, related prepaid expenses decreased by $3,100 and relevant accrued liabilities increased by $1,200. Determine the cash payments for operating expenses to suppliers of goods and services during 2014.

d. Vlieg's income tax expense for 2014 was $4,300. Income taxes payable decreased by $230 that year. Determine the cash payments for income taxes during 2014.

E2. Preparing a Schedule of Cash Flows from Operating Activities: Direct Method

Vasquez Corporation's income statement follows.

Vasquez Corporation
Income Statement
For the Year Ended June 30, 2014

Sales		$122,000
Cost of goods sold		60,000
Gross margin		$ 62,000
Operating expenses:		
Salaries expense	$32,000	
Rent expense	16,800	
Depreciation expense	2,000	50,800
Income before income taxes		$ 11,200
Income taxes		2,400
Net income		$ 8,800

Additional information: (a) Accounts receivable increased by $4,400 during the year; (b) inventories increased by $7,000, and accounts payable increased by $14,000 during the year; (c) prepaid rent decreased by $1,400, while salaries payable increased by $1,000; and (d) income taxes payable decreased by $600 during the year.

Using the direct method, prepare a schedule of cash flows from operating activities.

PROBLEMS

P1. Cash Flows from Operating Activities: Direct Method

✔ Total operating activities: $47,600 inflows

Tanucci Clothing Store's income statement follows.

Tanucci Clothing Store
Income Statement
For the Year Ended June 30, 2014

Net sales		$4,900,000
Cost of goods sold:		
Beginning inventory	$1,240,000	
Net cost of purchases	3,040,000	
Goods available for sale	$4,280,000	
Ending inventory	1,400,000	
Cost of goods sold		2,880,000
Gross margin		$2,020,000
Operating expenses:		
Sales and administrative salaries expense	$1,112,000	
Other sales and administrative expenses	624,000	
Total operating expenses		1,736,000
Income before income taxes		$ 284,000
Income taxes		78,000
Net income		$ 206,000

Additional information: (a) other sales and administrative expenses include depreciation expense of $104,000 and amortization expense of $36,000; (b) accrued liabilities for salaries were $24,000 less than the previous year, and prepaid expenses were $40,000 more than the previous year; and (c) during the year accounts receivable (net) increased by $288,000, accounts payable increased by $228,000, and income taxes payable decreased by $14,400.

REQUIRED

Using the direct method, prepare a schedule of cash flows from operating activities.

P2. Statement of Cash Flows: Direct Method

RATIO

SPREADSHEET

✔ 1: Total operating activities: $548,000 inflows
✔ 1: Total financing activities: $260,000 outflows

Flanders Corporation's 2014 income statement and comparative balance sheet as of June 30, 2014 and 2013 follow.

Flanders Corporation
Income Statement
For the Year Ended June 30, 2014

Sales		$2,081,800
Cost of goods sold		1,312,600
Gross margin		$ 769,200
Operating expenses (including depreciation expense of $120,000)		378,400
Income from operations		$ 390,800
Other income (expenses):		
Loss on disposal of equipment	$ 8,000	
Interest expense	75,200	83,200
Income before income taxes		$ 307,600
Income taxes		68,400
Net income		$ 239,200

Flanders Corporation
Comparative Balance Sheets
For Years Ended June 30, 2014 and 2013

	2014	2013
Assets		
Cash	$ 334,000	$ 40,000
Accounts receivable (net)	200,000	240,000
Inventory	360,000	440,000
Prepaid expenses	1,200	2,000
Property, plant, and equipment	1,256,000	1,104,000
Accumulated depreciation—property, plant, and equipment	(366,000)	(280,000)
Total assets	$1,785,200	$1,546,000
Liabilities and Stockholders' Equity		
Accounts payable	$ 128,000	$ 84,000
Notes payable (due in 90 days)	60,000	160,000
Income taxes payable	52,000	36,000
Mortgage payable	720,000	560,000
Common stock, $5 par value	400,000	400,000
Retained earnings	425,200	306,000
Total liabilities and stockholder's equity	$ 1,785,200	$1,546,000

The following is additional information about 2014: (a) equipment that cost $48,000 with accumulated depreciation of $34,000 was sold at a loss of $8,000; (b) land and building were purchased in the amount of $200,000 through an increase of $200,000 in the mortgage payable; (c) a $40,000 payment was made on the mortgage; (d) the notes were repaid, but the company borrowed an additional $60,000 through the issuance of a new note payable; and (e) a $120,000 cash dividend was declared and paid.

REQUIRED

1. Use the direct method to prepare a statement of cash flows. Include a supporting schedule of noncash investing and financing transactions. Do not include a reconciliation of net income to net cash flows from operating activities.
2. What are the primary reasons for Flanders' large increase in cash from 2013 to 2014?
3. Compute and assess cash flow yield and free cash flow for 2014. (Round to one decimal place.)

P3. Statement of Cash Flows: Direct Method

Saudade Corporation's 2014 income statement and comparative balance sheet as of June 30, 2014 and 2013 follow.

✔ 1: Total operating activities:
$638,400 inflows
✔ 1: Total financing activities:
$303,000 outflows

Saudade Corporation
Income Statement
For the Year Ended June 30, 2014

Sales		$2,252,700
Cost of goods sold		1,451,200
Gross margin		$ 801,500
Operating expenses (including depreciation expense of $140,000)		397,300
Income from operations		$ 404,200
Other income (expenses):		
Loss on disposal of equipment	$ 7,500	
Interest expense	74,800	82,300
Income before income taxes		$ 321,900
Income taxes		69,200
Net income		$ 252,700

Saudade Corporation
Comparative Balance Sheets
For Years Ended June 30, 2014 and 2013

	2014	2013
Assets		
Cash	$ 393,900	$ 50,000
Accounts receivable (net)	180,000	250,000
Inventory	330,000	420,000
Prepaid expenses	1,400	2,300
Property, plant, and equipment	1,365,000	1,213,000
Accumulated depreciation—property, plant, and equipment	(404,000)	(297,000)
Total assets	$1,866,300	$1,638,300
Liabilities and Stockholders' Equity		
Accounts payable	$ 148,000	$ 85,000
Notes payable (due in 90 days)	75,000	150,000
Income taxes payable	53,300	39,000
Mortgage payable	740,000	587,000
Common stock, $5 par value	415,000	415,000
Retained earnings	435,000	362,300
Total liabilities and stockholders' equity	$1,866,300	$1,638,300

The following is additional information about 2014: (a) equipment that cost $49,000 with accumulated depreciation of $33,000 was sold at a loss of $7,500; (b) land and building were purchased in the amount of $201,000 through an increase of $201,000 in the mortgage payable; (c) a $48,000 payment was made on the mortgage; (d) the notes were repaid, but the company borrowed an additional $75,000 through the issuance of a new note payable; and (e) a $180,000 cash dividend was declared and paid.

REQUIRED

1. Use the direct method to prepare a statement of cash flows. Include a supporting schedule of noncash investing and financing transactions. Do not include a reconciliation of net income to net cash flows from operating activities.
2. What are the primary reasons for Saudade's large increase in cash from 2013 to 2014?
3. Compute and assess cash flow yield and free cash flow for 2014. (Round to one decimal place.)

CHAPTER 16
Financial Statement Analysis

BUSINESS INSIGHT
Medal Investments

Having studied the eating habits of Americans for several months, Kate Medal, president of Medal Investments, has concluded that there is a trend toward eating out and that the trend will continue. She is, therefore, planning to invest in a fast-food restaurant chain, and she has narrowed her choice to two companies: Fast Burger and Tasty Steak. She is now thinking about how she should evaluate these companies and arrive at her final decision.

In this chapter, we discuss the various analytical tools and standards that Kate can use to measure and compare the financial performance of the two companies.

1. CONCEPT ▶ *What concepts underlie the standards that Kate can use to compare the performance of the two companies?*

2. ACCOUNTING APPLICATION ▶ *What analytical tools can Kate use to measure the financial performance of Fast Burger and Tasty Steak?*

3. BUSINESS APPLICATION ▶ *In what ways would having access to prior years' information aid this analysis? Why is earnings management important in your assessment?*

LEARNING OBJECTIVES

LO 1 Describe the concepts, standards of comparison, and sources of information used in measuring financial performance.

LO 2 Apply horizontal analysis, trend analysis, vertical analysis, and ratio analysis to financial statements.

LO 3 Apply financial ratio analysis in a comprehensive evaluation of a company's financial performance.

LO 4 Define *quality of earnings*, and identify the factors that affect quality of earnings and related management compensation issues.

CONCEPTS
- Relevance
- Predictive value
- Comparability
- Timeliness

RELEVANT LEARNING OBJECTIVE

LO 1 Describe the concepts, standards of comparison, and sources of information used in measuring financial performance.

LO 1 Concepts Underlying Financial Performance Measurement

Financial statement analysis (or *financial performance measurement*) is used to show how items in a company's financial statements relate to the company's financial performance objectives. Users of accounting information interested in measuring a company's financial performance fall into two groups:

- A company's top managers, who set and strive to achieve financial performance objectives; middle-level managers of business processes; and lower-level employees who own stock in the company
- Creditors and investors, as well as customers who have cooperative agreements with the company

Both these groups of users want measures of financial performance that meet these underlying concepts:

- **Relevance:** The measures need to make a difference in the analysis of a company's performance.
- **Predictive value:** The users want measures that will help them make decisions about future actions.
- **Comparability:** The users want measures that make useful comparison of one period of the company's performance with another and of the company's performance to other companies.
- **Timeliness:** The users want measures that enable them to make decisions made in time to have the desired effects.

In the analysis of accounting information, managers, creditors, and investors want measures that relate to the following objectives:

- **Profitability:** To continue operating, a company must earn a satisfactory net income. Management is responsible for monitoring and measuring net income, determining the causes of any deviations from financial performance plans, and correcting the deviations. Creditors and investors look at a company's past and present net income to identify trends and to judge potential earnings ability.
- **Total Asset Management:** A company uses its assets to generate revenues. These assets are part of the cost of operating a business. To maximize net income, management must use all of the company's assets in a way that maximizes revenues while minimizing the investment in these assets.
- **Liquidity:** A company must be able to pay its bills when they come due and meet unexpected needs for cash. Management must use cash, like other assets, to fund operations that generate maximum revenues. Creditors focus on liquidity because they expect to be paid what they are owed at the appropriate time.
- **Financial Risk:** Management must use debt and stockholders' investments effectively without jeopardizing the company's future. Creditors and stockholders judge the risk involved in making a loan or an investment by looking at a company's past performance and current position. The more difficult it is to predict future profitability and liquidity, the greater the risk.
- **Operating Asset Management:** Managing operating assets is much like managing total assets. Managers must use current assets and current liabilities in a way that supports revenue growth and minimizes investment.

Standards of Comparison

When analyzing financial statements, decision makers must judge whether the relationships they find in the statements are favorable or unfavorable. Three standards of comparison that they commonly use are rule-of-thumb measures, a company's past performance, and industry norms.

Rule-of-Thumb Measures Many financial analysts, investors, and lenders apply general standards, or *rule-of-thumb measures*, to key financial ratios. For example, the credit-rating firm of **Dun & Bradstreet** offers the following rules of thumb:

- **Current Ratio:** The higher the ratio, the more likely the company will be able to meet its liabilities. A ratio of 2 to 1 (2.0) or higher is desirable.
- **Current Liabilities to Net Worth Ratio (%):** Normally a business starts to have trouble when this relationship exceeds 80%.[1]

Past Performance Comparing financial measures or ratios of the same company over time is an improvement over using rule-of-thumb measures. Such a comparison gives the analyst some basis for judging whether the measure or ratio is getting better or worse. Thus, it may be helpful in showing future trends. However, such projections must be made with care. Trends reverse over time, and a company's needs may change. For example, even if a company improves its return on investment from 3 percent in one year to 4 percent the next year, the 4 percent return may not be adequate for the company's current needs. In addition, using a company's past performance as a standard of comparison is not helpful in judging its performance relative to that of other companies.

Industry Norms Using industry norms as a standard of comparison overcomes some of the limitations of comparing a company's measures over time. Industry norms show how a company compares with other companies in the same industry. For example, if companies in a particular industry have an average rate of return on investment of 8 percent, a 3 or 4 percent rate of return is probably not adequate. Using industry norms as standards has the following limitations:

- **Comparability:** Companies in the same industry may not be strictly comparable. For example, one company in the oil industry purchases oil products and markets them through service stations. The other, an international company, discovers, produces, refines, and markets its own oil products. Because of the disparity in their operations, these two companies cannot be directly compared.
- **Accounting differences:** Companies in the same industry with similar operations may not use the same accounting procedures. For example, they may use different methods of valuing inventories and of depreciating assets.
- **Diversity: Diversified companies** (or *conglomerates*) are large companies that have multiple segments and operate in more than one industry. They may not be comparable to any other company.

International Perspective
IFRS The Use and Evaluation of Performance Measures Must Change When Using IFRS

Financial statement users must carefully consider evaluations and comparisons of historical performance under IFRS for a variety of reasons. When a company switches from U.S. GAAP to IFRS, prior years' performance measures will not likely be comparable. In fact, 80 percent of companies surveyed in a research study of European companies reported higher net income for the same operations under IFRS than under U.S. GAAP. When this occurs, an IFRS profit margin will likely provide a more optimistic evaluation when compared with pre-IFRS results or with a U.S. GAAP-based competitor. Further, the definitions of assets, liabilities, and equity differ under IFRS. The combined effect is that debt to equity, return on equity, and return on assets ratios may not exhibit historical trends. Contracts and management compensation based on these IFRS measures also require a closer look.

The FASB provides a partial solution to the limitation posed by diversified companies. It requires a diversified company to report profit or loss, certain revenue and expense items, and assets for each of its segments. Segment information may be reported for operations in different industries or different geographical areas or for major customers.[2] Exhibit 1 shows how **Goodyear Tire & Rubber Company** reports data on sales, income, and assets for its tire products segments. These data allow the analyst to compute measures of profitability, such as profit margin, asset turnover, and return on assets, for each segment and to compare them with industry norms.

Exhibit 1

Selected Segment Information for Goodyear Tire & Rubber Company

(In millions)	2011	2010	2009
Sales:			
North American Tire	$ 9,859	$ 8,205	$ 6,977
Europe, Middle East and Africa Tire	8,040	6,407	5,801
Latin American Tire	2,472	2,158	1,814
Asia Pacific Tire	2,396	2,062	1,709
Net Sales	**$22,767**	**$18,832**	**$16,301**
Segment Operating Income:			
North American Tire	$ 276	$ 18	$ (305)
Europe, Middle East and Africa Tire	627	319	166
Latin American Tire	231	330	301
Asia Pacific Tire	234	250	210
Total Segment Operating Income	**$ 1,368**	**$ 917**	**$ 372**
Assets:			
North American Tire	$ 5,744	$ 5,243	$ 4,836
Europe, Middle East and Africa Tire	5,915	5,266	5,144
Latin American Tire	2,141	1,809	1,672
Asia Pacific Tire	2,482	2,150	1,548
Total Segment Assets	**$16,282**	**$14,468**	**$13,200**
Corporate	1,347	1,162	1,210
Total Assets	**$17,629**	**$15,630**	**$14,410**

Source: The Goodyear Tire & Rubber Company, Form 10-K, For the Fiscal Year Ended 2011 (adapted).

Despite these limitations, if little information about a company's past performance is available, industry norms probably offer the best available standards for judging current performance—as long as they are used with care.

Sources of Information

The major sources of information about public corporations follow.

- **Reports published by a corporation**: A public corporation's annual report is an important source of financial information. Most public corporations also publish **interim financial statements** each quarter and sometimes each month. These reports, which present limited information in the form of condensed financial statements, are not subject to a full audit by an independent auditor. The financial community watches interim statements closely for early signs of change in a company's earnings trend.
- **Reports filed with the Securities and Exchange Commission (SEC)**: Public corporations in the United States must file annual reports (**Form 10-K**), quarterly reports (**Form 10-Q**), and current reports (**Form 8-K**) with the SEC. If they have more than $10 million in assets and more than 500 shareholders, they must file these reports electronically at http://www.sec.gov/edgar/searchedgar/webusers .htm, where anyone can access them free of charge.

STUDY NOTE: *Publishers often redefine the content of the ratios that companies provide. While the general content is similar, variations occur. Be sure to ascertain and evaluate the information that a published source uses to calculate ratios.*

■ **Business periodicals and credit and investment advisory services:** Financial analysts must keep up with current events in the financial world. One leading source of financial news is *The Wall Street Journal*. It is the most complete financial newspaper in the United States and is published every business day. Credit and investment advisory services such as **Moody's Investors Service**, **Standard & Poor's**, and **Dun and Bradstreet** provide useful information, including details about a company's financial history, industry data, and credit ratings.

APPLY IT!

Identify each of the following as (a) an underlying concept, (b) an objective of financial statement analysis, (c) a standard for financial statement analysis, or (d) a source of information for financial statement analysis:

1. A company's past performance
2. Investment advisory services
3. Assessment of a company's future potential
4. Relevance
5. Industry norms
6. Annual report
7. Form 10-K
8. Timeliness

SOLUTION

1. c;   2. d;   3. b;   4. a;   5. c;   6. d;   7. d;   8. a

TRY IT! SE1, SE2, E1A, E1B

ACCOUNTING APPLICATIONS

LO 2 Tools and Techniques of Financial Analysis

To gain insight into a company's financial performance, one must look beyond the individual numbers to the relationship between the numbers and their change from one period to another. The tools of financial analysis—horizontal analysis, trend analysis, vertical analysis, and ratio analysis—are intended to show these relationships and changes.

Horizontal Analysis

Comparative financial statements provide financial information for the current year and the previous year. To gain insight into year-to-year changes, analysts use **horizontal analysis**, in which changes from the previous year to the current year are computed in both dollar amounts and percentages. The percentage change relates the size of the change to the size of the dollar amounts involved. Note that it is important to ascertain the base amount used when a percentage describes an item. For example, inventory may be 50 percent of total current assets but only 10 percent of total assets.

Exhibits 2 and 3 present **Starbucks Corporation**'s comparative balance sheets and income statements and show both the dollar and percentage changes.

The percentage change is computed as follows.

$$\text{Percentage Change} = 100 \times \frac{\text{Comparative Year Amount} - \text{Base Year Amount}}{\text{Base Year Amount}}$$

The **base year** is the first year considered in any set of data. For example, when comparing data for 2010 and 2011, 2010 is the base year. As the balance sheets in Exhibit 2 show, between 2010 and 2011, Starbucks' total current assets increased by $1,038.5 million, from $2,756.4 million to $3,794.9 million, or by 37.7 percent, computed as follows.

$$\text{Percentage Change} = 100 \times \frac{\$1,038.5 \text{ million}}{\$2,756.4 \text{ million}} = 37.7\%$$

When examining such changes, it is important to consider the dollar amount of the change as well as the percentage change in each component. For example, the difference between the percentage increase in accounts receivable, net (27.7 percent) and total current assets (37.7 percent) is 10 percent. However, the dollar increase in total current assets is more than twelve times the dollar increase in accounts receivable ($1,038.5 million versus $83.8 million). Thus, even though the percentage changes differ by 10 percent, current assets require much more cash than accounts receivable.

Starbucks' balance sheets for 2010 and 2011 also show the following:

▲ Total assets *increased* by $974.5 million, or 15.3 percent.

▲ Shareholders' equity *increased* by $710.2 million, or 19.3 percent.

Starbucks' income statements in Exhibit 3 show the following:

▲ Net revenues *increased* by $993.0 million, or 9.3 percent.

▲ Gross margin *increased* by $502.3 million, or 8.0 percent.

This indicates that the cost of sales grew faster than net revenues. In fact, the cost of sales increased 11.0 percent compared with the 9.3 percent increase in net revenues.

In addition,

▲ Total operating expenses *increased* by $249 million, or 5.0 percent, which is lower than the 9.3 percent increase in net revenues.

▲ Operating income *increased* by $309.1 million, or 21.8 percent.

▲ Net income *increased* by $299.7 million, or 31.6 percent.

Exhibit 2
Comparative Balance Sheets with Horizontal Analysis

Starbucks Corporation
Consolidated Balance Sheets
For the Years Ended October 2, 2011 and October 3, 2010

(Dollar amounts in millions)	2011	2010	Increase (Decrease) Amount*	Percentage*
Assets				
Current assets:				
Cash and cash equivalents	$1,148.1	$1,164.0	$(15.9)	(1.4)
Short-term investments – available-for-sale securities	855.0	236.5	618.5	261.5
Short-term investments – trading securities	47.6	49.2	(1.6)	(3.3)
Accounts receivable, net	386.5	302.7	83.8	27.7
Inventories	965.8	543.3	422.5	77.8
Prepaid and other current assets	161.5	156.5	5.0	3.2
Deferred income taxes, net	230.4	304.2	(73.8)	(24.3)
Total current assets	$3,794.9	$2,756.4	$1,038.5	37.7
Long-term investments – available-for-sale securities	107.0	191.8	(84.8)	(44.2)
Equity and cost investments	372.3	341.5	30.8	9.0
Property, plant, and equipment, net	2,355.0	2,416.5	(61.5)	(2.5)
Other assets	297.7	346.5	(48.8)	(14.1)
Other intangible assets	111.9	70.8	41.1	58.1
Goodwill	321.6	262.4	59.2	22.6
Total assets	$7,360.4	$6,385.9	$ 974.5	15.3
Liabilities and Shareholders' Equity				
Current liabilities:				
Accounts payable	540.0	282.6	257.4	91.1
Accrued compensation and related costs	364.4	400.0	(35.6)	(8.9)
Accrued occupancy costs	148.3	173.2	(24.9)	(14.4)
Accrued taxes	109.2	100.2	9.0	9.0
Insurance reserves	145.6	146.2	(0.6)	(0.4)
Other accrued liabilities	319.0	262.8	56.2	21.4
Deferred revenue	449.3	414.1	35.2	8.5
Total current liabilities	$2,075.8	$1,779.1	$ 296.7	16.7
Long-term debt	549.5	549.4	0.1	0.0
Other long-term liabilities	347.8	375.1	(27.3)	(7.3)
Total liabilities	2,973.1	2,703.6	269.5	10.0
Total shareholders' equity	4,384.9	3,674.7	710.2	19.3
Noncontrolling interests	2.4	7.6	(5.2)	(68.4)
Total equity	4,387.3	3,682.3	705.0	19.1
Total liabilities and shareholders' equity	$7,360.4	$6,385.9	$ 974.5	15.3

*Rounded
Source: Data from Starbucks Corporation, Form 10-K, For the Fiscal Year Ended October 2, 2011.

Exhibit 3
Comparative Income Statements with Horizontal Analysis

Starbucks Corporation
Consolidated Income Statements
For the Years Ended October 2, 2011 and October 3, 2010

(Dollar amounts in millions except per share amounts)	2011	2010	Increase (Decrease) Amount*	Increase (Decrease) Percentage*
Net revenues	$11,700.4	$10,707.4	$993.0	9.3
Cost of sales, including occupancy costs	4,949.3	4,458.6	490.7	11.0
Gross margin	$ 6,751.1	$ 6,248.8	$502.3	8.0
Operating expenses				
Store operating expenses	$ 3,665.1	$ 3,551.4	$113.7	3.2
Other operating expenses	402.0	293.2	108.8	37.1
Depreciation and amortization expenses	523.3	510.4	12.9	2.5
General and administrative expenses	636.1	569.5	66.6	11.7
Restructuring charges	—	53.0	(53.0)	(100.0)
Total operating expenses	$ 5,226.5	$ 4,977.5	$249.0	5.0
Gain on sale of properties	30.2	—	30.2	—
Income from equity investees	173.7	148.1	25.6	17.3
Operating income	$ 1,728.5	$ 1,419.4	$309.1	21.8
Interest income and other, net	115.9	50.3	65.6	130.4
Interest expense	(33.3)	(32.7)	(0.6)	1.8
Income before taxes	$ 1,811.1	$ 1,437.0	$374.1	26.0
Income taxes	563.1	488.7	74.4	15.2
Net income	$ 1,248.0	$ 948.3	$299.7	31.6

*Rounded
Source: Data from Starbucks Corporation, Form 10-K, For the Fiscal Year Ended October 2, 2011.

The primary reason for the increases in operating income and net income is that operating expenses increased at a slower rate (5.0 percent) than net revenues (9.3 percent).

Trend Analysis

STUDY NOTE: *To reflect the general five-year economic cycle of the U.S. economy, trend analysis usually covers a five-year period.*

Trend analysis is a variation of horizontal analysis. With this tool, the analyst calculates percentage changes for several successive years instead of for just two years. Because of its long-term view, trend analysis can highlight basic changes in the nature of a business.

Exhibit 4 shows a trend analysis of **Starbucks'** five-year summary of net revenues and operating income.

Trend analysis uses an **index number** to show changes in related items over time. For an index number, the base year is set at 100 percent. Other years are measured in relation to that amount. For example, the 2011 index for Starbucks' net revenues is figured as follows (dollar amounts are in millions).

Exhibit 4
Trend Analysis

Starbucks Corporation
Net Revenues and Operating Income
Trend Analysis

	2011	2010	2009	2008	2007
Dollar values (In millions)					
Net revenues	$11,700.4	$10,707.4	$9,774.6	$10,383.0	$9,411.5
Operating income	1,728.5	1,419.4	562.0	390.3	945.9
Trend analysis (In percentages)					
Net revenues	124.3	113.8	103.9	110.3	100.0
Operating income	182.7	150.1	59.4	41.3	100.0

Source: Data from Starbucks Corporation, Form 10-K, For the Fiscal Year Ended October 2, 2011.

$$\text{Index} = 100 \times \frac{\$11,700.4}{\$9,411.5} = 124.3\%$$

The trend analysis in Exhibit 4 shows the following:

▲ Net revenues *increased* over the five-year period.

▲ Overall, revenue *increased* 24.3 percent.

Net revenues grew faster than operating income in 2008 and 2009; however, operating income grew faster than net revenues in 2010 and 2011. Exhibit 5 illustrates these trends.

Exhibit 5
Graph of Trend Analysis
Shown in Exhibit 4

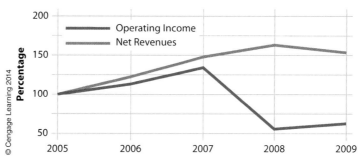

© Cengage Learning 2014

Vertical Analysis

Vertical analysis shows how the different components of a financial statement relate to a total figure in the statement. On the balance sheet, the figure would be total assets or total liabilities and stockholders' equity, and on the income statement, it would be net revenues or net sales. The analyst sets the total figure at 100 percent and computes each component's percentage of that total. The resulting financial statement, which is expressed entirely in percentages, is called a **common-size statement**. Common-size balance sheets and common-size income statements for **Starbucks** are shown in pie-chart form in Exhibits 6 and 8 and in financial statement form in Exhibits 7 and 9.

Exhibit 6
Common-Size Balance Sheets Presented Graphically

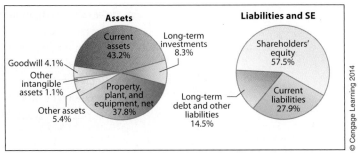

Rounding causes some additions not to total precisely.

Exhibit 7
Common-Size
Balance Sheets

	Starbucks Corporation **Common-Size Balance Sheets** **October 2, 2011, and October 3, 2010**	
	2011	**2010**
Assets		
Current assets	51.6%	43.2%
Long-term investments	6.6	8.3
Property, plant, and equipment, net	32.0	37.8
Other assets	4.0	5.4
Other intangible assets	1.5	1.1
Goodwill	4.4	4.1
Total assets	100.0%	100.0%
Liabilities and Shareholders' Equity		
Current liabilities	28.2%	27.9%
Long-term debt and other liabilities	12.2	14.5
Shareholders' equity	59.6	57.5
Total liabilities and shareholders' equity	100.0%	100.0%

Note: Amounts do not precisely total 100 percent in all cases due to rounding.
Source: Data from Starbucks Corporation, Form 10-K, For the Fiscal Year Ended October 2, 2011.

Vertical analysis and common-size statements are useful in comparing the importance of specific components in the operation of a business and in identifying important changes in the components from one year to the next. The main conclusions to be drawn from our analysis of Starbucks are the following:

- Starbucks' assets consist largely of current assets and property, plant, and equipment.
- Starbucks finances assets primarily through equity and current liabilities.
- Starbucks has few long-term liabilities.

Looking at the pie charts in Exhibit 6 and the common-size balance sheets in Exhibit 7, you can see the following:

- The composition of Starbucks' assets shifted from property, plant, and equipment (declined from 37.8% to 32.0%), long-term investments (from 8.3% to 6.6%), and other assets (from 5.4% to 4.0%) to current assets (from 43.2% to 51.6%).

■ The proportion of long-term debt and other liabilities decreased (from 14.5% to 12.2%) while current liabilities increased (from 27.9% to 28.2%) and shareholders' equity increased (from 57.5% to 59.6%).

The common-size income statements in Exhibit 9, illustrated as pie charts in Exhibit 8, show that Starbucks decreased its operating expenses from 2010 to 2011 by 1.9 percent of revenues (46.5% vs. 44.6%). In other words, revenues grew faster than operating expenses.

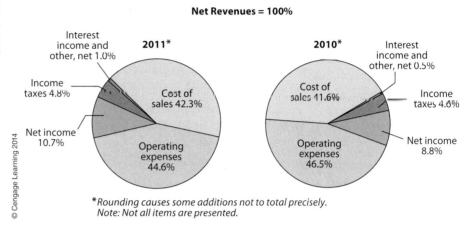

Exhibit 8
Common-Size Income Statements Presented Graphically

Rounding causes some additions not to total precisely.
Note: Not all items are presented.

© Cengage Learning 2014

Exhibit 9
Common-Size Income Statements

Starbucks Corporation
Common-Size Income Statements
For the Years Ended October 2, 2011, and October 3, 2010

	2011	2010
Net revenues	100.0%	100.0%
Cost of sales, including occupancy costs	42.3	41.6
Gross margin	57.7%	58.4%
Operating expenses:		
Store operating expenses	31.3%	33.2%
Other operating expenses	3.4	2.7
Depreciation and amortization expenses	4.5	4.8
General and administrative expenses	5.4	5.3
Restructuring charges	—	0.5
Total operating expenses	44.6%	46.5%
Gain on sales of properties	0.3%	—%
Income from equity investees	1.5	1.4
Operating income	14.9%	13.3%
Interest income and other, net	1.0	0.5
Interest expense	(0.3)	(0.3)
Income before taxes	15.5%	13.4%
Income taxes	4.8	4.6
Net income	10.7%	8.9%

Note: Amounts do not precisely total 100 percent in all cases due to rounding.
Source: Data from Starbucks Corporation, Form 10-K, For the Fiscal Year Ended October 2, 2011.

Common-size statements are often used to make comparisons between companies. They allow an analyst to compare the operating and financing characteristics of two companies of different size in the same industry. For example, the analyst might want to compare Starbucks with other specialty retailers in terms of percentage of total assets financed by debt or in terms of operating expenses as a percentage of net revenues. Common-size statements would show those and other relationships. These statements can also be used to compare the characteristics of companies that report in different currencies.

 ## Financial Ratio Analysis

Financial ratio analysis identifies key relationships between the components of the financial statements. Ratios are useful tools for evaluating a company's financial position and operations and may reveal areas that need further investigation. To interpret ratios correctly, the analyst must have:

- A general understanding of the company and its environment
- Financial data for several years or for several companies
- An understanding of the data underlying the numerator and denominator

Ratios can be expressed in several ways. For example, a ratio of net income of $100,000 to sales of $1,000,000 can be stated as follows.

- Net income is 1/10, or 10 percent, of sales.
- The ratio of sales to net income is 10 to 1 (10:1), or sales are 10 times net income.
- For every dollar of sales, the company has an average net income of 10 cents.

APPLY IT!

Using 2012 as the base year, prepare a trend analysis for the data that follows, and tell whether the results suggest a favorable or unfavorable trend. (Round to one decimal place.)

	2014	2013	2012
Net sales	$216,000	$152,000	$100,000
Accounts receivable (net)	40,000	29,000	20,000

SOLUTION

	2014	2013	2012
Net sales	216.0%	152.0%	100.0%
Accounts receivable (net)	200.0%	145.0%	100.0%

These results show favorable trends because the company is increasing sales at a faster pace than the amount of resources tied up in accounts receivable.

TRY IT! SE3, SE4, SE5, E2A, E3A, E4A, E2B, E3B, E4B

 ## LO3 Comprehensive Illustration of Financial Ratio Analysis

In this section, we perform a comprehensive financial ratio analysis of **Starbucks'** performance in 2010 and 2011. The following excerpt from the Management's Discussion and Analysis of Financial Condition section of Starbucks' 2011 annual report provides the context for our evaluation:

> *Starbucks results for fiscal 2011 reflect the strength and resiliency of our business model, the global power of our brand and the talent and dedication of our employees. Our business has performed well this year despite significant headwinds from commodity costs and a continuingly challenging consumer environment. Strong global comparable stores sales growth of 8% for the full year (US*

8% and International 5%) drove increased sales leverage and resulted in higher operating margins and net earnings. This helped mitigate the impact of higher commodity costs, which negatively impacted EPS by approximately $0.20 per share for the year, equivalent to approximately 220 basis points of operating margin. Most of the commodity pressure was related to coffee, with dairy, cocoa, sugar and fuel accounting for the rest. . . .

We are aggressively pursuing the profitable expansion opportunities that exist outside the US, including disciplined growth and scale in our more mature markets, and faster expansion in key emerging markets like China.

We will use the ratios introduced earlier in the text, as well as some commonly used supplemental financial ratios, to evaluate Starbucks' performance in relation to the five concepts: profitability, total asset management, liquidity, financial risk, and operating asset management. We will also evaluate Starbucks' market strength. The data that we use in computing all ratios are from Starbucks' Form 10-K, 2011, and Form 10-K, 2010. All dollar amounts shown in the computations are in millions.

Evaluating Profitability and Total Asset Management

Investors and creditors use profit margin to evaluate a company's ability to earn a satisfactory income (*profitability*). They use asset turnover to determine whether the company uses assets in a way that maximizes revenue (*total asset management*). These two ratios require only three numbers: revenue (or net revenue),* net income, and average total assets. Their combined effect is overall earning power—that is, return on assets.

Profit Margin **Profit margin** measures the net income produced by each dollar of sales. **Starbucks**' profit margins in 2011 and 2010 are computed as follows.

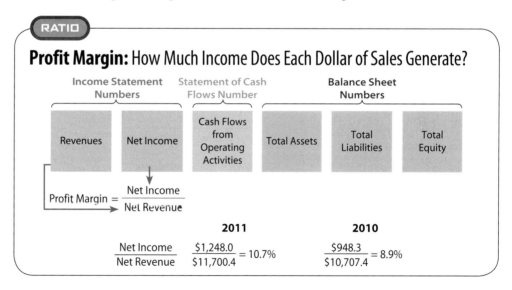

Starbucks' profit margin increased from 8.9 to 10.7 percent between 2011 and 2010 because as a percentage of revenue, operating expenses decreased, as shown in Exhibit 9.

Asset Turnover **Asset turnover** measures how efficiently assets are used to produce sales. **Starbucks**' asset turnover ratios in 2011 and 2010 are computed as follows.

---

* Starbucks refers to revenue as *net revenue*, and we use that term throughout our examples.

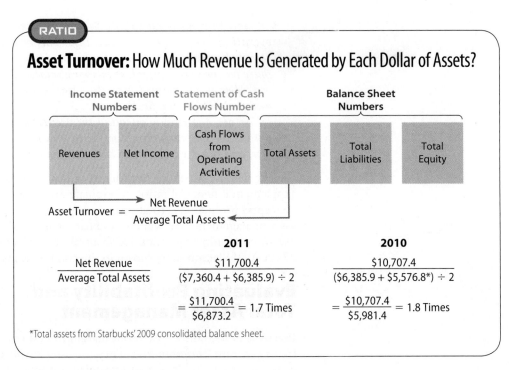

Asset Turnover: How Much Revenue Is Generated by Each Dollar of Assets?

Starbucks' asset turnover decreased slightly to 1.7 times from 1.8 times because net sales increased slightly less in relation to average total assets.

Return on Assets **Return on assets** measures a company's overall earning power, or profitability. **Starbucks'** return on assets ratios in 2011 and 2010 are computed as follows.

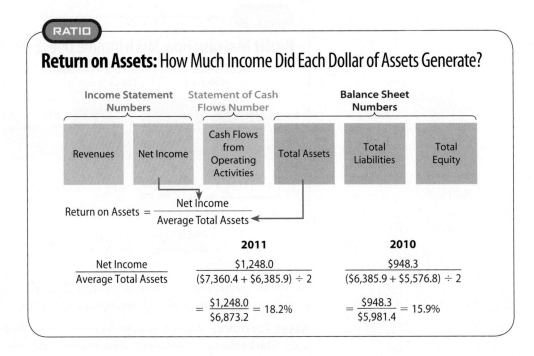

Return on Assets: How Much Income Did Each Dollar of Assets Generate?

Starbucks' return on assets increased from 15.9 percent in 2010 to 18.2 percent in 2011 because net income increased more in relation to average total assets.

Profitability Ratio Relationships The relationships of the three financial ratios for profitability are as follows.

	Profit Margin Net Income / Net Sales		Asset Turnover Net Sales / Average Total Assets		Return on Assets Net Income / Average Total Assets
2010	8.9%	×	1.8	=	16.0%
2011	10.7%	×	1.7	=	18.2%

Starbucks' return on assets increased in 2011 because of an increase in profit margin. Although Starbucks' profitability and total asset management ratios were relatively low, Starbucks is very good at generating cash from these returns on assets.

It is important to note that net income is sometimes not as useful in computing profitability ratios as it is for Starbucks. If a company has one-time items on its income statement, such as gains, or losses on the sale or disposal of discontinued operations, income from continuing operations may be a better measure of sustainable earnings than net income. Some analysts like to use earnings before interest and taxes (EBIT) for the earnings measure because it excludes the effects of the company's borrowings and the tax rates from the analysis. Whatever figure one uses for earnings, it is important to try to determine the effects of various components on future operations.

STUDY NOTE: *The analysis of both asset turnover and return on assets is improved if only productive assets are used in the calculations. For example, when investments in unfinished new plant construction or in nonoperating plants are removed from the asset base, the result is a better picture of the productivity of assets.*

Evaluating Liquidity

As mentioned, *liquidity* is a company's ability to pay bills when they are due and to meet unexpected needs for cash. Analysts compute cash flow yield, cash flows to sales, cash flows to assets, and free cash flow to evaluate a company's liquidity.

Cash Flow Yield **Cash flow yield** is the most important liquidity ratio because it measures a company's ability to generate operating cash flows in relation to net income. **Starbucks'** cash flow yields in 2011 and 2010 are computed as follows.

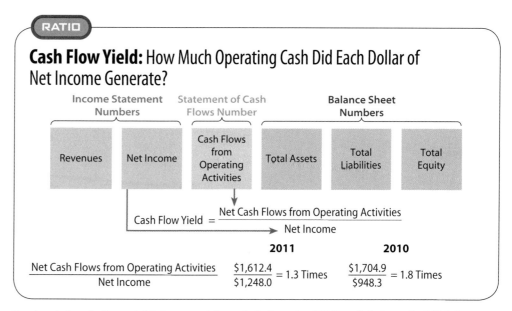

Starbucks' cash flow yield decreased from 1.8 times in 2010 to 1.3 times in 2011 because net cash flows from operating activities decreased while net income increased.

Cash Flows to Sales **Cash flows to sales** refers to the ability of sales to generate operating cash flows. **Starbucks'** cash flows to sales ratios in 2011 and 2010 are computed as follows.

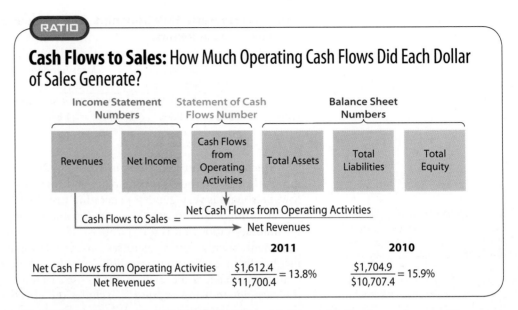

Cash Flows to Sales: How Much Operating Cash Flows Did Each Dollar of Sales Generate?

$$\text{Cash Flows to Sales} = \frac{\text{Net Cash Flows from Operating Activities}}{\text{Net Revenues}}$$

	2011	2010
$\dfrac{\text{Net Cash Flows from Operating Activities}}{\text{Net Revenues}}$	$\dfrac{\$1,612.4}{\$11,700.4} = 13.8\%$	$\dfrac{\$1,704.9}{\$10,707.4} = 15.9\%$

Starbucks' cash flows to sales decreased from 15.9 to 13.8 percent because the company's cash flows provided by its operations decreased while net revenues increased.

Cash Flows to Assets **Cash flows to assets** measures the ability of assets to generate operating cash flows. **Starbucks'** cash flows to assets ratios in 2011 and 2010 are computed as follows.

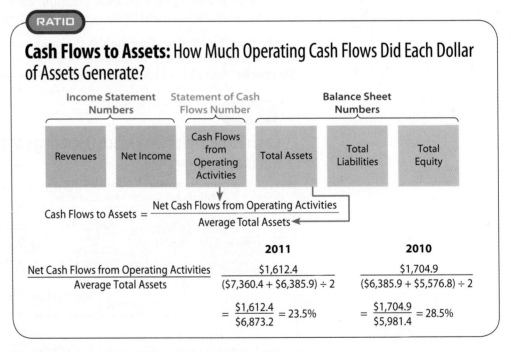

Cash Flows to Assets: How Much Operating Cash Flows Did Each Dollar of Assets Generate?

$$\text{Cash Flows to Assets} = \frac{\text{Net Cash Flows from Operating Activities}}{\text{Average Total Assets}}$$

	2011	2010
$\dfrac{\text{Net Cash Flows from Operating Activities}}{\text{Average Total Assets}}$	$\dfrac{\$1,612.4}{(\$7,360.4 + \$6,385.9) \div 2}$	$\dfrac{\$1,704.9}{(\$6,385.9 + \$5,576.8) \div 2}$
	$= \dfrac{\$1,612.4}{\$6,873.2} = 23.5\%$	$= \dfrac{\$1,704.9}{\$5,981.4} = 28.5\%$

Starbucks' cash flows to assets decreased from 28.5 to 23.5 percent. The cash flows provided by the company's operations decreased, while the average total assets increased.

Free Cash Flow **Free cash flow** is a measure of the cash remaining after providing for commitments. **Starbucks'** free cash flows in 2010 and 2011 are computed as follows.

	2011	2010
Net Cash Flows from Operating Activities	$\$1,612.4 - \$389.5 - \$531.9$	$\$1,704.9 - \$171.0 - \$440.7$
− Dividends	$= \$691.0$	$= \$1,093.2$
− Net Capital Expenditures*		

*From the consolidated statements of cash flows.

Starbucks' free cash flow decreased. While the company's net capital expenditures (the difference between purchases and sales of plant assets) increased by \$91.2 million (\$531.9 − \$440.7), the net cash provided by operating activities decreased by \$92.5 million (\$1,612.4 − \$1,704.9). Another unfavorable factor in Starbucks' free cash flow is that the company paid dividends in the past two years. In sum, Starbucks is very proficient in turning its income into cash. It has very good cash flow returns and strong free cash flow.

Evaluating Financial Risk

Financial risk refers to a company's ability to survive in good times and bad. The aim of evaluating financial risk is to detect early signs that a company is headed for financial difficulty through its use of debt, or *financial leverage*, to finance part of the company. Many companies use financial leverage positively. They take advantage of the fact that interest paid on debt is tax-deductible, whereas dividends on stock are not. Because debt usually carries a fixed interest charge and the cost of financing can be limited, leverage can be used to advantage. If a company can earn a return on assets greater than the cost of interest, it increases the return to its stockholders. However, increasing amounts of debt in a company's capital structure can mean that the company is becoming more heavily leveraged. When this occurs, the company runs the risk of not earning a return on assets equal to the cost of financing the assets, thereby incurring a loss. This condition has a negative effect because it represents increasing legal obligations to pay interest periodically and the principal at maturity. Failure to make those payments can result in bankruptcy.

STUDY NOTE: *Because of innovative financing plans and other means of acquiring assets, lease payments and similar types of fixed obligations should be considered when evaluating financial risk.*

Declining profitability and liquidity ratios together with increased leverage are key indicators of possible failure. Ratios related to financial risk include debt to equity, return on equity, and interest coverage.

Debt to Equity Ratio The **debt to equity ratio** measures financial risk by showing the amount of assets provided by creditors in relation to the amount provided by stockholders. A higher ratio indicates more financial risk because it indicates the company is reling more heavily on debt financing. **Starbucks'** debt to equity ratios in 2010 and 2011 are computed as follows.

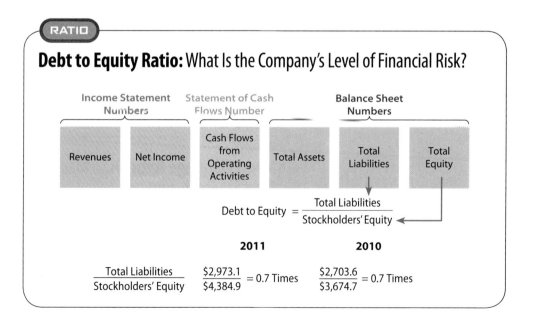

Starbucks' debt to equity ratio was stable at 0.7 times in both 2010 and 2011. Recall from Exhibit 2 that the company increased both its liabilities and its stockholders' equity from 2010 to 2011.

Return on Equity **Return on equity** measures the return to stockholders, or the profitability of stockholders' investments. **Starbucks'** return on equity ratios in 2010 and 2011 are computed as follows.

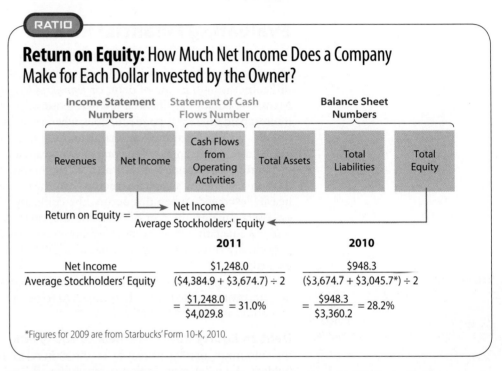

Return on Equity: How Much Net Income Does a Company Make for Each Dollar Invested by the Owner?

	Income Statement Numbers	Statement of Cash Flows Number	Balance Sheet Numbers
	Revenues Net Income	Cash Flows from Operating Activities	Total Assets Total Liabilities Total Equity

$$\text{Return on Equity} = \frac{\text{Net Income}}{\text{Average Stockholders' Equity}}$$

	2011	**2010**
$\dfrac{\text{Net Income}}{\text{Average Stockholders' Equity}}$	$\dfrac{\$1,248.0}{(\$4,384.9 + \$3,674.7) \div 2}$	$\dfrac{\$948.3}{(\$3,674.7 + \$3,045.7^*) \div 2}$
	$= \dfrac{\$1,248.0}{\$4,029.8} = 31.0\%$	$= \dfrac{\$948.3}{\$3,360.2} = 28.2\%$

*Figures for 2009 are from Starbucks' Form 10-K, 2010.

Starbucks' return on equity increased from 28.2 percent in 2010 to 31.0 percent in 2011. These are excellent returns compared to return on assets of 15.8 percent in 2010 and 18.1 percent in 2011. Note that both the overall profitability (return on assets) and the return to stockholders (return on equity) increased. The reason for this is that Starbucks' net income increased proportionally more than average stockholders' equity.

Interest Coverage The **interest coverage ratio** is a supplementary ratio that measures the degree of protection creditors have from default on interest payments. Analysts use this ratio to determine whether a company's interest payments are in peril. **Starbucks'** interest coverage ratios in 2010 and 2011 are computed as follows.

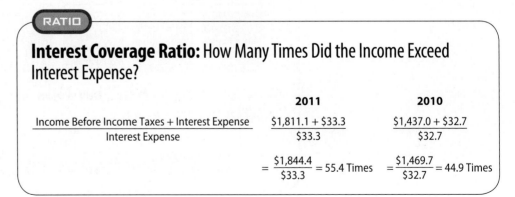

Interest Coverage Ratio: How Many Times Did the Income Exceed Interest Expense?

	2011	**2010**
$\dfrac{\text{Income Before Income Taxes} + \text{Interest Expense}}{\text{Interest Expense}}$	$\dfrac{\$1,811.1 + \$33.3}{\$33.3}$	$\dfrac{\$1,437.0 + \$32.7}{\$32.7}$
	$= \dfrac{\$1,844.4}{\$33.3} = 55.4 \text{ Times}$	$= \dfrac{\$1,469.7}{\$32.7} = 44.9 \text{ Times}$

Starbucks' interest coverage increased from 44.9 times to 55.4 times, due to an increase in income before income taxes. Therefore, the interest coverage is at a very safe level.

Evaluating Operating Asset Management

Research has shown that successful companies carefully manage the operating assets and payables in the **operating cycle**.[3] As discussed in an earlier chapter, the operating cycle involves inventories, accounts receivable, and accounts payable. It spans the time it takes to purchase inventory, sell it, and collect for it. The **financing period**—the period between the time a supplier must be paid and the end of the operating cycle—defines how much additional financing the company must have to support its operations. Because additional debt increases a company's financial risk, it is important to keep the financing period at a manageable level.

The financial ratios that measure operating asset management include inventory turnover, days' inventory on hand, receivables turnover, days' sales uncollected, payables turnover, and days' payable. To determine the days in each component of the cash cycle, the turnover must first be computed by relating the average for each balance sheet account—inventory, accounts receivable, and accounts payable—to the respective income statement account for the period—cost of goods sold and net sales or revenues. The average number of days of each component is then determined by dividing the turnover into 365 days.

Inventory Turnover **Inventory turnover** measures the relative size of inventories. **Starbucks'** inventory turnover ratios in 2010 and 2011 are computed as follows.

RATIO

Inventory Turnover: How Many Times Did the Company Sell Its Inventory During an Accounting Period?

	2011	**2010**
$\dfrac{\text{Cost of Goods Sold*}}{\text{Average Inventory}}$	$\dfrac{\$4{,}949.3}{(\$965.8 + \$543.3) \div 2}$	$\dfrac{\$4{,}458.6}{(\$543.3 + \$664.9^{**}) \div 2}$
	$= \dfrac{\$4{,}949.3}{\$754.6} = 6.6 \text{ Times}$	$= \dfrac{\$4{,}458.6}{\$604.1} = 7.4 \text{ Times}$

*Starbucks refers to Cost of Goods Sold as Cost of Sales.
**Inventory from Starbucks' 2009 consolidated balance sheet.

Starbucks' inventory turnover decreased from 7.4 times in 2010 to 6.6 times in 2011 because the average inventory increased more in relation to the cost of goods sold.

Days' Inventory on Hand **Days' inventory on hand** measures the average number of days that it takes to sell inventory. **Starbucks'** days' inventory on hand ratios in 2010 and 2011 are computed as follows.

RATIO

Days' Inventory on Hand: How Many Days Did It Take the Company to Sell Its Inventory?

	2011	**2010**
$\dfrac{\text{Days in Accounting Period}}{\text{Inventory Turnover}}$	$\dfrac{365 \text{ Days}}{6.6 \text{ Times}} = 55.3 \text{ Days}$	$\dfrac{365 \text{ Days}}{7.4 \text{ Times}} = 49.3 \text{ Days}$

Starbucks' days' inventory on hand increased from 49.3 days in 2010 to 55.3 days in 2011 due to the decrease in the inventory turnover.

Receivables Turnover **Receivables turnover** measures the relative size of accounts receivable and the effectiveness of credit policies. **Starbucks'** receivables turnover ratios in 2010 and 2011 are computed as follows.

RATIO

Receivables Turnover: How Many Times Did the Company Collect Its Accounts Receivable During an Accounting Period?

	2011	2010
$\dfrac{\text{Net Sales}}{\text{Average Accounts Receivable}}$	$\dfrac{\$11,700.4}{(\$386.5 + \$302.7) \div 2}$	$\dfrac{\$10,707.4}{(\$302.7 + \$271.0^*) \div 2}$
	$= \dfrac{\$11,700.4}{\$344.6} = 34.0 \text{ Times}$	$= \dfrac{\$10,707.4}{\$286.9} = 37.3 \text{ Times}$

*Accounts receivable from Starbucks' 2009 consolidated balance sheet.

Because most of Starbucks' sales are for cash or credit card, receivables are not a significant asset for Starbucks. Thus, its receivables turnover is very high. However, it declined slightly, from 37.3 times in 2010 to 34.0 times in 2011.

Days' Sales Uncollected **Days' sales uncollected** measures the average number of days it takes to collect receivables. **Starbucks'** days' sales uncollected ratios in 2010 and 2011 are computed as follows.

RATIO

Days' Sales Uncollected: How Many Days Does It Take to Collect Accounts Receivables?

	2011	2010
$\dfrac{\text{Days in Accounting Period}}{\text{Receivables Turnover}}$	$\dfrac{365 \text{ Days}}{34.0 \text{ Times}} = 10.7 \text{ Days}$	$\dfrac{365 \text{ Days}}{37.3 \text{ Times}} = 9.8 \text{ Days}$

Starbucks' high receivables turnover ratios resulted in an increase in days' sales uncollected from 9.8 days in 2010 to 10.7 days in 2011.

Payables Turnover **Payables turnover** measures the relative size of accounts payable and the credit terms extended to a company. **Starbucks'** payables turnover ratios in 2010 and 2011 are computed as follows.

RATIO

Payables Turnover: How Many Times Does a Company Pay Its Accounts Payable During an Accounting Period?

	2011	2010
$\dfrac{\text{Costs of Goods Sold } +/-\text{ Change in Inventory}}{\text{Average Accounts Payable}}$	$\dfrac{\$4,949.3 + \$422.5}{(\$540.0 + \$282.6) \div 2}$	$\dfrac{\$4,458.6 - \$121.6}{(\$282.6 + \$267.1^*) \div 2}$
	$= \dfrac{\$5,371.8}{\$411.3} = 13.1 \text{ Times}$	$= \dfrac{\$4,337.0}{\$274.9} = 15.8 \text{ Times}$

*Accounts Payable from Starbucks' 2009 consolidated balance sheet.

Starbucks' payables turnover decreased from 15.8 times in 2010 to 13.1 times in 2011.

Days' Payable **Days' payable** measures the average number of days it takes to pay accounts payable. Starbucks' days' payable ratios in 2010 and 2011 are computed as follows.

RATIO

Days' Payable: How Many Days Did It Take to Pay Accounts Payable?

	2011	2010
$\dfrac{\text{Days in Accounting Period}}{\text{Payables Turnover}}$	$\dfrac{365 \text{ Days}}{13.1 \text{ Times}} = 27.9 \text{ Days}$	$\dfrac{365 \text{ Days}}{15.8 \text{ Times}} = 23.1 \text{ Days}$

Strabucks' decrease in payables turnover resulted in an increase in days' payable from 23.1 days in 2010 to 27.9 days in 2011.

Financing Period We can now assess **Starbucks'** overall operating asset management by computing the financing period—the number of days of financing that must be provided. The financing period is computed by deducting the days' payable from the operating cycle (days' inventory on hand + days' sales uncollected). Starbucks' financing periods in 2010 and 2011 are computed as follows.

2011: 55.3 Days + 10.7 Days − 27.9 Days = 38.1 Days
2010: 49.3 Days + 9.8 Days − 23.1 Days = 36.0 Days

Since both days' inventory on hand and days' sales uncollected increased and days' payable increased, Starbucks had to provide 2.1 (38.1 − 36.0) more days of financing for its operating assets in 2011 than in 2010.

Supplemental Financial Ratios for Assessing Operating Asset Management and Liquidity

In evaluating operating asset management and liquidity, many analysts also consider two supplemental financial ratios: the current ratio and the quick ratio.

Current Ratio
The **current ratio** measures short-term debt-paying ability by comparing current assets with current liabilities. **Starbucks'** current ratios in 2010 and 2011 are computed as follows.

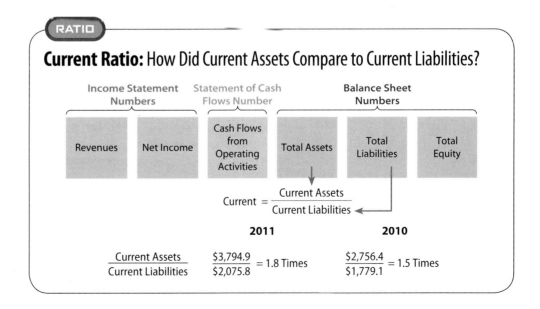

RATIO

Current Ratio: How Did Current Assets Compare to Current Liabilities?

Income Statement Numbers		Statement of Cash Flows Number	Balance Sheet Numbers		
Revenues	Net Income	Cash Flows from Operating Activities	Total Assets	Total Liabilities	Total Equity

$$\text{Current} = \frac{\text{Current Assets}}{\text{Current Liabilities}}$$

	2011	2010
$\dfrac{\text{Current Assets}}{\text{Current Liabilities}}$	$\dfrac{\$3,794.9}{\$2,075.8} = 1.8 \text{ Times}$	$\dfrac{\$2,756.4}{\$1,779.1} = 1.5 \text{ Times}$

Starbucks' current ratio was increased from 1.5 times in 2010 to 1.8 times in 2011. From 2010 to 2011, its current assets grew faster than its current liabilities.

Quick Ratio   The **quick ratio**, another measure of short-term debt-paying ability, differs from the current ratio in that the numerator of the quick ratio excludes inventories and prepaid expenses. Inventories and prepaid expenses take longer to convert to cash than the current assets included in the numerator of the quick ratio. **Starbucks**' quick ratios in 2010 and 2011 are computed as follows.

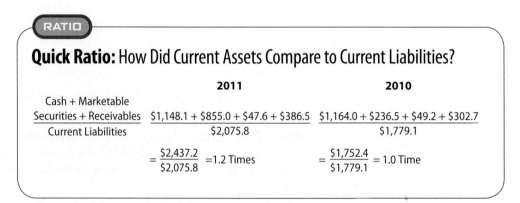

RATIO

Quick Ratio: How Did Current Assets Compare to Current Liabilities?

	2011	**2010**
$\dfrac{\text{Cash} + \text{Marketable Securities} + \text{Receivables}}{\text{Current Liabilities}}$	$\dfrac{\$1,148.1 + \$855.0 + \$47.6 + \$386.5}{\$2,075.8}$	$\dfrac{\$1,164.0 + \$236.5 + \$49.2 + \$302.7}{\$1,779.1}$
	$= \dfrac{\$2,437.2}{\$2,075.8} = 1.2 \text{ Times}$	$= \dfrac{\$1,752.4}{\$1,779.1} = 1.0 \text{ Time}$

Starbucks' quick ratio increased from 1.0 time in 2010 to 1.2 times in 2011.

Evaluating Market Strength with Financial Ratios

Market price is the price at which a company's stock is bought and sold. It indicates how investors view the potential return and risk connected with owning the stock. Market price by itself is not very informative, however, because companies have different numbers of shares outstanding, different earnings, and different dividend policies. Thus, market price must be related to earnings by considering the price/earnings (P/E) ratio and the dividend yield.

Price/Earnings (P/E)   **Price/earnings (P/E)**, which measures investors' confidence in a company, is the ratio of the market price per share to earnings per share. The P/E ratio is useful in comparing the earnings of different companies and the value of a company's shares in relation to values in the overall market. With a higher P/E ratio, the investor obtains less earnings per dollar invested. **Starbucks**' P/E ratios in 2010 and 2011 are computed as follows.

RATIO

Price/Earnings (P/E): What Value Does the Market Place on the Company's Earnings?

	2011	**2010**
$\dfrac{\text{Market Price per Share}}{\text{Earnings per Share**}}$	$\dfrac{\$37.86^{*}}{\$1.66} = 22.8 \text{ Times}$	$\dfrac{\$24.79^{*}}{\$1.27} = 19.5 \text{ Times}$

*Market price is the average for the fourth quarter reported in Starbucks' 2010 and 2011 annual reports.
**Earnings per share is Starbucks' basic EPS.

Starbucks' P/E ratio increased from 19.5 times in 2010 to 22.8 times in 2011 because the market value of its stock increased at a faster rate (from about $25 to about $38) than its earnings per share. The implication is that investors are confident that Starbucks' earnings will grow as fast in the future as it did in the past.

Dividend Yield **Dividend yield** measures a stock's current return to an investor in the form of dividends. **Starbucks'** dividend yields in 2010 and 2011 are computed as follows.

> **RATIO**
>
> ## Dividend Yield: What Is the Return from Dividends on Each Share of Stock?
>
> | | **2011** | **2010** |
> |---|---|---|
> | $\dfrac{\text{Dividends per Share}}{\text{Market Price per Share}}$ | $\dfrac{\$0.56}{\$37.86} = 1.5\%$ | $\dfrac{\$0.36}{\$24.79} = 1.5\%$ |

Starbucks's dividend yield was steady and rather low at 1.5 percent for both years 2010 and 2011. Because the dividend yield was rather low, we can conclude that those who invest in the company expect their return to come from increases in the stock's market value.

Financial Statement Analysis and Performance Assessment

The relationships of key financial ratios help the users of financial statements assess financial performance. These relationships are shown in Exhibit 10.

Exhibit 10
Relationships of Financial Ratios

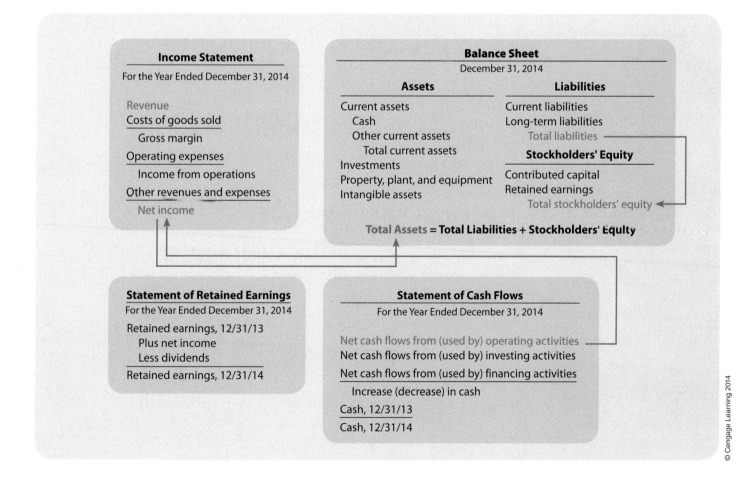

APPLY IT!

Kora's, a retail company, engaged in the transactions that follow. Opposite each transaction is a ratio and space to mark the effect of each transaction on the ratio. Show that you understand the effect of business activities on performance measures by placing an X in the appropriate column to show whether the transaction increased, decreased, or had no effect on the ratio.

		Effect		
Transaction	Ratio	Increase	Decrease	None
a. Accrued salaries.	Current ratio			
b. Purchased inventory.	Quick ratio			
c. Increased allowance for uncollectible accounts.	Receivables turnover			
d. Purchased inventory on credit.	Payables turnover			
e. Sold treasury stock.	Profit margin			
f. Borrowed cash by issuing bond payable.	Asset turnover			
g. Paid wages expense.	Return on assets			
h. Repaid bond payable.	Debt to equity ratio			
i. Accrued interest expense.	Interest coverage ratio			
j. Sold merchandise on account.	Return on equity			
k. Recorded depreciation expense.	Cash flow yield			
l. Sold equipment.	Free cash flow			

SOLUTION

		Effect		
Transaction	Ratio	Increase	Decrease	None
a. Accrued salaries.	Current ratio		X	
b. Purchased inventory.	Quick ratio		X	
c. Increased allowance for uncollectible accounts.	Receivables turnover	X		
d. Purchased inventory on credit.	Payables turnover		X	
e. Sold treasury stock.	Profit margin			X
f. Borrowed cash by issuing bond payable.	Asset turnover		X	
g. Paid wages expense.	Return on assets		X	
h. Repaid bond payable.	Debt to equity ratio	X		
i. Accrued interest expense.	Interest coverage ratio		X	
j. Sold merchandise on account.	Return on equity	X		
k. Recorded depreciation expense.	Cash flow yield	X		
l. Sold equipment.	Free cash flow	X		

TRY IT! SE6, SE7, SE8, SE9, SE10, E5A, E6A, E7A, E8A, E9A, E5B, E6B, E7B, E8B, E9B

LO 4 Evaluating Quality of Earnings

Net income (net earnings) is the measure most commonly used to evaluate a company's profitability. In fact, one survey indicated that the two important measures in evaluating common stocks were expected changes in earnings per share and return on assets.[4] Net income is a key component of both measures.

Because of the importance of net income, or the "bottom line," in measuring a company's prospects, there is significant interest in evaluating the quality of the net income. The **quality of earnings** refers to the substance of earnings and their sustainability into future periods. Quality of earnings is affected by the following:

- Accounting methods
- Accounting estimates
- One-time items

Accounting Methods

The accounting methods a firm uses affect its operating income. Generally accepted accounting methods include:

- Uncollectible receivables methods (percentage of net sales and aging of accounts receivable)
- Inventory methods (LIFO, FIFO, and average cost)
- Depreciation methods (accelerated, production, and straight-line)
- Revenue recognition methods

All these methods are designed to *match* revenues and expenses. However, the expenses are estimates, and the period or periods benefited cannot be demonstrated conclusively. In practice, it is hard to justify one method of estimation over another.

Different accounting methods have different effects on net income. Some methods are more conservative than others because they tend to produce a lower net income in the current period. For example, suppose that Rudy Company and Kanya Company have similar operations, but Rudy uses FIFO for inventory costing and the straight-line (SL) method for computing depreciation. Kanya uses LIFO for inventory costing and the double-declining-balance (DDB) method for computing depreciation. The income statements of the two companies might appear as shown in Exhibit 11.

Exhibit 11
Effects of Different Accounting Methods

	Rudy Company (FIFO and SL)	Kanya Company (LIFO and DDB)
Net sales	$462,500	$462,500
Cost of goods available for sale	$200,000	$200,000
Less ending inventory	30,000	25,000
Cost of goods sold	$170,000	$175,000
Gross margin	$292,500	$287,500
Less depreciation expense	$ 20,000	$ 40,000
Less other expenses	85,000	85,000
Total operating expenses	$105,000	$125,000
Income from continuing operations before income taxes	$187,500	$162,500

© Cengage Learning 2014

Impact of Different Accounting Methods on Income The income from continuing operations before income taxes for the firm that uses LIFO and DDB is lower because in periods of rising prices, the LIFO method produces a higher cost of goods sold. Also, in the early years of an asset's useful life, accelerated depreciation yields a higher depreciation expense. The result is lower operating income. However, future operating income should be higher.

Impact of Different Accounting Methods on Cash Flows Although the choice of accounting method does not affect cash flows except for possible differences in income taxes, the $25,000 difference in operating income stems solely from the choice of accounting methods. Estimates of the useful lives and residual values of plant assets could lead to an even greater difference. In practice, of course, differences in net income occur for many reasons; but the user of financial statements must be aware of the discrepancies that can occur as a result of the accounting methods used. In general, an accounting method or estimate that results in lower current earnings produces a better quality of operating income.

Impact of Different Accounting Methods on Financial Statements The latitude that companies have in their choice of accounting methods could cause problems in the interpretation of financial statements were it not for the conventions of *full disclosure* and *consistency*. As noted in an earlier chapter, **full disclosure** requires management to explain, in a note to the financial statements, the significant accounting policies used. For instance, in a note to its financial statements, **Starbucks** discloses that it uses the straight-line method for depreciation of property, plant, and equipment.[5] **Consistency** requires that the same accounting procedures be used from year to year. If a company changes its accounting procedure, it must explain the nature of the change and its monetary effect in a note to its statements.

Accounting Estimates

Users of financial statements also need to be aware of the impact that accounting estimates have on reported income. To comply with *accrual accounting* (the *matching rule*), accountants must assign revenues and expenses to the periods in which they occur. If they cannot establish a direct relationship between revenues and expenses, they systematically allocate the expenses among the periods that benefit from them. In doing so, they must make estimates and exercise judgment, based on realistic assumptions. However, there is latitude in making the estimate, and the final judgment will affect net income.

For example, when a company acquires an asset, the accountant must estimate the asset's useful life. Technological obsolescence could shorten the asset's expected useful life, and regular maintenance and repairs could lengthen it. Although the actual useful life cannot be known with certainty until some future date, the accountant's estimate of it affects both current and future operating income. Other areas that require accounting estimates include:

- Residual value of assets
- Uncollectible accounts receivable
- Sales returns
- Total units of production
- Total recoverable units of natural resources
- Amortization periods
- Warranty claims
- Environmental cleanup costs

The importance of accounting estimates depends on the industry in which a firm operates. For example, estimated uncollectible receivables for a credit card firm, such as **American Express**, or for a financial services firm, such as **Bank of America**, can have a material impact on earnings; but estimated useful life may be less important because depreciable assets represent a small percentage of the firm's total assets. **Starbucks** has few receivables, but it has major investments in depreciable assets. Thus, estimates of useful life and residual value are more important to Starbucks than an estimate of uncollectible accounts receivable. The company depreciates its equipment over 2 to 15 years and its buildings over 30 to 40 years.[6]

One-Time Items

If earnings increase because of one-time items, that portion of earnings will not be sustained in the future. In contrast, one-time decreases in earnings may not indicate that earnings will be poor in the future. Examples of one-time items include:

- Gains and losses
- Write-downs and restructurings
- Nonoperating items

Because management has choices in the content and positioning of these income statement components, there is a potential for managing earnings to achieve specific income targets. It is, therefore, critical for users of income statements to understand these factors and take them into consideration when evaluating a company's performance.

Exhibit 12 shows the components of a typical income statement. Net income or loss (the "bottom line" of the income statement) includes all revenues, expenses, gains, and losses over the period. When a company has both continuing and discontinued operations, the operating income section is called *income from continuing operations*. Income

Exhibit 12
Corporate Income Statement

Dingo Corporation
Income Statement
For the Year Ended December 31, 2014

Operating items before income taxes	Revenues		$ 1,850,000
	Costs and expenses		(1,100,000)
	Gain on sale of assets		300,000
	Write-downs of assets		(50,000)
	Restructurings		(150,000)
	Income from continuing operations before income taxes		$ 850,000
Income taxes	Income taxes expense		289,000
	Income from continuing operations		$ 561,000
Nonoperating items	Discontinued operations:		
	Income from operations of discontinued segment (net of taxes, $70,000)	$ 180,000	
	Loss on disposal of segment (net of taxes, $84,000)	(146,000)	34,000
	Net income		$ 595,000
Earnings per share information	Earnings per common share:		
	Income from continuing operations		$2.81
	Discontinued operations (net of taxes)		0.17
	Net income		$2.98

Business Perspective

Beware of the "Bottom Line!"

In the second quarter of 2007, **McDonald's** posted its second-ever loss: $711.7 million. Should this have been cause for concern? The answer is no because the loss resulted from a one-time noncash impairment (decline in value) of $1.6 billion related to investments in Latin America; the company was actually in a period of rapidly growing revenues and profits. In another example, **Campbell Soup** showed unrealistically positive results. Its income jumped by 31 percent due to a tax settlement and an accounting restatement. Without these items, its revenue and income would have been up less than 1 percent; soup sales—its main product—actually dropped by 6 percent. The lesson to be learned is to look beyond the "bottom line" to the components of the income statement when evaluating a company's performance.[7]

from continuing operations before income taxes may include gains or losses on the sale of assets, write-downs, and restructurings.

As you can see in Exhibit 12, the section of the income statement that follows income taxes may contain such nonoperating items as **discontinued operations**— segments that are no longer part of a company's operations—and gains (or losses) on the sale or disposal of these segments. Another item that may appear in this section is the write-off of goodwill when its value has been impaired. Earnings per share information appears at the bottom of the statement

Gains and Losses When a company sells or otherwise disposes of operating assets or marketable securities, a gain or loss generally results. Although these gains or losses appear in the operating section of the income statement, they usually represent one-time events. However, management often has some choice as to their timing. Thus, from an analyst's point of view, they should be ignored when considering operating income.

Write-Downs and Restructurings When management decides that an asset is no longer of value to the company, a write-down or restructuring occurs.

- A **write-down** (or *write-off*) is a reduction in the value of an asset below its carrying value on the balance sheet.
- A **restructuring** is the estimated cost of a change in a company's operations. It usually involves the closing of facilities and the laying off of personnel.

Both write-downs and restructurings reduce current operating income and boost future income by shifting future costs to the current period. They are often an indication of poor management decisions in the past, such as paying too much for the assets of another company or making operational changes that do not work out. Companies sometimes take all possible losses in the current year so that future years will be "clean" of these costs. Such "big baths," as they are called, commonly occur when a company is having a bad year. They also often occur in years when there is a change in management. The new management takes a "big bath" in the current year so it can show improved results in future years.

In a recent year, 34 percent of 500 large companies had write-downs of tangible assets, and 41 percent had restructurings. Another 19 percent had write-downs or charges related to intangible assets, often involving goodwill. In 2011, **Starbucks** did not have any restructuring costs, but in 2009 its restructuring costs were $332.4 million (compared with net income of only $390.8 million) in connection with the closing of a number of its stores.[8]

Nonoperating Items The nonoperating items that appear on the income statement include discontinued operations and gains or losses on the sale or disposal of these segments. These items can significantly affect net income. For example, in Exhibit 12, earnings per common share for income from continuing operations are $2.81; but when all the nonoperating items are taken into consideration, net income per share is $2.98. To

Business Perspective
Look Carefully at the Numbers

In recent years, companies have increasingly used pro forma statements—statements as they would appear without certain items—as a way of presenting a better picture of their operations than would be the case in reports prepared under GAAP. For example, in the first quarter of 2012, **GEO Group, Inc.**, reported pro forma net income of $18.8 million, even though its actual net income was $15.1 million. The higher pro forma figure came about by not deducting certain expenses which are required under GAAP. In addition, a common practice used by such companies as **Google**, **eBay**, and **Starbucks** is to provide in the notes to the financial statements income as it would be without the expense related to compensation for stock options.[9] Pro forma statements, which are unaudited, have come to mean whatever a company's management wants them to mean. As a result, the SEC issued rules that prohibit companies from giving more prominence to non-GAAP measures and from using terms that are similar to GAAP measures.[10] Nevertheless, companies still report pro forma results. Analysts should rely exclusively on financial statements that are prepared using GAAP and that are audited by an independent CPA.

make it easier to evaluate a company's ongoing operations, generally accepted accounting principles require that gains and losses from discontinued operations be reported separately on the income statement.

In Exhibit 12, the *disclosure* of discontinued operations has two parts:

- One part shows that after the decision to discontinue, the income from operations of the disposed segment was $180,000 (net of $70,000 taxes).
- The other part shows that the loss from the disposal of the segment was $146,000 (net of $84,000 tax savings). (The computation of the gains or losses involved in discontinued operations is covered in more advanced accounting courses.)

Management Compensation

Knowledge of performance measurement not only is important for evaluating a company, but also leads to an understanding of the criteria by which a board of directors evaluates and compensates management. Members of management are often paid based on the earnings of the company. As noted earlier, one intent of the Sarbanes-Oxley Act of 2002 was to strengthen the corporate governance of public corporations. Under this act, a public corporation's board of directors must establish a **compensation committee** made up of independent directors to determine how the company's top executives will be compensated. The company must file documents with the SEC, *disclosing* the components of compensation and the criteria used to remunerate top executives.

The components of **Starbucks**' compensation of executive officers are typical of those used by many companies. They include the following:

- Annual base salary
- Annual incentive bonuses
- Long-term incentive compensation (stock option awards)[11]

Incentive bonuses are based on financial performance measures that the compensation committee identifies as important to the company's long-term success, especially in terms of increasing the value of shareholders' investments in the company. Many companies tie incentive bonuses to measures such as growth in revenues and return on assets or return on equity. Starbucks bases 50 percent of its incentive bonus on an "adjusted consolidated operating income or adjusted business unit operating income," 30 percent on "adjusted earnings per share target approved by the compensation committee," and 20 percent on the executive's "specific individual performance goals."[12]

Stock option awards are usually based on how well the company is achieving its long-term strategic goals. In 2011, Starbucks' CEO received a base salary of $1,382,692 and a non-equity incentive plan compensation of $2,982,000. He also received a stock option awards of $11,479,494.[13]

From one vantage point, earnings per share is a "bottom-line" number that encompasses all the other performance measures. However, using a single performance measure as the basis for determining compensation has the potential of leading to practices that are not in the best interests of a company or its stockholders. For instance, management could boost earnings per share by reducing the number of shares outstanding (the denominator in the earnings per share equation) while not improving earnings. It could accomplish this by using cash to repurchase shares of the company's stock (treasury stock), rather than investing the cash in more profitable operations.

APPLY IT!

The following data apply to Kawa, Inc.: net sales, $180,000; cost of goods sold, $87,500; loss from discontinued operations (net of income tax benefit of $17,500), $50,000; loss on disposal of discontinued operations (net of income tax benefit of $4,000), $12,500; operating expenses, $32,500; income taxes expense on continuing operations, $18,000. Prepare the company's income statement for the year ended December 31, 2014. (*Note:* Ignore earnings per share information.)

SOLUTION

Kawa, Inc.
Income Statement
For the Year Ended December 31, 2014

Net sales		$180,000
Cost of goods sold		87,500
Gross margin		$ 92,500
Operating expenses		32,500
Income from continuing operations before income taxes		$ 60,000
Income taxes expense		18,000
Income from continuing operations		$ 42,000
Discontinued operations		
Loss from discontinued operations (net of income tax benefit of $17,500)	$(50,000)	
Loss on disposal of discontinued operations (net of income tax benefit of $4,000)	(12,500)	(62,500)
Net loss		$ (20,500)

TRY IT! SE11, SE12, E10A, E11A, E12A, E10B, E11B, E12B

TriLevel Problem

Monkey Business Images/Shutterstock.com

Medal Investments

The beginning of this chapter focused on Kate Medal, the president of Medal Investments, who was planning to invest in either Fast Burger or Tasty Steak. Complete the following requirements in order to answer the questions posed at the beginning of the chapter.

Section 1: Concepts
What concepts underlie the standards that Kate can use to compare the performance of the two companies?

Section 2: Accounting Applications
What analytical tools can Kate use to measure the financial performance of Fast Burger and Tasty Steak?

The 2014 income statements and balance sheets of the two companies follow.

		Income Statements	Fast Burger	Tasty Steak
		For the Year Ended December 31, 2014		
		(In thousands, except per share amounts)		
			Fast Burger	Tasty Steak
5	Net sales		$53,000	$86,000
6	Costs and expenses:			
7		Cost of goods sold	$37,000	$61,000
8		Selling expenses	7,000	10,000
9		Administrative expenses	4,000	5,000
10		Total costs and expenses	$48,000	$76,000
11	Income from operations		$ 5,000	$10,000
12	Interest expense		1,400	3,200
13	Income before income taxes		$ 3,600	$ 6,800
14	Income taxes expense		1,800	3,400
15	Net income		$ 1,800	$ 3,400
16	Earnings per share		$ 1.80	$ 1.13
17				

		Balance Sheets	Fast Burger	Tasty Steak
		December 31, 2014		
		(in thousands)		
			Fast Burger	Tasty Steak
5		Assets		
6	Cash		$ 2,000	$ 4,500
7	Accounts receivable (net)		2,000	6,500
8	Inventory		2,000	5,000
9	Property, plant, and equipment (net)		20,000	35,000
10	Other assets		4,000	5,000
11		Total assets	$30,000	$56,000
12				
13		Liabilities and Stockholders' Equity		
14	Accounts payable		$ 2,500	$ 3,000
15	Notes payable		1,500	4,000
16	Bonds payable		10,000	30,000
17	Common stock, $1 par value		1,000	3,000
18	Additional paid-in capital		9,000	9,000
19	Retained earnings		6,000	7,000
20		Total liabilities and stockholders' equity	$30,000	$56,000
21				

The following information pertaining to 2014 is also available to Kate:

- Fast Burger's statement of cash flows shows that it had net cash flows from operations of $2,200,000. Tasty Steak's statement of cash flows shows that its net cash flows from operations were $3,000,000.
- Net capital expenditures were $2,100,000 for Fast Burger and $1,800,000 for Tasty Steak.
- Fast Burger paid dividends of $500,000, and Tasty Steak paid dividends of $600,000.
- The market prices of the stocks of Fast Burger and Tasty Steak were $30 and $20, respectively.
- Kate does not have financial information pertaining to prior years. Thus, she used year-end amounts, rather than average amounts.

Perform a comprehensive ratio analysis of both Fast Burger and Tasty Steak using the steps that follow. Assume that all notes payable of the two companies are current liabilities and that all their bonds payable are long-term liabilities. Show dollar amounts in thousands, use end-of-year balances for averages, assume no change in inventory, and round all ratios and percentages to one decimal place.

1. Prepare an analysis of profitability and total asset management.

2. Prepare an analysis of liquidity.

3. Prepare an analysis of financial risk.

4. Prepare an analysis of operating asset management.

5. Prepare an analysis of market strength.

6. In each analysis, indicate which company apparently had the more favorable ratio. (Consider differences of 0.1 or less to be neutral.)

Section 3: Business Applications
In what ways would having access to prior years' information aid this analysis? Why is earnings management important in your assessment?

SOLUTION

Section 1: Concepts
Kate can use rule-of-thumb measures, a company's past performance, and industry norms as standards to compare financial performance of the two companies. Rule-of-thumb measures are weak because they often lack *relevance*. A company's past performance is more reliable and it can be used for measuring the improvement (or lack thereof) in a particular ratio, but can be lacking in *predictive value* and *timeliness* because past performance is not a guarantee of future performance and a company's past performance is not helpful in judging its performance relative to the performance of other companies. Finally, Kate can use industry norms to *compare* the financial performance of two companies, but she needs to remember that firms even in the same industry are not always *comparable* because of having different accounting procedures and diversity issues.

Section 2: Accounting Applications
1.

Ratio Name	Fast Burger	Tasty Steak	6. Company with More Favorable Ratio
Profit margin	$\dfrac{\$1,800}{\$53,000} = 3.4\%$	$\dfrac{\$3,400}{\$86,000} = 4.0\%$	Tasty Steak
Asset turnover	$\dfrac{\$53,000}{\$30,000} = 1.8$ Times	$\dfrac{\$86,000}{\$56,000} = 1.5$ Times	Fast Burger
Return on assets	$\dfrac{\$1,800}{\$30,000} = 6.0\%$	$\dfrac{\$3,400}{\$56,000} = 6.1\%$	Tasty Steak

2.

Ratio Name	Fast Burger	Tasty Steak	6. Company with More Favorable Ratio
Cash flow yield	$\dfrac{\$2,200}{\$1,800} = 1.2$ Times	$\dfrac{\$3,000}{\$3,400} = 0.9$ Time	Fast Burger
Cash flows to sales	$\dfrac{\$2,200}{\$53,000} = 4.2\%$	$\dfrac{\$3,000}{\$86,000} = 3.5\%$	Fast Burger
Cash flows to assets	$\dfrac{\$2,200}{\$30,000} = 7.3\%$	$\dfrac{\$3,000}{\$56,000} = 5.4\%$	Fast Burger
Free cash flow	$\$2,200 - \$500 - \$2,100$ $= (\$400)$	$\$3,000 - \$600 - \$1,800$ $= \$600$	Tasty Steak

3.

Ratio Name	Fast Burger	Tasty Steak	6. Company with More Favorable Ratio
Debt to equity ratio	$\dfrac{\$2,500 + \$1,500 + \$10,000}{\$1,000 + \$9,000 + \$6,000}$ $\dfrac{\$14,000}{\$16,000} = 0.9$ Time	$\dfrac{\$3,000 + \$4,000 + \$30,000}{\$3,000 + \$9,000 + \$7,000}$ $\dfrac{\$37,000}{\$19,000} = 1.9$ Times	Fast Burger
Return on equity	$\dfrac{\$1,800}{\$1,000 + \$9,000 + \$6,000}$ $\dfrac{\$1,800}{\$16,000} = 11.3\%$	$\dfrac{\$3,400}{\$3,000 + \$9,000 + \$7,000}$ $\dfrac{\$3,400}{\$19,000} = 17.9\%$	Tasty Steak
Interest coverage ratio	$\dfrac{\$3,600 + \$1,400}{\$1,400}$ $\dfrac{\$5,000}{\$1,400} = 3.6$ Times	$\dfrac{\$6,800 + \$3,200}{\$3,200}$ $\dfrac{\$10,000}{\$3,200} = 3.1$ Times	Fast Burger

4.

Ratio Name	Fast Burger	Tasty Steak	6. Company with More Favorable Ratio
Inventory turnover	$\dfrac{\$37,000}{\$2,000} = 18.5$ Times	$\dfrac{\$61,000}{\$5,000} = 12.2$ Times	Fast Burger
Days' inventory on hand	$\dfrac{365 \text{ Days}}{18.5 \text{ Times}} = 19.7$ Days	$\dfrac{365 \text{ Days}}{12.2 \text{ Times}} = 29.9$ Days	Fast Burger
Receivable turnover	$\dfrac{\$53,000}{\$2,000} = 26.5$ Times	$\dfrac{\$86,000}{\$6,500} = 13.2$ Times	Fast Burger
Day's sales uncollected	$\dfrac{365 \text{ Days}}{26.5 \text{ Times}} = 13.8$ Days	$\dfrac{365 \text{ Days}}{13.2 \text{ Times}} = 27.7$ Days	Fast Burger
Payables turnover	$\dfrac{\$37,000}{\$2,500} = 14.8$ Times	$\dfrac{\$61,000}{\$3,000} = 20.3$ Times	Tasty Steak
Days' payable	$\dfrac{365 \text{ Days}}{14.8 \text{ Times}} = 24.7$ Days	$\dfrac{365 \text{ Days}}{20.3 \text{ Times}} = 18.0$ Days	Fast Burger

Financing period

Fast Burger: 19.7 Days + 13.8 Days − 24.7 Days = 8.8 Days
Tasty Steak: 29.9 Days + 27.7 Days − 18.0 Days = 39.6 Days

Fast Burger's financing period of only 8.8 days is more favorable.

Current ratio	$\dfrac{\$2,000 + \$2,000 + \$2,000}{\$2,500 + \$1,500}$ $\dfrac{\$6,000}{\$4,000} = 1.5$ Times	$\dfrac{\$4,500 + \$6,500 + \$5,000}{\$3,000 + \$4,000}$ $\dfrac{\$16,000}{\$7,000} = 2.3$ Times	Tasty Steak
Quick ratio	$\dfrac{\$2,000 + \$2,000}{\$2,500 + \$1,500}$ $\dfrac{\$4,000}{\$4,000} = 1.0$ Time	$\dfrac{\$4,500 + \$6,500}{\$3,000 + \$4,000}$ $\dfrac{\$11,000}{\$7,000} = 1.6$ Times	Tasty Steak

Note: This analysis indicates the company with the apparently more favorable ratio.

5.

Ratio Name	Fast Burger	Tasty Steak	6. Company with More Favorable Ratio
Price/earnings ratio	$\dfrac{\$30}{\$1.80} = 16.7$ Times	$\dfrac{\$20}{\$1.13} = 17.7$ Times	Tasty Steak
Dividend yield	$\dfrac{\$500,000 \div 1,000,000}{\$30}$ $= \dfrac{\$0.50}{\$30} = 1.7\%$	$\dfrac{\$600,000 \div 3,000,000}{\$20}$ $= \dfrac{\$0.20}{\$20} = 1.0\%$	Fast Burger

Section 3: Business Applications
Prior years' information would be helpful in two ways. First, turnover, return, and cash flows to assets ratios could be based on average amounts. Second, a trend analysis could be performed for each company. Earnings management is important because it can be used to make a company look as if it is performing better than it is in reality.

Chapter Review

Describe the concepts, standards of comparison, and sources of information used in measuring financial performance. **LO 1**

Important to measuring financial performance are the concepts of relevance, predictive value, comparability, and timeliness, which underlie the objectives of profitability, total asset management, liquidity, financial risk, and operating asset management. Creditors and investors use financial performance measurement to judge a company's past performance and current position, as well as its future potential and the risk associated with it. Creditors use the information from their analyses to make reliable loans that will be repaid with interest. Investors use the information to make investments that will provide a return that is worth the risk.

Three standards of comparison commonly used in evaluating financial performance are rule-of-thumb measures, a company's past performance, and industry norms. Rule-of-thumb measures are weak because of a lack of evidence that they can be widely applied and that they have predictive value. A company's past performance can offer a guideline for measuring improvement, but it is not helpful in judging performance relative to the performance of other companies. Although the use of industry norms overcomes this last problem, firms are not always comparable, even in the same industry.

The main sources of information about public corporations are annual reports and interim financial statements, reports filed with the SEC, business periodicals, and credit and investment advisory services.

Apply horizontal analysis, trend analysis, vertical analysis, and ratio analysis to financial statements. **LO 2**

Horizontal analysis involves the computation of changes in both dollar amounts and percentages from year to year.

Trend analysis calculates percentage changes for several years. The analyst computes the changes by setting a base year equal to 100 and calculating the results for subsequent years as percentages of the base year.

Vertical analysis uses percentages to show the relationship of the component parts of a financial statement to a total figure in the statement. The resulting financial statements, which are expressed entirely in percentages, are called common-size statements.

Financial ratio analysis identifies key relationships between the components of the financial statements. To interpret ratios correctly, the analyst must have a general understanding of the company and its environment, financial data for several years or for several companies, and an understanding of the data underlying the numerators and denominators.

Apply financial ratio analysis in a comprehensive evaluation of a company's financial performance. **LO 3**

A comprehensive ratio analysis includes the evaluation of a company's profitability, total asset management, liquidity, financial risk, operating asset management, and market strength.

Define *quality of earnings*, and identify the factors that affect quality of earnings and related management compensation issues. **LO 4**

The quality of earnings refers to the substance of earnings and their sustainability into future accounting periods. The quality of a company's earnings may be affected by the accounting methods and estimates it uses and by one-time items that it reports on its income statement. One-time items include gains and losses, write-downs and restructurings, and nonoperating items.

When a company has both continuing and discontinued operations, the operating income section of its income statement is called income from continuing operations. Income from continuing operations before income taxes is affected by choices of accounting methods and estimates and may contain gains and losses on the sale of assets, write-downs, and restructurings. The lower part of the income statement may contain such nonoperating items as discontinued operations. Earnings per share information appears at the bottom of the statement.

In public corporations, a committee made up of independent directors appointed by the board of directors determines the compensation of top executives. Although earnings per share can be regarded as a "bottom-line" number that encompasses all the other performance measures, using it as the sole basis for determining executive compensation may lead to management practices that are not in the best interests of the company or its stockholders.

Key Terms and Ratios

base year 664 (LO2)
common-size statement 667 (LO2)
compensation committee 687 (LO4)
consistency 684 (LO4)
discontinued operations 686 (LO4)
diversified companies 661 (LO1)
financial ratio analysis 670 (LO2)
financial statement
  analysis 660 (LO1)
financing period 677 (LO3)
Form 8-K 662 (LO1)
Form 10-K 662 (LO1)
Form 10-Q 662 (LO1)
full disclosure 684 (LO4)
horizontal analysis 664 (LO2)
index number 666 (LO2)

interim financial
  statements 662 (LO1)
operating cycle 677 (LO3)
quality of earnings 683 (LO4)
restructuring 686 (LO4)
trend analysis 666 (LO2)
vertical analysis 667 (LO2)
write-down 686 (LO4)

RATIOS
asset turnover 671 (LO3)
cash flow yield 673 (LO3)
cash flows to assets 674 (LO3)
cash flows to sales 673 (LO3)
current ratio 679 (LO3)
days' inventory on hand 677 (LO3)

days' payable 679 (LO3)
days' sales uncollected 678 (LO3)
debt to equity ratio 675 (LO3)
dividend yield 681 (LO3)
free cash flow 674 (LO3)
interest coverage ratio 676 (LO3)
inventory turnover 677 (LO3)
payables turnover 678 (LO3)
price/earnings (P/E) 680 (LO3)
profit margin 671 (LO3)
quick ratio 680 (LO3)
receivables turnover 678 (LO3)
return on assets 672 (LO3)
return on equity 676 (LO3)

Chapter Assignments

DISCUSSION QUESTIONS

LO 1   **DQ1.** How are past performance and industry norms useful in evaluating a company's performance? What are their limitations?

LO 2   **DQ2.** In a five-year trend analysis, why do the dollar values remain the same for their respective years while the percentages usually change when a new five-year period is chosen?

LO 3   **DQ3.** Why does a decrease in receivables turnover create the need for cash from operating activities?
RATIO

LO 3   **DQ4.** Why would ratios that include one balance sheet account and one income statement account, such as receivables turnover or return on assets, be questionable if they came from quarterly or other interim financial reports?
RATIO

LO 3   **DQ5.** What is a limitation of free cash flow in comparing one company to another?

LO 4   **DQ6. BUSINESS APPLICATION** ▶ In what way is selling an investment for a gain potentially a negative in evaluating quality of earnings?

LO 4   **DQ7. BUSINESS APPLICATION** ▶ Is it unethical for new management to take an extra large write-off (a "big bath") in order to reduce future costs? Why or why not?

LO 4   **DQ8. BUSINESS APPLICATION** ▶ Why is it useful to disclose discontinued operations separately on the income statement?

LO 4   **DQ9. BUSINESS APPLICATION** ▶ Why is it essential that management compensation, including bonuses, be linked to financial goals and strategies that achieve shareholder value?

LO 4   **DQ10. BUSINESS APPLICATION** ▶ What is one way a company can improve its earnings per share without improving its earnings or net income?

SHORT EXERCISES

LO 1   **Objectives and Standards of Financial Performance Evaluation**

SE1. CONCEPT ▶ Indicate whether each of the following items is (a) an underlying concept, (b) an objective or (c) a standard of comparison of financial statement analysis:

1. Industry norms
2. Assessment of a company's past performance
3. Comparability
4. The company's past performance
5. Assessment of future potential and related risk
6. Predictive value

LO 1   **Sources of Information**

SE2. For each piece of information in the list that follows, indicate whether the best source would be (a) reports published by the company, (b) SEC reports, (c) business periodicals, or (d) credit and investment advisory services.

1. Current market value of a company's stock
2. Management's analysis of the past year's operations
3. Objective assessment of a company's financial performance
4. Most complete body of financial disclosures
5. Current events affecting the company

LO 2   **Trend Analysis**

SE3. ACCOUNTING CONNECTION ▶ Using 2012 as the base year, prepare a trend analysis for the data that follow, and tell whether the results suggest a favorable or unfavorable trend. (Round to one decimal place.)

	2014	2013	2012
Net sales	$316,000	$272,000	$224,000
Accounts receivable (net)	86,000	64,000	42,000

LO 2   **Horizontal Analysis**

SE4. ACCOUNTING CONNECTION ▶ Vision, Inc.'s comparative income statements follow. Compute the amount and percentage changes for the income statements, and comment on the changes from 2013 to 2014. (Round the percentage changes to one decimal place.)

(Continued)

Vision, Inc.
Comparative Income Statements
For the Years Ended December 31, 2014 and 2013

	2014	2013
Net sales	$360,000	$290,000
Cost of goods sold	224,000	176,000
Gross margin	$136,000	$114,000
Operating expenses	80,000	60,000
Operating income	$ 56,000	$ 54,000
Interest expense	14,000	10,000
Income before income taxes	$ 42,000	$ 44,000
Income taxes expense	14,000	16,000
Net income	$ 28,000	$ 28,000
Earnings per share	$ 2.80	$ 2.80

LO 2   **Vertical Analysis**

SE5. ACCOUNTING CONNECTION ▶ Vision, Inc.'s comparative balance sheets follow. Prepare common-size statements and comment on the changes from 2013 to 2014. (Round to one decimal place.)

Vision, Inc.
Comparative Balance Sheets
December 31, 2014 and 2013

	2014	2013
Assets		
Current assets	$ 48,000	$ 40,000
Property, plant, and equipment (net)	260,000	200,000
Total assets	$308,000	$240,000
Liabilities and Stockholders' Equity		
Current liabilities	$ 36,000	$ 44,000
Long-term liabilities	180,000	120,000
Stockholders' equity	92,000	76,000
Total liabilities and stockholders' equity	$308,000	$240,000

LO 3   **Operating Asset Management Analysis**

SE6. ACCOUNTING CONNECTION ▶ Using the information for Vision, Inc., in **SE4** and **SE5**, compute the current ratio, quick ratio, receivables turnover, days' sales uncollected, inventory turnover, days' inventory on hand, payables turnover, days' payable, and financing period for 2013 and 2014. Inventories were $8,000 in 2012, $10,000 in 2013, and $14,000 in 2014. Accounts receivable were $12,000 in 2012, $16,000 in 2013, and $20,000 in 2014. Accounts payable were $18,000 in 2012, $20,000 in 2013, and $24,000 in 2014. The company had no marketable securities or prepaid assets. Comment on the results. (Round to one decimal place.)

LO 3   **Profitability and Total Asset Management Analysis**

SE7. ACCOUNTING CONNECTION ▶ Using the information for Vision, Inc., in **SE4** and **SE5**, compute the profit margin, asset turnover, and return on assets for 2013 and 2014. In 2012, total assets were $200,000. Comment on the results. (Round to one decimal place.)

LO 3   **Financial Risk Analysis**

SE8. ACCOUNTING CONNECTION ▶ Using the information for Vision, Inc., in **SE4** and **SE5**, compute the debt to equity ratio, return on equity, and the interest coverage ratio for 2013 and 2014. In 2012 total stockholders' equity was $60,000. Comment on the results. (Round to one decimal place.)

LO **3** **Liquidity Analysis**

SE9. ACCOUNTING CONNECTION ▶ Using the information for Vision, Inc., in **SE4**, **SE5**, and **SE7**, compute the cash flow yield, cash flows to sales, cash flows to assets, and free cash flow for 2013 and 2014. Net cash flows from operating activities were $42,000 in 2013 and $32,000 in 2014. Net capital expenditures were $60,000 in 2013 and $80,000 in 2014. Cash dividends were $12,000 in both years. Comment on the results. (Round to one decimal place.)

LO **3** **Market Strength Analysis**

SE10. ACCOUNTING CONNECTION ▶ Using the information for Vision, Inc., in **SE4**, **SE5**, and **SE9**, compute the price/earnings (P/E) ratio and dividend yield for 2013 and 2014. The company had 10,000 shares of common stock outstanding in both years. The price of Vision's common stock was $60 in 2013 and $40 in 2014. Comment on the results. (Round to one decimal place.)

LO **4** **Quality of Earnings**

SE11. BUSINESS APPLICATION ▶ Each of the items that follow is a quality of earnings issue. Indicate whether the item is (a) an accounting method, (b) an accounting estimate, or (c) a nonoperating item. For any item for which the answer is (a) or (b), indicate which alternative is usually the more conservative choice.

1. LIFO versus FIFO
2. Extraordinary loss
3. 10-year useful life versus 15-year useful life
4. Straight-line versus accelerated method
5. Discontinued operations
6. Immediate write-off versus amortization
7. Increase versus decrease in percentage of uncollectible accounts

LO **4** **Corporate Income Statement**

SE12. BUSINESS APPLICATION ▶ Assume that Karib Corporation's chief financial officer gave you the following information: net sales, $720,000; cost of goods sold, $350,000; loss from discontinued operations (net of income tax benefit of $70,000), $200,000; loss on disposal of discontinued operations (net of income tax benefit of $16,000), $50,000; operating expenses, $130,000; income taxes expense on continuing operations, $100,000. Prepare the company's income statement for the year ended June 30, 2014. (Ignore earnings per share information.)

EXERCISES: SET A

LO **1** **Issues in Financial Performance Evaluation: Objectives, Standards, Sources of Information, and Executive Compensation**

E1A. CONCEPT ▶ Identify each of the following as (a) an underlying concept, (b) an objective of financial statement analysis, (c) a standard for financial statement analysis, (d) a source of information for financial statement analysis, or (e) an executive compensation issue:

1. Past ratios of the company
2. Linking performance to shareholder value
3. Average ratios of other companies in the same industry
4. Assessment of the future potential of an investment
5. Timeliness
6. Interim financial statements
7. SEC Form 10-K
8. Assessment of risk
9. Comparability
10. A company's annual report

LO 2   **Trend Analysis**

E2A. ACCOUNTING CONNECTION ▶ Using 2010 as the base year, prepare a trend analysis of the data that follow, and tell whether the situation shown by the trends is favorable or unfavorable. (Round to one decimal place.)

	2014	2013	2012	2011	2010
Net sales	$51,040	$47,960	$48,400	$45,760	$44,000
Cost of goods sold	34,440	30,800	31,080	29,400	28,000
General and administrative expenses	10,560	10,368	10,176	9,792	9,600
Operating income	6,040	6,792	7,144	6,568	6,400

LO 2   **Horizontal Analysis**

E3A. ACCOUNTING CONNECTION ▶ Compute the amount and percentage changes for Rivera Company's comparative balance sheets, and comment on the changes from 2013 to 2014. (Round the percentage changes to one decimal place.)

Rivera Company
Comparative Balance Sheets
December 31, 2014 and 2013

	2014	2013
Assets		
Current assets	$ 37,200	$ 25,600
Property, plant, and equipment (net)	218,928	194,400
Total assets	$256,128	$220,000
Liabilities and Stockholders' Equity		
Current liabilities	$ 22,400	$ 6,400
Long-term liabilities	70,000	80,000
Stockholders' equity	163,728	133,600
Total liabilities and stockholders' equity	$256,128	$220,000

LO 2   **Vertical Analysis**

E4A. ACCOUNTING CONNECTION ▶ Express Rivera Company's partial comparative income statements as common-size statements, and comment on the changes from 2013 to 2014.

Rivera Company
Partial Comparative Income Statements
For the Years Ended December 31, 2014 and 2013

	2014	2013
Net sales	$424,000	$368,000
Cost of goods sold	254,400	239,200
Gross margin	$169,600	$128,800
Selling expenses	$106,000	$ 73,600
General expenses	50,880	36,800
Total operating expenses	$156,880	$110,400
Operating income	$ 12,720	$ 18,400

LO 3   **Operating Asset Management Analysis**

RATIO   **E5A. ACCOUNTING CONNECTION** ▶ Partial comparative balance sheet and income statement information for Posad Company follows.

	2014	**2013**
Cash	$ 13,600	$ 10,400
Marketable securities	7,200	17,200
Accounts receivable (net)	44,800	35,600
Inventory	54,400	49,600
Total current assets	$120,000	$112,800
Accounts payable	$ 40,000	$ 28,200
Net sales	$322,560	$220,720
Cost of goods sold	217,600	203,360
Gross margin	$104,960	$ 17,360

In 2012, the year end balances for Accounts Receivable and Inventory were $32,400 and $51,200, respectively. Accounts Payable was $30,600 in 2012 and is the only current liability. Compute the current ratio, quick ratio, receivables turnover, days' sales uncollected, inventory turnover, days' inventory on hand, payables turnover, days' payable for each year, and financing period. (Round to one decimal place.) Comment on the change in the company's liquidity position, including its operating cycle and required days of financing from 2013 to 2014.

LO **3**   **Turnover Analysis**

E6A. ACCOUNTING CONNECTION ▶ Designer Suits Rental has been in business for four years. Because the company has recently had a cash flow problem, management wonders whether there is a problem with receivables or inventories. Selected figures from the company's financial statements (in thousands) follow.

	2014	**2013**	**2012**	**2011**
Net sales	$144.0	$112.0	$96.0	$80.0
Cost of goods sold	90.0	72.0	60.0	48.0
Accounts receivable (net)	24.0	20.0	16.0	12.0
Merchandise inventory	28.0	22.0	16.0	10.0
Accounts payable	13.0	10.0	8.0	5.0

Compute the receivables turnover, inventory turnover, and payables turnover for each of the four years, and comment on the results relative to the cash flow problem that the firm has been experiencing. Merchandise inventory was $11,000, accounts receivable were $11,000, and accounts payable were $4,000 in 2010. (Round to one decimal place.)

LO **3**   **Profitability and Total Asset Management Analysis**

E7A. ACCOUNTING CONNECTION ▶ Elm Company had total assets of $640,000 in 2012, $680,000 in 2013, and $760,000 in 2014. In 2013, Elm had net income of $77,112 on revenues of $1,224,000. In 2014, it had net income of $98,952 on revenues of $1,596,000. Compute the profit margin, asset turnover, and return on assets for 2013 and 2014. Comment on the apparent cause of the increase or decrease in profitability. (Round to one decimal place.)

LO **3**   **Financial Risk and Market Strength Ratios**

E8A. ACCOUNTING CONNECTION ▶ An investor is considering investing in the long-term bonds and common stock of Companies A and B. Both firms operate in the same industry. Both also pay a dividend per share of $8 and have a yield of 10 percent on their long-term bonds. Other data for the two firms follow.

(Continued)

	Company A	Company B
Total assets	$4,800,000	$2,160,000
Total liabilities	2,160,000	1,188,000
Prior year stockholders' equity	2,120,000	750,000
Income before income taxes	576,000	259,200
Interest expense	194,400	106,920
Net income	136,800	74,800
Earnings per share	6.40	10.00
Market price of common stock	80.00	95.00

Compute the debt to equity ratio, return on equity ratio, interest coverage ratio, and price/earnings (P/E) ratio, as well as the dividend yield, and comment on the results. (Round to one decimal place.)

LO 3

Liquidity Analysis

E9A. Using the data from the financial statements of Stanford, Inc., that follow, compute the company's cash flow yield, cash flows to sales, cash flows to assets, and free cash flow. (Round to one decimal place.)

Net sales	$3,200,000
Net income	352,000
Net cash flows from operating activities	456,000
Total assets, beginning of year	2,890,000
Total assets, end of year	3,120,000
Cash dividends	120,000
Net capital expenditures	298,000

LO 4

Effect of Alternative Accounting Methods

E10A. BUSINESS APPLICATION ▶ At the end of its first year of operations, a company calculated its ending merchandise inventory according to three different accounting methods, as follows: FIFO, $47,500; average-cost, $45,000; LIFO, $43,000. If the company used the average-cost method, its net income for the year would be $17,000.

1. Determine net income if the company used the FIFO method.
2. Determine net income if the company used the LIFO method.
3. Which method is more conservative?
4. **CONCEPT** ▶ Will the consistency convention be violated if the company chooses to use the LIFO method? Why or why not?
5. **CONCEPT** ▶ Does the full-disclosure convention require disclosure of the inventory method used in the financial statements?

LO 4

Corporate Income Statement

E11A. BUSINESS APPLICATION ▶ Assume that Stream Toy Corporation's chief financial officer gave you the following information: net sales, $3,800,000; cost of goods sold, $2,100,000; extraordinary gain (net of income taxes of $7,000), $25,000; loss from discontinued operations (net of income tax benefit of $60,000), $100,000; loss on disposal of discontinued operations (net of income tax benefit of $26,000), $70,000; selling expenses, $100,000; administrative expenses, $80,000; income taxes expense on continuing operations, $600,000. Prepare the company's income statement for the year ended June 30, 2014. (Ignore earnings per share information.)

LO **4** **Corporate Income Statement**

E12A. BUSINESS APPLICATION ▶ Components of Van Corporation's income statement for the year ended December 31, 2014 follow. Recast the income statement in multi-step form, including allocating income taxes to appropriate items (assume a 30 percent income tax rate) and showing earnings per share figures (200,000 shares outstanding). (Round earnings per share figures to the nearest cent.)

Sales	$1,110,000
Cost of goods sold	(550,000)
Operating expenses	(225,000)
Restructuring	(110,000)
Total income taxes expense for period	(179,100)
Income from discontinued operations	160,000
Gain on disposal of discontinued operations	140,000
Extraordinary gain	72,000
Net income	$ 417,900
Earnings per share	$ 2.09

EXERCISES: SET B

Visit the textbook companion website at www.cengagebrain.com to access Exercise Set B for this chapter.

PROBLEMS

LO **2** **Horizontal and Vertical Analysis**

SPREADSHEET

✔ 1: Net income: 34.9% increase
✔ 1: Total assets: 3.6% increase
✔ 2: 2014 Net income: 4.2%

P1. Obras Corporation's condensed comparative income statements and comparative balance sheets for 2014 and 2013 follow.

Obras Corporation
Comparative Income Statements
For the Years Ended December 31, 2014 and 2013

	2014	2013
Net sales	$3,276,800	$3,146,400
Cost of goods sold	2,088,800	2,008,400
Gross margin	$1,188,000	$1,138,000
Operating expenses:		
Selling expenses	$ 476,800	$ 518,000
Administrative expenses	447,200	423,200
Total operating expenses	$ 924,000	$ 941,200
Income from operations	$ 264,000	$ 196,800
Interest expense	65,600	39,200
Income before income taxes	$ 198,400	$ 157,600
Income taxes expense	62,400	56,800
Net income	$ 136,000	$ 100,800
Earnings per share	$ 3.40	$ 2.52

(Continued)

Obras Corporation
Comparative Balance Sheets
December 31, 2014 and 2013

	2014	2013
Assets		
Cash	$ 81,200	$ 40,800
Accounts receivable (net)	235,600	229,200
Inventory	574,800	594,800
Property, plant, and equipment (net)	750,000	720,000
Total assets	$1,641,600	$1,584,800
Liabilities and Stockholders' Equity		
Accounts payable	$ 267,600	$ 477,200
Notes payable (short-term)	200,000	400,000
Bonds payable	400,000	—
Common stock, $10 par value	400,000	400,000
Retained earnings	374,000	307,600
Total liabilities and stockholders' equity	$1,641,600	$1,584,800

REQUIRED

1. Prepare schedules showing the amount and percentage changes from 2013 to 2014 for the comparative income statements and the balance sheets. (Round to one decimal place.)
2. Prepare common-size income statements and balance sheets for 2013 and 2014. (Round to one decimal place.)
3. **ACCOUNTING CONNECTION** ▶ Comment on the results in requirements 1 and 2 by identifying favorable and unfavorable changes in the components and composition of the statements.

LO 3

Effects of Transactions on Ratios

P2. Davis Corporation, a clothing retailer, engaged in the transactions that follow. Opposite each transaction is a ratio and space to mark the effect of each transaction on the ratio.

		Effect		
Transaction	**Ratio**	**Increase**	**Decrease**	**None**
a. Issued common stock for cash.	Asset turnover	___	___	___
b. Declared cash dividend.	Current ratio	___	___	___
c. Sold treasury stock.	Return on equity	___	___	___
d. Borrowed cash by issuing note payable.	Debt to equity ratio	___	___	___
e. Paid salaries expense.	Inventory turnover	___	___	___
f. Purchased merchandise for cash.	Current ratio	___	___	___
g. Sold equipment for cash.	Receivables turnover	___	___	___
h. Sold merchandise on account.	Quick ratio	___	___	___
i. Paid current portion of long-term debt.	Return on assets	___	___	___
j. Gave sales discount.	Profit margin	___	___	___
k. Purchased marketable securities for cash.	Quick ratio	___	___	___
l. Declared 5% stock dividend.	Current ratio	___	___	___
m. Purchased a building.	Free cash flow	___	___	___

REQUIRED

ACCOUNTING CONNECTION ▶ Show that you understand the effect of business activities on performance measures by placing an *X* in the appropriate column to show whether the transaction increased, decreased, or had no effect on the indicated ratio.

Comprehensive Ratio Analysis

P3. Tuxedo Corporation's condensed comparative income statements and balance sheets follow. All figures are given in thousands of dollars, except earnings per share.

✔ 1a: 2014 Current ratio: 1.5 times
✔ 1e: 2014 Inventory turnover: 3.9 times
✔ 2c: 2014 Return on assets: 5.0%
✔ 3b: 2014 Return on equity: 8.2%
✔ 4a: 2014 Cash flow yield: 1.7 times
✔ 5b: 2014 Dividend yield: 1.3%

Tuxedo Corporation
Comparative Income Statements
For the Years Ended December 31, 2014 and 2013

	2014	2013
Net sales	$800,400	$742,600
Cost of goods sold	454,100	396,200
Gross margin	$346,300	$346,400
Operating expenses:		
Selling expenses	$130,100	$104,600
Administrative expenses	140,300	115,500
Total operating expenses	$270,400	$220,100
Income from operations	$ 75,900	$126,300
Interest expense	25,000	20,000
Income before income taxes	$ 50,900	$106,300
Income taxes expense	14,000	35,000
Net income	$ 36,900	$ 71,300
Earnings per share	$ 2.46	$ 4.76

Tuxedo Corporation
Comparative Balance Sheets
December 31, 2014 and 2013

	2014	2013
Assets		
Cash	$ 31,100	$ 27,200
Accounts receivable (net)	72,500	42,700
Inventory	122,600	107,800
Property, plant, and equipment (net)	577,700	507,500
Total assets	$803,900	$685,200
Liabilities and Stockholders' Equity		
Accounts payable	$104,700	$ 72,300
Notes payable (short-term)	50,000	50,000
Bonds payable	200,000	110,000
Common stock, $10 par value	300,000	300,000
Retained earnings	149,200	152,900
Total liabilities and stockholders' equity	$803,900	$685,200

Additional data for Tuxedo in 2014 and 2013 follow.

	2014	2013
Net cash flows from operating activities	$64,000	$99,000
Net capital expenditures	$119,000	$38,000
Dividends paid	$31,400	$35,000
Number of common shares	30,000	30,000
Market price per share	$80	$120

Balances of selected accounts at the end of 2012 were accounts receivable (net), $52,700; inventory, $99,400; accounts payable, $64,800; total assets, $647,800; and stockholders' equity, $376,600. All of the bonds payable were long-term liabilities.

(Continued)

REQUIRED

Perform the following analyses. (Round to one decimal place.)

1. Prepare an operating asset management analysis by calculating for each year the (a) current ratio, (b) quick ratio, (c) receivables turnover, (d) days' sales uncollected, (e) inventory turnover, (f) days' inventory on hand, (g) payables turnover, (h) days' payable, and (i) financing period.

2. Prepare a profitability and total asset management analysis by calculating for each year the (a) profit margin, (b) asset turnover, and (c) return on assets.

3. Prepare a financial risk analysis by calculating for each year the (a) debt to equity ratio, (b) return on equity, and (c) interest coverage ratio.

4. Prepare a liquidity analysis by calculating for each year the (a) cash flow yield, (b) cash flows to sales, (c) cash flows to assets, and (d) free cash flow.

5. Prepare an analysis of market strength by calculating for each year the (a) price/earnings (P/E) ratio and (b) dividend yield.

6. **ACCOUNTING CONNECTION ▶** After making the calculations, indicate whether each ratio improved or deteriorated from 2013 to 2014 (use *F* for favorable and *U* for unfavorable and consider changes of 0.1 or less to be neutral).

LO **3**   ## Comprehensive Ratio Analysis of Two Companies

P4. Mel Filbert is considering an investment in the common stock of a chain of retail department stores. She has narrowed her choice to two retail companies, Single Corporation and Design Corporation, whose income statements and balance sheets follow.

✔ 1b: Single quick ratio: 1.5 times
✔ 1g: Single payables turnover: 17.9 times
✔ 2b: Single asset turnover: 2.5 times
✔ 3a: Single debt to equity ratio: 1.0 time
✔ 4b: Single cash flows to sales: 2.2%
✔ 5a: Single price/earnings
ratio: 13.9 times

Income Statements

	Single	Design
Net sales	$12,560,000	$25,210,000
Costs and expenses:		
Cost of goods sold	$ 6,142,000	$14,834,000
Selling expenses	4,822,600	7,108,200
Administrative expenses	986,000	2,434,000
Total costs and expenses	$11,950,600	$24,376,200
Income from operations	$ 609,400	$ 833,800
Interest expense	194,000	228,000
Income before income taxes	$ 415,400	$ 605,800
Income taxes expense	200,000	300,000
Net income	$ 215,400	$ 305,800
Earnings per share	$ 4.31	$ 10.19

Balance Sheets

	Single	Design
Assets		
Cash	$ 80,000	$ 192,400
Marketable securities (at cost)	203,400	84,600
Accounts receivable (net)	552,800	985,400
Inventory	629,800	1,253,400
Prepaid expenses	54,400	114,000
Property, plant, and equipment (net)	2,913,600	6,552,000
Intangibles and other assets	553,200	144,800
Total assets	$4,987,200	$9,326,600

(Continued)

Liabilities and Stockholders' Equity

Accounts payable	$ 344,000	$ 572,600
Notes payable	150,000	400,000
Income taxes payable	50,200	73,400
Bonds payable	2,000,000	2,000,000
Common stock, $20 par value	1,000,000	600,000
Additional paid-in capital	609,800	3,568,600
Retained earnings	833,200	2,112,000
Total liabilities and stockholders' equity	$4,987,200	$9,326,600

During the year, Single paid a total of $50,000 in dividends. The market price per share of its stock is currently $60. In comparison, Design paid a total of $114,000 in dividends, and the current market price of its stock is $76 per share. Single had net cash flows from operations of $271,500 and net capital expenditures of $625,000. Design had net cash flows from operations of $492,500 and net capital expenditures of $1,050,000. Information for prior years is not readily available. Assume that all notes payable are current liabilities and all bonds payable are long-term liabilities and that there is no change in inventory.

REQUIRED

Conduct a comprehensive ratio analysis for each company, using the available information. Compare the results. (Round to one decimal place, and consider changes of 0.1 or less to be indeterminate.)

1. Prepare an operating asset management analysis by calculating for each company the (a) current ratio, (b) quick ratio, (c) receivables turnover, (d) days' sales uncollected, (e) inventory turnover, (f) days' inventory on hand, (g) payables turnover, (h) days' payable, and (i) financing period.
2. Prepare a profitability and total asset management analysis by calculating for each company the (a) profit margin, (b) asset turnover, and (c) return on assets.
3. Prepare a financial risk analysis by calculating for each company the (a) debt to equity ratio, (b) return on equity, and (c) interest coverage ratio.
4. Prepare a liquidity analysis by calculating for each company the (a) cash flow yield, (b) cash flows to sales, (c) cash flows to assets, and (d) free cash flow.
5. Prepare an analysis of market strength by calculating for each company the (a) price/earnings (P/E) ratio and (b) dividend yield.
6. **ACCOUNTING CONNECTION ▸** Compare the two companies by inserting the ratio calculations from 1 through 5 in a table with the following column headings: Ratio Name, Single, Design, and Company with More Favorable Ratio. Indicate in the last column which company had the more favorable ratio in each case.
7. **BUSINESS APPLICATION ▸** How could the analysis be improved if information about these companies' prior years were available?

LO **4**   **Effect of Alternative Accounting Methods**

✔ 1: Net income using FIFO and straight line: $190,800
✔ 1: Net income using LIFO and double-declining-balance: $93,200

P5. BUSINESS APPLICATION ▸ Furlong Corporation began operations in 2014. At the beginning of the year, the company purchased plant assets of $900,000, with an estimated useful life of 10 years and no residual value. During the year, the company had net sales of $1,300,000, salaries expense of $200,000, and other expenses of $80,000, excluding depreciation. In addition, Furlong purchased inventory as follows.

Jan. 15	400 units at $400	$160,000
Mar. 20	200 units at $408	81,600
June 15	800 units at $416	332,800
Sept. 18	600 units at $412	247,200
Dec. 9	300 units at $420	126,000
Total	2,300 units	$947,600

At the end of the year, a physical inventory disclosed 500 units still on hand. Furlong's managers know they have a choice of accounting methods, but they are unsure how those

(Continued)

methods will affect net income. They have heard of the FIFO and LIFO inventory methods and the straight-line and double-declining-balance depreciation methods.

REQUIRED

1. Prepare two income statements for Furlong, one using the FIFO and straight-line methods and the other using the LIFO and double-declining-balance methods. Ignore income taxes.
2. Prepare a schedule accounting for the difference in the two net income figures obtained in requirement **1**.
3. What effect does the choice of accounting method have on Furlong's inventory turnover? What conclusions can you draw? Use the year-end balance to compute the ratio. (Round to one decimal place.)
4. How does the choice of accounting methods affect Furlong's return on assets? Assume the company's only assets are cash of $80,000, inventory, and plant assets. Use year-end balances to compute the ratios. Is your evaluation of Furlong's profitability affected by the choice of accounting methods?

LO **4**

Corporate Income Statement

✔ 1: Net income: $145,000

P6. BUSINESS APPLICATION ▶ Information concerning Krall Corporation's operations during 2014 follows.

a. Administrative expenses, $90,000
b. Cost of goods sold, $420,000
c. Extraordinary loss from an earthquake (net of taxes, $36,000), $60,000
d. Sales (net), $900,000
e. Selling expenses, $80,000
f. Income taxes expense applicable to continuing operations, $105,000

REQUIRED

1. Prepare the corporation's income statement for the year ended December 31, 2014 (ignore earnings per share data).
2. Which item in Krall's income statement affects the company's quality of earnings? Why does it have an effect on quality of earnings?

ALTERNATE PROBLEMS

LO **2**

Horizontal and Vertical Analysis

SPREADSHEET

✔ 1: Net income: 34.9% increase
✔ 1: Total assets: 3.6% increase
✔ 2: 2014 Net income: 4.2%

P7. Rylander Corporation's condensed comparative income statements and balance sheets for 2014 and 2013 follow.

Rylander Corporation
Comparative Income Statements
For the Years Ended December 31, 2014 and 2013

	2014	2013
Net sales	$6,553,600	$6,292,800
Cost of goods sold	4,177,600	4,016,800
Gross margin	$2,376,000	$2,276,000
Operating expenses:		
Selling expenses	$ 953,600	$1,036,000
Administrative expenses	894,400	846,400
Total operating expenses	$1,848,000	$1,882,400
Income from operations	$ 528,000	$ 393,600
Interest expense	131,200	78,400
Income before income taxes	$ 396,800	$ 315,200
Income taxes expense	124,800	113,600
Net income	$ 272,000	$ 201,600
Earnings per share	$ 3.40	$ 2.52

Rylander Corporation
Comparative Balance Sheets
December 31, 2014 and 2013

	2014	2013
Assets		
Cash	$ 162,400	$ 81,600
Accounts receivable (net)	471,200	458,400
Inventory	1,149,600	1,189,600
Property, plant, and equipment (net)	1,500,000	1,440,000
Total assets	$3,283,200	$3,169,600
Liabilities and Stockholders' Equity		
Accounts payable	$ 535,200	$ 954,400
Notes payable (short-term)	400,000	800,000
Bonds payable	800,000	—
Common stock, $10 par value	800,000	800,000
Retained earnings	748,000	615,200
Total liabilities and stockholders' equity	$3,283,200	$3,169,600

REQUIRED

1. Prepare schedules showing the amount and percentage changes from 2013 to 2014 for the comparative income statements and the balance sheets. (Round to one decimal place.)
2. Prepare common-size income statements and balance sheets for 2013 and 2014. (Round to one decimal place.)
3. **ACCOUNTING CONNECTION** ▶ Comment on the results in requirements **1** and **2** by identifying favorable and unfavorable changes in the components and composition of the statements.

LO **3**   **Effects of Transactions on Ratios**

P8. Koz Corporation engaged in the transactions that follow. Opposite each transaction is a ratio and space to indicate the effect of each transaction on the ratio.

		Effect		
Transaction	**Ratio**	**Increase**	**Decrease**	**None**
a. Sold merchandise on account.	Current ratio	___	___	___
b. Sold merchandise on account.	Inventory turnover	___	___	___
c. Collected on accounts receivable.	Quick ratio	___	___	___
d. Wrote off an uncollectible account.	Receivables turnover	___	___	___
e. Paid on accounts payable.	Current ratio	___	___	___
f. Declared cash dividend.	Return on equity	___	___	___
g. Incurred advertising expense.	Profit margin	___	___	___
h. Issued stock dividend.	Debt to equity ratio	___	___	___
i. Issued bonds payable.	Asset turnover	___	___	___
j. Accrued interest expense.	Current ratio	___	___	___
k. Paid previously declared cash dividend.	Dividend yield	___	___	___
l. Purchased treasury stock.	Return on assets	___	___	___
m. Recorded depreciation expense.	Cash flow yield	___	___	___

REQUIRED

ACCOUNTING CONNECTION ▶ Show that you understand the effect of business activities on performance measures by placing an *X* in the appropriate column to show whether the transaction increased, decreased, or had no effect on the indicated ratio.

LO **3**

✔ 1a: 2014 Current ratio: 1.9 times
✔ 1e: 2014 Inventory turnover: 3.6 times
✔ 2c: 2014 Return on assets: 8.4%
✔ 3b: 2014 Return on equity: 18.4%
✔ 4d: 2014 Free cash flows: ($280,000)
✔ 5b: 2014 Dividend yield: 3.1%

Comprehensive Ratio Analysis

P9. Data for Obras Corporation in 2014 and 2013 follow. These data should be used in conjunction with the data in **P1**.

	2014	2013
Net cash flows from operating activities	$(196,000)	$144,000
Net capital expenditures	$40,000	$65,000
Dividends paid	$44,000	$34,400
Number of common shares	40,000	40,000
Market price per share	$36	$60

Selected balances at the end of 2012 were accounts receivable (net), $206,800; inventory, $547,200; total assets, $1,465,600; accounts payable, $386,600; and stockholders' equity, $641,200. All of Obras's notes payable were current liabilities; all its bonds payable were long-term liabilities.

REQUIRED

Perform a comprehensive ratio analysis following the steps outlined below. (Round to one decimal place.)

1. Prepare a operating asset management analysis by calculating for each year the (a) current ratio, (b) quick ratio, (c) receivables turnover, (d) days' sales uncollected, (e) inventory turnover, (f) days' inventory on hand, (g) payables turnover, (h) days' payable, and (i) financing period.
2. Prepare a profitability and total asset management analysis by calculating for each year the (a) profit margin, (b) asset turnover, and (c) return on assets.
3. Prepare a financial risk analysis by calculating for each year the (a) debt to equity ratio, (b) return on equity, and (c) interest coverage ratio.
4. Prepare a liquidity analysis by calculating for each year the (a) cash flow yield, (b) cash flows to sales, (c) cash flows to assets, and (d) free cash flow.
5. Prepare a market strength analysis by calculating for each year the (a) price/earnings (P/E) ratio and (b) dividend yield.
6. **ACCOUNTING CONNECTION** ▶ After making the calculations, indicate whether each ratio improved or deteriorated from 2013 to 2014 (use *F* for favorable and *U* for unfavorable and consider changes of 0.1 or less to be neutral).

LO **3**

✔ 1b: Lucent quick ratio: 1.5 times
✔ 1g: Lucent payables turnover: 17.9 times
✔ 2b: Lucent asset turnover: 2.5 times
✔ 3a: Lucent debt to equity ratio: 1.0 time
✔ 4b: Lucent cash flows to sales: 2.2%
✔ 5a: Lucent price/earnings
ratio: 13.9 times

Comprehensive Ratio Analysis of Two Companies

P10. Lucy Lee is considering an investment in the common stock of a chain of retail department stores. She has narrowed her choice to two retail companies, Lucent Corporation and Ranbaxy Corporation, whose income statements and balance sheets follow.

Income Statements

	Lucent	Ranbaxy
Net sales	$50,240,000	$100,840,000
Costs and expenses:		
Cost of goods sold	$24,568,000	$ 59,336,000
Selling expenses	19,290,400	28,432,800
Administrative expenses	3,944,000	9,736,000
Total costs and expenses	$47,802,400	$ 97,504,800
Income from operations	$ 2,437,600	$ 3,335,200
Interest expense	776,000	912,000
Income before income taxes	$ 1,661,600	$ 2,423,200
Income taxes expense	800,000	1,200,000
Net income	$ 861,600	$ 1,223,200
Earnings per share	$ 8.62	$ 20.38

Balance Sheets

	Lucent	Ranbaxy
Assets		
Cash	$ 320,000	$ 769,600
Marketable securities (at cost)	813,600	338,400
Accounts receivable (net)	2,211,200	3,941,600
Inventory	2,519,200	5,013,600
Prepaid expenses	217,600	456,000
Property, plant, and equipment (net)	11,654,400	26,208,000
Intangibles and other assets	2,212,800	579,200
Total assets	$19,948,800	$37,306,400
Liabilities and Stockholders' Equity		
Accounts payable	$ 1,376,000	$ 2,290,400
Notes payable	600,000	1,600,000
Income taxes payable	200,800	293,600
Bonds payable	8,000,000	8,000,000
Common stock, $20 par value	4,000,000	2,400,000
Additional paid-in capital	2,439,200	14,274,400
Retained earnings	3,332,800	8,448,000
Total liabilities and stockholders' equity	$19,948,800	$37,306,400

During the year, Lucent paid a total of $200,000 in dividends. The market price per share of its stock is currently $120. In comparison, Ranbaxy paid a total of $456,000 in dividends, and the current market price of its stock is $152 per share. Lucent had net cash flows from operations of $1,086,000 and net capital expenditures of $2,500,000. Ranbaxy had net cash flows from operations of $1,970,000 and net capital expenditures of $4,200,000. Information for prior years is not readily available. Assume that all notes payable are current liabilities and all bonds payable are long-term liabilities and that there is no change in inventory.

REQUIRED

Conduct a comprehensive ratio analysis for each company, following the steps below. Compare the results. (Round to one decimal place, and consider changes of 0.1 or less to be indeterminate.)

1. Prepare an operating asset management analysis by calculating for each company the (a) current ratio, (b) quick ratio, (c) receivables turnover, (d) days' sales uncollected, (e) inventory turnover, (f) days' inventory on hand, (g) payables turnover, (h) days' payable, and (i) financing period.
2. Prepare a profitability and total asset management analysis by calculating for each company the (a) profit margin, (b) asset turnover, and (c) return on assets.
3. Prepare a financial risk analysis by calculating for each company the (a) debt to equity ratio, (b) return on equity, and (c) interest coverage ratio.
4. Prepare a liquidity analysis by calculating for each company the (a) cash flow yield, (b) cash flows to sales, (c) cash flows to assets, and (d) free cash flow.
5. Prepare an analysis of market strength by calculating for each company the (a) price/earnings (P/E) ratio and (b) dividend yield.
6. **ACCOUNTING CONNECTION** ▶ Compare the two companies by inserting the ratio calculations from 1 through 5 in a table with the following column headings: Ratio Name, Lucent, Ranbaxy, and Company with More Favorable Ratio. Indicate in the last column which company had the more favorable ratio in each case.
7. **BUSINESS APPLICATION** ▶ How could the analysis be improved if information about these companies' prior years were available?

LO **4**

SPREADSHEET

✔ 1: Net income using FIFO and
straight line: $381,600
✔ 1: Net income using LIFO and
double-declining-balance: $186,400

Effect of Alternative Accounting Methods

P11. BUSINESS APPLICATION ▶ Minnows Corporation began operations in 2014. At the beginning of the year, the company purchased plant assets of $1,800,000, with an estimated useful life of 10 years and no residual value. During the year, the company had net sales of $2,600,000, salaries expense of $400,000, and other expenses of $160,000, excluding depreciation. In addition, Minnows purchased inventory as follows.

Jan. 15	800 units at $400	$ 320,000
Mar. 20	400 units at $408	163,200
June 15	1,600 units at $416	665,600
Sept. 18	1,200 units at $412	494,400
Dec. 9	600 units at $420	252,000
Total	4,600 units	$1,895,200

At the end of the year, a physical inventory disclosed 1,000 units still on hand. Minnows's managers know they have a choice of accounting methods, but they are unsure how those methods will affect net income. They have heard of the FIFO and LIFO inventory methods and the straight-line and double-declining-balance depreciation methods.

REQUIRED

1. Prepare two income statements for Minnows, one using the FIFO and straight-line methods and the other using the LIFO and double-declining-balance methods. Ignore income taxes.
2. Prepare a schedule accounting for the difference in the two net income figures obtained in requirement **1**.
3. What effect does the choice of accounting method have on Minnows's inventory turnover? What conclusions can you draw? Use the year-end balance to compute the ratio. (Round to one decimal place.)
4. How does the choice of accounting methods affect Minnows's return on assets? Assume the company's only assets are cash of $160,000, inventory, and plant assets. Use year-end balances to compute the ratios. Is your evaluation of Minnows's profitability affected by the choice of accounting methods? (Round to one decimal place.)

LO **4**

✔ 1: Net income: $176,000

Corporate Income Statement

P12. BUSINESS APPLICATION ▶ Income statement information for Linz Corporation in 2014 follows.

a. Administrative expenses, $220,000
b. Cost of goods sold, $880,000
c. Extraordinary loss from a storm (net of taxes, $20,000), $40,000
d. Income taxes expense, continuing operations, $84,000
e. Net sales, $1,780,000
f. Selling expenses, $380,000

REQUIRED

1. Prepare Linz's income statement for 2014 (ignore earnings per share data).
2. Which item in Linz's income statement affects the company's quality of earnings? Why does it have this effect?

CASES

LO **1, 3**   **Conceptual Understanding: Standards for Financial Performance Evaluation**

C1. In 2005, in a dramatic move, **Standard & Poor's Ratings Group**, the large financial company that evaluates the riskiness of companies' debt, downgraded its rating of **General Motors** and **Ford Motor Co.** debt to "junk" bond status because of concerns about the companies' profitability and cash flows. Despite aggressive cost cutting, both companies still face substantial future liabilities for health care and pension obligations. They are losing money or barely breaking even on auto operations that concentrate on slow-selling SUVs. High gas prices and competition force them to sell the cars at a discount. What standards do you think Standard & Poor's would use to evaluate General Motors' progress? What performance measures would Standard & Poor's most likely use in making its evaluation? Was Standard & Poor's right in light of future events?

LO **1**   **Interpreting Financial Reports: Using Segment Information**

C2. Refer to Exhibit 1, which shows the segment information of **Goodyear Tire & Rubber Company**. In what business segments does Goodyear operate? What is the relative size of its business segments in terms of sales and income in the most recent year shown? Which segment is most profitable in terms of return on assets? Which segment is largest, and which segment is most profitable in terms of return on assets? (Round to one decimal place.)

LO **2, 3**   **Interpreting Financial Reports: Effect of a One-Time Item on a Loan Decision**

C3. Apple a Day, Inc., and Unforgettable Edibles, Inc., are food catering businesses that operate in the same metropolitan area. Their customers include *Fortune* 500 companies, regional firms, and individuals. The two firms reported similar profit margins for the current year, and both base bonuses for managers on the achievement of a target profit margin and return on equity. Each firm has submitted a loan request to you, a loan officer for City National Bank. They have provided you with the following information:

	Apple a Day	**Unforgettable Edibles**
Net sales	$625,348	$717,900
Cost of goods sold	225,125	287,080
Gross margin	$400,223	$430,820
Operating expenses	281,300	371,565
Operating income	$118,923	$ 59,255
Gain on sale of real estate	—	81,923
Interest expense	(9,333)	(15,338)
Income before income taxes	$109,590	$125,840
Income taxes expense	25,990	29,525
Net income	$ 83,600	$ 96,315
Average stockholders' equity	$312,700	$390,560

1. Perform a vertical analysis and prepare a common-size income statement for each firm. Compute profit margin and return on equity. (Round to one decimal place.)
2. Discuss these results, the bonus plan for management, and loan considerations. Identify the company that is the better loan risk.

LO **3**   **Interpreting Financial Reports: Comprehensive Ratio Analysis**

C4. Using data from **CVS Corporation**'s annual report in the Supplement to Chapter 16, conduct a comprehensive ratio analysis that compares the company's performance in 2011 and 2010. If you have computed ratios for CVS in previous chapters, you may

(Continued)

prepare a table that summarizes the ratios and show calculations only for the ratios not previously calculated. If this is the first ratio analysis you have done for CVS, show all your computations. In either case, after each group of ratios, comment on the performance of CVS. (Round to one decimal place.) Prepare and comment on the following categories of ratios:

- Operating asset management analysis: current ratio, quick ratio, receivables turnover, days' sales uncollected, inventory turnover, days' inventory on hand, payables turnover, days' payable, and financing period (Accounts Receivable, Inventories, and Accounts Payable were [in millions] $5,457, $10,343, and $3,560, respectively, in 2009.)
- Profitability and total asset management analysis: profit margin, asset turnover, and return on assets (Total assets were [in millions] $61,641 in 2009.)
- Financial risk analysis: debt to equity ratio, return on equity, and interest coverage ratio (Total total shareholders' equity was [in millions] $35,768 in 2009.)
- Liquidity analysis: cash flow yield, cash flows to sales, cash flows to assets, and free cash flow
- Market strength analysis: price/earnings (P/E) ratio and dividend yield

LO 3   ### Interpreting Financial Reports: Comparison of Key Financial Performance Measures

C5. Refer to **CVS Corporation**'s annual report and **Southwest Airlines Co.**'s financial statements in the Supplement to Chapter 16. Prepare a table for the following key financial performance measures for the two most recent years for both companies. (Round to one decimal place.) Use your computations in **C4** or perform those analyses if you have not done so. Total assets for Southwest in 2009 were $14,269 million.

- Profitability and total asset management: profit margin, asset turnover, return on assets
- Financial risk: debt to equity ratio
- Liquidity: cash flow yield, free cash flow

Evaluate and comment on the relative performance of the two companies with respect to each of the above categories.

LO 4   ### Conceptual Understanding: Classic Quality of Earnings Case

C6. BUSINESS APPLICATION ▶ On January 19, 1988, **IBM** reported greatly increased earnings for the fourth quarter of 1987. Despite this reported gain in earnings, the price of IBM's stock on the New York Stock Exchange declined by $6 per share to $111.75. In sympathy with this move, most other technology stocks also declined.[14] IBM's fourth-quarter net earnings rose from $1.39 billion, or $2.28 a share, to $2.08 billion, or $3.47 a share, an increase of 49.6 percent and 52.2 percent over the same period a year earlier. Management declared that these results demonstrated the effectiveness of IBM's efforts to become more competitive and that, despite the economic uncertainties of 1988, the company was planning for growth. The apparent cause of the stock price decline was that the huge increase in income could be traced to nonrecurring gains. Investment analysts pointed out that IBM's high earnings stemmed primarily from such factors as a lower tax rate. Despite most analysts' expectations of a tax rate between 40 and 42 percent, IBM's was a low 36.4 percent, down from the previous year's 45.3 percent. Analysts were also disappointed in IBM's revenue growth. Revenues within the United States were down, and much of the company's growth in revenues came through favorable currency translations, increases that might not be repeated. In fact, some estimates of IBM's fourth-quarter earnings attributed $0.50 per share to currency translations and another $0.25 to tax-rate changes. Other factors contributing to IBM's rise in earnings were one-time transactions, such as the sale of **Intel Corporation** stock and bond redemptions, along with a corporate stock buyback program that reduced the amount of stock outstanding in the fourth quarter by 7.4 million shares. The analysts were concerned about the quality of IBM's earnings. Identify four quality of earnings issues reported in the case and the analysts' concern about each. In percentage terms, what is the impact of the currency changes on fourth quarter earnings? (Round to one decimal place.)

(*Optional*) Comment on management's assessment of IBM's performance.

Continuing Case: Annual Report Project

C7. Using the most recent annual report of the company you have chosen to study and that you have accessed online at the company's website, examine the financial statements and accompanying notes of your company. Conduct a comprehensive financial analysis for the past two years, as follows. (Round to one decimal place.)

- Operating asset management analysis: current ratio, quick ratio, receivables turnover, days' sales uncollected, inventory turnover, days' inventory on hand, payables turnover, days' payable, and financing period
- Profitability and total asset management analysis: profit margin, asset turnover, and return on assets
- Financial risk analysis: debt to equity ratio, return on equity, and interest coverage ratio
- Liquidity analysis: cash flow yield, cash flows to sales, cash flows to assets, and free cash flow
- Market strength analysis: price/earnings (P/E) ratio and dividend yield

More than 4 million corporations are chartered in the United States. Most of them are small, family-owned businesses. They are called *private* or *closely held corporations* because their common stock is held by only a few people and is not for sale to the public. Larger companies usually find it desirable to raise investment funds from many investors by issuing common stock to the public. These companies are called *public companies.* Although they are fewer in number than private companies, their total economic impact is much greater.

Public companies must register their common stock with the Securities and Exchange Commission (SEC), which regulates the issuance and subsequent trading of the stock of public companies. Public companies are required to report their financial performance annually to their stockholders. This report, called an *annual report*, contains the company's annual financial statements and other pertinent data. It must also be filed with the SEC on a Form 10-K.

The general public may obtain an annual report by calling or writing the company or accessing the report online at the company's website. If a company has filed its 10-K electronically with the SEC, it can be accessed at http://www.sec.gov/edgar/searchedgar/webusers.htm. Many libraries also maintain files of annual reports or have them available on electronic media, such as *Compact Disclosure.*

This supplement describes the major components of the typical annual report. We have included many of these components in the annual report of **CVS Caremark Corporation**, one of the country's most successful retailers. Case assignments in many chapters refer to this annual report. For purposes of comparison, the supplement also includes the financial statements and summary of significant accounting policies of **Southwest Airlines Co.**, one of the largest and most successful airlines in the United States.

The Components of an Annual Report

In addition to listing the corporation's directors and officers, an annual report usually contains a letter to the shareholders (or *stockholders*), a multiyear summary of financial highlights, a description of the company, management's discussion and analysis of the company's operating results and financial condition, the financial statements, notes to the financial statements, a statement about management's responsibilities, and the auditors' report.

Letter to the Shareholders

Traditionally, an annual report begins with a letter in which the top officers of the corporation tell shareholders (or stockholders) about the company's performance and prospects. In **CVS**'s 2011 annual report, the chairman and chief executive officer wrote to the shareholders about the highlights of the past year, the key priorities for the new year, and other aspects of the business. He reported as follows: "By capitalizing on CVS Caremark's best-in-class businesses as well as the power of our combined entity, we are well-positioned to deliver on our goal of reinventing pharmacy for better health ... and better shareholder value." CVS Caremark reported strong revenue and earnings and record free cash flow. Total revenue rose 11.8 percent to $107.1 billion, and generated $4.6 billion in free cash flow, a 39 percent increase over 2010's level.

Financial Highlights

The financial highlights section presents key statistics for at least a 5-year period but often for a 10-year period. It is often accompanied by graphs. **CVS**'s annual report, for example, gives critical figures for sales, operating profits, and other key measures. Note that the financial highlights section often includes nonfinancial data and graphs as well. For instance, CVS includes the number of its stores.

Description of the Company

An annual report contains a detailed description of the company's products and divisions. Although this section often contains glossy photographs and other image-building or marketing material, it may provide useful information about past results and future plans.

Management's Discussion and Analysis

In this section, management describes the company's financial condition and results of operations and explains the difference in results from one year to the next. For example, **CVS**'s management explains the effects of an acquisition and the length of its 2011 fiscal year on its net revenues as follows.

- Net revenues increased $11.3 billion and decreased $2.4 billion during 2011 and 2010, respectively.
- During 2011, the Longs Acquisition increased net revenues by $6.6 billion, compared to 2008.
- Three fewer days in the 2009 fiscal year negatively impacted net revenues by $671 million, compared to 2008.

This kind of detail is invaluable to understanding CVS's financial performance.

Financial Statements

All companies present the same four basic financial statements in their annual reports, but the names they use may vary. As you can see in Exhibits 1 through 4, **CVS** presents the following:

- Statements of income
- Balance sheets
- Statements of cash flows
- Statements of shareholders' equity (includes retained earnings)

(Note that the numbers given in the statements are in millions, but the last six digits are omitted. For example, $107,100,000,000 is shown as $107,100.) CVS's financial statement headings are preceded by the word *consolidated*. A corporation issues consolidated financial statements when it consists of more than one company and has combined the companies' data for reporting purposes.

CVS provides several years of data for each financial statement (two years for the balance sheet and three years for the others). Financial statements presented in this fashion are called *comparative financial statements*. Such statements are in accordance with generally accepted accounting principles and help readers assess the company's performance over several years.

CVS's fiscal year ends on the Saturday nearest the end of December (December 31, 2011 in the latest year). Retailers commonly end their fiscal years during a slow period, usually the end of January, which is in contrast to CVS's choosing the end of December.

Income Statements   As shown in Exhibit 1, **CVS** uses a multistep form of the income statement in that results are shown in several steps. The steps are gross profit, operating profit, earnings before income tax provision, and net earnings. The company also shows net earnings available to common shareholders, and discloses basic earnings per share and diluted earnings per share. *Basic earnings per share* is used for most analysis. *Diluted earnings per share* assumes that all rights that could be exchanged for common shares,

Exhibit 1
CVS's Income Statements

| Consolidated means that data from all companies owned by CVS are combined. → | | | |

CVS Caremark Corporation
Consolidated Statements of Income

(In millions, except per share amounts)	Year Ended December 31,		
	2011	**2010**	**2009**
Net revenues	$ 107,100	$ 95,778	$ 98,215
Cost of revenues	86,539	75,559	77,857
Gross profit	20,561	20,219	20,358
Operating expenses	14,231	14,082	13,933
Operating profit	6,330	6,137	6,425
Interest expense, net	584	536	525
Income before income tax provision	5,746	5,601	5,900
Income tax provision	2,258	2,179	2,200
Income from continuing operations	3,488	3,422	3,700
Income (loss) from discontinued operations, net of tax	(31)	2	(4)
Net income	3,457	3,424	3,696
Net loss attributable to noncontrolling interest	4	3	—
Net income attributable to CVS Caremark	$ 3,461	$ 3,427	$ 3,696
Basic earnings per common share:			
Income from continuing operations attributable to CVS Caremark	$ 2.61	$ 2.51	$ 2.58
Loss from discontinued operations attributable to CVS Caremark	(0.02)	—	—
Net income attributable to CVS Caremark	$ 2.59	$ 2.51	$ 2.58
Weighted average common shares outstanding	1,338	1,367	1,434
Diluted earnings per common share:			
Income from continuing operations attributable to CVS Caremark	$ 2.59	$ 2.49	$ 2.55
Loss from discontinued operations attributable to CVS Caremark	(0.02)	—	—
Net income attributable to CVS Caremark	$ 2.57	$ 2.49	$ 2.55
Weighted average common shares outstanding	1,347	1,377	1,450
Dividends declared per common share	$ 0.500	$ 0.350	$ 0.305

See accompanying notes to consolidated financial statements.

such as stock options, are in fact exchanged. The weighted average number of shares of common stock, used in calculating the per share figures, are shown at the bottom of the income statement.

Balance Sheets CVS has a typical balance sheet for a retail company, as shown in Exhibit 2. In the assets and liabilities sections, the company separates out the current assets and the current liabilities. *Current assets* will become available as cash or will be used up in the next year. *Current liabilities* will have to be paid or satisfied in the next year. These groupings are useful in assessing a company's liquidity.

The shareholders' equity section includes a number of items. *Common stock* represents the number of shares outstanding at par value. *Capital surplus* (*additional paid-in capital*) represents amounts invested by stockholders in excess of the par value of the common stock. *Preferred stock* is capital stock that has certain features that distinguish it from common stock. *Treasury stock* represents shares of common stock the company repurchased.

CASH FLOW

Statements of Cash Flows Whereas the income statement reflects CVS's profitability, the statement of cash flows reflects its liquidity. As shown in Exhibit 3, this statement provides information about a company's cash receipts, cash payments, and investing and financing activities during an accounting period.

Exhibit 2
CVS's Balance Sheets

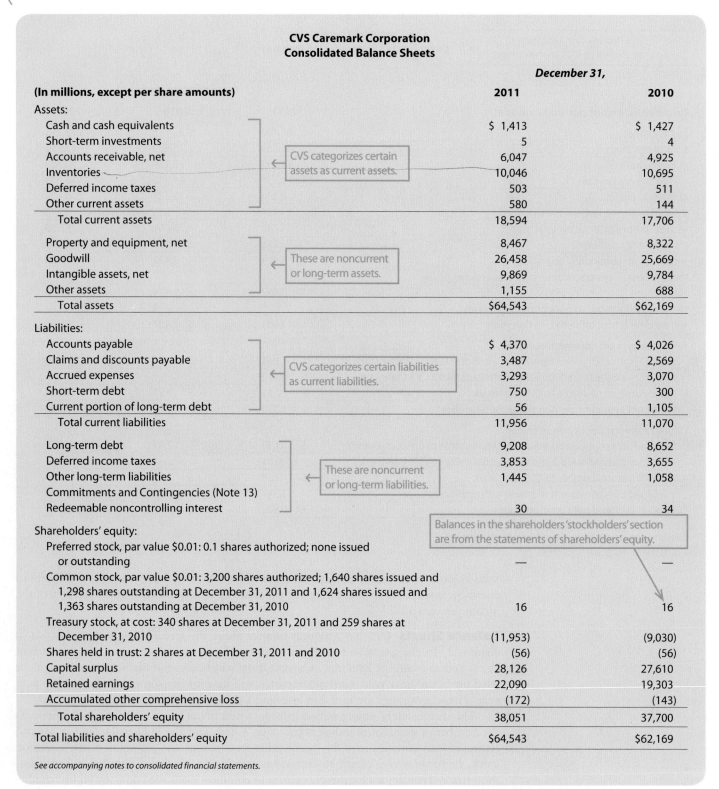

CVS Caremark Corporation
Consolidated Balance Sheets

(In millions, except per share amounts)	December 31, 2011	December 31, 2010
Assets:		
Cash and cash equivalents	$ 1,413	$ 1,427
Short-term investments	5	4
Accounts receivable, net	6,047	4,925
Inventories	10,046	10,695
Deferred income taxes	503	511
Other current assets	580	144
Total current assets	18,594	17,706
Property and equipment, net	8,467	8,322
Goodwill	26,458	25,669
Intangible assets, net	9,869	9,784
Other assets	1,155	688
Total assets	$64,543	$62,169
Liabilities:		
Accounts payable	$ 4,370	$ 4,026
Claims and discounts payable	3,487	2,569
Accrued expenses	3,293	3,070
Short-term debt	750	300
Current portion of long-term debt	56	1,105
Total current liabilities	11,956	11,070
Long-term debt	9,208	8,652
Deferred income taxes	3,853	3,655
Other long-term liabilities	1,445	1,058
Commitments and Contingencies (Note 13)		
Redeemable noncontrolling interest	30	34
Shareholders' equity:		
Preferred stock, par value $0.01: 0.1 shares authorized; none issued or outstanding	—	—
Common stock, par value $0.01: 3,200 shares authorized; 1,640 shares issued and 1,298 shares outstanding at December 31, 2011 and 1,624 shares issued and 1,363 shares outstanding at December 31, 2010	16	16
Treasury stock, at cost: 340 shares at December 31, 2011 and 259 shares at December 31, 2010	(11,953)	(9,030)
Shares held in trust: 2 shares at December 31, 2011 and 2010	(56)	(56)
Capital surplus	28,126	27,610
Retained earnings	22,090	19,303
Accumulated other comprehensive loss	(172)	(143)
Total shareholders' equity	38,051	37,700
Total liabilities and shareholders' equity	$64,543	$62,169

Callout boxes:
- CVS categorizes certain assets as current assets.
- These are noncurrent or long-term assets.
- CVS categorizes certain liabilities as current liabilities.
- These are noncurrent or long-term liabilities.
- Balances in the shareholders' stockholders' section are from the statements of shareholders' equity.

See accompanying notes to consolidated financial statements.

Exhibit 3
CVS's Statements of Cash Flows

| Cash flows are shown for operating activities, investing activities, and financing activities. |

CVS Caremark Corporation
Consolidated Statements of Cash Flows

Year Ended December 31,

(In millions)	2011	2010	2009
Cash flows from operating activities:			
Cash receipts from customers	$ 97,688	$ 94,503	$ 93,568
Cash paid for inventory and prescriptions dispensed by retail network pharmacies	(75,148)	(73,143)	(73,536)
Cash paid to other suppliers and employees	(13,635)	(13,778)	(13,121)
Interest received	4	4	5
Interest paid	(647)	(583)	(542)
Income taxes paid	(2,406)	(2,224)	(2,339)
Net cash provided by operating activities	5,856	4,779	4,035
Cash flows from investing activities:			
Purchases of property and equipment	(1,872)	(2,005)	(2,548)
Proceeds from sale-leaseback transactions	592	507	1,562
Proceeds from sale of property and equipment	4	34	23
Acquisitions (net of cash acquired) and other investments	(1,441)	(177)	(101)
Purchase of available-for-sale investments	(3)	—	(5)
Sale or maturity of available-for-sale investments	60	1	—
Proceeds from sale of subsidiary	250	—	—
Net cash used in investing activities	(2,410)	(1,640)	(1,069)
Cash flows from financing activities:			
Increase (decrease) in short-term debt	450	(15)	(2,729)
Proceeds from issuance of long-term debt	1,463	991	2,800
Repayments of long-term debt	(2,122)	(2,103)	(653)
Dividends paid	(674)	(479)	(439)
Derivative settlements	(19)	(5)	(3)
Proceeds from exercise of stock options	431	285	250
Excess tax benefits from stock-based compensation	21	28	19
Repurchase of common stock	(3,001)	(1,500)	(2,477)
Other	(9)	—	—
Net cash used in financing activities	(3,460)	(2,798)	(3,232)
Net increase (decrease) in cash and cash equivalents	(14)	341	(266)
Cash and cash equivalents at the beginning of the year	1,427	1,086	1,352
Cash and cash equivalents at the end of the year	$ 1,413	$ 1,427	$ 1,086
Reconciliation of net income to net cash provided by operating activities:			
Net income	$ 3,457	$ 3,424	$ 3,696
Adjustments required to reconcile net income to net cash provided by operating activities:			
Depreciation and amortization	1,568	1,469	1,389
Stock-based compensation	135	150	165
Gain on sale of subsidiary	(53)	—	—
Deferred income taxes and other noncash items	144	30	48
Change in operating assets and liabilities, net of effects from acquisitions:			
Accounts receivable, net	(748)	532	(86)
Inventories	607	(352)	(1,199)
Other current assets	(420)	(4)	48
Other assets	(49)	(210)	(2)
Accounts payable	1,128	(40)	4
Accrued expenses	85	(176)	(66)
Other long-term liabilities	2	(44)	38
Net cash provided by operating activities	$ 5,856	$ 4,779	$ 4,035

| Cash and cash equivalents move to balance sheets. |

| This section explains the difference between net earnings and net cash provided by operating activities. |

See accompanying notes to consolidated financial statements.

- The first major section of CVS's consolidated statements of cash flows shows cash flows from operating activities. It shows the cash received and paid for various items related to the company's operations.
- The second major section is cash flows from investing activities. The largest outflow in this category is additions for property and equipment. This figure demonstrates that CVS is a growing company.
- The third major section is cash flows from financing activities. CVS's largest cash inflows are for borrowing of long-term debt.

At the bottom of the statements of cash flows, you can see a reconciliation of net earnings to net cash provided by operating activities. This disclosure is important to the user because it relates the goal of profitability (net earnings) to liquidity (net cash provided). Most companies substitute this disclosure for the operating activities at the beginning of their statement of cash flows.

Statements of Shareholders' Equity Instead of a simple statement of retained earnings, **CVS** presents consolidated statements of shareholders' equity, as shown in Exhibit 4. These statements explain the changes in components of shareholders' equity (or stockholders' equity), including retained earnings.

Notes to the Financial Statements

To meet the requirements of *full disclosure*, a company must add notes to the financial statements to help users interpret some of the more complex items. The notes are an integral part of the financial statements. In recent years, the need for explanation and further details has become so great that the notes often take more space than the statements themselves. The notes to the financial statements include a summary of significant accounting policies, explanatory notes, and supplementary information.

Summary of Significant Accounting Policies Generally accepted accounting principles require that the financial statements include a *Summary of Significant Accounting Policies*. In most cases, this summary is presented in the first note to the financial statements or as a separate section just before the notes. In this summary, the company tells which generally accepted accounting principles it has followed in preparing the statements. For example, in **CVS**'s report, the company states the principles followed for revenue recognition for its Retail Pharmacy Segment:

> **Retail Pharmacy Segment.** *The RPS recognizes revenue from the sale of merchandise (other than prescription drugs) at the time the merchandise is purchased by the retail customer. Revenue from the sale of prescription drugs is recognized at the time the prescription is filled, which is or approximates when the retail customer picks up the prescription.*

Explanatory Notes Other notes explain some of the items in the financial statements. For example, **CVS** describes its commitments for future lease payments as follows.

> *Following is a summary of the future minimum lease payments under capital and operating leases as of December 31, 2011:*

(In millions)	Capital Leases	Operating Leases
2012	$ 20	$ 2,230
2013	20	2,143
2014	20	1,936
2015	20	1,880
2016	20	1,806
Thereafter	237	17,630
Total future lease payments	$337	$27,625

Information like this is very useful in determining the full scope of a company's liabilities and other commitments.

Exhibit 4
CVS's Statements of Shareholders' Equity

CVS Caremark Corporation
Consolidated Statements of Shareholders' Equity

Each component of shareholders' equity is explained.

(In millions)	Shares Year Ended December 31, 2011	2010	2009	Dollars Year Ended December 31, 2011	2010	2009
Preference stock:						
Beginning of year	—	—	4	$ —	$ —	$ 191
Conversion to common stock	—	—	(4)	—	—	(191)
End of year	—	—	—	$ —	$ —	$ —
Common stock:						
Beginning of year	1,624	1,612	1,603	$ 16	$ 16	$ 16
Stock options exercised and stock awards	16	12	9	—	—	—
End of year	1,640	1,624	1,612	$ 16	$ 16	$ 16
Treasury stock:						
Beginning of year	(259)	(219)	(165)	$ (9,030)	$ (7,610)	$ (5,812)
Purchase of treasury shares	(84)	(42)	(73)	(3,001)	(1,500)	(2,477)
Conversion of preference stock	—	—	17	—	—	583
Employee stock purchase plan issuances	3	2	2	78	80	96
End of year	(340)	(259)	(219)	$(11,953)	$ (9,030)	$ (7,610)
Shares held in trust:						
Beginning of year	(2)	(2)	(2)	$ (56)	$ (56)	$ (56)
End of year	(2)	(2)	(2)	$ (56)	$ (56)	$ (56)
Capital surplus:						
Beginning of year				$ 27,610	$ 27,198	$27,280
Stock option activity and stock awards				495	384	291
Tax benefit on stock options and stock awards				21	28	19
Conversion of preference stock				—	—	(392)
End of year				$ 28,126	$ 27,610	$ 27,198
Retained earnings:						
Beginning of year				$ 19,303	$ 16,355	$ 13,098
Net income attributable to CVS Caremark				3,461	3,427	3,696
Common stock dividends				(674)	(479)	(439)
End of year				$ 22,090	$ 19,303	$ 16,355
Accumulated other comprehensive loss:						
Beginning of year				$ (143)	$ (135)	$ (143)
Net cash flow hedges, net of income tax				(9)	(1)	1
Pension liability adjustment, net of income tax				(20)	(7)	7
End of year				$ (172)	$ (143)	$ (135)
Total shareholders' equity				$ 38,051	$ 37,700	$ 35,768
Comprehensive income:						
Net income				$ 3,457	$ 3,424	$ 3,696
Other comprehensive income:						
Net cash flow hedges, net of income tax				(9)	(1)	1
Pension liability adjustment, net of income tax				(20)	(7)	7
Comprehensive income				3,428	3,416	3,704
Comprehensive loss attributable to noncontrolling interest				4	3	—
Comprehensive income attributable to CVS Caremark				$ 3,432	$ 3,419	$ 3,704

Net income is from the income statement.

See accompanying notes to consolidated financial statements.

Supplementary Information Notes In recent years, the FASB and the SEC have ruled that certain supplemental information must be presented with financial statements. Examples are the quarterly reports that most companies present to their stockholders and to the SEC. These quarterly reports, called *interim financial statements*, are in most cases reviewed but not audited by a company's independent CPA firm. In its annual report, **CVS** presents unaudited quarterly financial data from its 2011 quarterly statements. The quarterly data also include the high and low price for the company's common stock during each quarter.

Statements of Management's Responsibilities

Separate statements of management's responsibility for the financial statements and for internal control structure accompany the financial statements as required by the Sarbanes-Oxley Act of 2002. In its reports, **CVS**'s management acknowledges its responsibility for the consistency, integrity, and presentation of the financial information and for the system of internal controls.

Auditors' Reports

The *registered independent auditors' report* deals with the credibility of the financial statements. This report, prepared by independent certified public accountants, gives the accountants' opinion about how fairly the statements have been presented. Because management is responsible for preparing the financial statements, issuing statements that have not been independently audited would be like having a judge hear a case in which he or she was personally involved. The certified public accountants add the necessary credibility to management's figures for interested third parties. They report to the board of directors and the stockholders rather than to the company's management.

In form and language, most auditors' reports are like the one shown in Exhibit 5. Usually, such a report is short, but its language is very important. It normally has four parts, but it can have a fifth part if an explanation is needed.

1. The first paragraph identifies the financial statements that have been audited. It also identifies responsibilities. The company's management is responsible for the financial statements, and the auditor is responsible for expressing an opinion on the financial statements based on the audit.

2. The second paragraph, or *scope section*, states that the examination was made in accordance with standards of the Public Company Accounting Oversight Board (PCAOB). This paragraph also contains a brief description of the objectives and nature of the audit.

3. The third paragraph, or *opinion section*, states the results of the auditors' examination. The use of the word *opinion* is very important because the auditor does not certify or guarantee that the statements are absolutely correct. To do so would go beyond the truth, because many items, such as depreciation, are based on estimates. Instead, the auditors simply give an opinion about whether, overall, the financial statements "present fairly," in all material respects, the company's financial position, results of operations, and cash flows. This means that the statements are prepared in accordance with generally accepted accounting principles. If, in the auditors' opinion, the statements do not meet accepted standards, the auditors must explain why and to what extent.

4. The fourth paragraph states whether in the auditor's opinion, the company's internal controls are effective in accordance with the standards set by the Committee of Sponsoring Organizations (COSO).

Exhibit 5
Auditors' Report for CVS

Report of Independent Registered Public Accounting Firm
The Board of Directors and Shareholders
CVS Caremark Corporation

(1) We have audited the accompanying consolidated balance sheets of CVS Caremark Corporation as of December 31, 2011 and 2010, and the related consolidated statements of income, shareholders' equity, and cash flows for each of the three years in the period ended December 31, 2011. These financial statements are the responsibility of the Company's management. Our responsibility is to express an opinion on these financial statements based on our audits.

(2) We conducted our audits in accordance with the standards of the Public Company Accounting Oversight Board (United States). Those standards require that we plan and perform the audit to obtain reasonable assurance about whether the financial statements are free of material misstatement. An audit includes examining, on a test basis, evidence supporting the amounts and disclosures in the financial statements. An audit also includes assessing the accounting principles used and significant estimates made by management, as well as evaluating the overall financial statement presentation. We believe that our audits provide a reasonable basis for our opinion.

(3) In our opinion, the financial statements referred to above present fairly, in all material respects, the consolidated financial position of CVS Caremark Corporation at December 31, 2011 and 2010, and the consolidated results of its operations and its cash flows for each of the three years in the period ended December 31, 2011, in conformity with U.S. generally accepted accounting principles.

(4) We also have audited, in accordance with the standards of the Public Company Accounting Oversight Board (United States), CVS Caremark Corporation's internal control over financial reporting as of December 31, 2011, based on criteria established in *Internal Control – Integrated Framework* issued by the Committee of Sponsoring Organizations of the Treadway Commission and our report dated February 17, 2012 expressed an unqualified opinion thereon.

Ernst & Young LLP

Boston, Massachusetts
February 17, 2012

Excerpts from
CVS Caremark Corporation's
2011 Annual Report

CVS Caremark is the largest pharmacy health care provider in the United States with integrated offerings across the entire spectrum of pharmacy care. Through our unique suite of assets, we are reinventing pharmacy to offer innovative solutions that help people on their path to better health. At the same time, we are highly focused on lowering overall health care costs for plan members and payors. CVS Caremark operates more than 7,300 CVS/pharmacy® stores; serves in excess of 60 million plan members as a leading pharmacy benefit manager (PBM); and cares for patients through the nation's largest retail health clinic system at our approximately 600 MinuteClinic® locations.

Financial Highlights

(in millions, except per share figures)	fiscal year 2011	fiscal year 2010	% change
Net revenues	$ 107,100	$ 95,778	11.8%
Operating profit	$ 6,330	$ 6,137	3.1%
Net income attributable to CVS Caremark	$ 3,461	$ 3,427	1.0%
Diluted EPS from continuing operations	$ 2.59	$ 2.49	4.0%
Stock price at year-end	$ 40.78	$ 34.77	17.3%
Market capitalization at year-end	$ 52,937	$ 47,426	11.6%

NET REVENUE
(in billions of dollars)

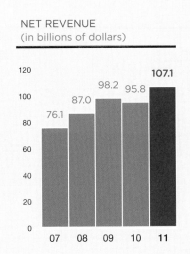

DILUTED EPS FROM
CONTINUING OPERATIONS
(in dollars)

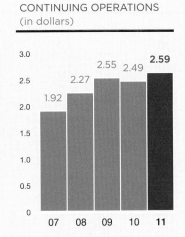

CASH DIVIDENDS
(in cents per common share)

Consolidated Statements of Income

	Year Ended December 31,		
in millions, except per share amounts	2011	2010	2009
Net revenues	$ 107,100	$ 95,778	$ 98,215
Cost of revenues	86,539	75,559	77,857
Gross profit	20,561	20,219	20,358
Operating expenses	14,231	14,082	13,933
Operating profit	6,330	6,137	6,425
Interest expense, net	584	536	525
Income before income tax provision	5,746	5,601	5,900
Income tax provision	2,258	2,179	2,200
Income from continuing operations	3,488	3,422	3,700
Income (loss) from discontinued operations, net of tax	(31)	2	(4)
Net income	3,457	3,424	3,696
Net loss attributable to noncontrolling interest	4	3	—
Net income attributable to CVS Caremark	$ 3,461	$ 3,427	$ 3,696
Basic earnings per common share:			
Income from continuing operations attributable to CVS Caremark	$ 2.61	$ 2.51	$ 2.58
Loss from discontinued operations attributable to CVS Caremark	(0.02)	—	—
Net income attributable to CVS Caremark	$ 2.59	$ 2.51	$ 2.58
Weighted average common shares outstanding	1,338	1,367	1,434
Diluted earnings per common share:			
Income from continuing operations attributable to CVS Caremark	$ 2.59	$ 2.49	$ 2.55
Loss from discontinued operations attributable to CVS Caremark	(0.02)	—	—
Net income attributable to CVS Caremark	$ 2.57	$ 2.49	$ 2.55
Weighted average common shares outstanding	1,347	1,377	1,450
Dividends declared per common share	$ 0.500	$ 0.350	$ 0.305

See accompanying notes to consolidated financial statements.

Consolidated Balance Sheets

		December 31,	
in millions, except per share amounts		2011	2010
Assets:			
Cash and cash equivalents	$	1,413	$ 1,427
Short-term investments		5	4
Accounts receivable, net		6,047	4,925
Inventories		10,046	10,695
Deferred income taxes		503	511
Other current assets		580	144
Total current assets		18,594	17,706
Property and equipment, net		8,467	8,322
Goodwill		26,458	25,669
Intangible assets, net		9,869	9,784
Other assets		1,155	688
Total assets	$	64,543	$ 62,169
Liabilities:			
Accounts payable	$	4,370	$ 4,026
Claims and discounts payable		3,487	2,569
Accrued expenses		3,293	3,070
Short-term debt		750	300
Current portion of long-term debt		56	1,105
Total current liabilities		11,956	11,070
Long-term debt		9,208	8,652
Deferred income taxes		3,853	3,655
Other long-term liabilities		1,445	1,058
Commitments and Contingencies (Note 13)			
Redeemable noncontrolling interest		30	34
Shareholders' equity:			
Preferred stock, par value $0.01: 0.1 shares authorized; none issued or outstanding		—	—
Common stock, par value $0.01: 3,200 shares authorized; 1,640 shares issued and 1,298 shares outstanding at December 31, 2011 and 1,624 shares issued and 1,363 shares outstanding at December 31, 2010		16	16
Treasury stock, at cost: 340 shares at December 31, 2011 and 259 shares at December 31, 2010		(11,953)	(9,030)
Shares held in trust: 2 shares at December 31, 2011 and 2010		(56)	(56)
Capital surplus		28,126	27,610
Retained earnings		22,090	19,303
Accumulated other comprehensive loss		(172)	(143)
Total shareholders' equity		38,051	37,700
Total liabilities and shareholders' equity	$	64,543	$ 62,169

See accompanying notes to consolidated financial statements.

Consolidated Statements of Cash Flows

	Year Ended December 31,		
in millions	2011	2010	2009
Cash flows from operating activities:			
Cash receipts from customers	$ 97,688	$ 94,503	$ 93,568
Cash paid for inventory and prescriptions dispensed by retail network pharmacies	(75,148)	(73,143)	(73,536)
Cash paid to other suppliers and employees	(13,635)	(13,778)	(13,121)
Interest received	4	4	5
Interest paid	(647)	(583)	(542)
Income taxes paid	(2,406)	(2,224)	(2,339)
Net cash provided by operating activities	5,856	4,779	4,035
Cash flows from investing activities:			
Purchases of property and equipment	(1,872)	(2,005)	(2,548)
Proceeds from sale-leaseback transactions	592	507	1,562
Proceeds from sale of property and equipment	4	34	23
Acquisitions (net of cash acquired) and other investments	(1,441)	(177)	(101)
Purchase of available-for-sale investments	(3)	—	(5)
Sale or maturity of available-for-sale investments	60	1	—
Proceeds from sale of subsidiary	250	—	—
Net cash used in investing activities	(2,410)	(1,640)	(1,069)
Cash flows from financing activities:			
Increase (decrease) in short-term debt	450	(15)	(2,729)
Proceeds from issuance of long-term debt	1,463	991	2,800
Repayments of long-term debt	(2,122)	(2,103)	(653)
Dividends paid	(674)	(479)	(439)
Derivative settlements	(19)	(5)	(3)
Proceeds from exercise of stock options	431	285	250
Excess tax benefits from stock-based compensation	21	28	19
Repurchase of common stock	(3,001)	(1,500)	(2,477)
Other	(9)	—	—
Net cash used in financing activities	(3,460)	(2,798)	(3,232)
Net increase (decrease) in cash and cash equivalents	(14)	341	(266)
Cash and cash equivalents at the beginning of the year	1,427	1,086	1,352
Cash and cash equivalents at the end of the year	$ 1,413	$ 1,427	$ 1,086
Reconciliation of net income to net cash provided by operating activities:			
Net income	$ 3,457	$ 3,424	$ 3,696
Adjustments required to reconcile net income to net cash provided by operating activities:			
Depreciation and amortization	1,568	1,469	1,389
Stock-based compensation	135	150	165
Gain on sale of subsidiary	(53)	—	—
Deferred income taxes and other noncash items	144	30	48
Change in operating assets and liabilities, net of effects from acquisitions:			
Accounts receivable, net	(748)	532	(86)
Inventories	607	(352)	(1,199)
Other current assets	(420)	(4)	48
Other assets	(49)	(210)	(2)
Accounts payable	1,128	(40)	4
Accrued expenses	85	(176)	(66)
Other long-term liabilities	2	(44)	38
Net cash provided by operating activities	$ 5,856	$ 4,779	$ 4,035

See accompanying notes to consolidated financial statements.

Consolidated Statements of Shareholders' Equity

	Shares			Dollars		
	Year Ended December 31,			Year Ended December 31,		
in millions	**2011**	2010	2009	**2011**	2010	2009
Preference stock:						
Beginning of year	**–**	–	4	**$ –**	$ –	$ 191
Conversion to common stock	**–**	–	(4)	**–**	–	(191)
End of year	**–**	–	–	**$ –**	$ –	$ –
Common stock:						
Beginning of year	**1,624**	1,612	1,603	**$ 16**	$ 16	$ 16
Stock options exercised and stock awards	**16**	12	9	**–**	–	–
End of year	**1,640**	1,624	1,612	**$ 16**	$ 16	$ 16
Treasury stock:						
Beginning of year	**(259)**	(219)	(165)	**$ (9,030)**	$ (7,610)	$ (5,812)
Purchase of treasury shares	**(84)**	(42)	(73)	**(3,001)**	(1,500)	(2,477)
Conversion of preference stock	**–**	–	17	**–**	–	583
Employee stock purchase plan issuances	**3**	2	2	**78**	80	96
End of year	**(340)**	(259)	(219)	**$(11,953)**	$ (9,030)	$ (7,610)
Shares held in trust:						
Beginning of year	**(2)**	(2)	(2)	**$ (56)**	$ (56)	$ (56)
End of year	**(2)**	(2)	(2)	**$ (56)**	$ (56)	$ (56)
Capital surplus:						
Beginning of year				**$ 27,610**	$ 27,198	$ 27,280
Stock option activity and stock awards				**495**	384	291
Tax benefit on stock options and stock awards				**21**	28	19
Conversion of preference stock				**–**	–	(392)
End of year				**$ 28,126**	$ 27,610	$ 27,198

See accompanying notes to consolidated financial statements.

Consolidated Statements of Shareholders' Equity

	Dollars		
	Year Ended December 31,		
in millions	**2011**	2010	2009
Retained earnings:			
Beginning of year	$ **19,303**	$ 16,355	$ 13,098
Net income attributable to CVS Caremark	**3,461**	3,427	3,696
Common stock dividends	**(674)**	(479)	(439)
End of year	¢ **22,090**	ⓢ 19,303	⑤ 10,355
Accumulated other comprehensive loss:			
Beginning of year	$ **(143)**	$ (135)	$ (143)
Net cash flow hedges, net of income tax	**(9)**	(1)	1
Pension liability adjustment, net of income tax	**(20)**	(7)	7
End of year	$ **(172)**	$ (143)	$ (135)
Total shareholders' equity	$ **38,051**	$ 37,700	$ 35,768
Comprehensive income:			
Net income	$ **3,457**	$ 3,424	$ 3,696
Other comprehensive income:			
Net cash flow hedges, net of income tax	**(9)**	(1)	1
Pension liability adjustment, net of income tax	**(20)**	(7)	7
Comprehensive income	**3,428**	3,416	3,704
Comprehensive loss attributable to noncontrolling interest	**4**	3	—
Comprehensive income attributable to CVS Caremark	$ **3,432**	$ 3,419	$ 3,704

See accompanying notes to consolidated financial statements.

Notes to Consolidated Financial Statements

1 SIGNIFICANT ACCOUNTING POLICIES

Description of business – CVS Caremark Corporation and its subsidiaries (the "Company") is the largest pharmacy health care provider in the United States based upon revenues and prescriptions filled. The Company currently has three reportable business segments, Pharmacy Services, Retail Pharmacy and Corporate, which are described below.

Pharmacy Services Segment (the "PSS") – The PSS provides a full range of pharmacy benefit management services including mail order pharmacy services, specialty pharmacy services, plan design and administration, formulary management and claims processing. The Company's clients are primarily employers, insurance companies, unions, government employee groups, managed care organizations and other sponsors of health benefit plans and individuals throughout the United States.

As a pharmacy benefits manager, the PSS manages the dispensing of pharmaceuticals through the Company's mail order pharmacies and national network of approximately 65,000 retail pharmacies to eligible members in the benefits plans maintained by the Company's clients and utilizes its information systems to perform, among other things, safety checks, drug interaction screenings and brand to generic substitutions.

The PSS' specialty pharmacies support individuals that require complex and expensive drug therapies. The specialty pharmacy business includes mail order and retail specialty pharmacies that operate under the CVS Caremark® and CarePlus CVS/pharmacy® names.

The PSS also provides health management programs, which include integrated disease management for 28 conditions, through our strategic alliance with Alere, L.L.C. and the Company's Accordant® health management offering.

In addition, through the Company's SilverScript Insurance Company ("SilverScript"), Accendo Insurance Company ("Accendo") and Pennsylvania Life Insurance Company ("Pennsylvania Life") subsidiaries, the PSS is a national provider of drug benefits to eligible beneficiaries under the Federal Government's Medicare Part D program.

The PSS generates net revenues primarily by contracting with clients to provide prescription drugs to plan members. Prescription drugs are dispensed by the mail order pharmacies, specialty pharmacies and national network of retail pharmacies. Net revenues are also generated by providing additional services to clients, including administrative services such as claims processing and formulary management, as well as health care related services such as disease management.

The pharmacy services business operates under the CVS Caremark® Pharmacy Services, Caremark®, CVS Caremark®, CarePlus CVS/pharmacy®, CarePlus™, RxAmerica® and Accordant® names. As of December 31, 2011, the PSS operated 31 retail specialty pharmacy stores, 12 specialty mail order pharmacies and 4 mail service pharmacies located in 22 states, Puerto Rico and the District of Columbia.

Retail Pharmacy Segment (the "RPS") – The RPS sells prescription drugs and a wide assortment of general merchandise, including over-the-counter drugs, beauty products and cosmetics, photo finishing, seasonal merchandise, greeting cards and convenience foods, through the Company's CVS/pharmacy® and Longs Drugs® retail stores and online through CVS.com®.

The RPS also provides health care services through its MinuteClinic® health care clinics. MinuteClinics are staffed by nurse practitioners and physician assistants who utilize nationally recognized protocols to diagnose and treat minor health conditions, perform health screenings, monitor chronic conditions and deliver vaccinations.

As of December 31, 2011, the retail pharmacy business included 7,327 retail drugstores (of which 7,271 operated a pharmacy) located in 41 states the District of Columbia and Puerto Rico operating primarily under the CVS/pharmacy® name, the online retail website, CVS.com and 657 retail health care clinics operating under the MinuteClinic® name (of which 648 were located in CVS/pharmacy stores).

Corporate Segment – The Corporate segment provides management and administrative services to support the Company. The Corporate segment consists of certain aspects of the Company's executive management, corporate relations, legal, compliance, human resources, corporate information technology and finance departments.

Principles of Consolidation – The consolidated financial statements include the accounts of the Company and its majority owned subsidiaries. All intercompany balances and transactions have been eliminated.

Use of estimates – The preparation of financial statements in conformity with accounting principles generally accepted in the United States of America requires management to make estimates and assumptions that affect the reported amounts in the consolidated financial statements and accompanying notes. Actual results could differ from those estimates.

Fair Value Hierarchy – The Company utilizes the three-level valuation hierarchy for the recognition and disclosure of fair value measurements. The categorization of assets and liabilities within this hierarchy is based upon the lowest level of input that is significant to the measurement of fair value. The three levels of the hierarchy consist of the following:

- Level 1 – Inputs to the valuation methodology are unadjusted quoted prices in active markets for identical assets or liabilities that the Company has the ability to access at the measurement date.

- Level 2 – Inputs to the valuation methodology are quoted prices for similar assets and liabilities in active markets, quoted prices in markets that are not active or inputs that are observable for the asset or liability, either directly or indirectly, for substantially the full term of the instrument.

- Level 3 – Inputs to the valuation methodology are unobservable inputs based upon management's best estimate of inputs market participants could use in pricing the asset or liability at the measurement date, including assumptions about risk.

Cash and cash equivalents – Cash and cash equivalents consist of cash and temporary investments with maturities of three months or less when purchased. The Company invests in short-term money market funds, commercial paper, time deposits, as well as other debt securities that are classified as cash equivalents within the accompanying consolidated balance sheets, as these funds are highly liquid and readily convertible to known amounts of cash. These investments are classified within Level 1 of the fair value hierarchy because they are valued using quoted market prices.

Short-term investments – The Company's short-term investments consist of certificate of deposits with initial maturities of greater than three months when purchased. These investments, which were classified as available-for-sale within Level 1 of the fair value hierarchy, were carried at historical cost, which approximated fair value at December 31, 2011 and 2010.

Fair value of financial instruments – As of December 31, 2011, the Company's financial instruments include cash and cash equivalents, accounts receivable, accounts payable and short-term debt. Due to the short-term nature of these instruments, the Company's carrying value approximates fair value. The carrying amount and estimated fair value of total long-term debt was $9.3 billion and $10.8 billion, respectively, as of December 31, 2011. The fair value of long-term debt was estimated based on rates currently offered to the Company for debt with similar terms and maturities. The Company had outstanding letters of credit, which guaranteed foreign trade purchases, with a fair value of $6 million as of December 31, 2011 and 2010. There were no outstanding derivative financial instruments as of December 31, 2011 and 2010.

Accounts receivable – Accounts receivable are stated net of an allowance for doubtful accounts. The accounts receivable balance primarily includes trade amounts due from third party providers (e.g., pharmacy benefit managers, insurance companies and governmental agencies), clients and members, as well as vendors and manufacturers.

The activity in the allowance for doubtful trade accounts receivable is as follows:

	Year Ended December 31,		
in millions	2011	2010	2009
Beginning balance	$ 182	$ 224	$ 189
Additions charged to bad debt expense	129	73	135
Write-offs charged to allowance	(122)	(115)	(100)
Ending balance	$ 189	$ 182	$ 224

Notes to Consolidated Financial Statements

Inventories – Inventories are stated at the lower of cost or market on a first-in, first-out basis using the retail inventory method in the retail pharmacy stores, the weighted average cost method in the mail service and specialty pharmacies, and the cost method on a first-in, first-out basis in the distribution centers. Physical inventory counts are taken on a regular basis in each store and a continuous cycle count process is the primary procedure used to validate the inventory balances on hand in each distribution center and mail facility to ensure that the amounts reflected in the accompanying consolidated financial statements are properly stated. During the interim period between physical inventory counts, the Company accrues for anticipated physical inventory losses on a location-by-location basis based on historical results and current trends.

Property and equipment – Property, equipment and improvements to leased premises are depreciated using the straight-line method over the estimated useful lives of the assets, or when applicable, the term of the lease, whichever is shorter. Estimated useful lives generally range from 10 to 40 years for buildings, building improvements and leasehold improvements and 3 to 10 years for fixtures, equipment and internally developed software. Repair and maintenance costs are charged directly to expense as incurred. Major renewals or replacements that substantially extend the useful life of an asset are capitalized and depreciated. Application development stage costs for significant internally developed software projects are capitalized and depreciated.

The following are the components of property and equipment at December 31:

in millions	2011	2010
Land	$ 1,295	$ 1,247
Building and improvements	2,404	2,265
Fixtures and equipment	7,582	7,148
Leasehold improvements	3,021	2,866
Software	1,098	757
	15,400	14,283
Accumulated depreciation and amortization	(6,933)	(5,961)
	$ 8,467	$ 8,322

The gross amount of property and equipment under capital leases was $211 million and $191 million as of December 31, 2011 and 2010, respectively.

Goodwill – Goodwill and other indefinite-lived assets are not amortized, but are subject to impairment reviews annually, or more frequently if necessary. See Note 4 for additional information on goodwill.

Intangible assets – Purchased customer contracts and relationships are amortized on a straight-line basis over their estimated useful lives between 10 and 20 years. Purchased customer lists are amortized on a straight-line basis over their estimated useful lives of up to 10 years. Purchased leases are amortized on a straight-line basis over the remaining life of the lease. See Note 4 for additional information about intangible assets.

Impairment of long-lived assets – The Company groups and evaluates fixed and finite-lived intangible assets, excluding goodwill, for impairment at the lowest level at which individual cash flows can be identified. When evaluating assets for potential impairment, the Company first compares the carrying amount of the asset group to the estimated future cash flows associated with the asset group (undiscounted and without interest charges). If the estimated future cash flows used in this analysis are less than the carrying amount of the asset group, an impairment loss calculation is prepared. The impairment loss calculation compares the carrying amount of the asset group to the asset group's estimated future cash flows (discounted and with interest charges). If required, an impairment loss is recorded for the portion of the asset group's carrying value that exceeds the asset group's estimated future cash flows (discounted and with interest charges).

Redeemable noncontrolling interest – The Company has an approximately 60% ownership interest in Generation Health, Inc. ("Generation Health") and consolidates Generation Health in its consolidated financial statements. The noncontrolling shareholders of Generation Health hold put rights for the remaining interest in Generation Health that if exercised would require the Company to purchase the remaining interest in Generation Health in 2015 for a minimum of $27 million and a maximum of $159 million, depending on certain financial metrics of Generation Health in 2014. Since the noncontrolling shareholders of Generation Health have a redemption feature as a result of the put rights, the Company has classified the redeemable noncontrolling interest in Generation Health in the mezzanine section of the consolidated balance sheet outside of shareholders' equity. The Company initially recorded the redeemable noncontrolling interest at a fair value of $37 million on the date of acquisition which was determined using inputs classified as Level 3 in the fair value hierarchy. At the end of each reporting period, if the estimated accreted redemption value exceeds the carrying value of the noncontrolling interest, the difference is recorded as a reduction of retained earnings. Any such reductions in retained earnings would also reduce income attributable to CVS Caremark in the Company's earnings per share calculations.

The following is a reconciliation of the changes in the redeemable noncontrolling interest:

in millions	2011	2010	2009
Beginning balance	$ 34	$ 37	$ —
Acquisition of Generation Health	—	—	37
Net loss attributable to noncontrolling interest	(4)	(3)	—
Ending balance	$ 30	$ 34	$ 37

Revenue Recognition

Pharmacy Services Segment – The PSS sells prescription drugs directly through its mail service pharmacies and indirectly through its retail pharmacy network. The PSS recognizes revenues from prescription drugs sold by its mail service pharmacies and under retail pharmacy network contracts where the PSS is the principal using the gross method at the contract prices negotiated with its clients. Net revenue from the PSS includes: (i) the portion of the price the client pays directly to the PSS, net of any volume-related or other discounts paid back to the client (see "Drug Discounts" later in this document), (ii) the price paid to the PSS ("Mail Co-Payments") or a third party pharmacy in the PSS' retail pharmacy network ("Retail Co-Payments") by individuals included in its clients' benefit plans, and (iii) administrative fees for retail pharmacy network contracts where the PSS is not the principal as discussed below.

The PSS recognizes revenue when: (i) persuasive evidence of an arrangement exists, (ii) delivery has occurred or services have been rendered, (iii) the seller's price to the buyer is fixed or determinable, and (iv) collectability is reasonably assured.

The Company has established the following revenue recognition policies for the PSS:

- Revenues generated from prescription drugs sold by mail service pharmacies are recognized when the prescription is shipped. At the time of shipment, the Company has performed substantially all of its obligations under its client contracts and does not experience a significant level of reshipments.

- Revenues generated from prescription drugs sold by third party pharmacies in the PSS' retail pharmacy network and associated administrative fees are recognized at the PSS' point-of-sale, which is when the claim is adjudicated by the PSS' online claims processing system.

The PSS determines whether it is the principal or agent for its retail pharmacy network transactions on a contract by contract basis. In the majority of its contracts, the PSS has determined it is the principal due to it: (i) being the primary obligor in the arrangement, (ii) having latitude in establishing the price, changing the product or performing part of the service, (iii) having discretion in supplier selection, (iv) having involvement in the determination of product or service specifications, and (v) having credit risk. The PSS' obligations under its client contracts for which revenues are reported using the gross method are separate and distinct from its obligations to the third party pharmacies included in its retail pharmacy

Notes to Consolidated Financial Statements

network contracts. Pursuant to these contracts, the PSS is contractually required to pay the third party pharmacies in its retail pharmacy network for products sold, regardless of whether the PSS is paid by its clients. The PSS' responsibilities under its client contracts typically include validating eligibility and coverage levels, communicating the prescription price and the co-payments due to the third party retail pharmacy, identifying possible adverse drug interactions for the pharmacist to address with the physician prior to dispensing, suggesting clinically appropriate generic alternatives where appropriate and approving the prescription for dispensing. Although the PSS does not have credit risk with respect to Retail Co-Payments, management believes that all of the other indicators of gross revenue reporting are present. For contracts under which the PSS acts as an agent, the PSS records revenues using the net method.

Drug Discounts – The PSS deducts from its revenues any rebates, inclusive of discounts and fees, earned by its clients. The PSS pays rebates to its clients in accordance with the terms of its client contracts, which are normally based on fixed rebates per prescription for specific products dispensed or a percentage of manufacturer discounts received for specific products dispensed. The liability for rebates due to the PSS' clients is included in "Claims and discounts payable" in the accompanying consolidated balance sheets.

Medicare Part D – The PSS participates in the Federal Government's Medicare Part D program as a Prescription Drug Plan ("PDP"). The PSS' net revenues include insurance premiums earned by the PDP, which are determined based on the PDP's annual bid and related contractual arrangements with the Centers for Medicare and Medicaid Services ("CMS"). The insurance premiums include a beneficiary premium, which is the responsibility of the PDP member, but is subsidized by CMS in the case of low-income members, and a direct premium paid by CMS. Premiums collected in advance are initially deferred in accrued expenses and are then recognized in net revenues over the period in which members are entitled to receive benefits.

In addition to these premiums, the PSS' net revenues include co-payments, coverage gap benefits, deductibles and co-insurance (collectively, the "Member Co-Payments") related to PDP members' actual prescription claims. In certain cases, CMS subsidizes a portion of these Member Co-Payments and pays the PSS an estimated prospective Member Co-Payment subsidy amount each month. The prospective Member Co-Payment subsidy amounts received from CMS are also included in the PSS' net revenues. The Company assumes no risk for these amounts, which represented 3.1%, 2.6% and 3.5% of consolidated net revenues in 2011, 2010 and 2009, respectively. If the prospective Member Co-Payment subsidies received differ from the amounts based on actual prescription claims, the difference is recorded in either accounts receivable or accrued expenses.

The PSS accounts for CMS obligations and Member Co-Payments (including the amounts subsidized by CMS) using the gross method consistent with its revenue recognition policies for Mail Co-Payments and Retail Co-Payments (discussed previously in this document). See Note 8 for additional information about Medicare Part D.

Retail Pharmacy Segment – The RPS recognizes revenue from the sale of merchandise (other than prescription drugs) at the time the merchandise is purchased by the retail customer. Revenue from the sale of prescription drugs is recognized at the time the prescription is filled, which is or approximates when the retail customer picks up the prescription. Customer returns are not material. Revenue generated from the performance of services in the RPS' health care clinics is recognized at the time the services are performed. See Note 14 for additional information about the revenues of the Company's business segments.

Cost of Revenues

Pharmacy Services Segment – The PSS' cost of revenues includes: (i) the cost of prescription drugs sold during the reporting period directly through its mail service pharmacies and indirectly through its retail pharmacy network, (ii) shipping and handling costs, and (iii) the operating costs of its mail service pharmacies and client service operations and related information technology support costs including depreciation and amortization. The cost of prescription drugs sold component of cost of revenues includes: (i) the cost of the prescription drugs purchased from manufacturers or distributors and shipped to members in clients' benefit plans from the PSS' mail service pharmacies, net of any volume-related or other discounts (see "Drug Discounts" previously in this document) and (ii) the cost of prescription drugs sold (including Retail Co-Payments) through the PSS' retail pharmacy network under contracts where it is the principal, net of any volume-related or other discounts.

Retail Pharmacy Segment – The RPS' cost of revenues includes: the cost of merchandise sold during the reporting period and the related purchasing costs, warehousing and delivery costs (including depreciation and amortization) and actual and estimated inventory losses. See Note 14 for additional information about the cost of revenues of the Company's business segments.

Vendor Allowances and Purchase Discounts

The Company accounts for vendor allowances and purchase discounts as follows:

Pharmacy Services Segment – The PSS receives purchase discounts on products purchased. The PSS' contractual arrangements with vendors, including manufacturers, wholesalers and retail pharmacies, normally provide for the PSS to receive purchase discounts from established list prices in one, or a combination of, the following forms: (i) a direct discount at the time of purchase, (ii) a discount for the prompt payment of invoices, or (iii) when products are purchased indirectly from a manufacturer (e.g., through a wholesaler or retail pharmacy), a discount (or rebate) paid subsequent to dispensing. These rebates are recognized when prescriptions are dispensed and are generally calculated and billed to manufacturers within 30 days of the end of each completed quarter. Historically, the effect of adjustments resulting from the reconciliation of rebates recognized to the amounts billed and collected has not been material to the PSS' results of operations. The PSS accounts for the effect of any such differences as a change in accounting estimate in the period the reconciliation is completed. The PSS also receives additional discounts under its wholesaler contract if it exceeds contractually defined annual purchase volumes. In addition, the PSS receives fees from pharmaceutical manufacturers for administrative services. Purchase discounts and administrative service fees are recorded as a reduction of "Cost of revenues".

Retail Pharmacy Segment – Vendor allowances received by the RPS reduce the carrying cost of inventory and are recognized in cost of revenues when the related inventory is sold, unless they are specifically identified as a reimbursement of incremental costs for promotional programs and/or other services provided. Amounts that are directly linked to advertising commitments are recognized as a reduction of advertising expense (included in operating expenses) when the related advertising commitment is satisfied. Any such allowances received in excess of the actual cost incurred also reduce the carrying cost of inventory. The total value of any upfront payments received from vendors that are linked to purchase commitments is initially deferred. The deferred amounts are then amortized to reduce cost of revenues over the life of the contract based upon purchase volume. The total value

of any upfront payments received from vendors that are not linked to purchase commitments is also initially deferred. The deferred amounts are then amortized to reduce cost of revenues on a straight-line basis over the life of the related contract. The total amortization of these upfront payments was not material to the accompanying consolidated financial statements.

Insurance – The Company is self-insured for certain losses related to general liability, workers' compensation and auto liability. The Company obtains third party insurance coverage to limit exposure from these claims. The Company is also self-insured for certain losses related to health and medical liabilities. The Company's self-insurance accruals, which include reported claims and claims incurred but not reported, are calculated using standard insurance industry actuarial assumptions and the Company's historical claims experience.

Facility opening and closing costs – New facility opening costs, other than capital expenditures, are charged directly to expense when incurred. When the Company closes a facility, the present value of estimated unrecoverable costs, including the remaining lease obligation less estimated sublease income and the book value of abandoned property and equipment, are charged to expense. The long-term portion of the lease obligations associated with facility closings was $327 million and $368 million in 2011 and 2010, respectively.

Advertising costs – Advertising costs are expensed when the related advertising takes place. Advertising costs, net of vendor funding (included in operating expenses), were $211 million, $234 million and $317 million in 2011, 2010 and 2009, respectively.

Interest expense, net – Interest expense, net of capitalized interest, was $588 million, $539 million and $530 million, and interest income was $4 million, $3 million and $5 million in 2011, 2010 and 2009, respectively. Capitalized interest totaled $37 million, $47 million and $39 million in 2011, 2010 and 2009, respectively.

Shares held in trust – The Company maintains grantor trusts, which held approximately 2 million shares of its common stock at December 31, 2011 and 2010. These shares are designated for use under various employee compensation plans. Since the Company holds these shares, they are excluded from the computation of basic and diluted shares outstanding.

Notes to Consolidated Financial Statements

Accumulated other comprehensive loss – Accumulated other comprehensive loss consists of changes in the net actuarial gains and losses associated with pension and other postretirement benefit plans, and unrealized losses on derivatives. The amount included in accumulated other comprehensive loss related to the Company's pension and postretirement plans was $250 million pre-tax ($152 million after-tax) as of December 31, 2011 and $217 million pre-tax ($132 million after-tax) as of December 31, 2010. The net impact on cash flow hedges totaled $32 million pre-tax ($20 million after-tax) and $18 million pre-tax ($11 million after-tax) as of December 31, 2011 and 2010, respectively.

Stock-based compensation – Stock-based compensation expense is measured at the grant date based on the fair value of the award and is recognized as expense over the applicable requisite service period of the stock award (generally 3 to 5 years) using the straight-line method. Stock-based compensation costs are included in selling, general and administrative expenses.

Income taxes – The Company provides for federal and state income taxes currently payable, as well as for those deferred because of timing differences between reported income and expenses for financial statement purposes versus tax purposes. Federal and state tax credits are recorded as a reduction of income taxes. Deferred tax assets and liabilities are recognized for the future tax consequences attributable to differences between the carrying amount of assets and liabilities for financial reporting purposes and the amounts used for income tax purposes. Deferred tax assets and liabilities are measured using the enacted tax rates expected to apply to taxable income in the years in which those temporary differences are expected to be recoverable or settled. The effect of a change in tax rates is recognized as income or expense in the period of the change.

Earnings per common share – Basic earnings per common share is computed by dividing: (i) net earnings by (ii) the weighted average number of common shares outstanding during the year (the "Basic Shares").

Diluted earnings per common share is computed by dividing: (i) net earnings by (ii) Basic Shares plus the additional shares that would be issued assuming that all dilutive stock awards are exercised. Options to purchase 30.5 million, 34.3 million and 37.7 million shares of common stock were outstanding as of December 31, 2011, 2010 and 2009, respectively, but were not included in the calculation of diluted earnings per share because the options' exercise prices were greater than the average market price of the common shares and, therefore, the effect would be antidilutive.

16 QUARTERLY FINANCIAL INFORMATION (UNAUDITED)

in millions, except per share amounts	First Quarter[1]	Second Quarter[1]	Third Quarter	Fourth Quarter	Year
2011:					
Net revenues	$ 25,695	$ 26,414	$ 26,674	$ 28,317	$ 107,100
Gross profit	4,742	5,086	5,178	5,555	20,561
Operating profit	1,305	1,484	1,584	1,957	6,330
Income from continuing operations	709	813	867	1,099	3,488
Income (loss) from discontinued operations, net of tax	3	2	—	(36)	(31)
Net income	712	815	867	1,063	3,457
Net loss attributable to noncontrolling interest	1	1	1	1	4
Net income attributable to CVS Caremark	$ 713	$ 816	$ 868	$ 1,064	$ 3,461
Basic earnings per common share:					
Income from continuing operations attributable to CVS Caremark	$ 0.52	$ 0.60	$ 0.65	$ 0.84	$ 2.61
Loss from discontinued operations attributable to CVS Caremark	$ —	$ —	$ —	$ (0.03)	$ (0.02)
Net income attributable to CVS Caremark	$ 0.52	$ 0.60	$ 0.65	$ 0.82	$ 2.59
Diluted Earnings per common share:					
Income from continuing operations attributable to CVS Caremark	$ 0.52	$ 0.60	$ 0.65	$ 0.84	$ 2.59
Loss from discontinued operations attributable to CVS Caremark	$ —	$ —	$ —	$ (0.03)	$ (0.02)
Net income attributable to CVS Caremark	$ 0.52	$ 0.60	$ 0.65	$ 0.81	$ 2.57
Dividends per common share	$ 0.125	$ 0.125	$ 0.125	$ 0.125	$ 0.500
Stock price: (New York Stock Exchange)					
High	$ 35.95	$ 39.50	$ 38.82	$ 41.35	$ 41.35
Low	$ 32.08	$ 34.21	$ 31.30	$ 32.28	$ 31.30

(1) The results of operations previously filed have been revised to reflect the results of TheraCom as discontinued operations. See Note 3.

Notes to Consolidated Financial Statements

in millions, except per share amounts	First Quarter [1]	Second Quarter [1]	Third Quarter [1]	Fourth Quarter [1]	Year [1]
2010:					
Net revenues	$ 23,593	$ 23,885	$ 23,711	$ 24,589	$ 95,778
Gross profit	4,738	5,012	5,015	5,454	20,219
Operating profit	1,404	1,494	1,478	1,761	6,137
Income from continuing operations	768	819	815	1,020	3,422
Income (loss) from discontinued operations, net of tax	2	2	(7)	5	2
Net income	770	821	808	1,025	3,424
Net loss attributable to noncontrolling interest	1	—	1	1	3
Net income attributable to CVS Caremark	$ 771	$ 821	$ 809	$ 1,026	$ 3,427
Basic earnings per common share:					
Income from continuing operations attributable to CVS Caremark	$ 0.56	$ 0.60	$ 0.60	$ 0.75	$ 2.51
Income (loss) from discontinued operations attributable to CVS Caremark	$ —	$ —	$ (0.01)	$ —	$ —
Net income attributable to CVS Caremark	$ 0.56	$ 0.61	$ 0.59	$ 0.75	$ 2.51
Diluted Earnings per common share:					
Income from continuing operations attributable to CVS Caremark	$ 0.55	$ 0.60	$ 0.60	$ 0.74	$ 2.49
Income (loss) from discontinued operations attributable to CVS Caremark	$ —	$ —	$ (0.01)	$ —	$ —
Net income attributable to CVS Caremark	$ 0.55	$ 0.60	$ 0.59	$ 0.75	$ 2.49
Dividends per common share	$ 0.0875	$ 0.0875	$ 0.0875	$ 0.0875	$ 0.3500
Stock price: (New York Stock Exchange)					
High	$ 37.32	$ 37.82	$ 32.09	$ 35.46	$ 37.82
Low	$ 30.36	$ 29.22	$ 26.84	$ 29.45	$ 26.84

(1) The results of operations previously filed have been revised to reflect the results of TheraCom as discontinued operations. See Note 3.

Five-Year Financial Summary

in millions, except per share amounts	2011 [1]	2010 [1]	2009 [1]	2008 [1]	2007 [1] [2]
Statement of operations data:					
Net revenues	$ 107,100	$ 95,778	$ 98,215	$ 87,005	$ 76,078
Gross profit	20,561	20,219	20,358	18,272	16,098
Operating expenses	14,231	14,082	13,933	12,237	11,309
Operating profit	6,330	6,137	6,425	6,035	4,789
Interest expense, net	584	536	525	509	435
Income tax provision [3]	2,258	2,179	2,200	2,189	1,720
Income from continuing operations	3,488	3,422	3,700	3,337	2,634
Income (loss) from discontinued operations, net of tax benefit [4]	(31)	2	(4)	(125)	3
Net income	3,457	3,424	3,696	3,212	2,637
Net loss attributable to noncontrolling interest [5]	4	3	—	—	—
Preference dividends, net of income tax benefit	—	—	—	(14)	(14)
Net income attributable to CVS Caremark	$ 3,461	$ 3,427	$ 3,696	$ 3,198	$ 2,623
Per common share data:					
Basic earnings per common share:					
Income from continuing operations attributable to CVS Caremark	$ 2.61	$ 2.51	$ 2.58	$ 2.32	$ 1.97
Loss from discontinued operations attributable to CVS Caremark	(0.02)	—	—	(0.09)	—
Net income attributable to CVS Caremark	$ 2.59	$ 2.51	$ 2.58	$ 2.23	$ 1.97
Diluted earnings per common share:					
Income from continuing operations attributable to CVS Caremark	$ 2.59	$ 2.49	$ 2.55	$ 2.27	$ 1.92
Loss from discontinued operations attributable to CVS Caremark	(0.02)	—	—	(0.09)	—
Net income attributable to CVS Caremark	$ 2.57	$ 2.49	$ 2.55	$ 2.18	$ 1.92
Cash dividends per common share	$ 0.50000	$ 0.35000	$ 0.30500	$ 0.25800	$ 0.22875
Balance sheet and other data:					
Total assets	$ 64,543	$ 62,169	$ 61,641	$ 60,960	$ 54,722
Long-term debt	$ 9,208	$ 8,652	$ 8,756	$ 8,057	$ 8,350
Total shareholders' equity	$ 38,051	$ 37,700	$ 35,768	$ 34,574	$ 31,322
Number of stores (at end of year)	7,388	7,248	7,095	6,997	6,301

(1) On December 23, 2008, our Board of Directors approved a change in our fiscal year-end from the Saturday nearest December 31 of each year to December 31 of each year to better reflect our position in the health care, rather than the retail, industry. The fiscal year change was effective beginning with the fourth quarter of fiscal 2008. As you review our operating performance, please consider that 2011, 2010 and 2009 include 365 days; fiscal 2008 includes 368 days, and fiscal 2007 includes 364 days.

(2) Effective March 22, 2007, Caremark Rx, Inc. was merged into a newly formed subsidiary of CVS Corporation, with Caremark Rx, L.L.C., continuing as the surviving entity (the "Caremark Merger"). Following the Caremark Merger, the name of the Company was changed to "CVS Caremark Corporation." By virtue of the Caremark Merger, each issued and outstanding share of Caremark common stock, par value $0.001 per share, was converted into the right to receive 1.67 shares of CVS Caremark's common stock, par value $0.01 per share. Cash was paid in lieu of fractional shares.

(3) Income tax provision includes the effect of the following: (i) in 2010, the recognition of $47 million of previously unrecognized tax benefits, including interest, relating to the expiration of various statutes of limitation and settlements with tax authorities and (ii) in 2009, the recognition of $167 million of previously unrecognized tax benefits, including interest, relating to the expiration of various statutes of limitation and settlements with tax authorities.

(4) As discussed in Note 3 to the consolidated financial statements, the results of the Theracom business are presented as discontinued operations and have been excluded from continuing operations for all periods presented.

In connection with certain business dispositions completed between 1991 and 1997, the Company retained guarantees on store lease obligations for a number of former subsidiaries, including Linens 'n Things which filed for bankruptcy in 2008. The Company's income (loss) from discontinued operations includes lease-related costs which the Company believes it will likely be required to satisfy pursuant to its Linens 'n Things lease guarantees.

Below is a summary of the results of discontinued operations:

in millions		Fiscal Year			
	2011	2010	2009	2008	2007
Income from operations of TheraCom	$ 18	$ 28	$ 13	$ 11	$ 5
Gain on disposal of TheraCom	53	—	—	—	—
Loss on disposal of Linens 'n Things	(7)	(24)	(19)	(214)	—
Income tax benefit (provision)	(95)	(2)	2	78	(2)
Income (loss) from discontinued operations, net of tax	$ (31)	$ 2	$ (4)	$ (125)	$ 3

(5) Represents the minority shareholders' portion of the net loss from our majority owned subsidiary, Generation Health, Inc., acquired in the fourth quarter of 2009.

Report of Independent Registered Public Accounting Firm

The Board of Directors and Shareholders
CVS Caremark Corporation

We have audited the accompanying consolidated balance sheets of CVS Caremark Corporation as of December 31, 2011 and 2010, and the related consolidated statements of income, shareholders' equity, and cash flows for each of the three years in the period ended December 31, 2011. These financial statements are the responsibility of the Company's management. Our responsibility is to express an opinion on these financial statements based on our audits.

We conducted our audits in accordance with the standards of the Public Company Accounting Oversight Board (United States). Those standards require that we plan and perform the audit to obtain reasonable assurance about whether the financial statements are free of material misstatement. An audit includes examining, on a test basis, evidence supporting the amounts and disclosures in the financial statements. An audit also includes assessing the accounting principles used and significant estimates made by management, as well as evaluating the overall financial statement presentation. We believe that our audits provide a reasonable basis for our opinion.

In our opinion, the financial statements referred to above present fairly, in all material respects, the consolidated financial position of CVS Caremark Corporation at December 31, 2011 and 2010, and the consolidated results of its operations and its cash flows for each of the three years in the period ended December 31, 2011, in conformity with U.S. generally accepted accounting principles.

We also have audited, in accordance with the standards of the Public Company Accounting Oversight Board (United States), CVS Caremark Corporation's internal control over financial reporting as of December 31, 2011, based on criteria established in *Internal Control – Integrated Framework* issued by the Committee of Sponsoring Organizations of the Treadway Commission and our report dated February 17, 2012 expressed an unqualified opinion thereon.

Ernst + Young LLP

Boston, Massachusetts
February 17, 2012

Excerpts from
Southwest Airlines Co.'s
2011 Annual Report

Item 8.   *Financial Statements and Supplementary Data*

SOUTHWEST AIRLINES CO.

CONSOLIDATED BALANCE SHEET

(in millions, except share data)

	DECEMBER 31,	
	2011	**2010**
ASSETS		
Current assets:		
Cash and cash equivalents	$ 829	$ 1,261
Short-term investments	2,315	2,277
Accounts and other receivables	299	195
Inventories of parts and supplies, at cost	401	243
Deferred income taxes	263	214
Prepaid expenses and other current assets	238	89
Total current assets	4,345	4,279
Property and equipment, at cost:		
Flight equipment	15,542	13,991
Ground property and equipment	2,423	2,122
Deposits on flight equipment purchase contracts	456	230
	18,421	16,343
Less allowance for depreciation and amortization	6,294	5,765
	12,127	10,578
Goodwill	970	—
Other assets	626	606
	$18,068	$15,463
LIABILITIES AND STOCKHOLDERS' EQUITY		
Current liabilities:		
Accounts payable	$ 1,057	$ 739
Accrued liabilities	996	863
Air traffic liability	1,836	1,198
Current maturities of long-term debt	644	505
Total current liabilities	4,533	3,305
Long-term debt less current maturities	3,107	2,875
Deferred income taxes	2,566	2,493
Deferred gains from sale and leaseback of aircraft	75	88
Other noncurrent liabilities	910	465
Stockholders' equity:		
Common stock, $1.00 par value: 2,000,000,000 shares authorized; 807,611,634 shares issued in 2011 and 2010	808	808
Capital in excess of par value	1,222	1,183
Retained earnings	5,395	5,399
Accumulated other comprehensive loss	(224)	(262)
Treasury stock, at cost: 35,050,991 and 60,177,362 shares in 2011 and 2010 respectively	(324)	(891)
Total stockholders' equity	6,877	6,237
	$18,068	$15,463

See accompanying notes.

SOUTHWEST AIRLINES CO.

CONSOLIDATED STATEMENT OF INCOME

(in millions, except per share amounts)

	YEAR ENDED DECEMBER 31,		
	2011	**2010**	**2009**
OPERATING REVENUES:			
Passenger	$14,735	$11,489	$ 9,892
Freight	139	125	118
Other	784	490	340
Total operating revenues	15,658	12,104	10,350
OPERATING EXPENSES:			
Salaries, wages, and benefits	4,371	3,704	3,468
Fuel and oil	5,644	3,620	3,044
Maintenance materials and repairs	955	751	719
Aircraft rentals	308	180	186
Landing fees and other rentals	959	807	718
Depreciation and amortization	715	628	616
Acquisition and integration	134	8	—
Other operating expenses	1,879	1,418	1,337
Total operating expenses	14,965	11,116	10,088
OPERATING INCOME	693	988	262
OTHER EXPENSES (INCOME):			
Interest expense	194	167	186
Capitalized interest	(12)	(18)	(21)
Interest income	(10)	(12)	(13)
Other (gains) losses, net	198	106	(54)
Total other expenses	370	243	98
INCOME BEFORE INCOME TAXES	323	745	164
PROVISION FOR INCOME TAXES	145	286	65
NET INCOME	$ 178	$ 459	$ 99
NET INCOME PER SHARE, BASIC	$ .23	$ .62	$ .13
NET INCOME PER SHARE, DILUTED	$ .23	$ .61	$ .13
Cash dividends declared per common share	$ .0180	$ .0180	$ .0180

See accompanying notes.

SOUTHWEST AIRLINES CO.

CONSOLIDATED STATEMENT OF STOCKHOLDERS' EQUITY

YEAR ENDED DECEMBER 31, 2011, 2010, AND 2009

(in millions, except per share amounts)	Common Stock	Capital in excess of par value	Retained earnings	Accumulated other comprehensive income (loss)	Treasury stock	Total
Balance at December 31, 2008	$808	$1,215	$4,907	$(984)	$(1,005)	$4,941
Issuance of common and treasury stock pursuant to Employee stock plans	—	—	(22)	—	42	20
Net tax benefit (expense) of options exercised	—	(13)	—	—	—	(13)
Share-based compensation	—	14	—	—	—	14
Cash dividends, $.018 per share	—	—	(13)	—	—	(13)
Comprehensive income (loss):						
Net income	—	—	99	—	—	99
Unrealized gain on fuel derivative instruments	—	—	—	366	—	366
Other	—	—	—	40	—	40
Total comprehensive income						505
Balance at December 31, 2009	$808	$1,216	$4,971	$(578)	$ (963)	$5,454
Issuance of common and treasury stock pursuant to Employee stock plans	—	—	(18)	—	72	54
Net tax benefit (expense) of options exercised	—	(45)	—	—	—	(45)
Share-based compensation	—	12	—	—	—	12
Cash dividends, $.018 per share	—	—	(13)	—	—	(13)
Comprehensive income (loss):						
Net income	—	—	459	—	—	459
Unrealized gain on fuel derivative instruments	—	—	—	330	—	330
Other	—	—	—	(14)	—	(14)
Total comprehensive income						775
Balance at December 31, 2010	$808	$1,183	$5,399	$(262)	$ (891)	$6,237
Repurchase of common stock	—	—	—	—	(225)	(225)
Issuance of common and treasury stock pursuant to Employee stock plans	—	(3)	(14)	—	37	20
Issuance of stock to acquire AirTran	—	—	(127)	—	650	523
Issuance of stock for conversion of debt	—	34	(27)	—	105	112
Net tax benefit (expense) of options exercised	—	(5)	—	—	—	(5)
Share-based compensation	—	13	—	—	—	13
Cash dividends, $.018 per share	—	—	(14)	—	—	(14)
Comprehensive income (loss):						
Net income	—	—	178	—	—	178
Unrealized gain on fuel derivative instruments	—	—	—	67	—	67
Other	—	—	—	(29)	—	(29)
Total comprehensive income						216
Balance at December 31, 2011	$808	$1,222	$5,395	$(224)	$ (324)	$6,877

See accompanying notes.

SOUTHWEST AIRLINES CO.

CONSOLIDATED STATEMENT OF CASH FLOWS

(in millions)	YEAR ENDED DECEMBER 31,		
	2011	2010	2009
CASH FLOWS FROM OPERATING ACTIVITIES:			
Net income	$ 178	$ 459	$ 99
Adjustments to reconcile net income to cash provided by operating activities:			
Depreciation and amortization	715	628	616
Unrealized (gain) loss on fuel derivative instruments	90	139	14
Deferred income taxes	123	133	72
Amortization of deferred gains on sale and leaseback of aircraft	(13)	(14)	(12)
Changes in certain assets and liabilities (excluding the effects of acquired business):			
Accounts and other receivables	(26)	(26)	40
Other current assets	(196)	(8)	(27)
Accounts payable and accrued liabilities	253	193	59
Air traffic liability	262	153	81
Cash collateral received from (provided to) derivative counterparties	(195)	265	(90)
Other, net	194	(361)	133
Net cash provided by operating activities	1,385	1,561	985
CASH FLOWS FROM INVESTING ACTIVITIES:			
Payment to acquire AirTran, net of AirTran cash on hand	(35)	—	—
Payments for purchase of property and equipment, net	(968)	(493)	(585)
Purchases of short-term investments	(5,362)	(5,624)	(6,106)
Proceeds from sales of short-term investments	5,314	4,852	5,120
Other, net	—	—	2
Net cash used in investing activities	(1,051)	(1,265)	(1,569)
CASH FLOWS FROM FINANCING ACTIVITIES:			
Issuance of long-term debt	—	—	455
Proceeds from credit line borrowing	—	—	83
Proceeds from sale leaseback transactions	—	—	381
Proceeds from Employee stock plans	20	55	20
Proceeds from termination of interest rate derivative instrument	76	—	—
Payments of long-term debt and capital lease obligations	(540)	(155)	(86)
Payments of convertible debt obligations	(81)	—	—
Payment of revolving credit facility obligations	—	—	(400)
Payment of credit line borrowing obligations	—	(44)	(97)
Payments of cash dividends	(14)	(13)	(13)
Repurchase of common stock	(225)	—	—
Other, net	(2)	8	(13)
Net cash provided by (used in) financing activities	(766)	(149)	330
NET CHANGE IN CASH AND CASH EQUIVALENTS	(432)	147	(254)
CASH AND CASH EQUIVALENTS AT BEGINNING OF PERIOD	1,261	1,114	1,368
CASH AND CASH EQUIVALENTS AT END OF PERIOD	$ 829	$ 1,261	$ 1,114
CASH PAYMENTS FOR:			
Interest, net of amount capitalized	$ 185	$ 135	$ 152
Income taxes	$ 13	$ 274	$ 5
SUPPLEMENTAL DISCLOSURE OF NONCASH TRANSACTIONS:			
Fair value of equity consideration given to acquire AirTran	$ 523	$ —	$ —
Fair value of common stock issued for conversion of debt	$ 78	$ —	$ —

See accompanying notes.

NOTES TO CONSOLIDATED FINANCIAL STATEMENTS
DECEMBER 31, 2011

1. Summary of Significant Accounting Policies

Basis of Presentation

Southwest Airlines Co. (the "Company") operates Southwest Airlines, a major domestic airline that provides point-to-point, low-fare service. The Consolidated Financial Statements include the accounts of the Company and its wholly owned subsidiaries, which include AirTran Holdings, LLC. On May 2, 2011 (the "acquisition date"), the Company acquired all of the outstanding equity of AirTran Holdings, Inc. ("AirTran Holdings"), the former parent company of AirTran Airways, Inc. ("AirTran Airways"), in exchange for common stock of the Company and cash. Throughout these Notes, the Company makes reference to AirTran, which is meant to be inclusive of the following: (i) for periods prior to the acquisition date, AirTran Holdings and its subsidiaries, including, among others, AirTran Airways; and (ii) for periods on and after the acquisition date, AirTran Holdings, LLC, the successor to AirTran Holdings, and its subsidiaries, including among others, AirTran Airways. The accompanying Consolidated Financial Statements include the results of operations and cash flows for AirTran from May 2, 2011 through December 31, 2011. See Note 2. All significant inter-entity balances and transactions have been eliminated. The preparation of financial statements in conformity with generally accepted accounting principles in the United States (GAAP) requires management to make estimates and assumptions that affect the amounts reported in the financial statements and accompanying notes. Actual results could differ from these estimates.

Cash and cash equivalents

Cash in excess of that necessary for operating requirements is invested in short-term, highly liquid, income-producing investments. Investments with original maturities of three months or less when purchased are classified as cash and cash equivalents, which primarily consist of certificates of deposit, money market funds, and investment grade commercial paper issued by major corporations and financial institutions. Cash and cash equivalents are stated at cost, which approximates fair value.

As of December 31, 2011 and 2010, the Company had provided cash collateral deposits to its fuel hedge counterparties totaling $226 million and $125 million, respectively. As of December 31, 2010, the Company also held cash collateral deposits of $60 million from a counterparty. Cash collateral amounts provided or held associated with fuel derivative instruments are not restricted in any way and earn interest income at an agreed upon rate that approximates the rates earned on short-term securities issued by the U.S. Government. Depending on the fair value of the Company's fuel derivative instruments, the amounts of collateral deposits held or provided at any point in time can fluctuate significantly. See Note 10 for further information on these collateral deposits and fuel derivative instruments.

Short-term and noncurrent investments

Short-term investments consist of investments with original maturities of greater than three months but less than twelve months when purchased. These are primarily short-term securities issued by the U.S. Government and certificates of deposit issued by domestic banks. All of these investments are classified as available-for-sale securities and are stated at fair value, which approximates cost. For all short-term investments, at each reset period or upon reinvestment, the Company accounts for the transaction as Proceeds from sales of short-term investments for the security relinquished, and Purchases of short-investments for the security purchased, in the accompanying Consolidated Statement of Cash Flows. Unrealized gains and losses, net of tax, if any, are recognized in Accumulated other comprehensive income (loss) ("AOCI") in the accompanying Consolidated Balance Sheet. Realized net gains and losses on specific investments, if any, are reflected in Interest income in the accompanying Consolidated Statement of Income. Both unrealized and realized gains and/or losses associated with investments were immaterial for all years presented.

Noncurrent investments consist of investments with maturities of greater than twelve months. At December 31, 2011, these primarily consisted of the Company's auction rate security instruments that it expects will not be redeemed during 2012. See Note 11 for further information. Noncurrent investments are included as a component of Other assets in the Consolidated Balance Sheet.

Accounts and other receivables

Accounts and other receivables are carried at cost. They primarily consist of amounts due from credit card companies associated with sales of tickets for future travel, amounts due from business partners in the Company's frequent flyer program, and amounts due from counterparties associated with fuel derivative instruments that have settled. The allowance for doubtful accounts was immaterial at December 31, 2011, 2010, and 2009. In addition, the provision for doubtful accounts and write-offs for 2011, 2010, and 2009 were each immaterial.

Inventories

Inventories consist primarily of aircraft fuel, flight equipment expendable parts, materials, and supplies. All of these items are carried at average cost, less an allowance for obsolescence. These items are generally charged to expense when issued for use. The reserve for obsolescence was immaterial at December 31, 2011, 2010, and 2009. In addition, the Company's provision for obsolescence and write-offs for 2011, 2010, and 2009 were each immaterial.

Property and equipment

Property and equipment is stated at cost. Depreciation is provided by the straight-line method to estimated residual values over periods generally ranging from 23 to 30 years for flight equipment and 5 to 30 years for ground property and equipment once the asset is placed in service. Residual values estimated for aircraft generally range from 5 to 15 percent and for ground property and equipment generally range from 0 to 10 percent. Property under capital leases and related obligations are initially recorded at an amount equal to the present value of future minimum lease payments computed on the basis of the Company's incremental borrowing rate or, when known, the interest rate implicit in the lease. Amortization of property under capital leases is on a straight-line basis over the lease term and is included in Depreciation and amortization expense. Leasehold improvements generally are amortized on a straight-line basis over the shorter of the estimated useful life of the improvement or the remaining term of the lease.

The Company evaluates its long-lived assets used in operations for impairment when events and circumstances indicate that the undiscounted cash flows to be generated by that asset are less than the carrying amounts of the asset and may not be recoverable. Factors that would indicate potential impairment include, but are not limited to, significant decreases in the market value of the long-lived asset(s), a significant change in the long-lived asset's physical condition, and operating or cash flow losses associated with the use of the long-lived asset. If an asset is deemed to be impaired, an impairment loss is recorded for the excess of the asset book value in relation to its estimated fair value.

Aircraft and engine maintenance

The cost of scheduled inspections and repairs and routine maintenance costs for all aircraft and engines are charged to Maintenance materials and repairs expense as incurred. The Company has "power-by-the-hour" agreements related to its Boeing 737-700 engines and AirTran's Boeing 717-200 engines with external service providers. Under these agreements, which the Company has determined effectively transfer the risk associated with the maintenance on such engines to the counterparty, expense is recorded commensurate with each hour flown on an engine. The Company modified its engine maintenance contract for its Classic fleet (737-300/500s) during fourth quarter 2011 and although payments made under this contract are made under a "power-by-the-hour" basis, the risk-transfer concept under this agreement is no longer met, and the Company now records expense on a time and materials basis when an engine repair event takes place.

Modifications that significantly enhance the operating performance or extend the useful lives of aircraft or engines are capitalized and amortized over the remaining life of the asset.

Goodwill and intangible assets

Goodwill represents the excess of the consideration transferred over the fair value of AirTran's assets and liabilities on the acquisition date. See Note 2. Goodwill is not amortized, but it is evaluated for impairment at least annually, or more frequently if events or circumstances indicate impairment may exist. A fair value-based methodology is utilized in testing the carrying value to Goodwill, utilizing assumptions including: (1) a long-term projection of revenues and expenses; (2) estimated discounted future cash flows; (3) observable earnings multiples of publicly-traded airlines; (4) weighted-average cost of capital; and (5) expected tax rate. Factors used in the valuation of goodwill include, but are not limited to, management's plans for future operations, recent operating results and discounted projected future cash flows. These factors are considered Level 3 inputs within the fair value hierarchy. No goodwill impairment was noted during 2011.

Intangible assets primarily consist of acquired leasehold rights to certain airport owned gates at Chicago's Midway International Airport, take-off and landing slots at certain domestic slot-controlled airports, and certain intangible assets recognized from the AirTran acquisition. See Note 2 for further information on acquired identifiable intangible assets. The following table is a summary of the Company's intangible assets, weighted-average useful lives, and balance of accumulated amortization as of December 31, 2011:

	Gross carrying amount (in millions)	Weighted-average useful life (in years)	Accumulated amortization (in millions)
Customer relationships/marketing agreements	$ 39	4	$14
Trademarks/trade names	36	3	8
Domestic slots	63	23	4
Internally developed software	2	2	1
Noncompete agreements	5	2	1
Gate leasehold rights	60	19	22
Total	$205	14	$50

Estimated aggregate amortization expense for the five succeeding years and thereafter is as follows: 2012 – $25 million, 2013 – $19 million, 2014 – $15 million, 2015 – $13 million, 2016 – $10 million, 2017 and thereafter – $73 million.

Revenue recognition

Tickets sold are initially deferred as Air traffic liability. Passenger revenue is recognized when transportation is provided. Air traffic liability primarily represents tickets sold for future travel dates and estimated refunds and exchanges of tickets sold for past travel dates. The majority of the Company's tickets sold are nonrefundable. Tickets that are sold but not flown on the travel date (whether refundable or nonrefundable) can be reused for another flight, up to a year from the date of sale, or refunded (if the ticket is refundable). A small percentage of tickets (or partial tickets) expire unused. The Company estimates the amount of tickets that expire unused and recognizes such amounts in Passenger revenue once the scheduled flight date has passed. Amounts collected from passengers for ancillary services such as baggage and other fees are generally recognized as Other revenue when the service is provided, which is typically the flight date.

The Company is also required to collect certain taxes and fees from Customers on behalf of government agencies and remit these back to the applicable governmental entity on a periodic basis. These taxes and fees include U.S. federal transportation taxes, federal security charges, and airport passenger facility charges.

These items are collected from Customers at the time they purchase their tickets, but are not included in Passenger revenue. The Company records a liability upon collection from the Customer and relieves the liability when payments are remitted to the applicable governmental agency.

Frequent flyer programs

The Company records a liability for the estimated incremental cost of providing free travel under its (and AirTran's) frequent flyer program for all amounts earned from flight activity that are expected to be redeemed for future travel. The estimated incremental cost includes direct passenger costs such as fuel, food, and other operational costs, but does not include any contribution to overhead or profit.

Southwest and AirTran also sell frequent flyer points and/or credits and related services to companies participating in their respective frequent flyer programs. Funds received from the sale of these points and/or credits are accounted for using the residual method. Under this method, the Company has determined the portion of funds received that relate to free travel, currently estimated at 92 percent of the amount received under Southwest's Rapid Reward program and 100 percent of amounts received under AirTran's A+ Reward program as of December 31, 2011. These amounts are deferred and recognized as Passenger revenue when the ultimate free travel awards are flown or the amounts expire unused. The remainder of the amount received per points sold (the residual), which is assumed not to be associated with future travel, includes items such as access to the Company's frequent flyer program population for marketing/solicitation purposes on a monthly or quarterly basis, use of the Company's logo on co-branded credit cards, and other trademarks, designs, images, etc. of the Company for use in marketing materials. This residual portion is recognized in Other revenue in the period earned, which the Company has determined is the period in which it has fulfilled its obligation under the contract signed with the particular business partner, which is on a monthly or quarterly basis, upon sale, as the related marketing services are performed or provided.

Advertising

Advertising costs are charged to expense as incurred. Advertising and promotions expense for the years ended December 31, 2011, 2010, and 2009 was $237 million, $202 million, and $204 million, respectively, and was recorded as a component of Other operating expense in the accompanying Consolidated Statement of Income.

Share-based Employee compensation

The Company has share-based compensation plans covering several of its Employee groups, including plans covering the Company's Board of Directors. The Company accounts for share-based compensation based on its grant date fair value. See Note 15

Financial derivative instruments

The Company accounts for financial derivative instruments at fair value and applies hedge accounting rules where appropriate. The Company utilizes various derivative instruments, including crude oil, unleaded gasoline, and heating oil-based derivatives, to attempt to reduce the risk of its exposure to jet fuel price increases. These instruments consist primarily of purchased call options, collar structures, call spreads, and fixed-price swap agreements, and upon proper qualification are accounted for as cash-flow hedges. The Company also has interest rate swap agreements to convert a portion of its fixed-rate debt to floating rates and, including instruments acquired from AirTran, has swap agreements that convert certain floating-rate debt to a fixed-rate. These interest rate hedges are appropriately designated as either fair value hedges or as cash flow hedges.

Since the majority of the Company's financial derivative instruments are not traded on a market exchange, the Company estimates their fair values. Depending on the type of instrument, the values are determined by the use of present value methods or option value models with assumptions about commodity prices based on those observed in underlying markets. Also, since there is not a reliable forward market for jet fuel, the Company must estimate the future prices of jet fuel in order to measure the effectiveness of the hedging instruments in offsetting changes to those prices. Forward jet fuel prices are estimated through utilization of a statistical-based regression equation with data from market forward prices of like commodities. This equation is then adjusted for certain items, such as transportation costs, that are stated in the Company's fuel purchasing contracts with its vendors.

For the effective portion of settled fuel hedges, the Company records the associated gains or losses as a component of Fuel and oil expense in the Consolidated Statement of Income. For amounts representing ineffectiveness, as defined, or changes in fair value of derivative instruments for which hedge accounting is not applied, the Company records any gains or losses as a component of Other (gains) losses, net, in the Consolidated Statement of Income. Amounts that are paid or received in connection with the purchase or sale of financial derivative instruments (i.e., premium costs of option contracts) are classified as a component of Other (gains) losses, net, in the Consolidated Statement of Income in the period in which the instrument settles or expires. All cash flows associated with purchasing and selling derivatives are classified as operating cash flows in the Consolidated Statement of Cash Flows, within Changes in certain assets and liabilities. See Note 10 for further information on hedge accounting and financial derivative instruments.

The Company classifies its cash collateral provided to or held from counterparties in a "net" presentation on the Consolidated Balance Sheet against the fair value of the derivative positions with those counterparties. See Note 10 for further information.

Software capitalization

The Company capitalizes certain internal and external costs related to the acquisition and development of internal use software during the application development stages of projects. The Company amortizes these costs using the straight-line method over the estimated useful life of the software, which ranges from five to fifteen years. Costs incurred during the preliminary project or the post-implementation/operation stages of the project are expensed as incurred.

Income taxes

The Company accounts for deferred income taxes utilizing an asset and liability method, whereby deferred tax assets and liabilities are recognized based on the tax effect of temporary differences between the financial statements and the tax basis of assets and liabilities, as measured by current enacted tax rates. The Company also evaluates the need for a valuation allowance to reduce deferred tax assets to estimated recoverable amounts.

The Company's policy for recording interest and penalties associated with uncertain tax positions is to record such items as a component of income before income taxes. Penalties are recorded in Other (gains) losses, net, and interest paid or received is recorded in Interest expense or Interest income, respectively, in the Consolidated Statement of Income. Amounts recorded for penalties and interest related to uncertain tax positions were immaterial for all years presented.

Concentration risk

Approximately 82 percent of the Company's fulltime equivalent Employees are unionized and are covered by collective bargaining agreements, including 82 percent of Southwest's Employees and 81 percent of AirTran's Employees. Historically, the Company has managed this risk by maintaining positive relationships with its Employees and its Employee's Representatives. Southwest's Ramp, Operations, Provisioning, and Freight Agents, Aircraft Appearance Technicians, and Dispatchers are under agreements that have become amendable and are in discussions on new agreements. In addition, Southwest's Pilots, Mechanics, and Customer Service

Agents and Customer Service Representatives are subject to agreements that become amendable during 2012, which represent approximately 29 percent of the Company's (including AirTran's) fulltime equivalent Employees.

The Company attempts to minimize its concentration risk with regards to its cash, cash equivalents, and its investment portfolio. This is accomplished by diversifying and limiting amounts among different counterparties, the type of investment, and the amount invested in any individual security or money market fund.

To manage risk associated with financial derivative instruments held, the Company selects and will periodically review counterparties based on credit ratings, limits its exposure to a single counterparty, and monitors the market position of the program and its relative market position with each counterparty. The Company also has agreements with counterparties containing early termination rights and/or bilateral collateral provisions whereby security is required if market risk exposure exceeds a specified threshold amount or credit ratings fall below certain levels. Collateral deposits provided to or held from counterparties serve to decrease, but not totally eliminate, the credit risk associated with the Company's hedging program. See Note 10 for further information.

The Company (including AirTran) currently operates an all-Boeing fleet, the majority of which are variations of the Boeing 737. If the Company were unable to acquire additional aircraft or associated aircraft parts from Boeing, or Boeing were unable or unwilling to make timely deliveries of aircraft or to provide adequate support for its products, the Company's operations would be materially adversely impacted. In addition, the Company would be materially adversely impacted in the event of a mechanical or regulatory issue associated with the Boeing 737 or Boeing 717 aircraft type, whether as a result of downtime for part or all of the Company's fleet or because of a negative perception by the flying public. The Company is also dependent on sole suppliers for aircraft engines and certain other aircraft parts and would, therefore, also be materially adversely impacted in the event of the unavailability of, or a mechanical or regulatory issue associated with, engines and other parts. The Company considers its relationship with Boeing and other suppliers to be excellent and believes the advantages of operating with a single aircraft supplier currently outweigh the risks of such a strategy.

The Company has historically entered into agreements with some of its co-brand, payment, and loyalty partners that contain exclusivity aspects which place certain confidential restrictions on the Company from entering into certain arrangements with other payment and loyalty partners. These arrangements generally extend for the terms of the partnerships, none of which currently extend beyond May 2017. The Company believes the financial benefits generated by the exclusivity aspects of these arrangements outweigh the risks involved with such agreements.

APPENDIX A

Accounting for Investments

A company invests in the stock or debt securities of other firms for one or more of the following reasons:

- A company may temporarily have excess funds on which it can earn a return.
- Investments may be an integral part of the company's business, as in the case of a bank.
- A company may invest in other firms for the purpose of partnering with or controlling them.

Concepts and Management Issues Related to Investments

Recognition, *valuation*, *classification*, *disclosure*, and ethics apply to accounting for investments.

Recognition

Recognition of investments as assets follows the general rule for recording transactions described earlier in the text. Purchases of investments are recorded on the date on which they are made, and sales of investments are reported on the date of sale. At the time of the transaction, there is either a transfer of funds or a definite obligation to pay. Income from investments is reported as other income on the income statement. Any gains or losses on investments are also reported on the income statement. Gains and losses appear as adjustments in the operating activities section of the statement of cash flows. The cash amounts of purchases and sales of investments appear in the investing activities section of the statement of cash flows.

Valuation

Like other purchase transactions, investments are *valued* according to the *cost principle*—that is, their cost at the time they are purchased. This cost includes any commissions or fees. However, after the purchase, the value of investments on the balance sheet is adjusted to reflect subsequent conditions, including the following:

- Changes in the market value or fair value of the investments
- Changes caused by the passage of time (as in amortization)
- Changes in the operations of the investee companies

Long-term investments must be evaluated annually for any impairment or decline in value that is more than temporary. If such an impairment exists, a loss on the investment must be recorded.

IFRS
Under certain conditions, companies are required to measure investments at fair value. Recall that *fair value* is defined as the *exchange price* associated with an actual or potential business transaction between market participants. This requirement applies to all types of investments, except an investment in a subsidiary that is consolidated with

the parent's financial statements. Fair value is not difficult to determine when there is a ready market in which there are buyers and sellers for an asset. However, if a ready market does not exist, another valuation technique must be used. For example, valuation might be determined by referring to the current fair value of another investment that is substantially the same. If that option is not available, valuation might be determined through discounted cash flow analysis.[1] Through the convergence project of the FASB and IASB, valuation practices under GAAP have come more in line with international financial reporting standards (IFRS).

Classification

Investments in debt and equity securities are *classified* as either short-term or long-term. **Short-term investments** (or *marketable securities*) have a maturity of more than 90 days but are intended to be held only until cash is needed for current operations. (As pointed out in an earlier chapter, investments with a maturity of *less* than 90 days are classified as cash equivalents.) **Long-term investments**, which are intended to be held for more than one year, are reported in the investments section of the balance sheet. Although long-term investments may be just as marketable as short-term assets, management intends to hold them for an indefinite time.

Short-term and long-term investments must be further classified as trading securities, available-for-sale securities, or held-to-maturity securities.[2]

■ **Trading securities** are debt or equity securities bought and held principally for the purpose of being sold in the near term.
■ **Available-for-sale securities** are debt or equity securities that do not meet the criteria for either trading or held-to-maturity securities. They may be short- or long-term, depending on what management intends to do with them.
■ **Held-to-maturity securities** are debt securities that management intends to hold until their maturity date.

Exhibit 1 illustrates the classification of short- and long-term investments.

Exhibit 1
Classification of Equity Investments

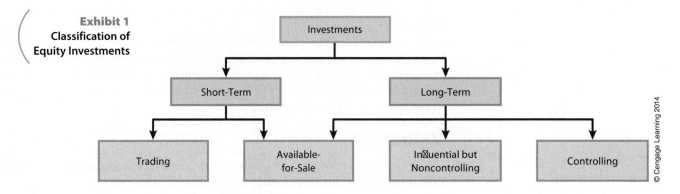

© Cengage Learning 2014

Exhibit 2 shows the accounting treatment of various levels of equity investments, that is, ownership of another company's stock. It also shows the relationship between the percentage of ownership in a company's stock and the investing company's level of control.

In general, the percentage of ownership in another company's stock has the following effects:

■ **Noninfluential and noncontrolling investment:** A firm that owns less than 20 percent of the stock of another company has no influence on the other company's operations.
■ **Influential but noncontrolling investment:** A firm that owns between 20 to 50 percent of another company's stock can exercise *significant influence* over that company's operating and financial policies, even though it holds 50 percent or less of

Exhibit 2
Accounting for
Equity Investments

Level of Control	Percentage of Ownership	Classification	Accounting Treatment
Noninfluential and noncontrolling	Less than 20%	Short-term investments— trading securities	Recorded at cost initially; cost adjusted after purchase for changes in market value; unrealized gains and losses reported on income statement
		Short-term or long-term investments— available-for-sale securities	Recorded at cost initially; cost adjusted for changes in market value with unrealized gains and losses to other comprehensive income
Influential but noncontrolling	Between 20% and 50%	Long-term investments	Equity method: recorded at cost initially; cost subsequently adjusted for investor's share of net income or loss and for dividends received
Controlling	More than 50%	Long-term investments	Financial statements consolidated

the voting stock. Indications of significant influence include representation on the board of directors, participation in policymaking, exchange of managerial personnel, and technological dependency between the two companies.

■ **Controlling investment:** A firm that owns more than 50 percent of another company's stock.

Disclosure

Companies provide detailed information about their investments and how they account for them in the notes to their financial statements. Such *disclosures* help users assess the impact of the investments.

Ethics of Investing

When a company engages in investment transactions, there is always the possibility that its employees may use their knowledge about the transactions for personal gain. In the United States, **insider trading**, or making use of inside information for personal gain, is unethical and illegal. Before a publicly held company releases significant information about an investment to its stockholders and the general public, its officers and employees are not allowed to buy or sell stock in the company or in the firm whose shares the company is buying. Only after the information is released to the public can insiders engage in such trading. The Securities and Exchange Commission vigorously prosecutes any individual, whether employed by the company in question or not, who buys or sells shares of a publicly held company based on information not yet available to the public.

Not all countries prohibit insider trading. Until recently, insider trading was legal in Germany; but with the goal of expanding its securities markets, that country reformed its securities laws. It established the Federal Authority for Securities Trading (FAST), in part to oversee insider trading. However, historically, FAST devotes few staff members to investigations of insider trading, whereas the SEC has a much larger staff for these types of investigations.[3] Other countries continue to permit insider trading.

Short-Term Investments in Trading Securities

As pointed out earlier, all trading securities are short-term investments, while available-for-sale securities may be either short-term or long-term.

Trading Securities

Trading securities are always short-term investments and are frequently bought and sold to generate profits on short-term changes in their prices. They are *classified* as current assets on the balance sheet and are *valued* at fair value, which is usually the same as market value. An increase or decrease in the fair value of a company's total trading portfolio (the group of securities it holds for trading purposes) is included in net income in the period in which the increase or decrease occurs.

Purchase of Trading Securities

Transaction Jackson Company buys 10,000 shares of **IBM** for $900,000 ($90 per share) and 10,000 shares of **Microsoft** for $300,000 ($30 per share) on October 25, 2014. The purchase is made for trading purposes—that is, Jackson's management intends to realize a gain by holding the shares for only a short period.

Analysis The journal entry to record the investment at cost

> ▲ *increases Short-Term Investments* with a debit for the cost of $1,200,000 ($900,000 + $300,000)
>
> ▼ *decreases Cash* with a credit of $1,200,000

Journal Entry

A	=	L	+	OE
+1,200,000				
−1,200,000				

2014			
Oct. 25	Short-Term Investments	1,200,000	
	Cash		1,200,000
	To record investment in stocks for trading		
	($900,000 + $300,000 = $1,200,000)		

Comment This investment is *classified* as short-term, because the intent is to resell the securities in the near future rather than to hold them for more than one year.

Year-End Valuation and Adjustment

Transaction At year-end, **IBM**'s stock price has decreased to $80 per share and **Microsoft**'s has risen to $32 per share. The trading portfolio is now *valued* at $1,120,000:

Security	Market Value	Cost	Gain (Loss)
IBM (10,000 shares)	$ 800,000	$ 900,000	$(100,000)
Microsoft (10,000 shares)	320,000	300,000	20,000
Totals	$1,120,000	$1,200,000	$ (80,000)

Analysis Because the current fair value of the portfolio is $80,000 less than the original cost of $1,200,000, an *unrealized loss* has occurred. The journal entry to record the year-end adjustment

> ▲ *increases Unrealized Loss on Short-Term Investments* with a debit for the cost of $80,000
>
> ▲ *increases Allowance to Adjust Short-Term Investments to Market* with a credit of $80,000

A	=	L	+	OE
−80,000				−80,000

Journal Entry

2014			
Dec. 31	Unrealized Loss on Short-Term Investments	80,000	
	Allowance to Adjust Short-Term Investments to Market		80,000
	To record unrealized loss on trading portfolio		

Comment The unrealized loss will appear on the income statement as a reduction in income. The loss is unrealized because the securities have not been sold. If unrealized gains occur due to the increase in *value* of the portfolio, they are treated the same way.

The Allowance to Adjust Short-Term Investments to Market account appears on the balance sheet as a contra-asset, as follows.

Short-term investments (at cost)	$1,200,000
Less allowance to adjust short-term investments to market	80,000
Short-term investments (at market)	$1,120,000

Or, more simply:

Short-term investments (at market value, cost is $1,200,000)	$1,120,000

Sale of Trading Securities

Transaction Jackson sells its 10,000 shares of **Microsoft** for $35 per share on March 2, 2015.

Analysis The journal entry to record a realized gain on trading securities

▲ *increases Cash* with a debit for the selling price of $350,000

▼ *decreases Short-Term Investments* with a credit of $300,000

▲ *increases Gain on Sale of Investments* with a credit for the difference of $50,000

Journal Entry

A	=	L	+	OE
+350,000				+50,000
−300,000				

2015			
Mar. 2	Cash	350,000	
	Short-Term Investments		300,000
	Gain on Sale of Investments		50,000
	To record sale of 10,000 shares of Microsoft for $35 per share; cost was $30 per share		

Comment The realized gain will appear on the income statement. The realized gain is unaffected by the adjustment for the unrealized loss at the end of 2014. The two transactions are treated independently. If the stock had been sold for less than cost, a realized loss on investments would have been recorded. Realized losses also appear on the income statement.

Year-End Valuation and Adjustment

Transaction During 2015, Jackson buys 4,000 shares of **Apple** at $32 per share and has no transactions involving its shares of **IBM**. By December 31, 2015, the price of IBM's stock has risen to $95 per share, or $5 per share more than the original cost, and Apple's stock price has fallen to $29, or $3 less than the original cost. We can now analyze Jackson's trading portfolio as follows.

Security	Market Value	Cost	Gain (Loss)
IBM (10,000 shares)	$ 950,000	$ 900,000	$ 50,000
Apple (4,000 shares)	116,000	128,000	(12,000)
Totals	$1,066,000	$1,028,000	$ 38,000

Analysis The market value of Jackson's trading portfolio now exceeds the cost by $38,000 ($1,066,000 − $1,028,000). This amount represents the targeted ending balance for the Allowance to Adjust Short-Term Investments to Market account. Recall that at the end of 2014, that account had a credit balance of $80,000, meaning that the market value of the trading portfolio was less than the cost. Because no entries are made to the account during 2015, it retains its balance until adjusting entries are made at the end of the year. The adjustment for 2015 must be $118,000—enough to result in a debit balance of $38,000 in the allowance account. The journal entry to record the year-end adjustment

▼ *decreases Allowance to Adjust Short-Term Investments to Market* with a debit of $118,000

▲ *increases Unrealized Gain on Short-Term Investments* with a credit of $118,000

Journal Entry

A	=	L	+	OE
+118,000				+118,000

2015			
Dec. 31	Allowance to Adjust Short-Term		
	Investments to Market	118,000	
	Unrealized Gain on Short-Term Investments		118,000
	To record unrealized gain on trading portfolio		
	($80,000 + $38,000 = $118,000)		

Comment The 2015 ending balance of Jackson's allowance account can be determined as follows.

Allowance to Adjust Short-Term Investments to Market			
Dec. 31, 2015 Adj.	118,000	Dec. 31, 2014 Bal.	80,000
Dec. 31, 2015 Bal.	38,000		

Short-term investments are presented on the balance sheet as follows.

Short-term investments (at cost)	$1,028,000
Plus allowance to adjust short-term investments to market	38,000
Short-term investments (at market)	$1,066,000

Or, more simply:

Short-term investments (at market value, cost is $1,028,000)	$1,066,000

Available-for-Sale Securities

Short-term available-for-sale securities are accounted for in the same way as trading securities, with two exceptions:

- An unrealized gain or loss is reported as other comprehensive income (loss).
- If a decline in the value of a security is considered permanent, it is charged as a loss on the income statement.

Long-Term Investments in Equity Securities

The accounting treatment of long-term investments in equity securities, such as common stock, depends on the extent to which the investing company can exercise control over the other company.

Noninfluential and Noncontrolling Investment

As noted earlier, available-for-sale securities are debt or equity securities that cannot be *classified* as trading or held-to-maturity securities. When long-term equity securities are involved, a further criterion for classifying them as available for sale is that they be non-influential and noncontrolling investments of less than 20 percent of the voting stock. Accounting for long-term available-for-sale securities requires using the **cost-adjusted-to-market method**. With this method, the securities are initially recorded at cost and are thereafter adjusted periodically for changes in market value by using an allowance account.[4]

Available-for-sale securities are *classified* as long term if management *intends* to hold them for more than one year. When accounting for long-term available-for-sale securities, the unrealized gain or loss resulting from the adjustment is reported as other comprehensive income (loss).

At the end of each accounting period, the total cost and the total market value of these long-term investments must be determined. If the total market value is less than the total cost, the difference must be credited to a contra-asset account called Allowance to Adjust Long-Term Investments to Market. Because of the long-term nature of the investment, the debit part of the entry, which represents a decrease in value below cost, is treated as a temporary decrease and does not appear as a loss on the income statement. It is shown in an account called Unrealized Loss on Long-Term Investments.* This account is reported on a statement of other comprehensive income. If the market value exceeds the cost, the allowance account is added to Long-Term Investments, and the unrealized gain appears on the statement of other comprehensive income.

When a company sells its long-term investments in stock, the difference between the sale price and the cost of the stock is recorded and reported as a realized gain or loss on the income statement. Dividend income from such investments is recorded by a debit to Cash and a credit to Dividend Income.

In the sections that follow, we show how to account for Nardini Corporation's purchase and sale of long-term investments in equity securities of two corporations—Herald and Taza.

Purchase of a Long-Term Investment

Transaction On June 1, 2014, Nardini Corporation paid cash for the following long-term investments: 10,000 shares of Herald Corporation common stock (representing 2 percent of outstanding stock) at $25 per share; 5,000 shares of Taza Corporation common stock (representing 3 percent of outstanding stock) at $15 per share.

Analysis The journal entry to record the investment at cost

▲ *increases Long-Term Investments* with a debit of $325,000

▼ *decreases Cash* with a credit of $325,000

Journal Entry

A	=	L	+	OE				
+325,000					2014			
−325,000					June 1	Long-Term Investments	325,000	
						Cash		325,000
						To record investments in Herald common stock (10,000 shares × $25 = $250,000) and Taza common stock (5,000 shares × $15 = $75,000)		

---

* If the decrease in market value of a long-term investment is deemed permanent or if the investment is deemed impaired, the decline or impairment is recorded by debiting a loss account that will affect the income statement instead of the Unrealized Loss account.

Comment These investments are *classified* as long term because of management's intent to hold them more than one year.

Year-End Adjustment

Transaction At the end of 2014, the market price of Herald's common stock is $21; the market price of Taza's is $17.

Analysis Nardini Corporation's trading portfolio is now *valued* at $295,000:

Company	Shares	Market Price	Total Market	Total Cost
Herald	10,000	$21	$210,000	$250,000
Taza	5,000	17	85,000	75,000
			$295,000	$325,000

Because the current fair value of the portfolio is $30,000 less than the original cost of $325,000, an *unrealized* loss has occurred. The journal entry to record the year-end adjustment

- ▲ *increases Unrealized Loss on Long-Term Investments* with a debit of $30,000
- ▲ *increases Allowance to Adjust Long-Term Investments to Market* with a credit of $30,000

Journal Entry

A	=	L	+	OE
−30,000				−30,000

2014			
Dec. 31	Unrealized Loss on Long-Term Investments	30,000	
	Allowance to Adjust Long-Term Investments to Market		30,000
	To record reduction of long-term investment		
	to market		

Comment As noted previously, the Unrealized Loss on Long-Term Investments does not appear on the income statement but appears on the statement of other comprehensive income. The Allowance to Adjust Long-Term Investments to Market is a contra-asset account that reduces investments on the balance sheet.

Sale of a Long-Term Investment

Transaction On April 1, 2015, a change in policy required the sale of 2,000 shares of Herald common stock at $23.

Analysis The journal entry to record this sale

- ▲ *increases Cash* with a debit for the selling price of $46,000
- ▲ *increases Loss on Sale of Investments* with a debit of $4,000
- ▼ *decreases Long-Term Investments* with a credit of $50,000

Journal Entry

A	=	L	+	OE
+46,000				−4,000
−50,000				

2015			
Apr. 1	Cash	46,000	
	Loss on Sale of Investments	4,000	
	Long-Term Investments*		50,000
	To record sale of 2,000 shares of Herald common stock		

*2,000 × $23 = $46,000
2,000 × $25 =   50,000
Loss $ 4,000

Comment Nardini's sale of stock was the result of a change in policy. This illustrates that *intent* is often the only difference between long-term investments and short-term investments.

Cash Dividend Received

Transaction On July 1, 2015, Nardini received a cash dividend from Taza equal to $0.20 per share.

Analysis The journal entry to record the cash dividend received

▲ *increases Cash* with a debit of $1,000 ($0.20 × 5,000 shares)

▲ *increases Dividend Income* with a credit of $1,000

Journal Entry

2015			
July 1	Cash	1,000	
	Dividend Income		1,000
	To record receipt of cash dividend from Taza stock		
	(5,000 × $0.20 = $1,000)		

Comment Dividend Income is *classified* on the income statement as other income below operating income.

Year-End Adjustment

Transaction At the end of 2015, the market price of Herald's common stock was $24; the market price of Taza's was $13.

Analysis The trading portfolio is now *valued* at $257,000:

Company	Shares	Market Price	Total Market	Total Cost
Herald	8,000	$24	$192,000	$200,000
Taza	5,000	13	65,000	75,000
			$257,000	$275,000

The adjustment will equal the previous balance ($30,000 from the December 31, 2014, entry) minus the new balance ($18,000), or $12,000. The new balance of $18,000 is the difference at the present time between the total market value and the total cost of all investments ($257,000). The journal entry to record the year-end adjustment

▲ *increases Allowance to Adjust Long-Term Investments to Market* with a debit of $12,000

▼ *decreases Unrealized Loss on Long-Term Investments* with a credit of $12,000

Journal Entry

2015			
Dec. 31	Allowance to Adjust Long-Term		
	Investments to Market	12,000	
	Unrealized Loss on Long-Term Investments		12,000
	To record the adjustment in long-term		
	investment so it is reported at market		

Comment Even though the portfolio increased in value from last year, it did not result in a credit to unrealized gain. It reduced the unrealized loss from last year. Only if the entire unrealized loss had been eliminated would an unrealized gain be recorded for the difference.

Also, the Allowance to Adjust Long-Term Investments to Market and the Unrealized Loss on Long-Term Investments are reciprocal accounts, each with the same dollar balance:

▼ The *Allowance* account *reduces* long-term investments by the amount by which the cost of the investments exceeds market.

▼ The *Unrealized Loss* account *reduces* other comprehensive income by a similar amount.

The effects of these transactions on T accounts are as follows.

Allowance to Adjust Long-Term Investments to Market (A Contra-Asset Account)			
Dec. 31, 2015 Adj.	12,000	Dec. 31, 2014 Bal.	30,000
		Dec. 31, 2015 Bal.	18,000

Unrealized Loss on Long-Term Investments (A Contra-Equity Account)			
Dec. 31, 2014 Bal.	30,000	Dec. 31, 2015 Adj.	12,000
Dec. 31, 2015 Bal.	18,000		

The opposite effects will exist if market value exceeds cost, resulting in an unrealized gain.

An Influential but Noncontrolling Investment

As noted, ownership of 20 percent or more of a company's voting stock is considered sufficient to influence the company's operations. When that is the case, the **equity method** should be used to account for the stock investment. The equity method presumes that an investment of 20 percent or more is not a passive investment and that the investor should therefore share proportionately in the success or failure of the company. The three main features of this method are as follows.

■   The investor records the original purchase of the stock at cost.
■   The investor records its share of the company's periodic net income as an increase in the Investment account, with a corresponding credit to an income account. Similarly, it records its share of a periodic loss as a decrease in the Investment account, with a corresponding debit to a loss account.
■   When the investor receives a cash dividend, the Cash account is increased, and the Investment account is decreased.

In the sections that follow, we use the equity method to account for ITO Corporation's purchase and sale of long-term investments in equity securities.

Purchase of an Equity Investment

Transaction   On January 1 2014, ITO Corporation acquired 40 percent of Quay Corporation's voting common stock for $180,000.

Analysis   The journal entry to record the investment at cost

▲ *increases Investment in Quay Corporation* with a debit of $180,000

▼ *decreases Cash* with a credit of $180,000

Journal Entry

A	=	L +	OE
+180,000			
−180,000			

2014			
Jan. 1	Investment in Quay Corporation	180,000	
	Cash		180,000
	To record investment in Quay Corporation common stock for a 40 percent ownership		

Comment   This entry is similar to the entries made for other investments, but note that with a 40 percent share of ownership, ITO can exert significant influence over Quay's operations.

Recognition of Income

Transaction On December 31, 2014, Quay reported income of $80,000.

Analysis Because ITO can exert significant influence over Quay, 40 percent of Quay's earnings, or $32,000 (40% × $80,000), is considered to be ITO's. The journal entry to recognize income

▲ *increases Investment in Quay Corporation* with a debit of $32,000

▲ *increases Income, Quay Corporation Investment* with a credit of $32,000

Journal Entry

A = **L** + **OE**	
+32,000 +32,000	

2014			
Dec. 31	Investment in Quay Corporation	32,000	
	Income, Quay Corporation Investment		32,000
	To record 40% of income reported by Quay		
	Corporation (40% × $80,000 = $32,000)		

Comment Note that ITO's share of Quay's income will appear on ITO's income statement.

Receipt of Cash Dividend

Transaction Quay paid cash dividends of $8,000 on December 31, 2014.

Analysis Because ITO can exert significant influence over Quay, the amount of the cash dividend, or $8,000 (40% × $20,000), received from Quay is considered a reduction of ITO's investment in Quay. The journal entry to record the dividend

▲ *increases Cash* with a debit of $8,000

▼ *decreases Investment in Quay Corporation* with a credit of $8,000

Journal Entry

A = **L** + **OE**	
+8,000	
−8,000	

2014			
Dec. 31	Cash	8,000	
	Investment in Quay Corporation		8,000
	To record cash dividend from Quay Corporation		
	(40% × $20,000 = $8,000)		

Comment The balance of the Investment in Quay Corporation account after these transactions is $204,000, as follows.

Investment in Quay Corporation			
Jan. 1, 2014 Investment	180,000	Dec. 31, 2014 Dividend received	8,000
Dec. 31, 2014 Share of income	32,000		
Dec. 31, 2014 Balance	204,000		

The share of income is reported as a separate line item on the income statement as a part of income from operations. The dividends received affect cash flows from operating activities on the statement of cash flows. The reported income of $32,000 exceeds the cash received by $24,000.

A Controlling Investment

Some firms that own less than 50 percent of another company's voting stock exercise such powerful influence that, for all practical purposes, they control the other company's policies. Nevertheless, ownership of more than 50 percent of the voting stock is required for accounting recognition of control. When a firm has a controlling interest in another company, a parent-subsidiary relationship is said to exist. The investing company is the **parent company**; the other company is a **subsidiary**.

Because a parent company and its subsidiaries are separate legal entities, each prepares separate financial statements. However, because of their special relationship, they are viewed for external financial reporting purposes as a single economic entity. For this reason, the FASB requires that they combine their financial statements into a single set of statements called **consolidated financial statements**.**

Investments in Debt Securities

As noted in previous chapters, debt securities are considered financial instruments because they are claims that will be paid in cash. When a company purchases debt securities, it records them at cost plus any commissions and fees. Like investments in equity securities, short-term investments in debt securities are *valued* at fair value at the end of the period and are accounted for as trading securities or available-for-sale securities. However, the accounting treatment is different if they qualify as held-to-maturity securities.

Held-to-Maturity Securities

As noted earlier, held-to-maturity securities are debt securities that management intends to hold to their maturity date. Such securities are recorded at cost and are *valued* on the balance sheet at cost adjusted for the effects of interest. In the sections that follow, we show how to account for the purchase and sale of investments in debt securities for Webber Company.

Purchase of Held-to-Maturity Securities

Transaction On December 1, 2014, Webber Company pays $97,000 for U.S. Treasury bills, which are short-term debt of the federal government. The bills will mature in 120 days at $100,000.

Analysis Webber would record the purchase much as it would other short-term investments. Thus, the journal entry to record the investment at cost

▲ *increases Short-Term Investments* with a debit for the cost of $97,000

▼ *decreases Cash* with a credit for $97,000

Journal Entry

2014		
Dec. 1	Short-Term Investments	97,000
	Cash	97,000
	To record purchase of U.S. Treasury bills that mature in 120 days	

A = **L** + **OE**
+97,000
−97,000

Comment If the maturity date of the treasury bills were less than 90 days, they would be *classified* as cash equivalents, rather than short-term investments.

Year-End Accrual of Interest

Transaction At Webber's year-end on December 31, the interest income earned to date must be accrued in an adjusting entry.

Analysis The journal entry to record the year-end adjustment

▲ *increases Short-Term Investments* with a debit for the accrued interest of $750 ($3,000 × 30/120)

▲ *increases Interest Income* with a credit for $750

**The concepts and procedures related to the preparation of consolidated financial statements are the subject of more advanced courses.

Journal Entry

A	=	L	+	OE
+750				+750

2014			
Dec. 31	Short-Term Investments	750	
	Interest Income		750
	To record accrual of interest on U.S. Treasury bills		
	($3,000 × 30/120 = $750)		

Comment On December 31, the U.S. Treasury bills would be shown on the balance sheet as a short-term investment at their amortized cost of $97,750 ($97,000 + $750). The market *value* of the investment is ignored.

Receipt of Interest

Transaction On March 31, 2015, Webber receives the maturity value of the treasury notes.

Analysis The journal entry to record the receipt of interest

▲ *increases Cash* with a debit for the maturity value of $100,000

▼ *decreases Short-Term Investments* with a credit for $97,750

▲ *increases Interest Income* by a credit of the difference of $2,250

Journal Entry

A	=	L	+	OE
+100,000				+2,250
−97,750				

2015			
Mar. 31	Cash	100,000	
	Short-Term Investments		97,750
	Interest Income		2,250
	To record receipt of cash at maturity of U.S. Treasury		
	bills and recognition of related income		

Comment Note that the total interest income of $3,000 has been divided into the amount earned in 2014 ($750) and the amount earned in 2015 ($2,250). There is no gain or loss on the transaction.

Long-Term Investments in Bonds

Like all investments, investments in bonds are recorded at cost, which, in this case, is the price of the bonds plus the broker's commission. When bonds are purchased between interest payment dates, the purchaser must also pay an amount equal to the interest that has accrued on the bonds since the last interest payment date. Then, on the next interest payment date, the purchaser receives an interest payment for the whole period. The payment for accrued interest should be recorded as a debit to Interest Income, which will be offset by a credit to Interest Income when the semiannual interest is received.

Subsequent accounting for a corporation's long-term bond investments depends on the *classification* of the bonds. If the company plans to hold the bonds until they are paid off on their maturity date, they are considered held-to-maturity securities. Except in industries like insurance and banking, it is unusual for companies to buy the bonds of other companies with the express purpose of holding them until they mature, which can be in 10 to 30 years. Thus, most long-term bond investments are classified as available-for-sale securities, meaning that the company plans to sell them at some point before their maturity date. Such bonds are accounted for at fair value, much as equity or stock investments are. Fair value is usually the market value. When bonds are intended to be held to maturity, they are accounted for not at fair value but at cost, adjusted for the amortization of their discount or premium. The procedure is similar to accounting for long-term bond liabilities, except that separate accounts for discounts and premiums are not used.

Key Terms

Chapter Assignments

DISCUSSION QUESTIONS

1. What is the role of fair value in accounting for investments?

2. What are the differences between trading securities, available-for-sale securities, and held-to-maturity securities?

3. Why are the level and percentage of ownership important in accounting for equity investments?

4. How are trading securities valued at the balance sheet date?

5. What are unrealized gains and losses on trading securities? On what statement are they reported?

6. How does accounting for available-for-sale securities differ from accounting for trading securities?

7. At what value are held-to-maturity securities shown on the balance sheet?

PROBLEMS

Trading Securities

✔ 2: Total cost: $408,000
✔ 2: Total market: $442,000

P1. Omar Corporation, which has begun investing in trading securities, engaged in the following transactions:

Jan.   6   Purchased 7,000 shares of Quaker Oats stock, $30 per share.
Feb. 15   Purchased 9,000 shares of EG&G, $22 per share.

At year-end on June 30, Quaker Oats was trading at $40 per share, and EG&G was trading at $18 per share.

REQUIRED

1. Prepare journal entries to record the purchases.
2. Record the necessary year-end adjusting entry. (Include a schedule of the trading portfolio cost and market in the explanation.)
3. Prepare the journal entry to record the sale of all the EG&G shares on August 20 for $16 per share. Is this entry affected by the June 30 adjustment?

Methods of Accounting for Long-Term Investments

P2. L Teague Corporation has the following long-term investments:

Investment	Percentage of Ownership
1. Ariel Corporation common stock	60%
2. Copper, Inc. common stock	13%
3. Staffordshire Corporation nonvoting preferred stock	50%
4. EQ, Inc. common stock	100%
5. Rue de le Brasseur (of France) common stock	35%
6. Nova Scotia Cannery (of Canada) common stock	70%

REQUIRED

For each of these investments, tell which of the following methods should be used for external financial reporting, and why:

a. Cost-adjusted-to-market method

b. Equity method

c. Consolidation of parent and subsidiary financial statements

Long-Term Investments

✔ Total unrealized loss: $60,000

P3. Fulco Corporation has the following portfolio of long-term available-for-sale securities at year-end, December 31, 2014:

Company	Percentage of Voting Stock Held	Cost	Year-End Market Value
A Corporation	4%	$ 80,000	$ 95,000
B Corporation	12%	375,000	275,000
C Corporation	5%	30,000	55,000
Total		$485,000	$425,000

Both the Unrealized Loss on Long-Term Investments account and the Allowance to Adjust Long-Term Investments to Market account currently have a balance of $40,000 from the last accounting period.

REQUIRED

Prepare T accounts with a beginning balance for each of these accounts. Record the effects of the above information on the accounts, and determine the ending balances.

Long-Term Investments: Cost-Adjusted-to-Market and Equity Methods

✔ Value of Curry: $2,045,000

P4. On January 1, Rourke Corporation purchased, as long-term investments, 8 percent of the voting stock of Taglia Corporation for $250,000 and 45 percent of the voting stock of Curry Corporation for $2 million. During the year, Taglia had earnings of $100,000 and paid dividends of $40,000. Curry had earnings of $300,000 and paid dividends of $200,000. The market value did not change for either investment during the year.

REQUIRED

Which of these investments should be accounted for using the cost-adjusted-to-market method? Which should be accounted for using the equity method? At what amount should each investment be carried on the balance sheet at year-end? Give your reasoning for each choice.

Held-to-Maturity Securities

SPREADSHEET

✔ 2014 Interest Income: $2,000

P5. Dale Company experiences heavy sales in the summer and early fall, after which time it has excess cash to invest until the next spring. On November 1, 2014, the company invested $194,000 in U.S. Treasury bills. The bills mature in 180 days at $200,000.

REQUIRED

Prepare journal entries to record the purchase on November 1; the adjustment to accrue interest on December 31, which is the end of the fiscal year; and the receipt of cash at the maturity date of April 30, 2015.

Comprehensive: Accounting for Investments

P6. Gulf Coast Corporation is a successful oil and gas exploration business in the south-western United States. At the beginning of 2014, the company made investments in three companies that perform services in the oil and gas industry. The details of each of these investments follow.

Gulf Coast purchased 100,000 shares of Marsh Service Corporation at a cost of $16 per share. Marsh has 1.5 million shares outstanding and, during 2014, paid dividends of $0.80 per share on earnings of $1.60 per share. At the end of the year, Marsh's shares were selling for $24 per share.

Gulf Coast also purchased 2 million shares of Crescent Drilling Company at $8 per share. Crescent has 10 million shares outstanding. In 2014, Crescent paid a dividend of $0.40 per share on earnings of $0.80 per share. During the year, the president of Gulf Coast was appointed to Crescent's board of directors. At the end of the year, Crescent's stock was selling for $12 per share.

In another action, Gulf Coast purchased 1 million shares of Logan Oil Field Supplies Company's 5 million outstanding shares at $12 per share. The president of Gulf Coast sought membership on Logan's board of directors but was rebuffed when a majority of shareholders stated they did not want to be associated with Gulf Coast. Therefore, Gulf Coast did not gain a significant influence over Logan. Logan paid a dividend of $0.80 per share and reported a net income of only $0.40 per share for the year. By the end of the year, its stock price had dropped to $4 per share.

REQUIRED

1. For each investment, prepare journal entries to record the (a) initial investment, (b) receipt of cash dividend, and (c) recognition of income (if appropriate).
2. What adjusting entry (if any) is required at the end of the year?
3. Assuming that Gulf Coast sells its investment in Logan after the first of the year for $6 per share, what journal entry would be made?
4. Assuming no other transactions occur and that the market value of Gulf Coast's investment in Marsh exceeds cost by $2,400,000 at the end of the second year, what adjusting entry (if any) would be required?
5. What principal factors were considered in determining how to account for Gulf Coast's investments? Should they be shown on the balance sheet as short-term or long-term investments? What factors affect this decision?

Long-Term Investments: Equity Method

P7. Rylander Corporation owns 35 percent of the voting stock of Waters Corporation. The Investment account on Rylander's books as of January 1, 2014 was $720,000. During 2014, Waters reported the following quarterly earnings and dividends:

Quarter	Earnings	Dividends Paid
1	$160,000	$100,000
2	240,000	100,000
3	120,000	100,000
4	(80,000)	100,000
	$440,000	$400,000

Because of the percentage of voting shares Rylander owns, it can exercise significant influence over Waters' operations. Therefore, Rylander must account for the investment using the equity method.

REQUIRED

1. Prepare a T account for Rylander's investment in Waters, and enter the beginning balance, the relevant entries for the year in total, and the ending balance.
2. What is the effect and placement of the entries in requirement 1 on Rylander's earnings as reported on the income statement?
3. What is the effect and placement of the entries in requirement 1 on the statement of cash flows?
4. How would the effects on the statements differ if Rylander's ownership represented only a 15 percent share of Waters?

APPENDIX B

The Time Value of Money

The **time value of money** is the concept that cash flows of equal dollar amounts separated by an interval of time have different present values because of the effect of compound interest. The notions of interest, present value, present value of an ordinary annuity, and annuity due are all related to the time value of money.

Interest

Interest is the cost associated with the use of money for a specific period of time.

Simple Interest

Measure **Simple interest** is the interest cost for one or more periods when the amount on which the interest is computed stays the same from period to period.

Example If you accept an 8 percent, $30,000 note due in 90 days, how much will you receive in total when the note comes due?

$$\text{Interest Expense} = \text{Principal} \times \text{Rate} \times \text{Time}$$
$$= \$30,000 \times 8/100 \times 90/360$$
$$= \underline{\$600}$$

The total that you will receive is computed as follows.

$$\text{Total} = \text{Principal} + \text{Interest}$$
$$= \$30,000 + \$600$$
$$= \underline{\$30,600}$$

Compound Interest

Measure **Compound interest** is the interest cost for two or more periods when the amount on which interest is computed includes all interest paid in previous periods.

Example You make a deposit of $5,000 in a savings account that pays 6 percent interest. You expect to leave the principal and accumulated interest in the account for three years. What will be your account balance at the end of the three years? Assuming that the interest is paid at the end of the year, that the interest is added to the principal at that time, and that this total in turn earns interest, the amount at the end of three years is computed as follows.

(1) Year	(2) Principal Amount at Beginning of Year	(3) Annual Amount of Interest (Col. 2 × 0.06)	(4) Accumulated Amount at End of Year (Col. 2 + Col. 3)
1	$5,000.00	$300.00	$5,300.00
2	5,300.00	318.00	5,618.00
3	5,618.00	337.08	5,955.08

At the end of three years, you will have $5,955.08 in your savings account.

Present Value

Present Value

Measure **Present value** is the amount that must be invested today at a given rate of compound interest to produce a given value at a future date.

Example Home State Bank needs $1,000 one year from now. How much should it invest today to achieve that goal if the interest rate is 5 percent?

$$\text{Present Value} \times (1.0 + \text{Interest Rate}) = \text{Future Value}$$
$$\text{Present Value} \times 1.05 = \$1,000.00$$
$$\text{Present Value} = \$1,000.00 \div 1.05$$
$$= \$952.38^*$$

*Rounded

Thus, to achieve a future value of $1,000.00, a present value of $952.38 must be invested. Interest of 5 percent on $952.38 for one year equals $47.62, and the two amounts added together equal $1,000.00.

Present Value of a Single Sum Due in the Future

Measure Present value that must be invested today at a given rate of compound interest to produce a given value at a date multiple time periods in the future.

Example Home State Bank wants to be sure of having $4,000 at the end of three years. How much must the company invest today in a 5 percent savings account to achieve that goal?

Manual Computation By adapting the preceding equation, the present value of $4,000 at compound interest of 5 percent for three years in the future may be computed as follows.

Year	Amount at End of Year	÷	1.0 + Interest Rate	=	Present Value at Beginning of Year
3	$4,000.00	÷	1.05	=	$3,809.52
2	3,809.52	÷	1.05	=	3,628.11
1	3,628.11	÷	1.05	=	3,455.34

Home State Bank must invest a present value of $3,455.34 to achieve a future value of $4,000 in three years.

Table Computation Table 1 is used to compute the value today of a single amount of cash to be received sometime in the future. To use Table 1, you must first know (1) the time period in years until funds will be received, (2) the stated annual rate of interest, and (3) the dollar amount to be received at the end of the time period.

In Table 1, look down the 5 percent column, finding the row for period 3. The factor there is 0.864. Multiplied by $1, this factor gives the present value of $1 to be received three years from now at 5 percent interest. For Home State Bank, the present value would be solved as follows.

$$\text{Present Value} = \text{Future Value} \times \text{Present Value Factor}$$
$$= \$4,000 \times 0.864$$
$$= \$3,456$$

Except for a rounding difference of $0.66, this gives the same result as the previous calculation.

The factor values for Table 1 are:

$$\text{PV Factor} = (1 + r)^{-n}$$

Where r is the rate of interest and n is the number of time periods.

Present Value of an Ordinary Annuity

STUDY NOTE: *The first payment of an ordinary annuity is always made at the end of the first year.*

Measure When we calculate the present value of equal amounts equally spaced over a period of time, we are computing the present value of an ordinary annuity. An **ordinary annuity** is a series of equal payments or receipts that will begin one time period from the current date.

Example Home State Bank has sold a piece of property and is to receive $15,000 in three equal annual cash payments of $5,000, beginning one year from today. What is the present value of this sale, assuming a current interest rate of 5 percent?

Manual Computation This present value can be determined by calculating a separate present value for each of the three payments (using Table 1) and summing the results, as follows.

Future Cash Receipts (Annuity)						
Year 1	Year 2	Year 3		Present Value Factor at 5 Percent (from Table 1)		Present Value
$5,000			×	0.952	=	$ 4,760
	$5,000		×	0.907	=	4,535
		$5,000	×	0.864	=	4,320
Total present value						$13,615

The present value of this sale is $13,615. Thus, there is an implied interest cost (given the 5 percent rate) of $1,385 associated with the payment plan that allows the purchaser to pay in three installments.

Table Computation Table 2 is used to compute the present value of a *series* of *equal* annual cash flows. Using Table 2, look down the 5 percent column, finding the row for period 3. The factor there is 2.723. That factor, when multiplied by $1, gives the present value of a series of three $1 payments, spaced one year apart, at compound interest of 5 percent. For Home State Bank, the present value would be solved as follows.

$$\text{Present Value} = \text{Periodic Payment} \times \text{Present Value Factor}$$
$$= \$5,000 \times 2.723$$
$$= \underline{\$13,615}$$

This result is the same as the one computed earlier.

The factor values for Table 2 are:

$$\text{PV Factor} = \frac{1 - (1+r)^{-n}}{r}$$

Where r is the rate of interest and n is the number of time periods.

To summarize, if Home State Bank is willing to accept a 5 percent rate of return, management will be equally satisfied to receive a single cash payment of $13,615 today or three equal annual cash payments of $5,000 spread over the next three years.

Present Value of an Annuity Due

Measure An **annuity due** is a series of equal cash flows for N time periods, but the first payment occurs immediately. The present value of the first payment equals the face value of the cash flow; Table 2 then is used to measure the present value of N − 1 remaining cash flows.

Table Computation Home State Bank will make 20 lease payments; each payment of $10,000 is due on January 1, beginning in 2014. Determine the present value on January 1, 2014, assuming an interest rate of 8 percent.

$$\text{Present Value} = \text{Immediate Payment} + \text{Present Value of 19 Subsequent Payments at 8\%}$$
$$= \$10,000 + (\$10,000 \times 9.604)$$
$$= \underline{\$106,040}$$

APPLY IT!

For each of the following situations, identify the correct factor(s) to use from Table 1 or 2. Then use the factor(s) to compute the appropriate present value.

1. Annual net cash inflows of $35,000 for five years, discounted at 16 percent
2. An amount of $25,000 to be received at the end of ten years, discounted at 12 percent
3. The amount of $28,000 to be received at the end of two years, and $15,000 to be received at the end of years 4, 5, and 6, discounted at 10 percent.
4. The amount of 10 payments of $5,000 due on January 1, beginning immediately in 2014. Assume an interest rate of 10 percent.

SOLUTION

1. From Table 2, use factor 3.274, as follows.

   $35,000 × 3.274 = $114,590 present value

TABLE 1

Present Value of $1 to Be Received at the End of a Given Number of Time Periods

Periods	1%	2%	3%	4%	5%	6%	7%	8%	9%	10%	12%
1	0.990	0.980	0.971	0.962	0.952	0.943	0.935	0.926	0.917	0.909	0.893
2	0.980	0.961	0.943	0.925	0.907	0.890	0.873	0.857	0.842	0.826	0.797
3	0.971	0.942	0.915	0.889	0.864	0.840	0.816	0.794	0.772	0.751	0.712
4	0.961	0.924	0.888	0.855	0.823	0.792	0.763	0.735	0.708	0.683	0.636
5	0.951	0.906	0.883	0.822	0.784	0.747	0.713	0.681	0.650	0.621	0.567
6	0.942	0.888	0.837	0.790	0.746	0.705	0.666	0.630	0.596	0.564	0.507
7	0.933	0.871	0.813	0.760	0.711	0.665	0.623	0.583	0.547	0.513	0.452
8	0.923	0.853	0.789	0.731	0.677	0.627	0.582	0.540	0.502	0.467	0.404
9	0.914	0.837	0.766	0.703	0.645	0.592	0.544	0.500	0.460	0.424	0.361
10	0.905	0.820	0.744	0.676	0.614	0.558	0.508	0.463	0.422	0.386	0.322
11	0.896	0.804	0.722	0.650	0.585	0.527	0.475	0.429	0.388	0.350	0.287
12	0.887	0.788	0.701	0.625	0.557	0.497	0.444	0.397	0.356	0.319	0.257
13	0.879	0.773	0.681	0.601	0.530	0.469	0.415	0.368	0.326	0.290	0.229
14	0.870	0.758	0.661	0.577	0.505	0.442	0.388	0.340	0.299	0.263	0.205
15	0.861	0.743	0.642	0.555	0.481	0.417	0.362	0.315	0.275	0.239	0.183
16	0.853	0.728	0.623	0.534	0.458	0.394	0.339	0.292	0.252	0.218	0.163
17	0.844	0.714	0.605	0.513	0.436	0.371	0.317	0.270	0.231	0.198	0.146
18	0.836	0.700	0.587	0.494	0.416	0.350	0.296	0.250	0.212	0.180	0.130
19	0.828	0.686	0.570	0.475	0.396	0.331	0.277	0.232	0.194	0.164	0.116
20	0.820	0.673	0.554	0.456	0.377	0.312	0.258	0.215	0.178	0.149	0.104
21	0.811	0.660	0.538	0.439	0.359	0.294	0.242	0.199	0.164	0.135	0.093
22	0.803	0.647	0.522	0.422	0.342	0.278	0.226	0.184	0.150	0.123	0.083
23	0.795	0.634	0.507	0.406	0.326	0.262	0.211	0.170	0.138	0.112	0.074
24	0.788	0.622	0.492	0.390	0.310	0.247	0.197	0.158	0.126	0.102	0.066
25	0.780	0.610	0.478	0.375	0.295	0.233	0.184	0.146	0.116	0.092	0.059
26	0.772	0.598	0.464	0.361	0.281	0.220	0.172	0.135	0.106	0.084	0.053
27	0.764	0.586	0.450	0.347	0.268	0.207	0.161	0.125	0.098	0.076	0.047
28	0.757	0.574	0.437	0.333	0.255	0.196	0.150	0.116	0.090	0.069	0.042
29	0.749	0.563	0.424	0.321	0.243	0.185	0.141	0.107	0.082	0.063	0.037
30	0.742	0.552	0.412	0.308	0.231	0.174	0.131	0.099	0.075	0.057	0.033
40	0.672	0.453	0.307	0.208	0.142	0.097	0.067	0.046	0.032	0.022	0.011
50	0.608	0.372	0.228	0.141	0.087	0.054	0.034	0.021	0.013	0.009	0.003

2. From Table 1, use factor 0.322, as follows.

$25,000 × 0.322 = $8,050 present value

3. From Table 1, use the factors indicated in the table below.

Amount to Be Received	×	Present Value Factor	=	Present Value
$28,000	×	0.826	=	$23,128
15,000	×	0.683	=	10,245
15,000	×	0.621	=	9,315
15,000	×	0.564	=	8,460
Total				$51,148

4. From Table 2, use factor 5.759 as follows.

$5,000 + ($5,000 × 5.759) = $33,795

TABLE 1
Present Value of $1 to Be Received at the End of a Given Number of Time Periods (*Continued*)

14%	15%	16%	18%	20%	25%	30%	35%	40%	45%	50%	Periods
0.877	0.870	0.862	0.847	0.833	0.800	0.769	0.741	0.714	0.690	0.667	1
0.769	0.756	0.743	0.718	0.694	0.640	0.592	0.549	0.510	0.476	0.444	2
0.675	0.658	0.641	0.609	0.579	0.512	0.455	0.406	0.364	0.328	0.296	3
0.592	0.572	0.552	0.516	0.482	0.410	0.350	0.301	0.260	0.226	0.198	4
0.519	0.497	0.476	0.437	0.402	0.328	0.269	0.223	0.186	0.156	0.132	5
0.456	0.432	0.410	0.370	0.335	0.262	0.207	0.165	0.133	0.108	0.088	6
0.400	0.376	0.354	0.314	0.279	0.210	0.159	0.122	0.095	0.074	0.059	7
0.351	0.327	0.305	0.266	0.233	0.168	0.123	0.091	0.068	0.051	0.039	8
0.308	0.284	0.263	0.225	0.194	0.134	0.094	0.067	0.048	0.035	0.026	9
0.270	0.247	0.227	0.191	0.162	0.107	0.073	0.050	0.035	0.024	0.017	10
0.237	0.215	0.195	0.162	0.135	0.086	0.056	0.037	0.025	0.017	0.012	11
0.208	0.187	0.168	0.137	0.112	0.069	0.043	0.027	0.018	0.012	0.008	12
0.182	0.163	0.145	0.116	0.093	0.055	0.033	0.020	0.013	0.008	0.005	13
0.160	0.141	0.125	0.099	0.078	0.044	0.025	0.015	0.009	0.006	0.003	14
0.140	0.123	0.108	0.084	0.065	0.035	0.020	0.011	0.006	0.004	0.002	15
0.123	0.107	0.093	0.071	0.054	0.028	0.015	0.008	0.005	0.003	0.002	16
0.108	0.093	0.080	0.060	0.045	0.023	0.012	0.006	0.003	0.002	0.001	17
0.095	0.081	0.069	0.051	0.038	0.018	0.009	0.005	0.002	0.001	0.001	18
0.083	0.070	0.060	0.043	0.031	0.014	0.007	0.003	0.002	0.001		19
0.073	0.061	0.051	0.037	0.026	0.012	0.005	0.002	0.001	0.001		20
0.064	0.053	0.044	0.031	0.022	0.009	0.004	0.002	0.001			21
0.056	0.046	0.038	0.026	0.018	0.007	0.003	0.001	0.001			22
0.049	0.040	0.033	0.022	0.015	0.006	0.002	0.001				23
0.043	0.035	0.028	0.019	0.013	0.005	0.002	0.001				24
0.038	0.030	0.024	0.016	0.010	0.004	0.001	0.001				25
0.033	0.026	0.021	0.014	0.009	0.003	0.001					26
0.029	0.023	0.018	0.011	0.007	0.002	0.001					27
0.026	0.020	0.016	0.010	0.006	0.002	0.001					28
0.022	0.017	0.014	0.008	0.005	0.002						29
0.020	0.015	0.012	0.007	0.004	0.001						30
0.005	0.004	0.003	0.001	0.001							40
0.001	0.001	0.001									50

TABLE 2
Present Value of $1 Received Each Period for a Given Number of Time Periods

Periods	1%	2%	3%	4%	5%	6%	7%	8%	9%	10%	12%
1	0.990	0.980	0.971	0.962	0.952	0.943	0.935	0.926	0.917	0.909	0.893
2	1.970	1.942	1.913	1.886	1.859	1.833	1.808	1.783	1.759	1.736	1.690
3	2.941	2.884	2.829	2.775	2.723	2.673	2.624	2.577	2.531	2.487	2.402
4	3.902	3.808	3.717	3.630	3.546	3.465	3.387	3.312	3.240	3.170	3.037
5	4.853	4.713	4.580	4.452	4.329	4.212	4.100	3.993	3.890	3.791	3.605
6	5.795	5.601	5.417	5.242	5.076	4.917	4.767	4.623	4.486	4.355	4.111
7	6.728	6.472	6.230	6.002	5.786	5.582	5.389	5.206	5.033	4.868	4.564
8	7.652	7.325	7.020	6.733	6.463	6.210	5.971	5.747	5.535	5.335	4.968
9	8.566	8.162	7.786	7.435	7.108	6.802	6.515	6.247	5.995	5.759	5.328
10	9.471	8.983	8.530	8.111	7.722	7.360	7.024	6.710	6.418	6.145	5.650
11	10.368	9.787	9.253	8.760	8.306	7.887	7.499	7.139	6.805	6.495	5.938
12	11.255	10.575	9.954	9.385	8.863	8.384	7.943	7.536	7.161	6.814	6.194
13	12.134	11.348	10.635	9.986	9.394	8.853	8.358	7.904	7.487	7.103	6.424
14	13.004	12.106	11.296	10.563	9.899	9.295	8.745	8.244	7.786	7.367	6.628
15	13.865	12.849	11.938	11.118	10.380	9.712	9.108	8.559	8.061	7.606	6.811
16	14.718	13.578	12.561	11.652	10.838	10.106	9.447	8.851	8.313	7.824	6.974
17	15.562	14.292	13.166	12.166	11.274	10.477	9.763	9.122	8.544	8.022	7.120
18	16.398	14.992	13.754	12.659	11.690	10.828	10.059	9.372	8.756	8.201	7.250
19	17.226	15.678	14.324	13.134	12.085	11.158	10.336	9.604	8.950	8.365	7.366
20	18.046	16.351	14.878	13.590	12.462	11.470	10.594	9.818	9.129	8.514	7.469
21	18.857	17.011	15.415	14.029	12.821	11.764	10.836	10.017	9.292	8.649	7.562
22	19.660	17.658	15.937	14.451	13.163	12.042	11.061	10.201	9.442	8.772	7.645
23	20.456	18.292	16.444	14.857	13.489	12.303	11.272	10.371	9.580	8.883	7.718
24	21.243	18.914	16.936	15.247	13.799	12.550	11.469	10.529	9.707	8.985	7.784
25	22.023	19.523	17.413	15.622	14.094	12.783	11.654	10.675	9.823	9.077	7.843
26	22.795	20.121	17.877	15.983	14.375	13.003	11.826	10.810	9.929	9.161	7.896
27	23.560	20.707	18.327	16.330	14.643	13.211	11.987	10.935	10.027	9.237	7.943
28	24.316	21.281	18.764	16.663	14.898	13.406	12.137	11.051	10.116	9.307	7.984
29	25.066	21.844	19.189	16.984	15.141	13.591	12.278	11.158	10.198	9.370	8.022
30	25.808	22.396	19.600	17.292	15.373	13.765	12.409	11.258	10.274	9.427	8.055
40	32.835	27.355	23.115	19.793	17.159	15.046	13.332	11.925	10.757	9.779	8.244
50	39.196	31.424	25.730	21.482	18.256	15.762	13.801	12.234	10.962	9.915	8.305

TABLE 2
Present Value of $1 Received Each Period for a Given Number of Time Periods (*Continued*)

14%	15%	16%	18%	20%	25%	30%	35%	40%	45%	50%	Periods
0.877	0.870	0.862	0.847	0.833	0.800	0.769	0.741	0.714	0.690	0.667	1
1.647	1.626	1.605	1.566	1.528	1.440	1.361	1.289	1.224	1.165	1.111	2
2.322	2.283	2.246	2.174	2.106	1.952	1.816	1.696	1.589	1.493	1.407	3
2.914	2.855	2.798	2.690	2.589	2.362	2.166	1.997	1.849	1.720	1.605	4
3.433	3.352	3.274	3.127	2.991	2.689	2.436	2.220	2.035	1.876	1.737	5
3.889	3.784	3.685	3.498	3.326	2.951	2.643	2.385	2.168	1.983	1.824	6
4.288	4.160	4.039	3.812	3.605	3.161	2.802	2.508	2.263	2.057	1.883	7
4.639	4.487	4.344	4.078	3.837	3.329	2.925	2.598	2.331	2.109	1.922	8
4.946	4.772	4.607	4.303	4.031	3.463	3.019	2.665	2.379	2.144	1.948	9
5.216	5.019	4.833	4.494	4.192	3.571	3.092	2.715	2.414	2.168	1.965	10
5.453	5.234	5.029	4.656	4.327	3.656	3.147	2.752	2.438	2.185	1.977	11
5.660	5.421	5.197	4.793	4.439	3.725	3.190	2.779	2.456	2.197	1.985	12
5.842	5.583	5.342	4.910	4.533	3.780	3.223	2.799	2.469	2.204	1.990	13
6.002	5.724	5.468	5.008	4.611	3.824	3.249	2.814	2.478	2.210	1.993	14
6.142	5.847	5.575	5.092	4.675	3.859	3.268	2.825	2.484	2.214	1.995	15
6.265	5.954	5.669	5.162	4.730	3.887	3.283	2.834	2.489	2.216	1.997	16
6.373	6.047	5.749	5.222	4.775	3.910	3.295	2.840	2.492	2.218	1.998	17
6.467	6.128	5.818	5.273	4.812	3.928	3.304	2.844	2.494	2.219	1.999	18
6.550	6.198	5.877	5.316	4.844	3.942	3.311	2.848	2.496	2.220	1.999	19
6.623	6.259	5.929	5.353	4.870	3.954	3.316	2.850	2.497	2.221	1.999	20
6.687	6.312	5.973	5.384	4.891	3.963	3.320	2.852	2.498	2.221	2.000	21
6.743	6.359	6.011	5.410	4.909	3.970	3.323	2.853	2.498	2.222	2.000	22
6.792	6.399	6.044	5.432	4.925	3.976	3.325	2.854	2.499	2.222	2.000	23
6.835	6.434	6.073	5.451	4.973	3.981	3.327	2.855	2.499	2.222	2.000	24
6.873	6.464	6.097	5.467	4.948	3.985	3.329	2.856	2.499	2.222	2.000	25
6.906	6.491	6.118	5.480	4.956	3.988	3.330	2.856	2.500	2.222	2.000	26
6.935	6.514	6.136	5.492	4.964	3.990	3.331	2.856	2.500	2.222	2.000	27
6.961	6.534	6.152	5.502	4.970	3.992	3.331	2.857	2.500	2.222	2.000	28
6.983	6.551	6.166	5.510	4.975	3.994	3.332	2.857	2.500	2.222	2.000	29
7.003	6.566	6.177	5.517	4.979	3.995	3.332	2.857	2.500	2.222	2.000	30
7.105	6.642	6.234	5.548	4.997	3.999	3.333	2.857	2.500	2.222	2.000	40
7.133	6.661	6.246	5.554	4.999	4.000	3.333	2.857	2.500	2.222	2.000	50

ENDNOTES

Chapter 1

1 Based on *Statement of Financial Accounting Concepts No.1*, "Objectives of Financial Reporting by Business Enterprises" (Norwalk, Conn.: Financial Accounting Standards Board, 1978), par. 9.
2 Ibid.
3 Information based on ExxonMobil, Form 10-K, For the Fiscal Year Ended December 31, 2011, and International Monetary Fund's World Economic Outlook Database.
4 *Accounting Principles Board Statement No. 4*, "Basic Concepts and Accounting Principles Underlying Financial Statements of Business Enterprises" (New York: AICPA, 1970), par. 138.
5 Based on Securities and Exchange Commission, *Roadmap for the Potential Use of Financial Statements Prepared in Accordance with International Financial Reporting Standards by US Issuers*, August 2008.
6 Based on "Brand Research Shows CPAs Viewed Positively in Marketplace," *AICPA News Update*, October 20, 2008.
7 Based on *Statement Number 1C*, "Standards of Ethical Conduct for Management Accountants" (Montvale, N.J.: Institute of Management Accountants, 1983; revised 1997).
8 CVS Corporation, Earnings Release, February 8, 2012.
9 Based on National Commission on Fraudulent Financial Reporting, *Report of the National Commission on Fraudulent Financial Reporting* (Washington, D.C.: 1987), p. 2.
10 Target Corporation, Form 10-K, For the Fiscal Year Ended January 29, 2011.
11 Costco Wholesale Corporation, *Annual Report*, 2011.
12 Southwest Airlines Co., *Annual Report*, 1996.

Chapter 2

1 ASC 820 and IFRS 13.
2 Based on *Statement of Financial Accounting Standards No. 157*, "Fair Value Measurements" (Norwalk, Conn.: Financial Accounting Standards Board, 2007).
3 The Boeing Company, Form 10-K, For the Fiscal Year Ended December 31, 2011.
4 Ibid.
5 Data from The Bank of New York Mellon Corporation, Form 10-K, For the Fiscal Year Ended December 31, 2011.

Chapter 3

1 Based on Securities and Exchange Commission, *Staff Accounting Bulletin No. 10*, 1999.
2 In our discussion, we assume that the amount of depreciation has been established.
3 Based on Netflix, Inc., Form 10-K, For the Fiscal Year Ended December 31, 2011.
4 Based on Ken Brown, "Wall Street Plays Numbers Games with Savings, Despite Reforms," *The Wall Street Journal*, July 22, 2003.
5 Based on Mark S. Beasley and others, "Fraudulent Financial Reporting 1998–2007: An Analysis of U.S. Companies," *Committee of Sponsoring Organizations*, 2010, p. 3.
6 Based on "Microsoft Settles with SEC," *CBSNews.com*, June 5, 2002.
7 Data from Lyric Opera of Chicago, Financial Statements, April 30, 2011.
8 Data from The Walt Disney Company, Form 10-K, For the Fiscal Year Ended October 1, 2011.

Chapter 4

1 Based on Zahary Coffin, "The Top Ten Effects of XBRL: The Future of Internet Reporting," p. 1, circa.europa.eu/irc.

Chapter 5

1 http://www.fasb.org, July 12, 2008.
2 *Statement of Financial Accounting Concepts No. 1*, "Objectives of Financial Reporting by Business Enterprises" (Norwalk, Conn.: Financial Accounting Standards Board, 1978), pars. 32–54.

3 *Statement of Financial Accounting Concepts No. 2*, "Qualitative Characteristics of Accounting Information" (Norwalk, Conn.: Financial Accounting Standards Board, 1980), par. 20.
4 Based on L. Todd Johnson, "Relevance and Reliability," *The FASB Report*, February 28, 2005.
5 Based on Securities and Exchange Commission, *Staff Accounting Bulletin No. 99*, 1999.
6 *Accounting Principles Board, Opinion No. 20*, "Accounting Changes" (New York: AICPA, 1971), par. 17.
7 Based on Ray J. Groves, "Here's the Annual Report. Got a Few Hours?" *The Wall Street Journal Europe*, August 26–27, 1994.
8 Roger Lowenstein, "Intrinsic Value: Investors Will Fish for Footnotes in 'Abbreviated' Annual Reports," *The Wall Street Journal*, September 14, 1995.
9 Dell Computer Corporation, Form 10-K, For the Fiscal Year Ended January 31, 2011.
10 Based on "Ex-Chief of WorldCom Is Found Guilty in $11 Billion Fraud," *The New York Times*, March 16, 2005.
11 Based on Roger Lowenstein, "Intrinsic Value: The '20% Club' No Longer Is Exclusive," *The Wall Street Journal*, May 4, 1995.
12 Based on Securities and Exchange Commission, *Staff Accounting Bulletin No. 99*, 1999.

Chapter 6

1 Based on "Credit Card Statistics," *CreditCards.com*, April 21, 2012.
2 For a comparison of complete journal entries made under the perpetual and periodic inventory systems, see the Review Problem in this chapter.
3 Based on Rafael Solorzano, "Forecast of E-Commerce Sales for 2011 and Beyond," *www.fortune3.com*, January 27, 2011.
4 Based on Joel Millman, "Here's What Happens to Many Lovely Gifts After Santa Rides Off," *The Wall Street Journal*, December 26, 2001.
5 Based on Matthew Rose, "Magazine Revenue at Newsstands Falls in Worst Year Ever," *The Wall Street Journal*, May 15, 2001.
6 Helpful ratios for calculating the three components of the financing period will be covered in subsequent chapters on inventories, receivables, and current liabilities.

Chapter 7

1 Data from Toyota Motor Corporation, Form 10-K, For the Fiscal Year Ended March 31, 2011.
2 Based on American Institute of Certified Public Accountants, *Accounting Trends & Techniques* (New York: AICPA, 2011).
3 Toyota Motor Corporation, Form 10-K, For the Fiscal Year Ended March 31, 2011.
4 Based on Ernst & Young, *U.S. GAAP vs. IFRS: The Basics*, 2007.
5 Based on American Institute of Certified Public Accountants, *Accounting Trends & Techniques* (New York: AICPA, 2011).
6 Based on Dell Computer, Form 10-K, For the Fiscal Year Ended February 3, 2012.
7 Based on Securities and Exchange Commission, SEC Announces Fraud Charges Against Former Rite Aid Senior Management, June 21, 2002.
8 Based on Highbeam Research, "Former Rent-Way Executive Gets Prison, Fine in Fraud Case," November 23, 2003.
9 Based on American Institute of Certified Public Accountants, *Accounting Trends & Techniques* (New York: AICPA, 2008).
10 Data from ExxonMobil Corporation, Form 10-K, For the Fiscal Year Ended December 31, 2006.
11 Data from ExxonMobil Corporation, Form 10-K, For the Fiscal Year Ended Decmber 31, 2011.
12 Data from Walgreen Co., Form 10-K, For the Fiscal Year Ended August 31, 2011.

Chapter 8

1 Based on Committee of Sponsoring Organizations of the Treadway Commission (COSO), *Internal Control—Integrated Framework*, 1985–2012.
2 Based on *Professional Standards*, vol. 1, Sec. AU 325.16.

3   Based on Elizabeth Woyke, "Attention Shoplifters," *BusinessWeek*, September 11, 2006.
4   Based on Grant Thornton, "Understanding and Preventing Retail Fraud," National Retail Federation, April 2009.
5   Based on Tom Lauricella, Shafali Anand, and Valerie Bauerlein, "A $34 Billion Cash Fund to Close Up," *The Wall Street Journal*, December 11, 2007.
6   Nike, Inc., Form 10-K, For the Fiscal Year Ended May 31, 2012.
7   Based on American Institute of Certified Public Accountants, *Accounting Trends & Techniques* (New York: AICPA, 2011).
8   Based on "Credit Card Statistics," *CreditCards.com*, April 21, 2011.
9   Costco Wholesale Corporation, Form 10-K, For the Fiscal Year Ended August 28, 2011.
10 Ibid.
11 Based on Committee of Sponsoring Organizations of the Treadway Commission, "Press Release: Financial Fraud at U.S. Public Companies," May 20, 2010.
12 Based on Amy Merrick, "Starbucks Accuses Employee, Husband of Embezzling $3.7 Million from Firm," *The Wall Street Journal*, November 20, 2000.

Chapter 9

1   Based on Jesse Drucker, "Sprint Expects Loss of Subscribers," *The Wall Street Journal*, September 24, 2002.
2   Based on International Accounting Standards Board, *Framework for the Preparation and Presentation of Financial Statements* (October 2008).
3   Based on American Institute of Certified Public Accountants, *Accounting Trends & Techniques* (New York: AICPA, 2010).
4   Based on "Bad Loans Rattle Telecom Vendors," *BusinessWeek*, February 19, 2001.
5   Based on Scott Thurm, "Better Debt Bolsters Bottom Lines," *The Wall Street Journal*, August 18, 2003.
6   Based on Circuit City Stores, Inc., Form 10-K, For the Fiscal Year Ended February 28, 2005.
7   Based on Deborah Solomon and Damian Paletta, "U.S. Drafts Sweeping Plans to Fight Crisis as Turmoil worsens in Credit Markets," *The Wall Street Journal*, September 19, 2008.
8   Based on Heather Timmons, "Do Household's Numbers Add Up?" *BusinessWeek*, December 10, 2001.
9   Based on Steve Daniels, "Bank One Reserves Feed Earnings," *Crain's Chicago Business*, December 15, 2003.
10 Based on Jonathon Weil, "Accounting Scheme Was Straightforward but Hard to Detect," *The Wall Street Journal*, March 20, 2003.
11 Nike, Inc., Form 10-K, For the Fiscal Year Ended May 31, 2012.
12 Information based on promotional brochures of Mitsubishi Corp.
13 Based on Elizabeth McDonald, "Unhatched Chickens," *Forbes*, February 19, 2001.
14 Based on CompuCredit Holdings Corporation, Form 10-K, For the Fiscal Year Ended December 31, 2009.
15 Data from Walgreen Co., Form 10-K, For the Fiscal Year Ended August 31, 2011.

Chapter 10

1   Based on *Statement of Financial Accounting Standard No. 144*, "Accounting for the Impairment or Disposal of Long-Lived Assets" (Norwalk, Conn.: Financial Accounting Standards Board, 2001).
2   Based on Edward J. Riedl, "An Examination of Long-lived Asset Impairments," *The Accounting Review*, Vol. 79, No. 3, pp. 823–852.
3   Based on *Statement of Financial Accounting Standards No. 34*, "Capitalization of Interest Cost" (Norwalk, Conn.: Financial Accounting Standards Board, 1979), pars. 9–11.
4   Leasehold improvements are sometimes included in the intangible assets section because they revert to the lessor and are therefore more of a right than a physical asset.
5   Based on American Institute of Certified Public Accountants, *Accounting Trends & Techniques* (New York: AICPA, 2011).
6   Ibid.
7   This method of revising depreciation is used widely in industry and is supported by *Opinion No. 9* and *Opinion No. 20* of the Accounting Principles Board.
8   Some special rules apply and are addressed in more advanced courses.

9   If the useful life of a plant asset is less than the expected life of the resource, the shorter life should be used to compute depreciation, using straight-line or declining-balance methods.
10 Based on *Statement of Financial Accounting Standards No. 25*, "Suspension of Certain Accounting Requirements for Oil and Gas Producing Companies" (Norwalk, Conn.: Financial Accounting Standards Board, 1979).
11 Based on Jonathan Weil, "Oil Reserves Can Sure Be Slick," *The Wall Street Journal*, March 11, 2004.
12 Based on *Statement of Financial Accounting Standards No. 142*, "Goodwill and Other Intangible Assets" (Norwalk, Conn.: Financial Accounting Standards Board, 2001), pars. 11–17.
13 Based on "BrandZ Top 100 Most Valuable Global Brands 2011," *www.millardbrown.com*, 2011.
14 Note that if the company developed the bottle cap internally instead of purchasing the patent, the costs of developing the cap—such as researchers' salaries and the costs of supplies and equipment used in testing—would be expensed as incurred.
15 Data from General Motors Corporation, Form 10-K, For the Fiscal Year Ended December 31, 2011.
16 Data from Abbott Laboratories, Form 10-K, For the Fiscal Year Ended December 31, 2011.
17 Based on *Statement of Financial Accounting Standards No. 2*, "Accounting for Research and Development Costs" (Norwalk, Conn.: Financial Accounting Standards Board, 1974), par. 12.
18 Based on *Statement of Financial Accounting Standards No. 86*, "Accounting for the Costs of Computer Software to Be Sold, Leased, or Otherwise Marketed" (Norwalk, Conn.: Financial Accounting Standards Board, 1985).
19 Based on *Statement of Financial Accounting Standards No. 142*, "Goodwill and Other Intangible Assets" (Norwalk, Conn.: Financial Accounting Standards Board, 2001), pars. 11–17.
20 Based on American Institute of Certified Public Accountants, *Accounting Trends & Techniques* (New York: AICPA, 2011).
21 Data from General Mills, Inc., *Quarterly Report*, 2012; H.J. Heinz Company, Form 10-K, For the Fiscal Year Ended April 29, 2012; Cisco Systems, *Quarterly Report*, 2012.
22 Based on Southwest Airlines Co., *Annual Report*, 2002.
23 Costco Wholesale Corporation, Form 10-K, For the Fiscal Year Ended August 28, 2011.
24 International Business Machines Corporation, Form 10-K, For the Fiscal Year Ended December 31, 2011.
25 Data from Starwood Hotel & Resorts Worldwide, Inc., Form 10-K, For the Fiscal Year Ended December 21, 2011; Marriot International, Inc., Form 10-K, For the Fiscal Year Ended December 30, 2011.

Chapter 11

1   The Hershey Company, Form 10-K, For the Fiscal Year Ended December 31, 2011.
2   Based on "Small Business Poll on Compensating Employees," quoted on sbinformation.about.com, June 6, 2010.
3   The Hershey Company, Form 10-K, For the Fiscal Year Ended December 31, 2011.
4   Based on "Press Room," *www.webfyer.com*, January 4, 2010.
5   Based on "Overview of U.S. Coupon Distribution and Redemption Trends," March 29, 2012, NCH Marketing Services, www.nchmarketing.com.
6   Based on *Statement of Financial Accounting Standards No. 5*, "Accounting for Contingencies" (Norwalk, Conn.: Financial Accounting Standards Board, 1975).
7   Based on American Institute of Certified Public Accountants, *Accounting Trends & Techniques* (New York: AICPA, 2012).
8   Microsoft Corporation, Form 10-K, For the Fiscal Year Ended June 30, 2011.
9   Based on American Institute of Certified Public Accountants, *Accounting Trends & Techniques* (New York: AICPA, 2012).
10 Data from Microsoft Corporation, Form 10-K, For the Fiscal Year Ended June 30, 2011.
11 Based on *Accounting Standards Codification (ASC) 820*, "Fair Value Measurements and Disclosures [Norwalk, Conn.: Financial Accounting Standards Board, revised by Accounting Standards Update (ASU 2011-04 in 2011)].
12 Based on *Accounting Standards Codification (ASC) 820*, "Fair Value Measurements and Disclosures [Norwalk, Conn.: Financial Accounting Standards Board, revised by Accounting Standards Update (ASU 2011-04 in 2011)] and IFRS 13, "Fair Value Measurement," International Accounting Standards Board, (2011).

13 Based on "Clarifications on Fair-Value Accounting," U.S. Securities and Exchange Commission, *Release 2008-234*, October 1, 2008.

14 Data from WorldCom (MCI, Inc.), Form 10-K, For the Fiscal Year Ended December 31, 2004.

15 Advertisement, *Chicago Tribune*, December 2007.

16 Data from Oracle Corporation, Form 10-K, For the Fiscal Year Ended May 31, 2011; Cisco Systems, Inc., Form 10-K, For the Fiscal Year Ended July 30, 2011.

Chapter 12

1 Based on "Nokia Unveils Plans for Chinese Centre," *Financial Times London*, May 9, 2000.

Chapter 13

1 Based on "Key Stats," Securities Industry and Financial Markets Association, April 2012.

2 Based on "The FASB's Basic Ownership Approach and a Reclassification of Preferred Stock as a Liability," *www.cfo.com*, July 18, 2008.

3 Based on Amir Efrati, "Google Preserves Cash and Control," *The Wall Street Journal*, April 13, 2012.

4 Based on Michael Rapaport and Jonathan Weil, "More Truth-in-Labeling for Accounting Carries Liabilities," *The Wall Street Journal*, August 23, 2003.

5 Based on American Institute of Certified Public Accountants, *Accounting Trends & Techniques* (New York: AICPA, 2011).

6 Data from Abbott Laboratories, Form 10-K, For the Fiscal Year Ended December 31, 2011.

7 Based on American Institute of Certified Public Accountants, *Accounting Research Bulletin No. 43* (New York: AICPA, 1953), chap. 7, sec. B, par. 10.

8 Based on American Institute of Certified Public Accountants, *Accounting Research Bulletin No. 43* (New York: AICPA, 1953), chap. 7, sec. B, par. 13.

9 Based on Nike, Inc., Form 10-K, For the Fiscal Year Ended May 31, 2007.

10 Based on Yahoo! Finance.com, June 3, 2012.

11 Based on "General Mills Declares Two-for-One Stock Split," *MarketWatch.com*, May 3, 2010.

12 Data from Microsoft Corporation, Form 10-K, For the Fiscal Year Ended June 30, 2011.

13 Ibid.

14 Based on American Institute of Certified Public Accountants, *Accounting Trends & Techniques* (New York: AICPA, 2011).

15 Data from Google, Inc., Form 10-K, For the Fiscal Year Ended December 31, 2011.

16 Based on "Spotlight on Stock Options Backdating," *www.sec.gov*, 2010.

17 Based on Mariss Marr, "Dreamworks Shares Rise 38% on First Day," *The Wall Street Journal*, October 10, 2004; Yahoo! Finance.com, December 26, 2007.

18 Data from IBM Corporation, Form 10-K, For the Fiscal Year Ended December 31, 2009; Based on "IBM Board Approves $5 Billion for Stock Repurchase," *www.wopular.com*, June 17, 2010.

19 Based on Yahoo! Finance.com, 2007.

Chapter 14

1 Data from Southwest Airlines, Form 10-K, For the Fiscal Year Ended December 31, 2011. We cover deferred income taxes in greater detail in a later chapter.

2 Based on Mary Williams Walsh, "$53 Billion Shortfall for New Jersey Retiree Care," *The New York Times*, July 25, 2007.

3 Based on *www.morningstar.com*, May 9, 2012.

4 Based on Accounting Principles Board, *Opinion No. 21*, "Interest on Receivables and Payables" (New York: AICPA, 1971), par. 15.

5 Based on *Statement of Financial Accounting Standards No. 13*, "Accounting for Leases" (Norwalk, Conn.: Financial Accounting Standards Board, 1976), par. 10.

6 Based on *Statement of Financial Accounting Standards No. 158*, "Employers' Accounting for Defined Benefit Pension and Other Postretirement Plans" (Norwalk, Conn.: Financial Accounting Standards Board, 2007).

7 Based on Lee Hawkins, Jr., "S&P Cuts Rating on GM and Ford to Junk Status," *The Wall Street Journal*, May 6, 2005.

8 Data from McDonald's, Inc., Form 10-K, For the Fiscal Year Ended December 31, 2011.

9 Based on Tom Sullivan and Sonia Ryst, "Kodak $1Billion Issue Draws Crowds," *The Wall Street Journal*, October 8, 2003.

10 Adapted from quotations in *The Wall Street Journal Online*, December 18, 2007.

11 Data from Intel Corporation, Form 10-K, For the Fiscal Year Ended December 31, 2011.

Chapter 15

1 Based on American Institute of Certified Public Accountants, *Accounting Trends & Techniques* (New York: AICPA, 2011).

2 Based on Martin Peers and Robin Sidel, "WorldCom Causes Analysts to Evaluate EBITDA's Role," *The Wall Street Journal*, July 15, 2002.

3 Based on Ian McDonald, "Companies Are Rolling in Cash. Too Bad," *The Wall Street Journal*, August 20, 2006; Justin Lahart, "U.S. Firms Build Up Record Cash Piles," *The Wall Street Journal*, June 11, 2010.

4 Based on Lulu Chang, "Companies Hoarding Cash," *CNBC*, July 19, 2010.

5 Based on "Free Cash Flow Standouts," *Upside Newsletter*, October 3, 2005.

6 Amazon.com, *Form 10-K*, For the Fiscal Year Ended December 31, 2011.

7 Gary Slutsker, "Look at the Birdie and Say: 'Cash Flow'," *Forbes*, October 25, 1993.

8 Jonathan Clements, "Yacktman Fund Is Bloodied but Unbowed," *The Wall Street Journal*, November 8, 1993.

9 Jeffery Laderman, "Earnings, Schmearnings—Look at the Cash," *BusinessWeek*, July 24, 1989.

10 Amazon.com, *Form 10-K*, For the Fiscal Year Ended December 31, 2011.

11 Data from Fleetwood Enterprises, Inc., *10Q*, July 29, 2001.

12 Enron Corporation, *Press Release*, October 16, 2001.

Chapter 16

1 Based on "Fourteen Key Business Ratios," *dnb.com*, 2012.

2 Based on *Statement of Financial Accounting Standards No. 131*, "Segment Disclosures" (Norwalk, Conn.: Financial Accounting Standards Board, 1997).

3 Based on Belverd E. Needles, Jr., Anton Shigaev, Marian Powers, and Mark L. Frigo, "Strategy and Integrated Financial Ratio Performance Measures: A Longitudinal Multi-Country Study of High Performance Companies," in *Studies in Financial and Managerial Accounting*, vol. 20, edited by Marc Epstein and Jean-Francois Manzoni (London: JAI Elsevier Science Ltd., 2010), pp. 211–252.

4 Based on Belverd E. Needles, Jr., Marian Powers, and Mark L. Frigo, "Performance Measurement and Executive Compensation: Practices of High Performance Companies," in *Studies in Financial and Managerial Accounting*, vol. 18, edited by Marc Epstein and Jean-Francois Manzoni (London: JAI Elsevier Science Ltd., 2008).

5 Based on Starbucks Corporation, Form 10-K, For the Fiscal Year Ended October 2, 2011.

6 Ibid.

7 Based on "After Charge for Licensing, McDonald's Posts a Record Loss," *The New York Times*, July 25, 2007; Christina Cheddar Berk, "Campbell's Profit Jumps 31 Percent," *The Wall Street Journal*, November 22, 2005.

8 Based on American Institute of Certified Public Accountants, *Accounting Trends & Techniques* (New York: AICPA, 2011); Starbucks Corporation, Form 10-K, For the Fiscal Year Ended October 2, 2011. Starbucks Corporation, Form 10-K, For the Fiscal Year Ended September 27, 2009.

9 Based on Jonathan Weil, "Pro Forma in Earnings Reports?... As If," *The Wall Street Journal*, April 24, 2003.

10 Based on David Henry, "The Numbers Game," *BusinessWeek*, May 14, 2001.

11 Starbucks Corporation, *Proxy Statement*, 2011.

12 Ibid.

13 Ibid.

14 Based on "Technology Firms Post Strong Earnings but Stock Prices Decline Sharply," *The Wall Street Journal*, January 21, 1988; Donald R. Seace, "Industrials Plunge 57.2 Points—Technology Stocks' Woes Cited," *The Wall Street Journal*, January 21, 1988.

Appendix A

1   Based on *Statement of Financial Accounting Standards No. 157*, "Fair Value
    Measurements" (Norwalk, Conn.: Financial Accounting Standards Board,
    2007); *Statement of Financial Accounting Standards No. 159*, "The Fair
    Value Option for Financial Assets and Financial Liabilities" (Norwalk, Conn.:
    Financial Accounting Standards Board, 2007).

2   Based on *Statement of Financial Accounting Standards No. 115*, "Accounting
    for Certain Investments in Debt and Equity Securities" (Norwalk, Conn.:
    Financial Accounting Standards Board, 1993).

3   Based on Greg Steinmetz and Cacilie Rohwedder, SAP Insider Probe Points to
    Reforms Needed in Germany," *The Wall Street Journal*, May 8, 1997.

4   Based on *Statement of Financial Accounting Standards No. 115*, "Accounting
    for Certain Investments in Debt and Equity Securities" (Norwalk, Conn.:
    Financial Accounting Standards Board, 1993).

GLOSSARY

A

Accelerated method A method of depreciation that allocates relatively large amounts of the depreciable cost of an asset to earlier years and smaller amounts to later years. (p. 377)

Account balance The difference in dollars between the total debit footing and the total credit footing of an account. (p. 44)

Accounting An information system that measures, processes, and communicates financial information about an economic entity. (p. 2)

Accounting conventions Rules of thumb, or general principles, for recording transactions and preparing financial statements. Also called *constraints*. (p. 172)

Accounting cycle A series of steps whose basic purpose is to produce financial statements for decision makers. (p. 46)

Accounting equation Assets = Liabilities + Owner's Equity. (p. 6)

Accounts Basic units for accumulating and storing accounting data from similar transactions. (p. 42)

Accounts payable Short-term obligations to suppliers for goods and services. Also called *trade accounts payable*. (p. 412)

Accounts receivable Short-term financial assets that arise from sales on credit at the wholesale or retail level. (p. 336)

Accounts receivable aging method A method of estimating uncollectible accounts based on the assumption that a predictable proportion of each dollar of accounts receivable outstanding will not be collected. (p. 341)

Accrual The recognition of an expense or revenue that has arisen but has not yet been recorded. (p. 91)

Accrual accounting Recording transactions in the periods in which they occur, rather than in the periods in which cash is received or paid. Also called the *matching rule*. (p. 87)

Accrued expenses Expenses incurred but not recorded in the accounts; unrecorded expenses. (p. 94)

Accrued liabilities Liabilities that are not already in the accounting records. (p. 414)

Accrued revenues Revenues for which a service has been performed or goods delivered but for which no entry has been made; unrecorded revenues. (p. 97)

Accumulated Depreciation Contra-asset accounts used to accumulate depreciation on specific long-term assets. (p. 93)

Additions Enlargements to the physical layout of a plant asset. (p. 370)

Adjusted trial balance A trial balance prepared after all adjusting entries have been recorded and posted to the accounts. (p. 99)

Adjusting entries Entries made to apply accrual accounting to transactions that span accounting periods. (p. 90)

Aging of accounts receivable The process of listing each customer's receivable account according to the due date of the account. (p. 341)

Allowance for Uncollectible Accounts A contra-asset account that reduces accounts receivable to the amount expected to be collected in cash. Also called *Allowance for Doubtful Accounts* and *Allowance for Bad Debts*. (p. 339)

Allowance method A method of accounting for uncollectible accounts by expensing estimated uncollectible accounts in the period in which the related sales take place. (p. 338)

American Institute of Certified Public Accountants (AICPA) The professional association of certified public accountants. (p. 13)

Amortization The periodic allocation of the cost of an intangible asset to the periods it benefits. (p. 368)

Articles of incorporation An official document filed with and approved by a state that authorizes the incorporators to do business as a corporation. (p. 492)

Asset impairment Loss of revenue-generating potential of a long-lived asset before the end of its useful life; the difference between an asset's carrying value and its fair value, as measured by the present value of the expected cash flows. (p. 369)

Asset turnover A measure of profitability that shows how efficiently assets are used to produce sales; calculated as Net Revenue ÷ Average Total Assets. (pp. 182, 671)

Assets The economic resources of a company that are expected to benefit future operations. (p. 6)

Audit An examination of a company's financial statements and the accounting systems, controls, and records that produced them in order to render an independent professional opinion about whether they have been presented fairly, in all material respects, in conformity with GAAP. (p. 12)

Authorization The approval of transactions or activities. (p. 303)

Authorized shares The maximum number of shares a corporation can issue without a change in its state charter. (p. 497)

Average-cost method An inventory costing method in which inventory is priced at the average cost of the goods available for sale during the period. (p. 269)

B

Balance sheet The financial statement that shows a business's assets, liabilities, and owner's equity as of a specific date. Also called the *statement of financial position*. (p. 8)

Bank reconciliation The process of accounting for the difference between the balance appearing on a company's bank statement and the balance in its Cash account. (p. 312)

Bank statement A printed or electronic record of the balance in a bank account and the amounts that have been paid into it and withdrawn from it over a given period of time. (p. 310)

Base year In financial analysis, the first year to be considered in any set of data. (p. 664)

Betterments Improvements that do not add to the physical layout of a plant asset. (p. 370)

Board of directors A group of individuals that are elected or appointed to oversee the activities of a corporation. (p. 492)

Bond A security, usually long term, representing money that a corporation or other entity borrows from the investing public. (p. 549)

Bond certificate Evidence of an organization's debt to a bondholder. (p. 549)

Bond indenture A contract that defines the terms of a bond issue. (p. 549)

Bond issue The total value of bonds issued at one time. (p. 549)

Bonding The process of carefully checking an employee's background and insuring the company against theft by that person. (p. 304)

Bonds payable The most common type of long-term debt for companies. (p. 546)

Bonus An amount that accrues to the original partners when a new partner pays more to the partnership than the interest received or that accrues to the new partner when the amount paid to the partnership is less than the interest received. (p. 463)

Book value A company's total assets less its liabilities; stockholders' equity or net assets. (p. 518)

Book value per share The equity of the owner of one share of stock in a corporation's net assets. (p. 518)

Bookkeeping The process of recording financial transactions and keeping financial records. (p. 3)

Brand name A registered name that can be used only by its owner to identify a product or service. (p. 387)

Business An economic unit that aims to sell goods and services to customers at prices that will provide an adequate return to its owners. (p. 17)

Business transactions Economic events that affect a business's financial position and that should be recorded in the accounting records. (pp. 3, 40)

C

Call price A specified price, usually above face value, at which a corporation can buy back its bonds before maturity. (p. 550)

Callable bonds Bonds that the issuing corporation can buy back and retire at a call price before their maturity dates. (p. 550)

Callable preferred stock Preferred stock that the issuing corporation can redeem or retire at a stated price. (p. 499)

Capital expenditure An expenditure for the purchase or expansion of a long-term asset, which is recorded in an asset account. (p. 370)

Capital lease A long-term lease that resembles a purchase or sale on installment and in which the lessee assumes the risk of ownership. (p. 548)

Carrying value The unexpired portion of an asset's cost. Also called *book value*. (pp. 93, 369)

Cash Coins and currency on hand, checks and money orders from customers, and deposits in checking and savings accounts; for purposes of the statement of cash flows, both cash and cash equivalents. (p. 602)

Cash basis of accounting Accounting for revenues and expenses on a cash-received and cash-paid basis. (p. 88)

Cash dividends A distribution of earnings to a corporation's stockholders; a corporation's board of directors has the sole authority to declare them. (p. 414)

Cash equivalents Short-term investments that will revert to cash in 90 days or less from the time they are purchased; examples include money market accounts, commercial paper, and U.S. Treasury bills. (pp. 311, 602)

Cash flow yield A measure of a company's ability to generate operating cash flows in relation to net income; calculated as Net Cash Flows from Operating Activities ÷ Net Income. (pp. 622, 673)

Cash flows The inflows and outflows of cash into and out of a business. (p. 10)

Cash flows to assets A measure of the ability of assets to generate operating cash flows; calculated as Net Cash Flows from Operating Activities ÷ Average Total Assets. (pp. 624, 674)

Cash flows to sales A measure of the ability of sales to generate operating cash flows; calculated as Net Cash Flows from Operating Activities ÷ Net Sales. (pp. 623, 673)

Cash-generating efficiency A company's ability to generate cash from its current or continuing operations. (p. 622)

Cash payments journal A journal used to record transactions involving payments of cash. Also called a *cash disbursements journal*. (p. 257)

Cash receipts journal A journal used to record transactions involving receipts of cash. (p. 254)

Certified public accountant (CPA) A public accountant who has met stringent state licensing requirements. (p. 12)

Chart of accounts A list of account numbers and titles that facilitates finding accounts in the ledger. (p. 42)

Check An authorization for the bank to pay the vendor in the amount of the invoice less any applicable discount. (p. 310)

Check authorization A form that an accounting department prepares after it has compared a receiving report with a purchase order and invoice and that authorizes the issuance of a check to pay the invoice. (p. 310)

Classification The process of assigning transactions to the appropriate accounts. (p. 41)

Classified financial statements General-purpose external financial statements that are divided into subcategories. (p. 175)

Closing entries Entries made at the end of an accounting period that set the stage for the next period by clearing temporary accounts of their balances and transferring them to the owner's Capital account; they summarize a period's revenues and expenses. (p. 132)

Commercial paper Unsecured loans sold to the public, usually through professionally managed investment firms, as a means of borrowing short-term funds. (p. 413)

Commitment A legal obligation that does not meet the technical requirements for recognition as a liability. (p. 425)

Common-size statement A financial statement in which the components are expressed as percentages of a total figure in the statement. (p. 667)

Common stock Shares of stock that carry voting rights but that rank below preferred stock in terms of dividends and the distribution of assets. (p. 497)

Comparability The convention of presenting information in a way that enables decision makers to recognize similarities, differences, and trends over different periods in the same company and among different companies. (p. 172)

Compensation committee A committee of independent directors appointed by a public corporation's board of directors to determine how top executives will be compensated. (p. 687)

Complete information All the information necessary for a reliable decision. (p. 172)

Compound entry A journal entry in which more than two accounts are involved. (p. 50)

Compound interest The interest cost for two or more periods when, after each period, the interest of that period is added to the amount on which interest is computed in future periods. (p. 426)

Confirmative value Information that confirms or changes previous evaluations. (p. 171)

Conservatism The convention that when faced with two equally acceptable alternatives, the accountant chooses the one least likely to overstate assets and income. (p. 173)

Consignment Merchandise that its owner (the consignor) places on the premises of another company (the consignee) with the understanding that payment is expected only when the merchandise is sold and that unsold items may be returned to the consignor. (p. 265)

Consistency The convention requiring that once a company has adopted an accounting procedure, it must use it from one period to the next unless a note to the financial statements informs users of a change in procedure. (pp. 172, 684)

Contingent liability A potential liability that arises from a past transaction and is dependent on a future event. (pp. 351, 424)

Continuity The difficulty associated with not knowing how long a business will survive. (p. 87)

Contra account An account whose balance is subtracted from an associated account in the financial statements. (p. 93)

Contributed Capital Assets that stockholders have invested in a corporation. Also called *Paid-in Capital*. (pp. 178, 492)

Control activities Policies and procedures that management

establishes to ensure that the objectives of internal control are met. (p. 303)

Control environment A company's ethics, philosophy and operating style, organizational structure, method of assigning authority and responsibility, and personnel policies and practices. (p. 303)

Controlling account An account in the general ledger that maintains the total of the individual account balances in a subsidiary ledger. Also called *control account*. (p. 249)

Convertible bonds Bonds that can be exchanged for the issuing corporation's common stock. (p. 550)

Convertible preferred stock Preferred stock that the owner can exchange for common stock. (p. 499)

Copyright An exclusive right granted by the federal government to reproduce and sell literary, musical, and other artistic materials and computer programs for a period of the author's life plus 70 years. (p. 387)

Corporation A business unit granted a state charter recognizing it as a separate legal entity having its own rights, privileges, and liabilities distinct from those of its owners. (p. 5)

Cost The net purchase price of an asset plus all reasonable and necessary expenditures to get it in place and ready for use. (p. 375)

Cost-benefit The convention that the benefits gained from providing accounting information should be greater than the costs of providing that information. Also called *cost constraint*. (p. 172)

Cost constraint The convention that the benefits gained from providing accounting information should be greater than the costs of providing that information. Also called *cost-benefit*. (p. 172)

Cost flow The association of costs with their assumed flow versus their actual goods flow in the operations of a company. (p. 265)

Cost of goods available for sale The sum of beginning inventory and the net cost of purchases during an accounting period. (p. 221)

Cost of goods sold The amount a merchandiser paid for the merchandise it sold during an accounting period or the cost to a manufacturer of making the products it sold during an

accounting period. Also called *cost of sales* or *cost of revenue*. (p. 209)

Cost principle The practice of recording transactions at the exchange price at the point of recognition. (p. 41)

Coupon bonds Bonds not registered with the issuing organization that bear coupons stating the amount of interest due and the payment date. (p. 551)

Credit The right side of an account. (p. 44)

Creditors Those who lend money or deliver goods and services to a company before being paid. (p. 16)

Crossfooting Adding and subtracting numbers across a row. (p. 145)

Cumulative preferred stock Preferred stock on which unpaid dividends accumulate over time and that must be satisfied before a dividend can be paid to common stockholders. (p. 498)

Current assets Cash and other assets that a company can reasonably expect to convert to cash, sell, or consume within one year or its normal operating cycle, whichever is longer. (p. 175)

Current liabilities Obligations due to be paid or performed within one year or within the normal operating cycle, whichever is longer. (pp. 177, 410)

Current ratio A measure of liquidity, or short-term debt-paying ability; calculated as Current Assets ÷ Current Liabilities. (pp. 180, 679)

Customer list A list of customers or subscribers. (p. 387)

D

Days' inventory on hand A measure that shows the average number of days taken to sell inventory; calculated as Days in Accounting Period ÷ Inventory Turnover. (pp. 281, 677)

Days' payable A measure that shows the average number of days a company takes to pay its accounts payable; calculated as Days in Accounting Period ÷ Payables Turnover. (pp. 434, 679)

Days' sales uncollected A measure that shows the number of days, on average, that a company must wait to receive payment for credit sales; calculated as Days in Accounting Period ÷ Receivables Turnover. (pp. 350, 678)

Debit   The left side of an account. (p. 44)

Debt to equity ratio   A measure of profitability that shows the proportion of a company's assets that is financed by creditors and the proportion financed by the owner or owners (stockholders); calculated as Total Liabilities ÷ Total Owner's/Stockholders' Equity. (pp. 185, 579, 675)

Declaration date   The date on which a board of directors declares a dividend. (p. 511)

Declining-balance method   An accelerated method of depreciation in which depreciation is computed by applying a fixed rate to the carrying value (the declining balance) of a tangible long-lived asset. (p. 377)

Deferral   The postponement of the recognition of an expense already paid or of revenue received in advance. (p. 91)

Deferred income taxes   A postponement in paying taxes as the result of using different methods to calculate income taxes for financial reporting and tax purposes. (p. 548)

Defined benefit plan   A pension plan in which the employer contributes an amount annually to fund estimated future pension liability. (p. 576)

Defined contribution plan   A pension plan in which the employer makes a fixed annual contribution, usually a percentage of the employee's gross pay. (p. 576)

Definitely determinable liabilities   Current liabilities that are set by contract or statute and that can be measured exactly. (p. 412)

Delivery expense   The transportation cost of delivering merchandise incurred by the seller. Also called *freight-out*. (p. 214)

Depletion   The exhaustion of a natural resource through mining, cutting, pumping, or other extraction, and the way in which the cost is allocated. (p. 368)

Deposits in transit   Deposits a company has sent to its bank but that the bank did not receive in time to enter on the bank statement. (p. 312)

Depreciable cost   The cost of an asset less its residual value. (p. 375)

Depreciation   The portion of the cost of a long-term asset allocated to any one accounting period. Also called *depreciation expense*. (pp. 93, 368)

Direct charge-off method   A method of accounting for uncollectible accounts by directly debiting an expense account when bad debts are discovered; it violates the matching rule but is required for computing federal income tax. (p. 337)

Direct method   The procedure for converting the income statement from an accrual basis to a cash basis by adjusting each item on the income statement. (p. 605)

Discontinued operations   Segments that are no longer part of a company's operations. (p. 686)

Discount   The amount by which a bond's face value exceeds its issue price, which occurs when the market interest rate is higher than the face interest rate. (p. 550)

Discounting   A method of selling notes receivable to a bank in which the bank derives its profit by deducting the interest from the maturity value of the note. (p. 352)

Dishonored note   A promissory note that the maker cannot or will not pay at the maturity date. (p. 347)

Dissolution   The loss of authority to continue a partnership as a separate entity due to a change in the original association of partners. (p. 461)

Diversified companies   Companies that operate in more than one industry. Also called *conglomerates*. (p. 661)

Dividend yield   A measure of a stock's current return to an investor in the form of dividends; calculated as Dividends per Share ÷ Market Price per Share. (pp. 520, 681)

Dividends   A distribution of a corporation's assets (usually cash generated by past earnings) to its stockholders. (pp. 179, 493)

Dividends in arrears   Past dividends on cumulative preferred stock that remain unpaid. (p. 498)

Double-declining-balance method   An accelerated method of depreciation in which a fixed rate equal to twice the straight-line percentage is applied to the carrying value (the declining balance) of a tangible long-lived asset. (p. 377)

Double-entry system   The accounting system in which each transaction is recorded with at least one debit and one credit so that the total amount of debits equals the total amount of credits. (p. 42)

Double taxation   Taxation of corporate earnings twice—once as income of the corporation and once as income to the stockholders in the form of dividends. (p. 494)

Due care   Competence and diligence in carrying out professional responsibilities. (p. 14)

Duration of a note   The time between a promissory note's issue date and its maturity date. (p. 346)

E

Early extinguishment of debt   The retirement of a bond issue before its maturity date. (p. 550)

Earnings management   The manipulation of revenues and expenses to achieve a specific outcome. (p. 102)

Economic entity   A unit that exists independently, such as a business, hospital, or a governmental body. (p. 2)

Economic Stimulus Act of 2008   A federal income tax law that allows a small company to expense the first $250,000 of equipment expenditures. (p. 379)

Effective interest method   A method of amortizing bond discounts or premiums that applies a constant interest rate (the market rate when the bonds were issued) to the bonds' carrying value at the beginning of each interest period. (p. 559)

Electronic funds transfer (EFT)   The transfer of funds from one bank to another through electronic communication. (p. 312)

Employee   A worker who is paid a wage or salary and who is under the organization's direct supervision and control. (p. 416)

Estimated liabilities   Definite debts or obligations whose exact amounts cannot be known until a later date. (p. 420)

Estimated useful life   The total number of service units expected from a long-term asset. (p. 375)

Ethics   A code of conduct that addresses whether actions are right or wrong. (p. 19)

Exchange gain or loss   A gain or loss due to exchange rate fluctuation between the date of sale and the date of payment; it is reported on the income statement. (p. 230)

Exchange rate   The value of one currency in terms of another. (p. 4)

Ex-dividend   A description of stock between the record date and the date of payment, during which the right to the dividend remains with the person who owned the stock on the record date. (p. 511)

Expenditure   A payment or an obligation to make future payment for an asset or a service. (p. 370)

Expenses   Decreases in owner's equity resulting from the costs of goods and services used in the course of earning revenues. Also called *cost of doing business* or *expired costs*. (pp. 7, 86)

Extraordinary repairs   Repairs that significantly enhance a plant asset's estimated useful life or residual value and thereby increase its carrying value. (p. 370)

F

Face interest rate   The fixed rate of interest paid to bondholders based on the face value of the bonds. (p. 549)

Face value   The principal amount of each share of stock; also called *par value*. (p. 549)

Factor   An entity that buys accounts receivable. (p. 351)

Factoring   The sale or transfer of accounts receivable. (p. 351)

Fair value   The exchange price of an actual or potential business transaction between market participants. (p. 40)

Faithful representation   The qualitative characteristic of information that financial information must be complete, neutral, and free from material error. (p. 172)

Financial accounting   The process of generating and communicating accounting information in the form of financial statements to those outside the organization. (p. 2)

Financial Accounting Standards Board (FASB)   The most important body for developing rules on accounting practice; it issues Statements of Financial Accounting Standards. (p. 13)

Financial analysis   The evaluation and interpretation of financial statements and related performance measures to determine whether a business is well managed and achieving its goals. (p. 18)

Financial leverage   A corporation's ability to increase earnings for stockholders by earning more on assets than it pays in interest on the debt it incurred to finance the assets. Also called *trading on equity*. (p. 578)

Financial position   The economic resources that belong to a company and the claims (equities) against those resources at a particular time. (p. 6)

Financial ratio analysis   A technique of financial performance evaluation that identifies key relationships between components of the financial statements. (p. 670)

Financial ratios   Comparisons between the elements on financial statements from one period to another and from one company to another. (p. 18)

Financial statement analysis   An evaluation method that shows how items in a company's financial statements relate to the company's financial performance objectives; Also called *financial performance measurement*. (p. 660)

Financial statements   The primary means of communicating important accounting information to users. They include the income statement, statement of owner's equity, balance sheet, and statement of cash flows. (p. 2)

Financing activities   Activities undertaken by management to obtain adequate funds (as from stockholders and creditors) to begin and to continue operating a business. (pp. 17, 603)

Financing period   The amount of time from the purchase of inventory until it is sold and payment is collected, less the amount of time creditors give the company to pay for the inventory. (pp. 228, 677)

First-in, first-out (FIFO) method   An inventory costing method based on the assumption that the costs of the first items acquired should be assigned to the first items sold. (p. 269)

Fiscal year   Any 12-month accounting period. (p. 87)

FOB destination   A term indicating that the seller retains title to the merchandise until it reaches its destination and that the seller bears the shipping costs. (p. 213)

FOB shipping point   A term indicating that the buyer assumes title to the merchandise at the shipping point and bears the shipping costs. (p. 213)

Footings   Working totals of columns of numbers. To foot means to total a column of numbers. (p. 44)

Form 8-K   Current reports filed by U.S. public corporations with the Securities and Exchange Commission. (p. 662)

Form 10-K   An annual report filed by U.S. public corporations with the Securities and Exchange Commission. (p. 662)

Form 10-Q   A quarterly report filed by U.S. public corporations with the Securities and Exchange Commission. (p. 662)

Franchise   The right to an exclusive territory or market. (p. 387)

Fraudulent financial reporting   The intentional preparation of misleading financial statements. (p. 19)

Free cash flow   The amount of cash that remains after deducting the funds a company must commit to continue operating at its planned level; calculated as Net Cash Flows from Operating Activities – Dividends – Purchases of Plant Assets + Sales of Plant Assets. (pp. 392, 624, 674)

Free from material error   Information that meets a minimum level of accuracy so it does not distort what is being reported. (p. 172)

Freight-in   The transportation cost of receiving merchandise. (p. 213)

Full-costing method   A method of accounting for the costs of exploring and developing oil and gas resources in which all costs are recorded as assets and depleted over the estimated life of the producing resources. (p. 386)

Full disclosure   The convention requiring that a company's financial statements and the accompanying notes present all information relevant to the users' understanding of the statements. Also called *transparency*. (pp. 173, 684)

Future value   The amount an investment will be worth at a future date if invested at simple interest or compound interest. (p. 426)

G

General and administrative expenses   Expenses for accounting, personnel, credit checking, collections, and any other expenses that apply to overall operations. (p. 210)

General journal The simplest and most flexible type of journal. (p. 58)

General ledger A book or file that contains all of a company's accounts arranged in the order of the chart of accounts. Also called the *ledger*. (p. 42)

Generally accepted accounting principles (GAAP) The conventions, rules, and procedures that define accepted accounting practice at a particular time. (p. 12)

Going concern The assumption that unless there is evidence to the contrary, a business will continue to operate indefinitely. (p. 87)

Goods flow The actual physical movement of goods in the operations of a company. (p. 265)

Goodwill The excess of the amount paid for a business over the fair market value of the business's net assets. (pp. 177, 387)

Governmental Accounting Standards Board (GASB) The board responsible for issuing accounting standards for state and local governments. (p. 14)

Gross margin The difference between net sales and cost of goods sold. Also called *gross profit*. (p. 209)

Gross profit method A method of inventory estimation based on the assumption that the ratio of gross margin for a business remains relatively stable from year to year. Also called *gross margin method*. (p. 278)

Gross sales Total revenue from cash and credit sales during an accounting period. (p. 209)

Group depreciation The grouping of similar items to calculate depreciation. (p. 379)

H

Horizontal analysis A technique for analyzing financial statements in which changes from the previous year to the current year are computed in both dollar amounts and percentages. (p. 664)

I

Imprest system A system for controlling small cash disbursements by establishing a fund at a fixed amount and periodically reimbursing the fund by the amount necessary to restore the original cash balance. (p. 312)

Income from operations Gross margin minus operating expenses. Also called *operating income*. (p. 211)

Income statement A financial statement that summarizes the revenues earned and expenses incurred by a business over an accounting period. (p. 8)

Income Summary account A temporary account used in the closing process that holds a summary of all revenues and expenses before the net income or loss is transferred to the owner's Capital account. (p. 132)

Independence The avoidance of all relationships that impair or appear to impair an accountant's objectivity. (p. 14)

Independent contractor An individual who offers services for a fee but who is not under the organization's direct control or supervision. (p. 416)

Index number In trend analysis, a number that shows changes in related items over time and that is calculated by setting the base year equal to 100 percent. (p. 666)

Indirect method The procedure for converting the income statement from an accrual basis to a cash basis by adjusting net income for items that do not affect cash flows, including depreciation, amortization, depletion, gains, losses, and changes in current assets and current liabilities. (p. 606)

Information and communication A component of internal control that refers to the way in which the accounting system gathers and treats information and how it communicates individual responsibilities within the system. (p. 303)

Initial public offering (IPO) A company's first issue of capital stock to the public. (p. 491)

Institute of Management Accountants (IMA) A professional organization made up primarily of managerial accountants. (p. 14)

Intangible assets Long-term assets with no physical substance whose value stems from the rights or privileges accruing to their owners. (pp. 177, 368)

Integrity Honesty, candidness, and the subordination of personal gain to service and the public trust. (p. 14)

Interest The cost of borrowing money or the return on lending money, depending on whether one is the borrower or the lender. (pp. 346, 426)

Interest coverage ratio A measure of the degree of protection a company has from default on interest payments; calculated as (Income Before Income Taxes + Interest Expense) ÷ Interest Expense. (pp. 580, 676)

Interest receivable Any interest accrued on promissory notes. (p. 339)

Interim financial statements Financial statements issued for a period of less than one year, usually a quarter or a month. (p. 662)

Interim periods Accounting periods of less than one year. (p. 87)

Internal control A process designed by a company to establish the reliability of the accounting records and financial statements in accordance with generally accepted accounting principles (GAAP) and to ensure that the company's assets are protected. (p. 302)

Internal Revenue Service (IRS) The agency that interprets and enforces the tax laws governing the assessment and collection of revenue for operating the federal government. (p. 14)

International Accounting Standards Board (IASB) An organization that encourages worldwide cooperation in the development of accounting principles; it has approved more than 40 international standards of accounting. (p. 13)

International financial reporting standards (IFRS) Accounting standards set by the IASB that are used in many parts of the world, including Europe, and by foreign companies registered in the United States. (p. 13)

Inventory accounting An accounting system in which the primary objective is to apply accrual accounting to the determination of cost of inventory sold during the accounting period. (p. 264)

Inventory cost The invoice price of an asset less purchases discounts, plus freight-in, plus applicable taxes and tariffs. (p. 264)

Inventory turnover A ratio indicating the number of times a company's average inventory is sold during an accounting period; calculated as Cost of Goods Sold ÷ Average Inventory. (pp. 280, 677)

Investing activities Activities undertaken by management to spend capital in productive ways that will help a business achieve its goals. (pp. 17, 603)

Investments Assets, usually long-term, that are not used in the normal operation of a business and that management does not intend to convert to cash within the next year. (p. 177)

Investors Stockholders who have a direct financial interest in the success of the company in which they have invested. (p. 16)

Invoice A form that a vendor sends to a purchaser describing the goods delivered and the quantity, price, and terms of payment. (p. 310)

Issued shares The shares of stock sold or otherwise transferred to stockholders. (p. 497)

J

Joint venture An association of two or more entities for the purpose of achieving a specific goal, such as the manufacture of a product in a new market. (p. 474)

Journal A chronological record of all transactions; the place where transactions first enter the accounting records. Also called *book of original entry*. (p. 47)

Journal entry A journal notation that records a single transaction. (p. 47)

Journal form A way of recording a transaction in which the date, debit account, and debit amount appear on one line and the credit account and credit amount appear on the next line. (p. 48)

Just-in-time (JIT) operating environment A method of reducing levels of inventory by working closely with suppliers to coordinate and schedule deliveries so that goods arrive just at the time they are needed. (p. 281)

L

Last-in, first-out (LIFO) method An inventory costing method based on the assumption that the costs of the last items purchased should be assigned to the first items sold. (p. 270)

Leasehold A right to occupy land or buildings under a long-term rental contract. (p. 387)

Leasehold improvements Improvements to leased property that become the property of the lessor at the end of the lease. (p. 373)

Ledger account form An account form that has four dollar amount columns: one column for debit entries, one column for credit entries, and two columns (debit and credit) for showing the balance of the account. (p. 59)

Legal capital The number of shares of stock issued times the par value; the minimum amount a corporation can report as contributed capital. (p. 494)

Liabilities A business's present obligations to pay cash, transfer assets, or provide services to other entities in the future. (p. 6)

License The right to use a formula, technique, process, or design. (p. 387)

LIFO liquidation The reduction of inventory below previous levels because sales of older, lower-priced units have exceeded the purchases of units for the current period. (p. 273)

Limited liability The limited risk of loss that applies to stockholders' investments in corporations. It is limited to the amount stockholders paid for their shares of stock (p. 5)

Limited liability company (LLC) A business organization in which the members are partners and their liability is limited to their investment in the business. (p. 475)

Limited life A characteristic of a partnership; the fact that any event that breaches the partnership agreement—including the admission, withdrawal, or death of a partner—terminates the partnership. (p. 452)

Limited partnership (LP) A form of partnership in which partners' liabilities are limited to their investment. (p. 474)

Line of credit An arrangement with a bank that allows a company to borrow funds as needed. (p. 411)

Liquidating dividend A dividend that exceeds retained earnings and that a corporation usually pays only when it is going out of business or reducing its operations. (p. 510)

Liquidation A special form of dissolution in which a business ends

by selling assets, paying liabilities, and distributing any remaining assets to the partners. (p. 467)

Liquidity Having enough cash available to pay debts when they are due and to take care of unexpected needs for cash. (pp. 17, 180)

Long-term assets Assets that have a useful life of more than one year, are used in the operation of a business, and are not intended for resale. Less commonly called fixed assets. (p. 368)

Long-term liabilities Debts and obligations due beyond one year or beyond the normal operating cycle. (pp. 178, 410, 546)

Lower-of-cost-or-market (LCM) rule A method of valuing inventory at an amount less than cost when the replacement cost falls below historical cost. (p. 266)

M

Management The people who have overall responsibility for operating a business and meeting its goals of profitability and liquidity. (p. 15)

Management information system (MIS) The interconnected subsystems that provide the information needed to run a business. (p. 3)

Managerial accounting The process of generating and communicating accounting information about operating, investing, and financing activities for internal use by managers. (p. 3)

Manufacturing company A company that makes and sells products. (p. 208)

Market Current replacement cost of inventory. (p. 266)

Market interest rate The rate of interest paid in the market on bonds of similar risk. Also called *effective interest rate*. (p. 549)

Marketable securities Short-term investments that have a maturity of more than 90 days but are intended to be held only until cash is needed for current operations. (p. 602)

Material Information that if omitted or misstated could influence economic decisions made by users of financial statements. (p. 171)

Materiality The convention that refers to the relative importance of an item or event in a financial statement and its influence on the decisions of the users of financial statements. (p. 171)

Maturity date The date on which a promissory note must be paid. (p. 346)

Maturity value The total proceeds of a promissory note—face value plus interest—at the maturity date. (p. 347)

Merchandise inventory The goods on hand at any one time that are available for sale to customers. (p. 206)

Merchandising company A business that earns income by buying and selling goods. (p. 208)

Money measure The recording of all business transactions in terms of money. (p. 3)

Monitoring Management's regular assessment of the quality of internal control. (p. 303)

Mortgage A debt secured by real property. (p. 547)

Multistep income statement An income statement that goes through a series of steps to arrive at net income. (p. 208)

Mutual agency A characteristic of a partnership; the authority of each partner to act as an agent of the partnership within the scope of the business's normal operations. (p. 452)

N

Natural resources Long-term assets purchased for the economic value that can be taken from the land and used up. (p. 368)

Net assets Assets minus liabilities; owner's equity. (p. 7)

Net cost of purchases Total purchases plus freight-in less any deductions such as purchases returns and allowances and discounts from suppliers for early payment. (p. 221)

Net income The difference between revenues and expenses when revenues exceed expenses. Also called *net earnings*. (pp. 7, 86, 211)

Net loss The difference between expenses and revenues when expenses exceed revenues. (pp. 7, 86)

Net sales The gross proceeds from sales of merchandise (gross sales) less sales returns and allowances and any discounts allowed. Also called *net revenue*. (p. 209)

Neutral information Information that is free from bias intended to achieve a certain result or to bring about a particular behavior. (p. 172)

No-par stock Capital stock that does not have a par value. (p. 501)

Noncash investing and financing transactions Significant investing and financing transactions involving only long-term assets, long-term liabilities, or stockholders' equity that do not affect current cash inflows or outflows. (p. 605)

Noncompete covenant A contract limiting the rights of others to compete in a specific industry or line of business for a specified period. (p. 387)

Noncumulative preferred stock Preferred stock that does not oblige the issuer to make up a missed dividend in a subsequent year. (p. 498)

Normal balance The usual balance of an account; the side (debit or credit) that increases the account. (p. 45)

Normal operating cycle The average time a company needs to go from spending cash to receiving cash. (p. 175)

Notes payable A promissory note that represents a loan from a bank or other creditor; a long-term debt when due in more than one year. (p. 547)

Notes receivable Collective term for promissory notes held by the entity to which payment is promised (payee). (p. 337)

NSF (nonsufficient funds) checks Checks that a company has deposited but that are not paid when the bank presents them to the issuer's bank. (p. 312)

O

Objectivity Impartiality and intellectual honesty. (p. 14)

Obsolescence The process of becoming out of date, which is a factor in the limited useful life of tangible assets. (p. 374)

Off-balance-sheet financing Structuring long-term debts in such a way that they do not appear as liabilities on the balance sheet. (p. 580)

Operating activities Activities undertaken by management in the course of running a business. (pp. 17, 603)

Operating cycle The time it takes to sell products and collect payment for them. (pp. 206, 677)

Operating expenses Expenses other than cost of goods sold incurred in running a business. (p. 210)

Operating lease A short-term lease in which the risks of ownership remain with the lessor and for which payments are recorded as rent expense. (p. 573)

Ordinary annuity A series of equal payments made at the end of equal intervals of time, with compound interest on the payments. (p. 429)

Other assets A balance sheet category that some companies use to group all assets other than current assets and property, plant, and equipment. (p. 175)

Other revenues and expenses The section of a multistep income statement that includes revenues and expenses not related to a company's operating activities. Also called *nonoperating revenues and expenses*. (p. 211)

Outstanding checks Checks that a company has issued and recorded but that do not yet appear on its bank statement. (p. 312)

Outstanding shares Shares that have been issued and that are still in circulation. (p. 497)

Owner's equity The claims of the owner of a company to the assets of the business. (p. 7)

Owner's investments Assets that the owner puts into the business. (p. 7)

P

Par value An arbitrary amount assigned to each share of stock; constitutes a corporation's legal capital. (p. 494)

Partners' equity The equity section of a partnership's balance sheet. (pp. 178, 454)

Partnership A business that is owned by two or more people and that is not incorporated. (pp. 4, 452)

Partnership agreement The contractual relationship between partners that identifies the details of their partnership. (p. 452)

Patent An exclusive right granted by the federal government for a period of 20 years to make a particular product or use a specific process. (p. 387)

Payables turnover The number of times, on average, that a company pays its accounts payable in an accounting period; calculated as (Cost of Goods Sold +/− Change in Merchandise Inventory) ÷ Average Accounts Payable (pp. 433, 678)

Payment date The date on which a dividend is paid. (p. 511)

Pension fund A fund established by the contributions of an employer and often of employees from which payments are made to employees after retirement or upon disability or death. (p. 576)

Pension plan A contract requiring a company to pay benefits to its employees after they retire. (p. 576)

Percentage of gross margin The gross margin divided by net sales. (p. 210)

Percentage of net sales method A method of estimating uncollectible accounts based on the assumption that a predictable proportion of each dollar of sales will not be collected. (p. 340)

Performance measures Quantitative tools that gauge and compare an organization's performance in relation to a specific goal or an expected outcome. (p. 18)

Periodic independent verification A periodic check of records against assets by someone other than the person responsible for accounting records and assets. (p. 304)

Periodic inventory system A system for determining inventory on hand by periodically taking a physical count. (p. 206)

Periodicity The assumption that although the lifetime of a business is uncertain, it is still useful to estimate its net income in terms of accounting periods. (p. 87)

Permanent accounts Balance sheet accounts that carry their balances into the next accounting period. Also called *real accounts*. (p. 132)

Perpetual inventory system A system for determining inventory on hand by keeping continuous records of the quantity and, usually, the cost of individual items as they are bought and sold. (p. 206)

Petty cash fund A fund for making small payments of cash when it is inconvenient to pay by check. (p. 314)

Petty cash voucher A form signed by a person who receives cash from a petty cash fund; lists the date, amount, and purpose of the expenditure. (p. 315)

Physical controls Controls that limit access to assets. (p. 304)

Physical deterioration A decline in the useful life of a depreciable asset resulting from use and from exposure to the elements. (p. 374)

Physical inventory An actual count of all merchandise on hand. (pp. 206, 302)

Post-closing trial balance A trial balance prepared after all adjusting and closing entries have been posted to ensure that all temporary accounts have zero balances and that total debits equal total credits. (p. 140)

Posting The process of transferring journal entry information from the journal to the ledger. (p. 59)

Predictive value Information that helps capital providers make decisions about future actions. (p. 171)

Preferred stock Stock that has preference over common stock, usually in terms of dividends and the distribution of assets. (p. 497)

Premium The amount by which a bond's issue price exceeds its face value, which occurs when the market interest rate is lower than the face interest rate. (p. 550)

Prepaid expenses Expenses paid in advance that have not yet expired; an asset account. (p. 91)

Present value The amount that must be invested today at a given rate of interest to produce a given future value. (p. 427)

Price/earnings (P/E) ratio A measure of confidence in a company's future; calculated as Market Price per Share ÷ Earnings per Share. (pp. 521, 680)

Production method A method of depreciation that assumes depreciation is solely the result of use and that allocates depreciation based on the units of use or output during each period of an asset's useful life. Also called the *units of production method*. (p. 376)

Profit margin A measure of profitability that shows the percentage of each sales dollar that results in net income; calculated as Net Income ÷ Net Revenues (or Net Sales). (pp. 181, 671)

Profitability The ability to earn enough income to attract and hold investment capital. (pp. 17, 181)

Promissory note(s) An unconditional promise to pay a definite sum of money on demand or at a future date. (pp. 337, 412)

Property, plant, and equipment Tangible long-term assets used in the day-to-day operations of a business. Also called *operating assets*, *fixed assets*, *tangible assets*, *long-lived assets*, or *plant assets*. (pp. 177, 368)

Public Company Accounting Oversight Board (PCAOB) A governmental body created by the Sarbanes-Oxley Act to regulate the accounting profession. It has the power to determine the standards that auditors must follow. (p. 13)

Purchase discounts Discounts that buyers take for early payment of merchandise; the Purchases Discounts account is a contra-purchases account used under the periodic inventory system. (p. 213)

Purchase order A form that a company's purchasing department sends to a vendor describing the items ordered and the quantity, price, terms, and shipping date. (p. 310)

Purchase requisition A formal written request for a purchase that a company's credit office (requesting department) sends to the purchasing department. (p. 310)

Purchases account A temporary account used under the periodic inventory system to accumulate the cost of merchandise purchased for resale during an accounting period. (p. 222)

Purchases journal A journal used to record purchases on credit. (p. 252)

Purchases Returns and Allowances account A contra-purchases account used under the periodic inventory system to accumulate cash refunds, credits on account, and other allowances made by suppliers. (p. 223)

Q

Qualitative characteristics Standards for judging accounting information. (p. 171)

Quality of earnings The substance of earnings and their sustainability into future periods. (p. 683)

Quick ratio A measure of short-term debt-paying ability; calculated as (Cash + Marketable Securities + Receivables) ÷ Current Liabilities. (p. 680)

R

Receivables turnover A ratio for measuring the average number of times receivables are turned into cash during an accounting period; calculated as Net Sales ÷ Average Accounts Receivable. (pp. 349, 678)

Receiving report A form on which an employee in a company's receiving department notes the quantity, type of goods, and their condition upon delivery from the vendor. (p. 310)

Recognition The determination of when a business transaction should be recorded. (p. 40)

Recognition point The predetermined time at which a transaction should be recorded; usually, the point at which title passes to the buyer. (p. 62)

Record date The date on which ownership of stock, and thus the right to receive a dividend, is determined. (p. 511)

Registered bonds Bonds that the issuing company registers in the names of the bondholders. (p. 551)

Registrar An official responsible for keeping a register or official records of stock transfers for a corporation. (p. 494)

Relevance The qualitative characteristic of information that has a direct effect on a decision. (p. 171)

Residual value The portion of an asset's acquisition cost expected to be recovered at the date of its disposal. Also called *salvage value, disposal value,* or *trade-in value*. (p. 375)

Restructuring The estimated cost of a change in a company's operations, usually involving the closing of facilities and the laying off of personnel. (p. 686)

Retail method A method of inventory estimation, used in retail merchandising businesses, in which inventory at retail value is reduced by the ratio of cost to retail price. (p. 277)

Retained earnings Stockholders' claims to assets arising from the earnings of the business; the accumulated earnings of a corporation since its inception, minus any losses, dividends, or transfers to contributed capital. Also called *Earned Capital*. (pp. 179, 496)

Return on assets A measure of profitability that shows how efficiently a company uses its assets to produce income; calculated as Net Income ÷ Average Total Assets. (pp. 183, 672)

Return on equity A measure of how much income is earned on each dollar invested by the company's owners/stockholders; calculated as Net Income ÷ Average Owner's/ Stockholders' Equity. (pp. 186, 520, 676)

Revenue expenditure An expenditure for ordinary repairs and maintenance of a long-term asset, which is recorded by a debit to an expense account. (p. 370)

Revenue recognition The process of determining when revenue should be recorded. (p. 88)

Revenues Increases in owner's equity resulting from operating a business. (pp. 7, 86)

Reversing entry An optional journal entry made on the first day of an accounting period that is the exact opposite of an adjusting entry made at the end of the previous period. (p. 141)

Risk assessment The identification of areas in which risk of loss of assets or inaccuracies in accounting records is high. (p. 303)

S

S corporations Corporations that U.S. tax laws treat as partnerships. (p. 475)

Salaries Compensation of employees at a monthly or yearly rate. (p. 415)

Sales discount A discount given to a buyer for early payment of a sale made on credit; the Sales Discounts account is a contra-revenue account. (p. 212)

Sales journal A journal used to record credit sales. (p. 249)

Sales returns and allowances Refunds, credits, and discounts given to customers who have received defective goods. (p. 209)

Sales Returns and Allowances account A contra-revenue account used to accumulate cash refunds, credits on account, and other allowances made to customers who have received defective or otherwise unsatisfactory products. (p. 218)

Sarbanes-Oxley Act An act of Congress that regulates financial reporting in public corporations. (p. 19)

Secured bonds Bonds that carry a pledge of certain assets as a guarantee of repayment. (p. 550)

Securities and Exchange Commission (SEC) A governmental agency that regulates the issuing, buying, and selling of stocks. It has the legal power to set and enforce accounting practices for firms whose securities are sold to the general public. (p. 14)

Securitization The grouping of receivables into batches for sale at a discount to companies and investors. (p. 351)

Selling expenses The costs of storing goods and preparing them for sale; preparing displays, advertising, and otherwise promoting sales; and delivering goods to a buyer if the seller has agreed to pay the cost of delivery. (p. 210)

Separate entity A business that is treated as distinct from its creditors, customers, and owners. (p. 4)

Separation of duties No one person can authorize transactions, handle assets, or keep records of assets. (p. 304)

Serial bonds Bonds in one issue that mature on different dates. (p. 550)

Share of stock A unit of ownership in a corporation. (p. 492)

Short-term notes payable Promissory notes issued by companies to meet their short-term funding needs. (p. 412)

Simple interest The interest cost for one or more periods when the amount on which the interest is computed stays the same from period to period. (p. 426)

Single-step income statement An income statement that arrives at net income in a single step. (p. 211)

Software Capitalized costs associated with computer programs developed for sale, lease, or internal use and amortized over the estimated economic life of the programs. (p. 387)

Sole proprietorship A business that is owned by one person and that is not incorporated. (p. 4)

Source documents Invoices, checks, receipts, or contracts that support the details of a transaction. (p. 47)

Special-purpose entities (SPEs) Business organizations with limited lives that a company creates to achieve a specific objective, such as raising money by selling receivables. (p. 475)

Special-purpose journals Journals that are used to record transactions that fall into special categories such as sales, purchases, cash receipts, and cash payments. (p. 249)

Specific identification method An inventory costing method in which the cost of each item in ending inventory is identified as coming from a specific purchase. (p. 268)

Start-up and organization costs The costs of forming a corporation. (p. 495)

Statement of cash flows A financial statement that shows the inflows and outflows of cash from operating activities, investing activities, and financing activities over an accounting period. (pp. 10, 602)

Statement of owner's equity A financial statement that shows the changes in owner's equity over an accounting period. (p. 8)

Statement of stockholders' equity A financial statement that summarizes changes in the components of the stockholders' equity section of the balance sheet. Also called the *statement of changes in stockholders' equity*. (p. 516)

Stock dividend A proportional distribution of shares among a corporation's stockholders. (p. 513)

Stock option plans Plans that give employees the right to purchase their companies' stock under specified terms. (p. 522)

Stock split An increase in the number of outstanding shares of stock accompanied by a proportionate reduction in the par or stated value. (p. 515)

Stockholders The owners of a corporation whose ownership is represented by shares of stock but who do not directly control the corporation's operations. (p. 5)

Stockholders' equity The equity section of a balance sheet for a corporation; the owners' claims to the business. Also called *shareholders' equity*. (pp. 178, 496)

Straight-line method A method of depreciation that assumes depreciation depends only on the passage of time and that allocates an equal amount of depreciation to each accounting period in an asset's useful life. (pp. 375, 558)

Subsidiary ledger A ledger separate from the general ledger that contains a group of related accounts. (p. 249)

Successful efforts accounting A method of accounting for the costs of exploring and developing oil and gas resources in which successful exploration is recorded as an asset and depleted over the estimated life of the resource and all unsuccessful efforts are immediately written off as losses. (p. 385)

Supply-chain management A system of ordering and tracking inventory conducted over the Internet. (p. 281)

T

T account The simplest form of account, which is used to analyze transactions. (p. 44)

Temporary accounts Revenue and expense accounts whose balances are transferred to the owner's Capital account at the end of an accounting period. Also called *nominal accounts*. (p. 132)

Term bonds Bonds in one issue that mature at the same time. (p. 550)

Time value of money The costs or benefits derived from holding or not holding money over time. (p. 426)

Timeliness The qualitative characteristic of information that enables users to receive information in time to influence a decision. (p. 172)

Trade credit Credit granted to customers by wholesalers or retailers. (p. 336)

Trade discount A deduction (usually 30 percent or more) off a list or catalogue price, which is not recorded in the accounting records. (p. 212)

Trademark A registered symbol that can be used only by its owner to identify a product or service. (p. 387)

Trading securities A type of marketable security that a company buys and sells for making a profit in the near term as opposed to holding it indefinitely for investment purposes. (p. 603)

Transfer agents A trust company, bank, or similar financial institution assigned by a corporation to maintain records of investors and account balances and transactions. (p. 494)

Treasury stock Shares of the corporation's own stock that it has bought back on the open market, which reduces the ownership of the business. (p. 496)

Trend analysis A variation of horizontal analysis in which percentage changes are calculated for several successive years instead of for two years. (p. 666)

Trial balance A comparison of the total of debit and credit balances in the accounts to check that they are equal. (p. 56)

U

Uncollectible accounts Accounts receivable owed by customers who cannot or will not pay. Also called *bad debts*. (p. 337)

Understandability The qualitative characteristic of information that enables users to comprehend the meaning of the information they receive. (p. 172)

Underwriter An intermediary between the corporation and the investing public who facilitates an issue of stock or other securities for a fee. (p. 494)

Unearned revenues Revenues received in advance for which the goods have not yet been delivered or the services performed; a liability account. (pp. 96, 418)

Unlimited liability A characteristic of a partnership; the fact that each partner has personal liability for all the debts of the partnership. (p. 452)

Unsecured bonds Bonds issued on a corporation's general credit. Also called *debenture bonds*. (p. 550)

V

Valuation The process of assigning a monetary value to a business transaction and the resulting assets and liabilities. (p. 40)

Verifiability The qualitative characteristic of information that helps assure users that information faithfully represents what it purports to depict. (p. 172)

Vertical analysis A technique for analyzing financial statements that uses percentages to show how the different components of a statement relate to a total figure in the statement. (p. 667)

W

Wages Compensation of employees at an hourly rate. (p. 415)

Withdrawals Assets that the owner takes out of the business. (p. 7)

Work sheet A type of working paper used as a preliminary step in recording adjusting and closing entries and that is used in preparing the financial statements. (p. 143)

Working capital A measure of liquidity that shows the net current assets on hand to continue business operations; calculated as Total Current Assets − Total Current Liabilities. (p. 180)

Working papers Documents that accountants use to organize their work and that support the information in the financial statements. (p. 143)

Write-down A reduction in the value of an asset below its carrying value on the balance sheet. Also called a *write-off*. (p. 686)

Z

Zero coupon bonds Bonds that do not pay periodic interest but that pay a fixed amount on the maturity date. (p. 558)

COMPANY NAME INDEX

SUBJECT INDEX